# STAR WARS

## THE EMPIRE

### VOLUME 3

*STAR WARS: DARTH VADER AND THE GHOST PRISON #1-5, STAR WARS: DARK TIMES — FIRE CARRIER #1-5, STAR WARS: DARK TIMES — A SPARK REMAINS #1-5 & STAR WARS: DARTH VADER AND THE NINTH ASSASSIN #1-5*

WRITERS:

## HADEN BLACKMAN, RANDY STRADLEY & TIM SIEDELL

PENCILERS:

## AGUSTIN ALESSIO, GABRIEL GUZMAN, DOUGLAS WHEATLEY, STEPHEN THOMPSON & IVÁN FERNÁNDEZ

INKERS:
**AGUSTIN ALESSIO, GABRIEL GUZMAN, DOUGLAS WHEATLEY, MARK IRWIN & DENIS FREITAS** WITH **DREW GERACI &** JASON GORDER

COLORISTS:
**AGUSTIN ALESSIO, GARRY HENDERSON, DAN JACKSON & MICHAEL ATIYEH**

LETTERER:
**MICHAEL HEISLER**

ASSISTANT EDITOR:
**FREDDYE LINS**

EDITORS:
**RANDY STRADLEY & DAVE MARSHALL**

COVER ARTIST:
**DAVE WILKINS**

**COLLECTION EDITOR:** MARK D. BEAZLEY
**ASSOCIATE MANAGING EDITOR:** KATERI WOODY
**ASSOCIATE MANAGER, DIGITAL ASSETS:** JOE HOCHSTEIN
**SENIOR EDITOR, SPECIAL PROJECTS:** JENNIFER GRÜNWALD
**VP PRODUCTION & SPECIAL PROJECTS:** JEFF YOUNGQUIST
**RESEARCH:** MIKE HANSEN
**LAYOUT:** JEPH YORK
**PRODUCTION:** RYAN DEVALL
**BOOK DESIGNER:** RODOLFO MURAGUCHI
**SVP PRINT, SALES & MARKETING:** DAVID GABRIEL

**EDITOR IN CHIEF:** AXEL ALONSO
**CHIEF CREATIVE OFFICER:** JOE QUESADA
**PUBLISHER:** DAN BUCKLEY
**EXECUTIVE PRODUCER:** ALAN FINE

SPECIAL THANKS TO FRANK PARISI & LUCASFILM AND DEIDRE HANSEN

**STAR WARS LEGENDS EPIC COLLECTION: THE EMPIRE VOL. 5.** Contains material originally published in magazine form as STAR WARS: DARTH VADER AND THE GHOST PRISON #1-5, STAR WARS: DARK TIMES — FIRE CARRIER #1-5, STAR WARS: DARK TIMES — A SPARK REMAINS #1-5 and STAR WARS: DARTH VADER AND THE NINTH ASSASSIN #1-5. First printing 2017. ISBN# 978-1-302-90375-6. Published by MARVEL WORLDWIDE, INC., a subsidiary of MARVEL ENTERTAINMENT, LLC. OFFICE OF PUBLICATION: 135 West 50th Street, New York, NY 10020. STAR WARS and related text and illustrations are trademarks and/or copyrights, in the United States and other countries, of Lucasfilm Ltd. and/or its affiliates. © & TM Lucasfilm Ltd. No similarity between any of the names, characters, persons, and/or institutions in this magazine with those of any living or dead person or institution is intended, and any such similarity which may exist is purely coincidental. Marvel and its logos are TM Marvel Characters, Inc. **Printed in the U.S.A.** ALAN FINE, President, Marvel Entertainment; DAN BUCKLEY, President, TV, Publishing & Brand Management; JOE QUESADA, Chief Creative Officer; TOM BREVOORT, SVP of Publishing; DAVID BOGART, SVP of Business Affairs & Operations, Publishing & Partnership; C.B. CEBULSKI, VP of Brand Management & Development, Asia; DAVID GABRIEL, SVP of Sales & Marketing, Publishing; JEFF YOUNGQUIST, VP of Production & Special Projects; DAN CARR, Executive Director of Publishing Technology; ALEX MORALES, Director of Publishing Operations; SUSAN CRESPI, Production Manager; STAN LEE, Chairman Emeritus. For information regarding advertising in Marvel Comics or on Marvel.com, please contact Vit DeBellis, Integrated Sales Manager, at vdebellis@marvel.com. For Marvel subscription inquiries, please call 888-511-5480. **Manufactured between 12/16/2016 and 1/23/2017 by LSC COMMUNICATIONS INC., SALEM, VA, USA.**

# THE EMPIRE — VOLUME 3

# THE EMPIRE
## VOL. 3

With the rise of the Galactic Empire from the ashes of the old Republic, the evil Emperor Palpatine has taken control of the galaxy. Over the past three months, he has quickly consolidated military and political power and made Coruscant his throneworld.

The Emperor's deadly apprentice, Darth Vader, continues to hide his feelings of guilt over the slaughter of Jedi younglings, part of the Emperor's plan to exterminate the Jedi Order and prevent any threat against the dark side of the Force. After a failed attempt at finding an apprentice of his own, Vader now fears that the Emperor may dispose of him as well if his loyalty to the Empire is questioned.

Meanwhile, the fugitive Jedi Dass Jennir and his companion Ember Chankeli have reunited with his friends, the outlaw crew of the ship *Uhumele*, after narrowly escaping the assassin bounty hunter Falco Sang. Vader has captured Sang in the hope of finding Jennir and proving himself by hunting down remaining Jedi.

But the Emperor has told Darth Vader that he has his own plan to deal with the surviving Jedi — one that does not include Vader....

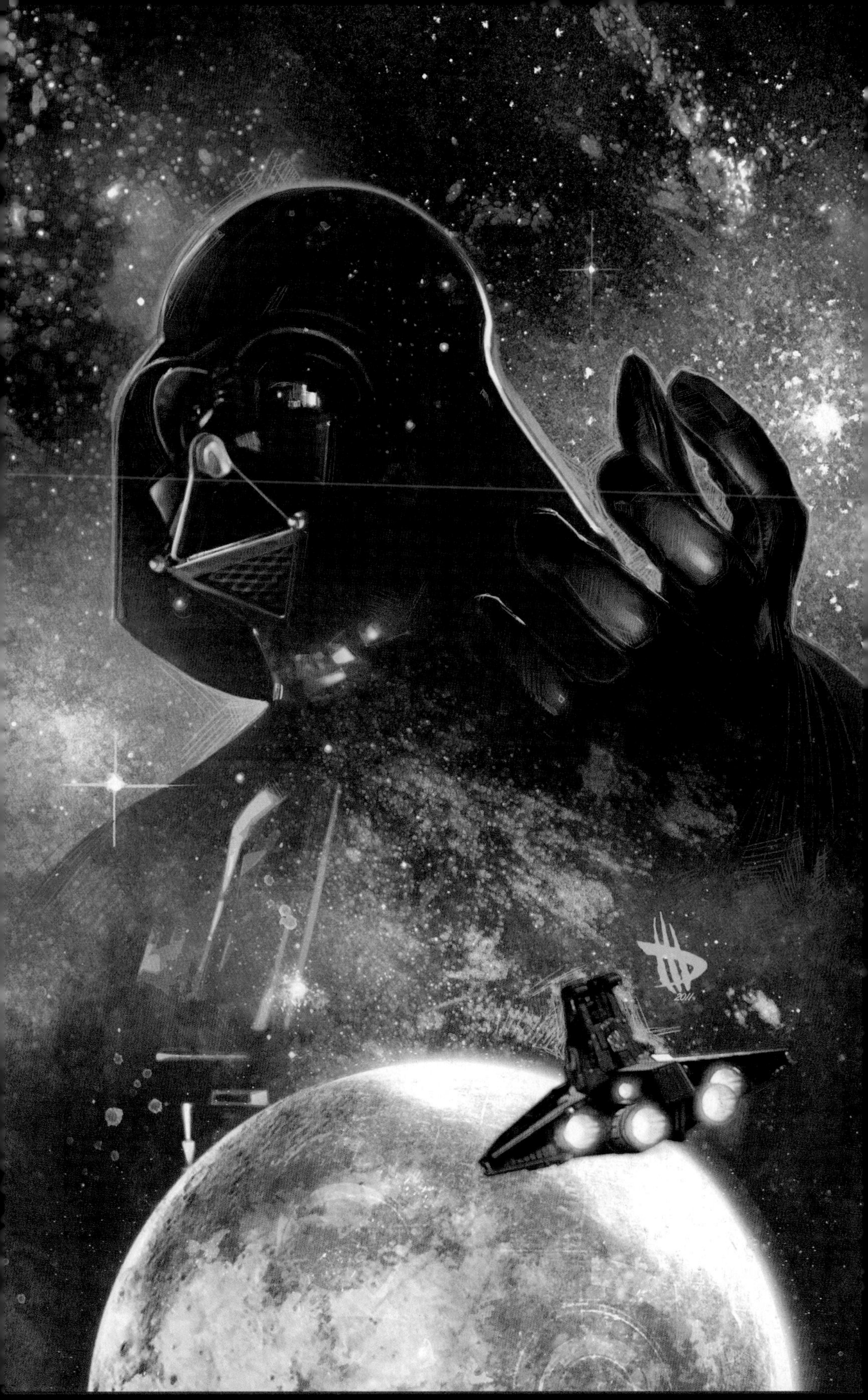

**STAR WARS: DARTH VADER AND THE GHOST PRISON #1**

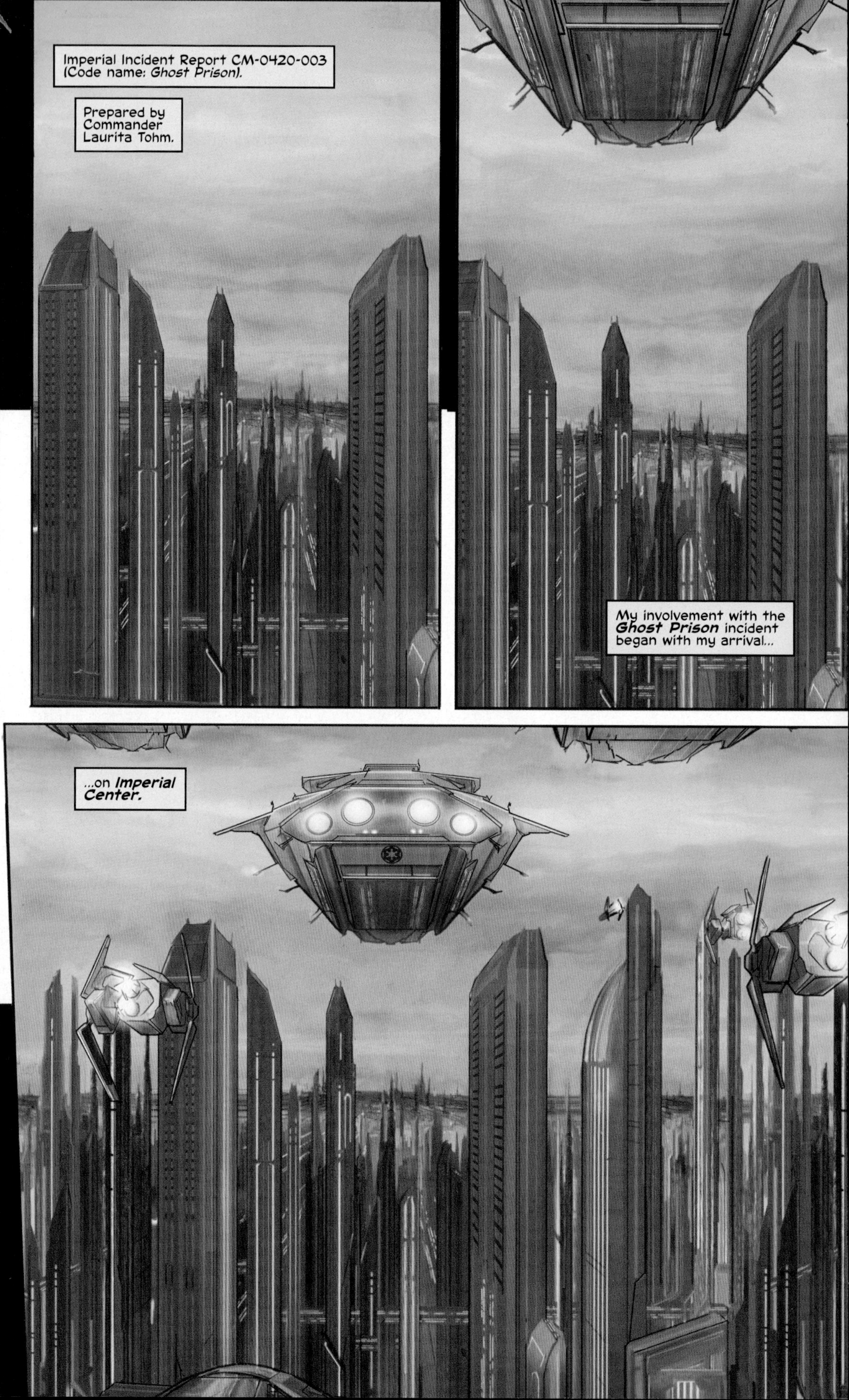
Imperial Incident Report CM-0420-003 (Code name: *Ghost Prison*).
Prepared by Commander Laurita Tohm.
My involvement with the ***Ghost Prison*** incident began with my arrival...
...on ***Imperial Center.***

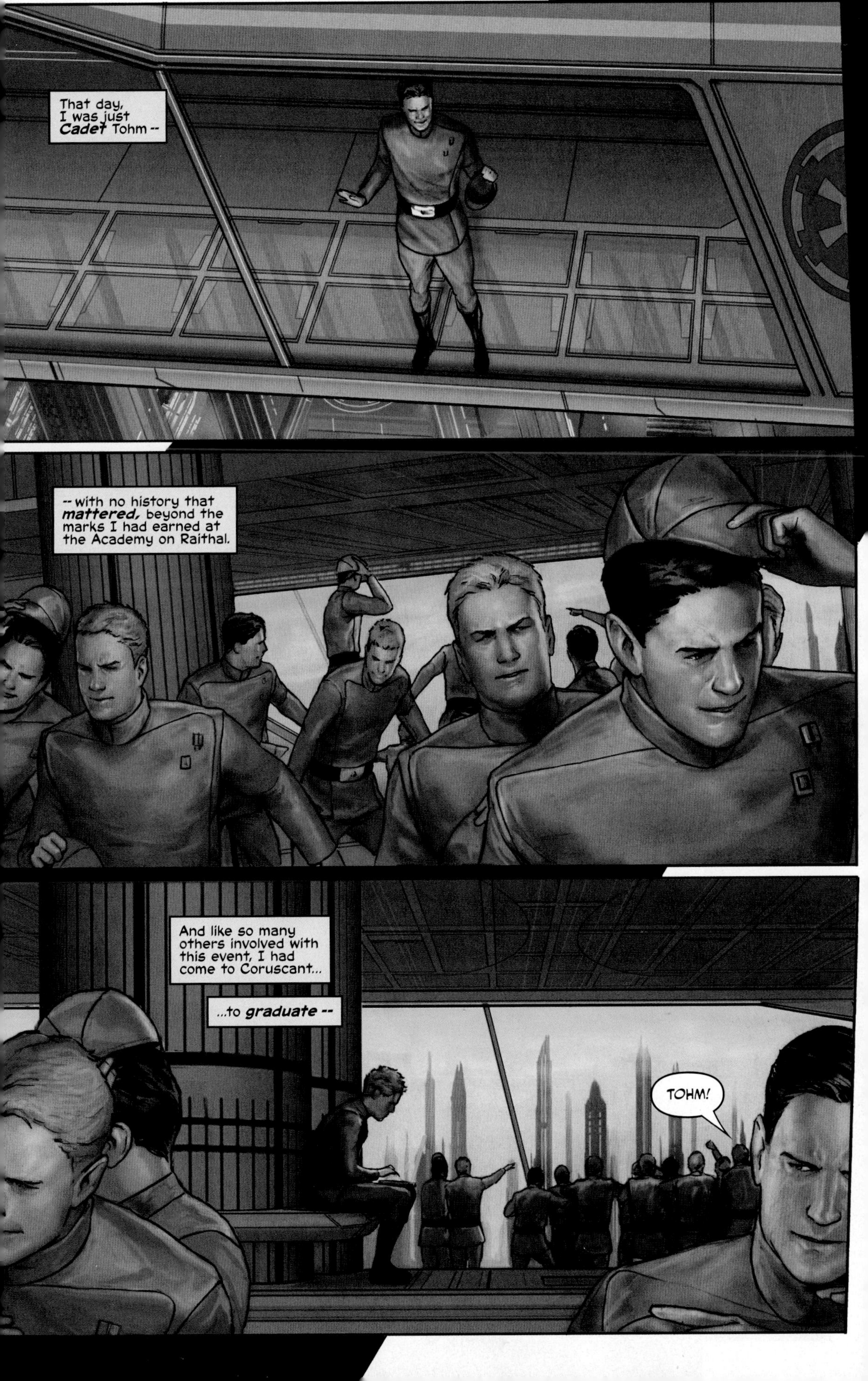
That day, I was just *Cadet* Tohm --
-- with no history that ***mattered,*** beyond the marks I had earned at the Academy on Raithal.
And like so many others involved with this event, I had come to Coruscant...
...to ***graduate --***
TOHM!

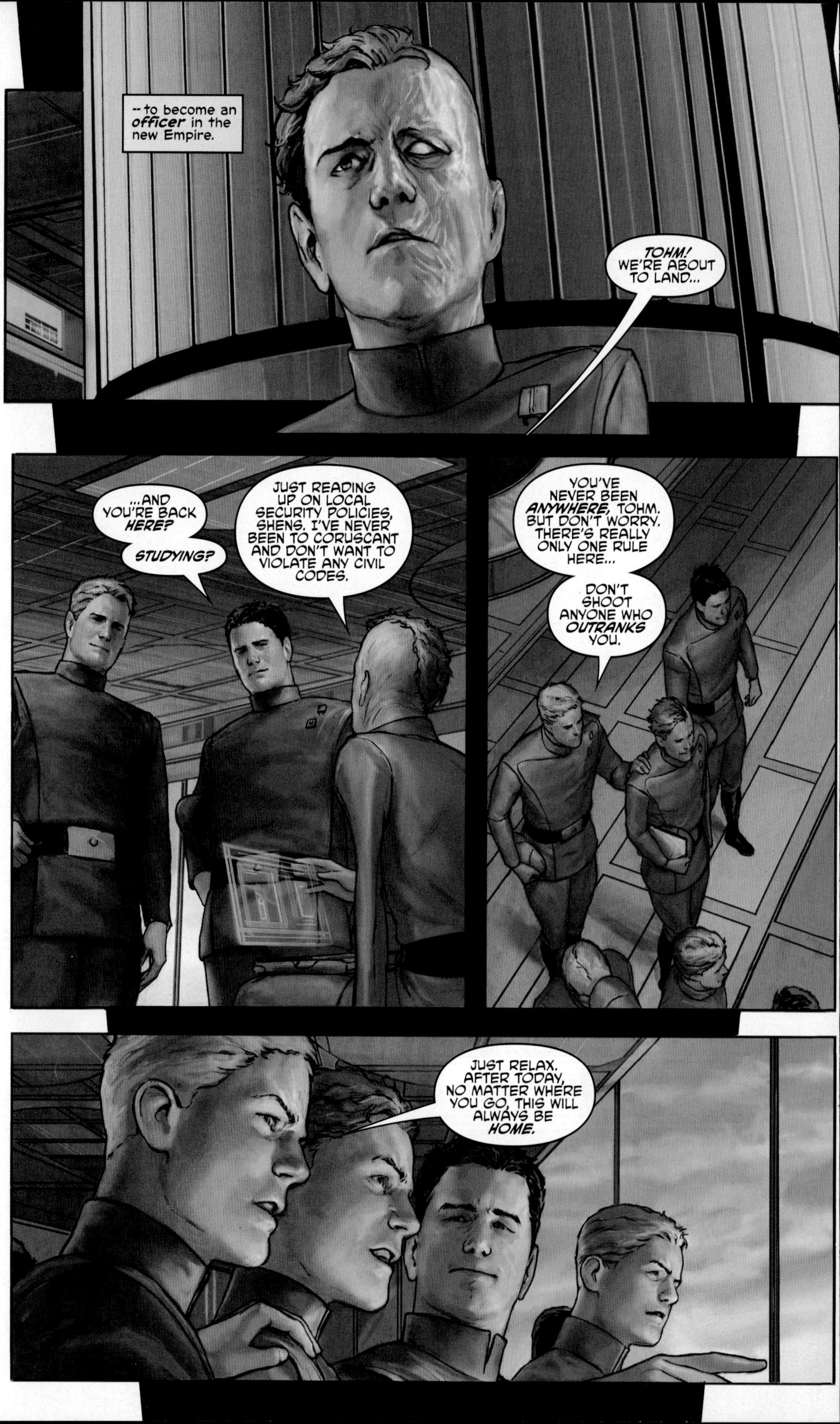
--to become an *officer* in the new Empire.
*TOHM!* WE'RE ABOUT TO LAND...
...AND YOU'RE BACK *HERE?*
*STUDYING?*
JUST READING UP ON LOCAL SECURITY POLICIES, SHENS. I'VE NEVER BEEN TO CORUSCANT AND DON'T WANT TO VIOLATE ANY CIVIL CODES.
YOU'VE NEVER BEEN *ANYWHERE,* TOHM. BUT DON'T WORRY. THERE'S REALLY ONLY ONE RULE HERE...
DON'T SHOOT ANYONE WHO *OUTRANKS* YOU.
JUST RELAX. AFTER TODAY, NO MATTER WHERE YOU GO, THIS WILL ALWAYS BE *HOME.*

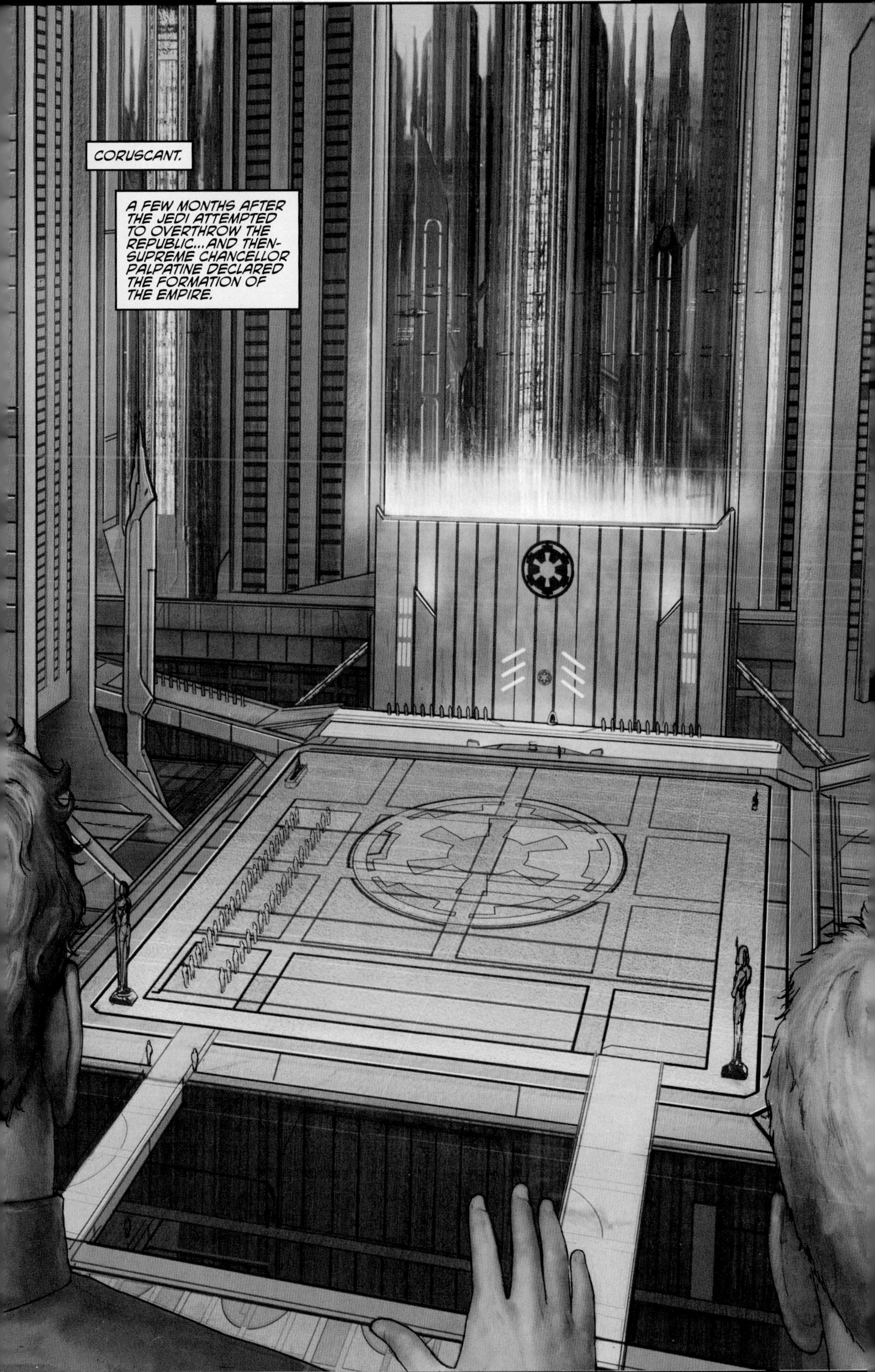
CORUSCANT.
A FEW MONTHS AFTER THE JEDI ATTEMPTED TO OVERTHROW THE REPUBLIC... AND THEN-SUPREME CHANCELLOR PALPATINE DECLARED THE FORMATION OF THE EMPIRE.

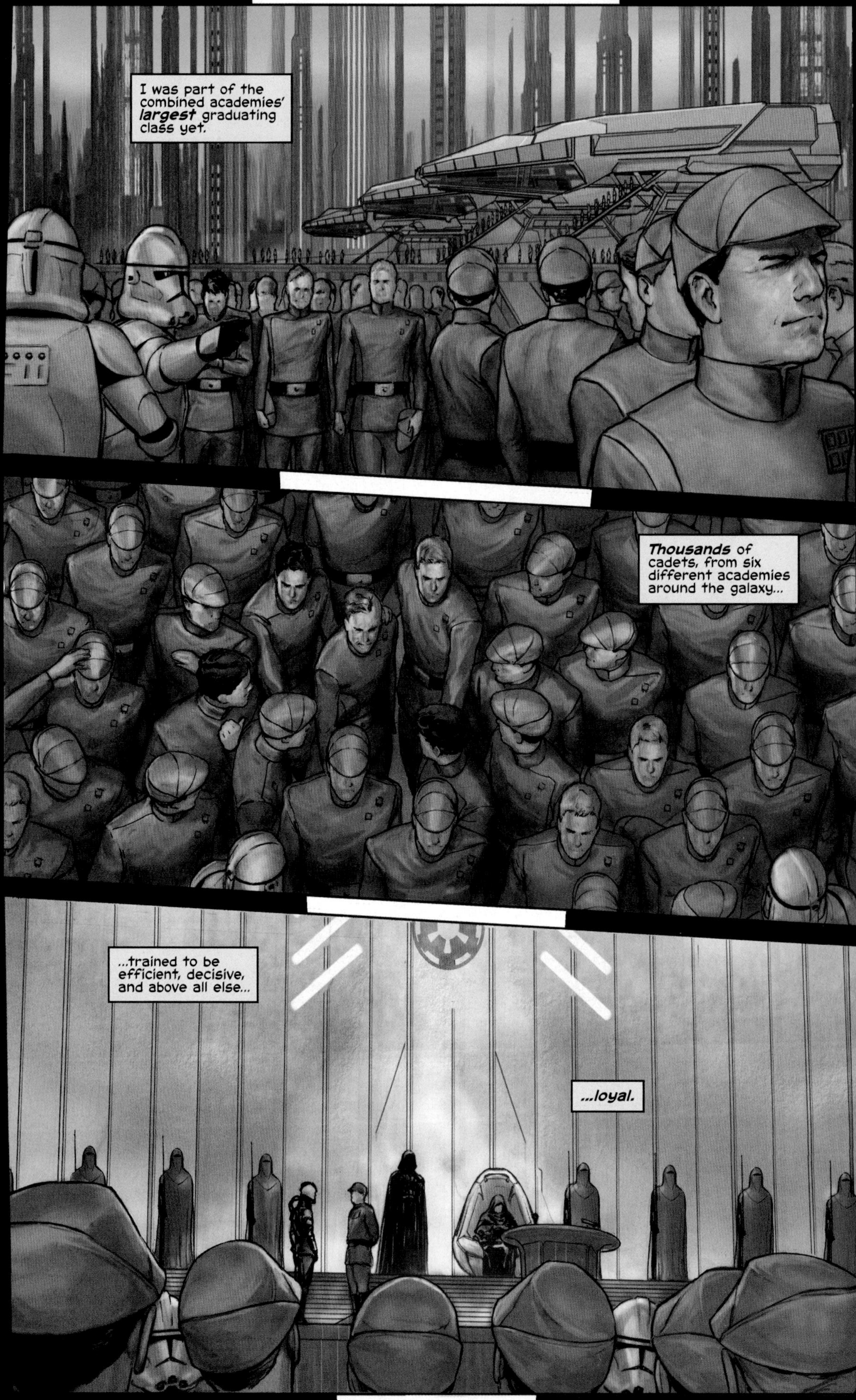
I was part of the combined academies' *largest* graduating class yet.
*Thousands* of cadets, from six different academies around the galaxy...
...trained to be efficient, decisive, and above all else...
...loyal.

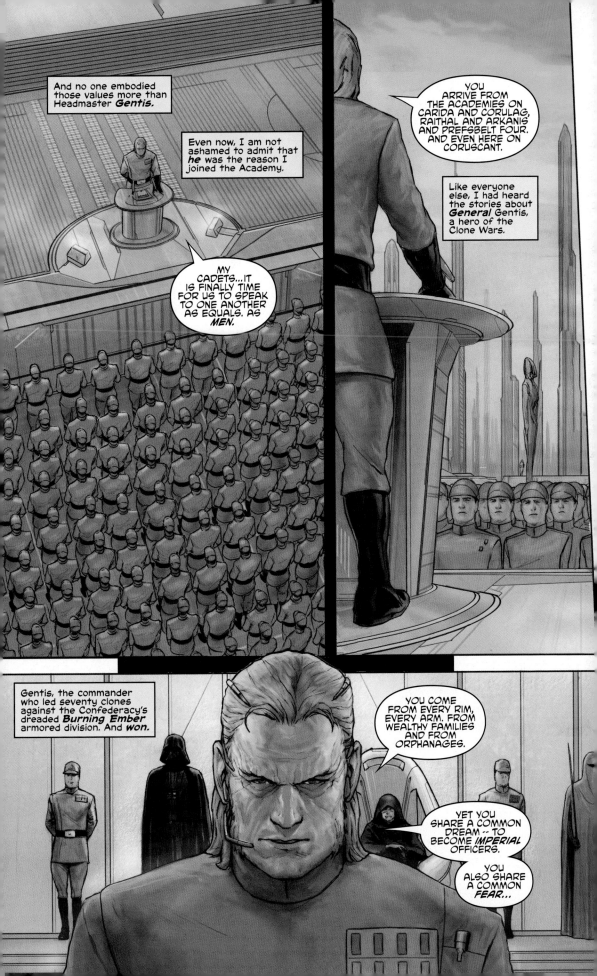

And no one embodied those values more than Headmaster *Gentis.*

Even now, I am not ashamed to admit that *he* was the reason I joined the Academy.

MY CADETS...IT IS FINALLY TIME FOR US TO SPEAK TO ONE ANOTHER AS EQUALS. AS *MEN.*

YOU ARRIVE FROM THE ACADEMIES ON CARIDA AND CORULAG, RAITHAL AND ARKANIS AND PREFSBELT FOUR. AND EVEN HERE ON CORUSCANT.

Like everyone else, I had heard the stories about *General* Gentis, a hero of the Clone Wars.

Gentis, the commander who led seventy clones against the Confederacy's dreaded *Burning Ember* armored division. And *won.*

YOU COME FROM EVERY RIM, EVERY ARM. FROM WEALTHY FAMILIES AND FROM ORPHANAGES.

YET YOU SHARE A COMMON DREAM -- TO BECOME *IMPERIAL* OFFICERS.

YOU ALSO SHARE A COMMON *FEAR...*

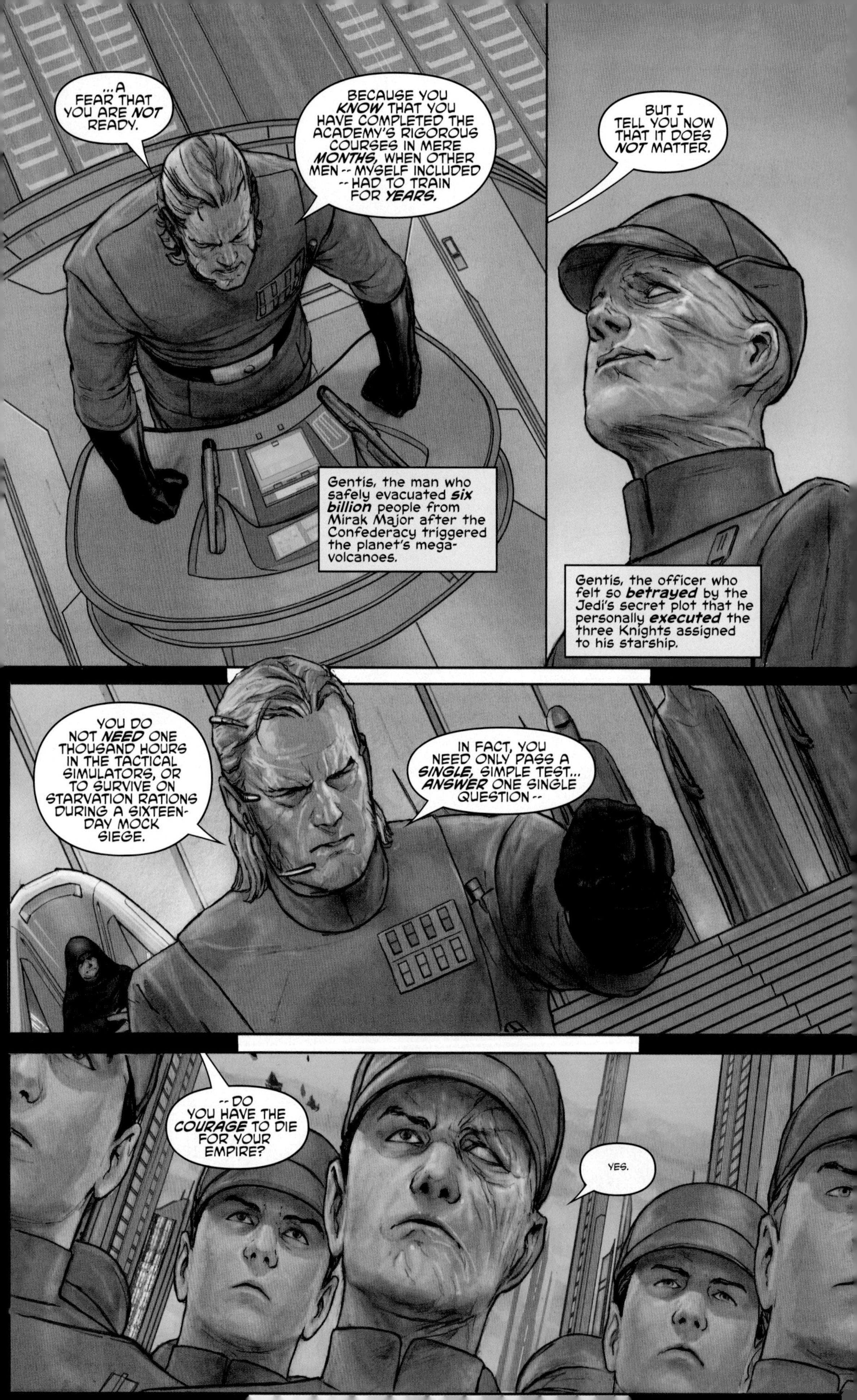
...A FEAR THAT YOU ARE NOT READY.
BECAUSE YOU KNOW THAT YOU HAVE COMPLETED THE ACADEMY'S RIGOROUS COURSES IN MERE MONTHS, WHEN OTHER MEN -- MYSELF INCLUDED -- HAD TO TRAIN FOR YEARS.
Gentis, the man who safely evacuated six billion people from Mirak Major after the Confederacy triggered the planet's mega-volcanoes.
BUT I TELL YOU NOW THAT IT DOES NOT MATTER.
Gentis, the officer who felt so betrayed by the Jedi's secret plot that he personally executed the three Knights assigned to his starship.
YOU DO NOT NEED ONE THOUSAND HOURS IN THE TACTICAL SIMULATORS, OR TO SURVIVE ON STARVATION RATIONS DURING A SIXTEEN-DAY MOCK SIEGE.
IN FACT, YOU NEED ONLY PASS A SINGLE, SIMPLE TEST... ANSWER ONE SINGLE QUESTION --
-- DO YOU HAVE THE COURAGE TO DIE FOR YOUR EMPIRE?
YES.

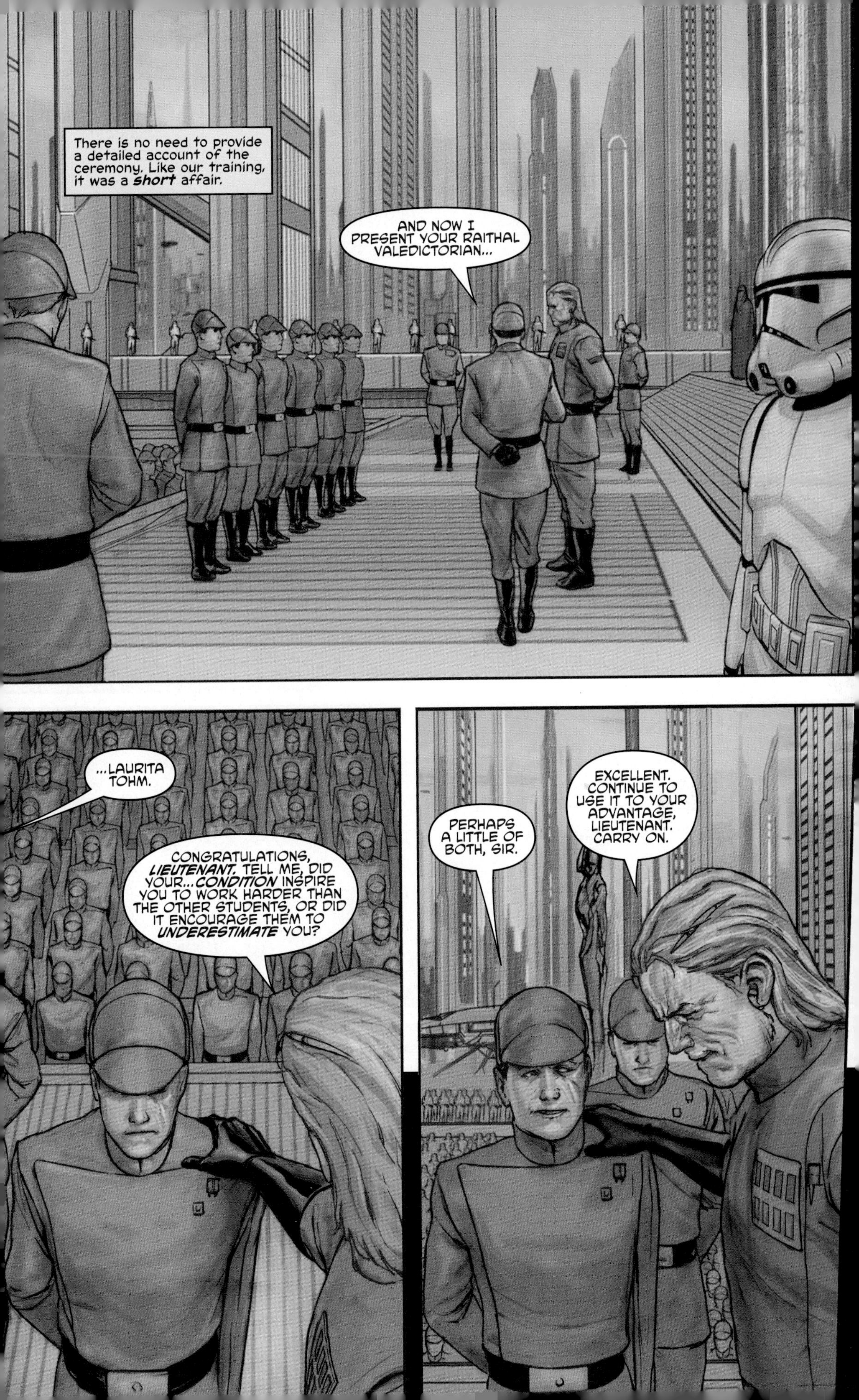
There is no need to provide a detailed account of the ceremony. Like our training, it was a *short* affair.
AND NOW I PRESENT YOUR RAITHAL VALEDICTORIAN...
...LAURITA TOHM.
CONGRATULATIONS, *LIEUTENANT.* TELL ME, DID YOUR... *CONDITION* INSPIRE YOU TO WORK HARDER THAN THE OTHER STUDENTS, OR DID IT ENCOURAGE THEM TO *UNDERESTIMATE* YOU?
PERHAPS A LITTLE OF BOTH, SIR.
EXCELLENT. CONTINUE TO USE IT TO YOUR ADVANTAGE, LIEUTENANT. CARRY ON.

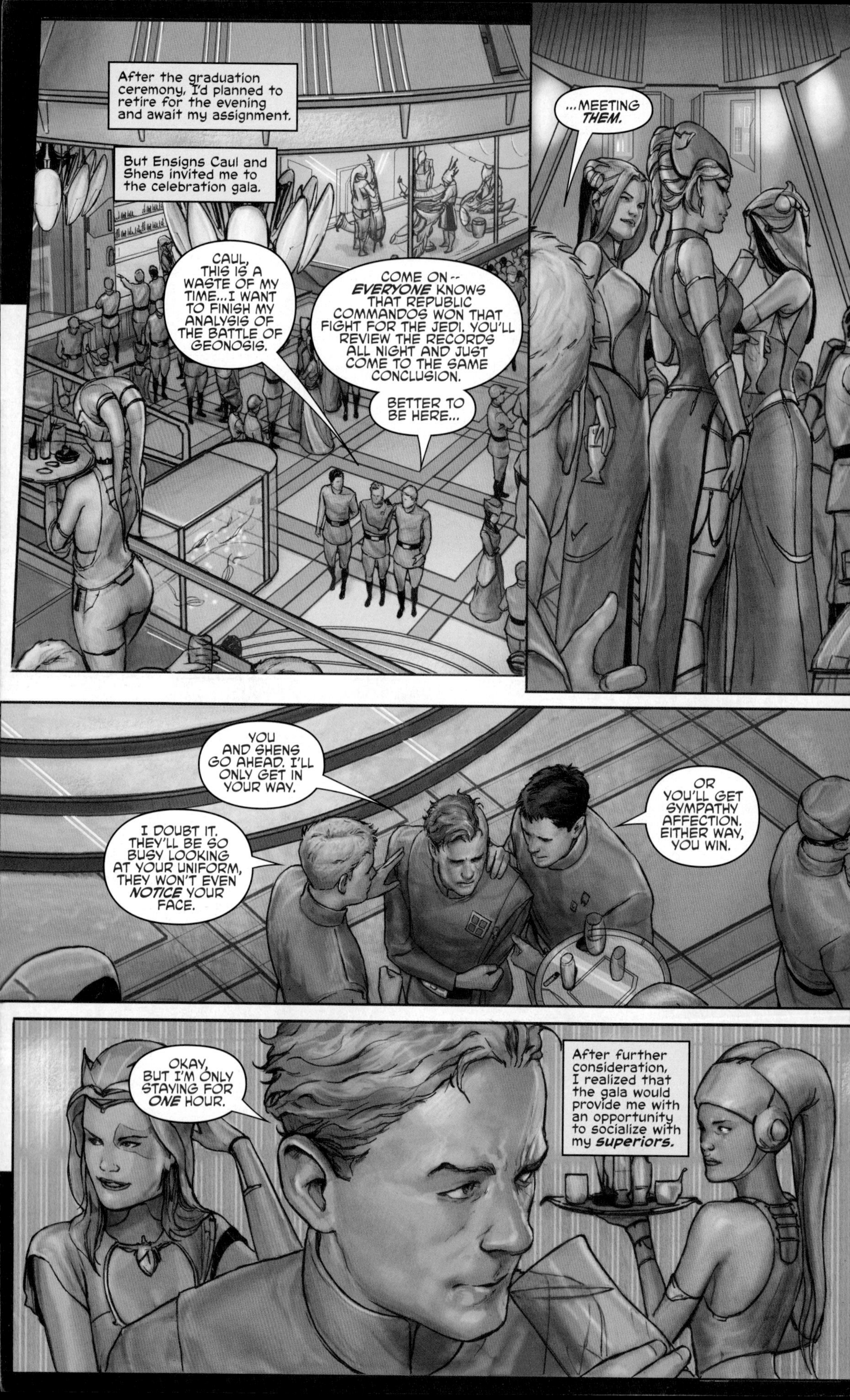

After the graduation ceremony, I'd planned to retire for the evening and await my assignment.
But Ensigns Caul and Shens invited me to the celebration gala.
CAUL, THIS IS A WASTE OF MY TIME...I WANT TO FINISH MY ANALYSIS OF THE BATTLE OF GEONOSIS.
COME ON -- ***EVERYONE*** KNOWS THAT REPUBLIC COMMANDOS WON THAT FIGHT FOR THE JEDI. YOU'LL REVIEW THE RECORDS ALL NIGHT AND JUST COME TO THE SAME CONCLUSION.
BETTER TO BE HERE...
...MEETING ***THEM.***
YOU AND SHENS GO AHEAD. I'LL ONLY GET IN YOUR WAY.
I DOUBT IT. THEY'LL BE SO BUSY LOOKING AT YOUR UNIFORM, THEY WON'T EVEN ***NOTICE*** YOUR FACE.
OR YOU'LL GET SYMPATHY AFFECTION. EITHER WAY, YOU WIN.
OKAY, BUT I'M ONLY STAYING FOR ***ONE*** HOUR.
After further consideration, I realized that the gala would provide me with an opportunity to socialize with my ***superiors.***

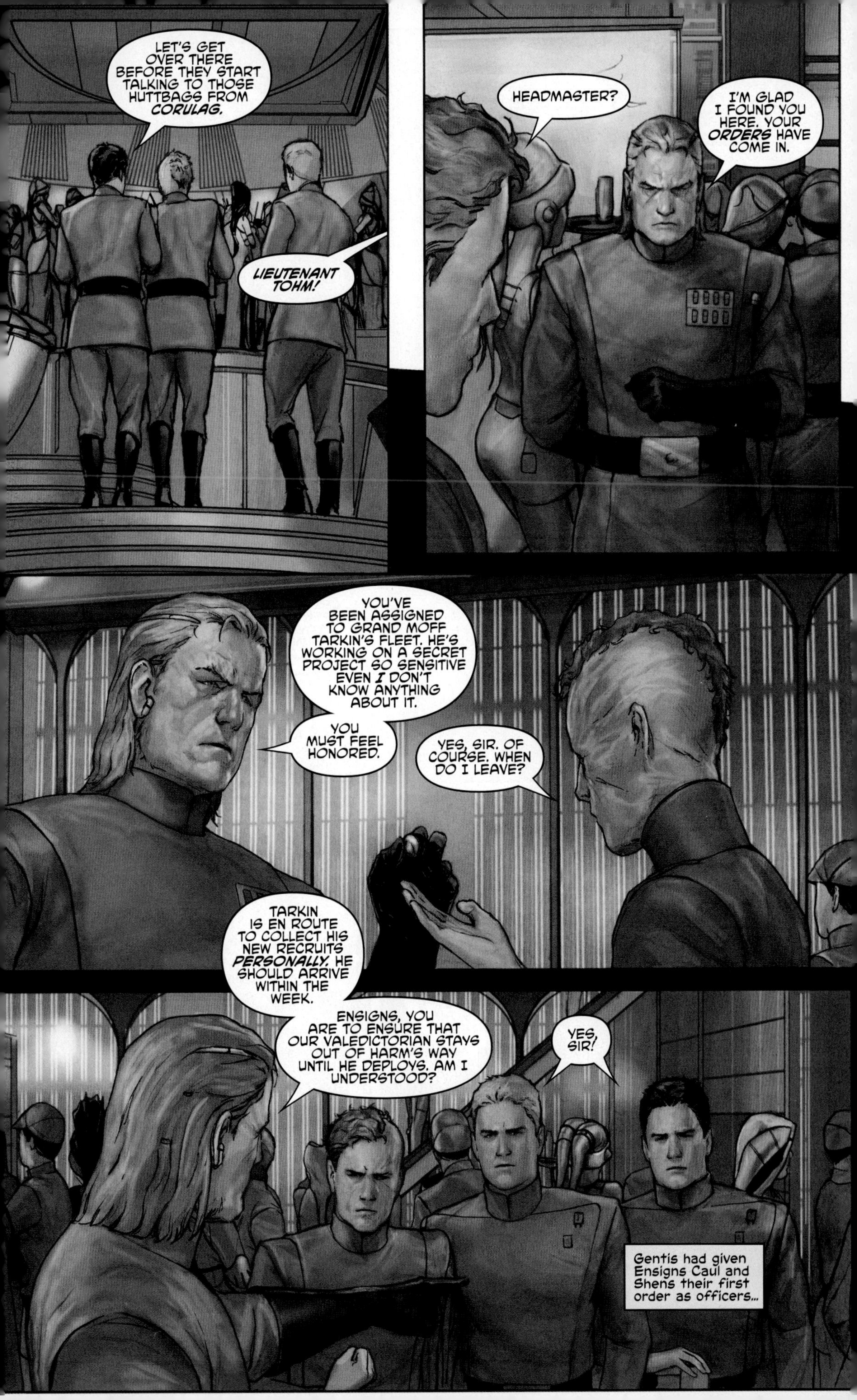
LET'S GET OVER THERE BEFORE THEY START TALKING TO THOSE HUTTBAGS FROM CORULAG.
LIEUTENANT TOHM!
HEADMASTER?
I'M GLAD I FOUND YOU HERE. YOUR ORDERS HAVE COME IN.
YOU'VE BEEN ASSIGNED TO GRAND MOFF TARKIN'S FLEET. HE'S WORKING ON A SECRET PROJECT SO SENSITIVE EVEN I DON'T KNOW ANYTHING ABOUT IT.
YOU MUST FEEL HONORED.
YES, SIR. OF COURSE. WHEN DO I LEAVE?
TARKIN IS EN ROUTE TO COLLECT HIS NEW RECRUITS PERSONALLY. HE SHOULD ARRIVE WITHIN THE WEEK.
ENSIGNS, YOU ARE TO ENSURE THAT OUR VALEDICTORIAN STAYS OUT OF HARM'S WAY UNTIL HE DEPLOYS. AM I UNDERSTOOD?
YES, SIR!
Gentis had given Ensigns Caul and Shens their first order as officers...

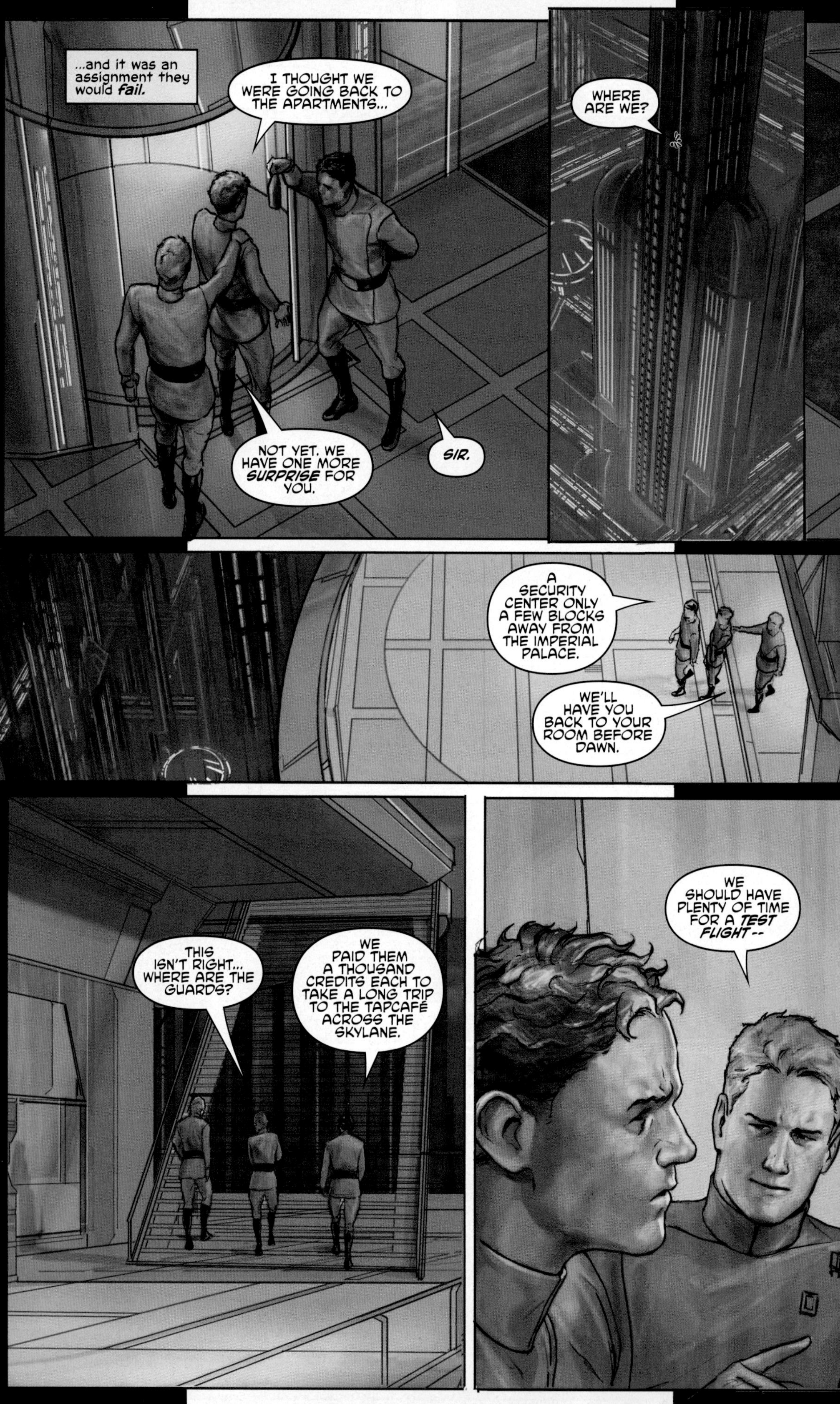
...and it was an assignment they would *fail.*
I THOUGHT WE WERE GOING BACK TO THE APARTMENTS...
NOT YET. WE HAVE ONE MORE *SURPRISE* FOR YOU.
*SIR.*
WHERE ARE WE?
A SECURITY CENTER ONLY A FEW BLOCKS AWAY FROM THE IMPERIAL PALACE.
WE'LL HAVE YOU BACK TO YOUR ROOM BEFORE DAWN.
THIS ISN'T RIGHT... WHERE ARE THE GUARDS?
WE PAID THEM A THOUSAND CREDITS EACH TO TAKE A LONG TRIP TO THE TAPCAFÉ ACROSS THE SKYLANE.
WE SHOULD HAVE PLENTY OF TIME FOR A *TEST FLIGHT* --

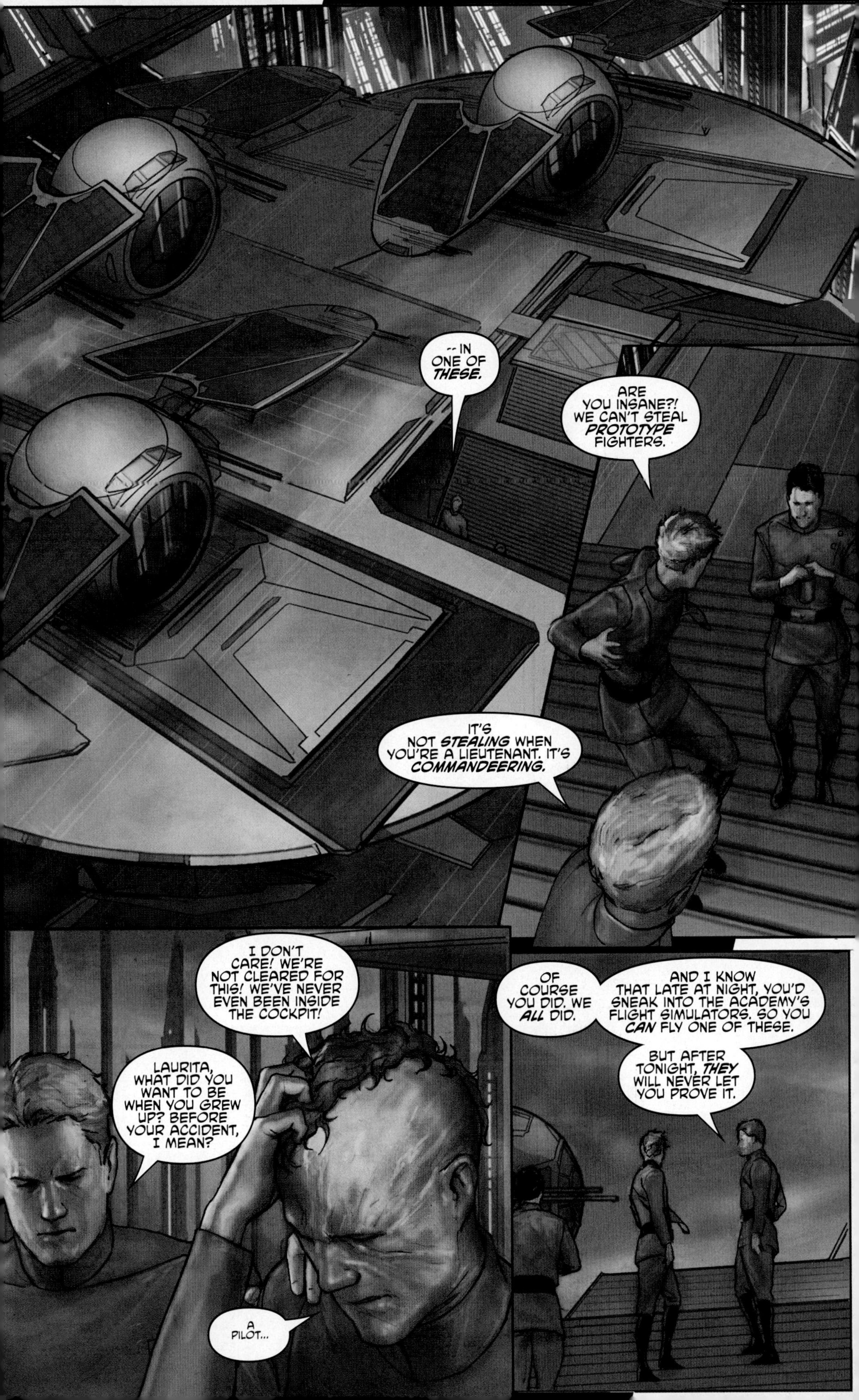
-- IN ONE OF *THESE.*
ARE YOU INSANE?! WE CAN'T STEAL *PROTOTYPE* FIGHTERS.
IT'S NOT *STEALING* WHEN YOU'RE A LIEUTENANT. IT'S *COMMANDEERING.*
I DON'T CARE! WE'RE NOT CLEARED FOR THIS! WE'VE NEVER EVEN BEEN INSIDE THE COCKPIT!
LAURITA, WHAT DID YOU WANT TO BE WHEN YOU GREW UP? BEFORE YOUR ACCIDENT, I MEAN?
A PILOT...
OF COURSE YOU DID. WE *ALL* DID.
AND I KNOW THAT LATE AT NIGHT, YOU'D SNEAK INTO THE ACADEMY'S FLIGHT SIMULATORS. SO YOU *CAN* FLY ONE OF THESE.
BUT AFTER TONIGHT, *THEY* WILL NEVER LET YOU PROVE IT.

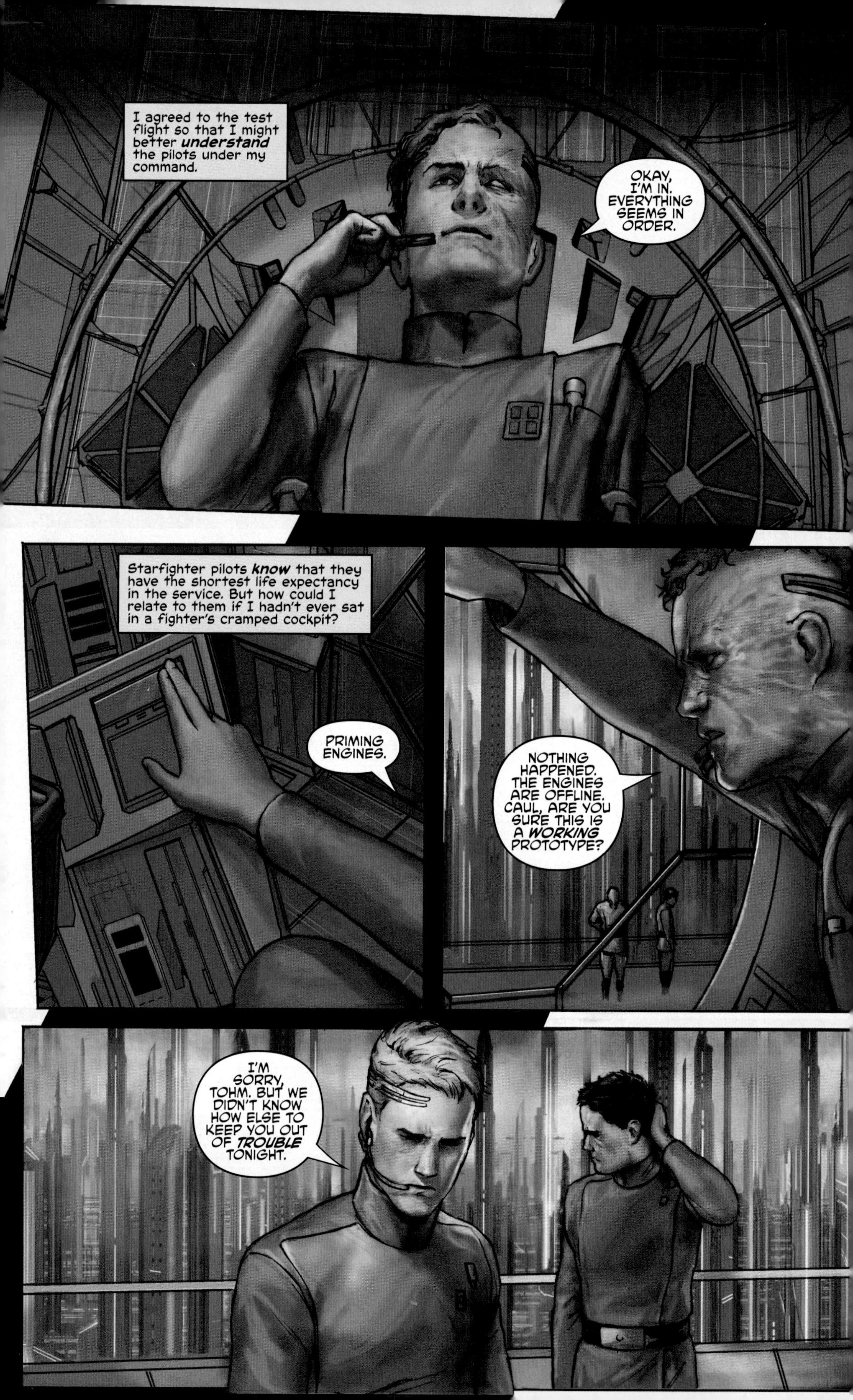

I agreed to the test flight so that I might better ***understand*** the pilots under my command.
OKAY, I'M IN. EVERYTHING SEEMS IN ORDER.
Starfighter pilots ***know*** that they have the shortest life expectancy in the service. But how could I relate to them if I hadn't ever sat in a fighter's cramped cockpit?
PRIMING ENGINES.
NOTHING HAPPENED. THE ENGINES ARE OFFLINE. CAUL, ARE YOU SURE THIS IS A ***WORKING*** PROTOTYPE?
I'M SORRY, TOHM. BUT WE DIDN'T KNOW HOW ELSE TO KEEP YOU OUT OF ***TROUBLE*** TONIGHT.

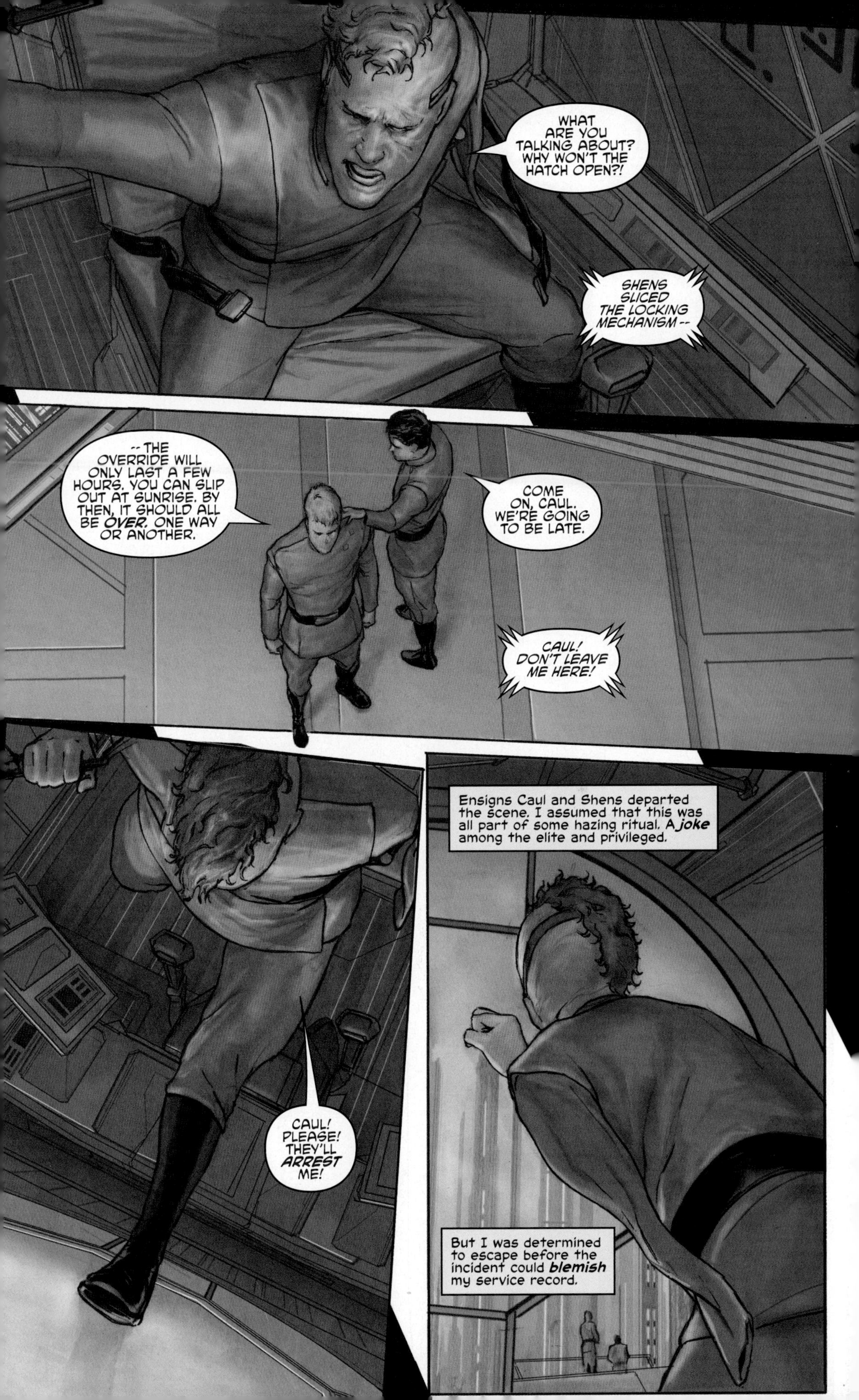
WHAT ARE YOU TALKING ABOUT? WHY WON'T THE HATCH OPEN?!
SHENS SLICED THE LOCKING MECHANISM --
-- THE OVERRIDE WILL ONLY LAST A FEW HOURS. YOU CAN SLIP OUT AT SUNRISE. BY THEN, IT SHOULD ALL BE OVER. ONE WAY OR ANOTHER.
COME ON, CAUL. WE'RE GOING TO BE LATE.
CAUL! DON'T LEAVE ME HERE!
CAUL! PLEASE! THEY'LL ARREST ME!
Ensigns Caul and Shens departed the scene. I assumed that this was all part of some hazing ritual. A joke among the elite and privileged.
But I was determined to escape before the incident could blemish my service record.

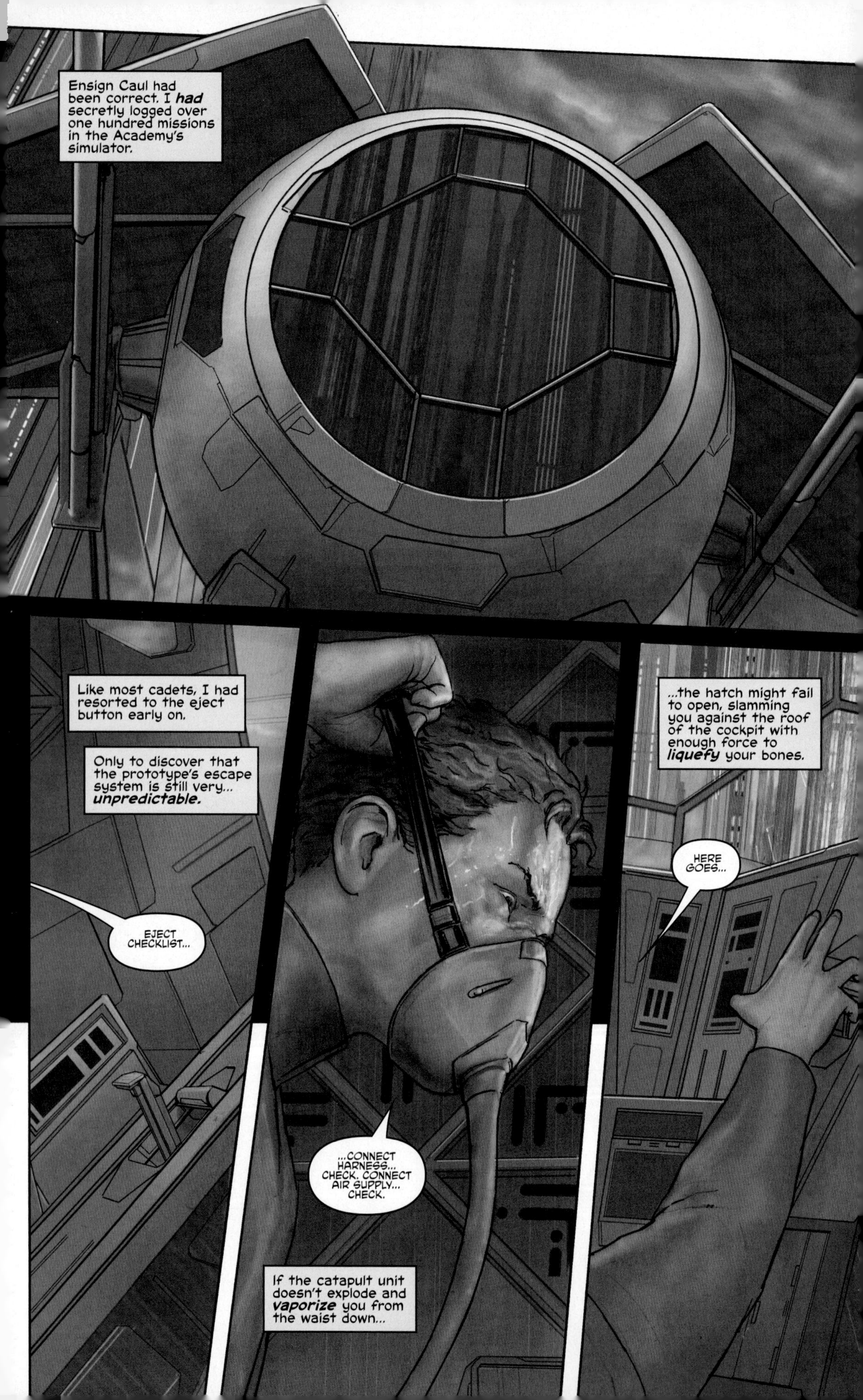
Ensign Caul had been correct. I ***had*** secretly logged over one hundred missions in the Academy's simulator.
Like most cadets, I had resorted to the eject button early on.
Only to discover that the prototype's escape system is still very... ***unpredictable.***
EJECT CHECKLIST...
...CONNECT HARNESS... CHECK. CONNECT AIR SUPPLY... CHECK.
If the catapult unit doesn't explode and ***vaporize*** you from the waist down...
...the hatch might fail to open, slamming you against the roof of the cockpit with enough force to ***liquefy*** your bones.
HERE GOES...

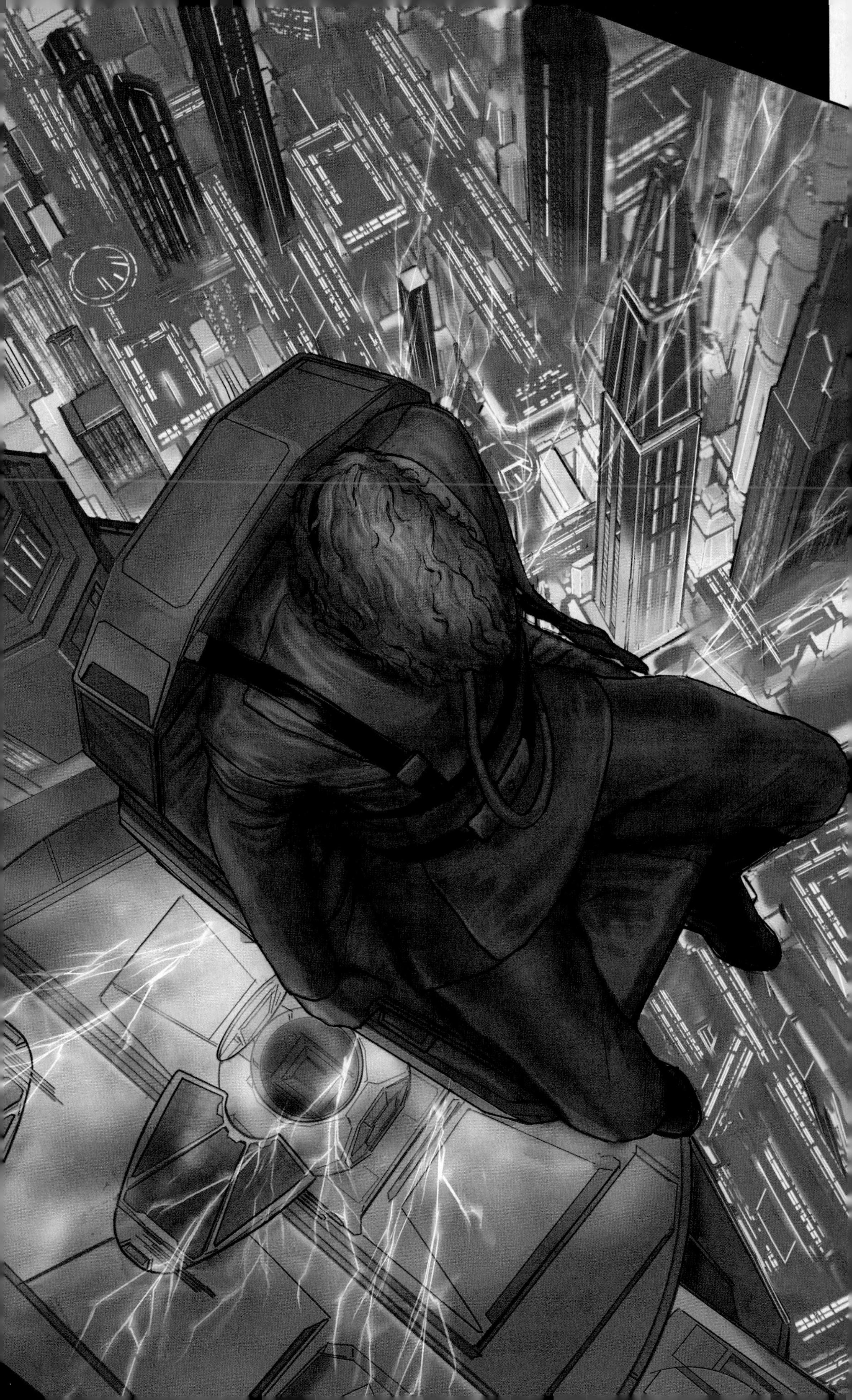

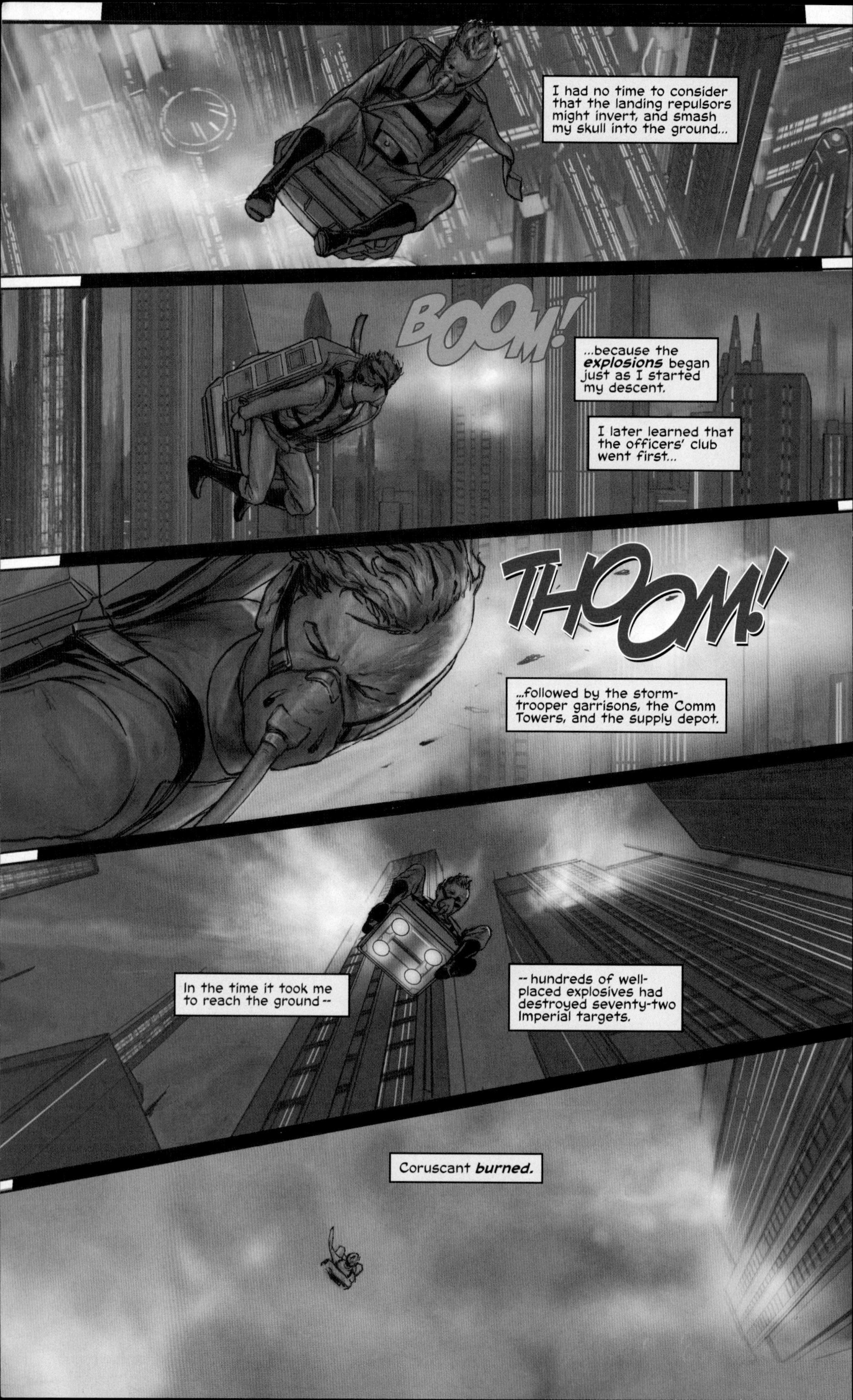
I had no time to consider that the landing repulsors might invert, and smash my skull into the ground...
BOOM!
...because the *explosions* began just as I started my descent.
I later learned that the officers' club went first...
THOOM!
...followed by the storm-trooper garrisons, the Comm Towers, and the supply depot.
In the time it took me to reach the ground --
-- hundreds of well-placed explosives had destroyed seventy-two Imperial targets.
Coruscant *burned.*

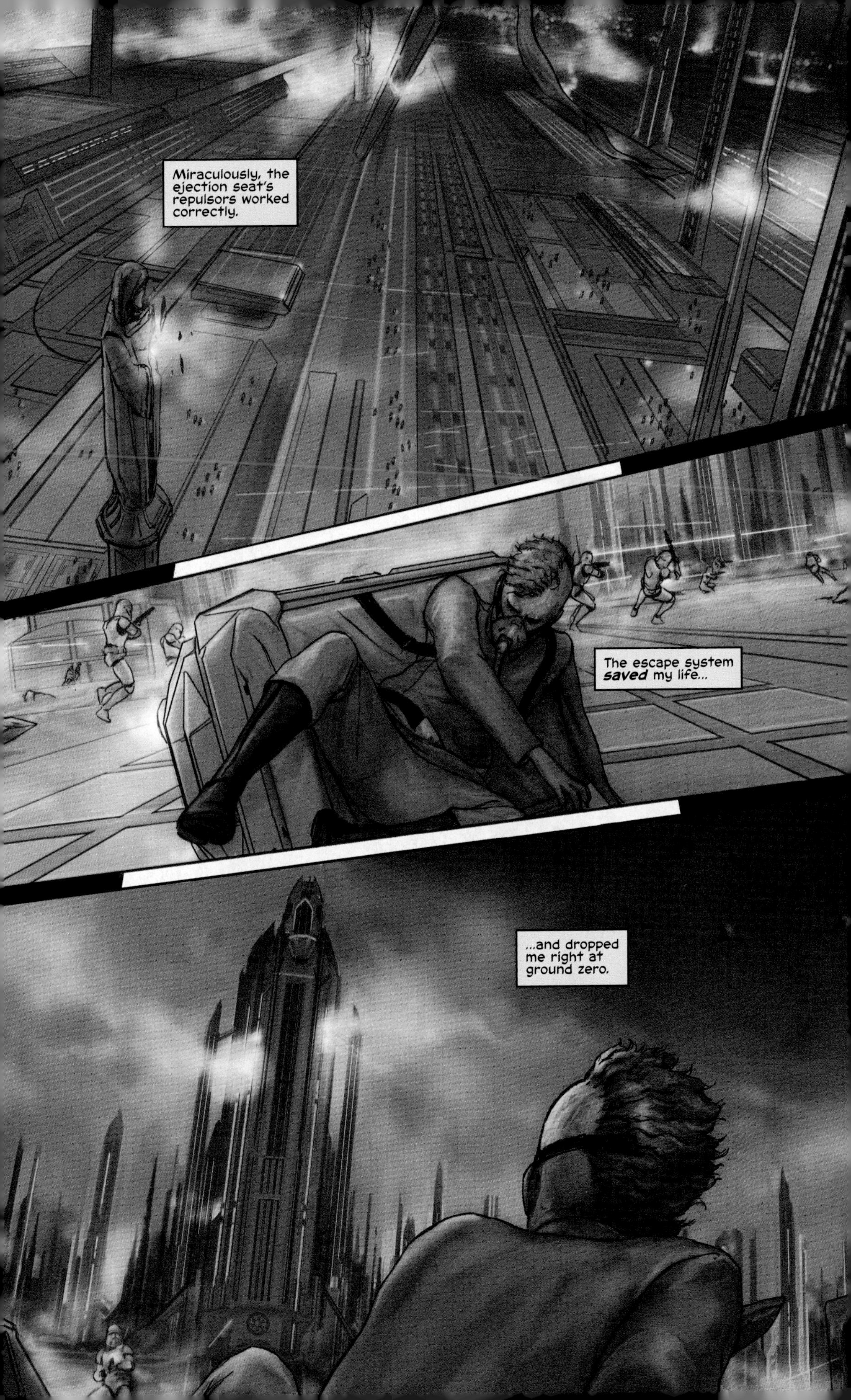
Miraculously, the ejection seat's repulsors worked correctly.
The escape system saved my life...
...and dropped me right at ground zero.

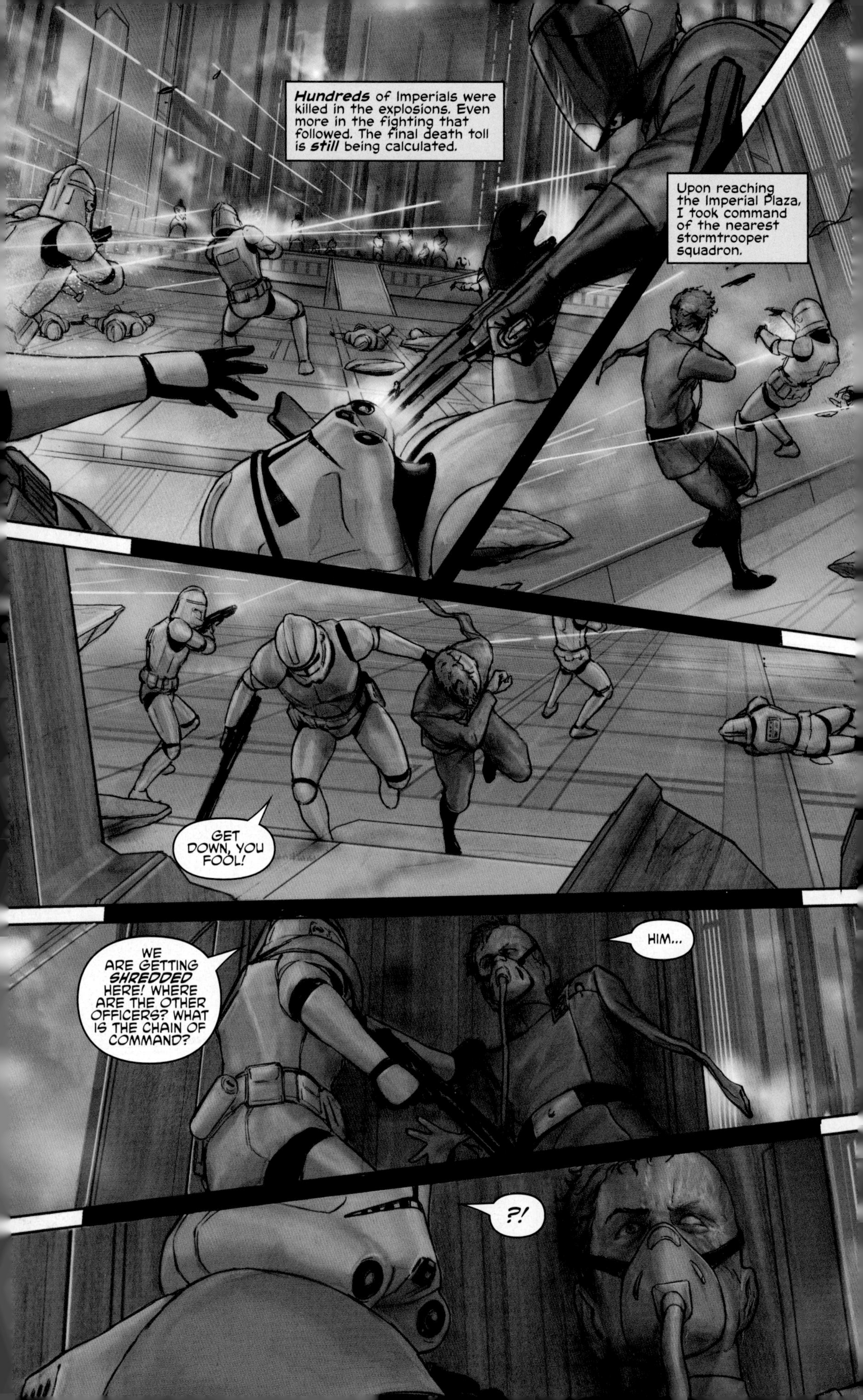
Hundreds of Imperials were killed in the explosions. Even more in the fighting that followed. The final death toll is still being calculated.
Upon reaching the Imperial Plaza, I took command of the nearest stormtrooper squadron.
GET DOWN, YOU FOOL!
WE ARE GETTING SHREDDED HERE! WHERE ARE THE OTHER OFFICERS? WHAT IS THE CHAIN OF COMMAND?
HIM...
?!

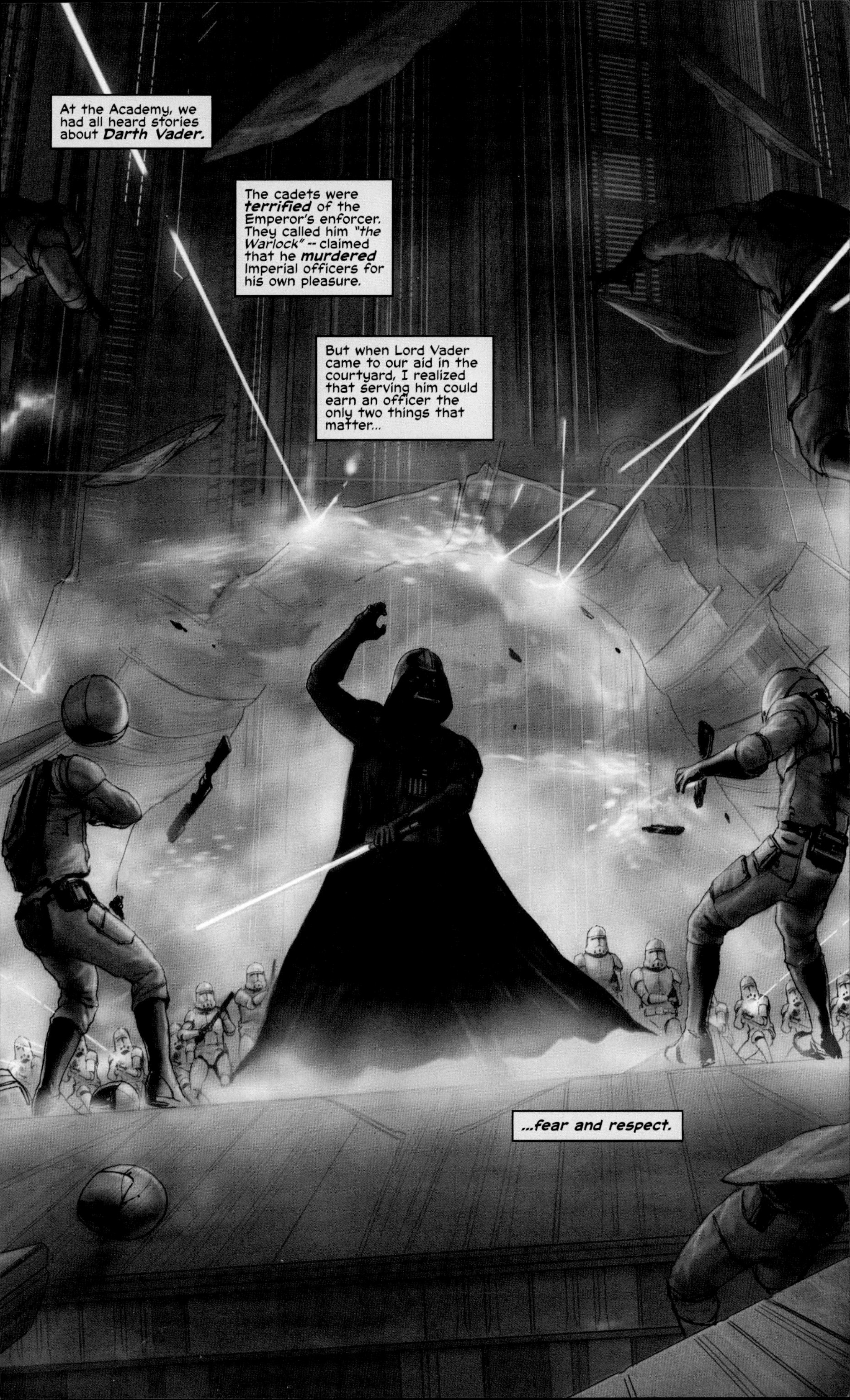
At the Academy, we had all heard stories about *Darth Vader.*
The cadets were ***terrified*** of the Emperor's enforcer. They called him *"the Warlock"* -- claimed that he ***murdered*** Imperial officers for his own pleasure.
But when Lord Vader came to our aid in the courtyard, I realized that serving him could earn an officer the only two things that matter...
*...fear and respect.*

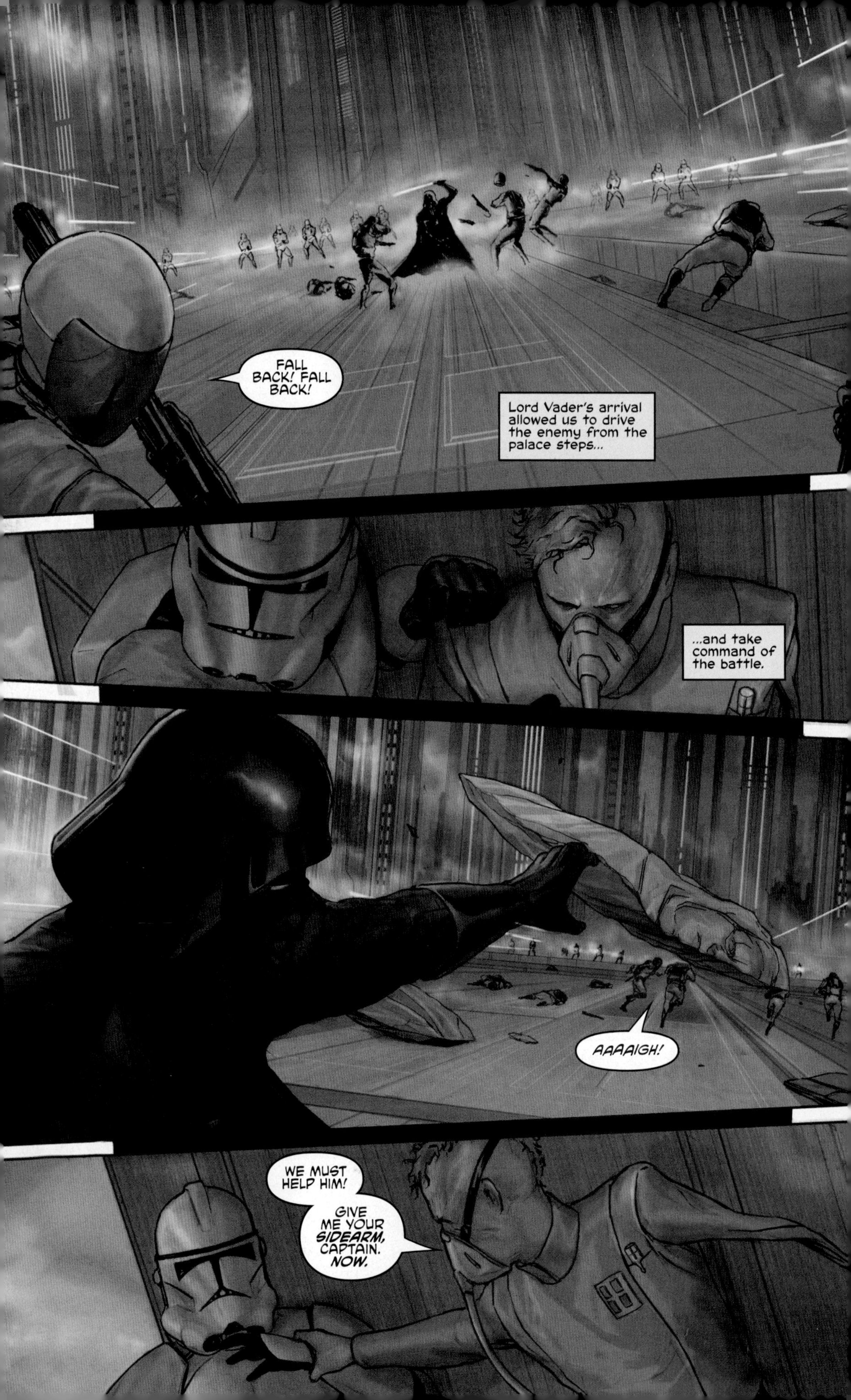
FALL BACK! FALL BACK!
Lord Vader's arrival allowed us to drive the enemy from the palace steps...
...and take command of the battle.
AAAAIGH!
WE MUST HELP HIM!
GIVE ME YOUR SIDEARM, CAPTAIN. NOW.

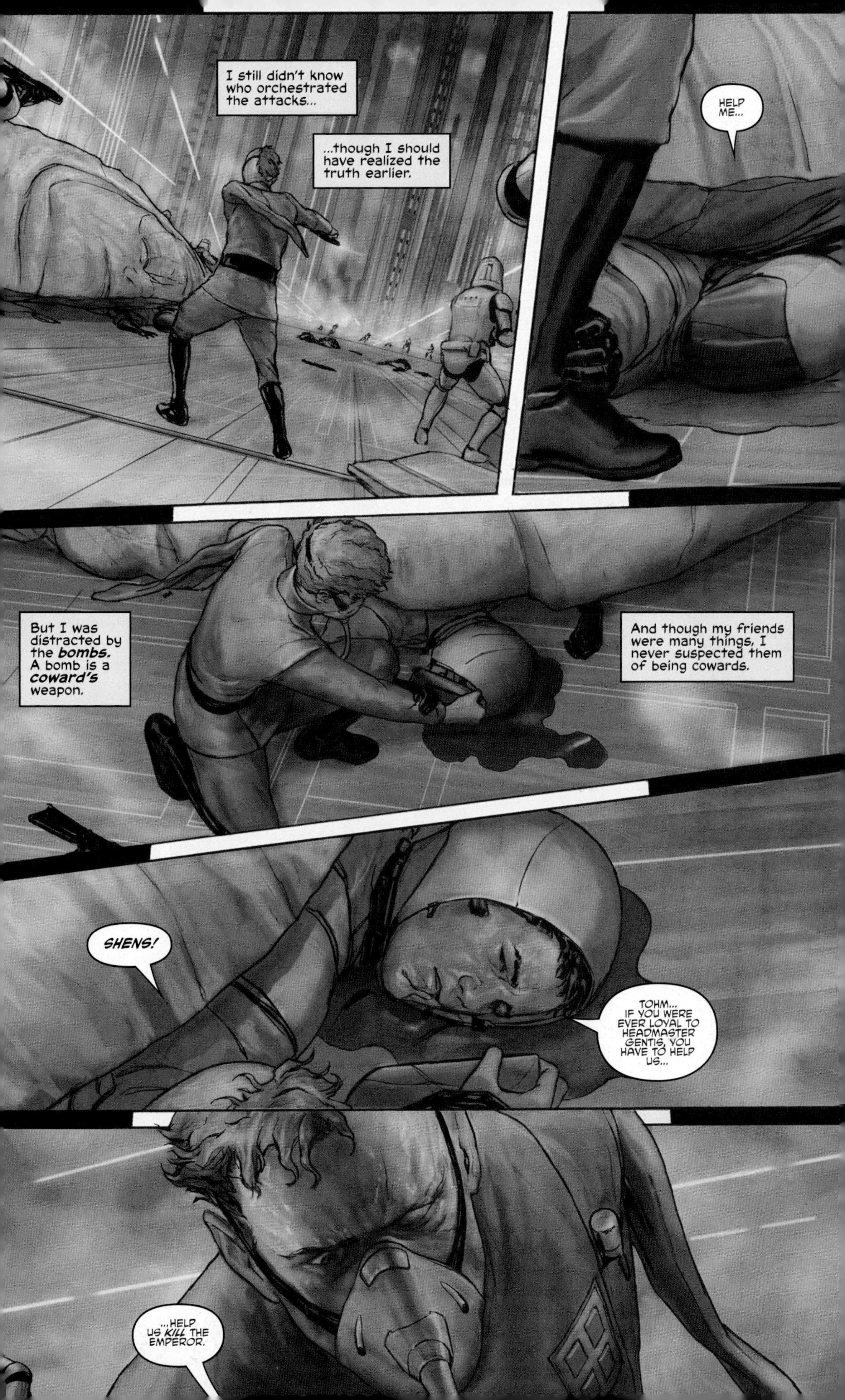

I still didn't know who orchestrated the attacks...
...though I should have realized the truth earlier.
HELP ME...
But I was distracted by the *bombs.* A bomb is a *coward's* weapon.
And though my friends were many things, I never suspected them of being cowards.
*SHENS!*
TOHM... IF YOU WERE EVER LOYAL TO HEADMASTER GENTIS, YOU HAVE TO HELP US...
...HELP US *KILL* THE EMPEROR.

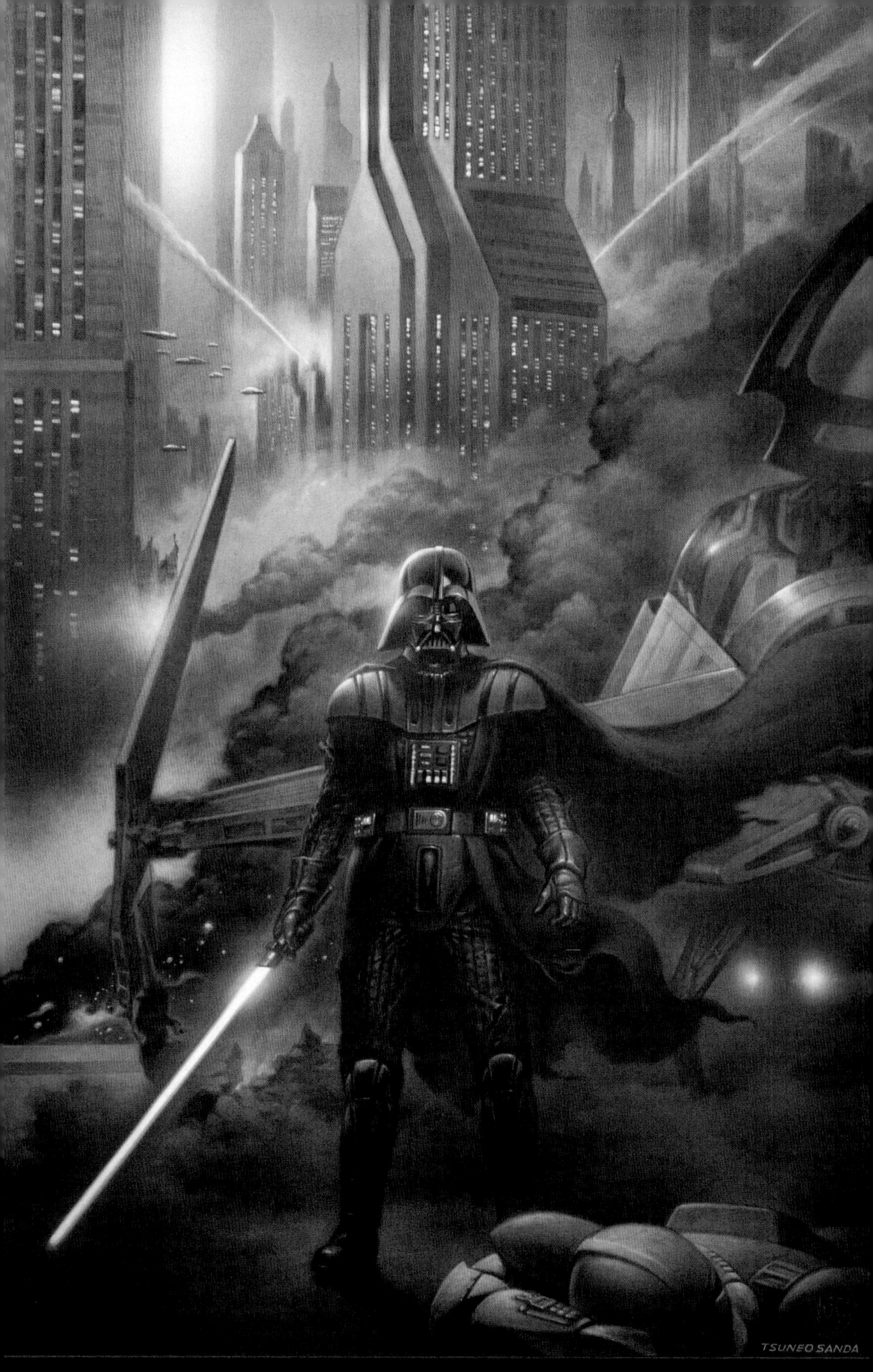
TSUNEO SANDA

STAR WARS: DARTH VADER AND THE GHOST PRISON # [illegible] COVER ART [illegible] NEO SANDA

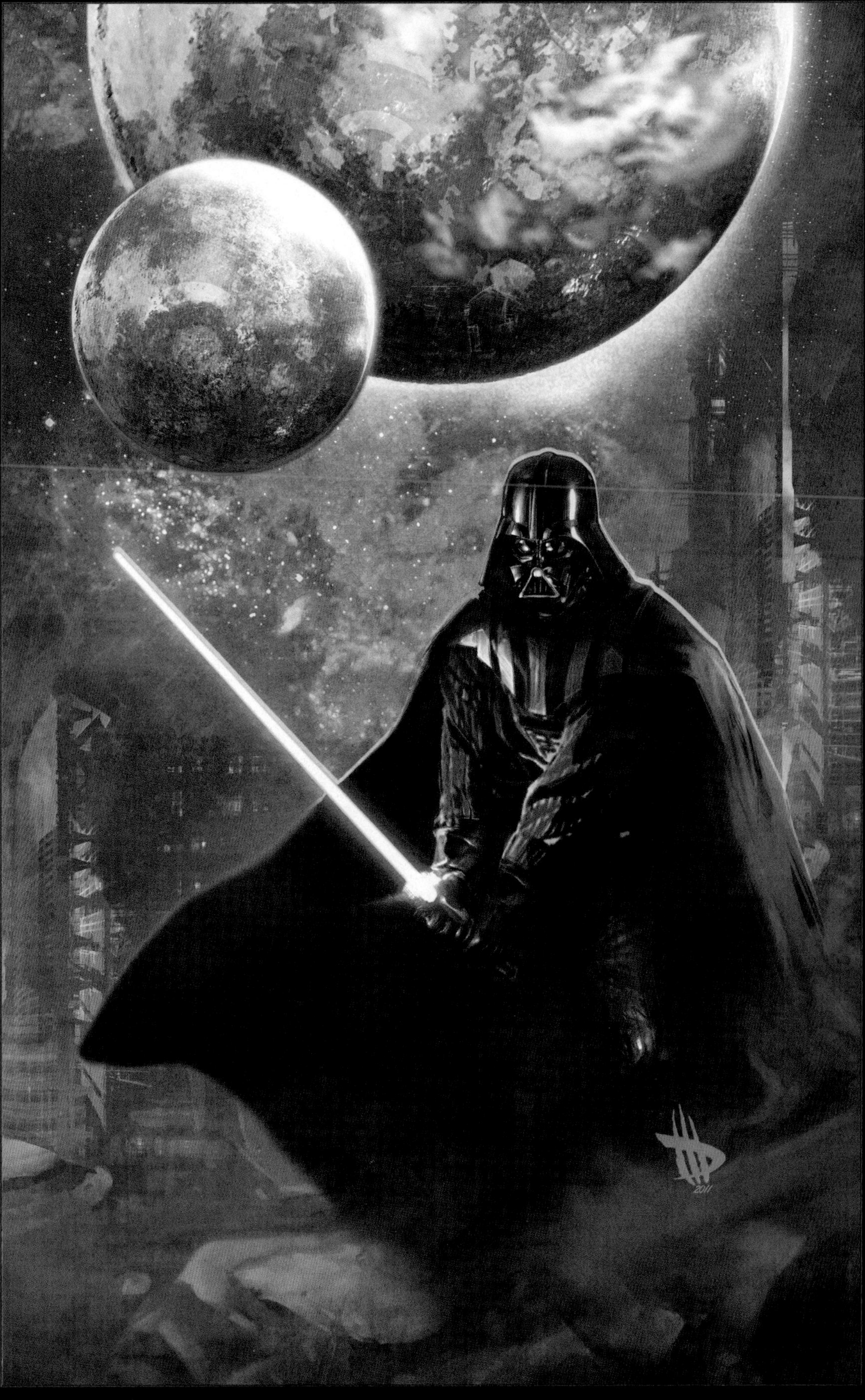

**STAR WARS: DARTH VADER AND THE GHOST PRISON #2**

WRITER: HADEN BLACKMAN • ARTIST & COLORIST: AGUSTIN ALESSIO • LETTERER: MICHAEL HEISLER
ASSISTANT EDITOR: FREDDYE LINS • EDITOR: RANDY STRADLEY • COVER ARTIST: DAVE WILKINS

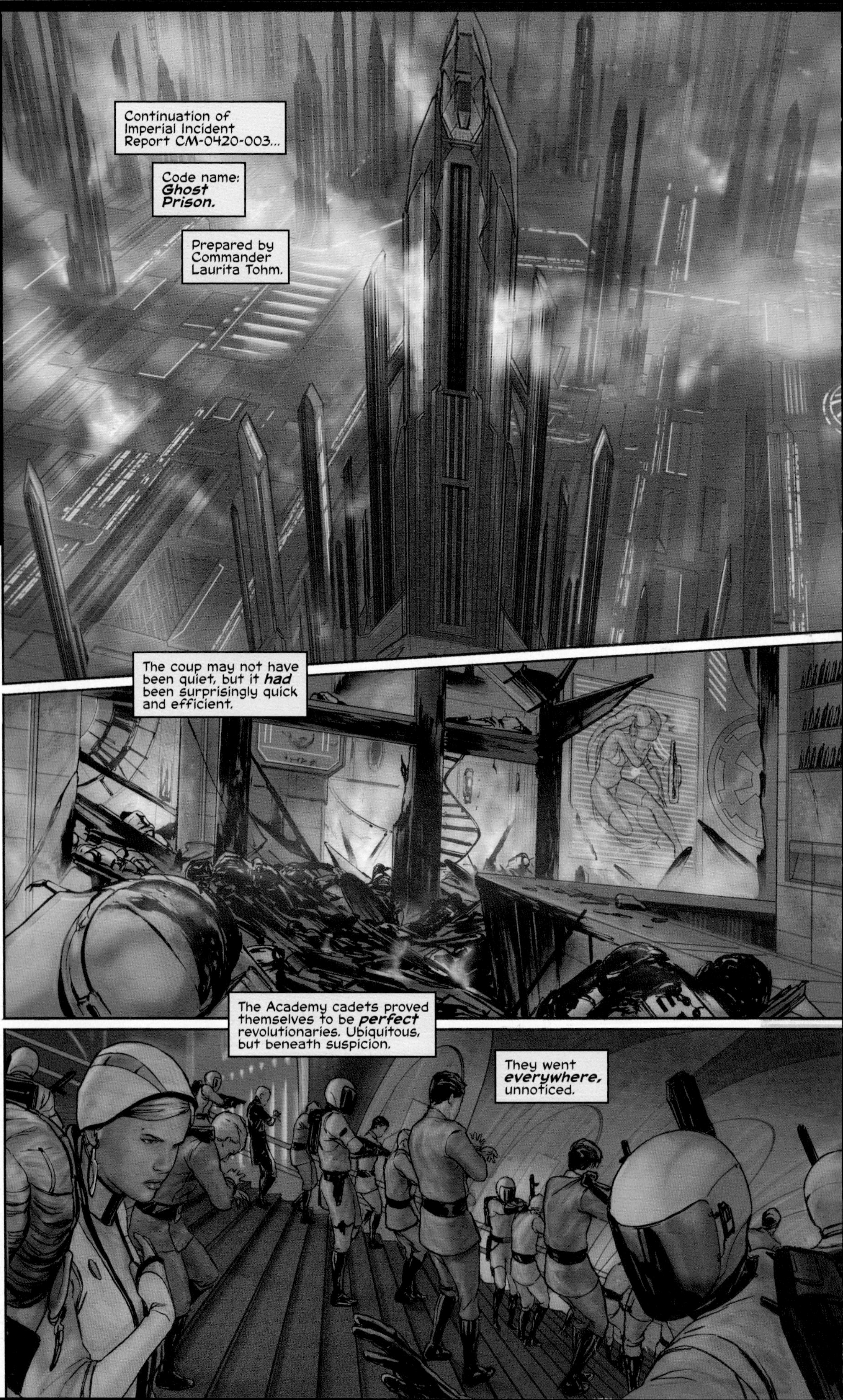
Continuation of Imperial Incident Report CM-0420-003...
Code name: *Ghost Prison.*
Prepared by Commander Laurita Tohm.
The coup may not have been quiet, but it *had* been surprisingly quick and efficient.
The Academy cadets proved themselves to be *perfect* revolutionaries. Ubiquitous, but beneath suspicion.
They went *everywhere,* unnoticed.

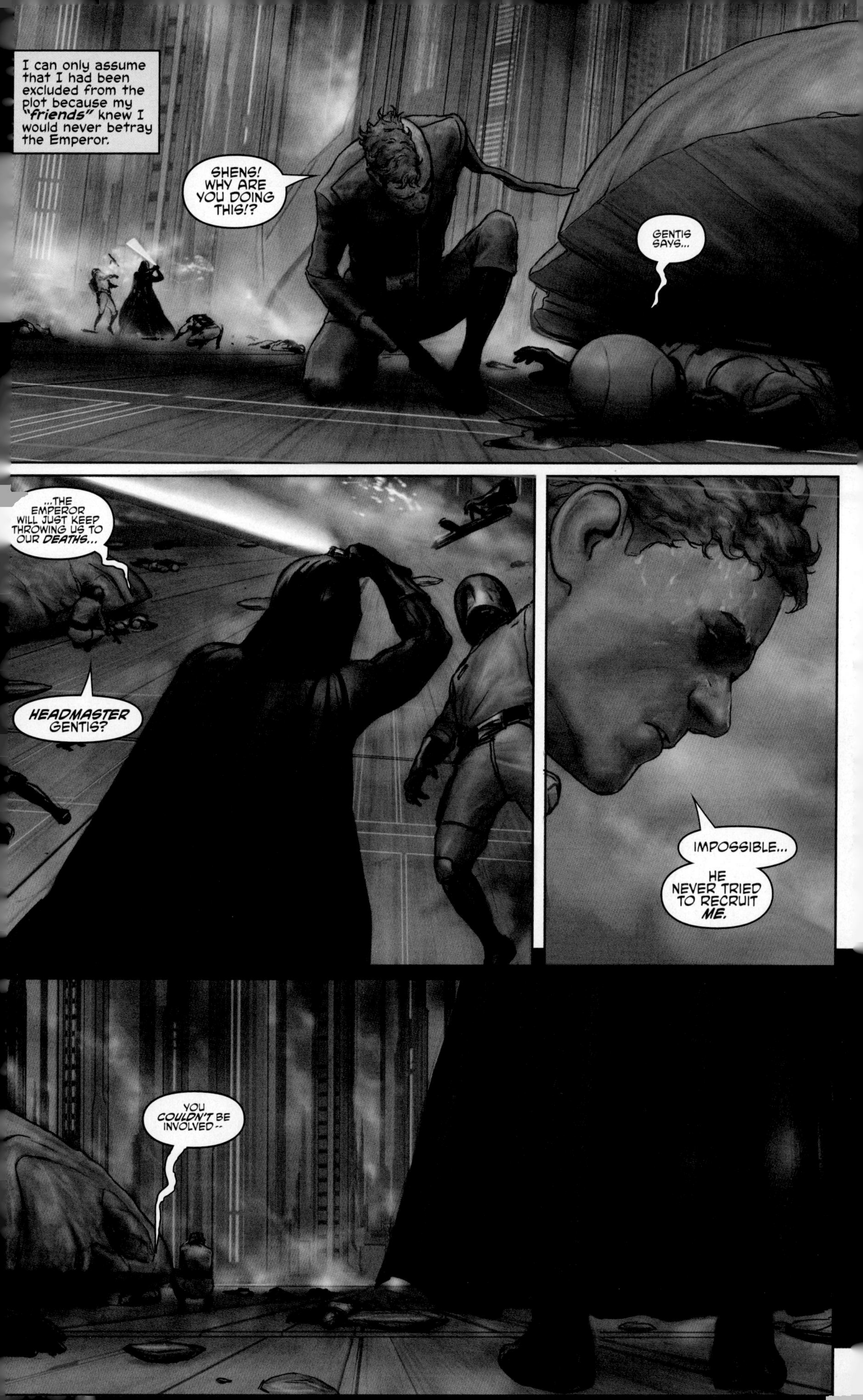
I can only assume that I had been excluded from the plot because my "friends" knew I would never betray the Emperor.
SHENS! WHY ARE YOU DOING THIS!?
GENTIS SAYS...
...THE EMPEROR WILL JUST KEEP THROWING US TO OUR DEATHS...
HEADMASTER GENTIS?
IMPOSSIBLE...
HE NEVER TRIED TO RECRUIT ME.
YOU COULDN'T BE INVOLVED--

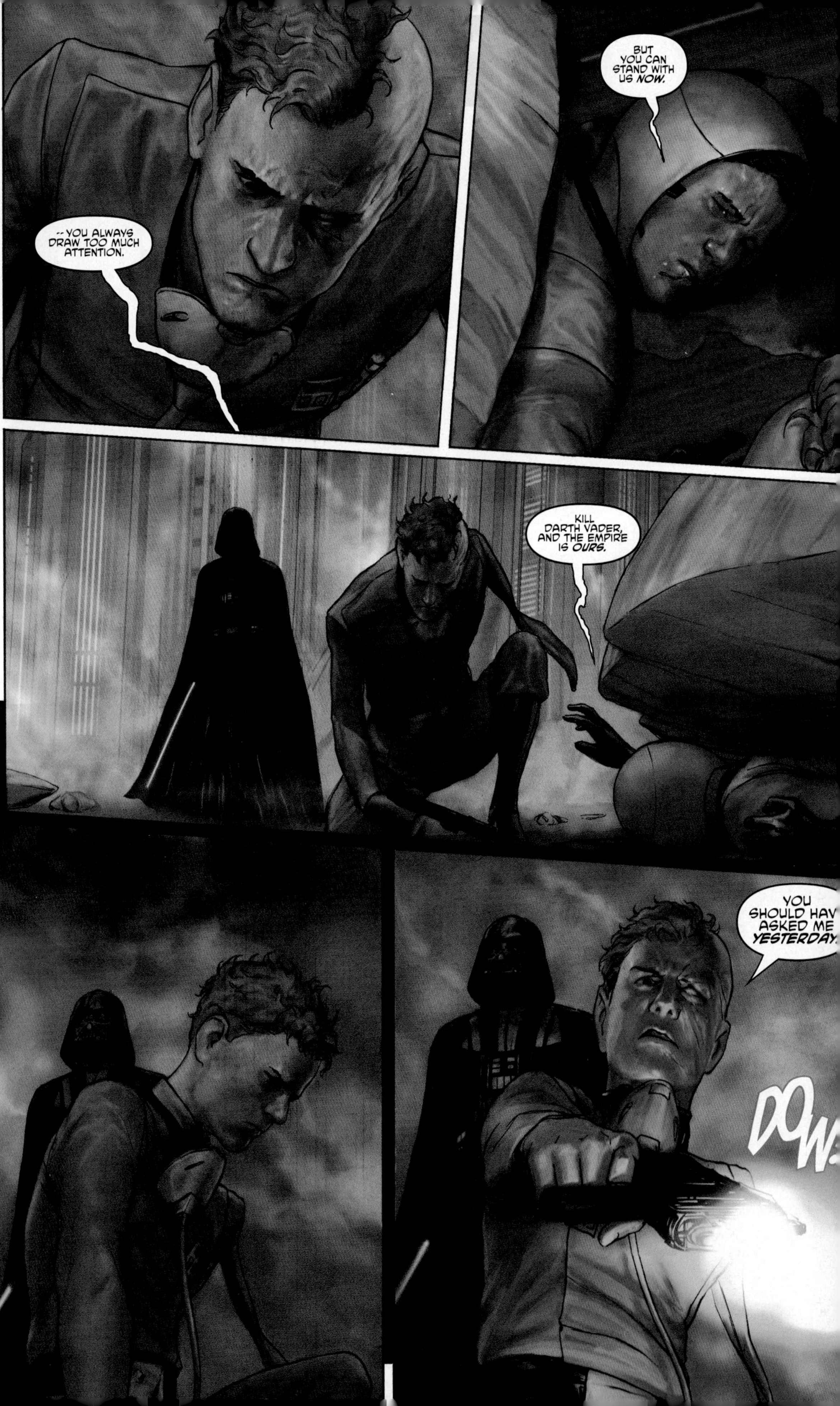
--YOU ALWAYS DRAW TOO MUCH ATTENTION.
BUT YOU CAN STAND WITH US NOW.
KILL DARTH VADER, AND THE EMPIRE IS OURS.
YOU SHOULD HAV ASKED ME YESTERDAY.

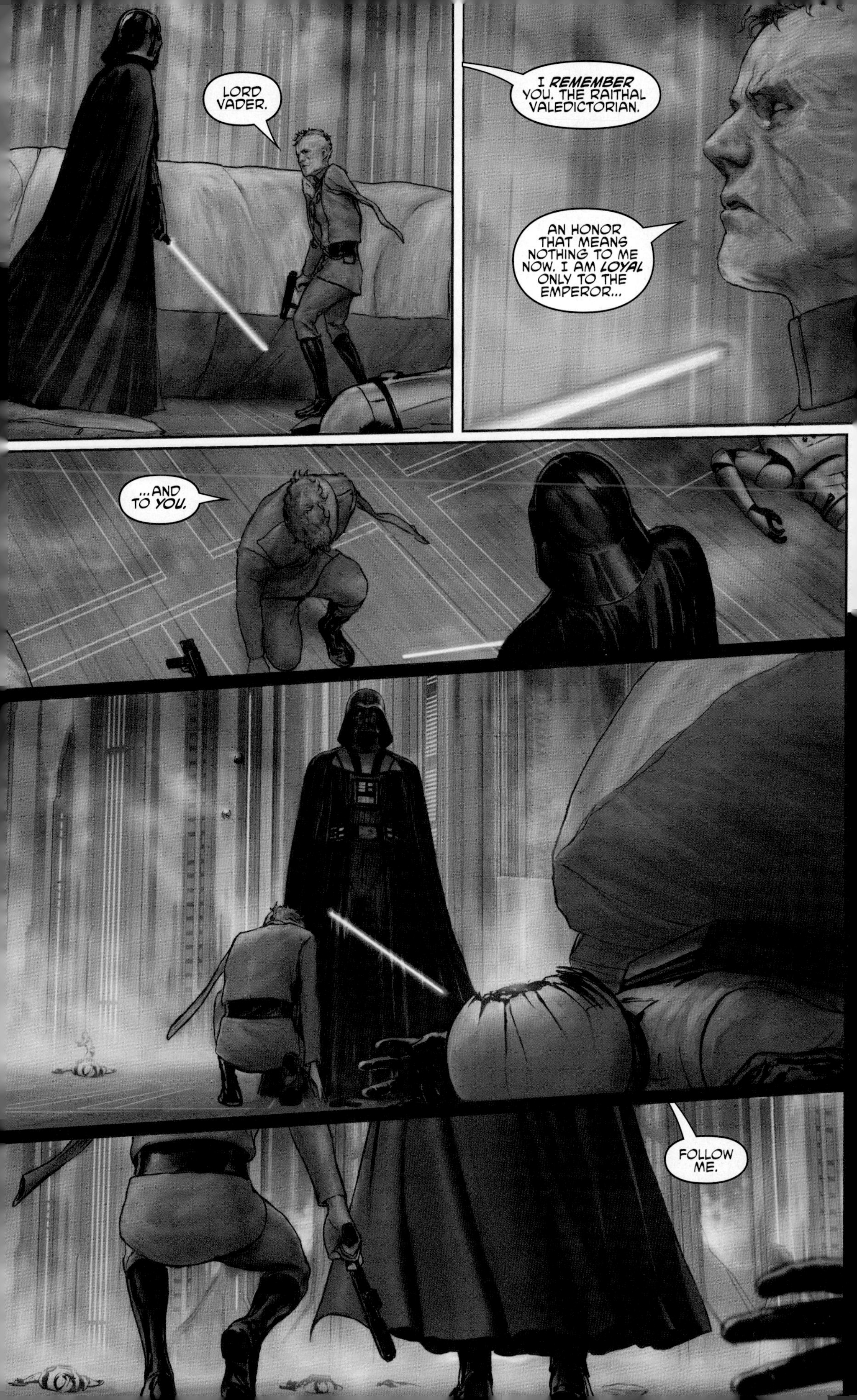
LORD VADER.
I *REMEMBER* YOU. THE RAITHAL VALEDICTORIAN.
AN HONOR THAT MEANS NOTHING TO ME NOW. I AM *LOYAL* ONLY TO THE EMPEROR...
...AND TO *YOU.*
FOLLOW ME.

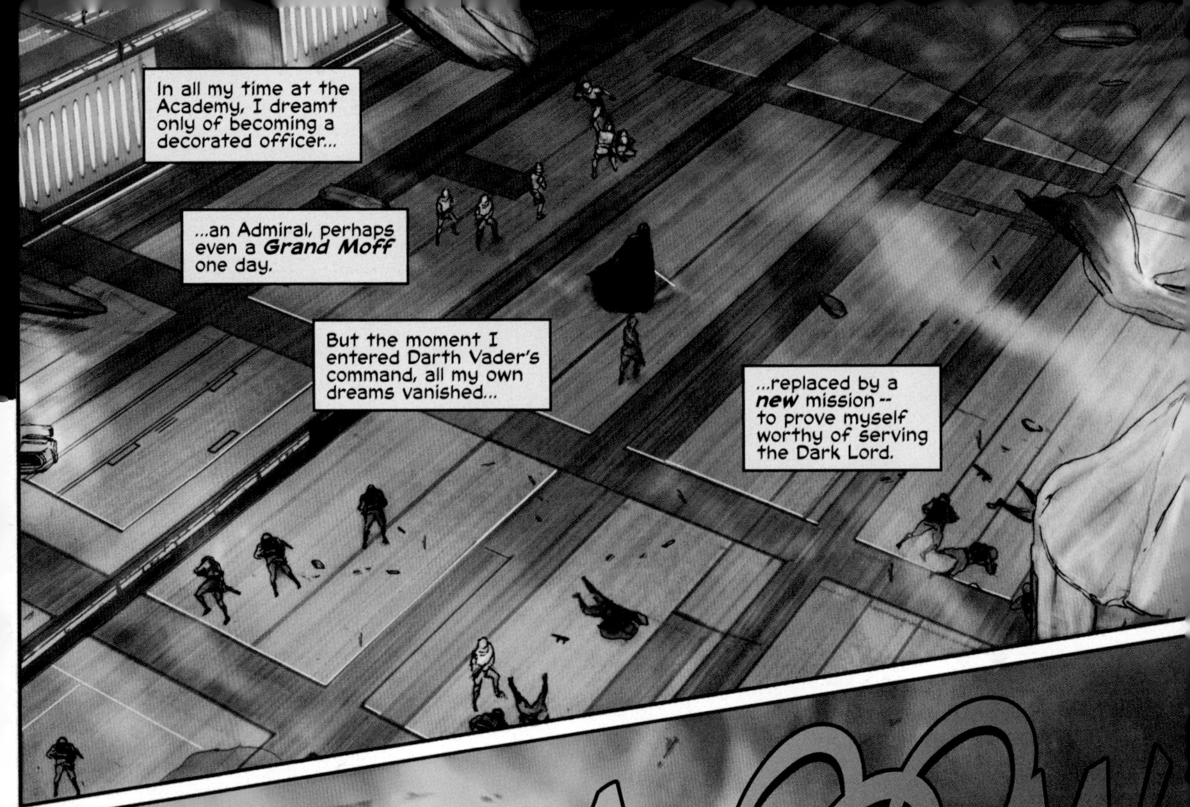
In all my time at the Academy, I dreamt only of becoming a decorated officer...
...an Admiral, perhaps even a Grand Moff one day.
But the moment I entered Darth Vader's command, all my own dreams vanished...
...replaced by a new mission -- to prove myself worthy of serving the Dark Lord.
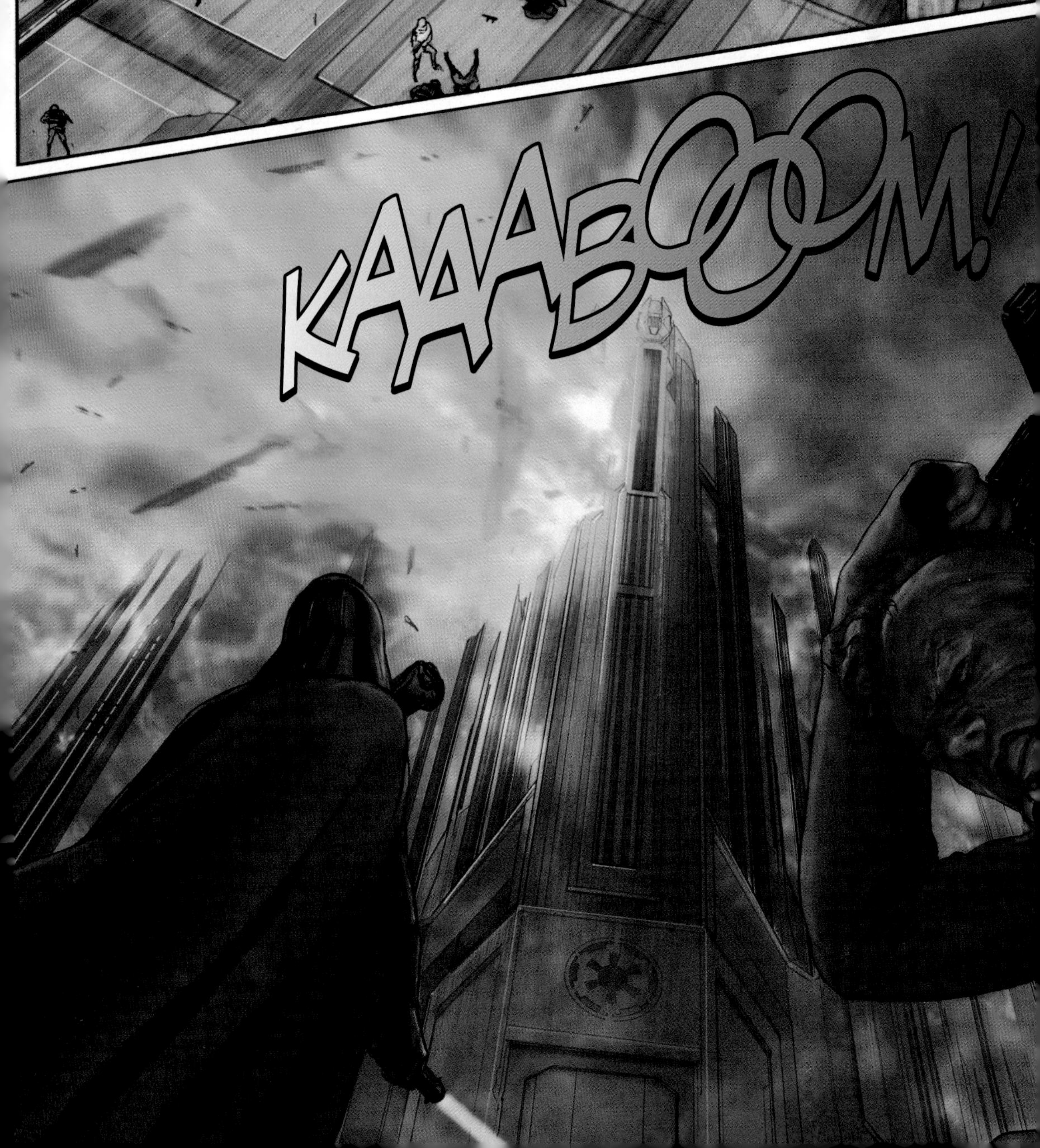
KAAABOOOM!

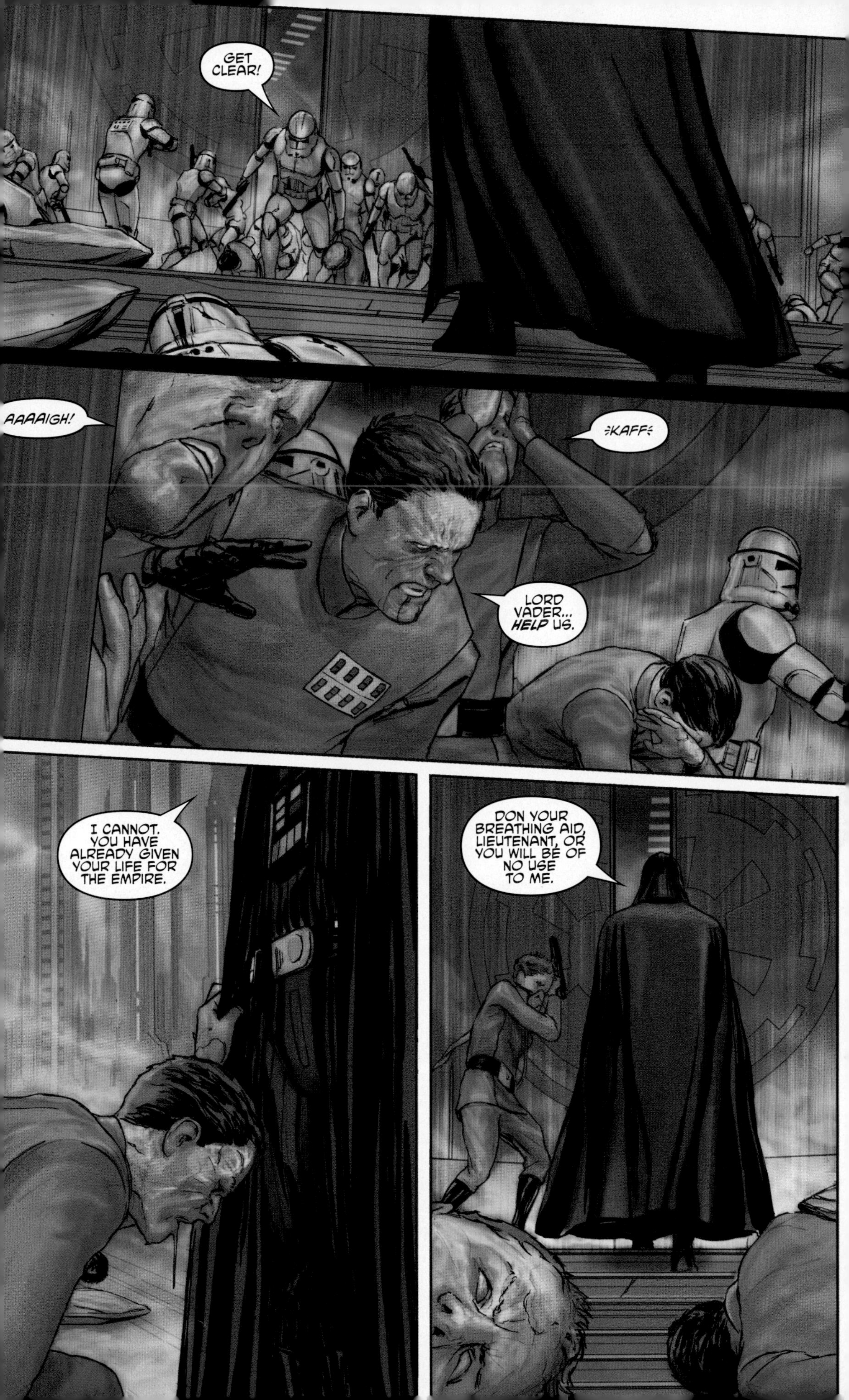
GET CLEAR!
AAAAIGH!
KAFF
LORD VADER... **HELP** US.
I CANNOT. YOU HAVE ALREADY GIVEN YOUR LIFE FOR THE EMPIRE.
DON YOUR BREATHING AID, LIEUTENANT, OR YOU WILL BE OF NO USE TO ME.

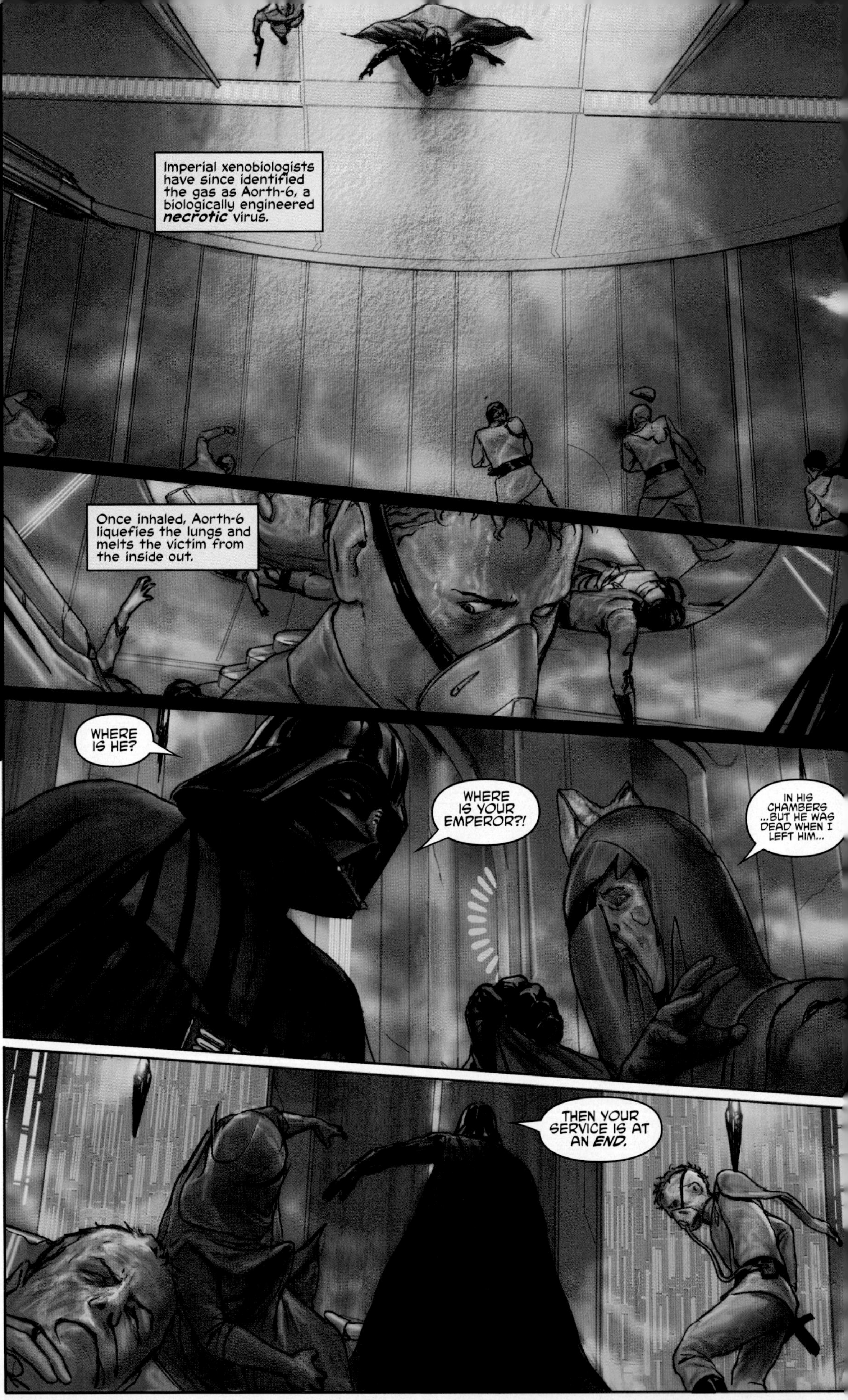

Imperial xenobiologists have since identified the gas as Aorth-6, a biologically engineered *necrotic* virus.
Once inhaled, Aorth-6 liquefies the lungs and melts the victim from the inside out.
WHERE IS HE?
WHERE IS YOUR EMPEROR?!
IN HIS CHAMBERS ...BUT HE WAS DEAD WHEN I LEFT HIM...
THEN YOUR SERVICE IS AT AN *END.*

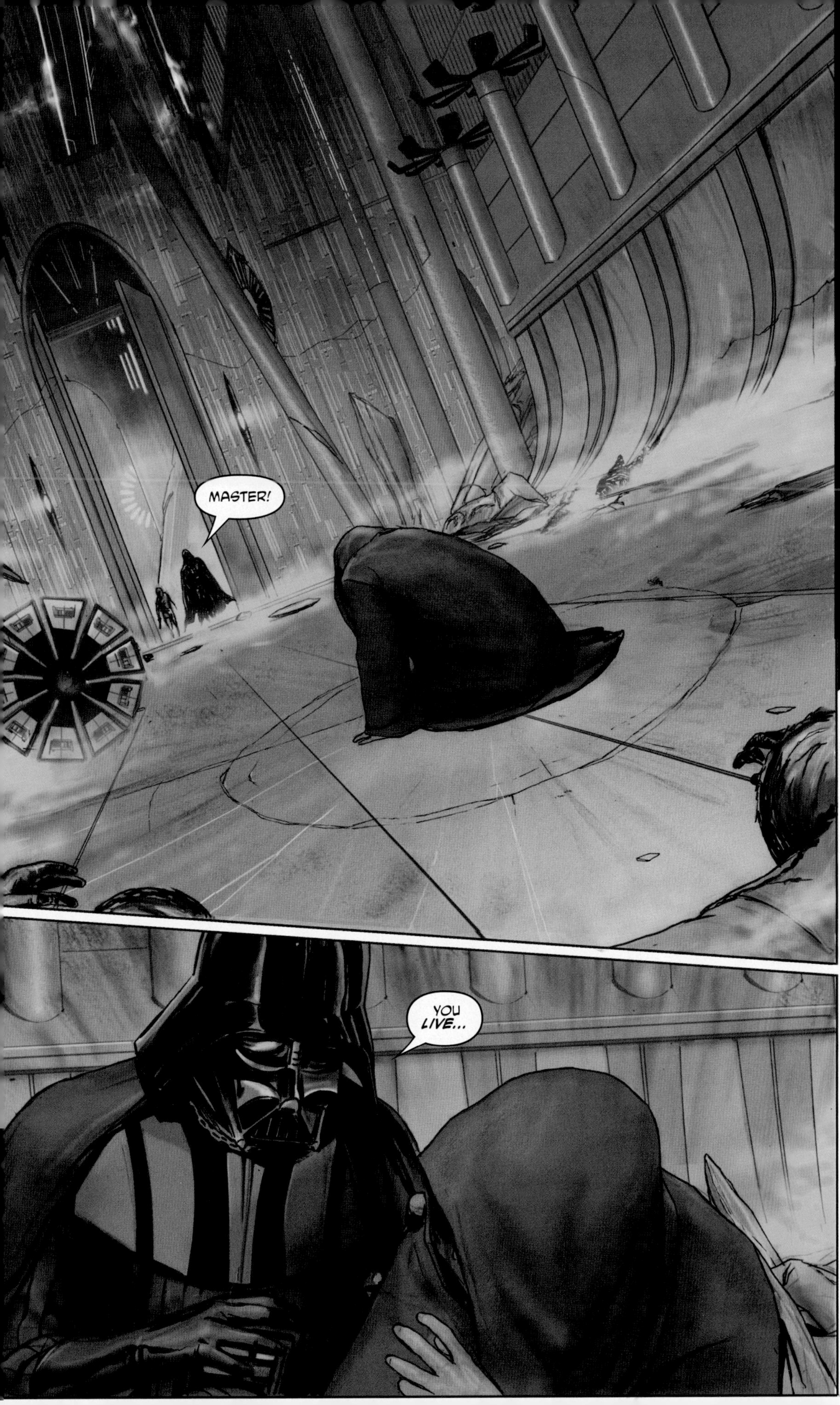
MASTER!
YOU LIVE...

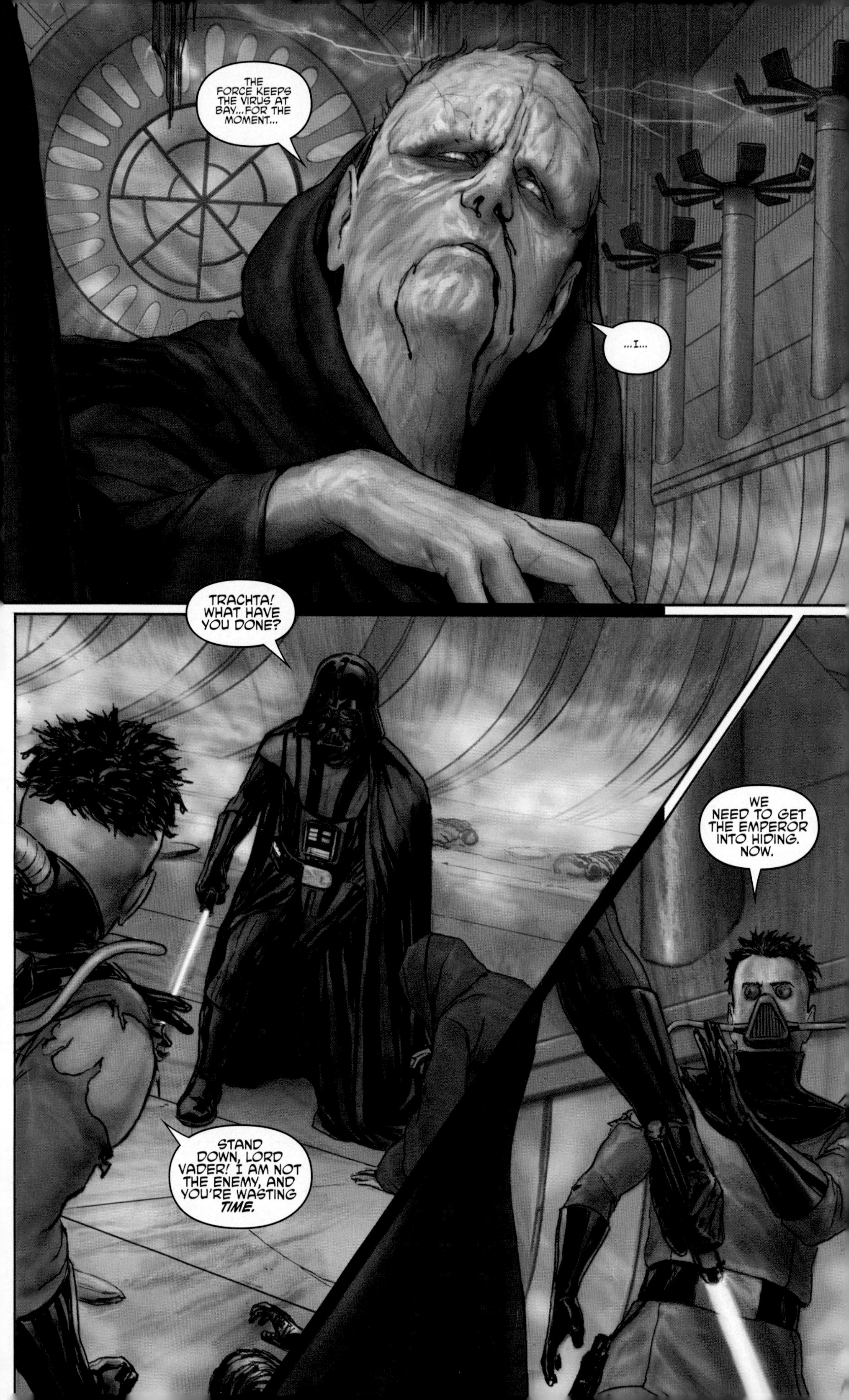
THE FORCE KEEPS THE VIRUS AT BAY...FOR THE MOMENT...
...I...
TRACHTA! WHAT HAVE YOU DONE?
WE NEED TO GET THE EMPEROR INTO HIDING. NOW.
STAND DOWN, LORD VADER! I AM NOT THE ENEMY, AND YOU'RE WASTING *TIME.*

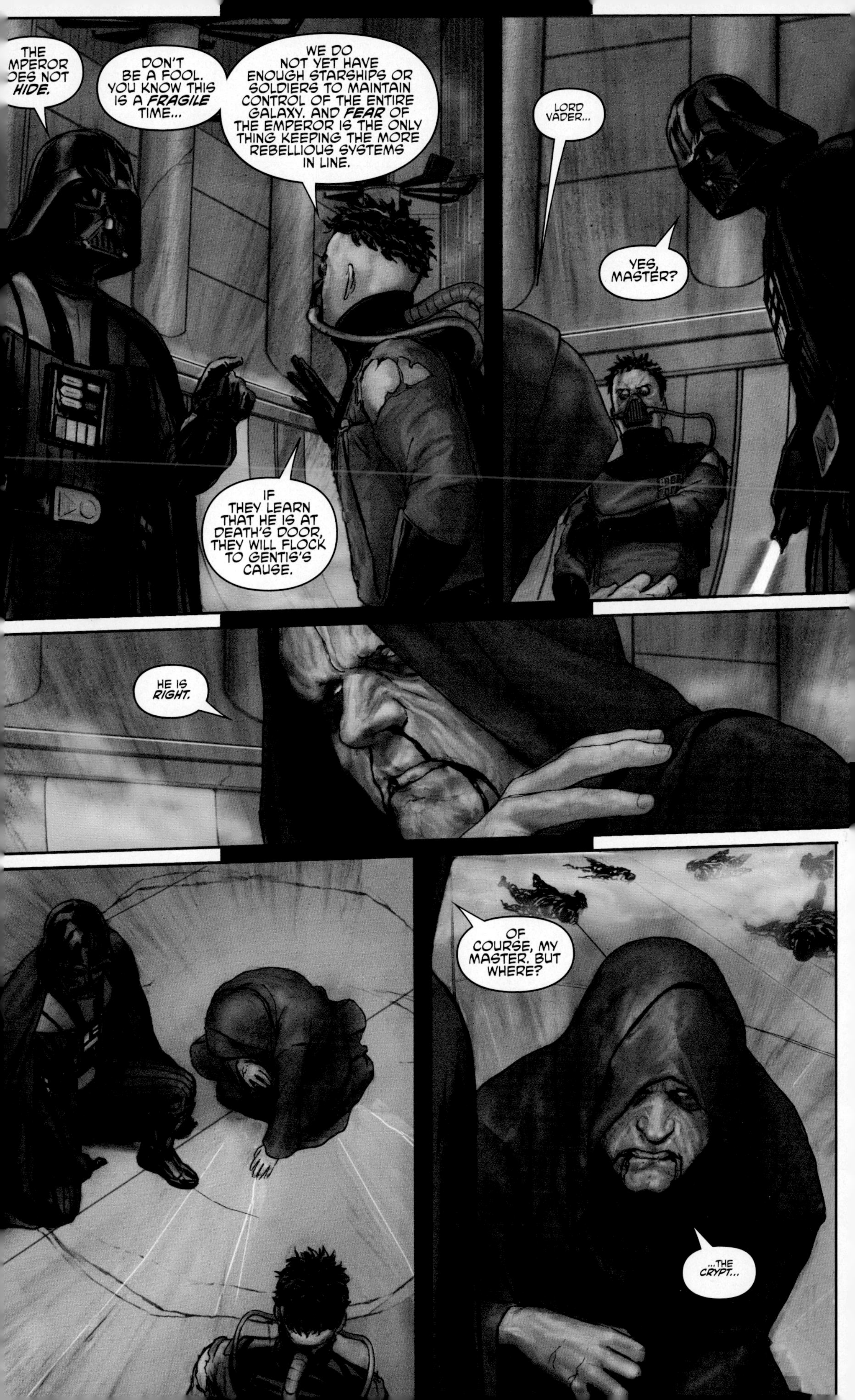
THE EMPEROR DOES NOT HIDE.
DON'T BE A FOOL. YOU KNOW THIS IS A FRAGILE TIME...
WE DO NOT YET HAVE ENOUGH STARSHIPS OR SOLDIERS TO MAINTAIN CONTROL OF THE ENTIRE GALAXY. AND FEAR OF THE EMPEROR IS THE ONLY THING KEEPING THE MORE REBELLIOUS SYSTEMS IN LINE.
IF THEY LEARN THAT HE IS AT DEATH'S DOOR, THEY WILL FLOCK TO GENTIS'S CAUSE.
LORD VADER...
YES, MASTER?
HE IS RIGHT.
OF COURSE, MY MASTER. BUT WHERE?
...THE CRYPT...

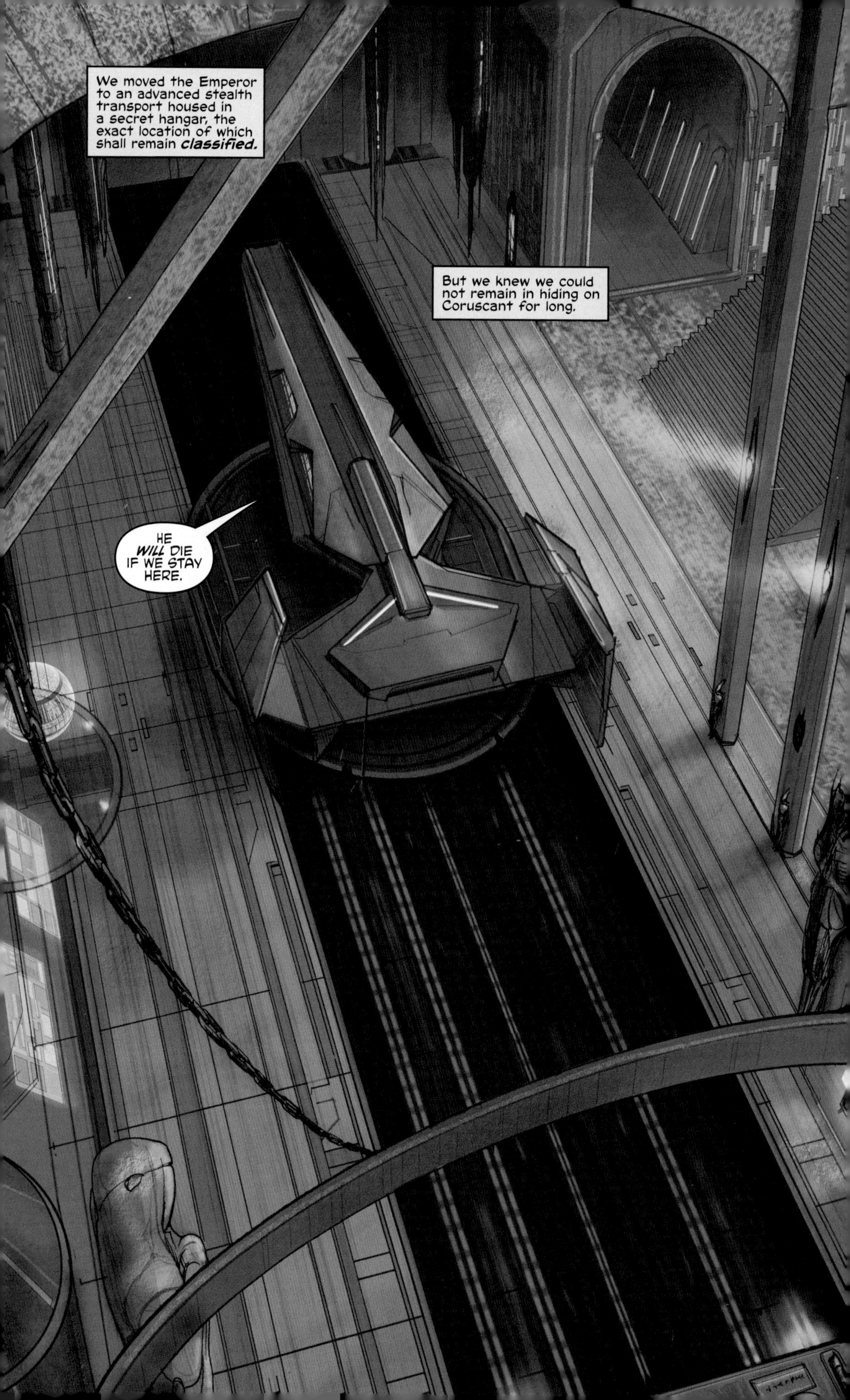
We moved the Emperor to an advanced stealth transport housed in a secret hangar, the exact location of which shall remain *classified.*
But we knew we could not remain in hiding on Coruscant for long.
HE *WILL* DIE IF WE STAY HERE.

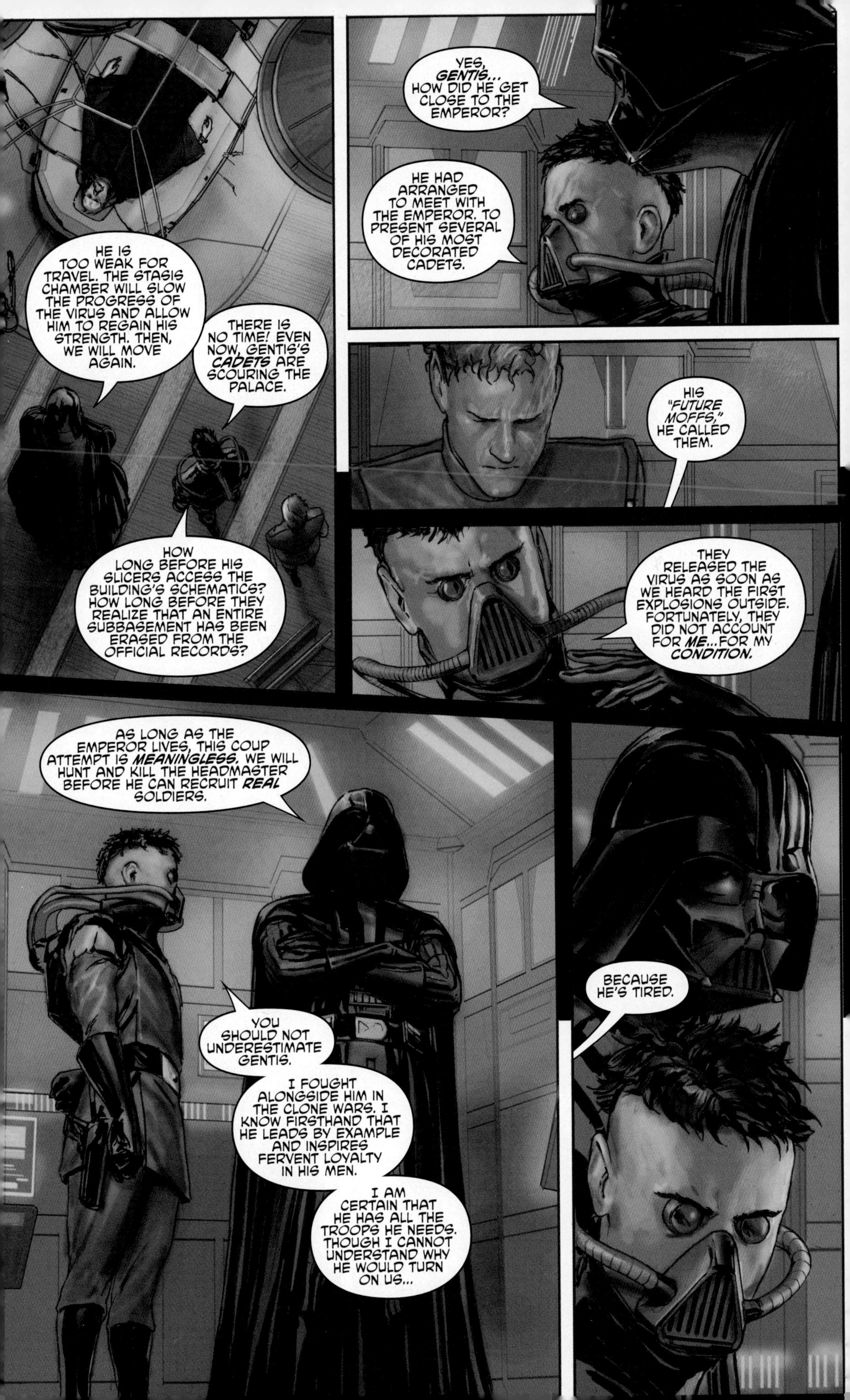
HE IS TOO WEAK FOR TRAVEL. THE STASIS CHAMBER WILL SLOW THE PROGRESS OF THE VIRUS AND ALLOW HIM TO REGAIN HIS STRENGTH. THEN, WE WILL MOVE AGAIN.
THERE IS NO TIME! EVEN NOW, GENTIS'S *CADETS* ARE SCOURING THE PALACE.
HOW LONG BEFORE HIS SLICERS ACCESS THE BUILDING'S SCHEMATICS? HOW LONG BEFORE THEY REALIZE THAT AN ENTIRE SUBBASEMENT HAS BEEN ERASED FROM THE OFFICIAL RECORDS?
YES, *GENTIS...* HOW DID HE GET CLOSE TO THE EMPEROR?
HE HAD ARRANGED TO MEET WITH THE EMPEROR. TO PRESENT SEVERAL OF HIS MOST DECORATED CADETS.
HIS *"FUTURE MOFFS,"* HE CALLED THEM.
THEY RELEASED THE VIRUS AS SOON AS WE HEARD THE FIRST EXPLOSIONS OUTSIDE. FORTUNATELY, THEY DID NOT ACCOUNT FOR *ME*...FOR MY *CONDITION.*
AS LONG AS THE EMPEROR LIVES, THIS COUP ATTEMPT IS *MEANINGLESS.* WE WILL HUNT AND KILL THE HEADMASTER BEFORE HE CAN RECRUIT *REAL* SOLDIERS.
YOU SHOULD NOT UNDERESTIMATE GENTIS.
I FOUGHT ALONGSIDE HIM IN THE CLONE WARS. I KNOW FIRSTHAND THAT HE LEADS BY EXAMPLE AND INSPIRES FERVENT LOYALTY IN HIS MEN.
I AM CERTAIN THAT HE HAS ALL THE TROOPS HE NEEDS. THOUGH I CANNOT UNDERSTAND WHY HE WOULD TURN ON US...
BECAUSE HE'S TIRED.

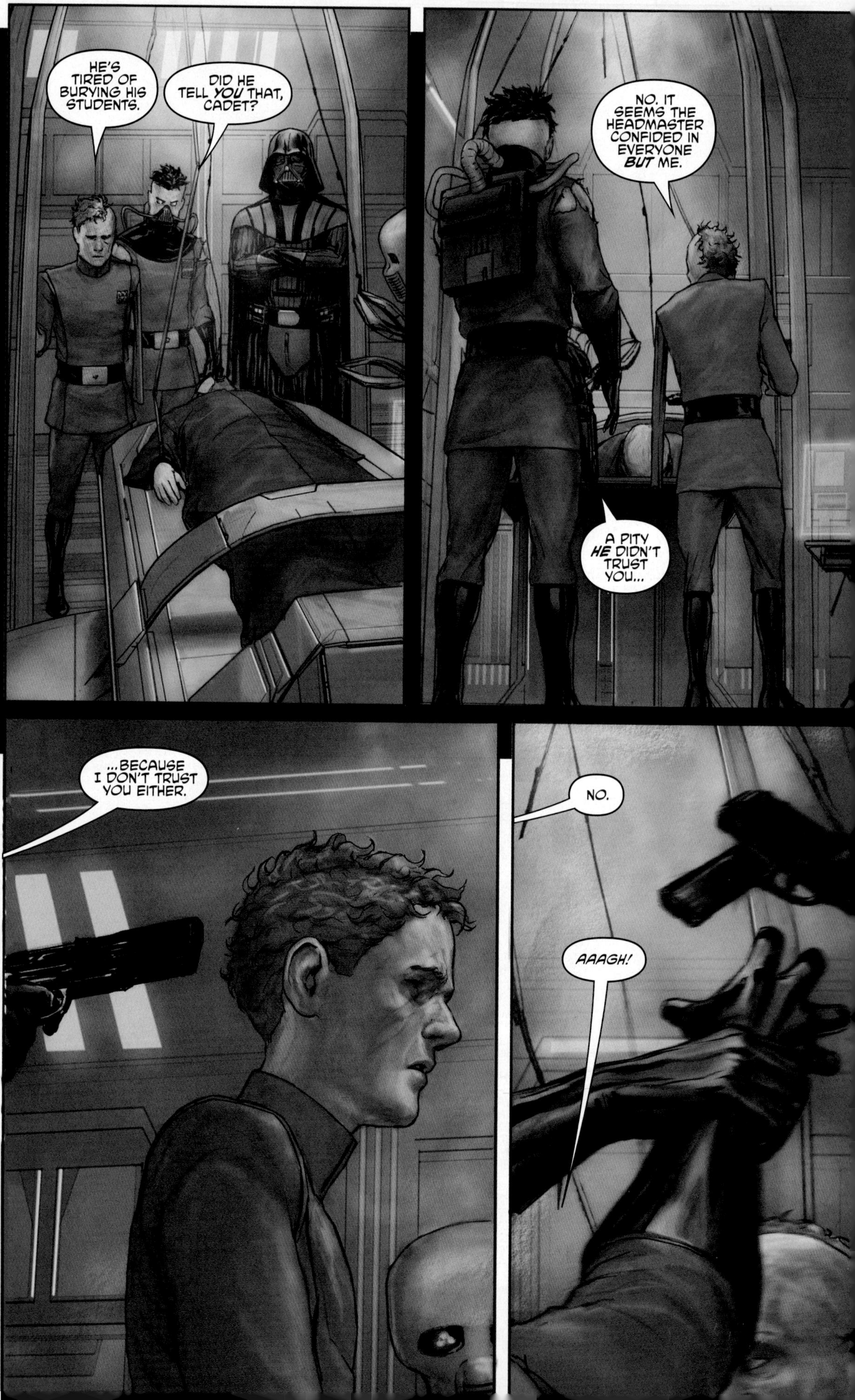
HE'S TIRED OF BURYING HIS STUDENTS.
DID HE TELL *YOU* THAT, CADET?
NO. IT SEEMS THE HEADMASTER CONFIDED IN EVERYONE *BUT* ME.
A PITY *HE* DIDN'T TRUST YOU...
...BECAUSE I DON'T TRUST YOU EITHER.
NO.
AAAGH!

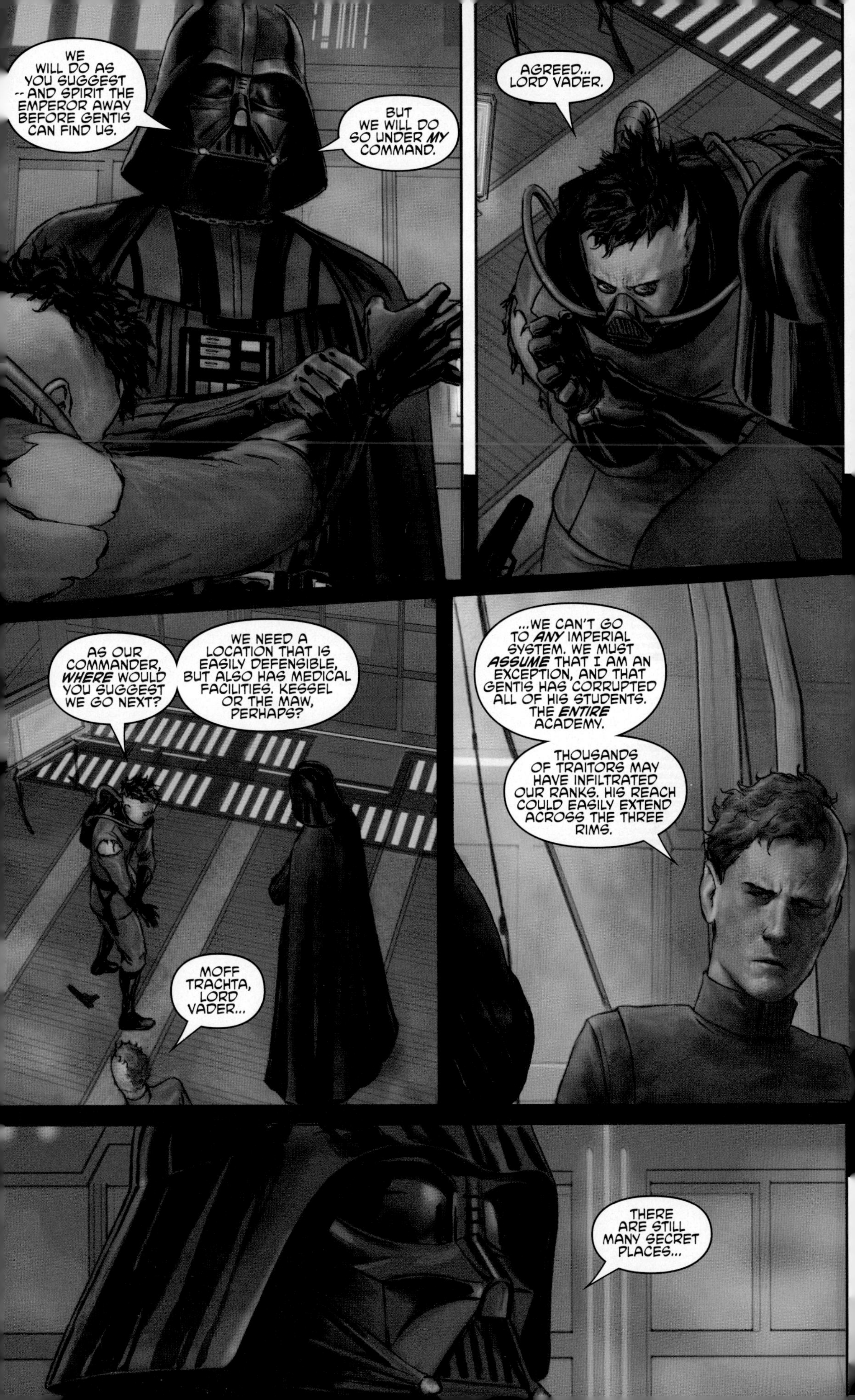
WE WILL DO AS YOU SUGGEST -- AND SPIRIT THE EMPEROR AWAY BEFORE GENTIS CAN FIND US.
BUT WE WILL DO SO UNDER *MY* COMMAND.
AGREED... LORD VADER.
AS OUR COMMANDER, *WHERE* WOULD YOU SUGGEST WE GO NEXT?
WE NEED A LOCATION THAT IS EASILY DEFENSIBLE, BUT ALSO HAS MEDICAL FACILITIES. KESSEL OR THE MAW, PERHAPS?
MOFF TRACHTA, LORD VADER...
...WE CAN'T GO TO *ANY* IMPERIAL SYSTEM. WE MUST *ASSUME* THAT I AM AN EXCEPTION, AND THAT GENTIS HAS CORRUPTED ALL OF HIS STUDENTS. THE *ENTIRE* ACADEMY.
THOUSANDS OF TRAITORS MAY HAVE INFILTRATED OUR RANKS. HIS REACH COULD EASILY EXTEND ACROSS THE THREE RIMS.
THERE ARE STILL MANY SECRET PLACES...

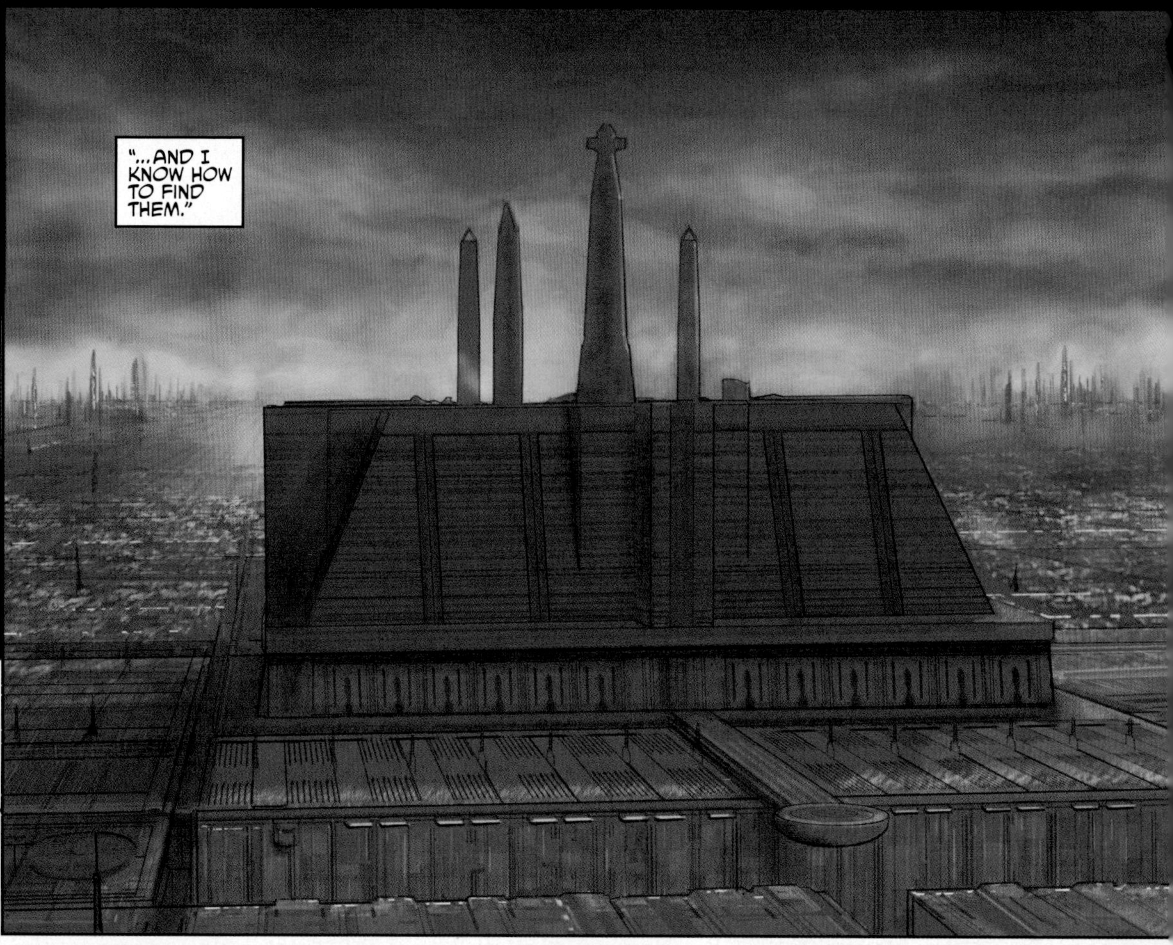
"...AND I KNOW HOW TO FIND THEM."

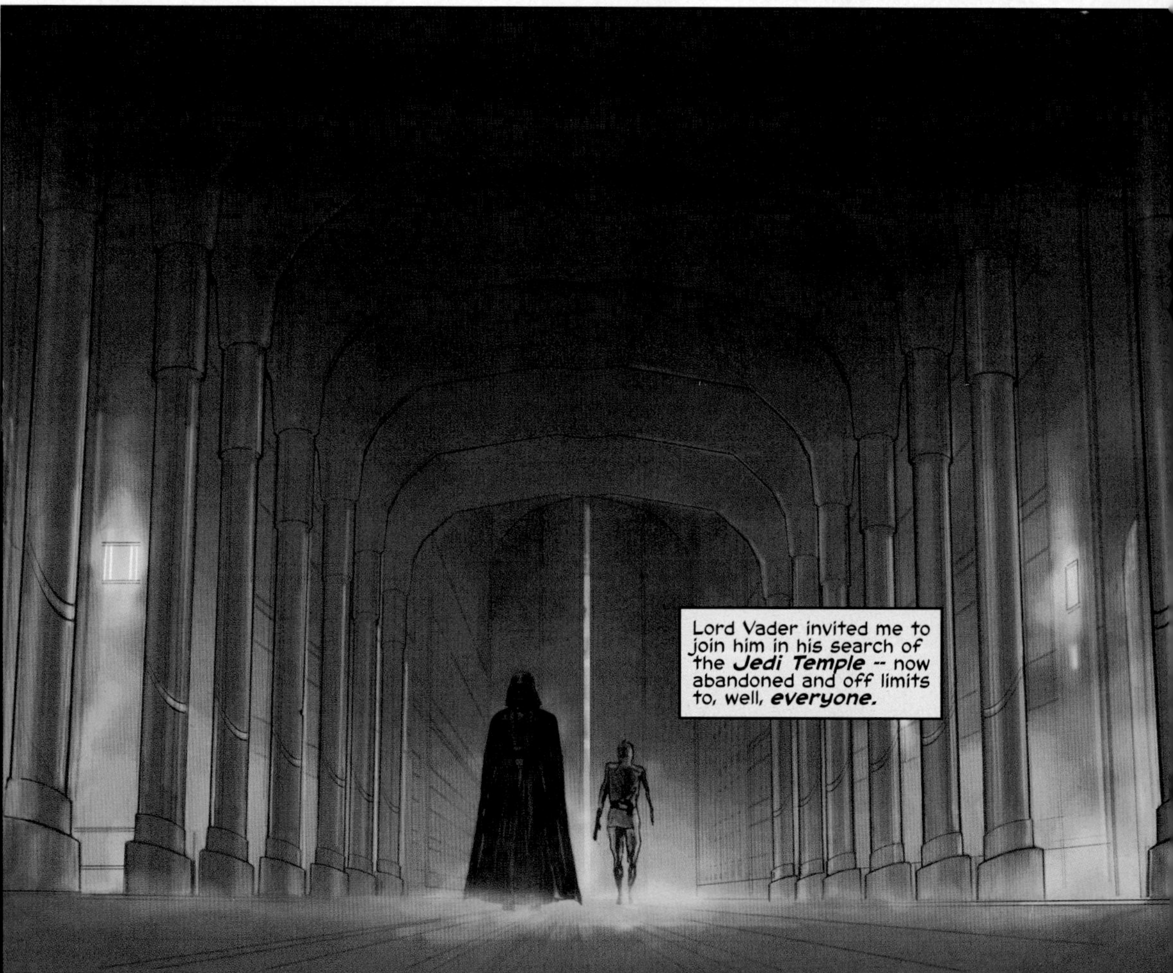
Lord Vader invited me to join him in his search of the *Jedi Temple* -- now abandoned and off limits to, well, *everyone.*

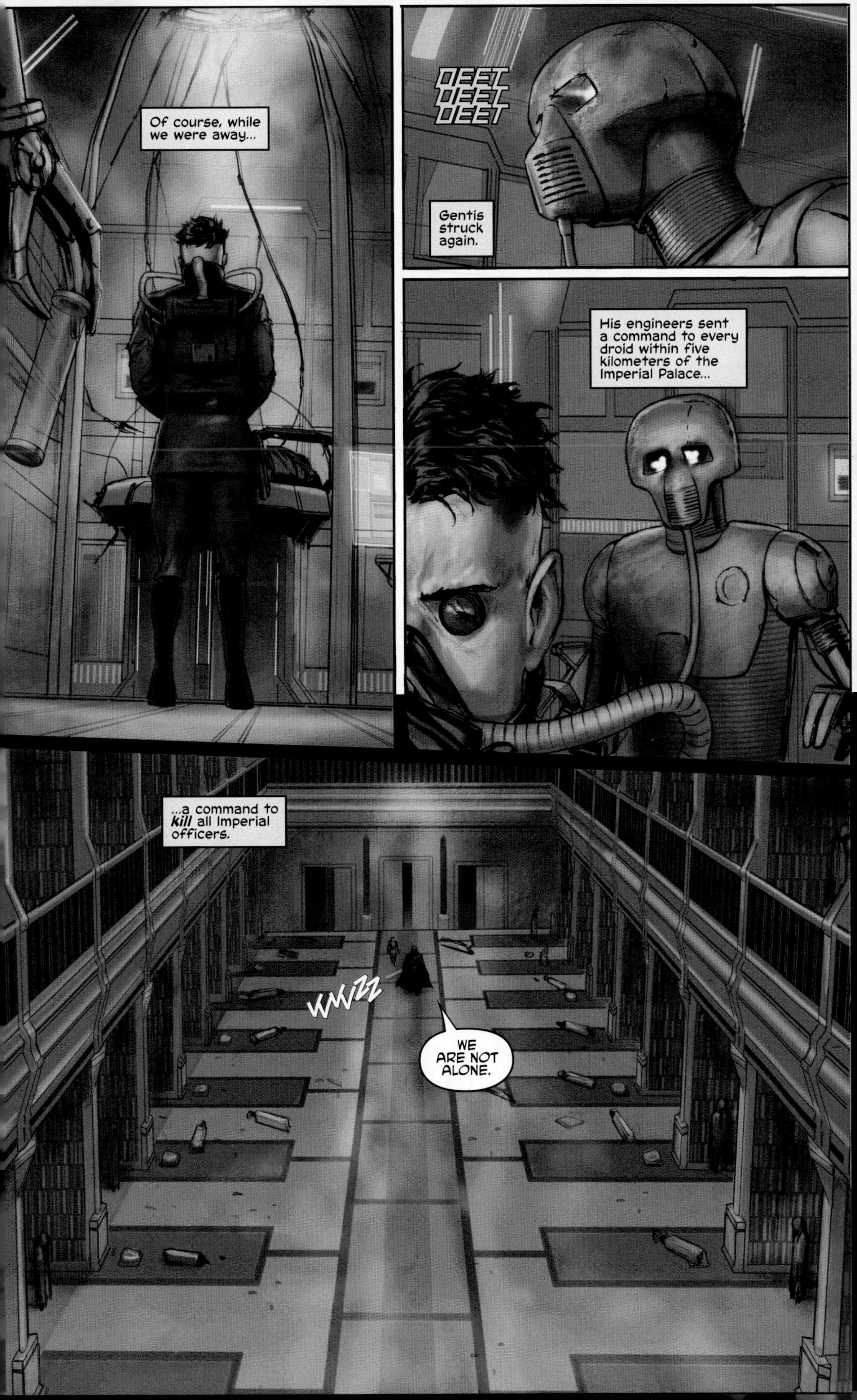

Of course, while we were away...
DEET DEET DEET
Gentis struck again.
His engineers sent a command to every droid within five kilometers of the Imperial Palace...
...a command to *kill* all Imperial officers.
WVVIZZ
WE ARE NOT ALONE.

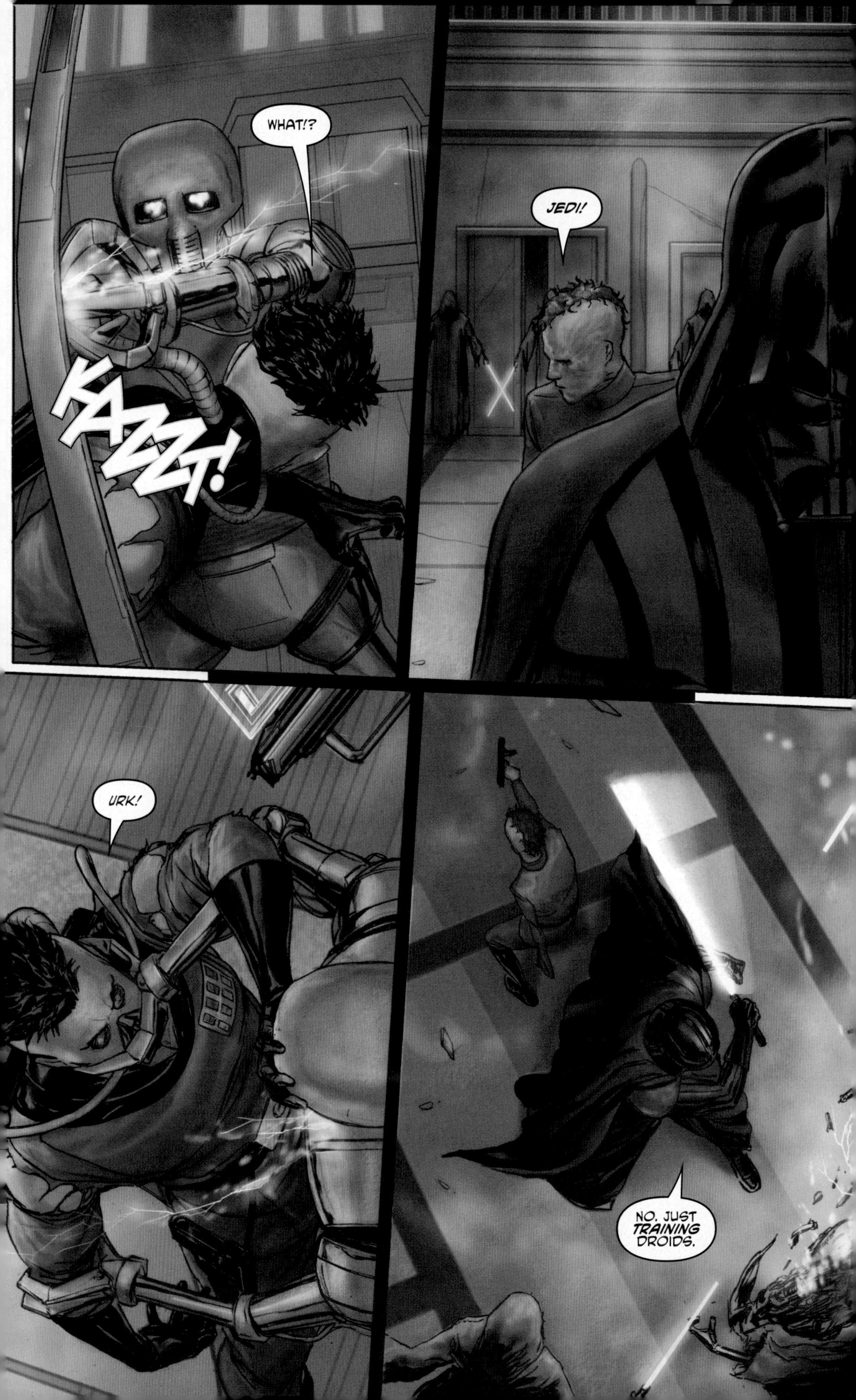
WHAT!?
KAZZZT!
JEDI!
URK!
NO. JUST TRAINING DROIDS.

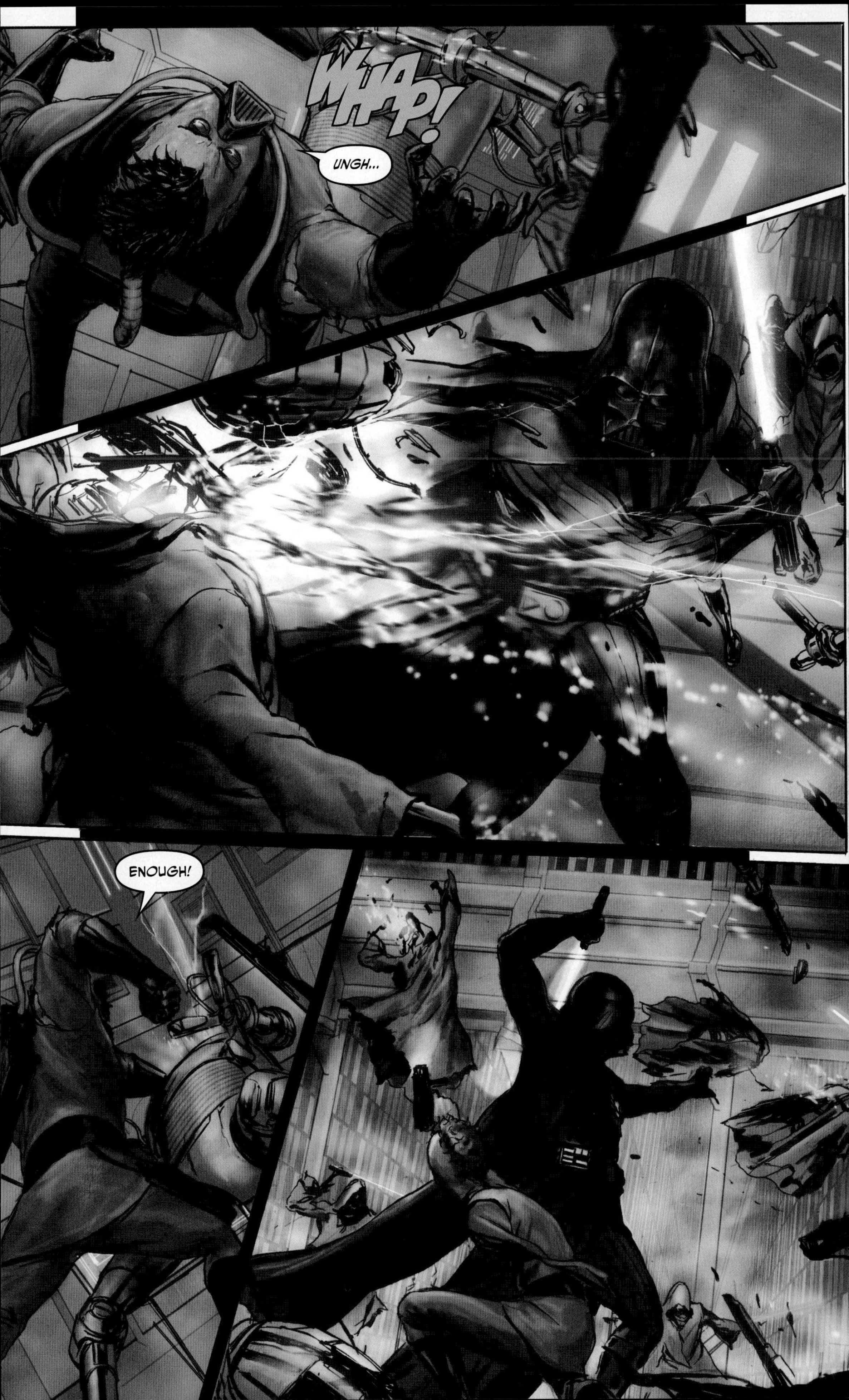
WHAP!
UNGH...
ENOUGH!

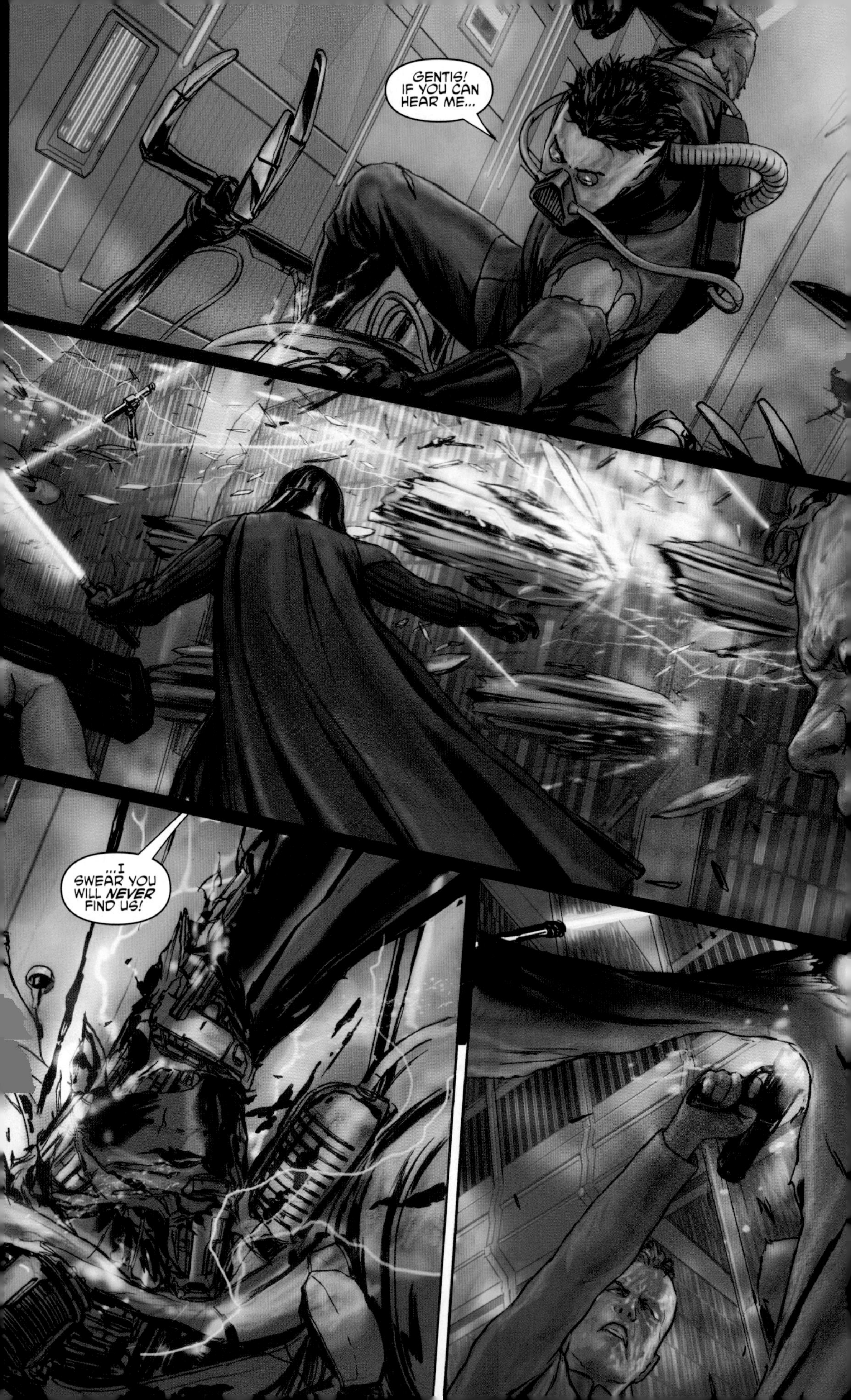
GENTIS! IF YOU CAN HEAR ME...
...I SWEAR YOU WILL *NEVER* FIND US!

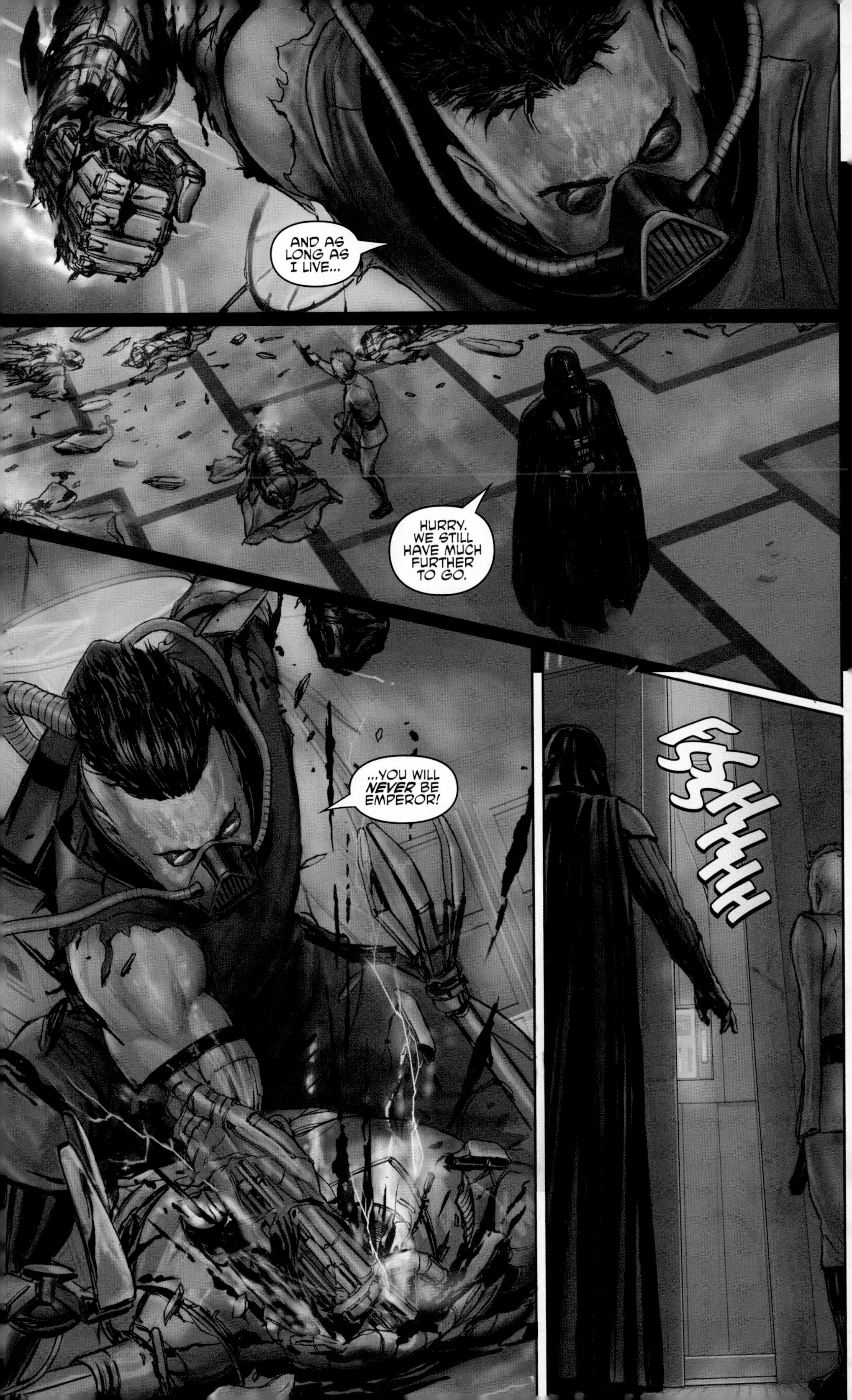
AND AS LONG AS I LIVE...
HURRY. WE STILL HAVE MUCH FURTHER TO GO.
...YOU WILL *NEVER* BE EMPEROR!
FSSHHHH

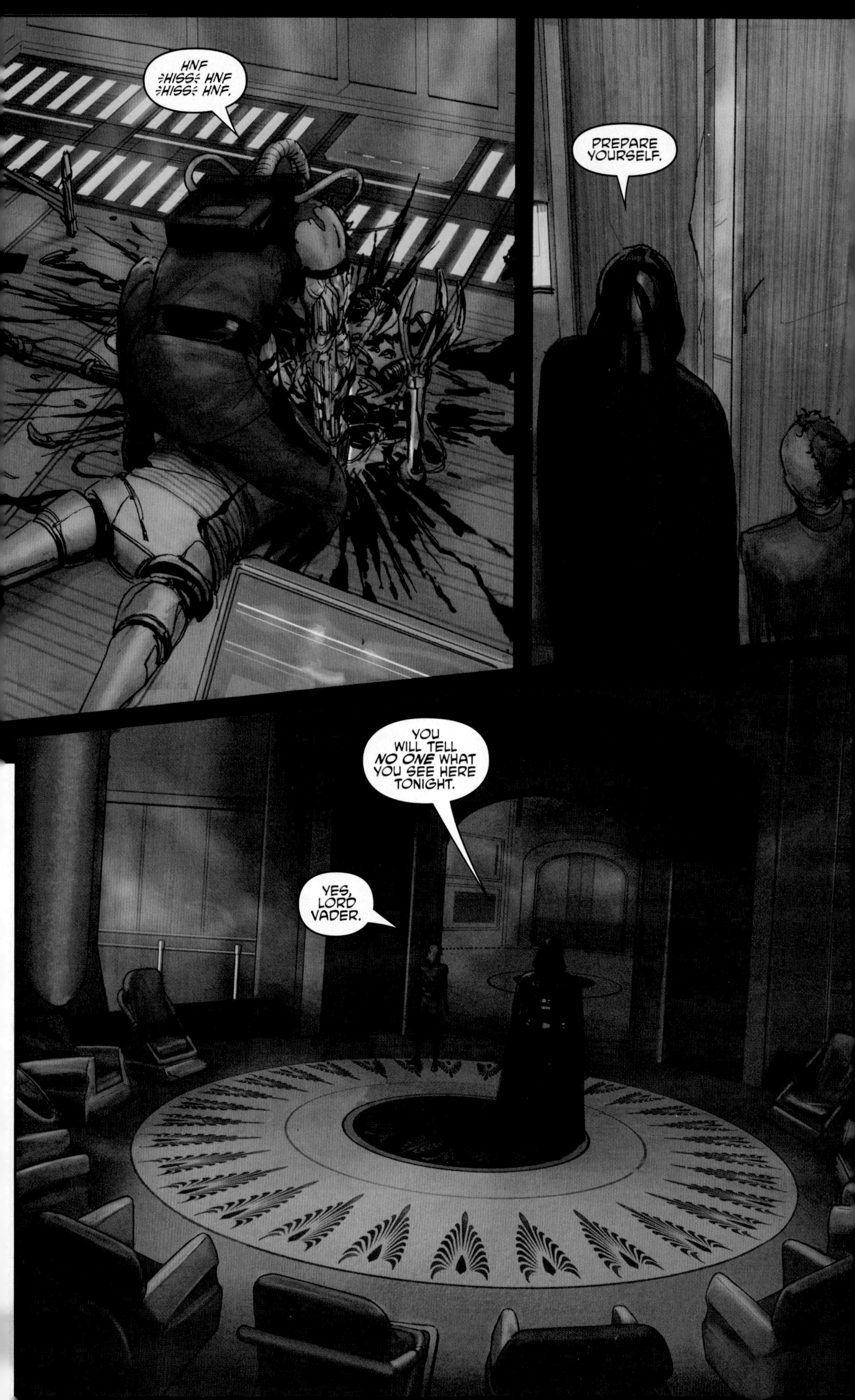
HNF
HISS HNF
HISS HNF.
PREPARE YOURSELF.
YOU WILL TELL NO ONE WHAT YOU SEE HERE TONIGHT.
YES, LORD VADER.

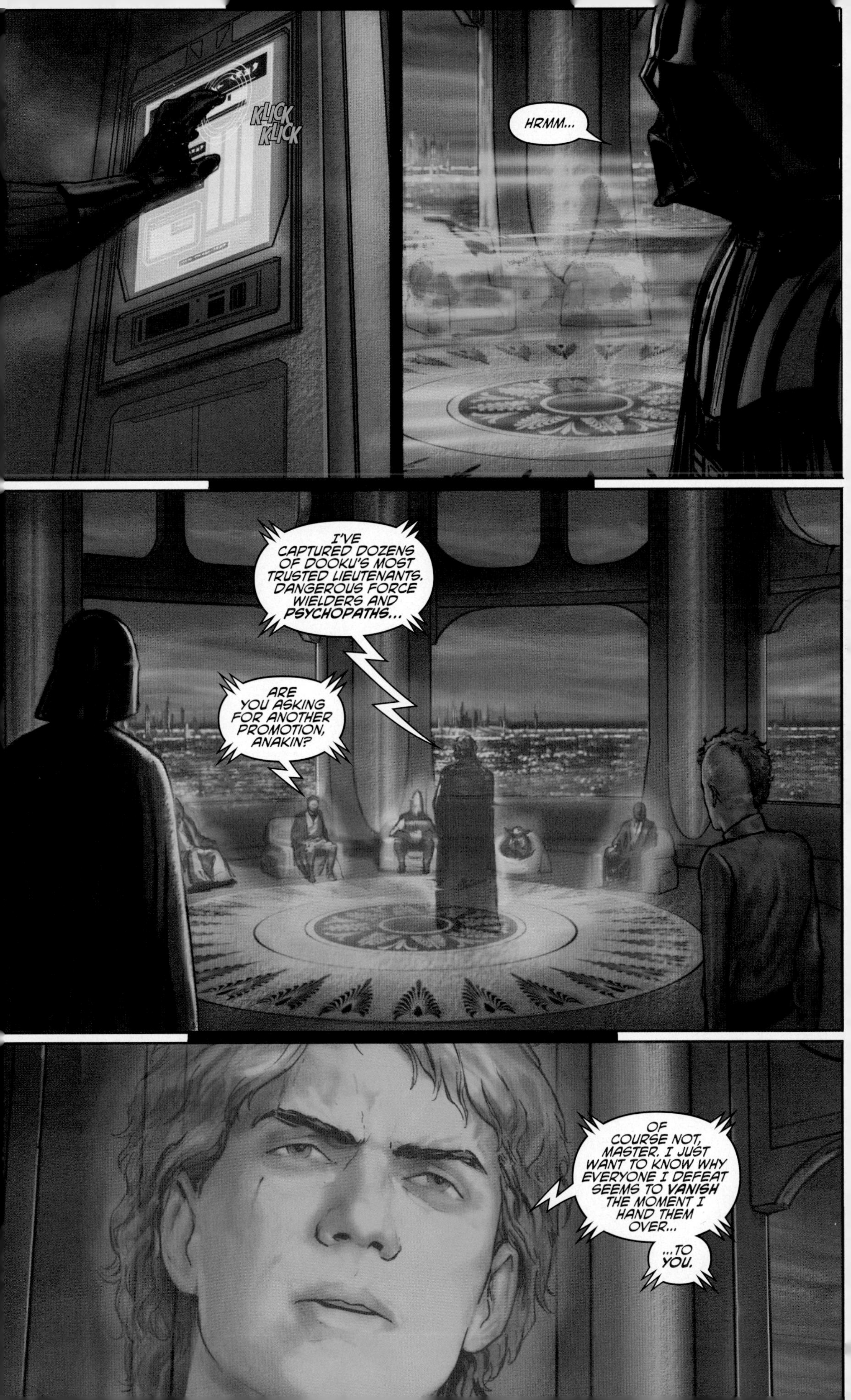
KLICK KLICK
HRMM...
I'VE CAPTURED DOZENS OF DOOKU'S MOST TRUSTED LIEUTENANTS, DANGEROUS FORCE WIELDERS AND PSYCHOPATHS...
ARE YOU ASKING FOR ANOTHER PROMOTION, ANAKIN?
OF COURSE NOT, MASTER. I JUST WANT TO KNOW WHY EVERYONE I DEFEAT SEEMS TO VANISH THE MOMENT I HAND THEM OVER...
...TO YOU.

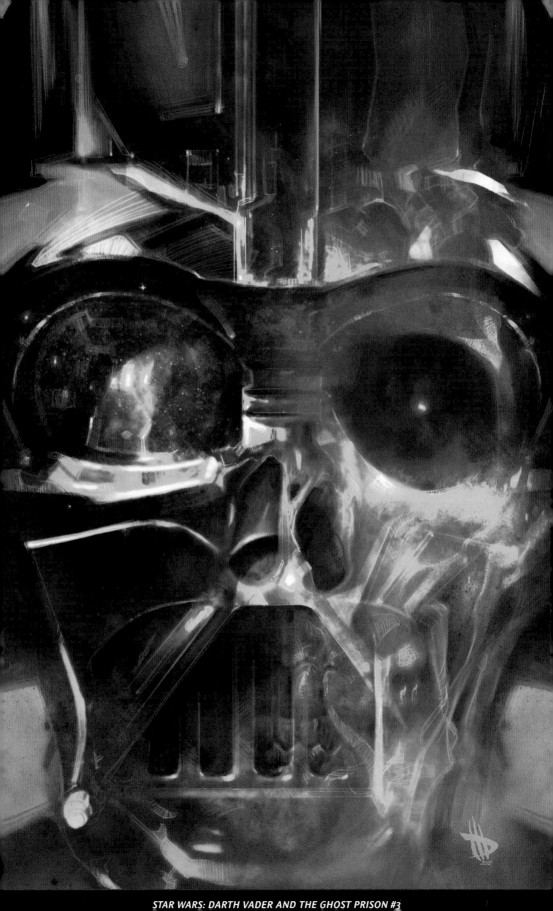

**STAR WARS: DARTH VADER AND THE GHOST PRISON #3**

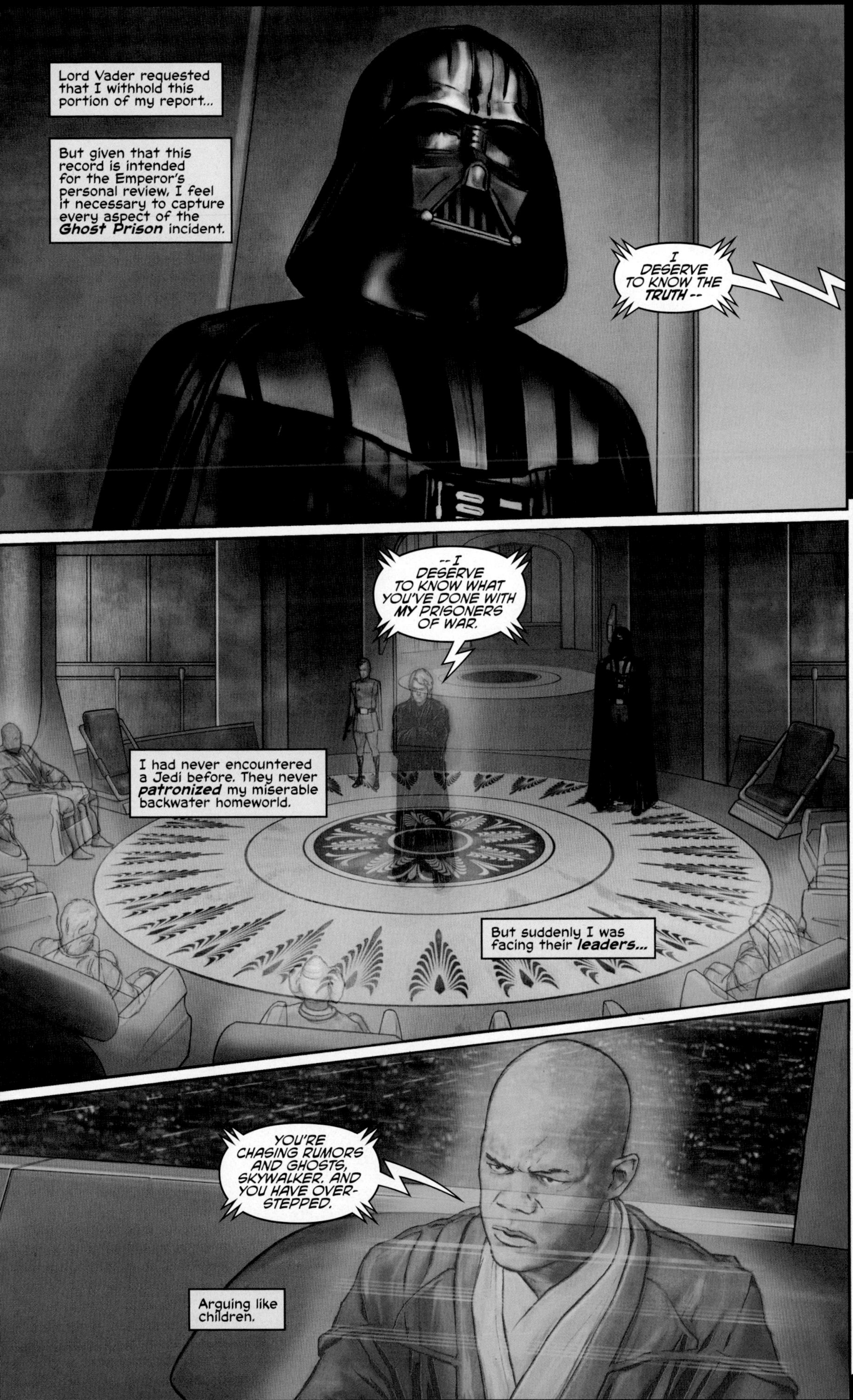
Lord Vader requested that I withhold this portion of my report...
But given that this record is intended for the Emperor's personal review, I feel it necessary to capture every aspect of the Ghost Prison incident.
I DESERVE TO KNOW THE TRUTH --
-- I DESERVE TO KNOW WHAT YOU'VE DONE WITH MY PRISONERS OF WAR.
I had never encountered a Jedi before. They never patronized my miserable backwater homeworld.
But suddenly I was facing their leaders...
YOU'RE CHASING RUMORS AND GHOSTS, SKYWALKER. AND YOU HAVE OVER-STEPPED.
Arguing like children.

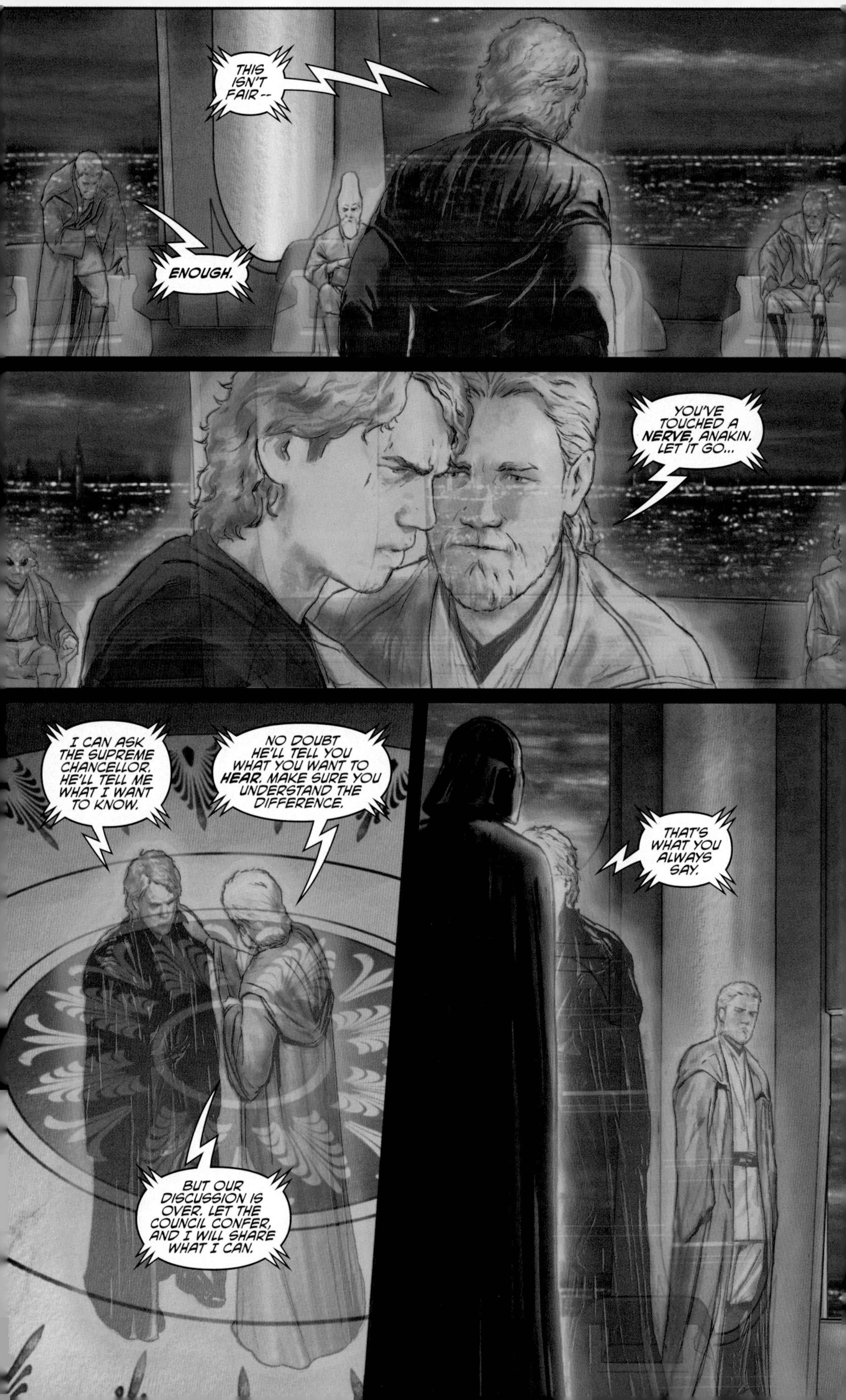
THIS ISN'T FAIR--
ENOUGH.
YOU'VE TOUCHED A NERVE, ANAKIN. LET IT GO...
I CAN ASK THE SUPREME CHANCELLOR. HE'LL TELL ME WHAT I WANT TO KNOW.
NO DOUBT HE'LL TELL YOU WHAT YOU WANT TO HEAR. MAKE SURE YOU UNDERSTAND THE DIFFERENCE.
BUT OUR DISCUSSION IS OVER. LET THE COUNCIL CONFER, AND I WILL SHARE WHAT I CAN.
THAT'S WHAT YOU ALWAYS SAY.

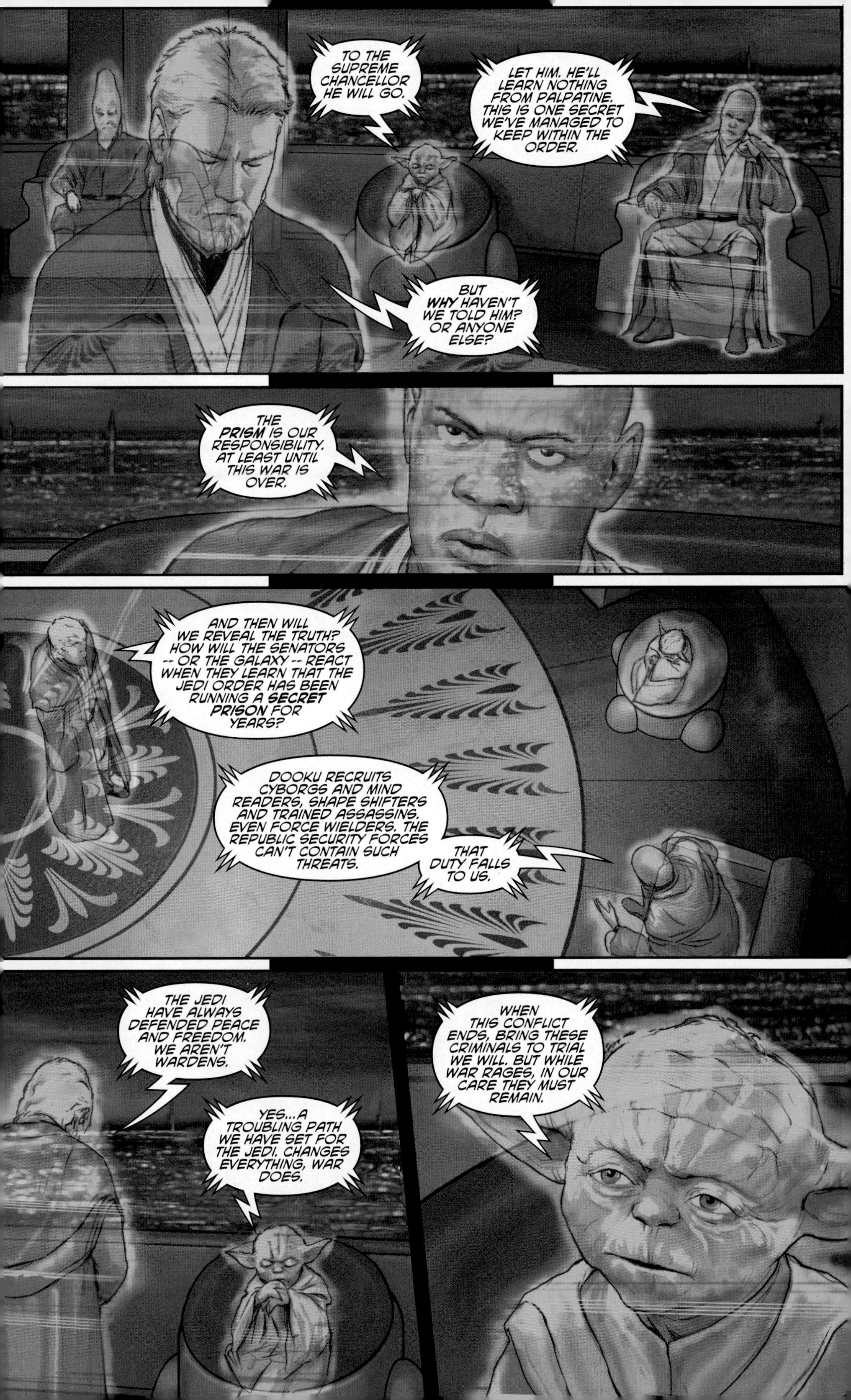
TO THE SUPREME CHANCELLOR HE WILL GO.
LET HIM. HE'LL LEARN NOTHING FROM PALPATINE. THIS IS ONE SECRET WE'VE MANAGED TO KEEP WITHIN THE ORDER.
BUT **WHY** HAVEN'T WE TOLD HIM? OR ANYONE ELSE?
THE **PRISM** IS OUR RESPONSIBILITY. AT LEAST UNTIL THIS WAR IS OVER.
AND THEN WILL WE REVEAL THE TRUTH? HOW WILL THE SENATORS -- OR THE GALAXY -- REACT WHEN THEY LEARN THAT THE JEDI ORDER HAS BEEN RUNNING A **SECRET PRISON** FOR YEARS?
DOOKU RECRUITS CYBORGS AND MIND READERS, SHAPE SHIFTERS AND TRAINED ASSASSINS. EVEN FORCE WIELDERS. THE REPUBLIC SECURITY FORCES CAN'T CONTAIN SUCH THREATS.
THAT DUTY FALLS TO US.
THE JEDI HAVE ALWAYS DEFENDED PEACE AND FREEDOM. WE AREN'T WARDENS.
YES...A TROUBLING PATH WE HAVE SET FOR THE JEDI. CHANGES EVERYTHING, WAR DOES.
WHEN THIS CONFLICT ENDS, BRING THESE CRIMINALS TO TRIAL WE WILL. BUT WHILE WAR RAGES, IN OUR CARE THEY MUST REMAIN.

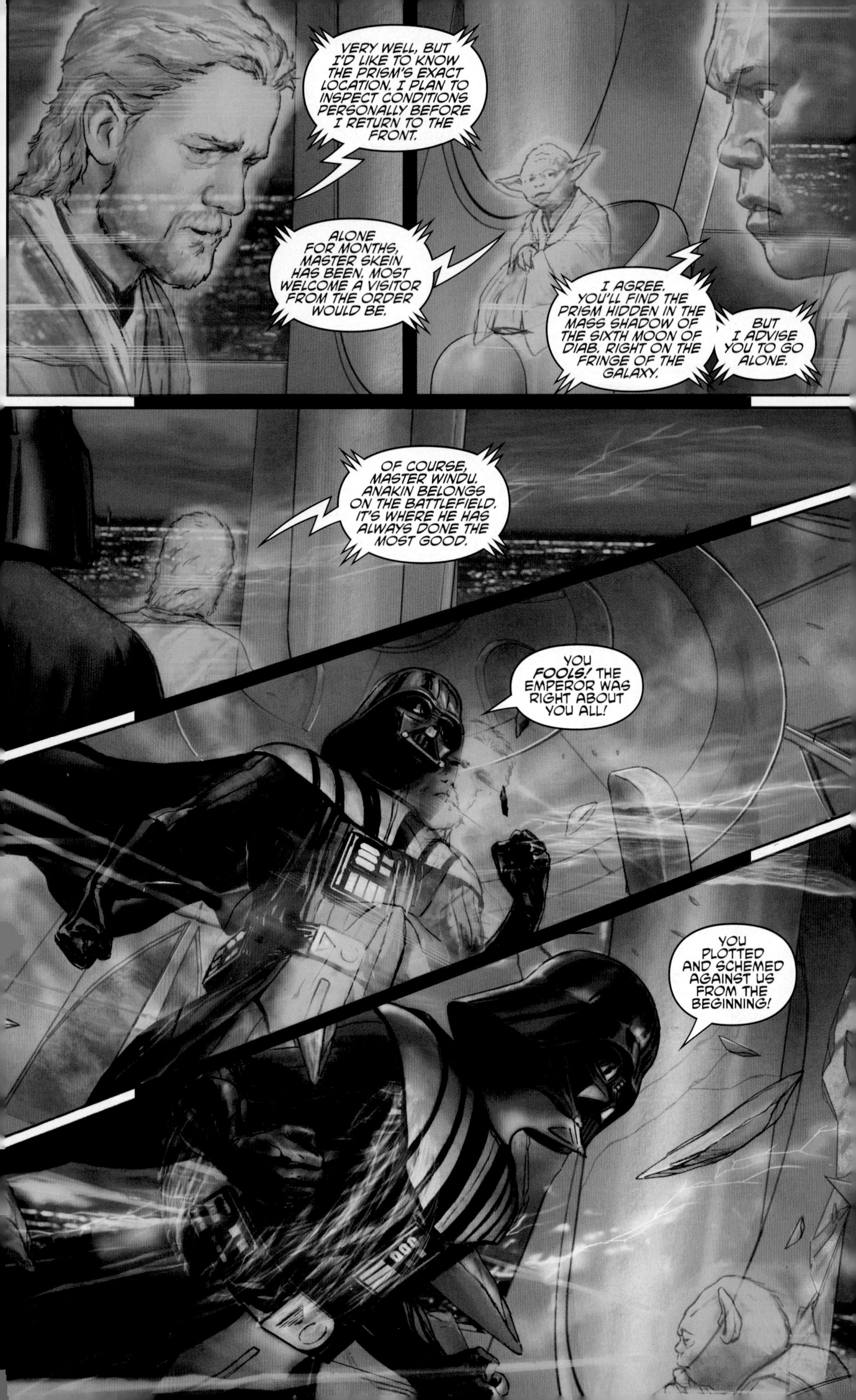
VERY WELL, BUT I'D LIKE TO KNOW THE PRISM'S EXACT LOCATION. I PLAN TO INSPECT CONDITIONS PERSONALLY BEFORE I RETURN TO THE FRONT.
ALONE FOR MONTHS, MASTER SKEIN HAS BEEN. MOST WELCOME A VISITOR FROM THE ORDER WOULD BE.
I AGREE. YOU'LL FIND THE PRISM HIDDEN IN THE MASS SHADOW OF THE SIXTH MOON OF DIAB. RIGHT ON THE FRINGE OF THE GALAXY.
BUT I ADVISE YOU TO GO ALONE.
OF COURSE, MASTER WINDU. ANAKIN BELONGS ON THE BATTLEFIELD. IT'S WHERE HE HAS ALWAYS DONE THE MOST GOOD.
YOU *FOOLS!* THE EMPEROR WAS RIGHT ABOUT YOU ALL!
YOU PLOTTED AND SCHEMED AGAINST US FROM THE BEGINNING!

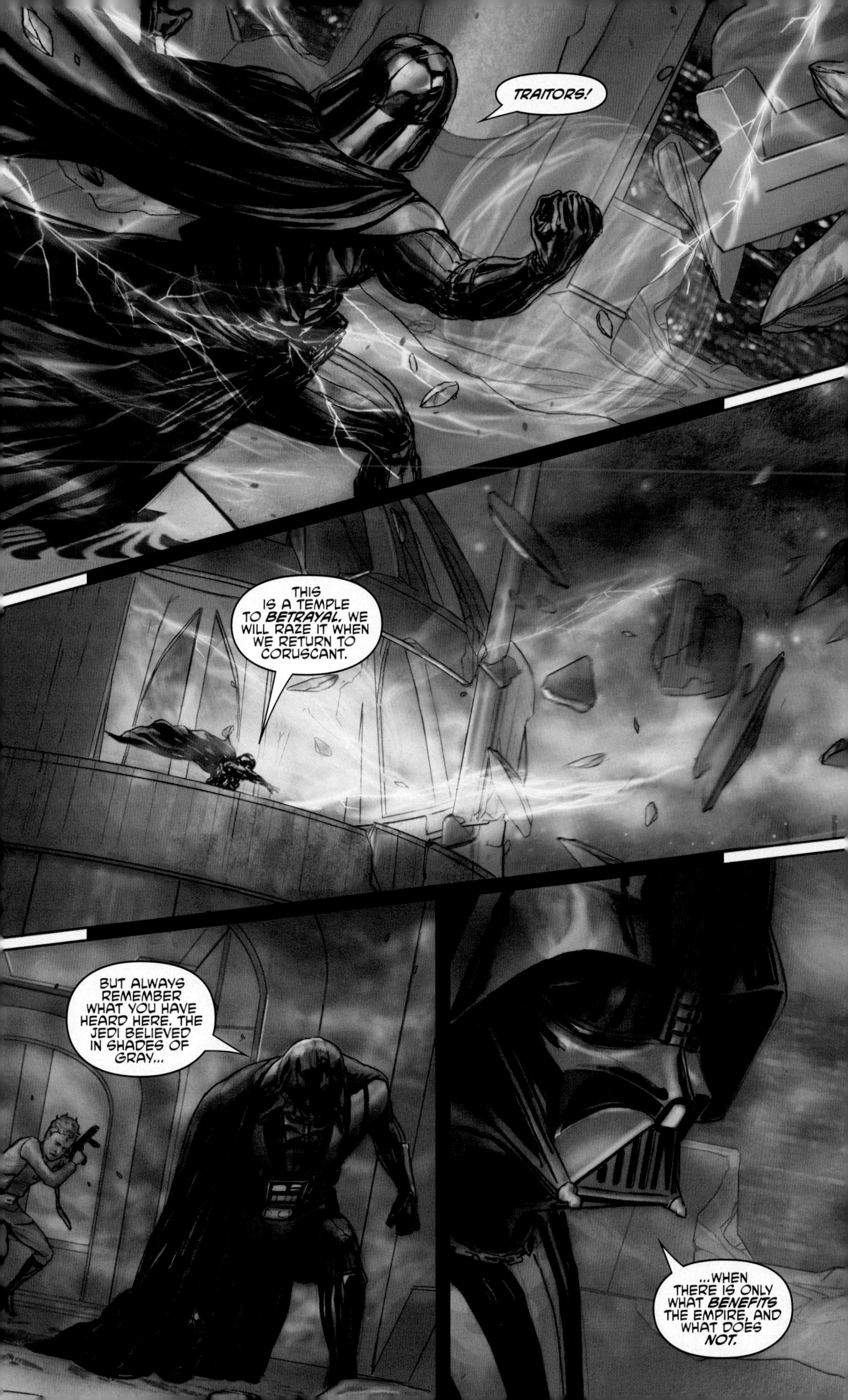
TRAITORS!
THIS IS A TEMPLE TO BETRAYAL. WE WILL RAZE IT WHEN WE RETURN TO CORUSCANT.
BUT ALWAYS REMEMBER WHAT YOU HAVE HEARD HERE. THE JEDI BELIEVED IN SHADES OF GRAY...
...WHEN THERE IS ONLY WHAT BENEFITS THE EMPIRE, AND WHAT DOES NOT.

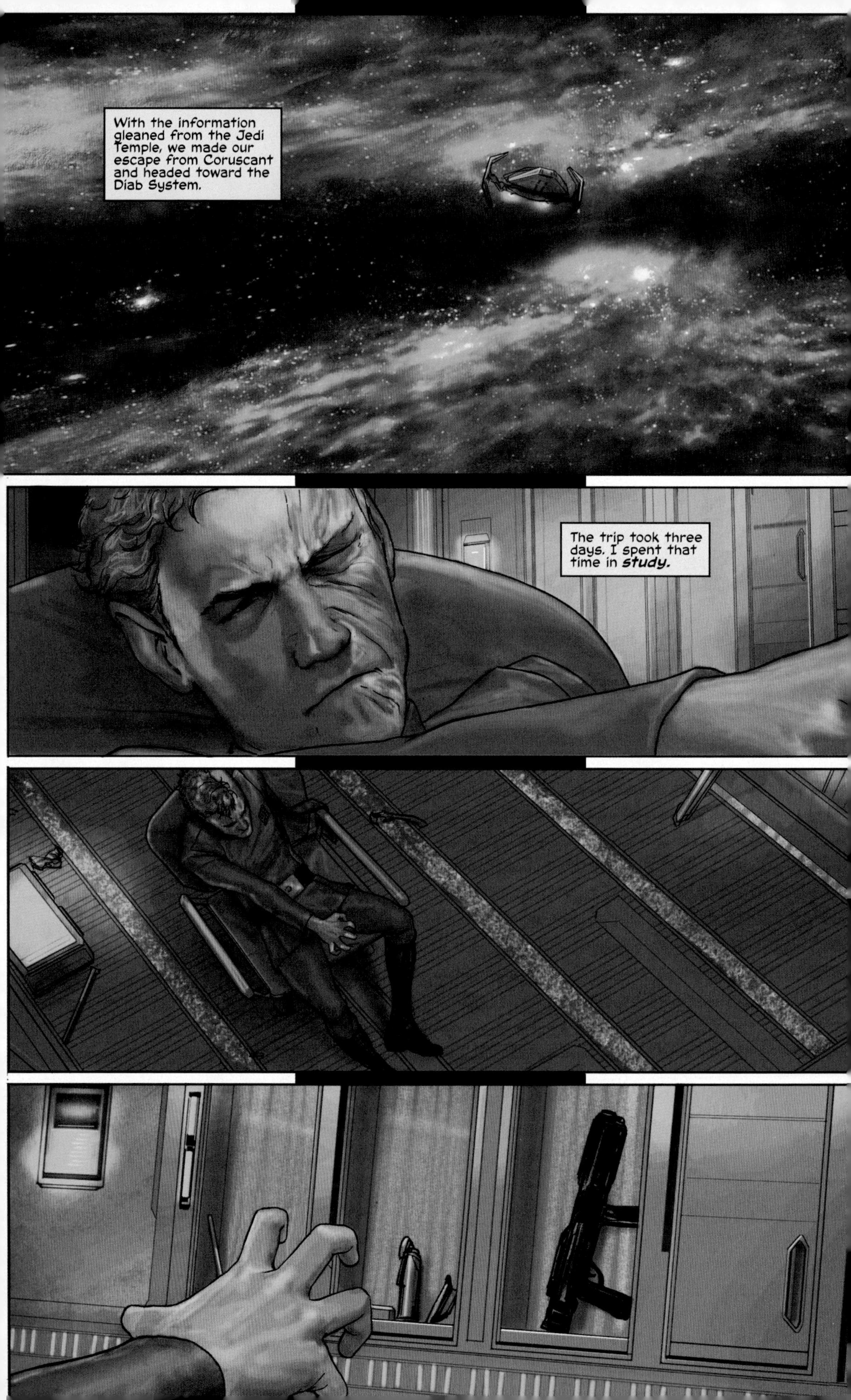
With the information gleaned from the Jedi Temple, we made our escape from Coruscant and headed toward the Diab System.
The trip took three days. I spent that time in *study.*

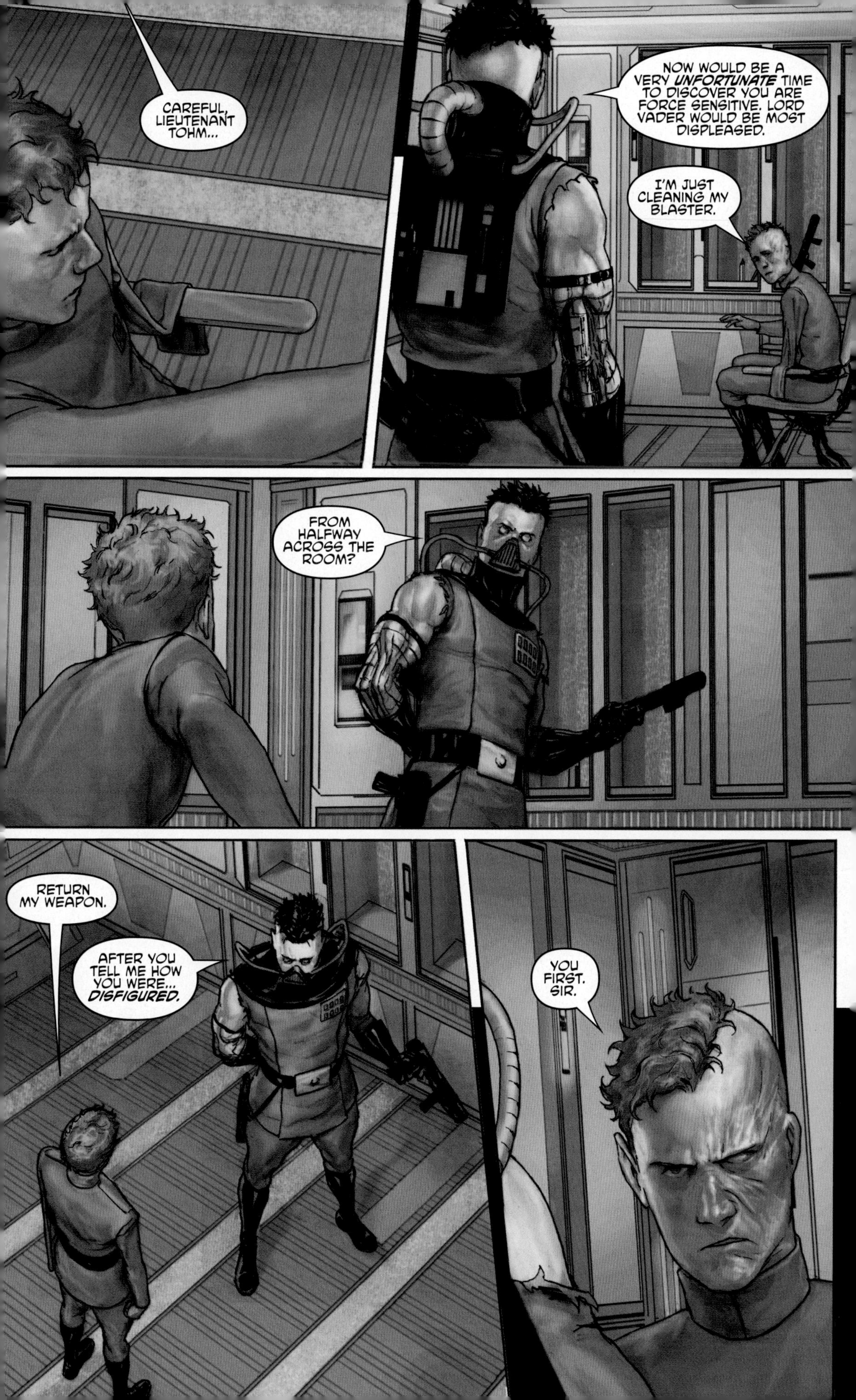
CAREFUL, LIEUTENANT TOHM...
NOW WOULD BE A VERY *UNFORTUNATE* TIME TO DISCOVER YOU ARE FORCE SENSITIVE. LORD VADER WOULD BE MOST DISPLEASED.
I'M JUST CLEANING MY BLASTER.
FROM HALFWAY ACROSS THE ROOM?
RETURN MY WEAPON.
AFTER YOU TELL ME HOW YOU WERE... *DISFIGURED.*
YOU FIRST. SIR.

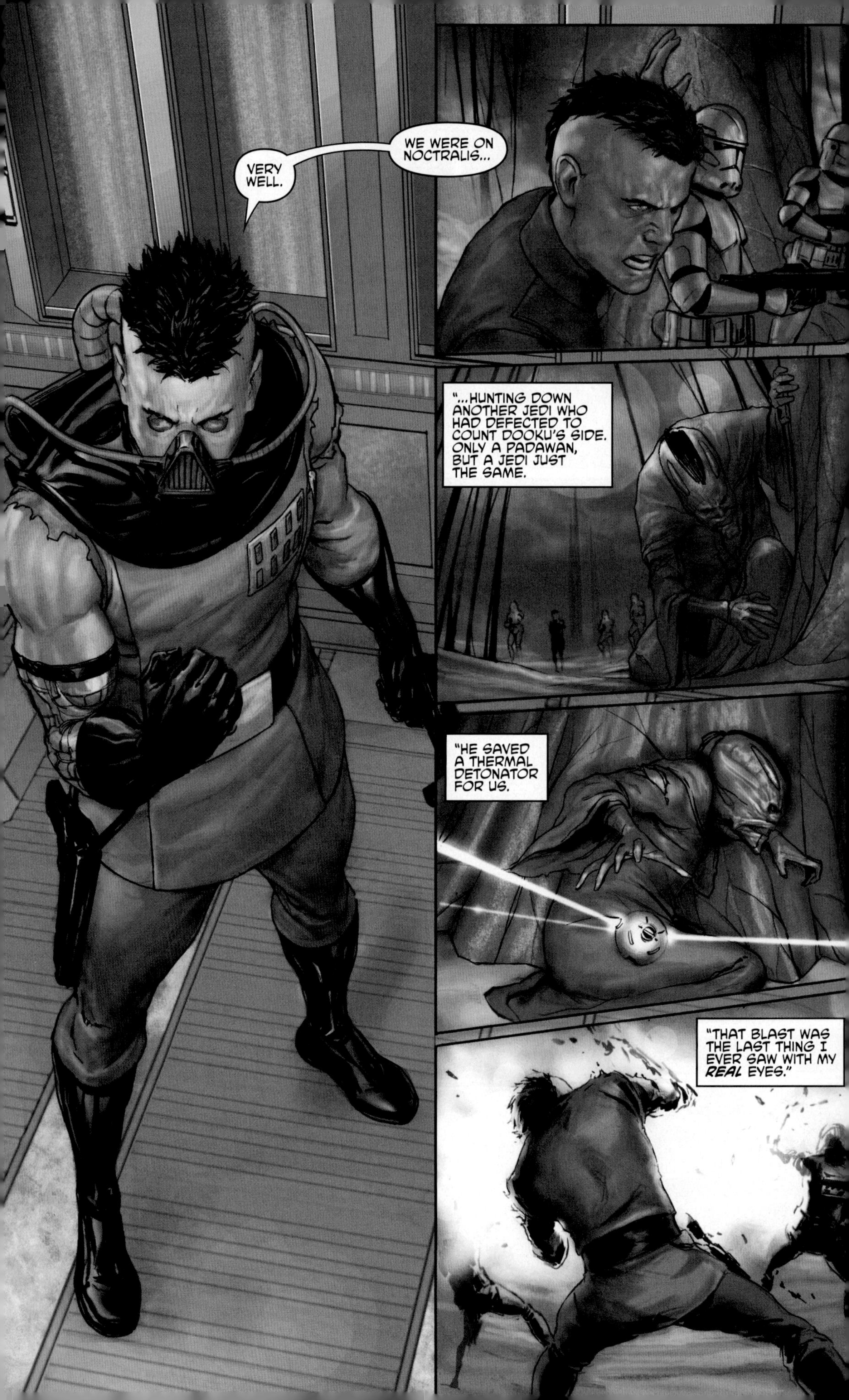
VERY WELL.
WE WERE ON NOCTRALIS...
"...HUNTING DOWN ANOTHER JEDI WHO HAD DEFECTED TO COUNT DOOKU'S SIDE. ONLY A PADAWAN, BUT A JEDI JUST THE SAME.
"HE SAVED A THERMAL DETONATOR FOR US.
"THAT BLAST WAS THE LAST THING I EVER SAW WITH MY REAL EYES."

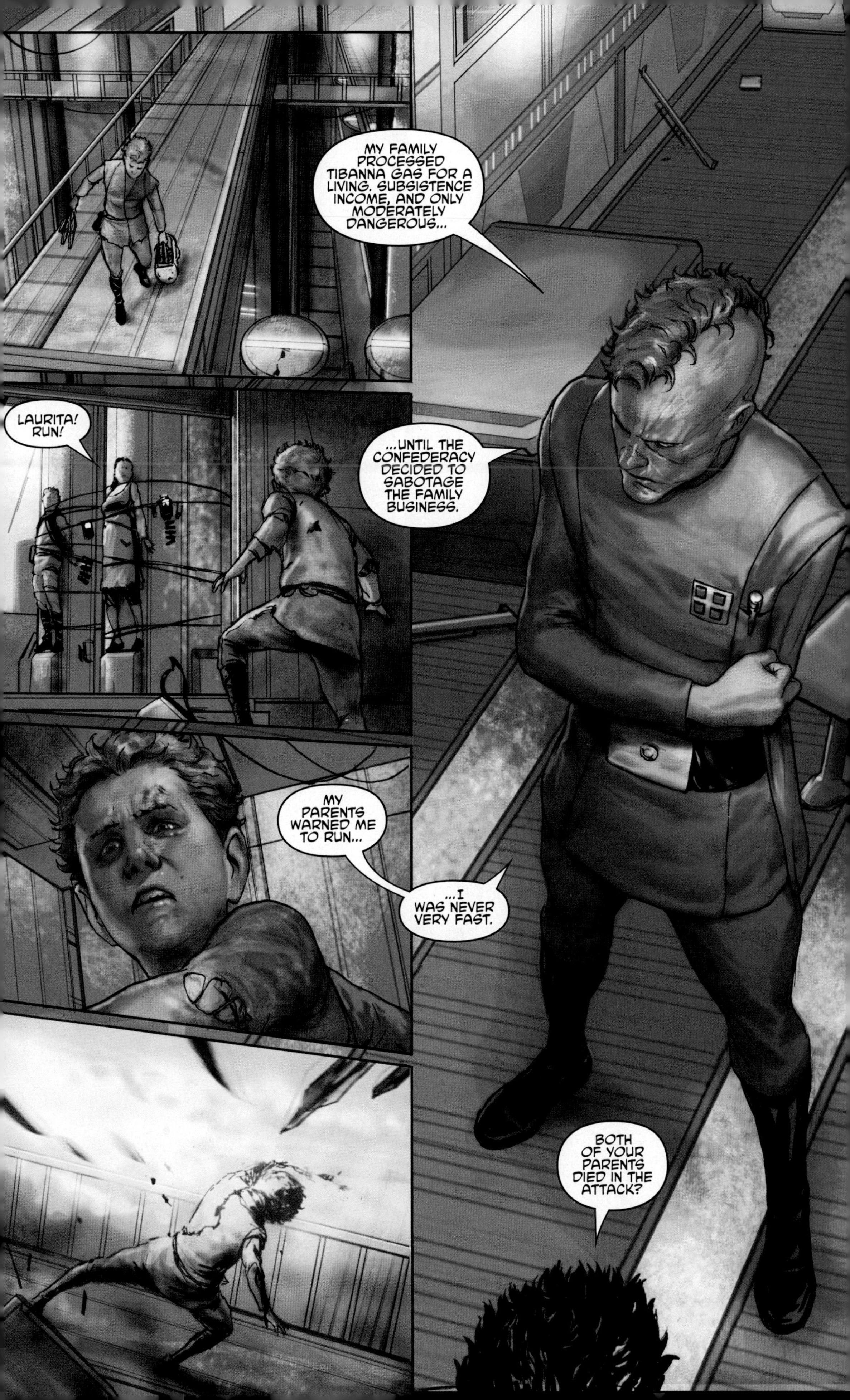
MY FAMILY PROCESSED TIBANNA GAS FOR A LIVING. SUBSISTENCE INCOME, AND ONLY MODERATELY DANGEROUS...
LAURITA! RUN!
...UNTIL THE CONFEDERACY DECIDED TO SABOTAGE THE FAMILY BUSINESS.
MY PARENTS WARNED ME TO RUN...
...I WAS NEVER VERY FAST.
BOTH OF YOUR PARENTS DIED IN THE ATTACK?

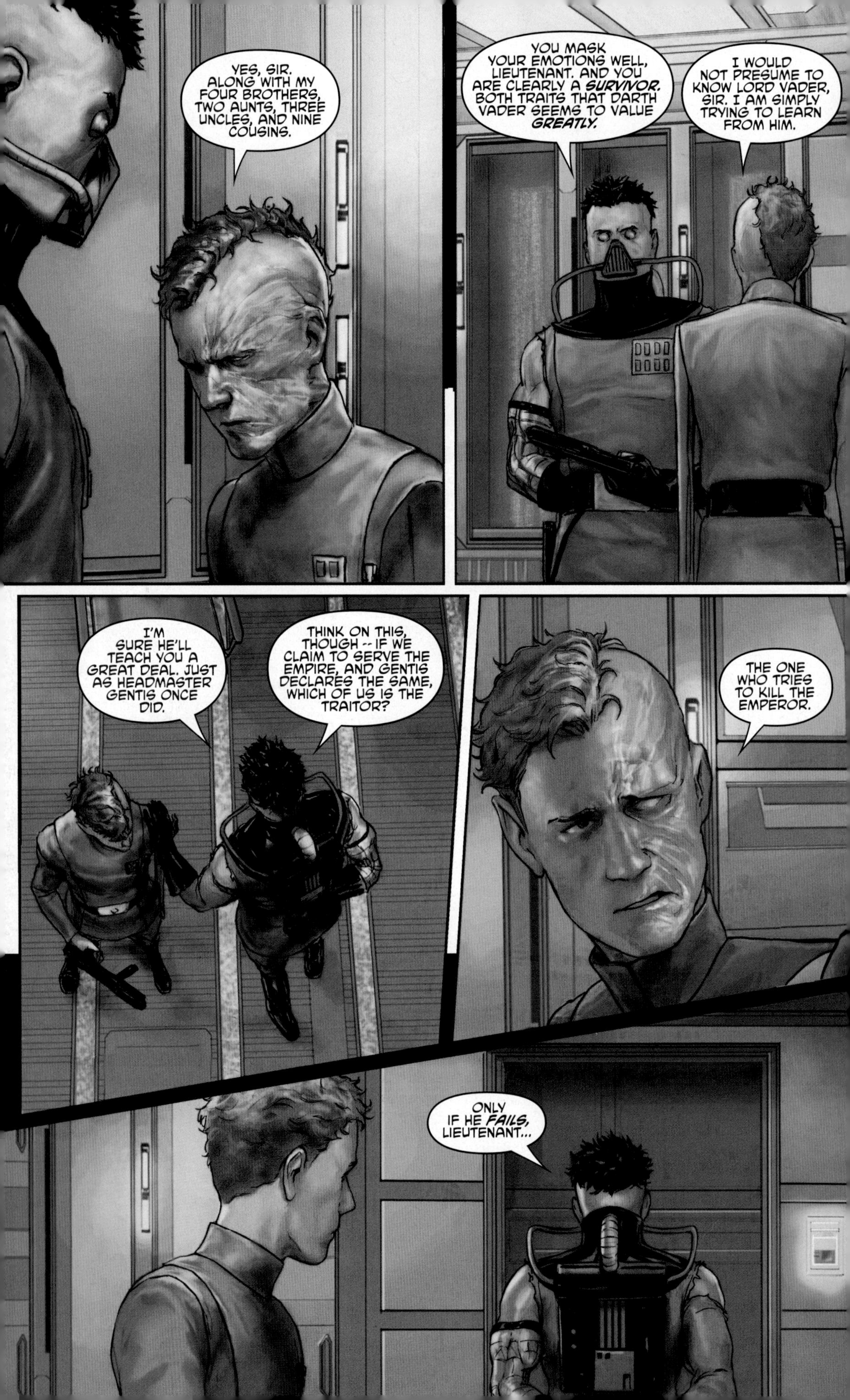
YES, SIR. ALONG WITH MY FOUR BROTHERS, TWO AUNTS, THREE UNCLES, AND NINE COUSINS.
YOU MASK YOUR EMOTIONS WELL, LIEUTENANT. AND YOU ARE CLEARLY A SURVIVOR. BOTH TRAITS THAT DARTH VADER SEEMS TO VALUE GREATLY.
I WOULD NOT PRESUME TO KNOW LORD VADER, SIR. I AM SIMPLY TRYING TO LEARN FROM HIM.
I'M SURE HE'LL TEACH YOU A GREAT DEAL. JUST AS HEADMASTER GENTIS ONCE DID.
THINK ON THIS, THOUGH -- IF WE CLAIM TO SERVE THE EMPIRE, AND GENTIS DECLARES THE SAME, WHICH OF US IS THE TRAITOR?
THE ONE WHO TRIES TO KILL THE EMPEROR.
ONLY IF HE FAILS, LIEUTENANT...

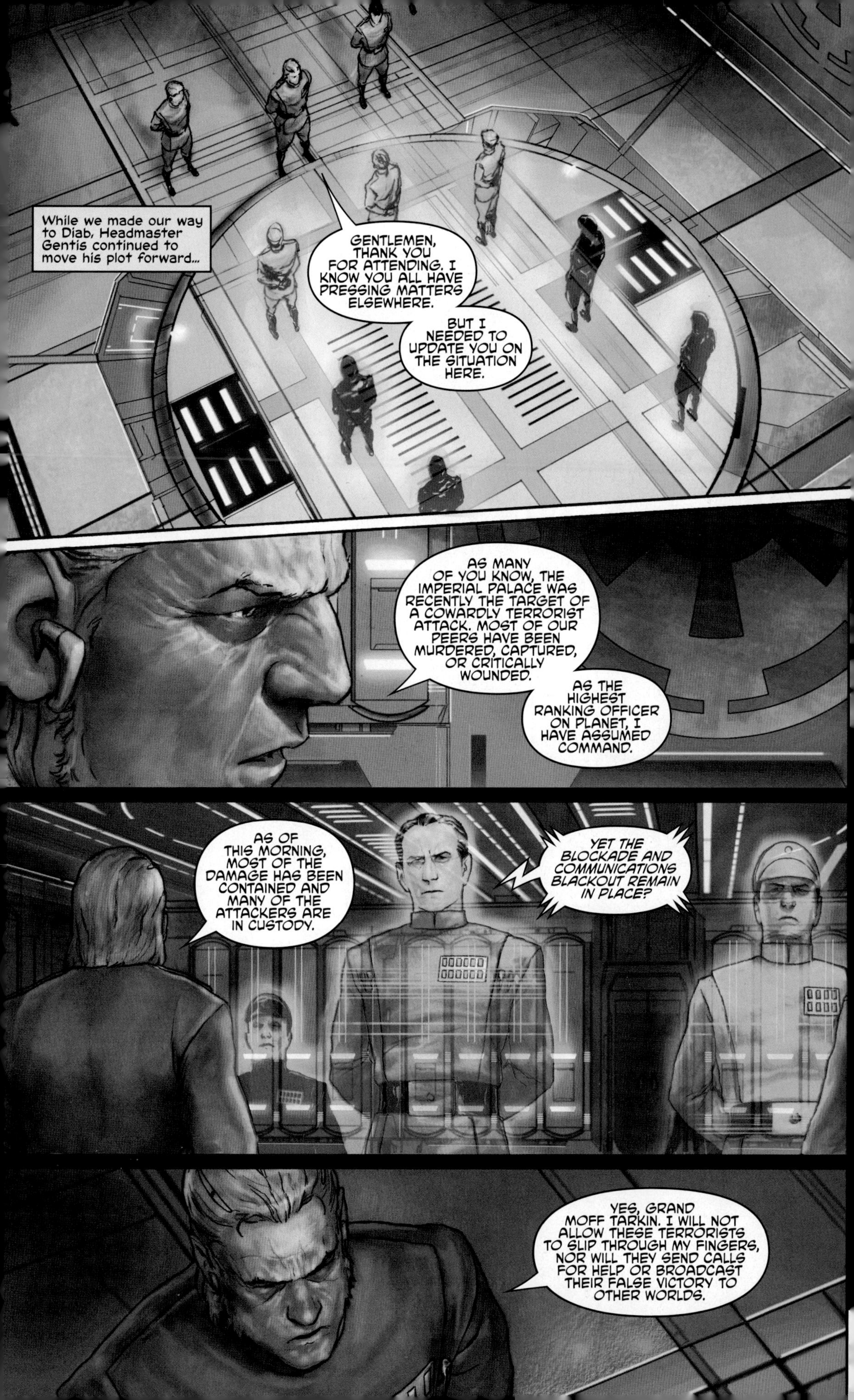
While we made our way to Diab, Headmaster Gentis continued to move his plot forward...
GENTLEMEN, THANK YOU FOR ATTENDING. I KNOW YOU ALL HAVE PRESSING MATTERS ELSEWHERE.
BUT I NEEDED TO UPDATE YOU ON THE SITUATION HERE.
AS MANY OF YOU KNOW, THE IMPERIAL PALACE WAS RECENTLY THE TARGET OF A COWARDLY TERRORIST ATTACK. MOST OF OUR PEERS HAVE BEEN MURDERED, CAPTURED, OR CRITICALLY WOUNDED.
AS THE HIGHEST RANKING OFFICER ON PLANET, I HAVE ASSUMED COMMAND.
AS OF THIS MORNING, MOST OF THE DAMAGE HAS BEEN CONTAINED AND MANY OF THE ATTACKERS ARE IN CUSTODY.
YET THE BLOCKADE AND COMMUNICATIONS BLACKOUT REMAIN IN PLACE?
YES, GRAND MOFF TARKIN. I WILL NOT ALLOW THESE TERRORISTS TO SLIP THROUGH MY FINGERS, NOR WILL THEY SEND CALLS FOR HELP OR BROADCAST THEIR FALSE VICTORY TO OTHER WORLDS.

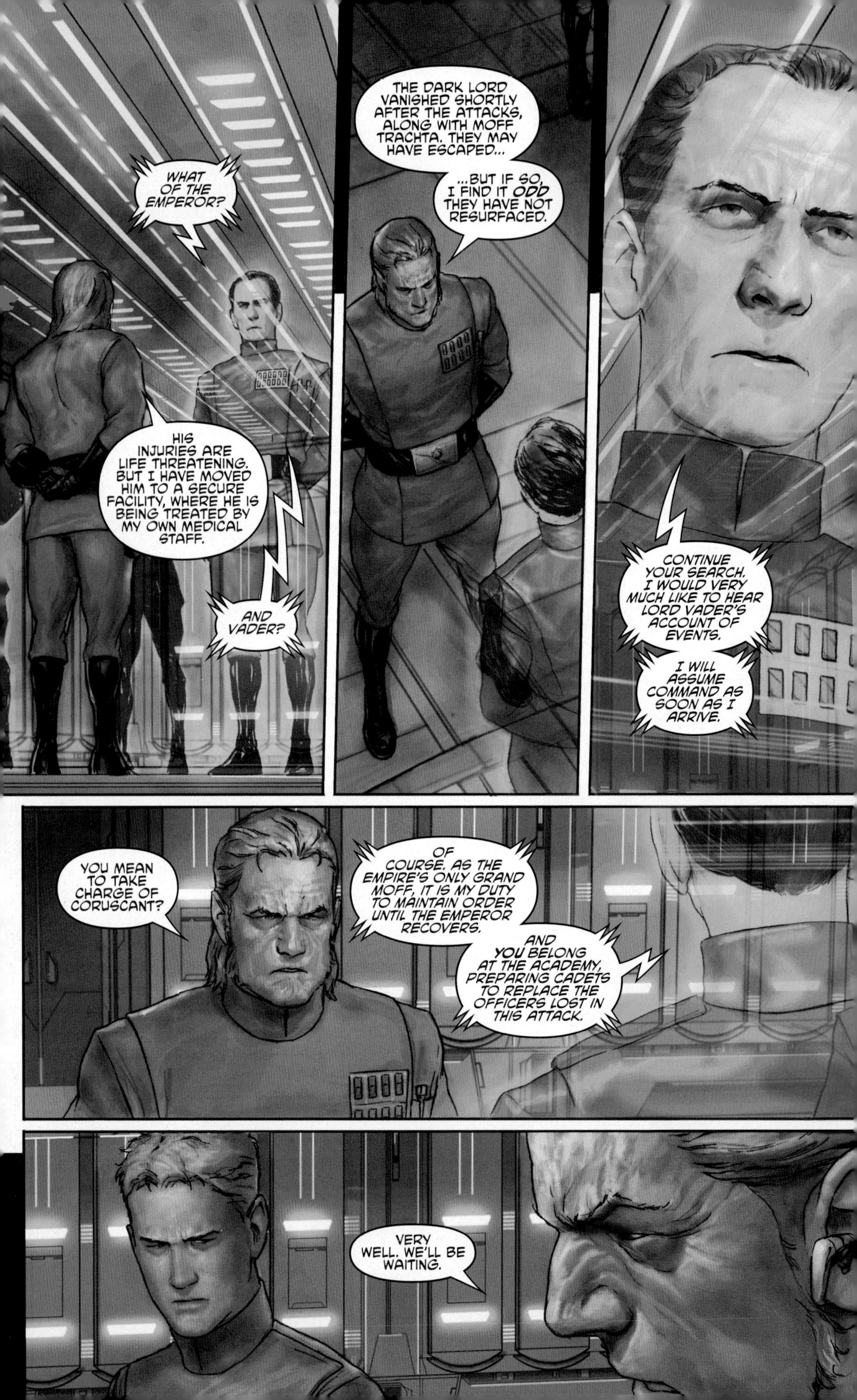
WHAT OF THE EMPEROR?
HIS INJURIES ARE LIFE THREATENING. BUT I HAVE MOVED HIM TO A SECURE FACILITY, WHERE HE IS BEING TREATED BY MY OWN MEDICAL STAFF.
AND VADER?
THE DARK LORD VANISHED SHORTLY AFTER THE ATTACKS, ALONG WITH MOFF TRACHTA. THEY MAY HAVE ESCAPED...
...BUT IF SO, I FIND IT ODD THEY HAVE NOT RESURFACED.
CONTINUE YOUR SEARCH. I WOULD VERY MUCH LIKE TO HEAR LORD VADER'S ACCOUNT OF EVENTS.
I WILL ASSUME COMMAND AS SOON AS I ARRIVE.
YOU MEAN TO TAKE CHARGE OF CORUSCANT?
OF COURSE. AS THE EMPIRE'S ONLY GRAND MOFF, IT IS MY DUTY TO MAINTAIN ORDER UNTIL THE EMPEROR RECOVERS.
AND YOU BELONG AT THE ACADEMY, PREPARING CADETS TO REPLACE THE OFFICERS LOST IN THIS ATTACK.
VERY WELL. WE'LL BE WAITING.

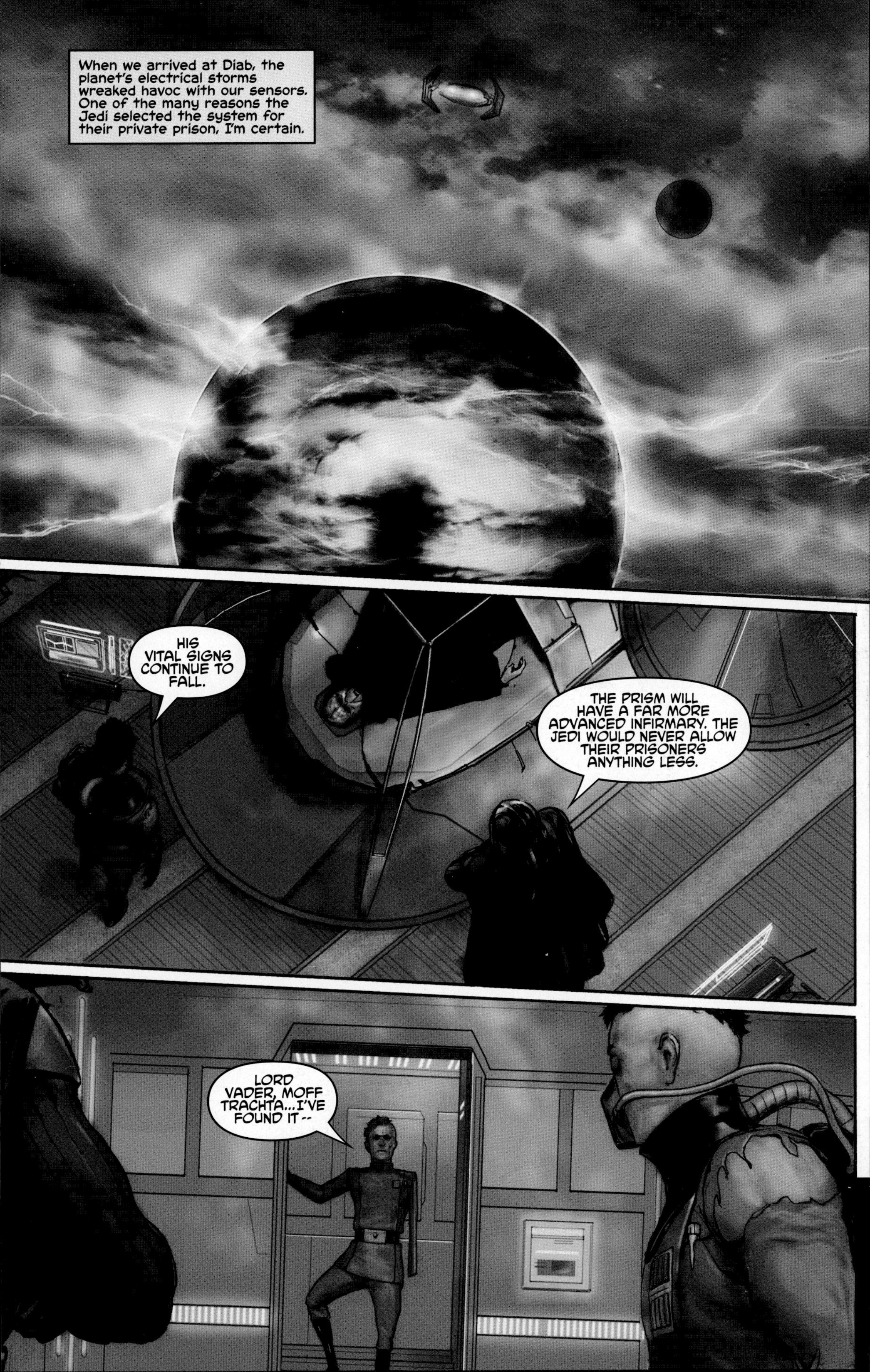
When we arrived at Diab, the planet's electrical storms wreaked havoc with our sensors. One of the many reasons the Jedi selected the system for their private prison, I'm certain.
HIS VITAL SIGNS CONTINUE TO FALL.
THE PRISM WILL HAVE A FAR MORE ADVANCED INFIRMARY. THE JEDI WOULD NEVER ALLOW THEIR PRISONERS ANYTHING LESS.
LORD VADER, MOFF TRACHTA...I'VE FOUND IT --

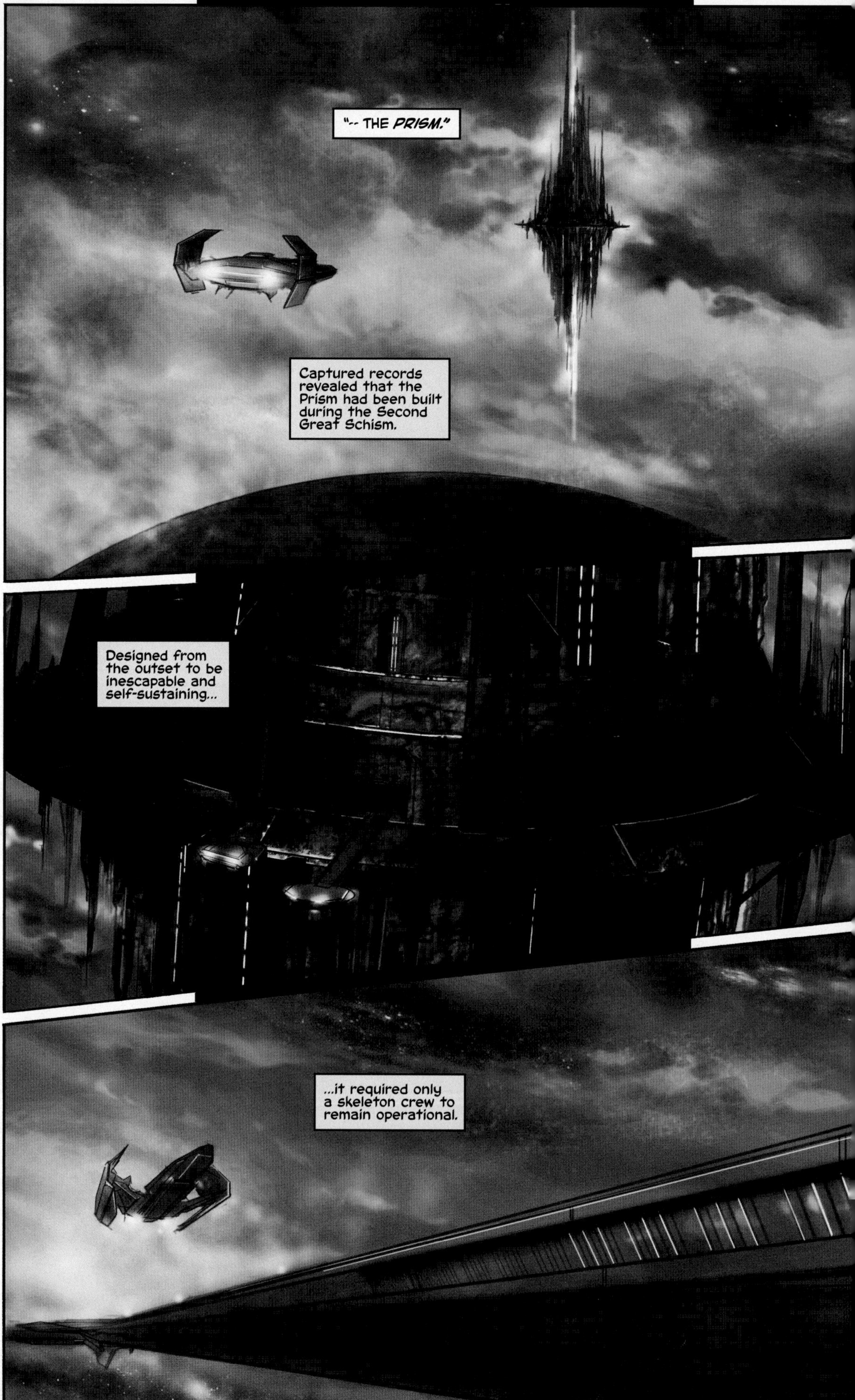
"-- THE *PRISM.*"
Captured records revealed that the Prism had been built during the Second Great Schism.
Designed from the outset to be inescapable and self-sustaining...
...it required only a skeleton crew to remain operational.

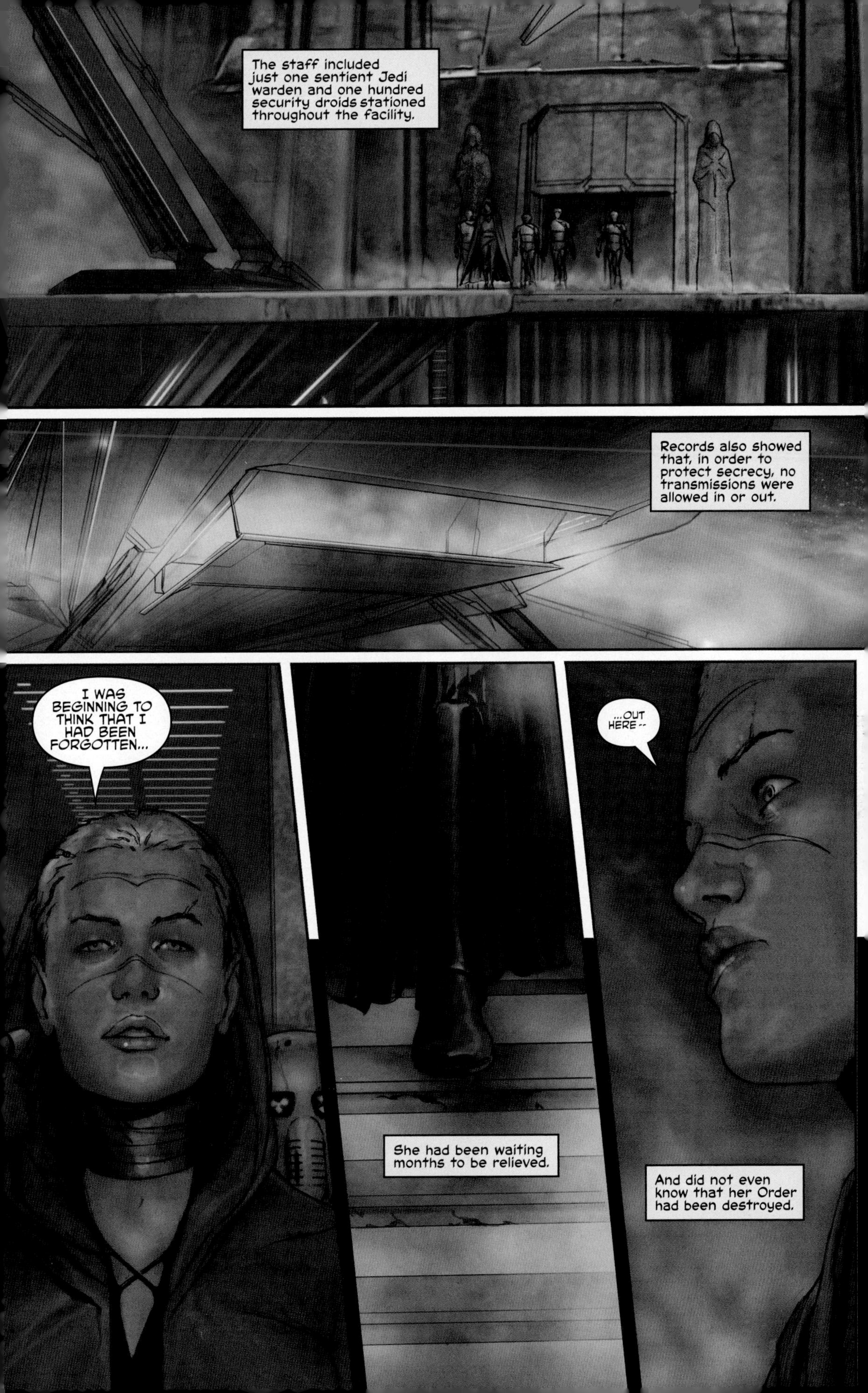
The staff included just one sentient Jedi warden and one hundred security droids stationed throughout the facility.
Records also showed that, in order to protect secrecy, no transmissions were allowed in or out.
I WAS BEGINNING TO THINK THAT I HAD BEEN FORGOTTEN...
She had been waiting months to be relieved.
...OUT HERE--
And did not even know that her Order had been destroyed.

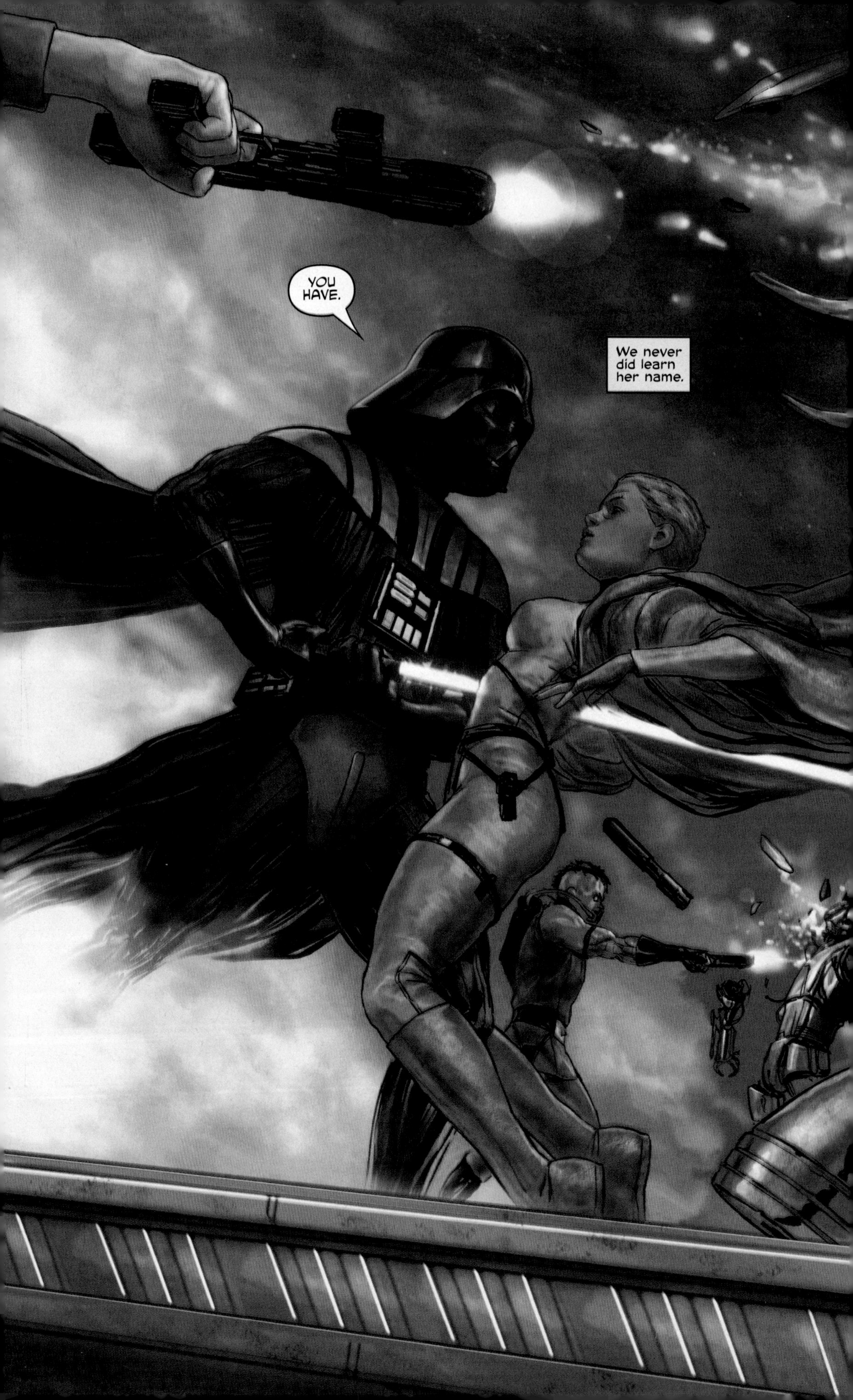
YOU HAVE.
We never did learn her name.

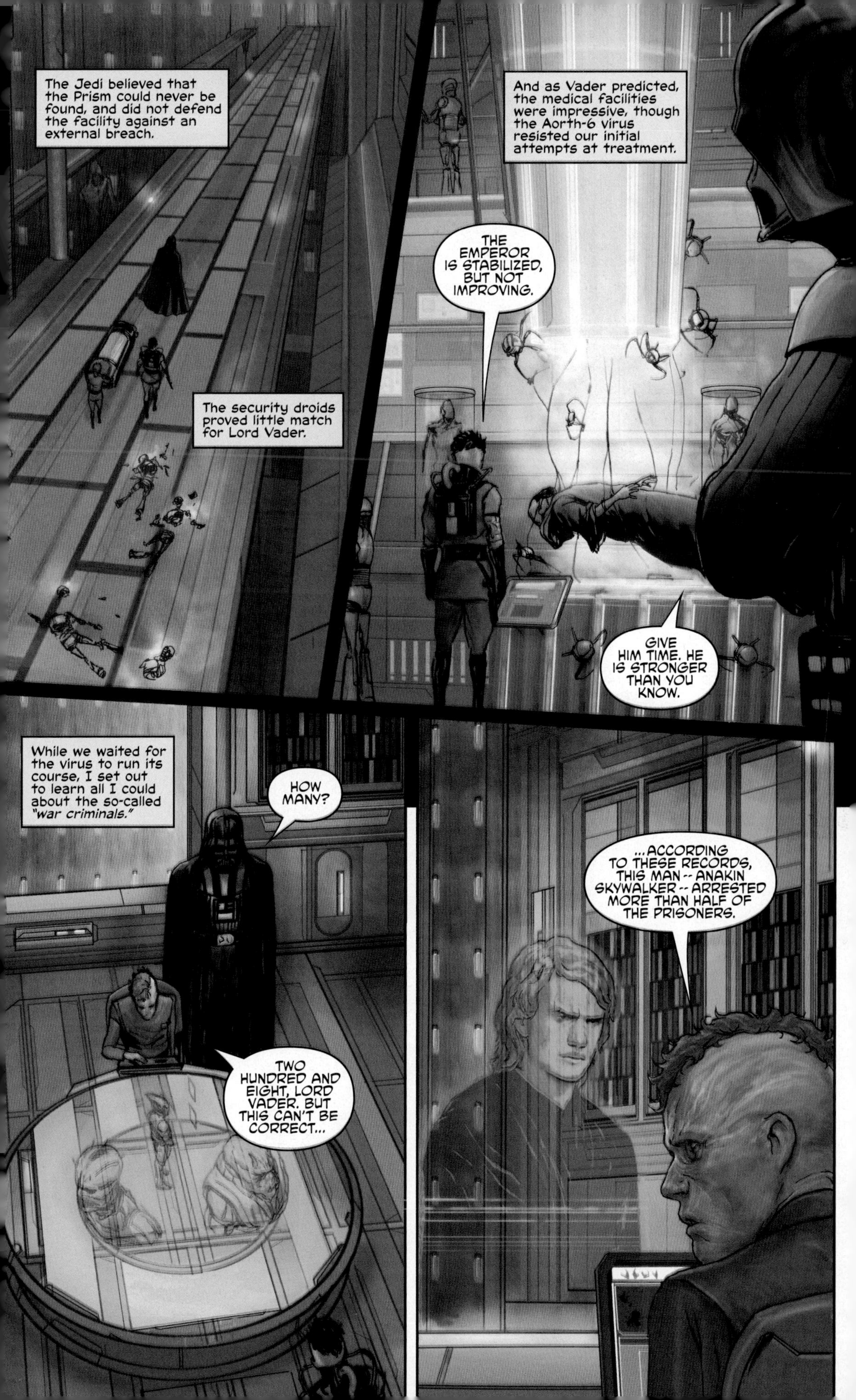

The Jedi believed that the Prism could never be found, and did not defend the facility against an external breach.
The security droids proved little match for Lord Vader.
And as Vader predicted, the medical facilities were impressive, though the Aorth-6 virus resisted our initial attempts at treatment.
THE EMPEROR IS STABILIZED, BUT NOT IMPROVING.
GIVE HIM TIME. HE IS STRONGER THAN YOU KNOW.
While we waited for the virus to run its course, I set out to learn all I could about the so-called *"war criminals."*
HOW MANY?
TWO HUNDRED AND EIGHT, LORD VADER. BUT THIS CAN'T BE CORRECT...
...ACCORDING TO THESE RECORDS, THIS MAN -- ANAKIN SKYWALKER -- ARRESTED MORE THAN HALF OF THE PRISONERS.

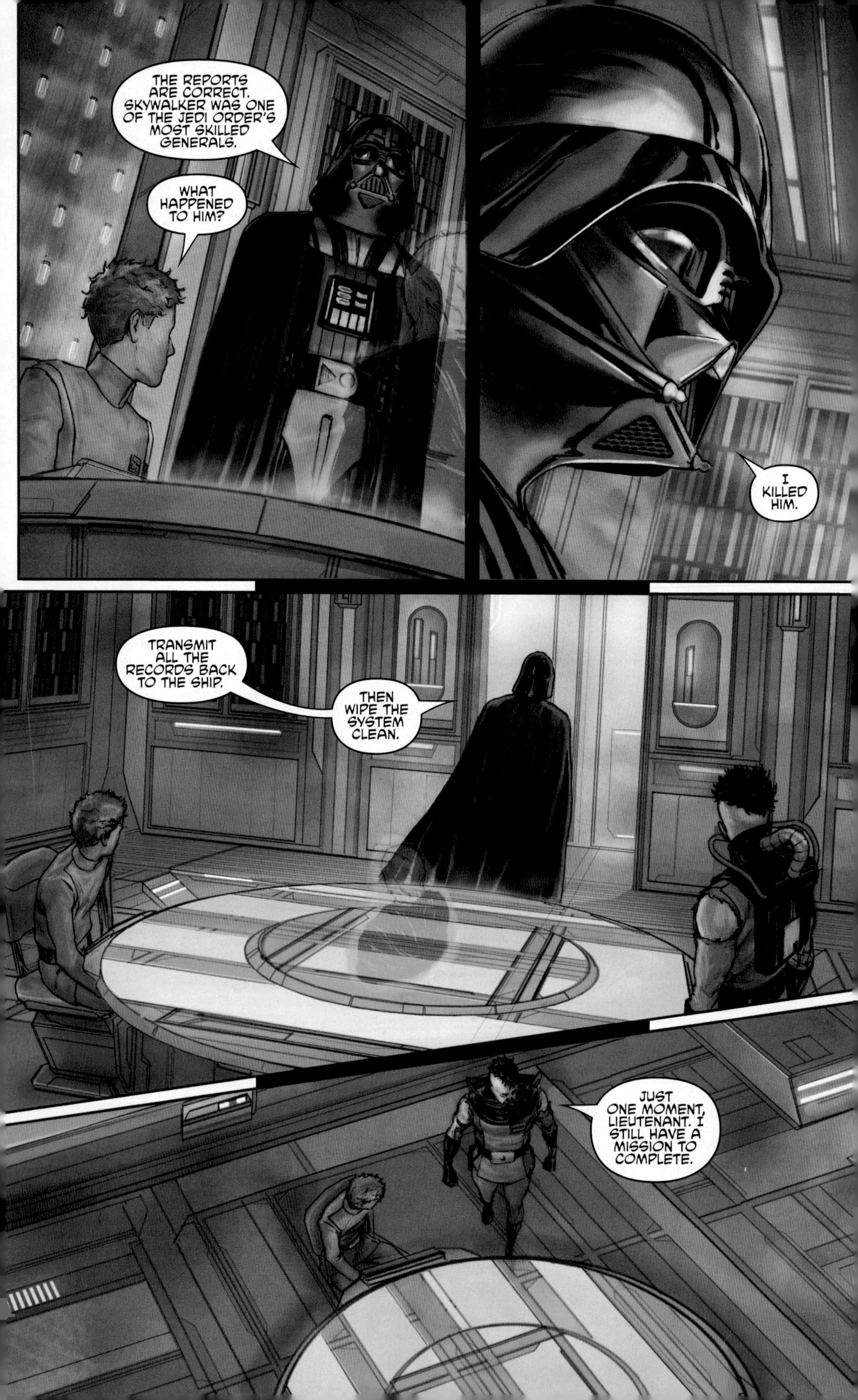
THE REPORTS ARE CORRECT. SKYWALKER WAS ONE OF THE JEDI ORDER'S MOST SKILLED GENERALS.
WHAT HAPPENED TO HIM?
I KILLED HIM.
TRANSMIT ALL THE RECORDS BACK TO THE SHIP.
THEN WIPE THE SYSTEM CLEAN.
JUST ONE MOMENT, LIEUTENANT. I STILL HAVE A MISSION TO COMPLETE.

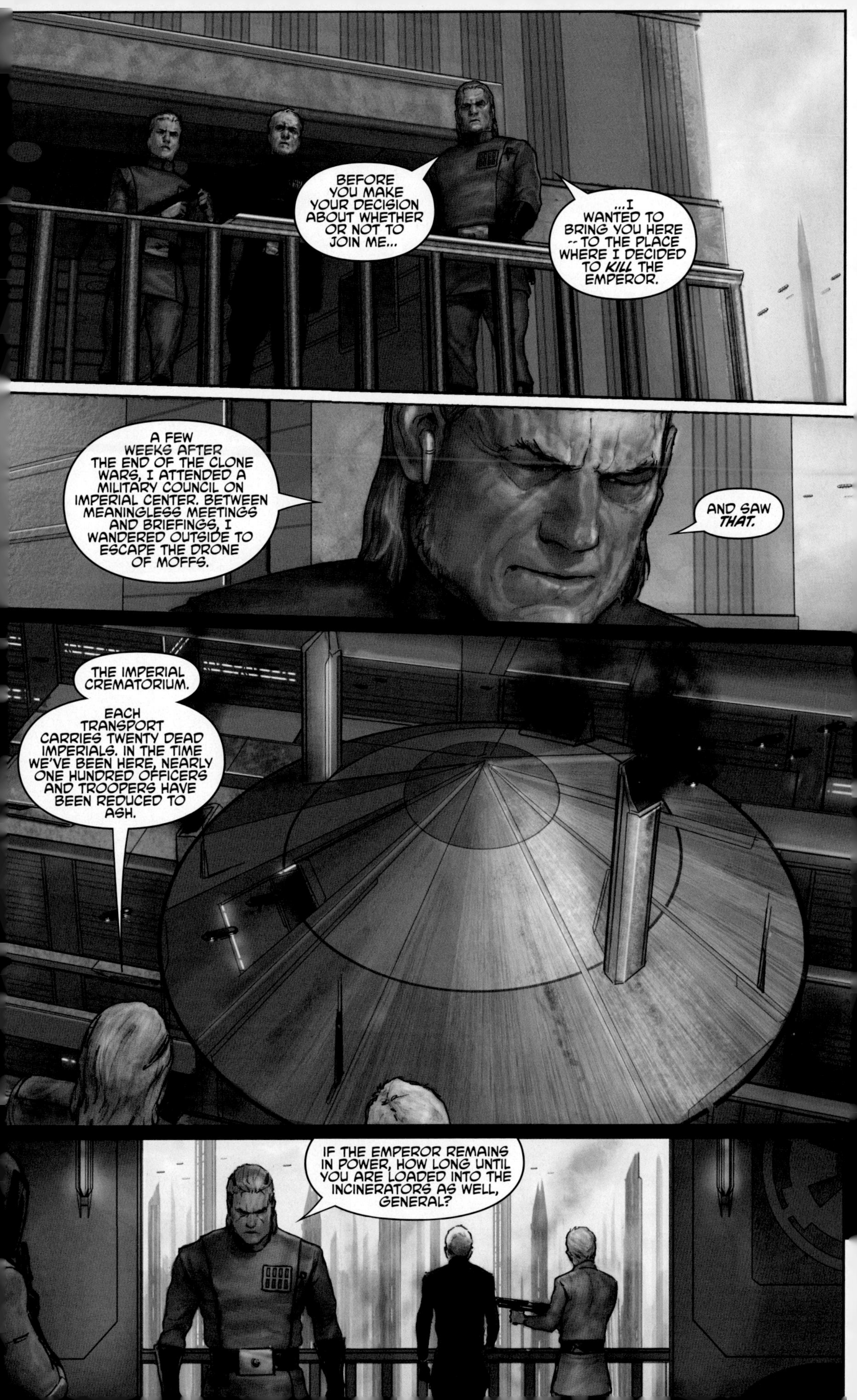
BEFORE YOU MAKE YOUR DECISION ABOUT WHETHER OR NOT TO JOIN ME...
...I WANTED TO BRING YOU HERE -- TO THE PLACE WHERE I DECIDED TO *KILL* THE EMPEROR.
A FEW WEEKS AFTER THE END OF THE CLONE WARS, I ATTENDED A MILITARY COUNCIL ON IMPERIAL CENTER. BETWEEN MEANINGLESS MEETINGS AND BRIEFINGS, I WANDERED OUTSIDE TO ESCAPE THE DRONE OF MOFFS.
AND SAW *THAT.*
THE IMPERIAL CREMATORIUM.
EACH TRANSPORT CARRIES TWENTY DEAD IMPERIALS. IN THE TIME WE'VE BEEN HERE, NEARLY ONE HUNDRED OFFICERS AND TROOPERS HAVE BEEN REDUCED TO ASH.
IF THE EMPEROR REMAINS IN POWER, HOW LONG UNTIL YOU ARE LOADED INTO THE INCINERATORS AS WELL, GENERAL?

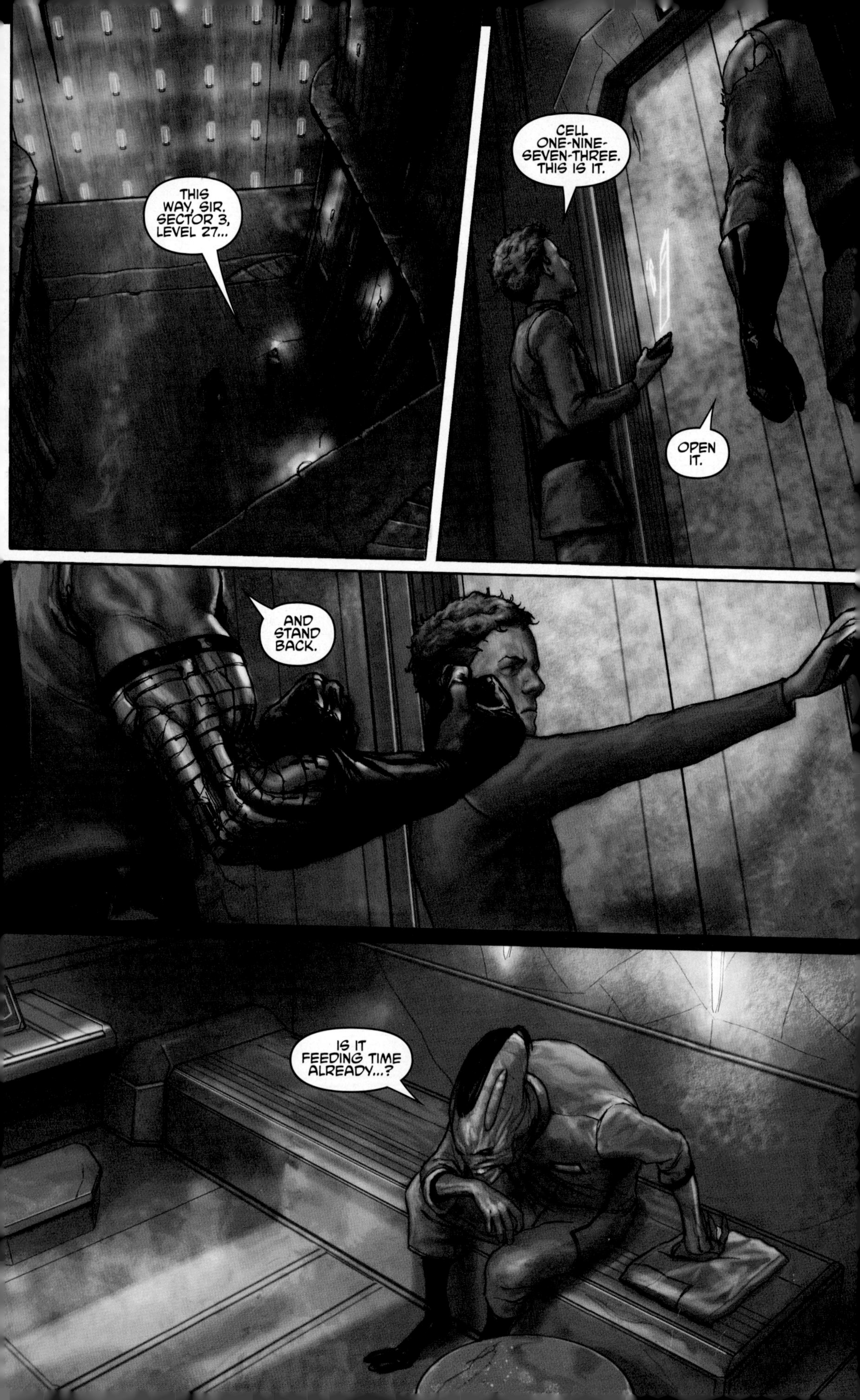

THIS WAY, SIR. SECTOR 3, LEVEL 27...
CELL ONE-NINE-SEVEN-THREE. THIS IS IT.
OPEN IT.
AND STAND BACK.
IS IT FEEDING TIME ALREADY...?

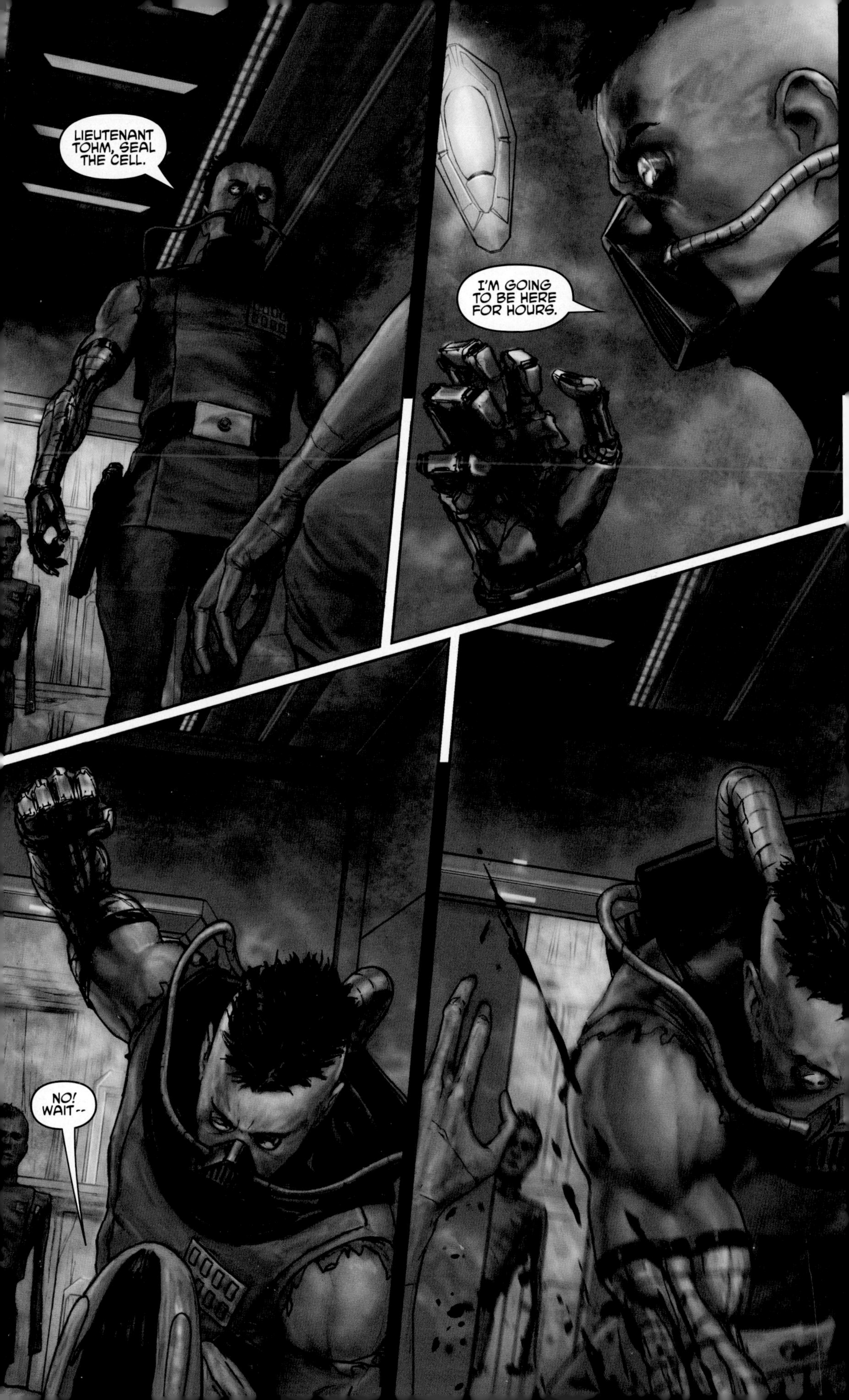
LIEUTENANT TOHM, SEAL THE CELL.
I'M GOING TO BE HERE FOR HOURS.
NO! WAIT--

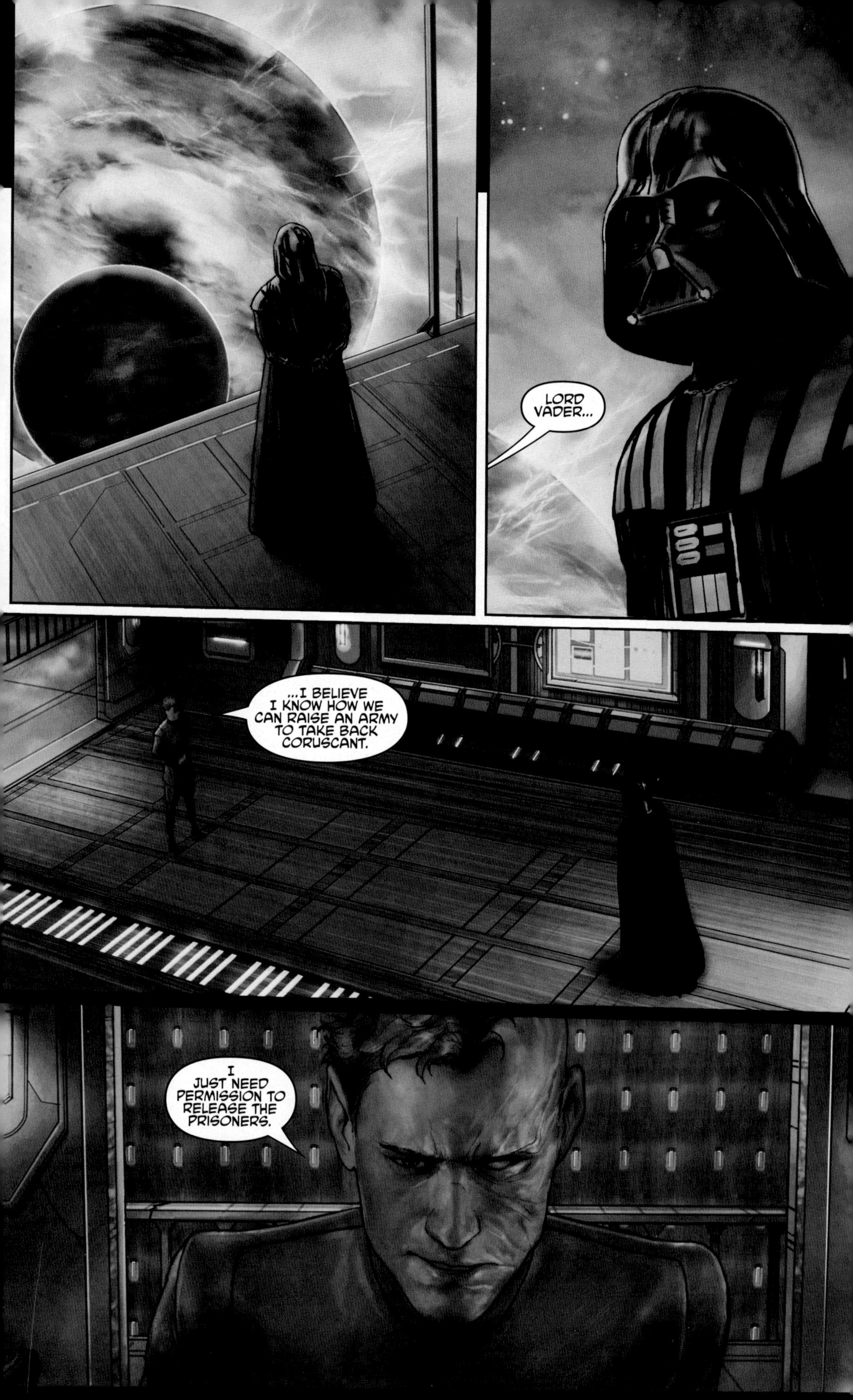
LORD VADER...
...I BELIEVE I KNOW HOW WE CAN RAISE AN ARMY TO TAKE BACK CORUSCANT.
I JUST NEED PERMISSION TO RELEASE THE PRISONERS.

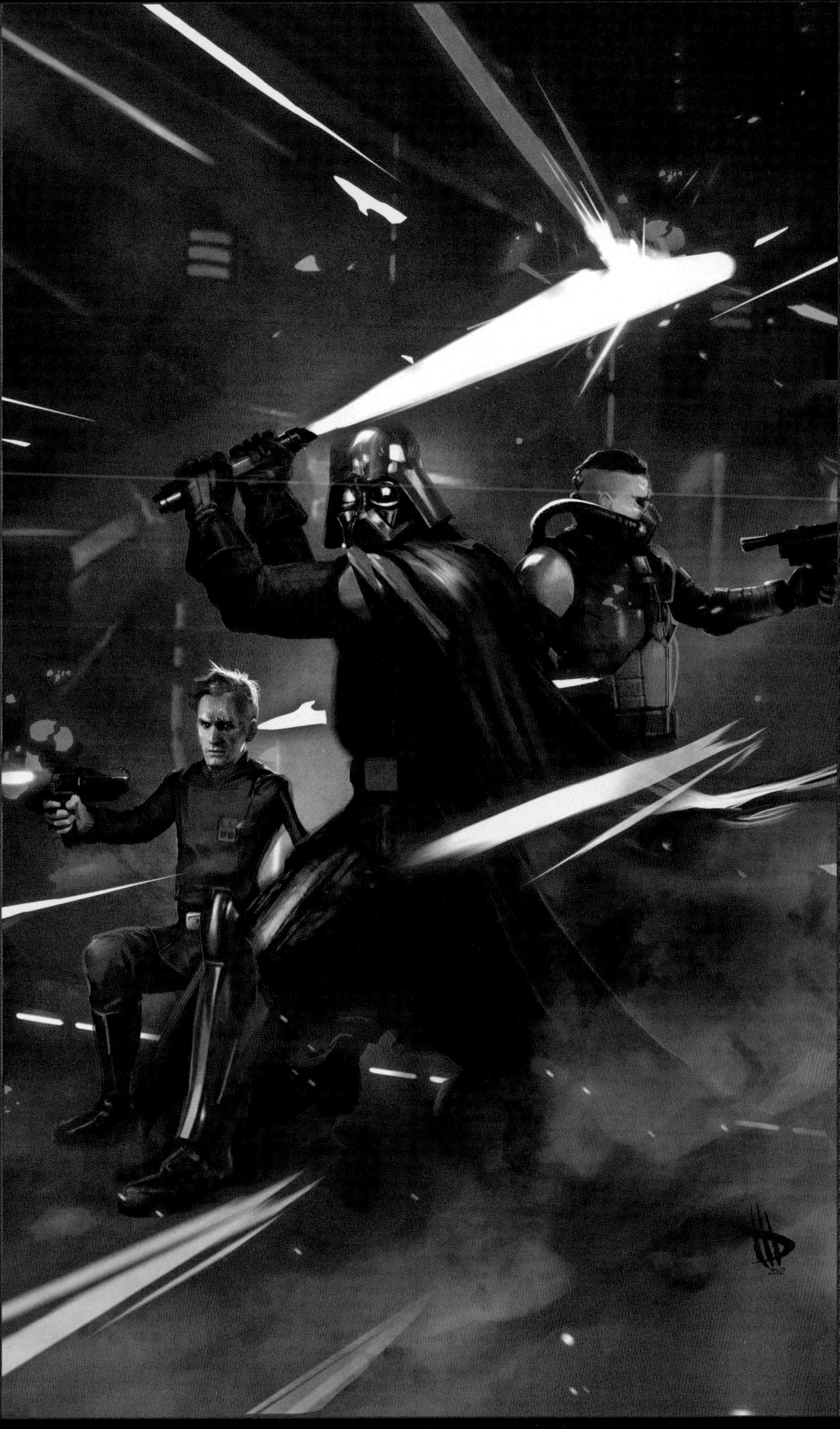

***STAR WARS: DARTH VADER AND THE GHOST PRISON #4***

WRITER: HADEN BLACKMAN • ARTIST & COLORIST: AGUSTIN ALESSIO • LETTERER: MICHAEL HEISLER
ASSISTANT EDITOR: FREDDYE LINS • EDITOR: RANDY STRADLEY • COVER ARTIST: DAVE WILKINS

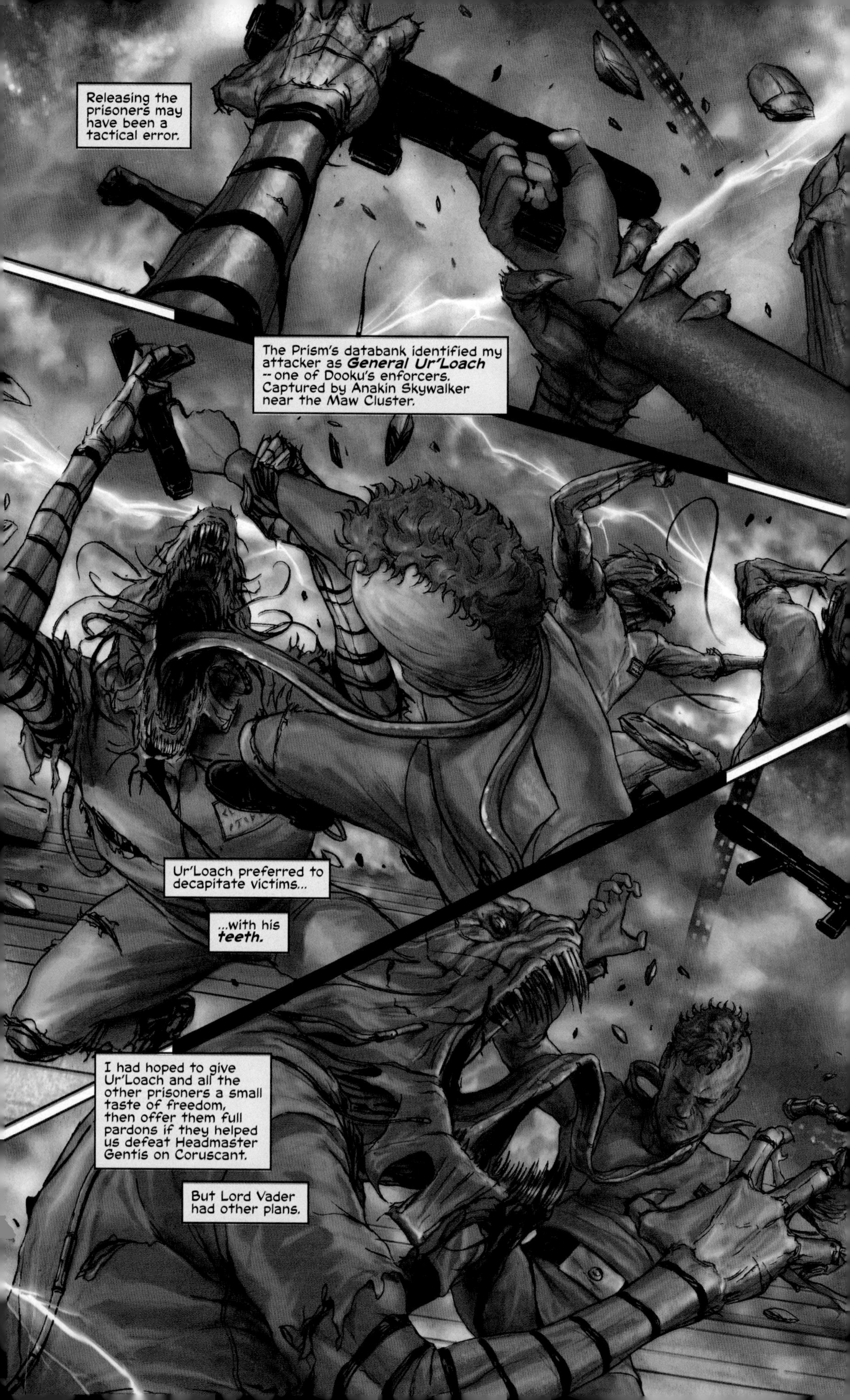
Releasing the prisoners may have been a tactical error.
The Prism's databank identified my attacker as *General Ur'Loach* -- one of Dooku's enforcers. Captured by Anakin Skywalker near the Maw Cluster.
Ur'Loach preferred to decapitate victims...
...with his *teeth.*
I had hoped to give Ur'Loach and all the other prisoners a small taste of freedom, then offer them full pardons if they helped us defeat Headmaster Gentis on Coruscant.
But Lord Vader had other plans.

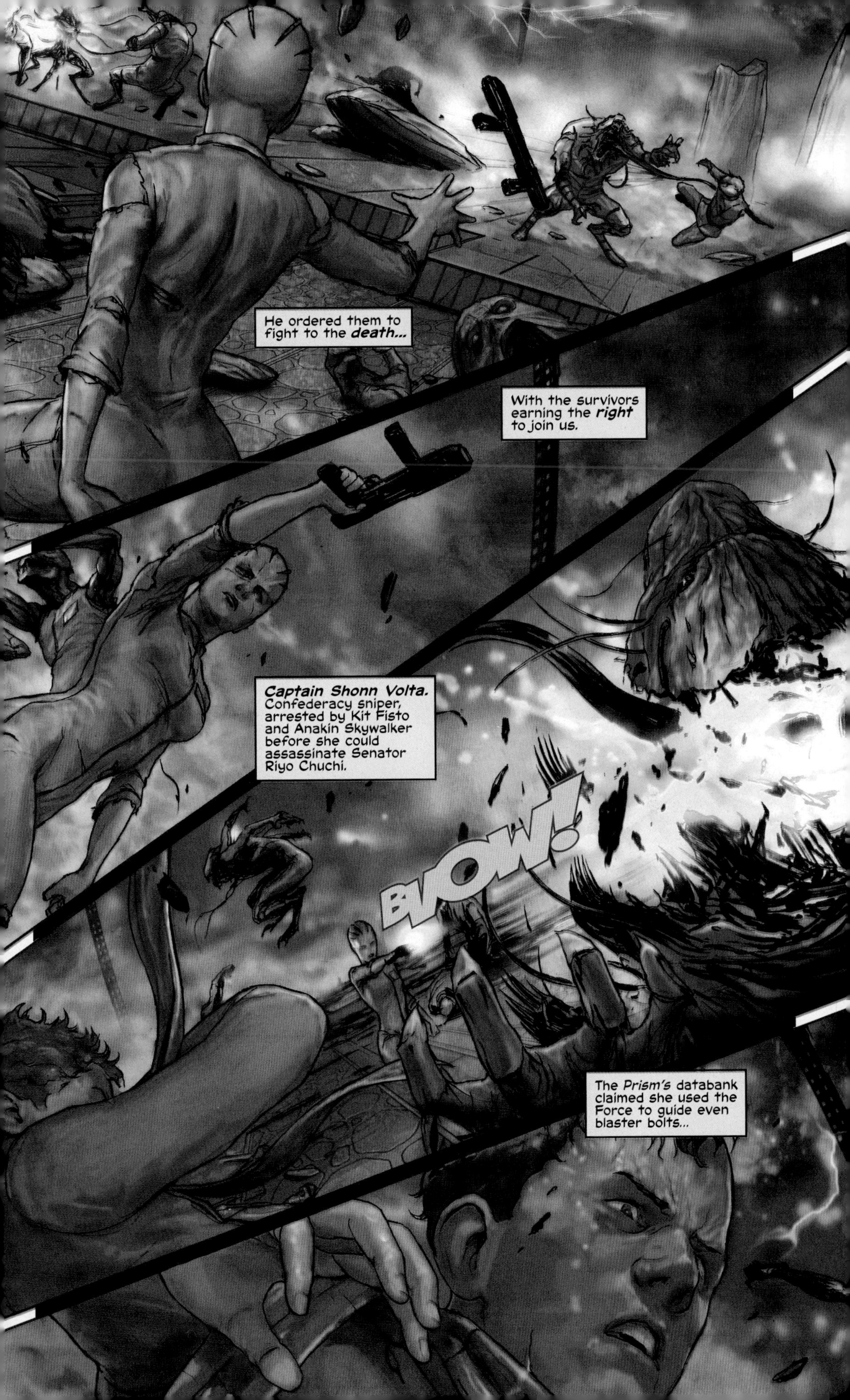
He ordered them to fight to the *death...*
With the survivors earning the *right* to join us.
***Captain Shonn Volta.*** Confederacy sniper, arrested by Kit Fisto and Anakin Skywalker before she could assassinate Senator Riyo Chuchi.
BVOW!
The *Prism's* databank claimed she used the Force to guide even blaster bolts...

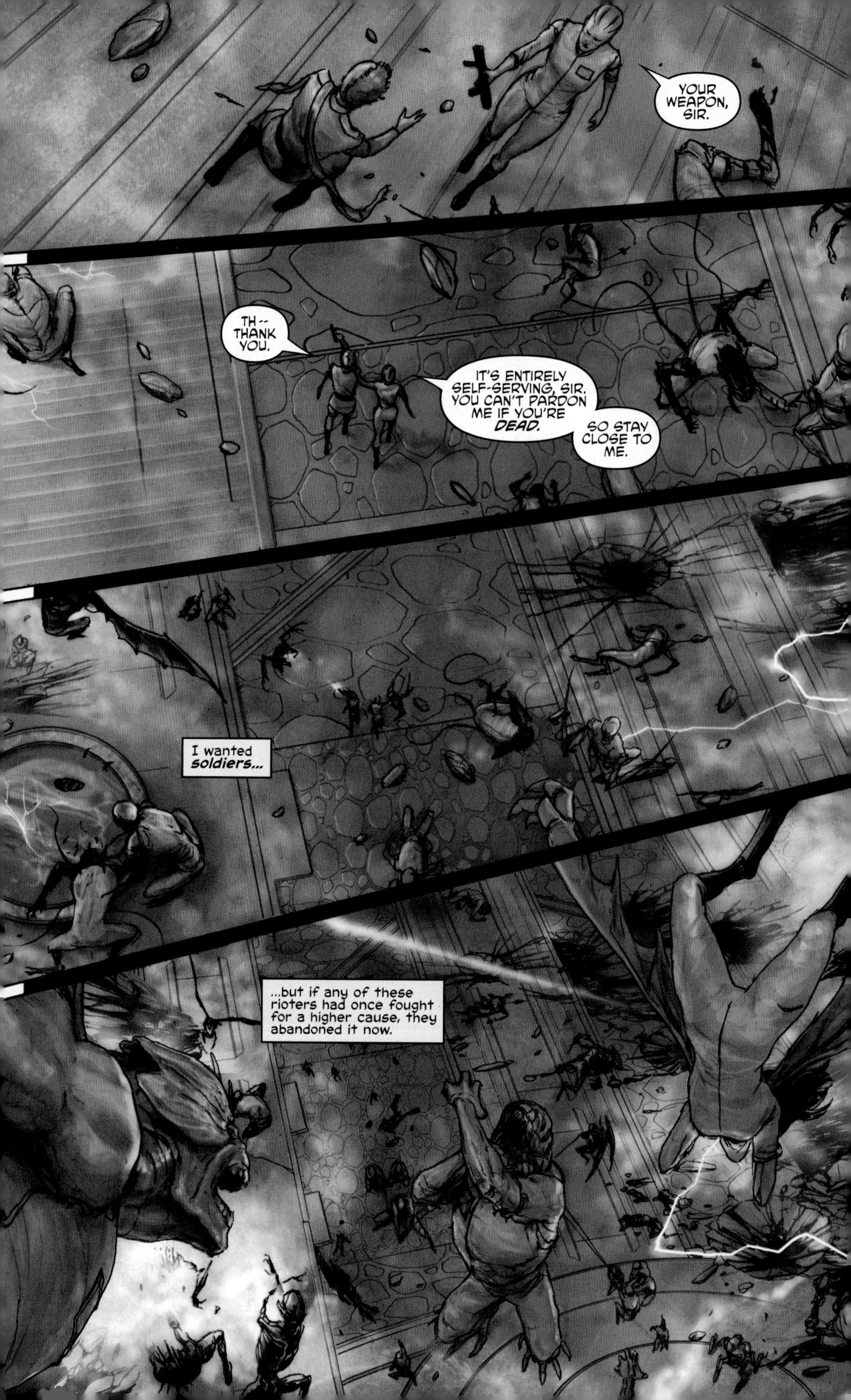

YOUR WEAPON, SIR.
TH -- THANK YOU.
IT'S ENTIRELY SELF-SERVING, SIR. YOU CAN'T PARDON ME IF YOU'RE *DEAD.*
SO STAY CLOSE TO ME.
I wanted *soldiers...*
...but if any of these rioters had once fought for a higher cause, they abandoned it now.

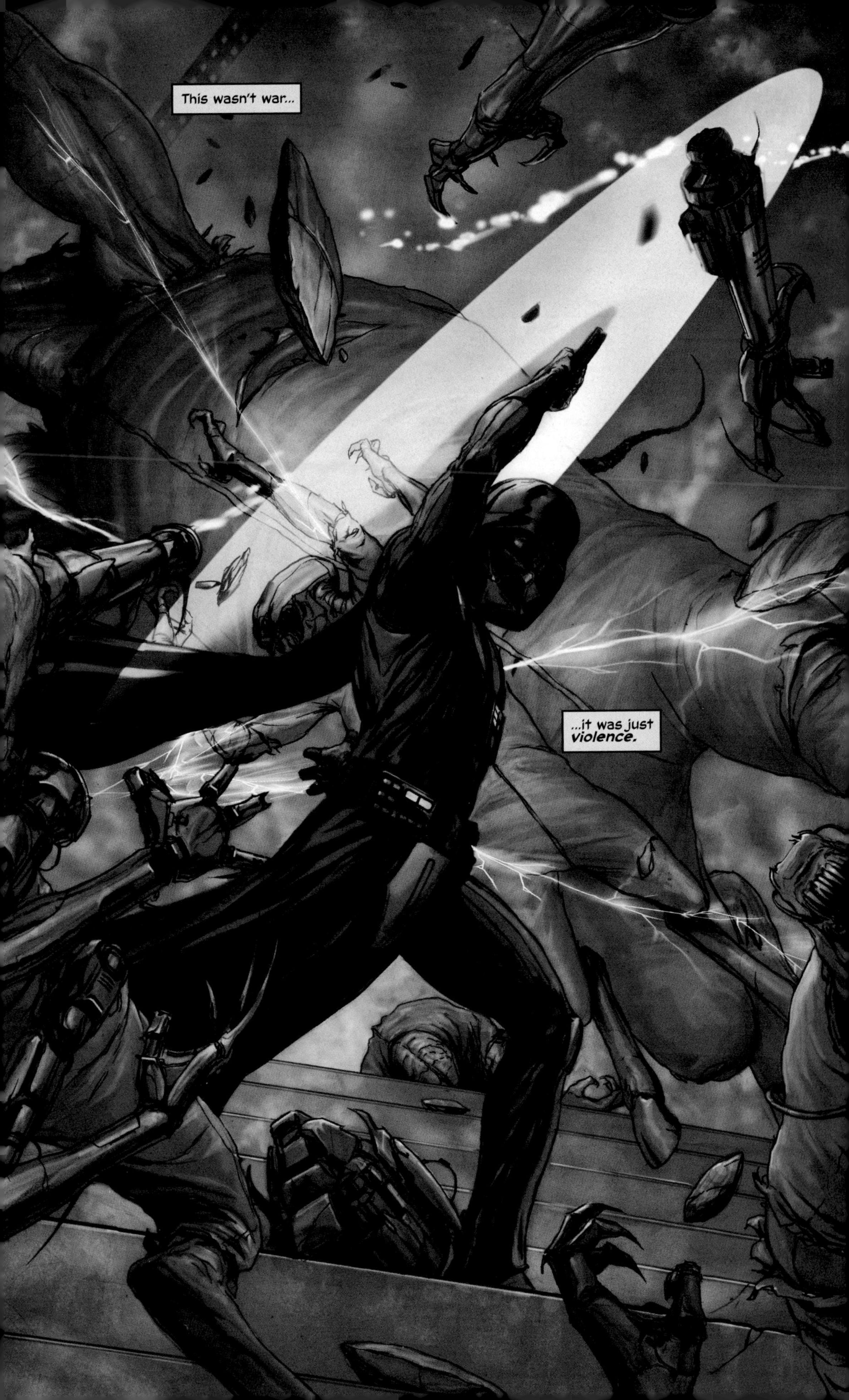
This wasn't war...
...it was just *violence.*

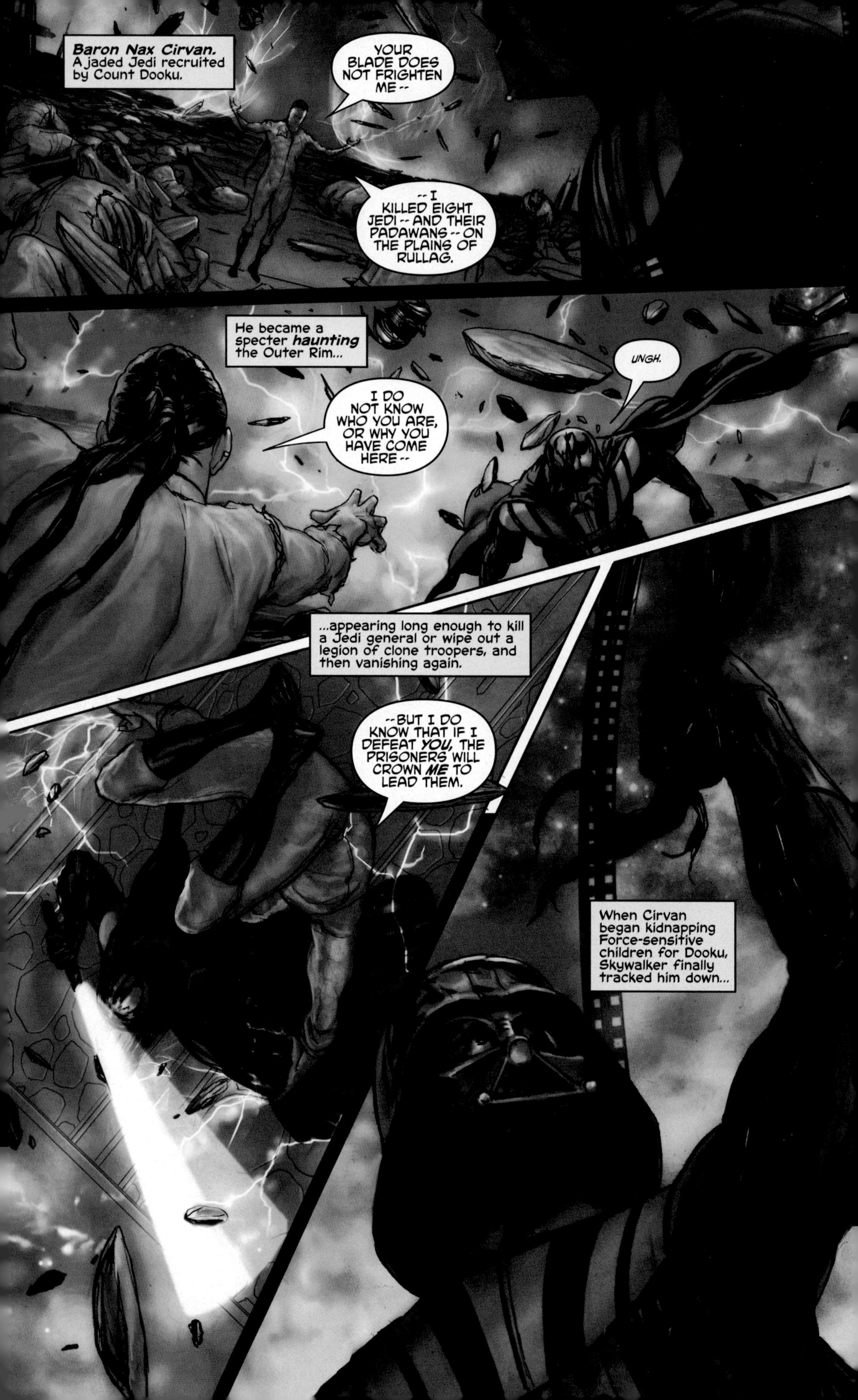

Baron Nax Cirvan. A jaded Jedi recruited by Count Dooku.
YOUR BLADE DOES NOT FRIGHTEN ME --
-- I KILLED EIGHT JEDI -- AND THEIR PADAWANS -- ON THE PLAINS OF RULLAG.
He became a specter haunting the Outer Rim...
I DO NOT KNOW WHO YOU ARE, OR WHY YOU HAVE COME HERE --
UNGH.
...appearing long enough to kill a Jedi general or wipe out a legion of clone troopers, and then vanishing again.
-- BUT I DO KNOW THAT IF I DEFEAT YOU, THE PRISONERS WILL CROWN ME TO LEAD THEM.
When Cirvan began kidnapping Force-sensitive children for Dooku, Skywalker finally tracked him down...

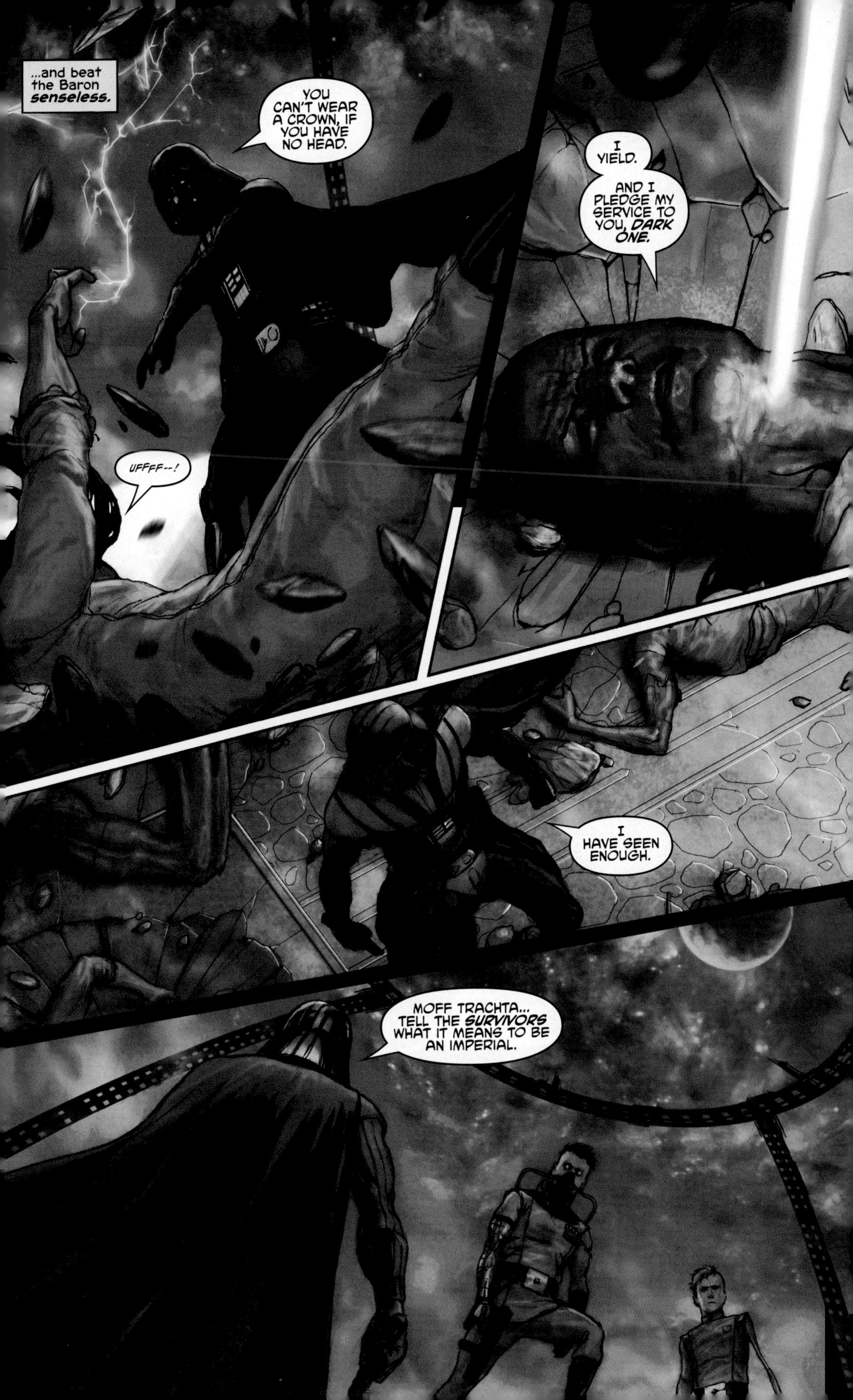

...and beat the Baron ***senseless.***
YOU CAN'T WEAR A CROWN, IF YOU HAVE NO HEAD.
UFFFF--!
I YIELD.
AND I PLEDGE MY SERVICE TO YOU, ***DARK ONE.***
I HAVE SEEN ENOUGH.
MOFF TRACHTA... TELL THE ***SURVIVORS*** WHAT IT MEANS TO BE AN IMPERIAL.

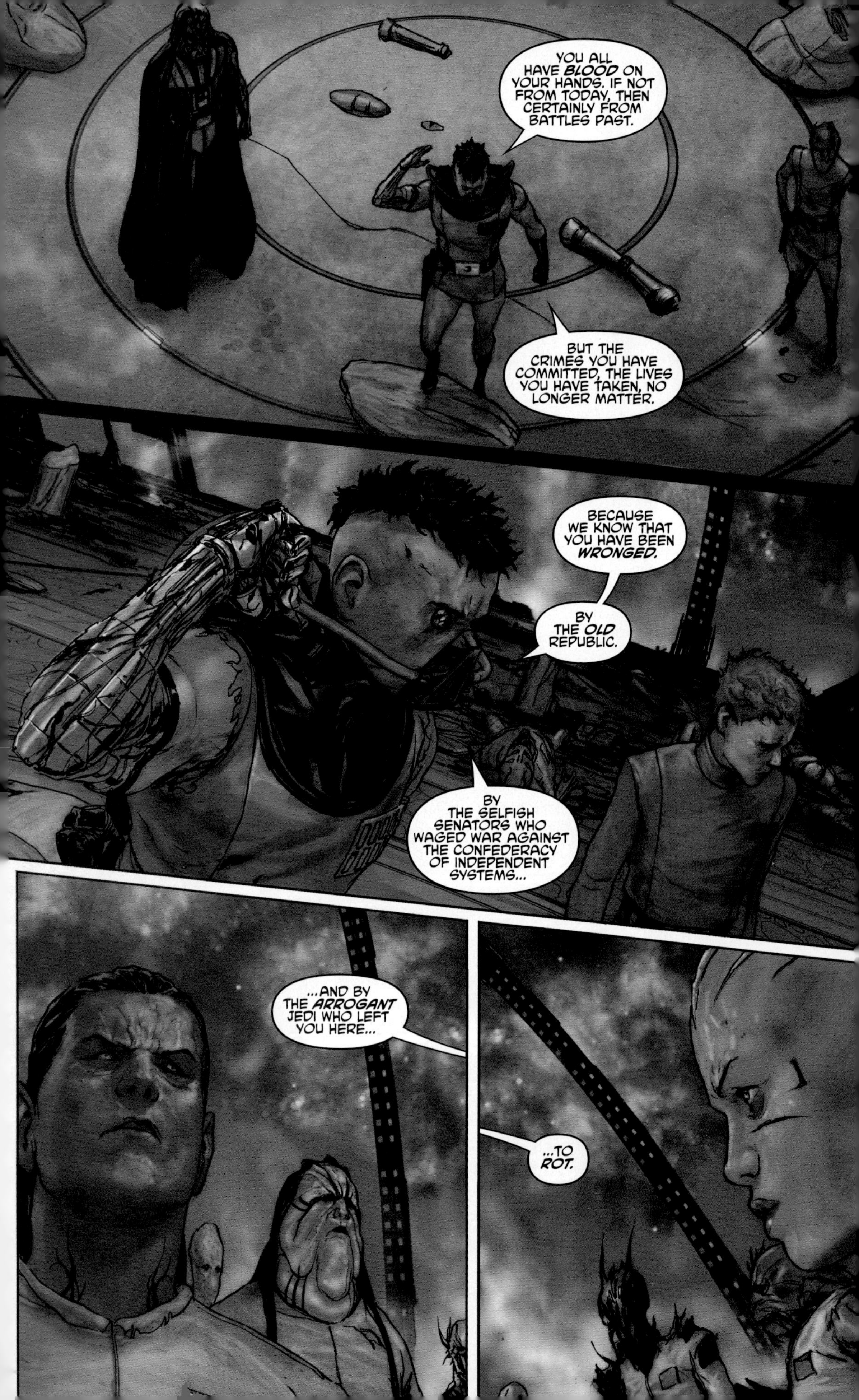
YOU ALL HAVE *BLOOD* ON YOUR HANDS. IF NOT FROM TODAY, THEN CERTAINLY FROM BATTLES PAST.
BUT THE CRIMES YOU HAVE COMMITTED, THE LIVES YOU HAVE TAKEN, NO LONGER MATTER.
BECAUSE WE KNOW THAT YOU HAVE BEEN *WRONGED.*
BY THE *OLD* REPUBLIC.
BY THE SELFISH SENATORS WHO WAGED WAR AGAINST THE CONFEDERACY OF INDEPENDENT SYSTEMS...
...AND BY THE *ARROGANT* JEDI WHO LEFT YOU HERE...
...TO *ROT.*

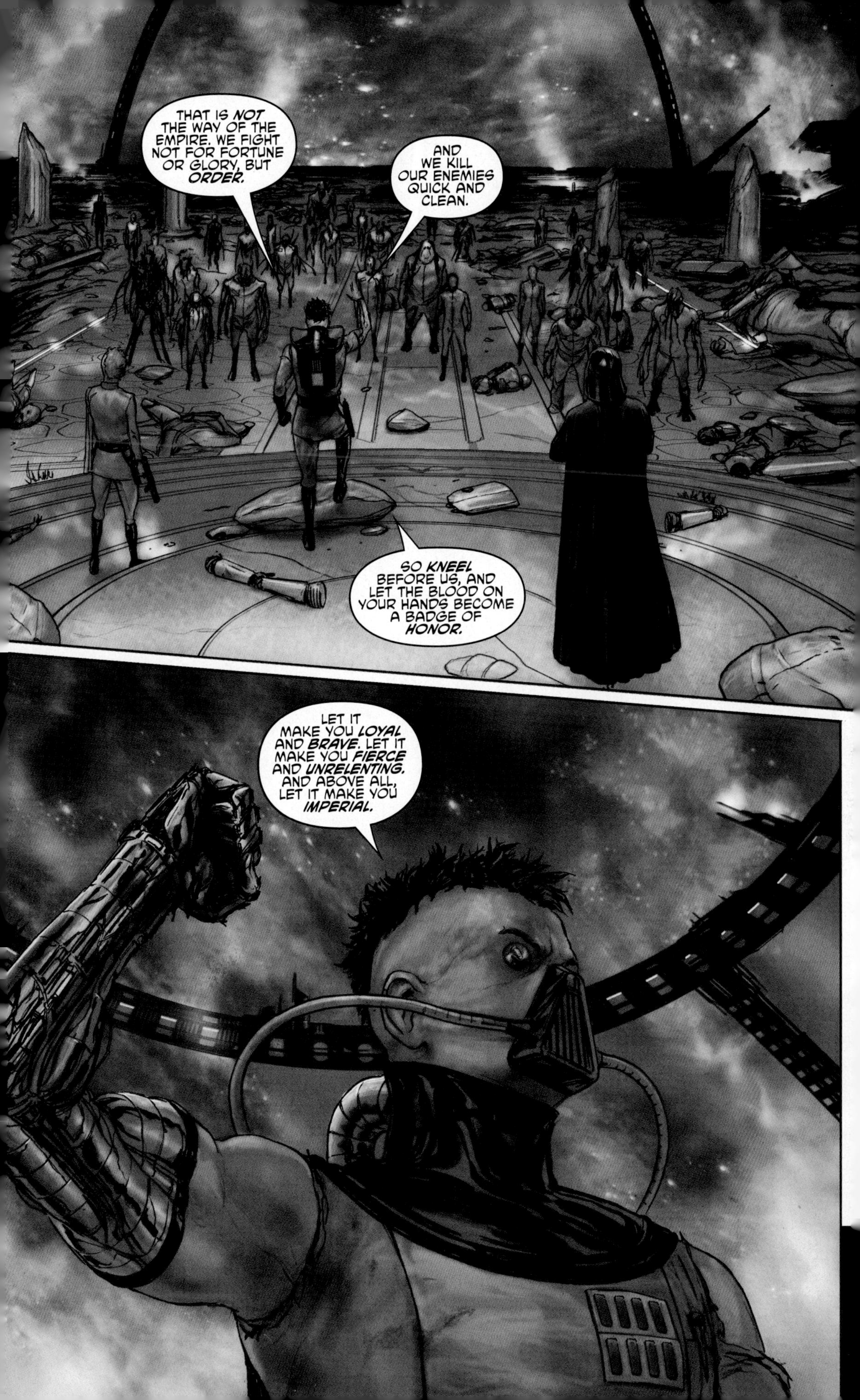
THAT IS NOT THE WAY OF THE EMPIRE. WE FIGHT NOT FOR FORTUNE OR GLORY, BUT ORDER.
AND WE KILL OUR ENEMIES QUICK AND CLEAN.
SO KNEEL BEFORE US, AND LET THE BLOOD ON YOUR HANDS BECOME A BADGE OF HONOR.
LET IT MAKE YOU LOYAL AND BRAVE. LET IT MAKE YOU FIERCE AND UNRELENTING. AND ABOVE ALL, LET IT MAKE YOU IMPERIAL.

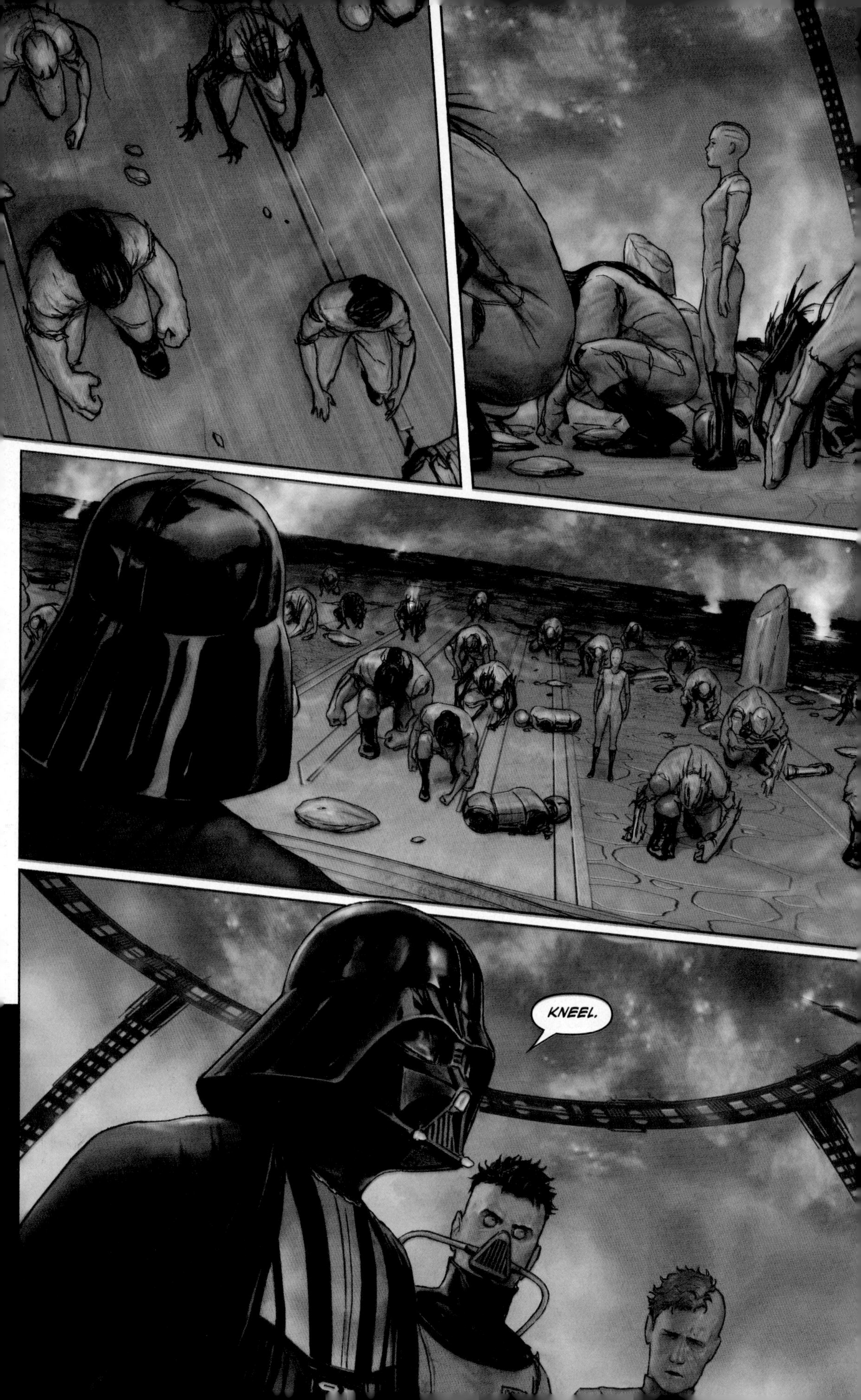
KNEEL.

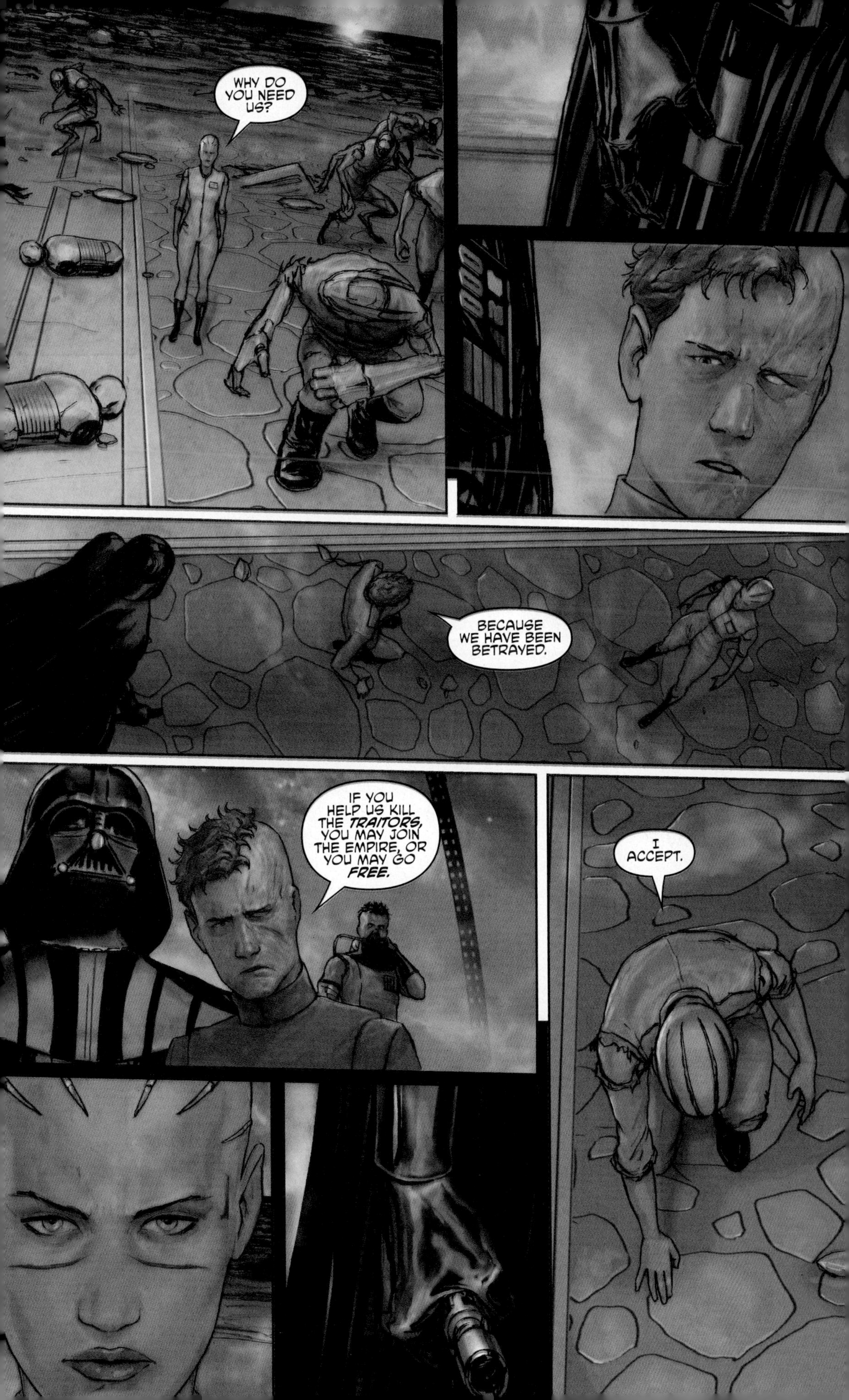
WHY DO YOU NEED US?
BECAUSE WE HAVE BEEN BETRAYED.
IF YOU HELP US KILL THE *TRAITORS,* YOU MAY JOIN THE EMPIRE, OR YOU MAY GO *FREE.*
I ACCEPT.

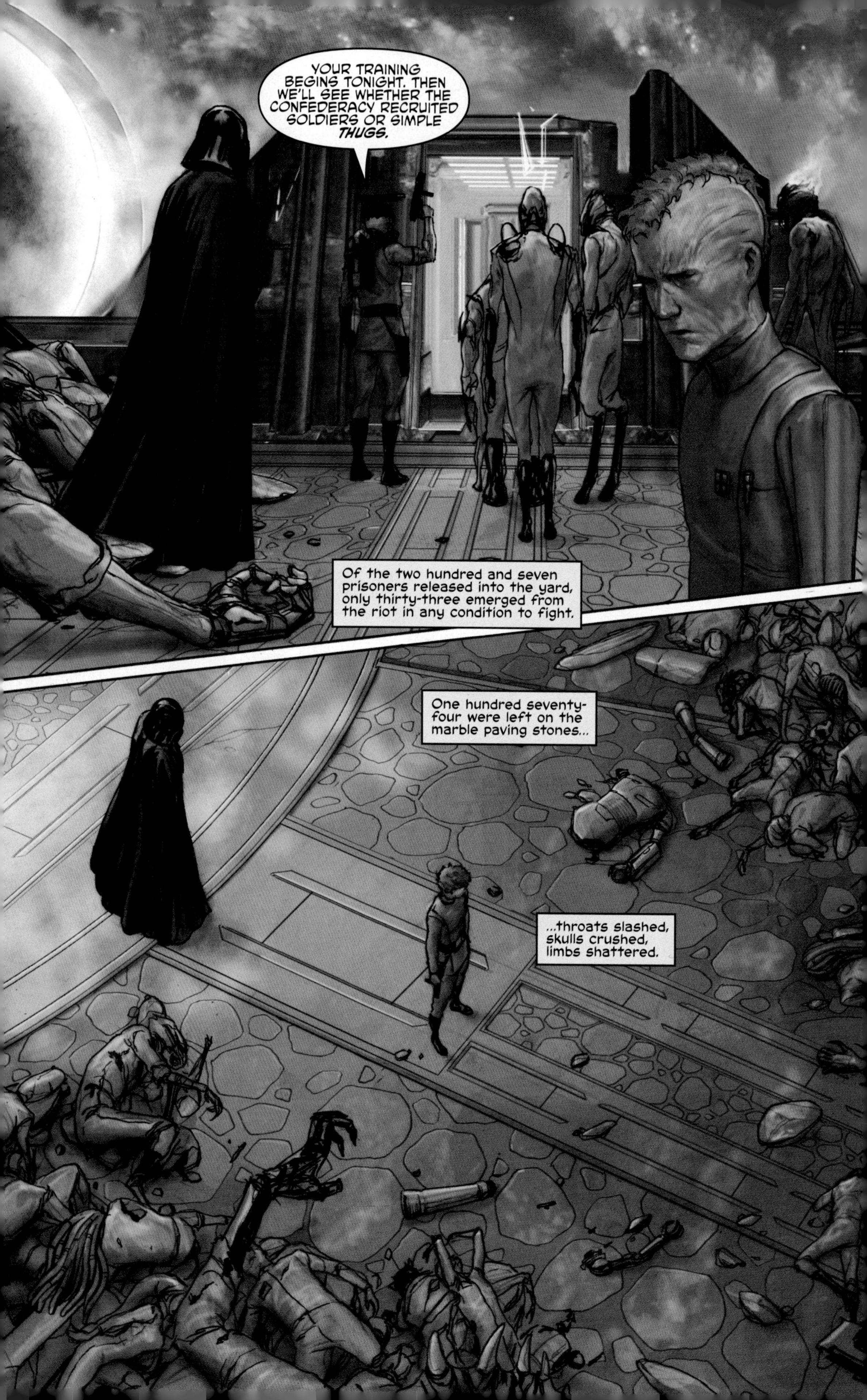
YOUR TRAINING BEGINS TONIGHT. THEN WE'LL SEE WHETHER THE CONFEDERACY RECRUITED SOLDIERS OR SIMPLE *THUGS.*
Of the two hundred and seven prisoners released into the yard, only thirty-three emerged from the riot in any condition to fight.
One hundred seventy-four were left on the marble paving stones...
...throats slashed, skulls crushed, limbs shattered.

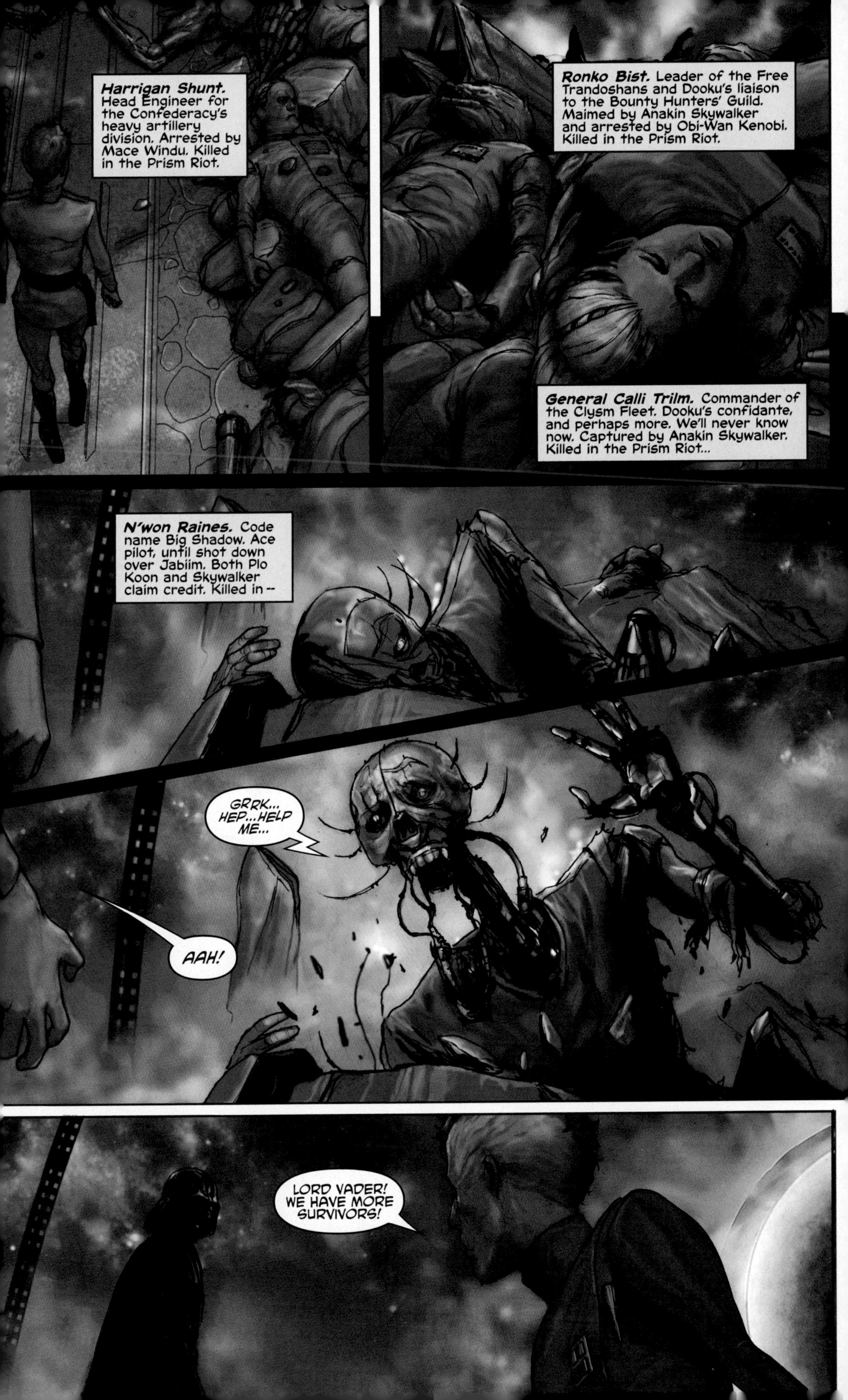

Harrigan Shunt. Head Engineer for the Confederacy's heavy artillery division. Arrested by Mace Windu. Killed in the Prism Riot.
Ronko Bist. Leader of the Free Trandoshans and Dooku's liaison to the Bounty Hunters' Guild. Maimed by Anakin Skywalker and arrested by Obi-Wan Kenobi. Killed in the Prism Riot.
General Calli Trilm. Commander of the Clysm Fleet. Dooku's confidante, and perhaps more. We'll never know now. Captured by Anakin Skywalker. Killed in the Prism Riot...
N'won Raines. Code name Big Shadow. Ace pilot, until shot down over Jabiim. Both Plo Koon and Skywalker claim credit. Killed in--
GRRK... HEP...HELP ME...
AAH!
LORD VADER! WE HAVE MORE SURVIVORS!

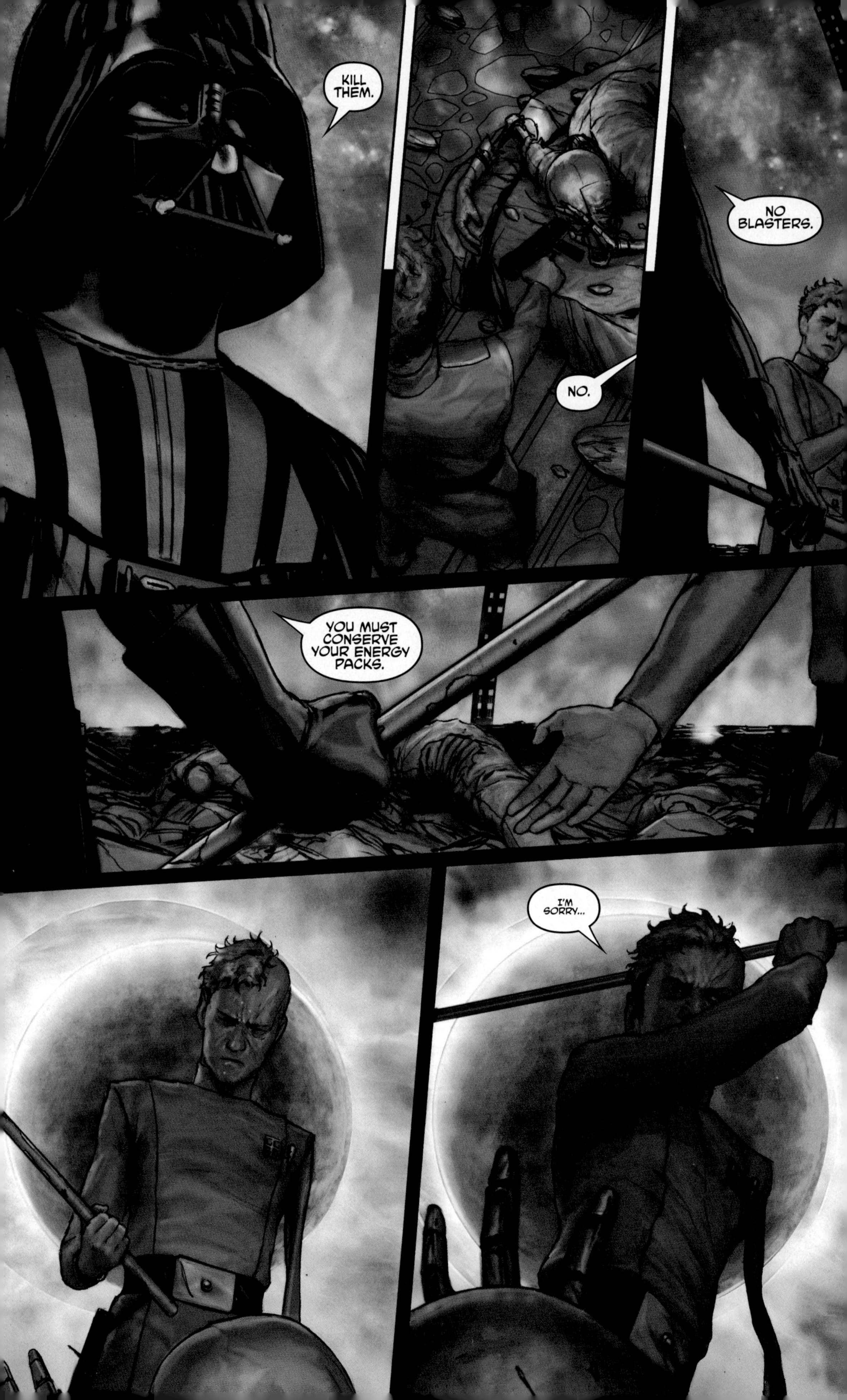
KILL THEM.
NO.
NO BLASTERS.
YOU MUST CONSERVE YOUR ENERGY PACKS.
I'M SORRY...

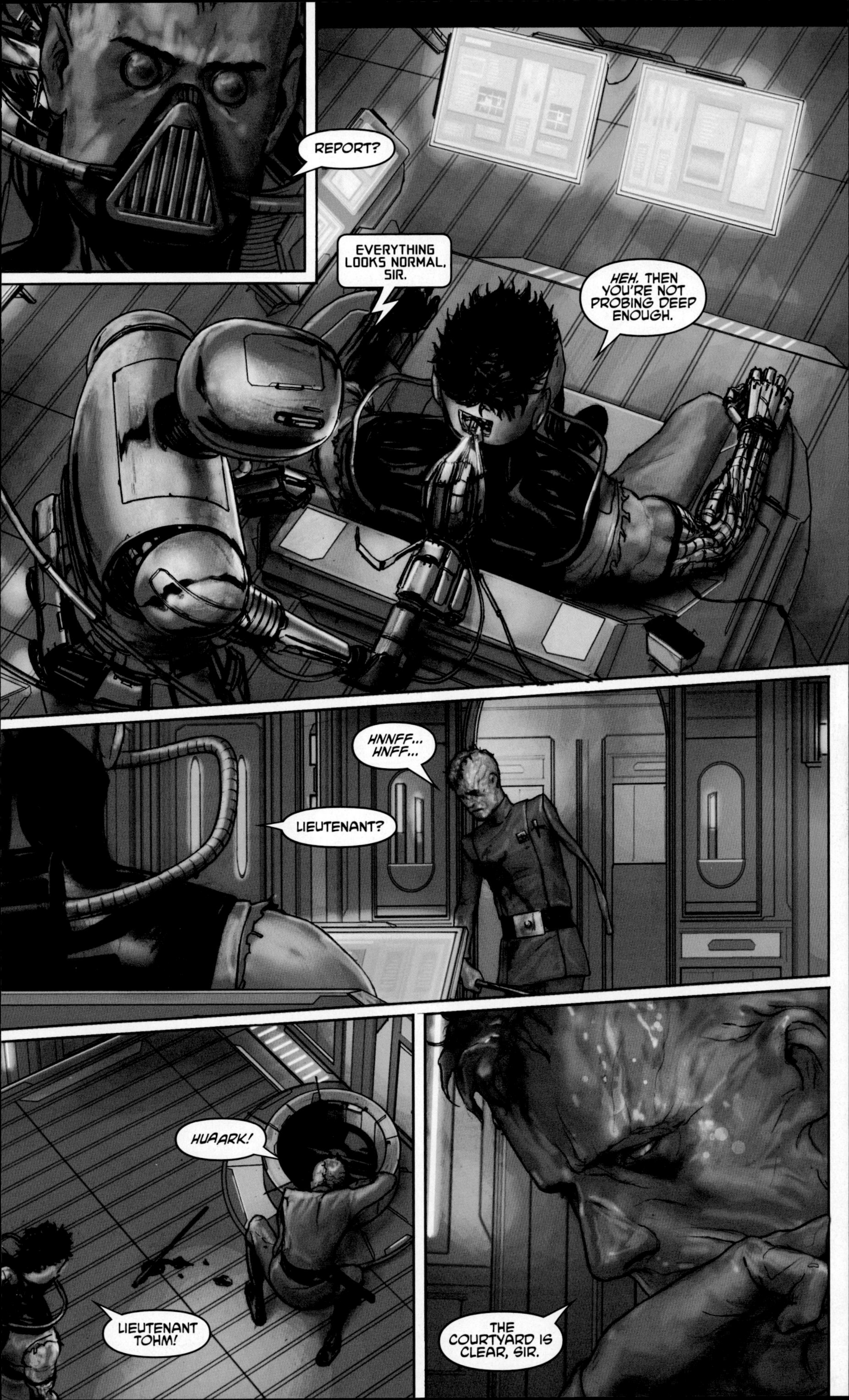
REPORT?
EVERYTHING LOOKS NORMAL, SIR.
HEH. THEN YOU'RE NOT PROBING DEEP ENOUGH.
HNNFF... HNFF...
LIEUTENANT?
HUAARK!
LIEUTENANT TOHM!
THE COURTYARD IS CLEAR, SIR.

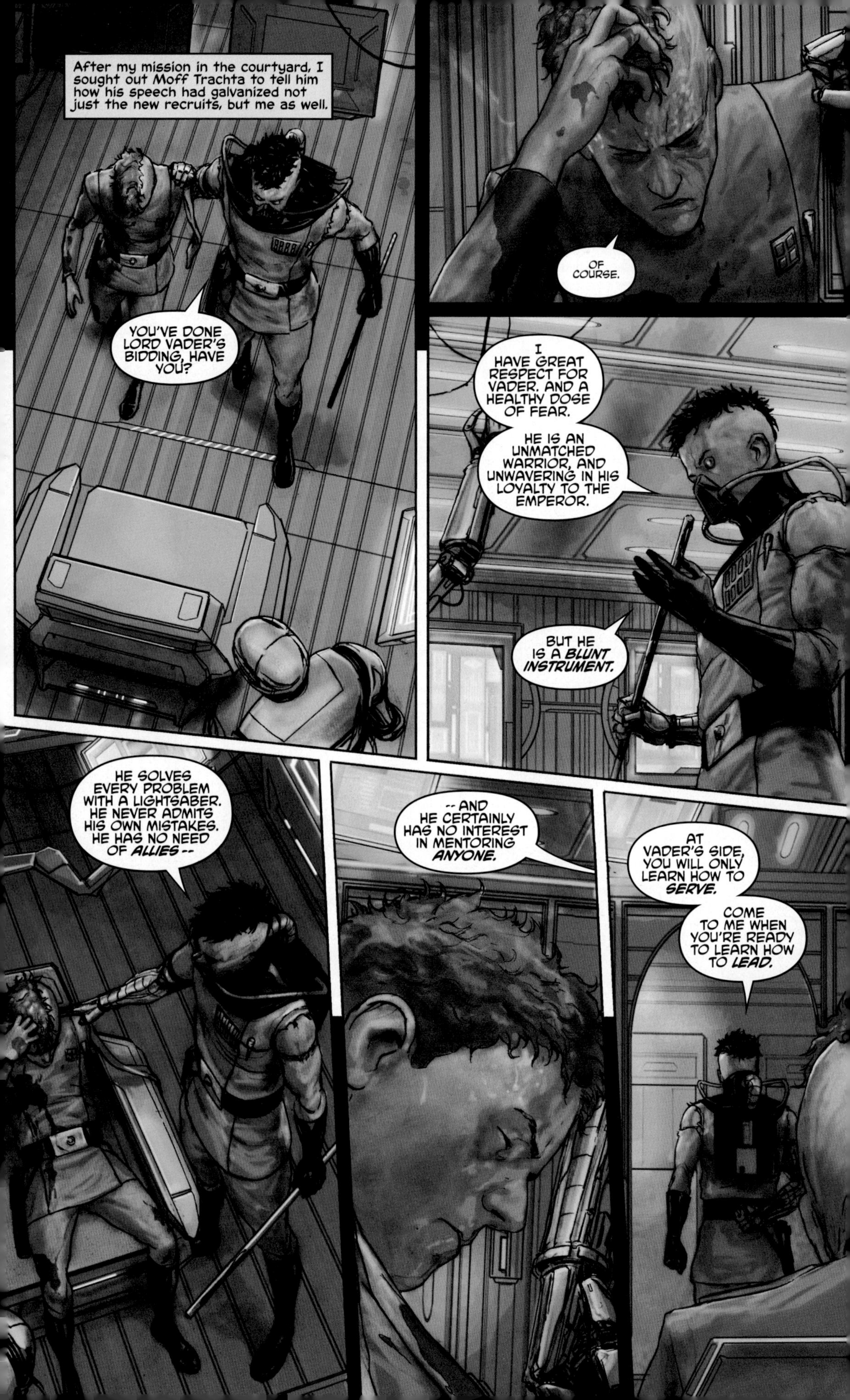
After my mission in the courtyard, I sought out Moff Trachta to tell him how his speech had galvanized not just the new recruits, but me as well.
YOU'VE DONE LORD VADER'S BIDDING, HAVE YOU?
OF COURSE.
I HAVE GREAT RESPECT FOR VADER. AND A HEALTHY DOSE OF FEAR.
HE IS AN UNMATCHED WARRIOR, AND UNWAVERING IN HIS LOYALTY TO THE EMPEROR.
BUT HE IS A *BLUNT INSTRUMENT.*
HE SOLVES EVERY PROBLEM WITH A LIGHTSABER. HE NEVER ADMITS HIS OWN MISTAKES. HE HAS NO NEED OF *ALLIES* --
-- AND HE CERTAINLY HAS NO INTEREST IN MENTORING *ANYONE.*
AT VADER'S SIDE, YOU WILL ONLY LEARN HOW TO *SERVE.*
COME TO ME WHEN YOU'RE READY TO LEARN HOW TO *LEAD.*

While Trachta and I plotted how best to serve Lord Vader, Headmaster Gentis prepared to make his coup complete.

THIS IS WHY WE STILL NEED MOFF TARKIN...

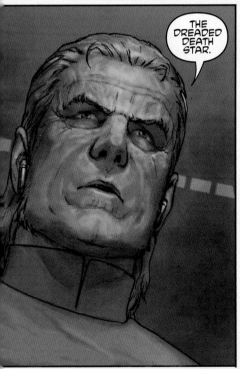

THE DREADED DEATH STAR.

I THOUGHT IT WAS JUST A RUMOR...

YOU'RE LURING TARKIN BACK HERE?

OF COURSE.

ACCORDING TO MY SPIES ABOARD THE DEATH STAR, TARKIN IS SO PARANOID ABOUT LEAVING HIS SECRET PROJECT UNPROTECTED, HE IS TRAVELING TO CORUSCANT WITH ONLY A SMALL SKELETON CREW.

WE'LL TAKE HIM INTO CUSTODY AND LEARN ALL WE CAN ABOUT THIS SUPERWEAPON, AND THEN EXECUTE HIM FOR CRIMES AGAINST THE TRUE EMPIRE.

ONLY THEN WILL WE ANNOUNCE TO THE GALAXY THAT THE EMPEROR HAS DIED FROM HIS INJURIES.

CAN THAT BE CONFIRMED?

IT DOESN'T MATTER. WITH TARKIN DEAD, YOU AND YOUR PEERS CAN DECLARE ME THE NEW EMPEROR. A PEACEFUL TRANSFER OF POWER...

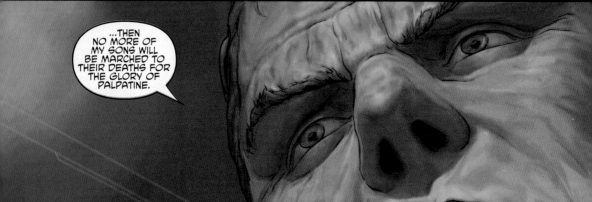

...THEN NO MORE OF MY SONS WILL BE MARCHED TO THEIR DEATHS FOR THE GLORY OF PALPATINE.

SPAKOOM!

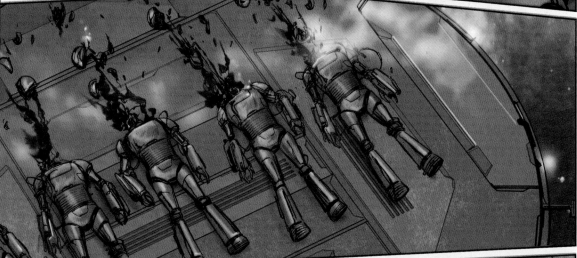

YOU'RE CERTAIN THAT YOU HAVE NO CYBERNETIC IMPLANTS?

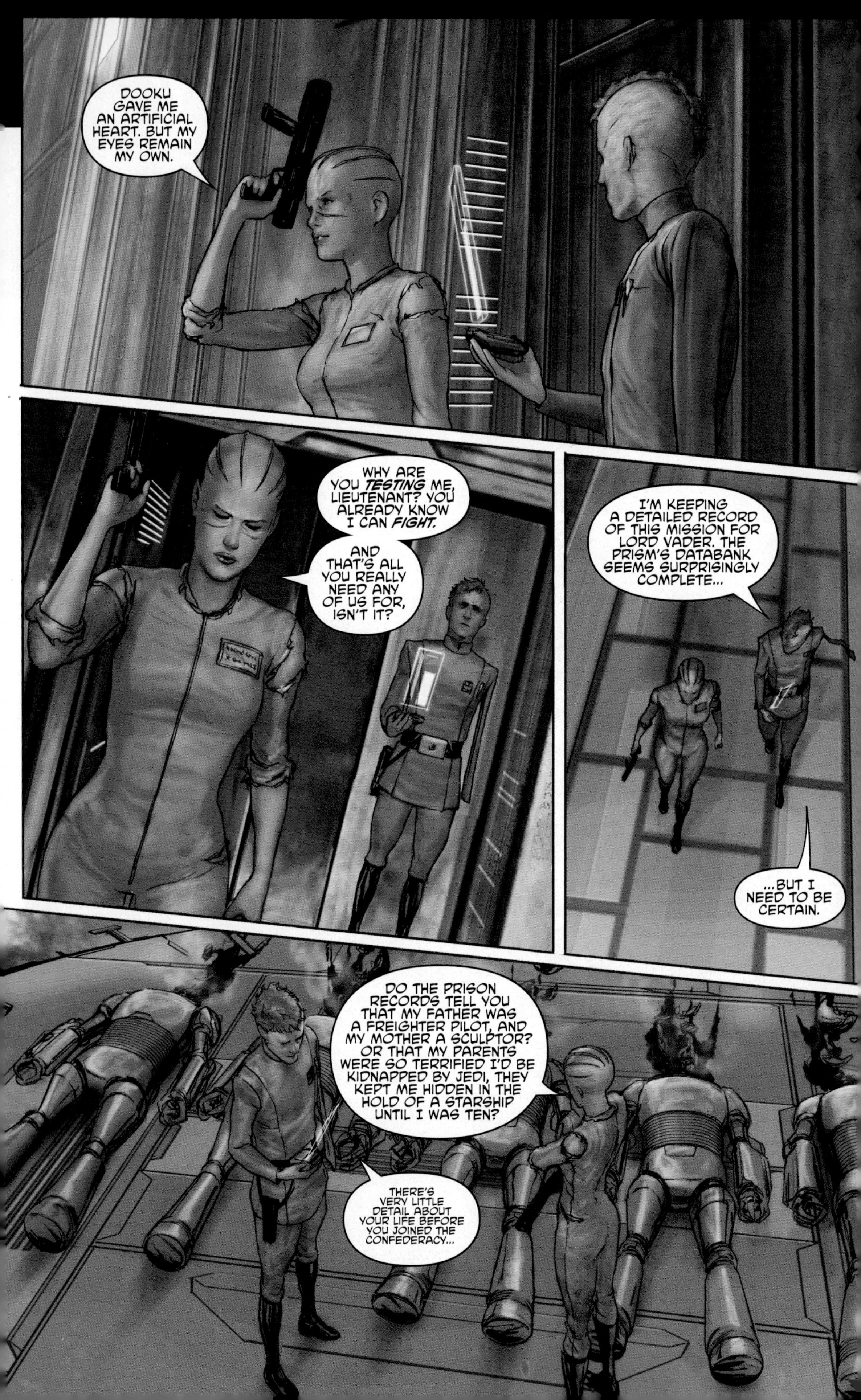
DOOKU GAVE ME AN ARTIFICIAL HEART. BUT MY EYES REMAIN MY OWN.
WHY ARE YOU *TESTING* ME, LIEUTENANT? YOU ALREADY KNOW I CAN *FIGHT.*
AND THAT'S ALL YOU REALLY NEED ANY OF US FOR, ISN'T IT?
I'M KEEPING A DETAILED RECORD OF THIS MISSION FOR LORD VADER. THE PRISM'S DATABANK SEEMS SURPRISINGLY COMPLETE...
...BUT I NEED TO BE CERTAIN.
DO THE PRISON RECORDS TELL YOU THAT MY FATHER WAS A FREIGHTER PILOT, AND MY MOTHER A SCULPTOR? OR THAT MY PARENTS WERE SO TERRIFIED I'D BE KIDNAPPED BY JEDI, THEY KEPT ME HIDDEN IN THE HOLD OF A STARSHIP UNTIL I WAS TEN?
THERE'S VERY LITTLE DETAIL ABOUT YOUR LIFE BEFORE YOU JOINED THE CONFEDERACY...

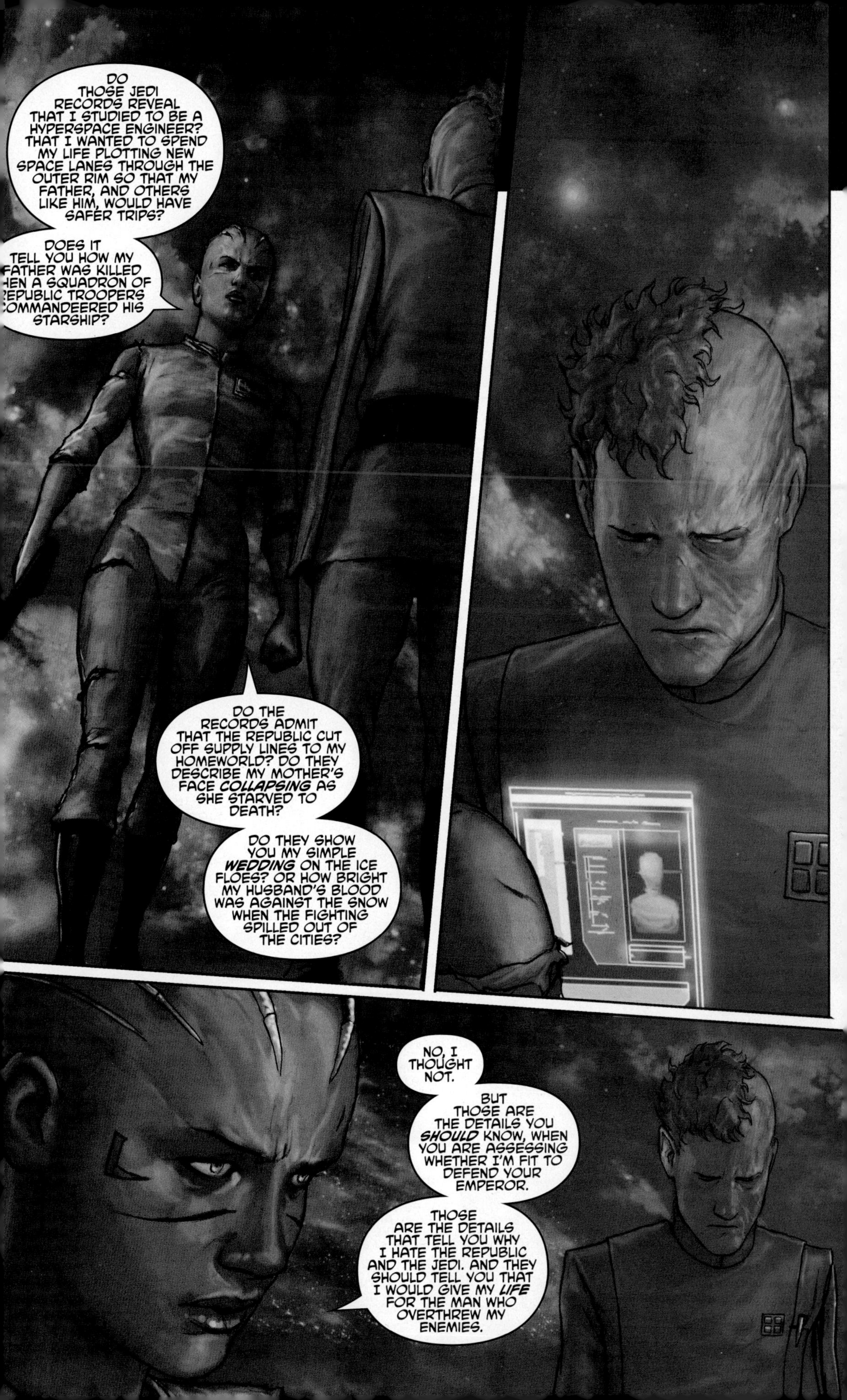
DO THOSE JEDI RECORDS REVEAL THAT I STUDIED TO BE A HYPERSPACE ENGINEER? THAT I WANTED TO SPEND MY LIFE PLOTTING NEW SPACE LANES THROUGH THE OUTER RIM SO THAT MY FATHER, AND OTHERS LIKE HIM, WOULD HAVE SAFER TRIPS?
DOES IT TELL YOU HOW MY FATHER WAS KILLED WHEN A SQUADRON OF REPUBLIC TROOPERS COMMANDEERED HIS STARSHIP?
DO THE RECORDS ADMIT THAT THE REPUBLIC CUT OFF SUPPLY LINES TO MY HOMEWORLD? DO THEY DESCRIBE MY MOTHER'S FACE COLLAPSING AS SHE STARVED TO DEATH?
DO THEY SHOW YOU MY SIMPLE WEDDING ON THE ICE FLOES? OR HOW BRIGHT MY HUSBAND'S BLOOD WAS AGAINST THE SNOW WHEN THE FIGHTING SPILLED OUT OF THE CITIES?
NO, I THOUGHT NOT.
BUT THOSE ARE THE DETAILS YOU SHOULD KNOW, WHEN YOU ARE ASSESSING WHETHER I'M FIT TO DEFEND YOUR EMPEROR.
THOSE ARE THE DETAILS THAT TELL YOU WHY I HATE THE REPUBLIC AND THE JEDI. AND THEY SHOULD TELL YOU THAT I WOULD GIVE MY LIFE FOR THE MAN WHO OVERTHREW MY ENEMIES.

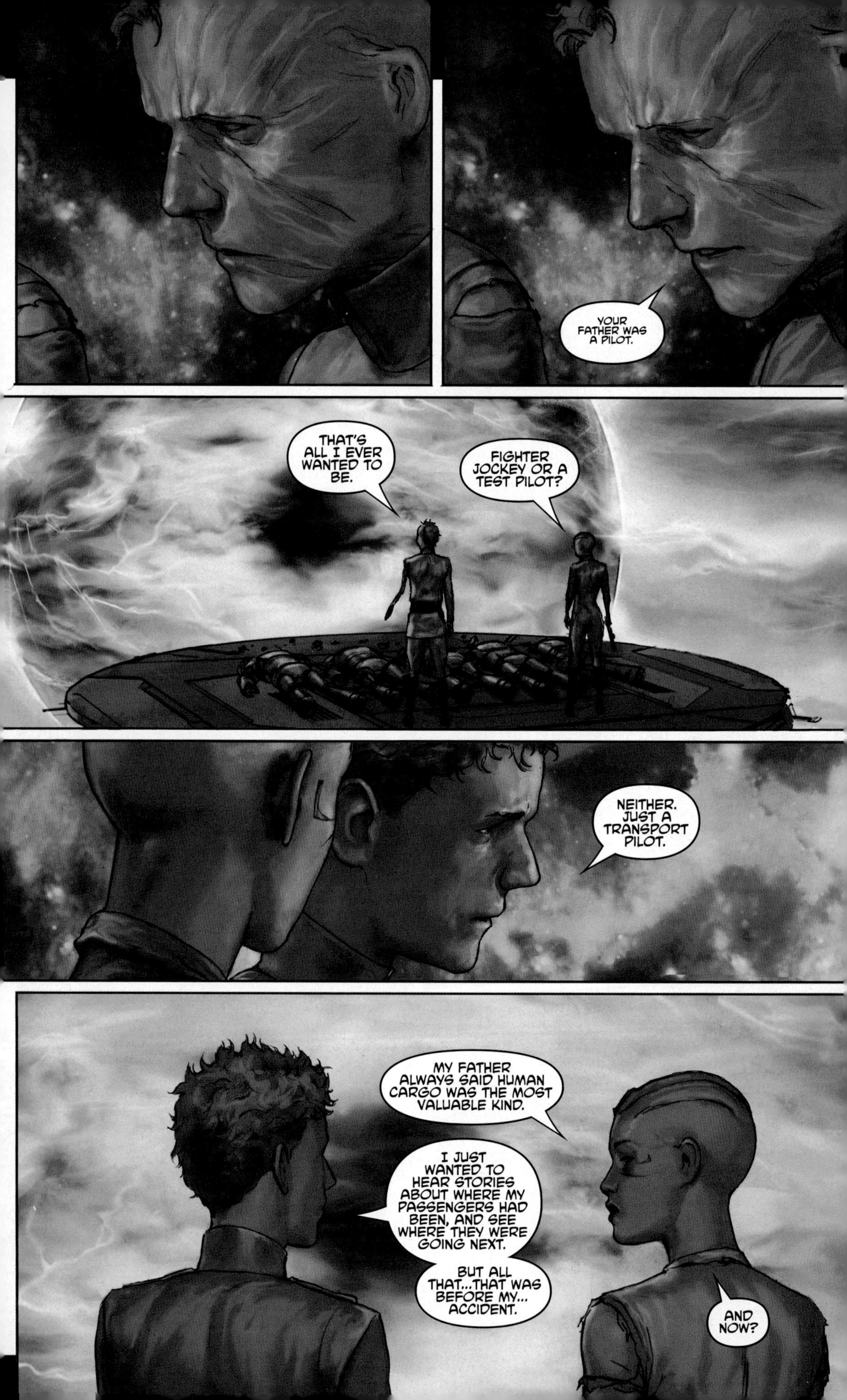
YOUR FATHER WAS A PILOT.
THAT'S ALL I EVER WANTED TO BE.
FIGHTER JOCKEY OR A TEST PILOT?
NEITHER. JUST A TRANSPORT PILOT.
MY FATHER ALWAYS SAID HUMAN CARGO WAS THE MOST VALUABLE KIND.
I JUST WANTED TO HEAR STORIES ABOUT WHERE MY PASSENGERS HAD BEEN, AND SEE WHERE THEY WERE GOING NEXT.
BUT ALL THAT...THAT WAS BEFORE MY... ACCIDENT.
AND NOW?

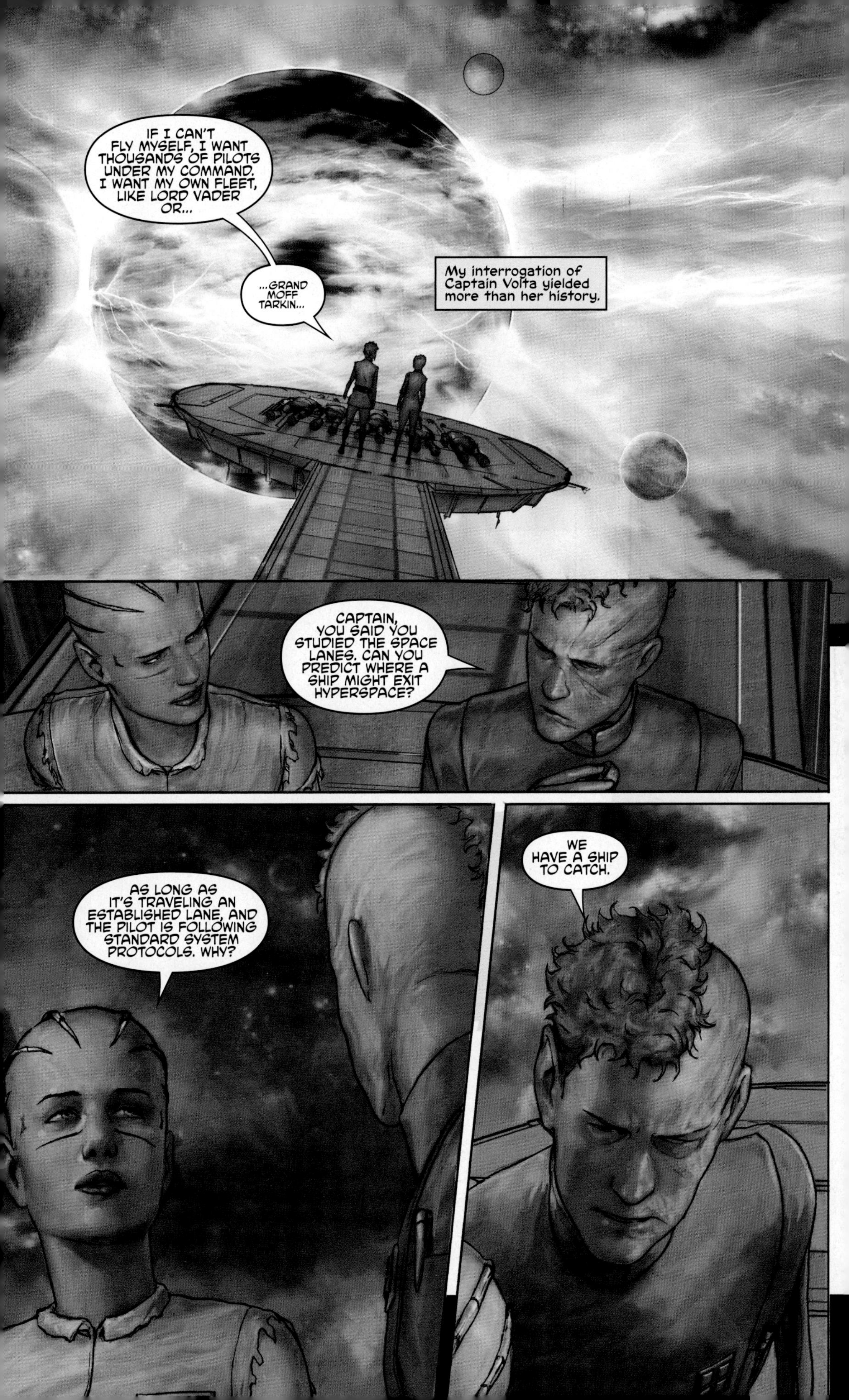
IF I CAN'T FLY MYSELF, I WANT THOUSANDS OF PILOTS UNDER MY COMMAND. I WANT MY OWN FLEET, LIKE LORD VADER OR...
...GRAND MOFF TARKIN...
My interrogation of Captain Volta yielded more than her history.
CAPTAIN, YOU SAID YOU STUDIED THE SPACE LANES. CAN YOU PREDICT WHERE A SHIP MIGHT EXIT HYPERSPACE?
AS LONG AS IT'S TRAVELING AN ESTABLISHED LANE, AND THE PILOT IS FOLLOWING STANDARD SYSTEM PROTOCOLS. WHY?
WE HAVE A SHIP TO CATCH.

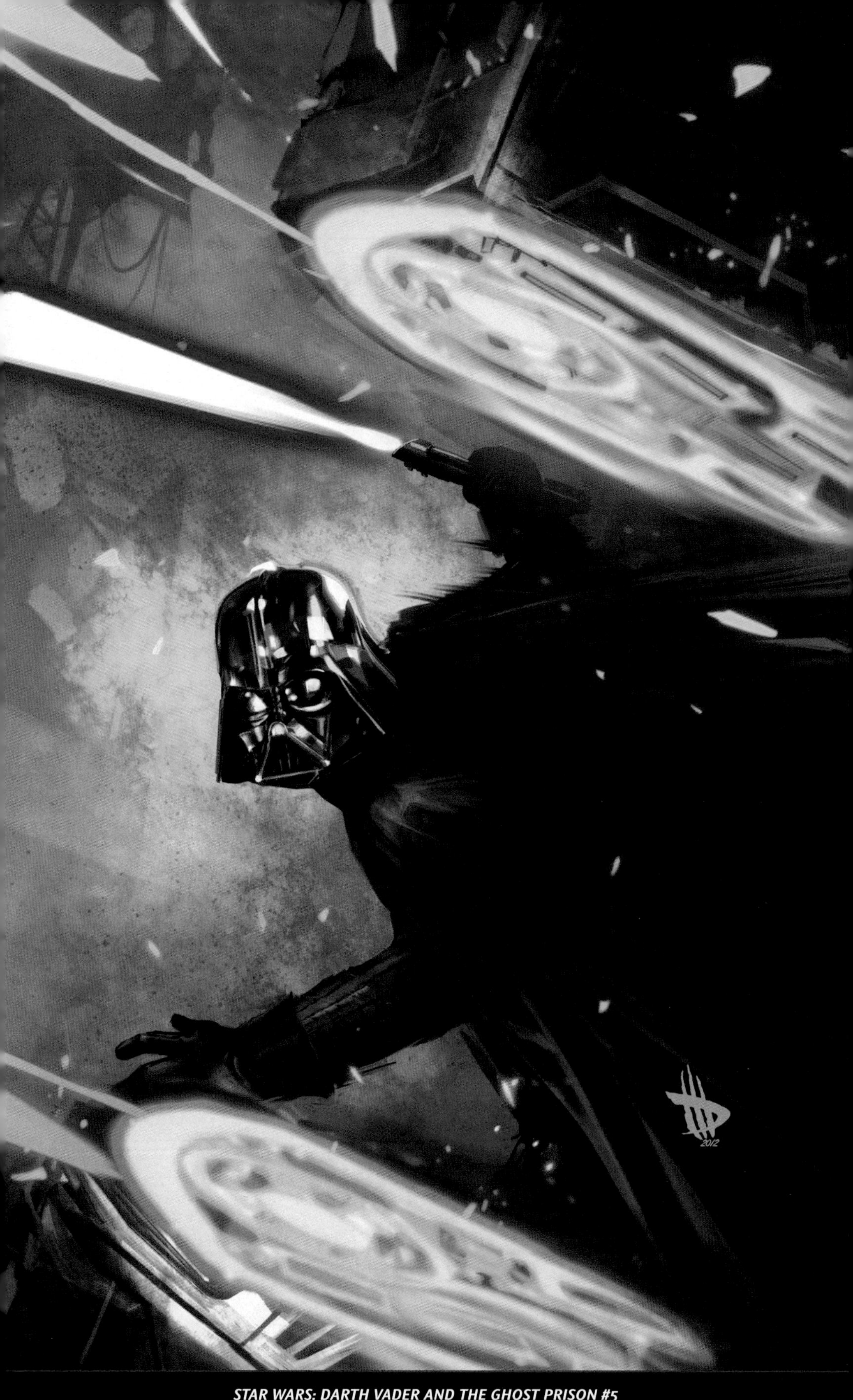
2012

*STAR WARS: DARTH VADER AND THE GHOST PRISON #5*

WRITER: HADEN BLACKMAN • ARTIST & COLORIST: AGUSTIN ALESSIO • LETTERER: MICHAEL HEISLER
ASSISTANT EDITOR: FREDDYE LINS • EDITOR: RANDY STRADLEY • COVER ARTIST: DAVE WILKINS

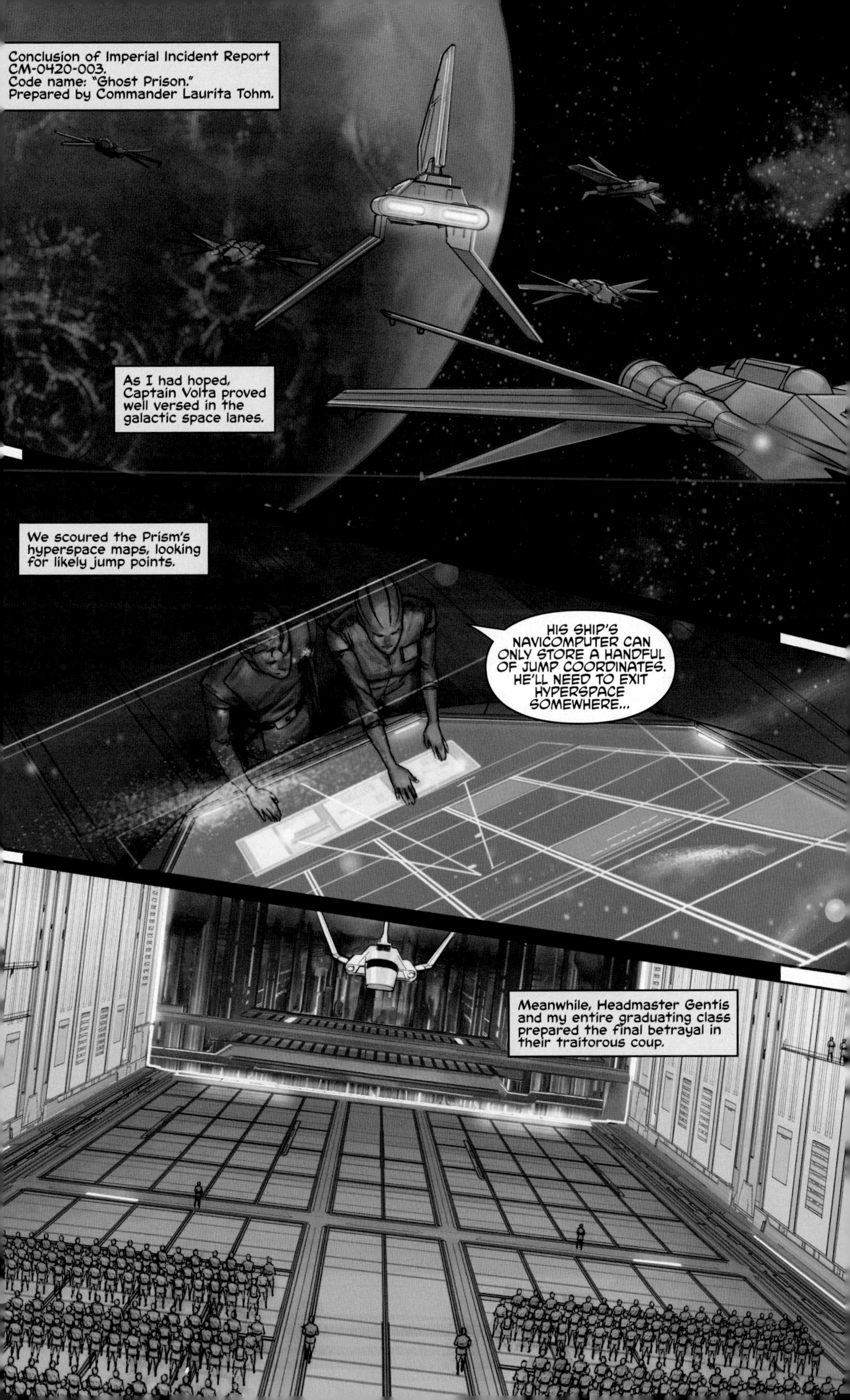
Conclusion of Imperial Incident Report CM-0420-003.
Code name: "Ghost Prison."
Prepared by Commander Laurita Tohm.
As I had hoped, Captain Volta proved well versed in the galactic space lanes.
We scoured the Prism's hyperspace maps, looking for likely jump points.
HIS SHIP'S NAVICOMPUTER CAN ONLY STORE A HANDFUL OF JUMP COORDINATES. HE'LL NEED TO EXIT HYPERSPACE SOMEWHERE...
Meanwhile, Headmaster Gentis and my entire graduating class prepared the final betrayal in their traitorous coup.

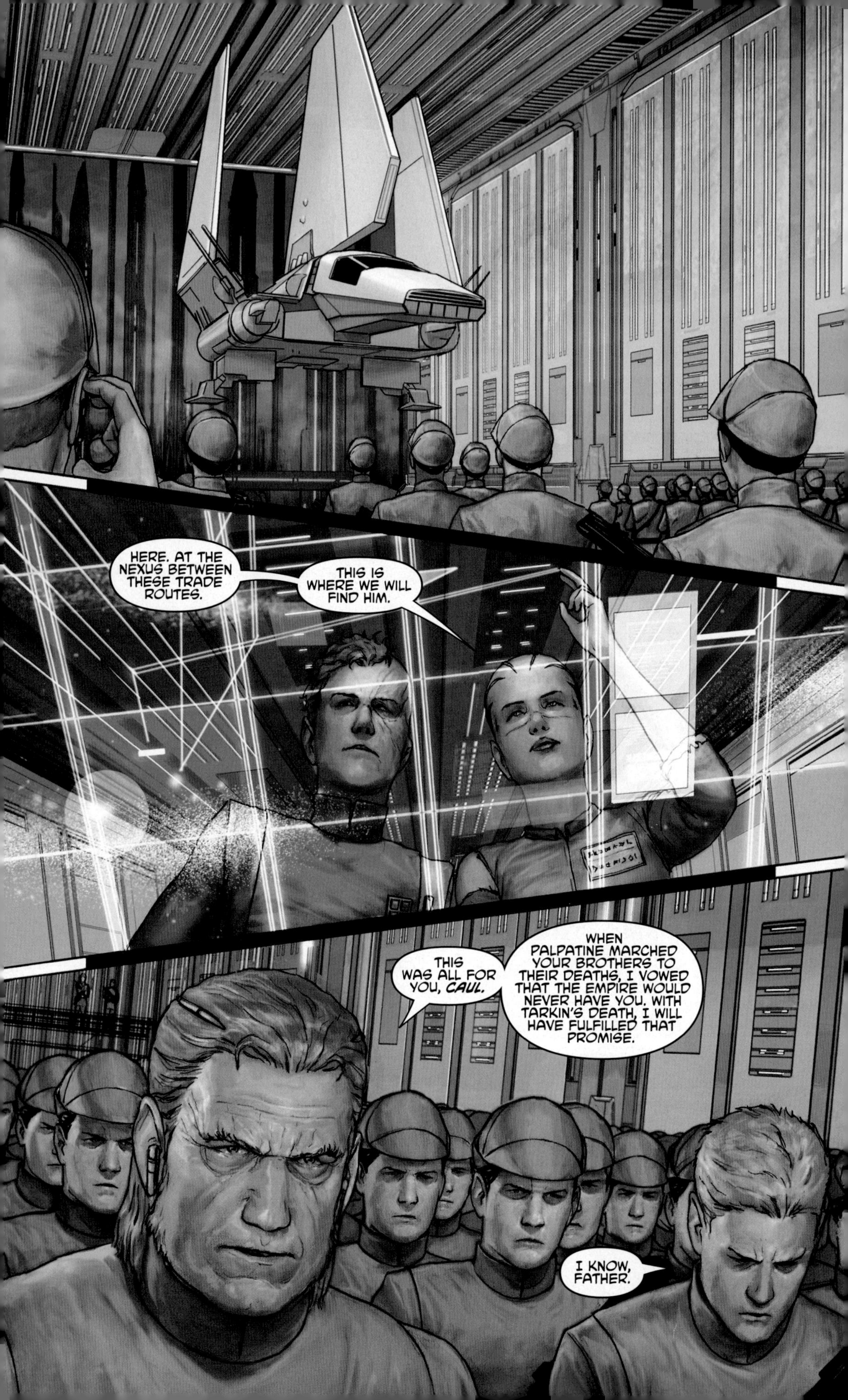
HERE. AT THE NEXUS BETWEEN THESE TRADE ROUTES.
THIS IS WHERE WE WILL FIND HIM.
THIS WAS ALL FOR YOU, CAUL.
WHEN PALPATINE MARCHED YOUR BROTHERS TO THEIR DEATHS, I VOWED THAT THE EMPIRE WOULD NEVER HAVE YOU. WITH TARKIN'S DEATH, I WILL HAVE FULFILLED THAT PROMISE.
I KNOW, FATHER.

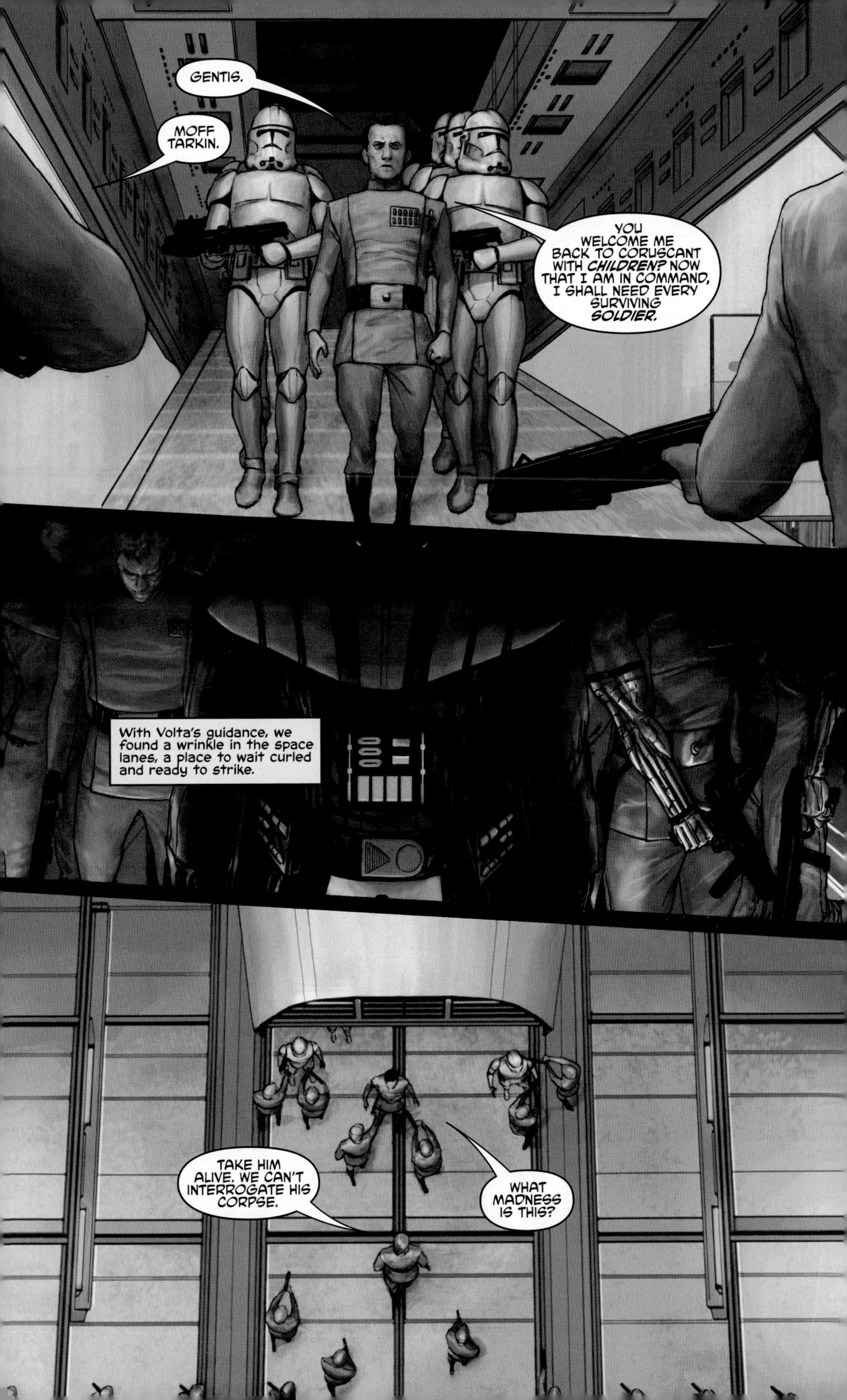
GENTIS.
MOFF TARKIN.
YOU WELCOME ME BACK TO CORUSCANT WITH CHILDREN? NOW THAT I AM IN COMMAND, I SHALL NEED EVERY SURVIVING SOLDIER.
With Volta's guidance, we found a wrinkle in the space lanes, a place to wait curled and ready to strike.
TAKE HIM ALIVE. WE CAN'T INTERROGATE HIS CORPSE.
WHAT MADNESS IS THIS?

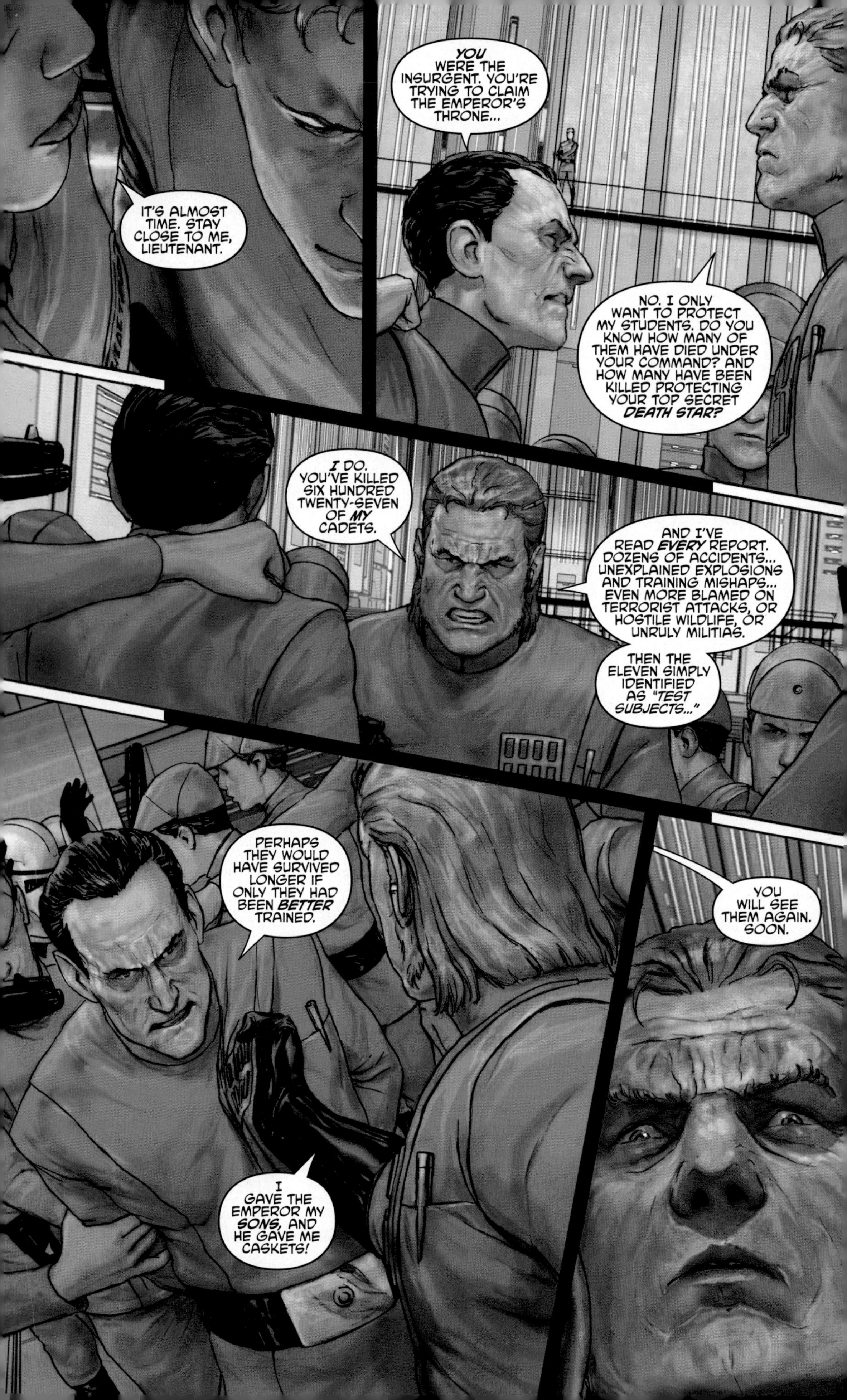

IT'S ALMOST TIME. STAY CLOSE TO ME, LIEUTENANT.
YOU WERE THE INSURGENT. YOU'RE TRYING TO CLAIM THE EMPEROR'S THRONE...
NO. I ONLY WANT TO PROTECT MY STUDENTS. DO YOU KNOW HOW MANY OF THEM HAVE DIED UNDER YOUR COMMAND? AND HOW MANY HAVE BEEN KILLED PROTECTING YOUR TOP SECRET DEATH STAR?
I DO. YOU'VE KILLED SIX HUNDRED TWENTY-SEVEN OF MY CADETS.
AND I'VE READ EVERY REPORT. DOZENS OF ACCIDENTS... UNEXPLAINED EXPLOSIONS AND TRAINING MISHAPS... EVEN MORE BLAMED ON TERRORIST ATTACKS, OR HOSTILE WILDLIFE, OR UNRULY MILITIAS.
THEN THE ELEVEN SIMPLY IDENTIFIED AS "TEST SUBJECTS..."
PERHAPS THEY WOULD HAVE SURVIVED LONGER IF ONLY THEY HAD BEEN BETTER TRAINED.
I GAVE THE EMPEROR MY SONS, AND HE GAVE ME CASKETS!
YOU WILL SEE THEM AGAIN. SOON.

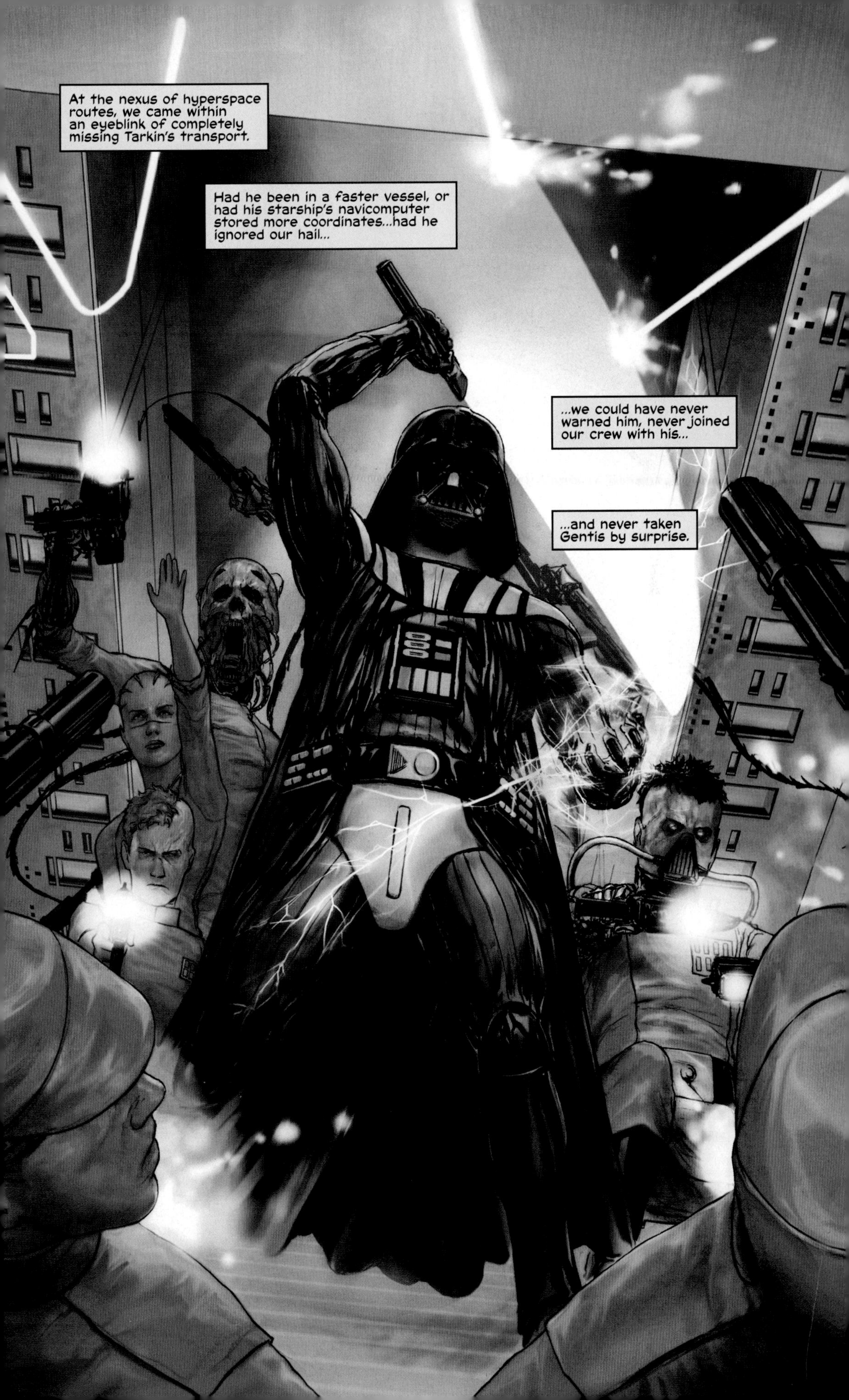
At the nexus of hyperspace routes, we came within an eyeblink of completely missing Tarkin's transport.
Had he been in a faster vessel, or had his starship's navicomputer stored more coordinates...had he ignored our hail...
...we could have never warned him, never joined our crew with his...
...and never taken Gentis by surprise.

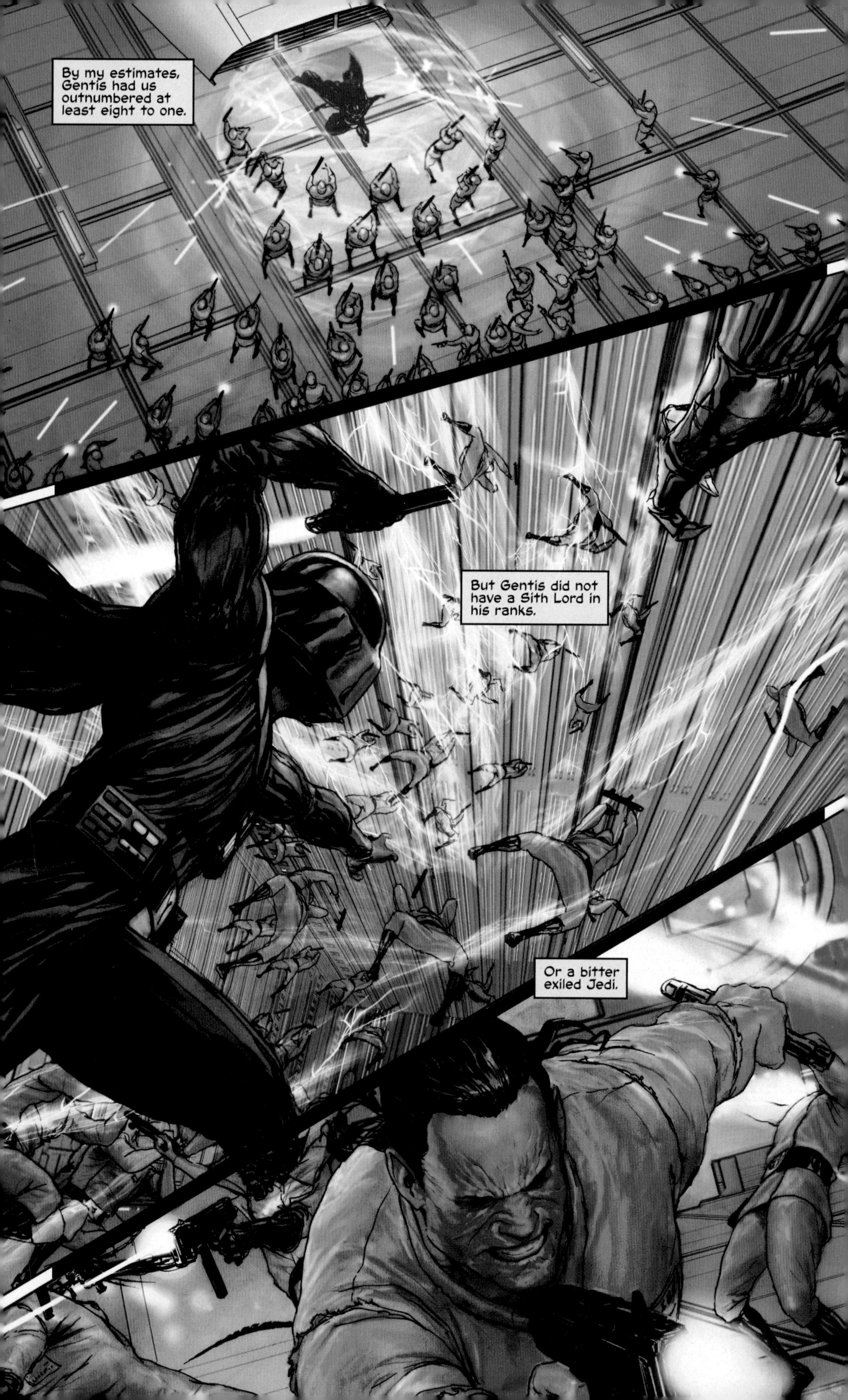

By my estimates, Gentis had us outnumbered at least eight to one.
But Gentis did not have a Sith Lord in his ranks.
Or a bitter exiled Jedi.

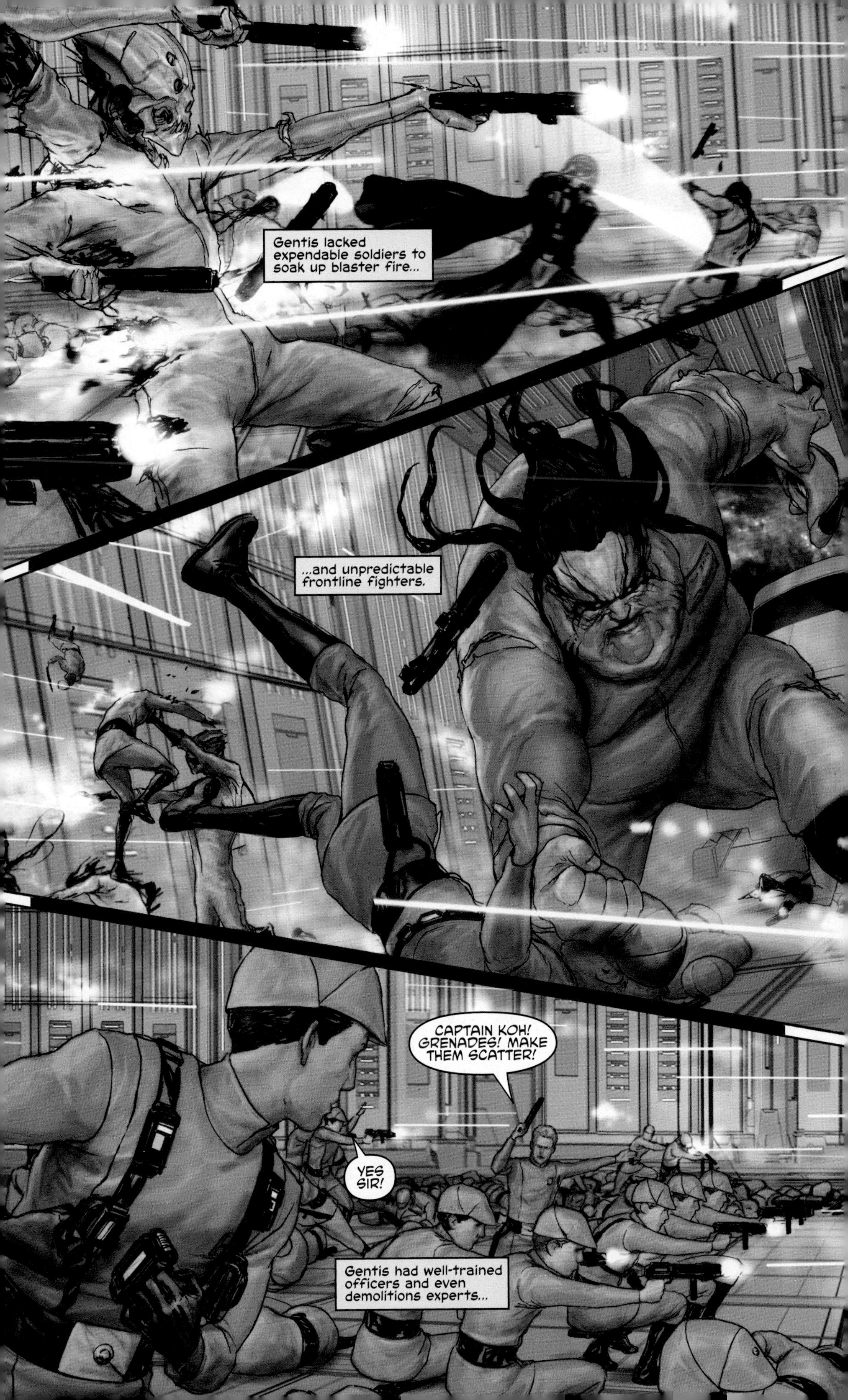
Gentis lacked expendable soldiers to soak up blaster fire...
...and unpredictable frontline fighters.
CAPTAIN KOH! GRENADES! MAKE THEM SCATTER!
YES SIR!
Gentis had well-trained officers and even demolitions experts...

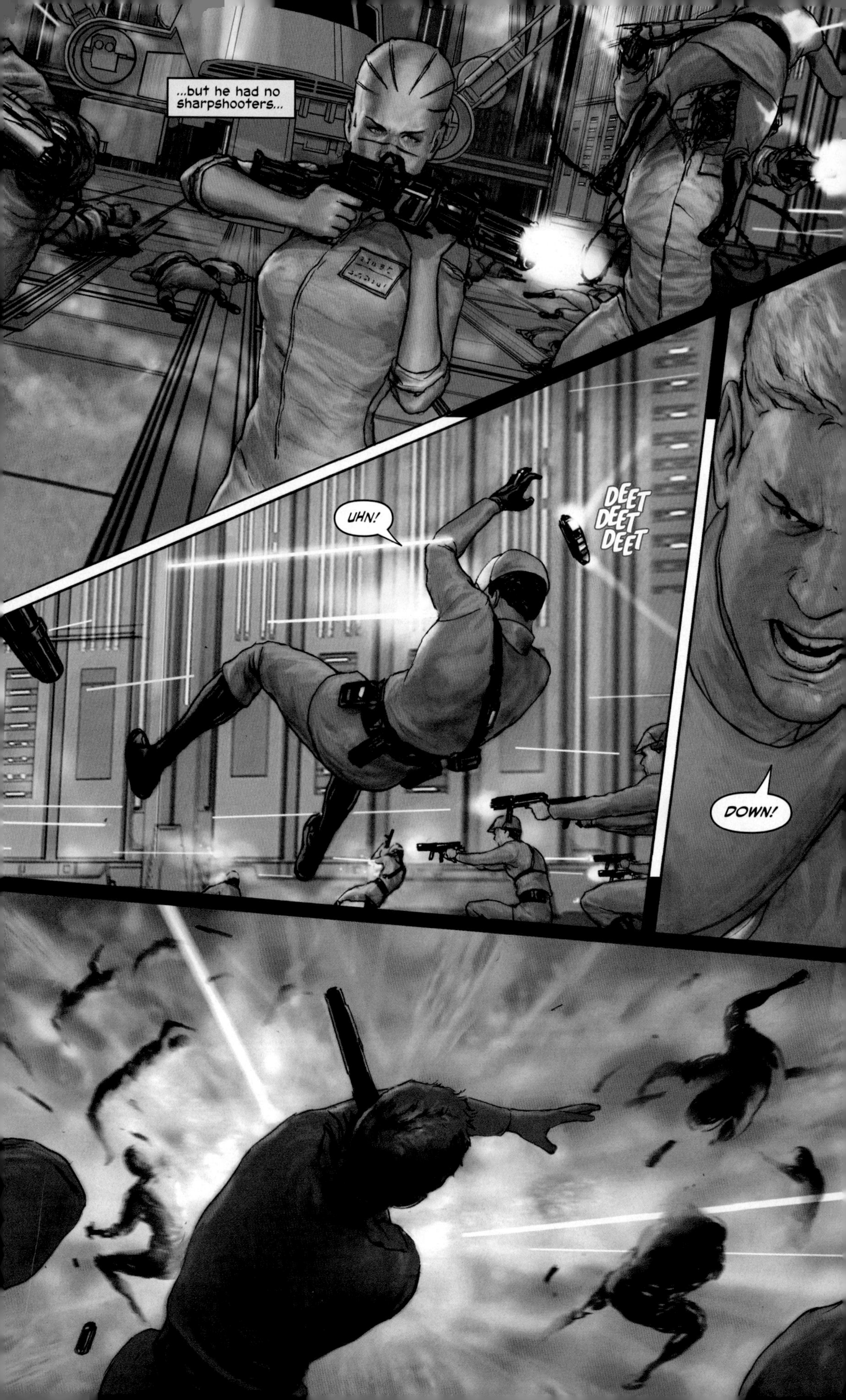
...but he had no sharpshooters...
UHN!
DEET DEET DEET
DOWN!

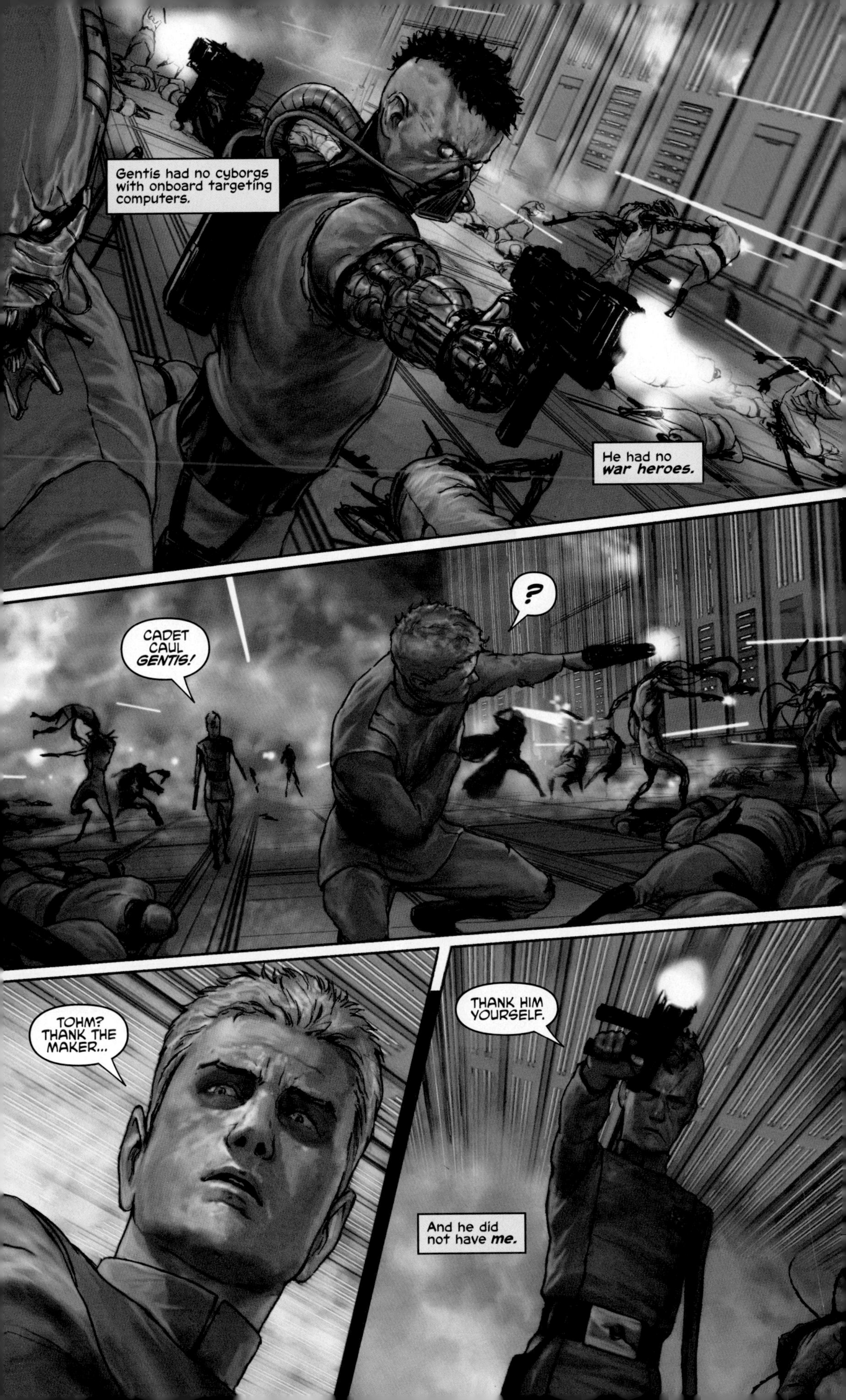
Gentis had no cyborgs with onboard targeting computers.
He had no *war heroes.*
CADET CAUL *GENTIS!*
?
TOHM? THANK THE MAKER...
THANK HIM YOURSELF.
And he did not have *me.*

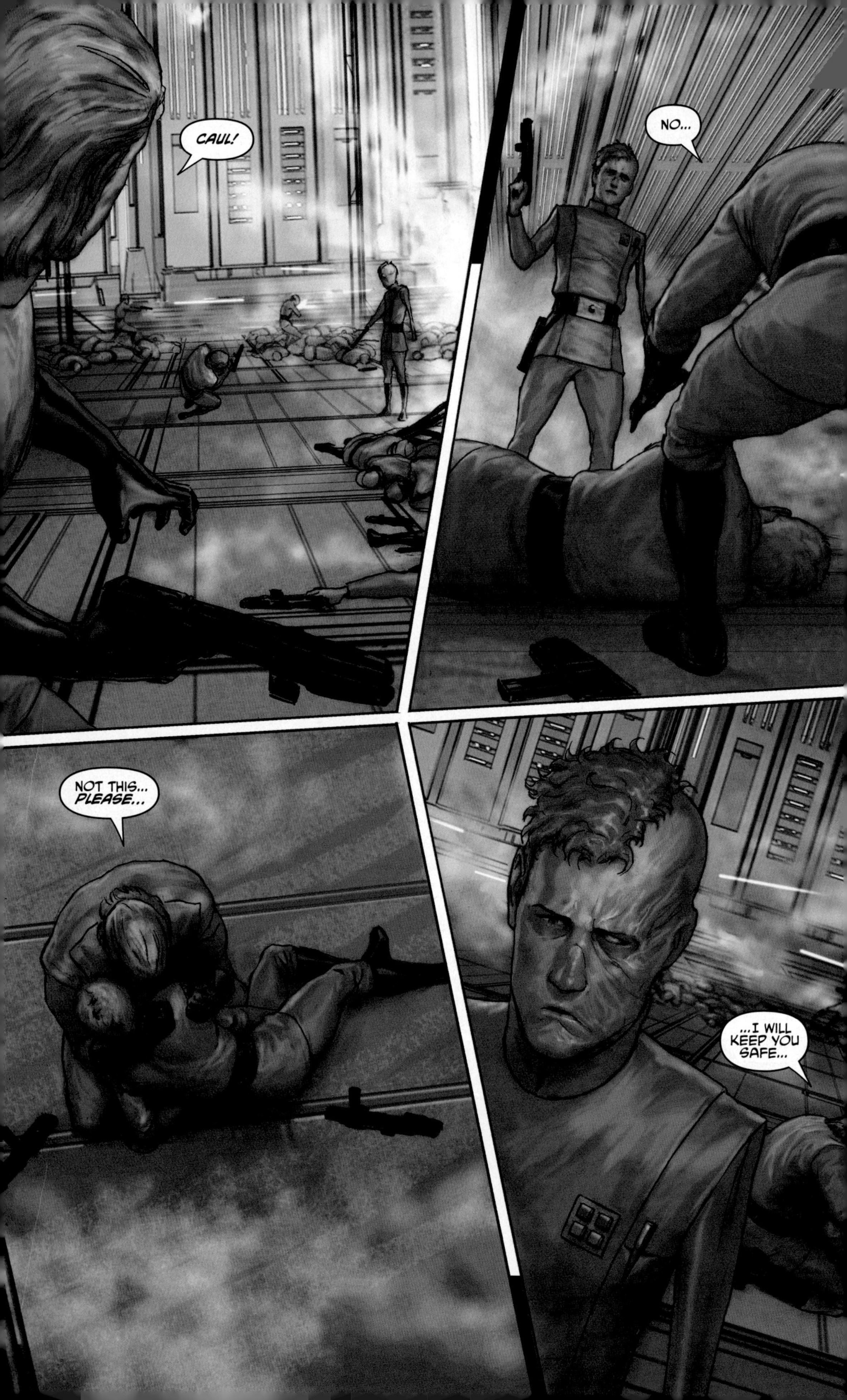
CAUL!
NO...
NOT THIS... *PLEASE...*
...I WILL KEEP YOU SAFE...

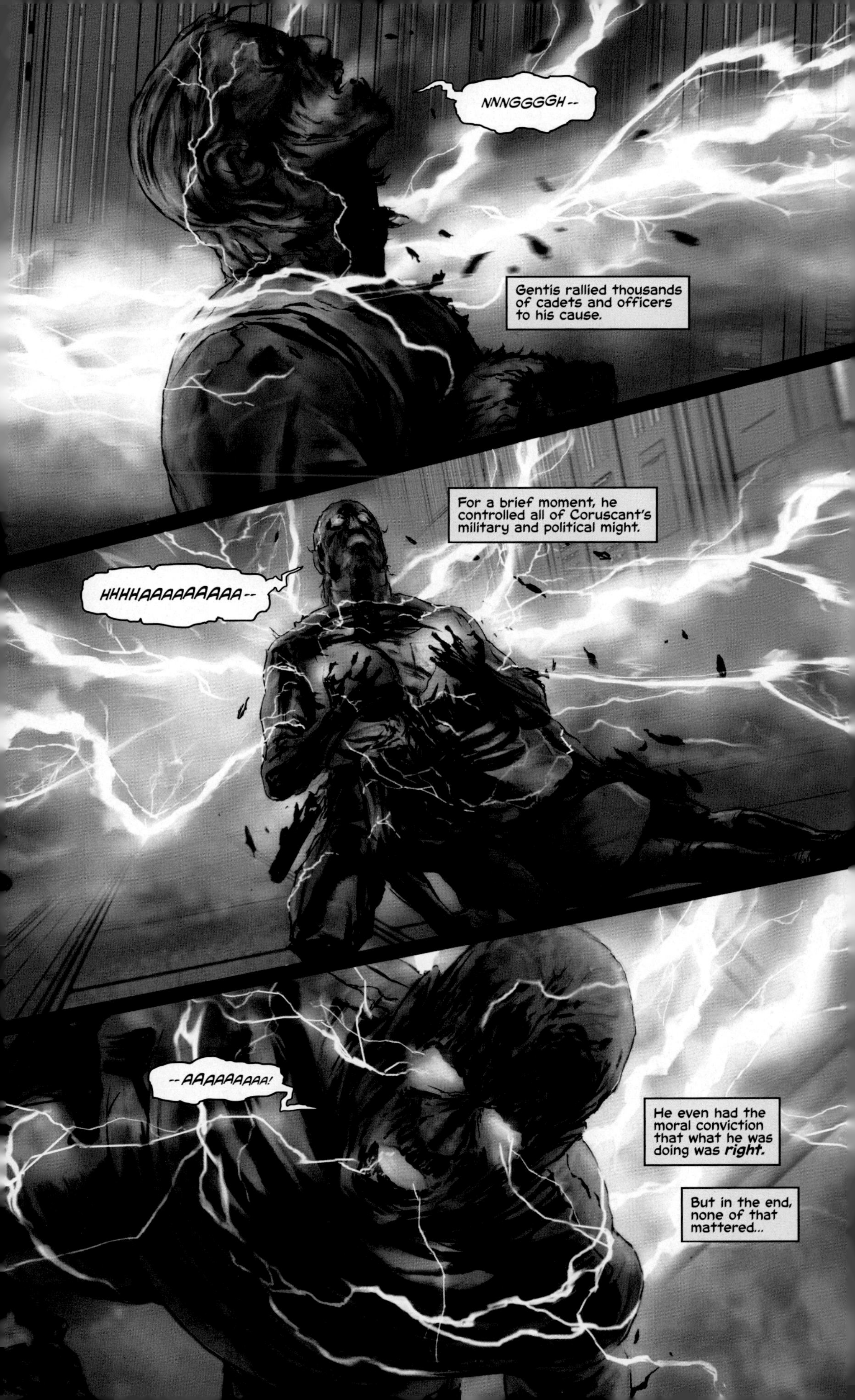

NNNGGGGH --
Gentis rallied thousands of cadets and officers to his cause.
For a brief moment, he controlled all of Coruscant's military and political might.
HHHHAAAAAAAAAA --
-- AAAAAAAAA!
He even had the moral conviction that what he was doing was *right.*
But in the end, none of that mattered...

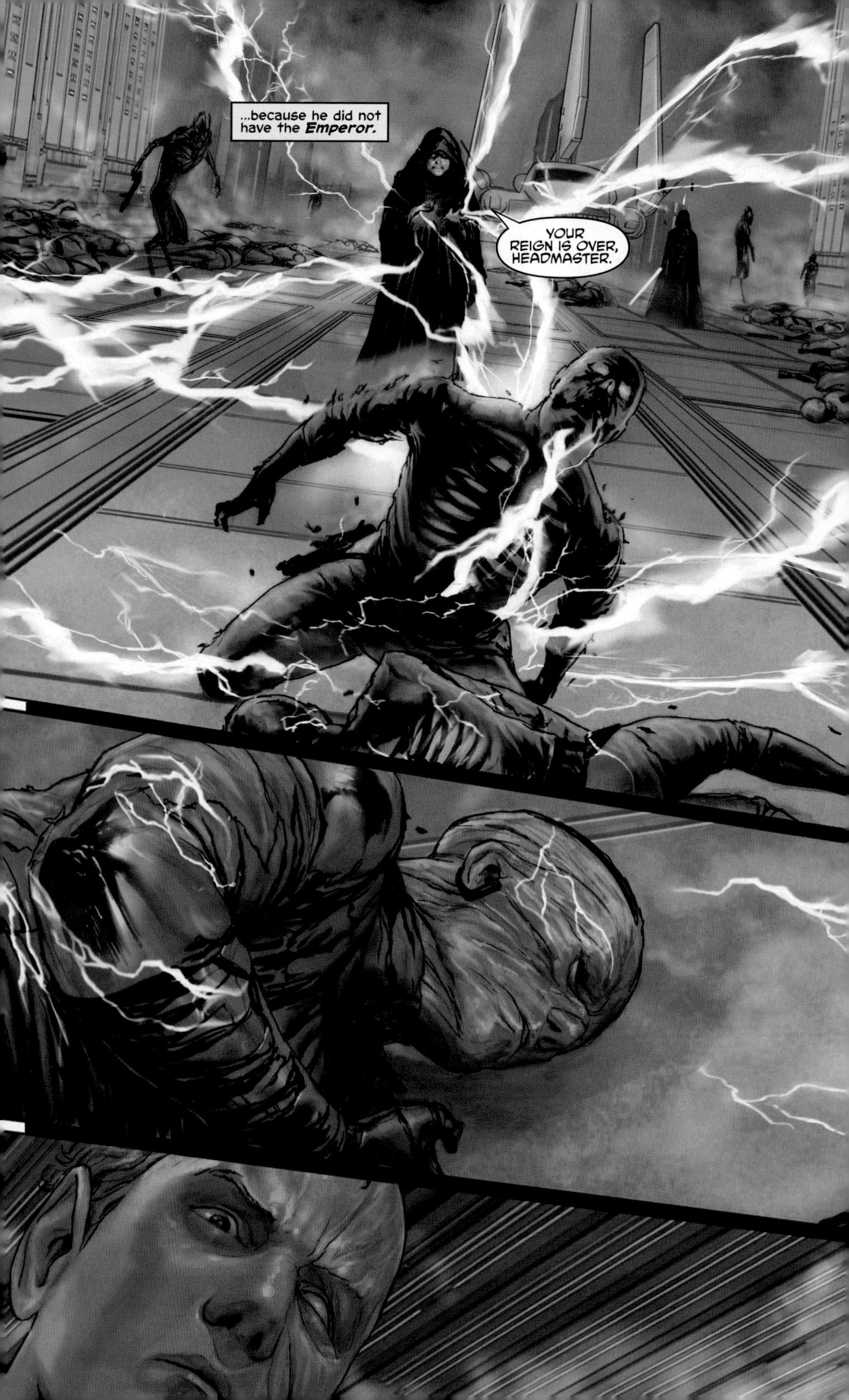
...because he did not have the Emperor.
YOUR REIGN IS OVER, HEADMASTER.

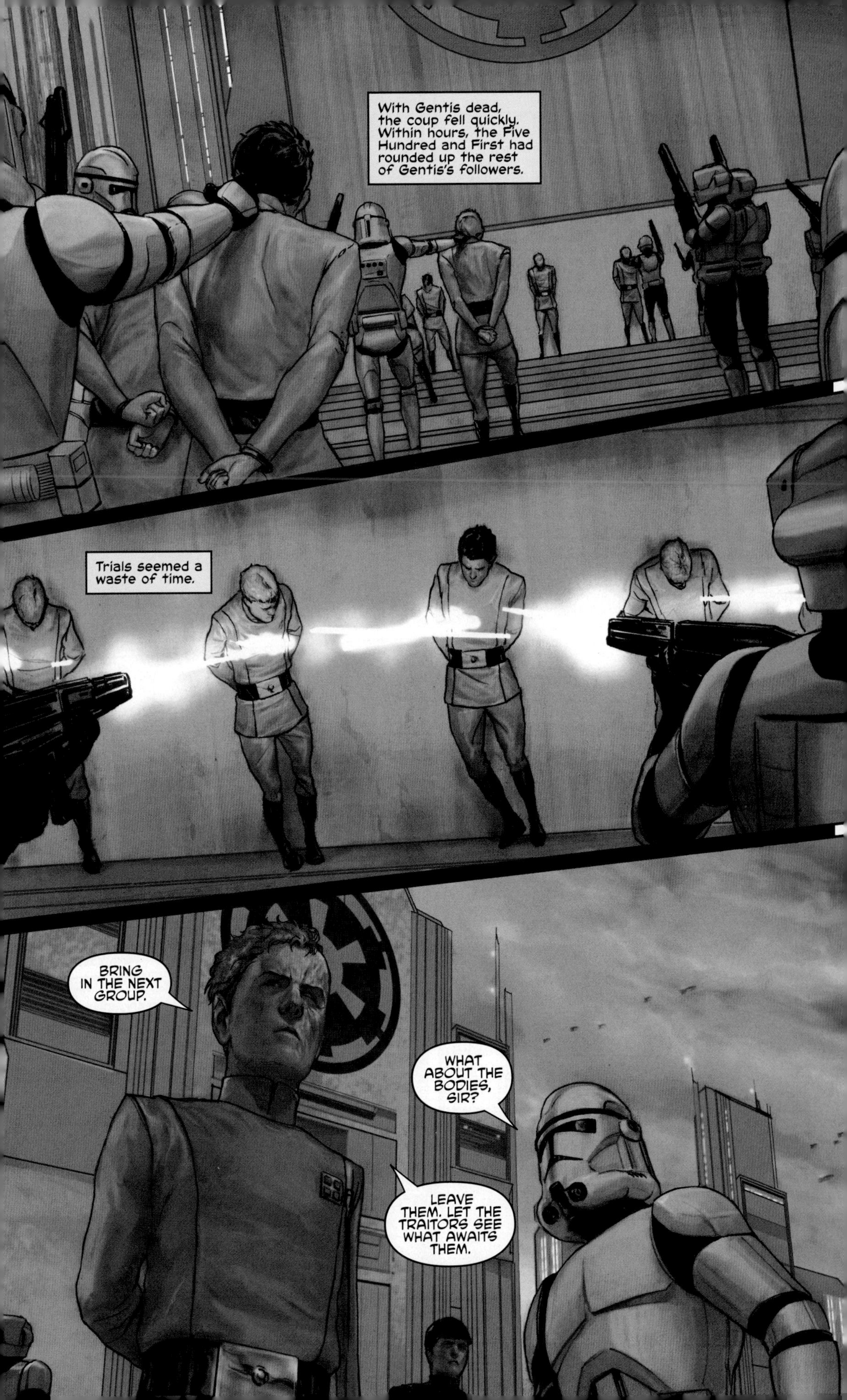
With Gentis dead, the coup fell quickly. Within hours, the Five Hundred and First had rounded up the rest of Gentis's followers.
Trials seemed a waste of time.
BRING IN THE NEXT GROUP.
WHAT ABOUT THE BODIES, SIR?
LEAVE THEM. LET THE TRAITORS SEE WHAT AWAITS THEM.

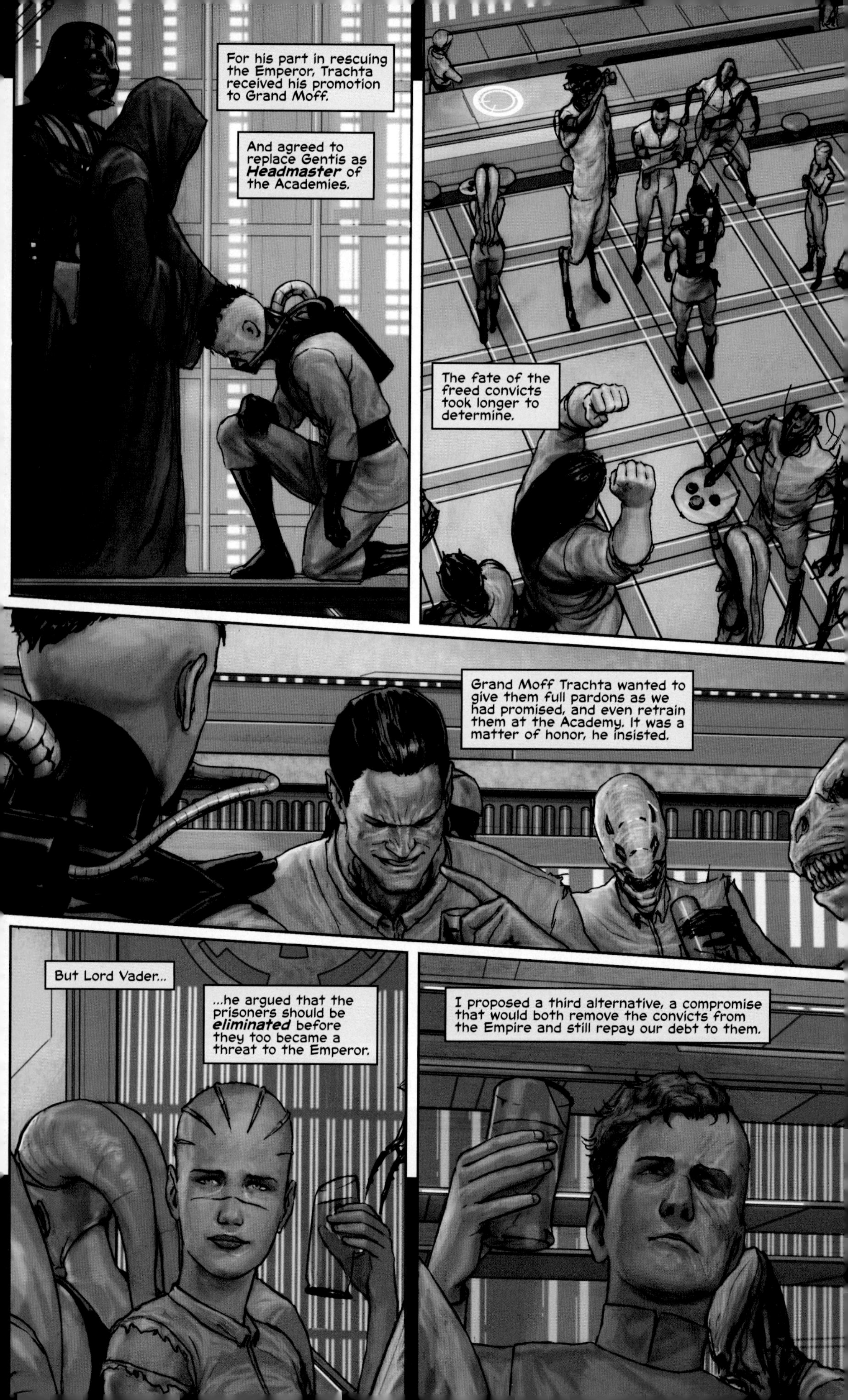
For his part in rescuing the Emperor, Trachta received his promotion to Grand Moff.
And agreed to replace Gentis as ***Headmaster*** of the Academies.
The fate of the freed convicts took longer to determine.
Grand Moff Trachta wanted to give them full pardons as we had promised, and even retrain them at the Academy. It was a matter of honor, he insisted.
But Lord Vader...
...he argued that the prisoners should be ***eliminated*** before they too became a threat to the Emperor.
I proposed a third alternative, a compromise that would both remove the convicts from the Empire and still repay our debt to them.

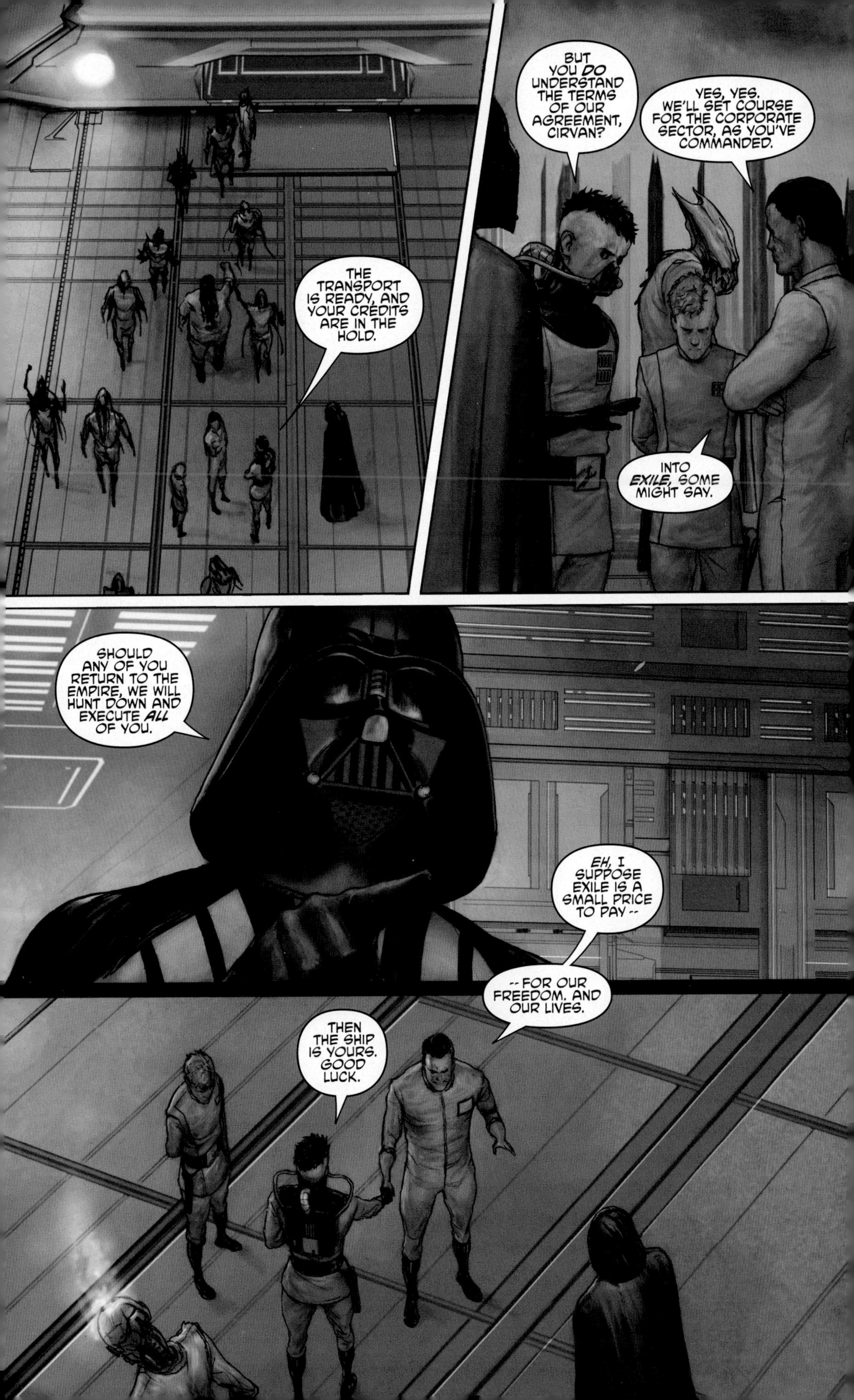
THE TRANSPORT IS READY, AND YOUR CREDITS ARE IN THE HOLD.
BUT YOU *DO* UNDERSTAND THE TERMS OF OUR AGREEMENT, CIRVAN?
YES, YES. WE'LL SET COURSE FOR THE CORPORATE SECTOR, AS YOU'VE COMMANDED.
INTO *EXILE,* SOME MIGHT SAY.
SHOULD ANY OF YOU RETURN TO THE EMPIRE, WE WILL HUNT DOWN AND EXECUTE *ALL* OF YOU.
*EH,* I SUPPOSE EXILE IS A SMALL PRICE TO PAY --
-- FOR OUR FREEDOM. AND OUR LIVES.
THEN THE SHIP IS YOURS. GOOD LUCK.

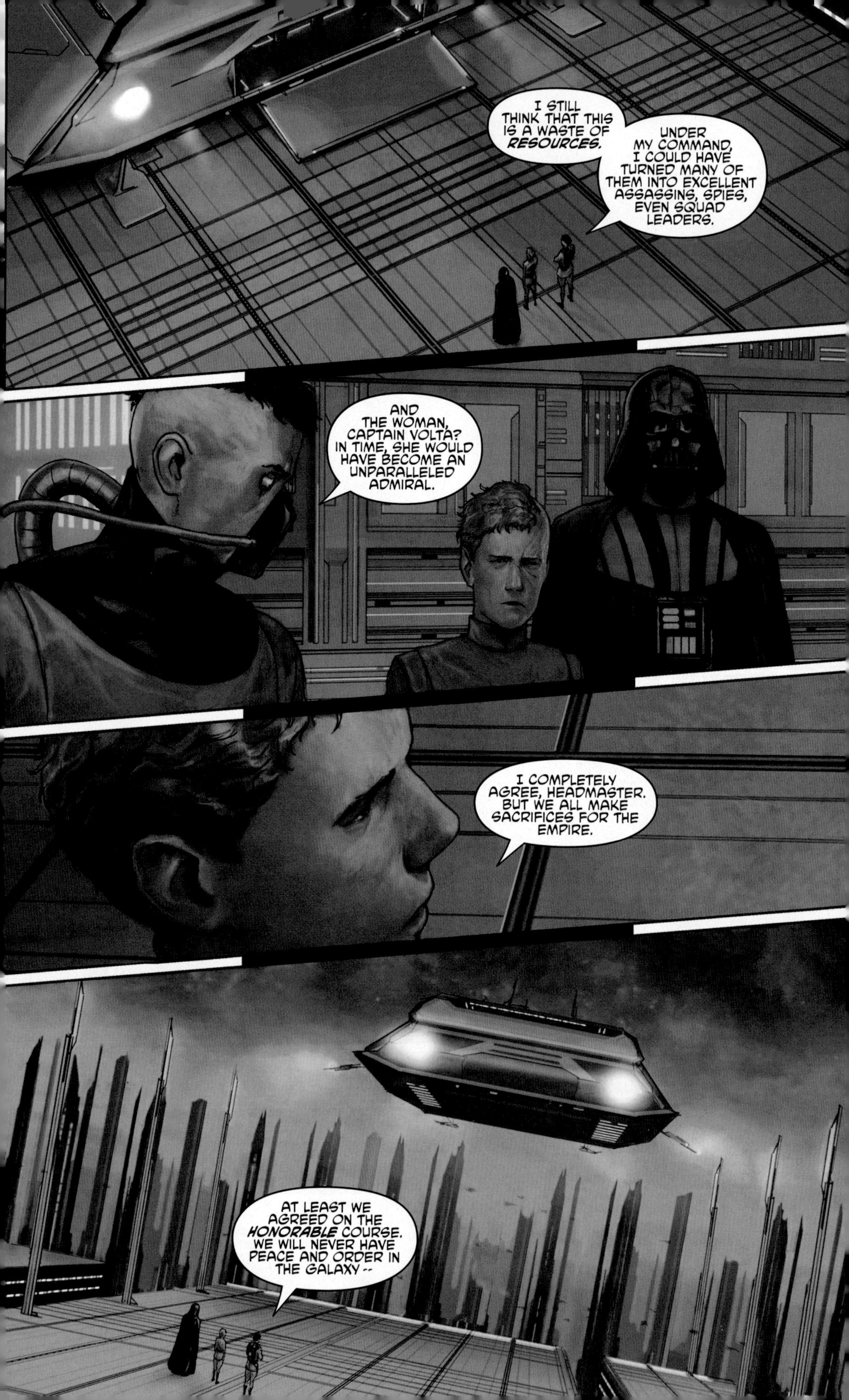
I STILL THINK THAT THIS IS A WASTE OF *RESOURCES.*
UNDER MY COMMAND, I COULD HAVE TURNED MANY OF THEM INTO EXCELLENT ASSASSINS, SPIES, EVEN SQUAD LEADERS.
AND THE WOMAN, CAPTAIN VOLTA? IN TIME, SHE WOULD HAVE BECOME AN UNPARALLELED ADMIRAL.
I COMPLETELY AGREE, HEADMASTER. BUT WE ALL MAKE SACRIFICES FOR THE EMPIRE.
AT LEAST WE AGREED ON THE *HONORABLE* COURSE. WE WILL NEVER HAVE PEACE AND ORDER IN THE GALAXY --

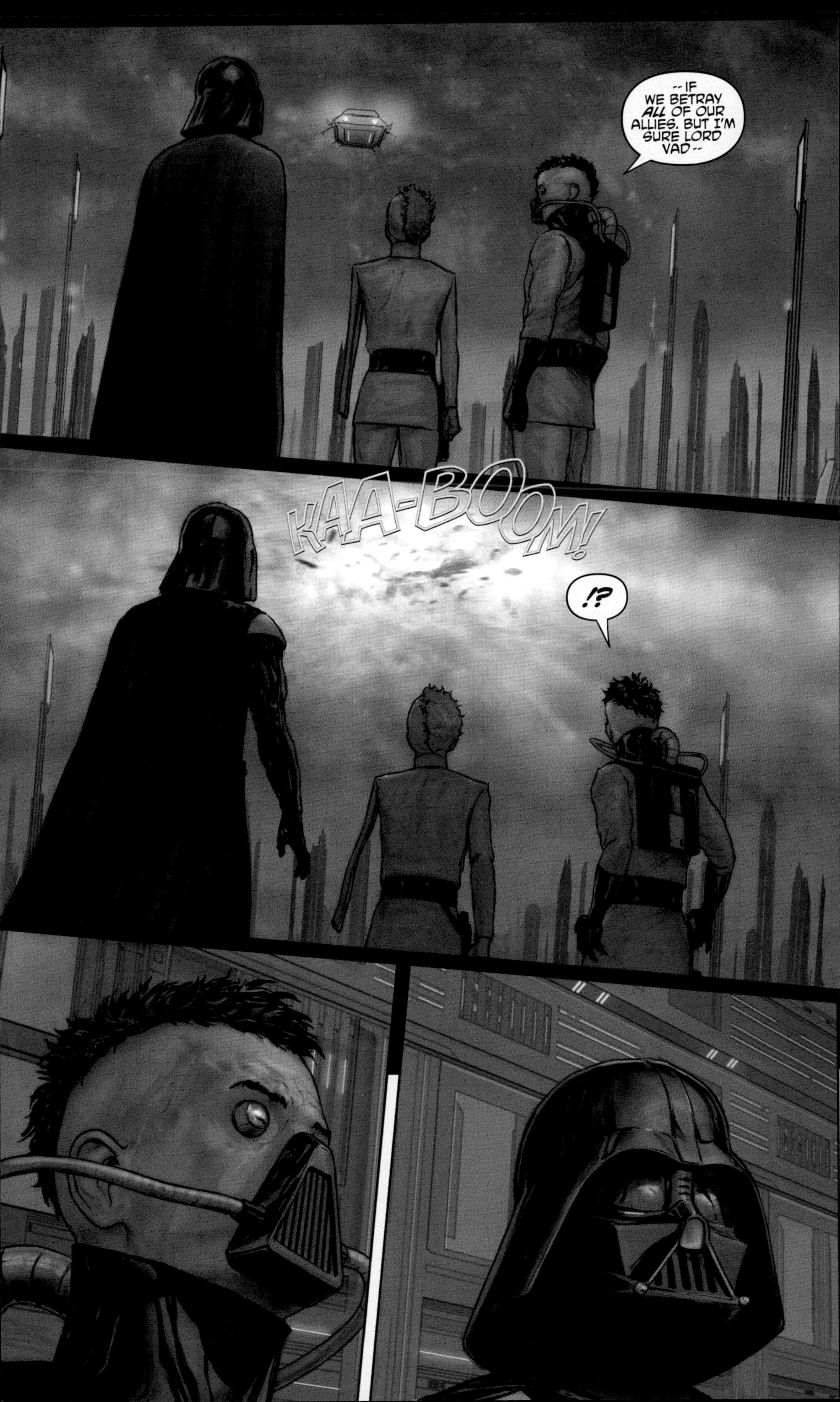

-- IF WE BETRAY ALL OF OUR ALLIES, BUT I'M SURE LORD VAD --
KAA-BOOM!
!?

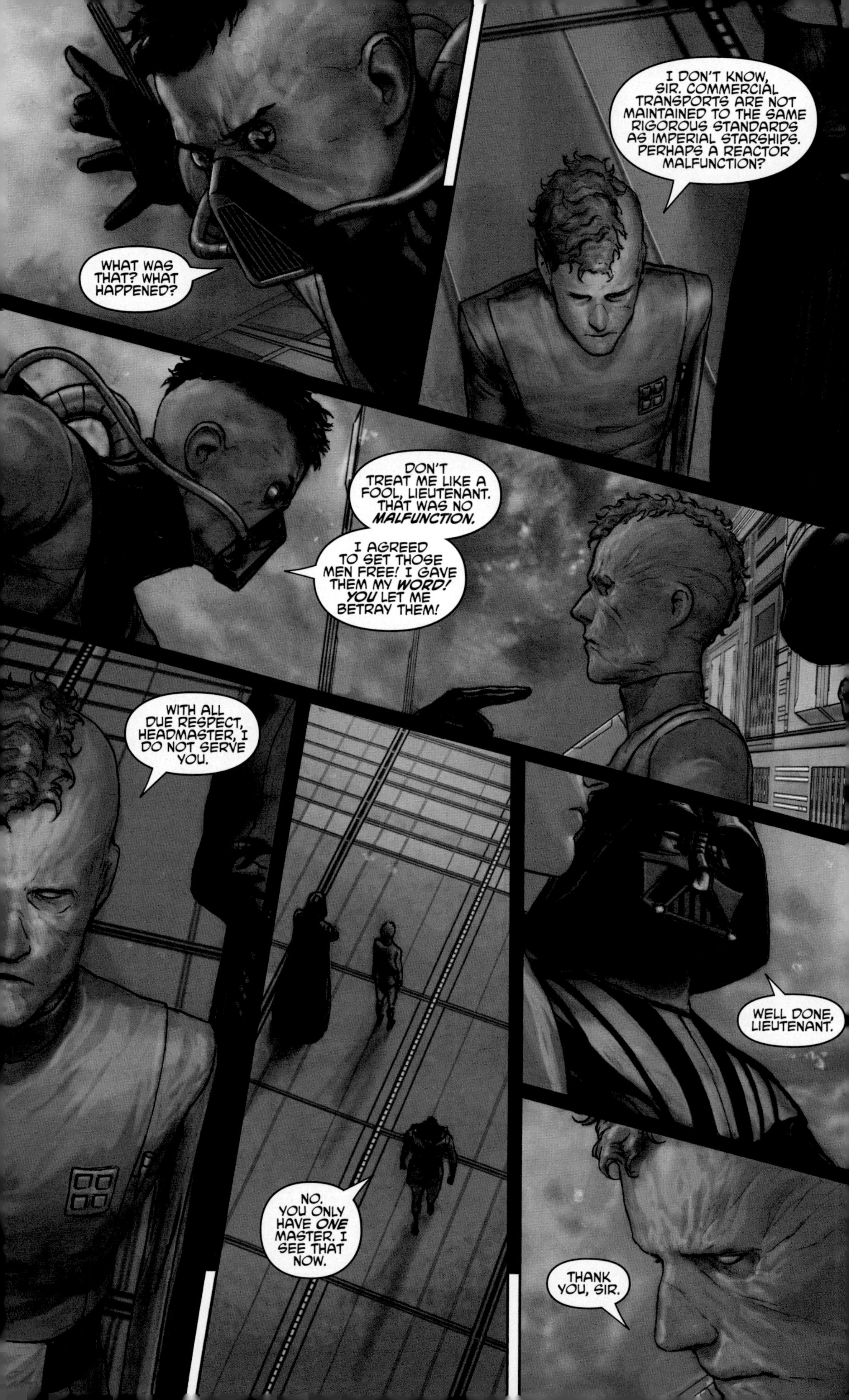
WHAT WAS THAT? WHAT HAPPENED?
I DON'T KNOW, SIR. COMMERCIAL TRANSPORTS ARE NOT MAINTAINED TO THE SAME RIGOROUS STANDARDS AS IMPERIAL STARSHIPS. PERHAPS A REACTOR MALFUNCTION?
DON'T TREAT ME LIKE A FOOL, LIEUTENANT. THAT WAS NO MALFUNCTION.
I AGREED TO SET THOSE MEN FREE! I GAVE THEM MY WORD! YOU LET ME BETRAY THEM!
WITH ALL DUE RESPECT, HEADMASTER, I DO NOT SERVE YOU.
NO. YOU ONLY HAVE ONE MASTER. I SEE THAT NOW.
WELL DONE, LIEUTENANT.
THANK YOU, SIR.

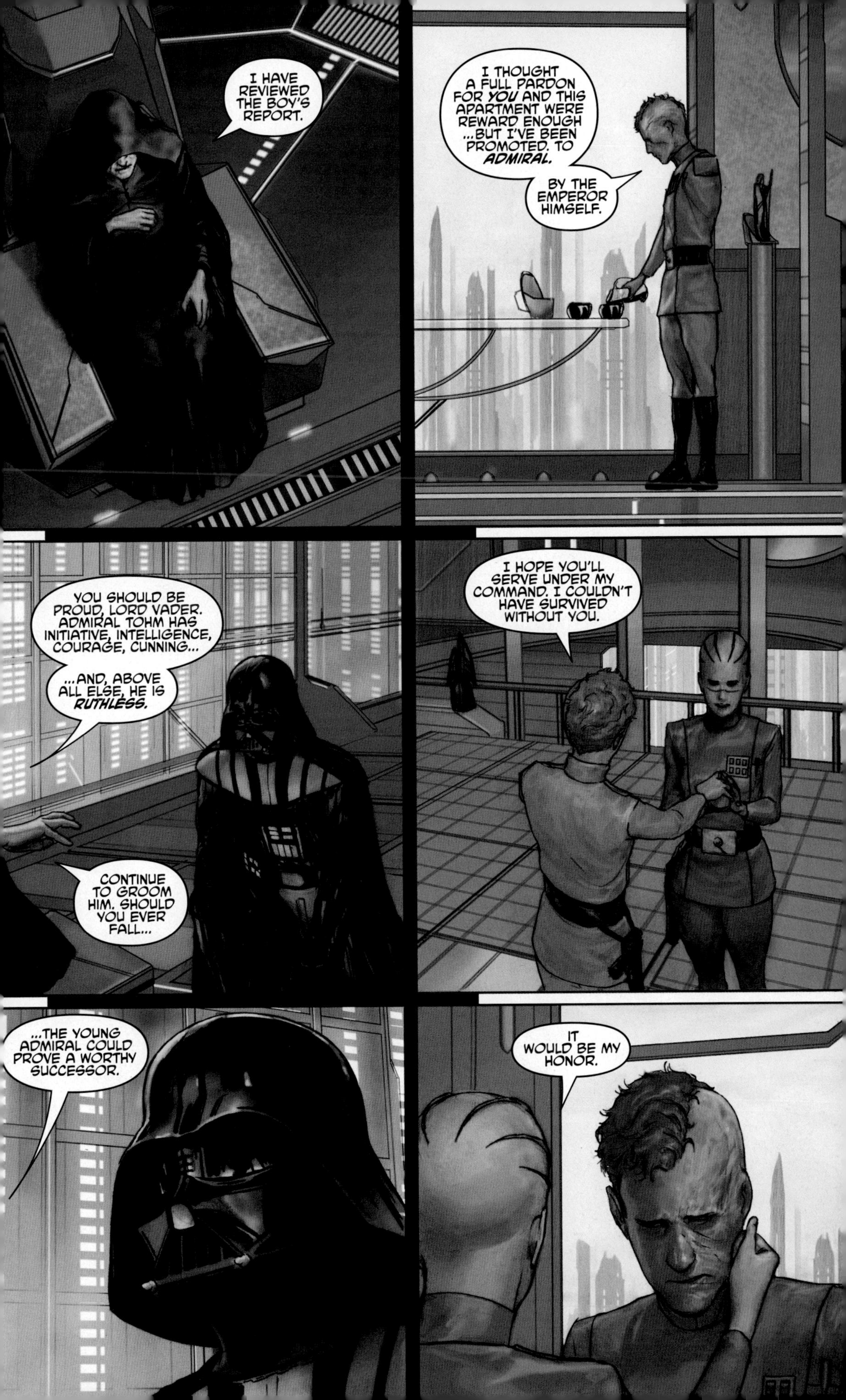
I HAVE REVIEWED THE BOY'S REPORT.
I THOUGHT A FULL PARDON FOR *YOU* AND THIS APARTMENT WERE REWARD ENOUGH ...BUT I'VE BEEN PROMOTED. TO ***ADMIRAL.***
BY THE EMPEROR HIMSELF.
YOU SHOULD BE PROUD, LORD VADER. ADMIRAL TOHM HAS INITIATIVE, INTELLIGENCE, COURAGE, CUNNING...
...AND, ABOVE ALL ELSE, HE IS ***RUTHLESS.***
CONTINUE TO GROOM HIM. SHOULD YOU EVER FALL...
I HOPE YOU'LL SERVE UNDER MY COMMAND. I COULDN'T HAVE SURVIVED WITHOUT YOU.
...THE YOUNG ADMIRAL COULD PROVE A WORTHY SUCCESSOR.
IT WOULD BE MY HONOR.

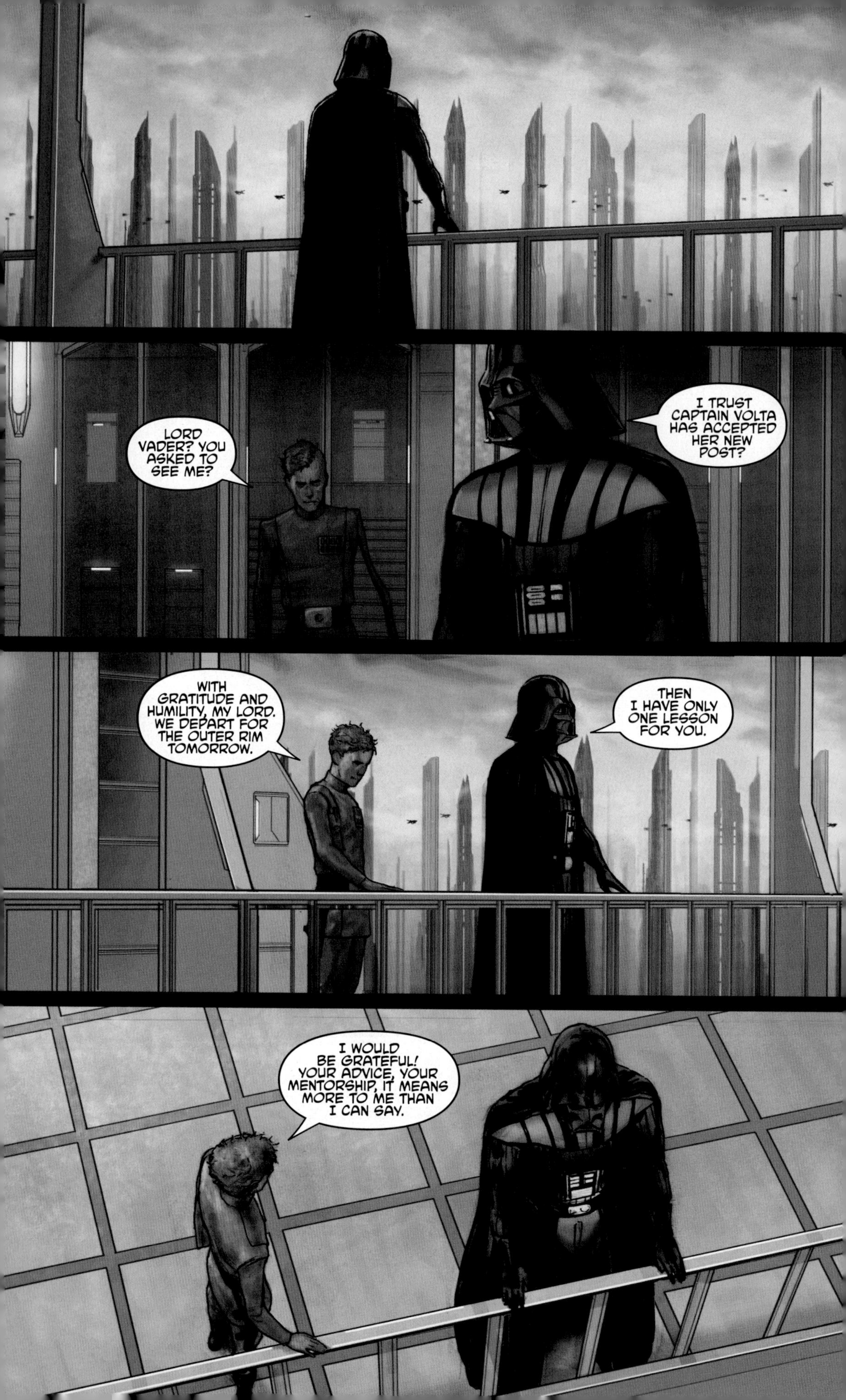
LORD VADER? YOU ASKED TO SEE ME?
I TRUST CAPTAIN VOLTA HAS ACCEPTED HER NEW POST?
WITH GRATITUDE AND HUMILITY, MY LORD. WE DEPART FOR THE OUTER RIM TOMORROW.
THEN I HAVE ONLY ONE LESSON FOR YOU.
I WOULD BE GRATEFUL! YOUR ADVICE, YOUR MENTORSHIP, IT MEANS MORE TO ME THAN I CAN SAY.

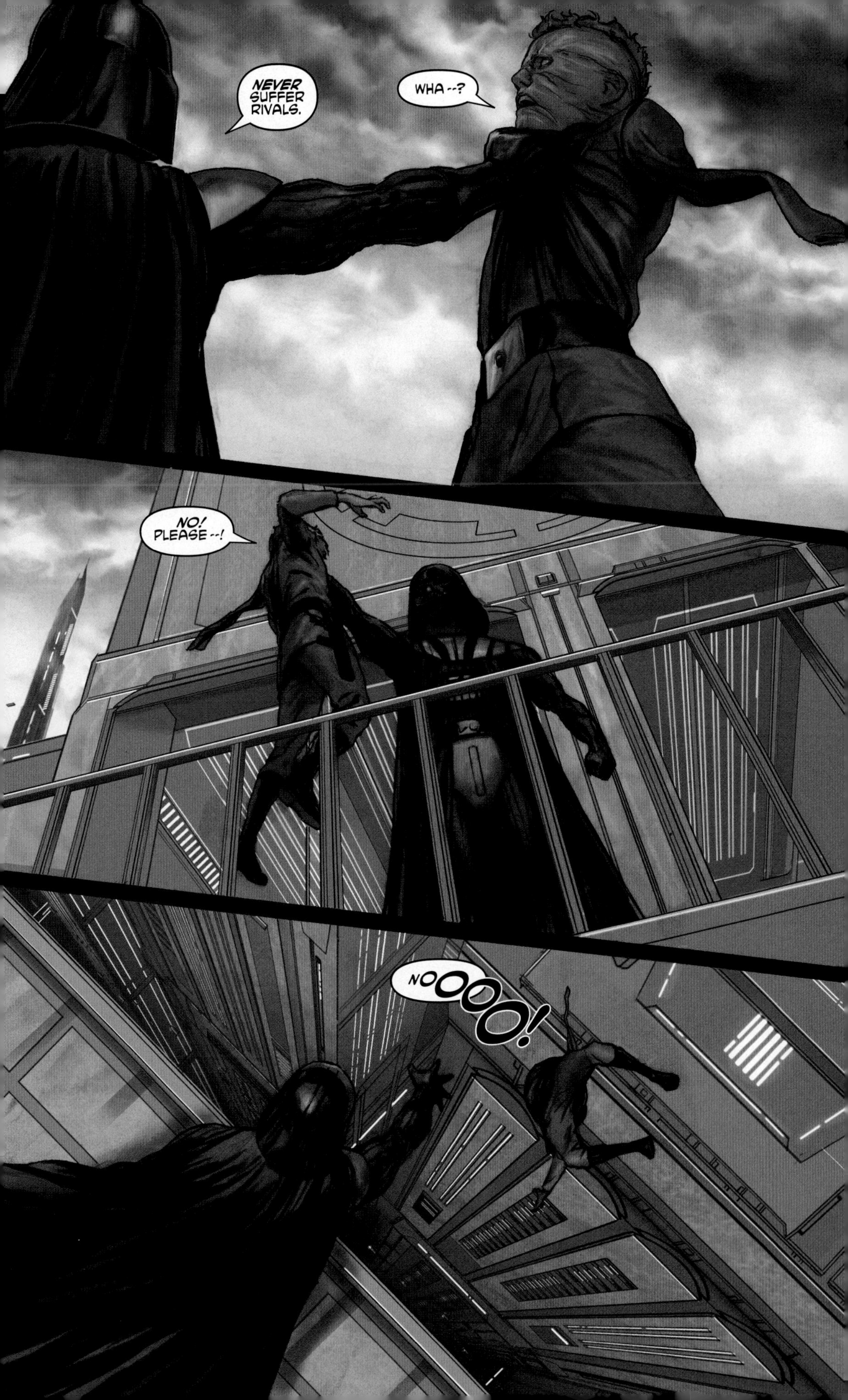
NEVER SUFFER RIVALS.
WHA --?
NO! PLEASE --!
NOOOO!

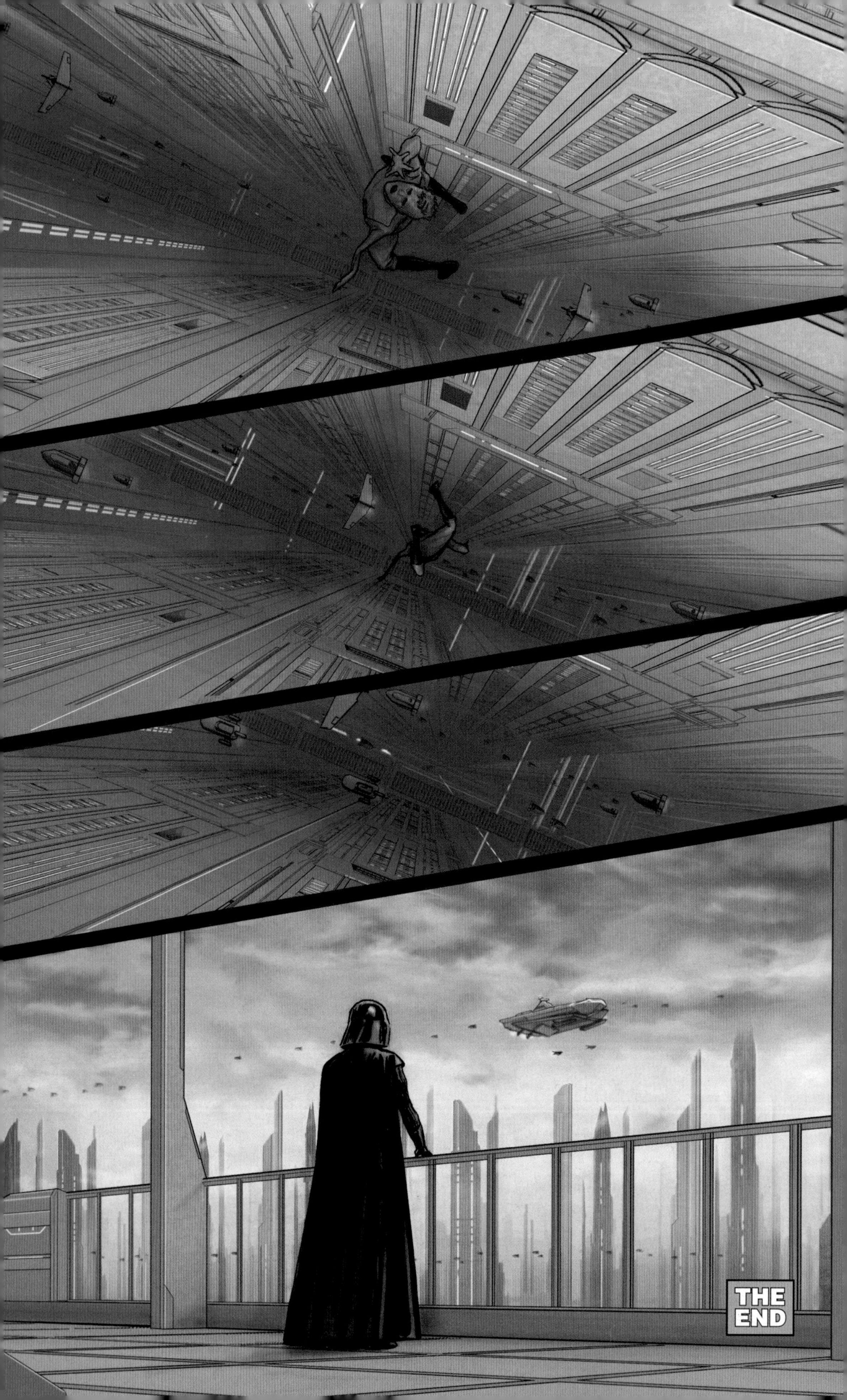
THE END

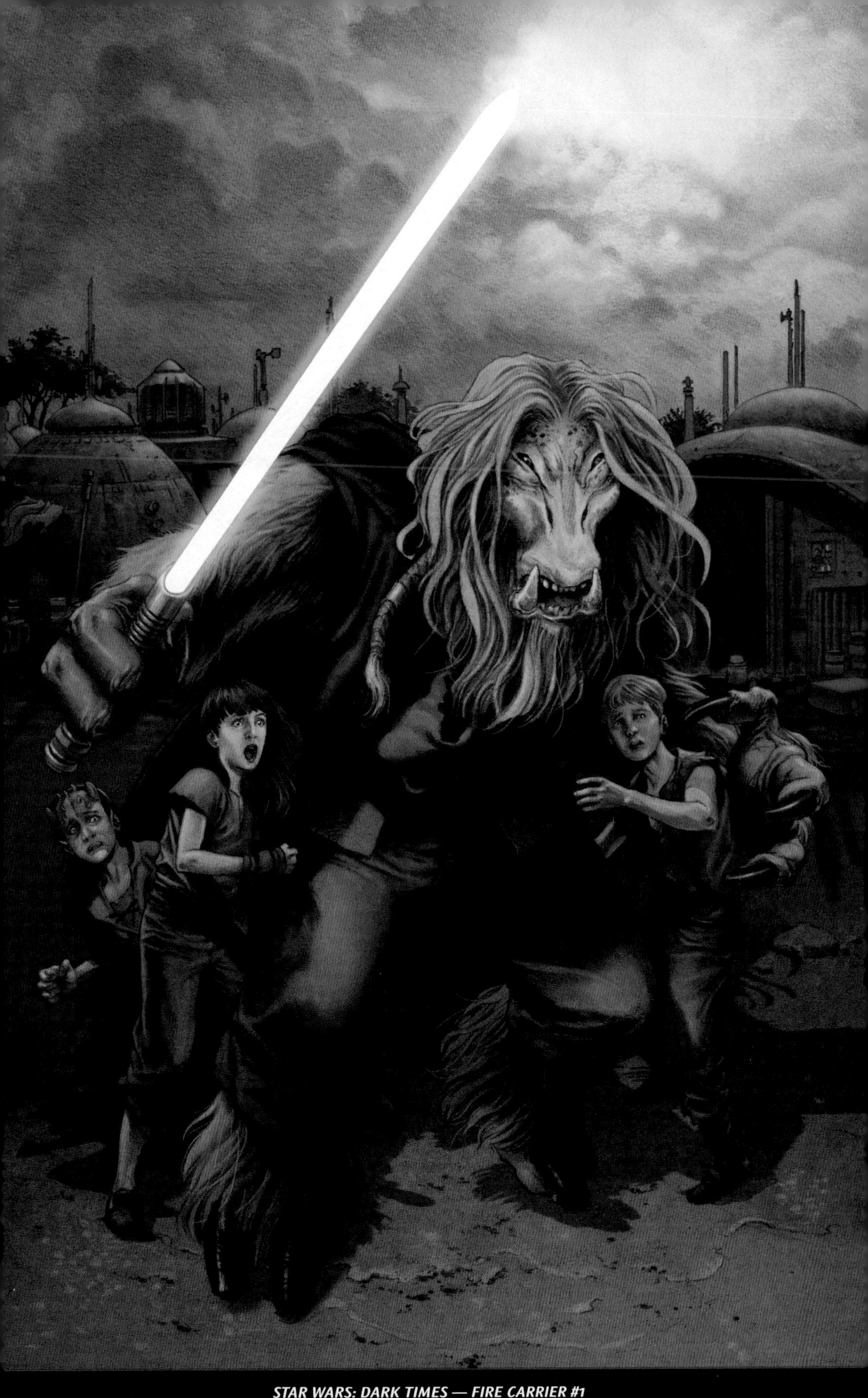

***STAR WARS: DARK TIMES — FIRE CARRIER #1***

WRITER: RANDY STRADLEY • ARTIST: GABRIEL GUZMAN • COLORIST: GARRY HENDERSON • LETTERER: MICHAEL HEISLER
ASSISTANT EDITOR: FREDDYE LINS • EDITOR: DAVE MARSHALL • COVER ARTIST: DOUGLAS WHEATLEY

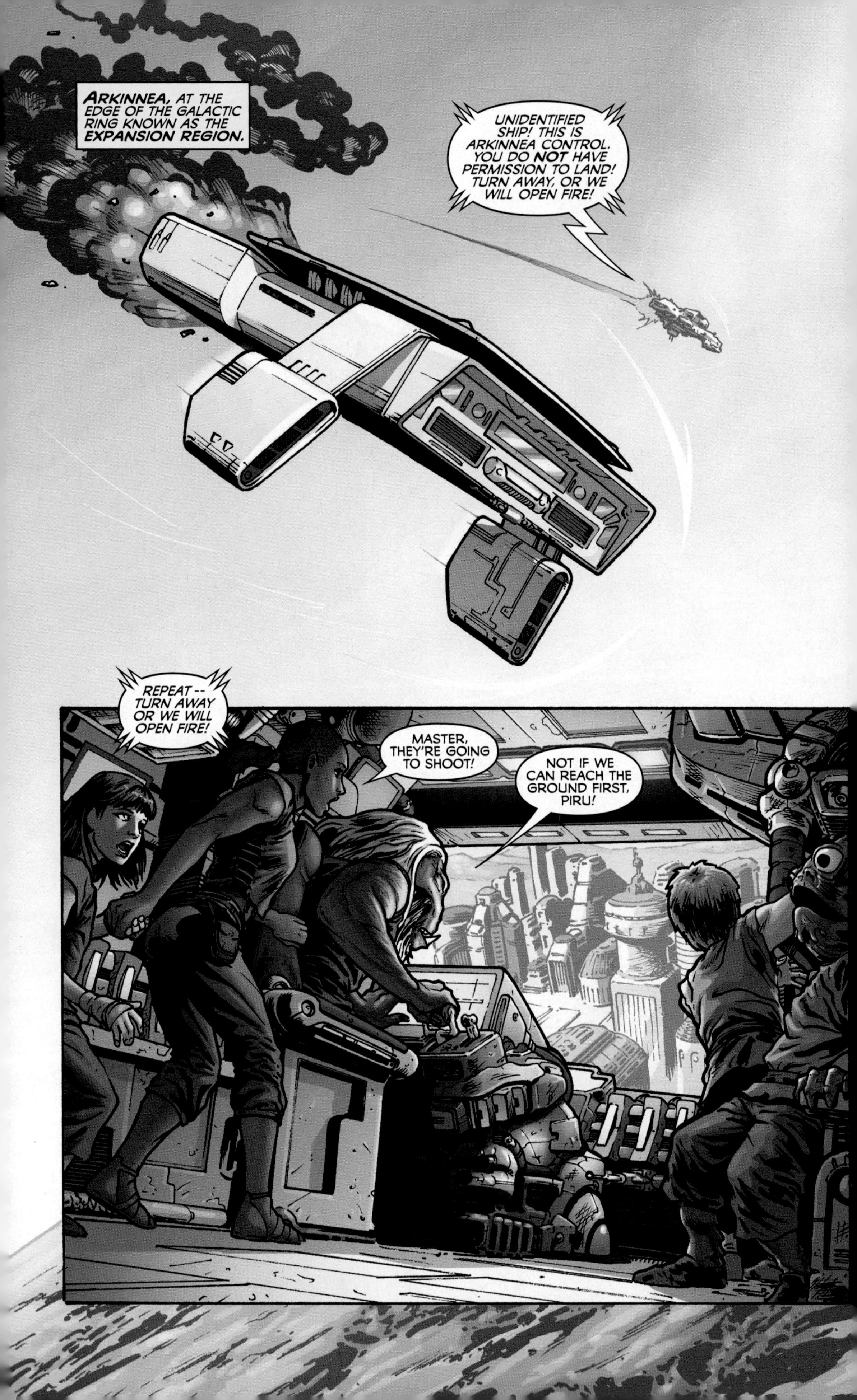
ARKINNEA, AT THE EDGE OF THE GALACTIC RING KNOWN AS THE EXPANSION REGION.
UNIDENTIFIED SHIP! THIS IS ARKINNEA CONTROL. YOU DO NOT HAVE PERMISSION TO LAND! TURN AWAY, OR WE WILL OPEN FIRE!
REPEAT -- TURN AWAY OR WE WILL OPEN FIRE!
MASTER, THEY'RE GOING TO SHOOT!
NOT IF WE CAN REACH THE GROUND FIRST, PIRU!

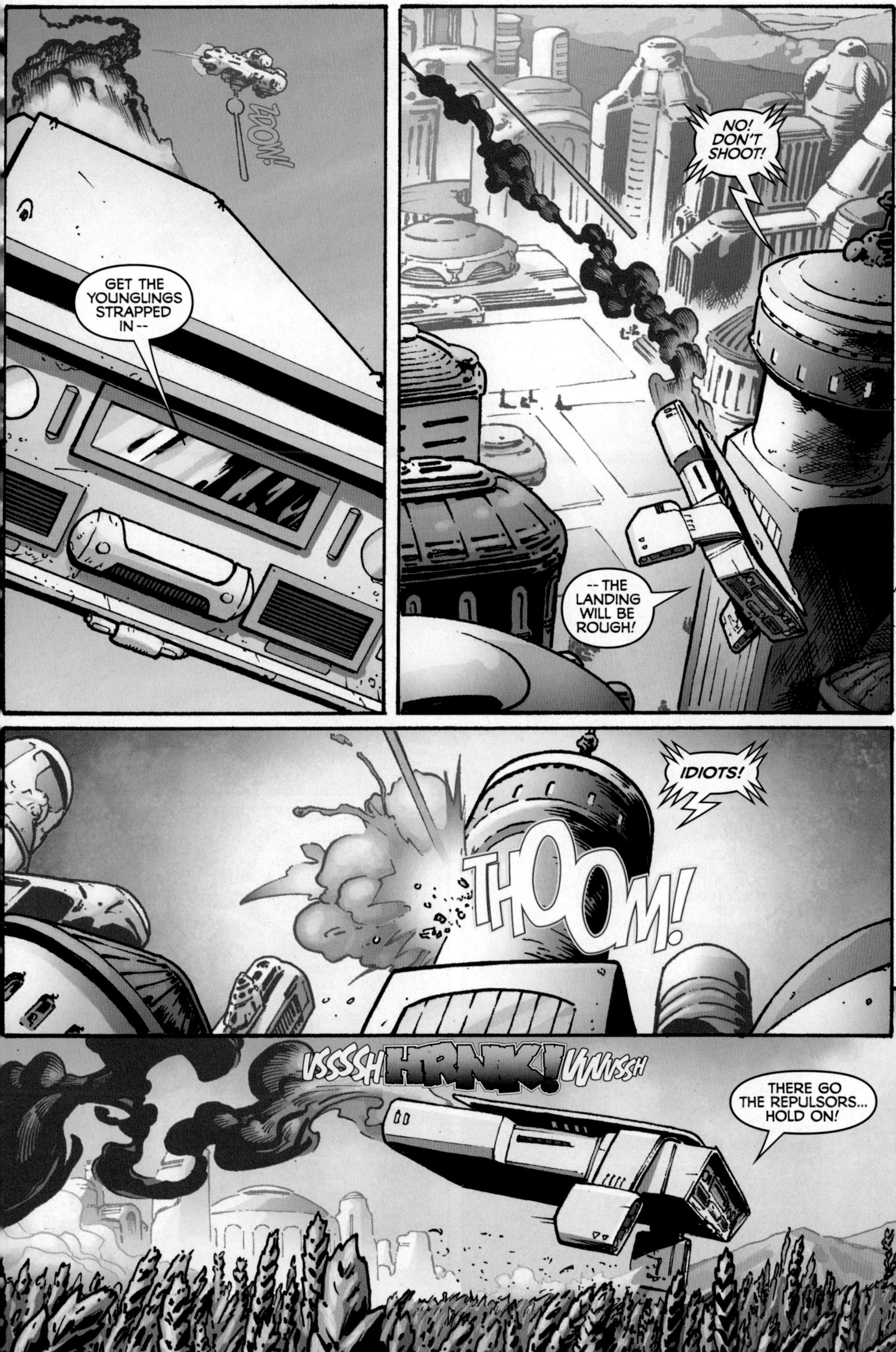
ZOOM!
GET THE YOUNGLINGS STRAPPED IN --
NO! DON'T SHOOT!
-- THE LANDING WILL BE ROUGH!
IDIOTS!
THOOOM!
VSSSSH HRNK! UWWSSH
THERE GO THE REPULSORS... HOLD ON!

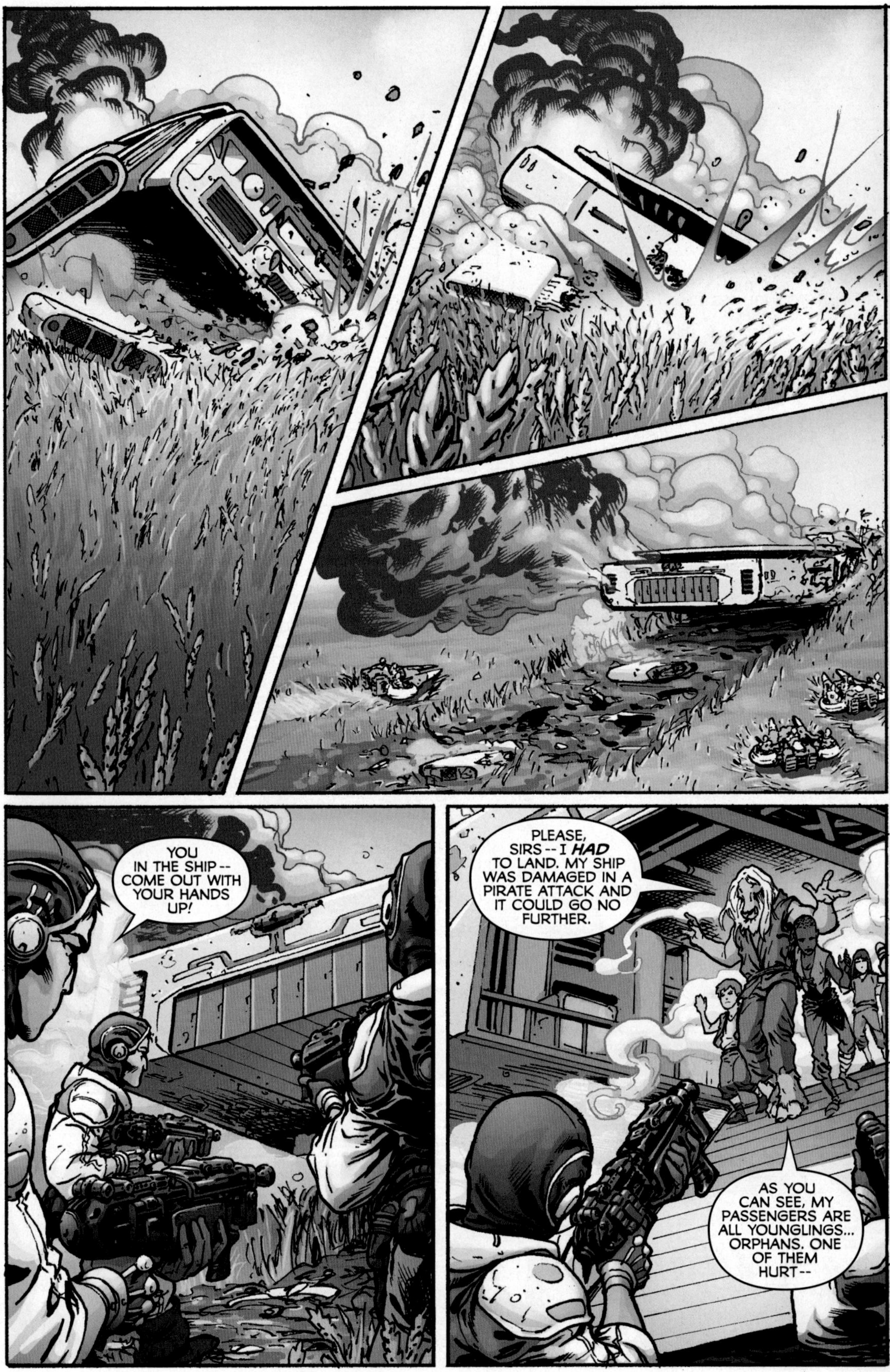
YOU IN THE SHIP-- COME OUT WITH YOUR HANDS UP!
PLEASE, SIRS--I HAD TO LAND. MY SHIP WAS DAMAGED IN A PIRATE ATTACK AND IT COULD GO NO FURTHER.
AS YOU CAN SEE, MY PASSENGERS ARE ALL YOUNGLINGS... ORPHANS. ONE OF THEM HURT--

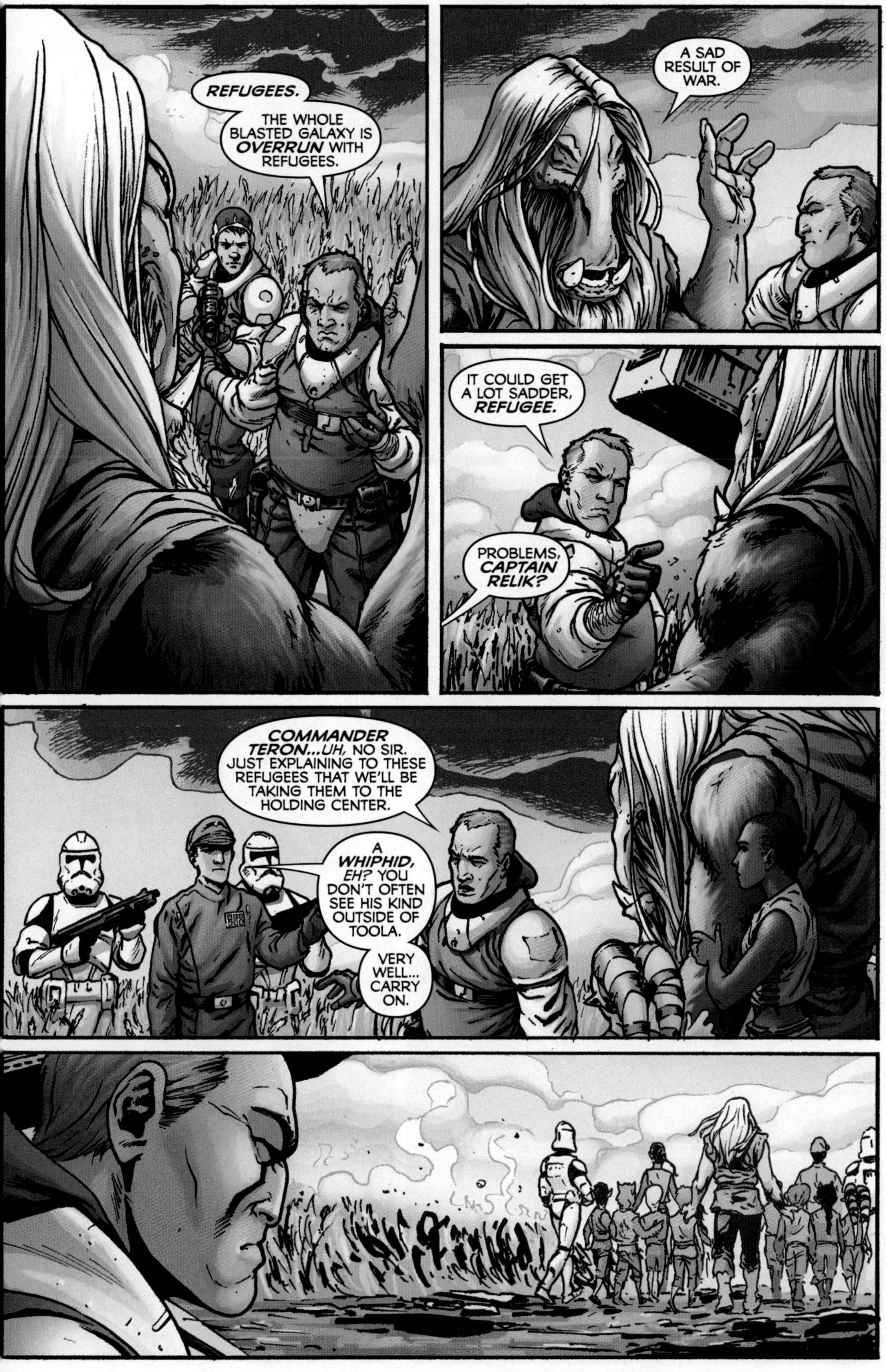
REFUGEES.
THE WHOLE BLASTED GALAXY IS OVERRUN WITH REFUGEES.
A SAD RESULT OF WAR.
IT COULD GET A LOT SADDER, REFUGEE.
PROBLEMS, CAPTAIN RELIK?
COMMANDER TERON...UH, NO SIR. JUST EXPLAINING TO THESE REFUGEES THAT WE'LL BE TAKING THEM TO THE HOLDING CENTER.
A WHIPHID, EH? YOU DON'T OFTEN SEE HIS KIND OUTSIDE OF TOOLA.
VERY WELL... CARRY ON.

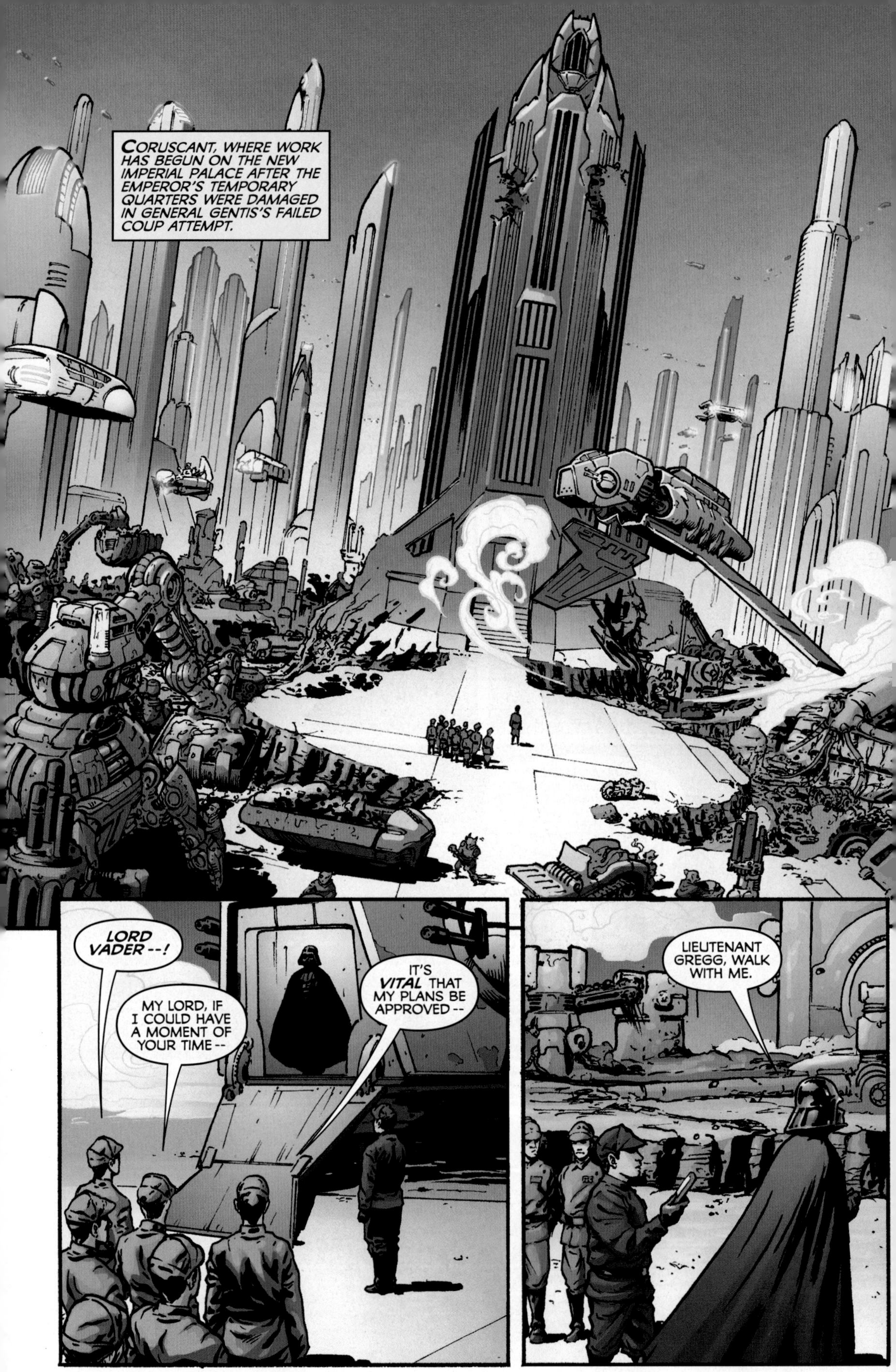
CORUSCANT, WHERE WORK HAS BEGUN ON THE NEW IMPERIAL PALACE AFTER THE EMPEROR'S TEMPORARY QUARTERS WERE DAMAGED IN GENERAL GENTIS'S FAILED COUP ATTEMPT.
LORD VADER --!
MY LORD, IF I COULD HAVE A MOMENT OF YOUR TIME --
IT'S VITAL THAT MY PLANS BE APPROVED --
LIEUTENANT GREGG, WALK WITH ME.

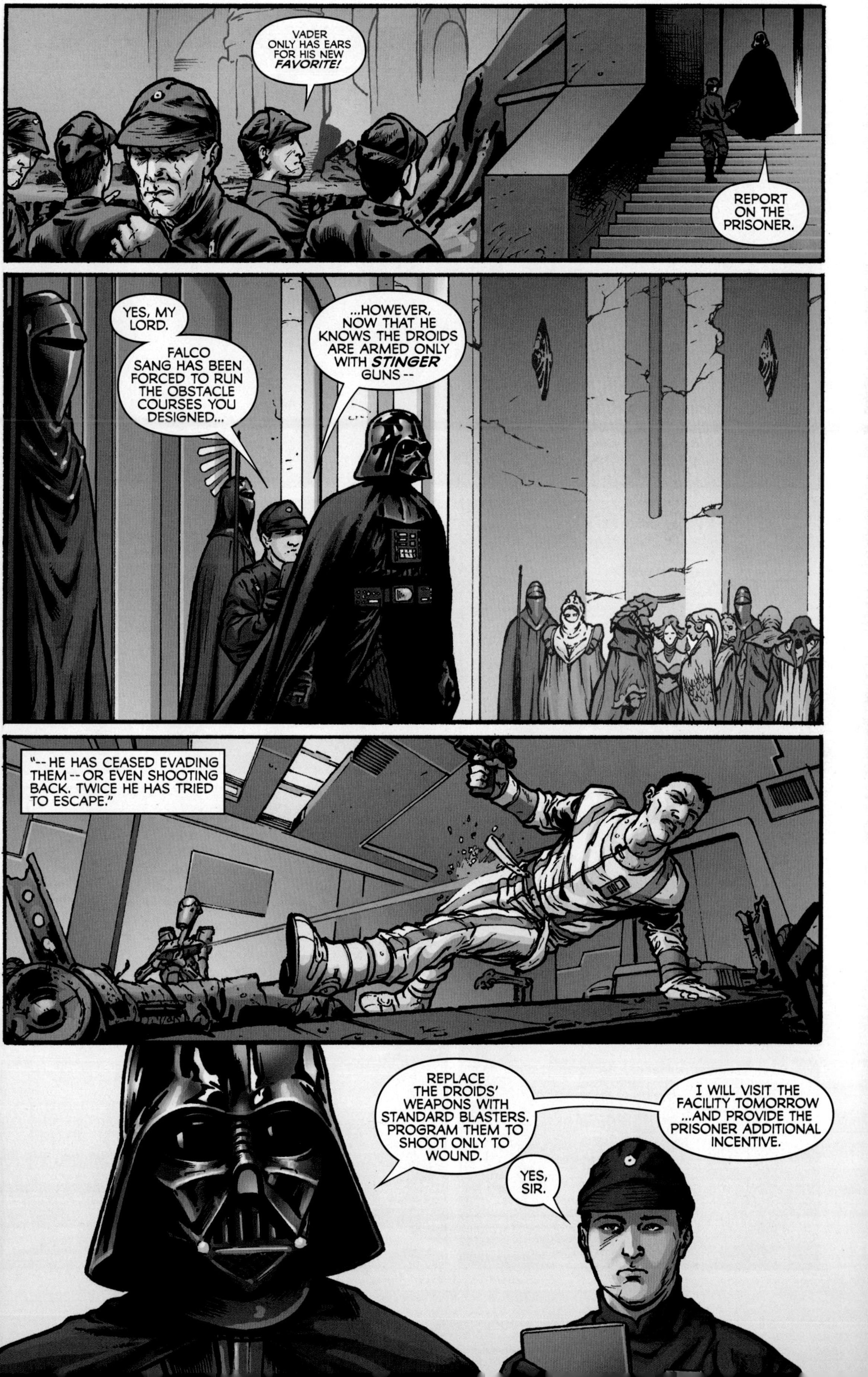
VADER ONLY HAS EARS FOR HIS NEW *FAVORITE!*
REPORT ON THE PRISONER.
YES, MY LORD.
FALCO SANG HAS BEEN FORCED TO RUN THE OBSTACLE COURSES YOU DESIGNED...
...HOWEVER, NOW THAT HE KNOWS THE DROIDS ARE ARMED ONLY WITH *STINGER* GUNS --
"-- HE HAS CEASED EVADING THEM -- OR EVEN SHOOTING BACK. TWICE HE HAS TRIED TO ESCAPE."
REPLACE THE DROIDS' WEAPONS WITH STANDARD BLASTERS. PROGRAM THEM TO SHOOT ONLY TO WOUND.
I WILL VISIT THE FACILITY TOMORROW ...AND PROVIDE THE PRISONER ADDITIONAL INCENTIVE.
YES, SIR.

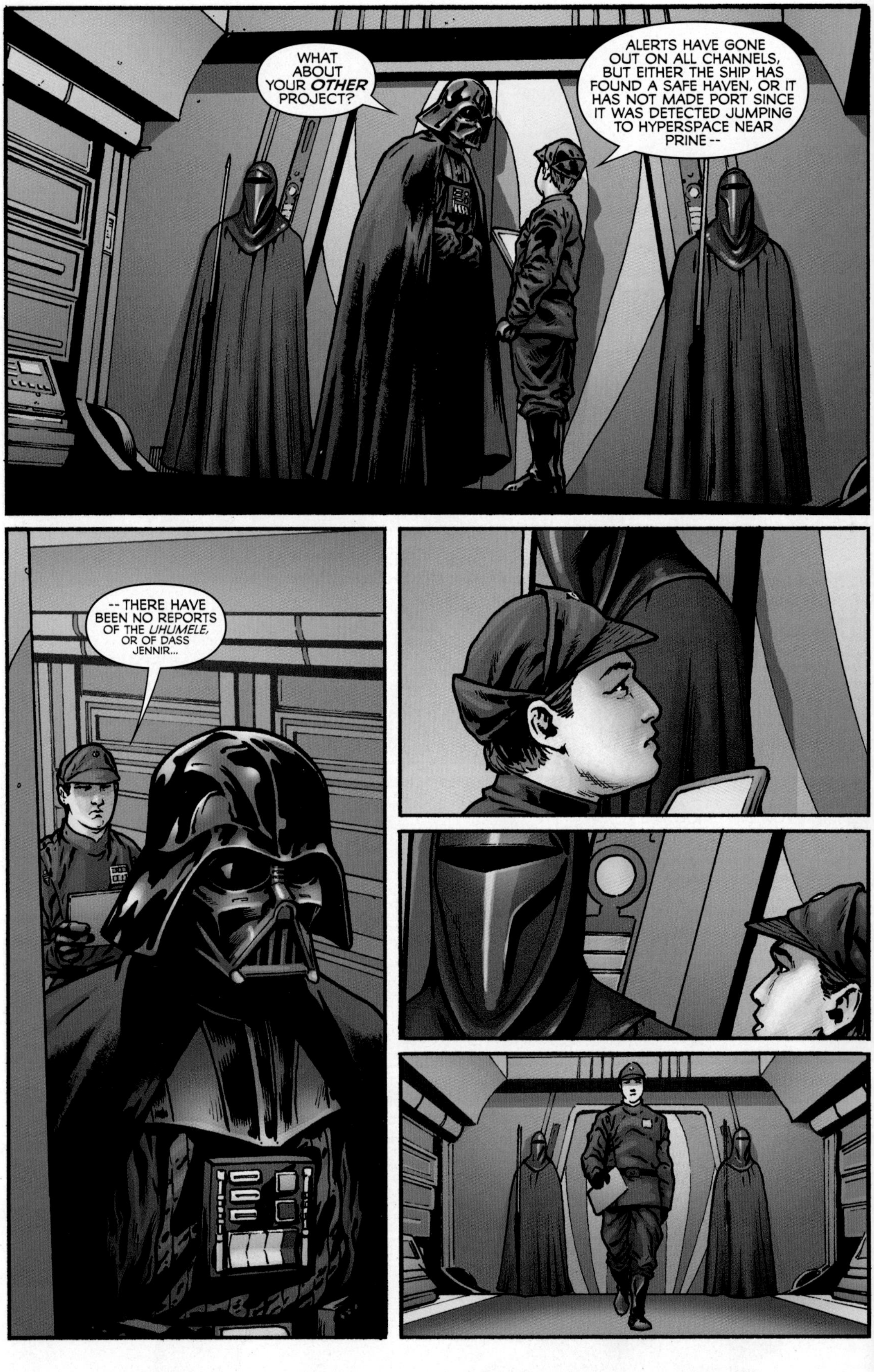
WHAT ABOUT YOUR *OTHER* PROJECT?
ALERTS HAVE GONE OUT ON ALL CHANNELS, BUT EITHER THE SHIP HAS FOUND A SAFE HAVEN, OR IT HAS NOT MADE PORT SINCE IT WAS DETECTED JUMPING TO HYPERSPACE NEAR PRINE --
-- THERE HAVE BEEN NO REPORTS OF THE *UHUMELE,* OR OF DASS JENNIR...

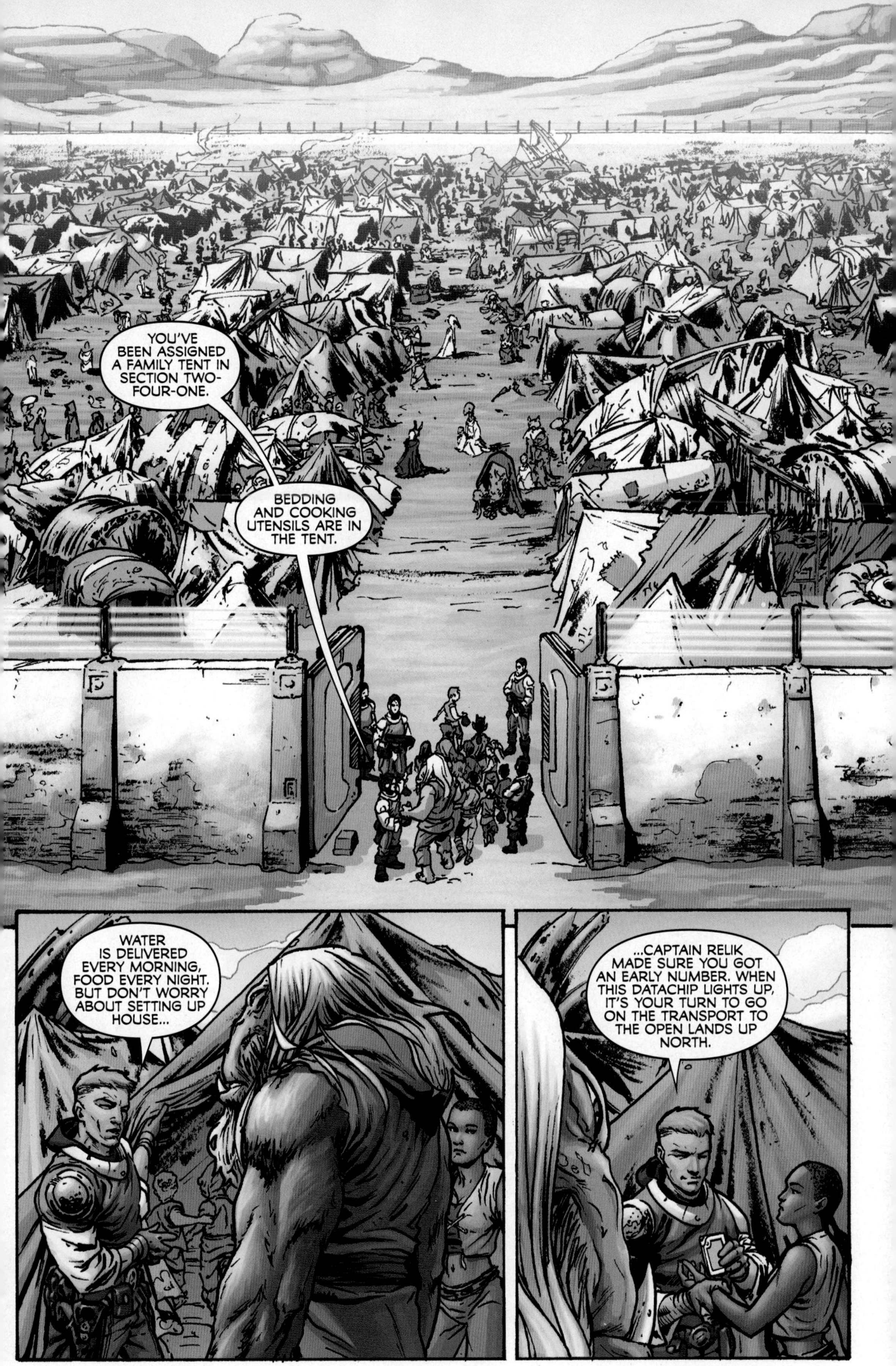
YOU'VE BEEN ASSIGNED A FAMILY TENT IN SECTION TWO-FOUR-ONE.
BEDDING AND COOKING UTENSILS ARE IN THE TENT.
WATER IS DELIVERED EVERY MORNING, FOOD EVERY NIGHT. BUT DON'T WORRY ABOUT SETTING UP HOUSE...
...CAPTAIN RELIK MADE SURE YOU GOT AN EARLY NUMBER. WHEN THIS DATACHIP LIGHTS UP, IT'S YOUR TURN TO GO ON THE TRANSPORT TO THE OPEN LANDS UP NORTH.

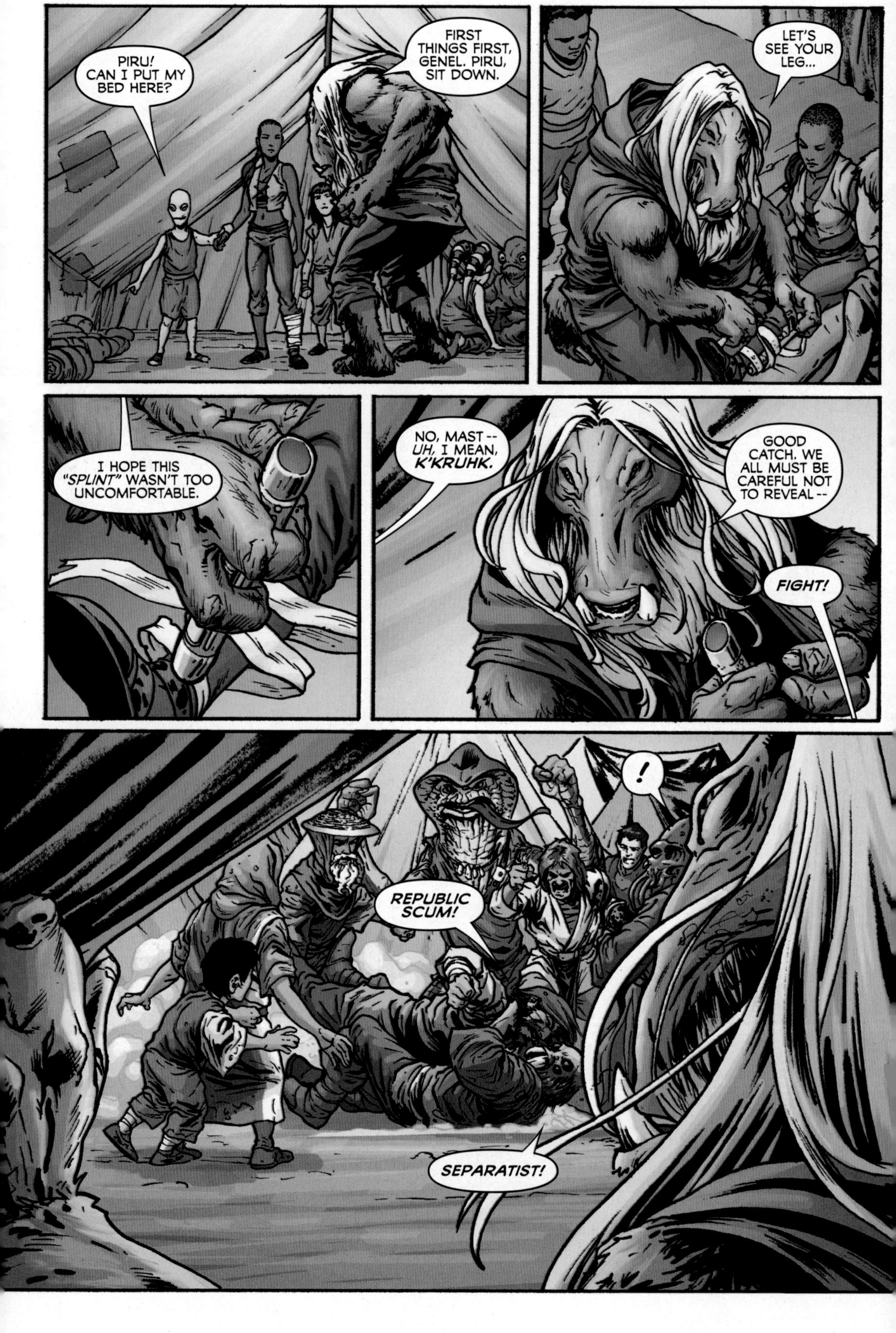
PIRU! CAN I PUT MY BED HERE?
FIRST THINGS FIRST, GENEL. PIRU, SIT DOWN.
LET'S SEE YOUR LEG...
I HOPE THIS "SPLINT" WASN'T TOO UNCOMFORTABLE.
NO, MAST -- UH, I MEAN, K'KRUHK.
GOOD CATCH. WE ALL MUST BE CAREFUL NOT TO REVEAL --
FIGHT!
!
REPUBLIC SCUM!
SEPARATIST!

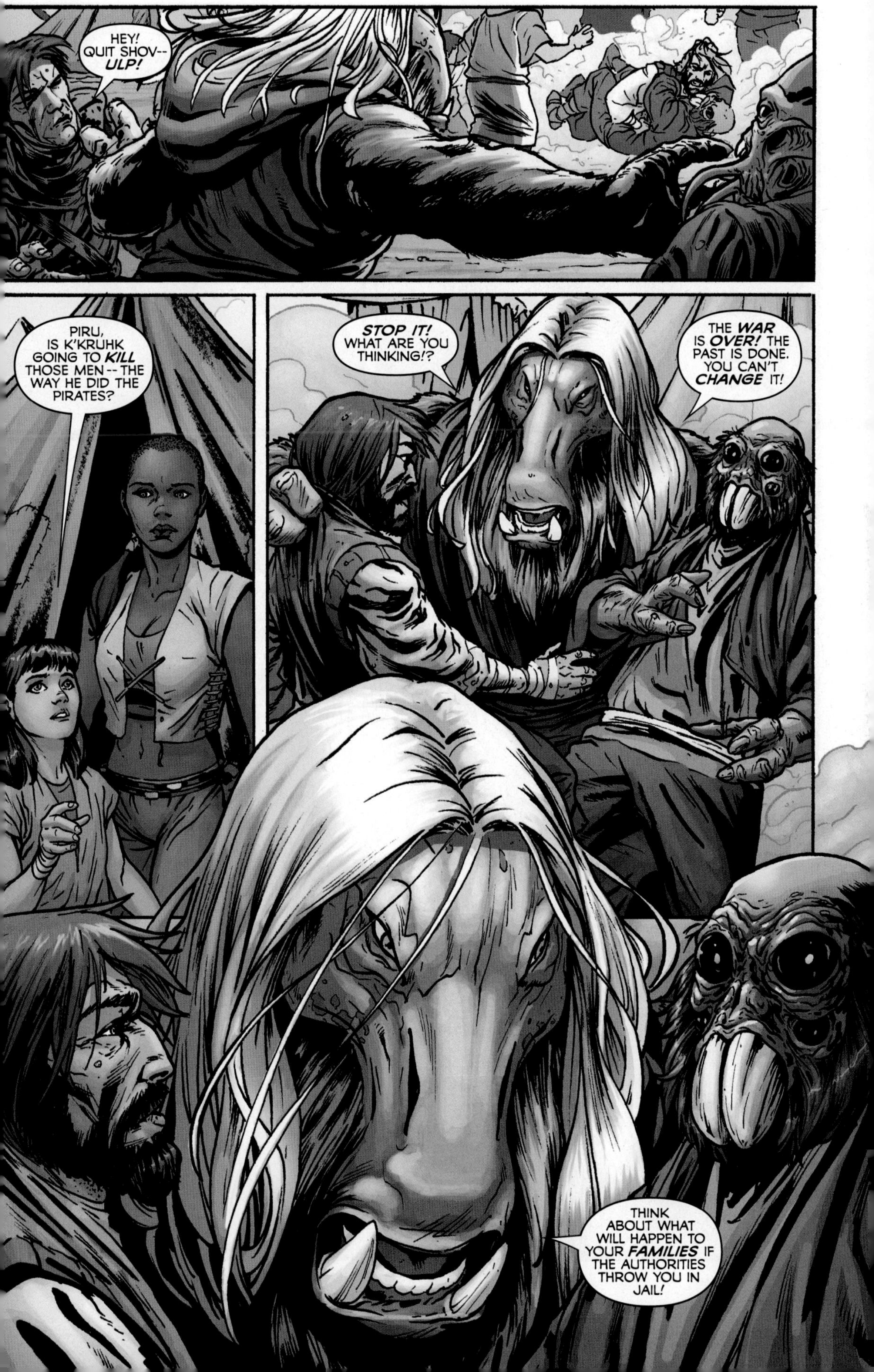
HEY! QUIT SHOV-- ULP!
PIRU, IS K'KRUHK GOING TO KILL THOSE MEN -- THE WAY HE DID THE PIRATES?
STOP IT! WHAT ARE YOU THINKING!?
THE WAR IS OVER! THE PAST IS DONE. YOU CAN'T CHANGE IT!
THINK ABOUT WHAT WILL HAPPEN TO YOUR FAMILIES IF THE AUTHORITIES THROW YOU IN JAIL!

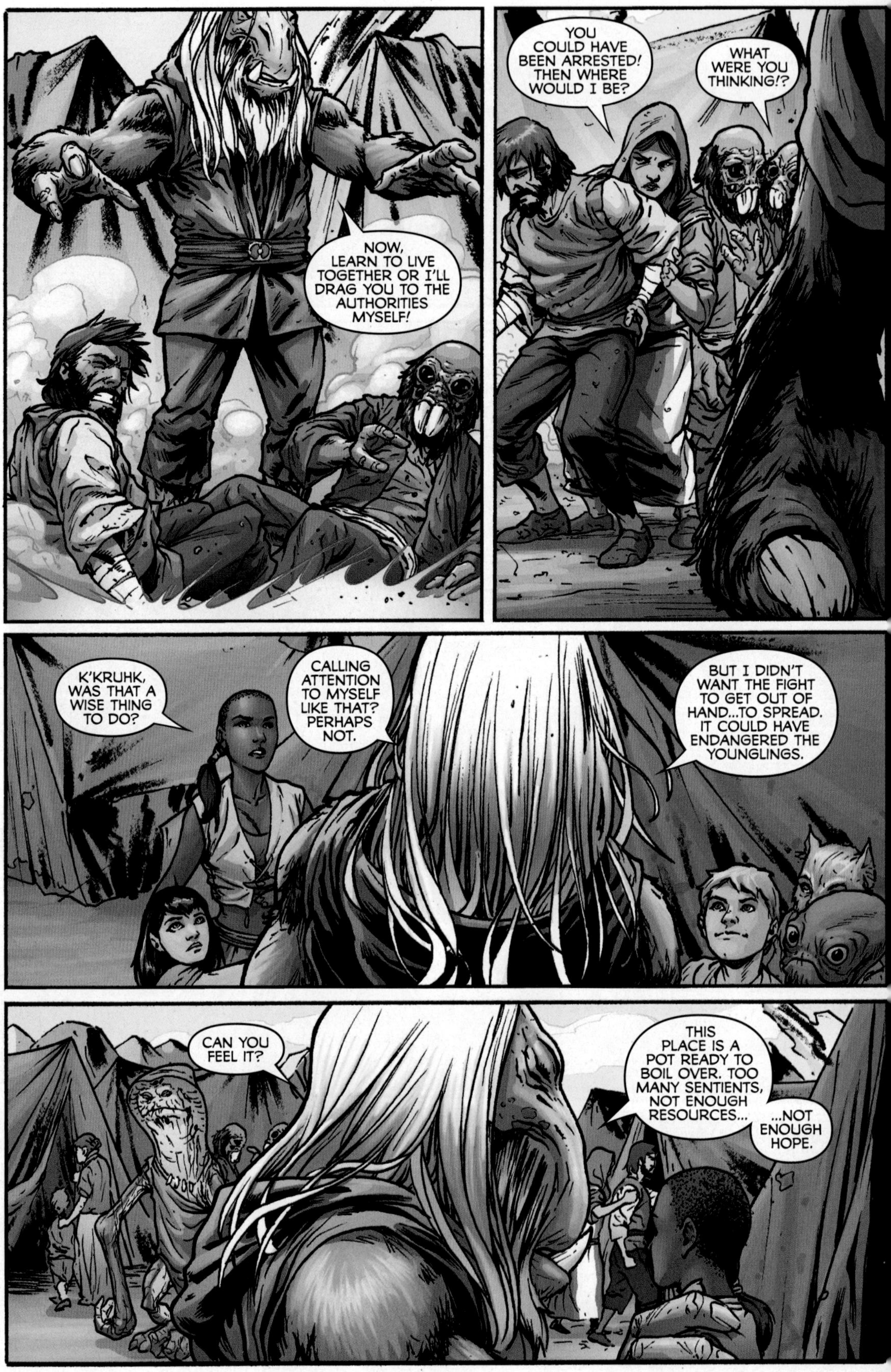
NOW, LEARN TO LIVE TOGETHER OR I'LL DRAG YOU TO THE AUTHORITIES MYSELF!
YOU COULD HAVE BEEN ARRESTED! THEN WHERE WOULD I BE?
WHAT WERE YOU THINKING!?
K'KRUHK, WAS THAT A WISE THING TO DO?
CALLING ATTENTION TO MYSELF LIKE THAT? PERHAPS NOT.
BUT I DIDN'T WANT THE FIGHT TO GET OUT OF HAND...TO SPREAD. IT COULD HAVE ENDANGERED THE YOUNGLINGS.
CAN YOU FEEL IT?
THIS PLACE IS A POT READY TO BOIL OVER. TOO MANY SENTIENTS, NOT ENOUGH RESOURCES...
...NOT ENOUGH HOPE.

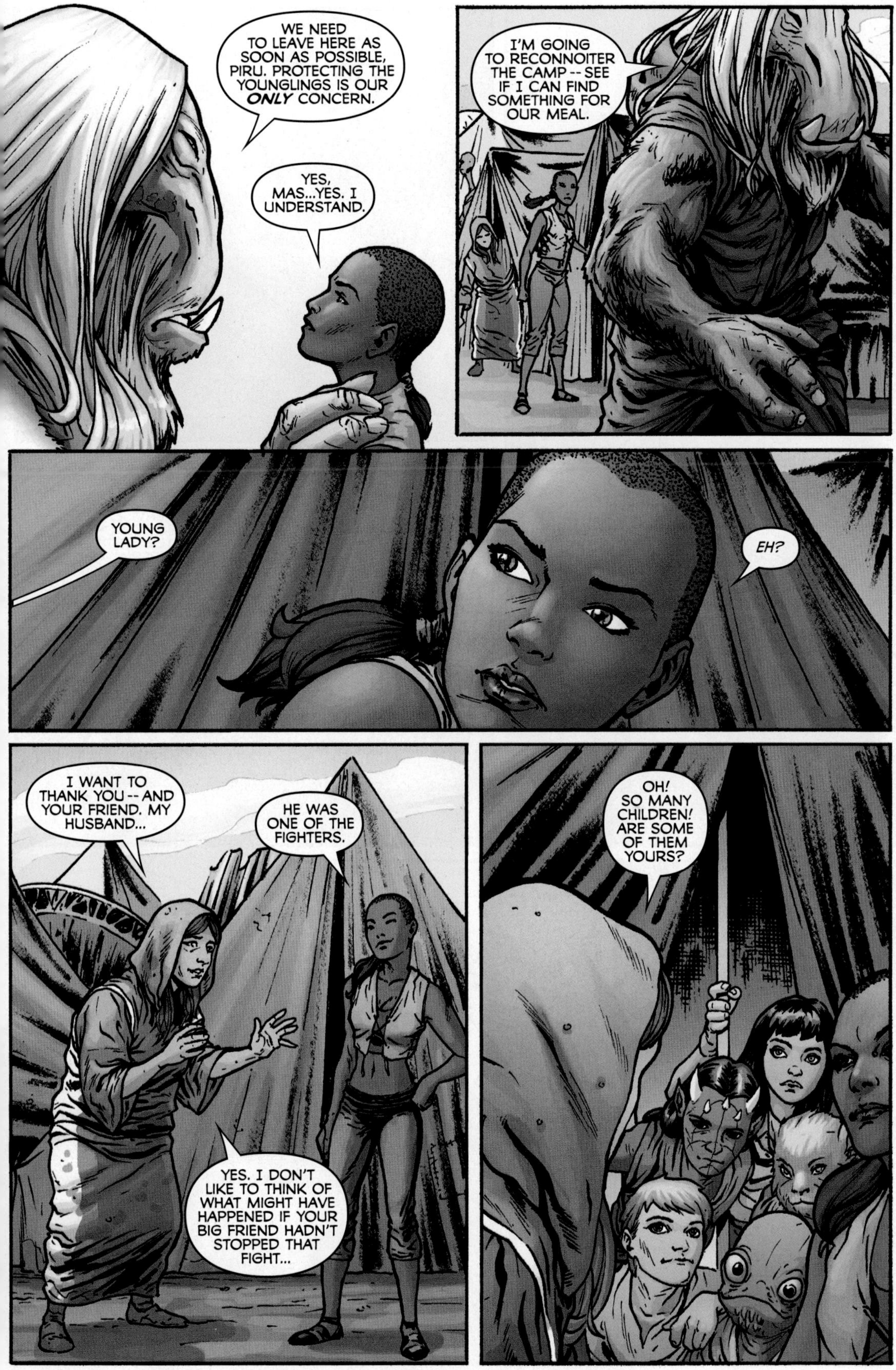

WE NEED TO LEAVE HERE AS SOON AS POSSIBLE, PIRU. PROTECTING THE YOUNGLINGS IS OUR *ONLY* CONCERN.
YES, MAS...YES. I UNDERSTAND.
I'M GOING TO RECONNOITER THE CAMP -- SEE IF I CAN FIND SOMETHING FOR OUR MEAL.
YOUNG LADY?
*EH?*
I WANT TO THANK YOU -- AND YOUR FRIEND. MY HUSBAND...
HE WAS ONE OF THE FIGHTERS.
YES. I DON'T LIKE TO THINK OF WHAT MIGHT HAVE HAPPENED IF YOUR BIG FRIEND HADN'T STOPPED THAT FIGHT...
OH! SO MANY CHILDREN! ARE SOME OF THEM YOURS?

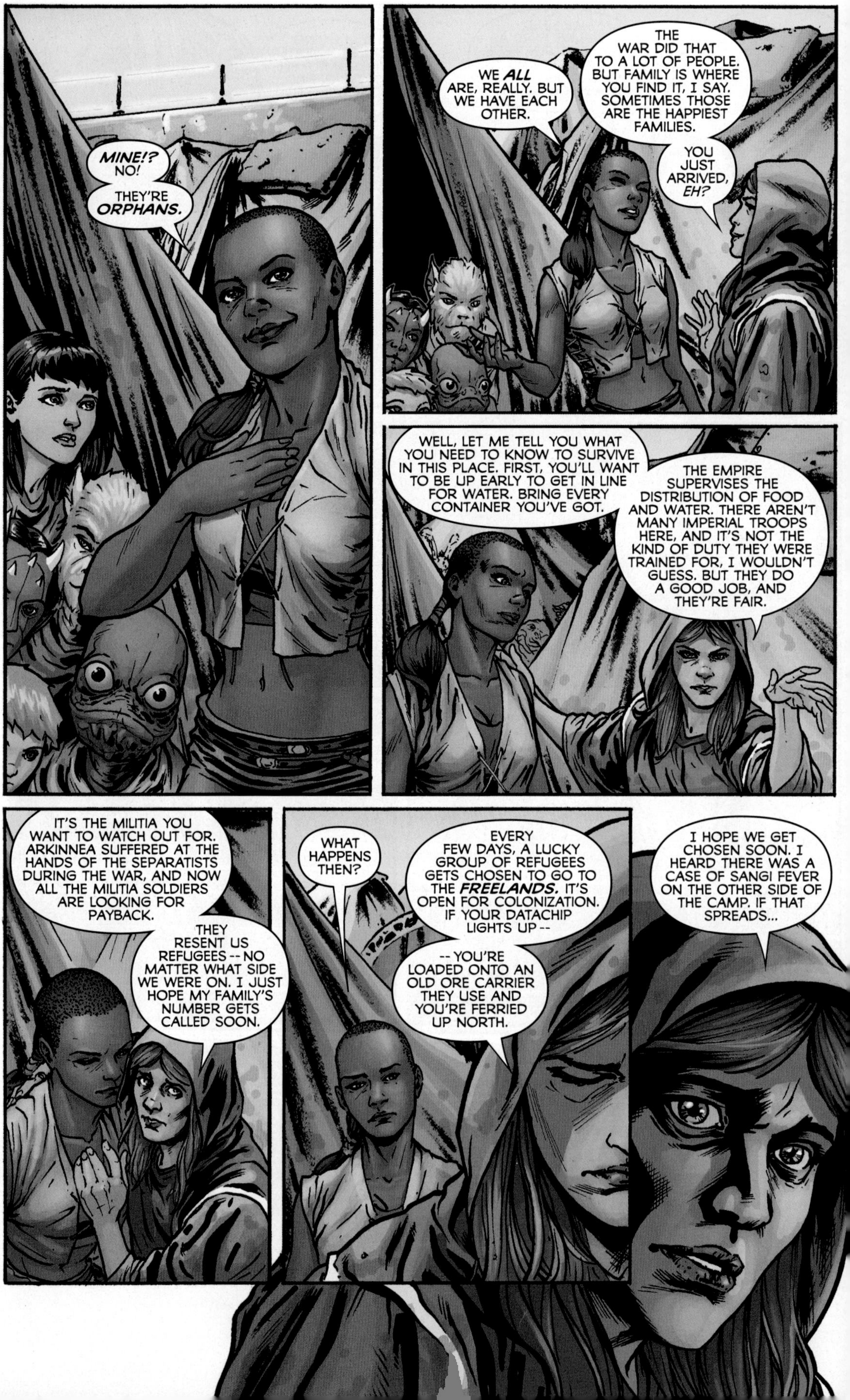
MINE!? NO!
THEY'RE ORPHANS.
WE ALL ARE, REALLY. BUT WE HAVE EACH OTHER.
THE WAR DID THAT TO A LOT OF PEOPLE. BUT FAMILY IS WHERE YOU FIND IT, I SAY. SOMETIMES THOSE ARE THE HAPPIEST FAMILIES.
YOU JUST ARRIVED, EH?
WELL, LET ME TELL YOU WHAT YOU NEED TO KNOW TO SURVIVE IN THIS PLACE. FIRST, YOU'LL WANT TO BE UP EARLY TO GET IN LINE FOR WATER. BRING EVERY CONTAINER YOU'VE GOT.
THE EMPIRE SUPERVISES THE DISTRIBUTION OF FOOD AND WATER. THERE AREN'T MANY IMPERIAL TROOPS HERE, AND IT'S NOT THE KIND OF DUTY THEY WERE TRAINED FOR, I WOULDN'T GUESS. BUT THEY DO A GOOD JOB, AND THEY'RE FAIR.
IT'S THE MILITIA YOU WANT TO WATCH OUT FOR. ARKINNEA SUFFERED AT THE HANDS OF THE SEPARATISTS DURING THE WAR, AND NOW ALL THE MILITIA SOLDIERS ARE LOOKING FOR PAYBACK.
THEY RESENT US REFUGEES -- NO MATTER WHAT SIDE WE WERE ON. I JUST HOPE MY FAMILY'S NUMBER GETS CALLED SOON.
WHAT HAPPENS THEN?
EVERY FEW DAYS, A LUCKY GROUP OF REFUGEES GETS CHOSEN TO GO TO THE FREELANDS. IT'S OPEN FOR COLONIZATION. IF YOUR DATACHIP LIGHTS UP --
-- YOU'RE LOADED ONTO AN OLD ORE CARRIER THEY USE AND YOU'RE FERRIED UP NORTH.
I HOPE WE GET CHOSEN SOON. I HEARD THERE WAS A CASE OF SANGI FEVER ON THE OTHER SIDE OF THE CAMP. IF THAT SPREADS...

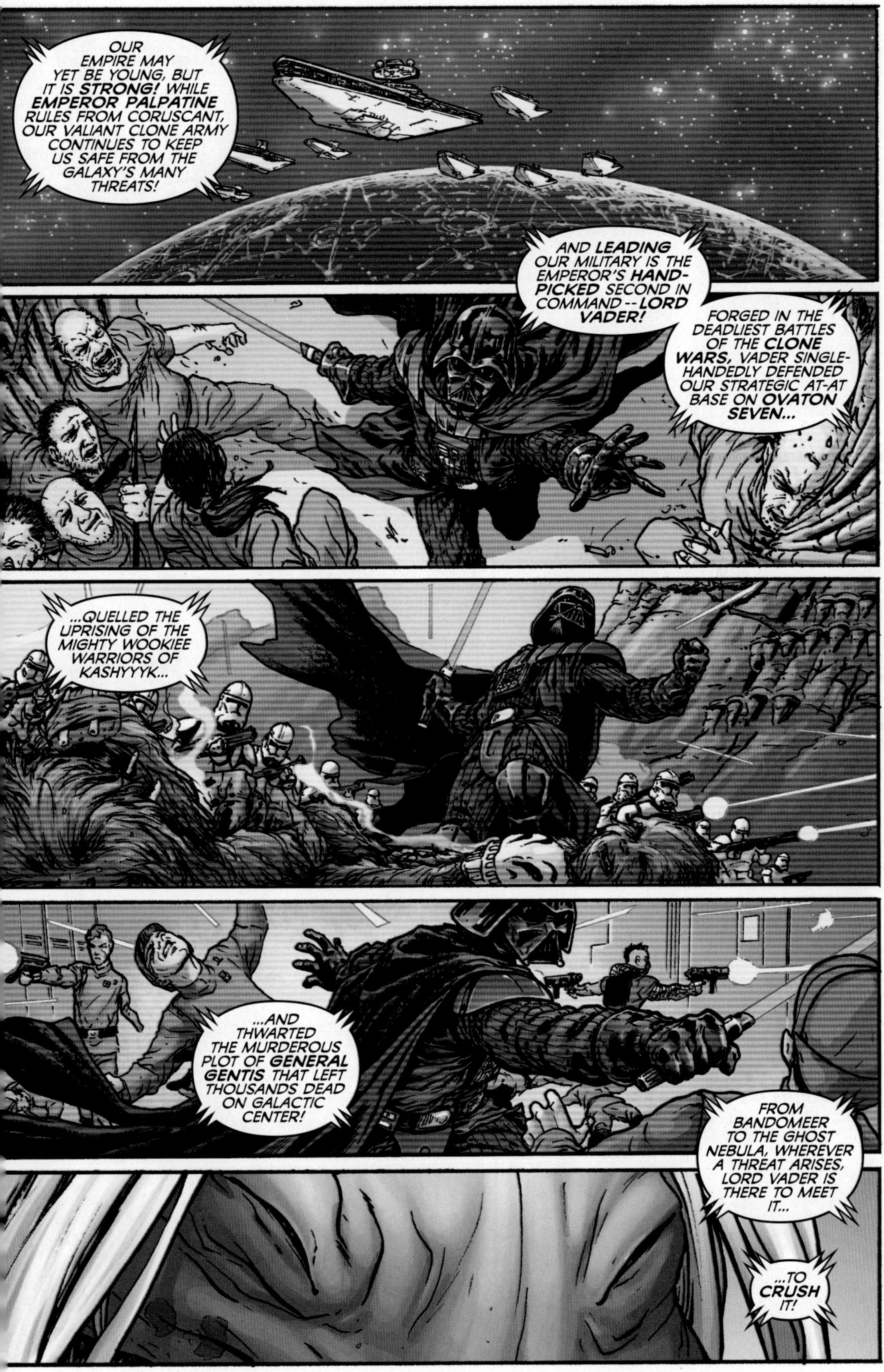
OUR EMPIRE MAY YET BE YOUNG, BUT IT IS STRONG! WHILE EMPEROR PALPATINE RULES FROM CORUSCANT, OUR VALIANT CLONE ARMY CONTINUES TO KEEP US SAFE FROM THE GALAXY'S MANY THREATS!
AND LEADING OUR MILITARY IS THE EMPEROR'S HAND-PICKED SECOND IN COMMAND -- LORD VADER!
FORGED IN THE DEADLIEST BATTLES OF THE CLONE WARS, VADER SINGLE-HANDEDLY DEFENDED OUR STRATEGIC AT-AT BASE ON OVATON SEVEN...
...QUELLED THE UPRISING OF THE MIGHTY WOOKIEE WARRIORS OF KASHYYYK...
...AND THWARTED THE MURDEROUS PLOT OF GENERAL GENTIS THAT LEFT THOUSANDS DEAD ON GALACTIC CENTER!
FROM BANDOMEER TO THE GHOST NEBULA, WHEREVER A THREAT ARISES, LORD VADER IS THERE TO MEET IT...
...TO CRUSH IT!

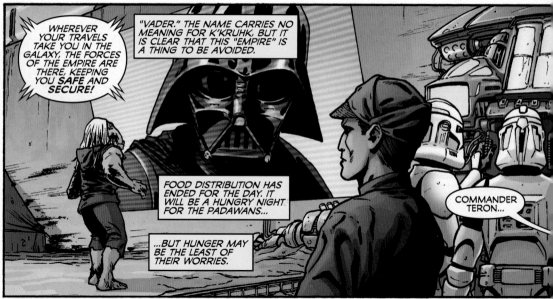

WHEREVER YOUR TRAVELS TAKE YOU IN THE GALAXY, THE FORCES OF THE EMPIRE ARE THERE, KEEPING YOU **SAFE** AND **SECURE!**

"VADER." THE NAME CARRIES NO MEANING FOR K'KRUHK, BUT IT IS CLEAR THAT THIS "EMPIRE" IS A THING TO BE AVOIDED.

FOOD DISTRIBUTION HAS ENDED FOR THE DAY. IT WILL BE A HUNGRY NIGHT FOR THE PADAWANS...

...BUT HUNGER MAY BE THE LEAST OF THEIR WORRIES.

COMMANDER TERON...

CAPTAIN RELIK.

A **TOOLAN!** WHAT NEXT, **EH?** THE SEPARATIST SCUM--

I AM WELL AWARE OF YOUR FEELING TOWARD THE SEPARATISTS, CAPTAIN...

...BUT THESE SENTIENTS WERE NOT ALL SEPARATISTS. AND THOSE WHO WERE ARE NOT **JUST** OUR DEFEATED FOES, BUT NOW **CITIZENS** OF THE **EMPIRE.**

AS SUCH THEY ARE DESERVING OF OUR RESPECT AND COMPASSION.

**COMPASSION?**

WHERE WAS THE SEPARATISTS' **COMPASSION** WHEN THEIR DROID ARMIES OVERRAN ARKINNEA, I ASK YOU?

I DON'T MIND SAYIN' IT, COMMANDER -- I CAN'T WAIT 'TILL **ALL** OF THESE OFF-WORLDERS ARE GONE!

AT LEAST THERE IS PLENTY OF OPEN LAND IN THE NORTH FOR THEM TO SETTLE.

YES, SIR. AT LEAST THERE'S **THAT**...

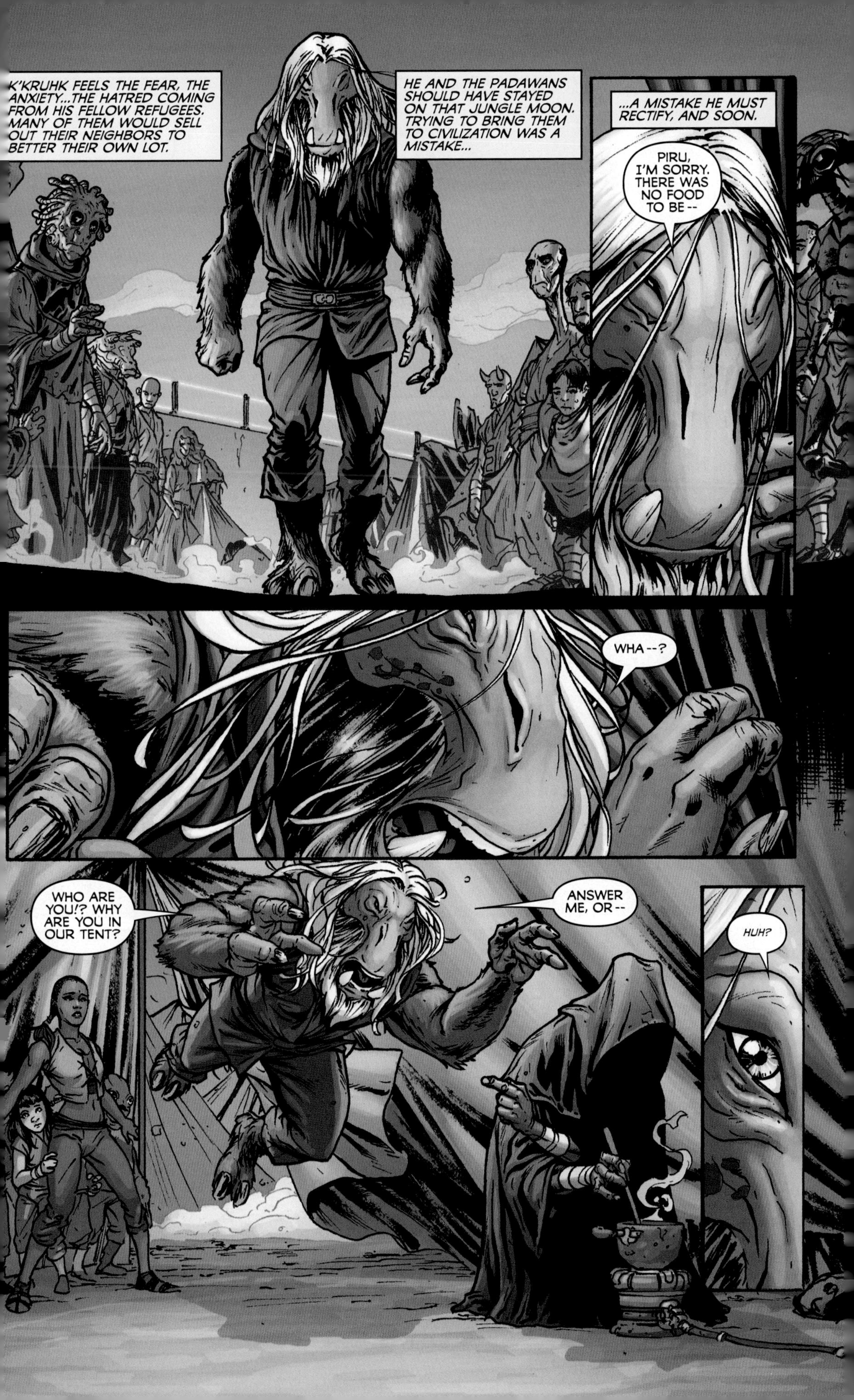
K'KRUHK FEELS THE FEAR, THE ANXIETY...THE HATRED COMING FROM HIS FELLOW REFUGEES. MANY OF THEM WOULD SELL OUT THEIR NEIGHBORS TO BETTER THEIR OWN LOT.
HE AND THE PADAWANS SHOULD HAVE STAYED ON THAT JUNGLE MOON. TRYING TO BRING THEM TO CIVILIZATION WAS A MISTAKE...
...A MISTAKE HE MUST RECTIFY, AND SOON.
PIRU, I'M SORRY. THERE WAS NO FOOD TO BE --
WHA --?
WHO ARE YOU!? WHY ARE YOU IN OUR TENT?
ANSWER ME, OR --
HUH?

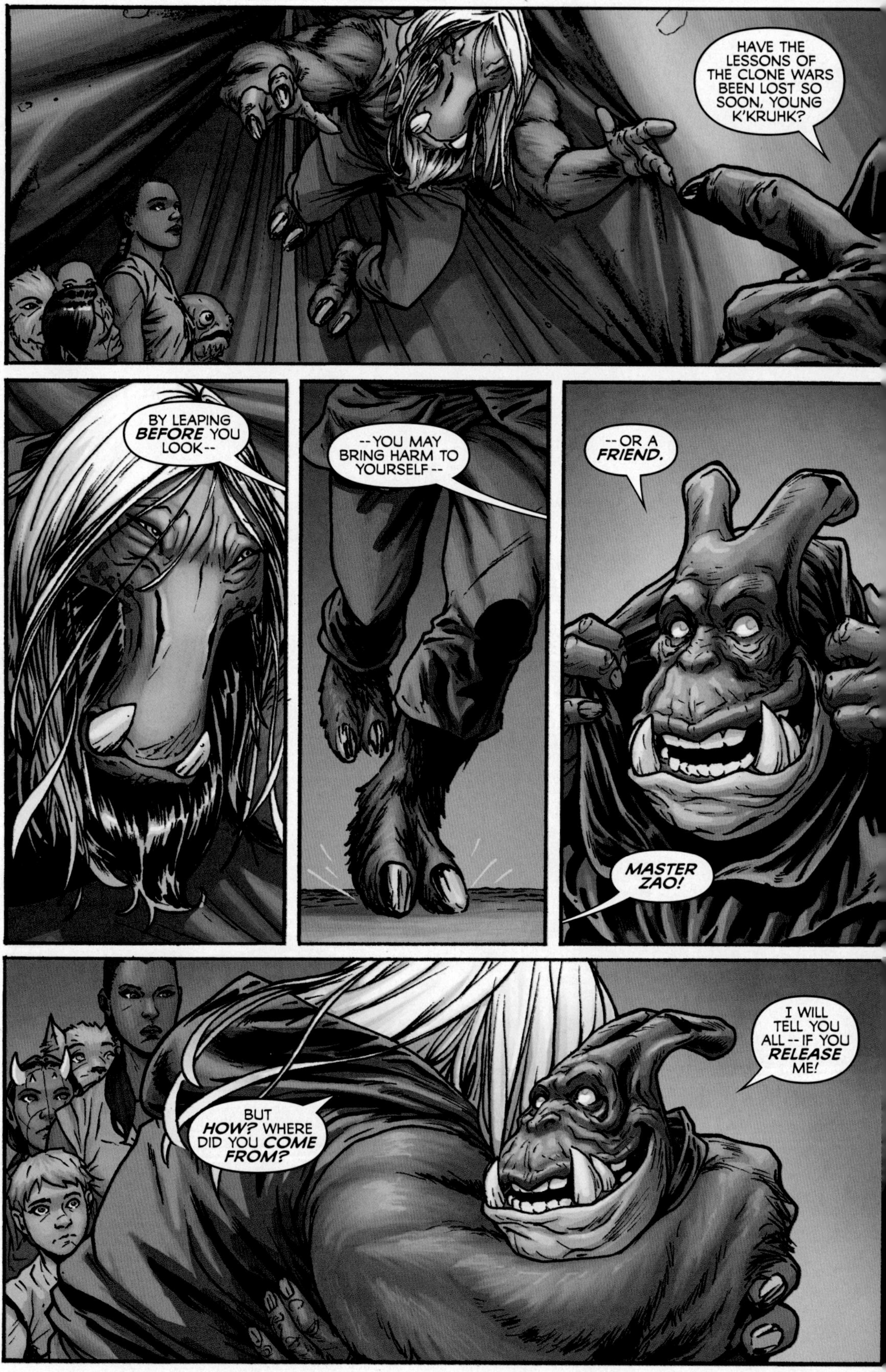
HAVE THE LESSONS OF THE CLONE WARS BEEN LOST SO SOON, YOUNG K'KRUHK?
BY LEAPING *BEFORE* YOU LOOK--
--YOU MAY BRING HARM TO YOURSELF--
--OR A *FRIEND.*
*MASTER ZAO!*
I WILL TELL YOU ALL--IF YOU *RELEASE* ME!
BUT *HOW?* WHERE DID YOU *COME FROM?*

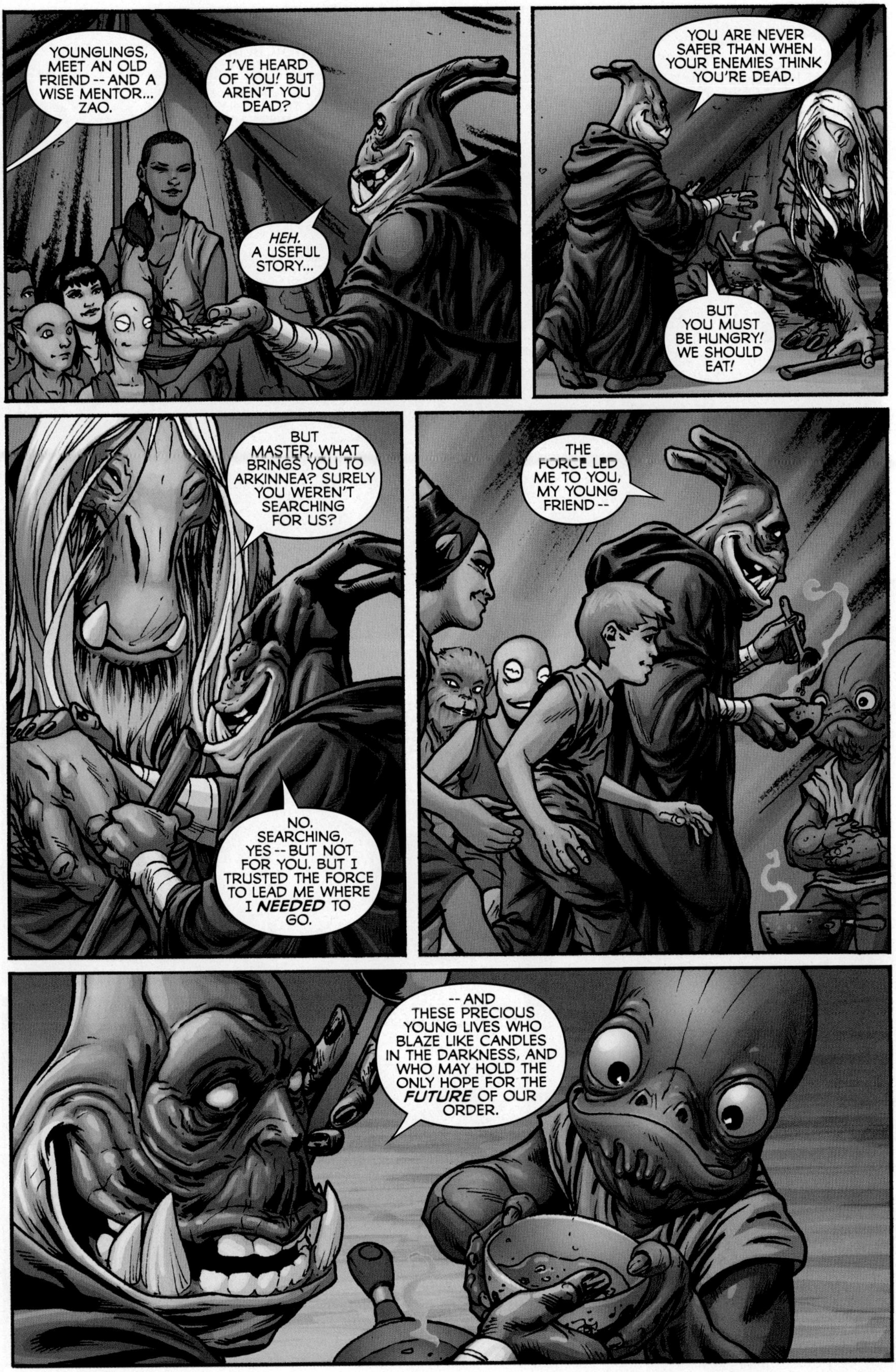
YOUNGLINGS, MEET AN OLD FRIEND -- AND A WISE MENTOR... ZAO.
I'VE HEARD OF YOU! BUT AREN'T YOU DEAD?
HEH. A USEFUL STORY...
YOU ARE NEVER SAFER THAN WHEN YOUR ENEMIES THINK YOU'RE DEAD.
BUT YOU MUST BE HUNGRY! WE SHOULD EAT!
BUT MASTER, WHAT BRINGS YOU TO ARKINNEA? SURELY YOU WEREN'T SEARCHING FOR US?
NO. SEARCHING, YES -- BUT NOT FOR YOU. BUT I TRUSTED THE FORCE TO LEAD ME WHERE I NEEDED TO GO.
THE FORCE LED ME TO YOU, MY YOUNG FRIEND --
-- AND THESE PRECIOUS YOUNG LIVES WHO BLAZE LIKE CANDLES IN THE DARKNESS, AND WHO MAY HOLD THE ONLY HOPE FOR THE FUTURE OF OUR ORDER.

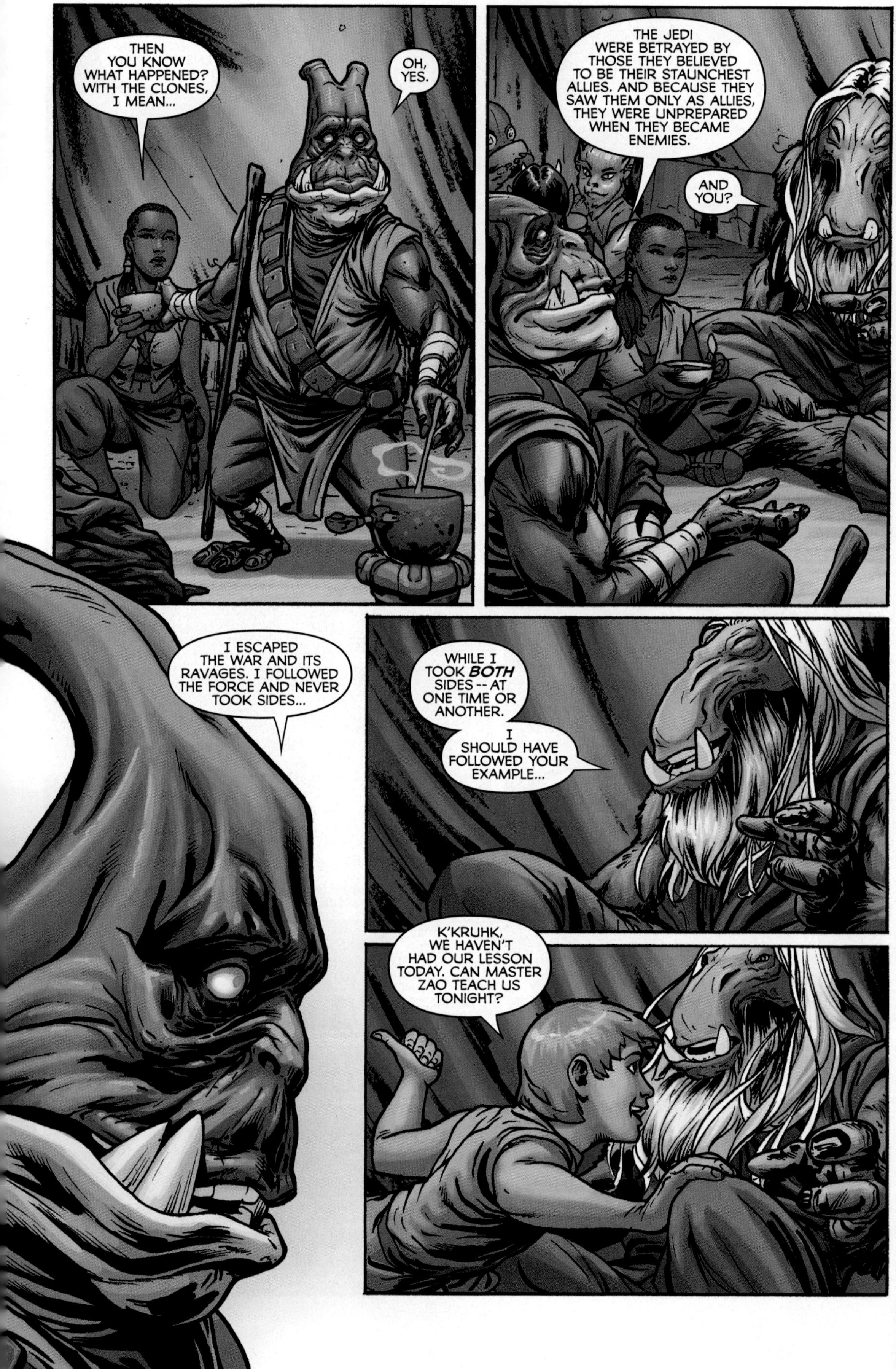
THEN YOU KNOW WHAT HAPPENED? WITH THE CLONES, I MEAN...
OH, YES.
THE JEDI WERE BETRAYED BY THOSE THEY BELIEVED TO BE THEIR STAUNCHEST ALLIES. AND BECAUSE THEY SAW THEM ONLY AS ALLIES, THEY WERE UNPREPARED WHEN THEY BECAME ENEMIES.
AND YOU?
I ESCAPED THE WAR AND ITS RAVAGES. I FOLLOWED THE FORCE AND NEVER TOOK SIDES...
WHILE I TOOK BOTH SIDES -- AT ONE TIME OR ANOTHER.
I SHOULD HAVE FOLLOWED YOUR EXAMPLE...
K'KRUHK, WE HAVEN'T HAD OUR LESSON TODAY. CAN MASTER ZAO TEACH US TONIGHT?

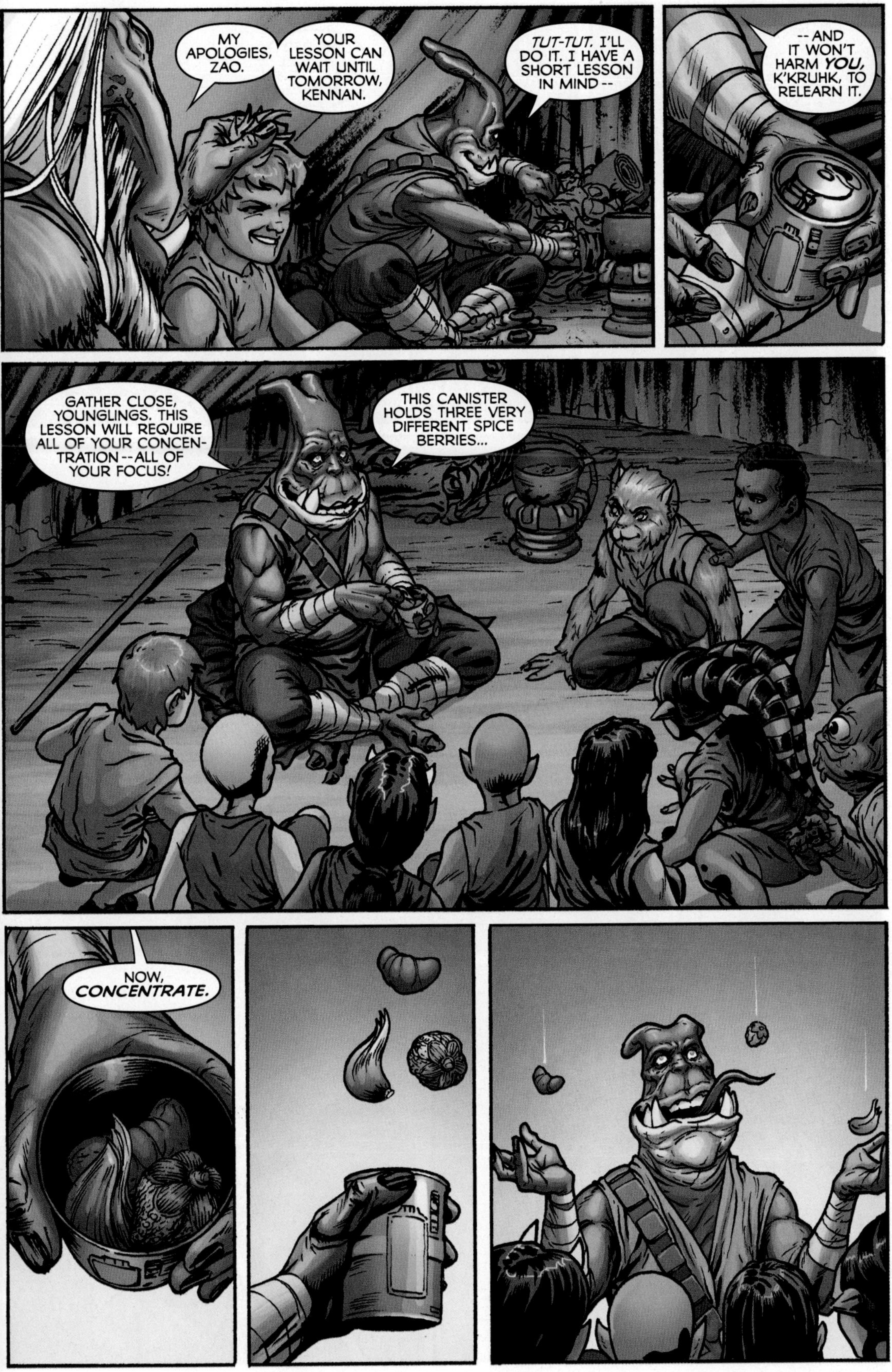
MY APOLOGIES, ZAO.
YOUR LESSON CAN WAIT UNTIL TOMORROW, KENNAN.
TUT-TUT. I'LL DO IT. I HAVE A SHORT LESSON IN MIND --
-- AND IT WON'T HARM YOU, K'KRUHK, TO RELEARN IT.
GATHER CLOSE, YOUNGLINGS. THIS LESSON WILL REQUIRE ALL OF YOUR CONCENTRATION -- ALL OF YOUR FOCUS!
THIS CANISTER HOLDS THREE VERY DIFFERENT SPICE BERRIES...
NOW, CONCENTRATE.

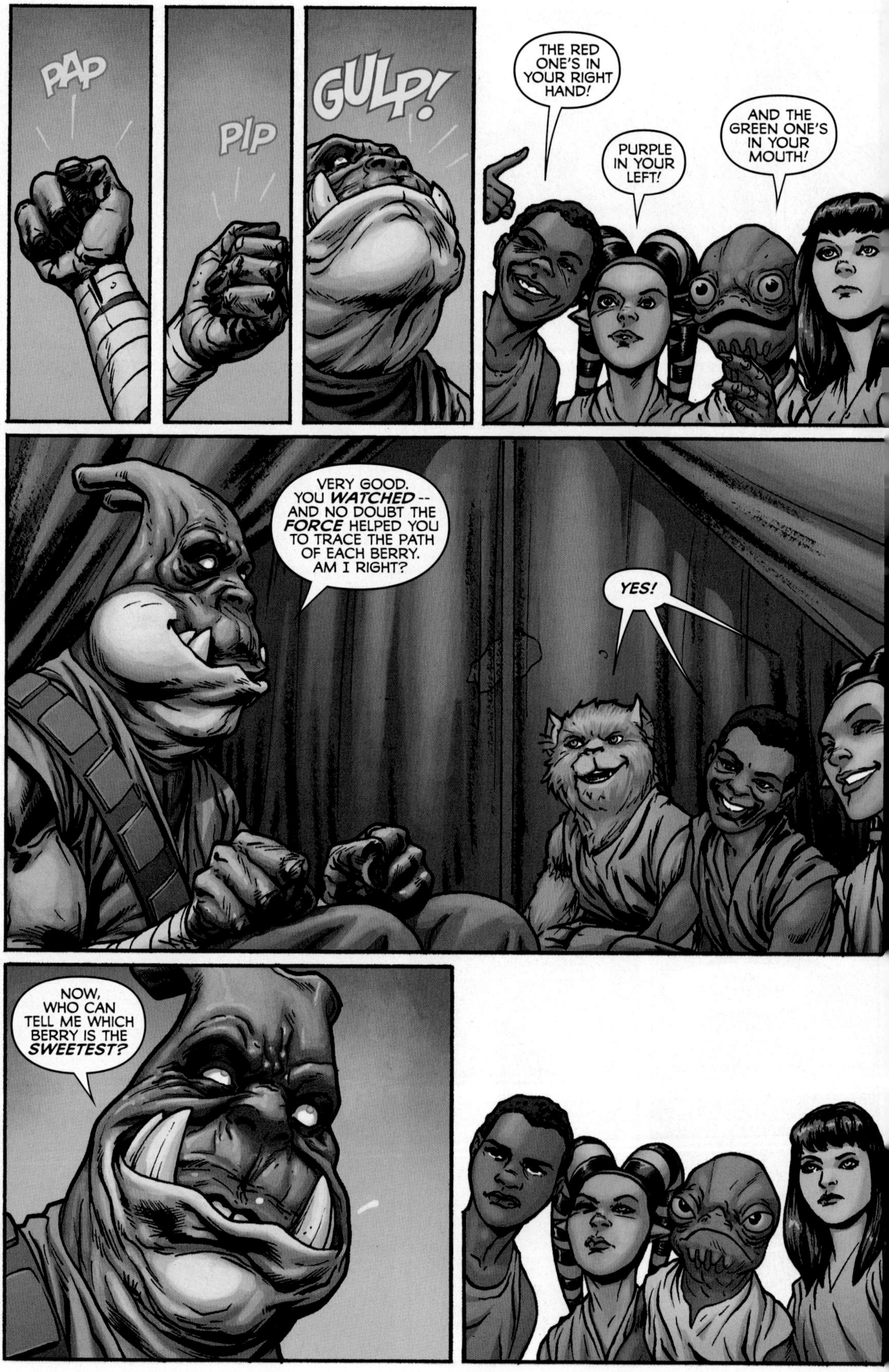
PAP
PIP
GULP!
THE RED ONE'S IN YOUR RIGHT HAND!
PURPLE IN YOUR LEFT!
AND THE GREEN ONE'S IN YOUR MOUTH!
VERY GOOD. YOU WATCHED -- AND NO DOUBT THE FORCE HELPED YOU TO TRACE THE PATH OF EACH BERRY. AM I RIGHT?
YES!
NOW, WHO CAN TELL ME WHICH BERRY IS THE SWEETEST?

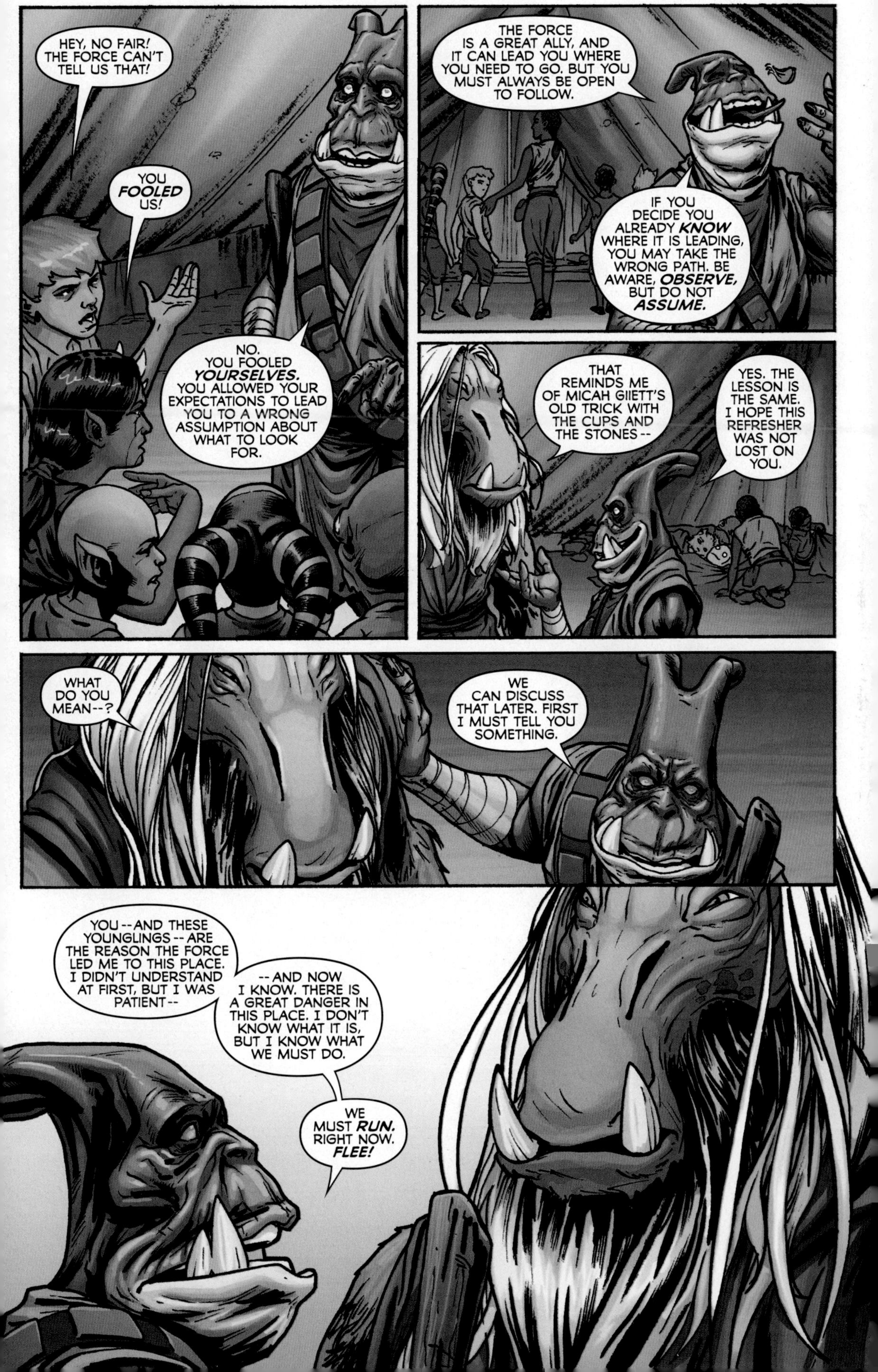
HEY, NO FAIR! THE FORCE CAN'T TELL US THAT!
YOU FOOLED US!
NO. YOU FOOLED YOURSELVES. YOU ALLOWED YOUR EXPECTATIONS TO LEAD YOU TO A WRONG ASSUMPTION ABOUT WHAT TO LOOK FOR.
THE FORCE IS A GREAT ALLY, AND IT CAN LEAD YOU WHERE YOU NEED TO GO. BUT YOU MUST ALWAYS BE OPEN TO FOLLOW.
IF YOU DECIDE YOU ALREADY KNOW WHERE IT IS LEADING, YOU MAY TAKE THE WRONG PATH. BE AWARE, OBSERVE, BUT DO NOT ASSUME.
THAT REMINDS ME OF MICAH GIIETT'S OLD TRICK WITH THE CUPS AND THE STONES--
YES. THE LESSON IS THE SAME. I HOPE THIS REFRESHER WAS NOT LOST ON YOU.
WHAT DO YOU MEAN--?
WE CAN DISCUSS THAT LATER. FIRST I MUST TELL YOU SOMETHING.
YOU--AND THESE YOUNGLINGS--ARE THE REASON THE FORCE LED ME TO THIS PLACE. I DIDN'T UNDERSTAND AT FIRST, BUT I WAS PATIENT--
--AND NOW I KNOW. THERE IS A GREAT DANGER IN THIS PLACE. I DON'T KNOW WHAT IT IS, BUT I KNOW WHAT WE MUST DO.
WE MUST RUN. RIGHT NOW. FLEE!

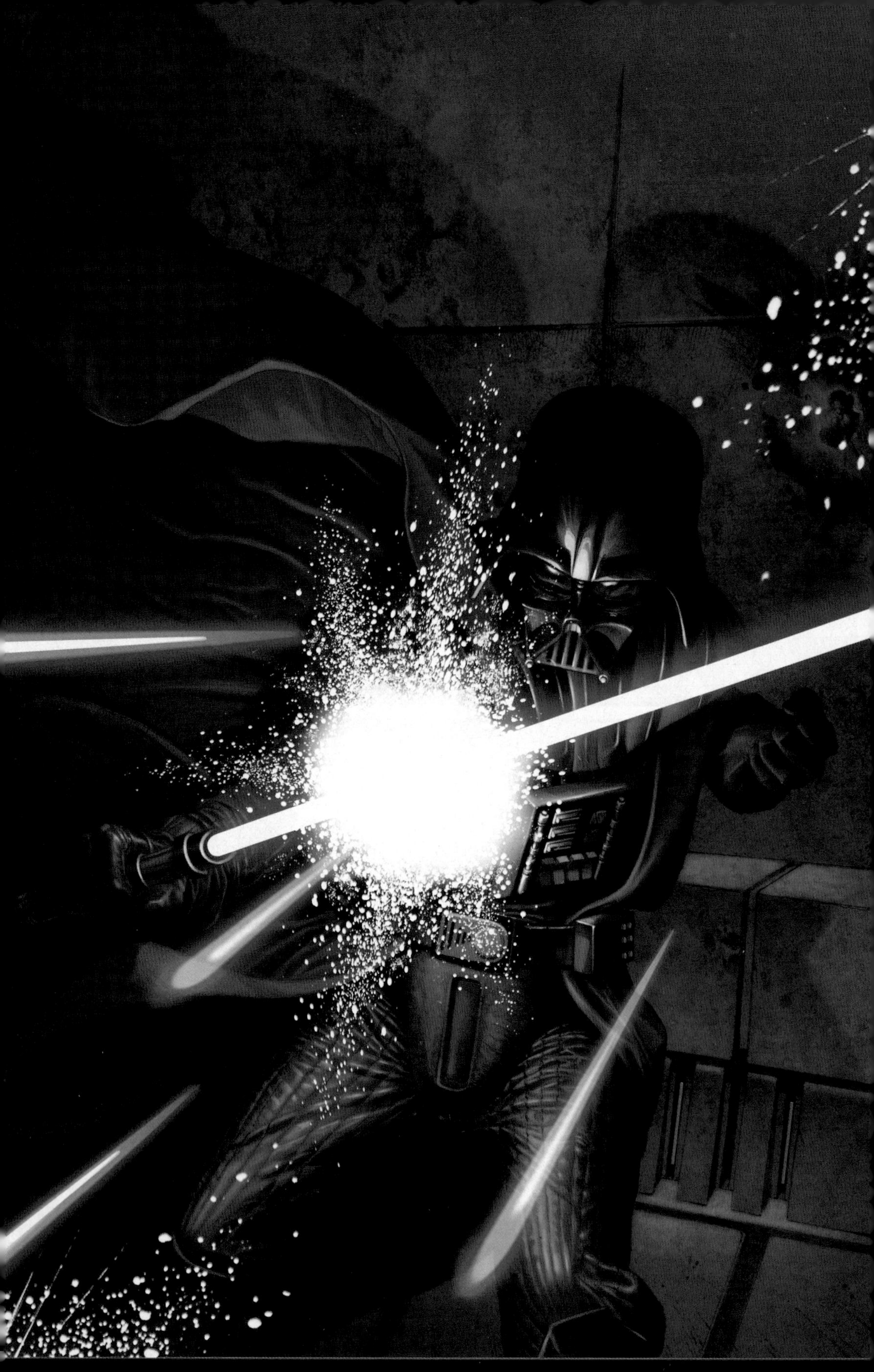

*STAR WARS: DARK TIMES — FIRE CARRIER #2*

WRITER: RANDY STRADLEY • ARTIST: GABRIEL GUZMAN • COLORIST: GARRY HENDERSON • LETTERER: MICHAEL HEISLER

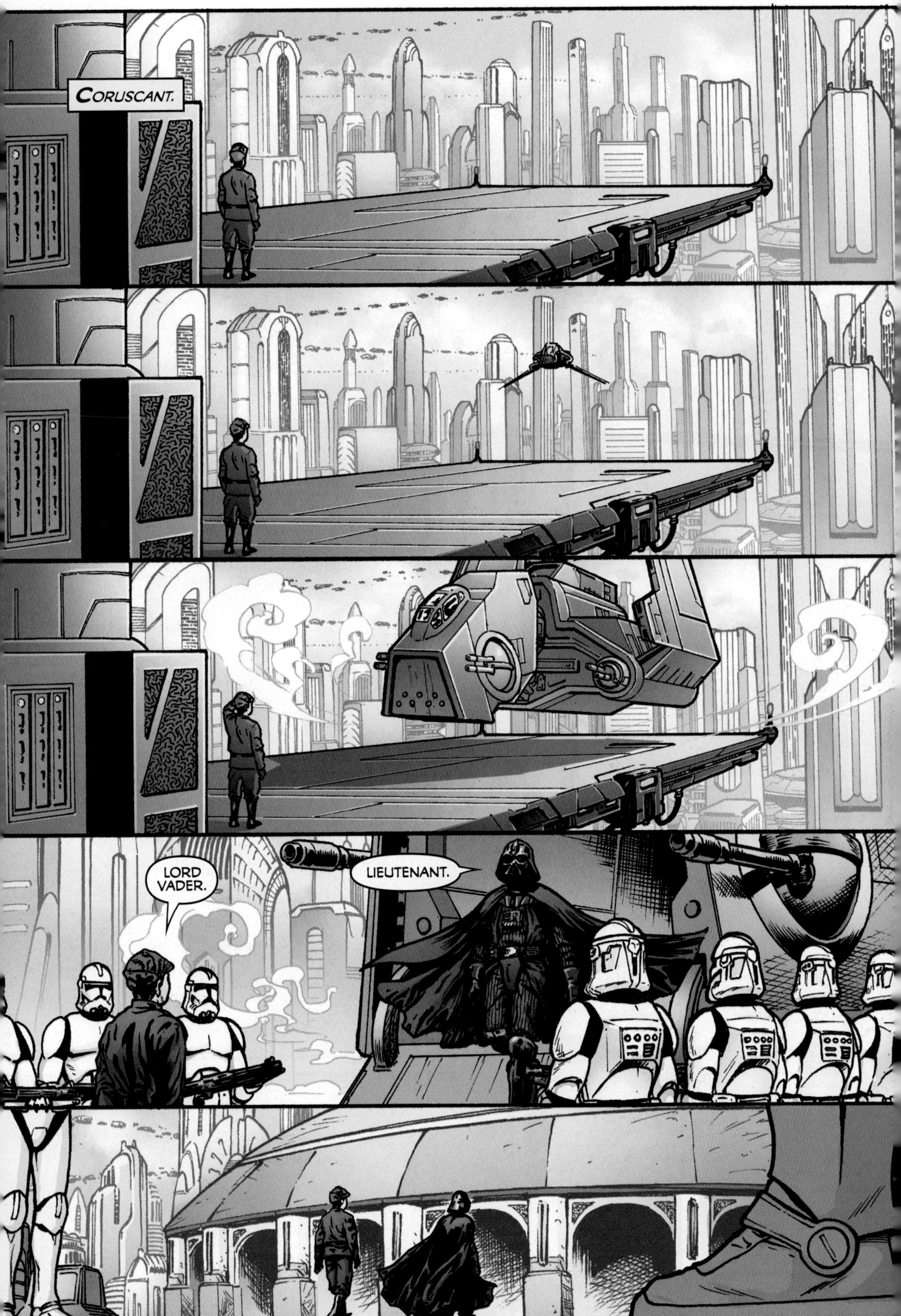
CORUSCANT.
LORD VADER.
LIEUTENANT.

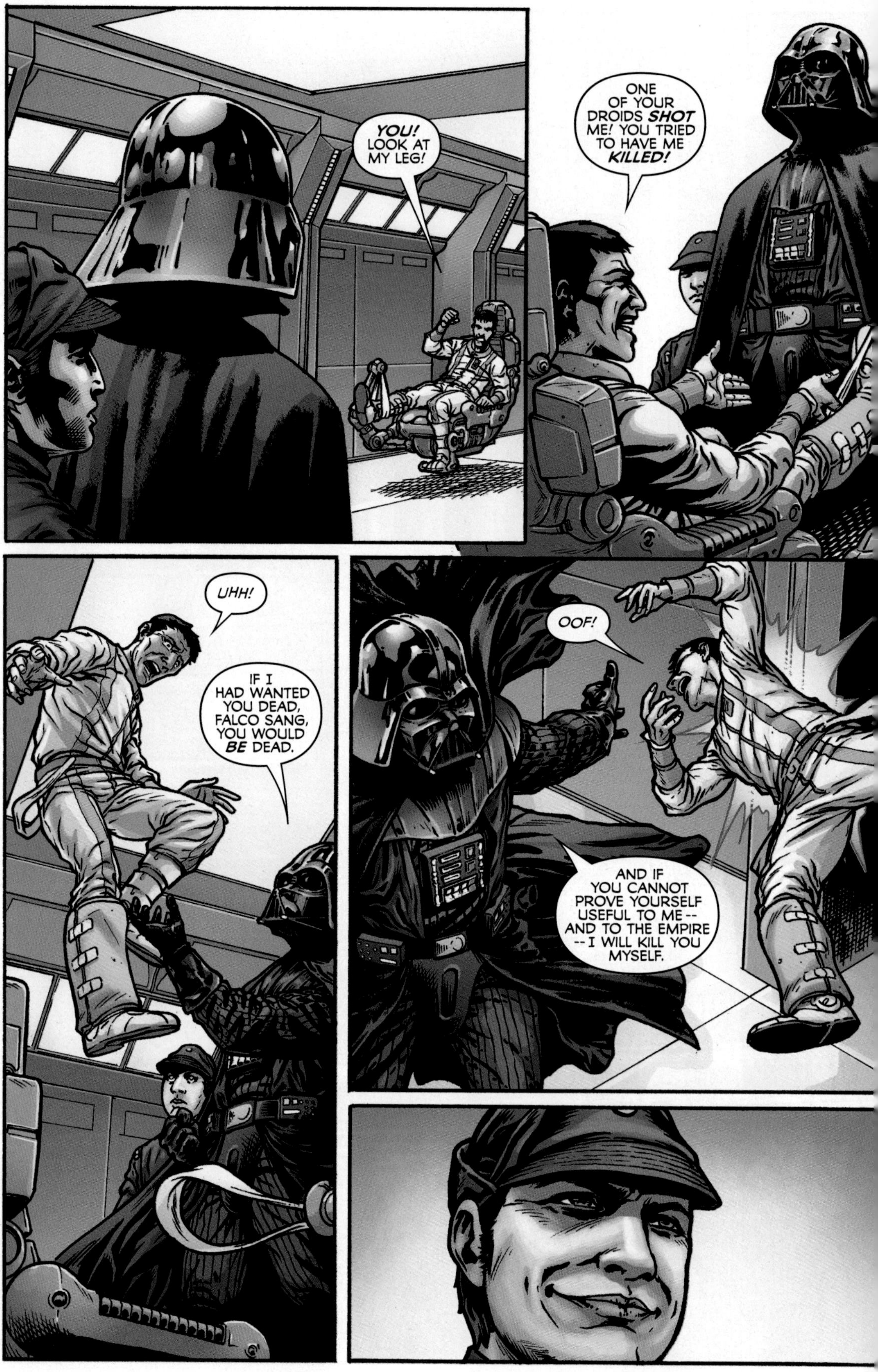

YOU! LOOK AT MY LEG!
ONE OF YOUR DROIDS SHOT ME! YOU TRIED TO HAVE ME KILLED!
UHH!
IF I HAD WANTED YOU DEAD, FALCO SANG, YOU WOULD BE DEAD.
OOF!
AND IF YOU CANNOT PROVE YOURSELF USEFUL TO ME -- AND TO THE EMPIRE -- I WILL KILL YOU MYSELF.

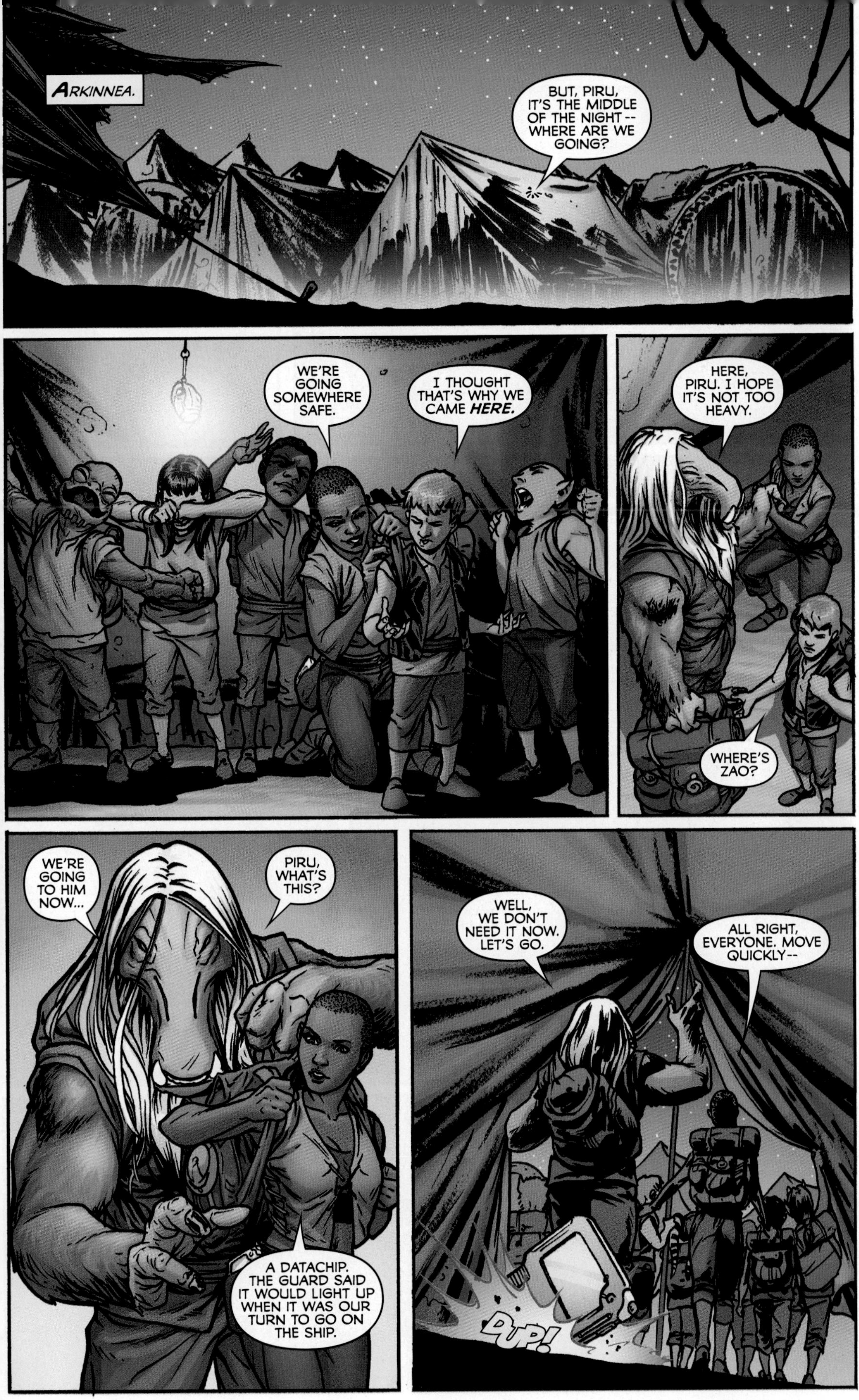
ARKINNEA.
BUT, PIRU, IT'S THE MIDDLE OF THE NIGHT -- WHERE ARE WE GOING?
WE'RE GOING SOMEWHERE SAFE.
I THOUGHT THAT'S WHY WE CAME HERE.
HERE, PIRU. I HOPE IT'S NOT TOO HEAVY.
WHERE'S ZAO?
WE'RE GOING TO HIM NOW...
PIRU, WHAT'S THIS?
A DATACHIP. THE GUARD SAID IT WOULD LIGHT UP WHEN IT WAS OUR TURN TO GO ON THE SHIP.
WELL, WE DON'T NEED IT NOW. LET'S GO.
ALL RIGHT, EVERYONE. MOVE QUICKLY--
DUP!

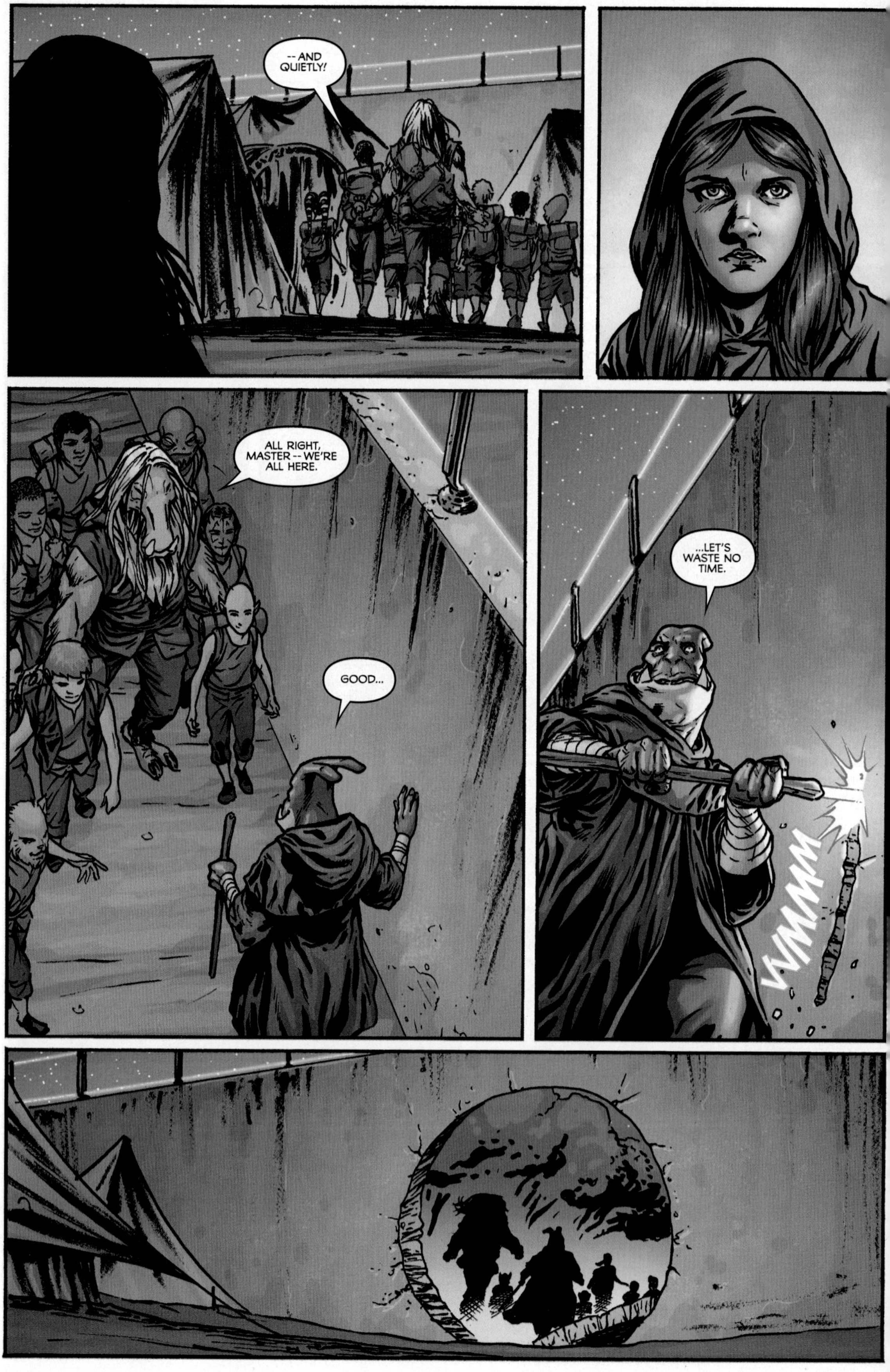
-- AND QUIETLY!
ALL RIGHT, MASTER -- WE'RE ALL HERE.
GOOD...
...LET'S WASTE NO TIME.
VWMMM

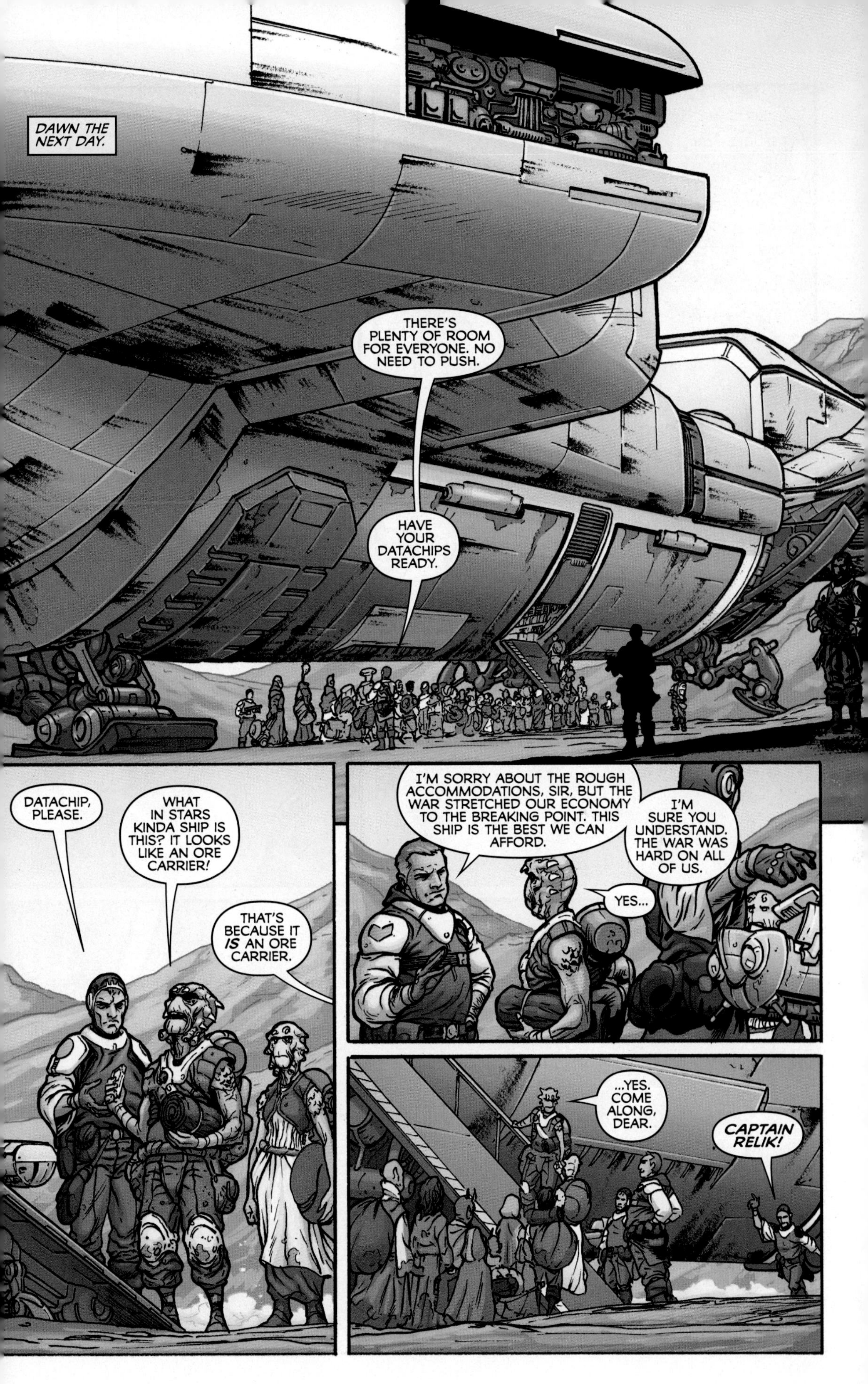
DAWN THE NEXT DAY.
THERE'S PLENTY OF ROOM FOR EVERYONE. NO NEED TO PUSH.
HAVE YOUR DATACHIPS READY.
DATACHIP, PLEASE.
WHAT IN STARS KINDA SHIP IS THIS? IT LOOKS LIKE AN ORE CARRIER!
THAT'S BECAUSE IT *IS* AN ORE CARRIER.
I'M SORRY ABOUT THE ROUGH ACCOMMODATIONS, SIR, BUT THE WAR STRETCHED OUR ECONOMY TO THE BREAKING POINT. THIS SHIP IS THE BEST WE CAN AFFORD.
I'M SURE YOU UNDERSTAND. THE WAR WAS HARD ON ALL OF US.
YES...
...YES. COME ALONG, DEAR.
*CAPTAIN RELIK!*

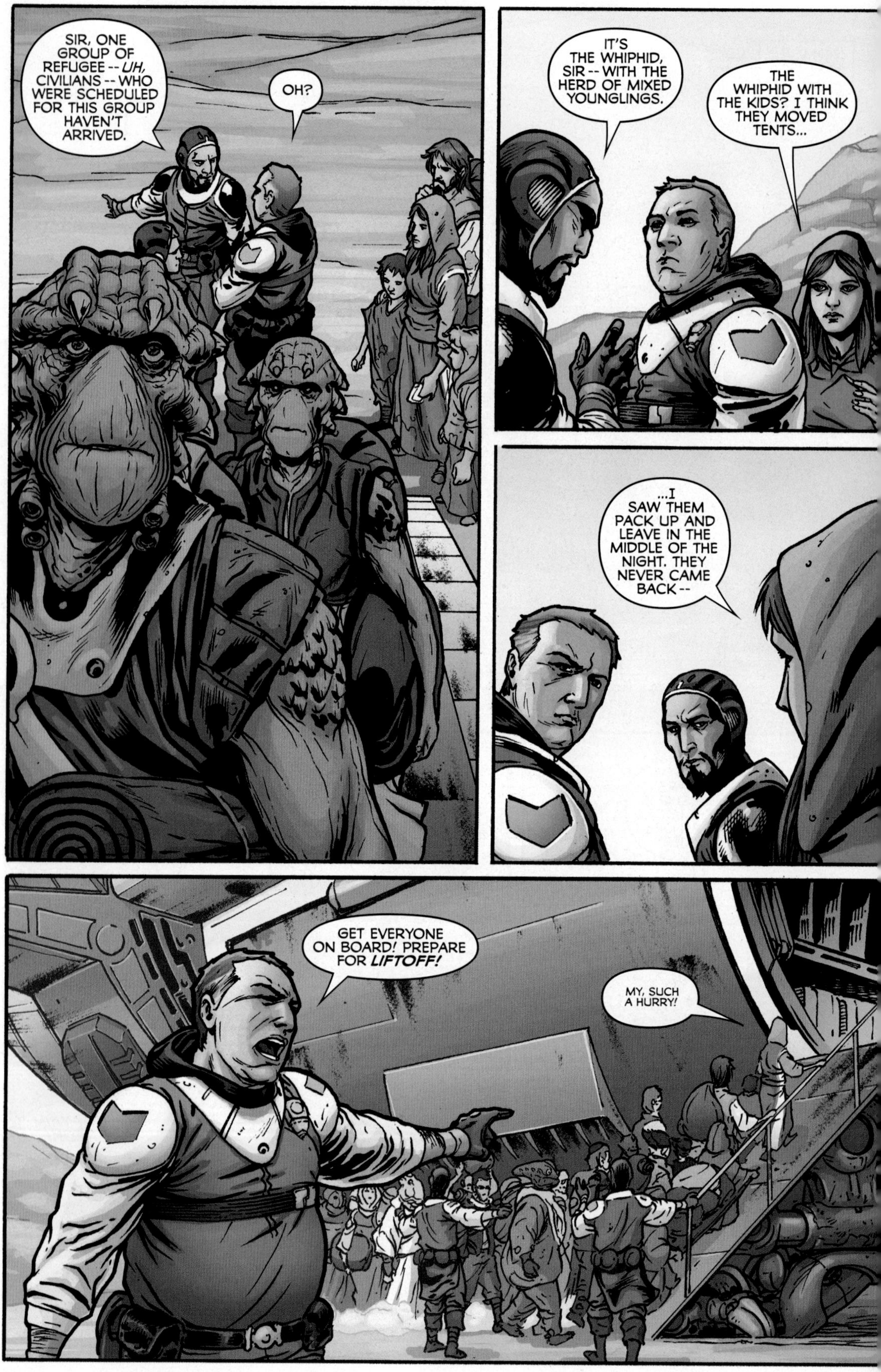
SIR, ONE GROUP OF REFUGEE -- *UH,* CIVILIANS -- WHO WERE SCHEDULED FOR THIS GROUP HAVEN'T ARRIVED.
OH?
IT'S THE WHIPHID, SIR -- WITH THE HERD OF MIXED YOUNGLINGS.
THE WHIPHID WITH THE KIDS? I THINK THEY MOVED TENTS...
...I SAW THEM PACK UP AND LEAVE IN THE MIDDLE OF THE NIGHT. THEY NEVER CAME BACK --
GET EVERYONE ON BOARD! PREPARE FOR *LIFTOFF!*
MY, SUCH A HURRY!

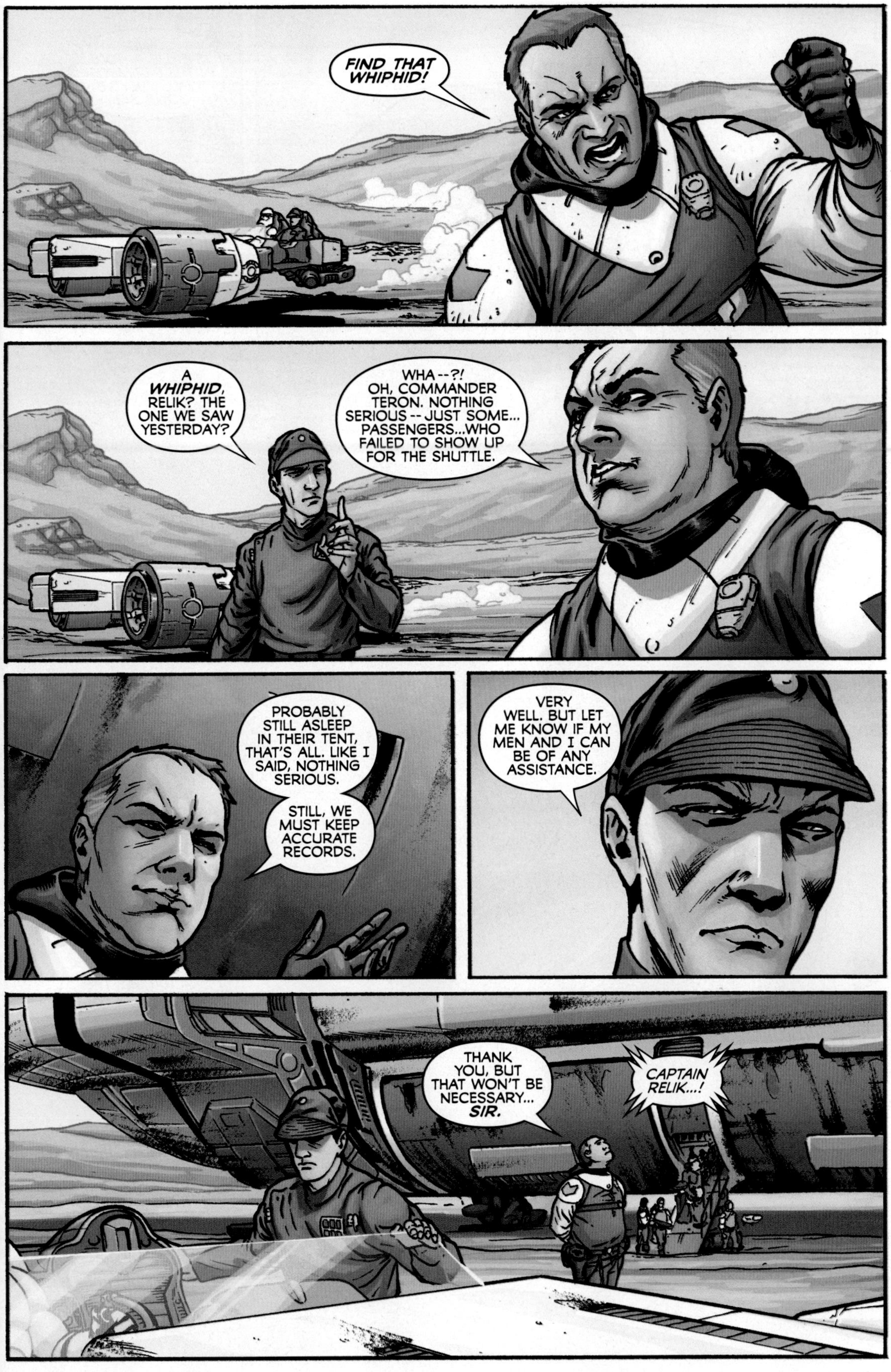
FIND THAT WHIPHID!
A WHIPHID, RELIK? THE ONE WE SAW YESTERDAY?
WHA--?! OH, COMMANDER TERON. NOTHING SERIOUS -- JUST SOME... PASSENGERS...WHO FAILED TO SHOW UP FOR THE SHUTTLE.
PROBABLY STILL ASLEEP IN THEIR TENT, THAT'S ALL. LIKE I SAID, NOTHING SERIOUS.
STILL, WE MUST KEEP ACCURATE RECORDS.
VERY WELL. BUT LET ME KNOW IF MY MEN AND I CAN BE OF ANY ASSISTANCE.
THANK YOU, BUT THAT WON'T BE NECESSARY... SIR.
CAPTAIN RELIK...!

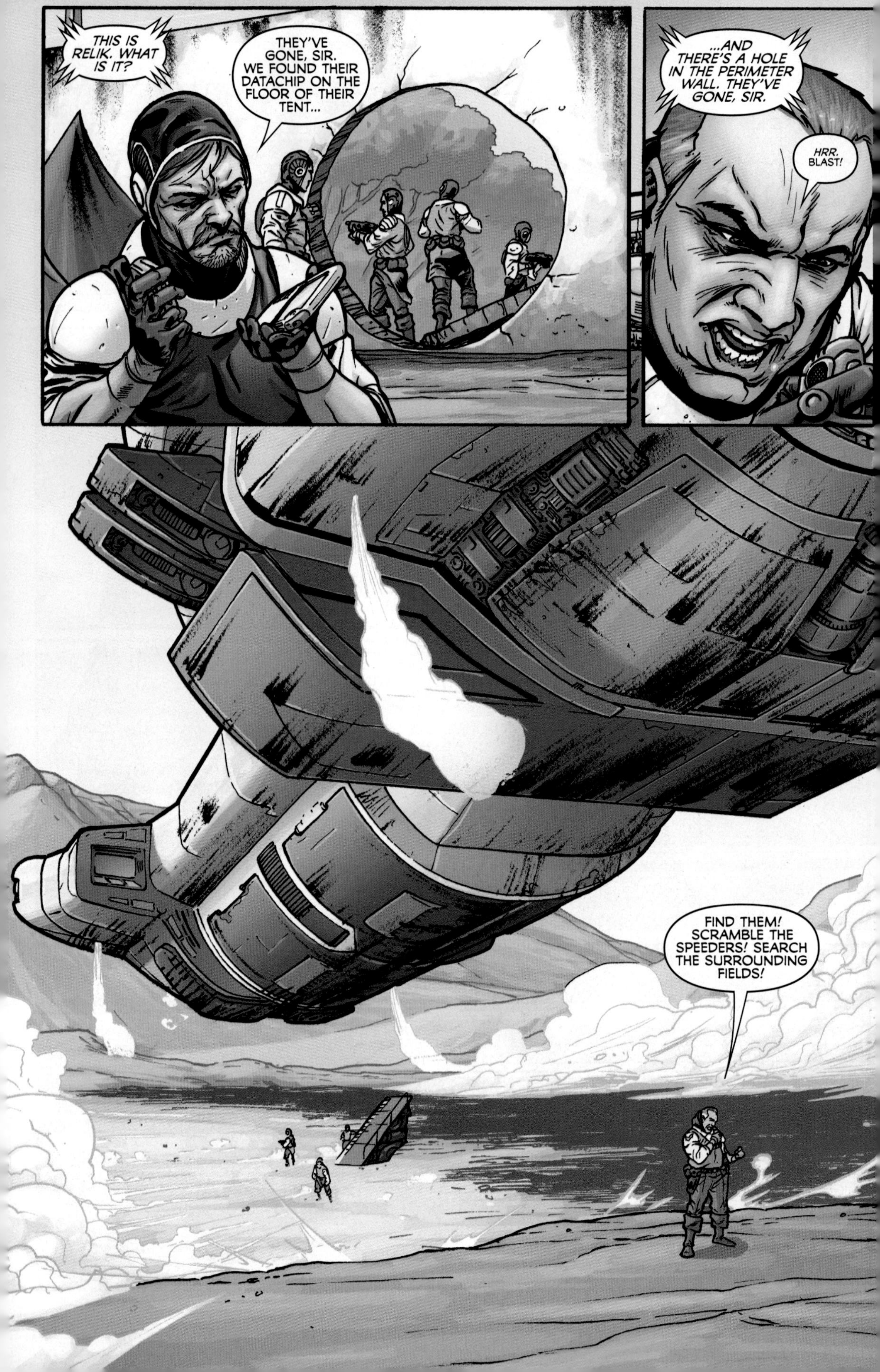
THIS IS RELIK. WHAT IS IT?
THEY'VE GONE, SIR. WE FOUND THEIR DATACHIP ON THE FLOOR OF THEIR TENT...
...AND THERE'S A HOLE IN THE PERIMETER WALL. THEY'VE GONE, SIR.
HRR. BLAST!
FIND THEM! SCRAMBLE THE SPEEDERS! SEARCH THE SURROUNDING FIELDS!

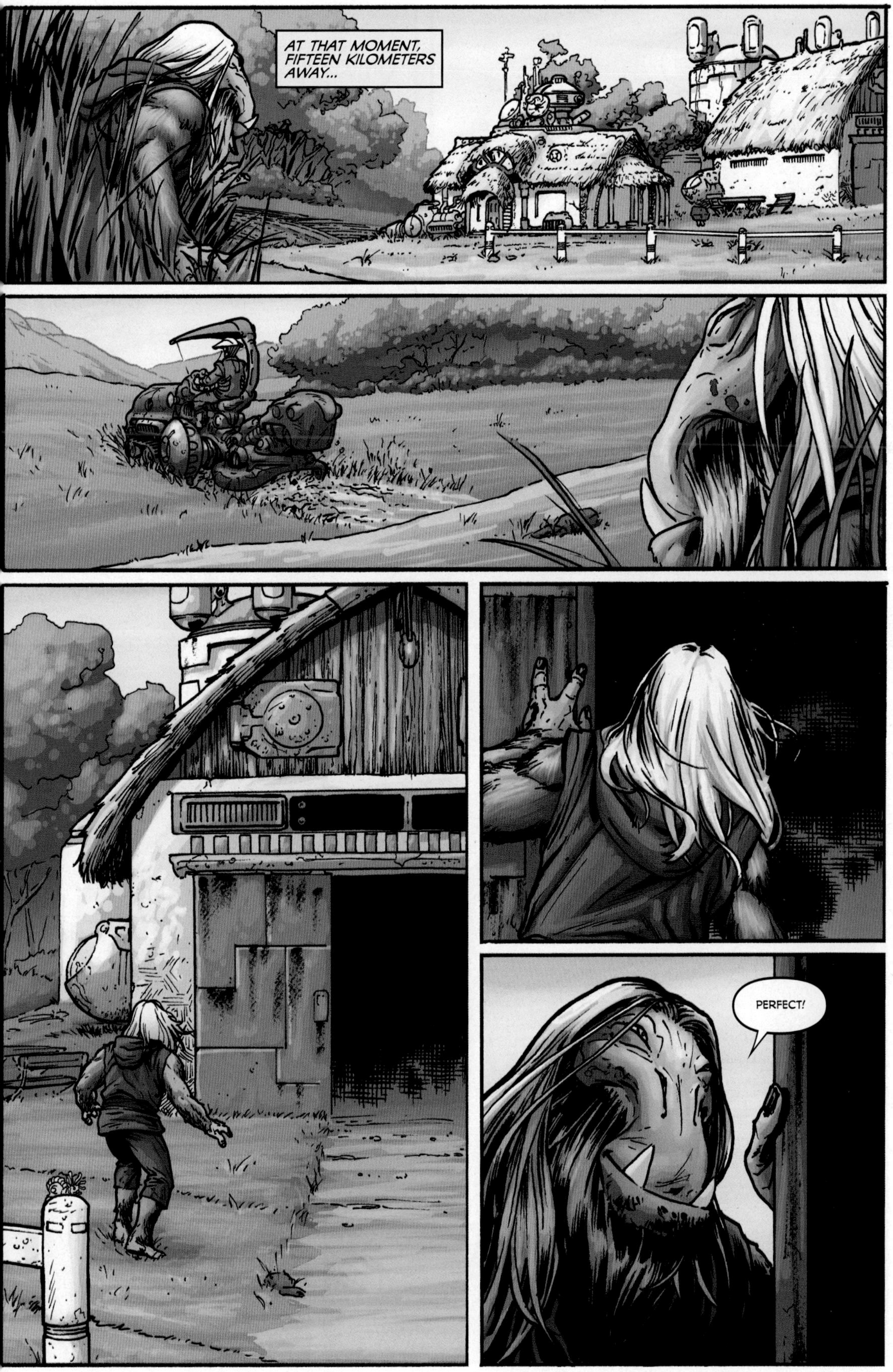
AT THAT MOMENT, FIFTEEN KILOMETERS AWAY...
PERFECT!

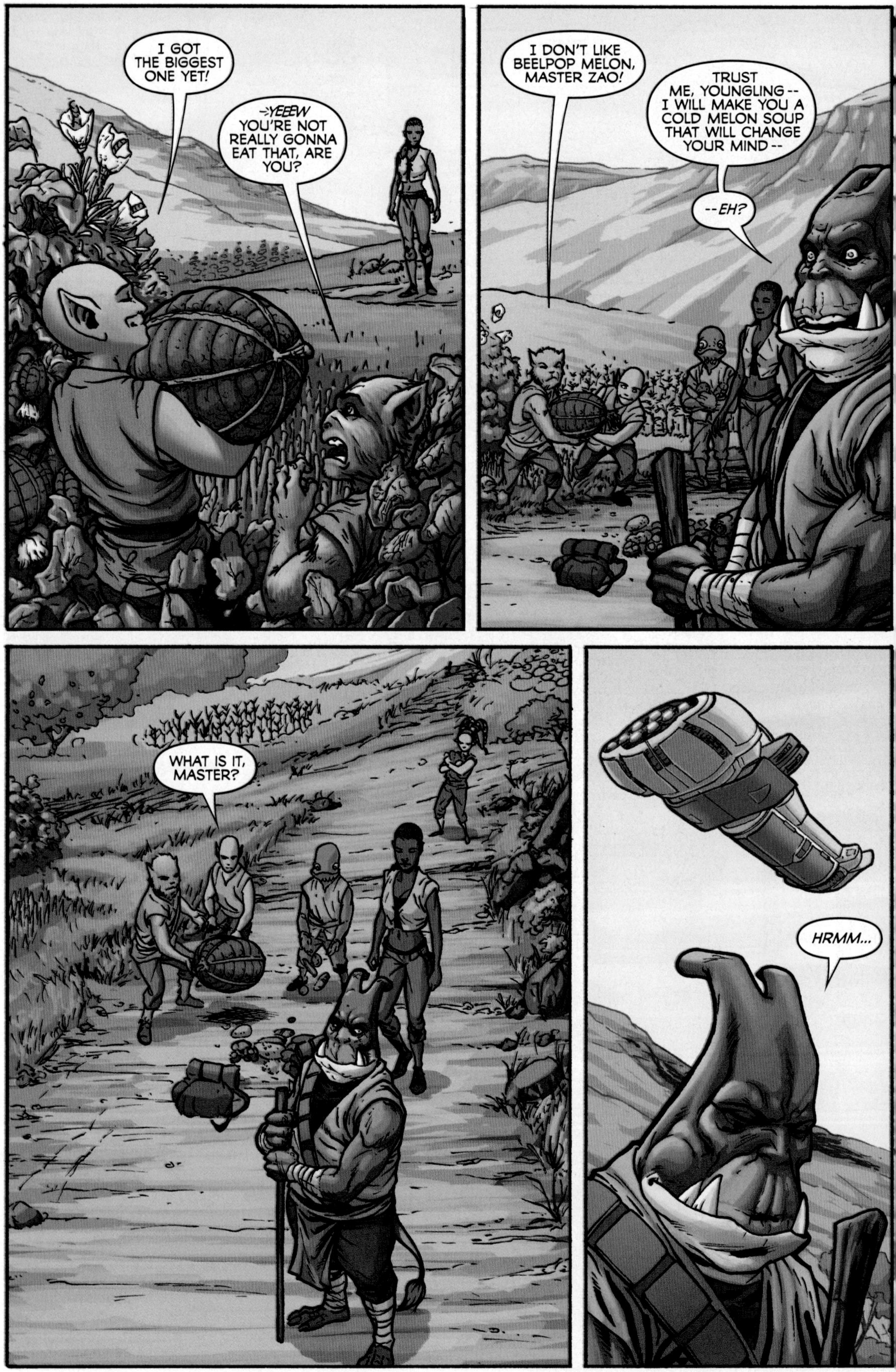
I GOT THE BIGGEST ONE YET!
-YEEEW YOU'RE NOT REALLY GONNA EAT THAT, ARE YOU?
I DON'T LIKE BEELPOP MELON, MASTER ZAO!
TRUST ME, YOUNGLING -- I WILL MAKE YOU A COLD MELON SOUP THAT WILL CHANGE YOUR MIND --
--EH?
WHAT IS IT, MASTER?
HRMM...

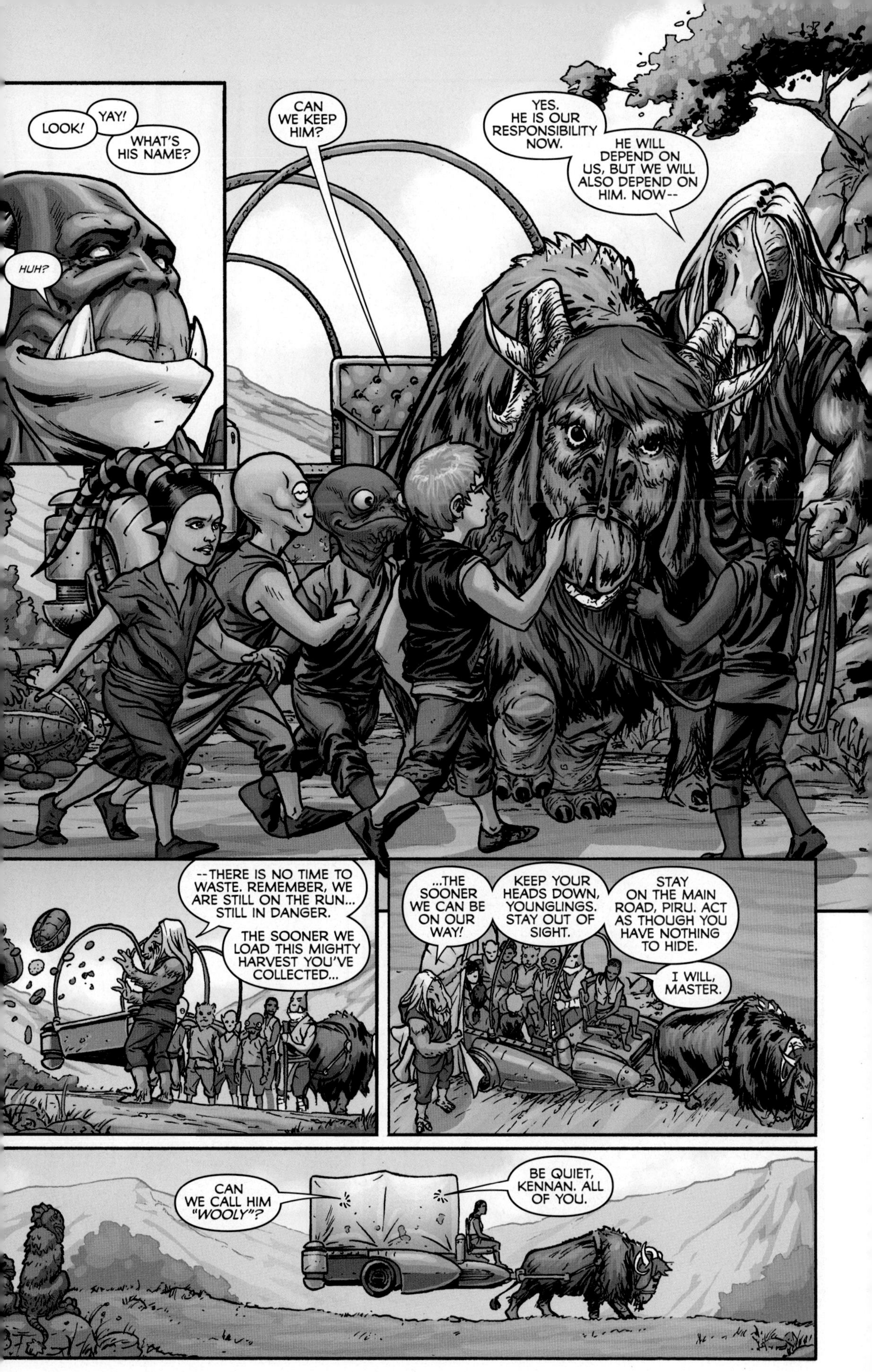
LOOK!
YAY!
WHAT'S HIS NAME?
HUH?
CAN WE KEEP HIM?
YES. HE IS OUR RESPONSIBILITY NOW.
HE WILL DEPEND ON US, BUT WE WILL ALSO DEPEND ON HIM. NOW--
--THERE IS NO TIME TO WASTE. REMEMBER, WE ARE STILL ON THE RUN... STILL IN DANGER.
THE SOONER WE LOAD THIS MIGHTY HARVEST YOU'VE COLLECTED...
...THE SOONER WE CAN BE ON OUR WAY!
KEEP YOUR HEADS DOWN, YOUNGLINGS. STAY OUT OF SIGHT.
STAY ON THE MAIN ROAD, PIRU. ACT AS THOUGH YOU HAVE NOTHING TO HIDE.
I WILL, MASTER.
CAN WE CALL HIM "WOOLY"?
BE QUIET, KENNAN. ALL OF YOU.

HOURS PASS.

MASTERS! TROUBLE...

...MILITIA SOLDIERS.

REMAIN CALM, PIRU. YOU ARE A SIMPLE FARM GIRL. YOU HAVE NOTHING THAT THESE SOLDIERS ARE SEEKING. ALLOW MASTER K'KRUHK AND I TO TAKE CARE OF THIS.

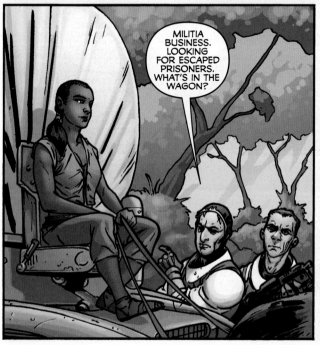

MILITIA BUSINESS. LOOKING FOR ESCAPED PRISONERS. WHAT'S IN THE WAGON?

JUST BEELPOP MELONS.

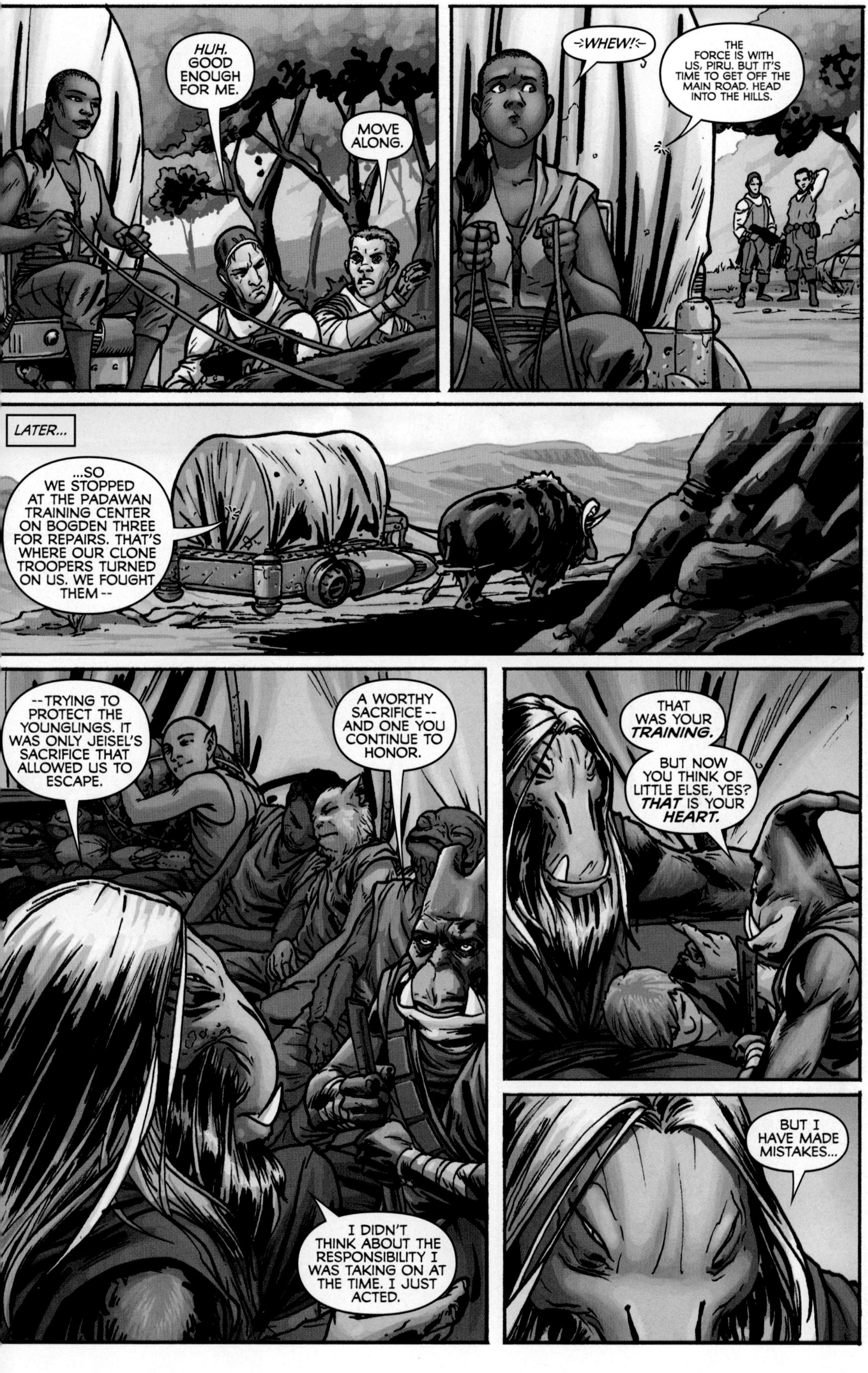
HUH. GOOD ENOUGH FOR ME.
MOVE ALONG.
WHEW!
THE FORCE IS WITH US, PIRU. BUT IT'S TIME TO GET OFF THE MAIN ROAD. HEAD INTO THE HILLS.
LATER...
...SO WE STOPPED AT THE PADAWAN TRAINING CENTER ON BOGDEN THREE FOR REPAIRS. THAT'S WHERE OUR CLONE TROOPERS TURNED ON US. WE FOUGHT THEM --
--TRYING TO PROTECT THE YOUNGLINGS. IT WAS ONLY JEISEL'S SACRIFICE THAT ALLOWED US TO ESCAPE.
A WORTHY SACRIFICE -- AND ONE YOU CONTINUE TO HONOR.
I DIDN'T THINK ABOUT THE RESPONSIBILITY I WAS TAKING ON AT THE TIME. I JUST ACTED.
THAT WAS YOUR TRAINING.
BUT NOW YOU THINK OF LITTLE ELSE, YES? THAT IS YOUR HEART.
BUT I HAVE MADE MISTAKES...

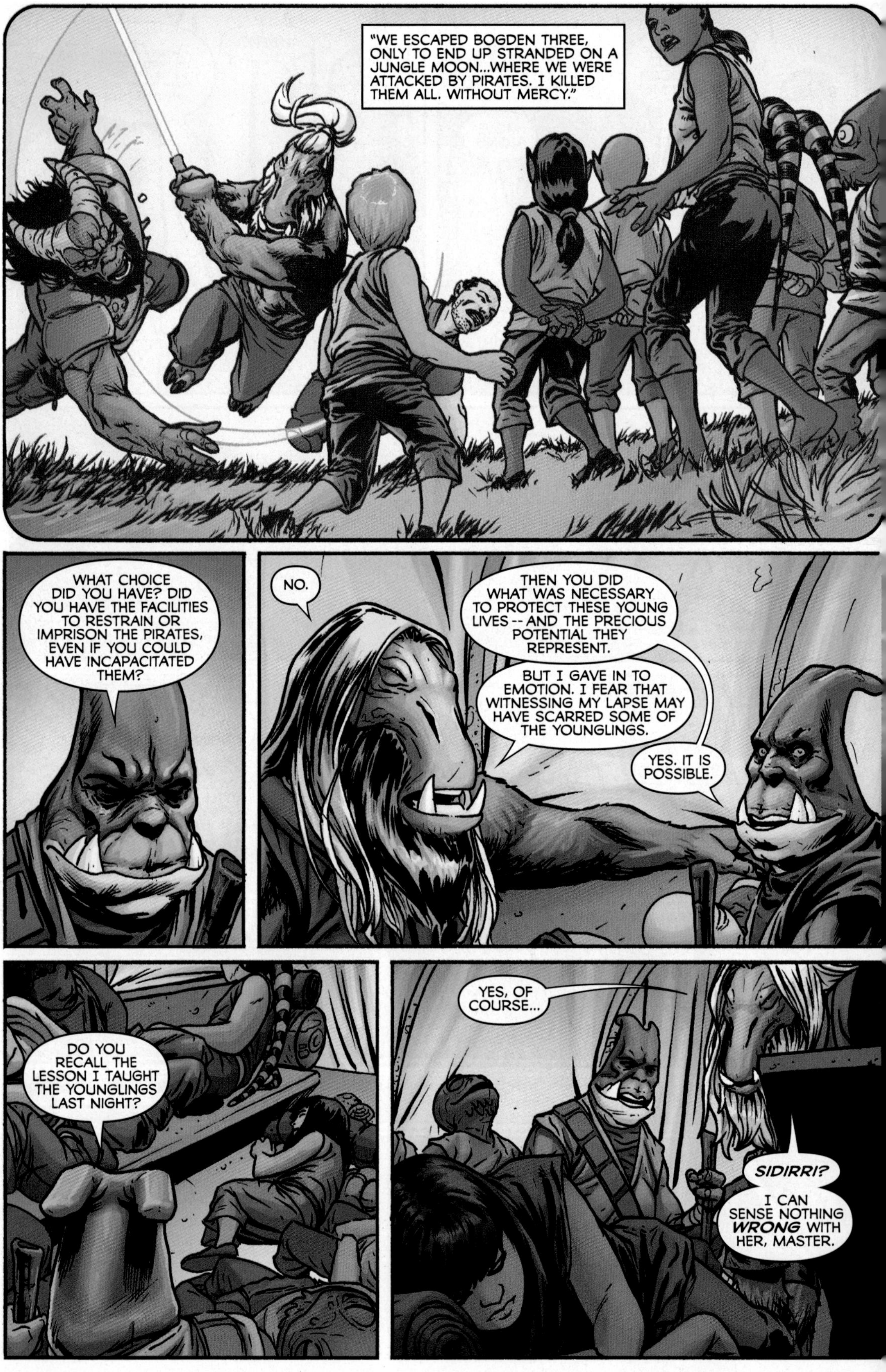

"WE ESCAPED BOGDEN THREE, ONLY TO END UP STRANDED ON A JUNGLE MOON...WHERE WE WERE ATTACKED BY PIRATES. I KILLED THEM ALL. WITHOUT MERCY."
WHAT CHOICE DID YOU HAVE? DID YOU HAVE THE FACILITIES TO RESTRAIN OR IMPRISON THE PIRATES, EVEN IF YOU COULD HAVE INCAPACITATED THEM?
NO.
THEN YOU DID WHAT WAS NECESSARY TO PROTECT THESE YOUNG LIVES -- AND THE PRECIOUS POTENTIAL THEY REPRESENT.
BUT I GAVE IN TO EMOTION. I FEAR THAT WITNESSING MY LAPSE MAY HAVE SCARRED SOME OF THE YOUNGLINGS.
YES. IT IS POSSIBLE.
DO YOU RECALL THE LESSON I TAUGHT THE YOUNGLINGS LAST NIGHT?
YES, OF COURSE...
*SIDIRRI?*
I CAN SENSE NOTHING ***WRONG*** WITH HER, MASTER.

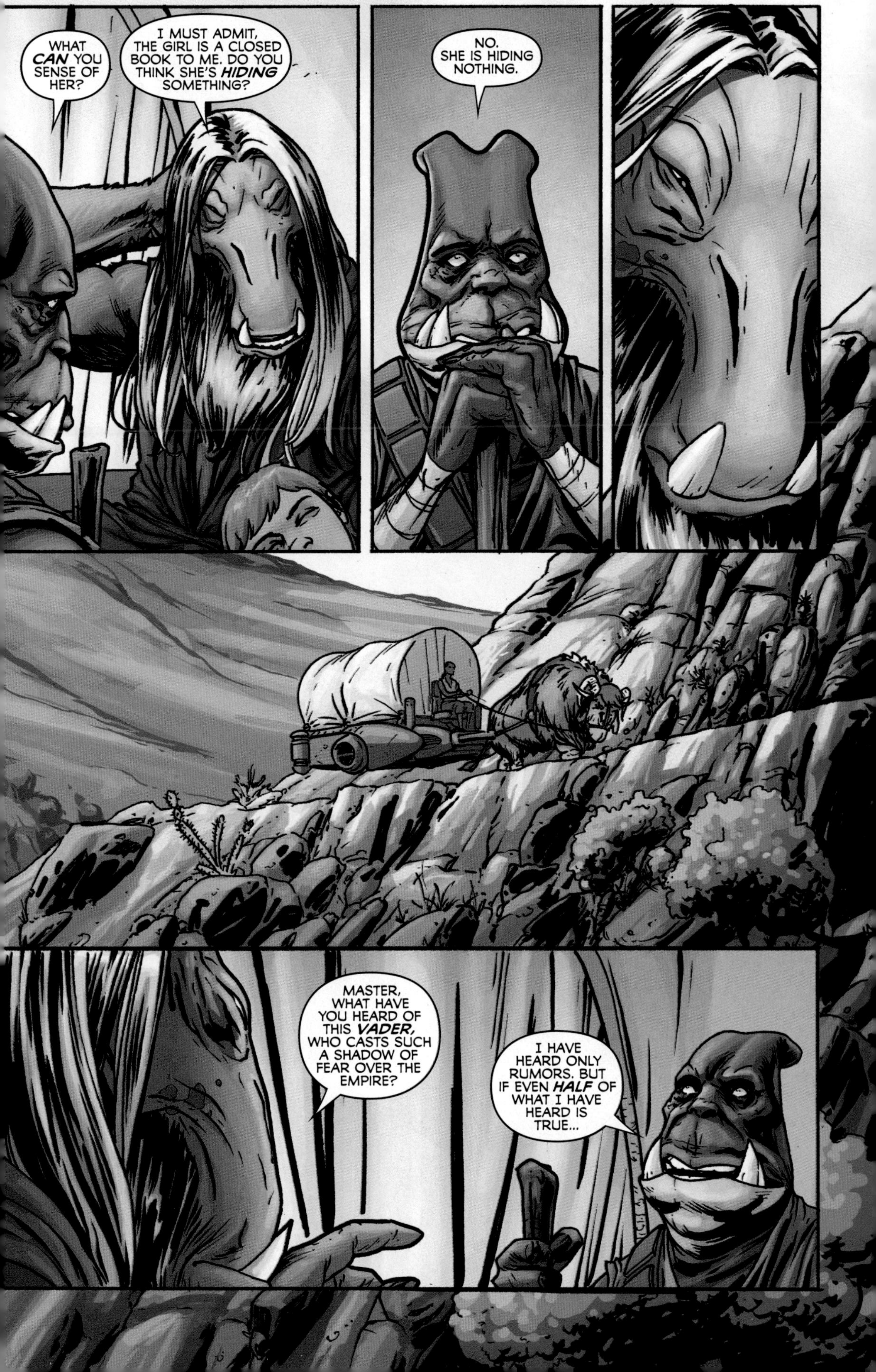

WHAT CAN YOU SENSE OF HER?
I MUST ADMIT, THE GIRL IS A CLOSED BOOK TO ME. DO YOU THINK SHE'S HIDING SOMETHING?
NO. SHE IS HIDING NOTHING.
MASTER, WHAT HAVE YOU HEARD OF THIS VADER, WHO CASTS SUCH A SHADOW OF FEAR OVER THE EMPIRE?
I HAVE HEARD ONLY RUMORS. BUT IF EVEN HALF OF WHAT I HAVE HEARD IS TRUE...

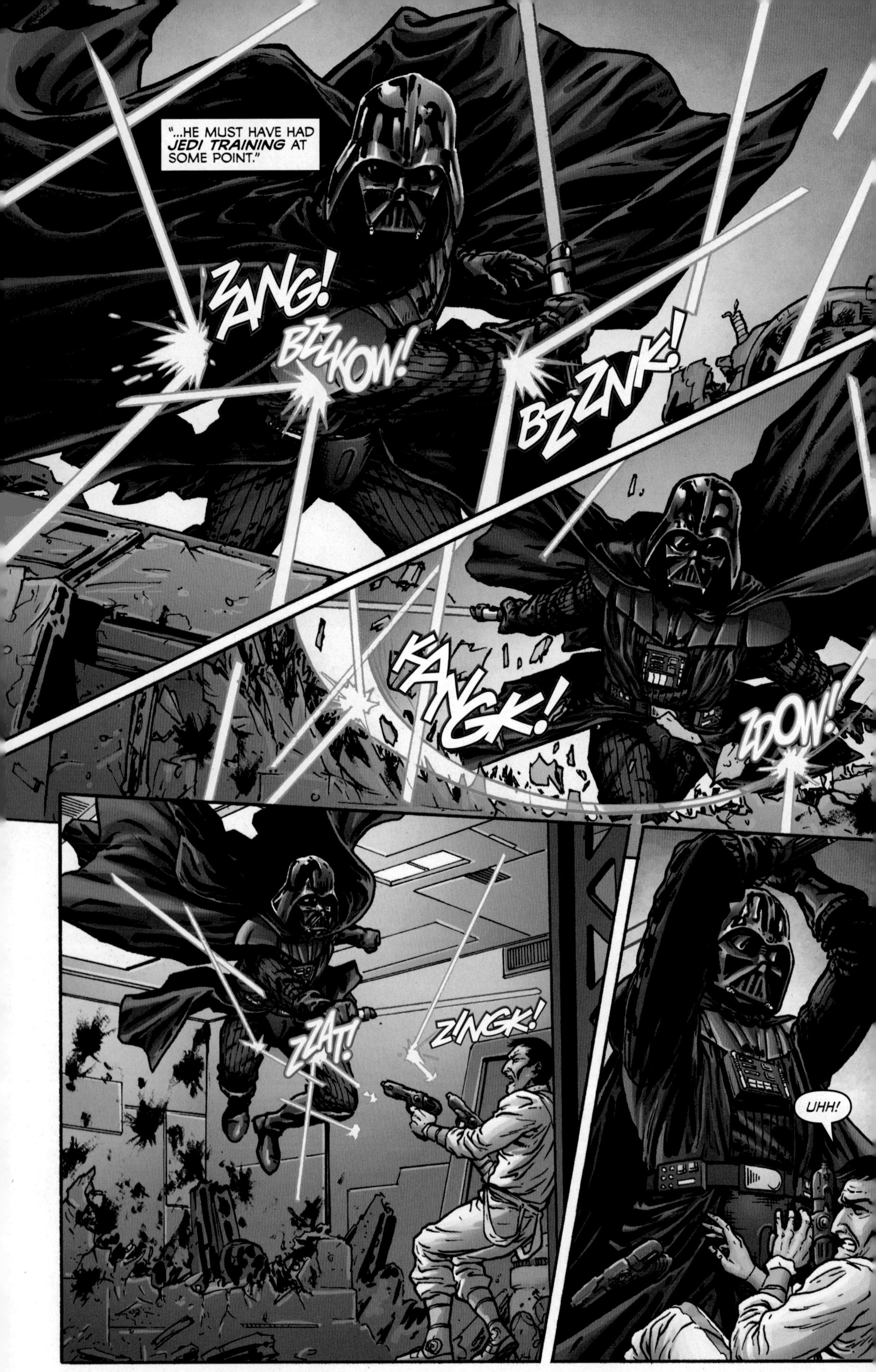
"...HE MUST HAVE HAD JEDI TRAINING AT SOME POINT."
ZANG!
BZZKOW!
BZZZNK!
KANGK!
ZDOW!!
ZZAT!
ZINGK!
UHH!

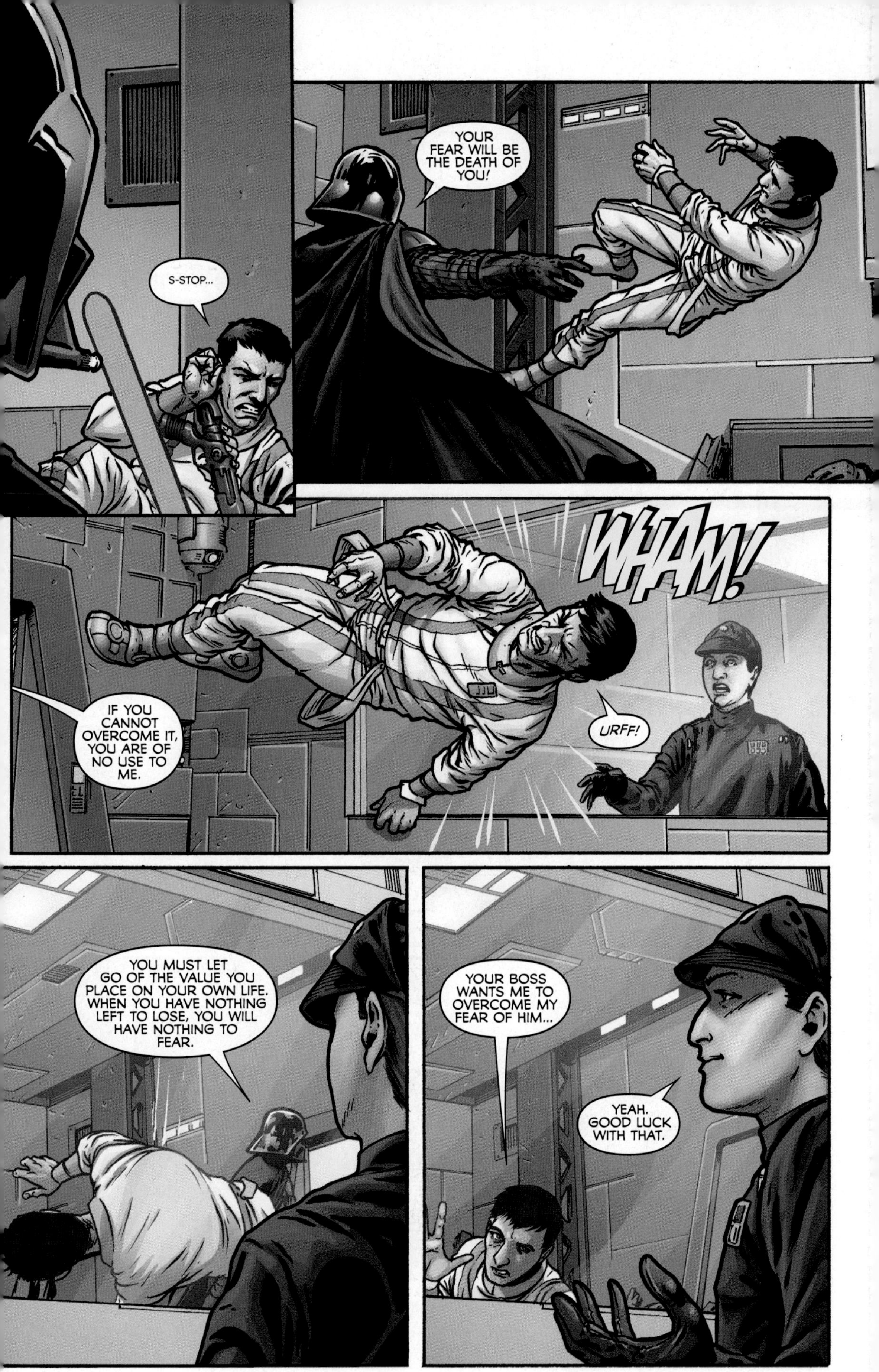
S-STOP...
YOUR FEAR WILL BE THE DEATH OF YOU!
WHAM!
IF YOU CANNOT OVERCOME IT, YOU ARE OF NO USE TO ME.
URFF!
YOU MUST LET GO OF THE VALUE YOU PLACE ON YOUR OWN LIFE. WHEN YOU HAVE NOTHING LEFT TO LOSE, YOU WILL HAVE NOTHING TO FEAR.
YOUR BOSS WANTS ME TO OVERCOME MY FEAR OF HIM...
YEAH. GOOD LUCK WITH THAT.

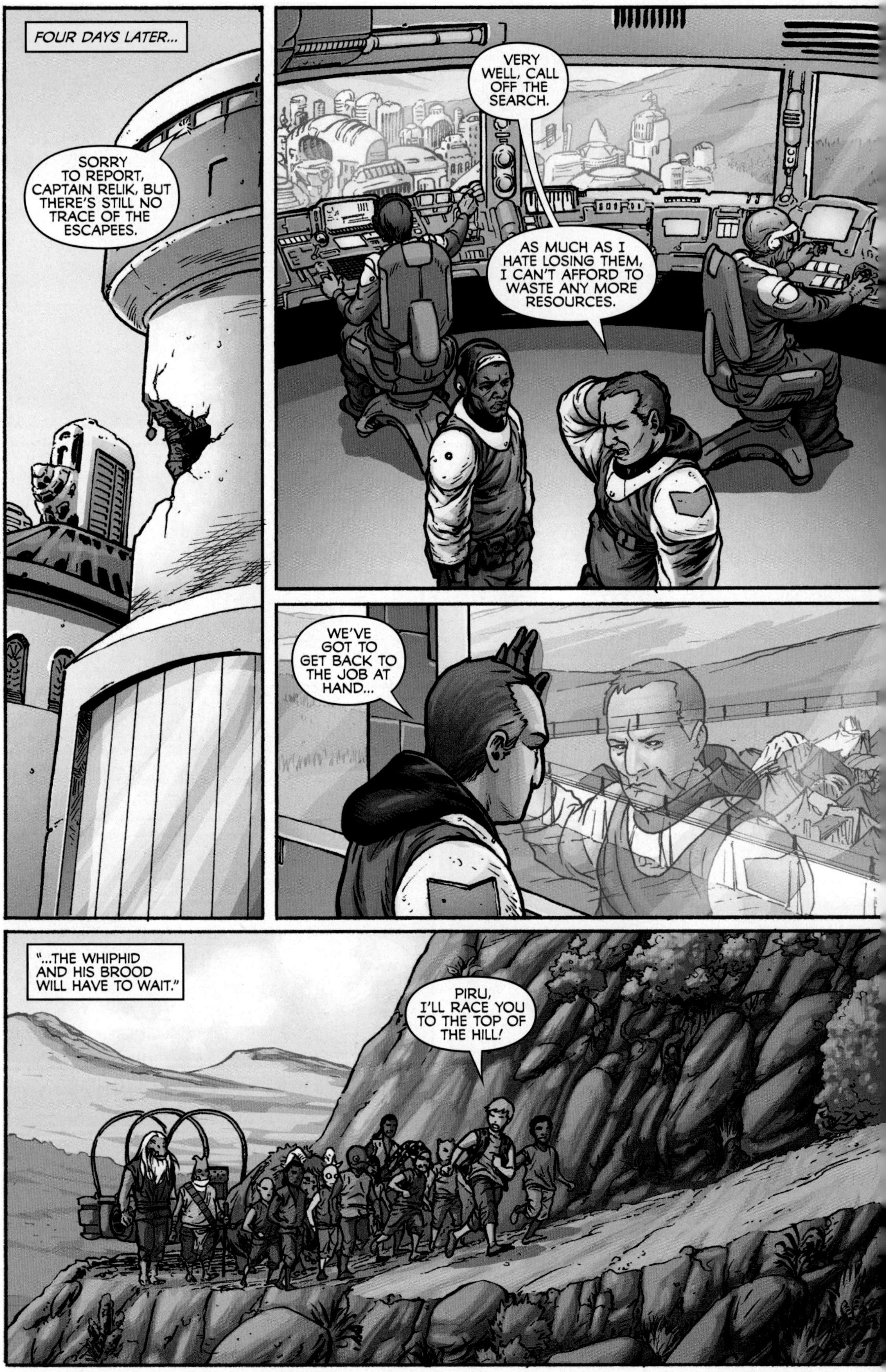
FOUR DAYS LATER...
SORRY TO REPORT, CAPTAIN RELIK, BUT THERE'S STILL NO TRACE OF THE ESCAPEES.
VERY WELL, CALL OFF THE SEARCH.
AS MUCH AS I HATE LOSING THEM, I CAN'T AFFORD TO WASTE ANY MORE RESOURCES.
WE'VE GOT TO GET BACK TO THE JOB AT HAND...
"...THE WHIPHID AND HIS BROOD WILL HAVE TO WAIT."
PIRU, I'LL RACE YOU TO THE TOP OF THE HILL!

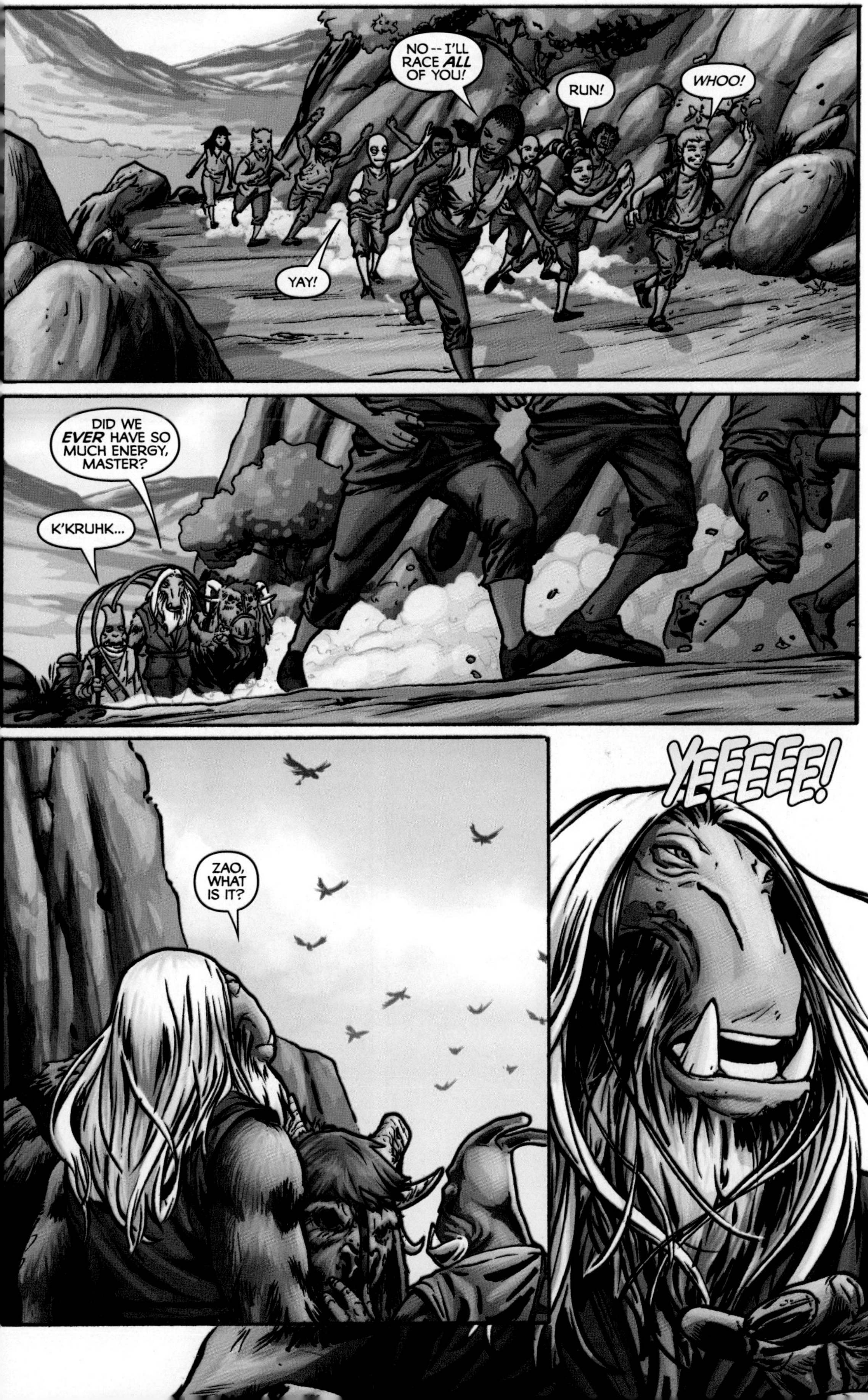
NO -- I'LL RACE ALL OF YOU!
RUN!
WHOO!
YAY!
DID WE EVER HAVE SO MUCH ENERGY, MASTER?
K'KRUHK...
YEEEEE!
ZAO, WHAT IS IT?

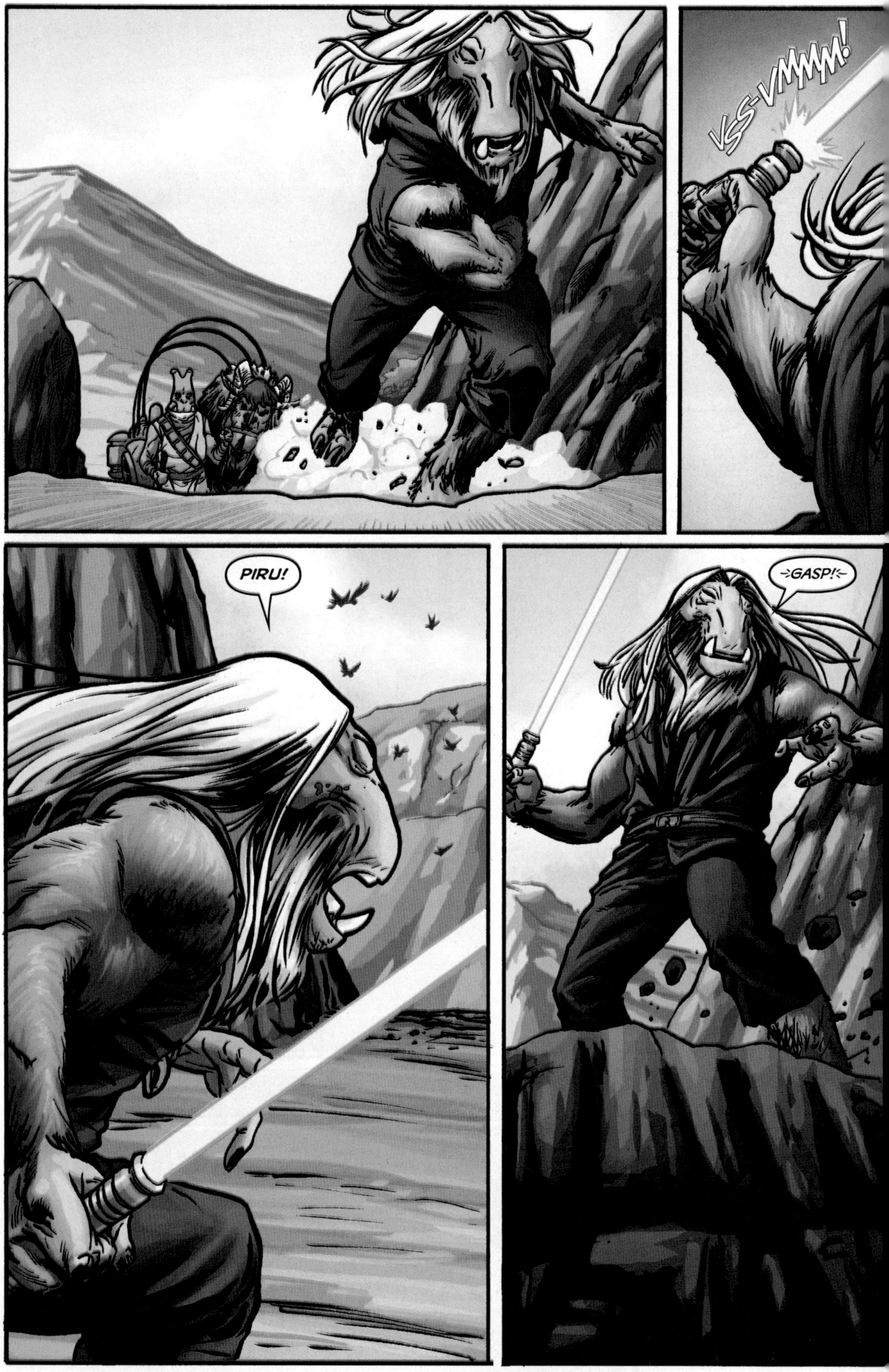
VSS-VMMM!
PIRU!
GASP!

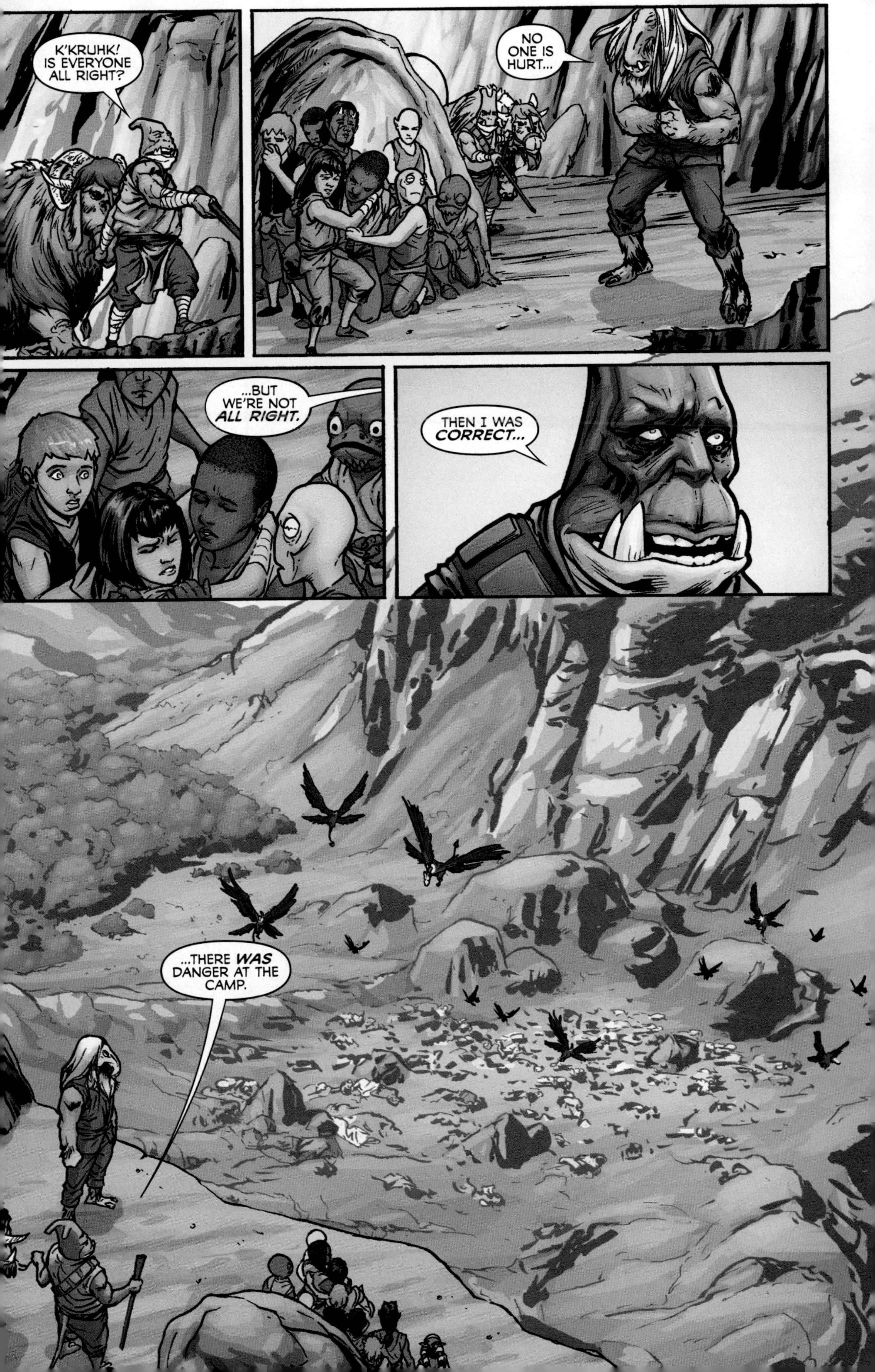
K'KRUHK! IS EVERYONE ALL RIGHT?
NO ONE IS HURT...
...BUT WE'RE NOT *ALL RIGHT.*
THEN I WAS *CORRECT...*
...THERE *WAS* DANGER AT THE CAMP.

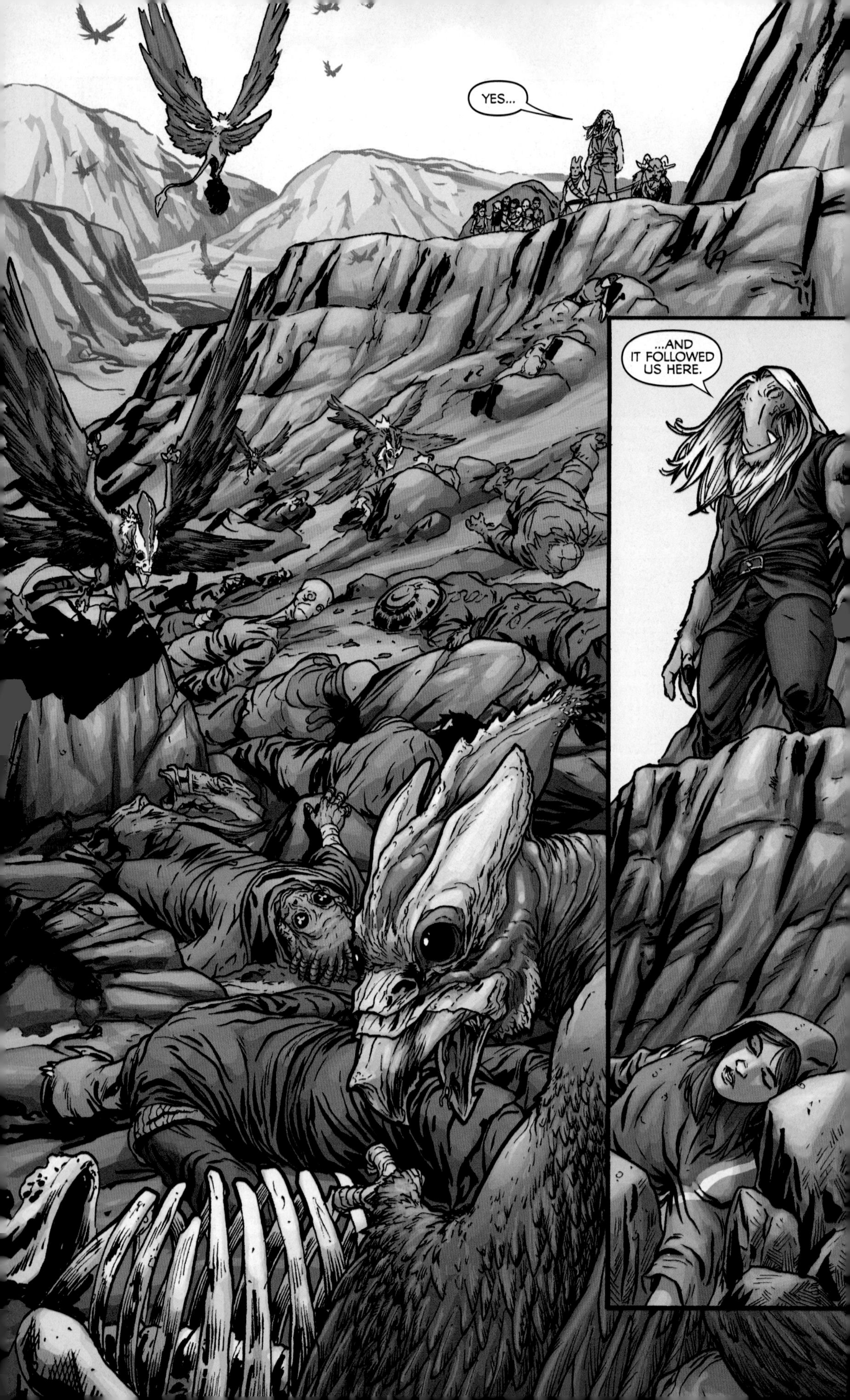
YES...
...AND IT FOLLOWED US HERE.

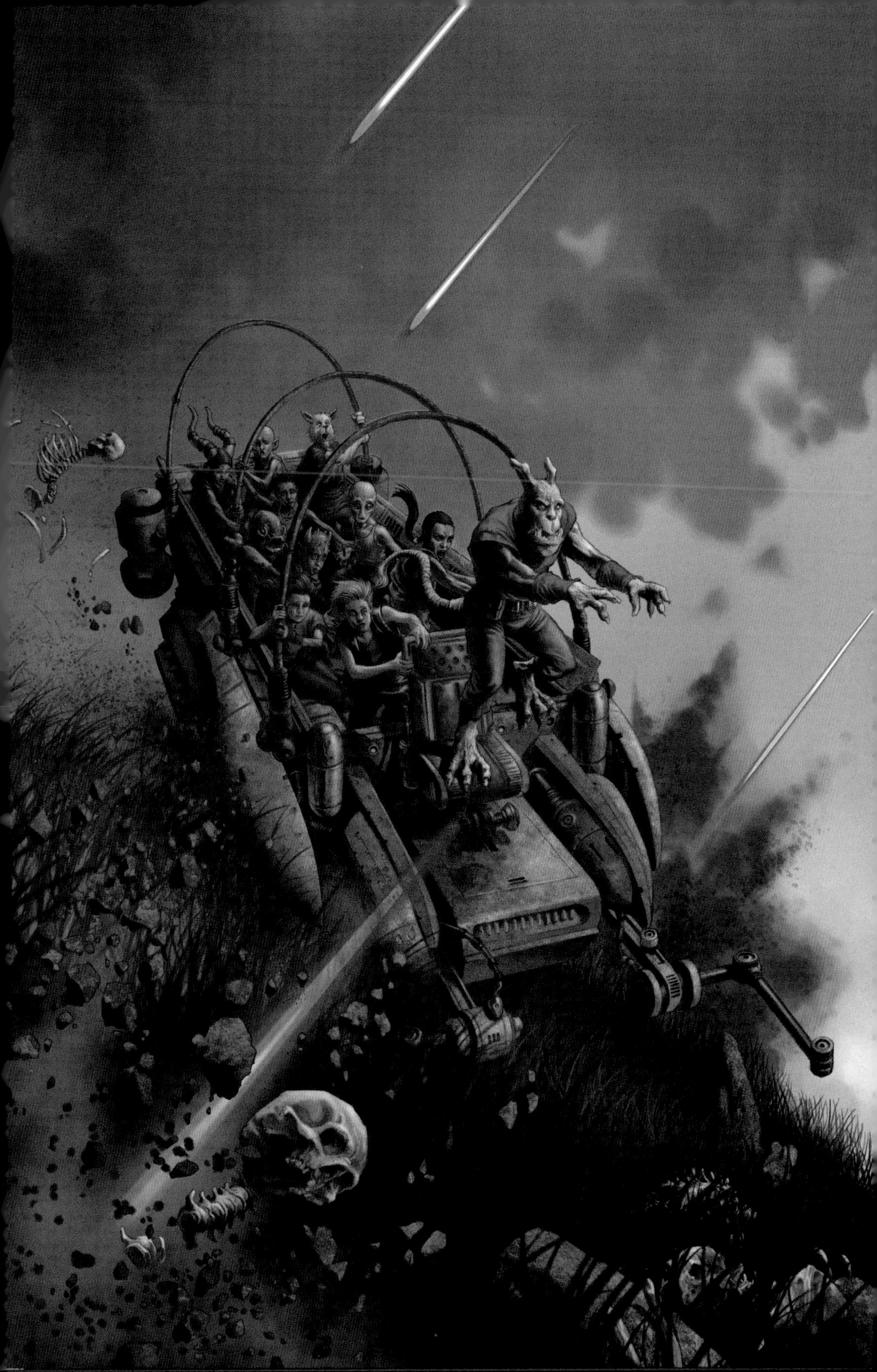

*STAR WARS: DARK TIMES — FIRE CARRIER #3*

WRITER: RANDY STRADLEY • ARTIST: GABRIEL GUZMAN • COLORIST: GARRY HENDERSON • LETTERER: MICHAEL HEISLER

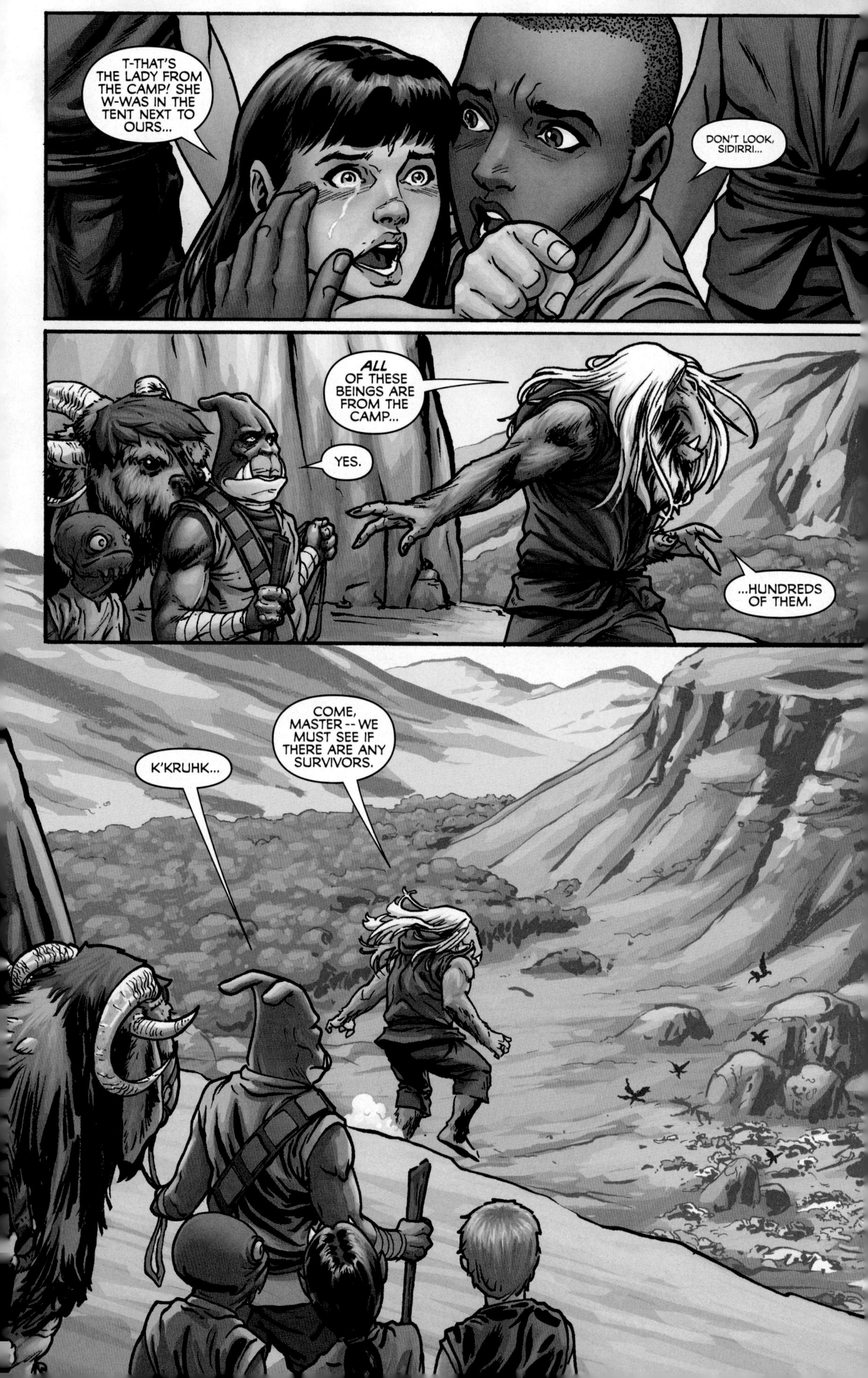
T-THAT'S THE LADY FROM THE CAMP! SHE W-WAS IN THE TENT NEXT TO OURS...
DON'T LOOK, SIDIRRI...
*ALL* OF THESE BEINGS ARE FROM THE CAMP...
YES.
...HUNDREDS OF THEM.
COME, MASTER -- WE MUST SEE IF THERE ARE ANY SURVIVORS.
K'KRUHK...

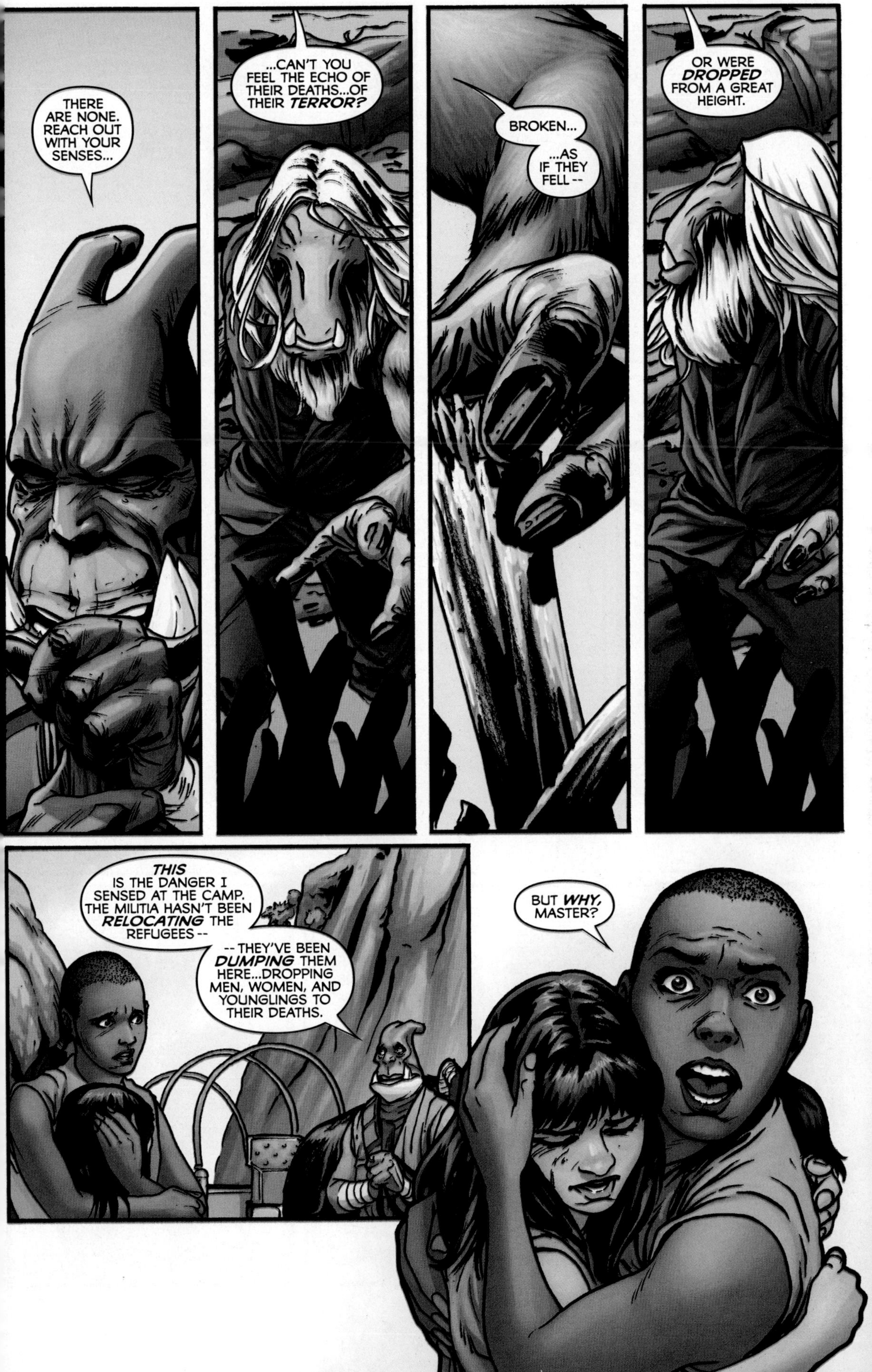
THERE ARE NONE. REACH OUT WITH YOUR SENSES...
...CAN'T YOU FEEL THE ECHO OF THEIR DEATHS...OF THEIR *TERROR?*
BROKEN...
...AS IF THEY FELL --
OR WERE *DROPPED* FROM A GREAT HEIGHT.
*THIS* IS THE DANGER I SENSED AT THE CAMP. THE MILITIA HASN'T BEEN *RELOCATING* THE REFUGEES --
-- THEY'VE BEEN *DUMPING* THEM HERE...DROPPING MEN, WOMEN, AND YOUNGLINGS TO THEIR DEATHS.
BUT *WHY,* MASTER?

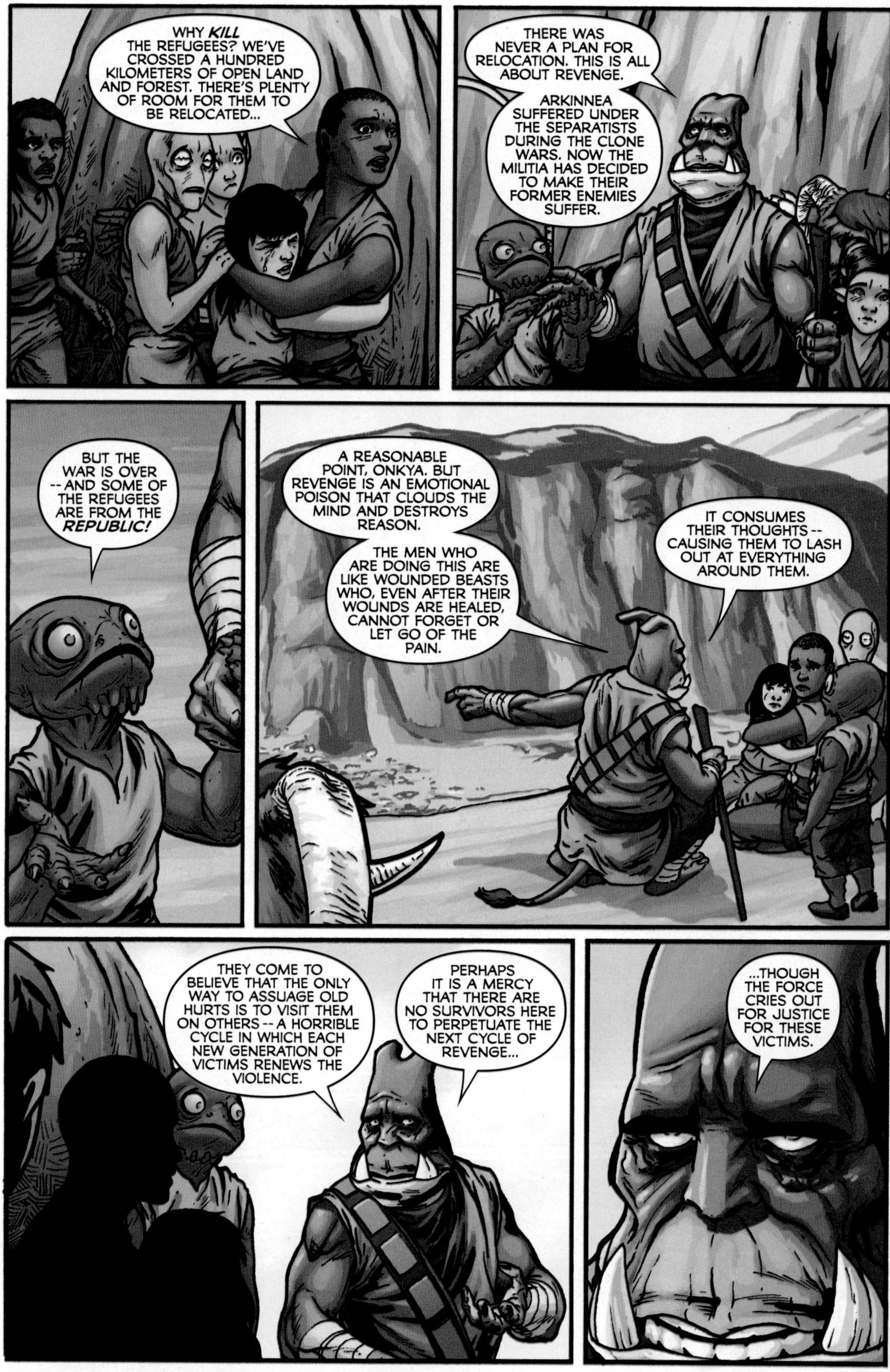
WHY KILL THE REFUGEES? WE'VE CROSSED A HUNDRED KILOMETERS OF OPEN LAND AND FOREST. THERE'S PLENTY OF ROOM FOR THEM TO BE RELOCATED...
THERE WAS NEVER A PLAN FOR RELOCATION. THIS IS ALL ABOUT REVENGE.
ARKINNEA SUFFERED UNDER THE SEPARATISTS DURING THE CLONE WARS. NOW THE MILITIA HAS DECIDED TO MAKE THEIR FORMER ENEMIES SUFFER.
BUT THE WAR IS OVER --AND SOME OF THE REFUGEES ARE FROM THE REPUBLIC!
A REASONABLE POINT, ONKYA. BUT REVENGE IS AN EMOTIONAL POISON THAT CLOUDS THE MIND AND DESTROYS REASON.
THE MEN WHO ARE DOING THIS ARE LIKE WOUNDED BEASTS WHO, EVEN AFTER THEIR WOUNDS ARE HEALED, CANNOT FORGET OR LET GO OF THE PAIN.
IT CONSUMES THEIR THOUGHTS -- CAUSING THEM TO LASH OUT AT EVERYTHING AROUND THEM.
THEY COME TO BELIEVE THAT THE ONLY WAY TO ASSUAGE OLD HURTS IS TO VISIT THEM ON OTHERS -- A HORRIBLE CYCLE IN WHICH EACH NEW GENERATION OF VICTIMS RENEWS THE VIOLENCE.
PERHAPS IT IS A MERCY THAT THERE ARE NO SURVIVORS HERE TO PERPETUATE THE NEXT CYCLE OF REVENGE...
...THOUGH THE FORCE CRIES OUT FOR JUSTICE FOR THESE VICTIMS.

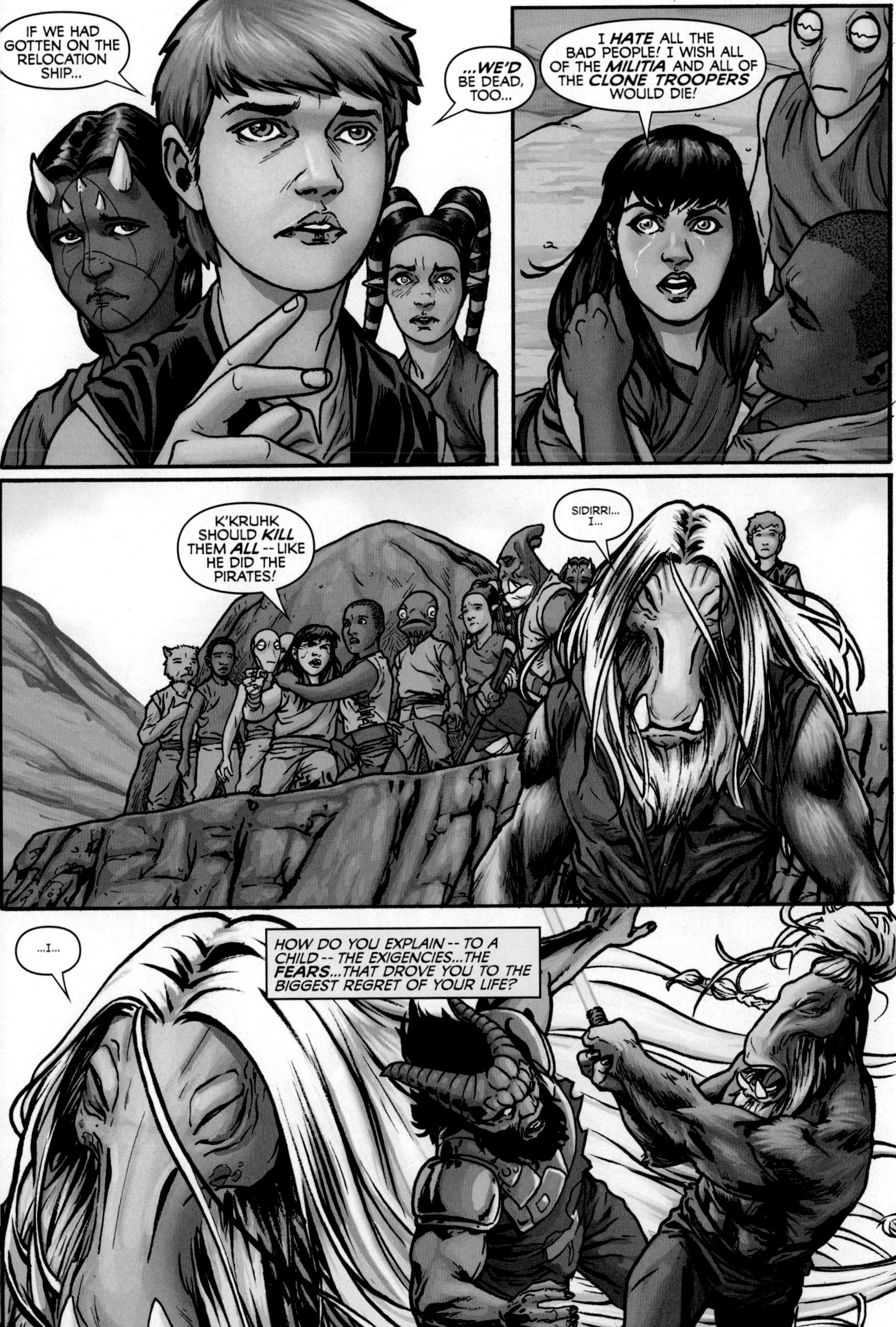

IF WE HAD GOTTEN ON THE RELOCATION SHIP...
...WE'D BE DEAD, TOO...
I HATE ALL THE BAD PEOPLE! I WISH ALL OF THE MILITIA AND ALL OF THE CLONE TROOPERS WOULD DIE!
K'KRUHK SHOULD KILL THEM ALL -- LIKE HE DID THE PIRATES!
SIDIRRI... I...
...I...
HOW DO YOU EXPLAIN -- TO A CHILD -- THE EXIGENCIES...THE FEARS...THAT DROVE YOU TO THE BIGGEST REGRET OF YOUR LIFE?

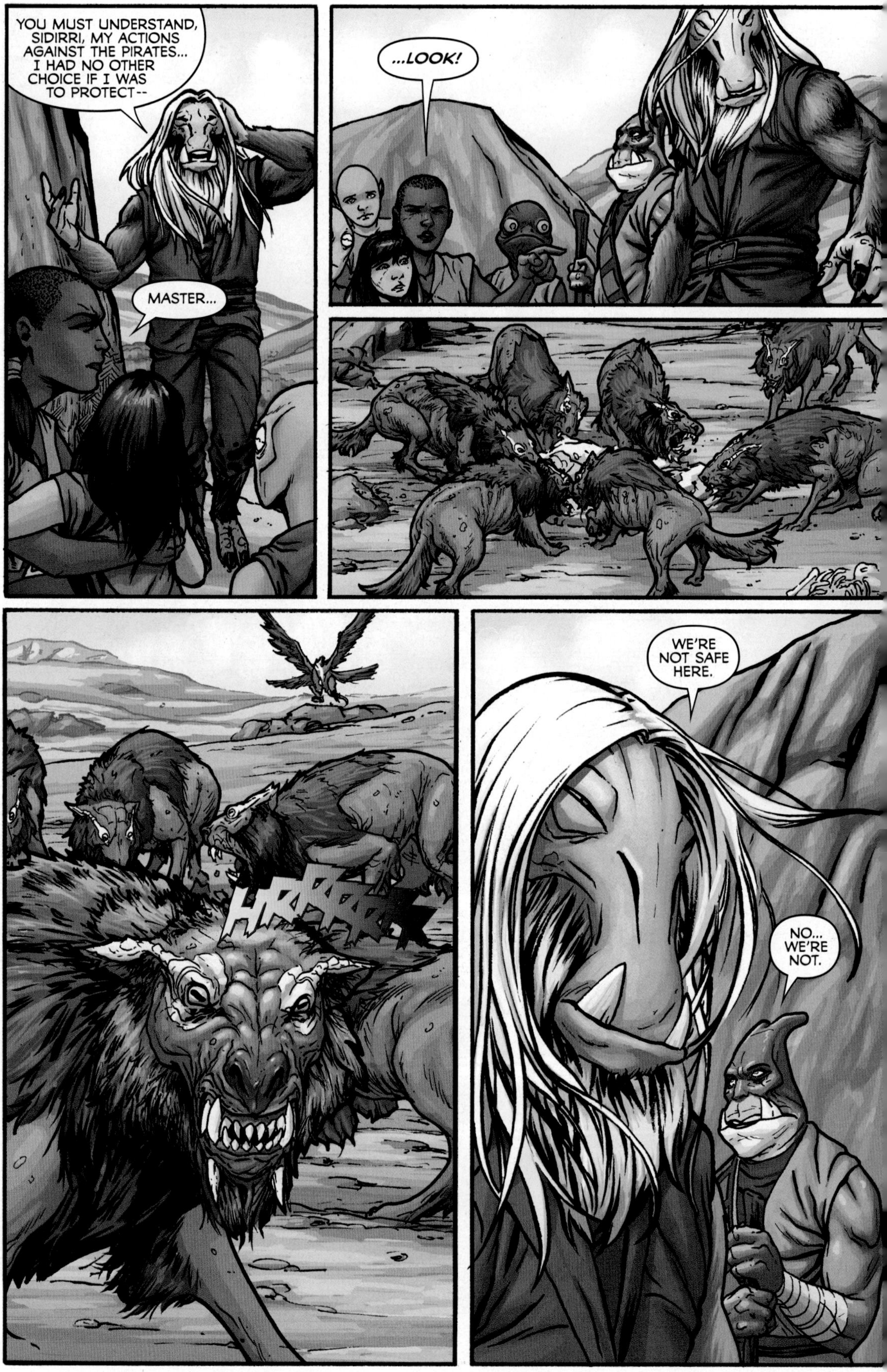

YOU MUST UNDERSTAND, SIDIRRI, MY ACTIONS AGAINST THE PIRATES... I HAD NO OTHER CHOICE IF I WAS TO PROTECT--
MASTER...
...LOOK!
HRRRRR
WE'RE NOT SAFE HERE.
NO... WE'RE NOT.

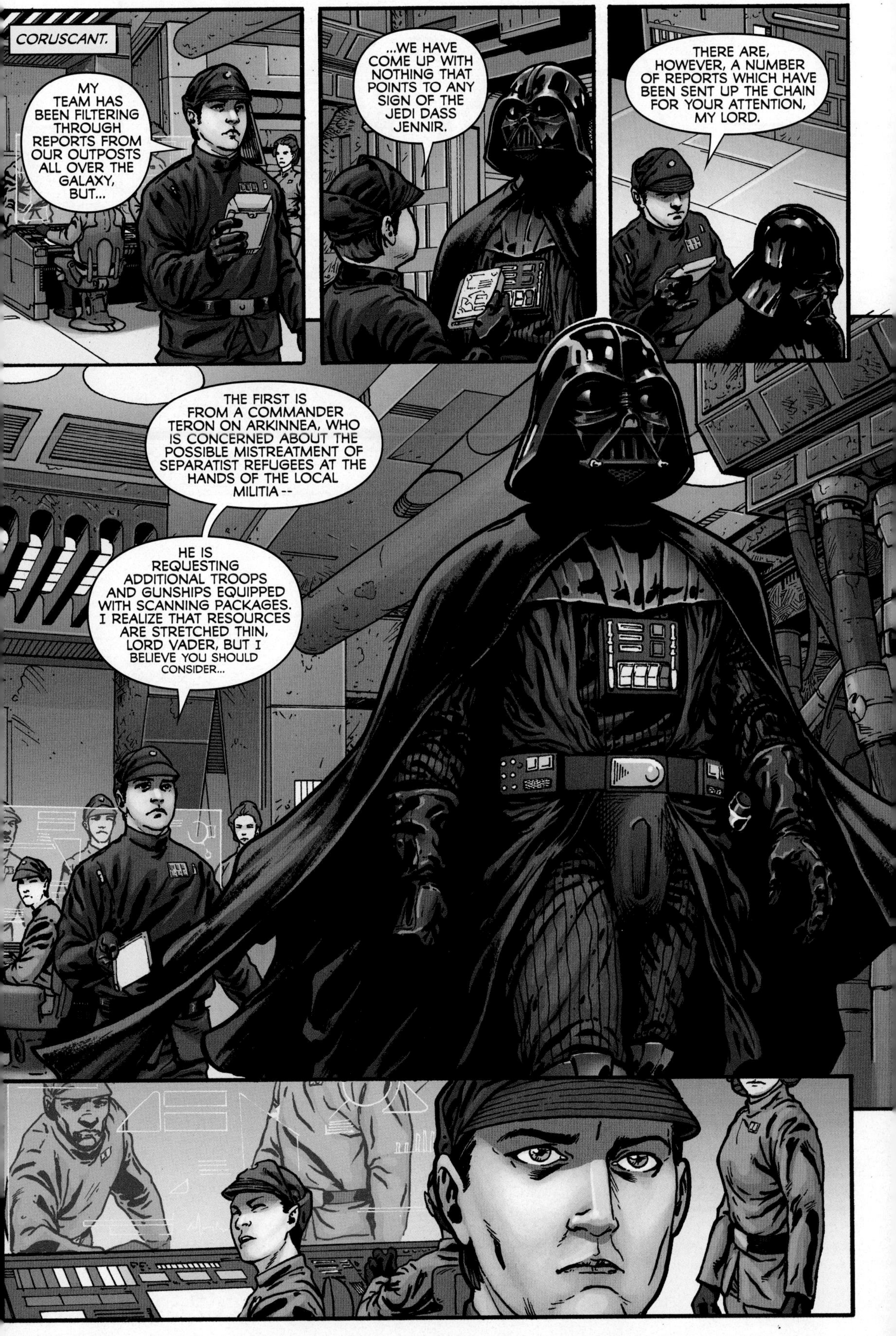
CORUSCANT.
MY TEAM HAS BEEN FILTERING THROUGH REPORTS FROM OUR OUTPOSTS ALL OVER THE GALAXY, BUT...
...WE HAVE COME UP WITH NOTHING THAT POINTS TO ANY SIGN OF THE JEDI DASS JENNIR.
THERE ARE, HOWEVER, A NUMBER OF REPORTS WHICH HAVE BEEN SENT UP THE CHAIN FOR YOUR ATTENTION, MY LORD.
THE FIRST IS FROM A COMMANDER TERON ON ARKINNEA, WHO IS CONCERNED ABOUT THE POSSIBLE MISTREATMENT OF SEPARATIST REFUGEES AT THE HANDS OF THE LOCAL MILITIA --
HE IS REQUESTING ADDITIONAL TROOPS AND GUNSHIPS EQUIPPED WITH SCANNING PACKAGES. I REALIZE THAT RESOURCES ARE STRETCHED THIN, LORD VADER, BUT I BELIEVE YOU SHOULD CONSIDER...

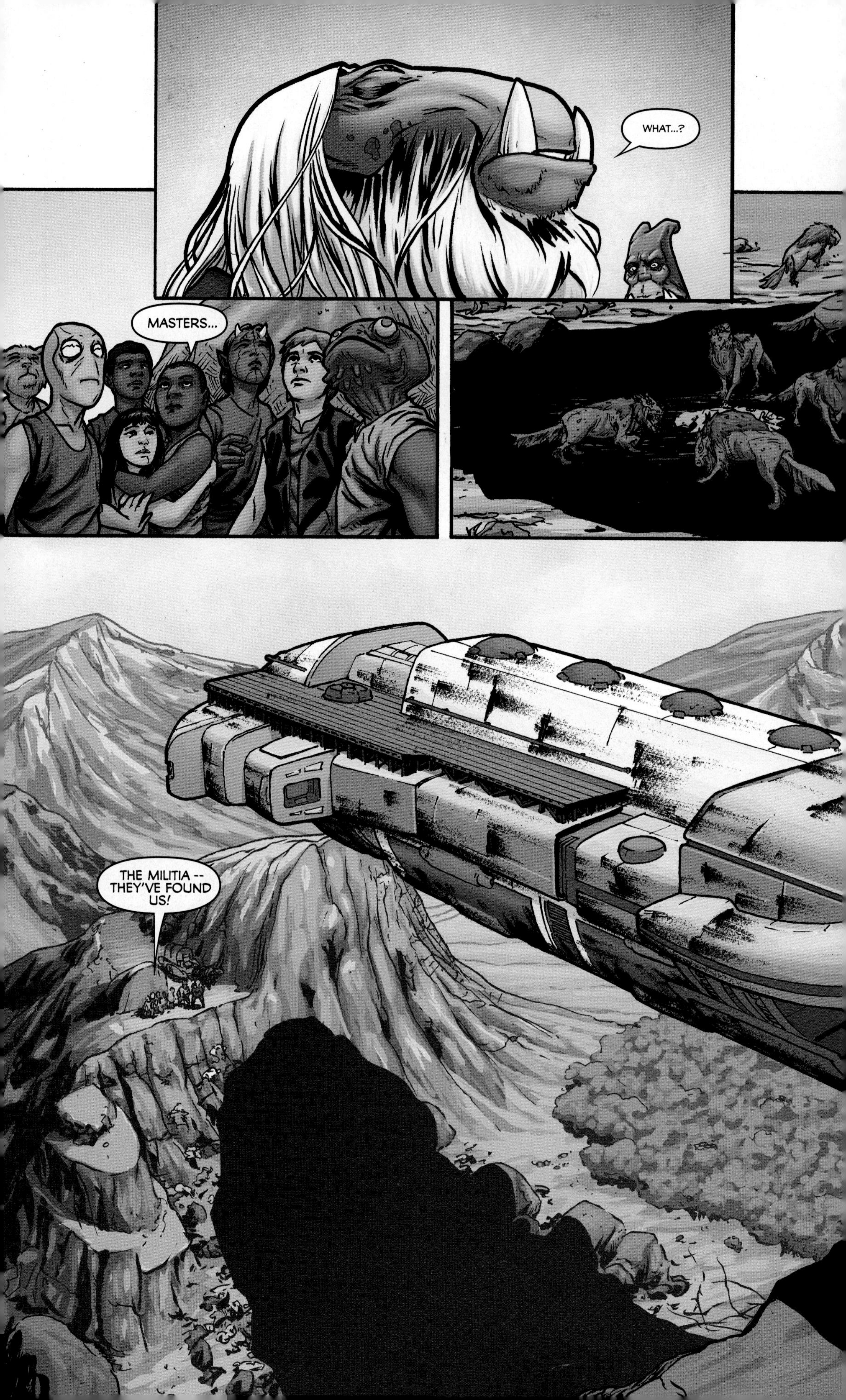
WHAT...?
MASTERS...
THE MILITIA -- THEY'VE FOUND US!

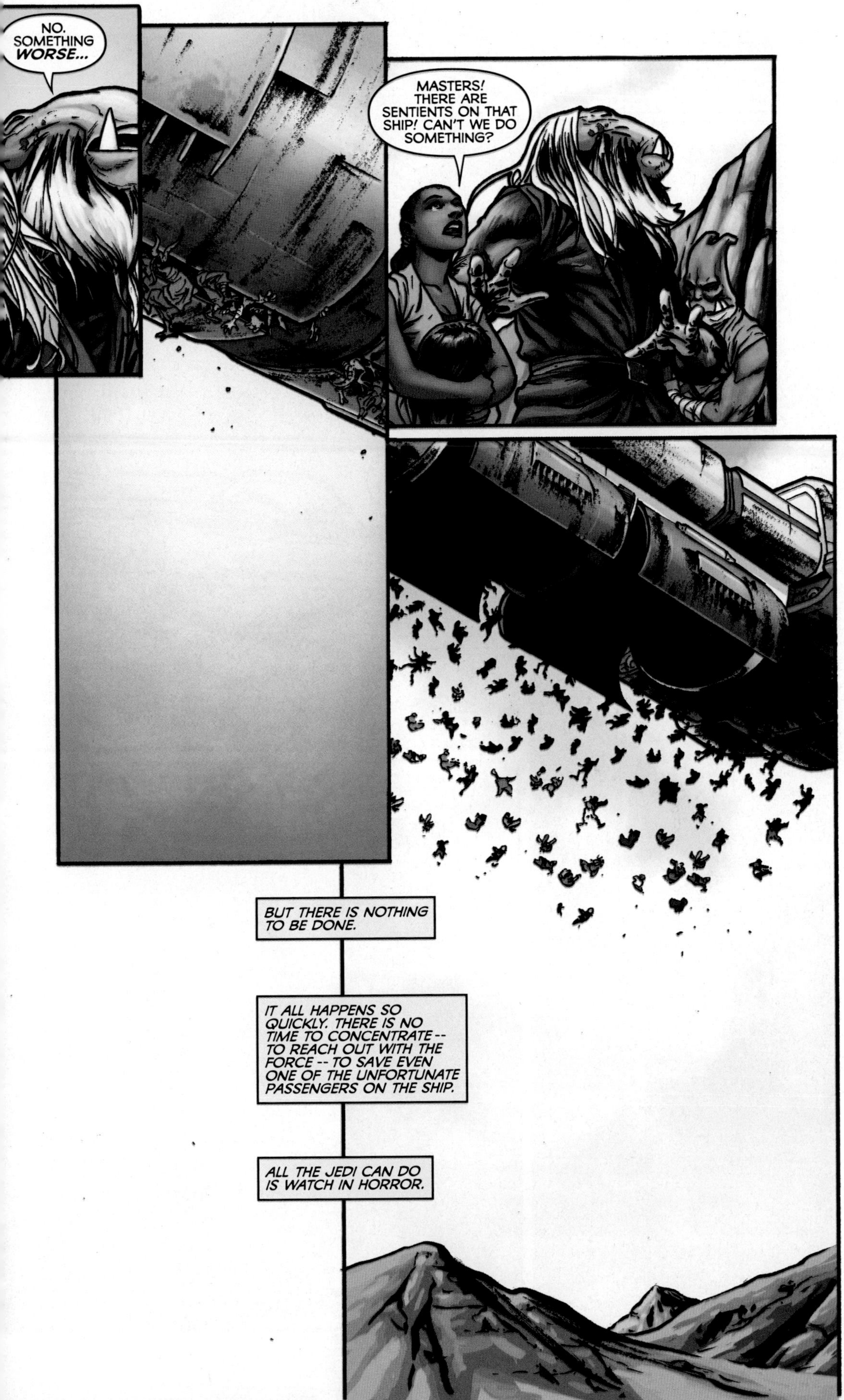
NO. SOMETHING WORSE...
MASTERS! THERE ARE SENTIENTS ON THAT SHIP! CAN'T WE DO SOMETHING?
BUT THERE IS NOTHING TO BE DONE.
IT ALL HAPPENS SO QUICKLY. THERE IS NO TIME TO CONCENTRATE -- TO REACH OUT WITH THE FORCE -- TO SAVE EVEN ONE OF THE UNFORTUNATE PASSENGERS ON THE SHIP.
ALL THE JEDI CAN DO IS WATCH IN HORROR.

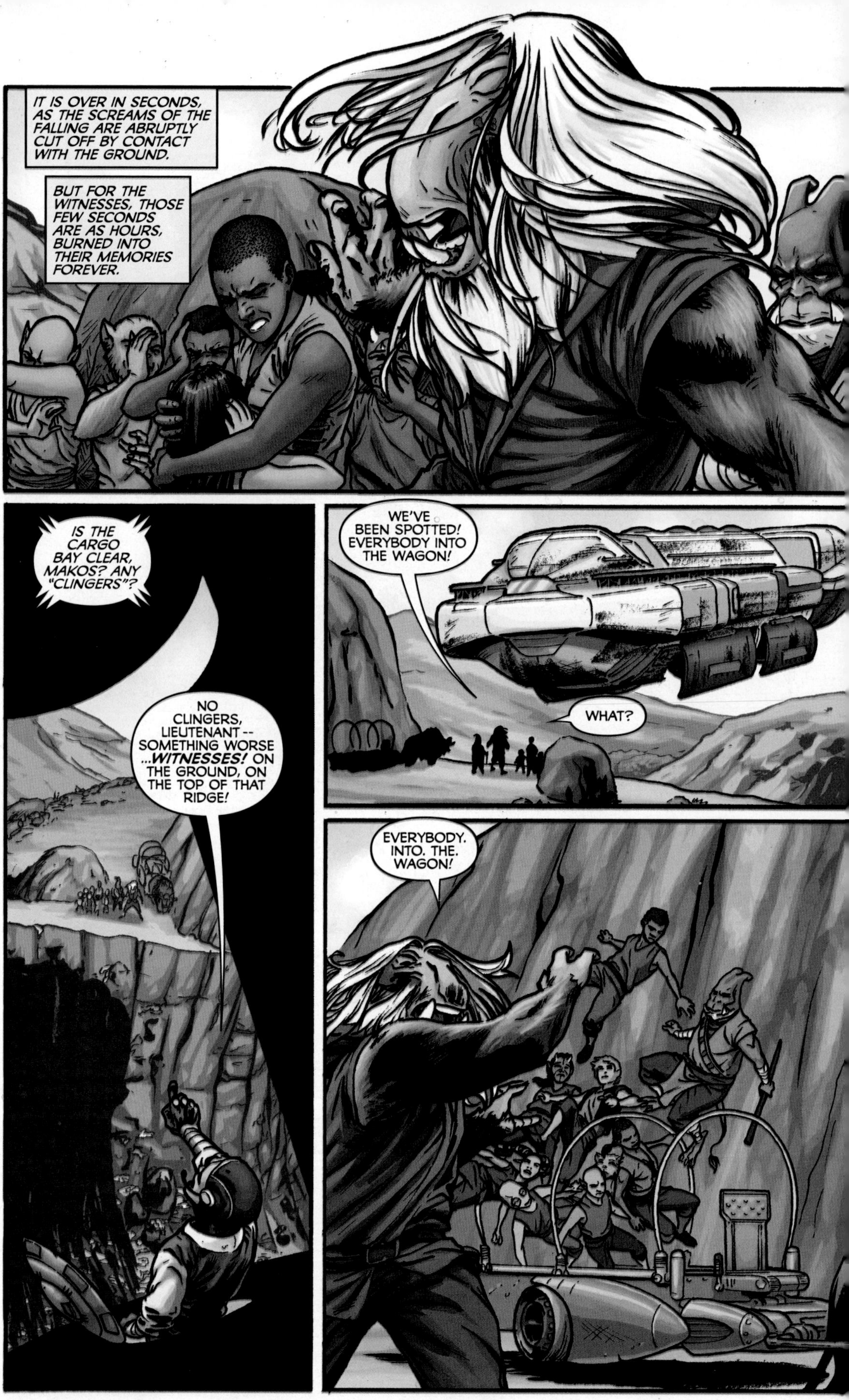
IT IS OVER IN SECONDS, AS THE SCREAMS OF THE FALLING ARE ABRUPTLY CUT OFF BY CONTACT WITH THE GROUND.
BUT FOR THE WITNESSES, THOSE FEW SECONDS ARE AS HOURS, BURNED INTO THEIR MEMORIES FOREVER.
IS THE CARGO BAY CLEAR, MAKOS? ANY "CLINGERS"?
NO CLINGERS, LIEUTENANT -- SOMETHING WORSE ...WITNESSES! ON THE GROUND, ON THE TOP OF THAT RIDGE!
WE'VE BEEN SPOTTED! EVERYBODY INTO THE WAGON!
WHAT?
EVERYBODY. INTO. THE. WAGON!

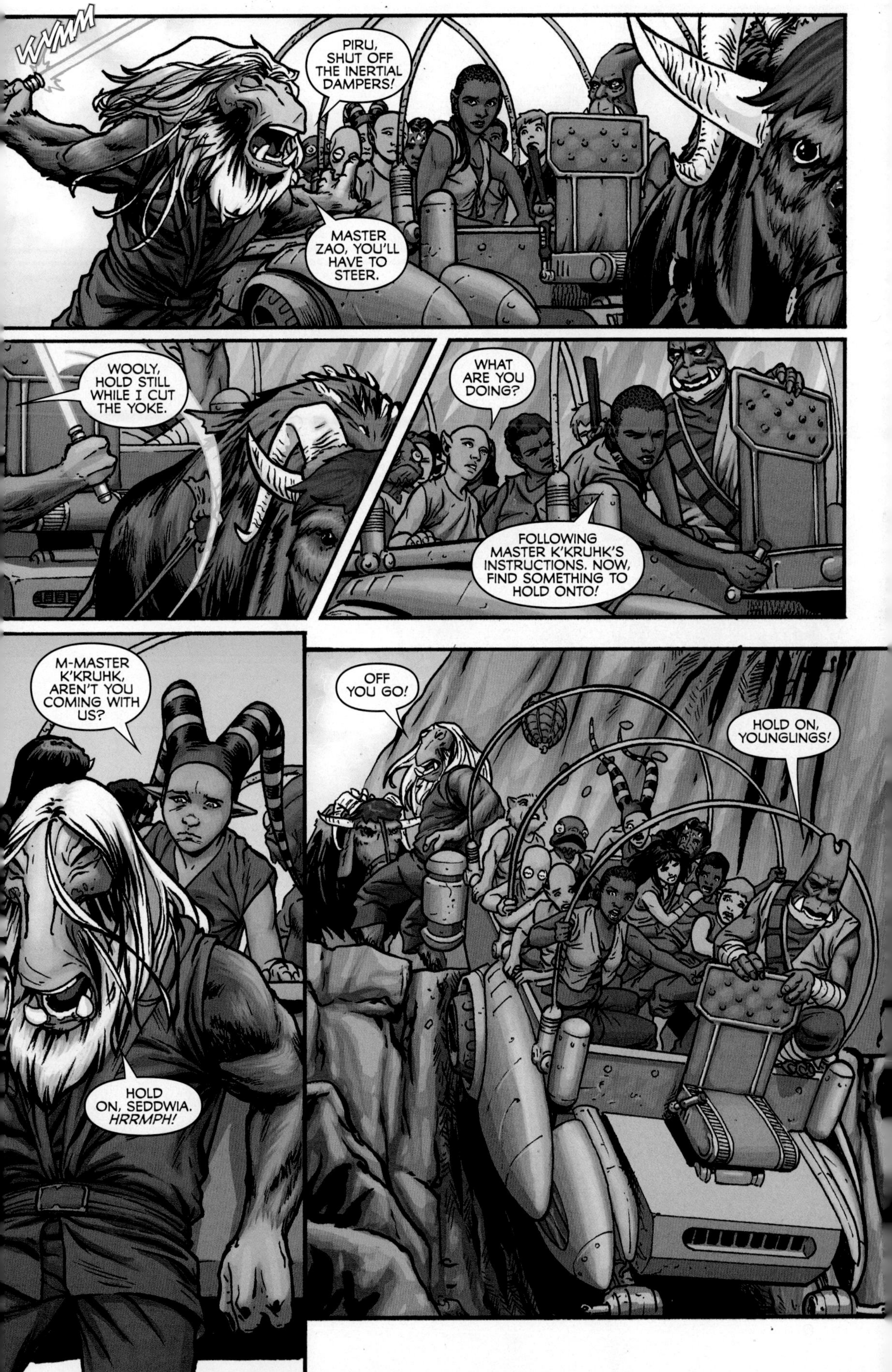
WVMM
PIRU, SHUT OFF THE INERTIAL DAMPERS!
MASTER ZAO, YOU'LL HAVE TO STEER.
WOOLY, HOLD STILL WHILE I CUT THE YOKE.
WHAT ARE YOU DOING?
FOLLOWING MASTER K'KRUHK'S INSTRUCTIONS. NOW, FIND SOMETHING TO HOLD ONTO!
M-MASTER K'KRUHK, AREN'T YOU COMING WITH US?
HOLD ON, SEDDWIA. *HRRMPH!*
OFF YOU GO!
HOLD ON, YOUNGLINGS!

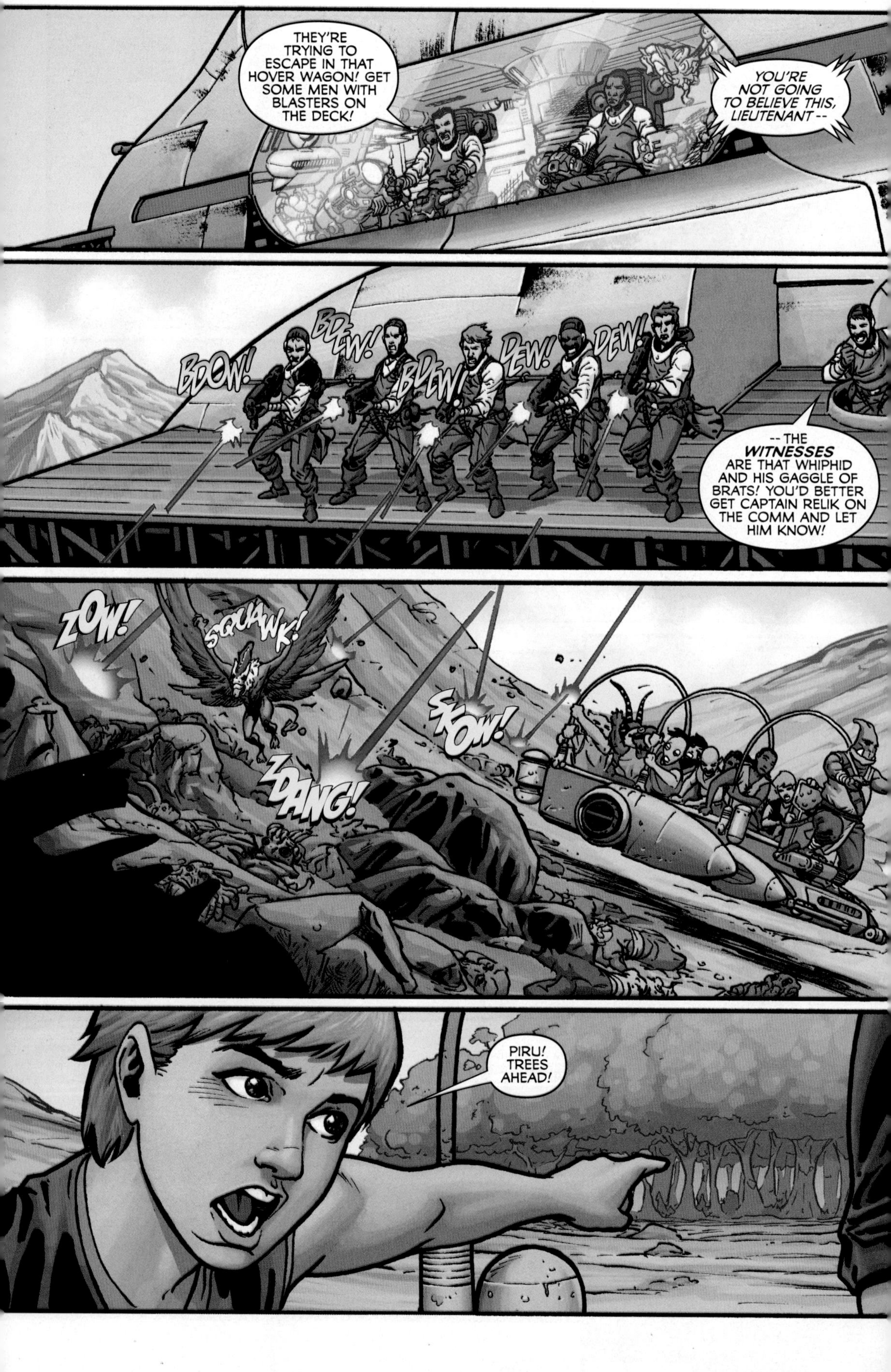
THEY'RE TRYING TO ESCAPE IN THAT HOVER WAGON! GET SOME MEN WITH BLASTERS ON THE DECK!
YOU'RE NOT GOING TO BELIEVE THIS, LIEUTENANT --
BDOW!
BDEW!
BDEW!
DEW!
DEW!
-- THE WITNESSES ARE THAT WHIPHID AND HIS GAGGLE OF BRATS! YOU'D BETTER GET CAPTAIN RELIK ON THE COMM AND LET HIM KNOW!
ZOW!
SQUAWK!
SKOW!
ZDANG!
PIRU! TREES AHEAD!

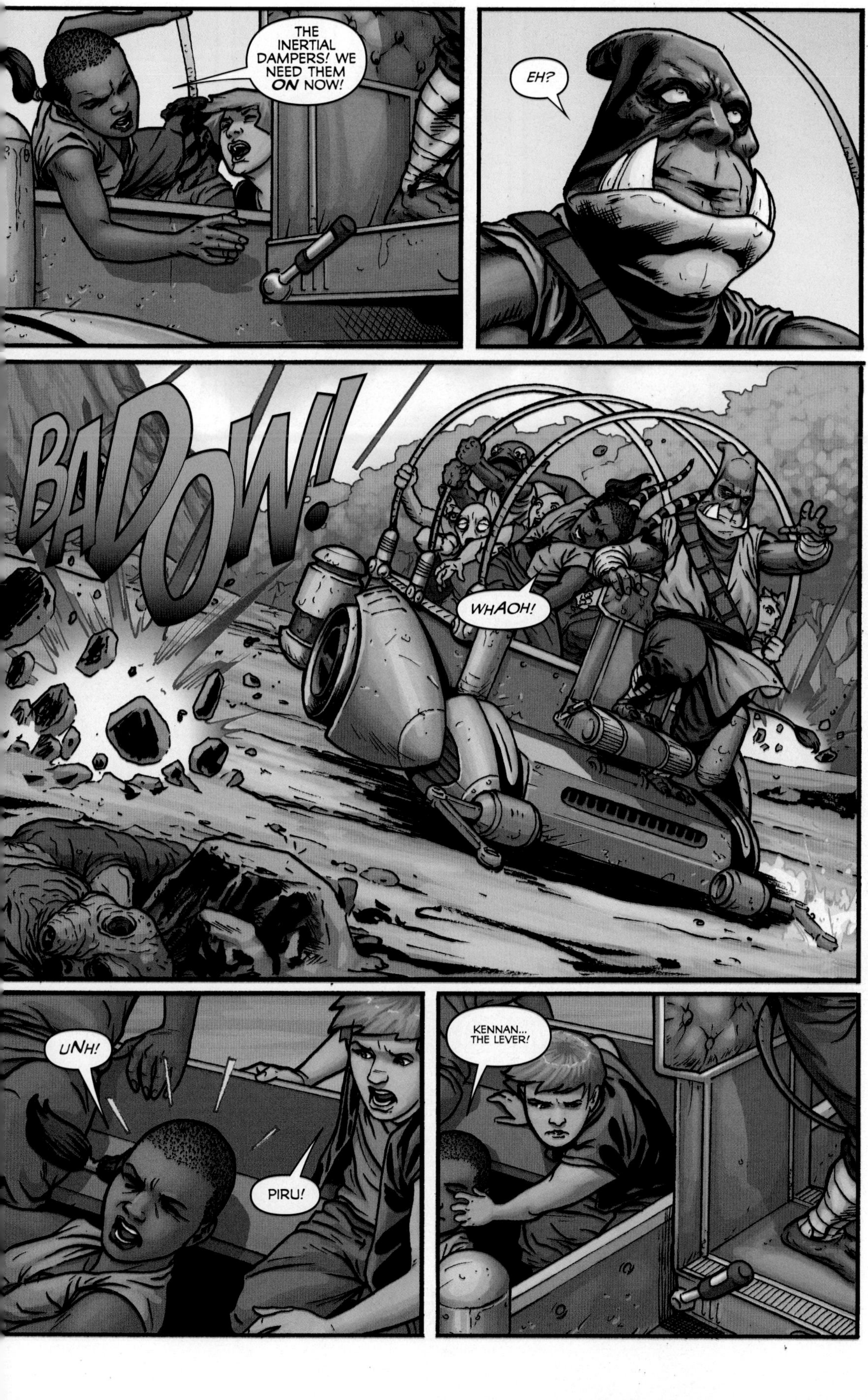
THE INERTIAL DAMPERS! WE NEED THEM ON NOW!
EH?
BADOW!!
WHAOH!
UNH!
PIRU!
KENNAN... THE LEVER!

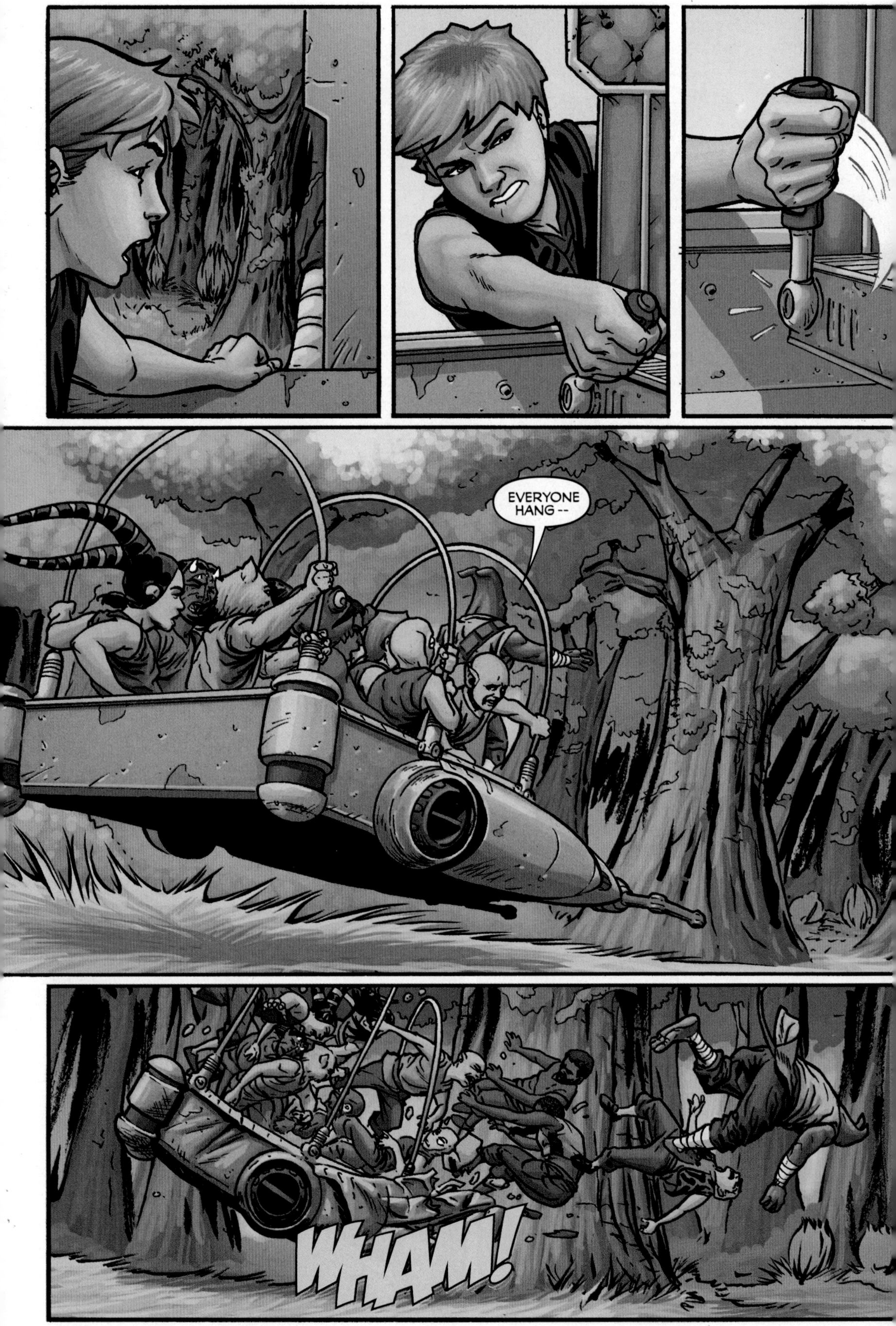
EVERYONE HANG --
WHAM!

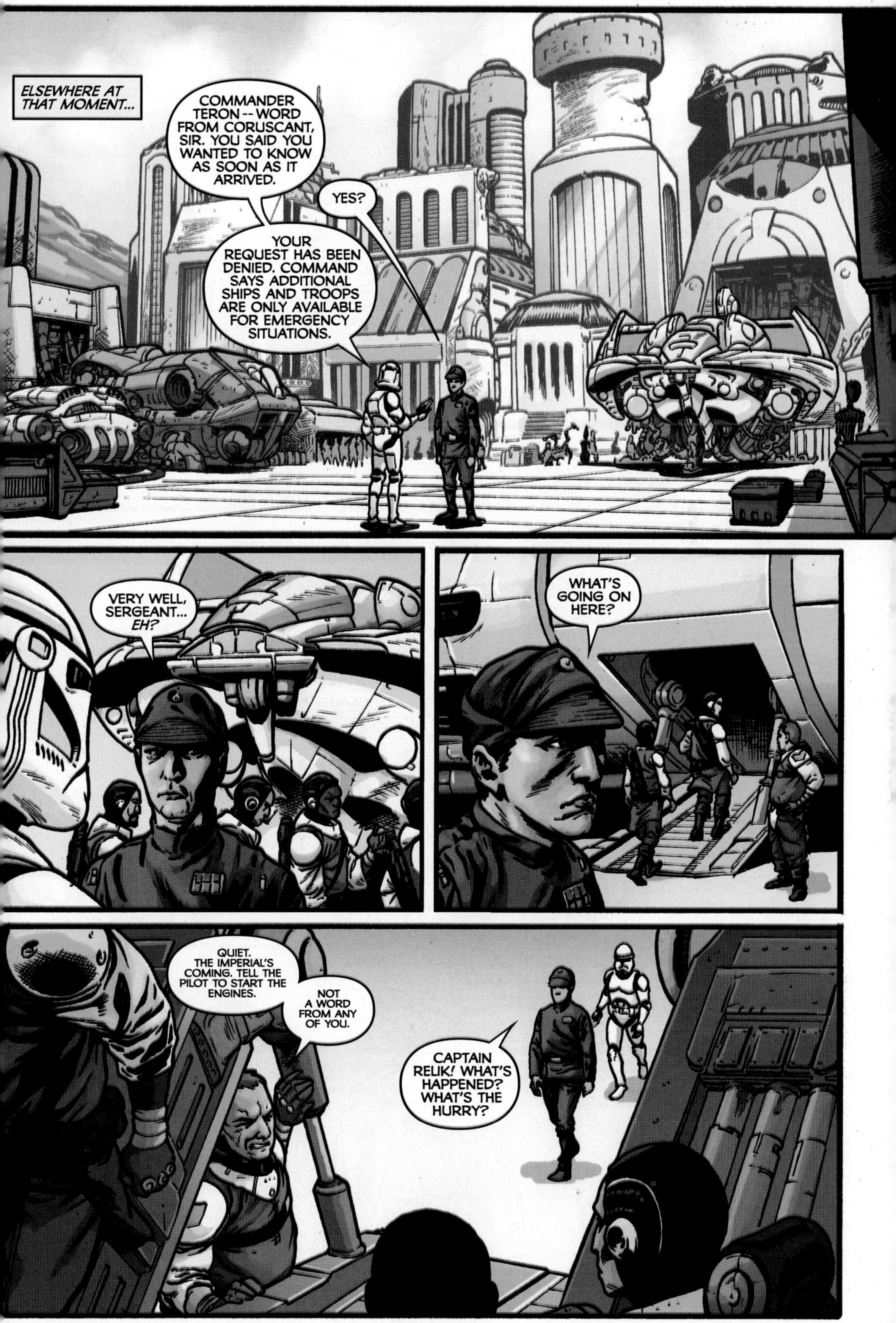
ELSEWHERE AT THAT MOMENT...
COMMANDER TERON -- WORD FROM CORUSCANT, SIR. YOU SAID YOU WANTED TO KNOW AS SOON AS IT ARRIVED.
YES?
YOUR REQUEST HAS BEEN DENIED. COMMAND SAYS ADDITIONAL SHIPS AND TROOPS ARE ONLY AVAILABLE FOR EMERGENCY SITUATIONS.
VERY WELL, SERGEANT... *EH?*
WHAT'S GOING ON HERE?
QUIET. THE IMPERIAL'S COMING. TELL THE PILOT TO START THE ENGINES.
NOT A WORD FROM ANY OF YOU.
CAPTAIN RELIK! WHAT'S HAPPENED? WHAT'S THE HURRY?

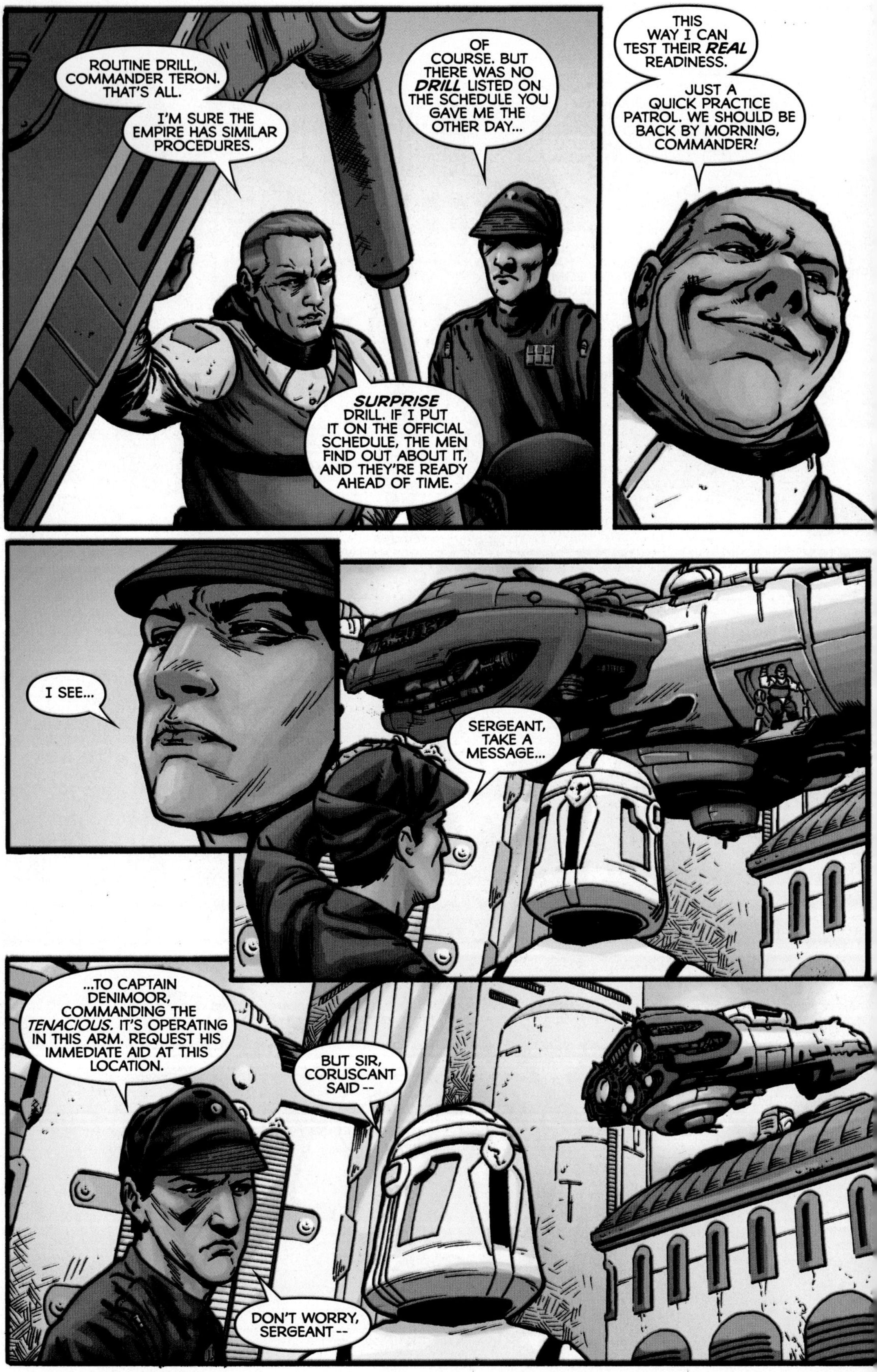
ROUTINE DRILL, COMMANDER TERON. THAT'S ALL.
I'M SURE THE EMPIRE HAS SIMILAR PROCEDURES.
OF COURSE. BUT THERE WAS NO *DRILL* LISTED ON THE SCHEDULE YOU GAVE ME THE OTHER DAY...
*SURPRISE* DRILL. IF I PUT IT ON THE OFFICIAL SCHEDULE, THE MEN FIND OUT ABOUT IT, AND THEY'RE READY AHEAD OF TIME.
THIS WAY I CAN TEST THEIR *REAL* READINESS.
JUST A QUICK PRACTICE PATROL. WE SHOULD BE BACK BY MORNING, COMMANDER!
I SEE...
SERGEANT, TAKE A MESSAGE...
...TO CAPTAIN DENIMOOR, COMMANDING THE *TENACIOUS.* IT'S OPERATING IN THIS ARM. REQUEST HIS IMMEDIATE AID AT THIS LOCATION.
BUT SIR, CORUSCANT SAID --
DON'T WORRY, SERGEANT --

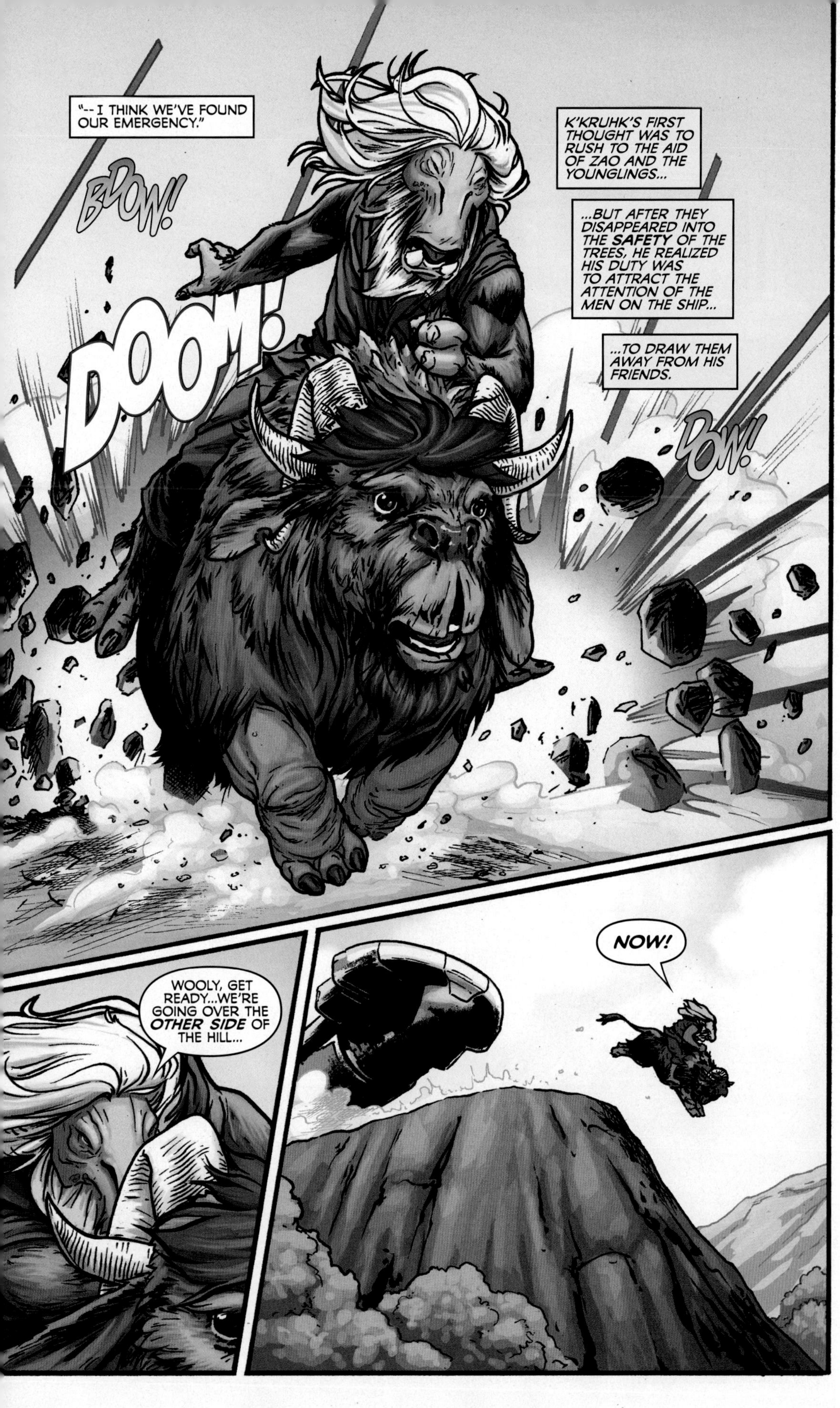
"-- I THINK WE'VE FOUND OUR EMERGENCY."
BDOW!
K'KRUHK'S FIRST THOUGHT WAS TO RUSH TO THE AID OF ZAO AND THE YOUNGLINGS...
...BUT AFTER THEY DISAPPEARED INTO THE SAFETY OF THE TREES, HE REALIZED HIS DUTY WAS TO ATTRACT THE ATTENTION OF THE MEN ON THE SHIP...
DOOM!
...TO DRAW THEM AWAY FROM HIS FRIENDS.
DOW!
WOOLY, GET READY...WE'RE GOING OVER THE OTHER SIDE OF THE HILL...
NOW!

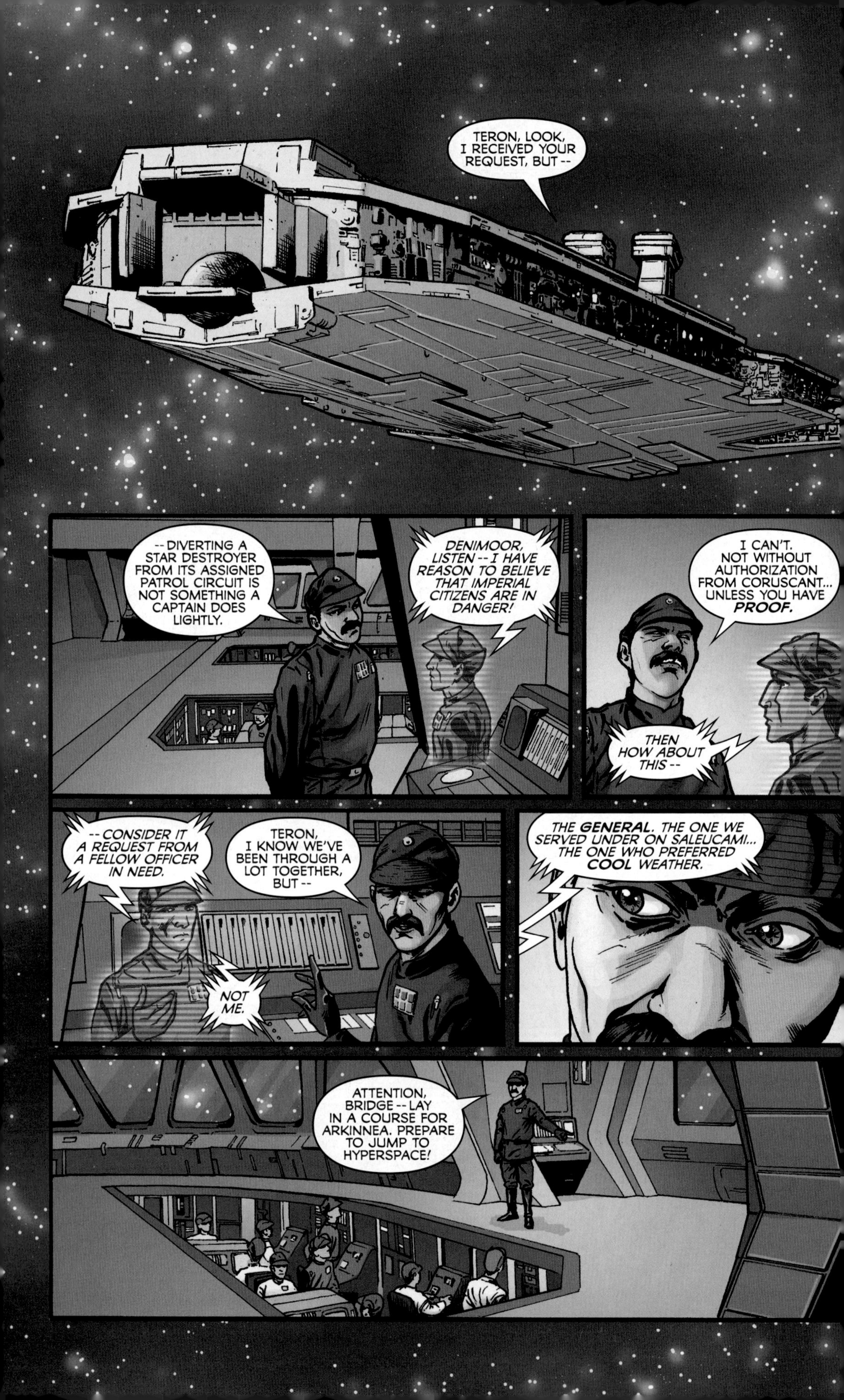
TERON, LOOK, I RECEIVED YOUR REQUEST, BUT --
-- DIVERTING A STAR DESTROYER FROM ITS ASSIGNED PATROL CIRCUIT IS NOT SOMETHING A CAPTAIN DOES LIGHTLY.
DENIMOOR, LISTEN -- I HAVE REASON TO BELIEVE THAT IMPERIAL CITIZENS ARE IN DANGER!
I CAN'T. NOT WITHOUT AUTHORIZATION FROM CORUSCANT... UNLESS YOU HAVE PROOF.
THEN HOW ABOUT THIS --
-- CONSIDER IT A REQUEST FROM A FELLOW OFFICER IN NEED.
TERON, I KNOW WE'VE BEEN THROUGH A LOT TOGETHER, BUT --
NOT ME.
THE GENERAL. THE ONE WE SERVED UNDER ON SALEUCAMI... THE ONE WHO PREFERRED COOL WEATHER.
ATTENTION, BRIDGE -- LAY IN A COURSE FOR ARKINNEA. PREPARE TO JUMP TO HYPERSPACE!

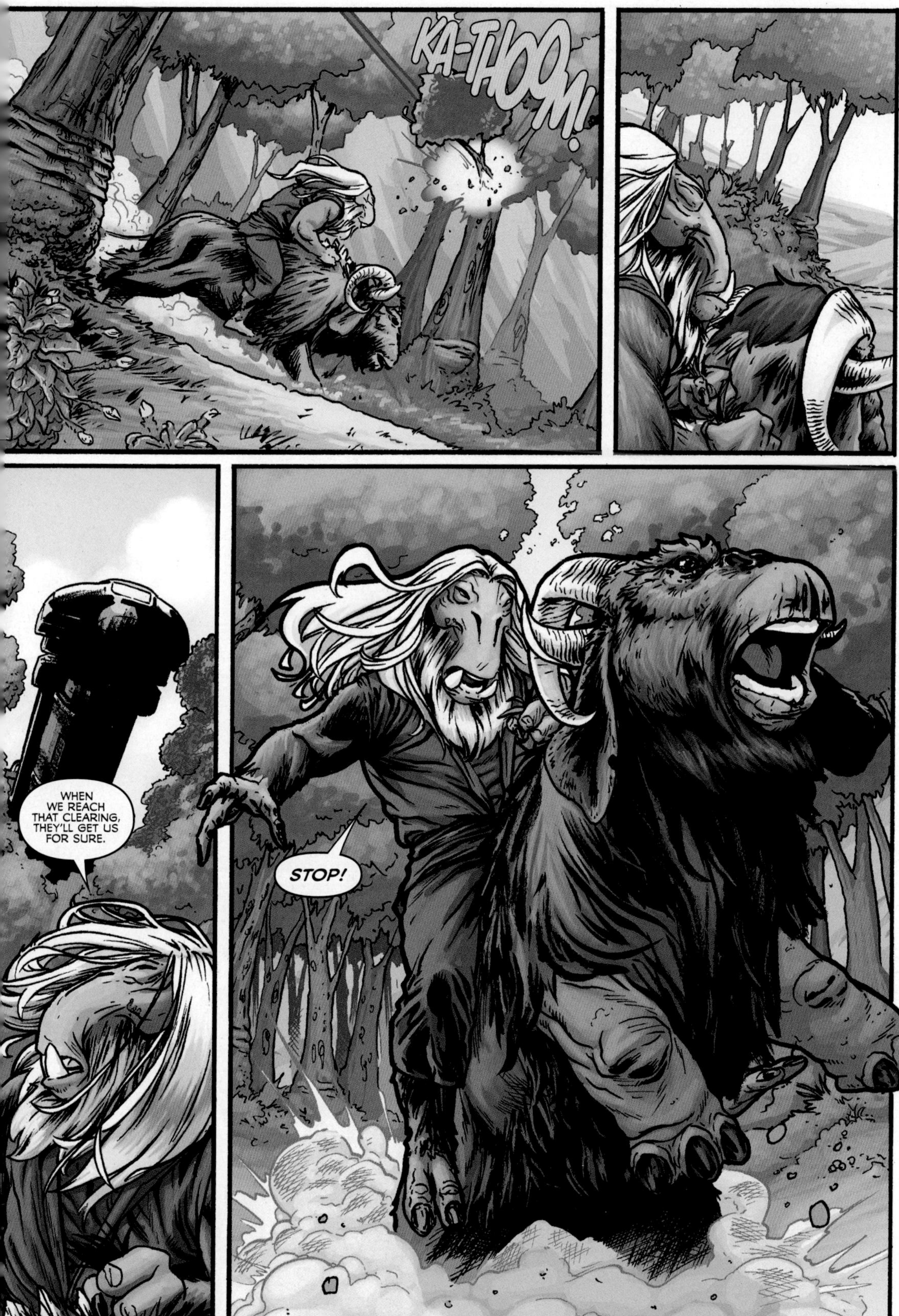
KA-THOOM!
WHEN WE REACH THAT CLEARING, THEY'LL GET US FOR SURE.
STOP!

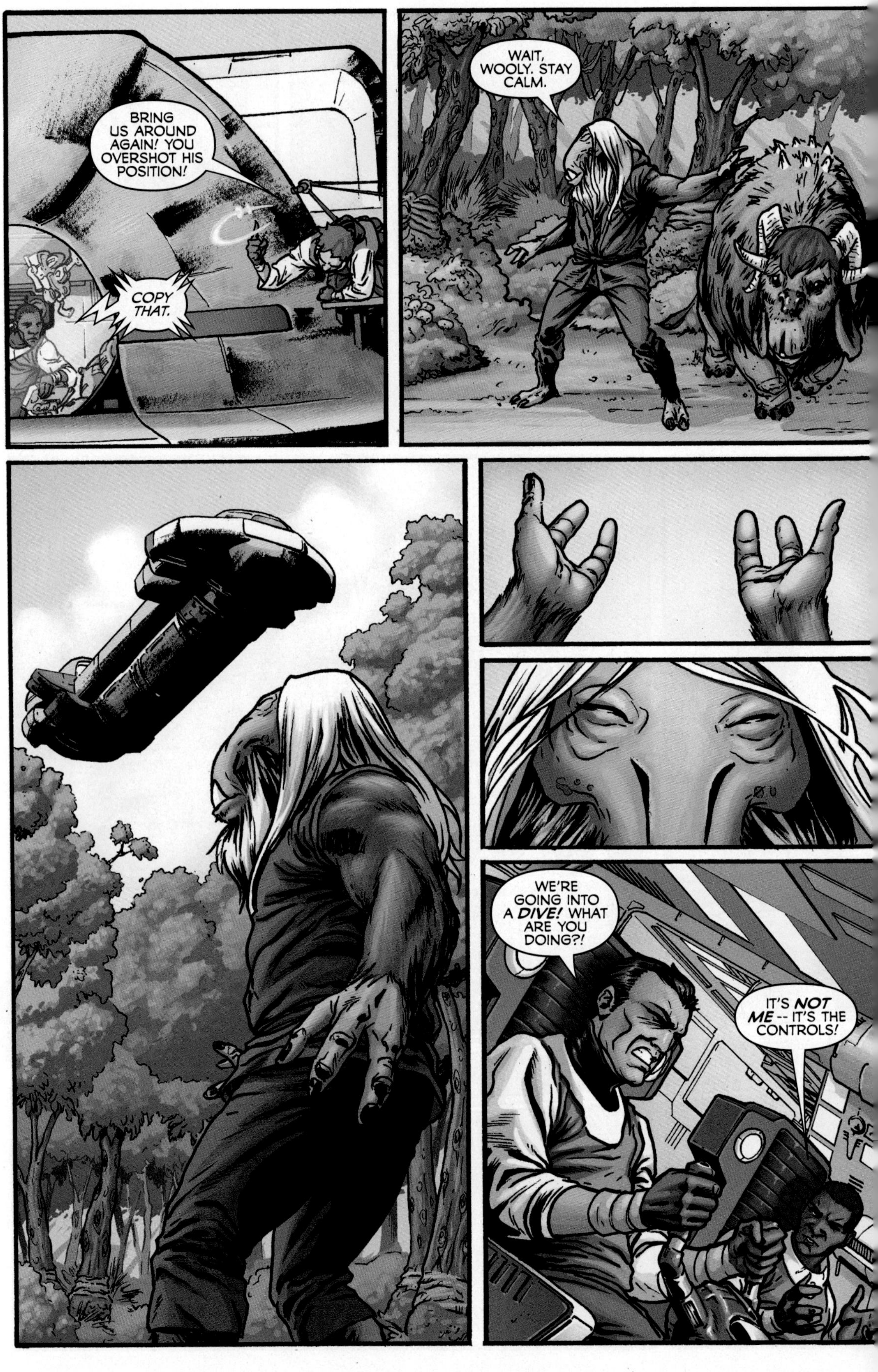
BRING US AROUND AGAIN! YOU OVERSHOT HIS POSITION!
COPY THAT.
WAIT, WOOLY. STAY CALM.
WE'RE GOING INTO A *DIVE!* WHAT ARE YOU DOING?!
IT'S ***NOT ME*** -- IT'S THE CONTROLS!

LIEUTENANT GREGG? I THOUGHT YOU'D WANT TO KNOW -- THE *TENACIOUS* HAS DEVIATED FROM ITS PATROL ROUTE AND IS EN ROUTE TO ARKINNEA.

AFTER LORD VADER HIMSELF TURNED DOWN ARKINNEA'S REQUEST FOR AID? INTERESTING...

THANK YOU, CORPORAL.

SO, THE EMPIRE'S GRIP ISN'T AS *TIGHT* AS EVERYONE THINKS. LOOKS LIKE I'M NOT THE *ONLY ONE* WHO DISOBEYS YOUR "*DARK LORD,*" EH, LIEUTENANT?

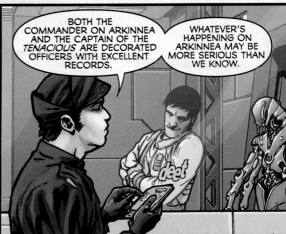

BOTH THE COMMANDER ON ARKINNEA AND THE CAPTAIN OF THE *TENACIOUS* ARE DECORATED OFFICERS WITH EXCELLENT RECORDS.

WHATEVER'S HAPPENING ON ARKINNEA MAY BE MORE SERIOUS THAN WE KNOW.

GET BACK TO YOUR TRAINING, SANG.

*AGGH!* BLAST YOU!

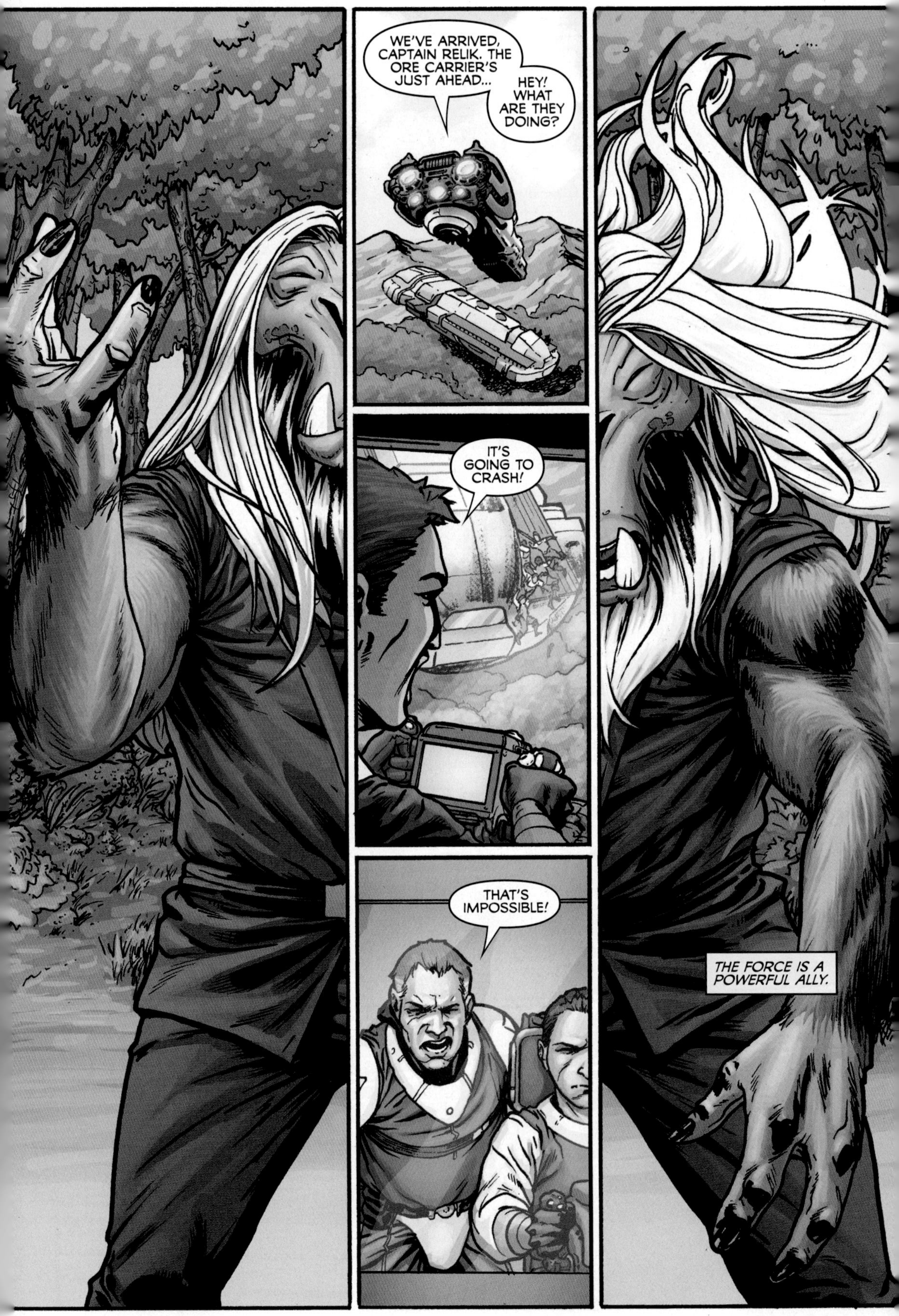
WE'VE ARRIVED, CAPTAIN RELIK. THE ORE CARRIER'S JUST AHEAD...
HEY! WHAT ARE THEY DOING?
IT'S GOING TO CRASH!
THAT'S IMPOSSIBLE!
THE FORCE IS A POWERFUL ALLY.

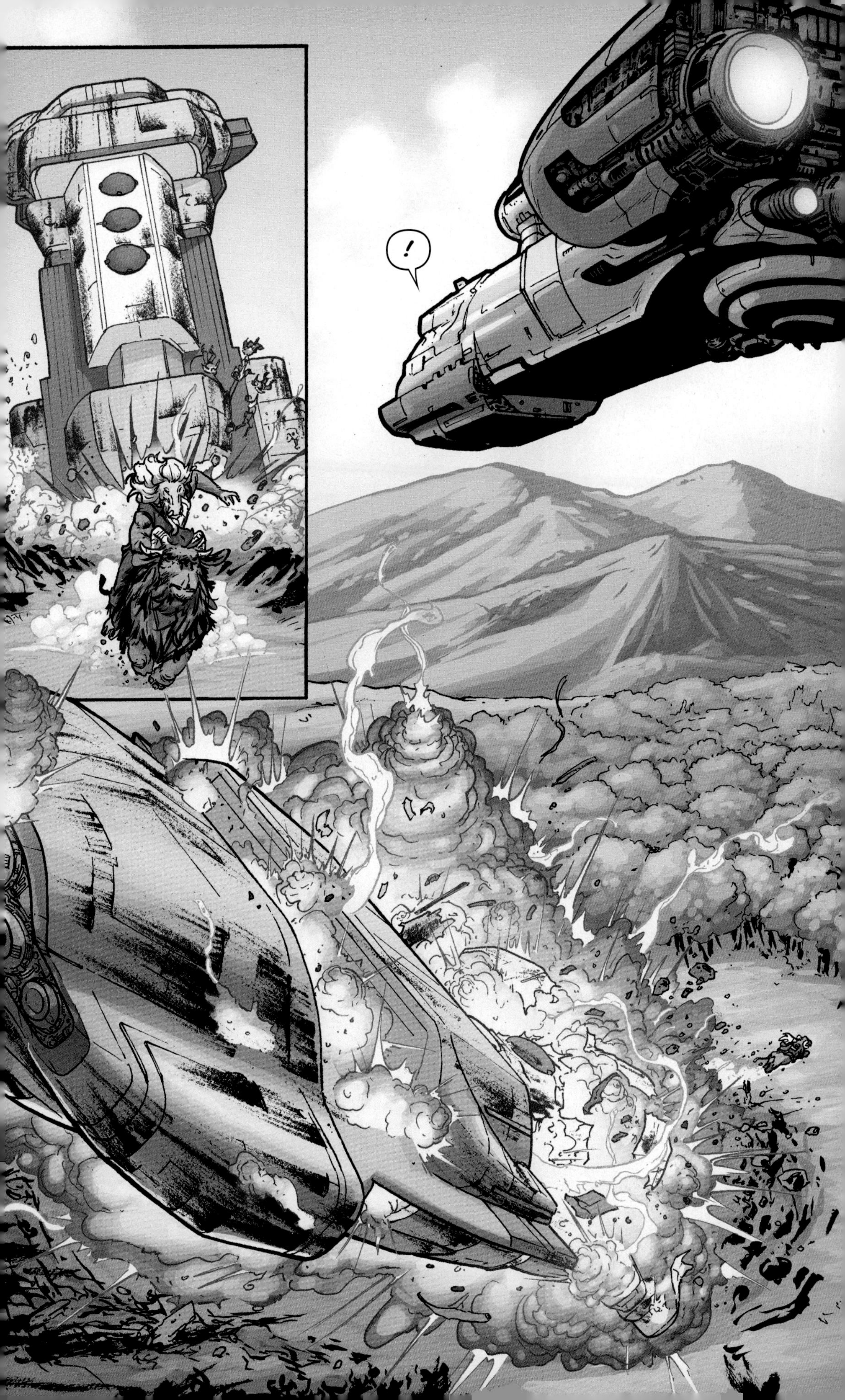
!

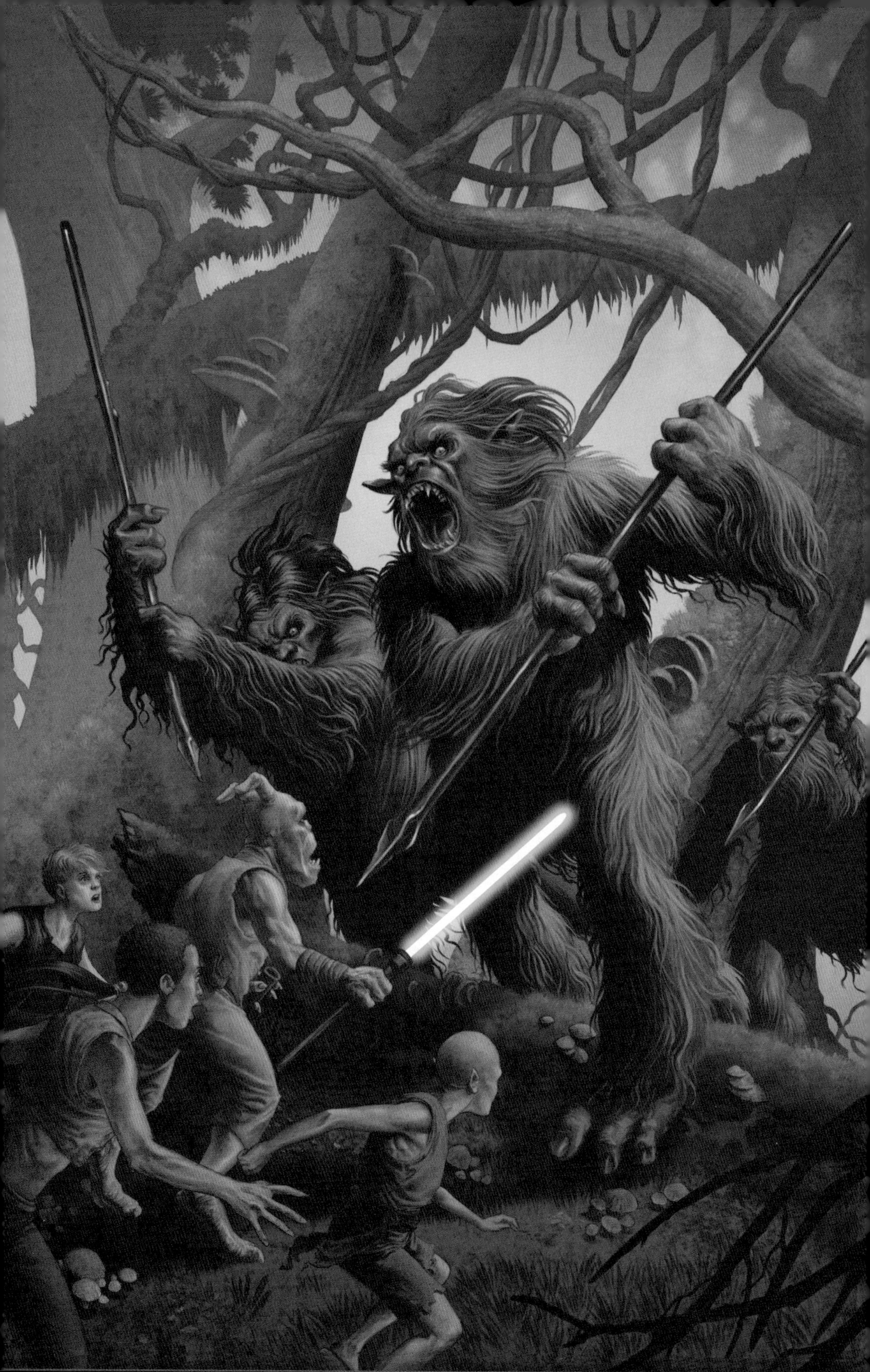

***STAR WARS: DARK TIMES — FIRE CARRIER #4***

WRITER: RANDY STRADLEY • ARTIST: GABRIEL GUZMAN • COLORIST: GARRY HENDERSON • LETTERER: MICHAEL HEISLER
ASSISTANT EDITOR: FREDDYE LINS • EDITOR: DAVE MARSHALL • COVER ARTIST: DOUGLAS WHEATLEY

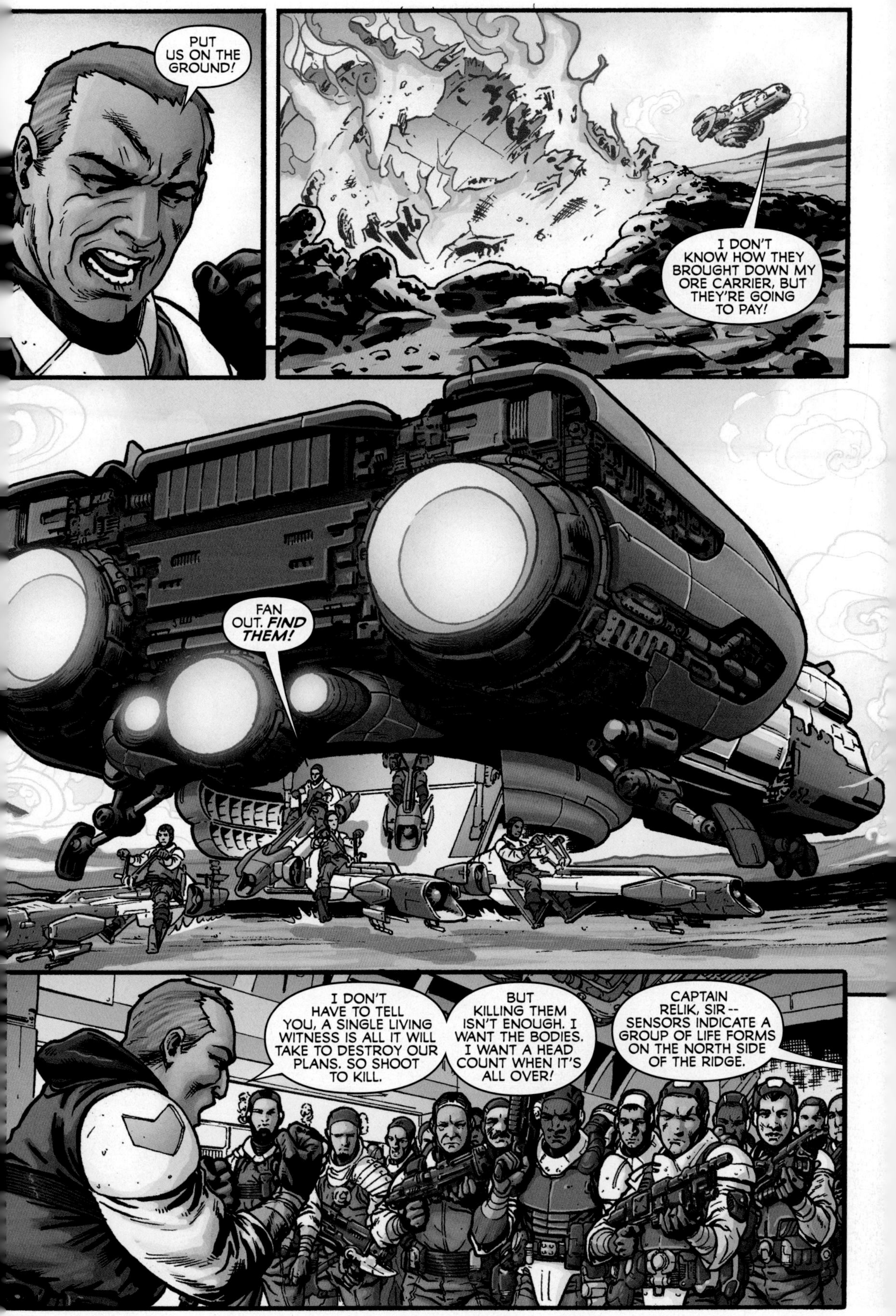
PUT US ON THE GROUND!
I DON'T KNOW HOW THEY BROUGHT DOWN MY ORE CARRIER, BUT THEY'RE GOING TO PAY!
FAN OUT. *FIND THEM!*
I DON'T HAVE TO TELL YOU, A SINGLE LIVING WITNESS IS ALL IT WILL TAKE TO DESTROY OUR PLANS. SO SHOOT TO KILL.
BUT KILLING THEM ISN'T ENOUGH. I WANT THE BODIES. I WANT A HEAD COUNT WHEN IT'S ALL OVER!
CAPTAIN RELIK, SIR -- SENSORS INDICATE A GROUP OF LIFE FORMS ON THE NORTH SIDE OF THE RIDGE.

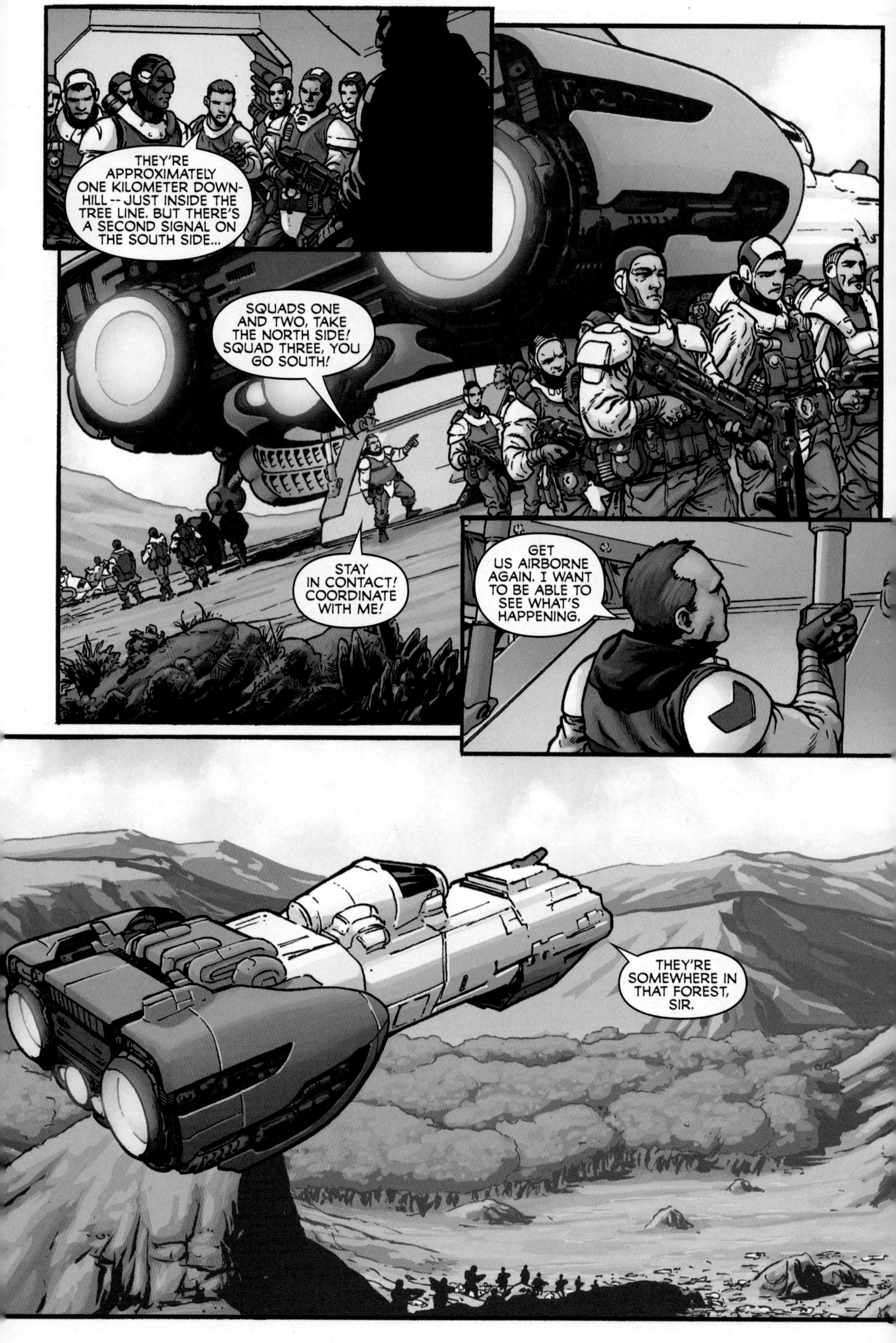
THEY'RE APPROXIMATELY ONE KILOMETER DOWN-HILL -- JUST INSIDE THE TREE LINE. BUT THERE'S A SECOND SIGNAL ON THE SOUTH SIDE...
SQUADS ONE AND TWO, TAKE THE NORTH SIDE! SQUAD THREE, YOU GO SOUTH!
STAY IN CONTACT! COORDINATE WITH ME!
GET US AIRBORNE AGAIN. I WANT TO BE ABLE TO SEE WHAT'S HAPPENING.
THEY'RE SOMEWHERE IN THAT FOREST, SIR.

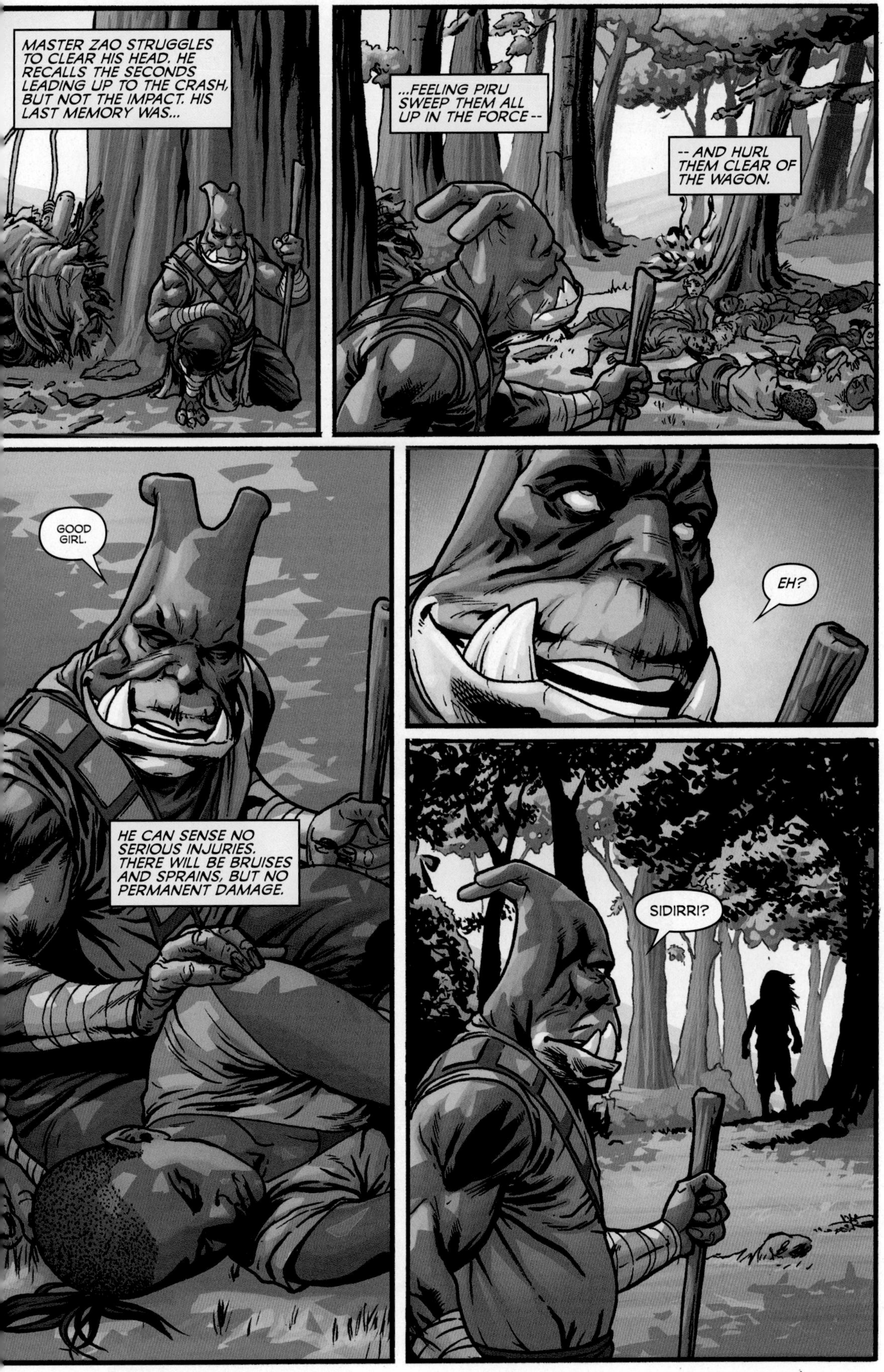
MASTER ZAO STRUGGLES TO CLEAR HIS HEAD. HE RECALLS THE SECONDS LEADING UP TO THE CRASH, BUT NOT THE IMPACT. HIS LAST MEMORY WAS...
...FEELING PIRU SWEEP THEM ALL UP IN THE FORCE --
-- AND HURL THEM CLEAR OF THE WAGON.
GOOD GIRL.
HE CAN SENSE NO SERIOUS INJURIES. THERE WILL BE BRUISES AND SPRAINS, BUT NO PERMANENT DAMAGE.
EH?
SIDIRRI?

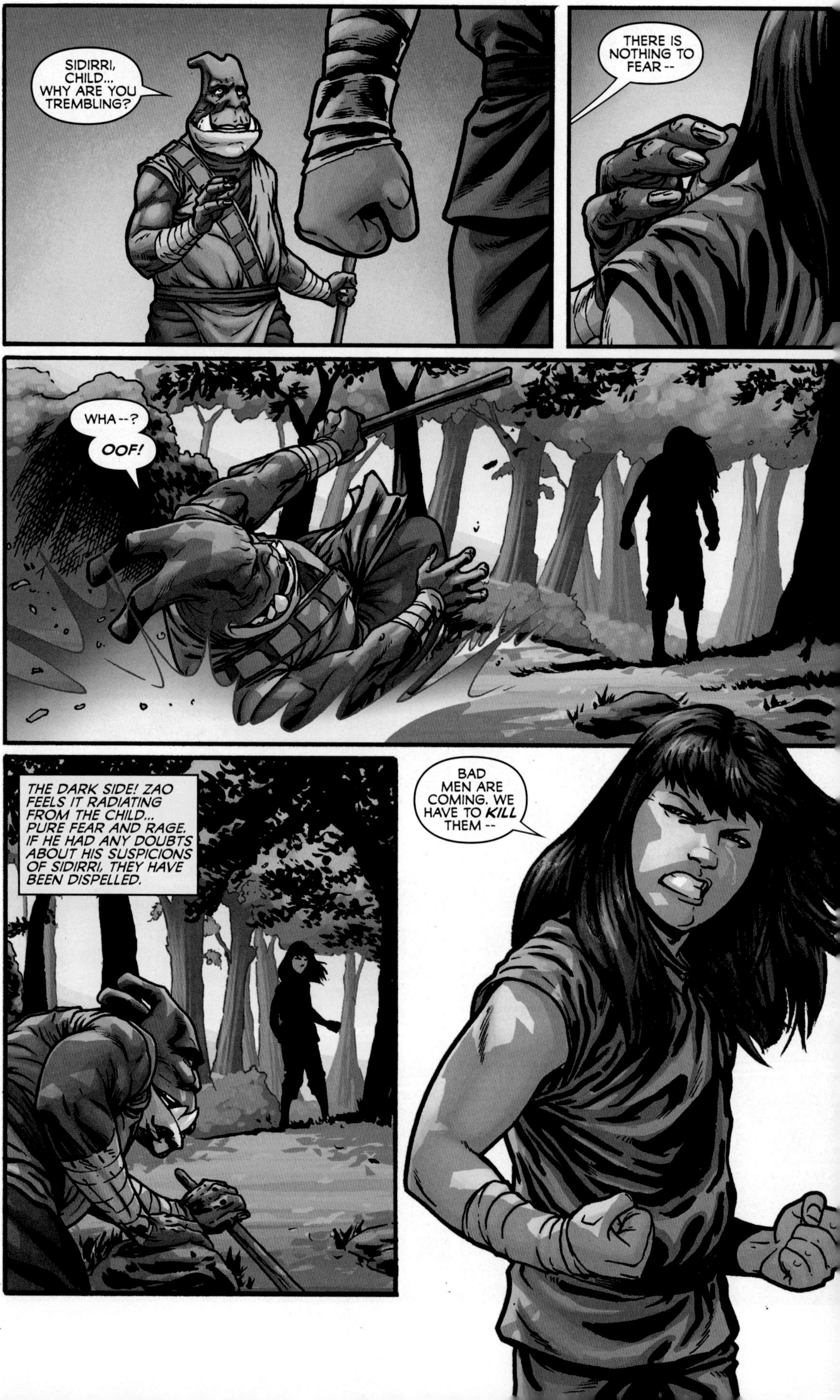
SIDIRRI, CHILD... WHY ARE YOU TREMBLING?
THERE IS NOTHING TO FEAR --
WHA --?
OOF!
THE DARK SIDE! ZAO FEELS IT RADIATING FROM THE CHILD... PURE FEAR AND RAGE. IF HE HAD ANY DOUBTS ABOUT HIS SUSPICIONS OF SIDIRRI, THEY HAVE BEEN DISPELLED.
BAD MEN ARE COMING. WE HAVE TO KILL THEM --

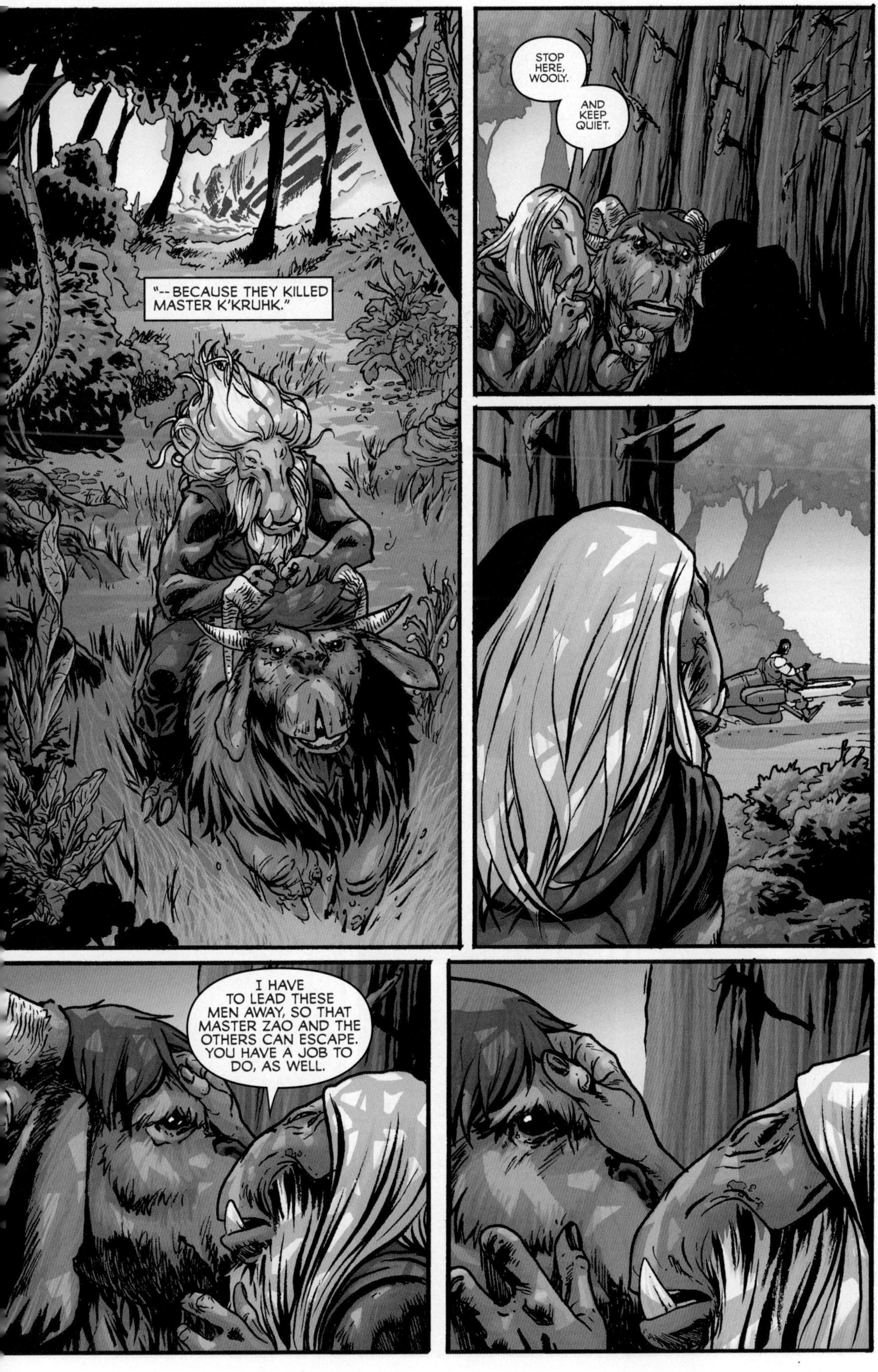
"-- BECAUSE THEY KILLED MASTER K'KRUHK."
STOP HERE, WOOLY.
AND KEEP QUIET.
I HAVE TO LEAD THESE MEN AWAY, SO THAT MASTER ZAO AND THE OTHERS CAN ESCAPE. YOU HAVE A JOB TO DO, AS WELL.

GO NOW.

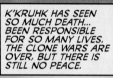

K'KRUHK HAS SEEN SO MUCH DEATH... BEEN RESPONSIBLE FOR SO MANY LIVES. THE CLONE WARS ARE OVER, BUT THERE IS STILL NO PEACE.

I WILL KILL AGAIN ONLY AS A LAST RESORT.

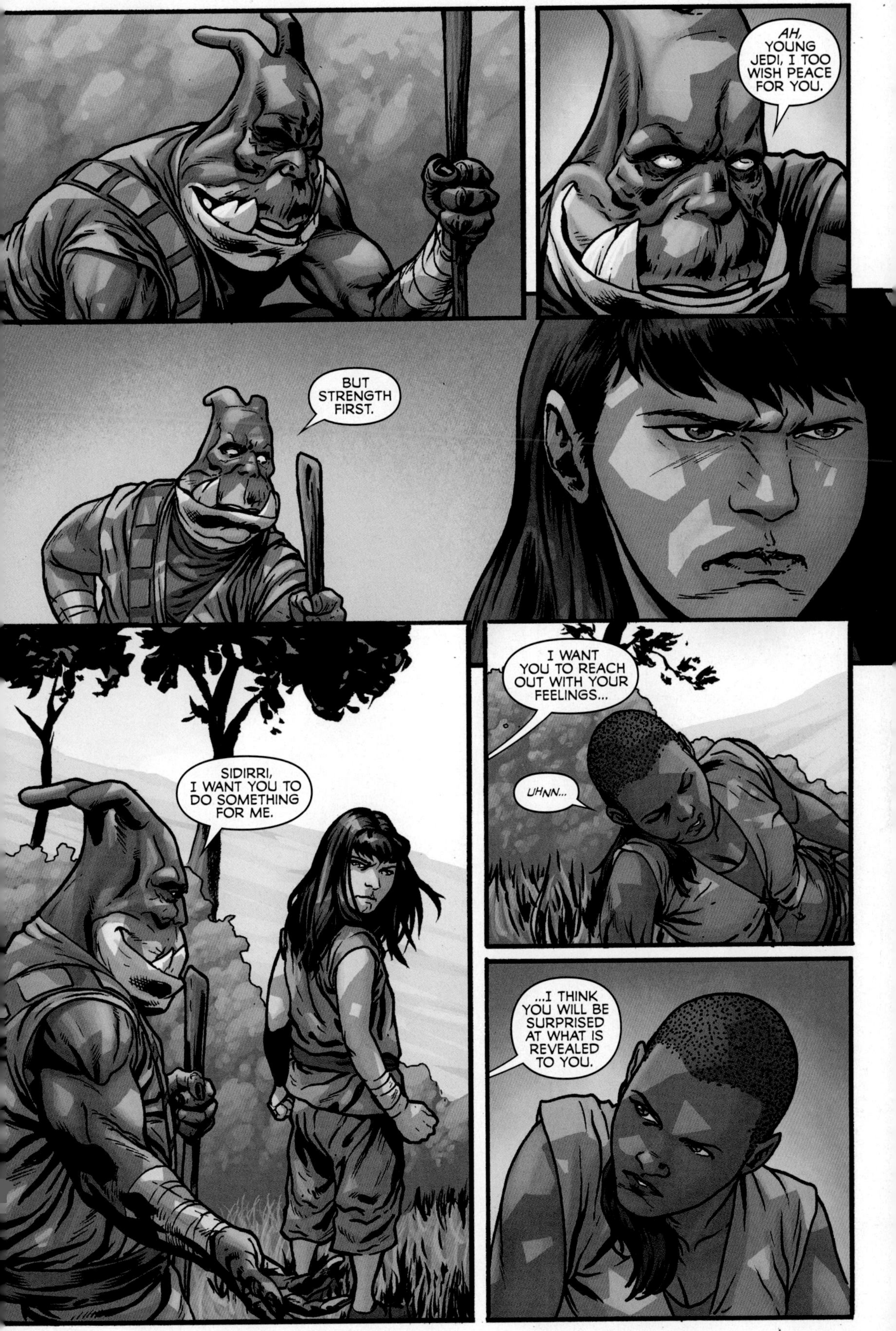
AH, YOUNG JEDI, I TOO WISH PEACE FOR YOU.
BUT STRENGTH FIRST.
SIDIRRI, I WANT YOU TO DO SOMETHING FOR ME.
I WANT YOU TO REACH OUT WITH YOUR FEELINGS...
UHNN...
...I THINK YOU WILL BE SURPRISED AT WHAT IS REVEALED TO YOU.

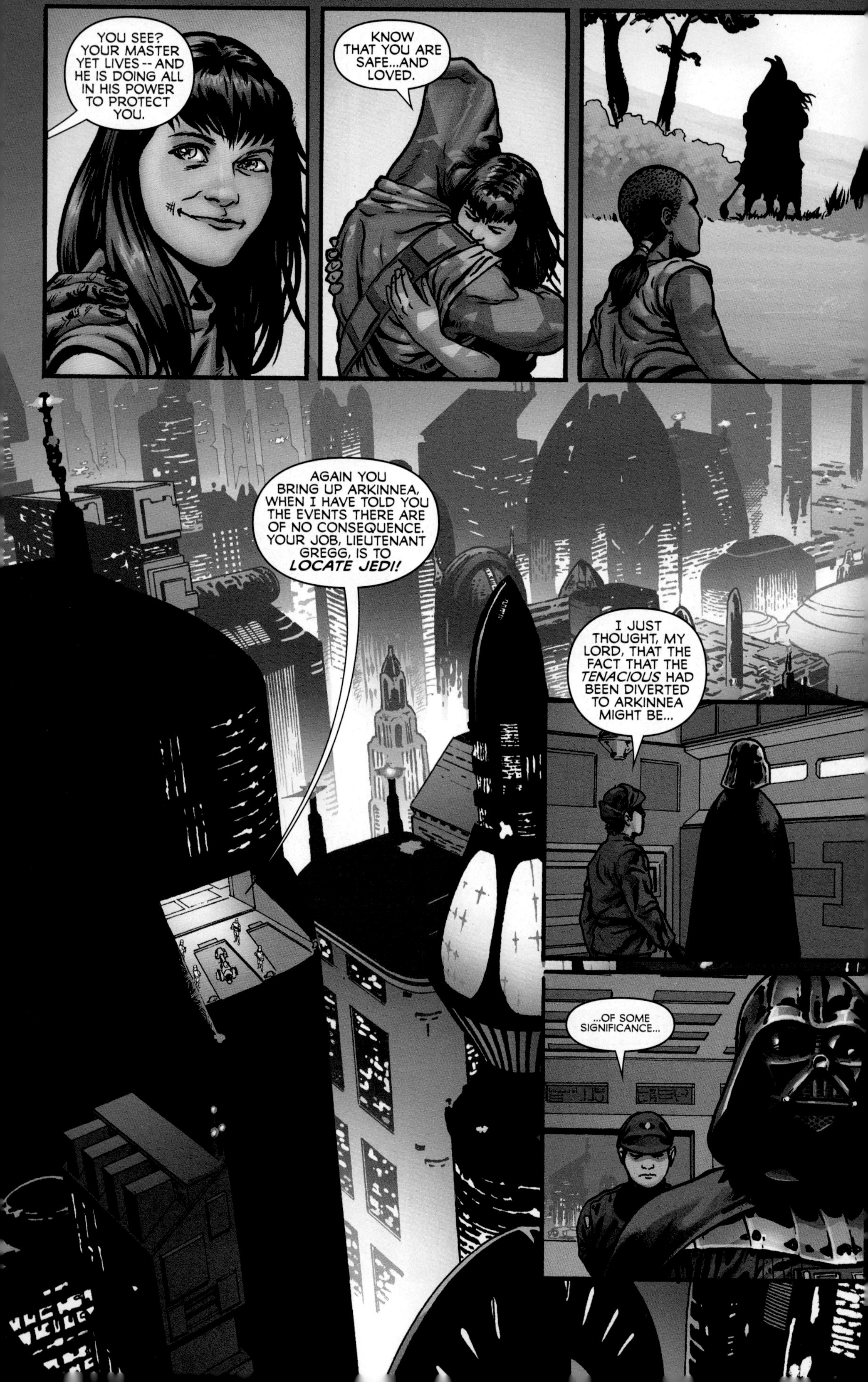
YOU SEE? YOUR MASTER YET LIVES -- AND HE IS DOING ALL IN HIS POWER TO PROTECT YOU.
KNOW THAT YOU ARE SAFE...AND LOVED.
AGAIN YOU BRING UP ARKINNEA, WHEN I HAVE TOLD YOU THE EVENTS THERE ARE OF NO CONSEQUENCE. YOUR JOB, LIEUTENANT GREGG, IS TO ***LOCATE JEDI!***
I JUST THOUGHT, MY LORD, THAT THE FACT THAT THE *TENACIOUS* HAD BEEN DIVERTED TO ARKINNEA MIGHT BE...
...OF SOME SIGNIFICANCE...

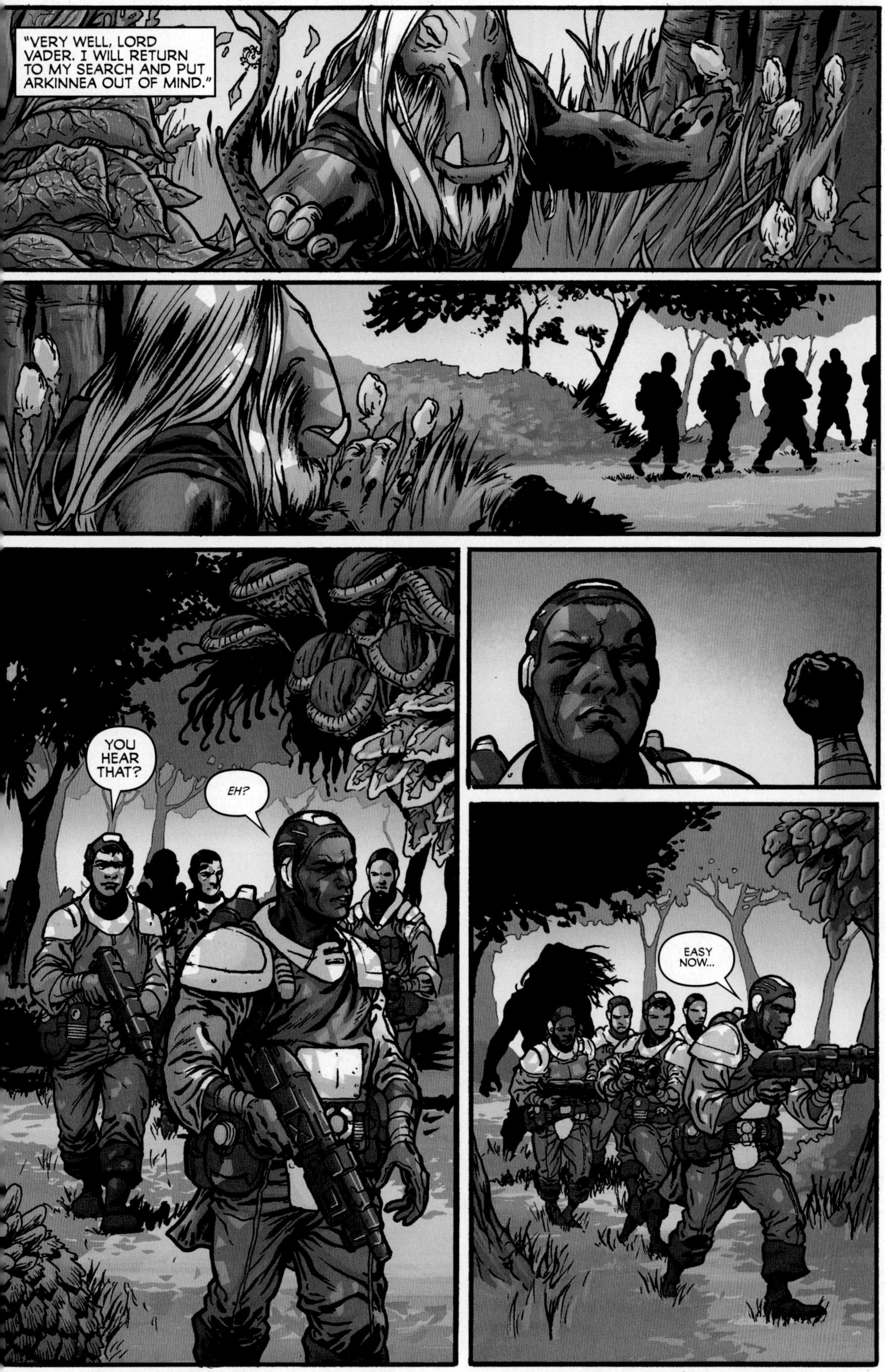
"VERY WELL, LORD VADER. I WILL RETURN TO MY SEARCH AND PUT ARKINNEA OUT OF MIND."
YOU HEAR THAT?
EH?
EASY NOW...

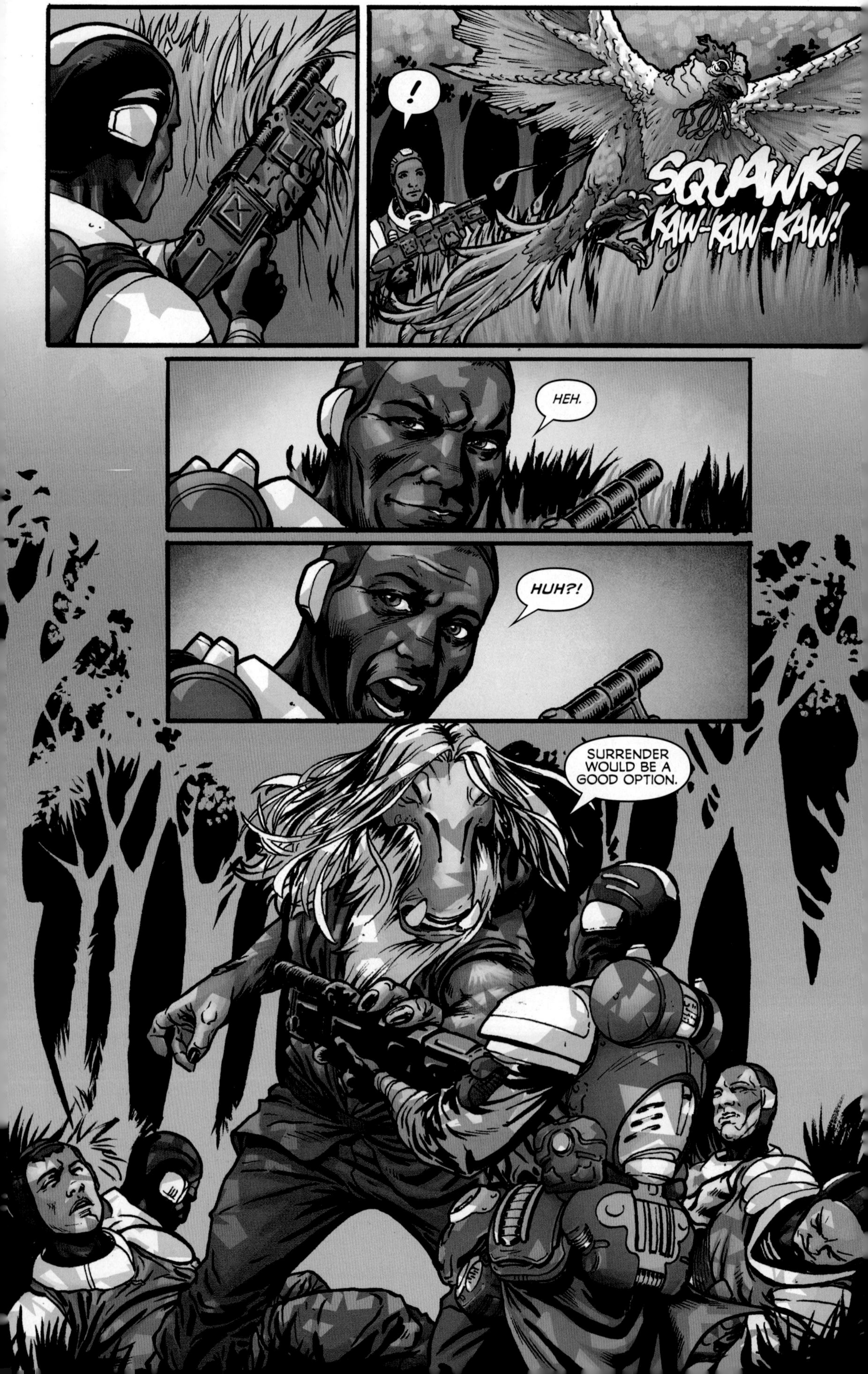
!
SQUAWK!
KAW-KAW-KAW!
HEH.
HUH?!
SURRENDER WOULD BE A GOOD OPTION.

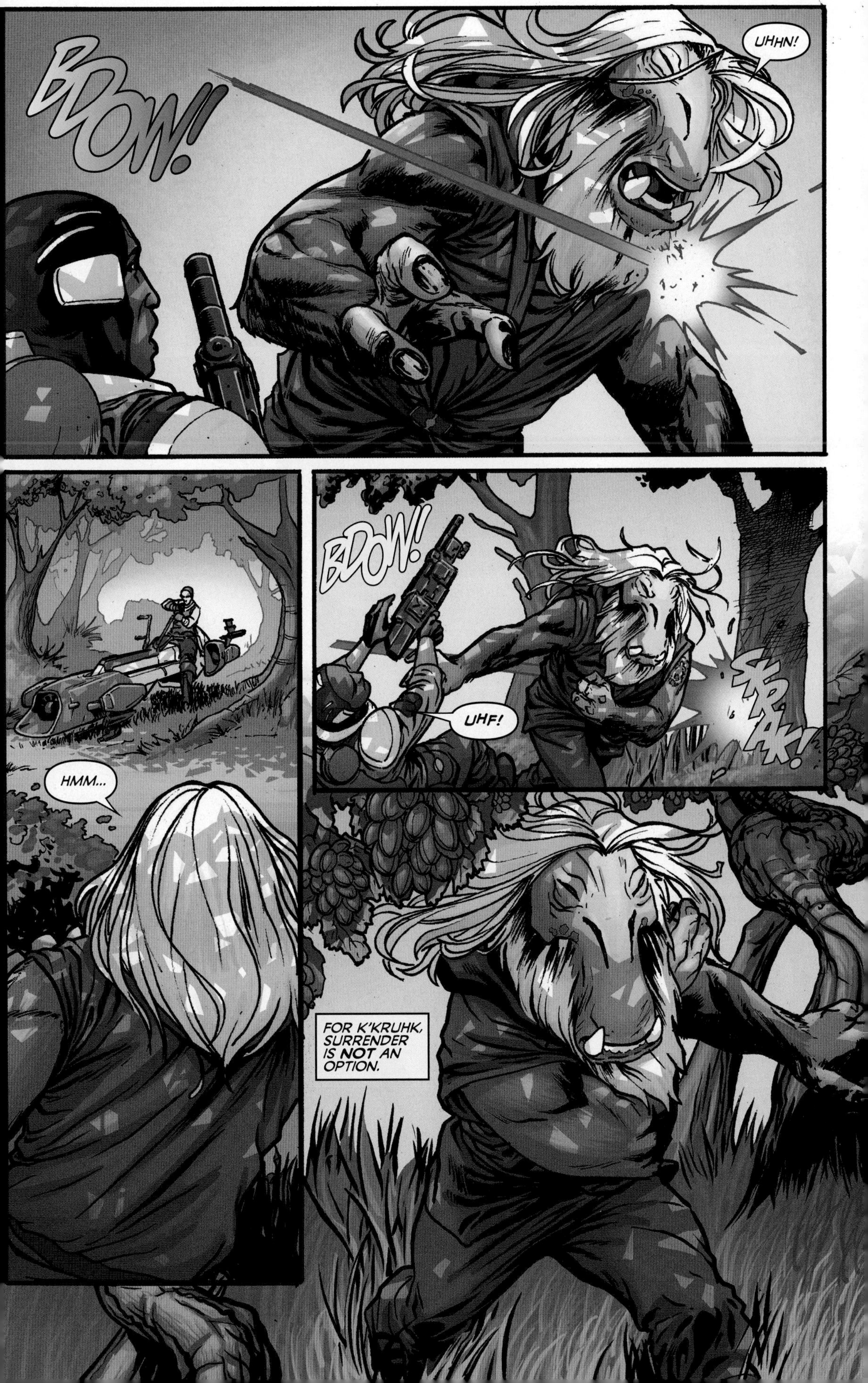
BDOW!
UHHN!
HMM...
BDOW!
UHF!
SKRAAK!
FOR K'KRUHK, SURRENDER IS NOT AN OPTION.

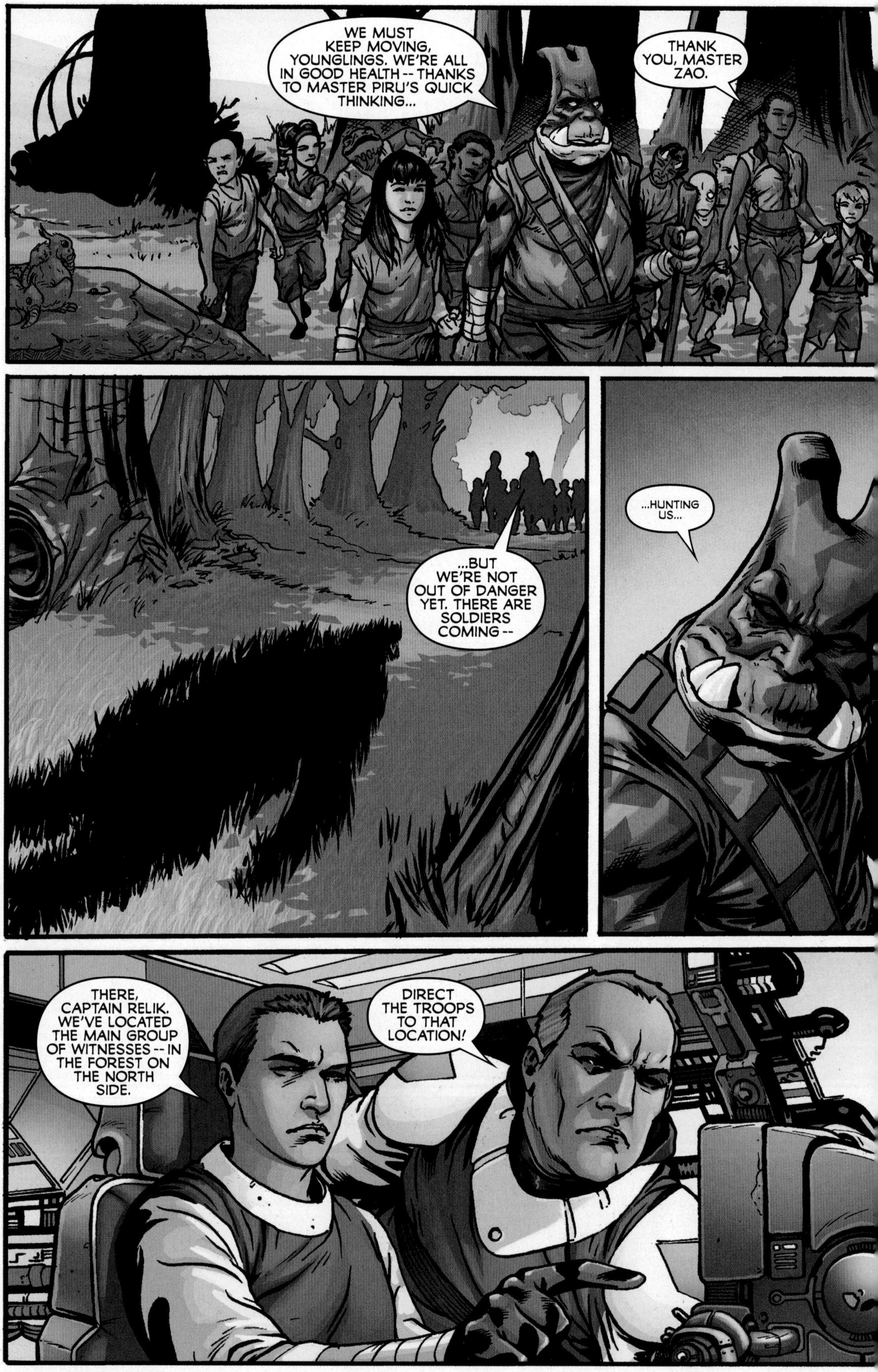
WE MUST KEEP MOVING, YOUNGLINGS. WE'RE ALL IN GOOD HEALTH -- THANKS TO MASTER PIRU'S QUICK THINKING...
THANK YOU, MASTER ZAO.
...BUT WE'RE NOT OUT OF DANGER YET. THERE ARE SOLDIERS COMING --
...HUNTING US...
THERE, CAPTAIN RELIK. WE'VE LOCATED THE MAIN GROUP OF WITNESSES -- IN THE FOREST ON THE NORTH SIDE.
DIRECT THE TROOPS TO THAT LOCATION!

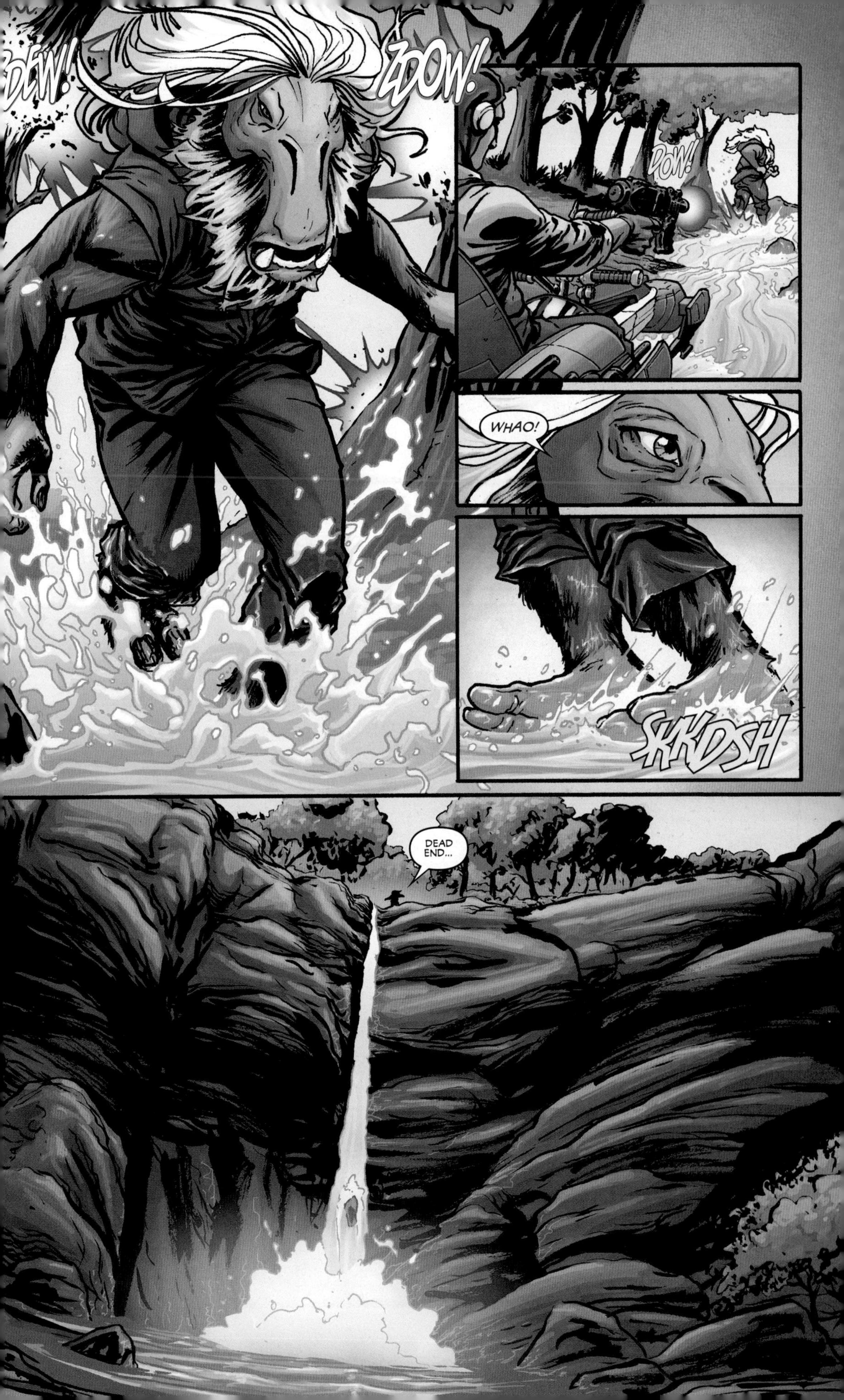
DEW!
ZDOW!
DOW!
WHAO!
SKKDSH
DEAD END...

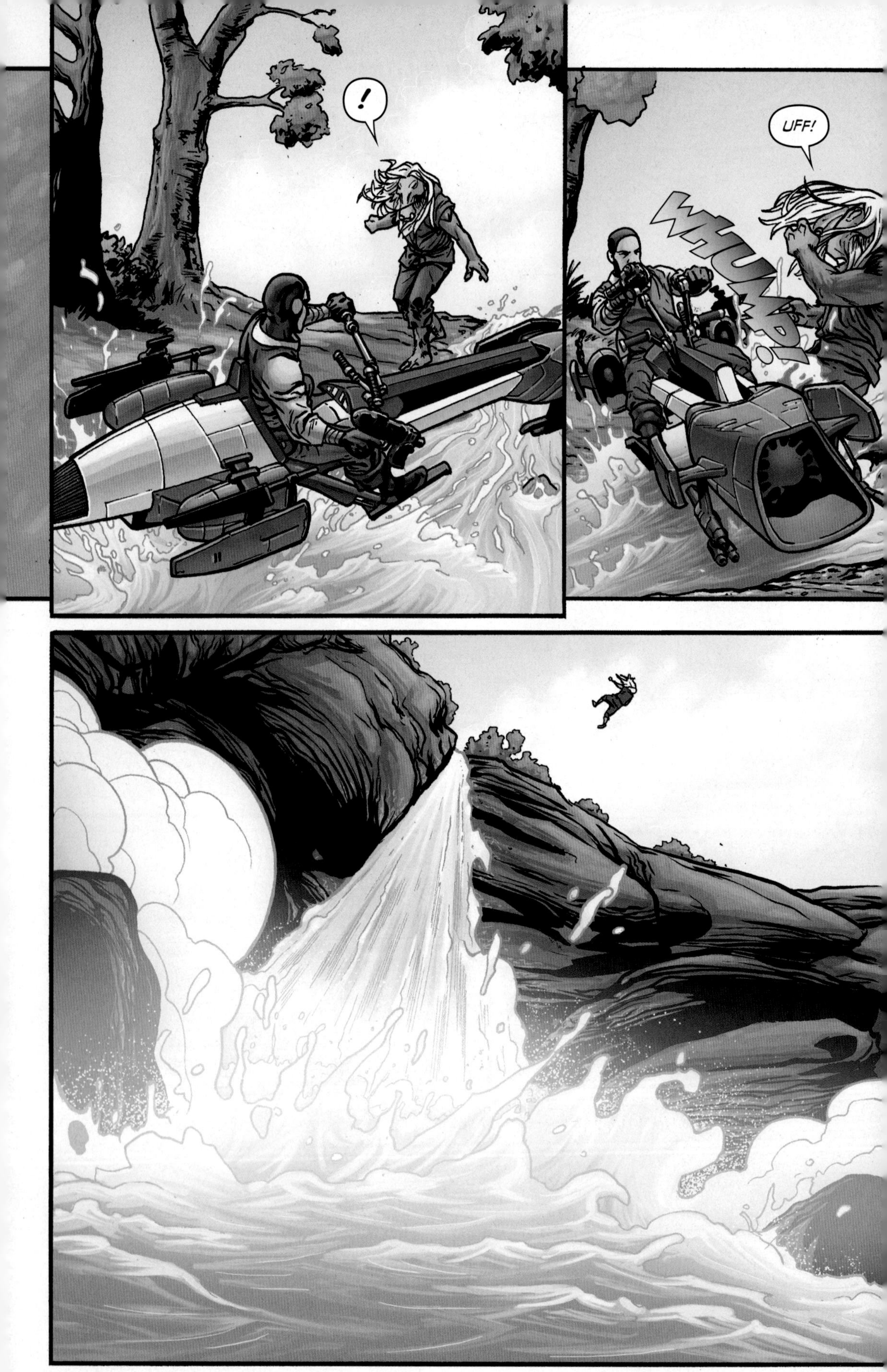
!
UFF!
WHUMP!

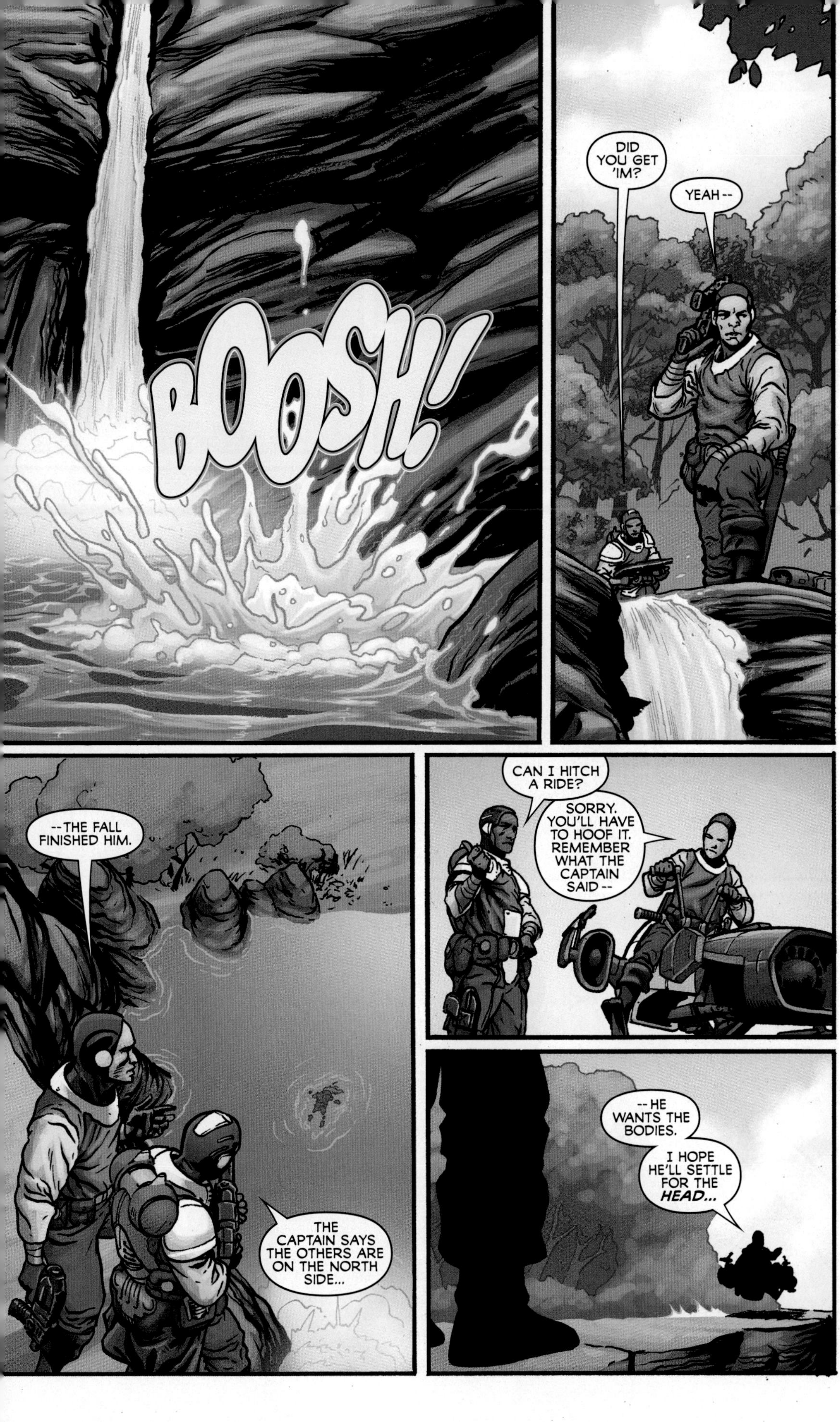
BOOSH!
DID YOU GET 'IM?
YEAH --
--THE FALL FINISHED HIM.
THE CAPTAIN SAYS THE OTHERS ARE ON THE NORTH SIDE...
CAN I HITCH A RIDE?
SORRY. YOU'LL HAVE TO HOOF IT. REMEMBER WHAT THE CAPTAIN SAID --
--HE WANTS THE BODIES.
I HOPE HE'LL SETTLE FOR THE *HEAD...*

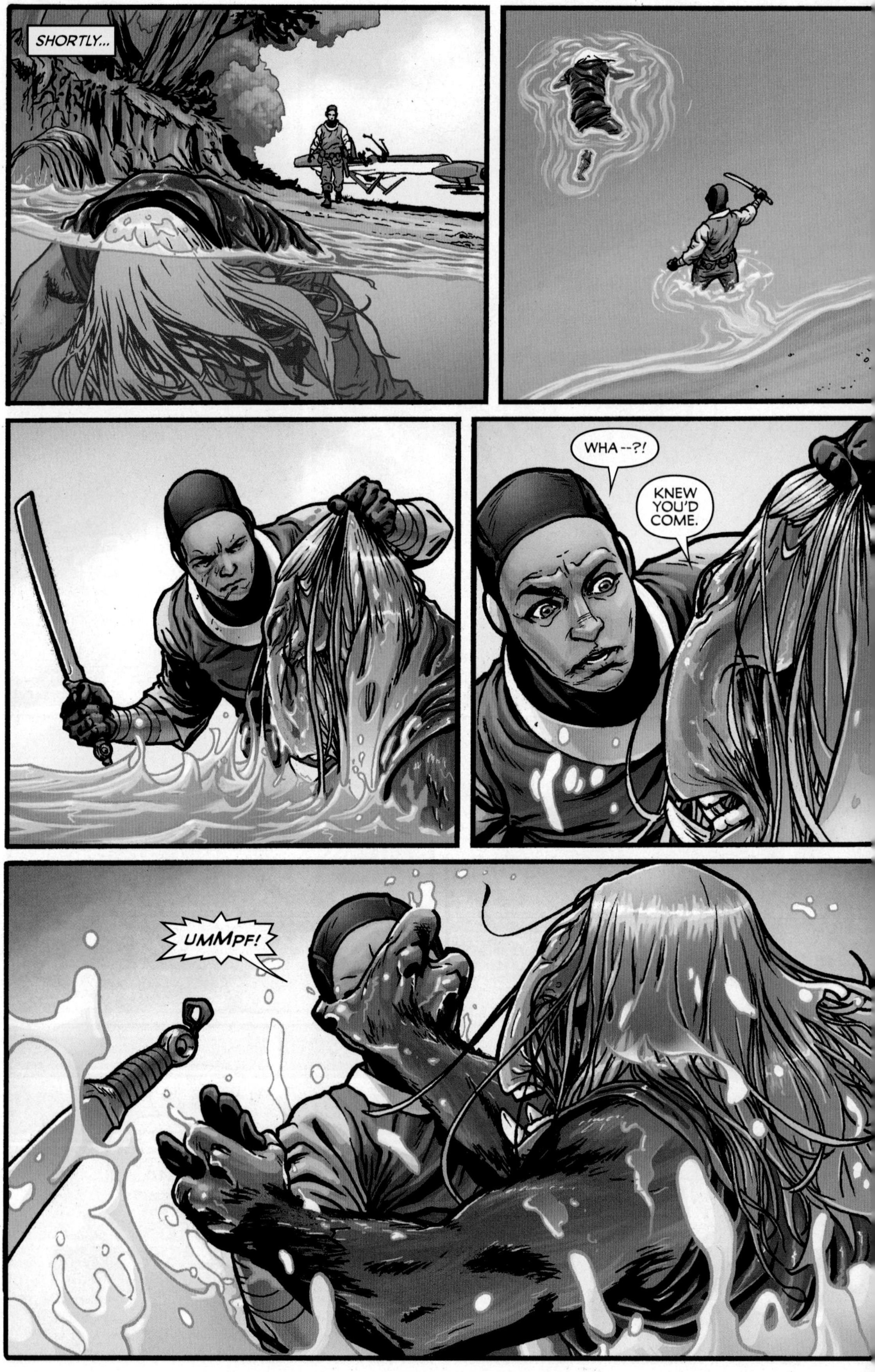
SHORTLY...
WHA--?!
KNEW YOU'D COME.
UMMPF!

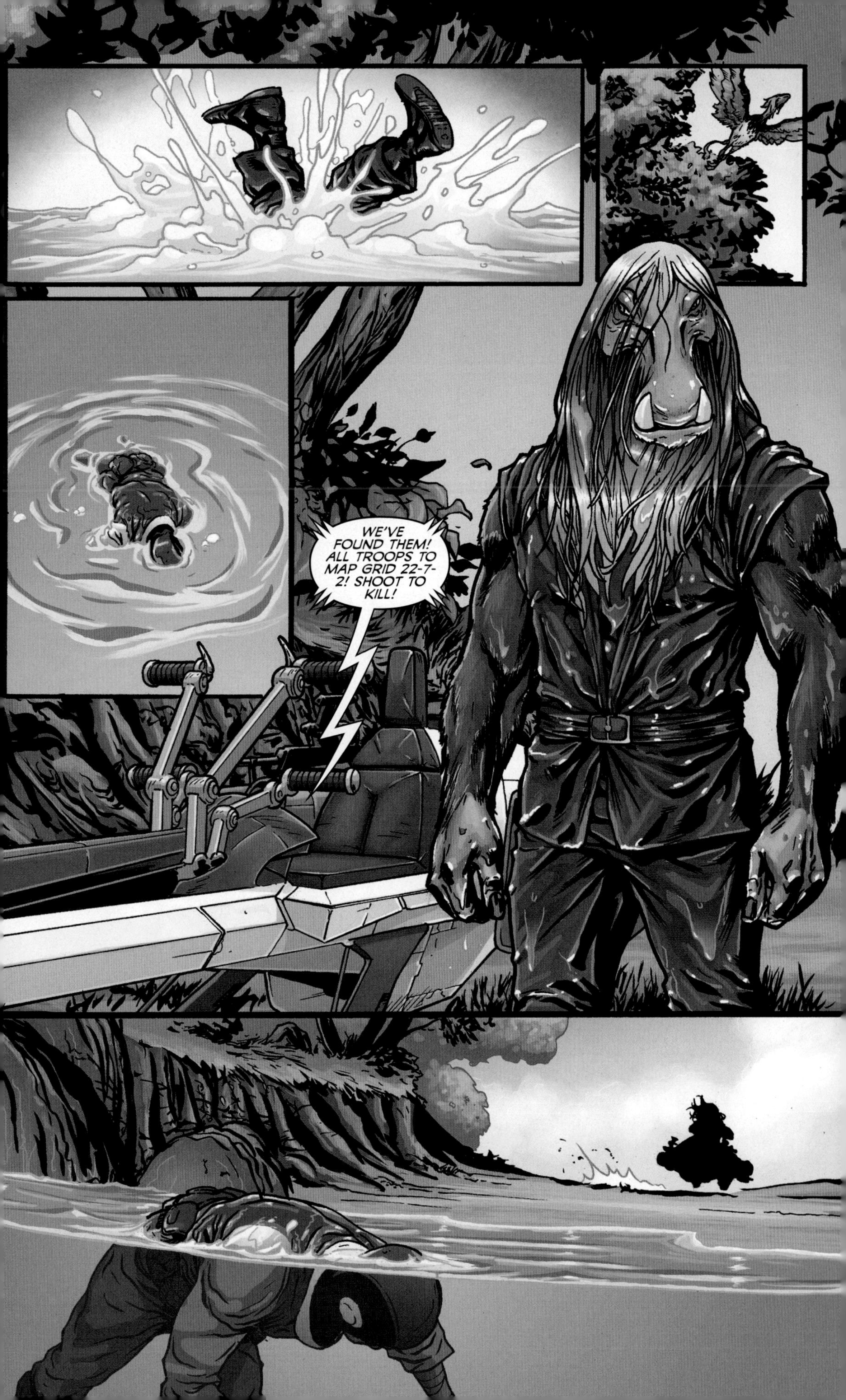
WE'VE FOUND THEM! ALL TROOPS TO MAP GRID 22-7-2! SHOOT TO KILL!

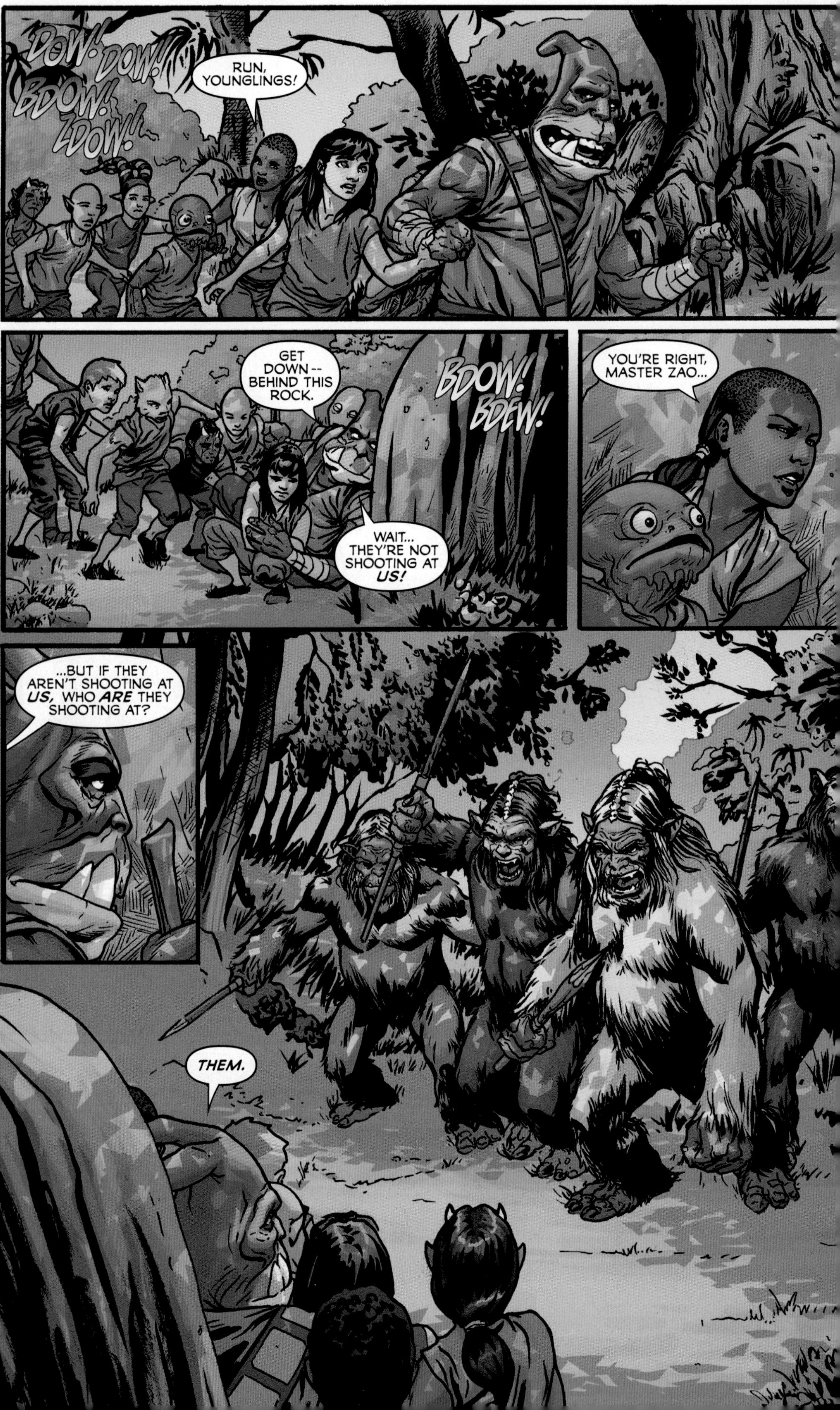
DOW! DOW!
BDOW!
ZDOW!
RUN, YOUNGLINGS!
GET DOWN -- BEHIND THIS ROCK.
BDOW! BDEW!
WAIT... THEY'RE NOT SHOOTING AT *US!*
YOU'RE RIGHT, MASTER ZAO...
...BUT IF THEY AREN'T SHOOTING AT *US,* WHO *ARE* THEY SHOOTING AT?
*THEM.*

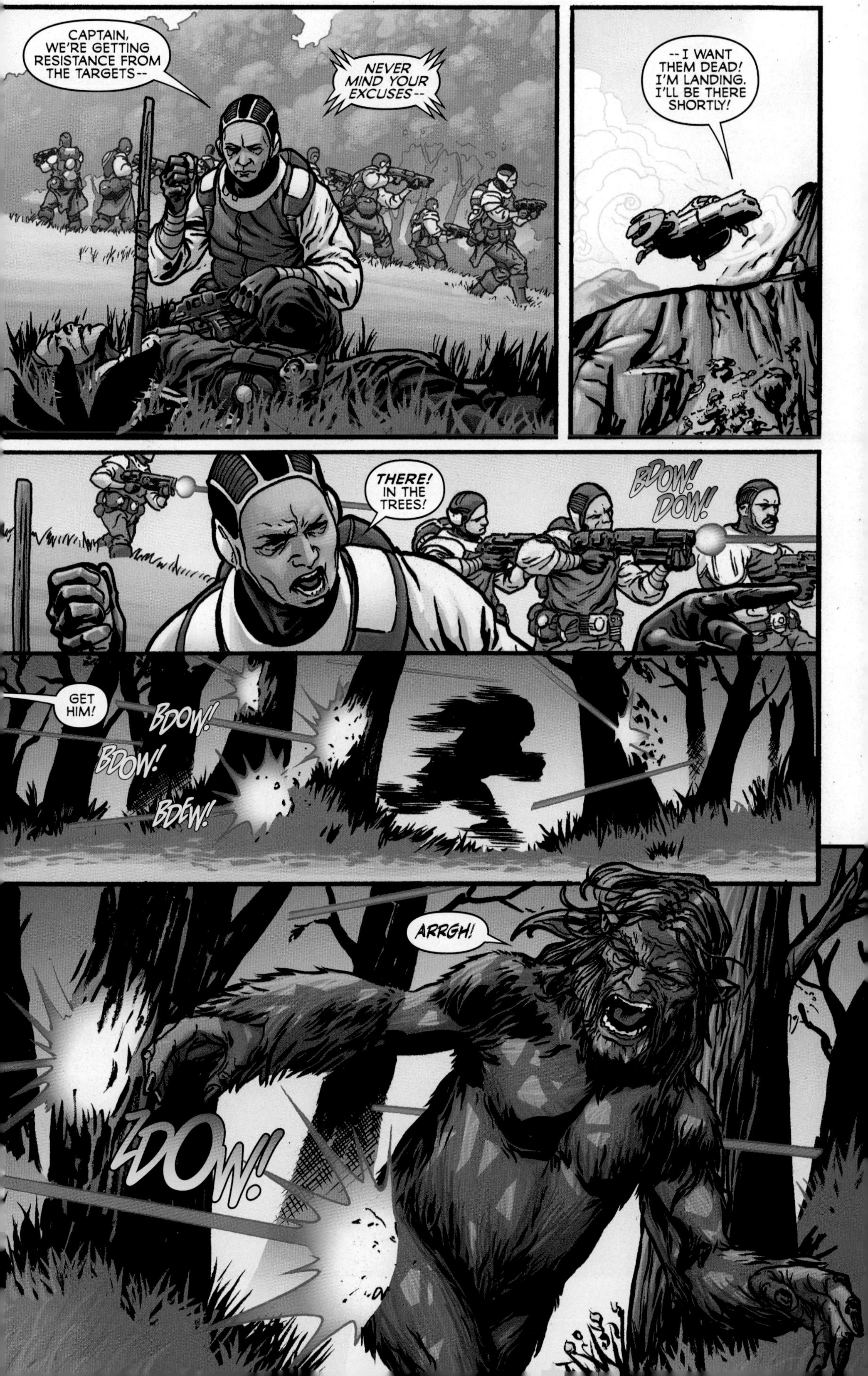
CAPTAIN, WE'RE GETTING RESISTANCE FROM THE TARGETS--
NEVER MIND YOUR EXCUSES--
--I WANT THEM DEAD! I'M LANDING. I'LL BE THERE SHORTLY!
THERE! IN THE TREES!
BDOW! DOW!
GET HIM!
BDOW!
BDOW!
BDEW!
ARRGH!
ZDOW!

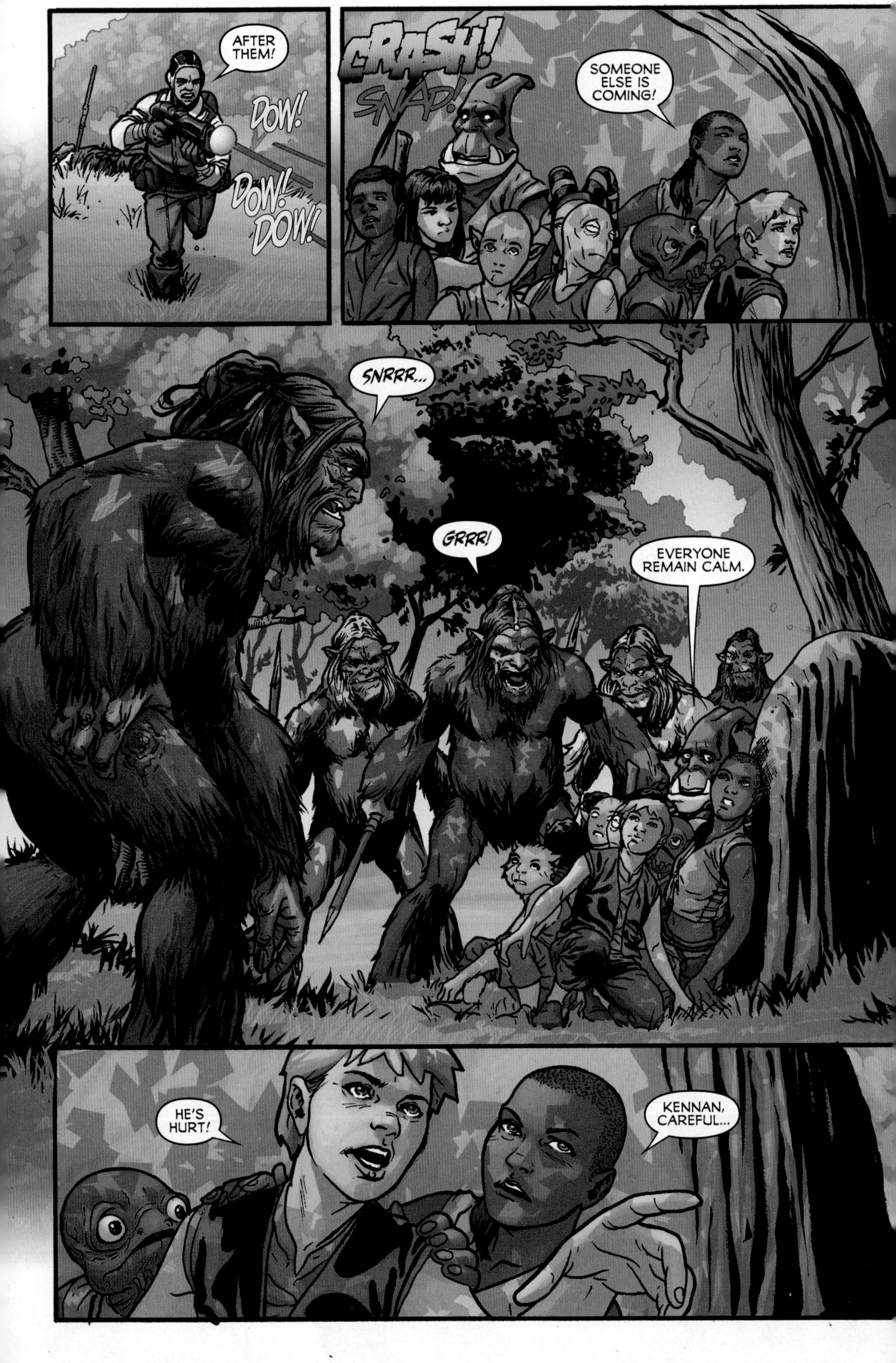
AFTER THEM!
DOW!
DOW!
DOW!
CRASH!
SNAP!
SOMEONE ELSE IS COMING!
SNRRR...
GRRR!
EVERYONE REMAIN CALM.
HE'S HURT!
KENNAN, CAREFUL...

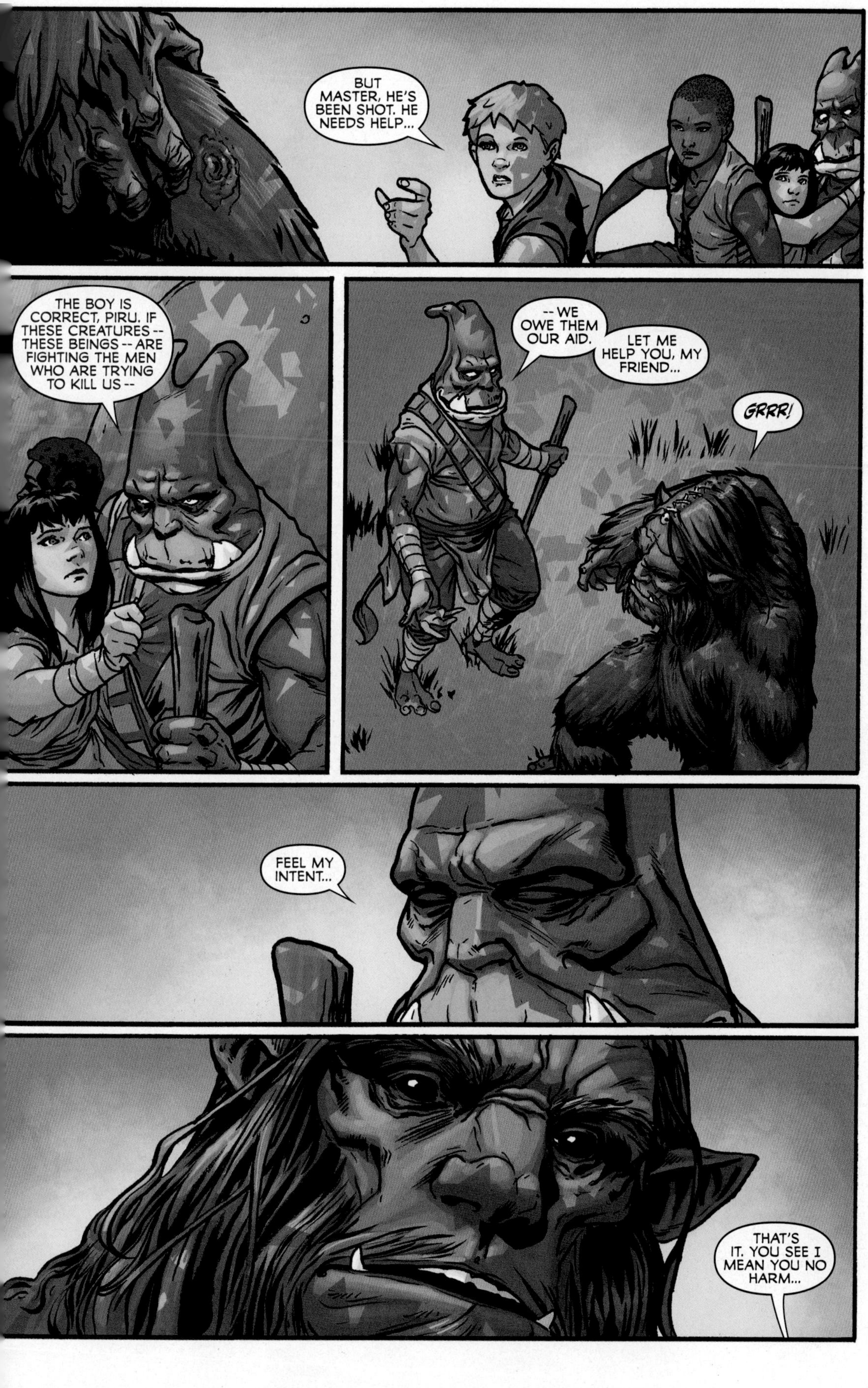
BUT MASTER, HE'S BEEN SHOT. HE NEEDS HELP...
THE BOY IS CORRECT, PIRU. IF THESE CREATURES -- THESE BEINGS -- ARE FIGHTING THE MEN WHO ARE TRYING TO KILL US --
-- WE OWE THEM OUR AID.
LET ME HELP YOU, MY FRIEND...
GRRR!
FEEL MY INTENT...
THAT'S IT. YOU SEE I MEAN YOU NO HARM...

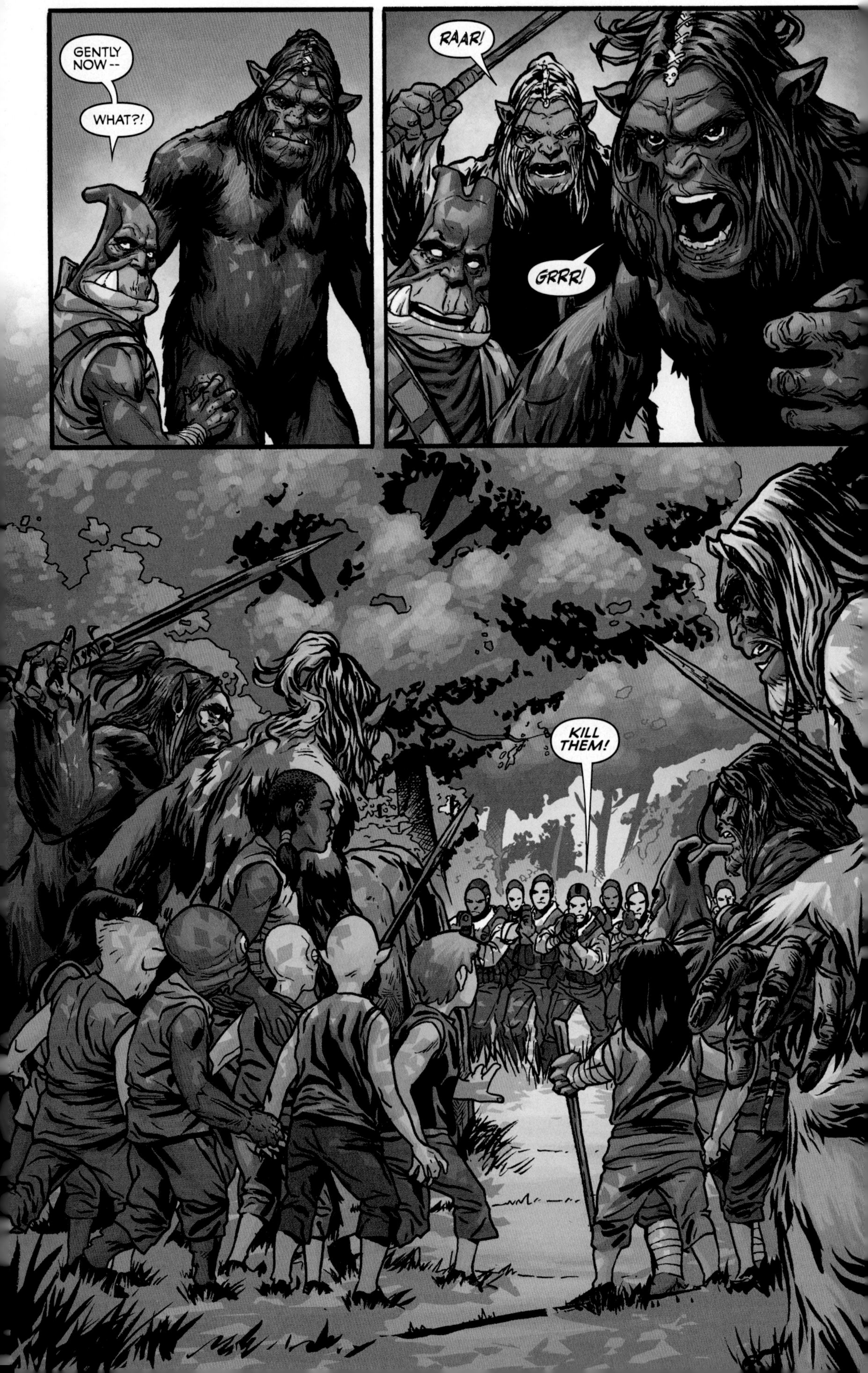
GENTLY NOW --
WHAT?!
RAAR!
GRRR!
KILL THEM!

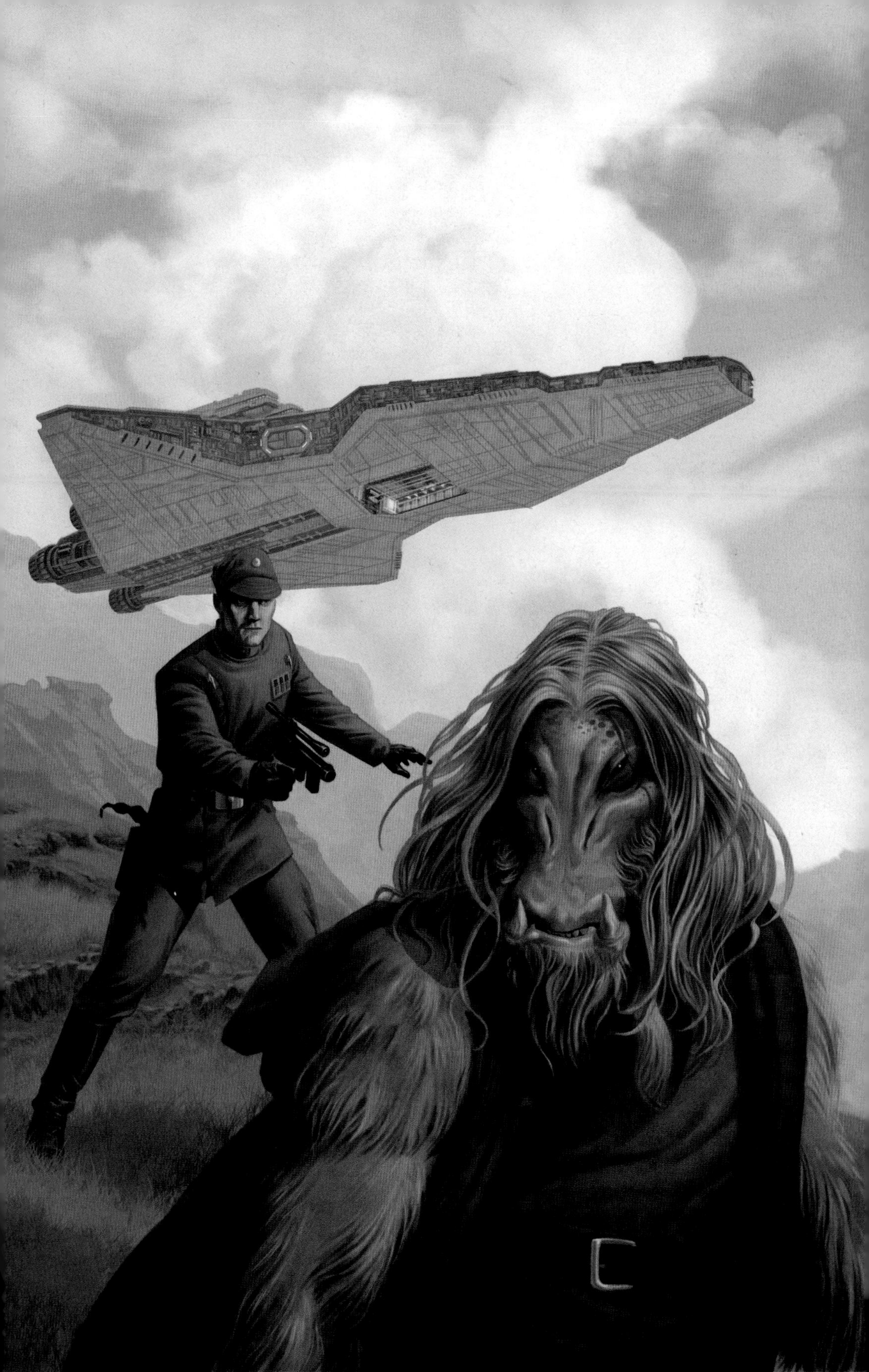

***STAR WARS: DARK TIMES — FIRE CARRIER #5***

WRITER: RANDY STRADLEY • ARTIST: GABRIEL GUZMAN • COLORIST: GARRY HENDERSON • LETTERER: MICHAEL HEISLER
ASSISTANT EDITOR: FREDDYE LINS • EDITOR: DAVE MARSHALL • COVER ARTIST: DOUGLAS WHEATLEY

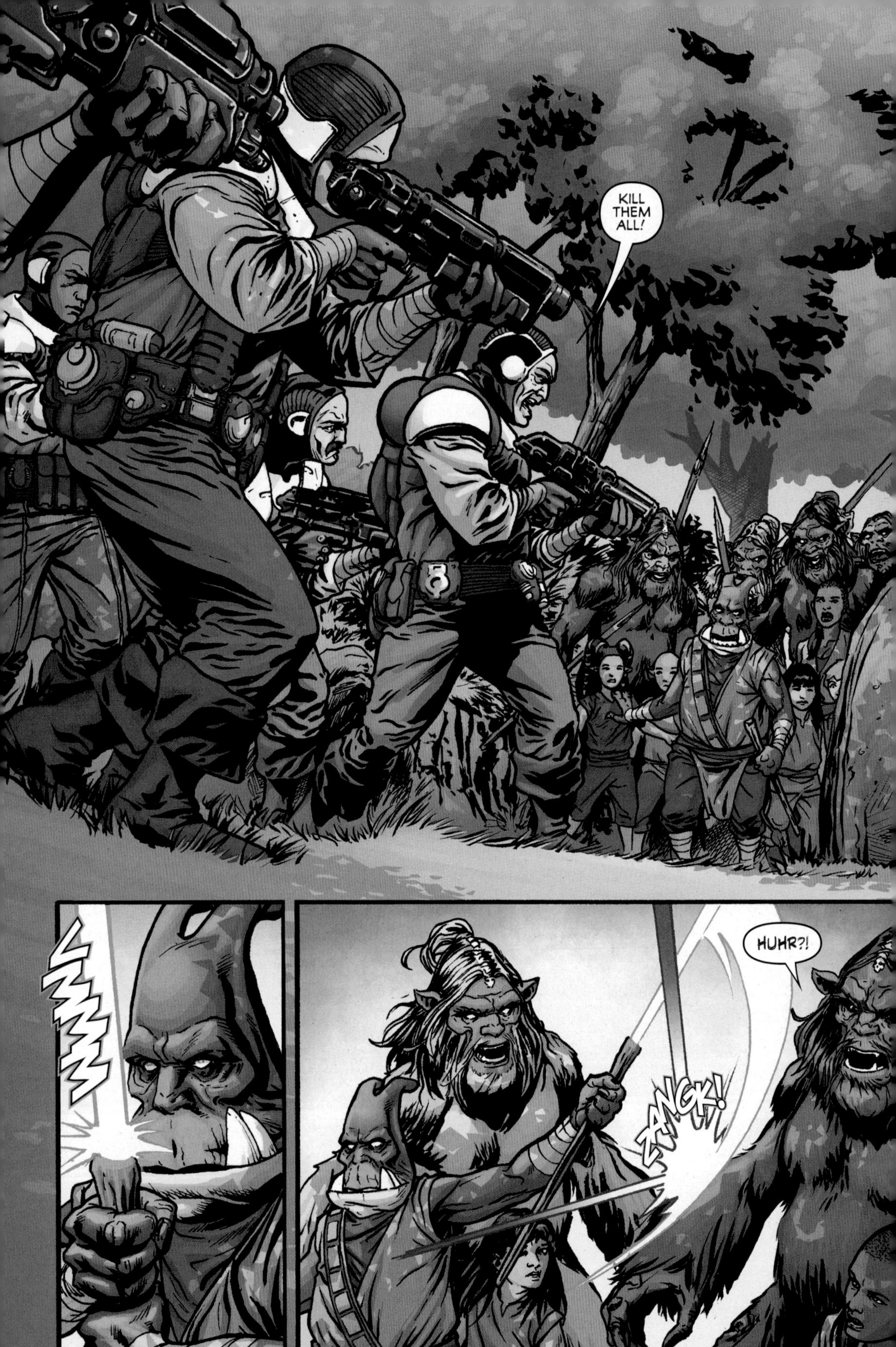
KILL THEM ALL!
VMMMM
HUHR?!
ZANGK!

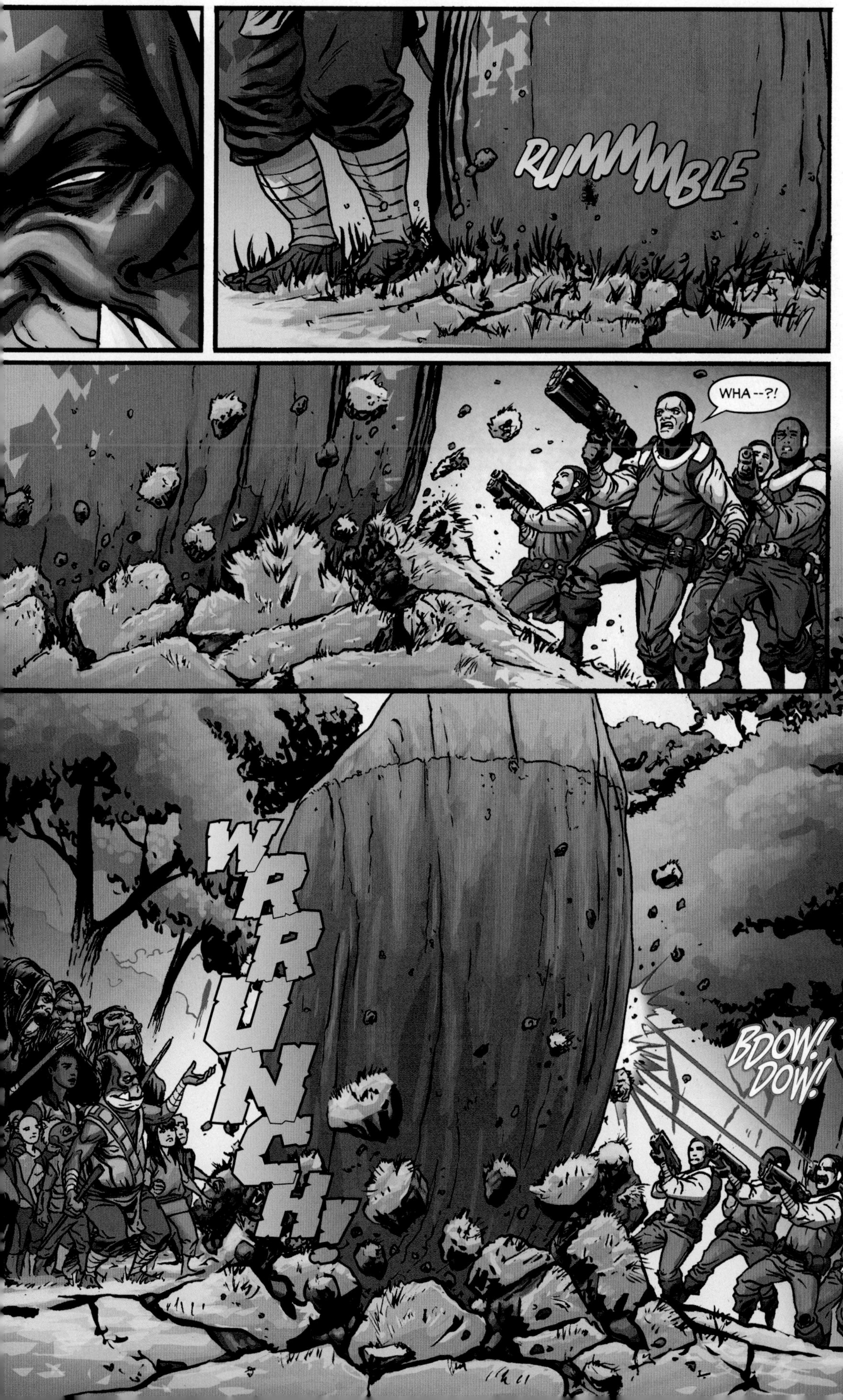
RUMMMMBLE
WHA --?!
WRRUNNCH!
BDOW! DOW!

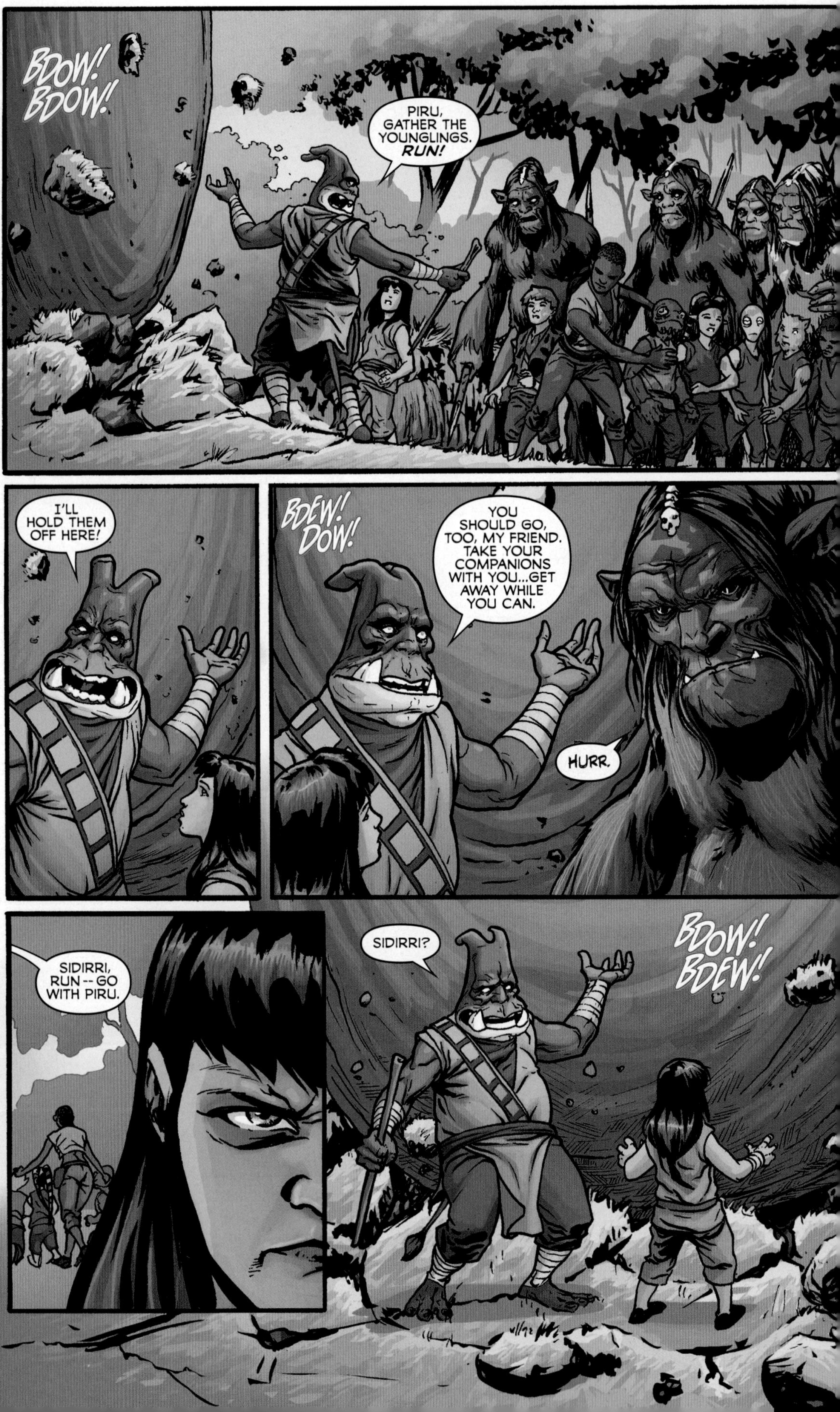
BDOW! BDOW!
PIRU, GATHER THE YOUNGLINGS. RUN!
I'LL HOLD THEM OFF HERE!
BDEW! DOW!
YOU SHOULD GO, TOO, MY FRIEND. TAKE YOUR COMPANIONS WITH YOU...GET AWAY WHILE YOU CAN.
HURR.
SIDIRRI, RUN -- GO WITH PIRU.
SIDIRRI?
BDOW! BDEW!

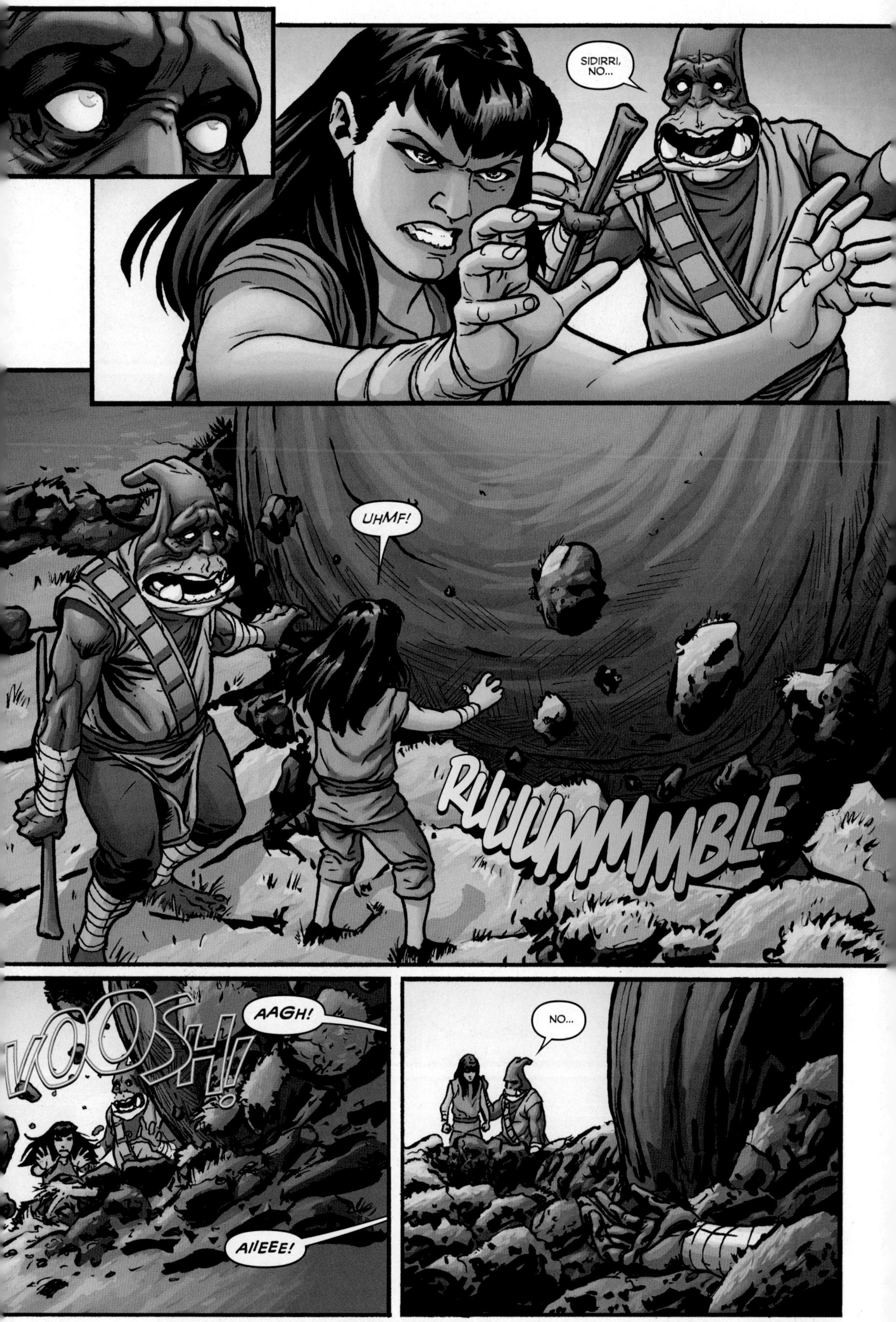
SIDIRRI, NO...
UHMF!
RUUUMMMBLE
VOOSH!
AAGH!
AIIEEE!
NO...

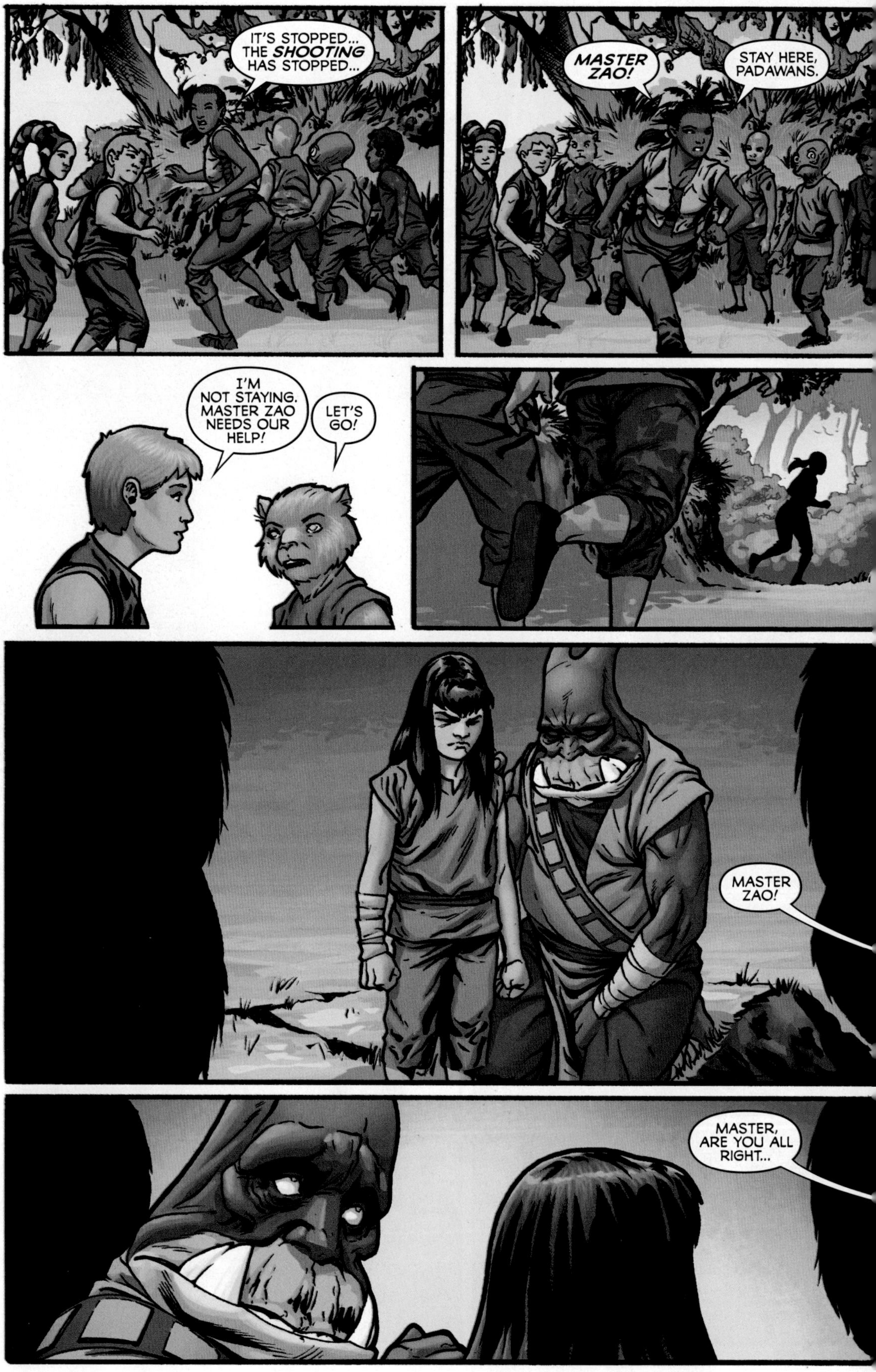

IT'S STOPPED... THE SHOOTING HAS STOPPED...
MASTER ZAO!
STAY HERE, PADAWANS.
I'M NOT STAYING. MASTER ZAO NEEDS OUR HELP!
LET'S GO!
MASTER ZAO!
MASTER, ARE YOU ALL RIGHT...

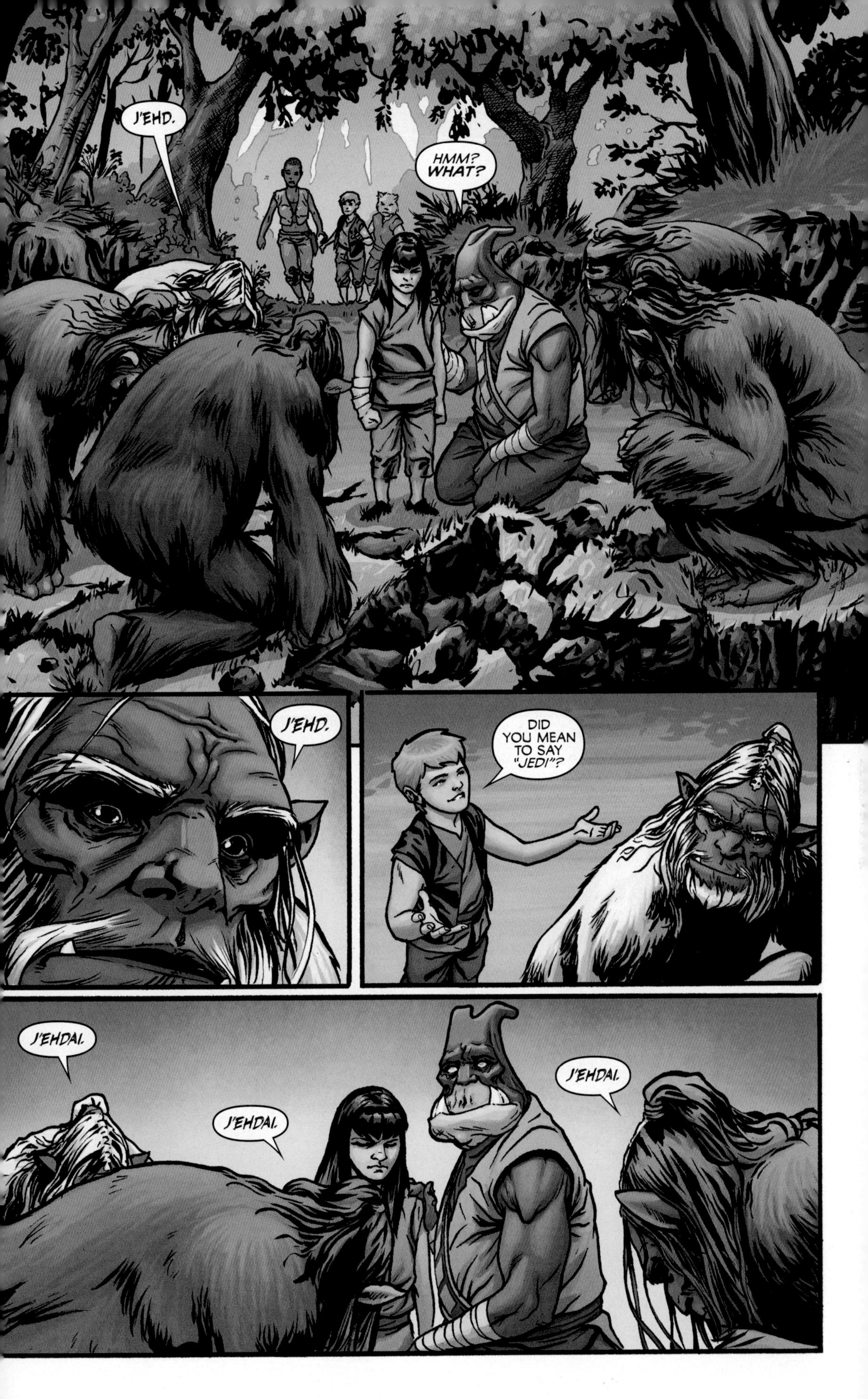
J'EHD.
HMM? WHAT?
J'EHD.
DID YOU MEAN TO SAY "JEDI"?
J'EHDAI.
J'EHDAI.
J'EHDAI.

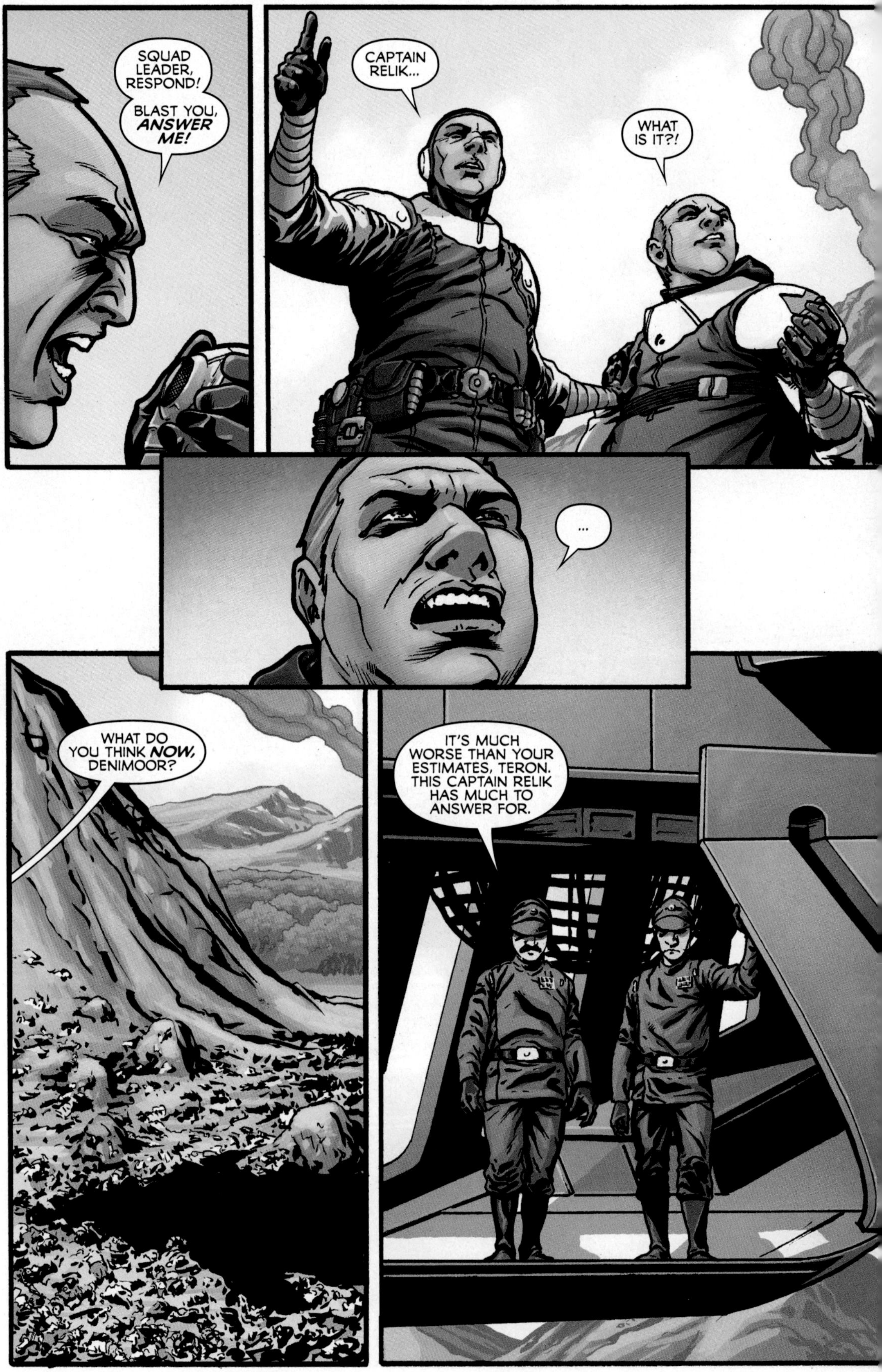
SQUAD LEADER, RESPOND!
BLAST YOU, ANSWER ME!
CAPTAIN RELIK...
WHAT IS IT?!
...
WHAT DO YOU THINK NOW, DENIMOOR?
IT'S MUCH WORSE THAN YOUR ESTIMATES, TERON. THIS CAPTAIN RELIK HAS MUCH TO ANSWER FOR.

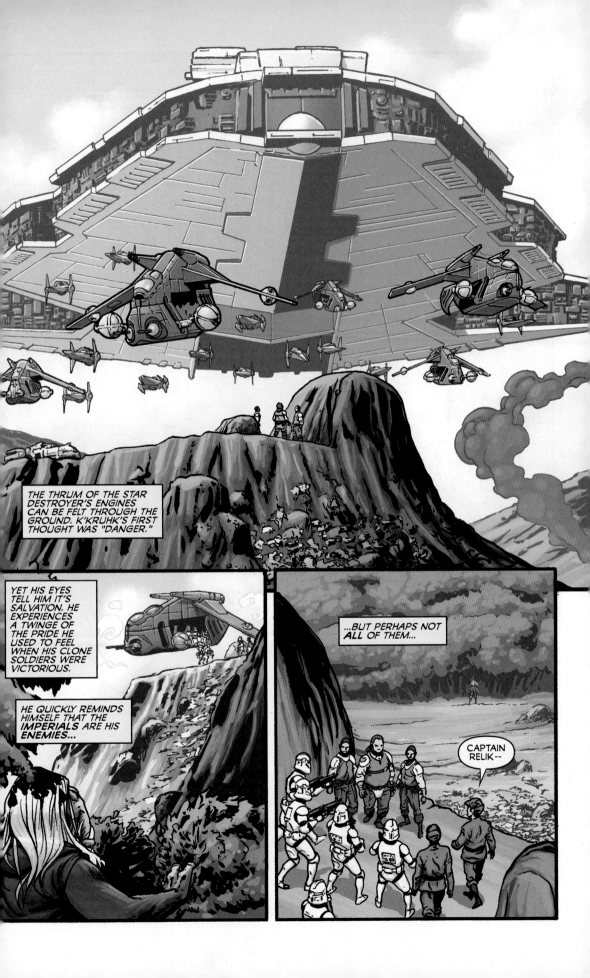

THE THRUM OF THE STAR DESTROYER'S ENGINES CAN BE FELT THROUGH THE GROUND. K'KRUHK'S FIRST THOUGHT WAS "DANGER."

YET HIS EYES TELL HIM IT'S SALVATION. HE EXPERIENCES A TWINGE OF THE PRIDE HE USED TO FEEL WHEN HIS CLONE SOLDIERS WERE VICTORIOUS.

HE QUICKLY REMINDS HIMSELF THAT THE IMPERIALS ARE HIS ENEMIES...

...BUT PERHAPS NOT ALL OF THEM...

CAPTAIN RELIK--

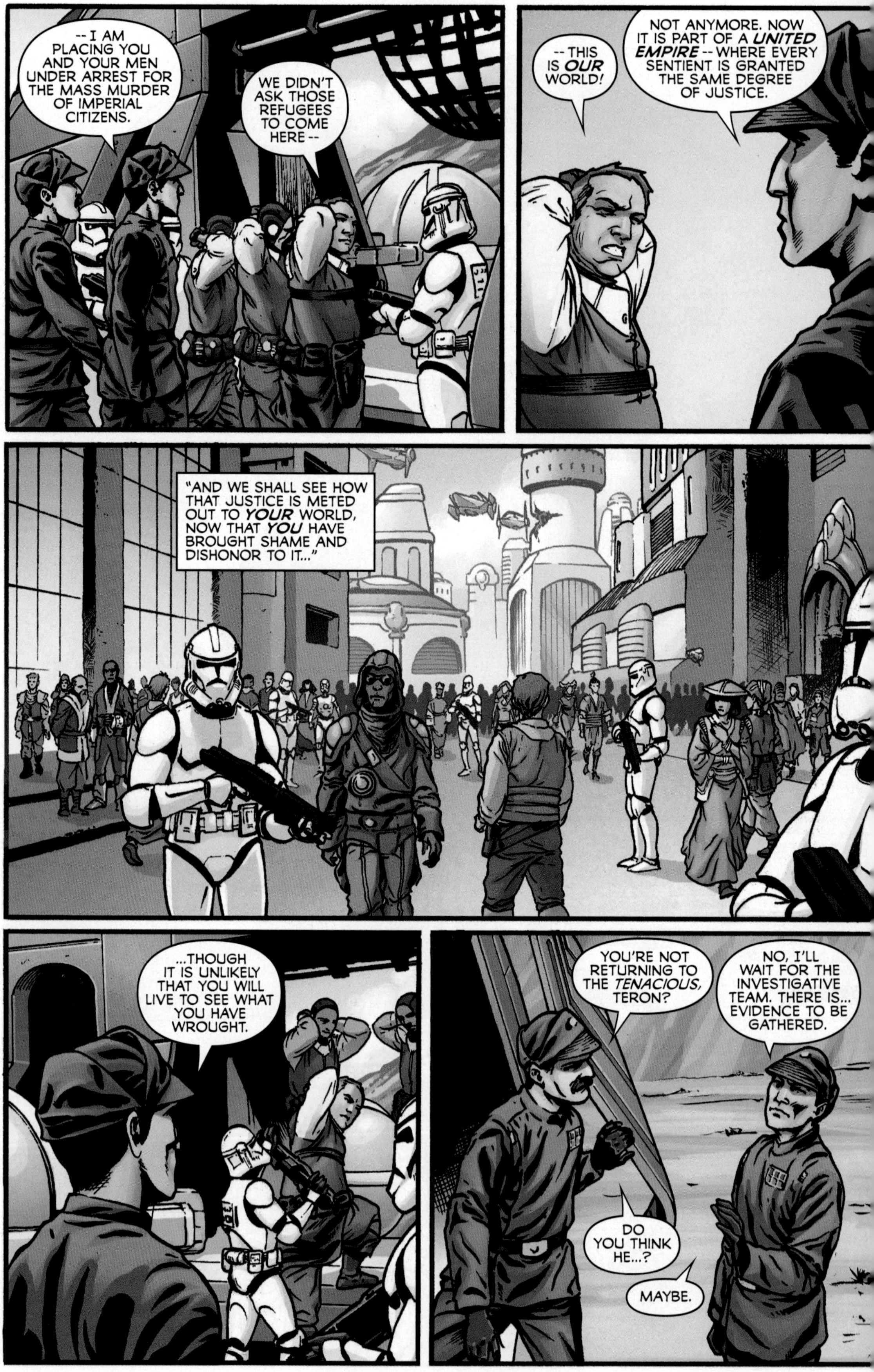
-- I AM PLACING YOU AND YOUR MEN UNDER ARREST FOR THE MASS MURDER OF IMPERIAL CITIZENS.
WE DIDN'T ASK THOSE REFUGEES TO COME HERE --
-- THIS IS *OUR* WORLD!
NOT ANYMORE. NOW IT IS PART OF A *UNITED EMPIRE* -- WHERE EVERY SENTIENT IS GRANTED THE SAME DEGREE OF JUSTICE.
"AND WE SHALL SEE HOW THAT JUSTICE IS METED OUT TO *YOUR* WORLD, NOW THAT *YOU* HAVE BROUGHT SHAME AND DISHONOR TO IT..."
...THOUGH IT IS UNLIKELY THAT YOU WILL LIVE TO SEE WHAT YOU HAVE WROUGHT.
YOU'RE NOT RETURNING TO THE *TENACIOUS,* TERON?
NO, I'LL WAIT FOR THE INVESTIGATIVE TEAM. THERE IS... EVIDENCE TO BE GATHERED.
DO YOU THINK HE...?
MAYBE.

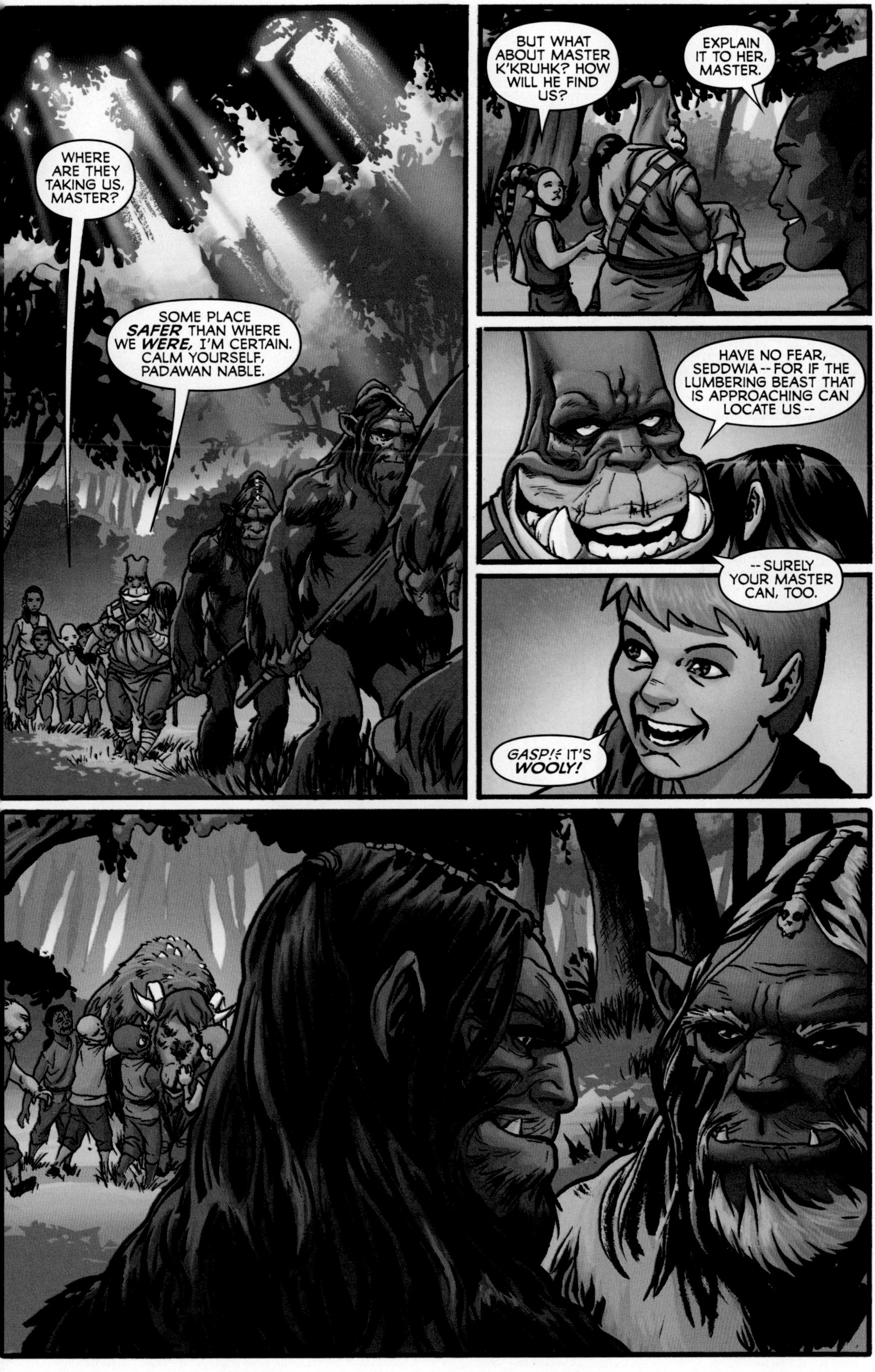
WHERE ARE THEY TAKING US, MASTER?
SOME PLACE SAFER THAN WHERE WE WERE, I'M CERTAIN. CALM YOURSELF, PADAWAN NABLE.
BUT WHAT ABOUT MASTER K'KRUHK? HOW WILL HE FIND US?
EXPLAIN IT TO HER, MASTER.
HAVE NO FEAR, SEDDWIA -- FOR IF THE LUMBERING BEAST THAT IS APPROACHING CAN LOCATE US --
-- SURELY YOUR MASTER CAN, TOO.
GASP!! IT'S WOOLY!

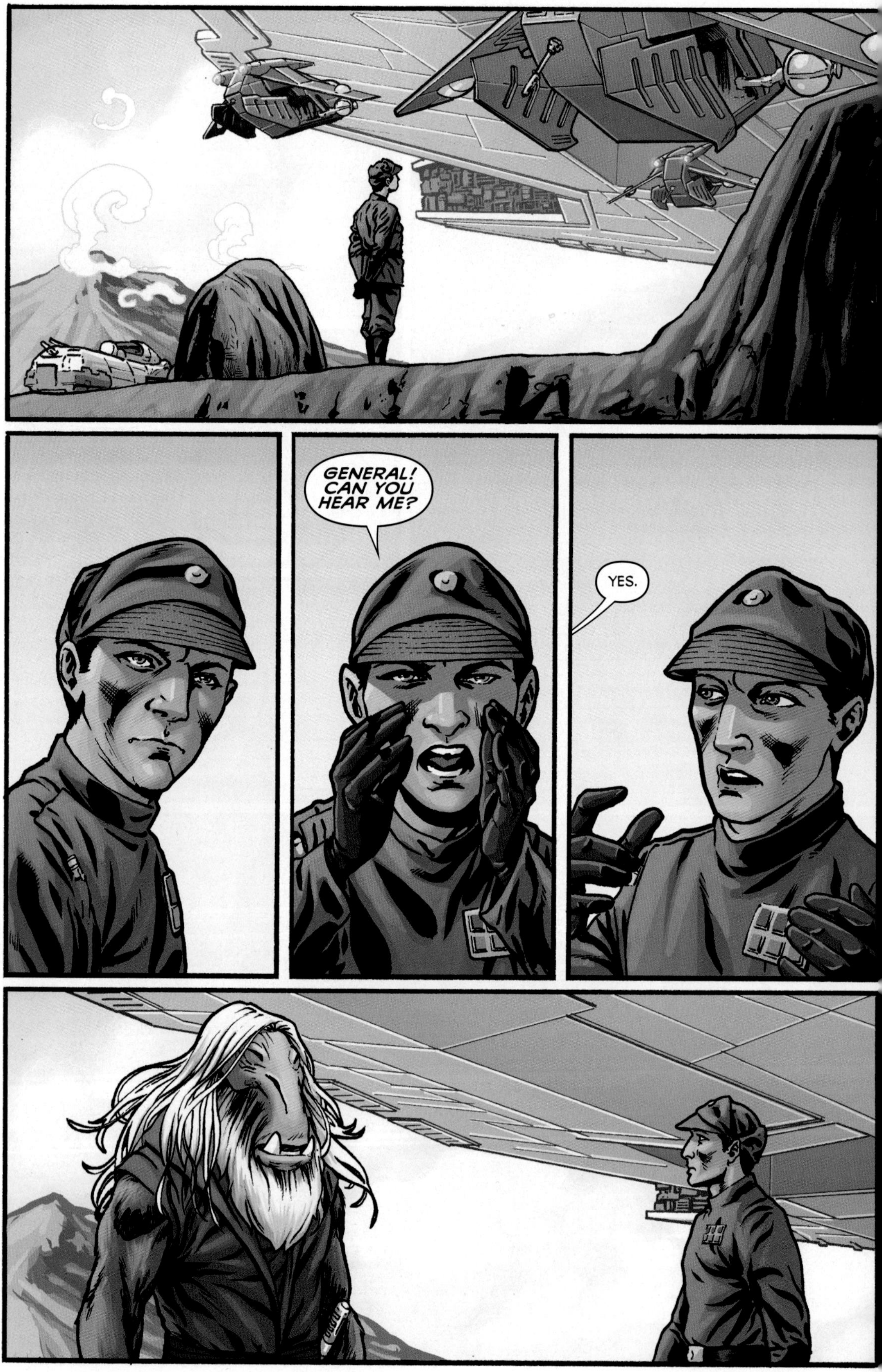
GENERAL! CAN YOU HEAR ME?
YES.

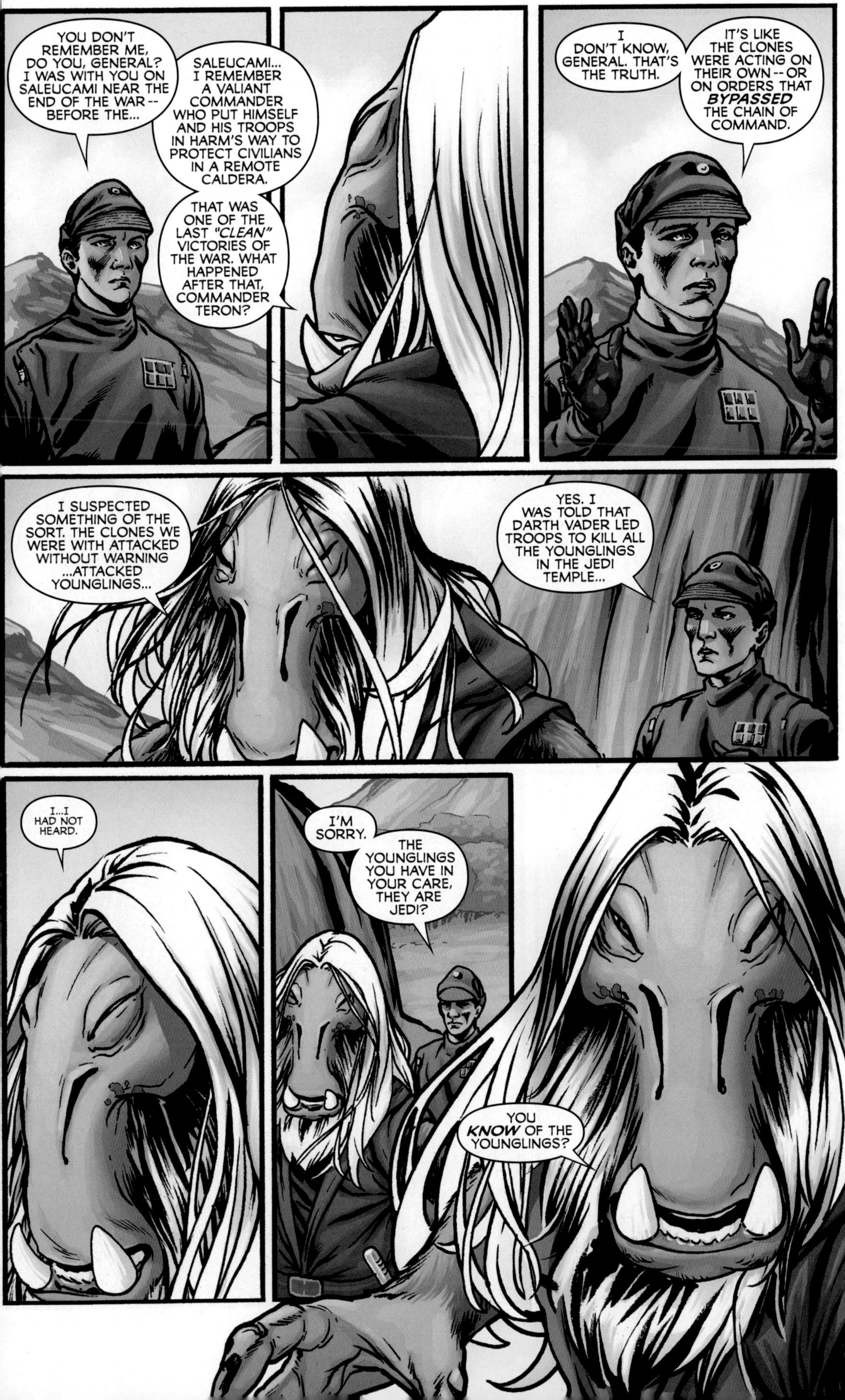
YOU DON'T REMEMBER ME, DO YOU, GENERAL? I WAS WITH YOU ON SALEUCAMI NEAR THE END OF THE WAR -- BEFORE THE...
SALEUCAMI... I REMEMBER A VALIANT COMMANDER WHO PUT HIMSELF AND HIS TROOPS IN HARM'S WAY TO PROTECT CIVILIANS IN A REMOTE CALDERA.
THAT WAS ONE OF THE LAST "CLEAN" VICTORIES OF THE WAR. WHAT HAPPENED AFTER THAT, COMMANDER TERON?
I DON'T KNOW, GENERAL. THAT'S THE TRUTH.
IT'S LIKE THE CLONES WERE ACTING ON THEIR OWN -- OR ON ORDERS THAT BYPASSED THE CHAIN OF COMMAND.
I SUSPECTED SOMETHING OF THE SORT. THE CLONES WE WERE WITH ATTACKED WITHOUT WARNING ...ATTACKED YOUNGLINGS...
YES. I WAS TOLD THAT DARTH VADER LED TROOPS TO KILL ALL THE YOUNGLINGS IN THE JEDI TEMPLE...
I...I HAD NOT HEARD.
I'M SORRY.
THE YOUNGLINGS YOU HAVE IN YOUR CARE, THEY ARE JEDI?
YOU KNOW OF THE YOUNGLINGS?

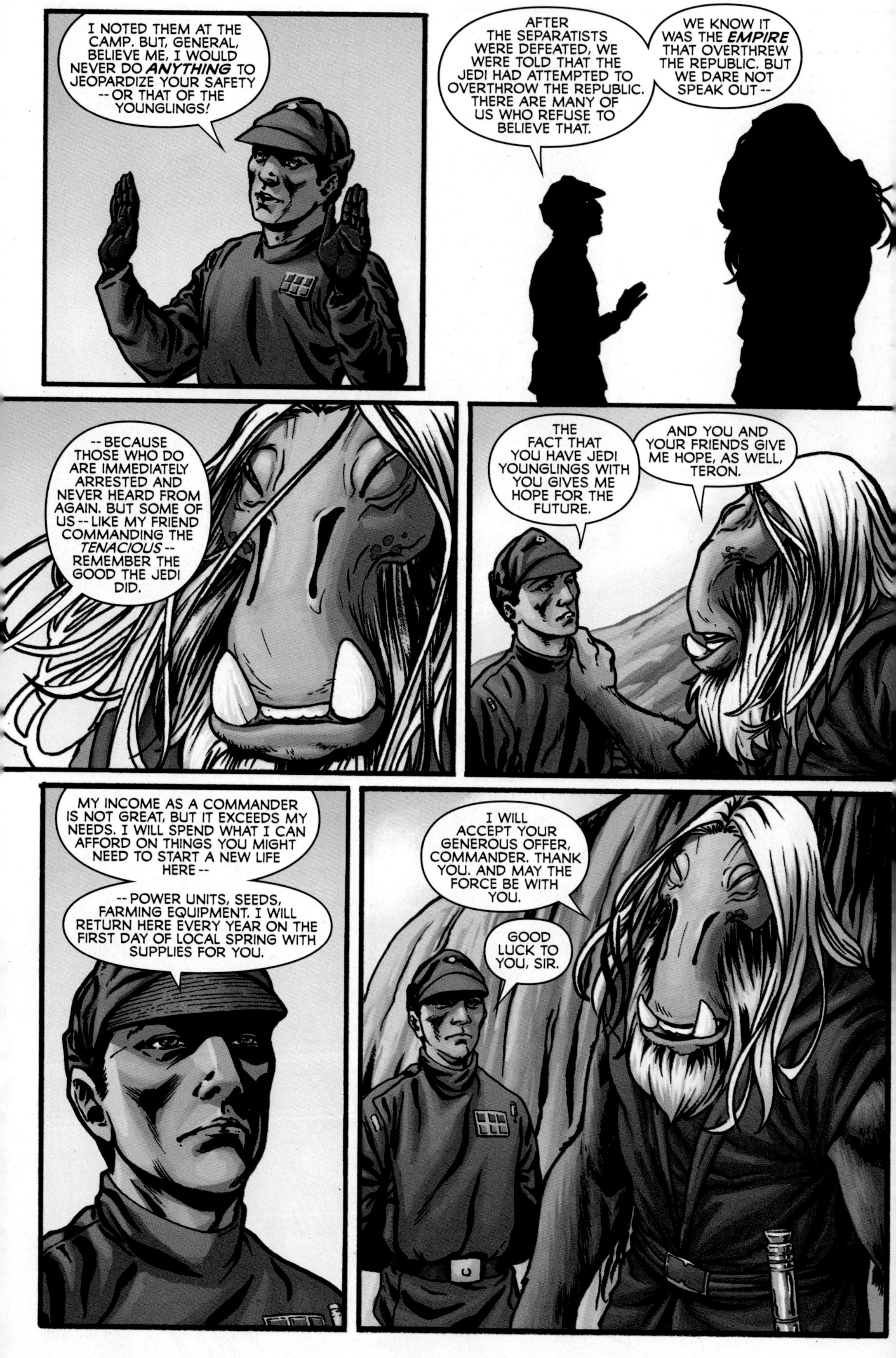
I NOTED THEM AT THE CAMP. BUT, GENERAL, BELIEVE ME, I WOULD NEVER DO *ANYTHING* TO JEOPARDIZE YOUR SAFETY -- OR THAT OF THE YOUNGLINGS!
AFTER THE SEPARATISTS WERE DEFEATED, WE WERE TOLD THAT THE JEDI HAD ATTEMPTED TO OVERTHROW THE REPUBLIC. THERE ARE MANY OF US WHO REFUSE TO BELIEVE THAT.
WE KNOW IT WAS THE *EMPIRE* THAT OVERTHREW THE REPUBLIC. BUT WE DARE NOT SPEAK OUT --
-- BECAUSE THOSE WHO DO ARE IMMEDIATELY ARRESTED AND NEVER HEARD FROM AGAIN. BUT SOME OF US -- LIKE MY FRIEND COMMANDING THE *TENACIOUS* -- REMEMBER THE GOOD THE JEDI DID.
THE FACT THAT YOU HAVE JEDI YOUNGLINGS WITH YOU GIVES ME HOPE FOR THE FUTURE.
AND YOU AND YOUR FRIENDS GIVE ME HOPE, AS WELL, TERON.
MY INCOME AS A COMMANDER IS NOT GREAT, BUT IT EXCEEDS MY NEEDS. I WILL SPEND WHAT I CAN AFFORD ON THINGS YOU MIGHT NEED TO START A NEW LIFE HERE --
-- POWER UNITS, SEEDS, FARMING EQUIPMENT. I WILL RETURN HERE EVERY YEAR ON THE FIRST DAY OF LOCAL SPRING WITH SUPPLIES FOR YOU.
I WILL ACCEPT YOUR GENEROUS OFFER, COMMANDER. THANK YOU. AND MAY THE FORCE BE WITH YOU.
GOOD LUCK TO YOU, SIR.

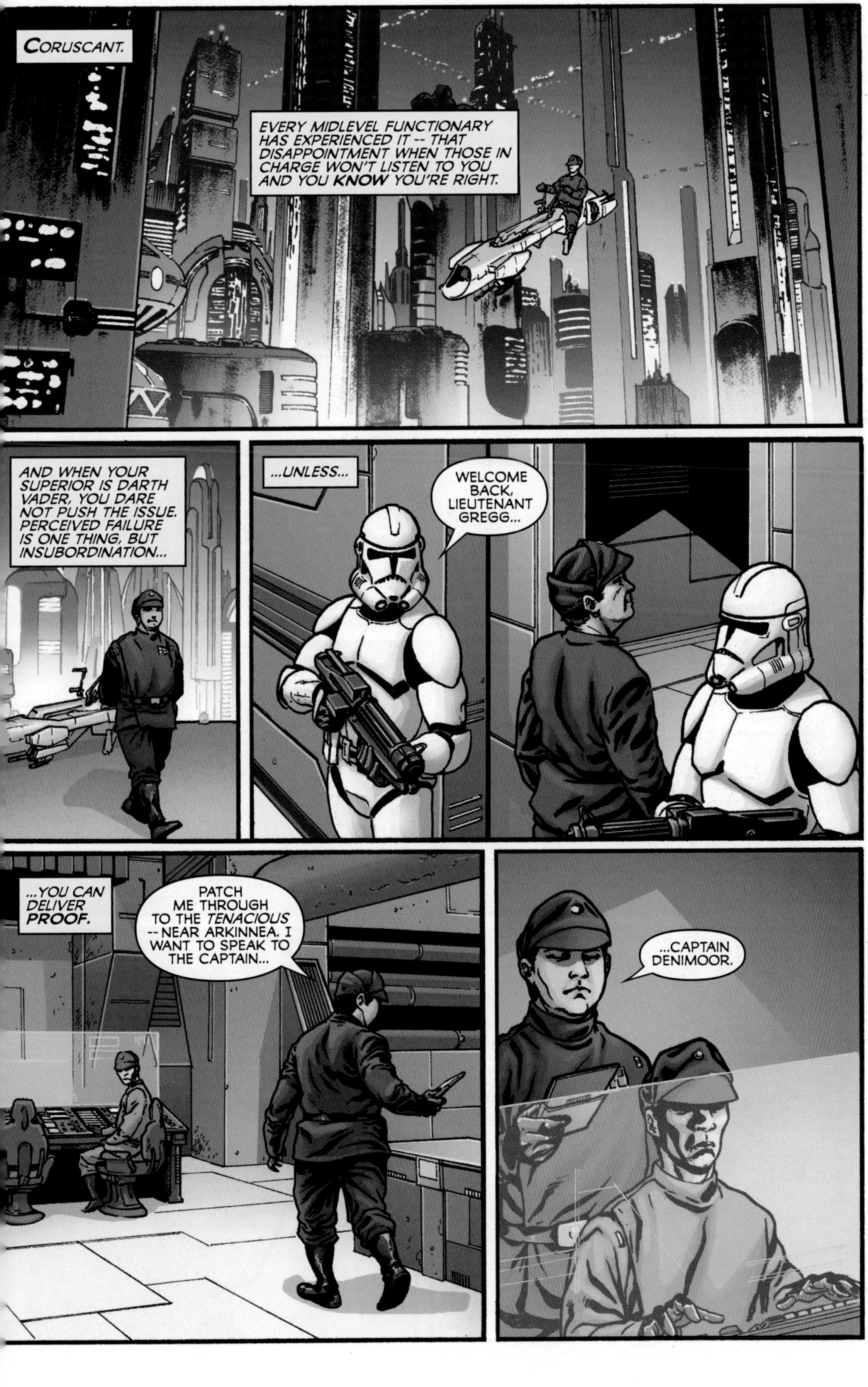
CORUSCANT.
EVERY MIDLEVEL FUNCTIONARY HAS EXPERIENCED IT -- THAT DISAPPOINTMENT WHEN THOSE IN CHARGE WON'T LISTEN TO YOU AND YOU **KNOW** YOU'RE RIGHT.
AND WHEN YOUR SUPERIOR IS DARTH VADER, YOU DARE NOT PUSH THE ISSUE. PERCEIVED FAILURE IS ONE THING, BUT INSUBORDINATION...
...UNLESS...
WELCOME BACK, LIEUTENANT GREGG...
...YOU CAN DELIVER **PROOF.**
PATCH ME THROUGH TO THE *TENACIOUS* -- NEAR ARKINNEA. I WANT TO SPEAK TO THE CAPTAIN...
...CAPTAIN DENIMOOR.

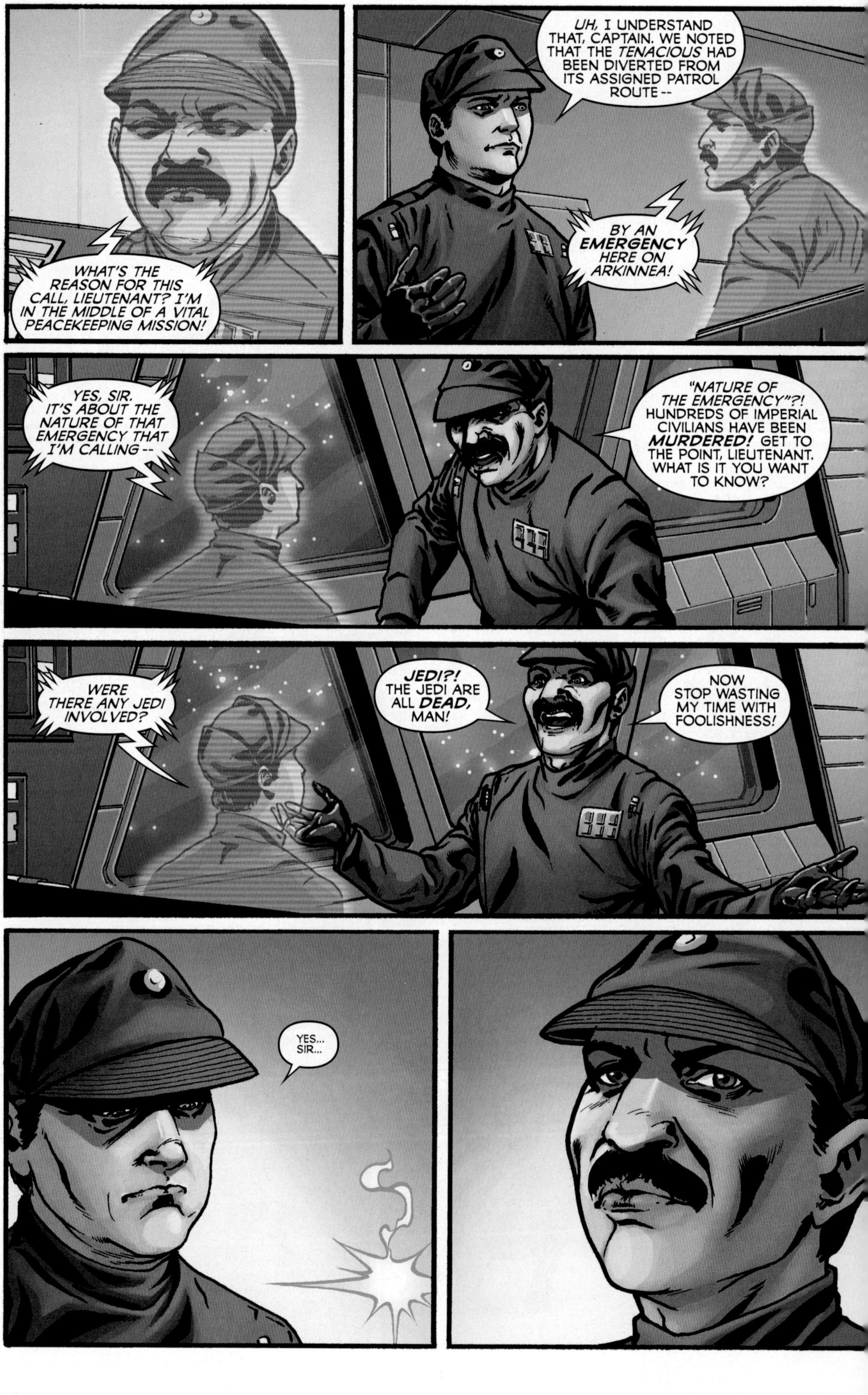
WHAT'S THE REASON FOR THIS CALL, LIEUTENANT? I'M IN THE MIDDLE OF A VITAL PEACEKEEPING MISSION!
UH, I UNDERSTAND THAT, CAPTAIN. WE NOTED THAT THE TENACIOUS HAD BEEN DIVERTED FROM ITS ASSIGNED PATROL ROUTE --
BY AN EMERGENCY HERE ON ARKINNEA!
YES, SIR. IT'S ABOUT THE NATURE OF THAT EMERGENCY THAT I'M CALLING --
"NATURE OF THE EMERGENCY"?! HUNDREDS OF IMPERIAL CIVILIANS HAVE BEEN MURDERED! GET TO THE POINT, LIEUTENANT. WHAT IS IT YOU WANT TO KNOW?
WERE THERE ANY JEDI INVOLVED?
JEDI?! THE JEDI ARE ALL DEAD, MAN!
NOW STOP WASTING MY TIME WITH FOOLISHNESS!
YES... SIR...

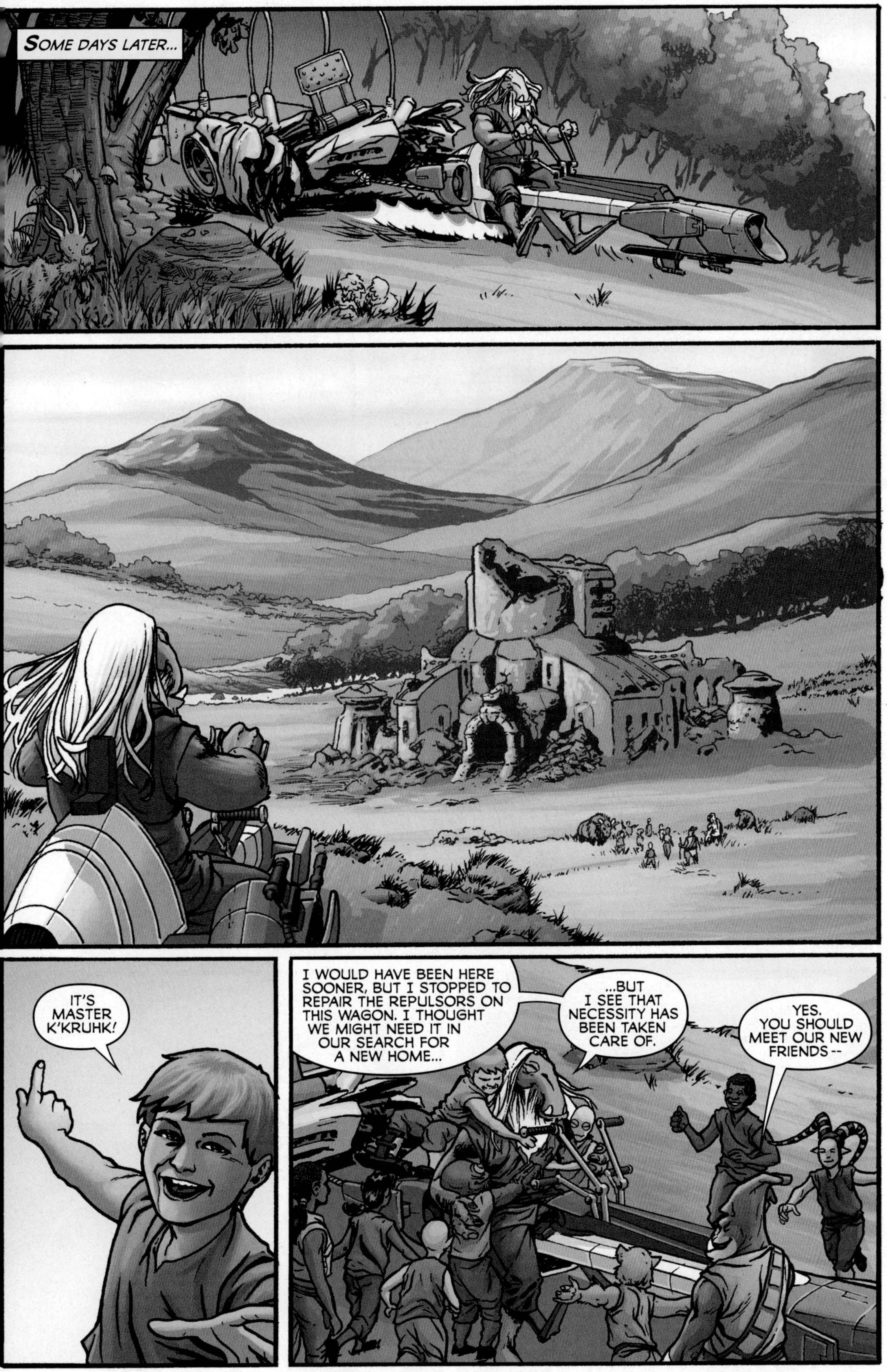
SOME DAYS LATER...
IT'S MASTER K'KRUHK!
I WOULD HAVE BEEN HERE SOONER, BUT I STOPPED TO REPAIR THE REPULSORS ON THIS WAGON. I THOUGHT WE MIGHT NEED IT IN OUR SEARCH FOR A NEW HOME...
...BUT I SEE THAT NECESSITY HAS BEEN TAKEN CARE OF.
YES. YOU SHOULD MEET OUR NEW FRIENDS --

"-- I THINK YOU'LL FIND THEM MOST INTERESTING."

J'EHDAI!

FROM WHAT I'VE BEEN ABLE TO PIECE TOGETHER, THIS WAS ONCE A JEDI OUTPOST. I'M GUESSING IT'S FROM NEAR THE MIDDLE OF THE OLD REPUBLIC.

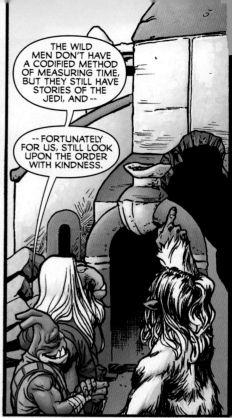

THE WILD MEN DON'T HAVE A CODIFIED METHOD OF MEASURING TIME, BUT THEY STILL HAVE STORIES OF THE JEDI, AND --

-- FORTUNATELY FOR US, STILL LOOK UPON THE ORDER WITH KINDNESS.

WHAT DO YOU THINK, MASTER?

I...

MASTER ZAO, PIRU -- WHERE IS SIDIRRI?! WAS SHE INJURED... OR...?

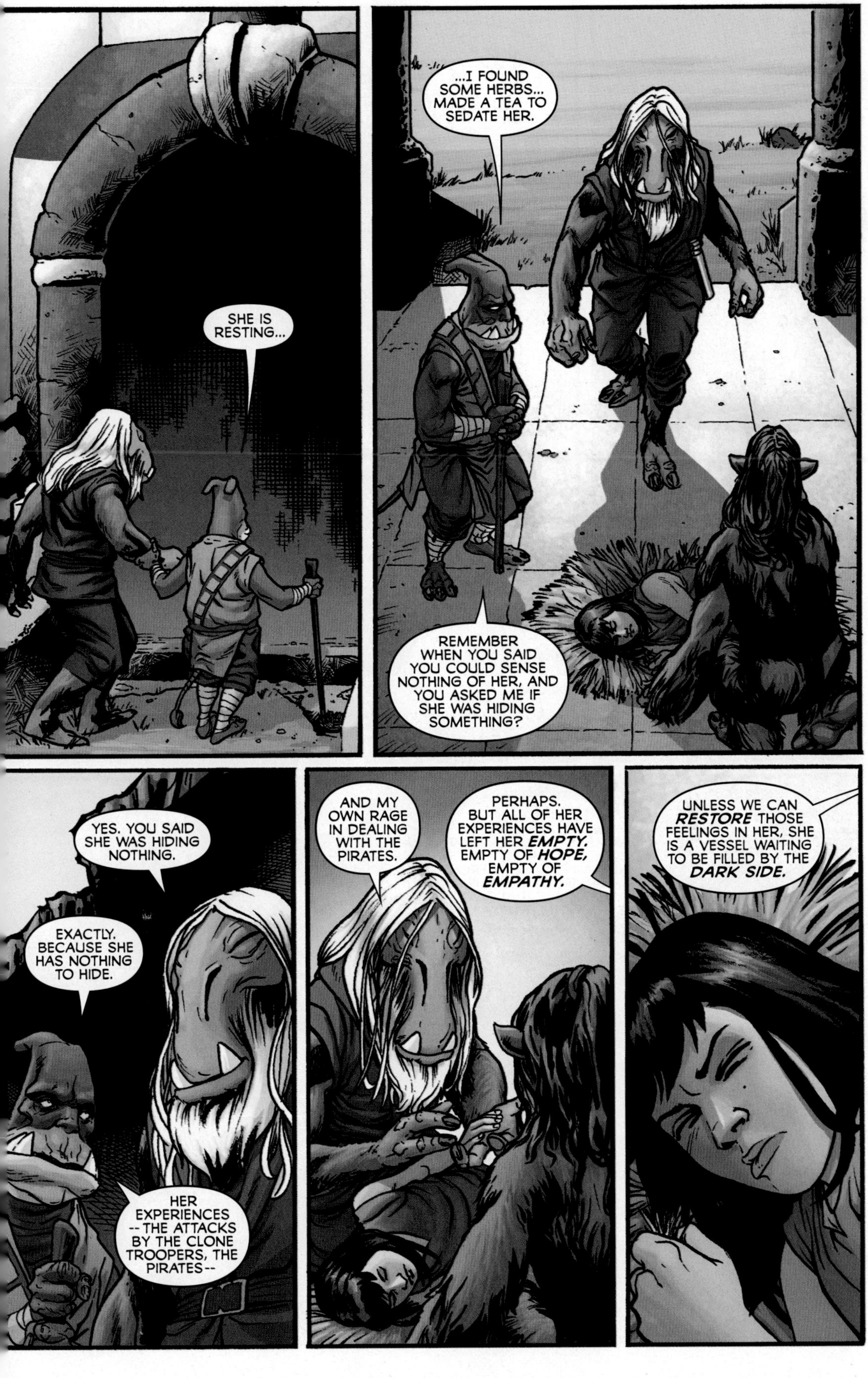
SHE IS RESTING...
...I FOUND SOME HERBS... MADE A TEA TO SEDATE HER.
REMEMBER WHEN YOU SAID YOU COULD SENSE NOTHING OF HER, AND YOU ASKED ME IF SHE WAS HIDING SOMETHING?
YES. YOU SAID SHE WAS HIDING NOTHING.
EXACTLY. BECAUSE SHE HAS NOTHING TO HIDE.
HER EXPERIENCES --THE ATTACKS BY THE CLONE TROOPERS, THE PIRATES--
AND MY OWN RAGE IN DEALING WITH THE PIRATES.
PERHAPS. BUT ALL OF HER EXPERIENCES HAVE LEFT HER *EMPTY.* EMPTY OF *HOPE,* EMPTY OF *EMPATHY.*
UNLESS WE CAN *RESTORE* THOSE FEELINGS IN HER, SHE IS A VESSEL WAITING TO BE FILLED BY THE *DARK SIDE.*

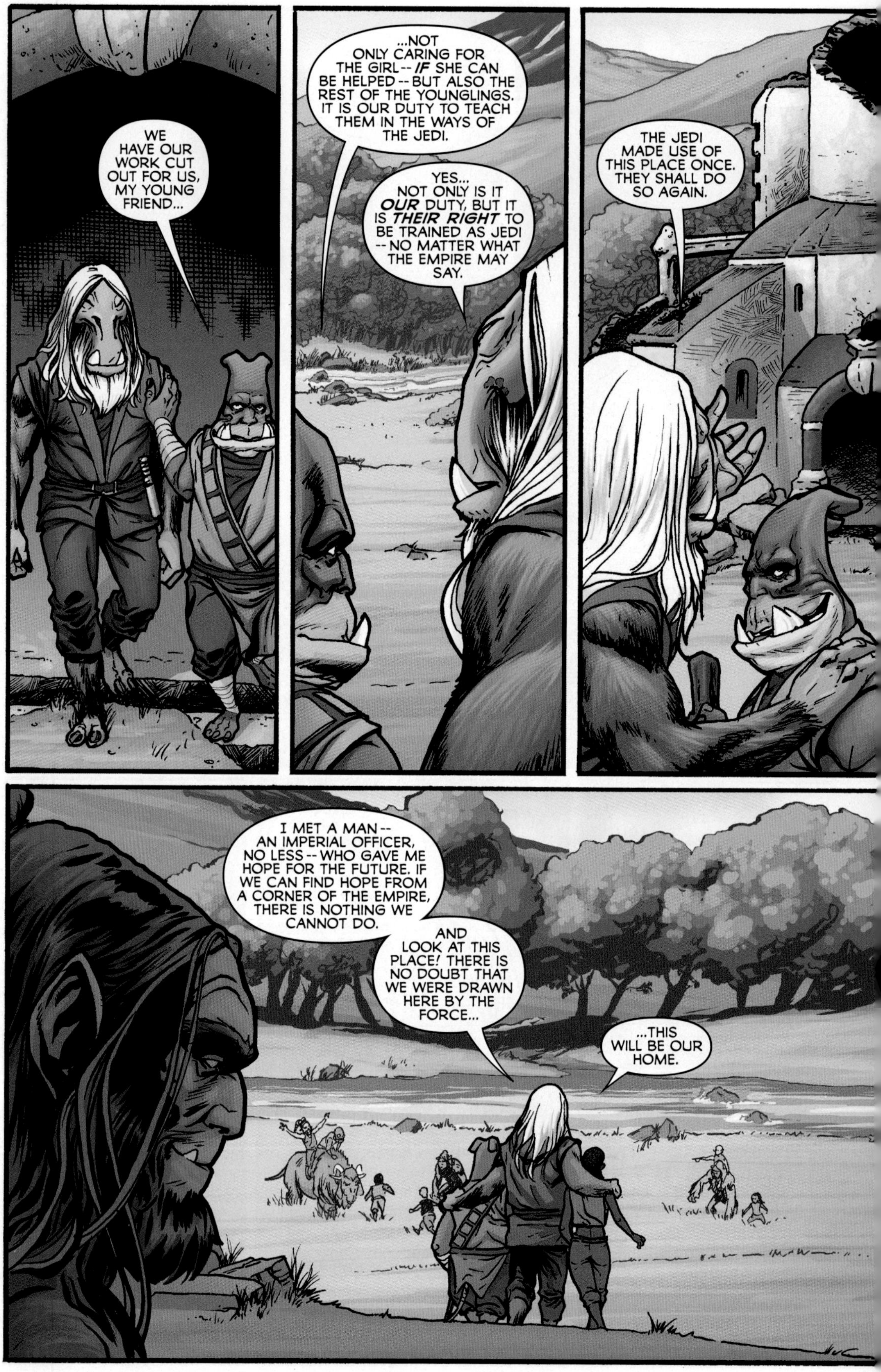
WE HAVE OUR WORK CUT OUT FOR US, MY YOUNG FRIEND...
...NOT ONLY CARING FOR THE GIRL--*IF* SHE CAN BE HELPED--BUT ALSO THE REST OF THE YOUNGLINGS. IT IS OUR DUTY TO TEACH THEM IN THE WAYS OF THE JEDI.
YES... NOT ONLY IS IT ***OUR*** DUTY, BUT IT IS ***THEIR RIGHT*** TO BE TRAINED AS JEDI--NO MATTER WHAT THE EMPIRE MAY SAY.
THE JEDI MADE USE OF THIS PLACE ONCE. THEY SHALL DO SO AGAIN.
I MET A MAN--AN IMPERIAL OFFICER, NO LESS--WHO GAVE ME HOPE FOR THE FUTURE. IF WE CAN FIND HOPE FROM A CORNER OF THE EMPIRE, THERE IS NOTHING WE CANNOT DO.
AND LOOK AT THIS PLACE! THERE IS NO DOUBT THAT WE WERE DRAWN HERE BY THE FORCE...
...THIS WILL BE OUR HOME.

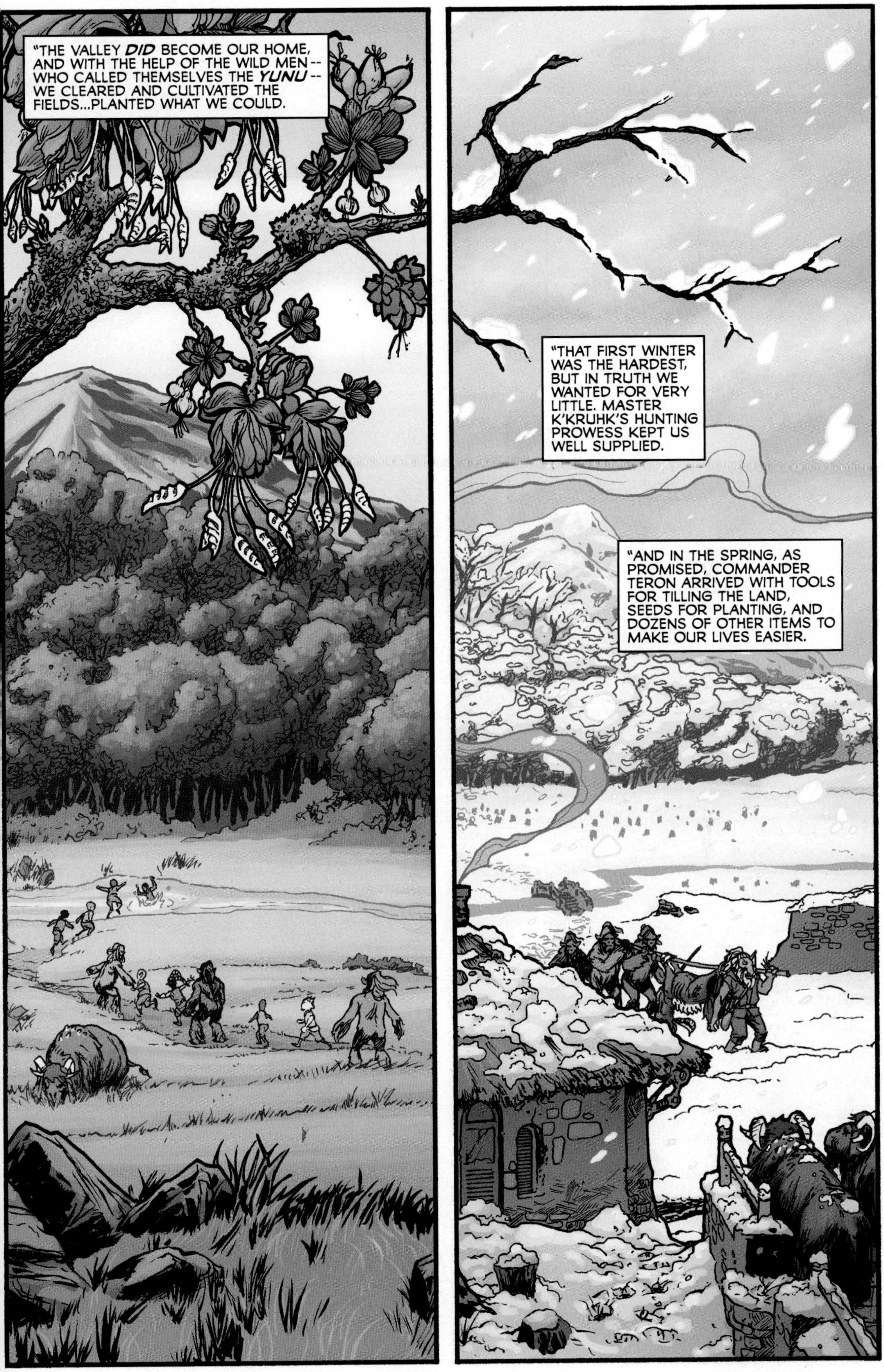
"THE VALLEY DID BECOME OUR HOME, AND WITH THE HELP OF THE WILD MEN -- WHO CALLED THEMSELVES THE YUNU -- WE CLEARED AND CULTIVATED THE FIELDS...PLANTED WHAT WE COULD.
"THAT FIRST WINTER WAS THE HARDEST, BUT IN TRUTH WE WANTED FOR VERY LITTLE. MASTER K'KRUHK'S HUNTING PROWESS KEPT US WELL SUPPLIED.
"AND IN THE SPRING, AS PROMISED, COMMANDER TERON ARRIVED WITH TOOLS FOR TILLING THE LAND, SEEDS FOR PLANTING, AND DOZENS OF OTHER ITEMS TO MAKE OUR LIVES EASIER.

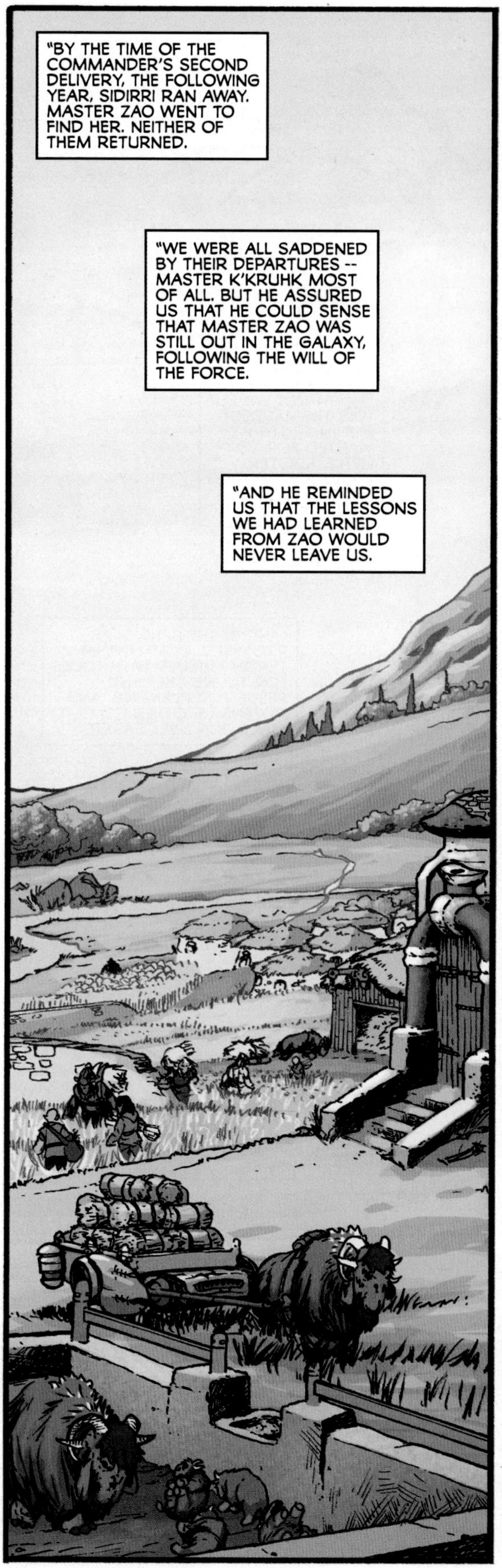
"BY THE TIME OF THE COMMANDER'S SECOND DELIVERY, THE FOLLOWING YEAR, SIDIRRI RAN AWAY. MASTER ZAO WENT TO FIND HER. NEITHER OF THEM RETURNED.
"WE WERE ALL SADDENED BY THEIR DEPARTURES -- MASTER K'KRUHK MOST OF ALL. BUT HE ASSURED US THAT HE COULD SENSE THAT MASTER ZAO WAS STILL OUT IN THE GALAXY, FOLLOWING THE WILL OF THE FORCE.
"AND HE REMINDED US THAT THE LESSONS WE HAD LEARNED FROM ZAO WOULD NEVER LEAVE US.

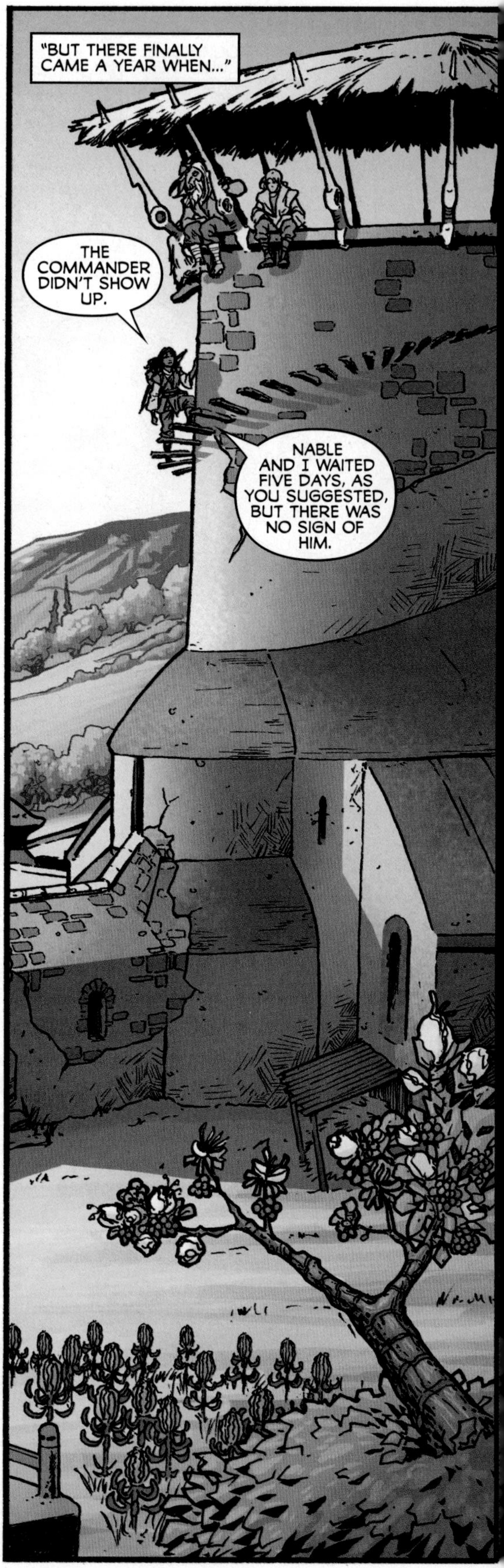
"BUT THERE FINALLY CAME A YEAR WHEN..."
THE COMMANDER DIDN'T SHOW UP.
NABLE AND I WAITED FIVE DAYS, AS YOU SUGGESTED, BUT THERE WAS NO SIGN OF HIM.

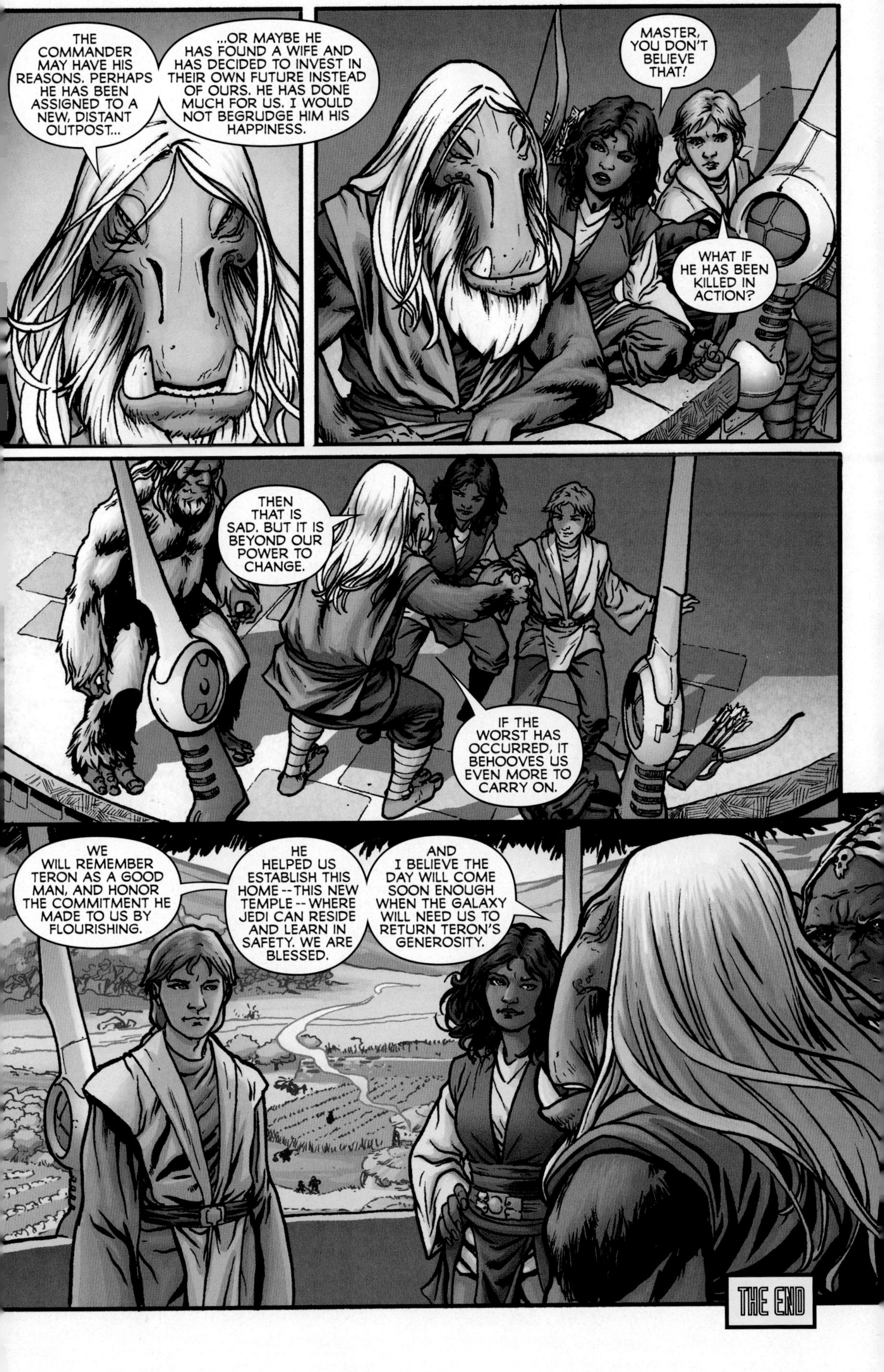
THE COMMANDER MAY HAVE HIS REASONS. PERHAPS HE HAS BEEN ASSIGNED TO A NEW, DISTANT OUTPOST...
...OR MAYBE HE HAS FOUND A WIFE AND HAS DECIDED TO INVEST IN THEIR OWN FUTURE INSTEAD OF OURS. HE HAS DONE MUCH FOR US. I WOULD NOT BEGRUDGE HIM HIS HAPPINESS.
MASTER, YOU DON'T BELIEVE THAT!
WHAT IF HE HAS BEEN KILLED IN ACTION?
THEN THAT IS SAD. BUT IT IS BEYOND OUR POWER TO CHANGE.
IF THE WORST HAS OCCURRED, IT BEHOOVES US EVEN MORE TO CARRY ON.
WE WILL REMEMBER TERON AS A GOOD MAN, AND HONOR THE COMMITMENT HE MADE TO US BY FLOURISHING.
HE HELPED US ESTABLISH THIS HOME -- THIS NEW TEMPLE -- WHERE JEDI CAN RESIDE AND LEARN IN SAFETY. WE ARE BLESSED.
AND I BELIEVE THE DAY WILL COME SOON ENOUGH WHEN THE GALAXY WILL NEED US TO RETURN TERON'S GENEROSITY.
THE END

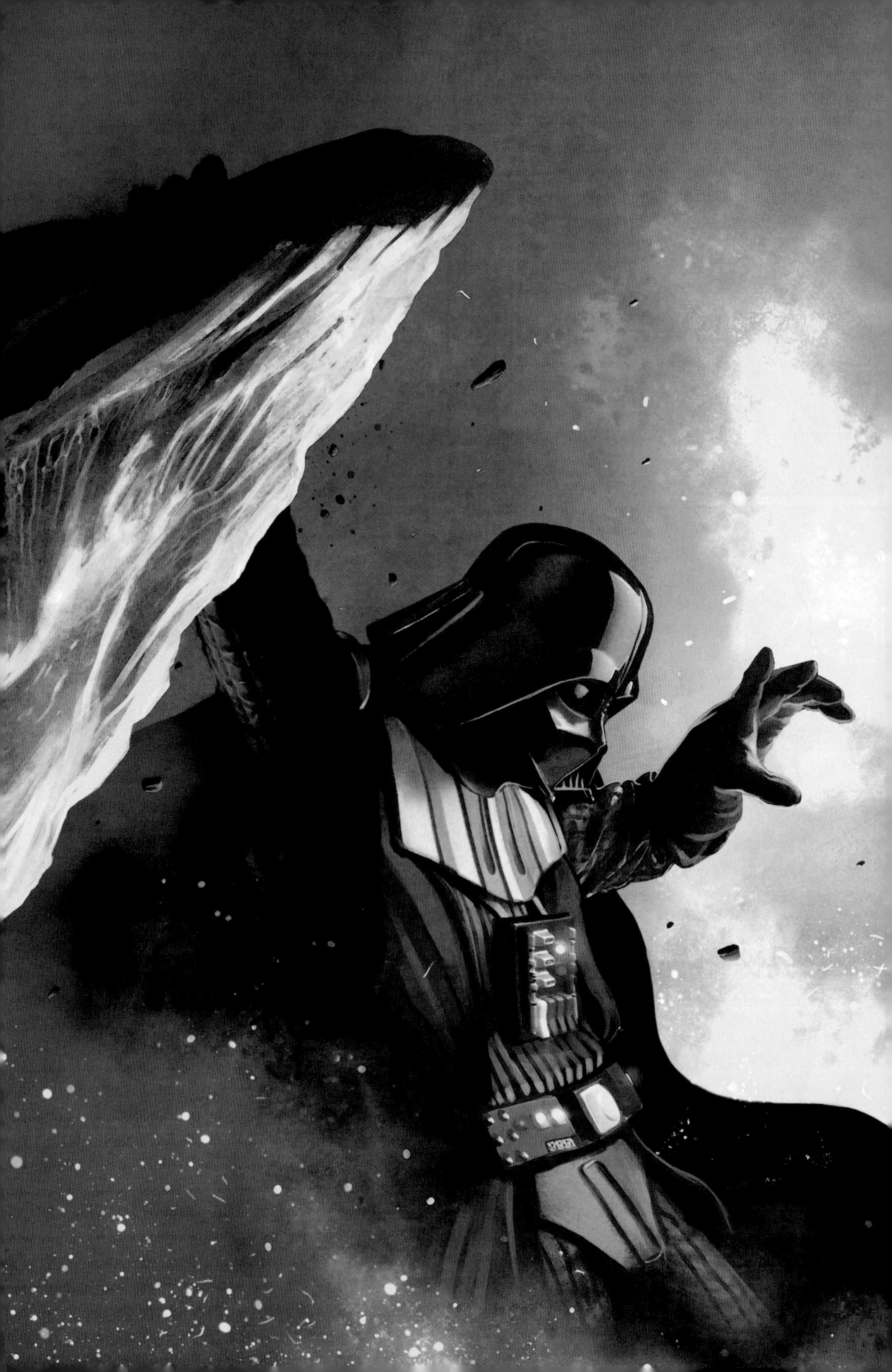

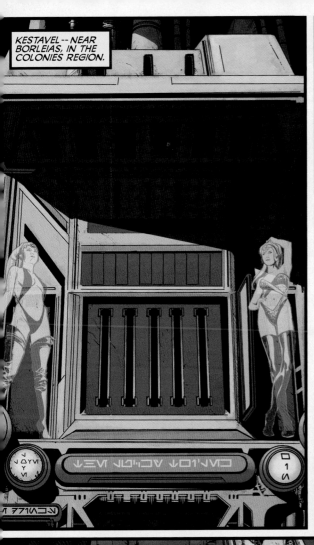

KESTAVEL -- NEAR BORLEIAS, IN THE COLONIES REGION.

THEY'RE APPROACHING THE SECOND ARCH!

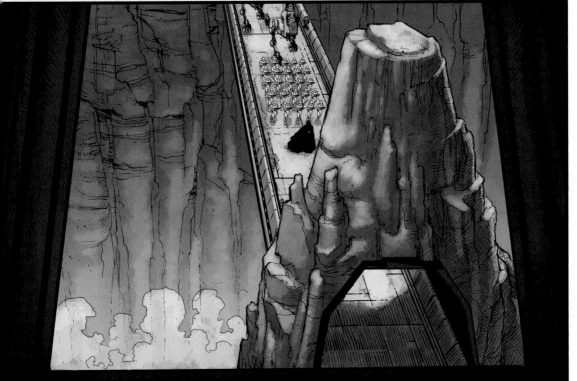

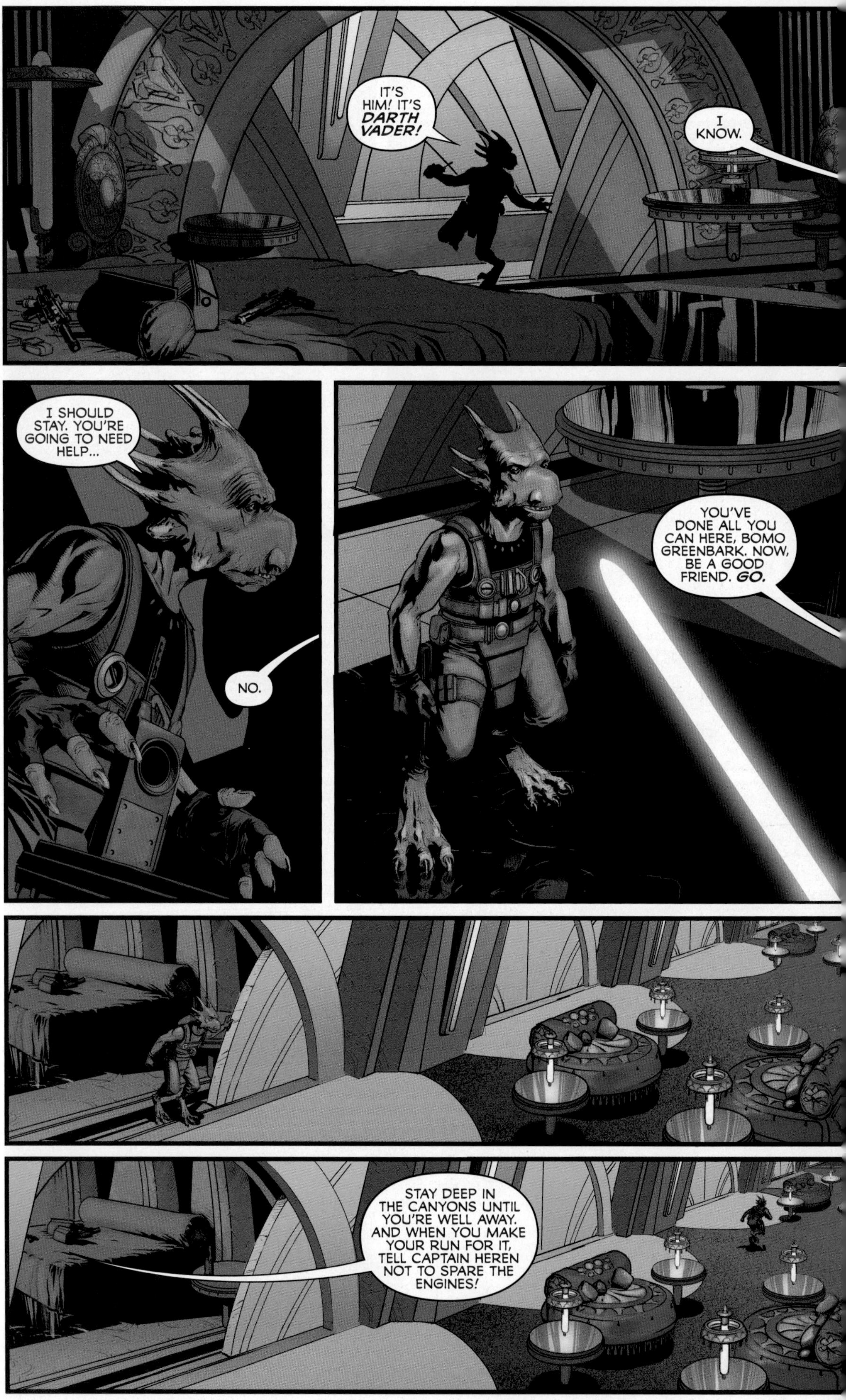
IT'S HIM! IT'S *DARTH VADER!*
I KNOW.
I SHOULD STAY. YOU'RE GOING TO NEED HELP...
NO.
YOU'VE DONE ALL YOU CAN HERE, BOMO GREENBARK. NOW, BE A GOOD FRIEND. *GO.*
STAY DEEP IN THE CANYONS UNTIL YOU'RE WELL AWAY. AND WHEN YOU MAKE YOUR RUN FOR IT, TELL CAPTAIN HEREN NOT TO SPARE THE ENGINES!

FORWARD!

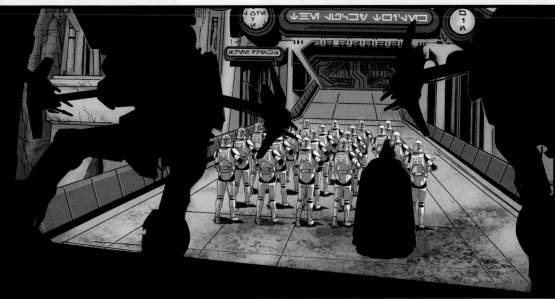

DRIP
DRIP
DRIP

FOOSH!

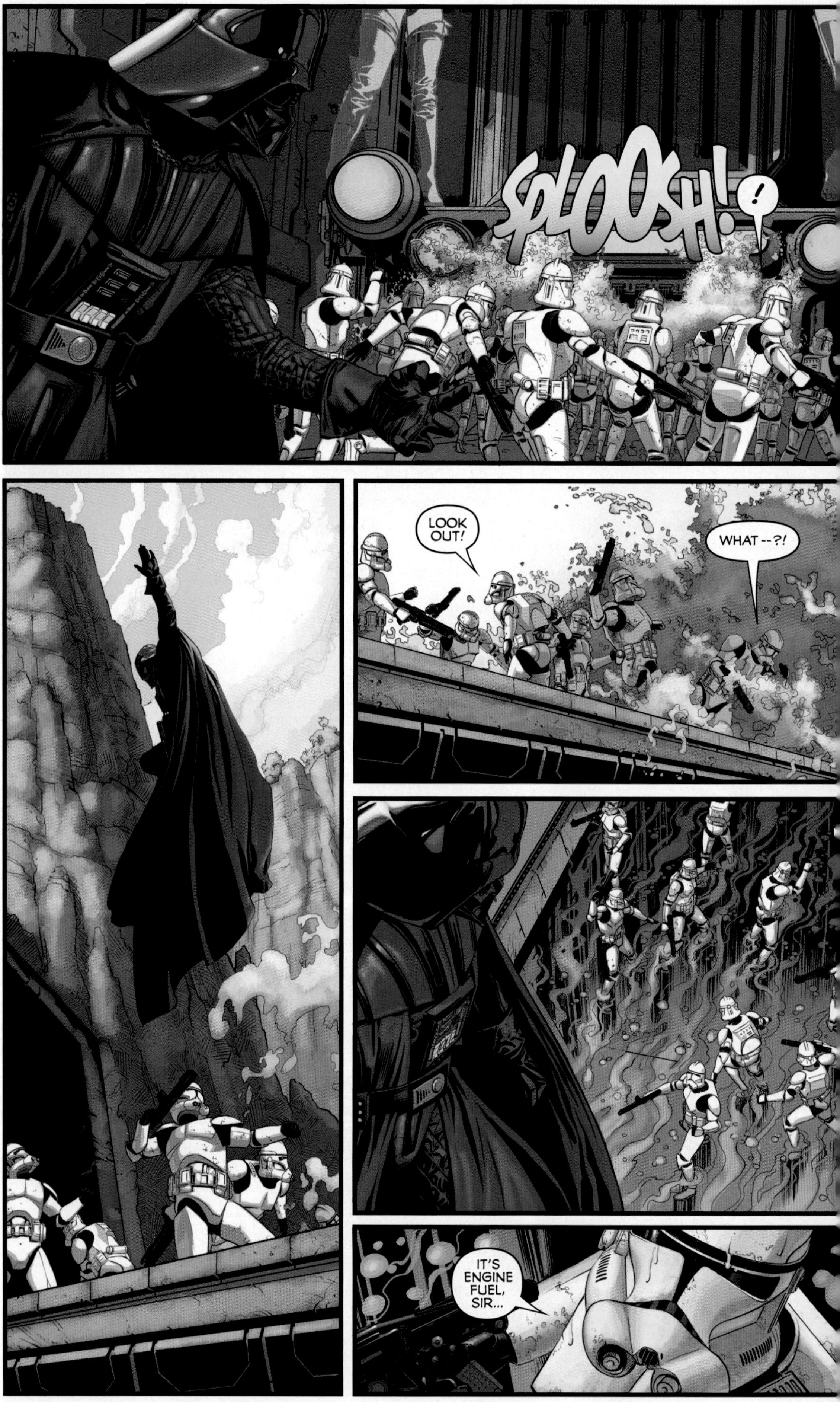
SPLOOSH!
!
LOOK OUT!
WHAT --?!
IT'S ENGINE FUEL, SIR...

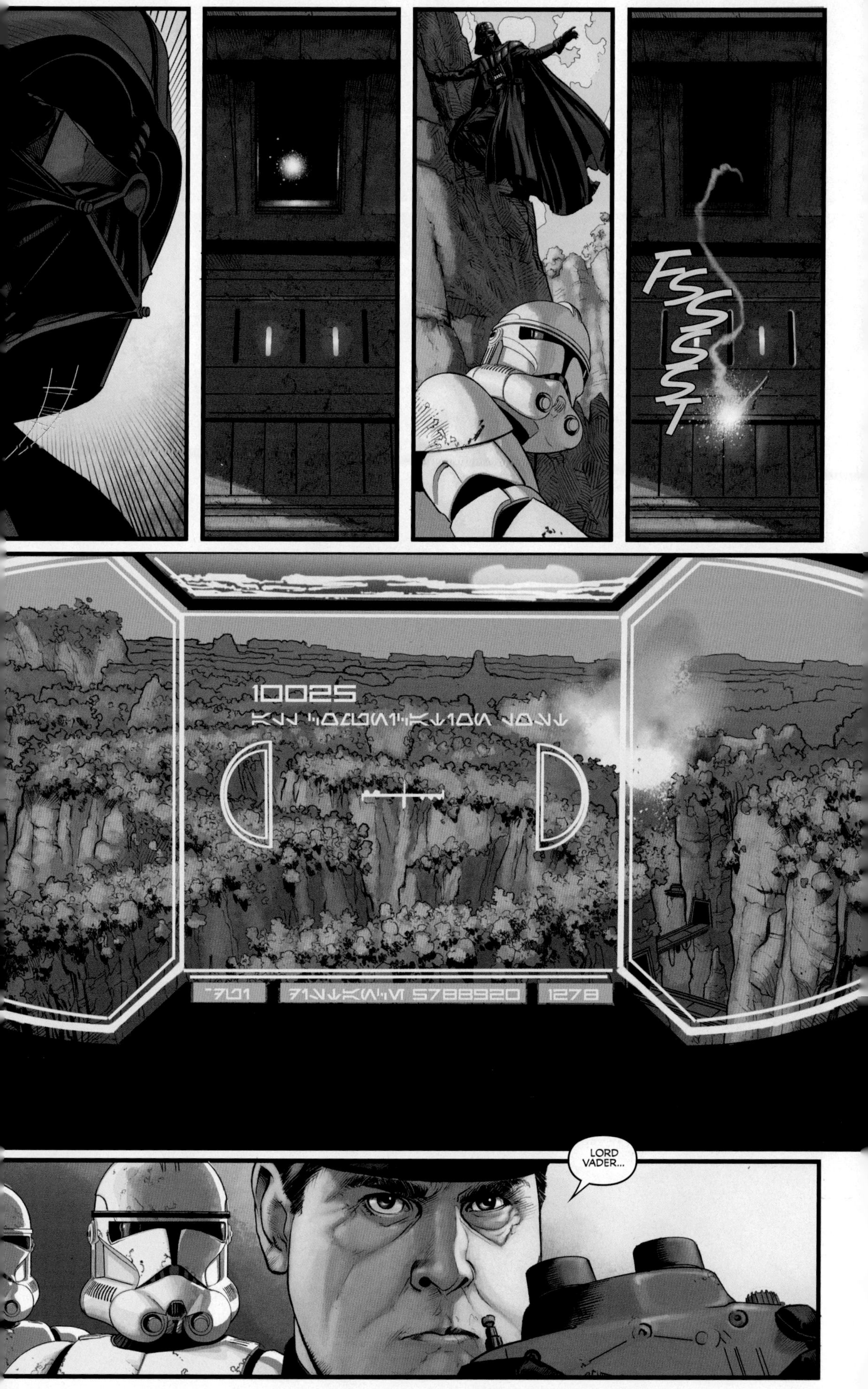
FSSSST
10025
5788920
1278
LORD VADER...

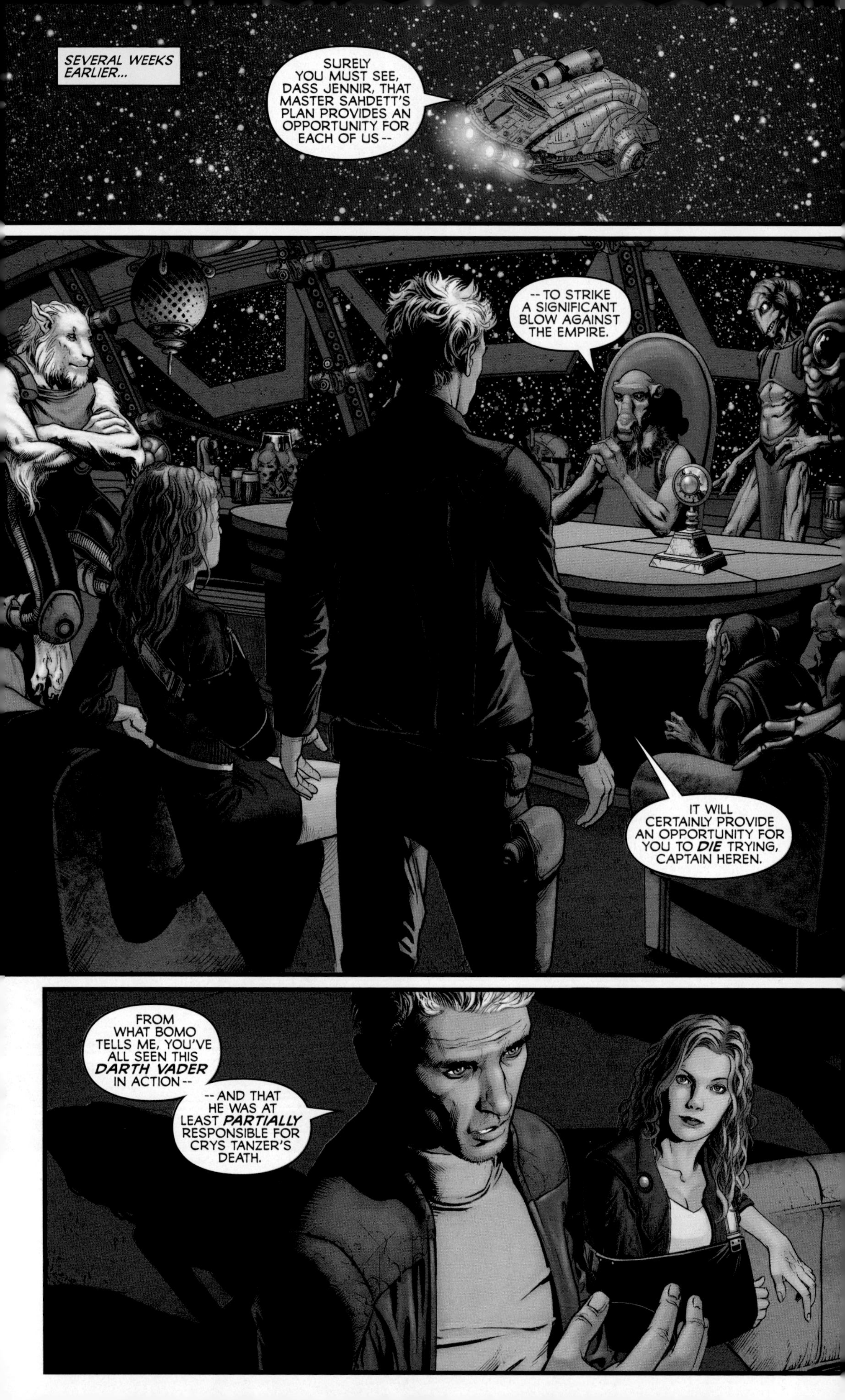
SEVERAL WEEKS EARLIER...
SURELY YOU MUST SEE, DASS JENNIR, THAT MASTER SAHDETT'S PLAN PROVIDES AN OPPORTUNITY FOR EACH OF US --
-- TO STRIKE A SIGNIFICANT BLOW AGAINST THE EMPIRE.
IT WILL CERTAINLY PROVIDE AN OPPORTUNITY FOR YOU TO *DIE* TRYING, CAPTAIN HEREN.
FROM WHAT BOMO TELLS ME, YOU'VE ALL SEEN THIS *DARTH VADER* IN ACTION --
-- AND THAT HE WAS AT LEAST *PARTIALLY* RESPONSIBLE FOR CRYS TANZER'S DEATH.

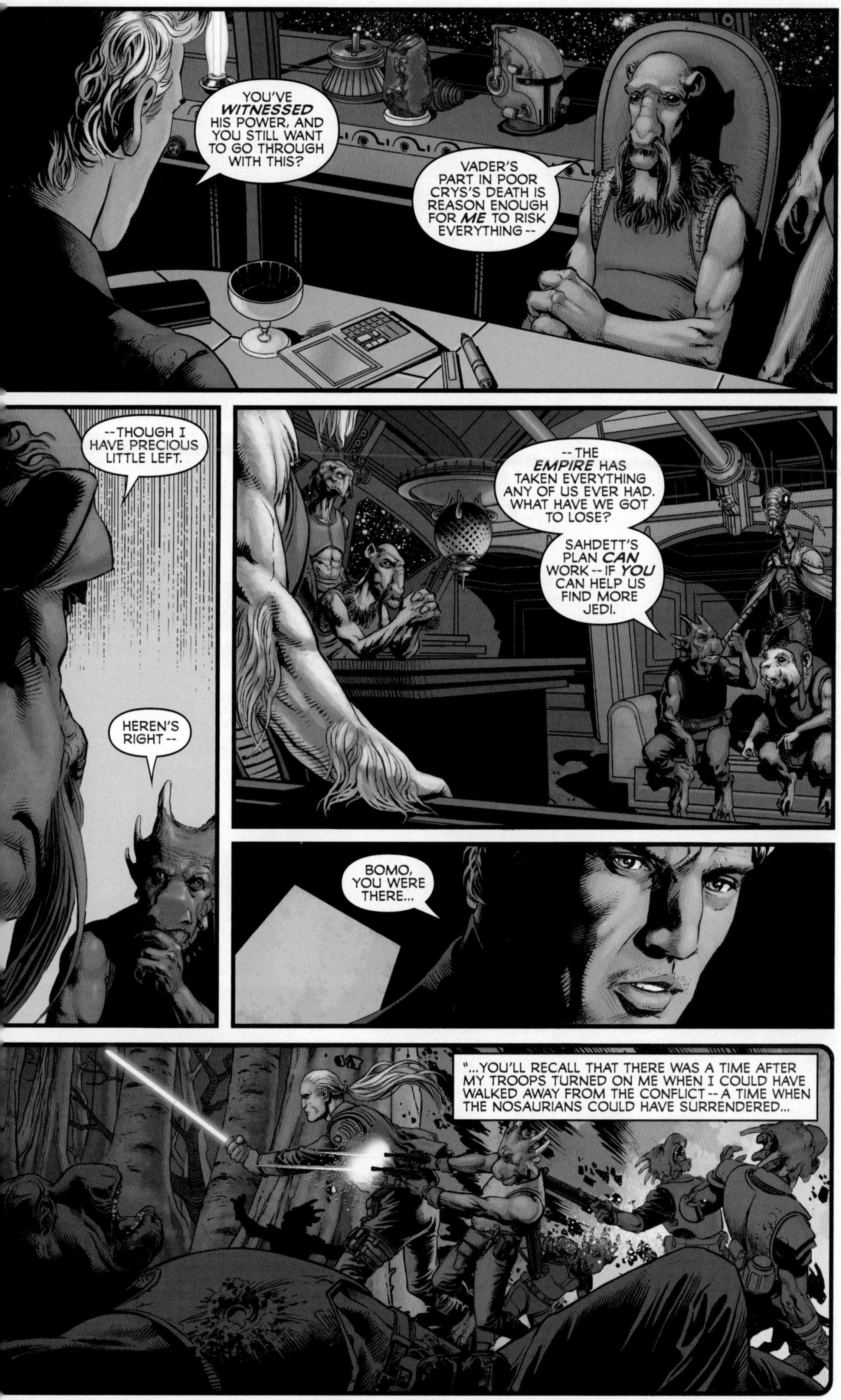
YOU'VE WITNESSED HIS POWER, AND YOU STILL WANT TO GO THROUGH WITH THIS?
VADER'S PART IN POOR CRYS'S DEATH IS REASON ENOUGH FOR ME TO RISK EVERYTHING --
--THOUGH I HAVE PRECIOUS LITTLE LEFT.
HEREN'S RIGHT --
-- THE EMPIRE HAS TAKEN EVERYTHING ANY OF US EVER HAD. WHAT HAVE WE GOT TO LOSE?
SAHDETT'S PLAN CAN WORK -- IF YOU CAN HELP US FIND MORE JEDI.
BOMO, YOU WERE THERE...
"...YOU'LL RECALL THAT THERE WAS A TIME AFTER MY TROOPS TURNED ON ME WHEN I COULD HAVE WALKED AWAY FROM THE CONFLICT -- A TIME WHEN THE NOSAURIANS COULD HAVE SURRENDERED...

"...BUT INSTEAD, WE ALL CHOSE TO FIGHT. DO NOT TELL ME THAT YOU HAVE FORGOTTEN THAT OUR DECISIONS LED TO THE ENSLAVEMENT OF *ALL* OF YOUR PEOPLE AND --"

-- THE DEATHS OF YOUR WIFE AND DAUGHTER.

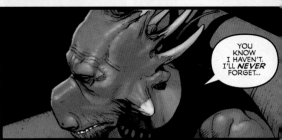

YOU KNOW I HAVEN'T. I'LL *NEVER* FORGET...

...BUT I'VE HAD TIME TO THINK.

I COULDN'T SEE IT AT THE TIME, BUT I REALIZE NOW THAT SURRENDERING TO THE EMPIRE WOULD NOT HAVE CHANGED THE FATE OF MY PEOPLE... OR OF MY MESA AND RESA. WE'D ALL BE ENSLAVED. OR DEAD.

WE MADE THE RIGHT DECISION TO KEEP ON FIGHTING. WE SURVIVED. AND NOW I WANT TO LIVE --

"-- AT LEAST LONG ENOUGH TO GET A BETTER REVENGE THAN THE ONE YOU ROBBED ME OF ON ESSELES."

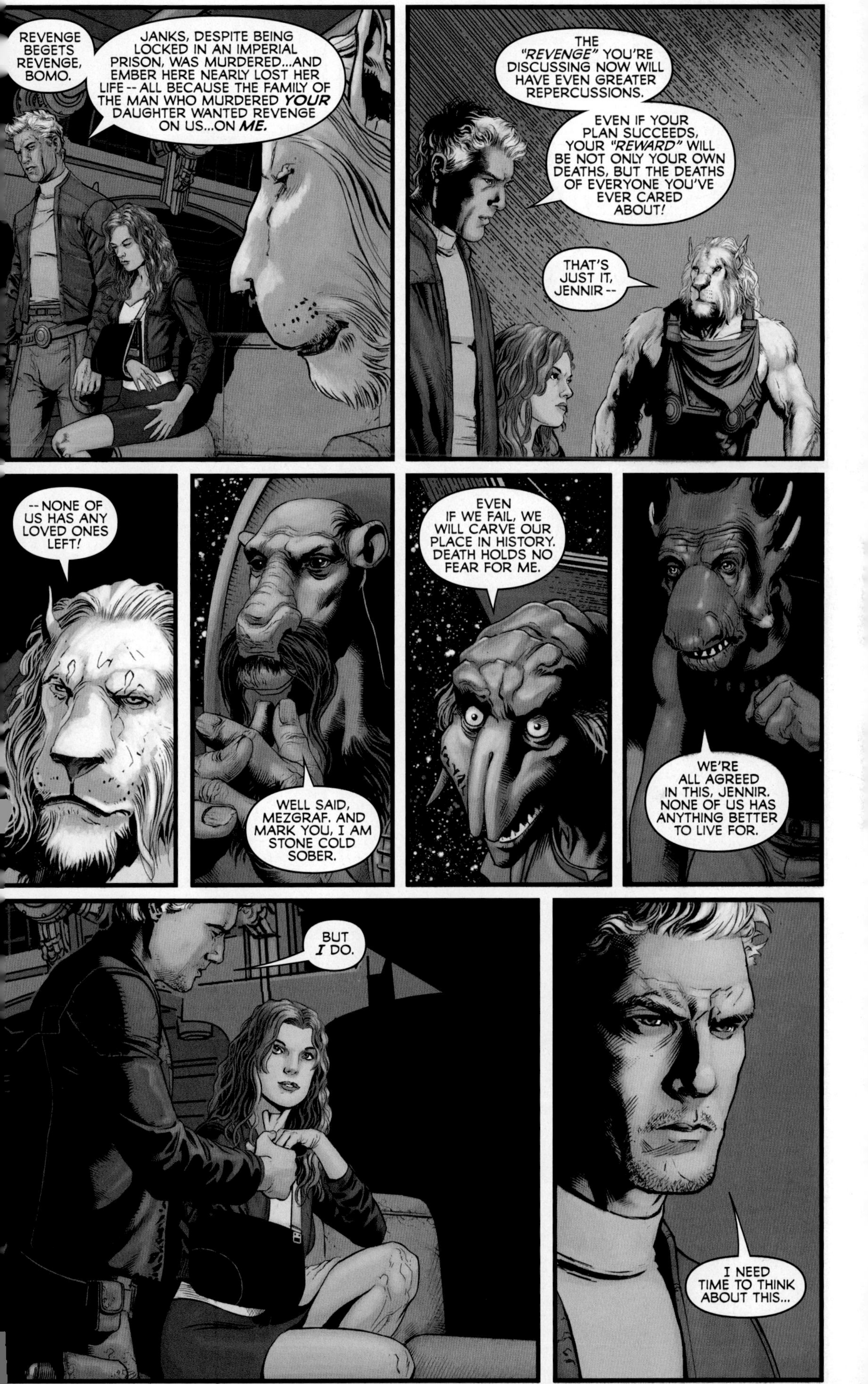
REVENGE BEGETS REVENGE, BOMO.
JANKS, DESPITE BEING LOCKED IN AN IMPERIAL PRISON, WAS MURDERED...AND EMBER HERE NEARLY LOST HER LIFE -- ALL BECAUSE THE FAMILY OF THE MAN WHO MURDERED YOUR DAUGHTER WANTED REVENGE ON US...ON ME.
THE "REVENGE" YOU'RE DISCUSSING NOW WILL HAVE EVEN GREATER REPERCUSSIONS.
EVEN IF YOUR PLAN SUCCEEDS, YOUR "REWARD" WILL BE NOT ONLY YOUR OWN DEATHS, BUT THE DEATHS OF EVERYONE YOU'VE EVER CARED ABOUT!
THAT'S JUST IT, JENNIR --
-- NONE OF US HAS ANY LOVED ONES LEFT!
WELL SAID, MEZGRAF. AND MARK YOU, I AM STONE COLD SOBER.
EVEN IF WE FAIL, WE WILL CARVE OUR PLACE IN HISTORY. DEATH HOLDS NO FEAR FOR ME.
WE'RE ALL AGREED IN THIS, JENNIR. NONE OF US HAS ANYTHING BETTER TO LIVE FOR.
BUT I DO.
I NEED TIME TO THINK ABOUT THIS...

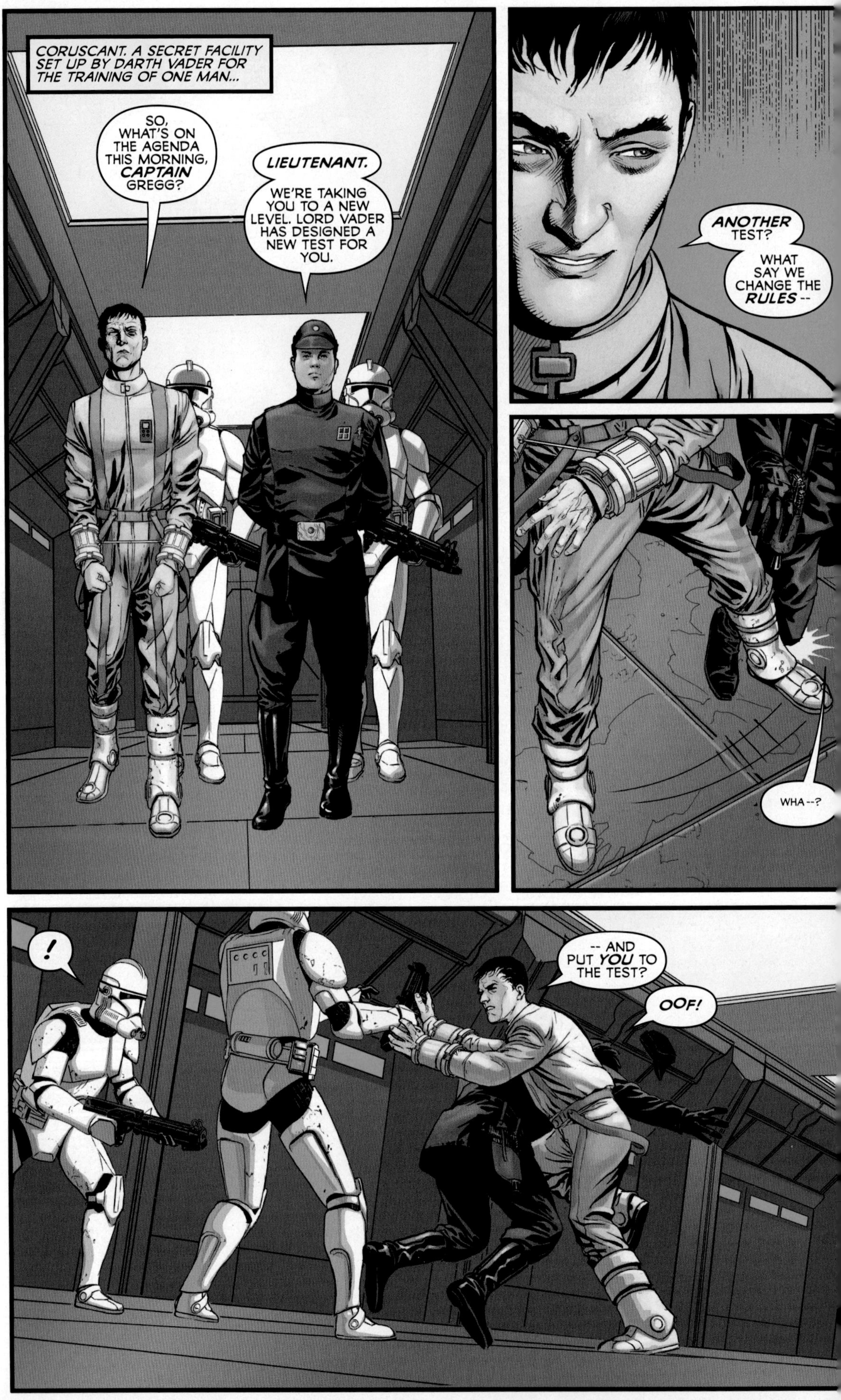
CORUSCANT. A SECRET FACILITY SET UP BY DARTH VADER FOR THE TRAINING OF ONE MAN...
SO, WHAT'S ON THE AGENDA THIS MORNING, CAPTAIN GREGG?
LIEUTENANT.
WE'RE TAKING YOU TO A NEW LEVEL. LORD VADER HAS DESIGNED A NEW TEST FOR YOU.
ANOTHER TEST?
WHAT SAY WE CHANGE THE RULES --
WHA--?
!
-- AND PUT YOU TO THE TEST?
OOF!

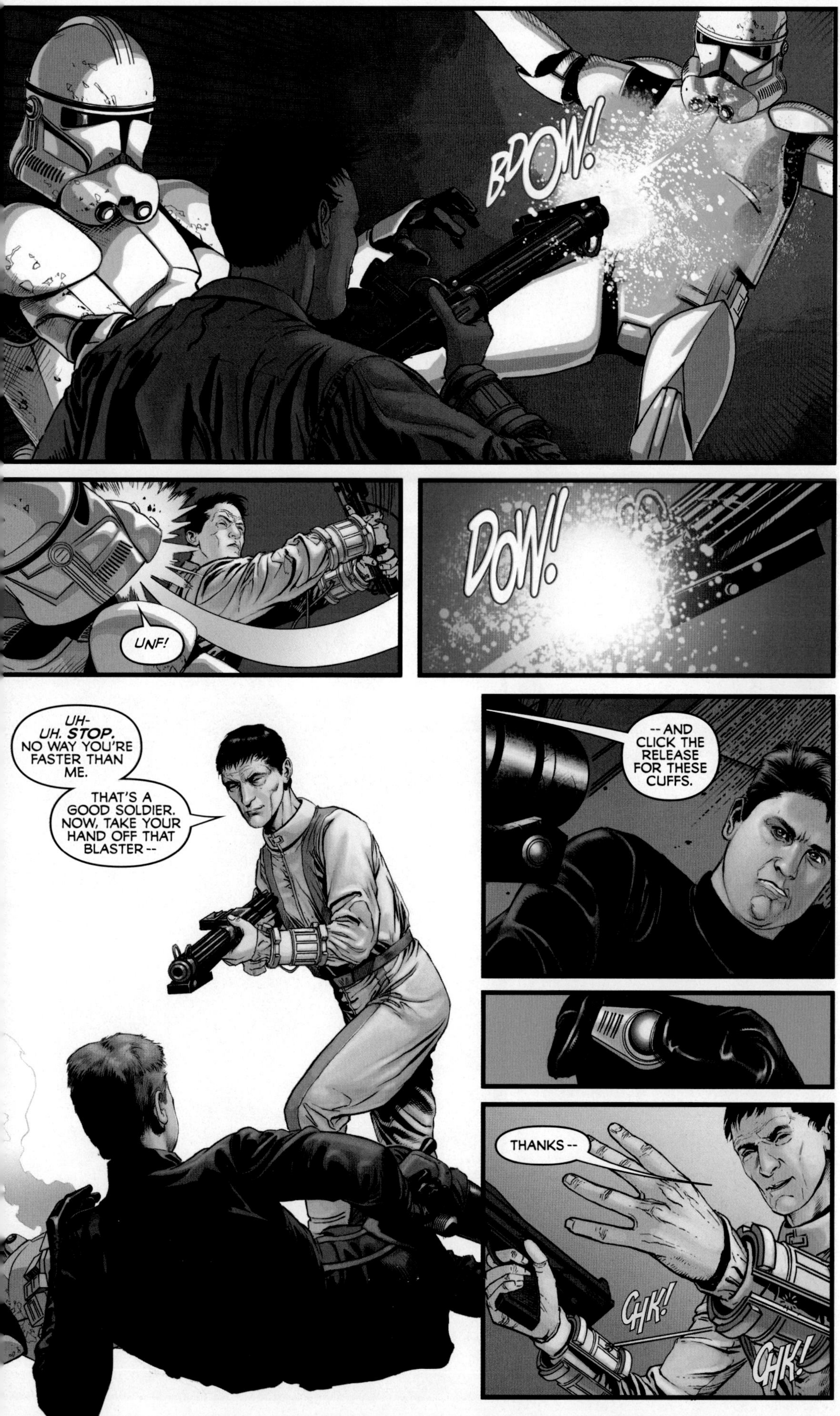
BDOW!
UNF!
DOW!
UH-UH. **STOP.** NO WAY YOU'RE FASTER THAN ME.
THAT'S A GOOD SOLDIER. NOW, TAKE YOUR HAND OFF THAT BLASTER --
-- AND CLICK THE RELEASE FOR THESE CUFFS.
THANKS --
CHK!
CHK!

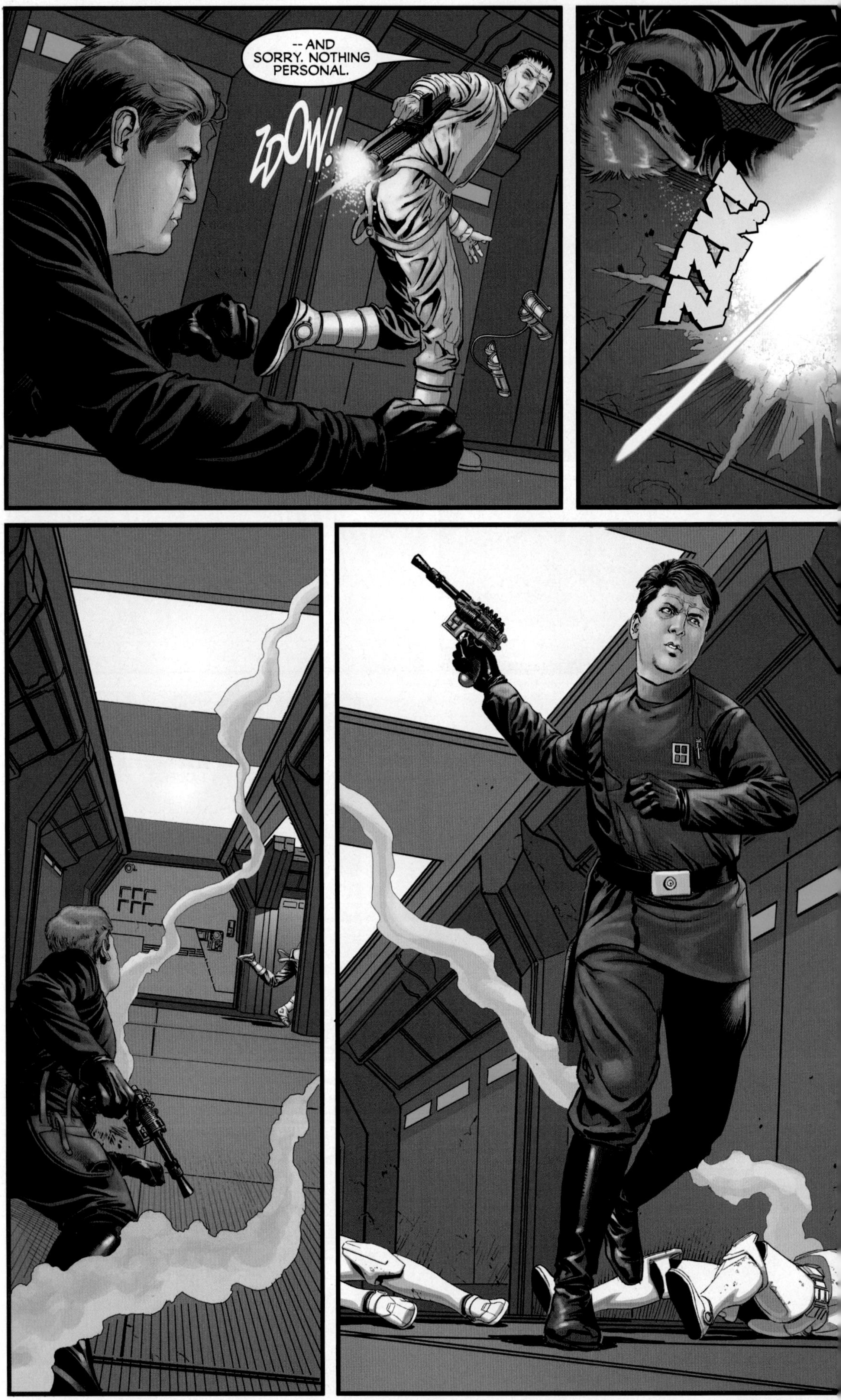
-- AND SORRY. NOTHING PERSONAL.
ZDOW!!
ZZK!

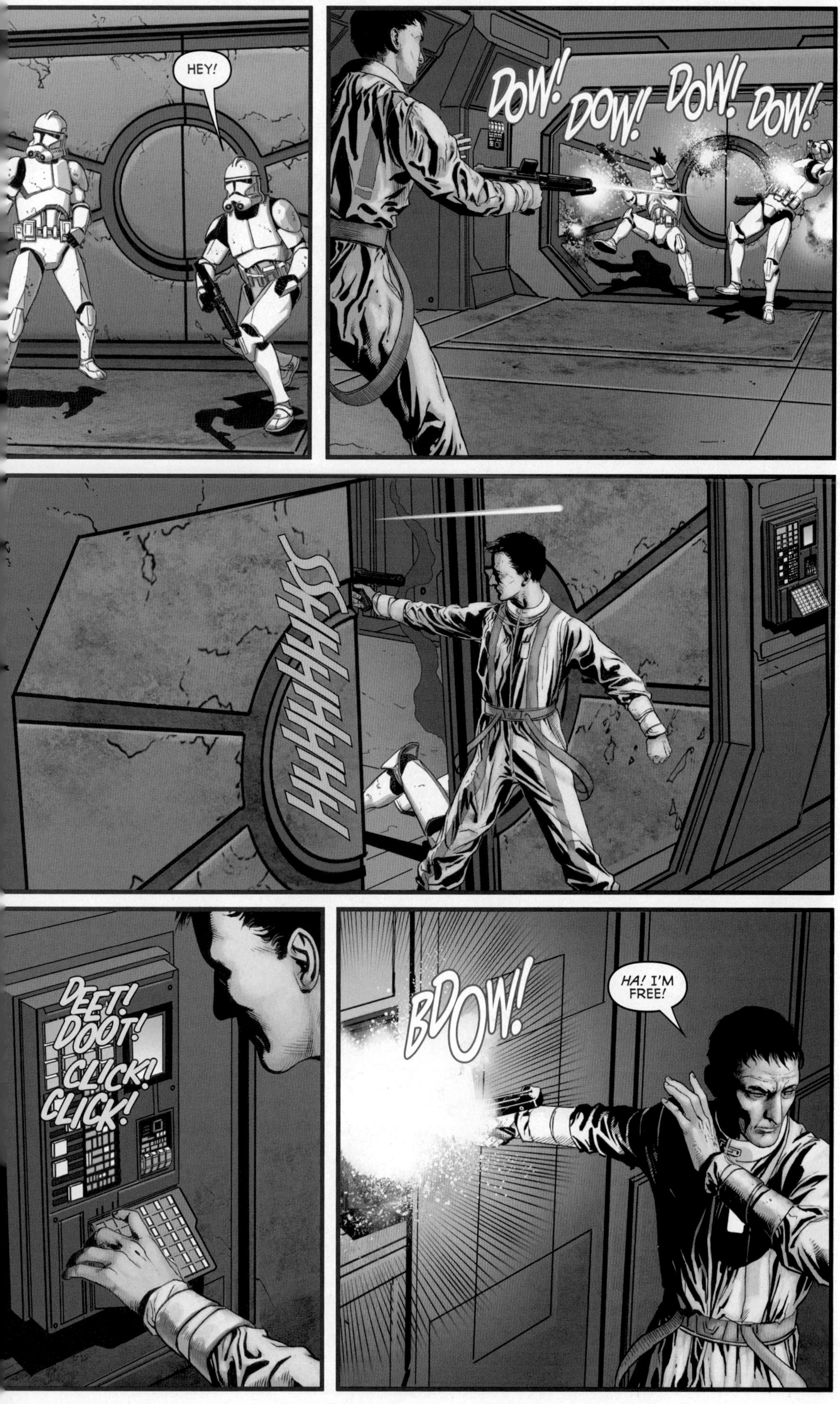
HEY!
DOW! DOW! DOW! DOW!
SHHHHHHH
DEET! DOOT! CLICK! CLICK!
BDOW!
HA! I'M FREE!

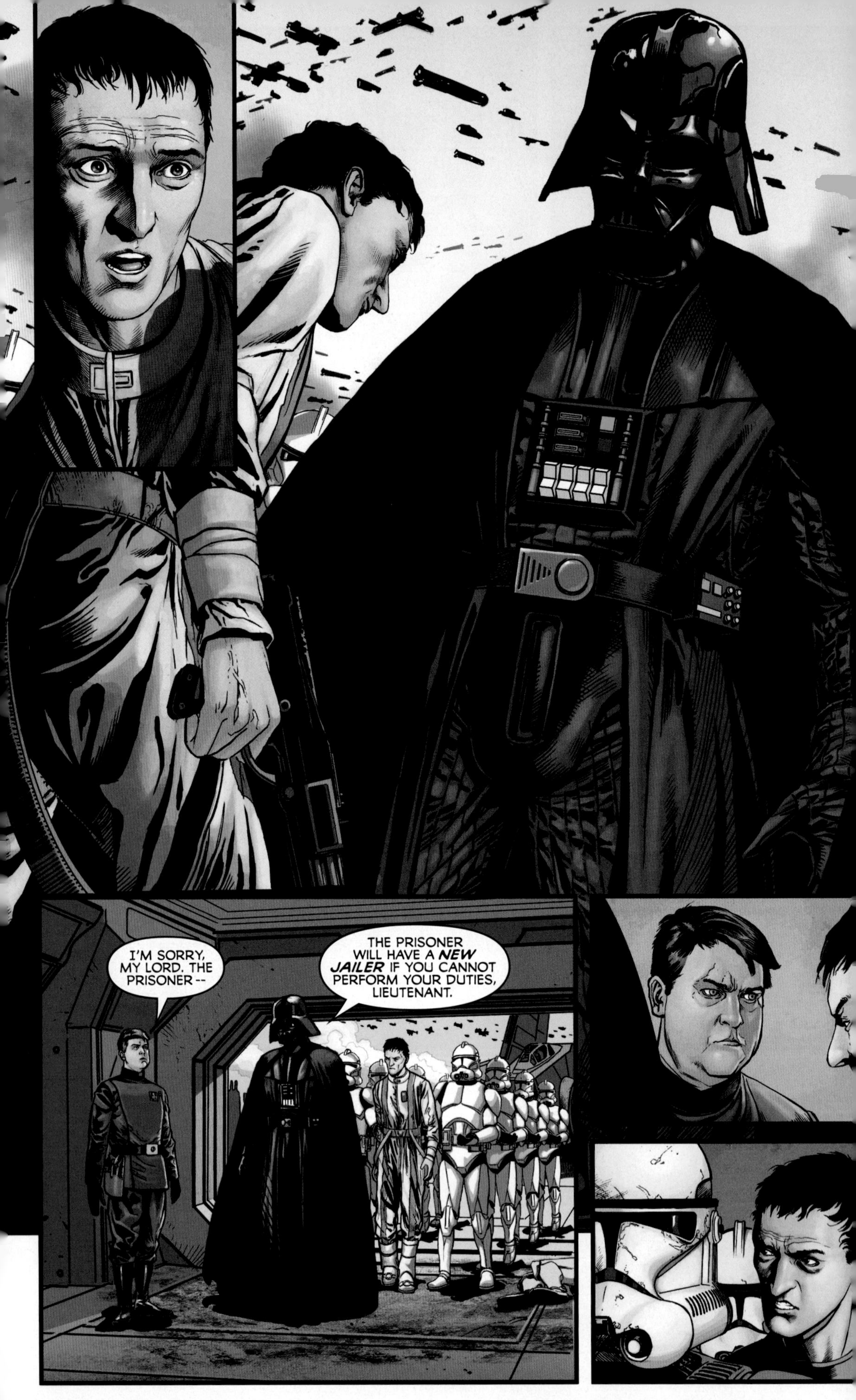
I'M SORRY, MY LORD. THE PRISONER --
THE PRISONER WILL HAVE A NEW JAILER IF YOU CANNOT PERFORM YOUR DUTIES, LIEUTENANT.

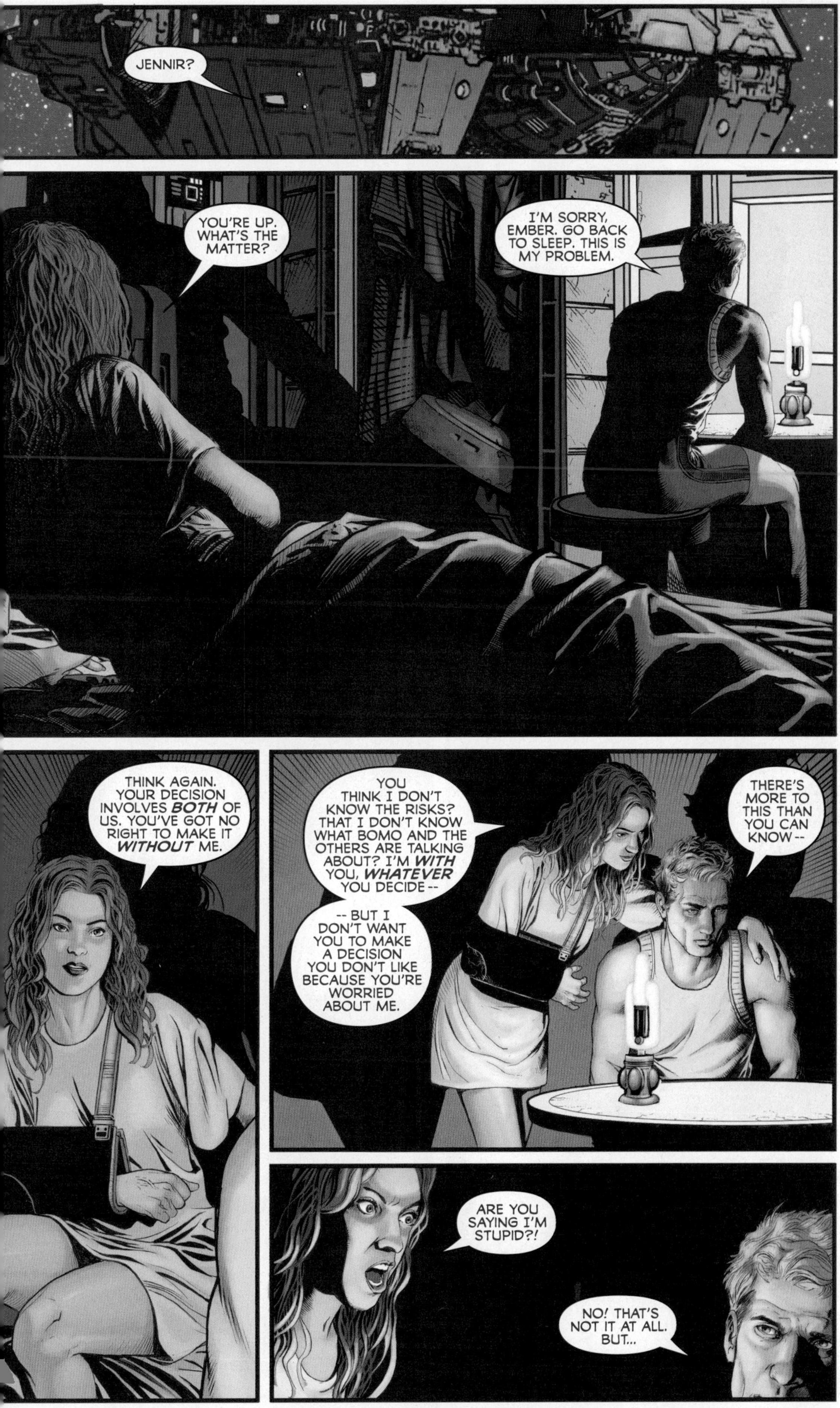
JENNIR?
YOU'RE UP. WHAT'S THE MATTER?
I'M SORRY, EMBER. GO BACK TO SLEEP. THIS IS MY PROBLEM.
THINK AGAIN. YOUR DECISION INVOLVES BOTH OF US. YOU'VE GOT NO RIGHT TO MAKE IT WITHOUT ME.
YOU THINK I DON'T KNOW THE RISKS? THAT I DON'T KNOW WHAT BOMO AND THE OTHERS ARE TALKING ABOUT? I'M WITH YOU, WHATEVER YOU DECIDE--
-- BUT I DON'T WANT YOU TO MAKE A DECISION YOU DON'T LIKE BECAUSE YOU'RE WORRIED ABOUT ME.
THERE'S MORE TO THIS THAN YOU CAN KNOW--
ARE YOU SAYING I'M STUPID?!
NO! THAT'S NOT IT AT ALL. BUT...

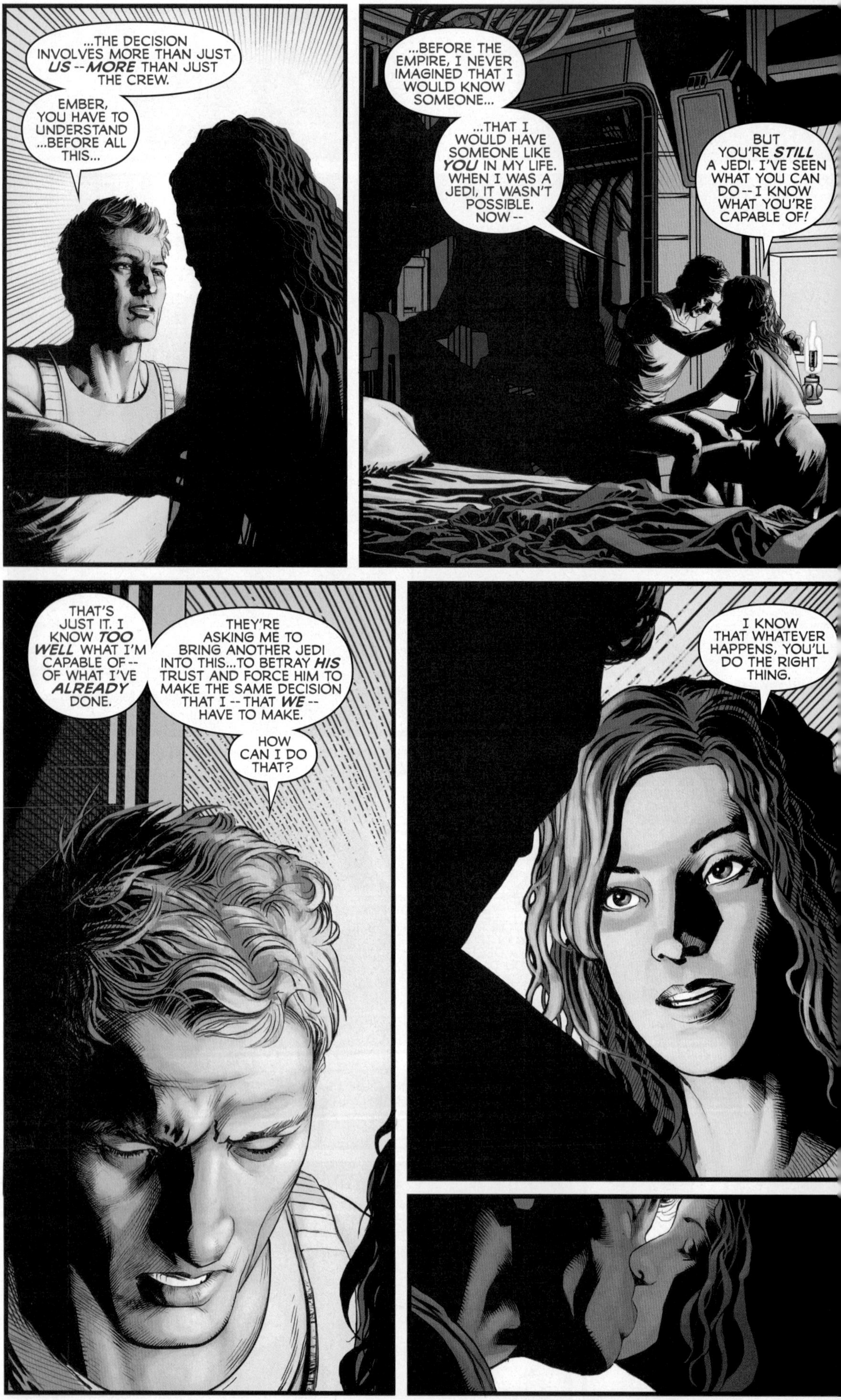
...THE DECISION INVOLVES MORE THAN JUST US--MORE THAN JUST THE CREW.
EMBER, YOU HAVE TO UNDERSTAND ...BEFORE ALL THIS...
...BEFORE THE EMPIRE, I NEVER IMAGINED THAT I WOULD KNOW SOMEONE...
...THAT I WOULD HAVE SOMEONE LIKE YOU IN MY LIFE. WHEN I WAS A JEDI, IT WASN'T POSSIBLE. NOW--
BUT YOU'RE STILL A JEDI. I'VE SEEN WHAT YOU CAN DO--I KNOW WHAT YOU'RE CAPABLE OF!
THAT'S JUST IT. I KNOW TOO WELL WHAT I'M CAPABLE OF--OF WHAT I'VE ALREADY DONE.
THEY'RE ASKING ME TO BRING ANOTHER JEDI INTO THIS...TO BETRAY HIS TRUST AND FORCE HIM TO MAKE THE SAME DECISION THAT I--THAT WE--HAVE TO MAKE.
HOW CAN I DO THAT?
I KNOW THAT WHATEVER HAPPENS, YOU'LL DO THE RIGHT THING.

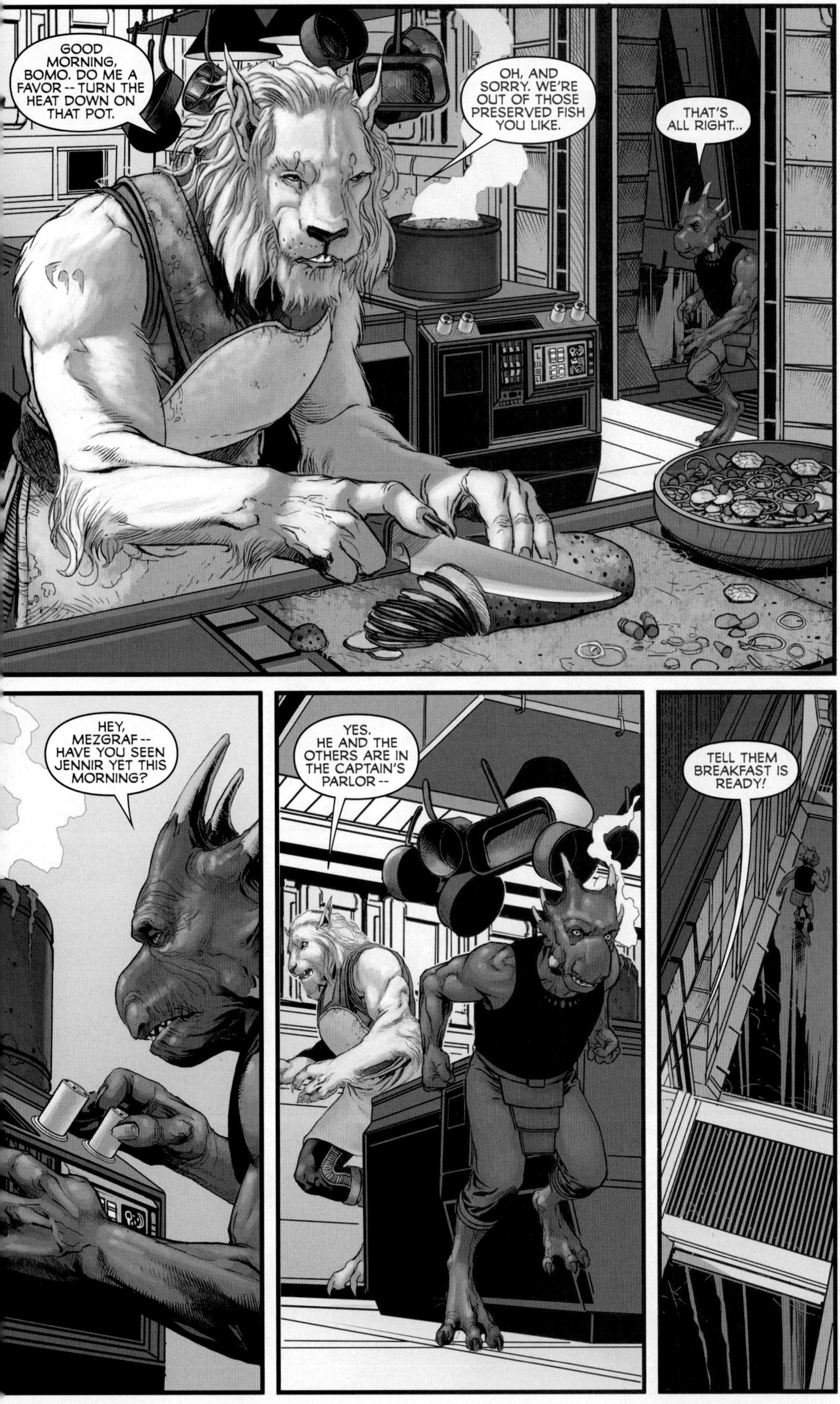
GOOD MORNING, BOMO. DO ME A FAVOR -- TURN THE HEAT DOWN ON THAT POT.
OH, AND SORRY. WE'RE OUT OF THOSE PRESERVED FISH YOU LIKE.
THAT'S ALL RIGHT...
HEY, MEZGRAF -- HAVE YOU SEEN JENNIR YET THIS MORNING?
YES. HE AND THE OTHERS ARE IN THE CAPTAIN'S PARLOR --
TELL THEM BREAKFAST IS READY!

OUR EMPIRE MAY YET BE YOUNG, BUT IT IS *STRONG!*

WHILE *EMPEROR PALPATINE* RULES FROM CORUSCANT, OUR VALIANT CLONE ARMY CONTINUES TO KEEPS US SAFE FROM THE GALAXY'S MANY THREATS!

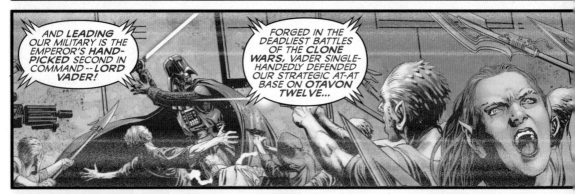

AND *LEADING* OUR MILITARY IS THE EMPEROR'S *HAND-PICKED* SECOND IN COMMAND -- *LORD VADER!*

FORGED IN THE DEADLIEST BATTLES OF THE *CLONE WARS,* VADER SINGLE-HANDEDLY DEFENDED OUR STRATEGIC AT-AT BASE ON *OTAVON TWELVE...*

...QUELLED THE UPRISING OF THE MIGHTY WOOKIEE WARRIORS OF *KASHYYYK...*

...AND *THWARTED* THE MURDEROUS PLOT OF *GENERAL GENTIS* THAT LEFT THOUSANDS DEAD ON GALACTIC CENTER!

FROM *BANDOMEER* TO THE *GHOST NEBULA,* WHEREVER A THREAT ARISES, LORD VADER IS THERE TO MEET IT...

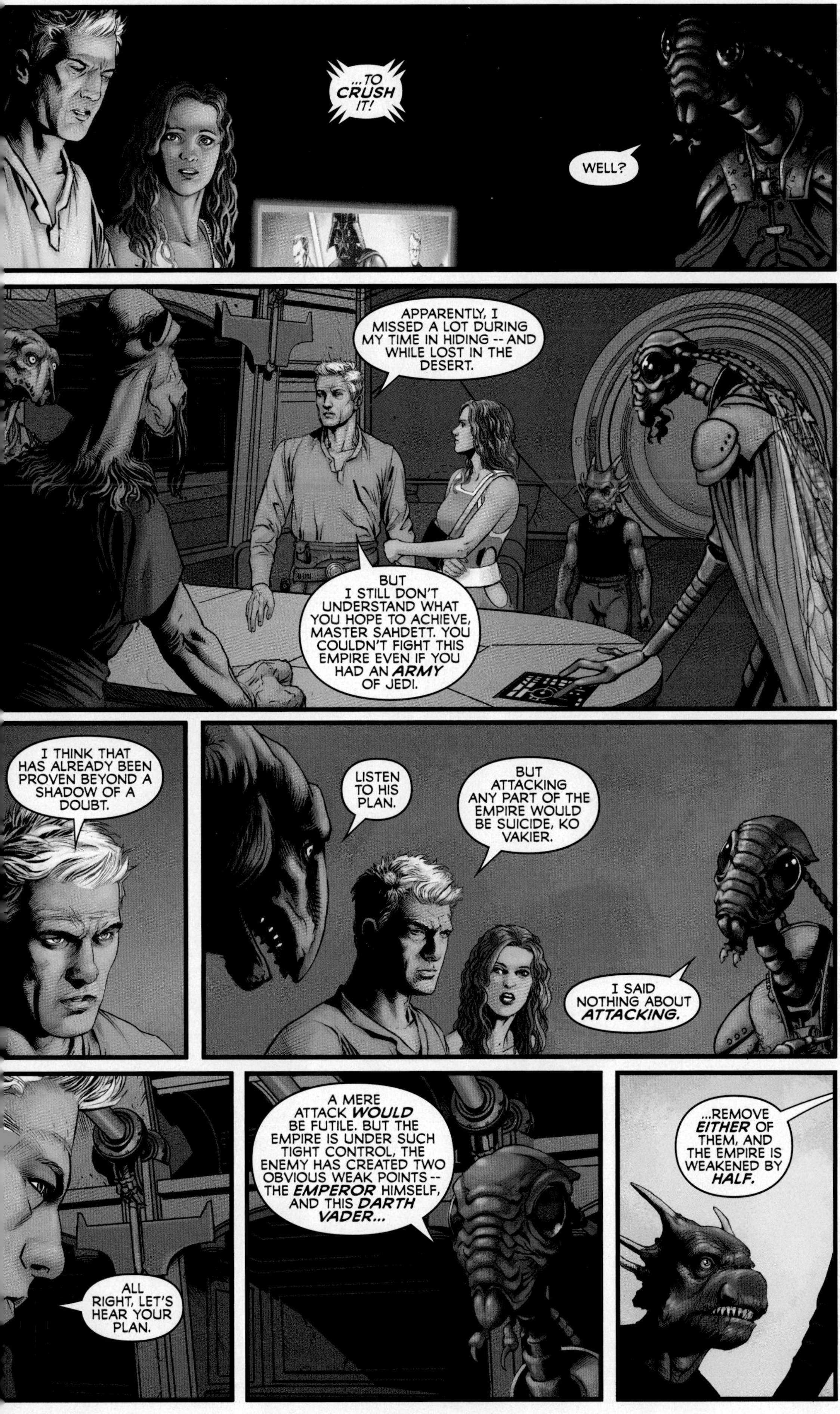
...TO CRUSH IT!
WELL?
APPARENTLY, I MISSED A LOT DURING MY TIME IN HIDING -- AND WHILE LOST IN THE DESERT.
BUT I STILL DON'T UNDERSTAND WHAT YOU HOPE TO ACHIEVE, MASTER SAHDETT. YOU COULDN'T FIGHT THIS EMPIRE EVEN IF YOU HAD AN ARMY OF JEDI.
I THINK THAT HAS ALREADY BEEN PROVEN BEYOND A SHADOW OF A DOUBT.
LISTEN TO HIS PLAN.
BUT ATTACKING ANY PART OF THE EMPIRE WOULD BE SUICIDE, KO VAKIER.
I SAID NOTHING ABOUT ATTACKING.
ALL RIGHT, LET'S HEAR YOUR PLAN.
A MERE ATTACK WOULD BE FUTILE. BUT THE EMPIRE IS UNDER SUCH TIGHT CONTROL, THE ENEMY HAS CREATED TWO OBVIOUS WEAK POINTS -- THE EMPEROR HIMSELF, AND THIS DARTH VADER...
...REMOVE EITHER OF THEM, AND THE EMPIRE IS WEAKENED BY HALF.

IF WE COULD CREATE A SITUATION...DRAW ONE OF THEM OUT SO THAT THEY WERE VULNERABLE --

RIDICULOUS. AFTER THE COUP ATTEMPT BY THAT GENERAL, THE EMPEROR WILL NEVER LEAVE CORUSCANT WITHOUT A LEGION OF TROOPERS.

RIGHT, BUT WHAT ABOUT THE *OTHER* ONE?

THIS VADER IS ALWAYS RUNNING ABOUT THE GALAXY ON HIS OWN. WHEN HE WAYLAID US, HE COULDN'T HAVE HAD MORE THAN TWENTY SOLDIERS WITH HIM.

AND TELL HIM THE OTHER PART, SAHDETT.

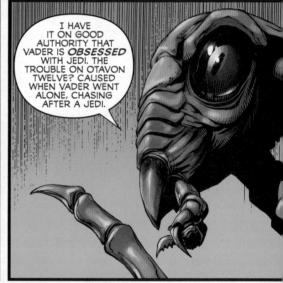

I HAVE IT ON GOOD AUTHORITY THAT VADER IS *OBSESSED* WITH JEDI. THE TROUBLE ON OTAVON TWELVE? CAUSED WHEN VADER WENT ALONE, CHASING AFTER A JEDI.

AND WHEN WE RAN INTO HIM -- HE WAS AFTER A JEDI WHO WAS IN STASIS INSIDE CAPTAIN HEREN'S BOX. I'M TELLING YOU, JENNIR, WE COULD DO THIS.

YOU'RE SUGGESTING WE USE *OURSELVES* AS BAIT...

*ONE* OF US -- WITH THE SURPRISE OF NUMBERS ON OUR SIDE.

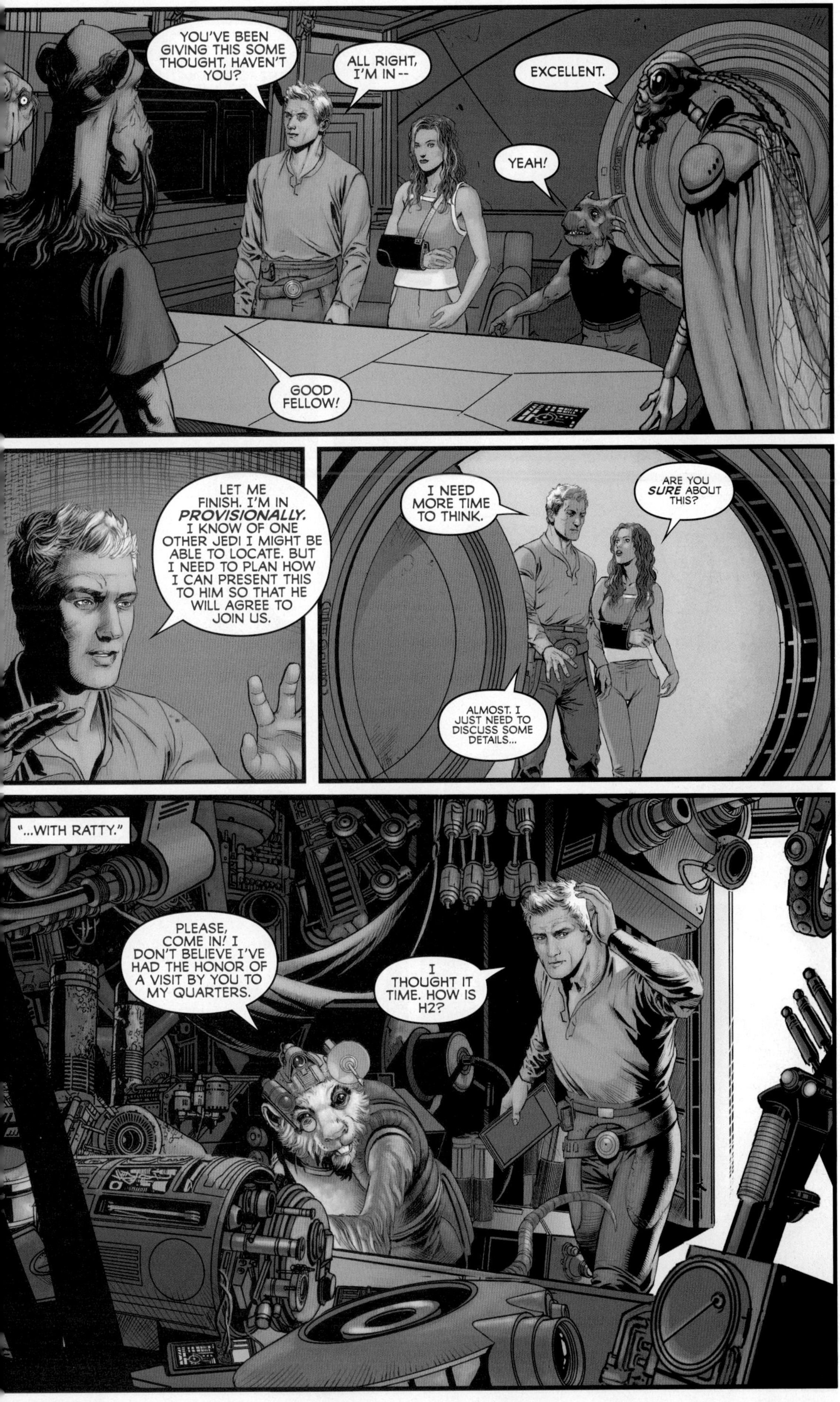
YOU'VE BEEN GIVING THIS SOME THOUGHT, HAVEN'T YOU?
ALL RIGHT, I'M IN --
EXCELLENT.
YEAH!
GOOD FELLOW!
LET ME FINISH. I'M IN *PROVISIONALLY.* I KNOW OF ONE OTHER JEDI I MIGHT BE ABLE TO LOCATE. BUT I NEED TO PLAN HOW I CAN PRESENT THIS TO HIM SO THAT HE WILL AGREE TO JOIN US.
I NEED MORE TIME TO THINK.
ARE YOU *SURE* ABOUT THIS?
ALMOST. I JUST NEED TO DISCUSS SOME DETAILS...
"...WITH RATTY."
PLEASE, COME IN! I DON'T BELIEVE I'VE HAD THE HONOR OF A VISIT BY YOU TO MY QUARTERS.
I THOUGHT IT TIME. HOW IS H2?

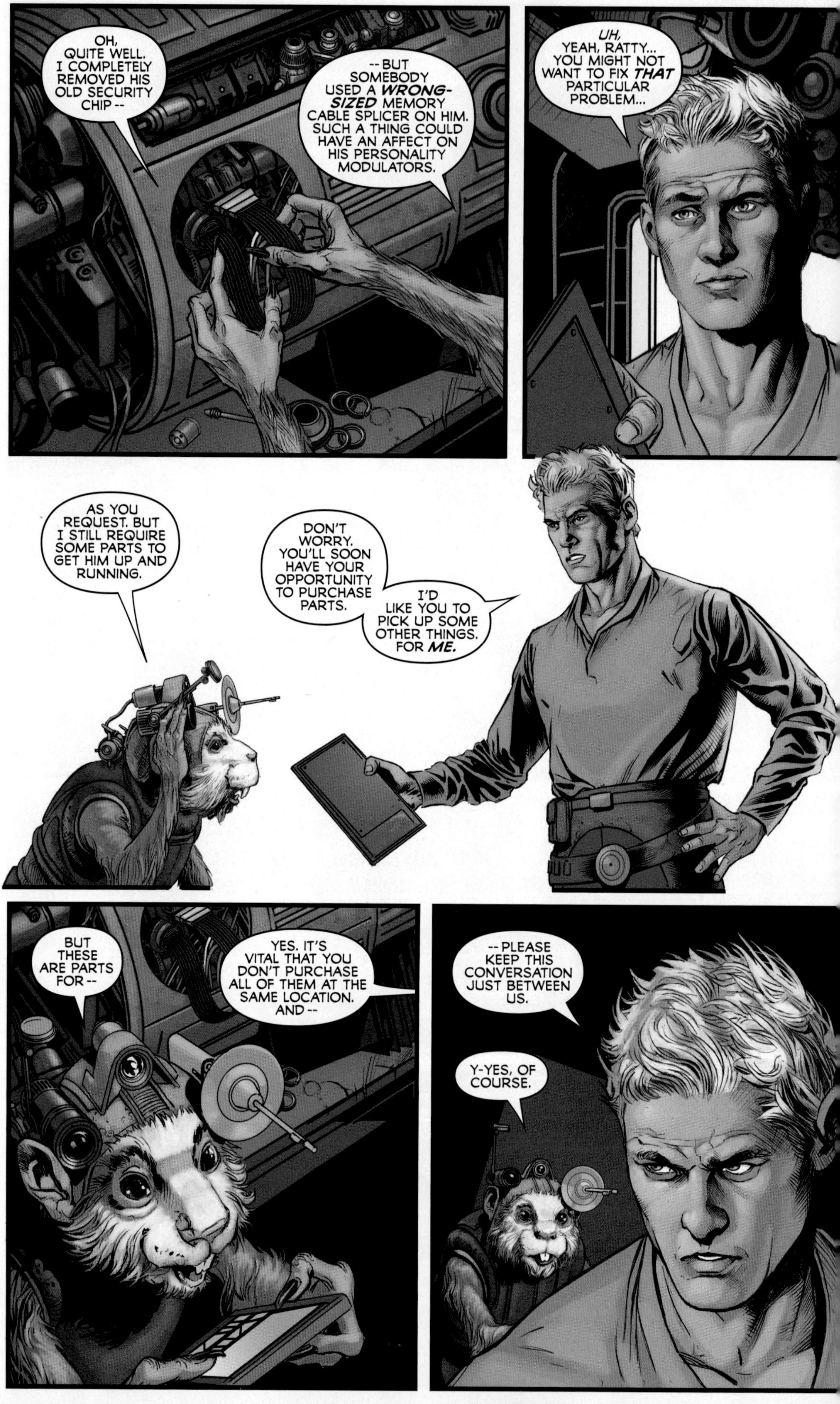
OH, QUITE WELL. I COMPLETELY REMOVED HIS OLD SECURITY CHIP --
-- BUT SOMEBODY USED A *WRONG-SIZED* MEMORY CABLE SPLICER ON HIM. SUCH A THING COULD HAVE AN AFFECT ON HIS PERSONALITY MODULATORS.
*UH,* YEAH, RATTY... YOU MIGHT NOT WANT TO FIX *THAT* PARTICULAR PROBLEM...
AS YOU REQUEST. BUT I STILL REQUIRE SOME PARTS TO GET HIM UP AND RUNNING.
DON'T WORRY. YOU'LL SOON HAVE YOUR OPPORTUNITY TO PURCHASE PARTS.
I'D LIKE YOU TO PICK UP SOME OTHER THINGS. FOR *ME.*
BUT THESE ARE PARTS FOR --
YES. IT'S VITAL THAT YOU DON'T PURCHASE ALL OF THEM AT THE SAME LOCATION. AND --
-- PLEASE KEEP THIS CONVERSATION JUST BETWEEN US.
Y-YES, OF COURSE.

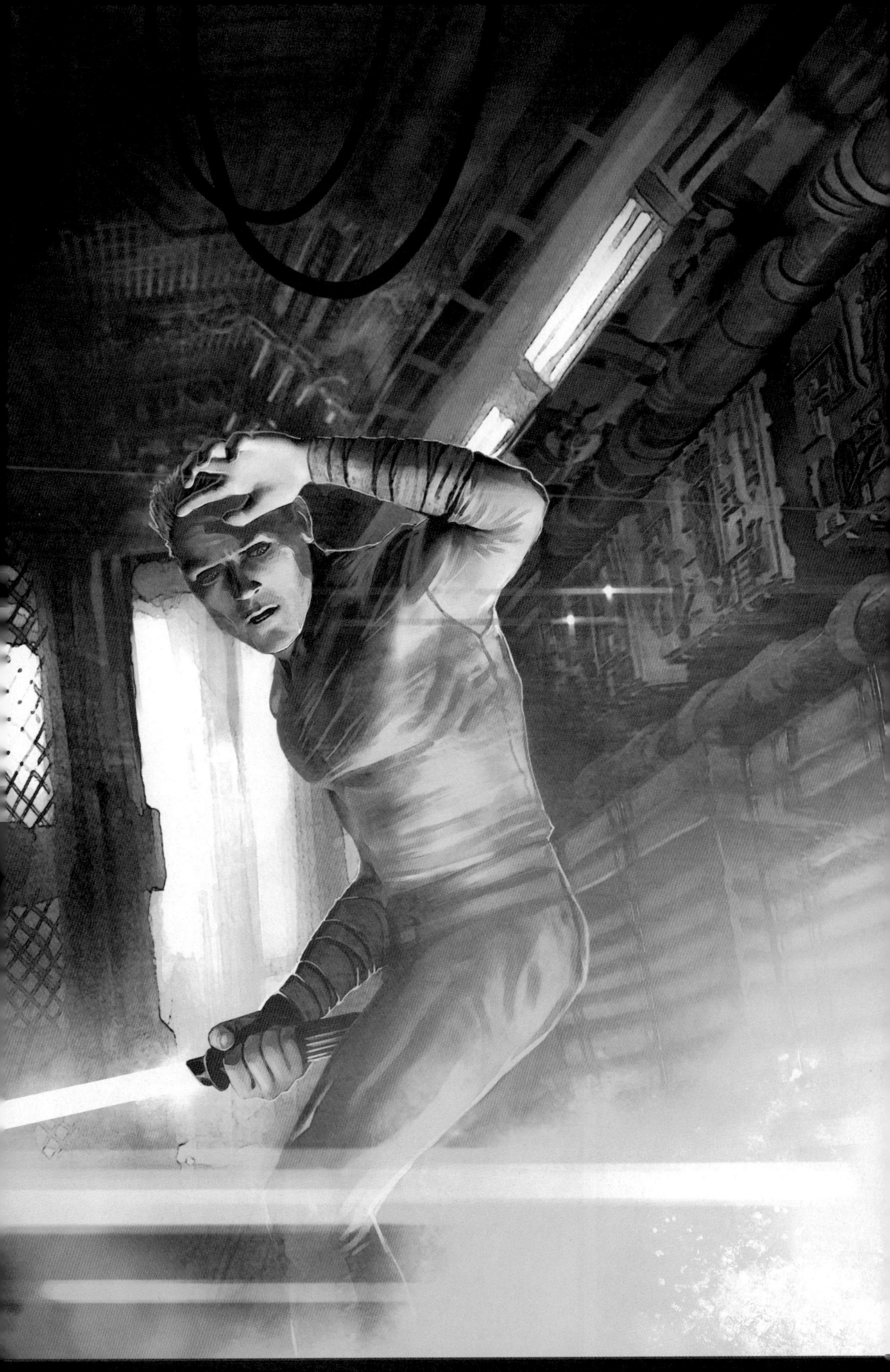

***STAR WARS: DARK TIMES — A SPARK REMAINS #2***

**WRITER: RANDY STRADLEY • ARTIST: DOUGLAS WHEATLEY • COLORIST: DAN JACKSON • LETTERER: MICHAEL HEISLER**
**ASSISTANT EDITOR: FREDDYE LINS • EDITOR: DAVE MARSHALL • COVER ARTIST: BENJAMIN CARRÉ**

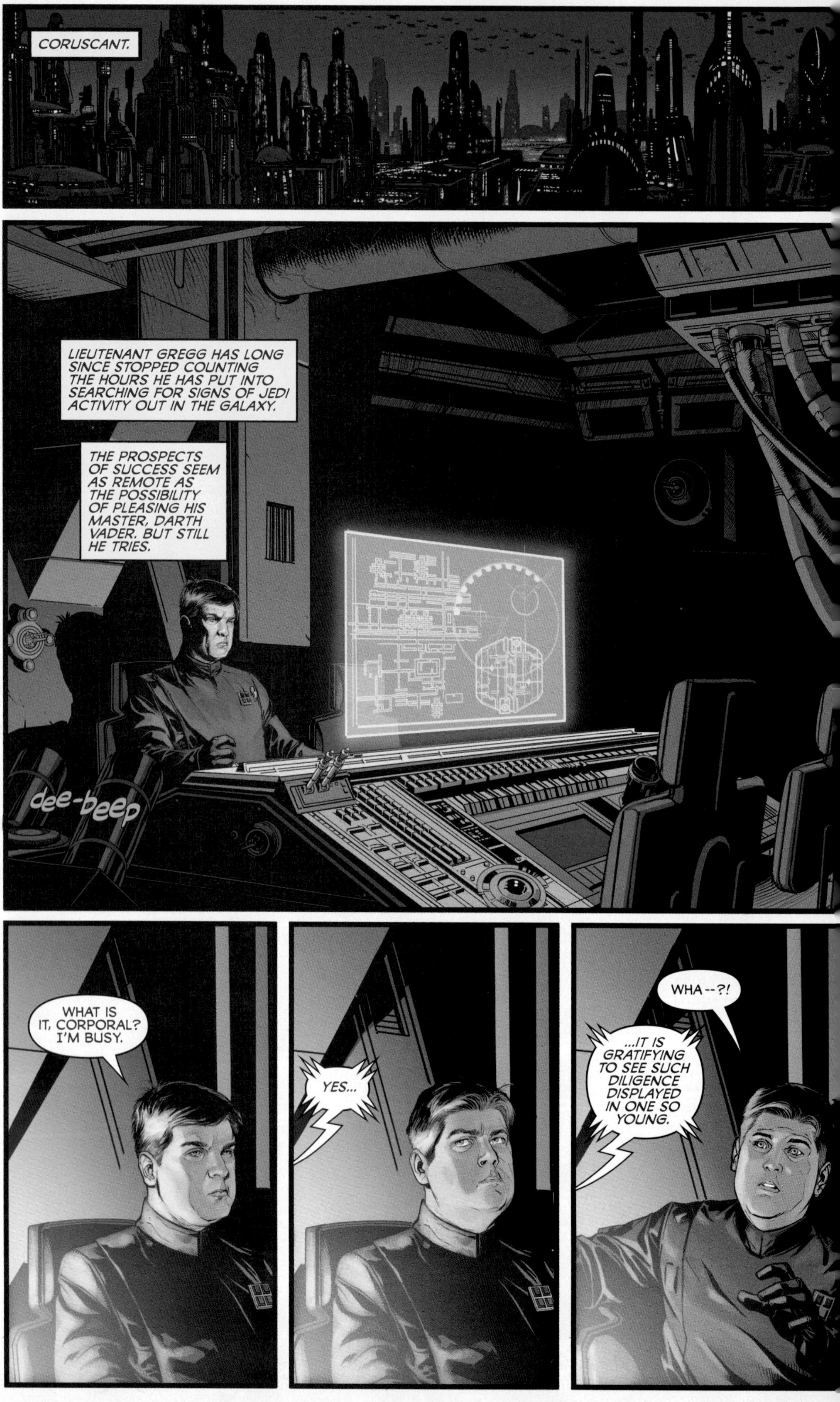
CORUSCANT.
LIEUTENANT GREGG HAS LONG SINCE STOPPED COUNTING THE HOURS HE HAS PUT INTO SEARCHING FOR SIGNS OF JEDI ACTIVITY OUT IN THE GALAXY.
THE PROSPECTS OF SUCCESS SEEM AS REMOTE AS THE POSSIBILITY OF PLEASING HIS MASTER, DARTH VADER. BUT STILL HE TRIES.
dee-beep
WHAT IS IT, CORPORAL? I'M BUSY.
YES...
WHA--?!
...IT IS GRATIFYING TO SEE SUCH DILIGENCE DISPLAYED IN ONE SO YOUNG.

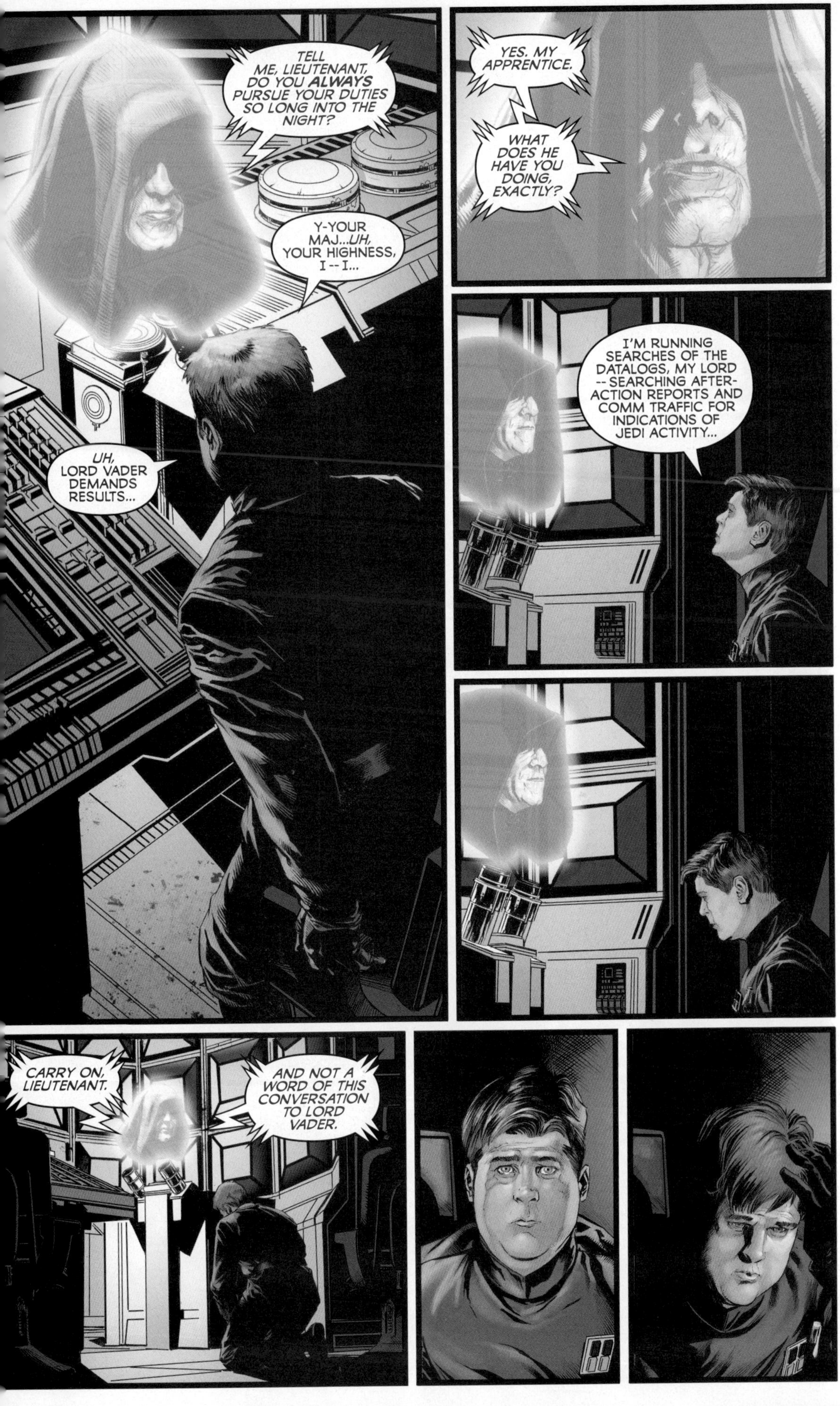
TELL ME, LIEUTENANT, DO YOU **ALWAYS** PURSUE YOUR DUTIES SO LONG INTO THE NIGHT?
Y-YOUR MAJ...*UH,* YOUR HIGHNESS, I -- I...
*UH,* LORD VADER DEMANDS RESULTS...
YES. MY APPRENTICE.
WHAT DOES HE HAVE YOU DOING, EXACTLY?
I'M RUNNING SEARCHES OF THE DATALOGS, MY LORD -- SEARCHING AFTER-ACTION REPORTS AND COMM TRAFFIC FOR INDICATIONS OF JEDI ACTIVITY...
CARRY ON, LIEUTENANT.
AND NOT A WORD OF THIS CONVERSATION TO LORD VADER.

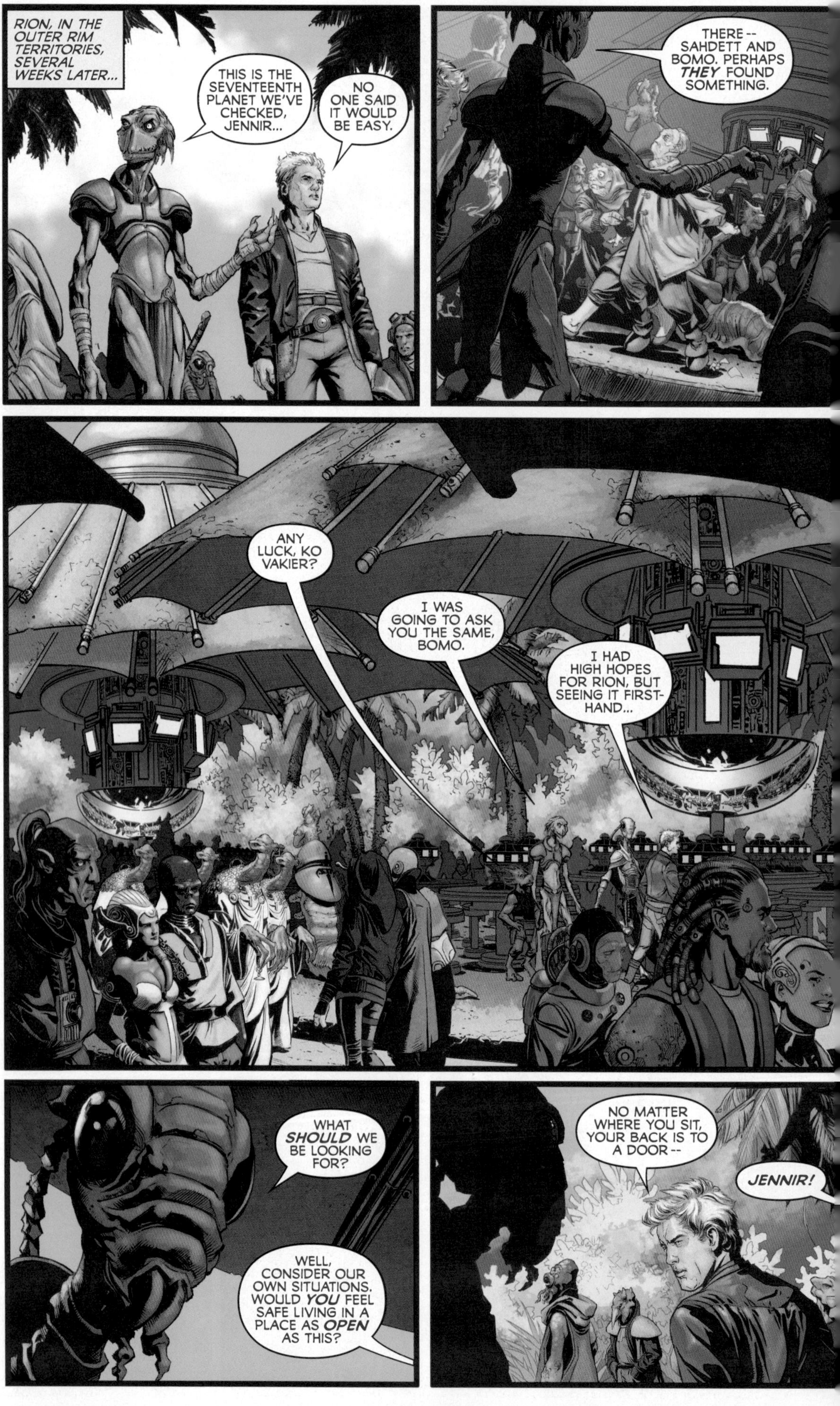

RION, IN THE OUTER RIM TERRITORIES, SEVERAL WEEKS LATER...
THIS IS THE SEVENTEENTH PLANET WE'VE CHECKED, JENNIR...
NO ONE SAID IT WOULD BE EASY.
THERE -- SAHDETT AND BOMO. PERHAPS THEY FOUND SOMETHING.
ANY LUCK, KO VAKIER?
I WAS GOING TO ASK YOU THE SAME, BOMO.
I HAD HIGH HOPES FOR RION, BUT SEEING IT FIRST-HAND...
WHAT SHOULD WE BE LOOKING FOR?
WELL, CONSIDER OUR OWN SITUATIONS. WOULD YOU FEEL SAFE LIVING IN A PLACE AS OPEN AS THIS?
NO MATTER WHERE YOU SIT, YOUR BACK IS TO A DOOR --
JENNIR!

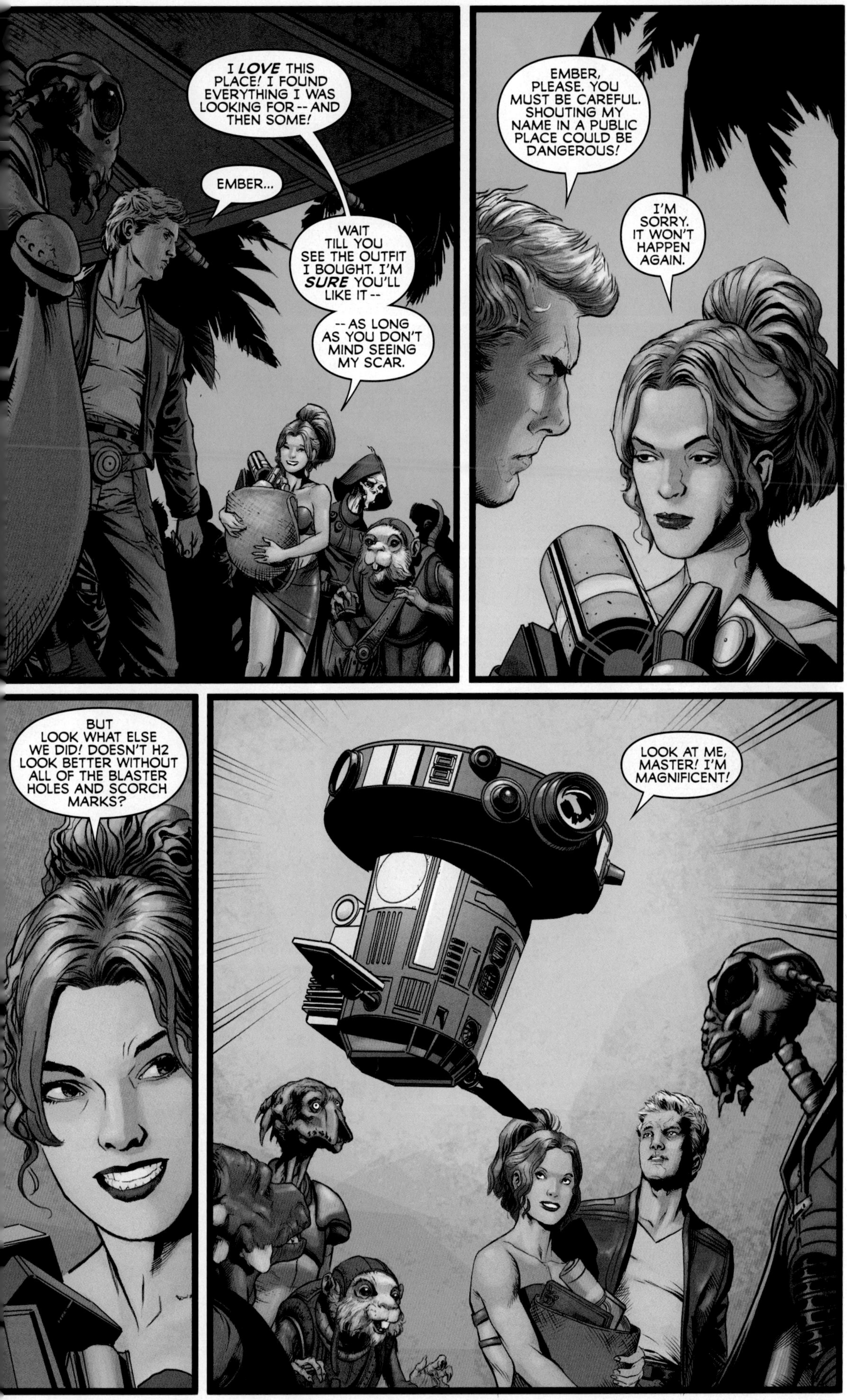
I LOVE THIS PLACE! I FOUND EVERYTHING I WAS LOOKING FOR -- AND THEN SOME!
EMBER...
WAIT TILL YOU SEE THE OUTFIT I BOUGHT. I'M SURE YOU'LL LIKE IT --
-- AS LONG AS YOU DON'T MIND SEEING MY SCAR.
EMBER, PLEASE. YOU MUST BE CAREFUL. SHOUTING MY NAME IN A PUBLIC PLACE COULD BE DANGEROUS!
I'M SORRY. IT WON'T HAPPEN AGAIN.
BUT LOOK WHAT ELSE WE DID! DOESN'T H2 LOOK BETTER WITHOUT ALL OF THE BLASTER HOLES AND SCORCH MARKS?
LOOK AT ME, MASTER! I'M MAGNIFICENT!

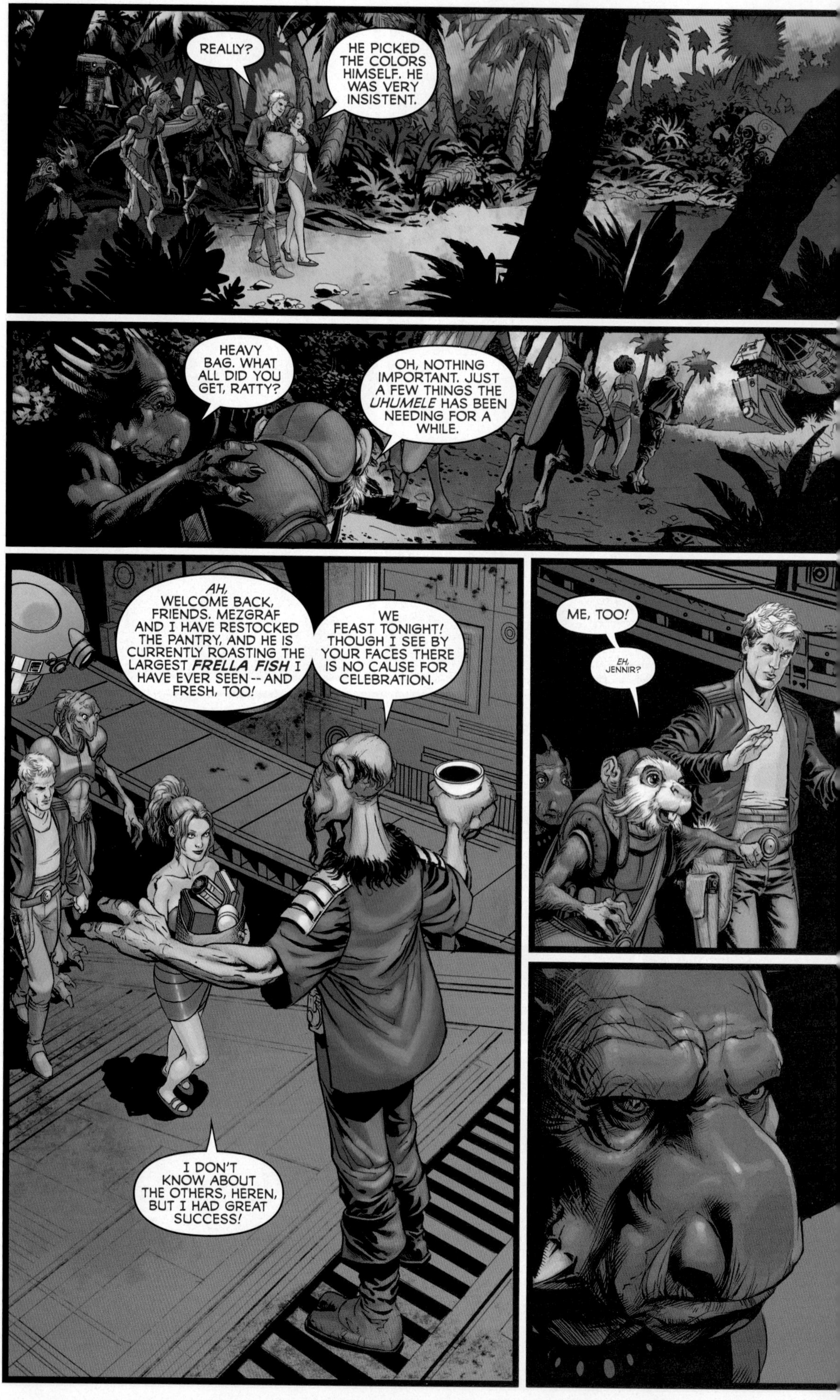
REALLY?
HE PICKED THE COLORS HIMSELF. HE WAS VERY INSISTENT.
HEAVY BAG. WHAT ALL DID YOU GET, RATTY?
OH, NOTHING IMPORTANT. JUST A FEW THINGS THE *UHUMELE* HAS BEEN NEEDING FOR A WHILE.
*AH,* WELCOME BACK, FRIENDS. MEZGRAF AND I HAVE RESTOCKED THE PANTRY, AND HE IS CURRENTLY ROASTING THE LARGEST ***FRELLA FISH*** I HAVE EVER SEEN -- AND FRESH, TOO!
WE FEAST TONIGHT! THOUGH I SEE BY YOUR FACES THERE IS NO CAUSE FOR CELEBRATION.
I DON'T KNOW ABOUT THE OTHERS, HEREN, BUT I HAD GREAT SUCCESS!
ME, TOO!
*EH,* JENNIR?

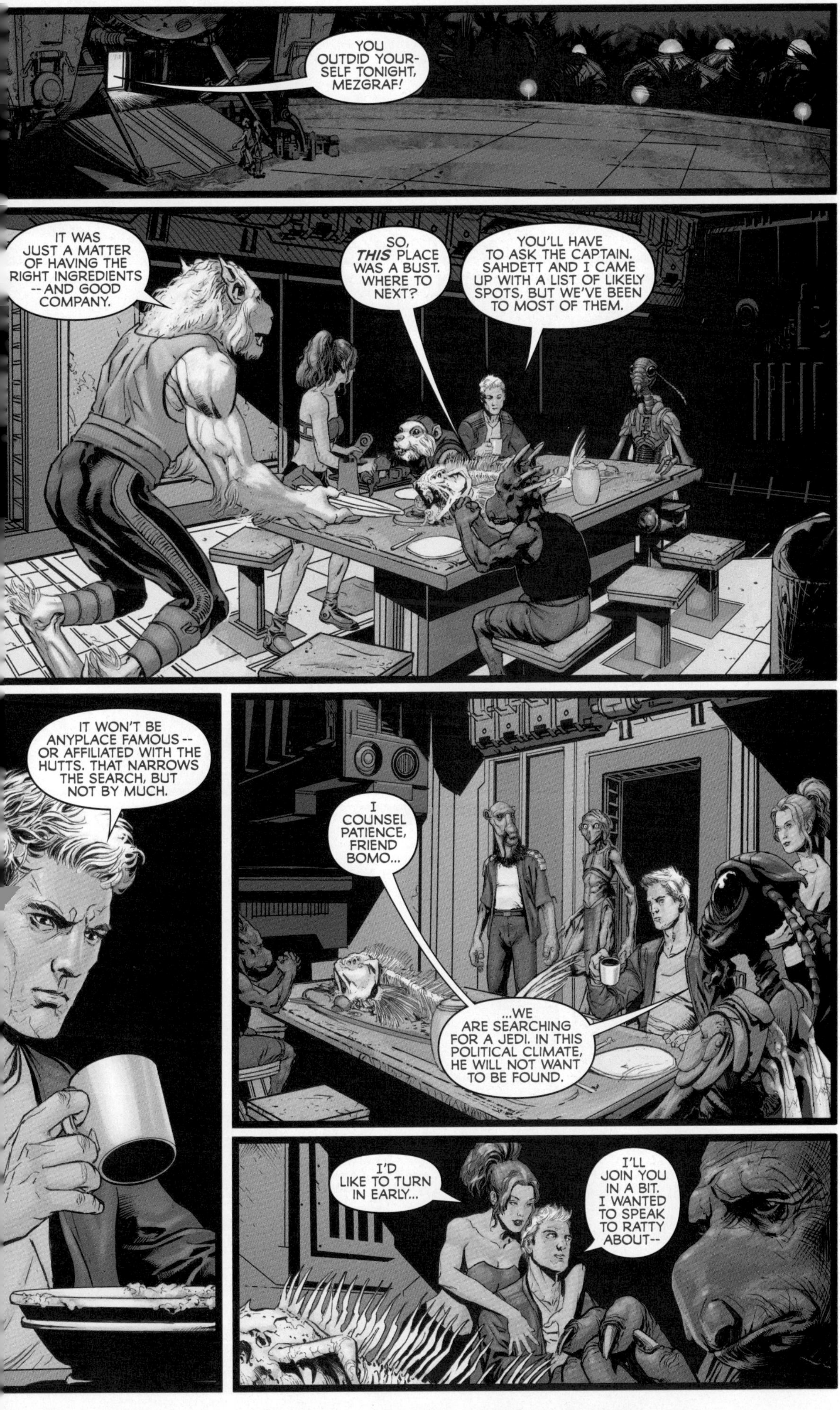
YOU OUTDID YOURSELF TONIGHT, MEZGRAF!
IT WAS JUST A MATTER OF HAVING THE RIGHT INGREDIENTS --AND GOOD COMPANY.
SO, *THIS* PLACE WAS A BUST. WHERE TO NEXT?
YOU'LL HAVE TO ASK THE CAPTAIN. SAHDETT AND I CAME UP WITH A LIST OF LIKELY SPOTS, BUT WE'VE BEEN TO MOST OF THEM.
IT WON'T BE ANYPLACE FAMOUS -- OR AFFILIATED WITH THE HUTTS. THAT NARROWS THE SEARCH, BUT NOT BY MUCH.
I COUNSEL PATIENCE, FRIEND BOMO...
...WE ARE SEARCHING FOR A JEDI. IN THIS POLITICAL CLIMATE, HE WILL NOT WANT TO BE FOUND.
I'D LIKE TO TURN IN EARLY...
I'LL JOIN YOU IN A BIT. I WANTED TO SPEAK TO RATTY ABOUT--

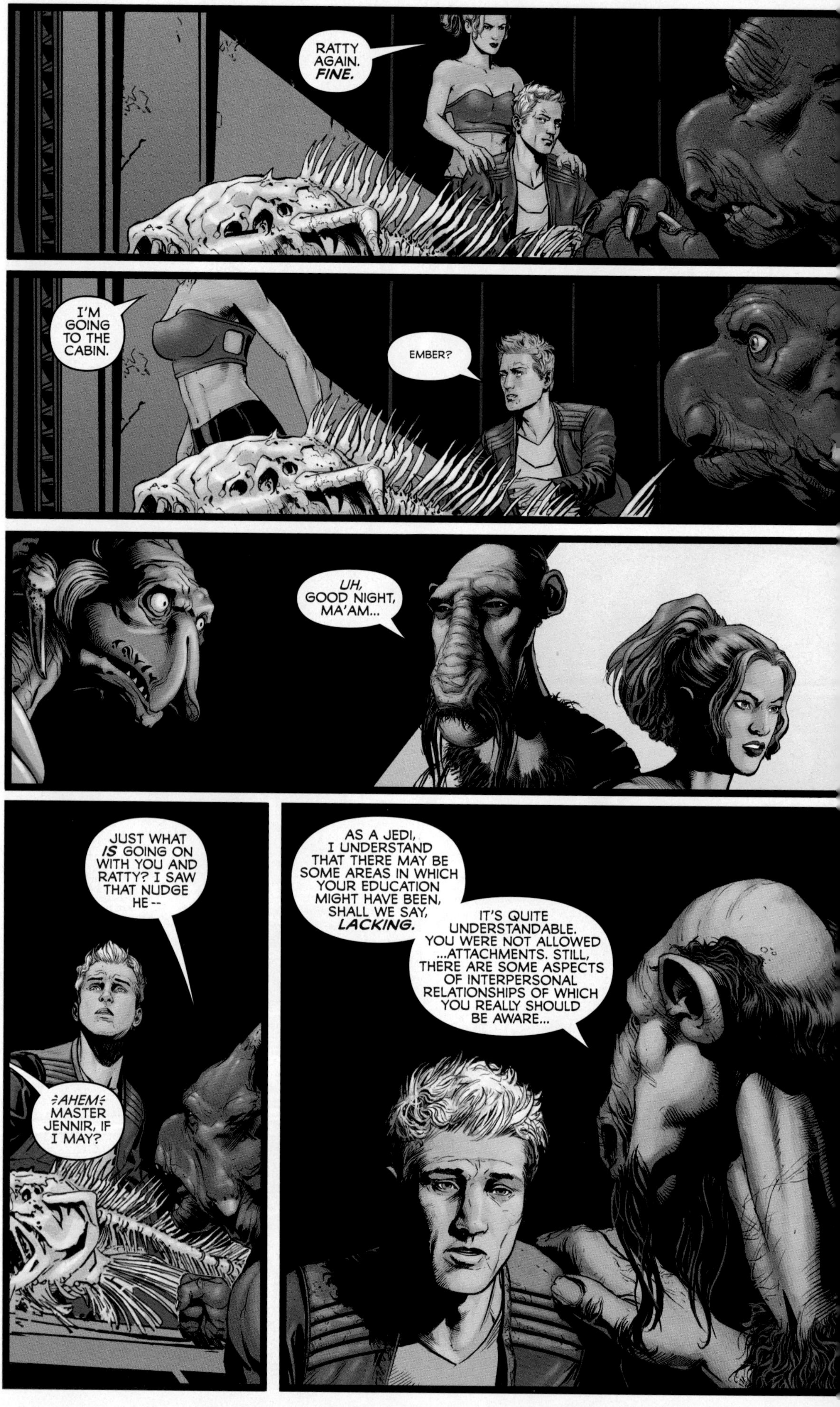
RATTY AGAIN. *FINE.*
I'M GOING TO THE CABIN.
EMBER?
*UH,* GOOD NIGHT, MA'AM...
JUST WHAT *IS* GOING ON WITH YOU AND RATTY? I SAW THAT NUDGE HE--
*AHEM* MASTER JENNIR, IF I MAY?
AS A JEDI, I UNDERSTAND THAT THERE MAY BE SOME AREAS IN WHICH YOUR EDUCATION MIGHT HAVE BEEN, SHALL WE SAY, *LACKING.*
IT'S QUITE UNDERSTANDABLE. YOU WERE NOT ALLOWED ...ATTACHMENTS. STILL, THERE ARE SOME ASPECTS OF INTERPERSONAL RELATIONSHIPS OF WHICH YOU REALLY SHOULD BE AWARE...

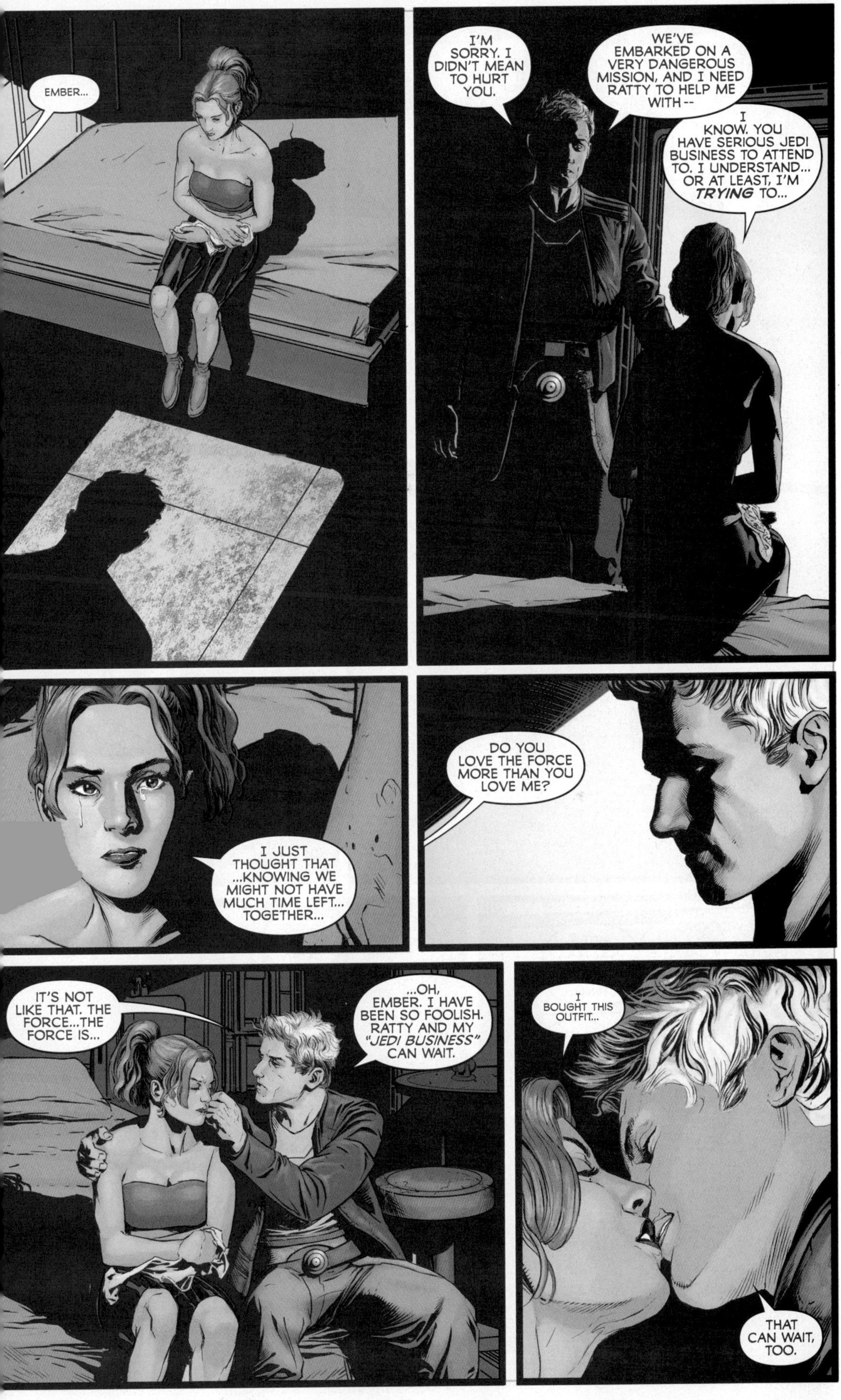
EMBER...
I'M SORRY. I DIDN'T MEAN TO HURT YOU.
WE'VE EMBARKED ON A VERY DANGEROUS MISSION, AND I NEED RATTY TO HELP ME WITH --
I KNOW. YOU HAVE SERIOUS JEDI BUSINESS TO ATTEND TO. I UNDERSTAND... OR AT LEAST, I'M *TRYING* TO...
I JUST THOUGHT THAT ...KNOWING WE MIGHT NOT HAVE MUCH TIME LEFT... TOGETHER...
DO YOU LOVE THE FORCE MORE THAN YOU LOVE ME?
IT'S NOT LIKE THAT. THE FORCE...THE FORCE IS...
...OH, EMBER. I HAVE BEEN SO FOOLISH. RATTY AND MY *"JEDI BUSINESS"* CAN WAIT.
I BOUGHT THIS OUTFIT...
THAT CAN WAIT, TOO.

WHAT'S GOING ON? NO CUFFS ON ME? NO GUN IN YOUR HAND?

TRYING SOMETHING NEW. I CAME UP WITH IT AFTER YOUR LAST ATTEMPT TO ESCAPE. ALL OF THE DOORS ARE VOICE CODED AND DEAD-LOCKED.

YOU COULD KILL ME, BUT THEN YOU'D BE LOCKED IN HERE ALONE...WITH *HIM*...

VADER.

I DON'T KNOW WHY YOU ALWAYS HAVE TO ANTAGONIZE HIM -- WHY YOU *INSIST* ON TREATING THIS LIKE A PRISON SENTENCE. YOU SHOULD FEEL HONORED.

*"HONORED"?!*

CLEARLY VADER SAW *SOMETHING* IN YOU WORTH PRESERVING -- OTHERWISE YOU'D STILL BE ON PRINE. AS ASHES.

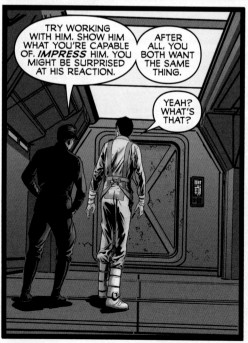

TRY WORKING WITH HIM. SHOW HIM WHAT YOU'RE CAPABLE OF. *IMPRESS* HIM. YOU MIGHT BE SURPRISED AT HIS REACTION.

AFTER ALL, YOU BOTH WANT THE SAME THING.

YEAH? WHAT'S THAT?

DASS JENNIR'S HEAD.

FORGET IT! I'M NOT SHARING MY BOUNTY!

DON'T WORRY. HE DOESN'T WANT THE BOUNTY-- JUST YOUR HELP.

THAT'S WHY HE HAD *THIS* BROUGHT HERE.

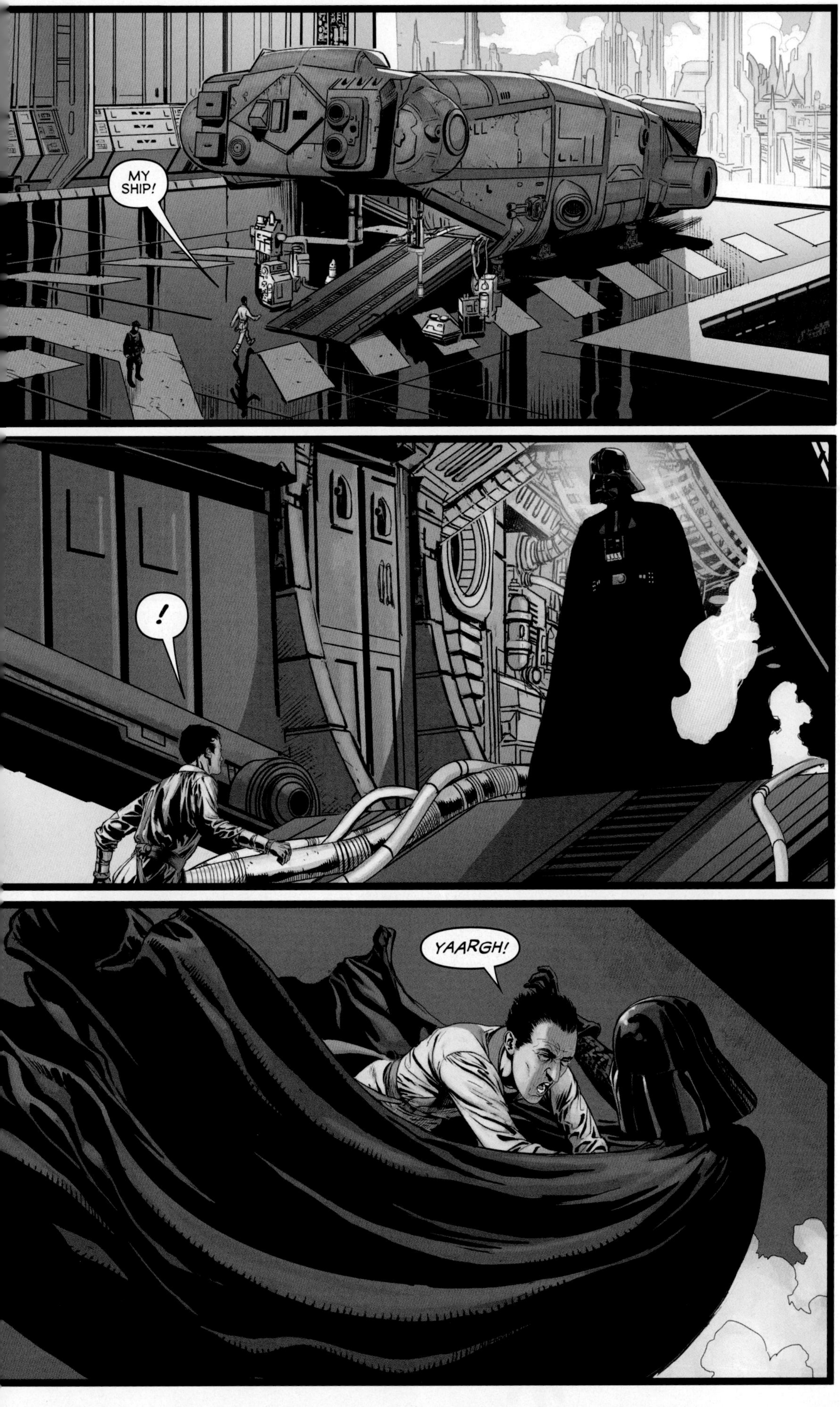
MY SHIP!
!
YAARGH!

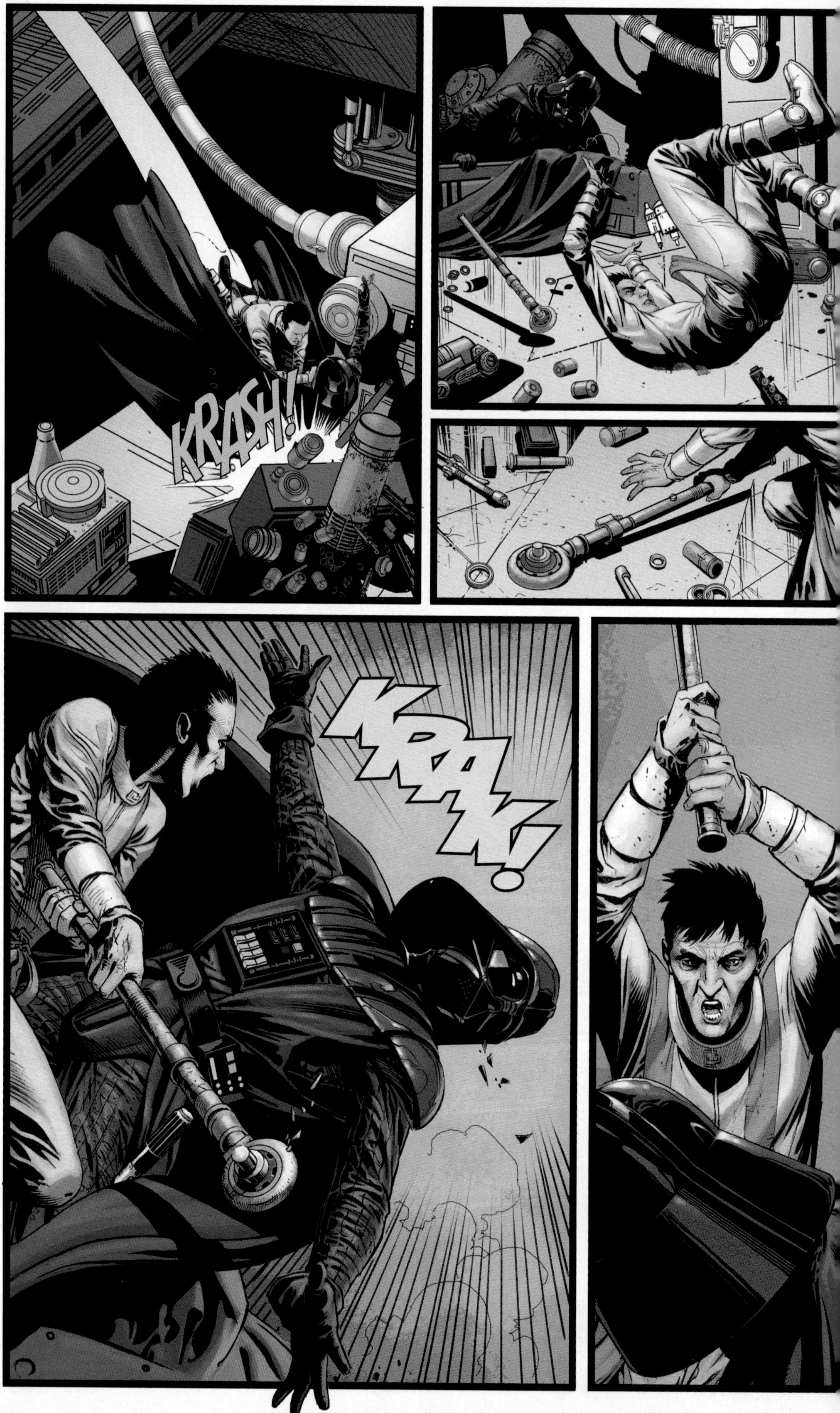
KRASH!
KRAK!

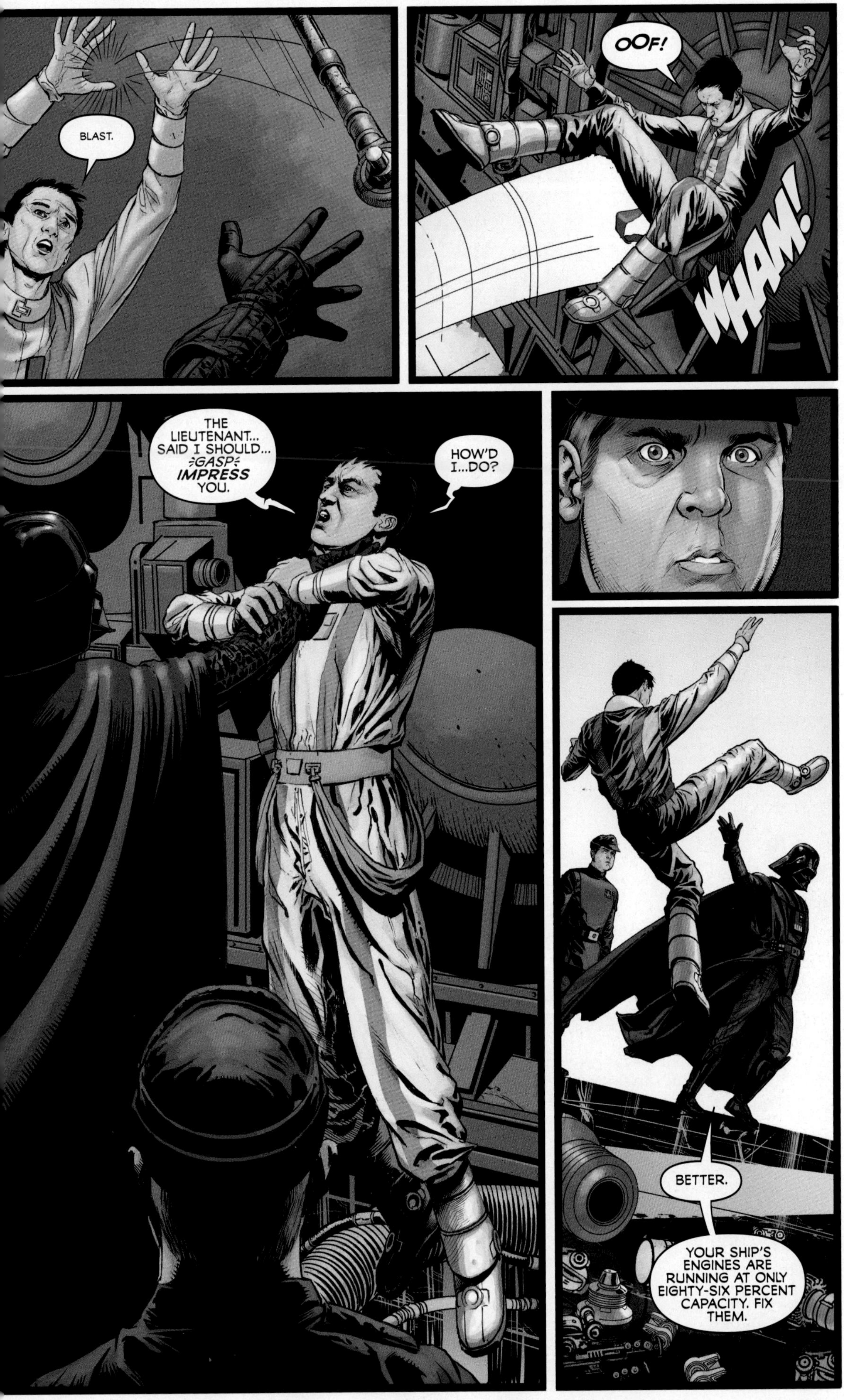
BLAST.
OOF!
WHAM!
THE LIEUTENANT... SAID I SHOULD... ≈GASP≈ IMPRESS YOU.
HOW'D I...DO?
BETTER.
YOUR SHIP'S ENGINES ARE RUNNING AT ONLY EIGHTY-SIX PERCENT CAPACITY. FIX THEM.

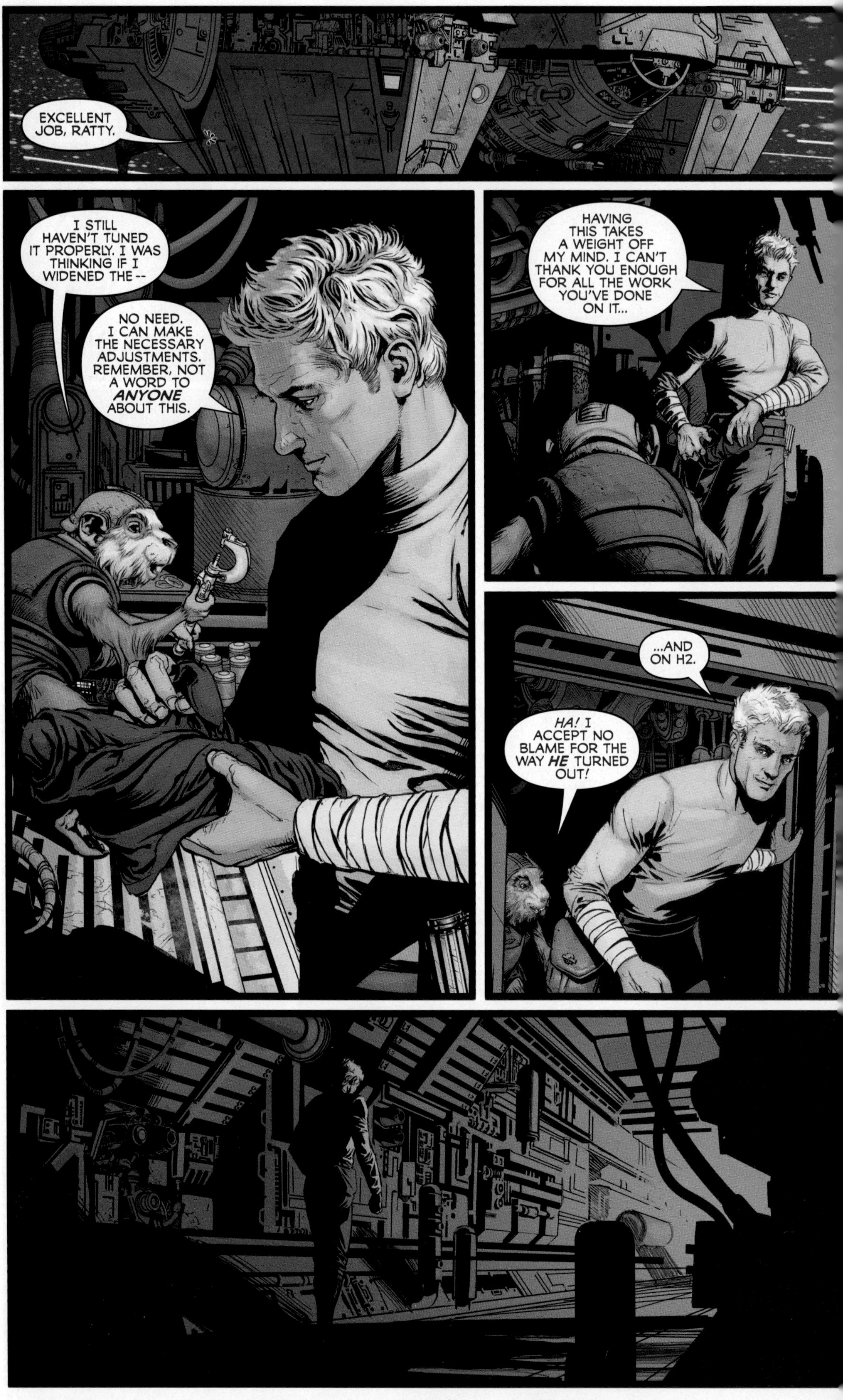
EXCELLENT JOB, RATTY.
I STILL HAVEN'T TUNED IT PROPERLY. I WAS THINKING IF I WIDENED THE --
NO NEED. I CAN MAKE THE NECESSARY ADJUSTMENTS. REMEMBER, NOT A WORD TO ***ANYONE*** ABOUT THIS.
HAVING THIS TAKES A WEIGHT OFF MY MIND. I CAN'T THANK YOU ENOUGH FOR ALL THE WORK YOU'VE DONE ON IT...
...AND ON H2.
*HA!* I ACCEPT NO BLAME FOR THE WAY ***HE*** TURNED OUT!

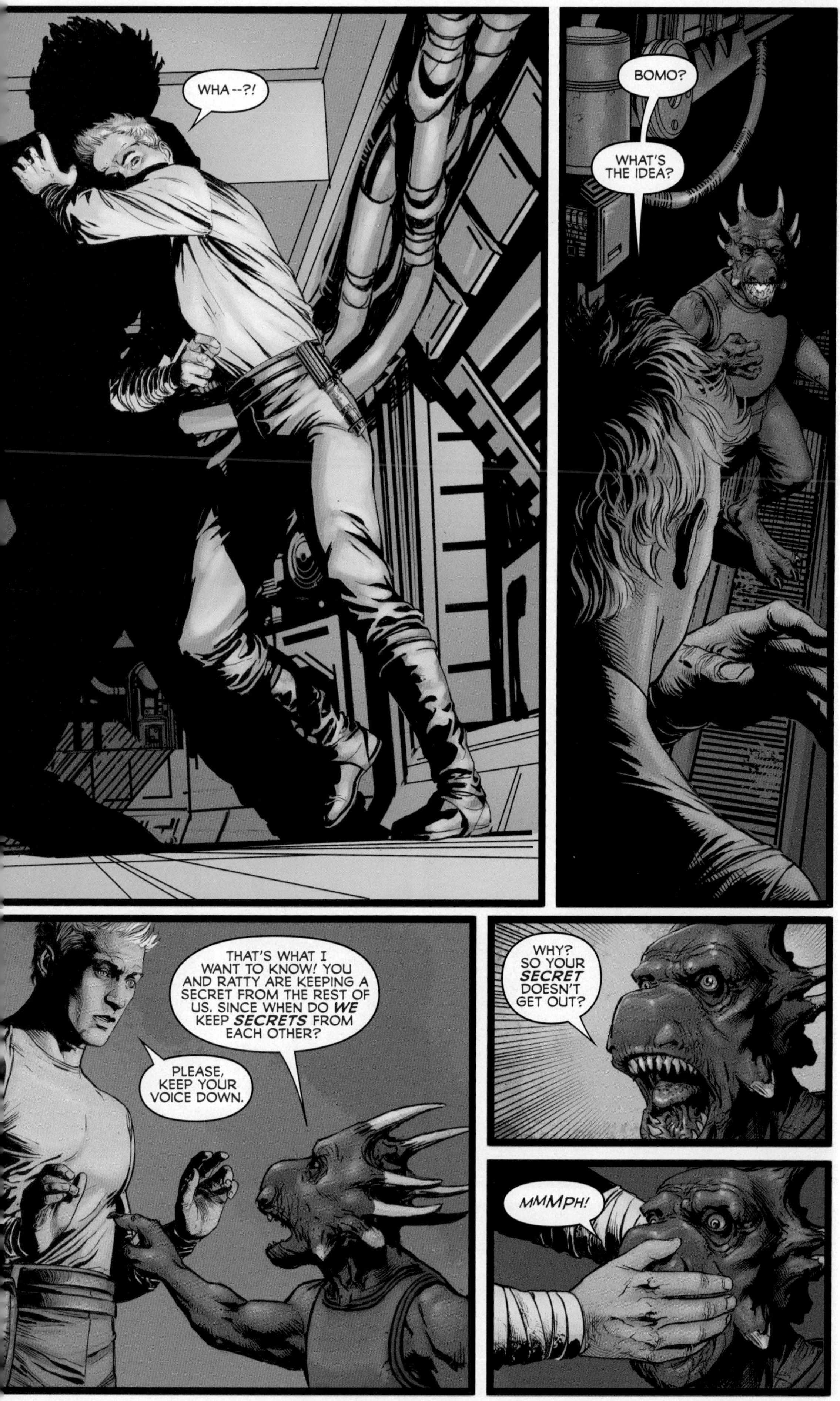
WHA--?!
BOMO?
WHAT'S THE IDEA?
THAT'S WHAT I WANT TO KNOW! YOU AND RATTY ARE KEEPING A SECRET FROM THE REST OF US. SINCE WHEN DO WE KEEP SECRETS FROM EACH OTHER?
PLEASE, KEEP YOUR VOICE DOWN.
WHY? SO YOUR SECRET DOESN'T GET OUT?
MMMPH!

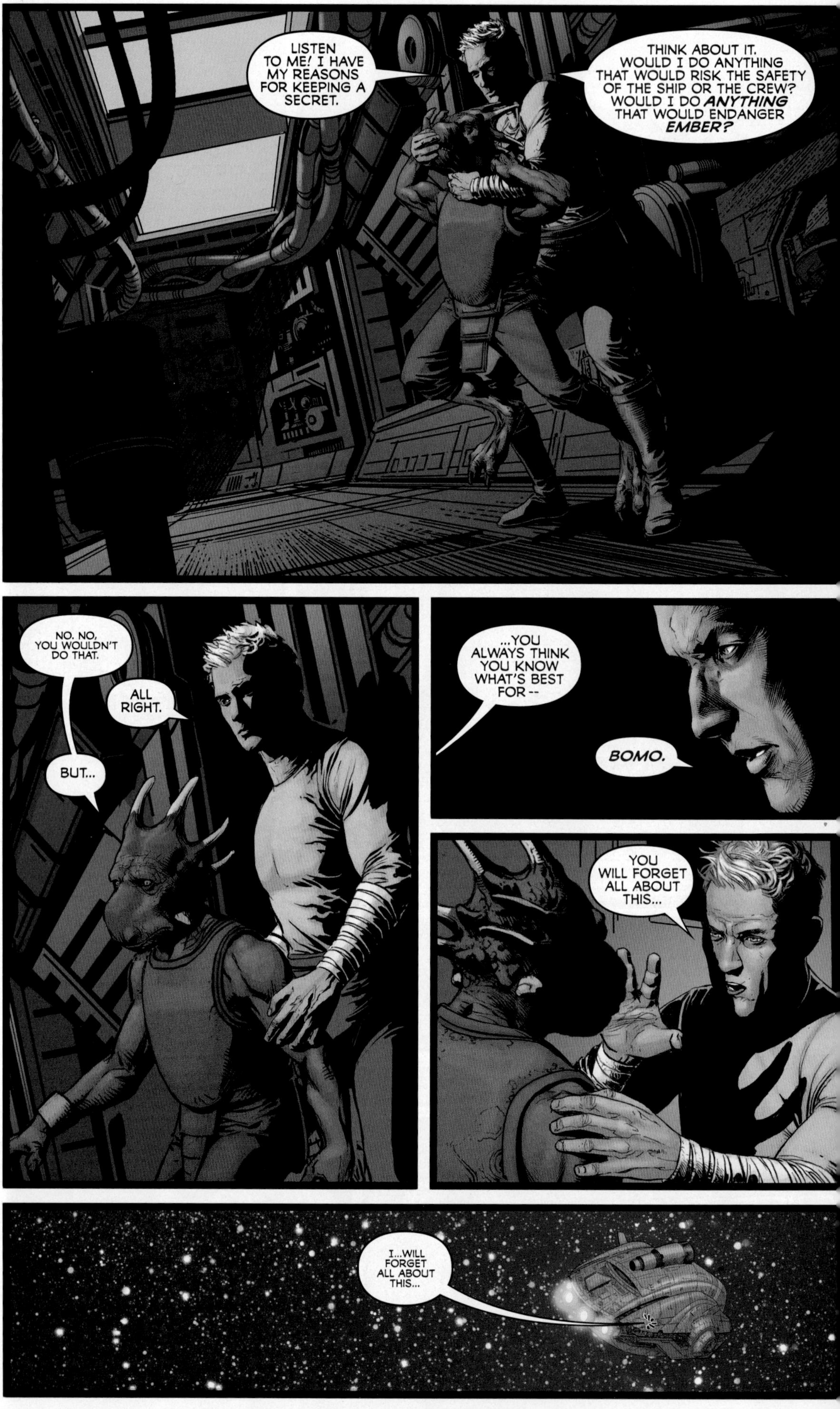
LISTEN TO ME! I HAVE MY REASONS FOR KEEPING A SECRET.
THINK ABOUT IT. WOULD I DO ANYTHING THAT WOULD RISK THE SAFETY OF THE SHIP OR THE CREW? WOULD I DO *ANYTHING* THAT WOULD ENDANGER *EMBER?*
NO. NO, YOU WOULDN'T DO THAT.
ALL RIGHT.
BUT...
...YOU ALWAYS THINK YOU KNOW WHAT'S BEST FOR --
*BOMO.*
YOU WILL FORGET ALL ABOUT THIS...
I...WILL FORGET ALL ABOUT THIS...

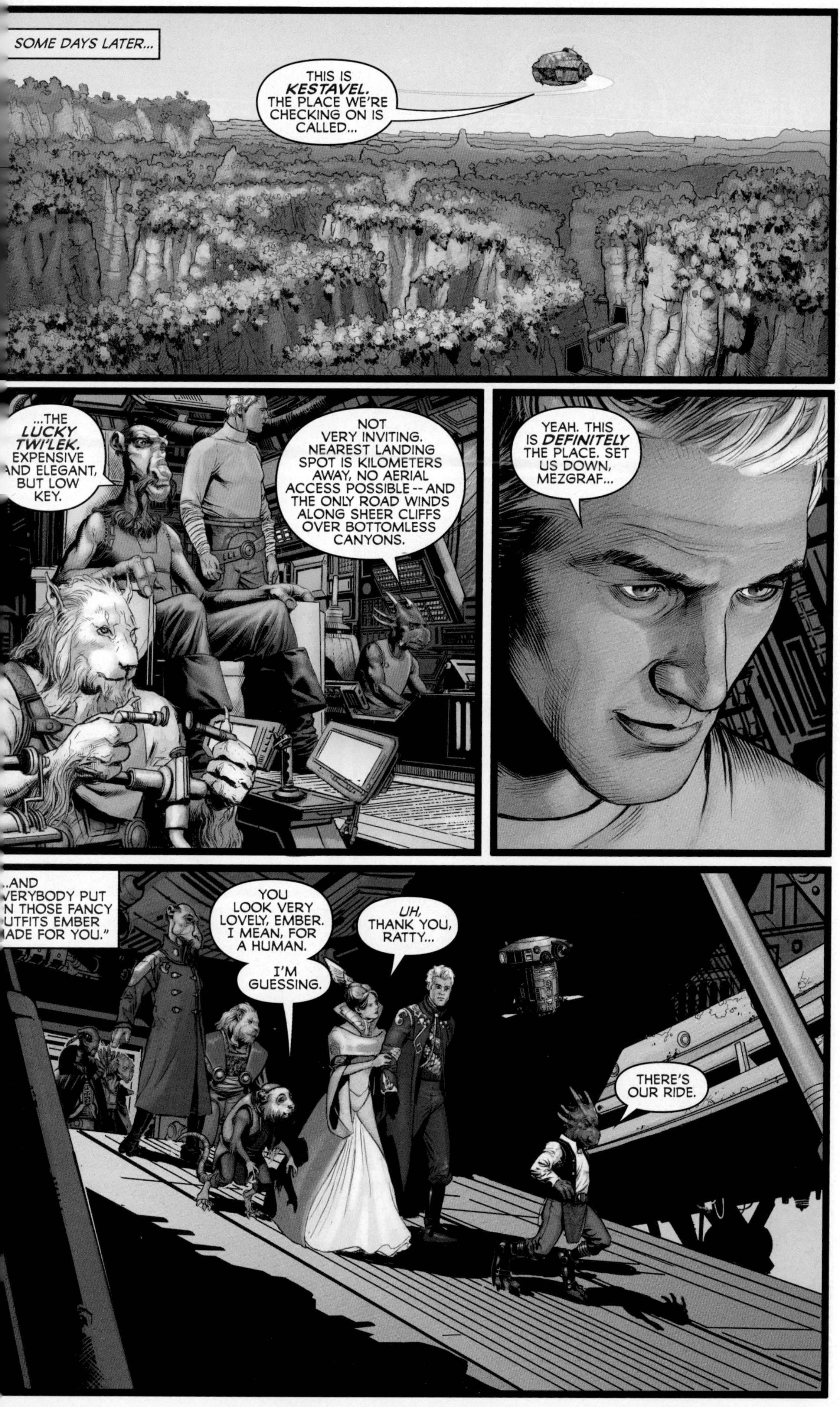

SOME DAYS LATER...
THIS IS KESTAVEL. THE PLACE WE'RE CHECKING ON IS CALLED...
...THE LUCKY TWI'LEK. EXPENSIVE AND ELEGANT, BUT LOW KEY.
NOT VERY INVITING. NEAREST LANDING SPOT IS KILOMETERS AWAY, NO AERIAL ACCESS POSSIBLE -- AND THE ONLY ROAD WINDS ALONG SHEER CLIFFS OVER BOTTOMLESS CANYONS.
YEAH. THIS IS DEFINITELY THE PLACE. SET US DOWN, MEZGRAF...
..AND VERYBODY PUT N THOSE FANCY UTFITS EMBER ADE FOR YOU."
YOU LOOK VERY LOVELY, EMBER. I MEAN, FOR A HUMAN.
I'M GUESSING.
UH, THANK YOU, RATTY...
THERE'S OUR RIDE.

WELCOME, GENTLE BEINGS. IT IS BUT A SHORT, SCENIC RIDE TO THE LUCKY TWI'LEK...

...WHERE ALL YOUR DREAMS MAY COME TRUE.

D-DRIVER, HOW F-FAR DOWN IS IT?

TO THE BOTTOM OF THE RAVINE? MANY KILOMETERS IN MOST PLACES...

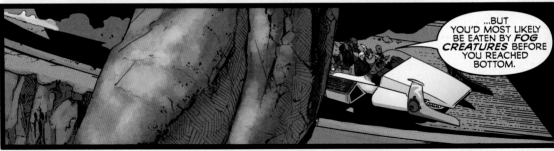

...BUT YOU'D MOST LIKELY BE EATEN BY FOG CREATURES BEFORE YOU REACHED BOTTOM.

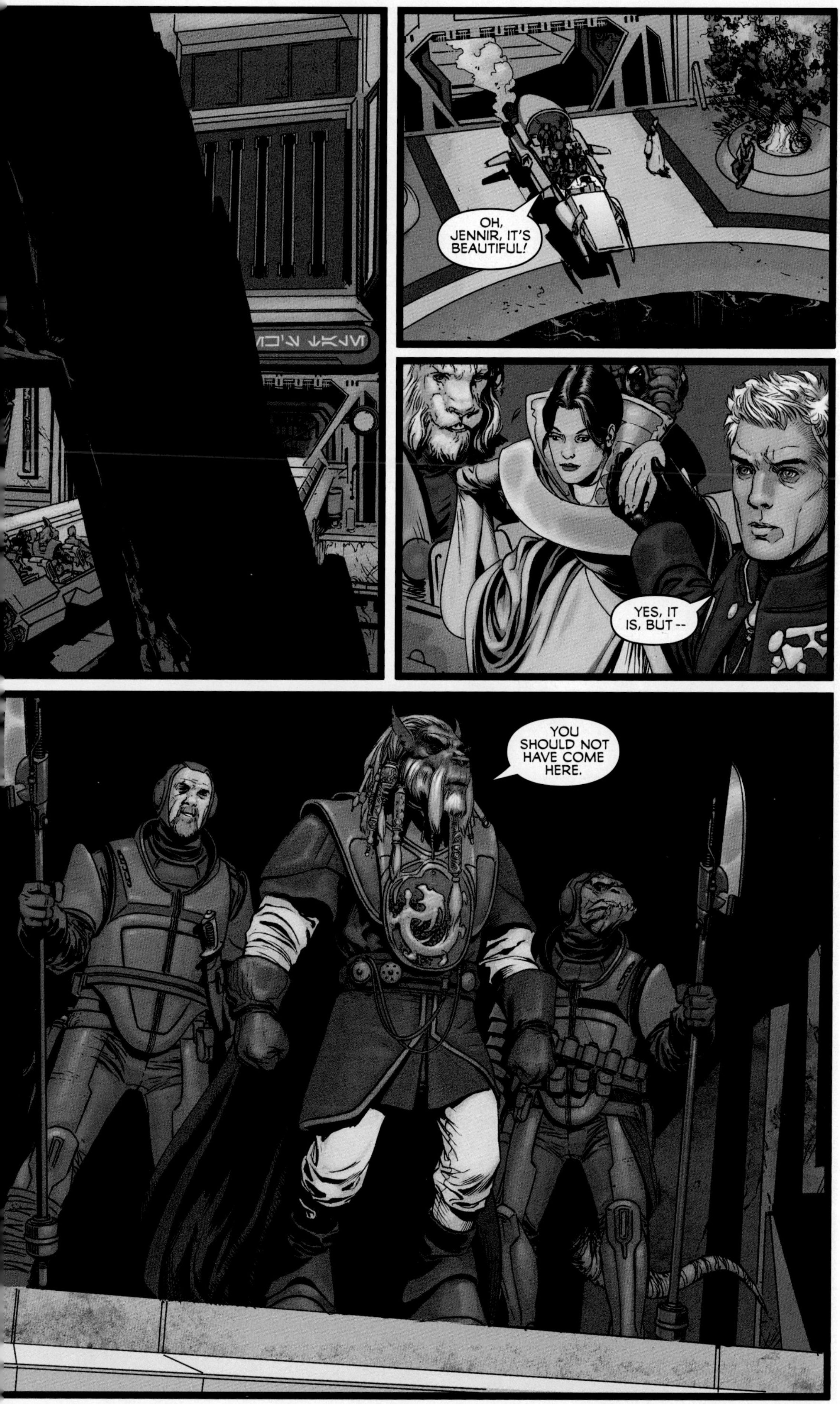
OH, JENNIR, IT'S BEAUTIFUL!
YES, IT IS, BUT --
YOU SHOULD NOT HAVE COME HERE.

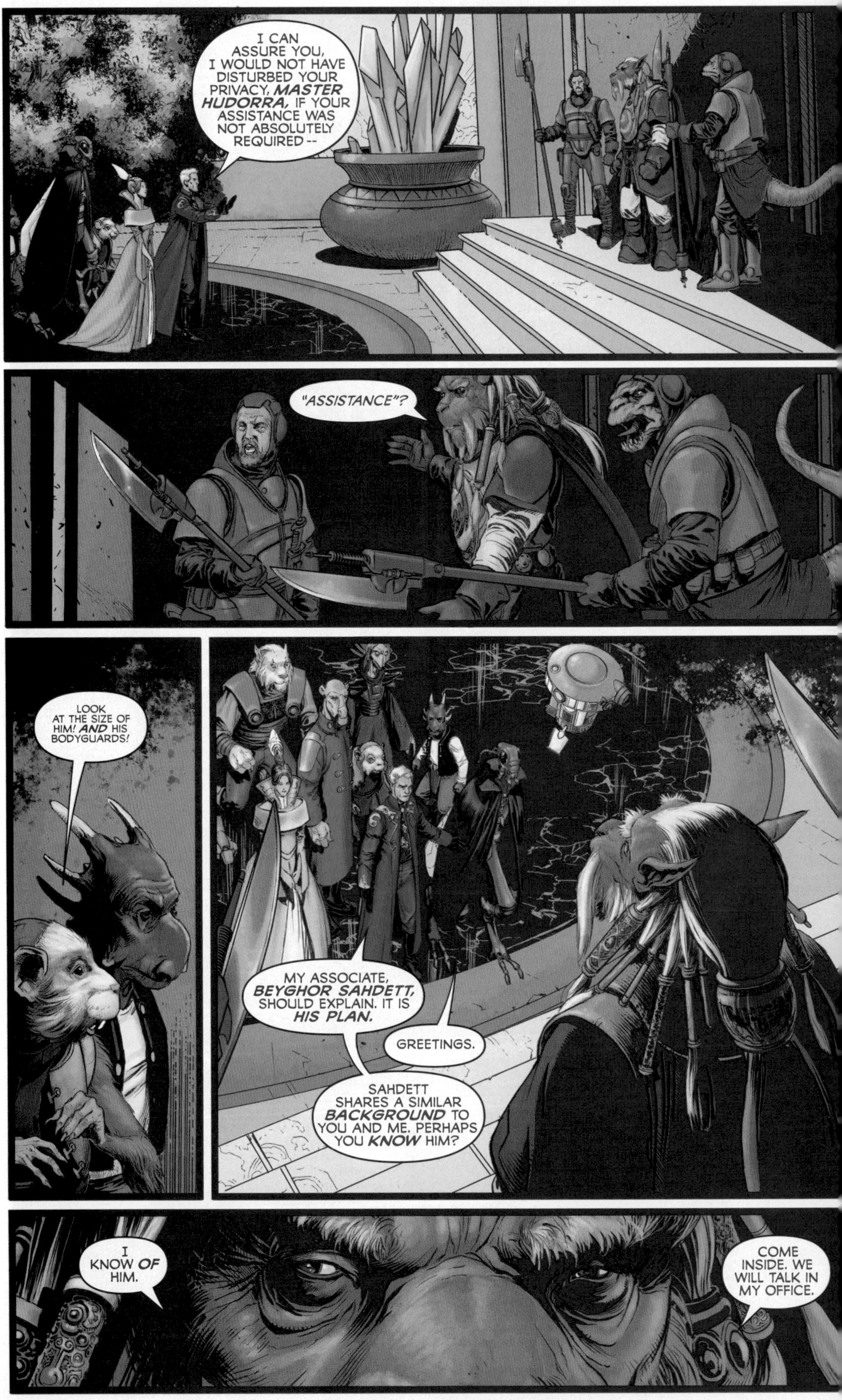
I CAN ASSURE YOU, I WOULD NOT HAVE DISTURBED YOUR PRIVACY, MASTER HUDORRA, IF YOUR ASSISTANCE WAS NOT ABSOLUTELY REQUIRED --
"ASSISTANCE"?
LOOK AT THE SIZE OF HIM! AND HIS BODYGUARDS!
MY ASSOCIATE, BEYGHOR SAHDETT, SHOULD EXPLAIN. IT IS HIS PLAN.
GREETINGS.
SAHDETT SHARES A SIMILAR BACKGROUND TO YOU AND ME. PERHAPS YOU KNOW HIM?
I KNOW OF HIM.
COME INSIDE. WE WILL TALK IN MY OFFICE.

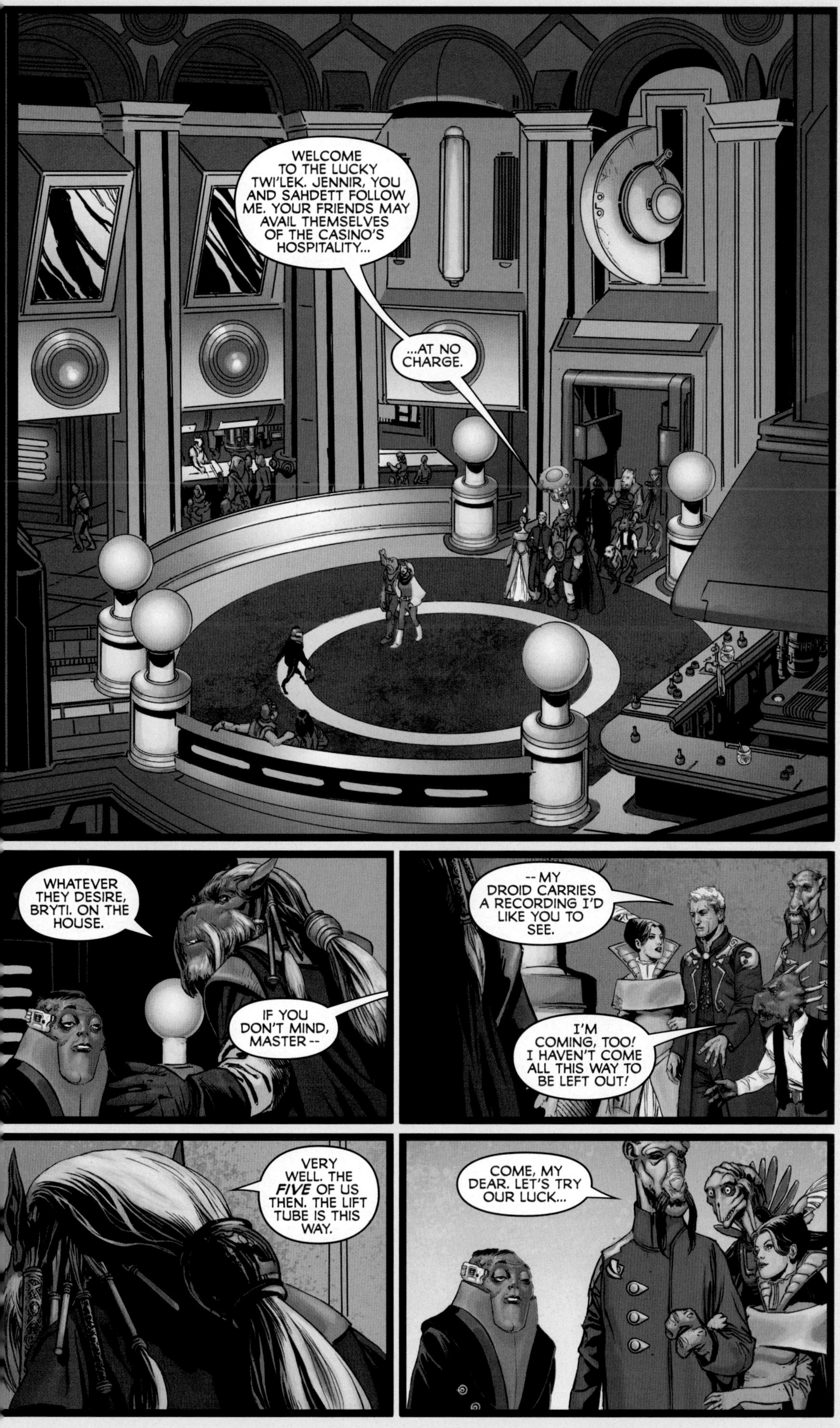
WELCOME TO THE LUCKY TWI'LEK. JENNIR, YOU AND SAHDETT FOLLOW ME. YOUR FRIENDS MAY AVAIL THEMSELVES OF THE CASINO'S HOSPITALITY...
...AT NO CHARGE.
WHATEVER THEY DESIRE, BRYTI. ON THE HOUSE.
IF YOU DON'T MIND, MASTER --
-- MY DROID CARRIES A RECORDING I'D LIKE YOU TO SEE.
I'M COMING, TOO! I HAVEN'T COME ALL THIS WAY TO BE LEFT OUT!
VERY WELL. THE *FIVE* OF US THEN. THE LIFT TUBE IS THIS WAY.
COME, MY DEAR. LET'S TRY OUR LUCK...

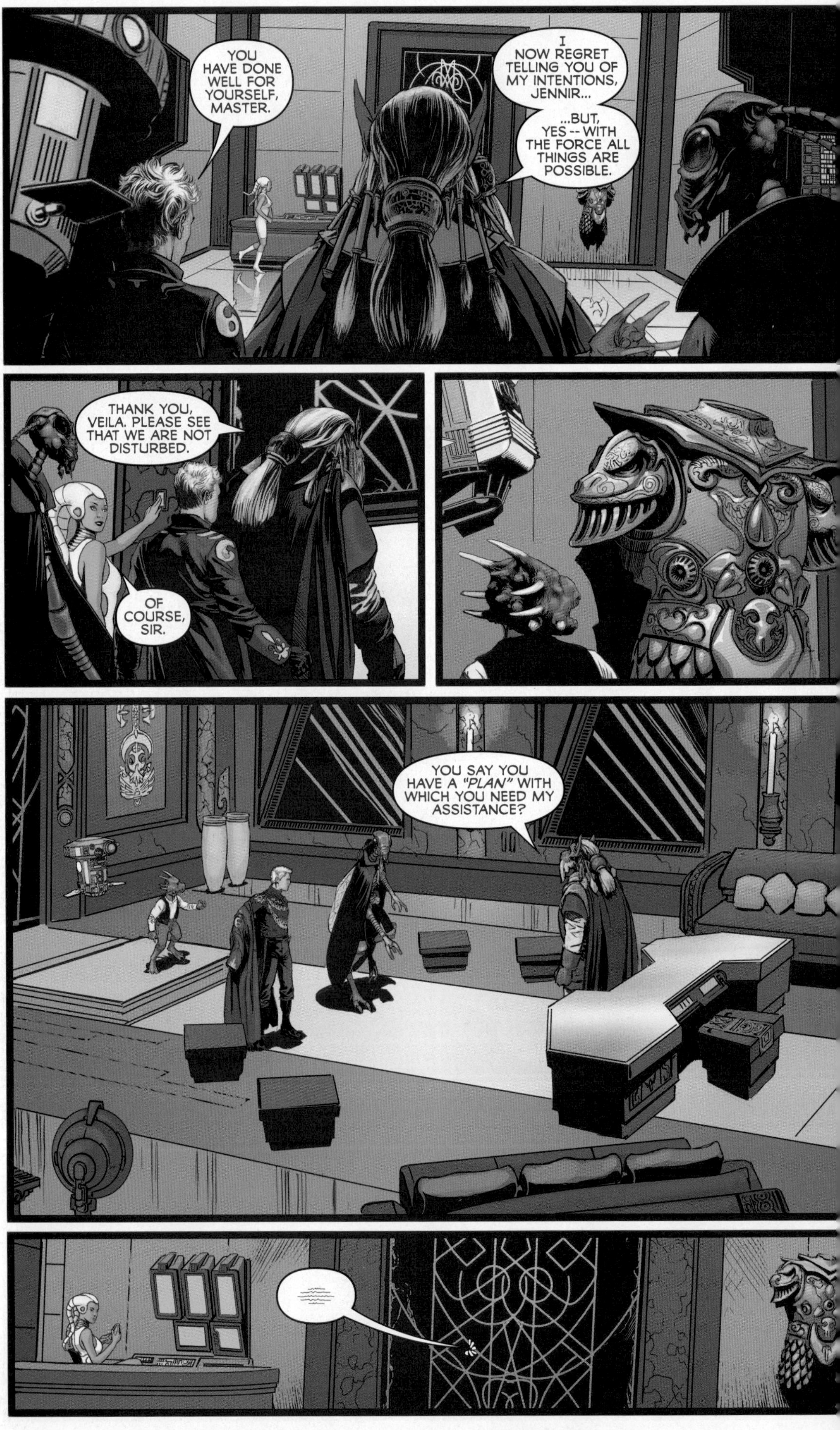
YOU HAVE DONE WELL FOR YOURSELF, MASTER.
I NOW REGRET TELLING YOU OF MY INTENTIONS, JENNIR...
...BUT, YES -- WITH THE FORCE ALL THINGS ARE POSSIBLE.
THANK YOU, VEILA. PLEASE SEE THAT WE ARE NOT DISTURBED.
OF COURSE, SIR.
YOU SAY YOU HAVE A "PLAN" WITH WHICH YOU NEED MY ASSISTANCE?

...A SURPRISE BY WHICH WE WILL OVERCOME THE ENEMY AND SIGNIFICANTLY WEAKEN THE EMPIRE.

YOU WOULD HAVE US SELL OUR LIVES -- BUT *DEARLY?*

YES. IF IT COMES TO THAT. THERE MAY BE NO OTHER WAY TO ACCOMPLISH OUR ENDS.

A BOLD PLAN, MASTER SAHDETT.

YOU KNOW HE'S *LYING,* DON'T YOU, JENNIR?

YES.

*WHAT?!*

I'VE KNOWN FOR SOME TIME. BUT I ALSO KNOW HIS REPUTATION WITH A LIGHTSABER. I KNEW I COULDN'T TAKE HIM MYSELF.

THAT'S WHY I NEEDED *YOUR* ASSISTANCE.

krik!

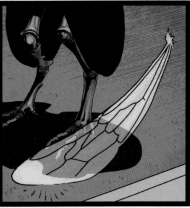

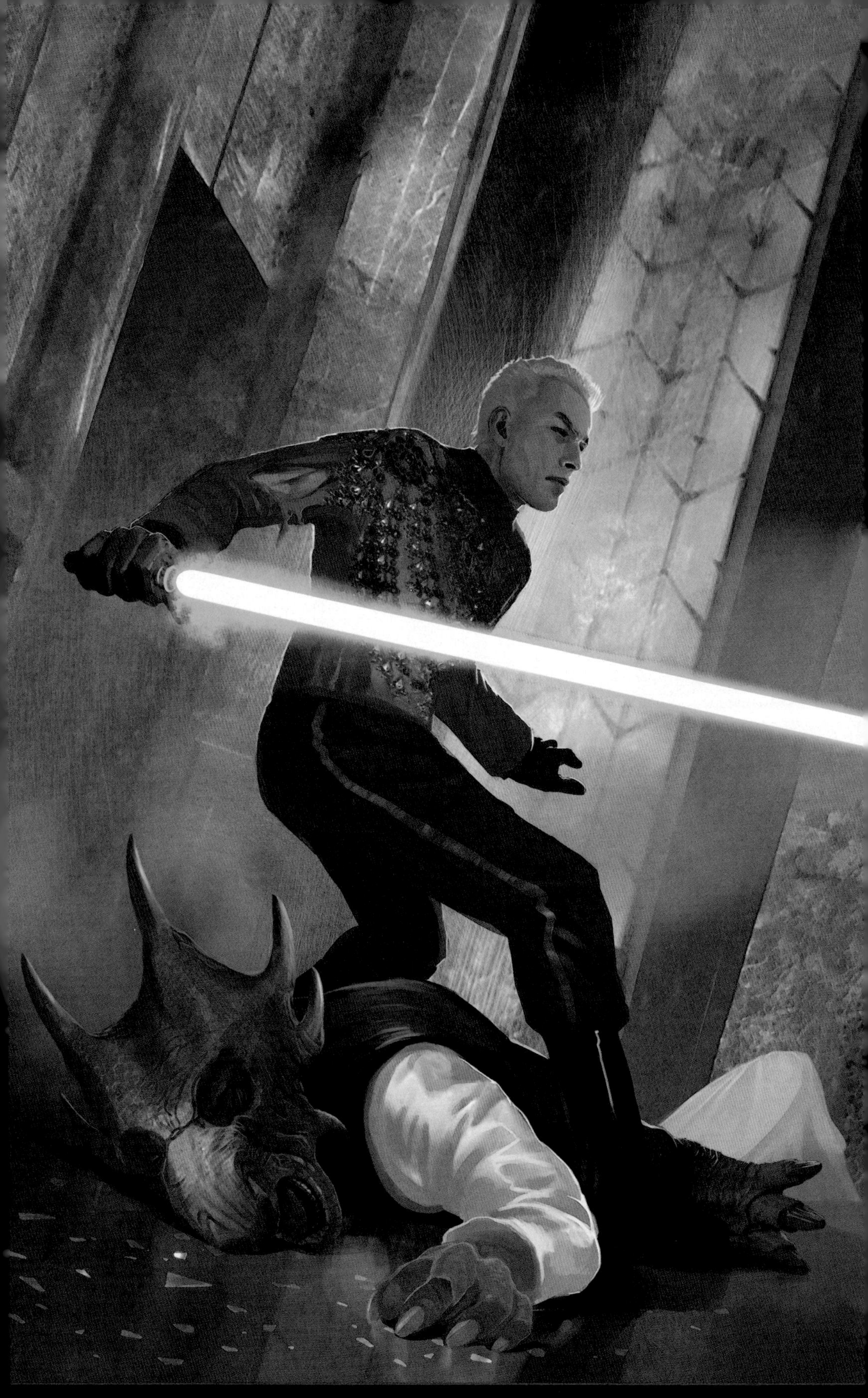

*STAR WARS: DARK TIMES — A SPARK REMAINS #3*

WRITER: RANDY STRADLEY • ARTIST: DOUGLAS WHEATLEY • COLORIST: DAN JACKSON • LETTERER: MICHAEL HEISLER
ASSISTANT EDITOR: FREDDYE LINS • EDITOR: DAVE MARSHALL • COVER ARTIST: BENJAMIN CARRÉ

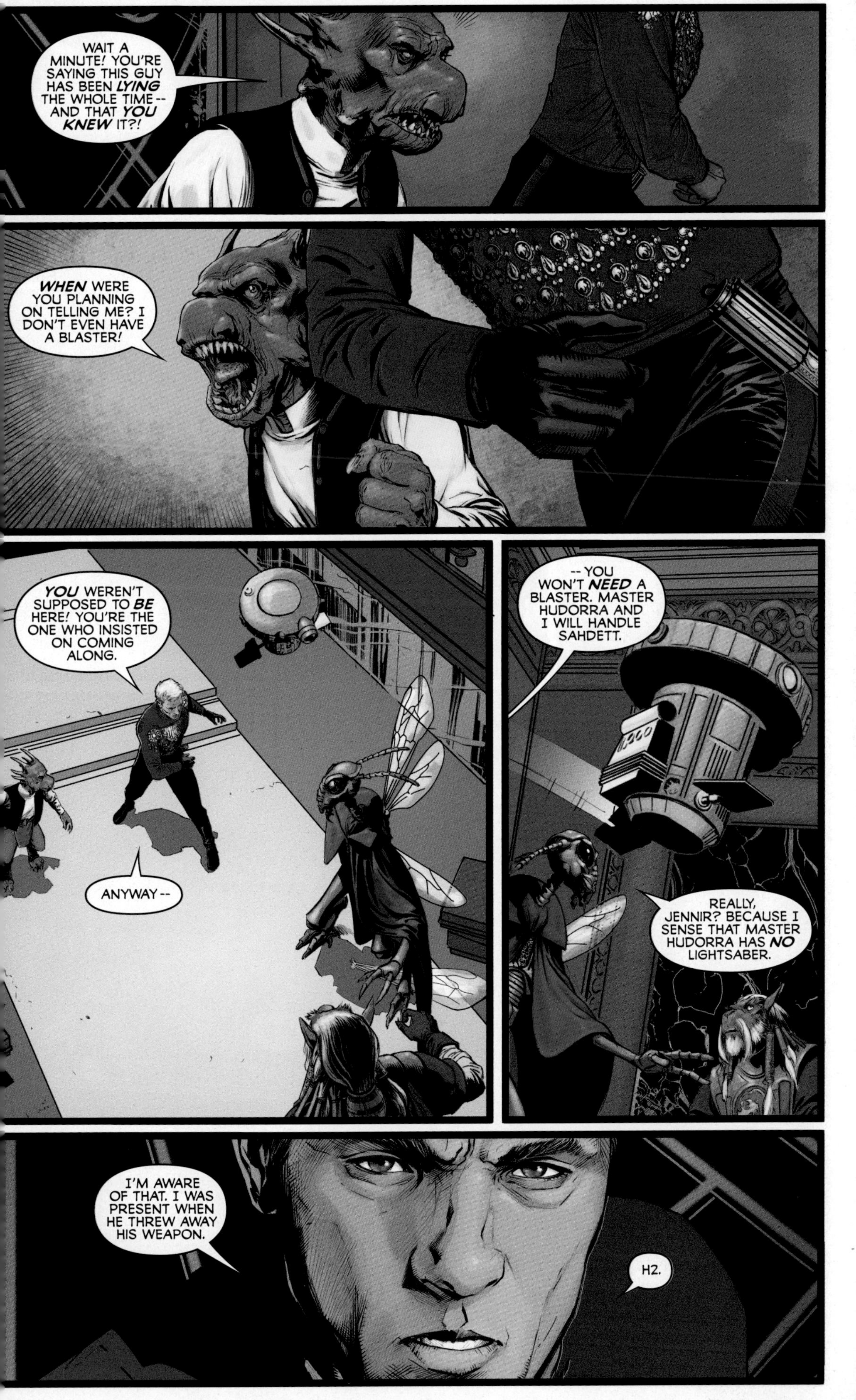
WAIT A MINUTE! YOU'RE SAYING THIS GUY HAS BEEN *LYING* THE WHOLE TIME -- AND THAT *YOU KNEW* IT?!
*WHEN* WERE YOU PLANNING ON TELLING ME? I DON'T EVEN HAVE A BLASTER!
*YOU* WEREN'T SUPPOSED TO *BE* HERE! YOU'RE THE ONE WHO INSISTED ON COMING ALONG.
ANYWAY --
-- YOU WON'T *NEED* A BLASTER. MASTER HUDORRA AND I WILL HANDLE SAHDETT.
REALLY, JENNIR? BECAUSE I SENSE THAT MASTER HUDORRA HAS *NO* LIGHTSABER.
I'M AWARE OF THAT. I WAS PRESENT WHEN HE THREW AWAY HIS WEAPON.
H2.

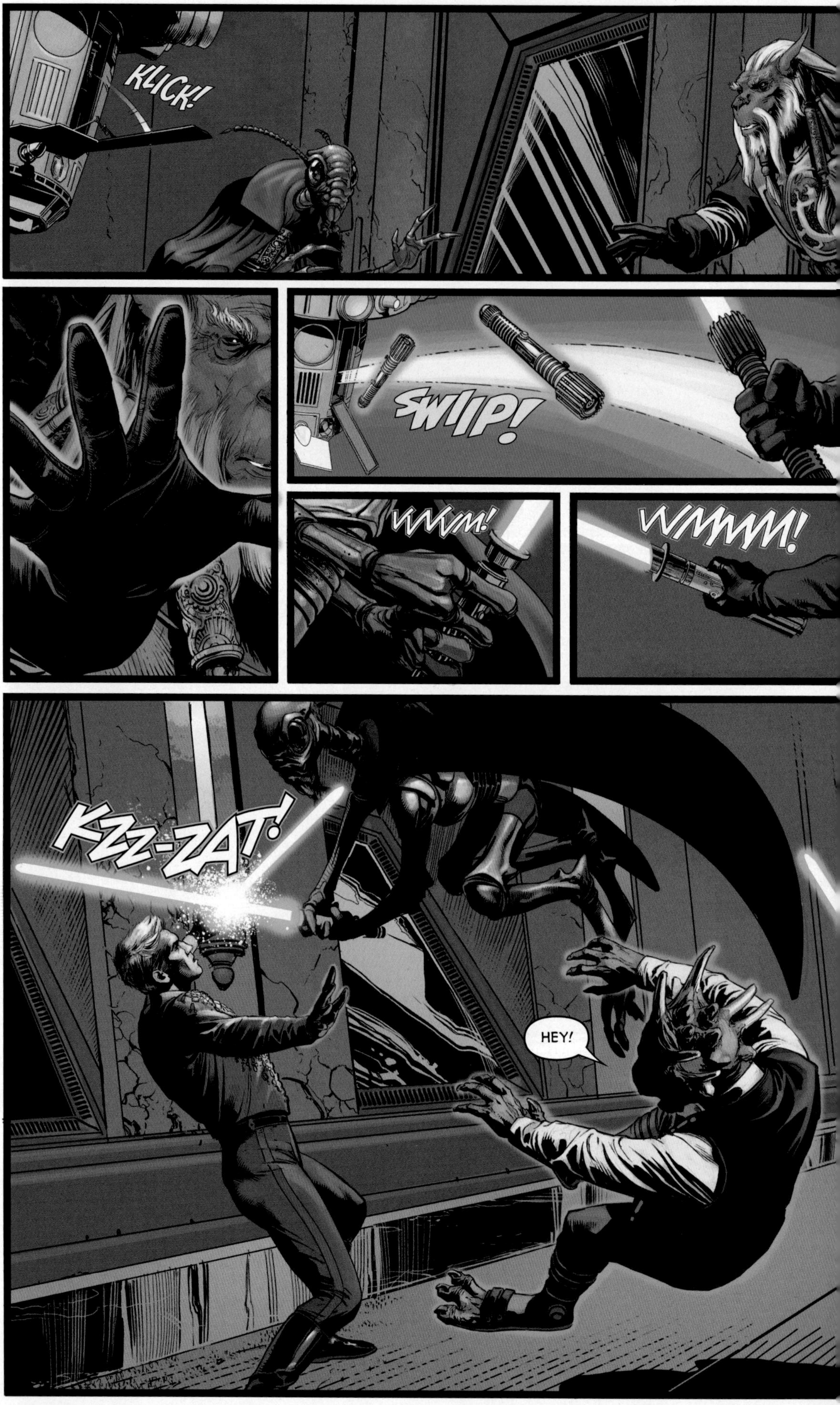

KLICK!
SWIP!
VVVVM!
VVMMM!
KZZ-ZAT!
HEY!

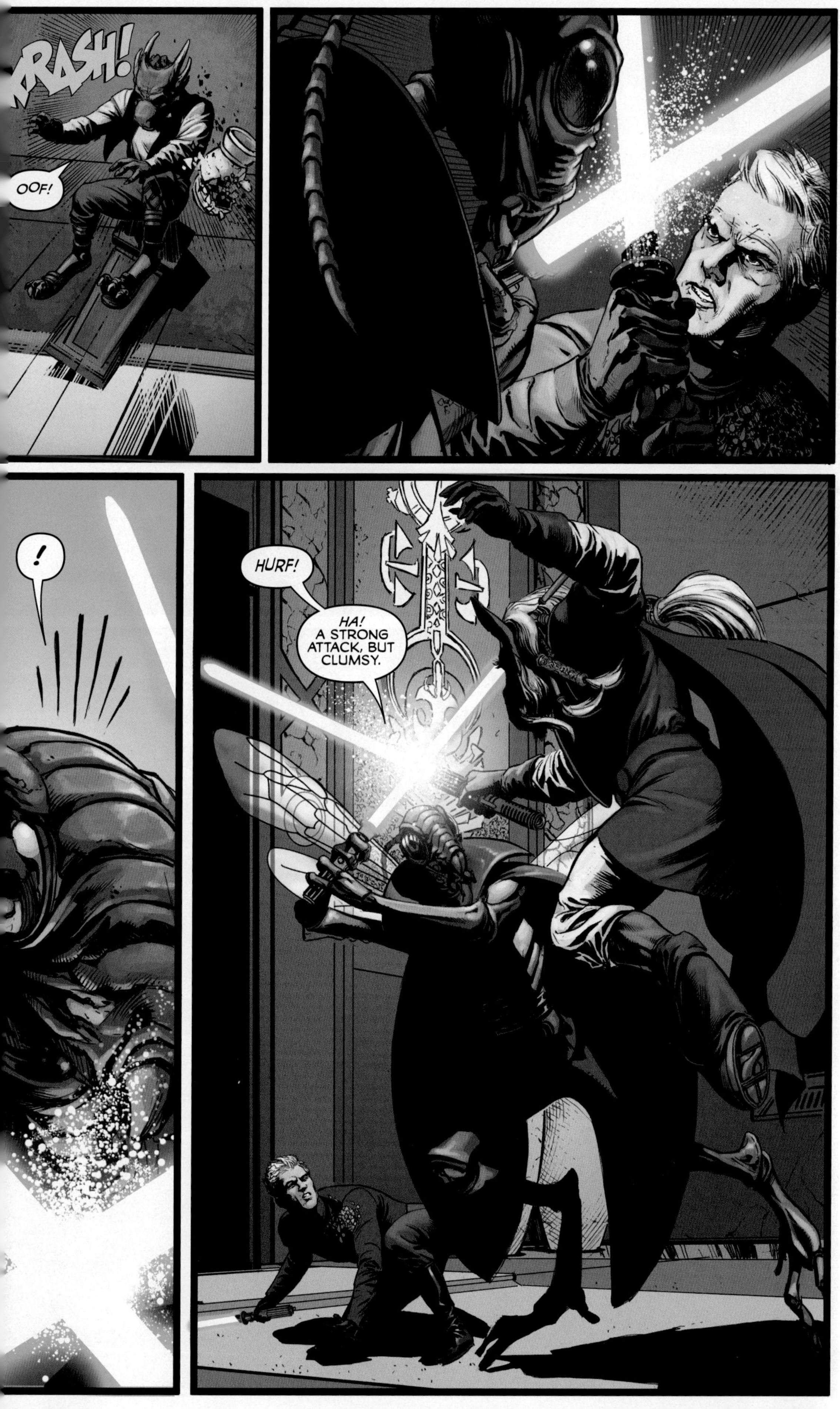

RASH!
OOF!
!
HURF!
HA! A STRONG ATTACK, BUT CLUMSY.

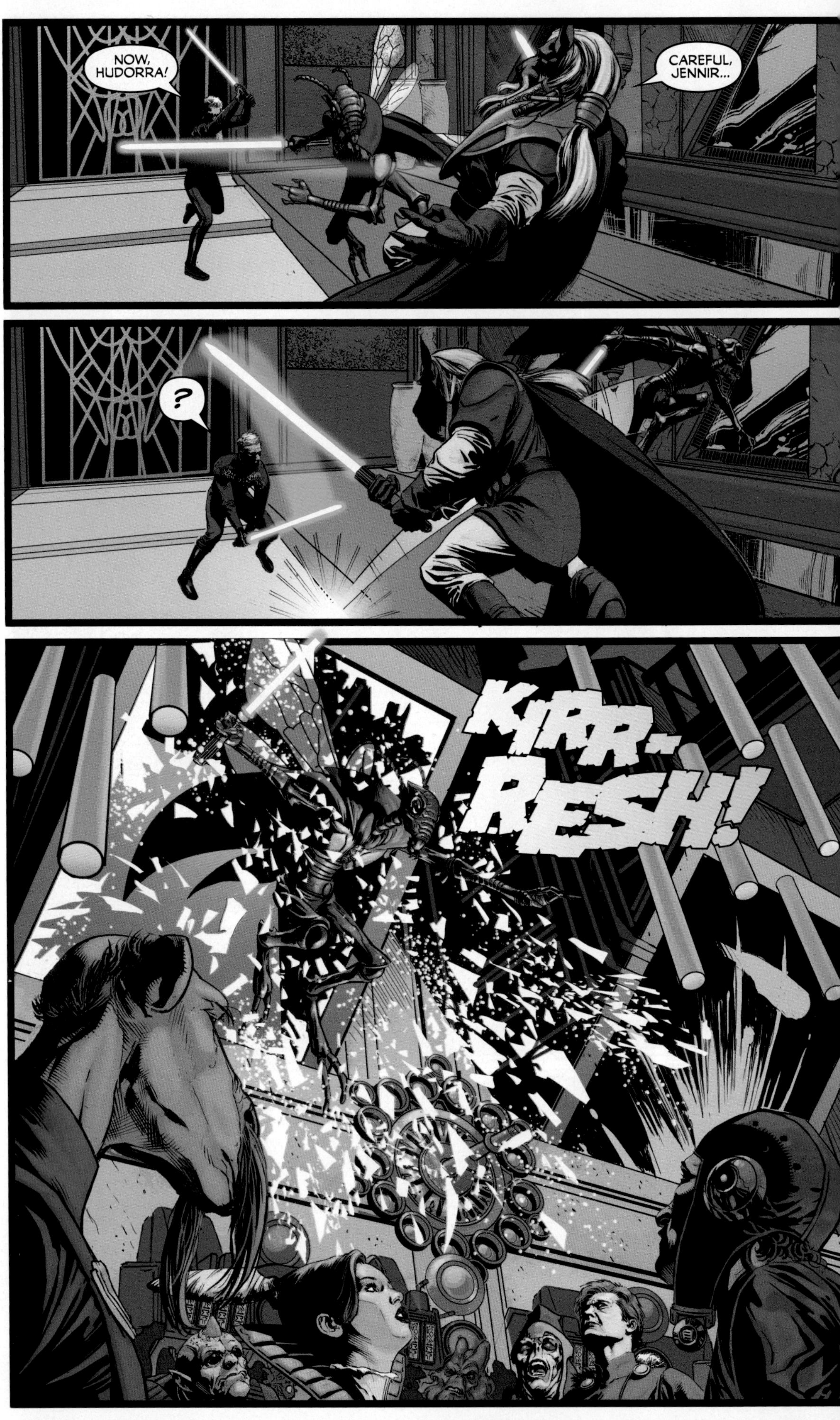
NOW, HUDORRA!
CAREFUL, JENNIR...
?
KIRR-RESH!

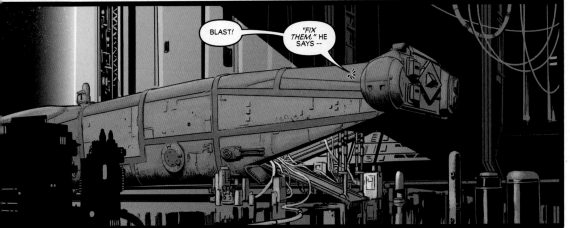

BLAST!

"FIX THEM," HE says --

--"YOUR ENGINES ARE ONLY RUNNING AT EIGHTY-SIX PERCENT!"

I'D LIKE TO SEE HIM DO BETTER...

TOGGLE YOUR REAR SHIELD POWER TO THE MAIN ENGINES --

STARS! YOU SCARED THE LIFE OUT OF ME!

--YOU WON'T NEED IT.

WHAT?

YOUR REAR SHIELD. YOU WON'T NEED IT. YOU'RE WORKING FOR THE EMPIRE NOW. FROM WHOM WILL YOU RUN?

SURE. THAT'S GREAT. BUT IN CASE YOU HADN'T NOTICED, THIS SHIP ISN'T EXACTLY OF IMPERIAL CONFIGURATION. WHAT IF WHOEVER'S SHOOTING DOESN'T KNOW THE EMPIRE HAS MY BACK?

THAT'S WHY I SAID TO TOGGLE THE POWER.

OH.

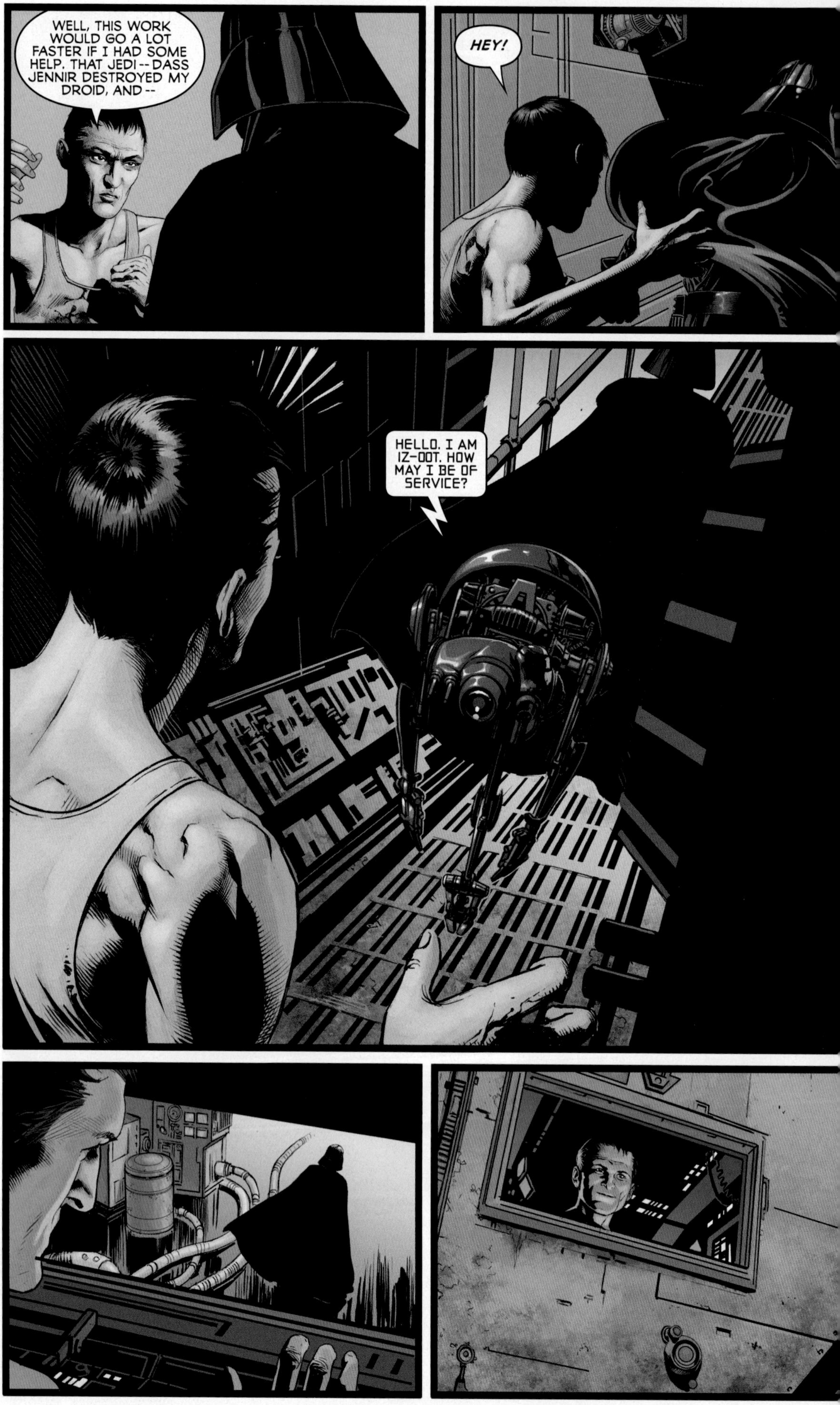
WELL, THIS WORK WOULD GO A LOT FASTER IF I HAD SOME HELP. THAT JEDI--DASS JENNIR DESTROYED MY DROID, AND--
HEY!
HELLO. I AM IZ-0OT. HOW MAY I BE OF SERVICE?

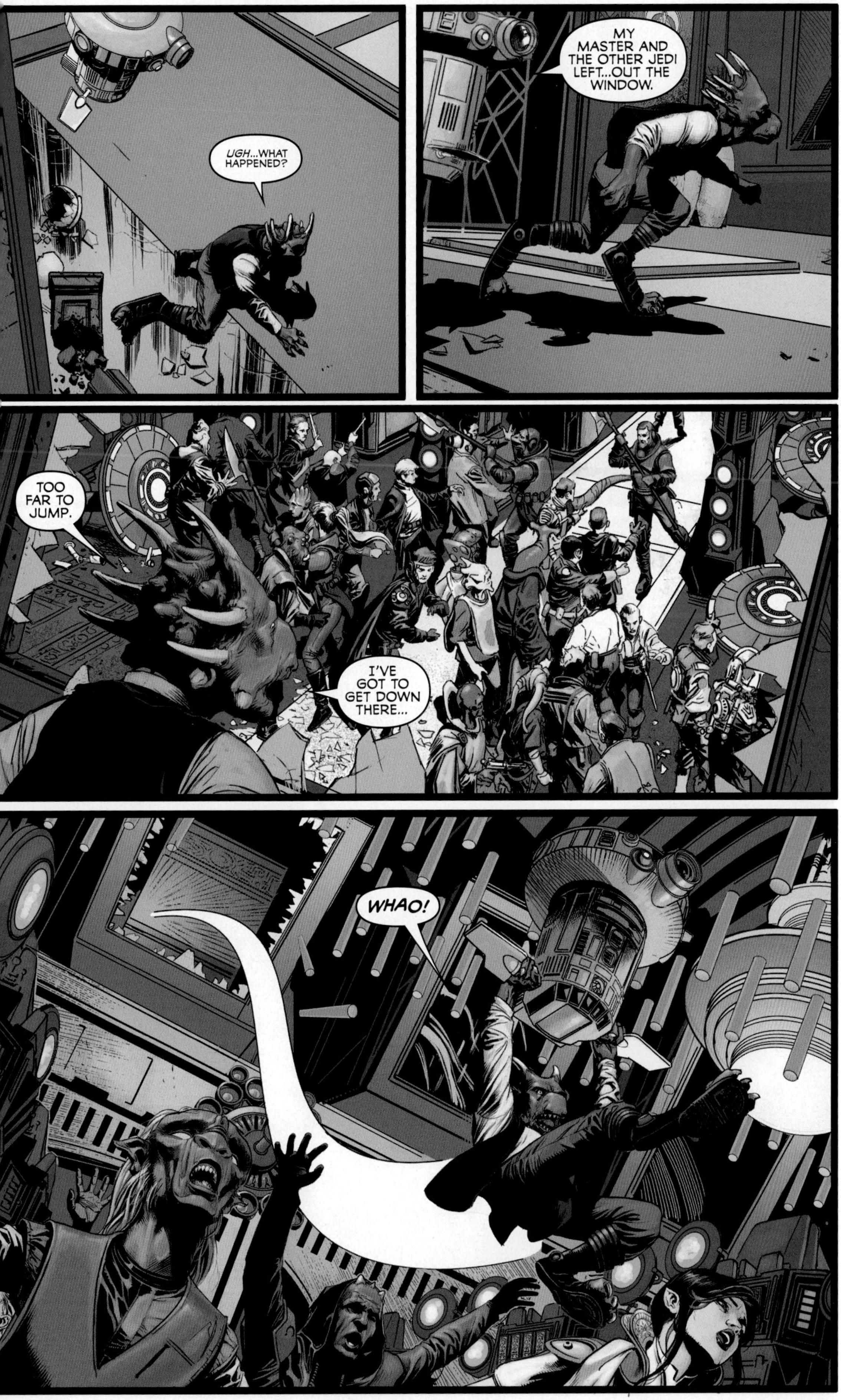

UGH...WHAT HAPPENED?
MY MASTER AND THE OTHER JEDI LEFT...OUT THE WINDOW.
TOO FAR TO JUMP.
I'VE GOT TO GET DOWN THERE...
WHAO!

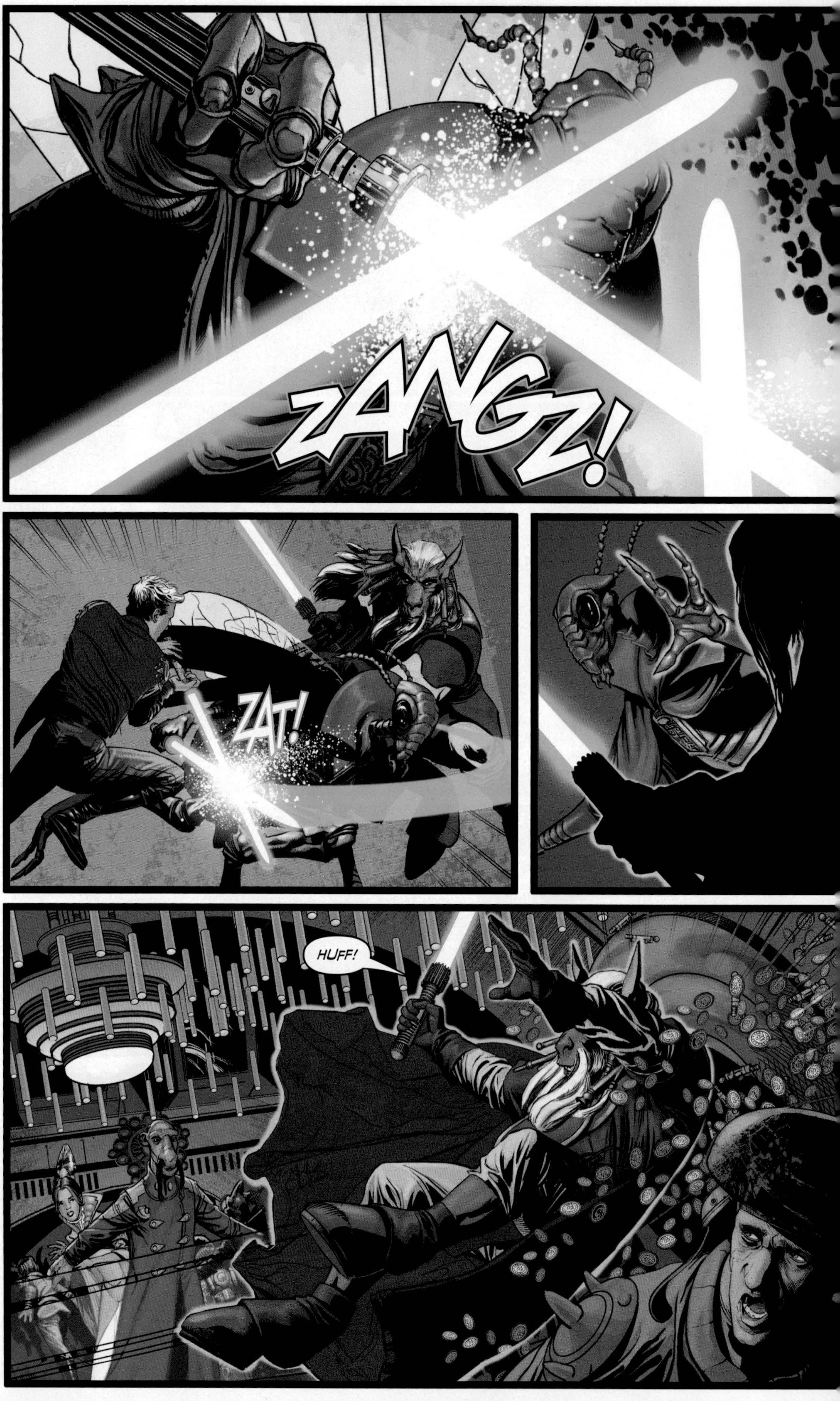
ZANGZ!
ZAT!
HUFF!

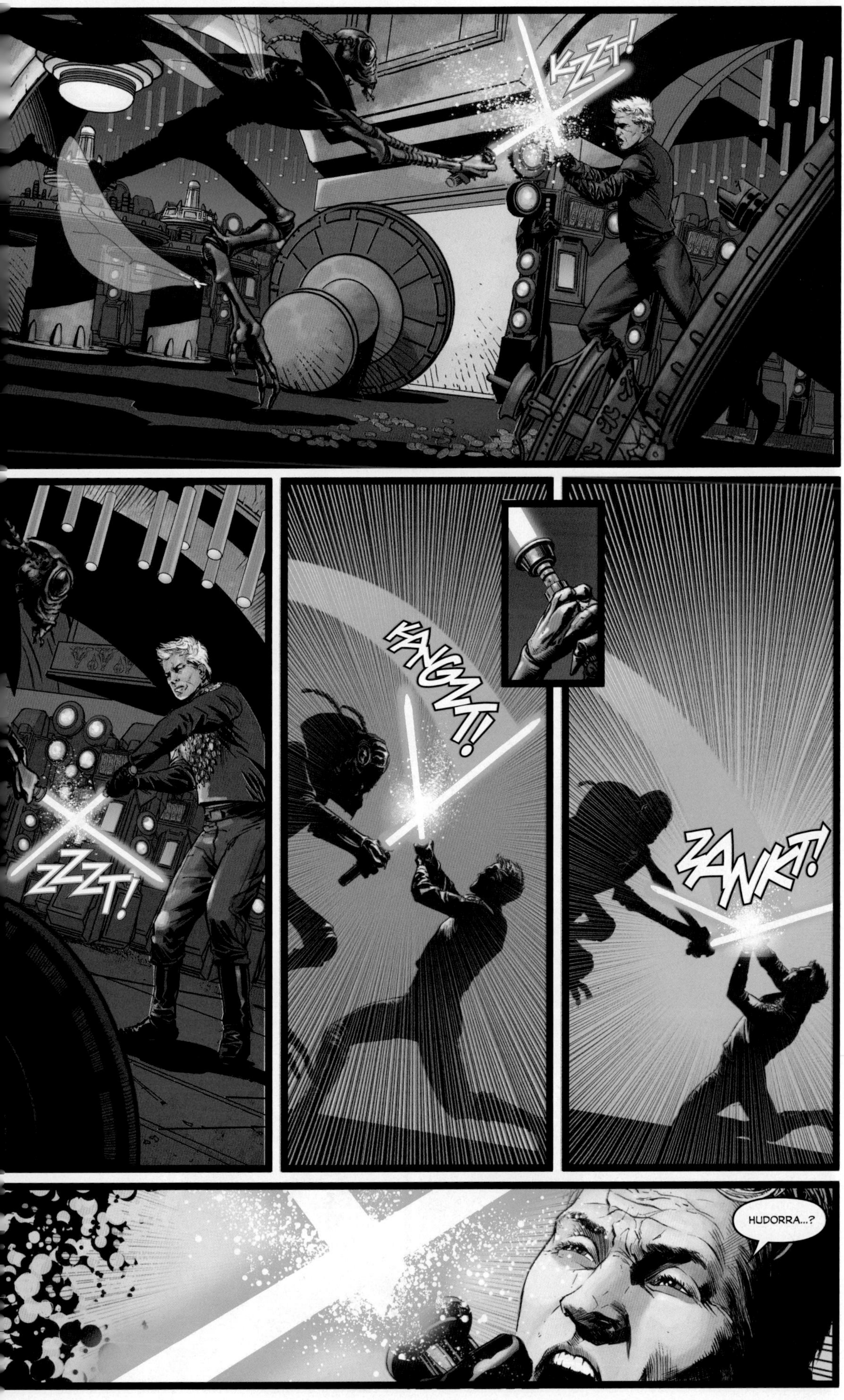
KZZZT!
ZZZZT!
KANGWT!
ZANKT!
HUDORRA...?

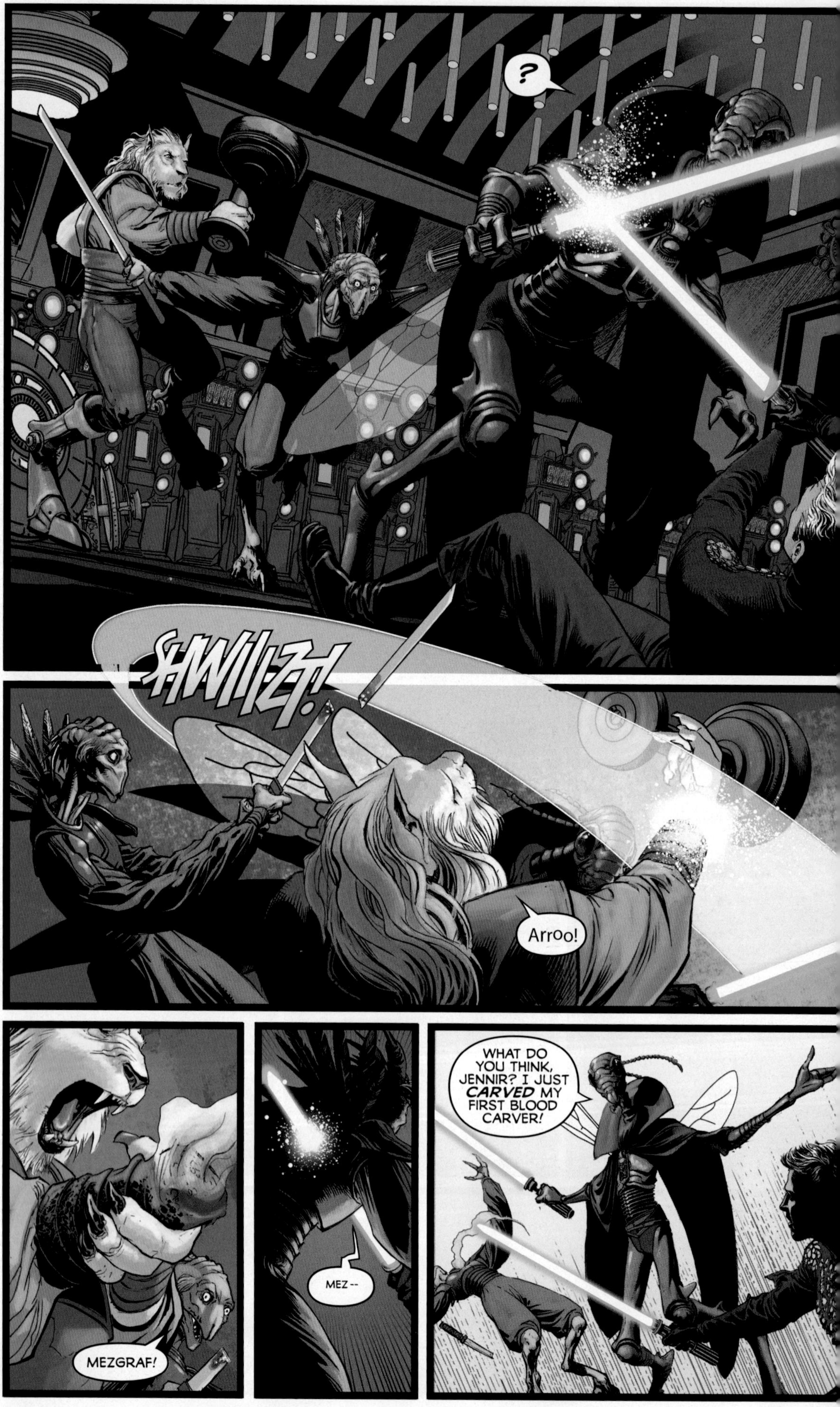
?
SHWIIZT!
Arroo!
MEZGRAF!
MEZ --
WHAT DO YOU THINK, JENNIR? I JUST *CARVED* MY FIRST BLOOD CARVER!

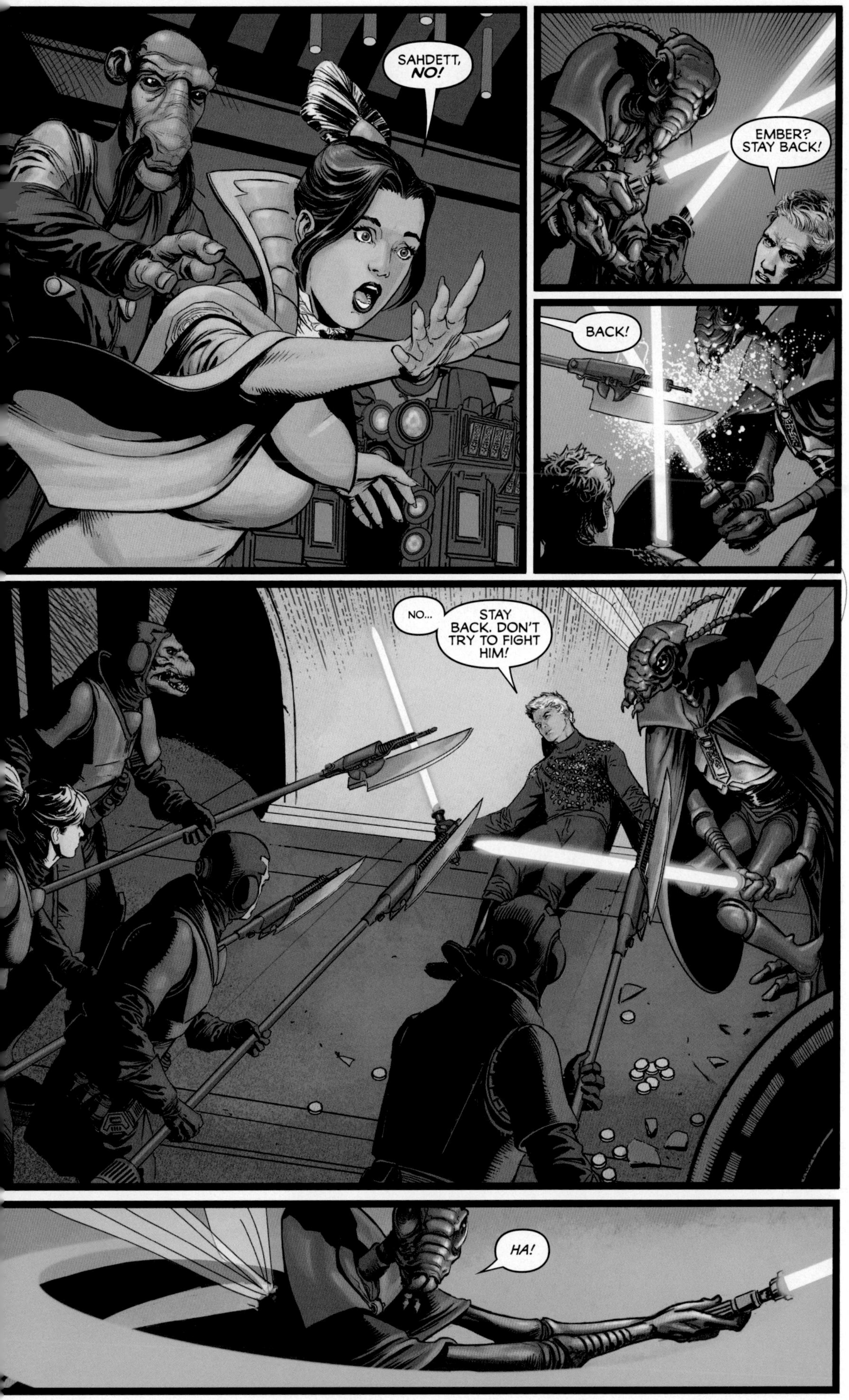
SAHDETT, NO!
EMBER? STAY BACK!
BACK!
NO...
STAY BACK. DON'T TRY TO FIGHT HIM!
HA!

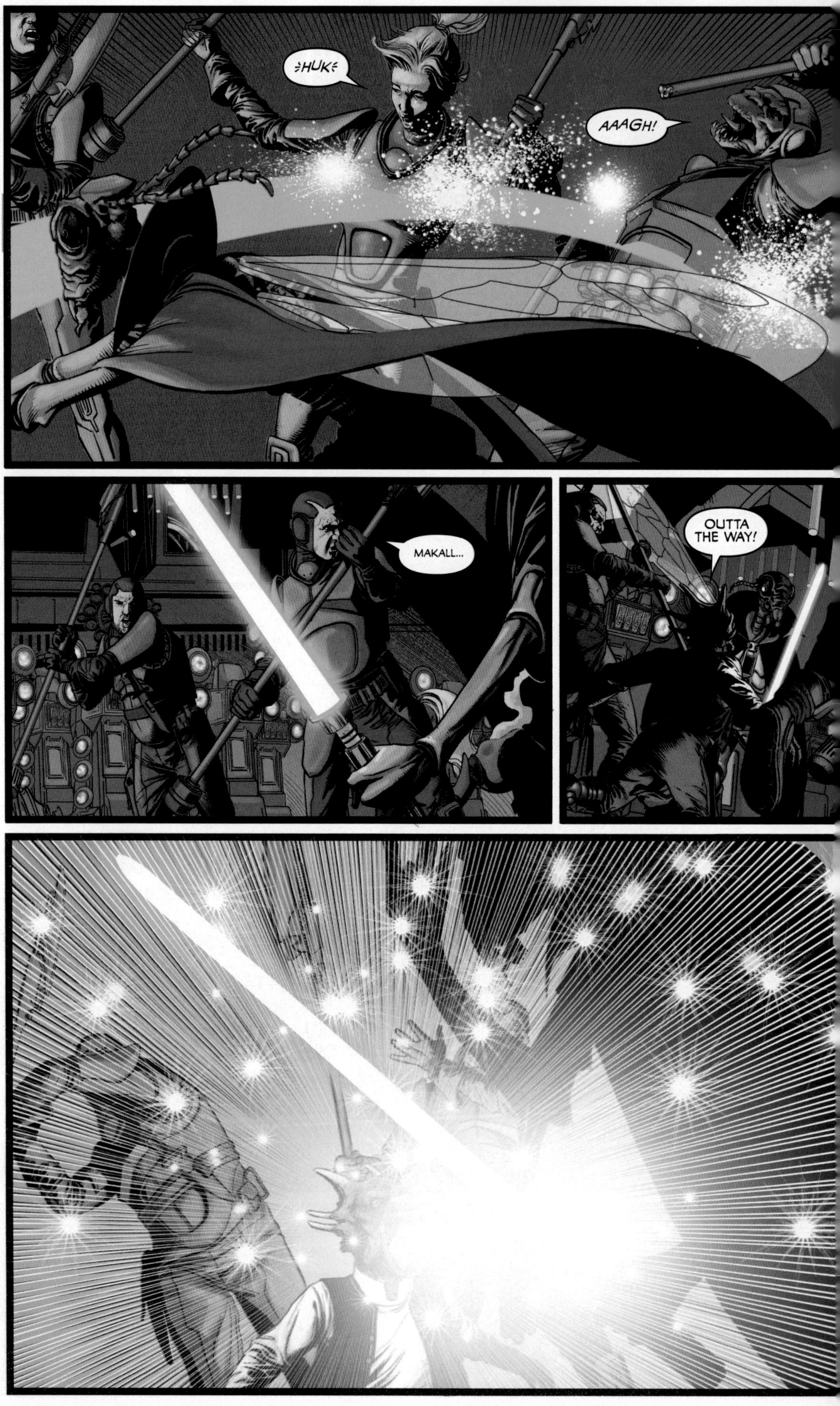
HUK
AAAGH!
MAKALL...
OUTTA THE WAY!

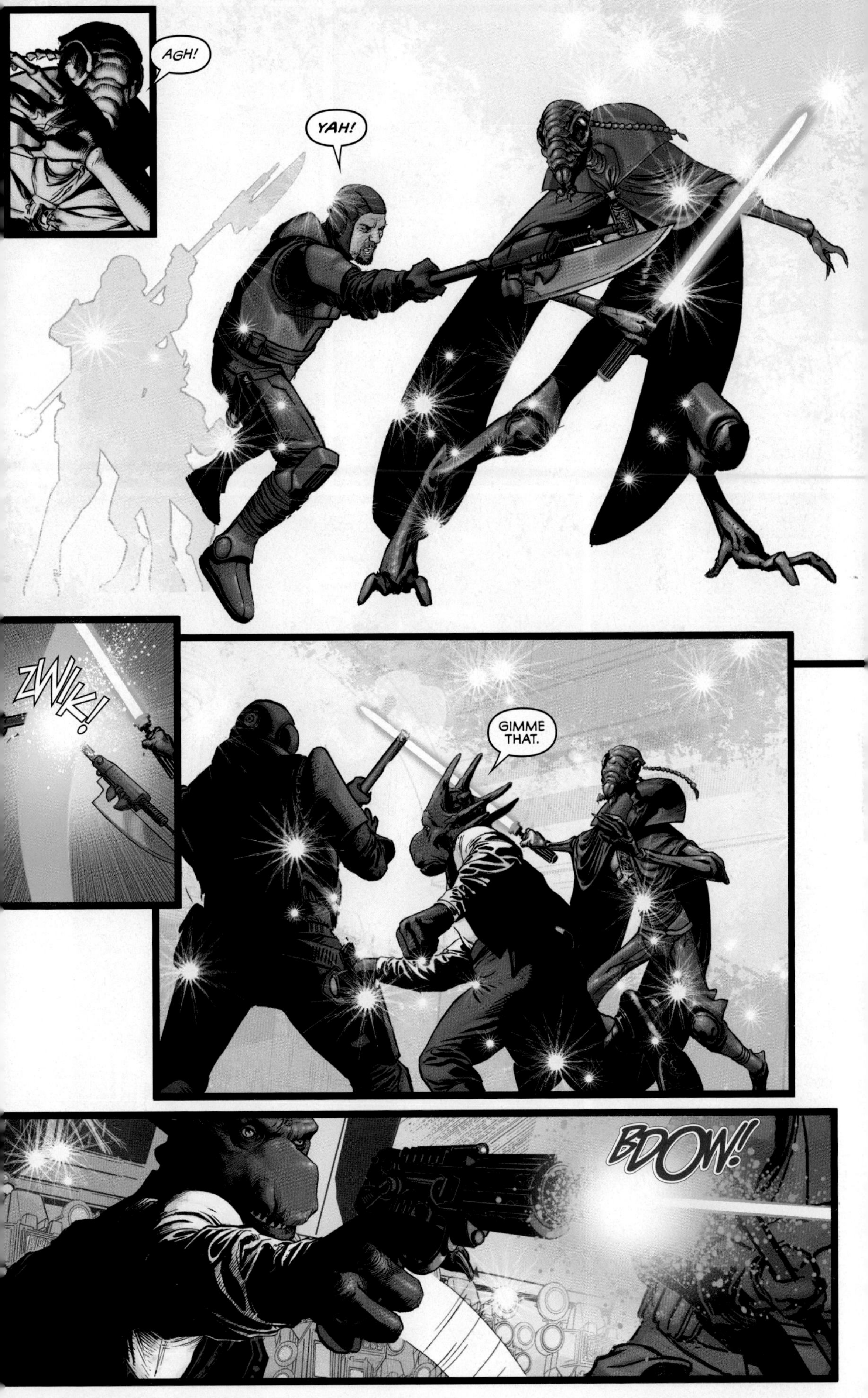
AGH!
YAH!
ZWIK!
GIMME THAT.
BDOW!

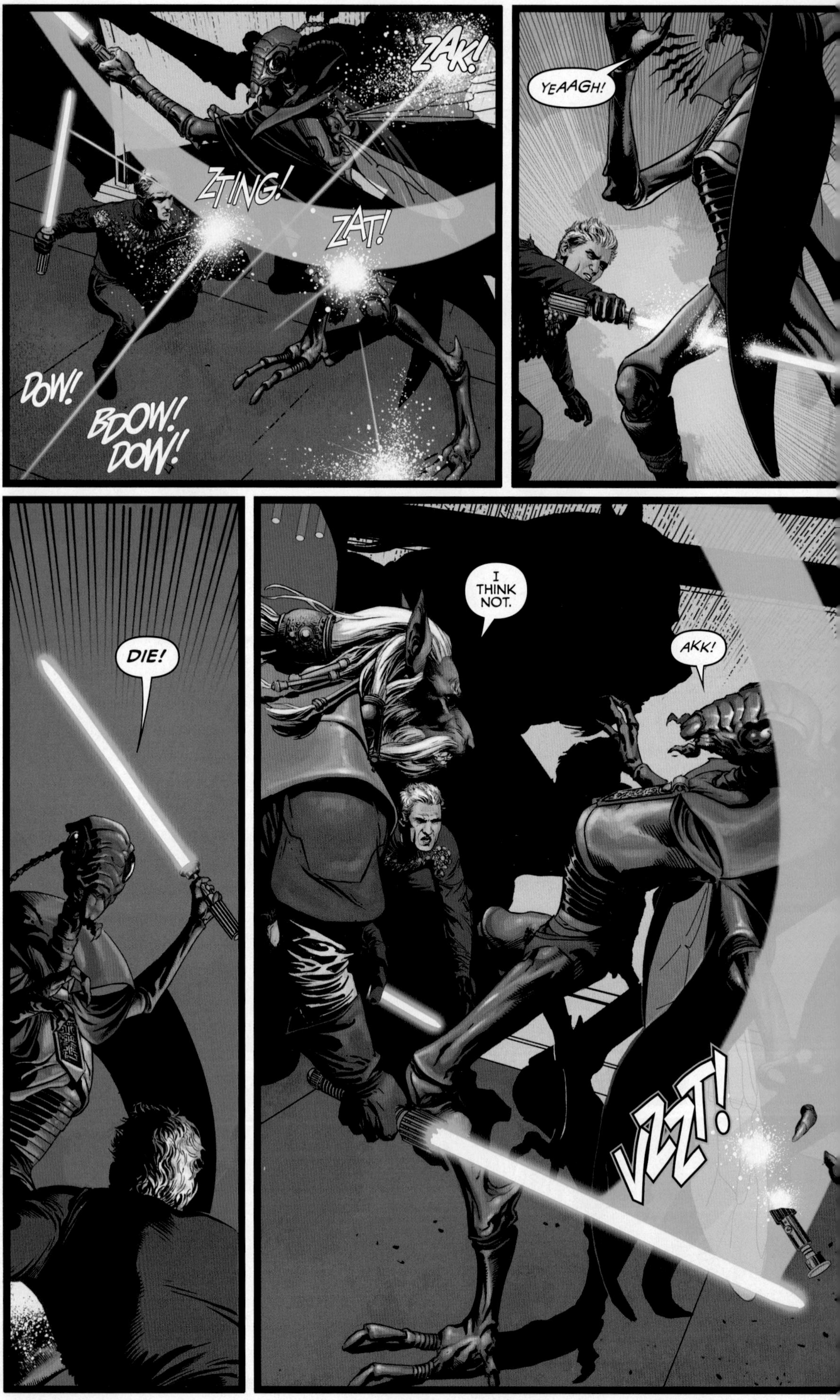
ZAK!
ZTING!
ZAT!
DOW!
BDOW!
DOW!
YEAAGH!
DIE!
I THINK NOT.
AKK!
VZZT!

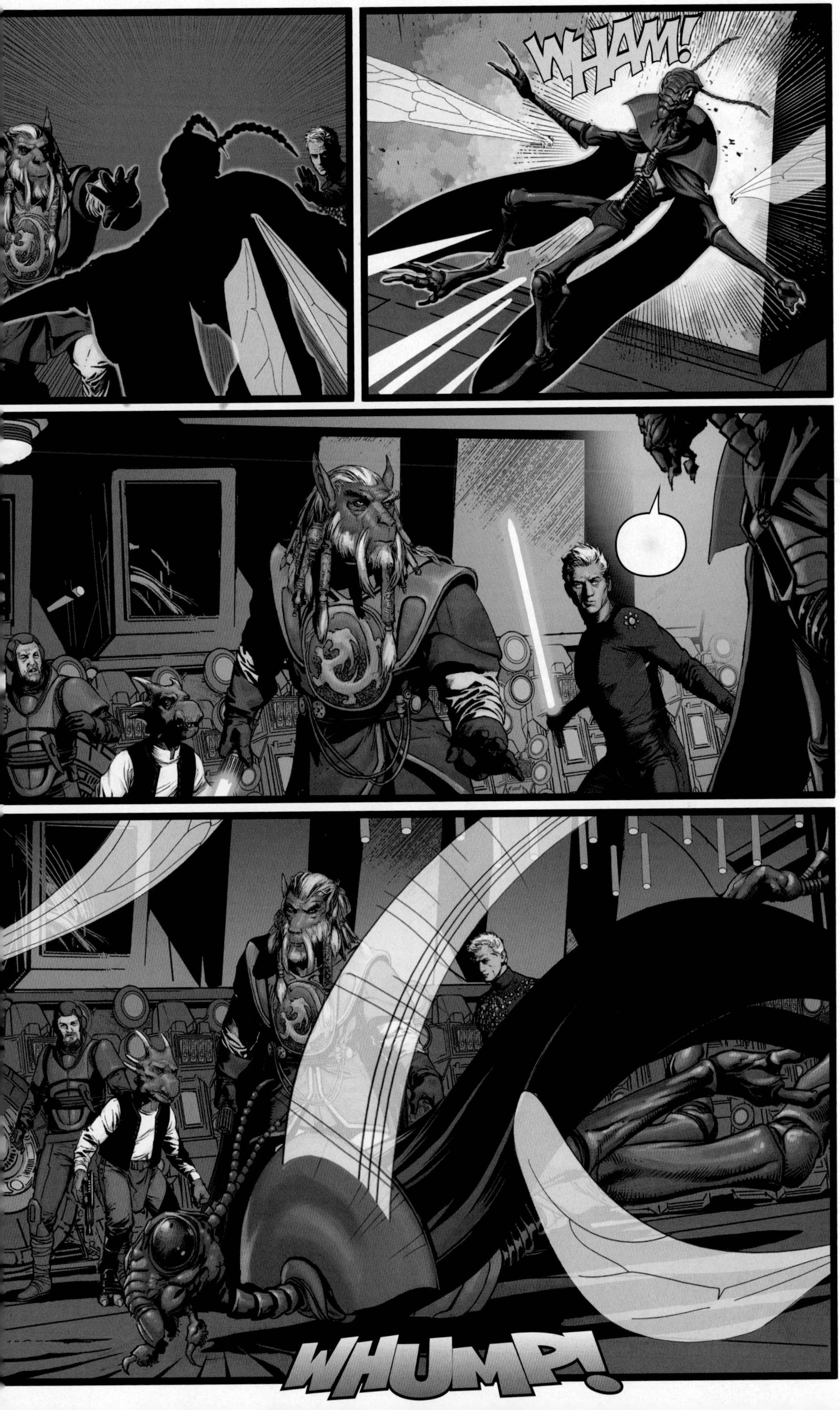
WHAM!
WHUMP!

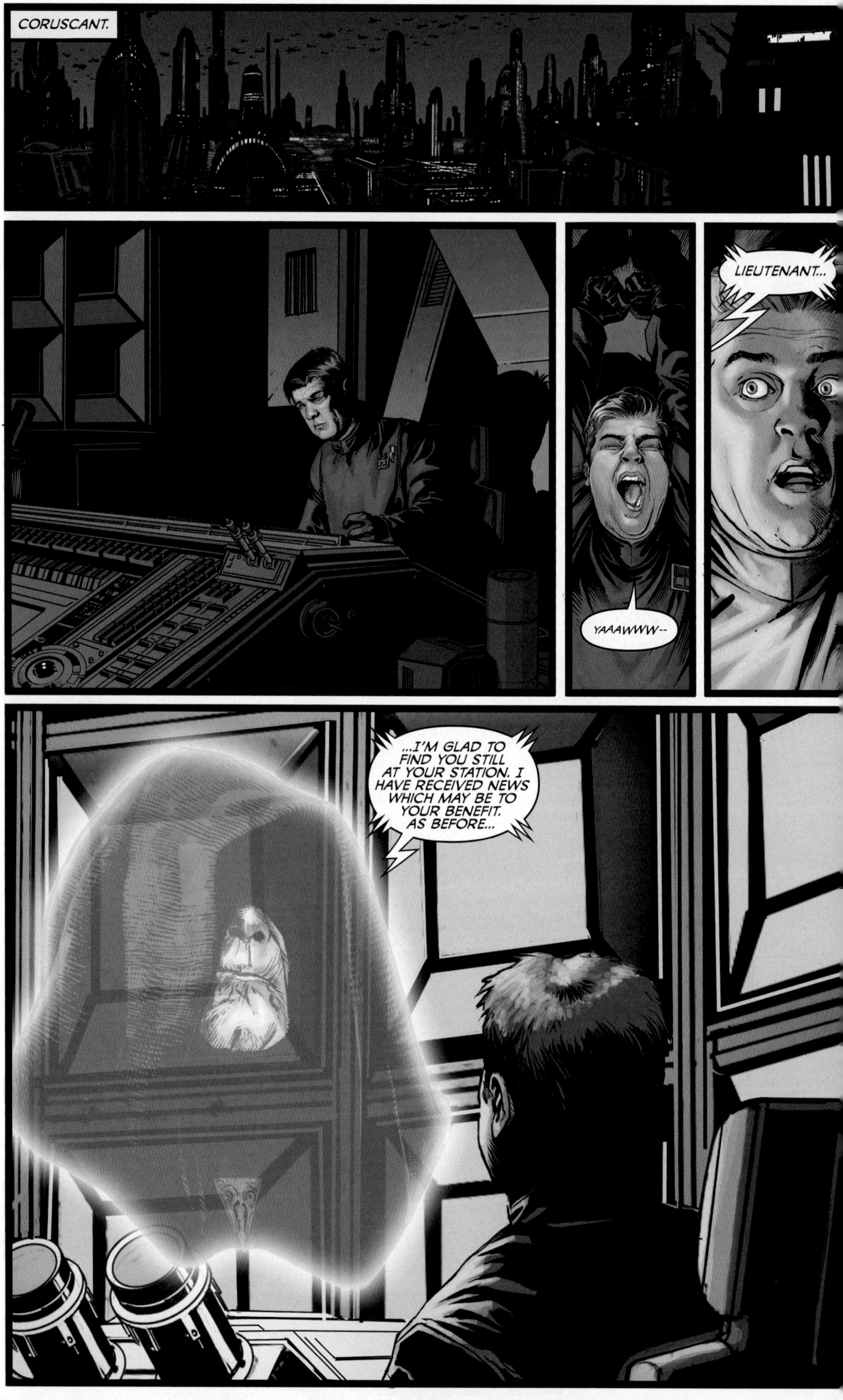
CORUSCANT.
YAAAWWW--
LIEUTENANT...
...I'M GLAD TO FIND YOU STILL AT YOUR STATION. I HAVE RECEIVED NEWS WHICH MAY BE TO YOUR BENEFIT. AS BEFORE...

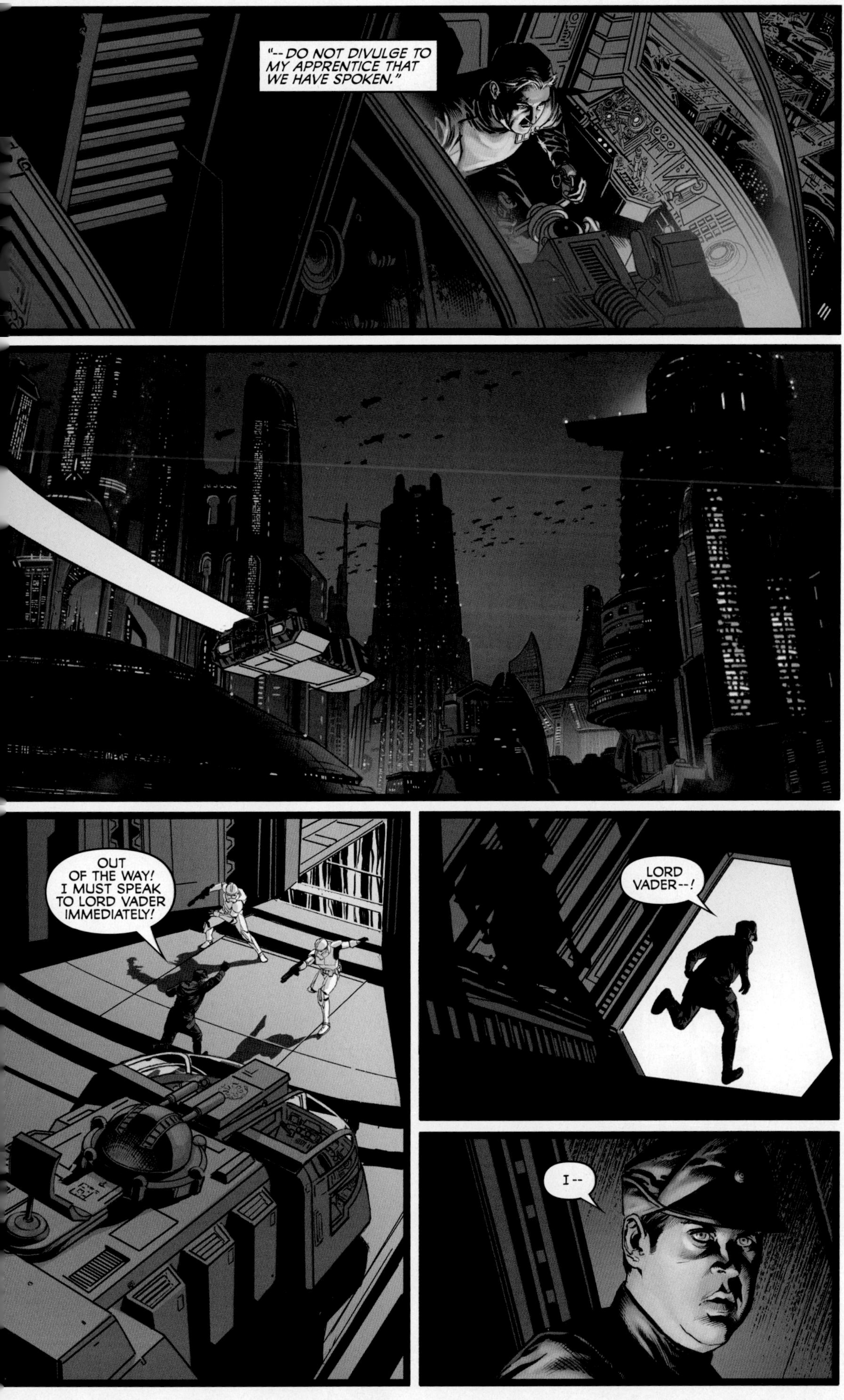
"-- DO NOT DIVULGE TO MY APPRENTICE THAT WE HAVE SPOKEN."
OUT OF THE WAY! I MUST SPEAK TO LORD VADER IMMEDIATELY!
LORD VADER--!
I --

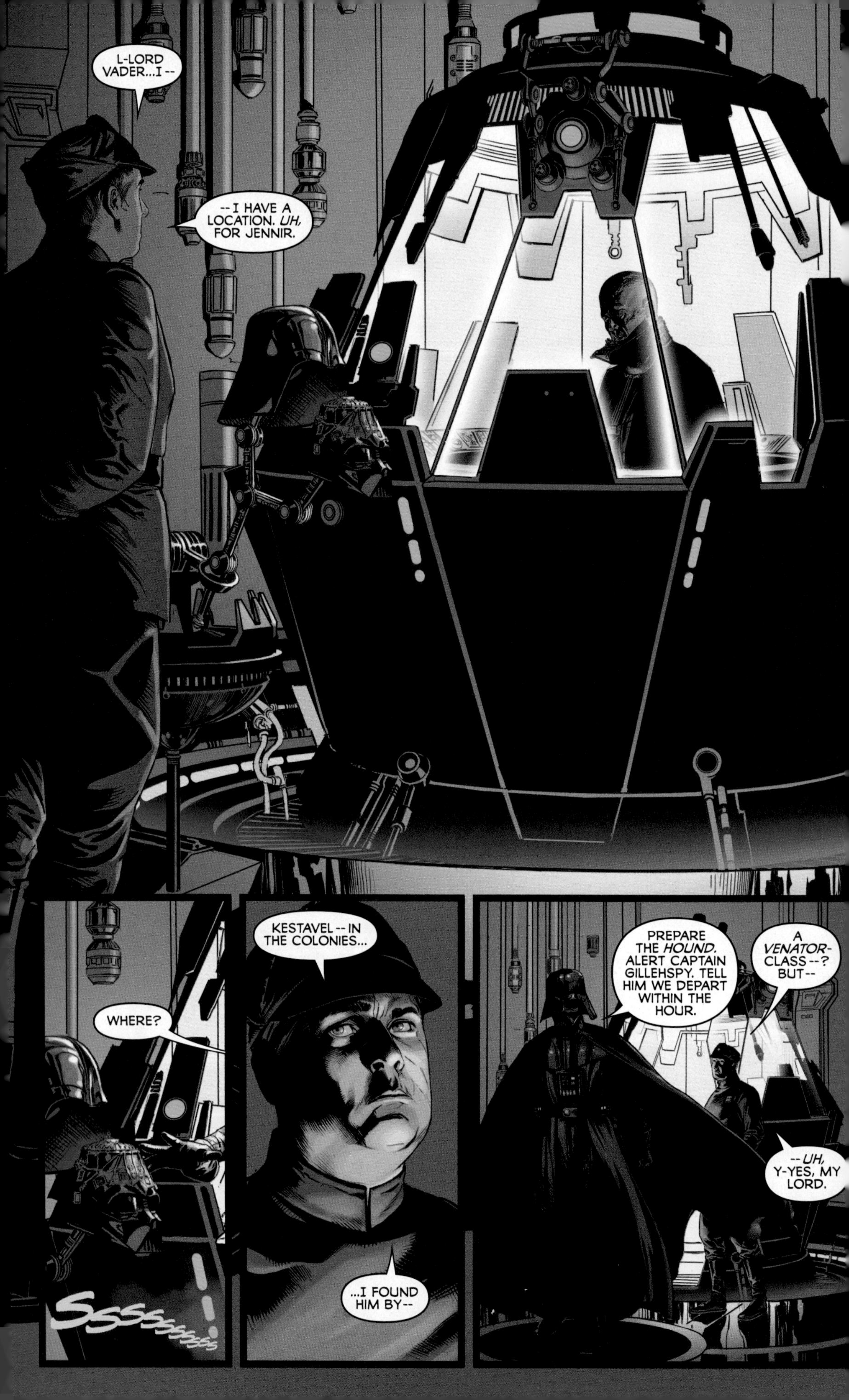
L-LORD VADER...I --
-- I HAVE A LOCATION. *UH,* FOR JENNIR.
WHERE?
SSSSSSSSSS
KESTAVEL -- IN THE COLONIES...
...I FOUND HIM BY--
PREPARE THE *HOUND.* ALERT CAPTAIN GILLEHSPY. TELL HIM WE DEPART WITHIN THE HOUR.
A *VENATOR*-CLASS --? BUT--
-- *UH,* Y-YES, MY LORD.

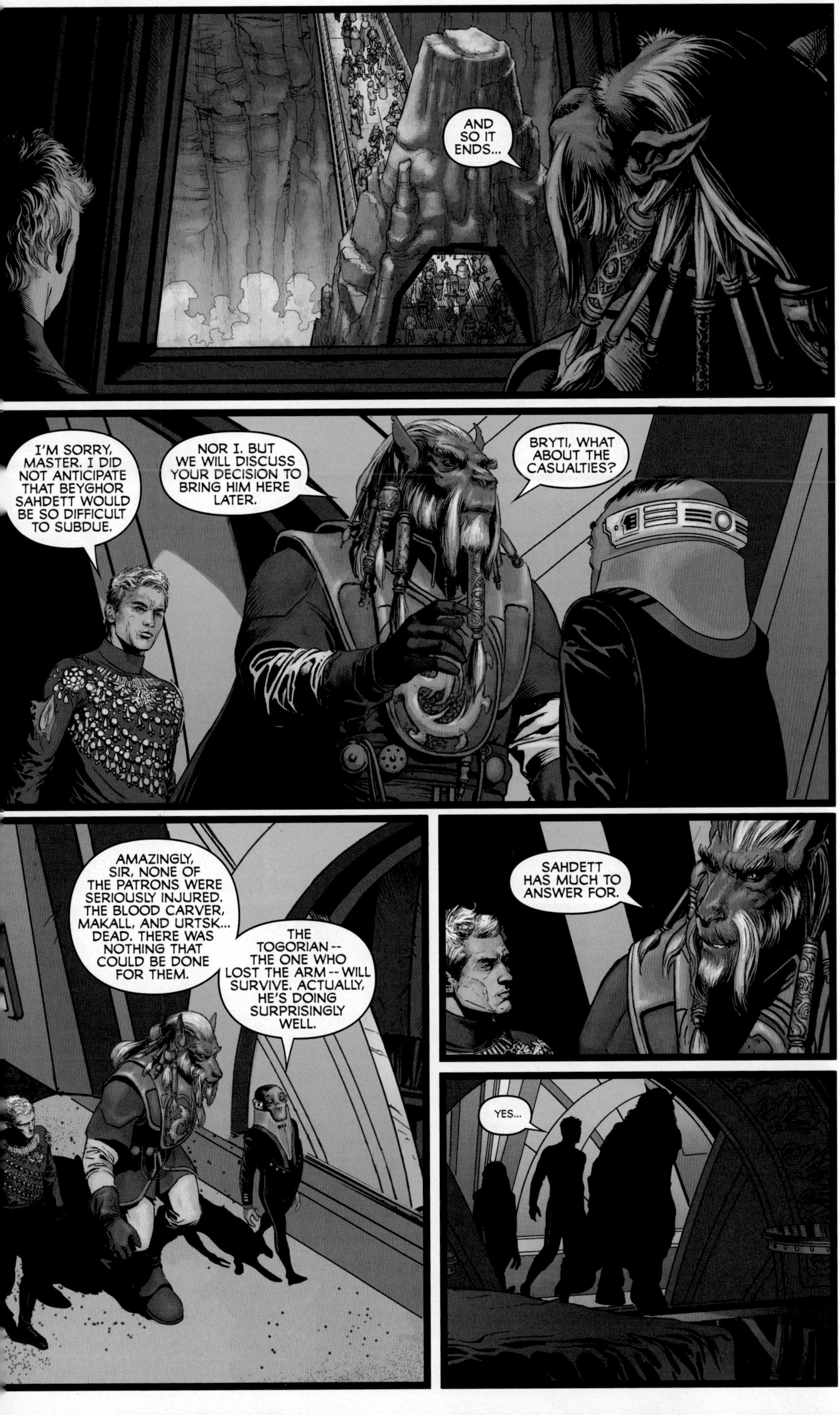
AND SO IT ENDS...
I'M SORRY, MASTER. I DID NOT ANTICIPATE THAT BEYGHOR SAHDETT WOULD BE SO DIFFICULT TO SUBDUE.
NOR I. BUT WE WILL DISCUSS YOUR DECISION TO BRING HIM HERE LATER.
BRYTI, WHAT ABOUT THE CASUALTIES?
AMAZINGLY, SIR, NONE OF THE PATRONS WERE SERIOUSLY INJURED. THE BLOOD CARVER, MAKALL, AND URTSK... DEAD. THERE WAS NOTHING THAT COULD BE DONE FOR THEM.
THE TOGORIAN -- THE ONE WHO LOST THE ARM -- WILL SURVIVE. ACTUALLY, HE'S DOING SURPRISINGLY WELL.
SAHDETT HAS MUCH TO ANSWER FOR.
YES...

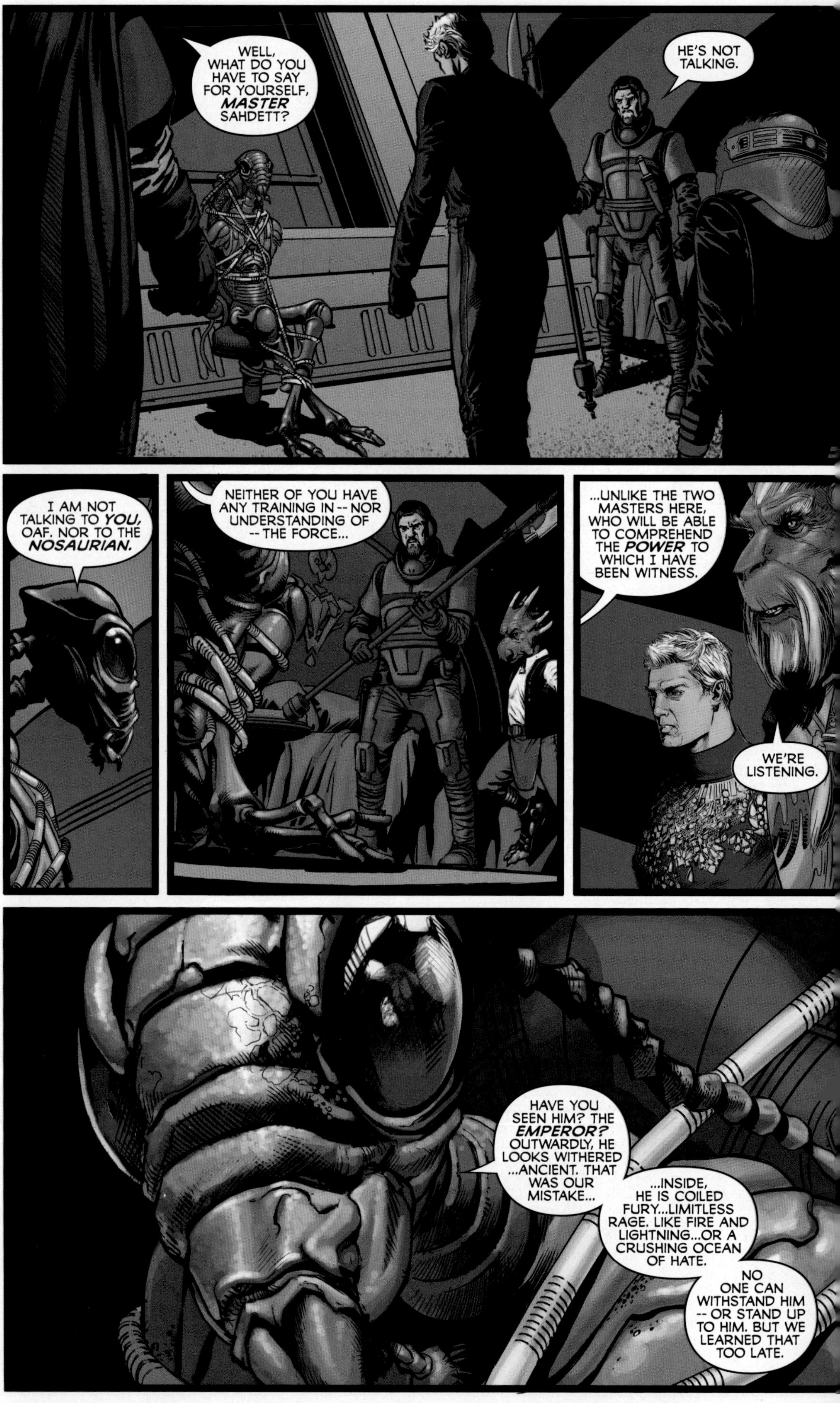
WELL, WHAT DO YOU HAVE TO SAY FOR YOURSELF, *MASTER* SAHDETT?
HE'S NOT TALKING.
I AM NOT TALKING TO *YOU,* OAF. NOR TO THE *NOSAURIAN.*
NEITHER OF YOU HAVE ANY TRAINING IN -- NOR UNDERSTANDING OF -- THE FORCE...
...UNLIKE THE TWO MASTERS HERE, WHO WILL BE ABLE TO COMPREHEND THE *POWER* TO WHICH I HAVE BEEN WITNESS.
WE'RE LISTENING.
HAVE YOU SEEN HIM? THE *EMPEROR?* OUTWARDLY, HE LOOKS WITHERED ...ANCIENT. THAT WAS OUR MISTAKE...
...INSIDE, HE IS COILED FURY...LIMITLESS RAGE. LIKE FIRE AND LIGHTNING...OR A CRUSHING OCEAN OF HATE.
NO ONE CAN WITHSTAND HIM -- OR STAND UP TO HIM. BUT WE LEARNED THAT TOO LATE.

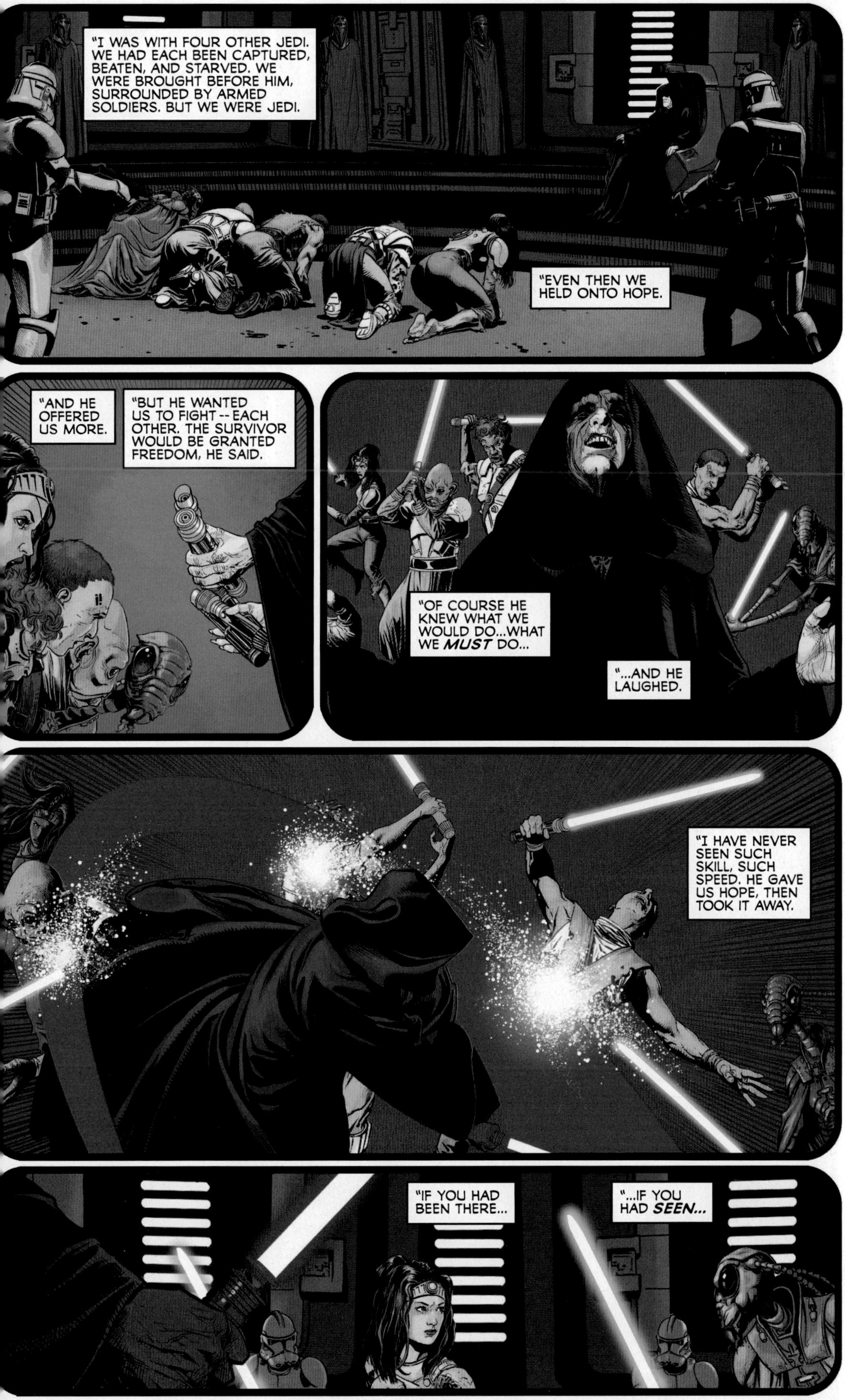
"I WAS WITH FOUR OTHER JEDI. WE HAD EACH BEEN CAPTURED, BEATEN, AND STARVED. WE WERE BROUGHT BEFORE HIM, SURROUNDED BY ARMED SOLDIERS. BUT WE WERE JEDI.
"EVEN THEN WE HELD ONTO HOPE.
"AND HE OFFERED US MORE.
"BUT HE WANTED US TO FIGHT -- EACH OTHER. THE SURVIVOR WOULD BE GRANTED FREEDOM, HE SAID.
"OF COURSE HE KNEW WHAT WE WOULD DO...WHAT WE *MUST* DO...
"...AND HE LAUGHED.
"I HAVE NEVER SEEN SUCH SKILL, SUCH SPEED. HE GAVE US HOPE, THEN TOOK IT AWAY.
"IF YOU HAD BEEN THERE...
"...IF YOU HAD *SEEN...*

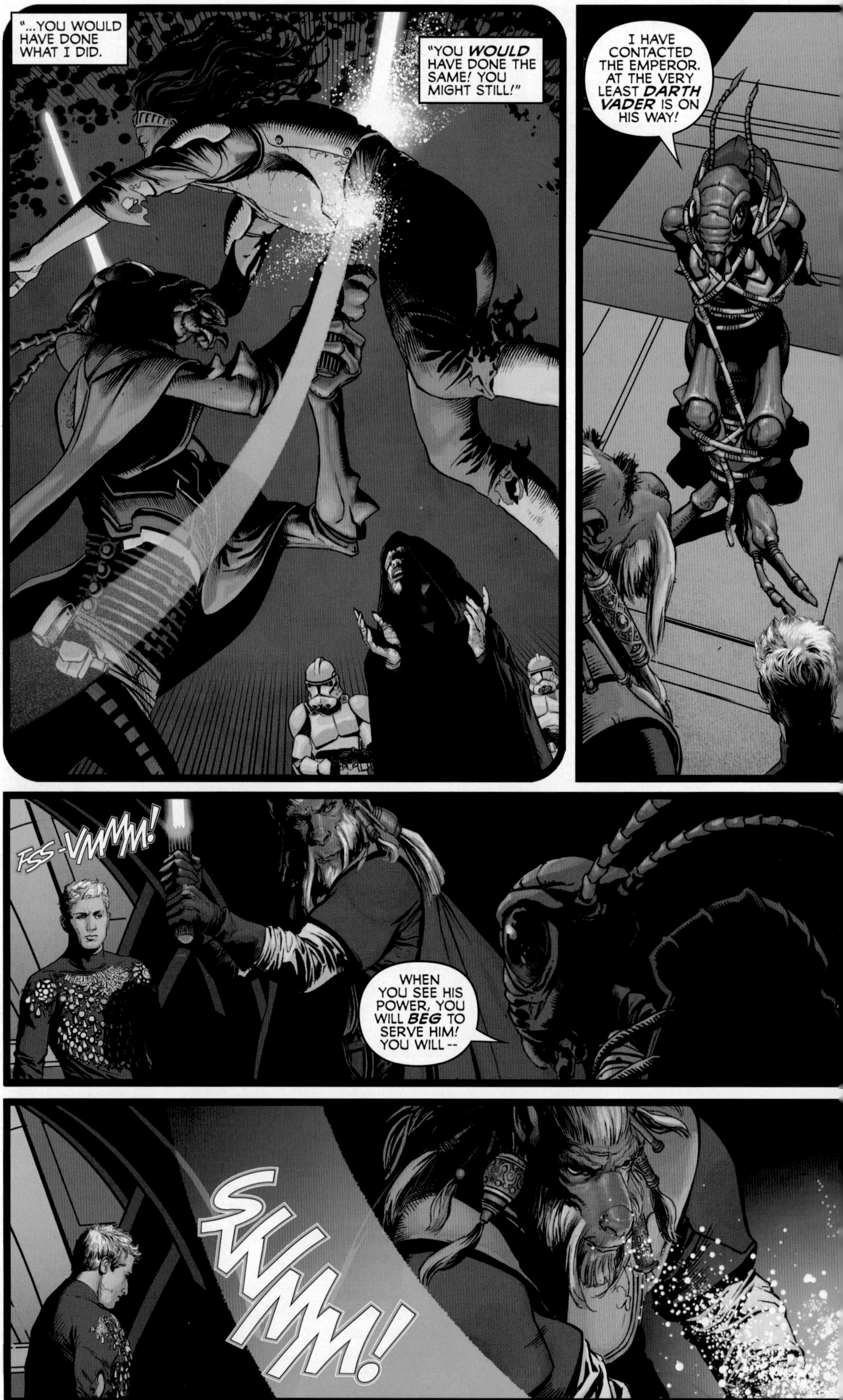
"...YOU WOULD HAVE DONE WHAT I DID.
"YOU WOULD HAVE DONE THE SAME! YOU MIGHT STILL!"
I HAVE CONTACTED THE EMPEROR. AT THE VERY LEAST DARTH VADER IS ON HIS WAY!
FSS-VMMM!
WHEN YOU SEE HIS POWER, YOU WILL BEG TO SERVE HIM! YOU WILL --
SKWMM!

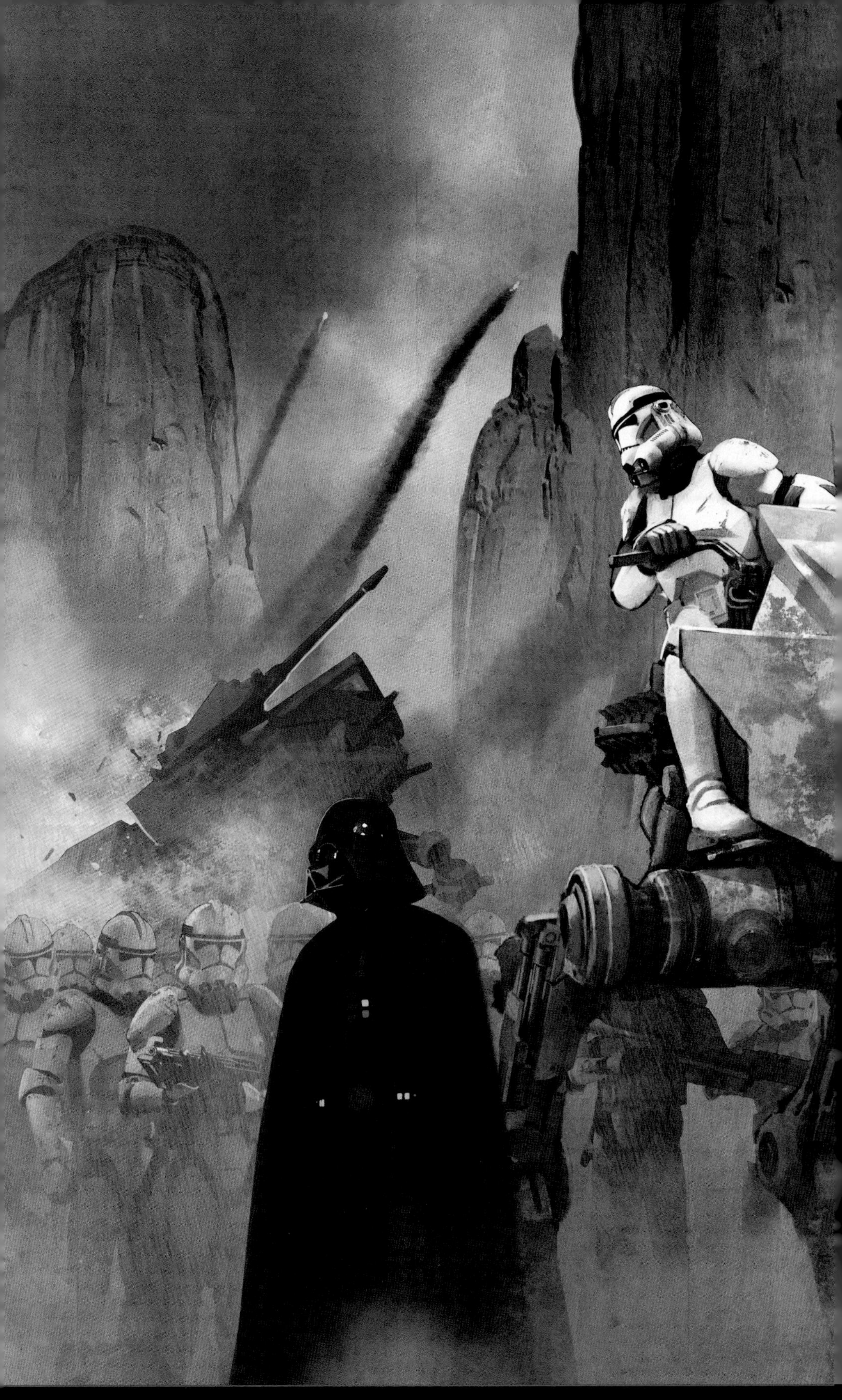

***STAR WARS: DARK TIMES — A SPARK REMAINS #4***

WRITER: RANDY STRADLEY • ARTIST: DOUGLAS WHEATLEY • COLORIST: DAN JACKSON • LETTERER: MICHAEL HEISLER

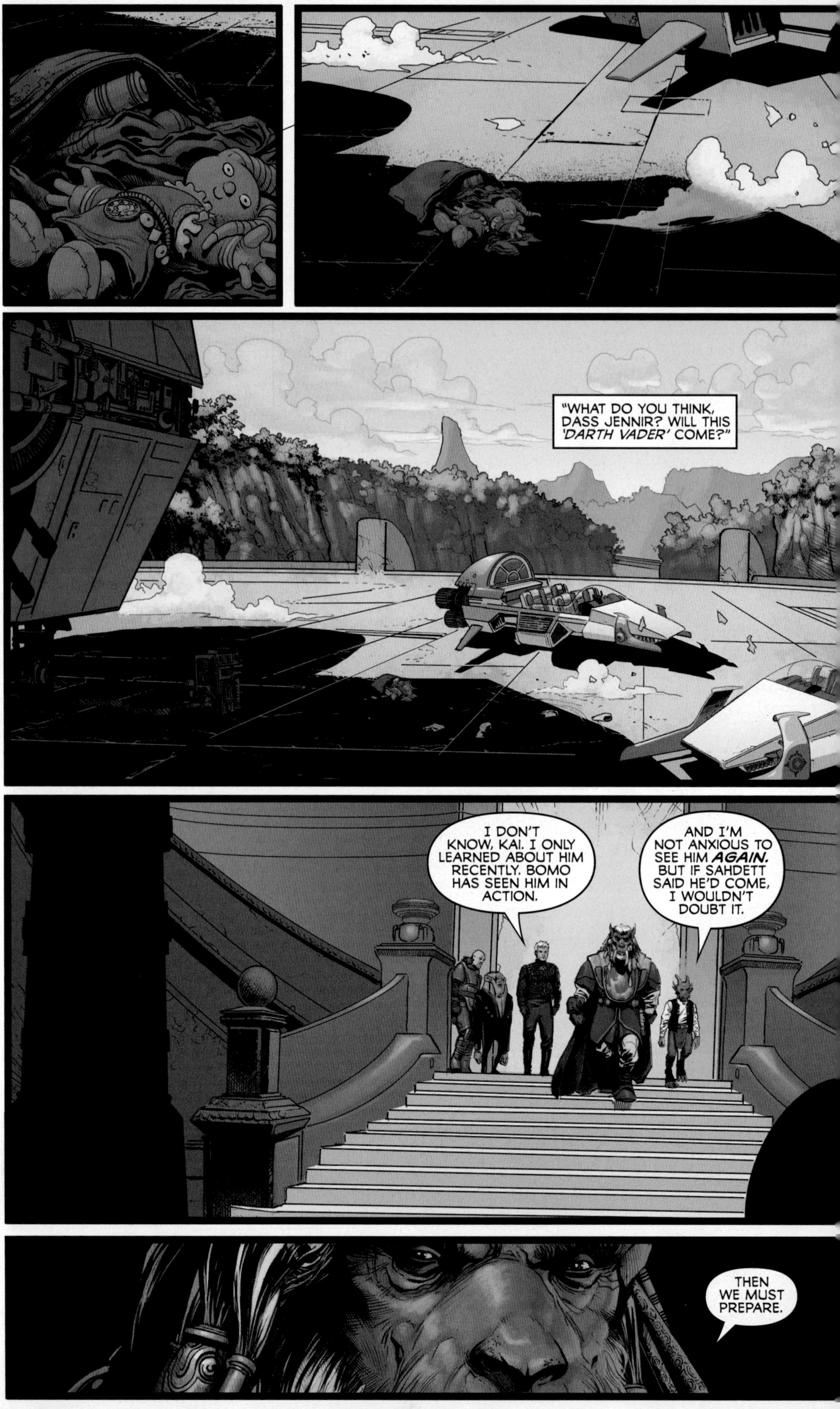
"WHAT DO YOU THINK, DASS JENNIR? WILL THIS *'DARTH VADER'* COME?"
I DON'T KNOW, KAI. I ONLY LEARNED ABOUT HIM RECENTLY. BOMO HAS SEEN HIM IN ACTION.
AND I'M NOT ANXIOUS TO SEE HIM ***AGAIN.*** BUT IF SAHDETT SAID HE'D COME, I WOULDN'T DOUBT IT.
THEN WE MUST PREPARE.

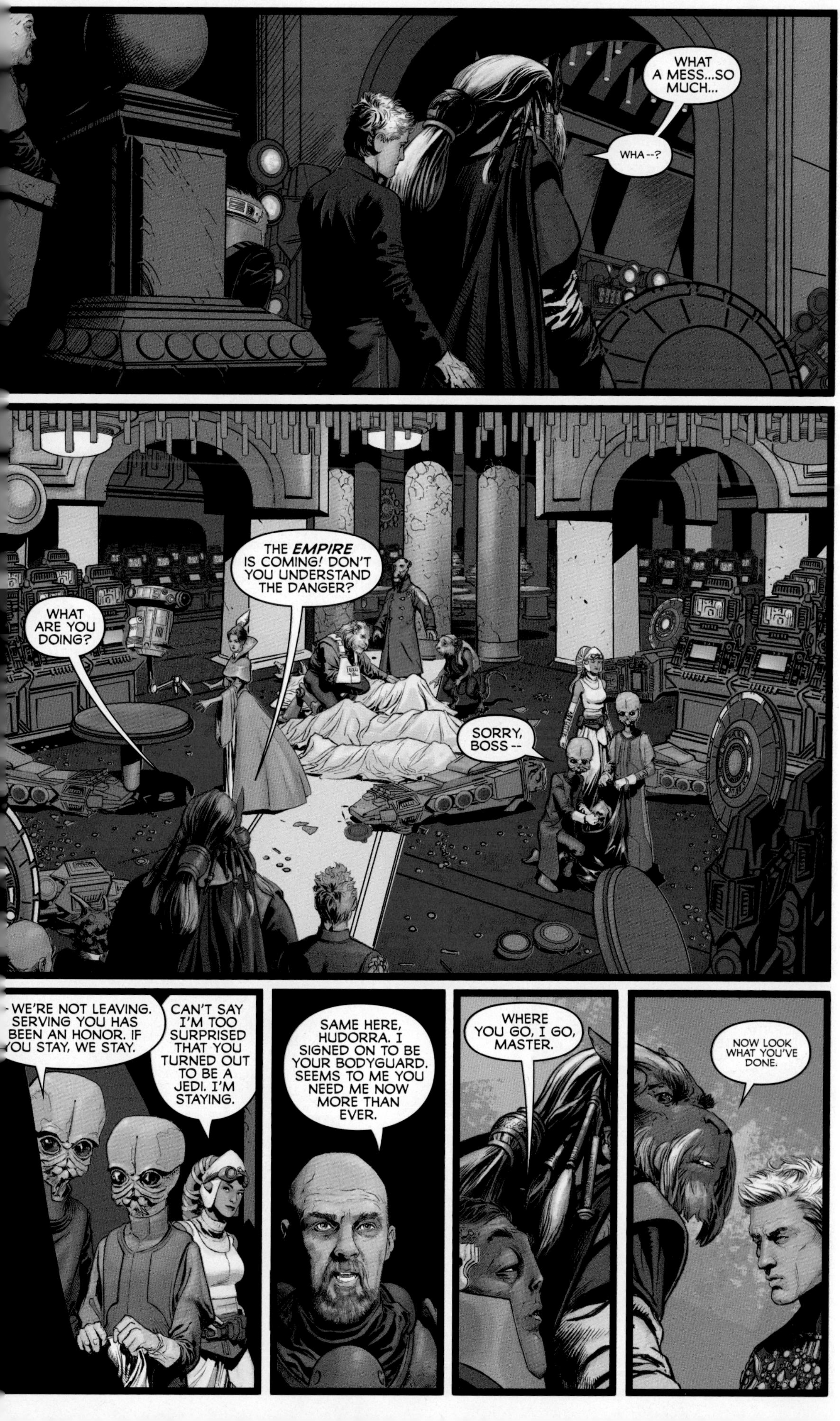
WHAT A MESS...SO MUCH...
WHA --?
THE EMPIRE IS COMING! DON'T YOU UNDERSTAND THE DANGER?
WHAT ARE YOU DOING?
SORRY, BOSS --
- WE'RE NOT LEAVING. SERVING YOU HAS BEEN AN HONOR. IF YOU STAY, WE STAY.
CAN'T SAY I'M TOO SURPRISED THAT YOU TURNED OUT TO BE A JEDI. I'M STAYING.
SAME HERE, HUDORRA. I SIGNED ON TO BE YOUR BODYGUARD. SEEMS TO ME YOU NEED ME NOW MORE THAN EVER.
WHERE YOU GO, I GO, MASTER.
NOW LOOK WHAT YOU'VE DONE.

THIS IS UNACCEPTABLE!

NO ONE IS *STAYING!* YOU'RE *ALL* GETTING OUT! YOU'RE ALL LEAVING -- *NOW!*

YOU CAN'T BE HERE WHEN THE EMPIRE ARRIVES! THERE WILL BE NO SURVIVORS FROM THAT FIGHT!

*WE* ALREADY *KNOW* THAT!

WE DIDN'T KNOW SAHDETT WAS A *TRAITOR* -- AND WE DIDN'T PLAN TO MAKE A STAND *HERE* --

-- BUT THE "*NO SURVIVORS*" THING CUTS BOTH WAYS.

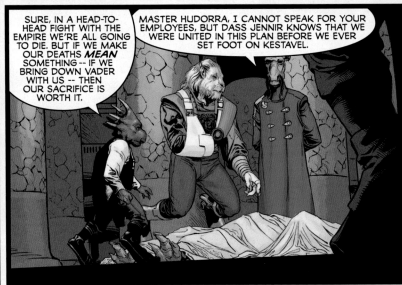

SURE, IN A HEAD-TO-HEAD FIGHT WITH THE EMPIRE WE'RE ALL GOING TO DIE. BUT IF WE MAKE OUR DEATHS *MEAN* SOMETHING -- IF WE BRING DOWN VADER WITH US -- THEN OUR SACRIFICE IS WORTH IT.

MASTER HUDORRA, I CANNOT SPEAK FOR YOUR EMPLOYEES, BUT DASS JENNIR KNOWS THAT WE WERE UNITED IN THIS PLAN BEFORE WE EVER SET FOOT ON KESTAVEL.

MY FRIEND KO VAKIER IS DEAD. I COULD NOT ASK *HIM* TO PAY A HIGHER PRICE THAN WHAT *I* AM WILLING TO PAY. IF VADER COMES, WE WILL FACE HIM.

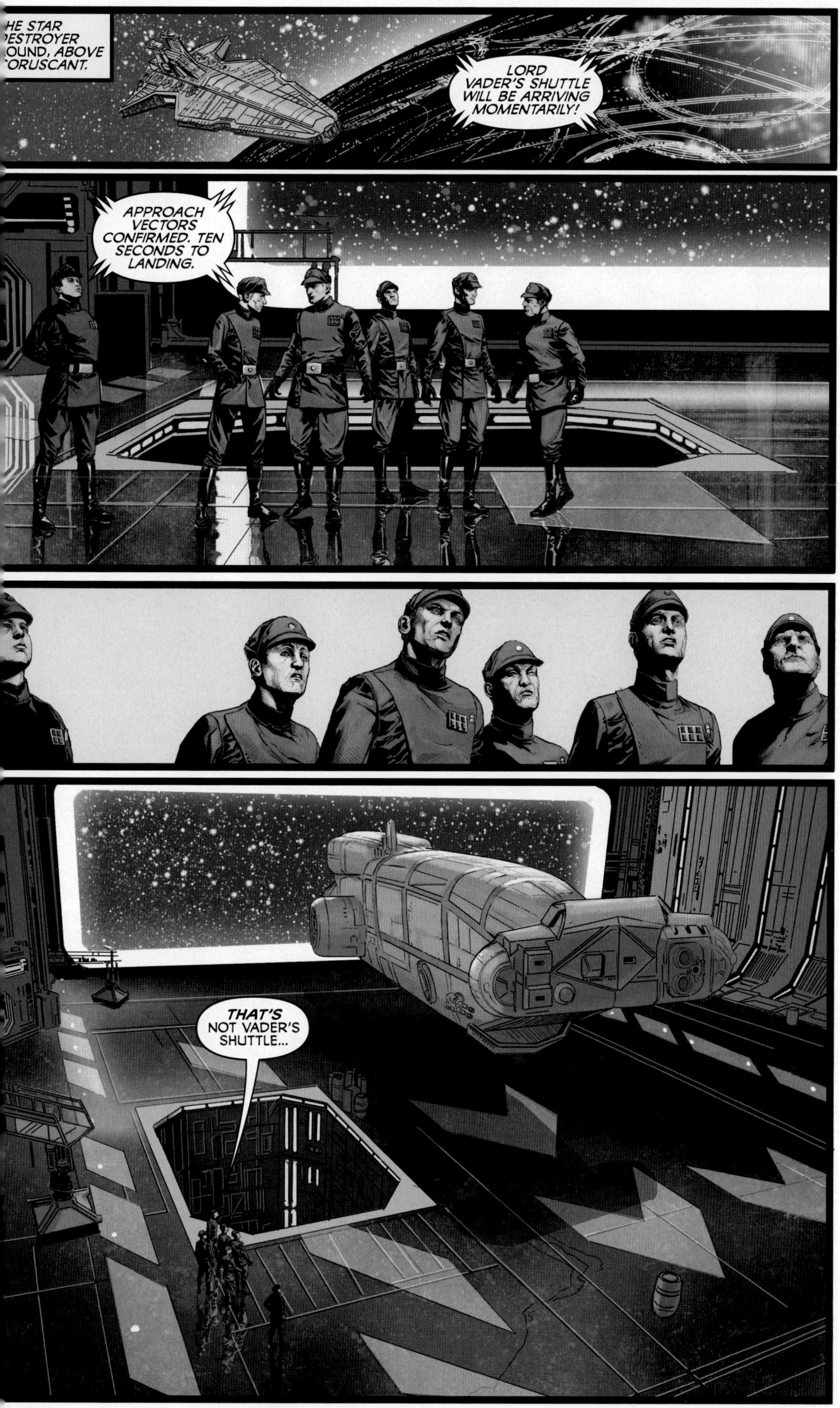
HE STAR
DESTROYER
OUND, ABOVE
ORUSCANT.
LORD VADER'S SHUTTLE WILL BE ARRIVING MOMENTARILY!
APPROACH VECTORS CONFIRMED. TEN SECONDS TO LANDING.
THAT'S NOT VADER'S SHUTTLE...

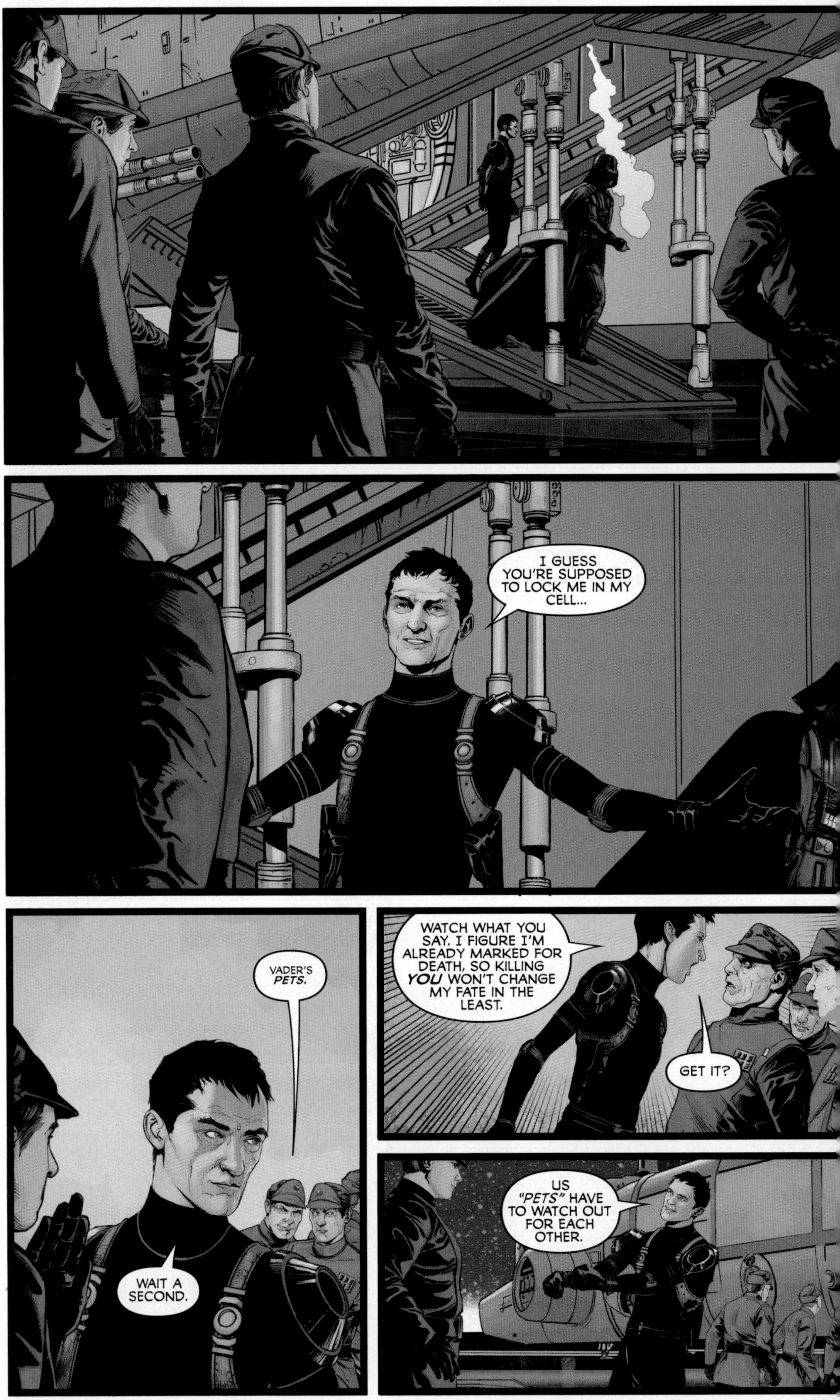
I GUESS YOU'RE SUPPOSED TO LOCK ME IN MY CELL...
VADER'S *PETS.*
WAIT A SECOND.
WATCH WHAT YOU SAY. I FIGURE I'M ALREADY MARKED FOR DEATH, SO KILLING *YOU* WON'T CHANGE MY FATE IN THE LEAST.
GET IT?
US *"PETS"* HAVE TO WATCH OUT FOR EACH OTHER.

WHERE -- *WHEN* -- DID YOU GET ALL OF THIS, HEREN? I DON'T BELIEVE IT!

I PICKED THINGS UP HERE AND THERE, BOMO. AFTER THE WAY YOU SAVED ALL OF US ON MIMBAN --

-- IT OCCURRED TO ME THAT HAVING A CACHE OF EXPLOSIVES ON HAND MIGHT BE USEFUL.

I'LL MAKE SURE OF IT.

THE ARCHWAY TUNNEL JUST BEFORE YOU REACH THE CASINO IS AN OBVIOUS CHOKE-POINT.

AS ARE THE TWO BRIDGES NEAR THE SPACEPORT. BUT I WOULD SUGGEST WE LEAVE THE FIRST BRIDGE ALONE -- LET THEM REACH THE SECOND BRIDGE BEFORE WE STRIKE...

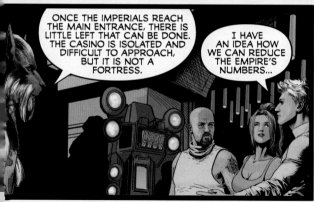

ONCE THE IMPERIALS REACH THE MAIN ENTRANCE, THERE IS LITTLE LEFT THAT CAN BE DONE. THE CASINO IS ISOLATED AND DIFFICULT TO APPROACH, BUT IT IS NOT A FORTRESS.

I HAVE AN IDEA HOW WE CAN REDUCE THE EMPIRE'S NUMBERS...

KAL, COME WITH ME.

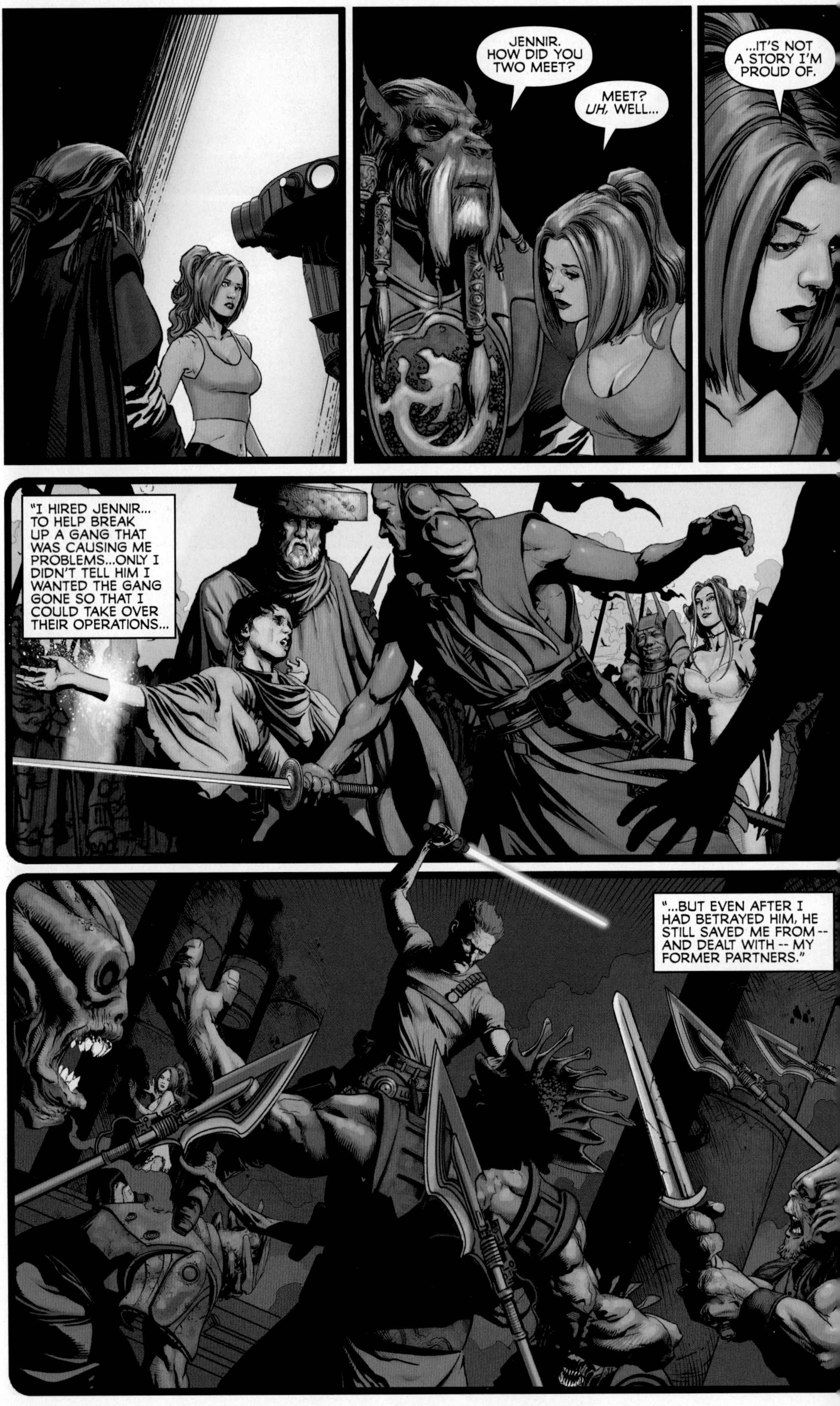
JENNIR. HOW DID YOU TWO MEET?
MEET? UH, WELL...
...IT'S NOT A STORY I'M PROUD OF.
"I HIRED JENNIR... TO HELP BREAK UP A GANG THAT WAS CAUSING ME PROBLEMS...ONLY I DIDN'T TELL HIM I WANTED THE GANG GONE SO THAT I COULD TAKE OVER THEIR OPERATIONS...
"...BUT EVEN AFTER I HAD BETRAYED HIM, HE STILL SAVED ME FROM -- AND DEALT WITH -- MY FORMER PARTNERS."

AND AFTER ALL OF THAT, I LIED TO HIM AGAIN. THAT TIME, MY LIE LED TO US CRASHING ON A DESERT MOON...

"...AND ME BEING CAPTURED BY A BAND OF PIRATES. JENNIR COULD HAVE GONE HIS OWN WAY AND BEEN SAFE -- BUT HE CAME TO MY RESCUE ...*TWICE.* FIRST HE FOUGHT THE PIRATES..."

"...THEN AN ASSASSIN WHO HAD BEEN HIRED TO KILL HIM."

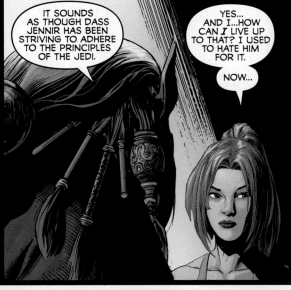

IT SOUNDS AS THOUGH DASS JENNIR HAS BEEN STRIVING TO ADHERE TO THE PRINCIPLES OF THE JEDI.

YES... AND I...HOW CAN *I* LIVE UP TO THAT? I USED TO HATE HIM FOR IT.

NOW...

YOU CARE FOR HIM. AND JENNIR -- DOES HE SHARE YOUR FEELINGS?

HE SAYS HE *DOES*... BUT...

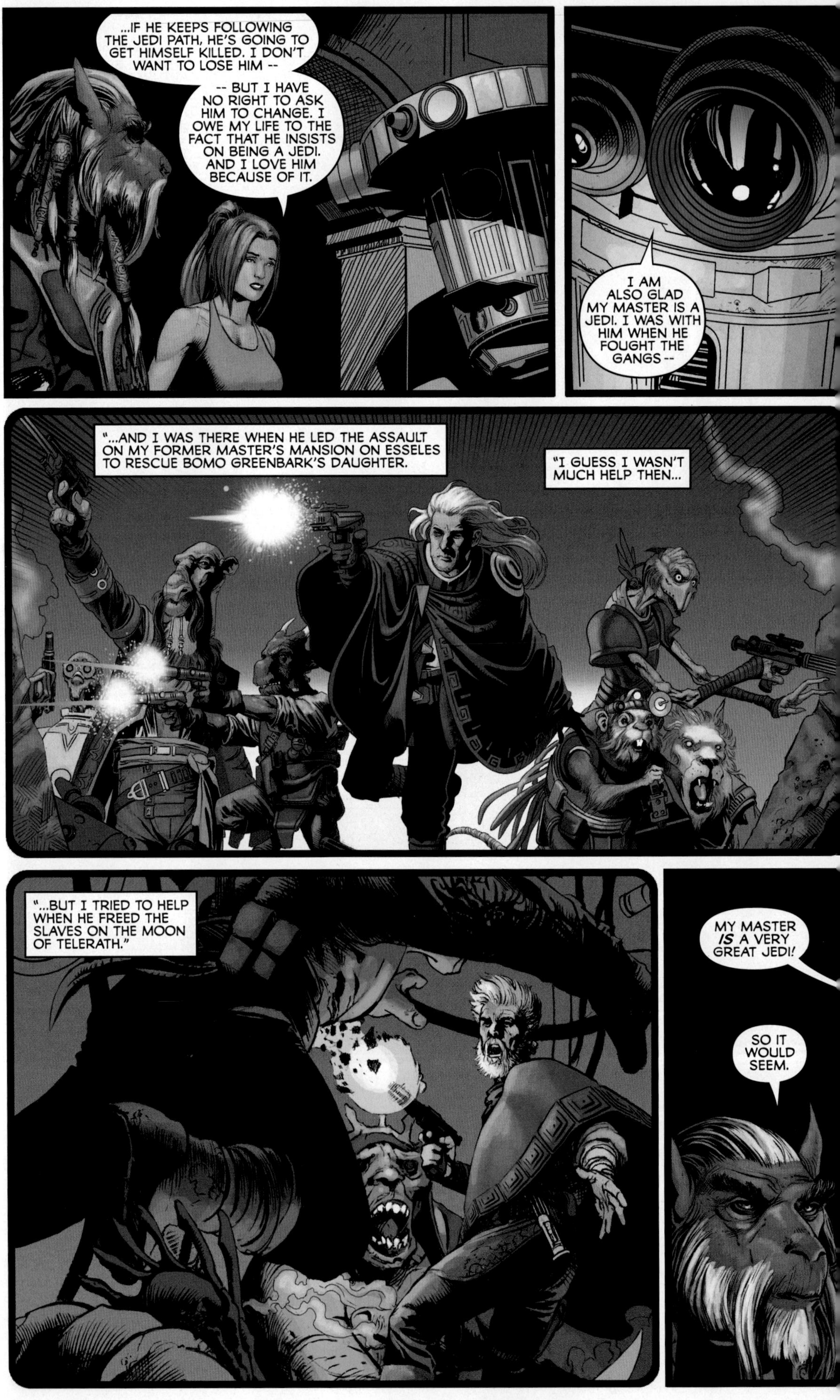
...IF HE KEEPS FOLLOWING THE JEDI PATH, HE'S GOING TO GET HIMSELF KILLED. I DON'T WANT TO LOSE HIM --
-- BUT I HAVE NO RIGHT TO ASK HIM TO CHANGE. I OWE MY LIFE TO THE FACT THAT HE INSISTS ON BEING A JEDI. AND I LOVE HIM BECAUSE OF IT.
I AM ALSO GLAD MY MASTER IS A JEDI. I WAS WITH HIM WHEN HE FOUGHT THE GANGS --
"...AND I WAS THERE WHEN HE LED THE ASSAULT ON MY FORMER MASTER'S MANSION ON ESSELES TO RESCUE BOMO GREENBARK'S DAUGHTER.
"I GUESS I WASN'T MUCH HELP THEN...
"...BUT I TRIED TO HELP WHEN HE FREED THE SLAVES ON THE MOON OF TELERATH."
MY MASTER *IS* A VERY GREAT JEDI!
SO IT WOULD SEEM.

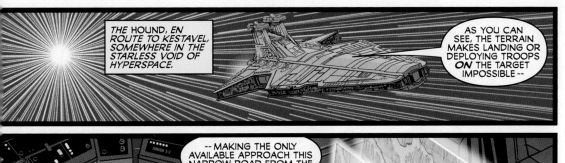

*THE HOUND, EN ROUTE TO KESTAVEL, SOMEWHERE IN THE STARLESS VOID OF HYPERSPACE.*

AS YOU CAN SEE, THE TERRAIN MAKES LANDING OR DEPLOYING TROOPS *ON* THE TARGET IMPOSSIBLE --

-- MAKING THE ONLY AVAILABLE APPROACH THIS NARROW ROAD FROM THE SPACEPORT.

THE ASSAULT FORCE WILL EMBARK FROM THERE -- TWO COMPANIES OF STORMTROOPERS, SUPPORTED BY AT-TE AND AT-RCT SQUADS --

WHY A GROUND ASSAULT? WHY RISK ALLOWING THE ENEMY TO ESCAPE? WHY NOT SIMPLY BOMBARD THE TARGET FROM ORBIT AND TURN THE SITE TO SLAG?

BECAUSE *I* WANT THE JEDI TO DIE BY *MY* HAND. BECAUSE *I* WANT TO LAY THEIR LIFELESS BODIES AT THE FEET OF THE EMPEROR.

FALCO SANG HAS INSTRUCTIONS ON WHAT TO DO SHOULD THE JEDI ATTEMPT TO FLEE.

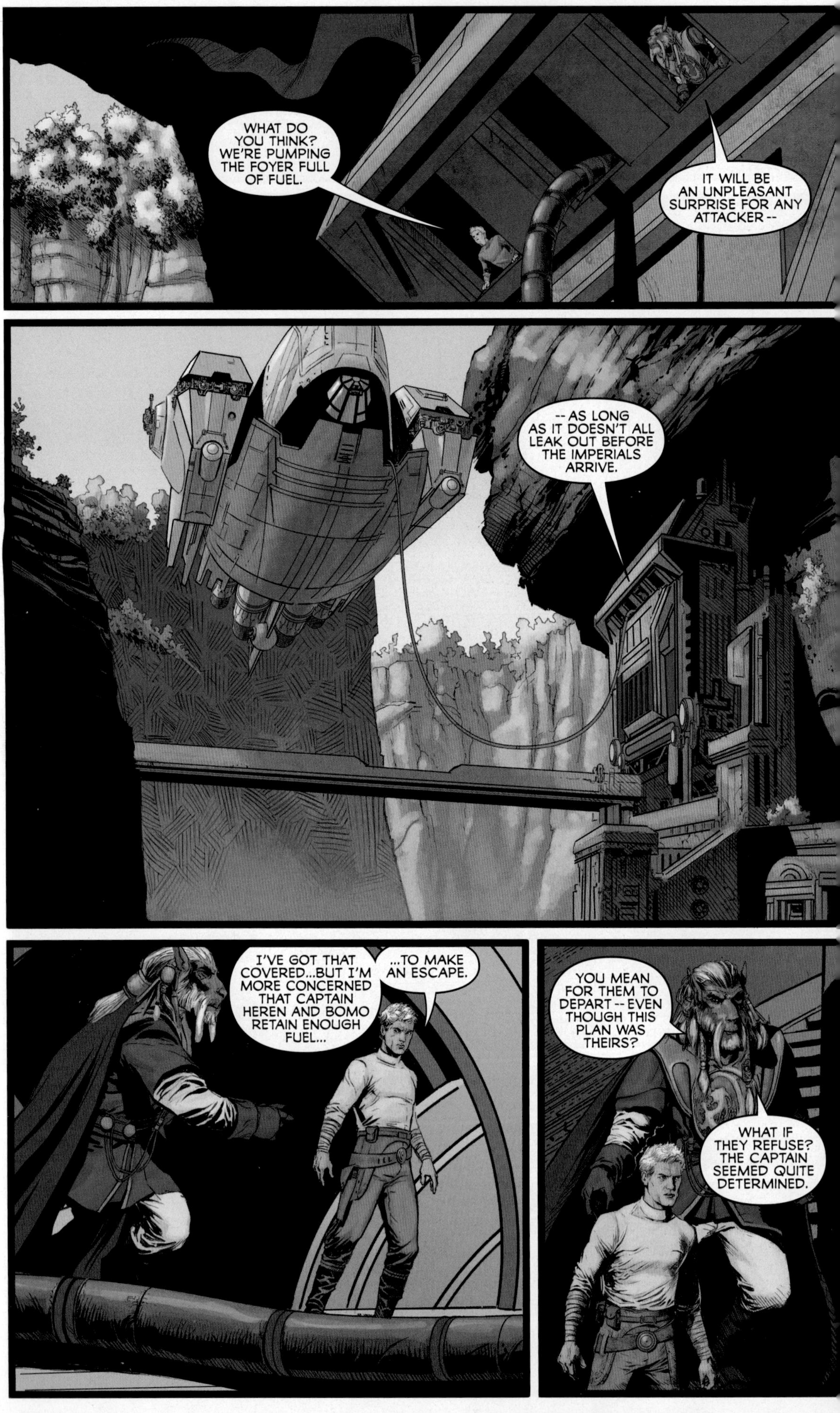
WHAT DO YOU THINK? WE'RE PUMPING THE FOYER FULL OF FUEL.
IT WILL BE AN UNPLEASANT SURPRISE FOR ANY ATTACKER --
-- AS LONG AS IT DOESN'T ALL LEAK OUT BEFORE THE IMPERIALS ARRIVE.
I'VE GOT THAT COVERED...BUT I'M MORE CONCERNED THAT CAPTAIN HEREN AND BOMO RETAIN ENOUGH FUEL...
...TO MAKE AN ESCAPE.
YOU MEAN FOR THEM TO DEPART -- EVEN THOUGH THIS PLAN WAS THEIRS?
WHAT IF THEY REFUSE? THE CAPTAIN SEEMED QUITE DETERMINED.

IF IT COMES TO IT, I'LL USE THE FORCE TO PERSUADE THEM.

I OWE THEM MORE THAN I CAN EVER REPAY. I WILL NOT PLACE MYSELF FURTHER IN THEIR DEBT -- ESPECIALLY OVER SOMETHING THAT IS, I THINK YOU'LL AGREE, A JEDI PROBLEM.

I AGREE THAT THE JEDI BEAR A GREAT RESPONSIBILITY. BUT THE *"PROBLEM"* -- THE EMPIRE -- AFFECTS ALL.

STILL, WHEN THE TIME COMES, MY PEOPLE WILL JOIN YOURS ON THE *UHUMELE.*

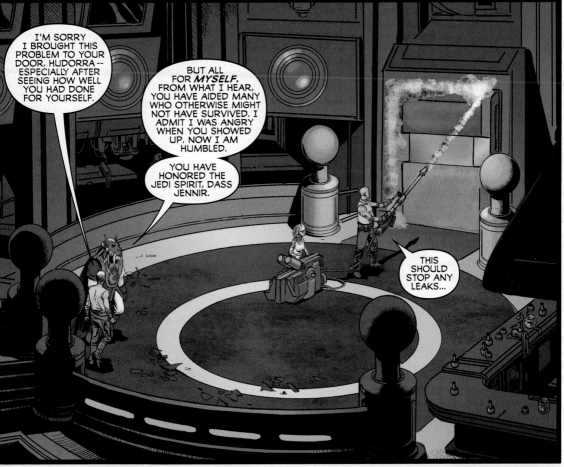

I'M SORRY I BROUGHT THIS PROBLEM TO YOUR DOOR, HUDORRA-- ESPECIALLY AFTER SEEING HOW WELL YOU HAD DONE FOR YOURSELF.

BUT ALL FOR *MYSELF.* FROM WHAT I HEAR, YOU HAVE AIDED MANY WHO OTHERWISE MIGHT NOT HAVE SURVIVED. I ADMIT I WAS ANGRY WHEN YOU SHOWED UP. NOW I AM HUMBLED.

YOU HAVE HONORED THE JEDI SPIRIT, DASS JENNIR.

THIS SHOULD STOP ANY LEAKS...

KAL, SHAYLAI -- YOU'VE DONE ENOUGH. GET CLEANED UP AND JOIN US IN THE DINING HALL. PASS THE WORD TO CAPTAIN HEREN AND BOMO GREENBARK.

I BELIEVE OUR CHEFS HAVE PREPARED A FEAST.

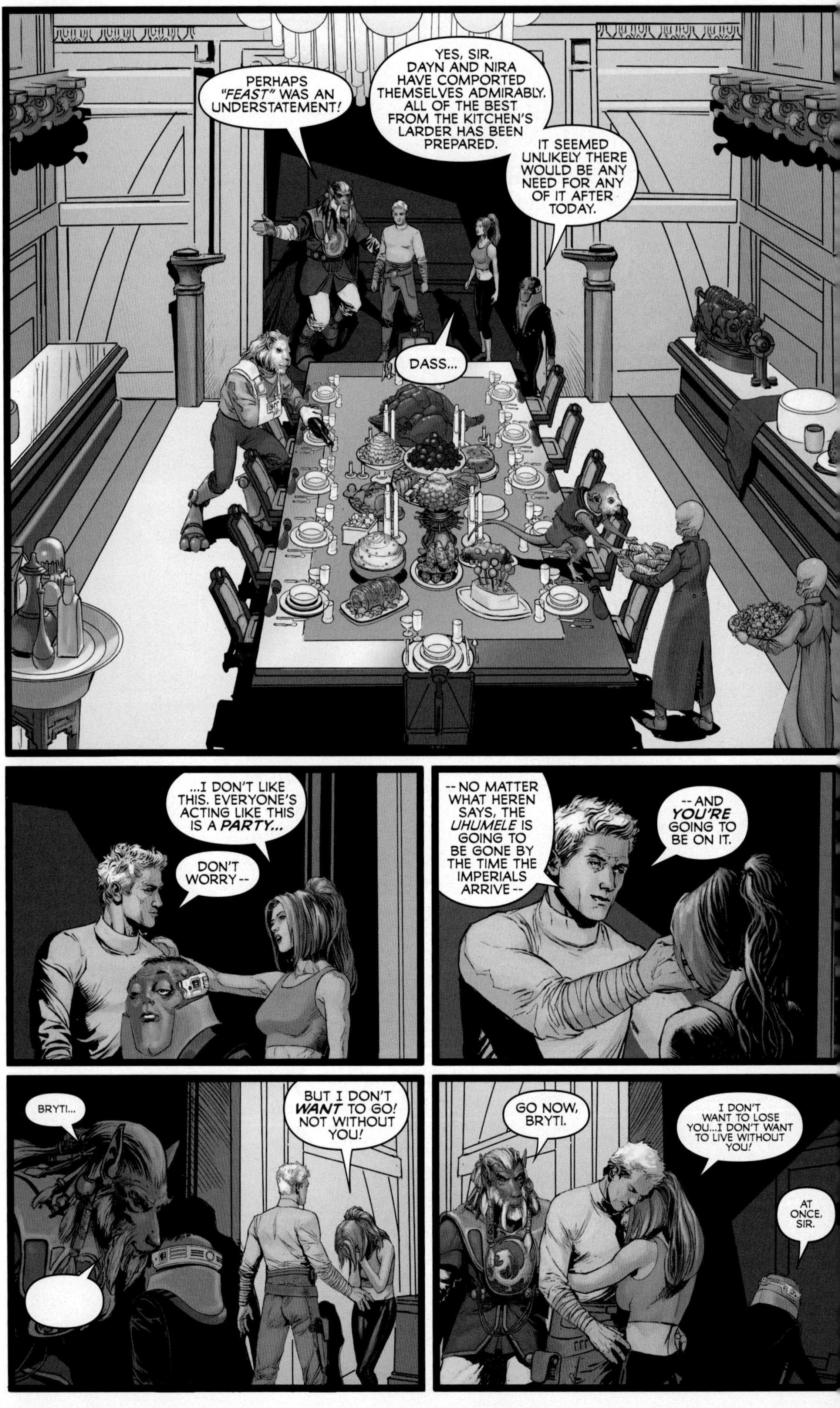
PERHAPS "FEAST" WAS AN UNDERSTATEMENT!
YES, SIR. DAYN AND NIRA HAVE COMPORTED THEMSELVES ADMIRABLY. ALL OF THE BEST FROM THE KITCHEN'S LARDER HAS BEEN PREPARED.
IT SEEMED UNLIKELY THERE WOULD BE ANY NEED FOR ANY OF IT AFTER TODAY.
DASS...
...I DON'T LIKE THIS. EVERYONE'S ACTING LIKE THIS IS A *PARTY*...
DON'T WORRY --
-- NO MATTER WHAT HEREN SAYS, THE *UHUMELE* IS GOING TO BE GONE BY THE TIME THE IMPERIALS ARRIVE --
-- AND ***YOU'RE*** GOING TO BE ON IT.
BRYTI...
BUT I DON'T ***WANT*** TO GO! NOT WITHOUT YOU!
GO NOW, BRYTI.
I DON'T WANT TO LOSE YOU...I DON'T WANT TO LIVE WITHOUT YOU!
AT ONCE, SIR.

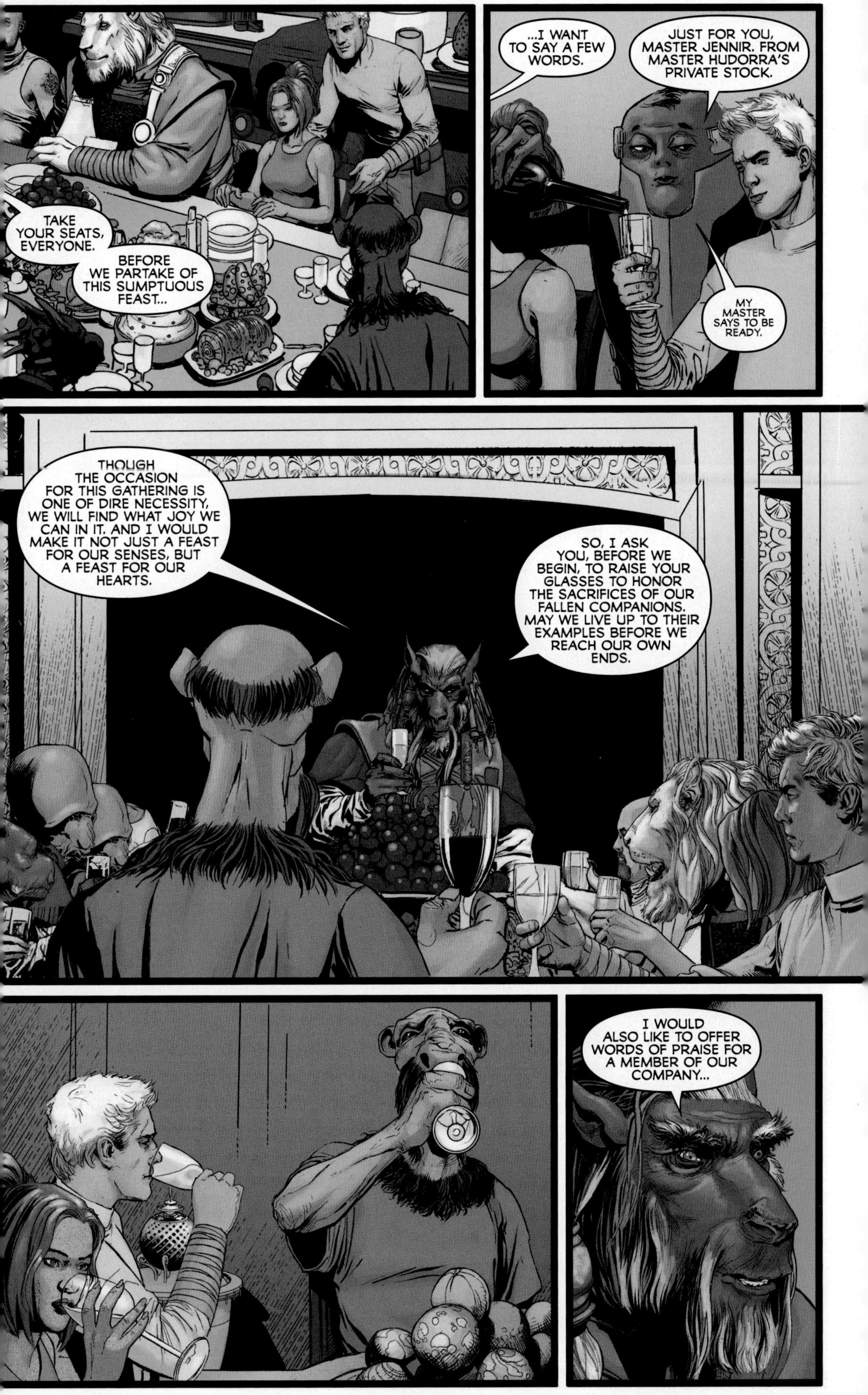
TAKE YOUR SEATS, EVERYONE.
BEFORE WE PARTAKE OF THIS SUMPTUOUS FEAST...
...I WANT TO SAY A FEW WORDS.
JUST FOR YOU, MASTER JENNIR. FROM MASTER HUDORRA'S PRIVATE STOCK.
MY MASTER SAYS TO BE READY.
THOUGH THE OCCASION FOR THIS GATHERING IS ONE OF DIRE NECESSITY, WE WILL FIND WHAT JOY WE CAN IN IT. AND I WOULD MAKE IT NOT JUST A FEAST FOR OUR SENSES, BUT A FEAST FOR OUR HEARTS.
SO, I ASK YOU, BEFORE WE BEGIN, TO RAISE YOUR GLASSES TO HONOR THE SACRIFICES OF OUR FALLEN COMPANIONS. MAY WE LIVE UP TO THEIR EXAMPLES BEFORE WE REACH OUR OWN ENDS.
I WOULD ALSO LIKE TO OFFER WORDS OF PRAISE FOR A MEMBER OF OUR COMPANY...

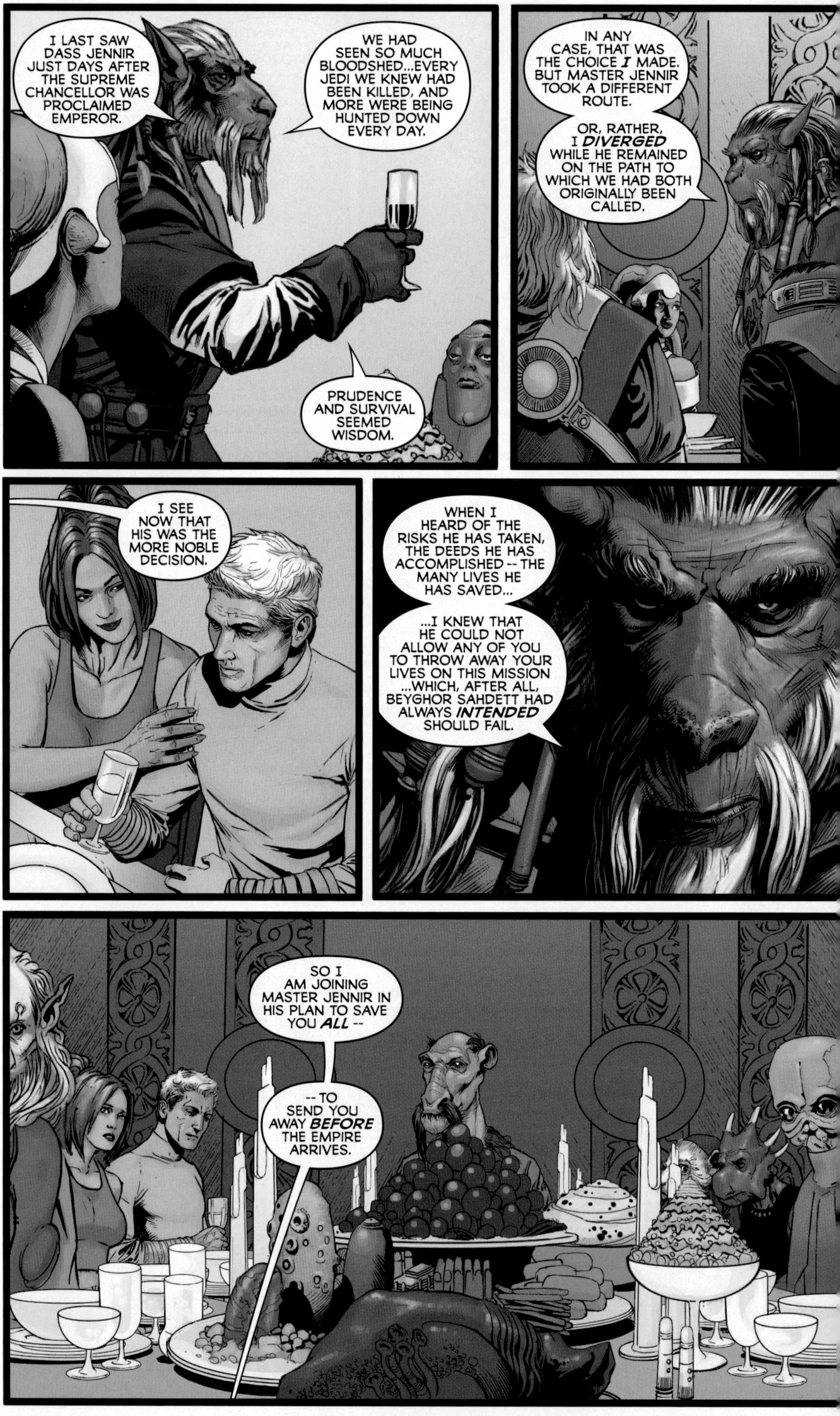
I LAST SAW DASS JENNIR JUST DAYS AFTER THE SUPREME CHANCELLOR WAS PROCLAIMED EMPEROR.
WE HAD SEEN SO MUCH BLOODSHED...EVERY JEDI WE KNEW HAD BEEN KILLED, AND MORE WERE BEING HUNTED DOWN EVERY DAY.
PRUDENCE AND SURVIVAL SEEMED WISDOM.
IN ANY CASE, THAT WAS THE CHOICE *I* MADE. BUT MASTER JENNIR TOOK A DIFFERENT ROUTE.
OR, RATHER, I *DIVERGED* WHILE HE REMAINED ON THE PATH TO WHICH WE HAD BOTH ORIGINALLY BEEN CALLED.
I SEE NOW THAT HIS WAS THE MORE NOBLE DECISION.
WHEN I HEARD OF THE RISKS HE HAS TAKEN, THE DEEDS HE HAS ACCOMPLISHED -- THE MANY LIVES HE HAS SAVED...
...I KNEW THAT HE COULD NOT ALLOW ANY OF YOU TO THROW AWAY YOUR LIVES ON THIS MISSION ...WHICH, AFTER ALL, BEYGHOR SAHDETT HAD ALWAYS *INTENDED* SHOULD FAIL.
SO I AM JOINING MASTER JENNIR IN HIS PLAN TO SAVE YOU *ALL* --
-- TO SEND YOU AWAY *BEFORE* THE EMPIRE ARRIVES.

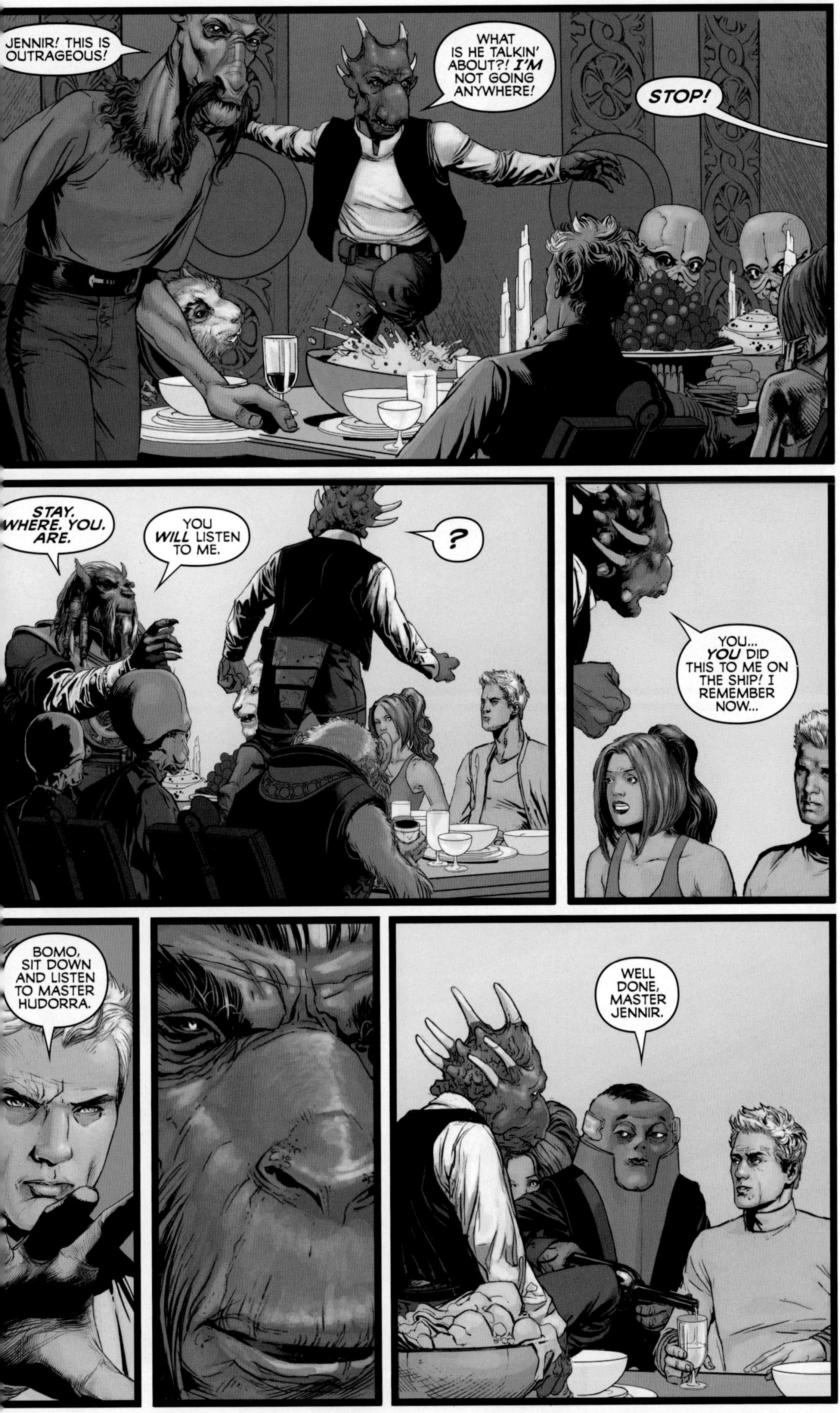
JENNIR! THIS IS OUTRAGEOUS!
WHAT IS HE TALKIN' ABOUT?! I'M NOT GOING ANYWHERE!
STOP!
STAY. WHERE. YOU. ARE.
YOU WILL LISTEN TO ME.
?
YOU... YOU DID THIS TO ME ON THE SHIP! I REMEMBER NOW...
BOMO, SIT DOWN AND LISTEN TO MASTER HUDORRA.
WELL DONE, MASTER JENNIR.

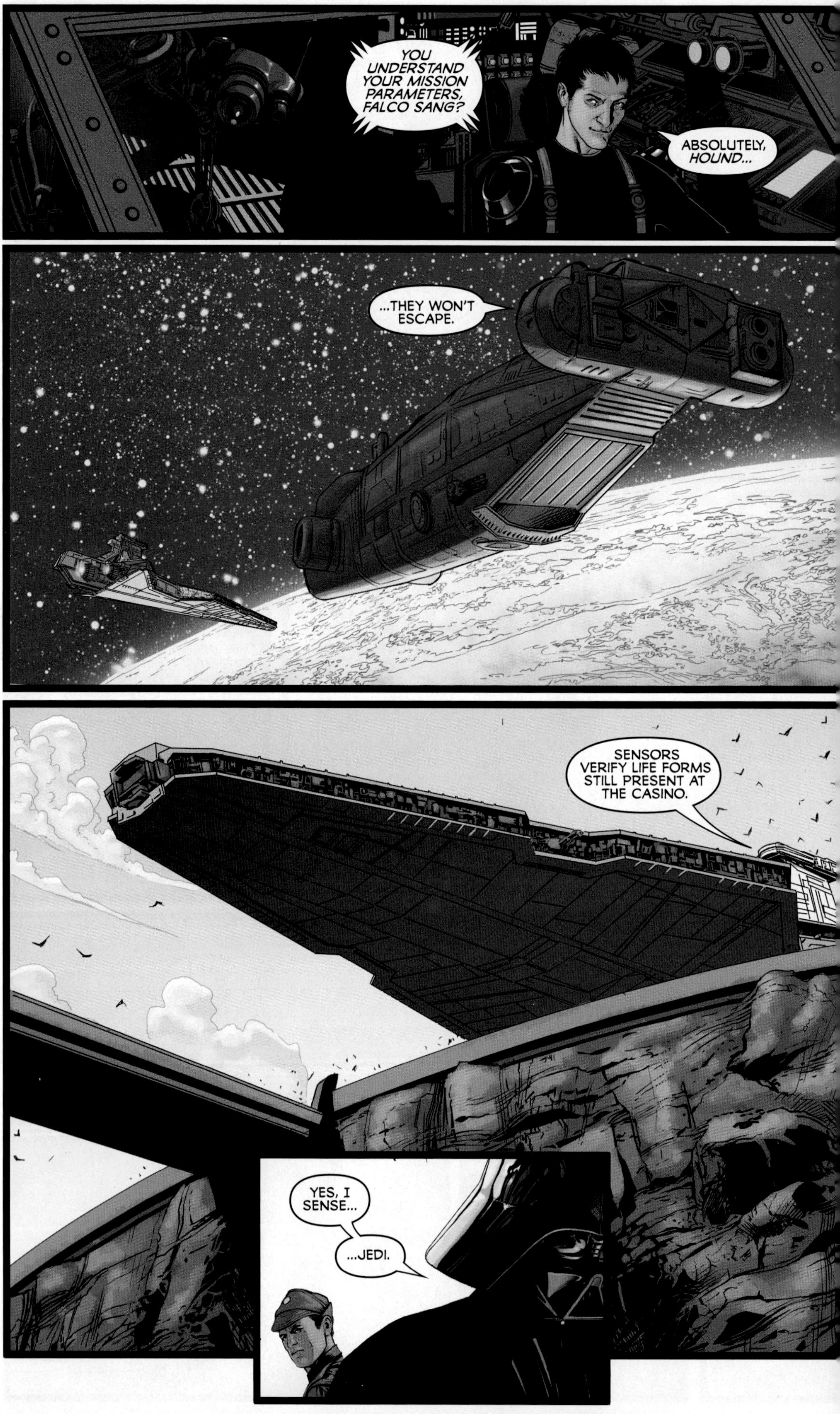
YOU UNDERSTAND YOUR MISSION PARAMETERS, FALCO SANG?
ABSOLUTELY, HOUND...
...THEY WON'T ESCAPE.
SENSORS VERIFY LIFE FORMS STILL PRESENT AT THE CASINO.
YES, I SENSE...
...JEDI.

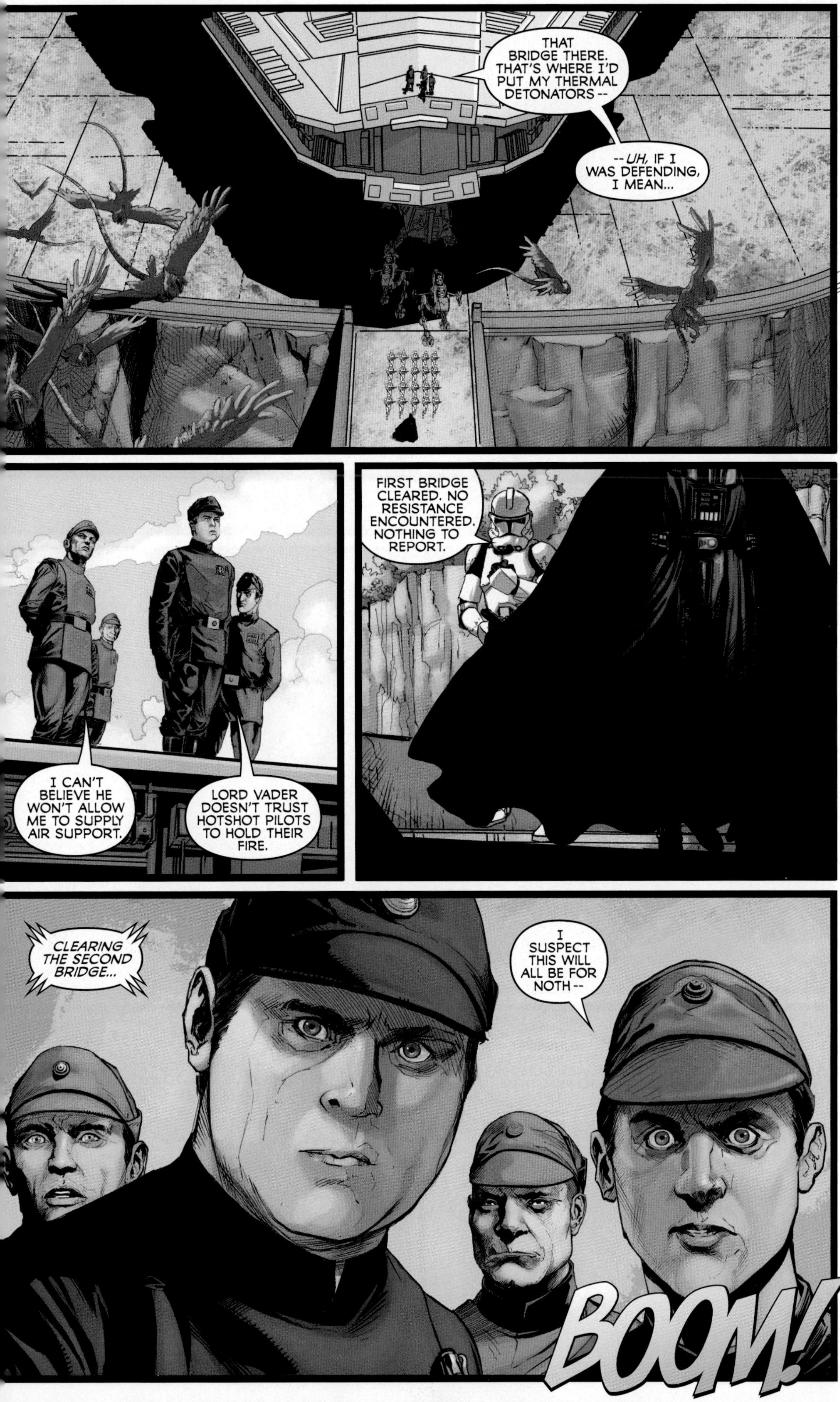
THAT BRIDGE THERE. THAT'S WHERE I'D PUT MY THERMAL DETONATORS --
--UH, IF I WAS DEFENDING, I MEAN...
I CAN'T BELIEVE HE WON'T ALLOW ME TO SUPPLY AIR SUPPORT.
LORD VADER DOESN'T TRUST HOTSHOT PILOTS TO HOLD THEIR FIRE.
FIRST BRIDGE CLEARED. NO RESISTANCE ENCOUNTERED. NOTHING TO REPORT.
CLEARING THE SECOND BRIDGE...
I SUSPECT THIS WILL ALL BE FOR NOTH --
BOOM!

BOOM!

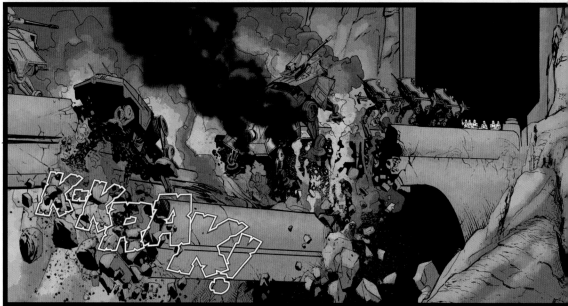

K-KRAK!

LORD VADER! ARE YOU ALL RIGHT?!

GUNSHIPS! TELL HIM WE'LL LAUNCH GUNSHIPS TO PICK THEM UP!

HOLD YOUR POSITION, CAPTAIN.

LIEUTENANT GREGG, IF THE CAPTAIN ATTEMPTS TO INTERFERE, YOUR ORDERS ARE TO SHOOT HIM.

Y-YES, LORD VADER.

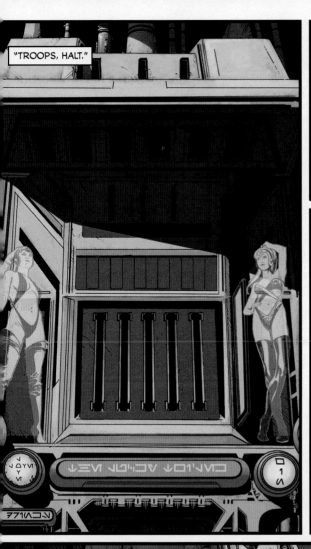

"TROOPS, HALT."

THEY'RE APPROACHING THE SECOND ARCH!

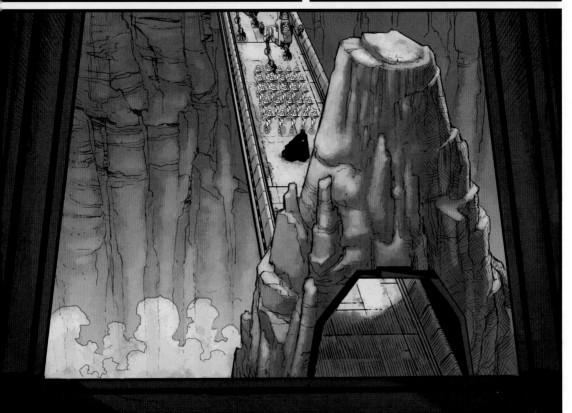

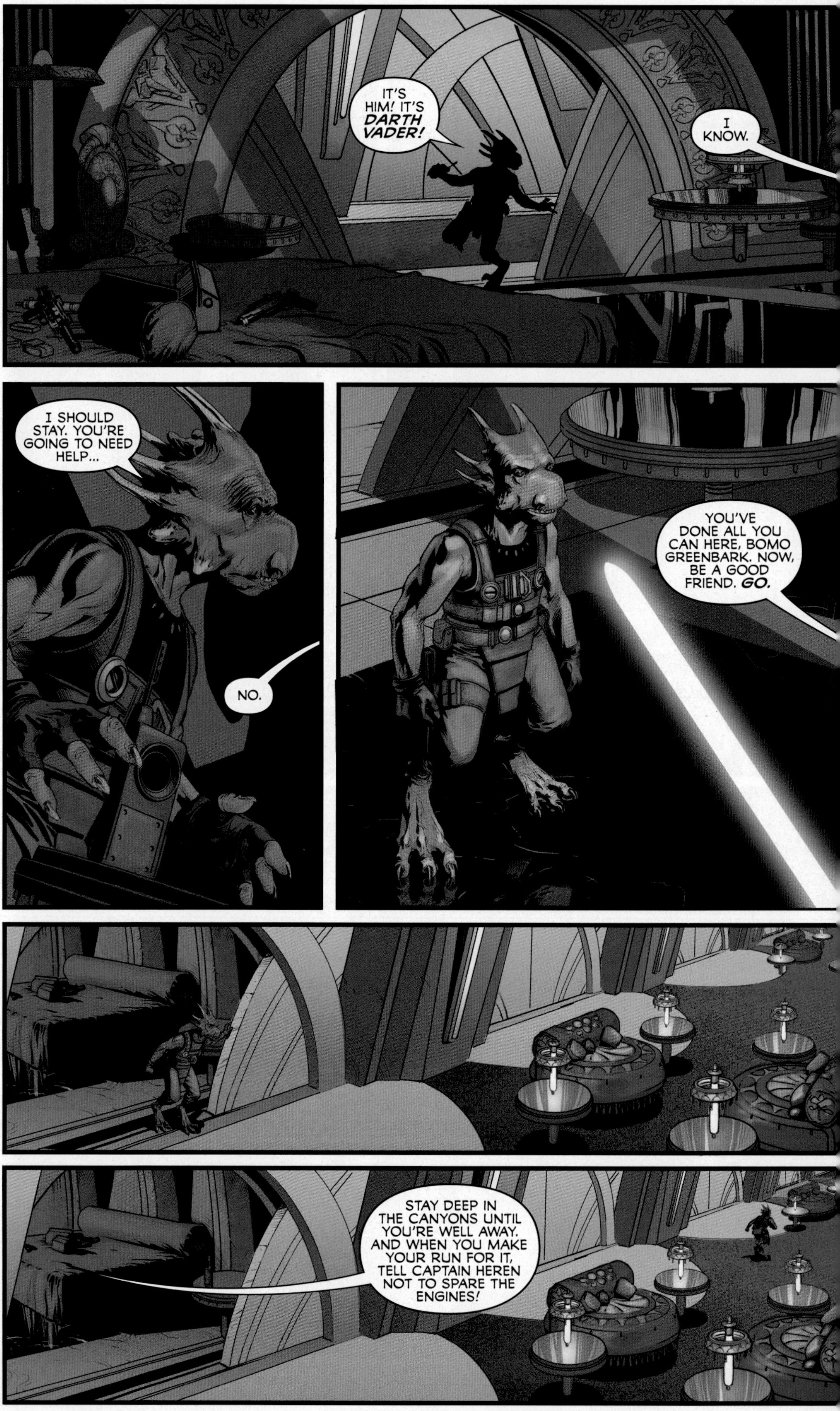
IT'S HIM! IT'S *DARTH VADER!*
I KNOW.
I SHOULD STAY. YOU'RE GOING TO NEED HELP...
NO.
YOU'VE DONE ALL YOU CAN HERE, BOMO GREENBARK. NOW, BE A GOOD FRIEND. ***GO.***
STAY DEEP IN THE CANYONS UNTIL YOU'RE WELL AWAY. AND WHEN YOU MAKE YOUR RUN FOR IT, TELL CAPTAIN HEREN NOT TO SPARE THE ENGINES!

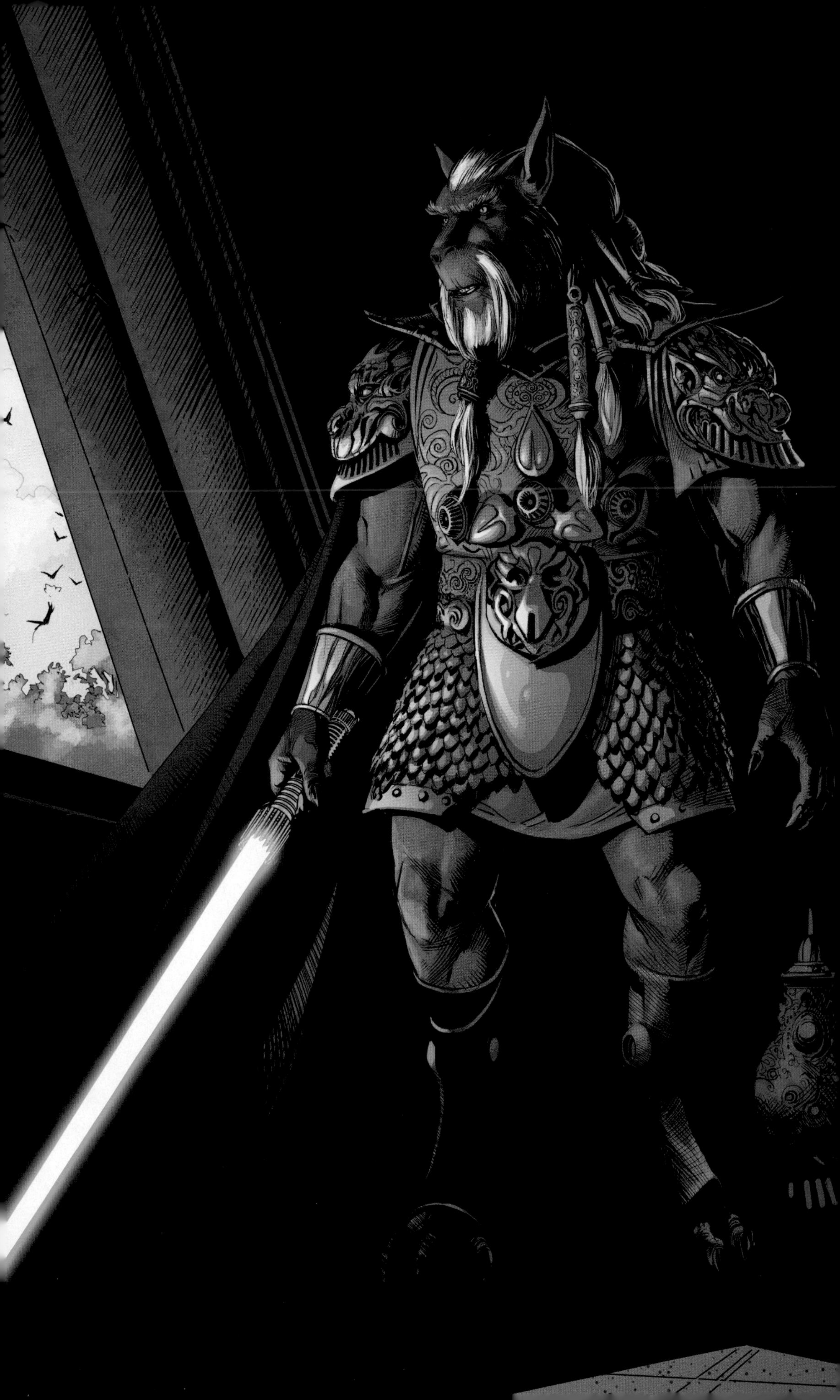

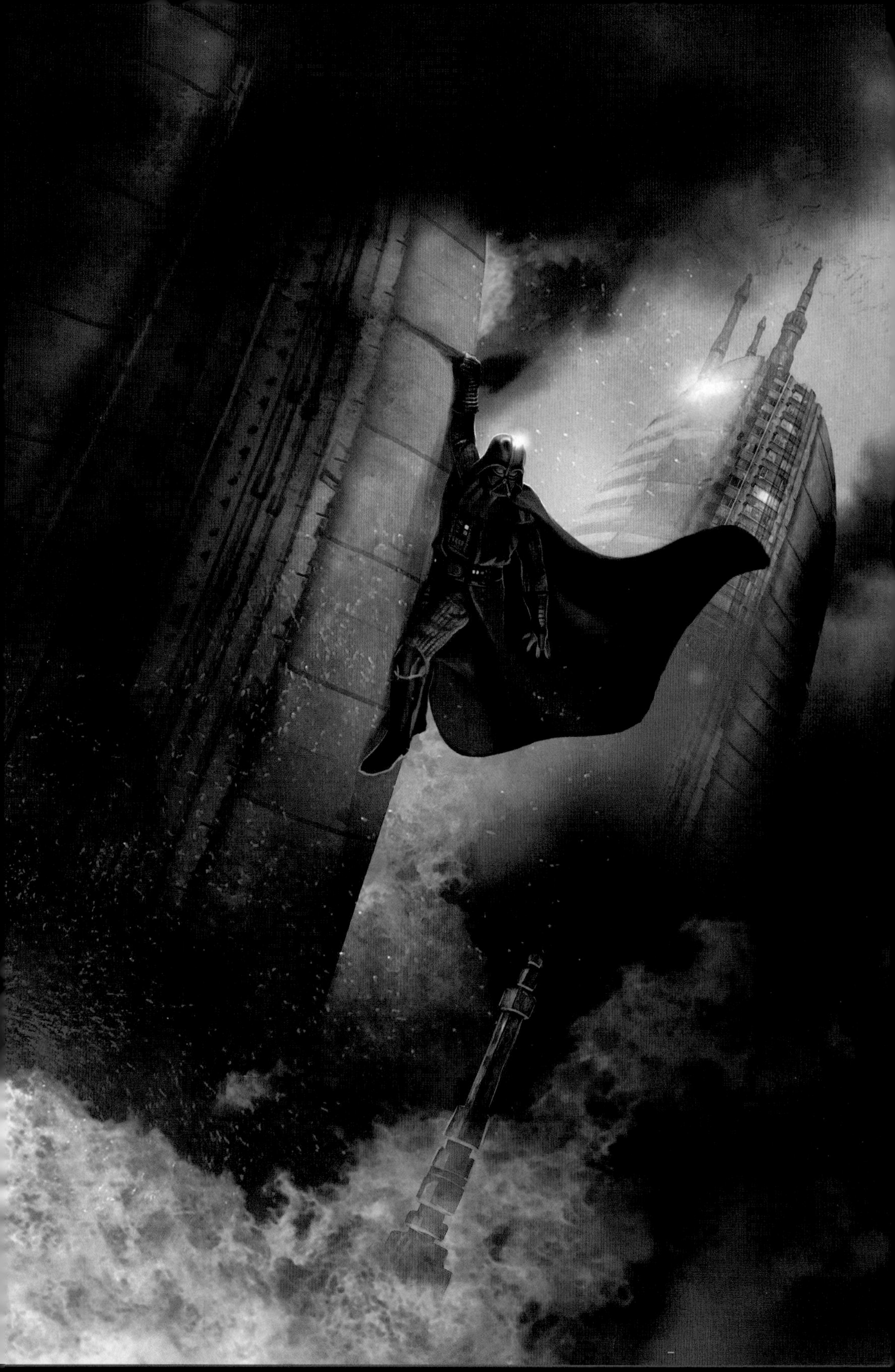

***STAR WARS: DARK TIMES — A SPARK REMAINS #5***

WRITER: RANDY STRADLEY • ARTIST: DOUGLAS WHEATLEY • COLORIST: DAN JACKSON • LETTERER: MICHAEL HEISLER
ASSISTANT EDITOR: FREDDYE LINS • EDITOR: DAVE MARSHALL • COVER ARTIST: BENJAMIN CARRÉ

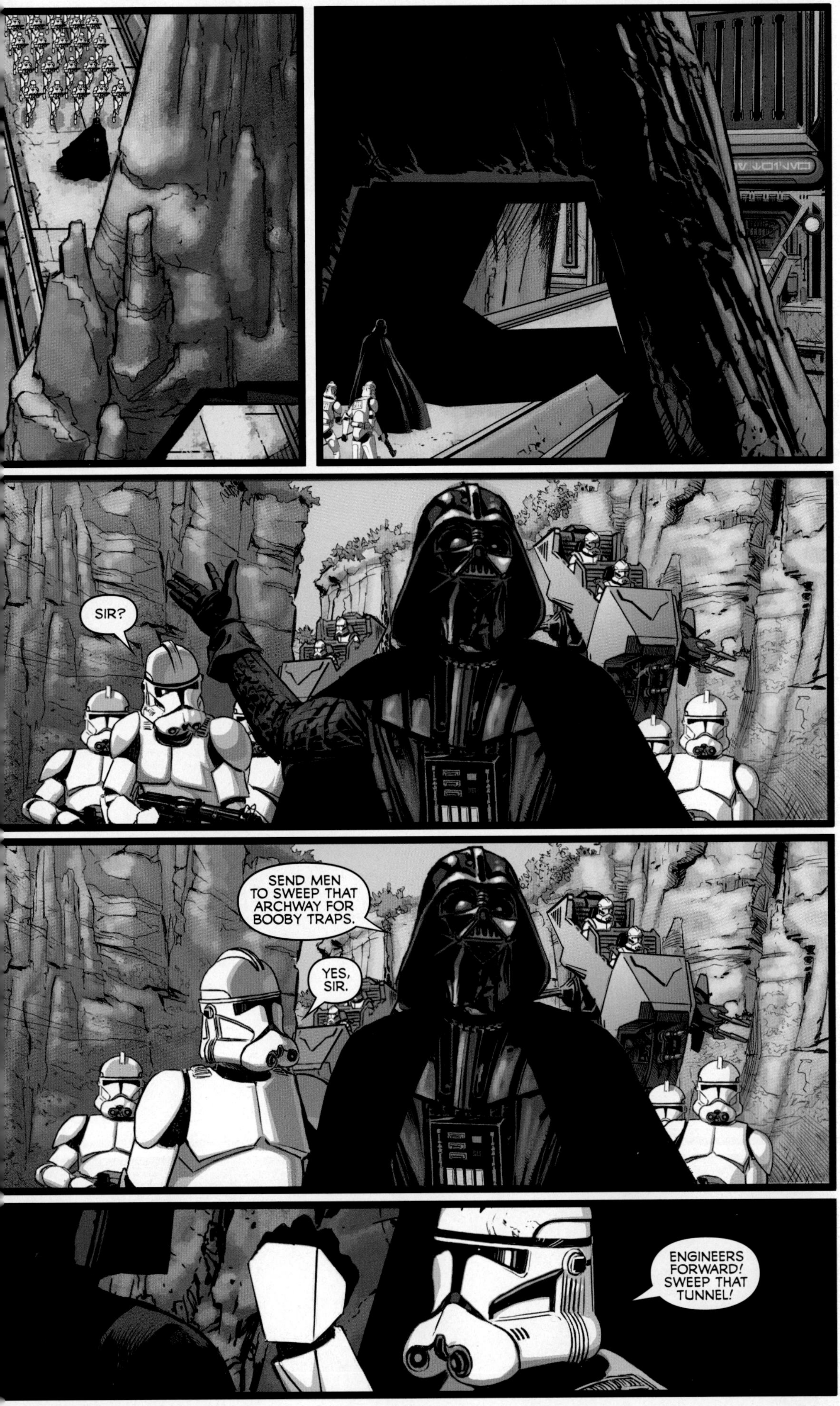
SIR?
SEND MEN TO SWEEP THAT ARCHWAY FOR BOOBY TRAPS.
YES, SIR.
ENGINEERS FORWARD! SWEEP THAT TUNNEL!

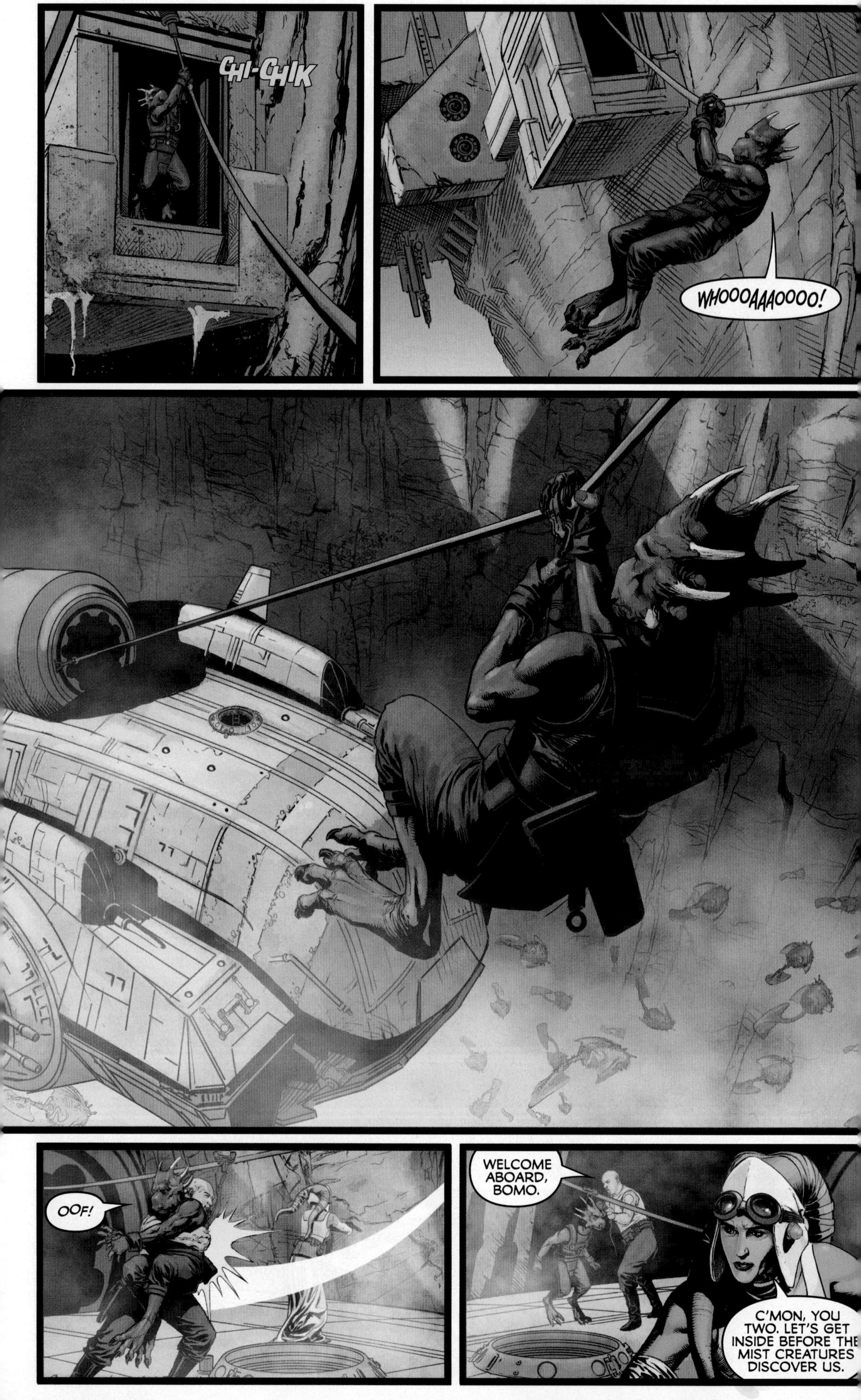
CHI-CHIK
WHOOOAAAOOOO!
OOF!
WELCOME ABOARD, BOMO.
C'MON, YOU TWO. LET'S GET INSIDE BEFORE THE MIST CREATURES DISCOVER US.

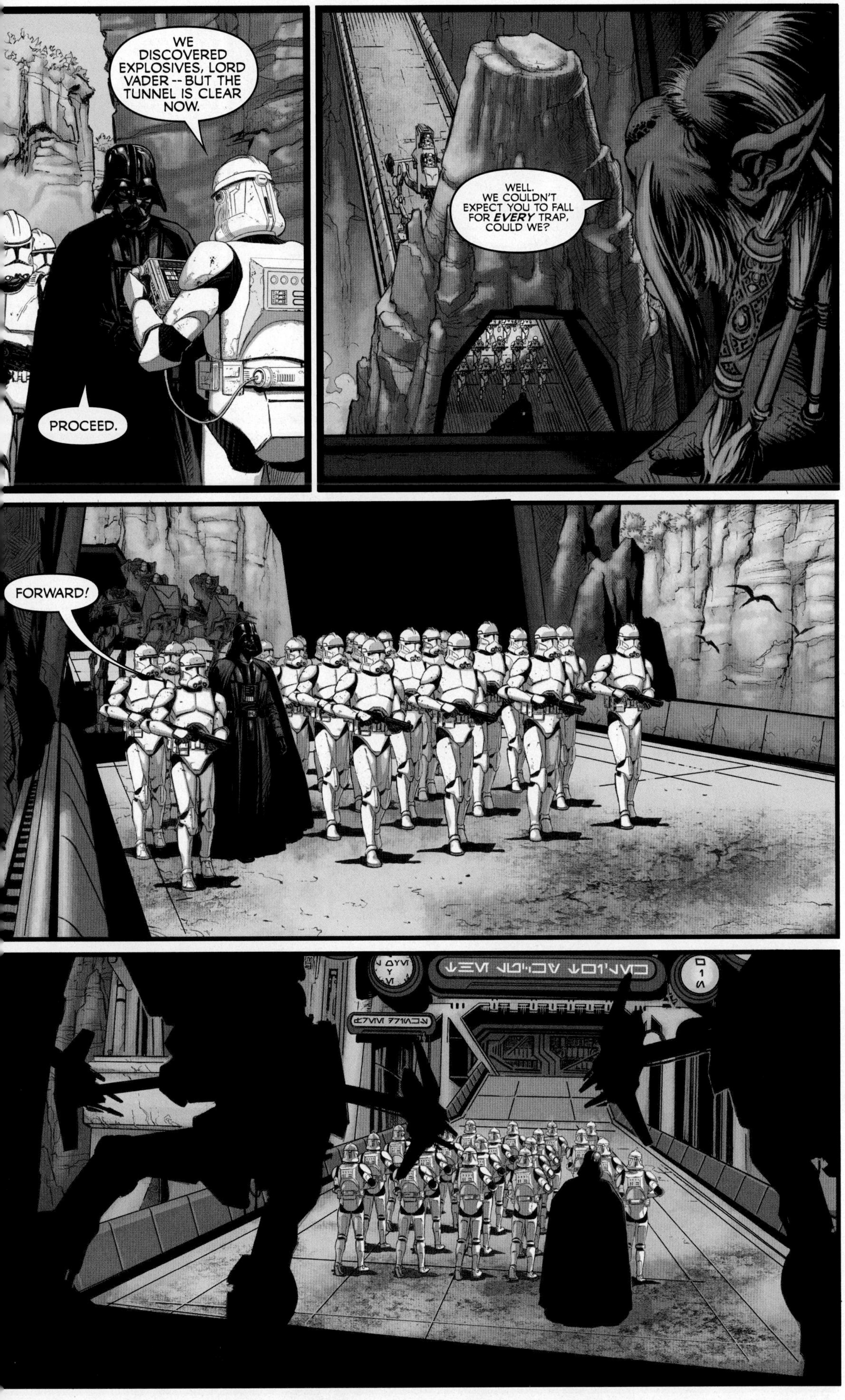

WE DISCOVERED EXPLOSIVES, LORD VADER -- BUT THE TUNNEL IS CLEAR NOW.
PROCEED.
WELL. WE COULDN'T EXPECT YOU TO FALL FOR *EVERY* TRAP, COULD WE?
FORWARD!

?...

JEDI... TWO OF THEM!

SO, DASS JENNIR HAS ENLISTED AN ALLY...

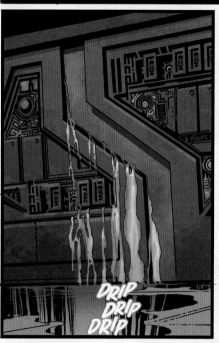
DRIP
DRIP
DRIP

FOOSH!

SPLOOSH!

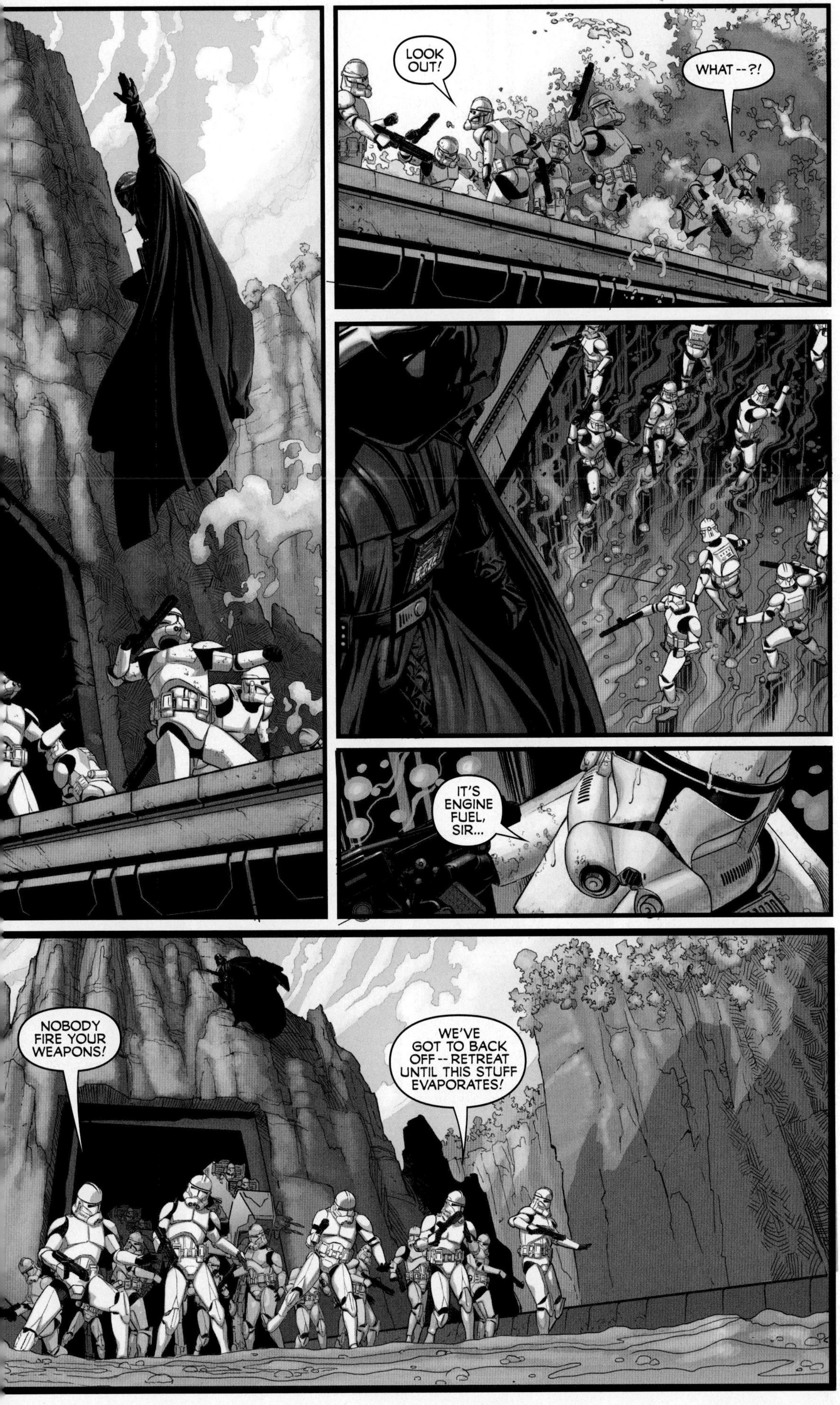
LOOK OUT!
WHAT --?!
IT'S ENGINE FUEL, SIR...
NOBODY FIRE YOUR WEAPONS!
WE'VE GOT TO BACK OFF -- RETREAT UNTIL THIS STUFF EVAPORATES!

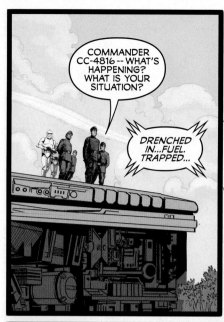

COMMANDER CC-4816 -- WHAT'S HAPPENING? WHAT IS YOUR SITUATION?

DRENCHED IN...FUEL. TRAPPED...

WE'VE GOT TO DO SOMETHING!

THIS IS RIDICULOUS! PATCH ME THROUGH TO THE FLIGHT DECK!

HUH?!

LORD VADER SAID NOT TO ALLOW YOU TO INTERFERE.

YOU HAVE *YOUR* ORDERS. I HAVE *MINE.*

FSSSSST

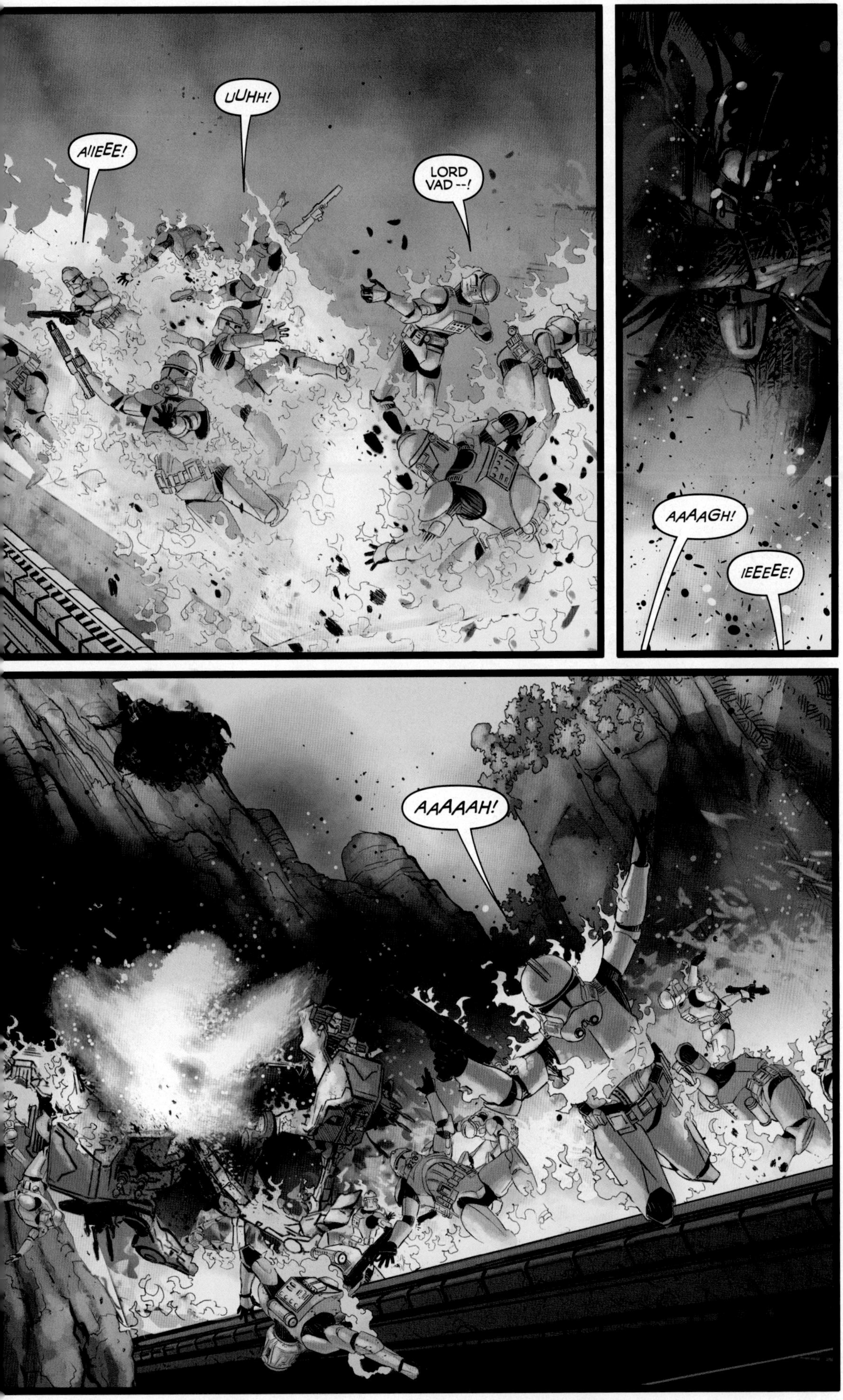
AIIEEE!
UUHH!
LORD VAD --!
AAAAGH!
IEEEEE!
AAAAAH!

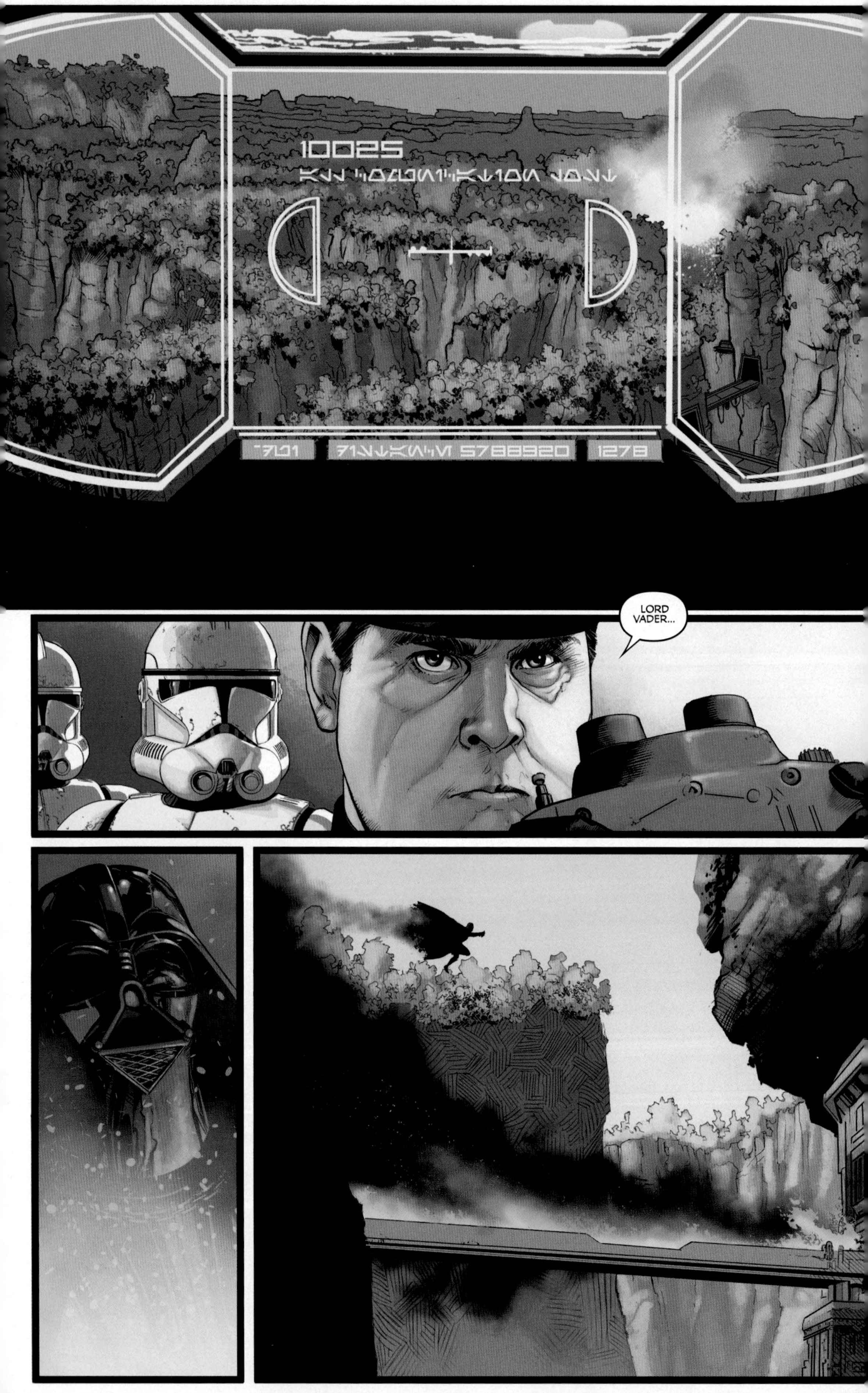
10025
5788920
1278
LORD VADER...

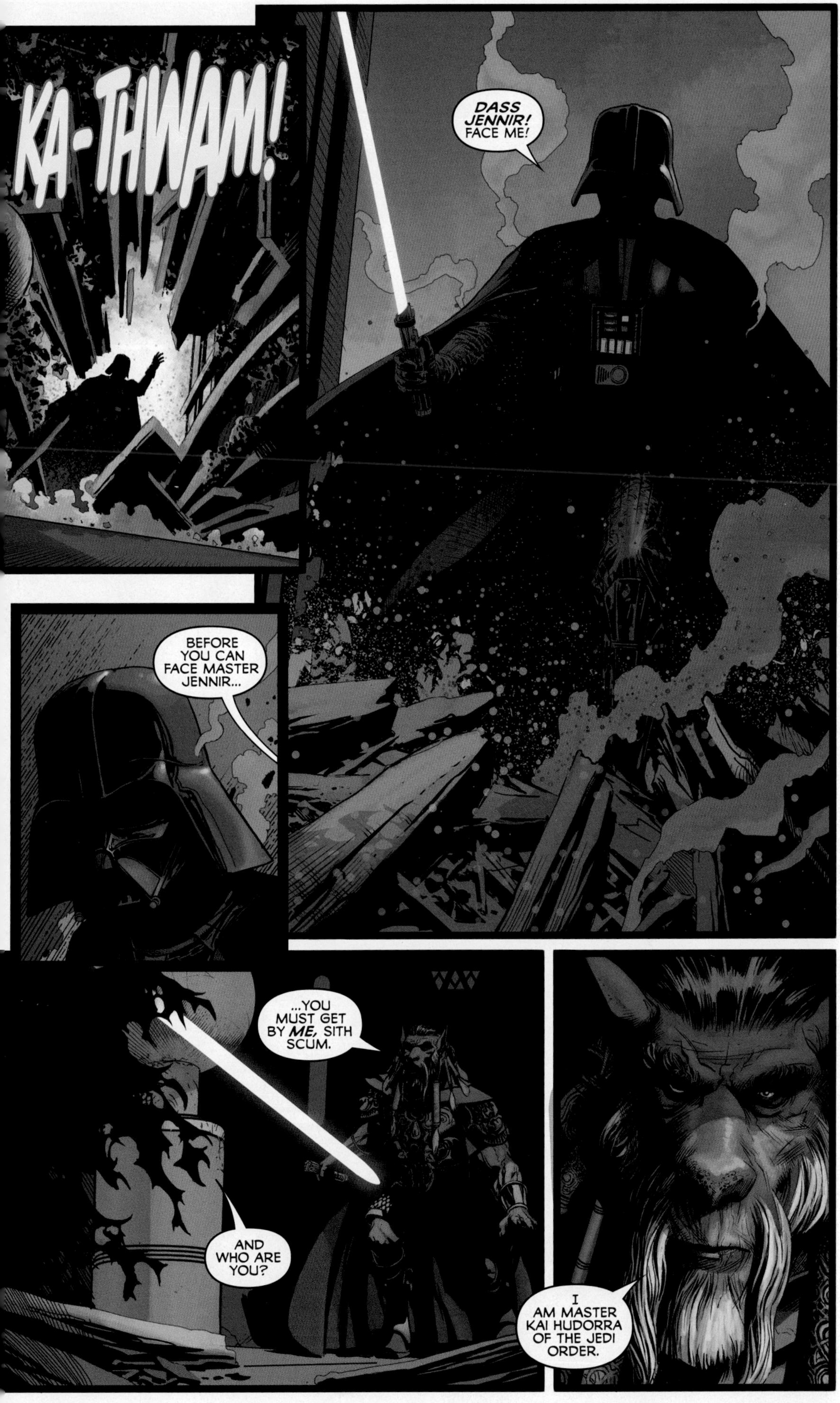
KA-THWAM!
DASS JENNIR! FACE ME!
BEFORE YOU CAN FACE MASTER JENNIR...
...YOU MUST GET BY *ME,* SITH SCUM.
AND WHO ARE YOU?
I AM MASTER KAI HUDORRA OF THE JEDI ORDER.

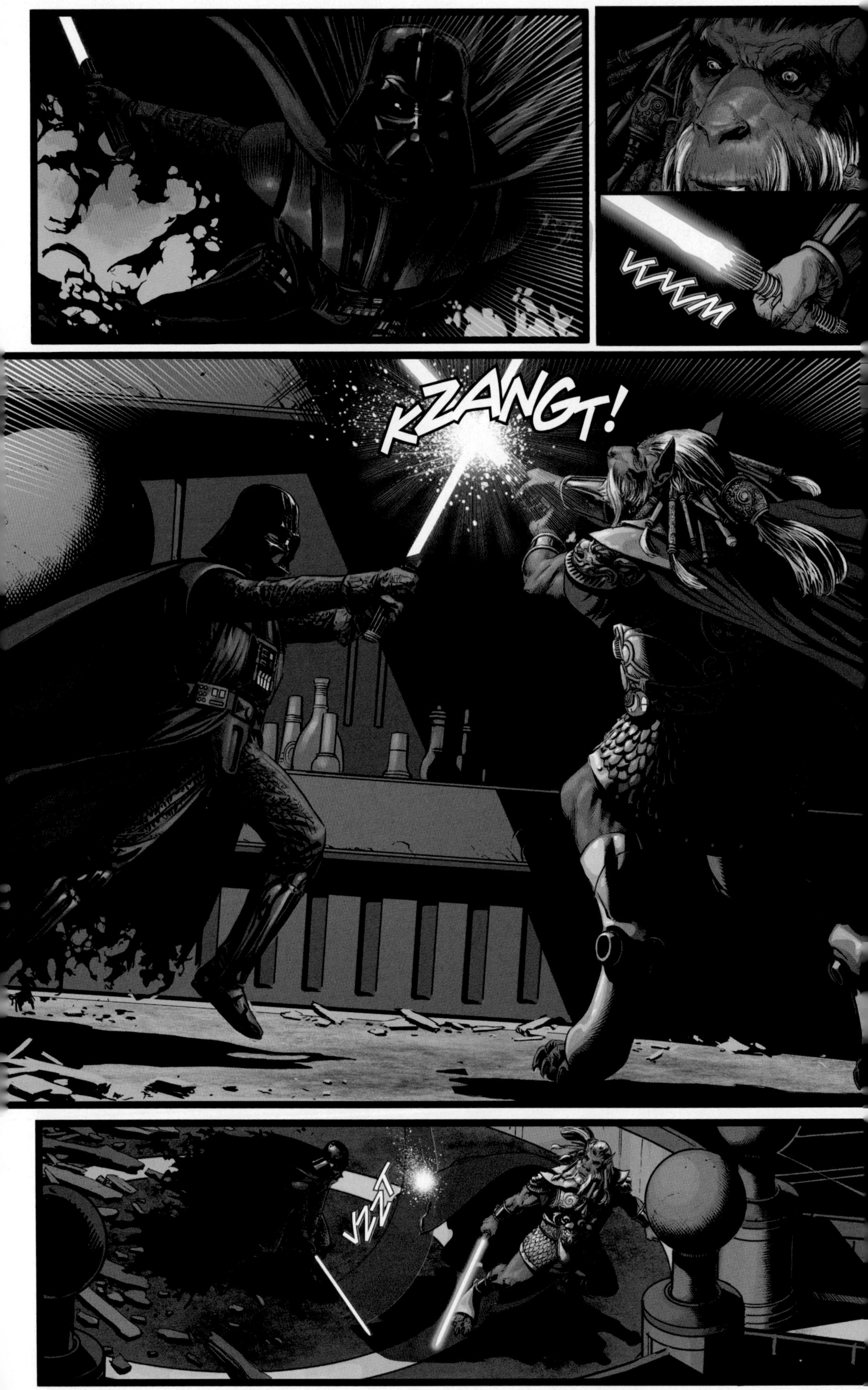

VVVVM
KZANGT!
VZZZT

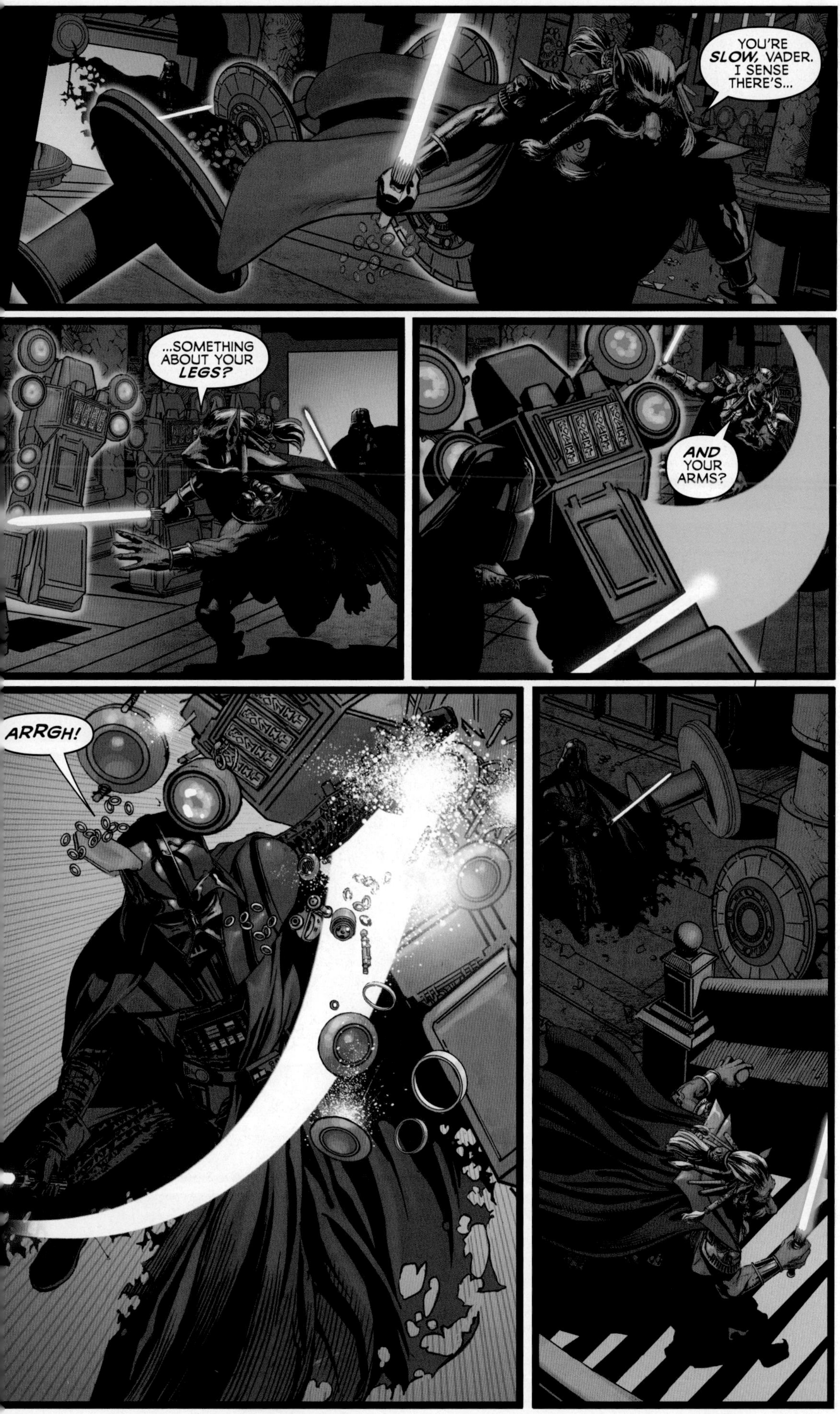
YOU'RE SLOW, VADER. I SENSE THERE'S...
...SOMETHING ABOUT YOUR LEGS?
AND YOUR ARMS?
ARRGH!

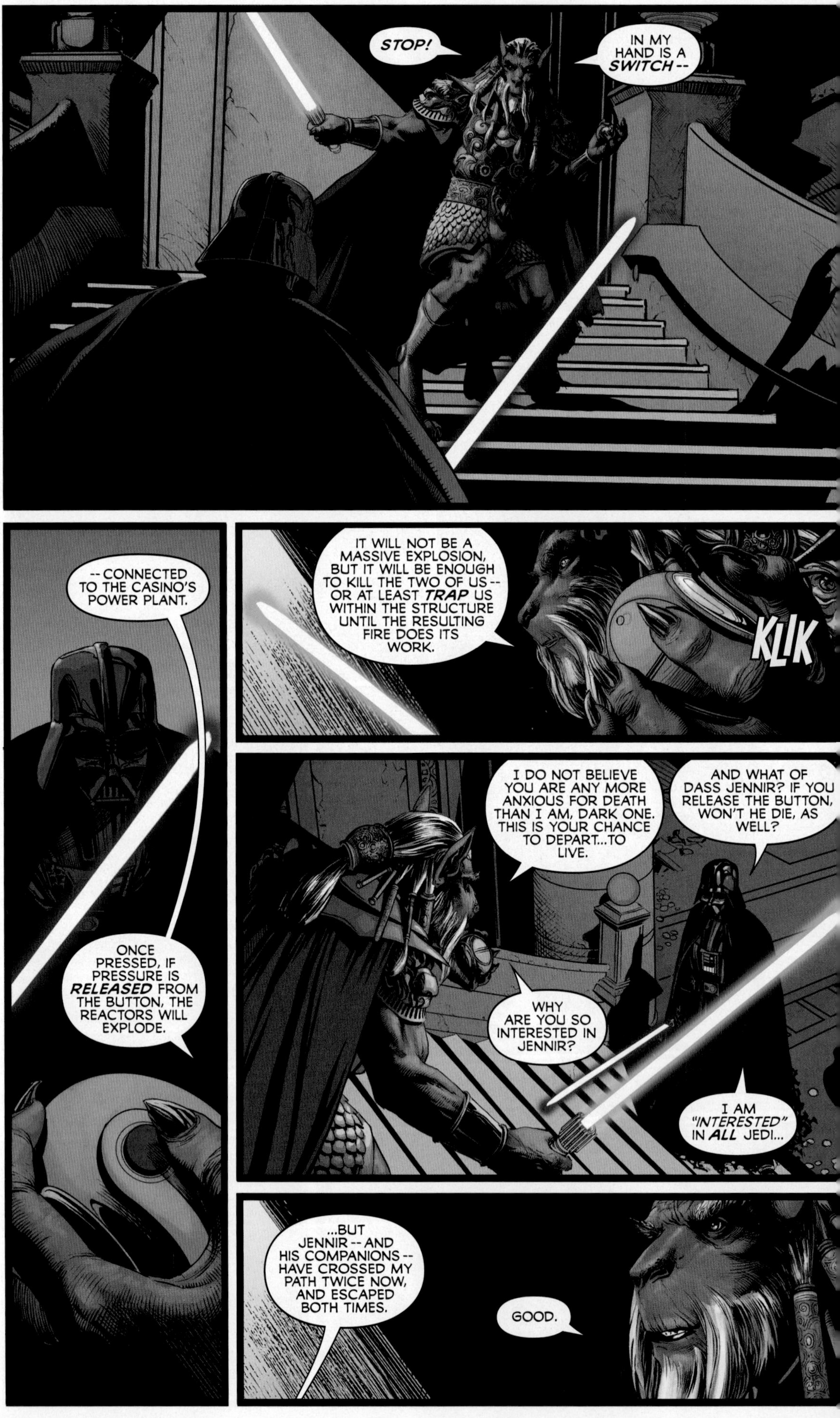
STOP!
IN MY HAND IS A *SWITCH* --
-- CONNECTED TO THE CASINO'S POWER PLANT.
IT WILL NOT BE A MASSIVE EXPLOSION, BUT IT WILL BE ENOUGH TO KILL THE TWO OF US -- OR AT LEAST *TRAP* US WITHIN THE STRUCTURE UNTIL THE RESULTING FIRE DOES ITS WORK.
KLIK
ONCE PRESSED, IF PRESSURE IS *RELEASED* FROM THE BUTTON, THE REACTORS WILL EXPLODE.
I DO NOT BELIEVE YOU ARE ANY MORE ANXIOUS FOR DEATH THAN I AM, DARK ONE. THIS IS YOUR CHANCE TO DEPART...TO LIVE.
AND WHAT OF DASS JENNIR? IF YOU RELEASE THE BUTTON, WON'T HE DIE, AS WELL?
WHY ARE YOU SO INTERESTED IN JENNIR?
I AM *"INTERESTED"* IN *ALL* JEDI...
...BUT JENNIR -- AND HIS COMPANIONS -- HAVE CROSSED MY PATH TWICE NOW, AND ESCAPED BOTH TIMES.
GOOD.

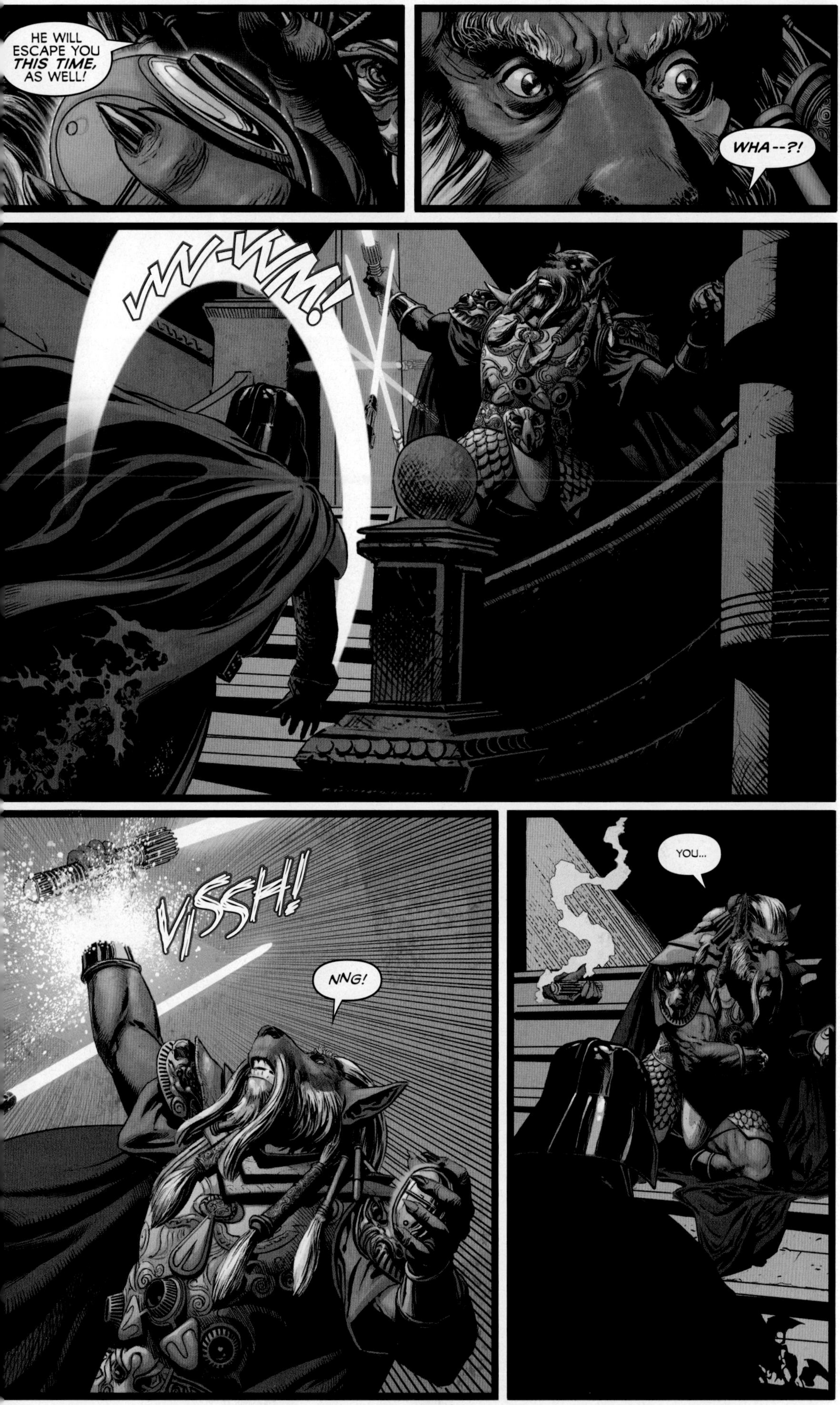
HE WILL ESCAPE YOU THIS TIME, AS WELL!
WHA--?!
VVV-VVM!
VISSH!
NNG!
YOU...

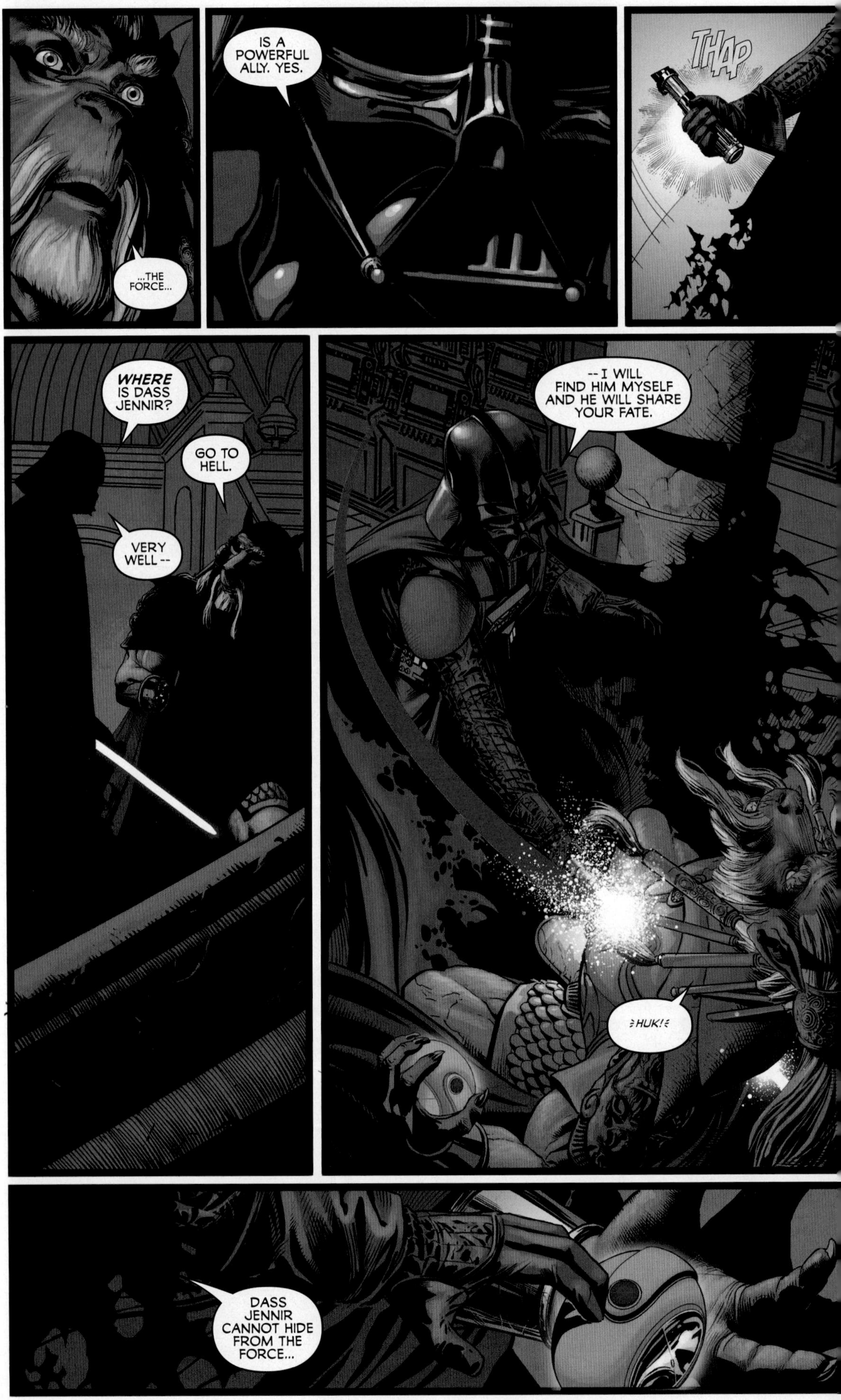
...THE FORCE...
IS A POWERFUL ALLY. YES.
THAP
WHERE IS DASS JENNIR?
GO TO HELL.
VERY WELL --
-- I WILL FIND HIM MYSELF AND HE WILL SHARE YOUR FATE.
HUK!
DASS JENNIR CANNOT HIDE FROM THE FORCE...

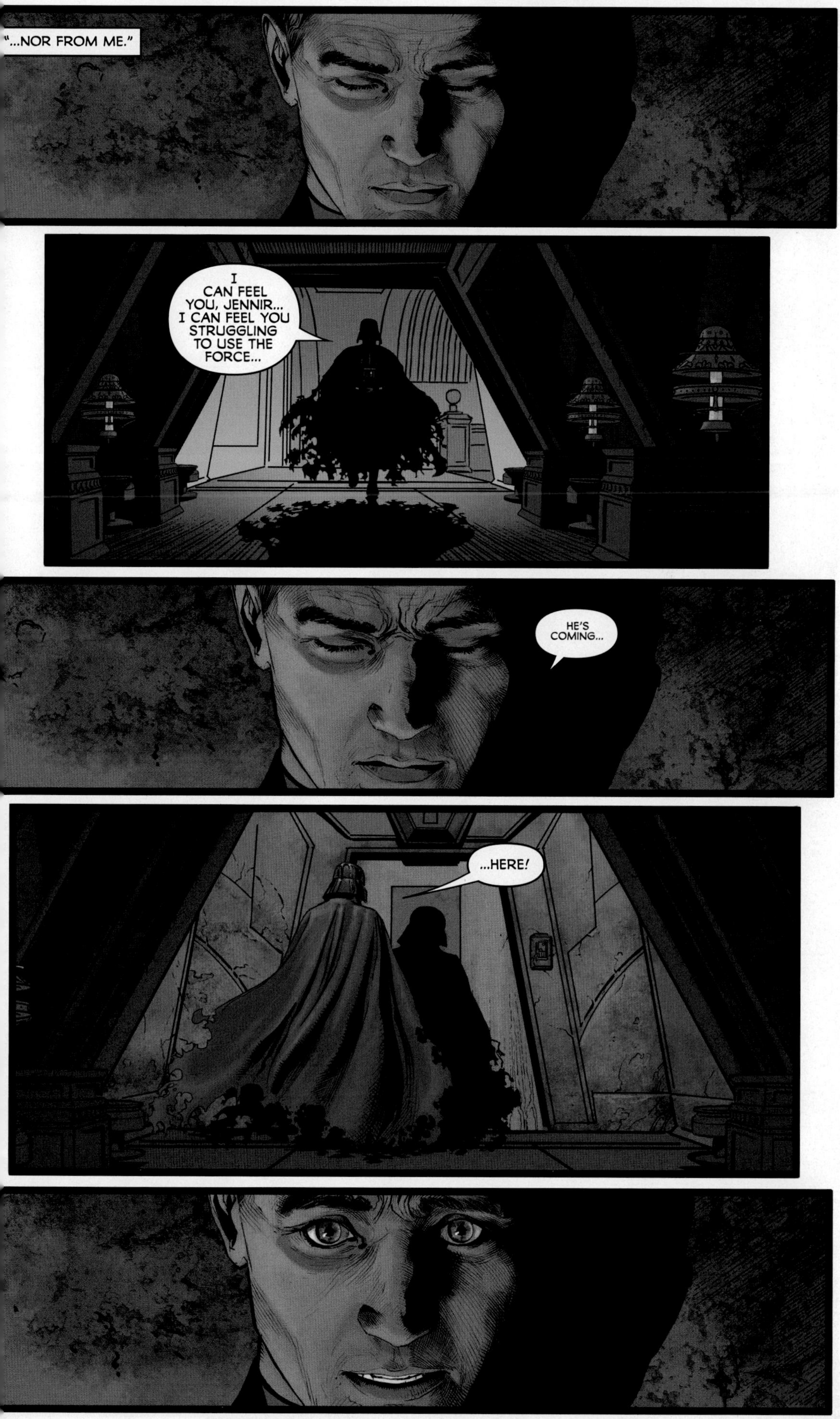
"...NOR FROM ME."
I CAN FEEL YOU, JENNIR... I CAN FEEL YOU STRUGGLING TO USE THE FORCE...
HE'S COMING...
...HERE!

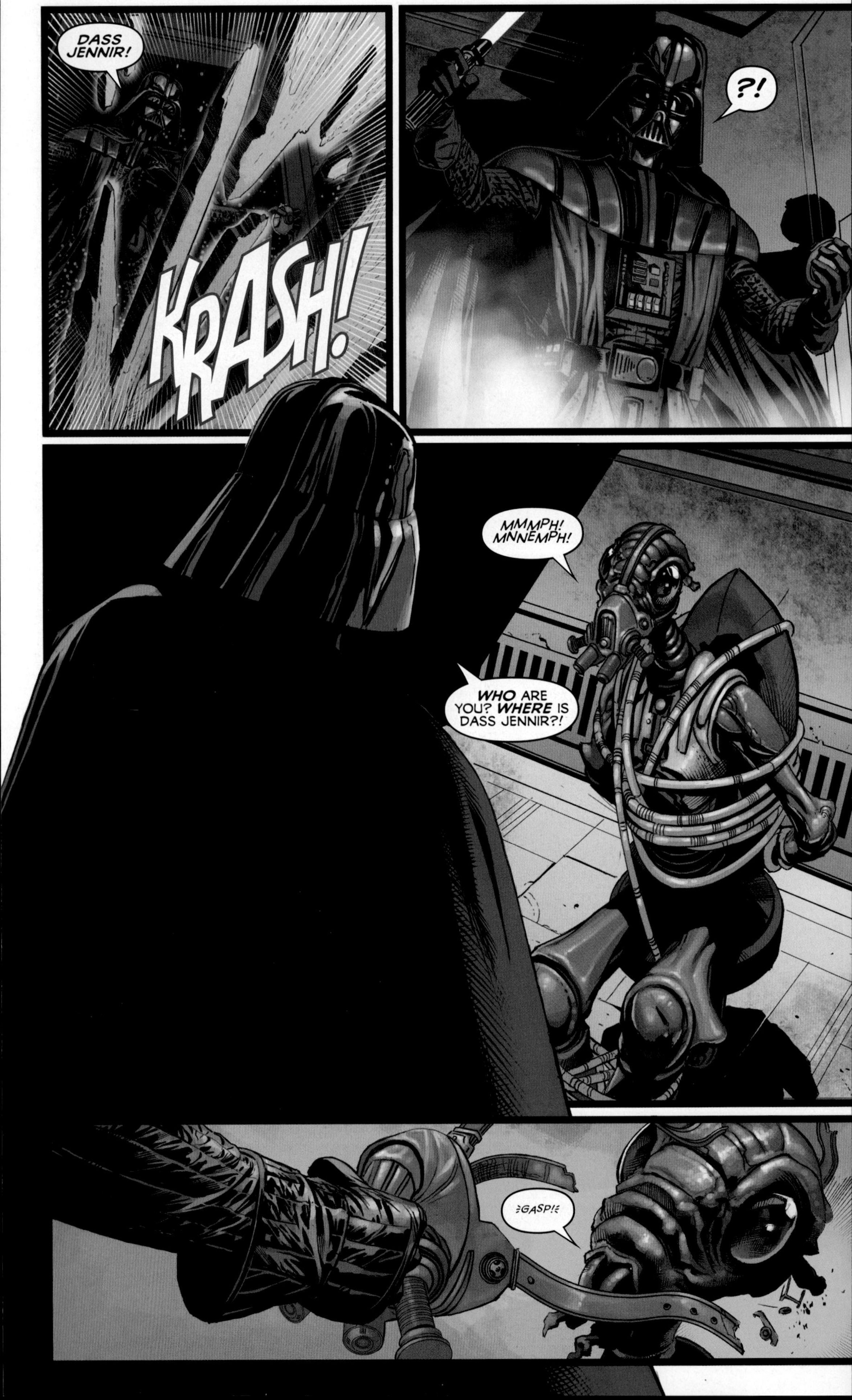
DASS JENNIR!
KRASH!
?!
MMMPH! MNNEMPH!
WHO ARE YOU? WHERE IS DASS JENNIR?!
GASP!

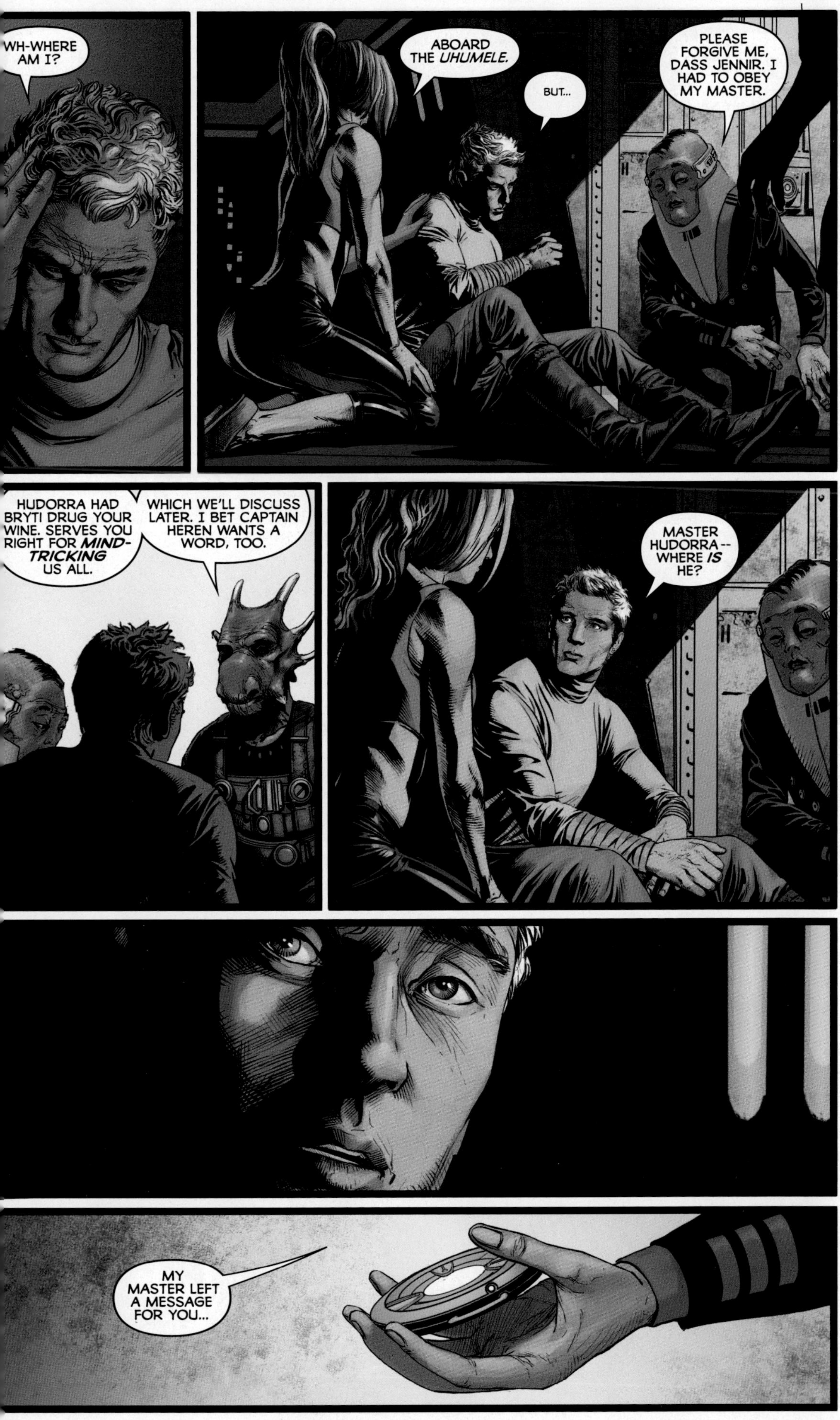
WH-WHERE AM I?
ABOARD THE *UHUMELE.*
BUT...
PLEASE FORGIVE ME, DASS JENNIR. I HAD TO OBEY MY MASTER.
HUDORRA HAD BRYTI DRUG YOUR WINE. SERVES YOU RIGHT FOR ***MIND-TRICKING*** US ALL.
WHICH WE'LL DISCUSS LATER. I BET CAPTAIN HEREN WANTS A WORD, TOO.
MASTER HUDORRA-- WHERE ***IS*** HE?
MY MASTER LEFT A MESSAGE FOR YOU...

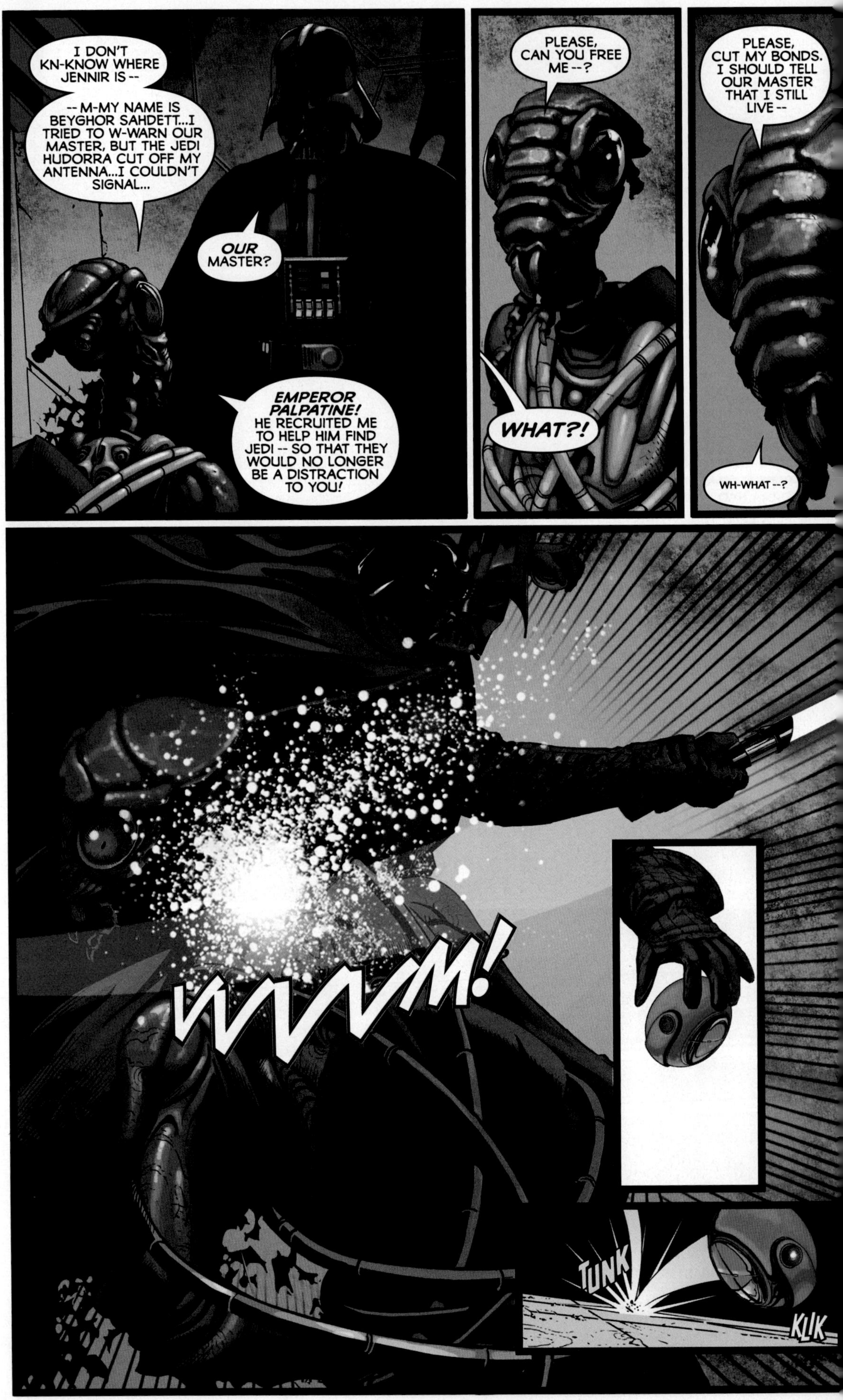

I DON'T KN-KNOW WHERE JENNIR IS --
-- M-MY NAME IS BEYGHOR SAHDETT...I TRIED TO W-WARN OUR MASTER, BUT THE JEDI HUDORRA CUT OFF MY ANTENNA...I COULDN'T SIGNAL...
OUR MASTER?
EMPEROR PALPATINE! HE RECRUITED ME TO HELP HIM FIND JEDI -- SO THAT THEY WOULD NO LONGER BE A DISTRACTION TO YOU!
PLEASE, CAN YOU FREE ME --?
WHAT?!
PLEASE, CUT MY BONDS. I SHOULD TELL OUR MASTER THAT I STILL LIVE --
WH-WHAT --?
VVVM!
TUNK
KLIK

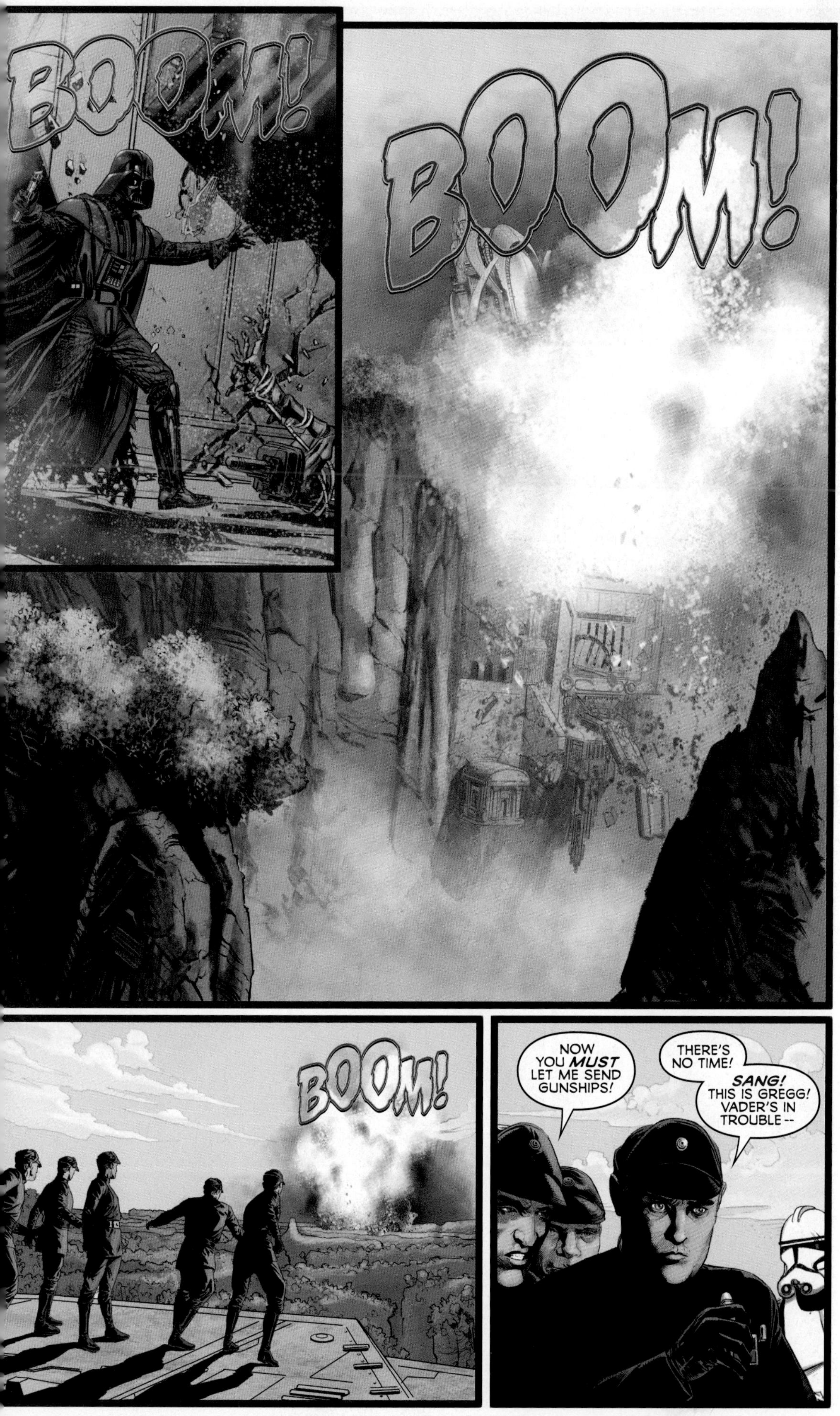
BOOM!
BOOM!
BOOM!
NOW YOU *MUST* LET ME SEND GUNSHIPS!
THERE'S NO TIME!
*SANG!* THIS IS GREGG! VADER'S IN TROUBLE --

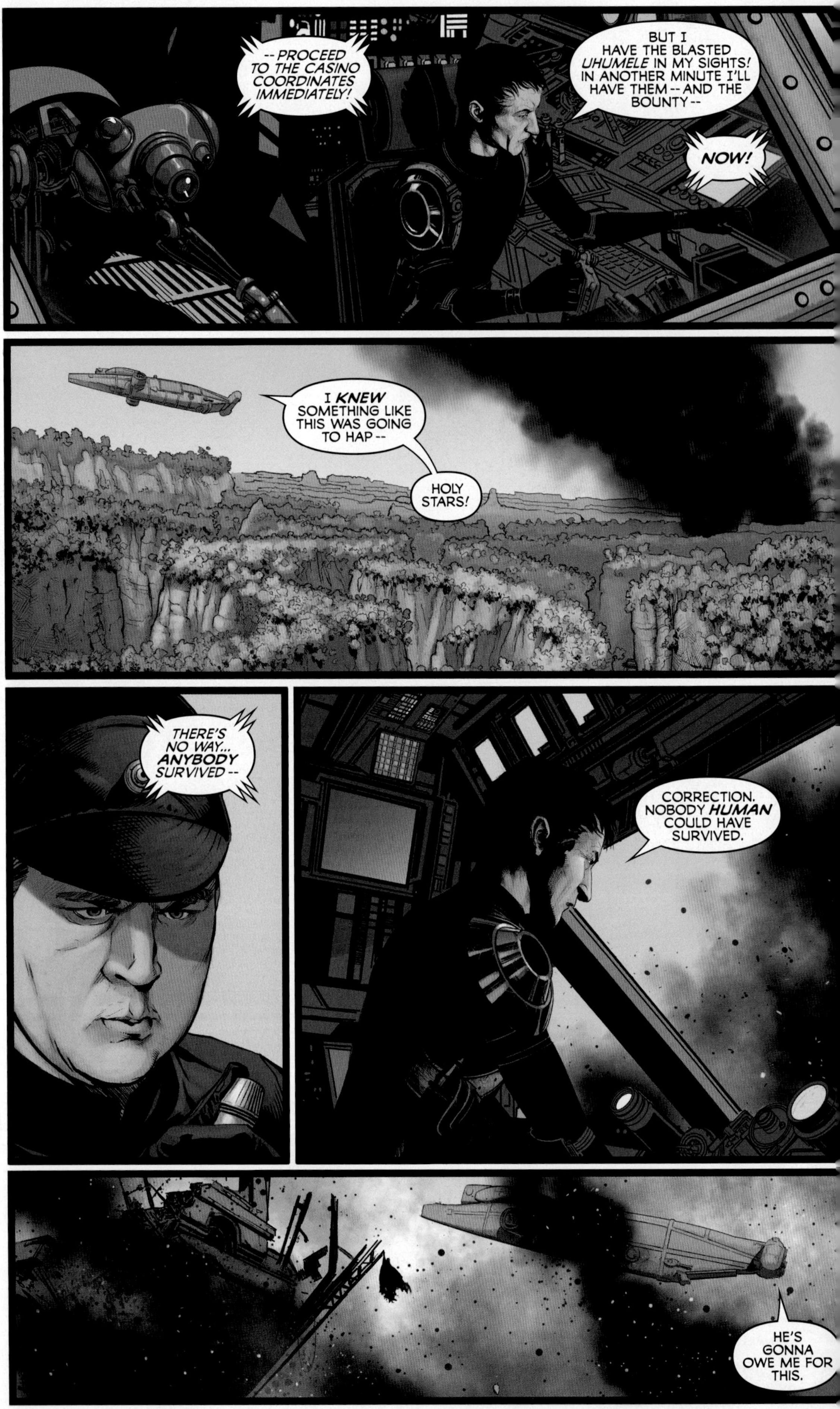
-- PROCEED TO THE CASINO COORDINATES IMMEDIATELY!
BUT I HAVE THE BLASTED UHUMELE IN MY SIGHTS! IN ANOTHER MINUTE I'LL HAVE THEM -- AND THE BOUNTY --
NOW!
I KNEW SOMETHING LIKE THIS WAS GOING TO HAP --
HOLY STARS!
THERE'S NO WAY... ANYBODY SURVIVED --
CORRECTION. NOBODY HUMAN COULD HAVE SURVIVED.
HE'S GONNA OWE ME FOR THIS.

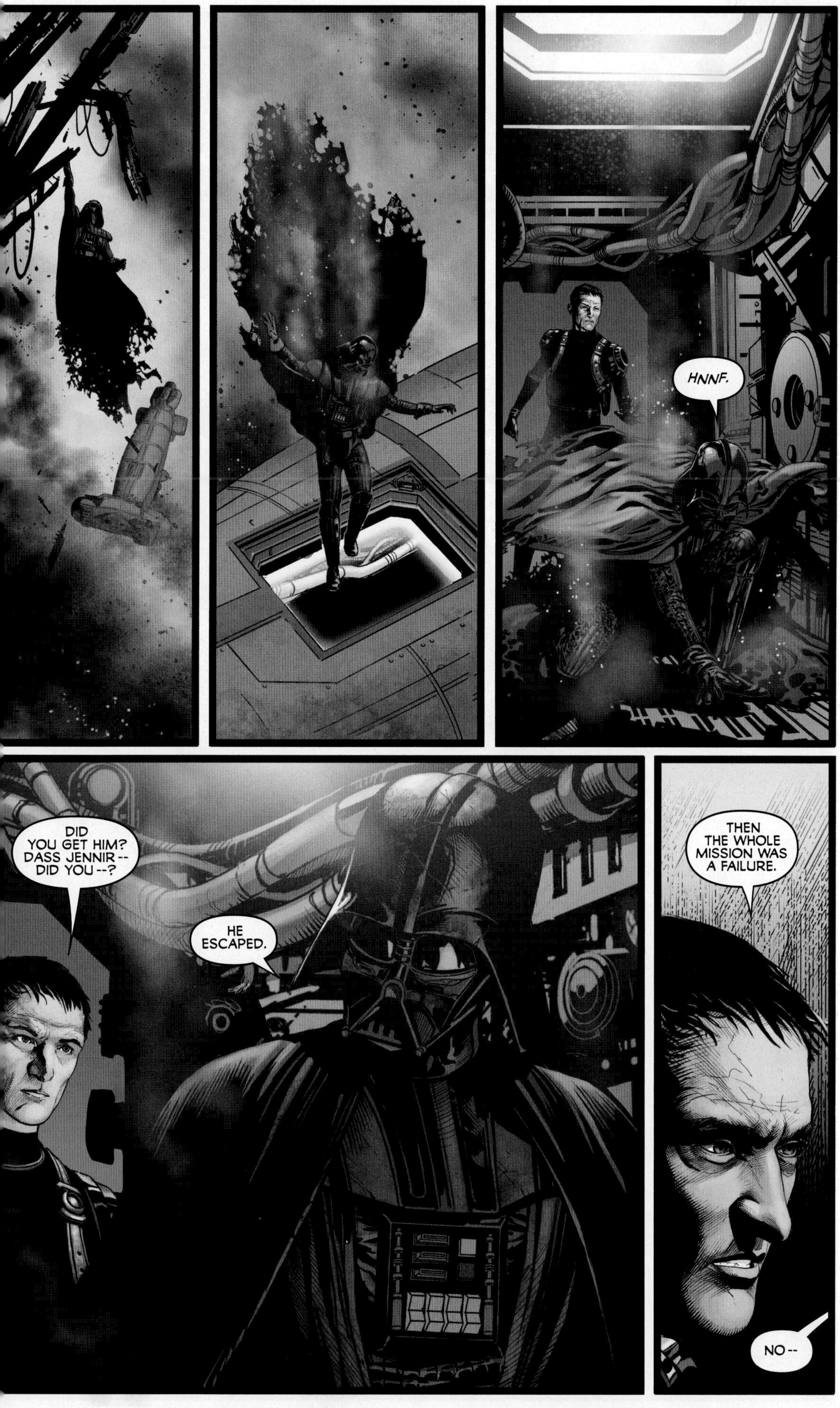
HNNF.
DID YOU GET HIM? DASS JENNIR -- DID YOU --?
HE ESCAPED.
THEN THE WHOLE MISSION WAS A FAILURE.
NO --

"--TWO JEDI DIED."

...BUT TODAY THE JEDI ORDER SURVIVED...

...EVEN IF YOU, DASS JENNIR, ARE THE **LAST** OF THAT ORDER. THOUGH I BELIEVE-- I **SENSE** -- THAT YOU ARE NOT. I HAVE HOPE.

I KNEW THAT WE COULD NOT BOTH RUN FROM THIS FIGHT. AT FIRST I RESENTED YOU FOR BRINGING THIS BATTLE TO MY DOORSTEP. BUT AFTER HEARING OF YOUR EXPLOITS -- AND YOUR SACRIFICES --

-- FROM EMBER CHANKELI AND THAT DROID OF YOURS, I KNEW THAT I COULD NOT ALLOW YOU TO THROW YOUR LIFE AWAY ON A FIGHT WE HAD SO LITTLE CHANCE OF WINNING.

IF YOU ARE VIEWING THIS, I AM DEAD.

BUT PLEASE, LET THERE BE NO SADNESS AT MY PASSING...

...FOR I CAN GO TO MY FATE SECURE IN THE KNOWLEDGE THAT IN THE GALAXY A VITAL SPARK OF THE JEDI REMAINS.

MAY THE FORCE BE WITH YOU ALL.

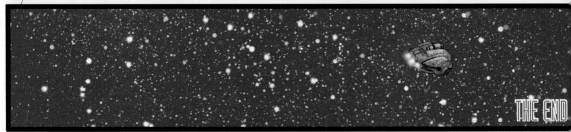

THE END

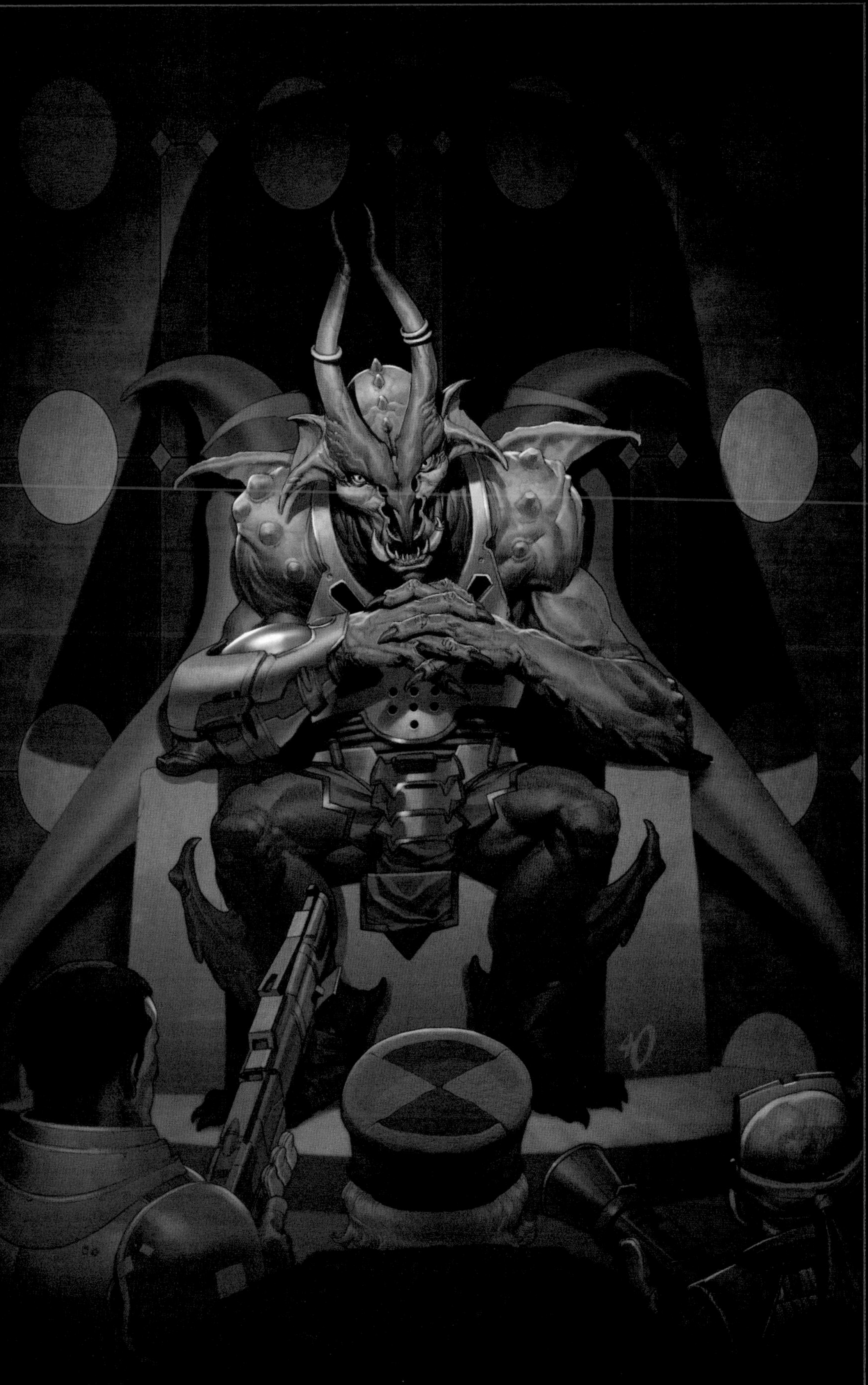

*STAR WARS: DARTH VADER AND THE NINTH ASSASSIN #1*

WRITER: TIM SIEDELL • PENCILER: STEPHEN THOMPSON • INKER: MARK IRWIN • COLORIST: MICHAEL ATIYEH • LETTERER: MICHAEL HEISLER
ASSISTANT EDITOR: FREDDYE LINS • EDITOR: DAVE MARSHALL • COVER ARTIST: ARIEL OLIVETTI

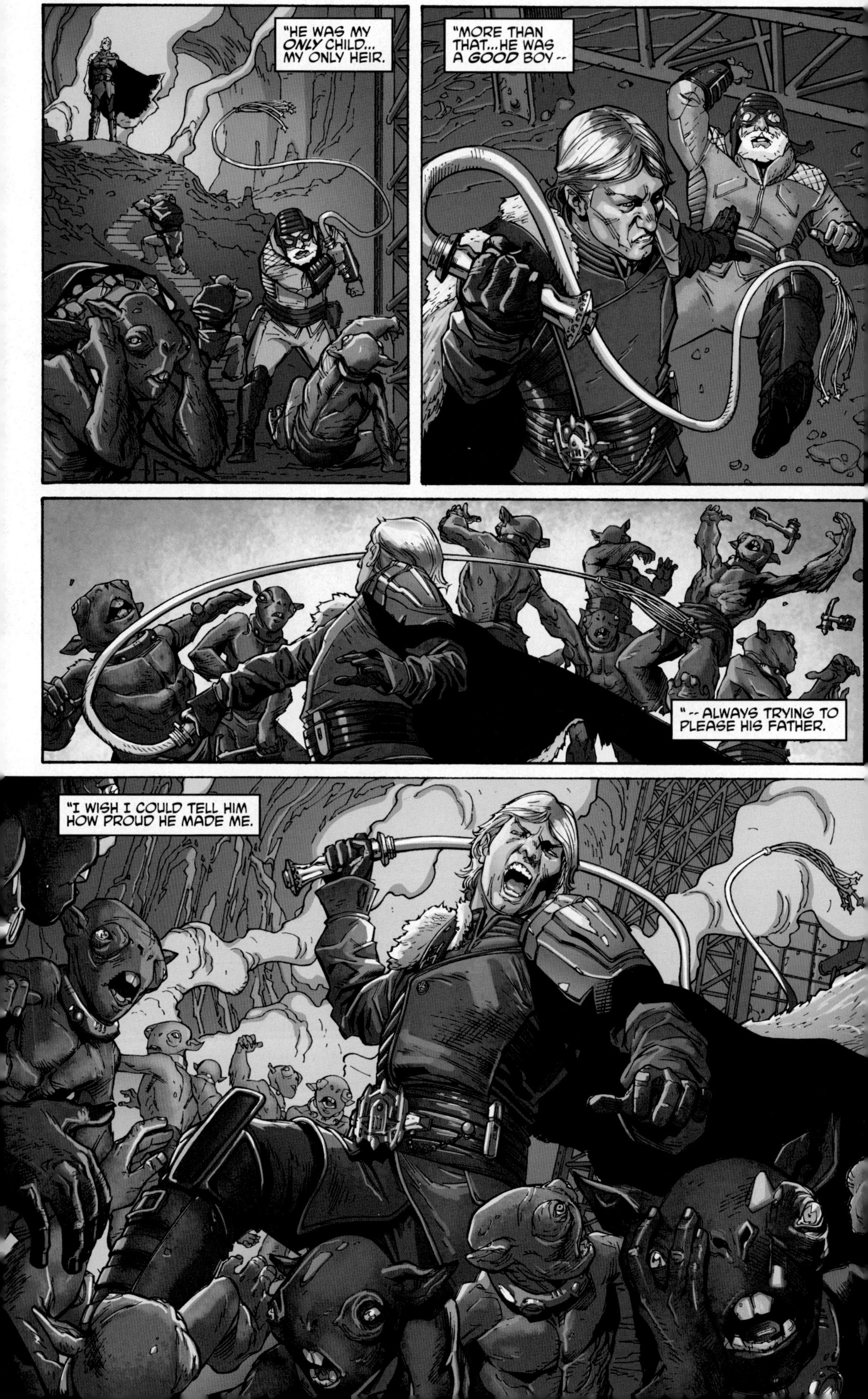
"HE WAS MY ONLY CHILD... MY ONLY HEIR.
"MORE THAN THAT...HE WAS A GOOD BOY --
"-- ALWAYS TRYING TO PLEASE HIS FATHER.
"I WISH I COULD TELL HIM HOW PROUD HE MADE ME.

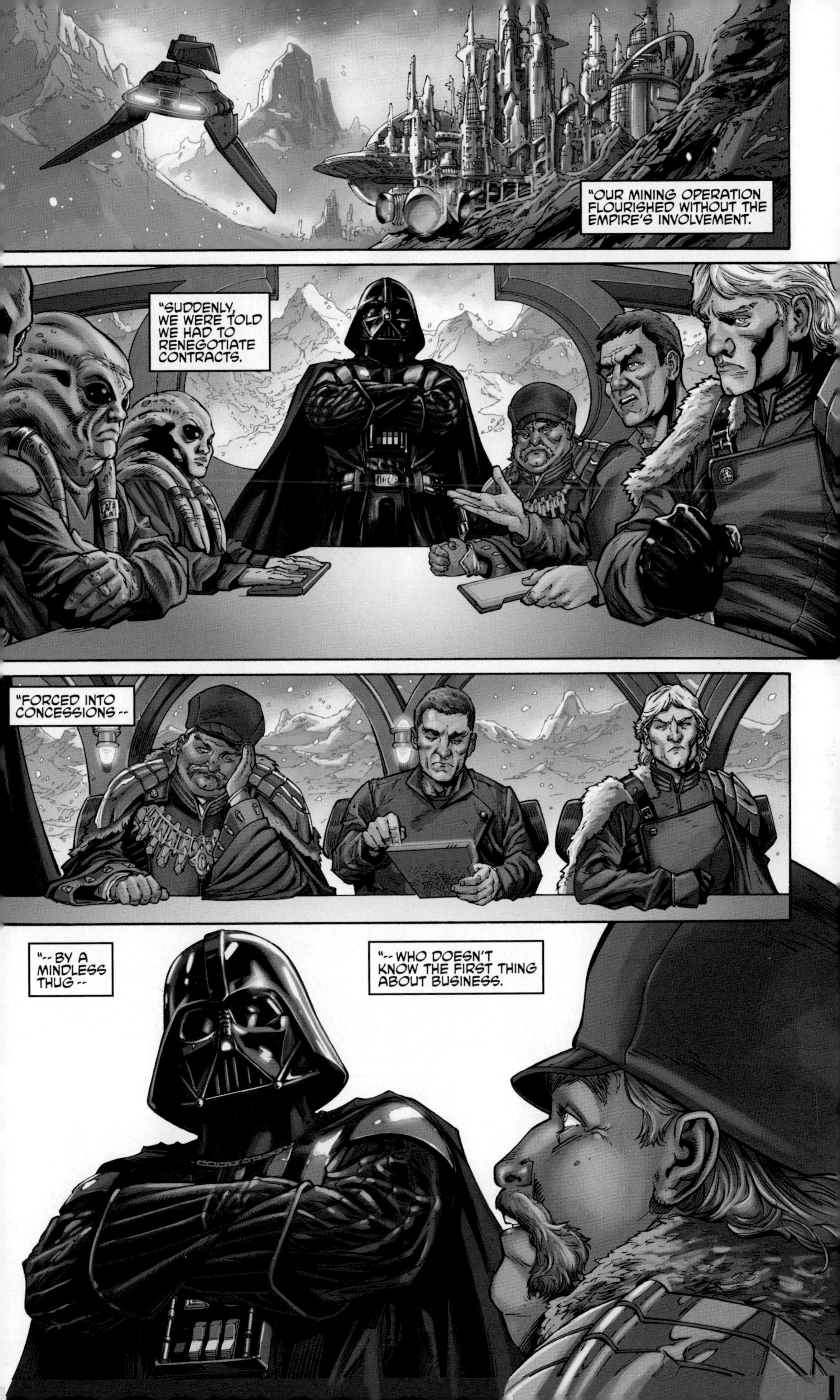
"OUR MINING OPERATION FLOURISHED WITHOUT THE EMPIRE'S INVOLVEMENT.
"SUDDENLY, WE WERE TOLD WE HAD TO RENEGOTIATE CONTRACTS.
"FORCED INTO CONCESSIONS --
"-- BY A MINDLESS THUG --
"-- WHO DOESN'T KNOW THE FIRST THING ABOUT BUSINESS.

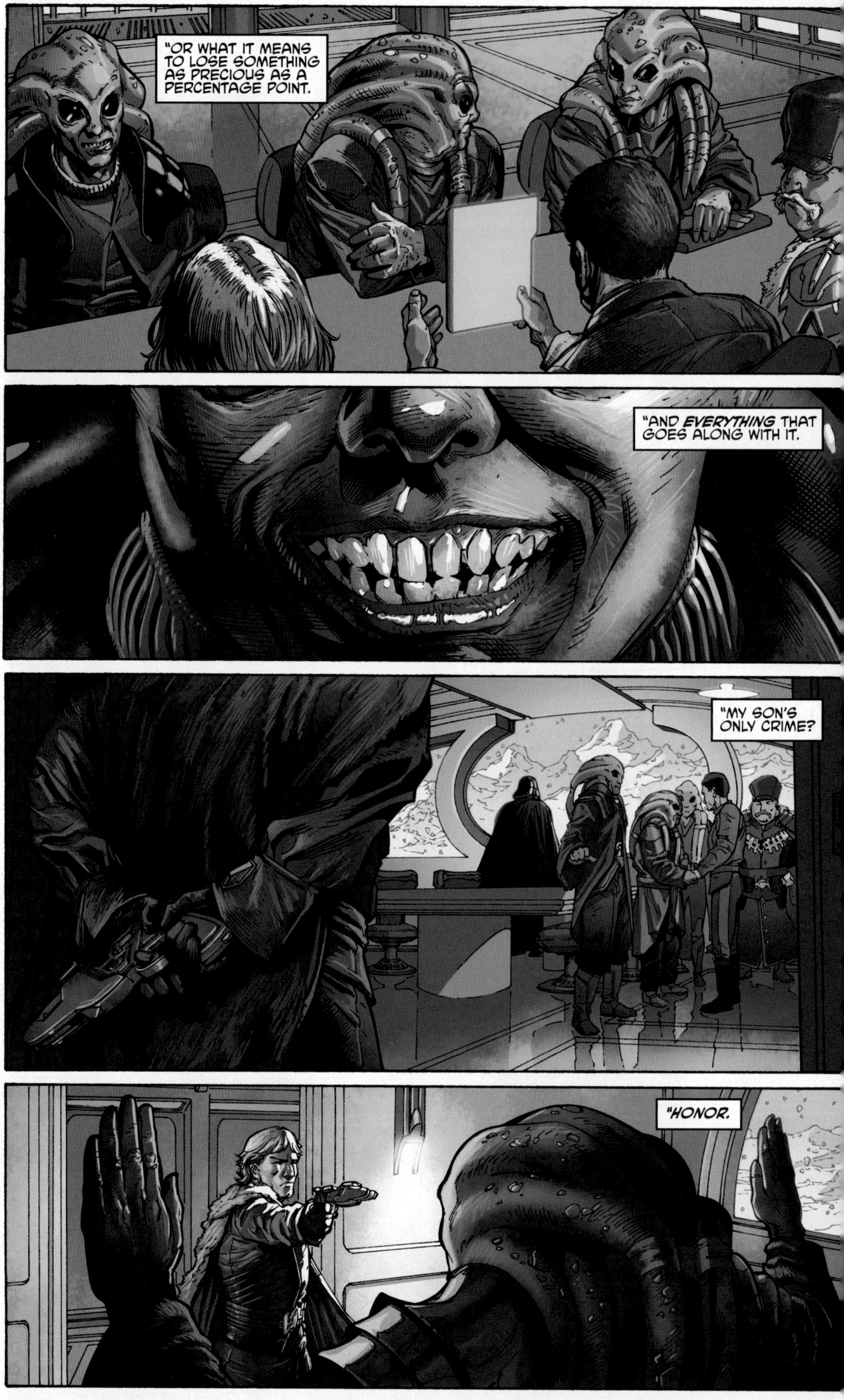
"OR WHAT IT MEANS TO LOSE SOMETHING AS PRECIOUS AS A PERCENTAGE POINT.
"AND *EVERYTHING* THAT GOES ALONG WITH IT.
"MY SON'S ONLY CRIME?
"HONOR.

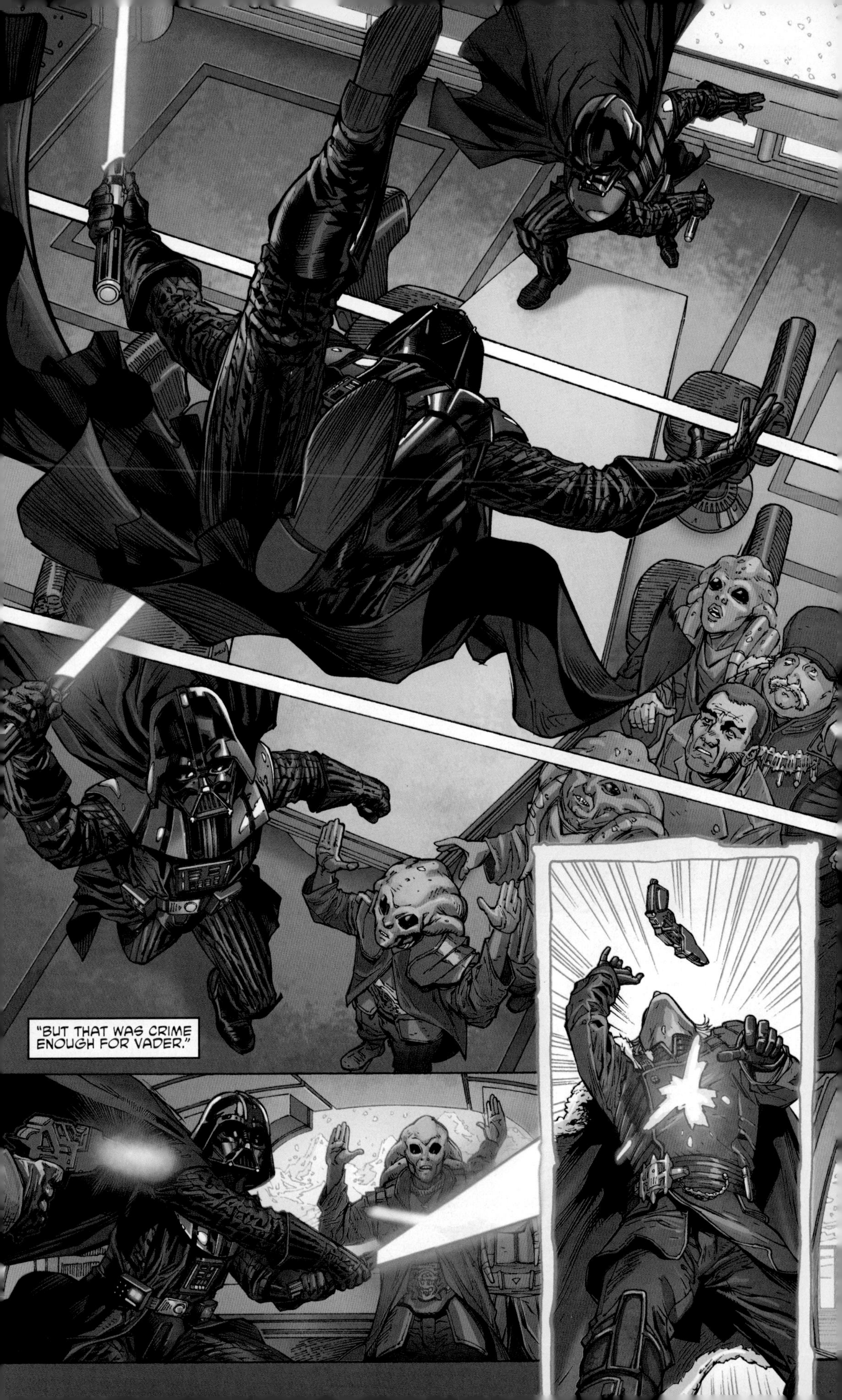
"BUT THAT WAS CRIME ENOUGH FOR VADER."

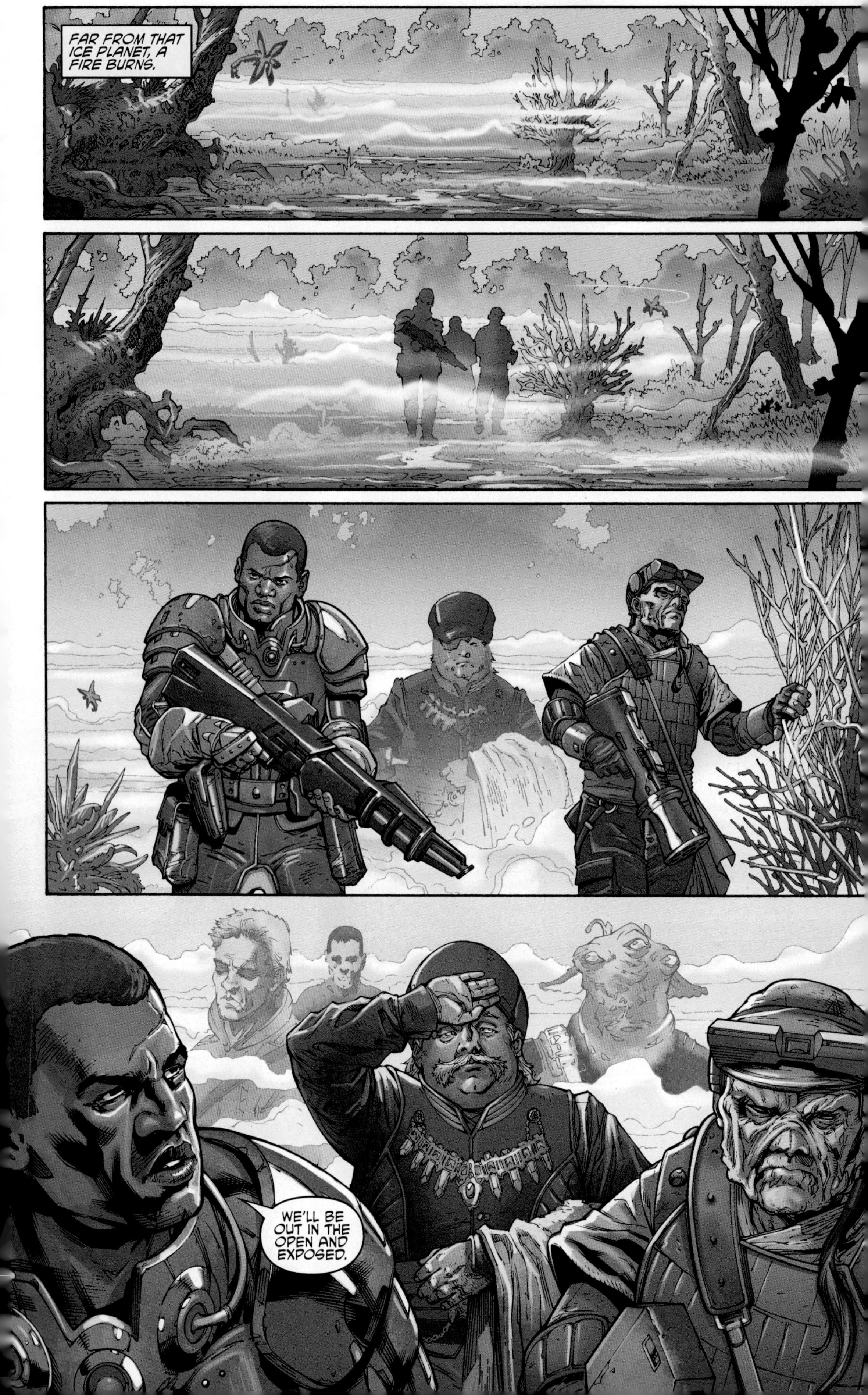
FAR FROM THAT ICE PLANET, A FIRE BURNS.
WE'LL BE OUT IN THE OPEN AND EXPOSED.

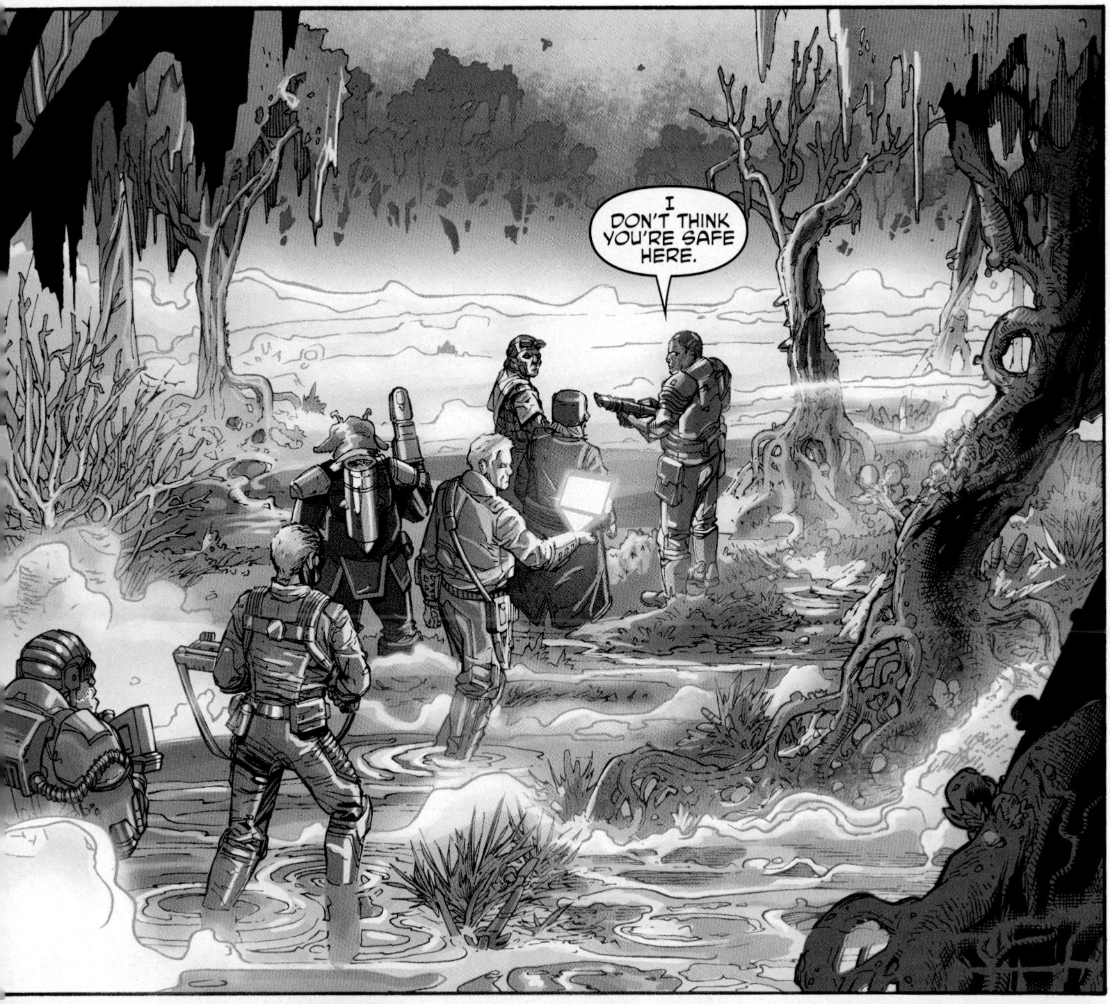
I DON'T THINK YOU'RE SAFE HERE.

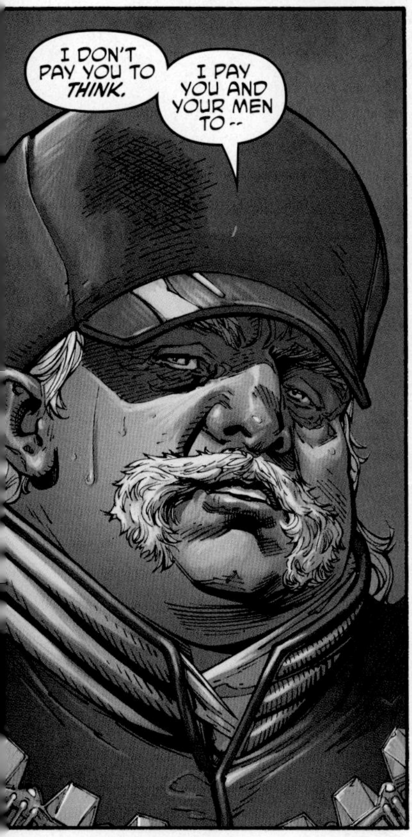
I DON'T PAY YOU TO *THINK.*
I PAY YOU AND YOUR MEN TO --

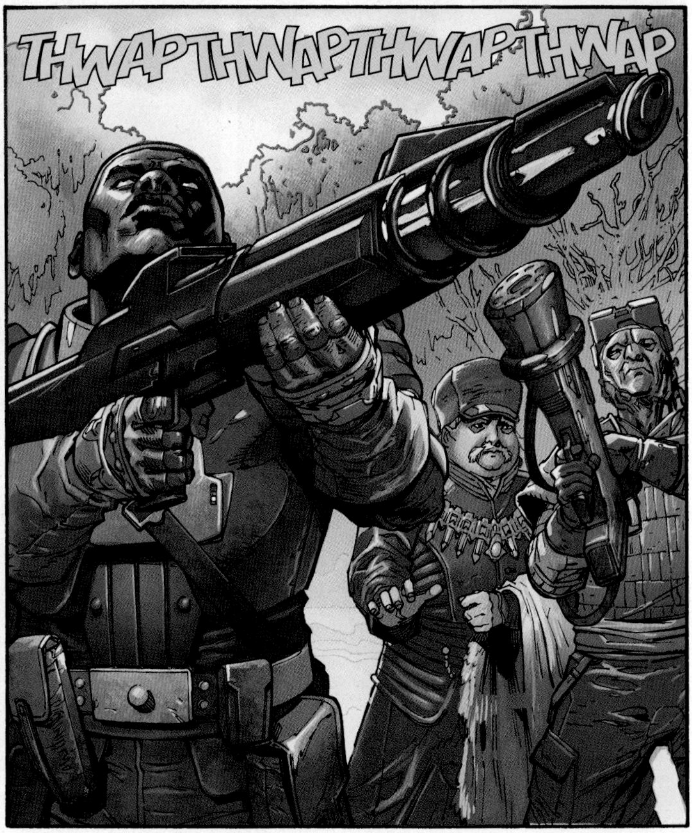
THWAPTHWAPTHWAPTHWAP

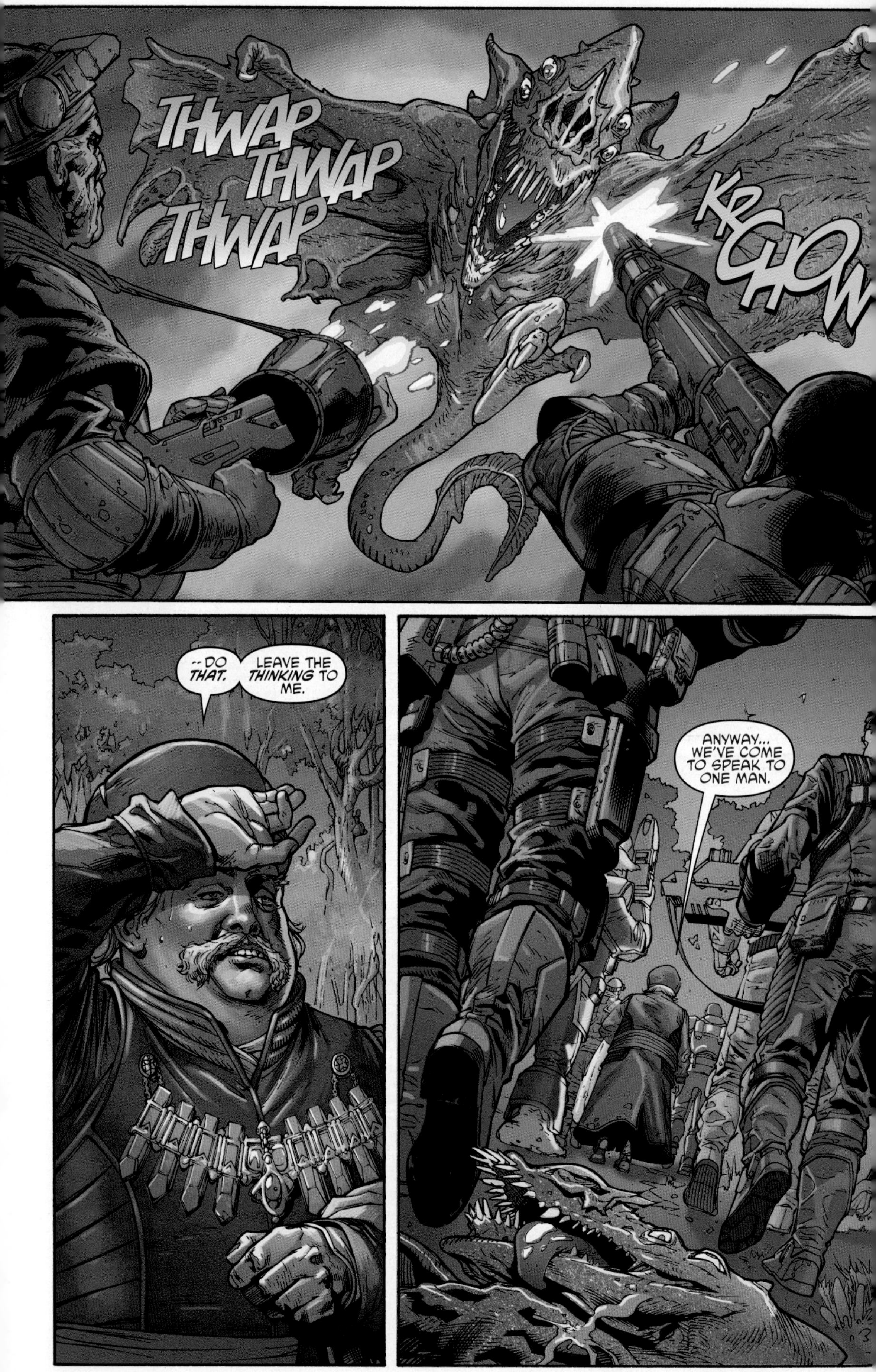
THWAP THWAP THWAP
KRCHOW
--DO *THAT.*
LEAVE THE *THINKING* TO ME.
ANYWAY... WE'VE COME TO SPEAK TO ONE MAN.

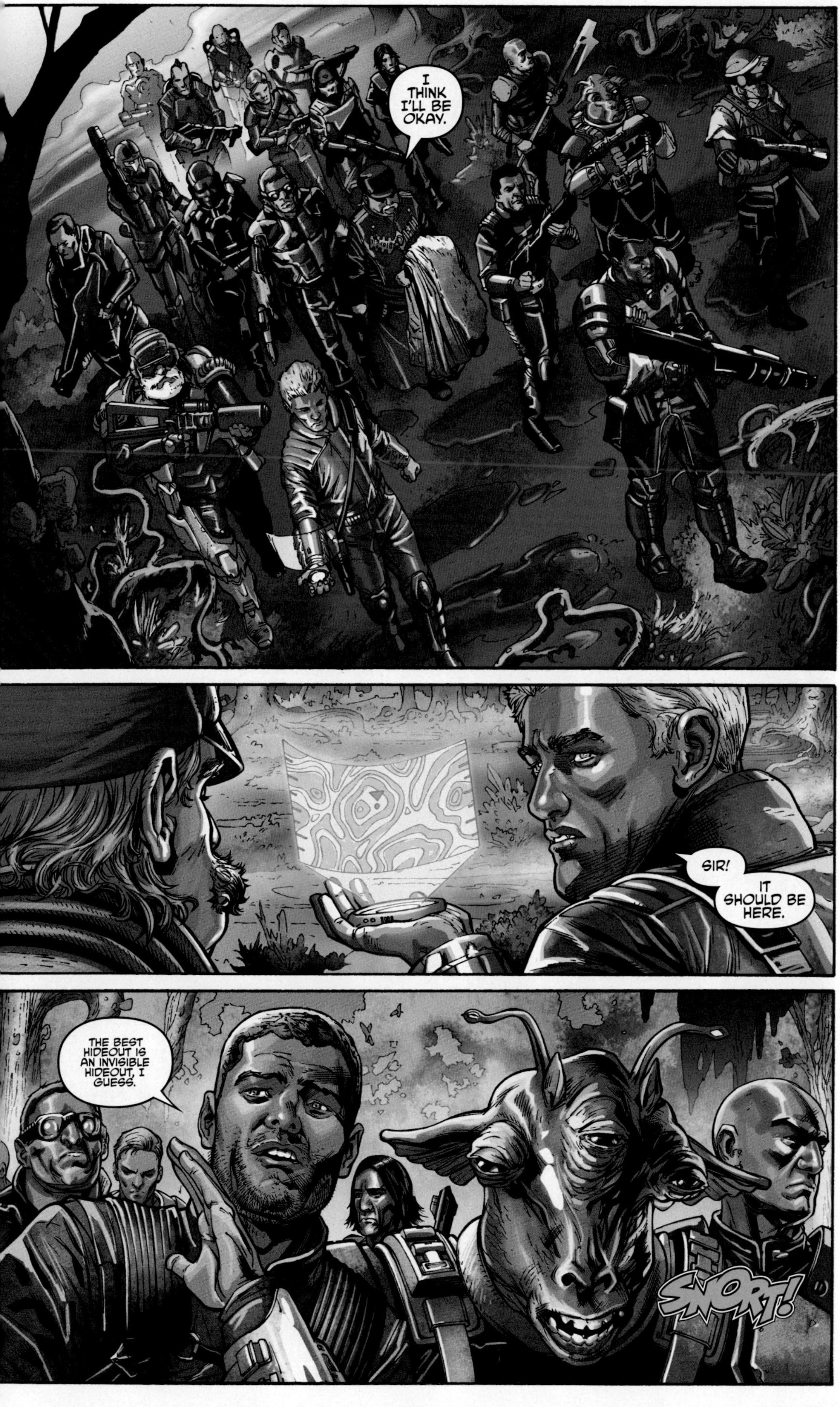
I THINK I'LL BE OKAY.
SIR!
IT SHOULD BE HERE.
THE BEST HIDEOUT IS AN INVISIBLE HIDEOUT, I GUESS.
SNORT!

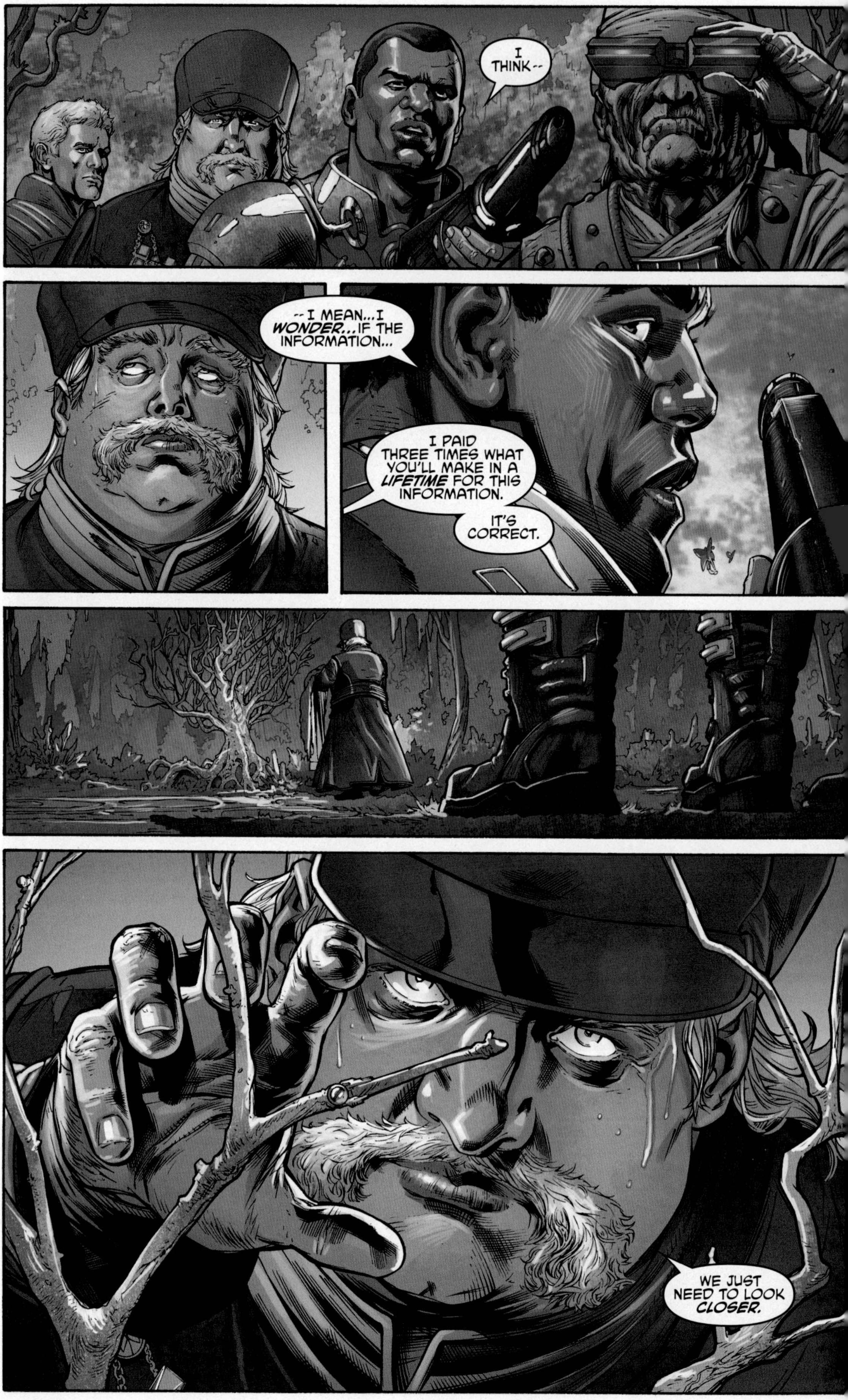
I THINK--
--I MEAN...I WONDER...IF THE INFORMATION...
I PAID THREE TIMES WHAT YOU'LL MAKE IN A LIFETIME FOR THIS INFORMATION.
IT'S CORRECT.
WE JUST NEED TO LOOK CLOSER.

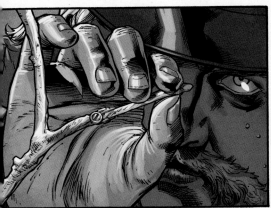
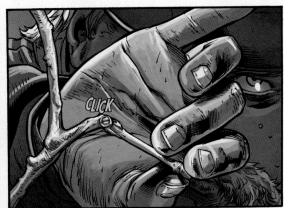

CLICK

QUICKLY.

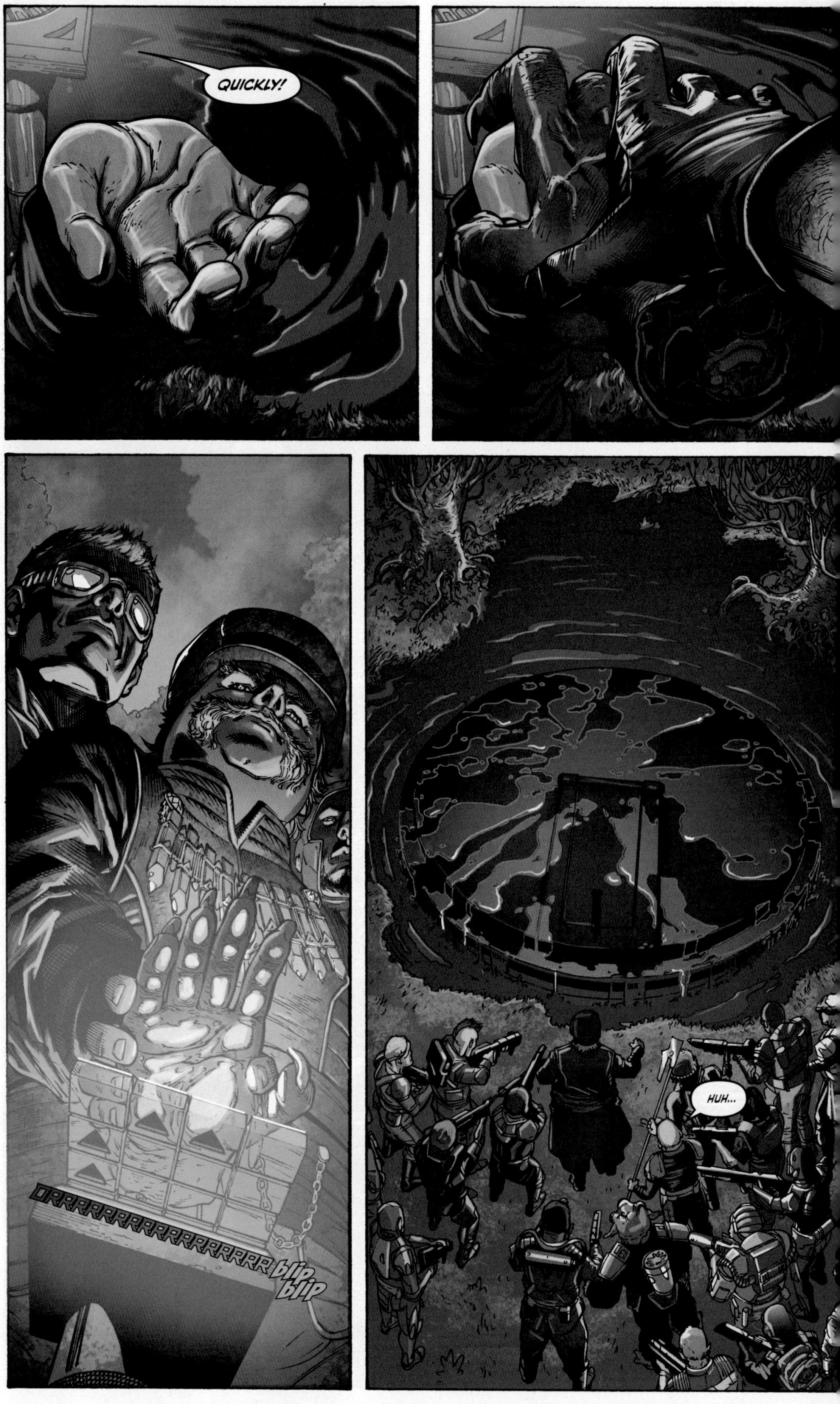
QUICKLY!
DRRRRRRRRRRRRRRRRRRRRRRR
blip blip
HUH...

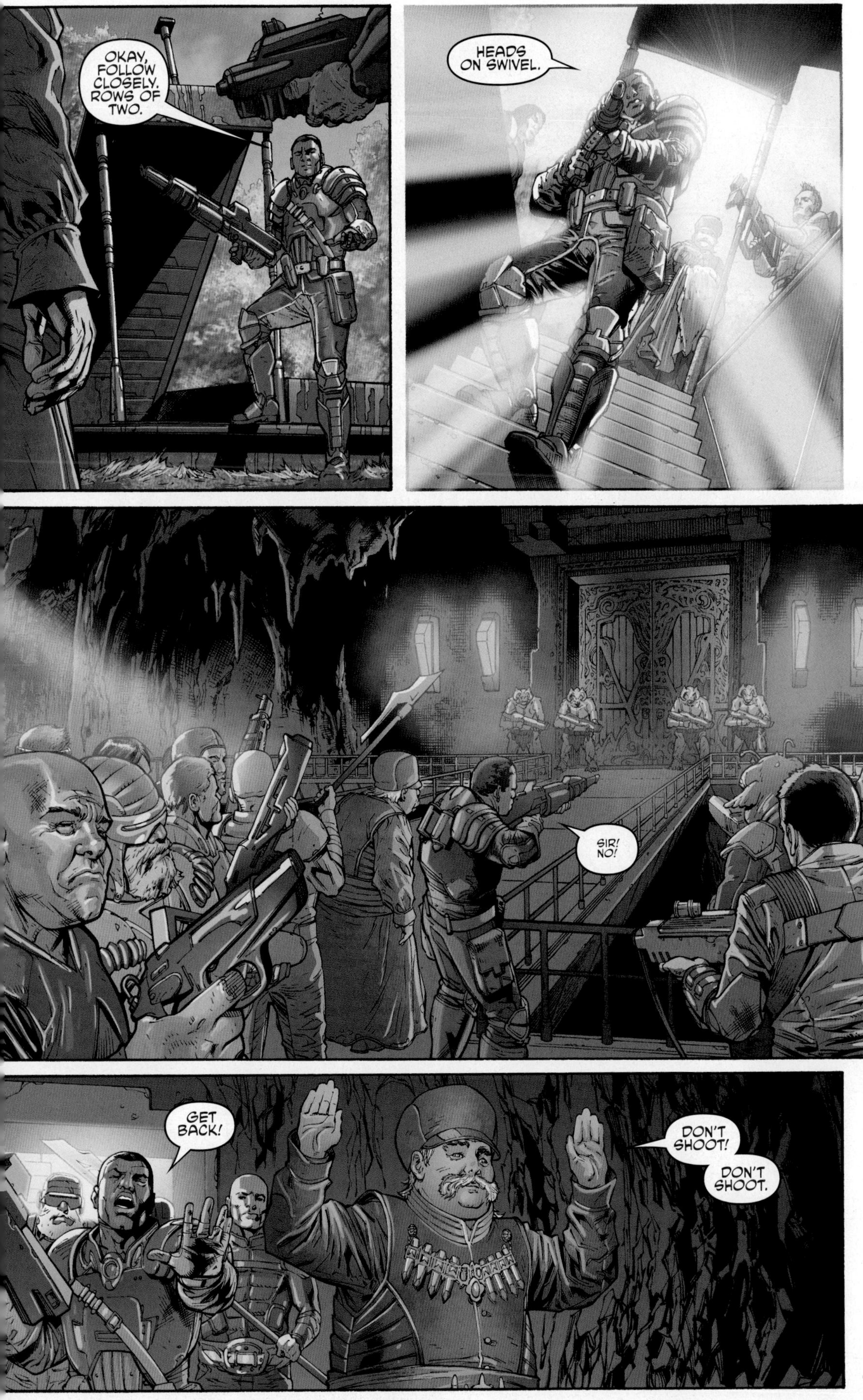
OKAY, FOLLOW CLOSELY. ROWS OF TWO.
HEADS ON SWIVEL.
SIR! NO!
GET BACK!
DON'T SHOOT!
DON'T SHOOT.

I COME SEEKING THE HELP OF YOUR MASTER.

NOBODY COMES TO HIM. HE COMES TO THOSE HE SEEKS.

AND ONLY THEN... AT A HIGH PRICE.

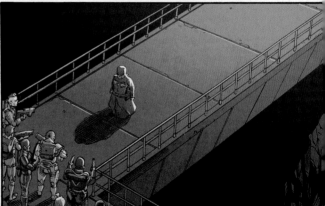

BADOW BADOW BADOW BADOW BADOW BADOW BADOW BADOW BADOW BADOW

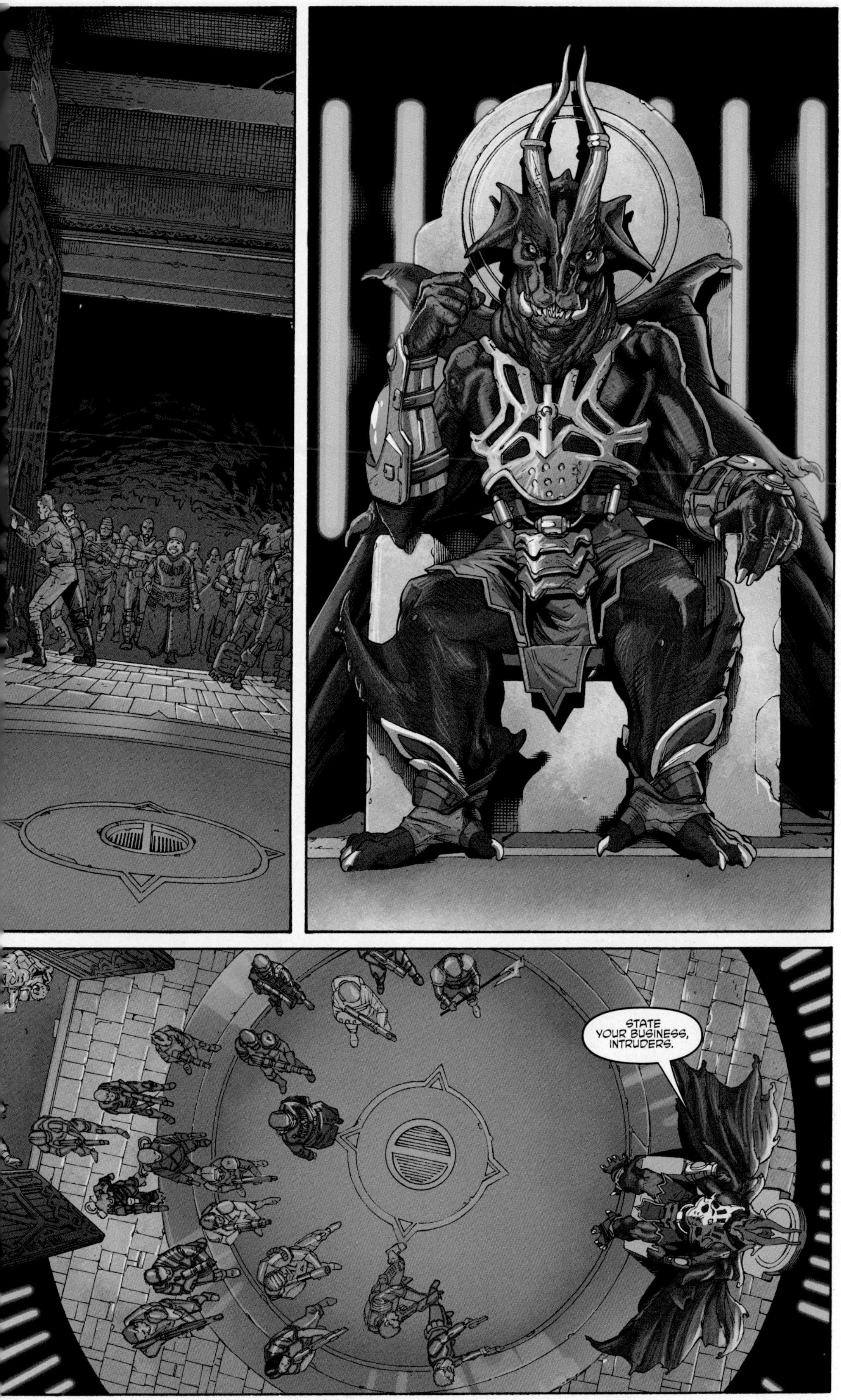
STATE YOUR BUSINESS, INTRUDERS.

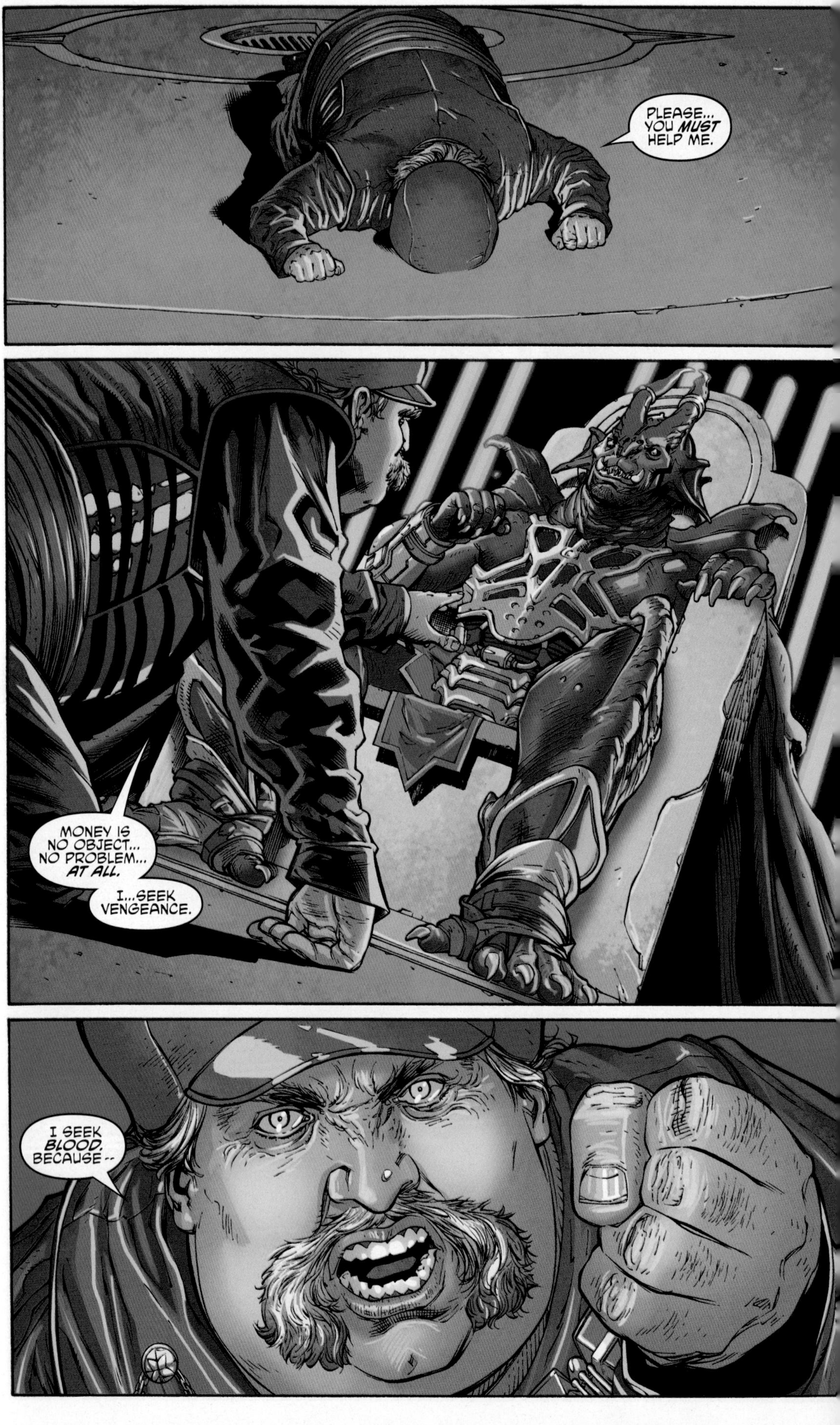
PLEASE... YOU *MUST* HELP ME.
MONEY IS NO OBJECT... NO PROBLEM... *AT ALL.*
I...SEEK VENGEANCE.
I SEEK *BLOOD.* BECAUSE--

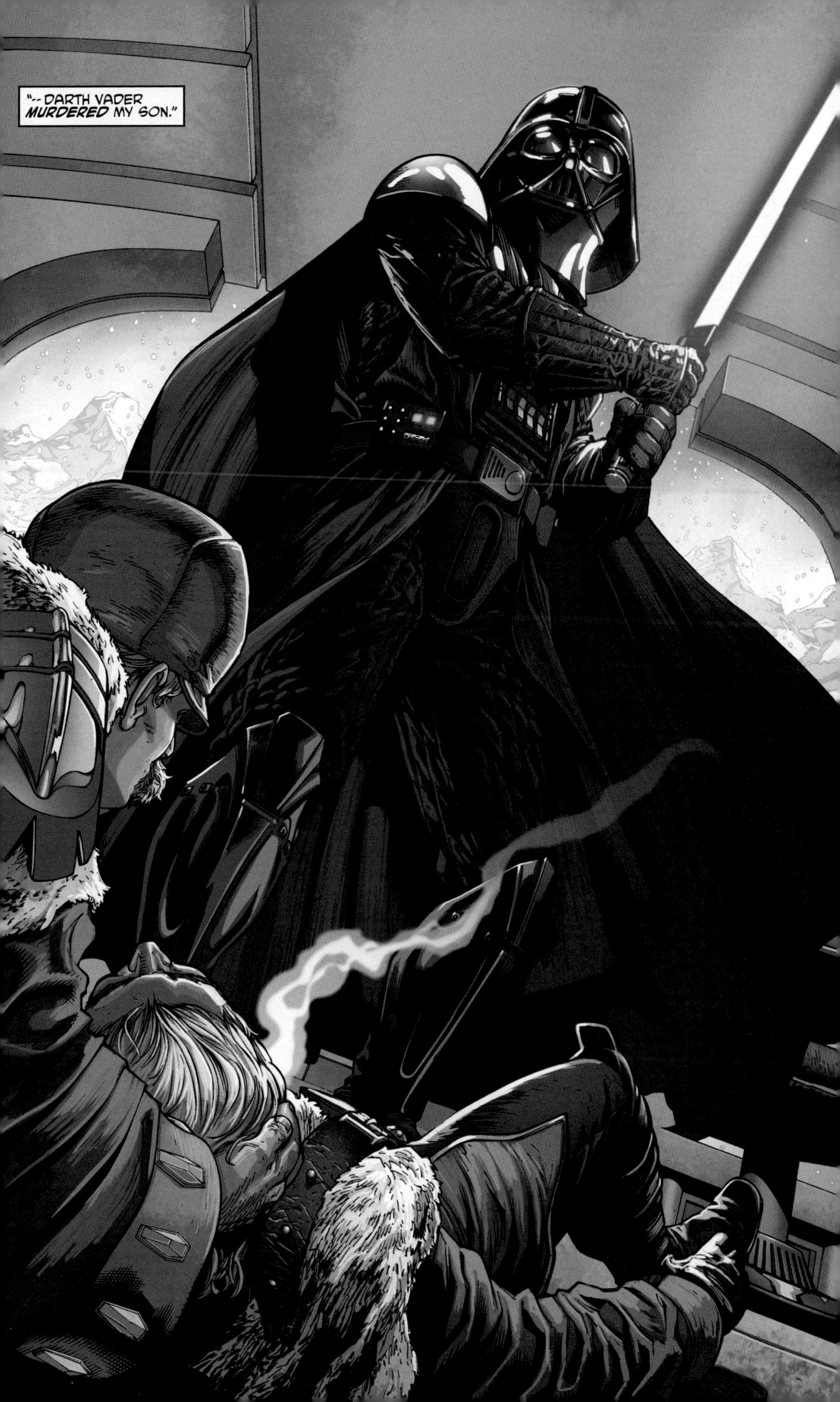
"-- DARTH VADER MURDERED MY SON."

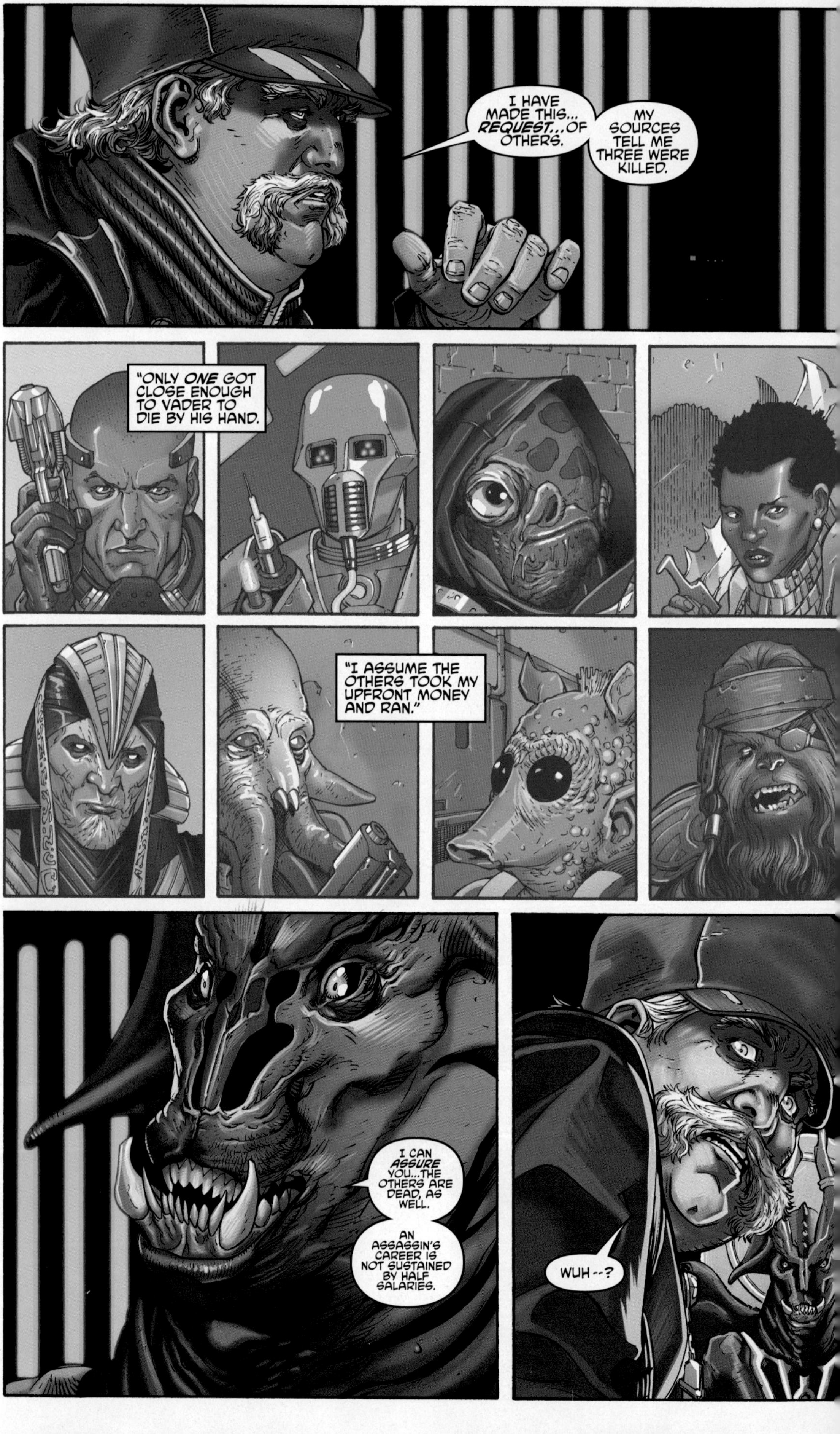
I HAVE MADE THIS... REQUEST... OF OTHERS.
MY SOURCES TELL ME THREE WERE KILLED.
"ONLY ONE GOT CLOSE ENOUGH TO VADER TO DIE BY HIS HAND.
"I ASSUME THE OTHERS TOOK MY UPFRONT MONEY AND RAN."
I CAN ASSURE YOU...THE OTHERS ARE DEAD, AS WELL.
AN ASSASSIN'S CAREER IS NOT SUSTAINED BY HALF SALARIES.
WUH --?

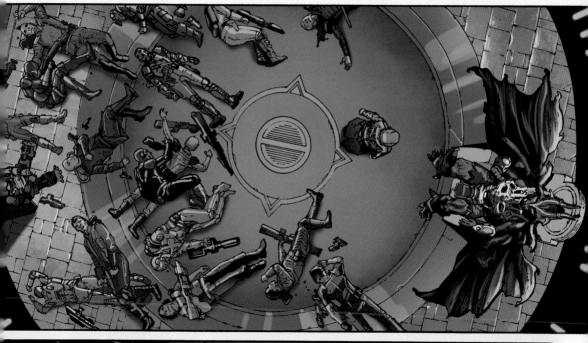

DON'T TURN AROUND.

YOU HAVE PAID A HIGH PRICE FOR COMING HERE.

YOU MAY NOT BE WILLING TO PAY THE PRICE TO SEE ME AND *LEAVE*.

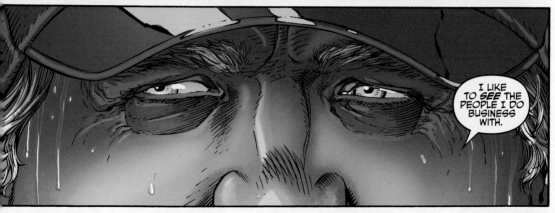

I LIKE TO *SEE* THE PEOPLE I DO BUSINESS WITH.

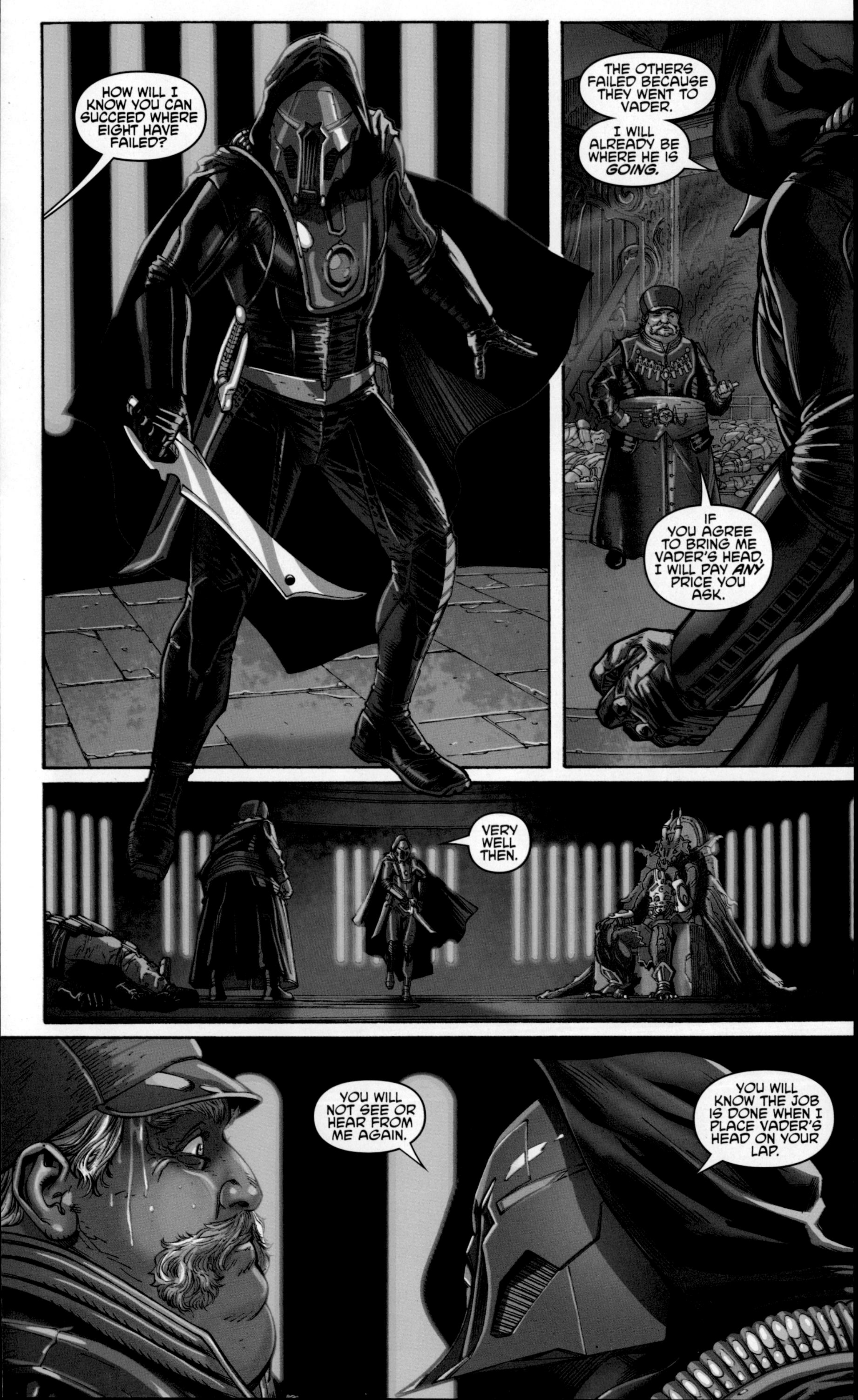
HOW WILL I KNOW YOU CAN SUCCEED WHERE EIGHT HAVE FAILED?
THE OTHERS FAILED BECAUSE THEY WENT TO VADER.
I WILL ALREADY BE WHERE HE IS GOING.
IF YOU AGREE TO BRING ME VADER'S HEAD, I WILL PAY ANY PRICE YOU ASK.
VERY WELL THEN.
YOU WILL NOT SEE OR HEAR FROM ME AGAIN.
YOU WILL KNOW THE JOB IS DONE WHEN I PLACE VADER'S HEAD ON YOUR LAP.

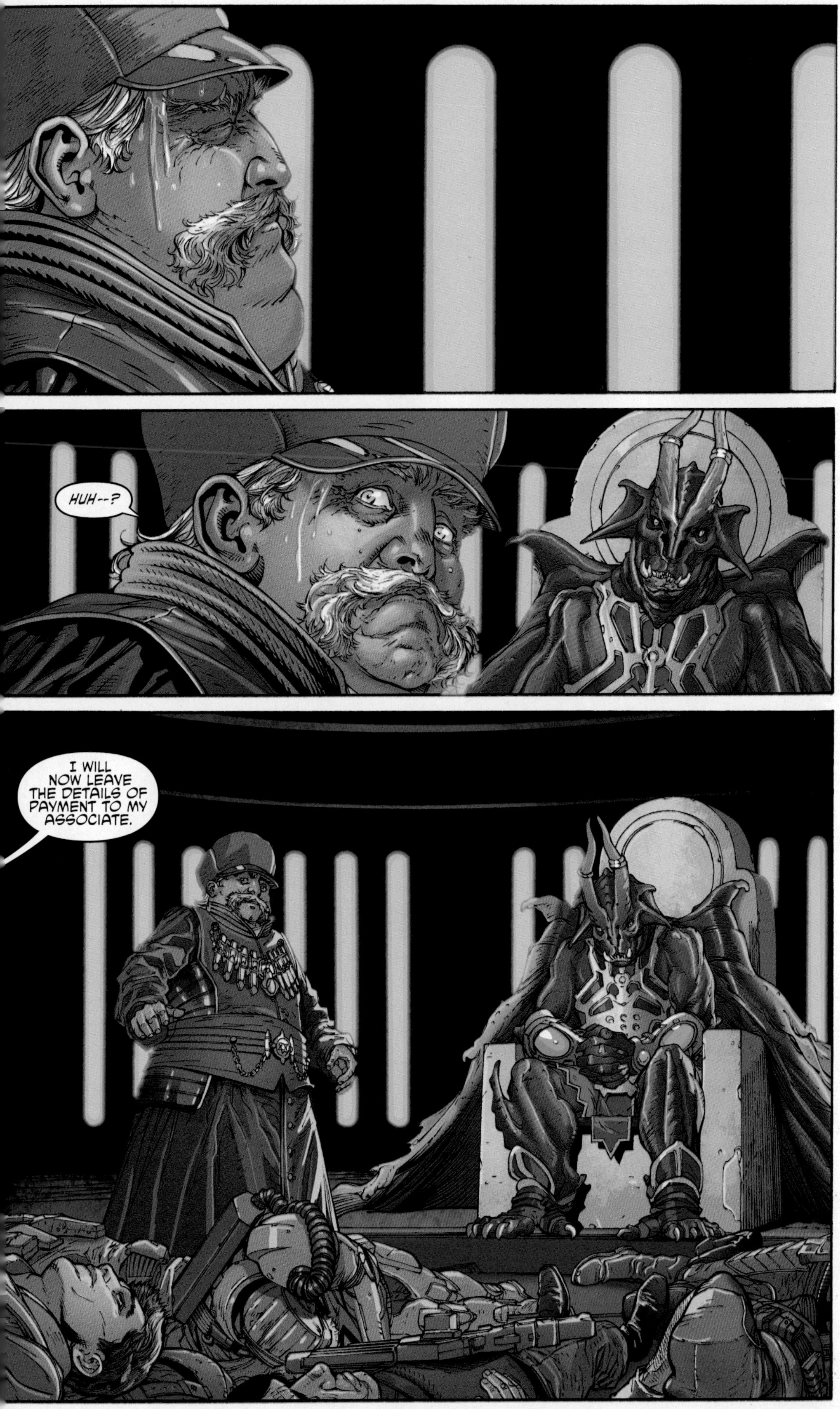
HUH--?
I WILL NOW LEAVE THE DETAILS OF PAYMENT TO MY ASSOCIATE.

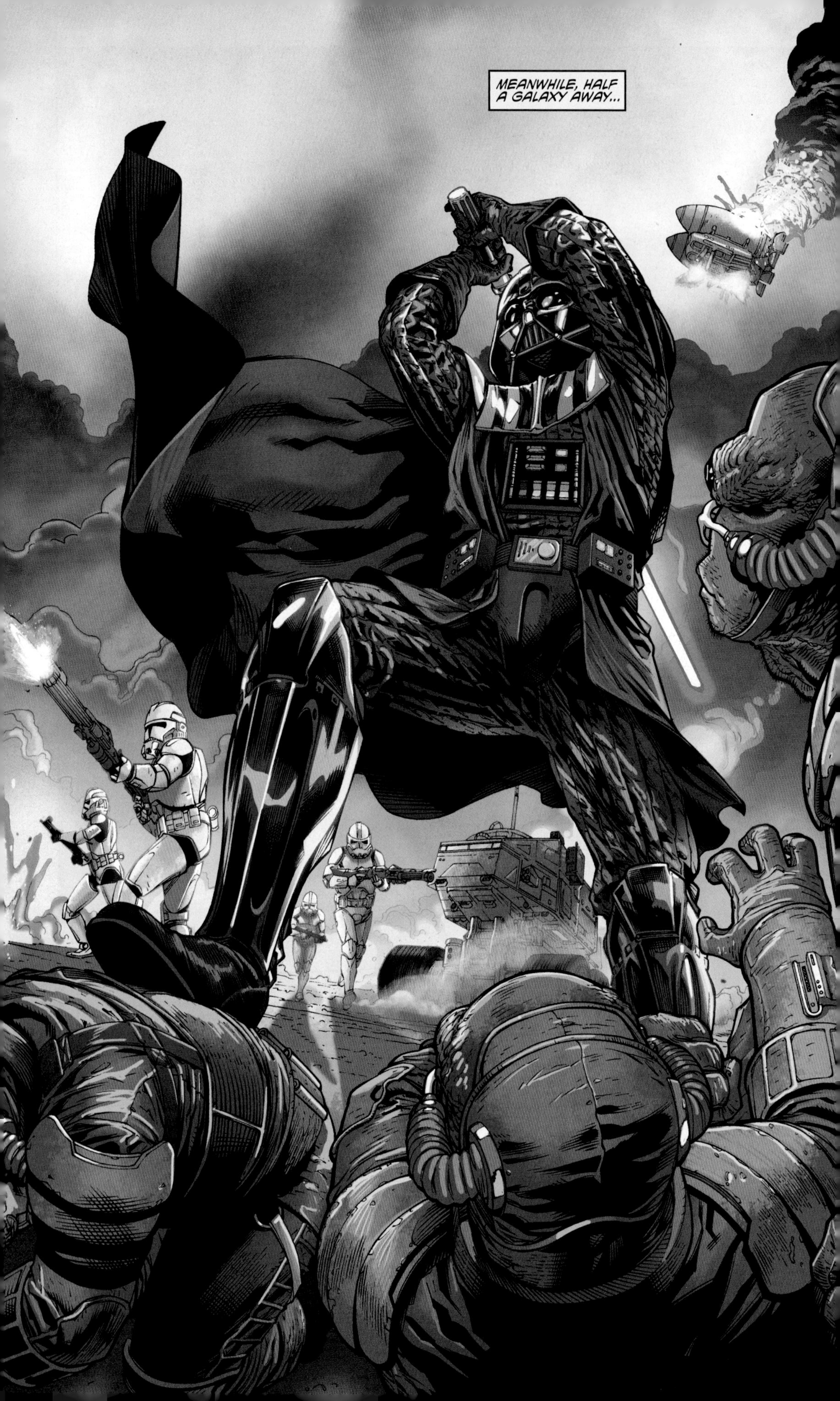
MEANWHILE, HALF A GALAXY AWAY...

DAYS LATER...

SOON, VADER.

VERY SOON.

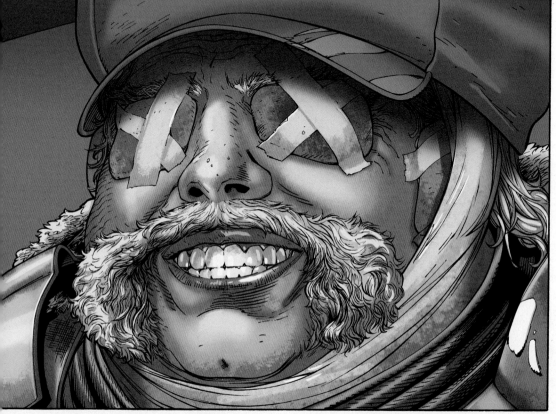

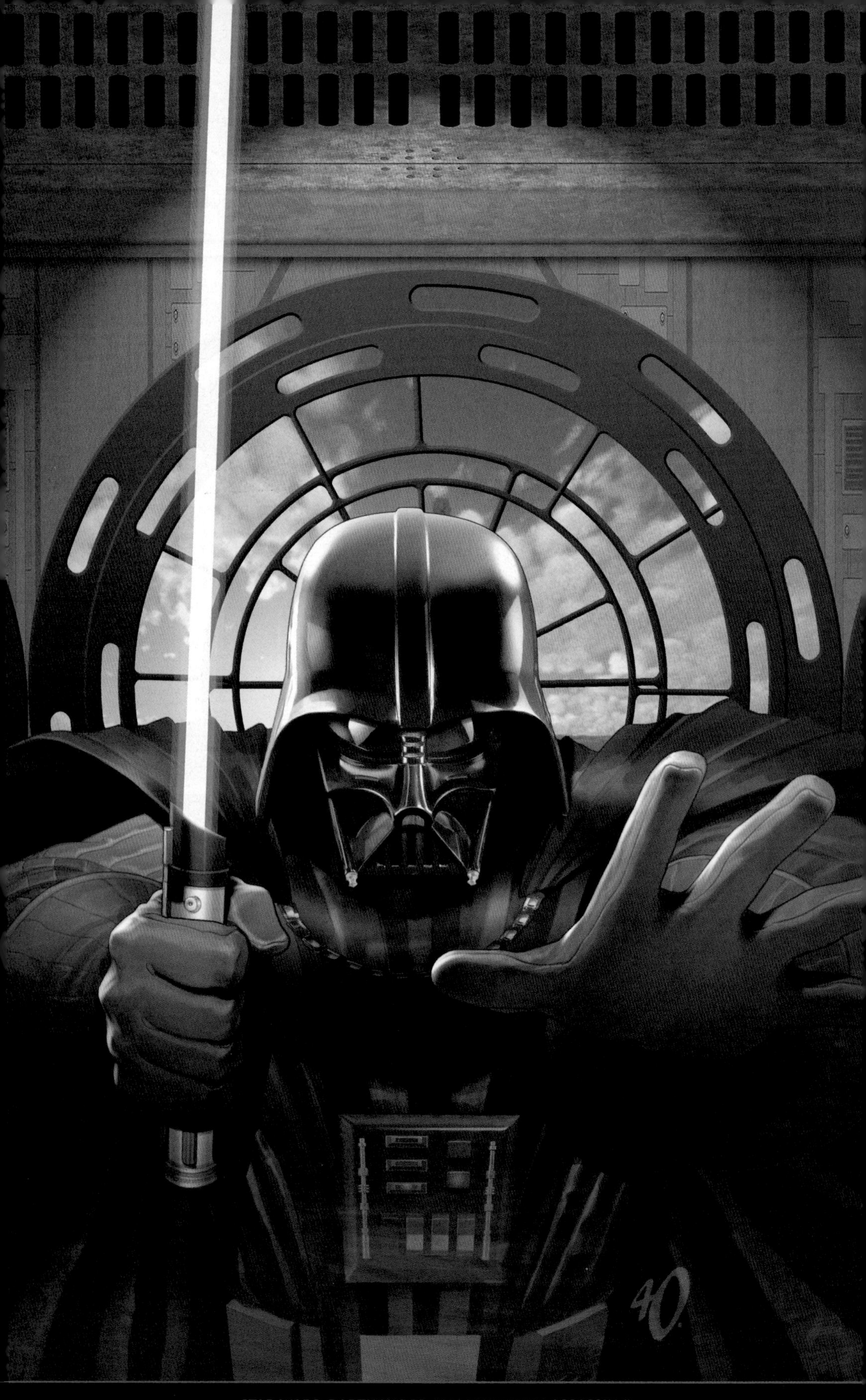

***STAR WARS: DARTH VADER AND THE NINTH ASSASSIN #2***

WRITER: TIM SIEDELL • PENCILER: STEPHEN THOMPSON • INKERS: MARK IRWIN & DREW GERACI • COLORIST: MICHAEL ATIYEH
LETTERER: MICHAEL HEISLER • ASSISTANT EDITOR: FREDDYE LINS • EDITOR: DAVE MARSHALL • CO[illegible]R ARTIST: ARIEL OLIVETTI

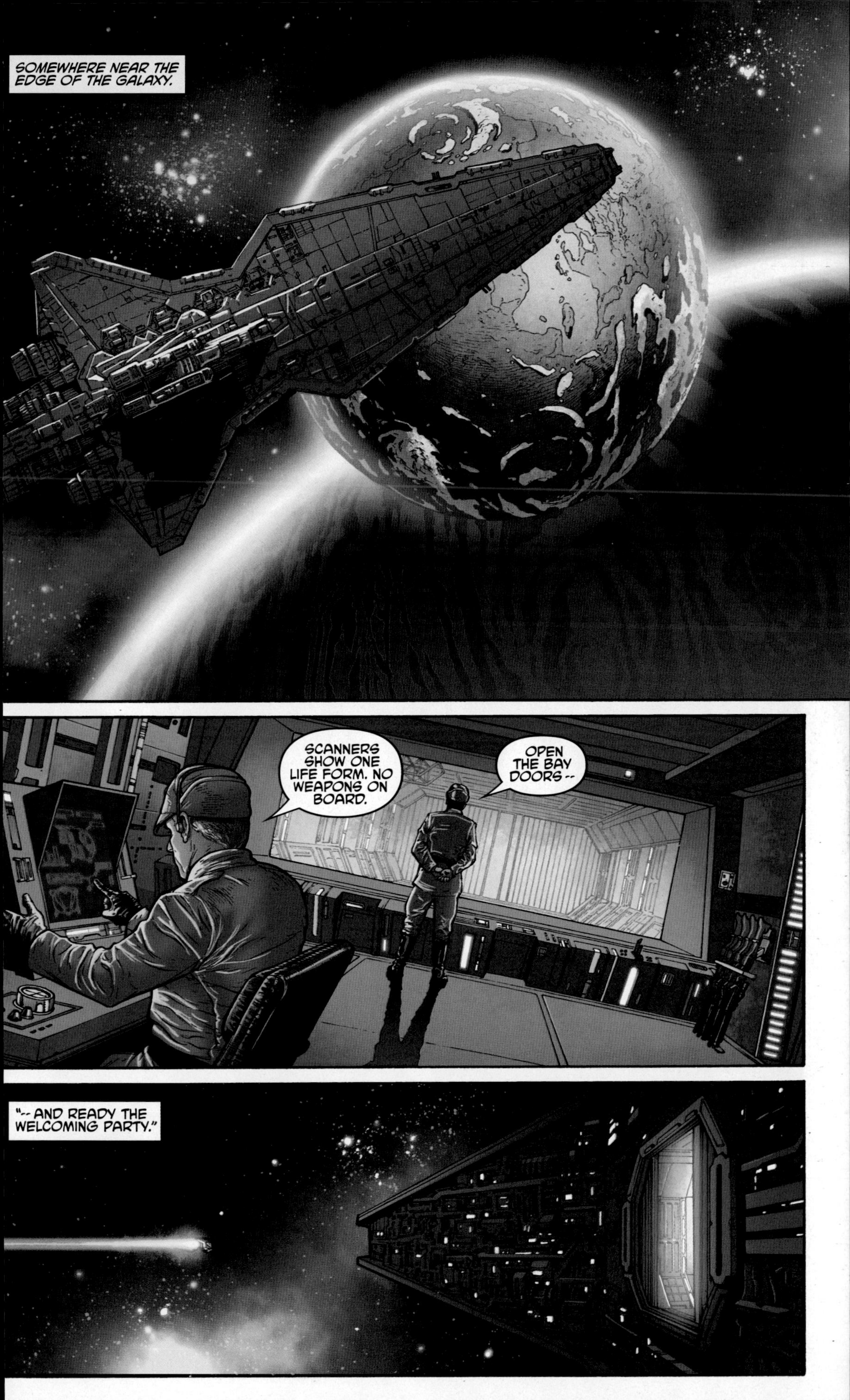
SOMEWHERE NEAR THE EDGE OF THE GALAXY.
SCANNERS SHOW ONE LIFE FORM. NO WEAPONS ON BOARD.
OPEN THE BAY DOORS --
"-- AND READY THE WELCOMING PARTY."

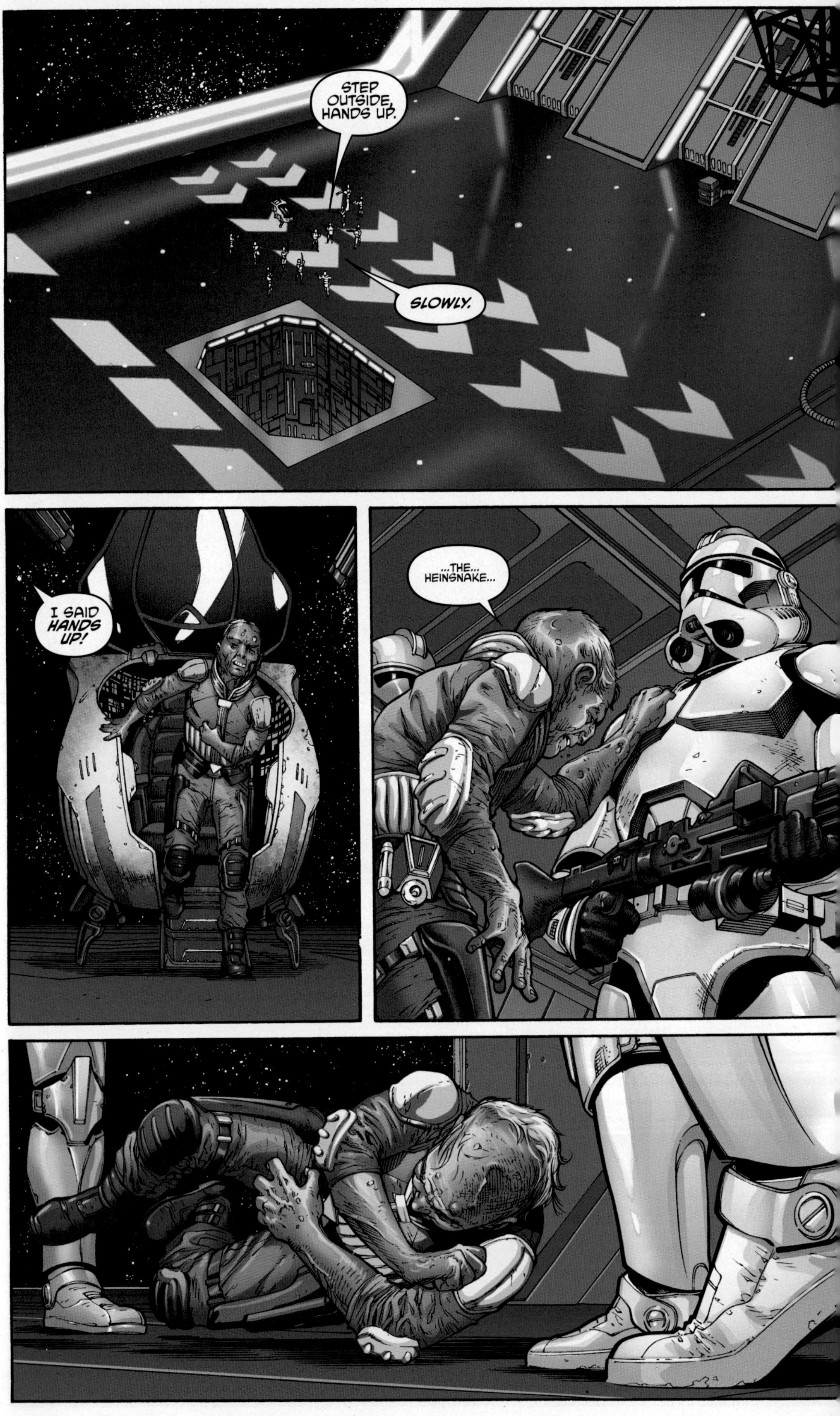
STEP OUTSIDE, HANDS UP.
SLOWLY.
I SAID HANDS UP!
...THE... HEINSNAKE...

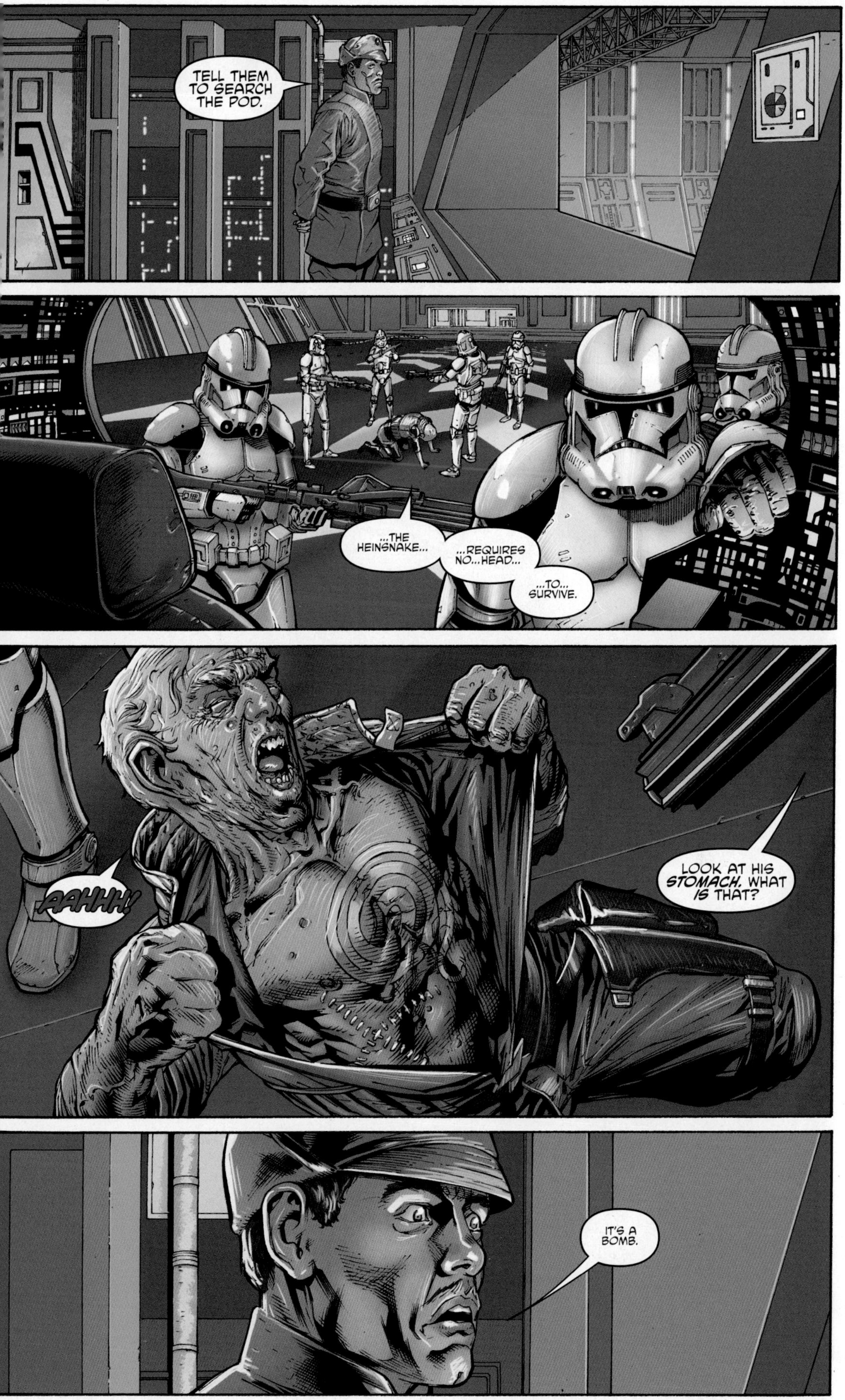
TELL THEM TO SEARCH THE POD.
...THE HEINSNAKE...
...REQUIRES NO...HEAD...
...TO... SURVIVE.
AAHHH!
LOOK AT HIS STOMACH. WHAT IS THAT?
IT'S A BOMB.

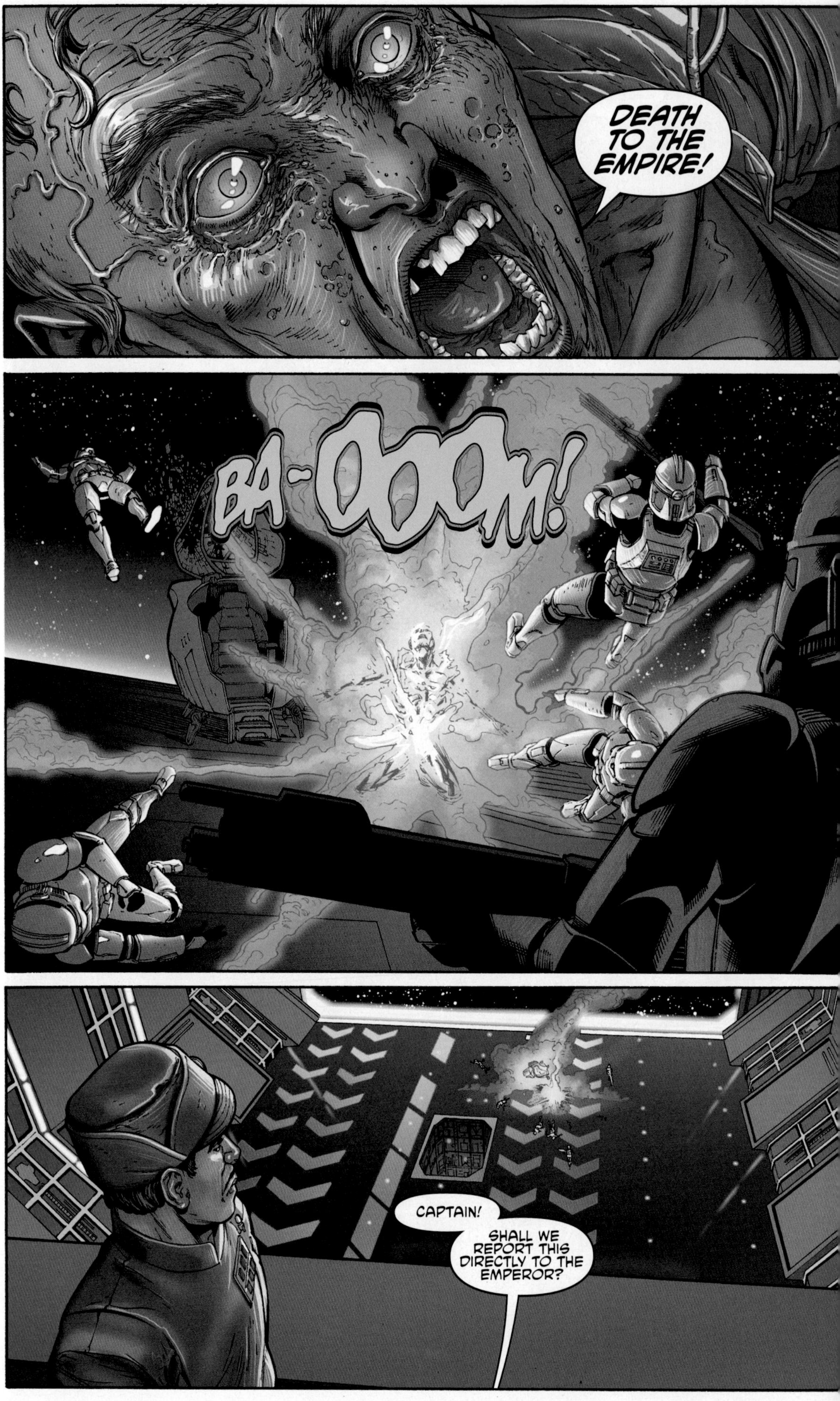
DEATH TO THE EMPIRE!
BA-OOOM!
CAPTAIN!
SHALL WE REPORT THIS DIRECTLY TO THE EMPEROR?

DEPENDS --

-- HOW MANY *BILLION* PODS DO YOU SUPPOSE THESE PEOPLE HAVE?

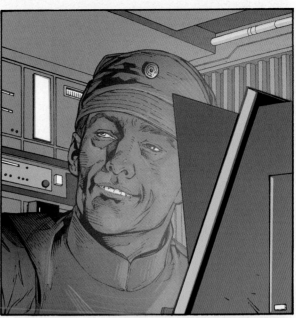

*UH, SIR. THESE READINGS...*

THE POD WAS A HOMING DEVICE.

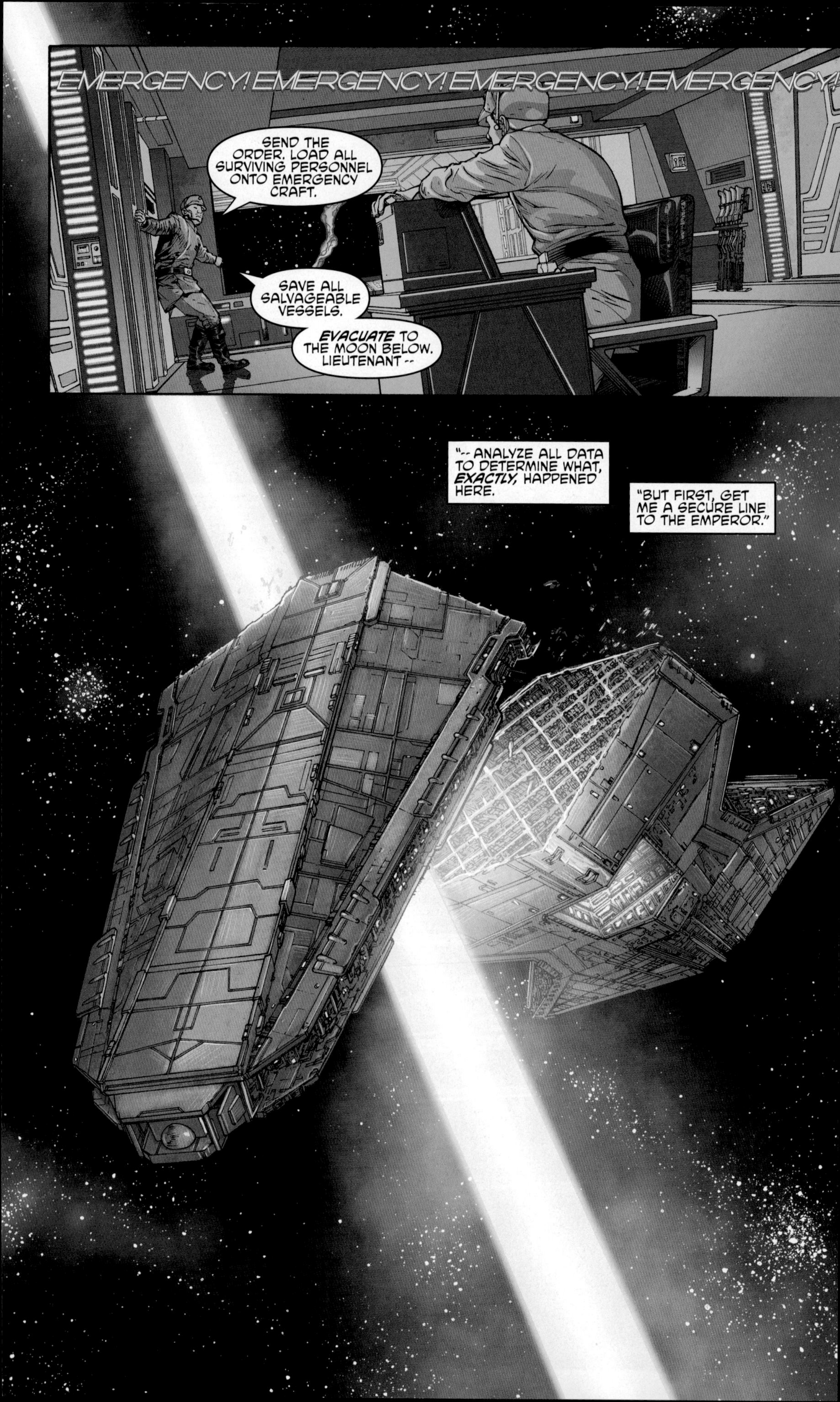
EMERGENCY! EMERGENCY! EMERGENCY! EMERGENCY!
SEND THE ORDER. LOAD ALL SURVIVING PERSONNEL ONTO EMERGENCY CRAFT.
SAVE ALL SALVAGEABLE VESSELS.
EVACUATE TO THE MOON BELOW. LIEUTENANT --
"-- ANALYZE ALL DATA TO DETERMINE WHAT, EXACTLY, HAPPENED HERE.
"BUT FIRST, GET ME A SECURE LINE TO THE EMPEROR."

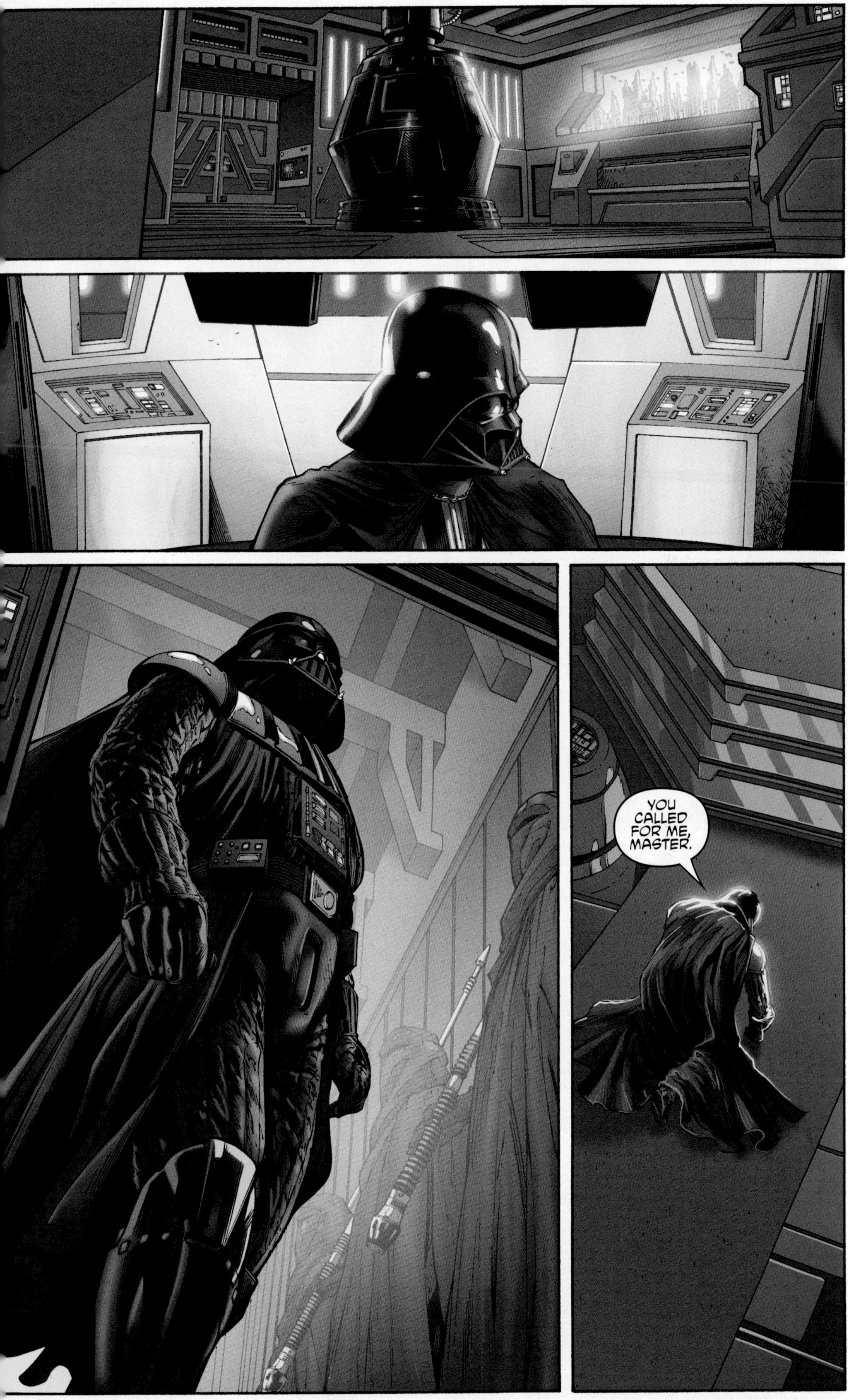
YOU CALLED FOR ME, MASTER.

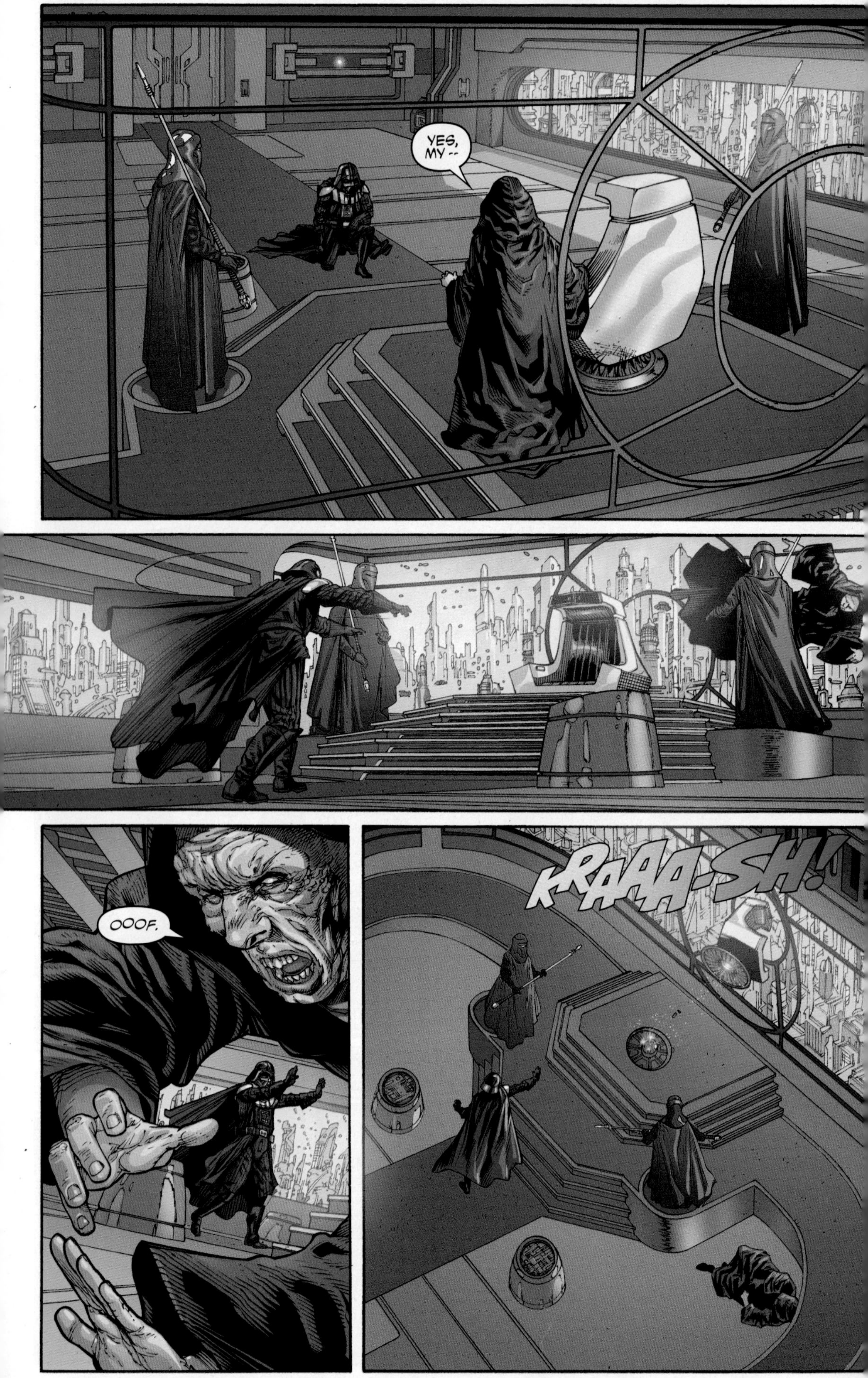
YES, MY --
OOOF.
KRAAA-SH!

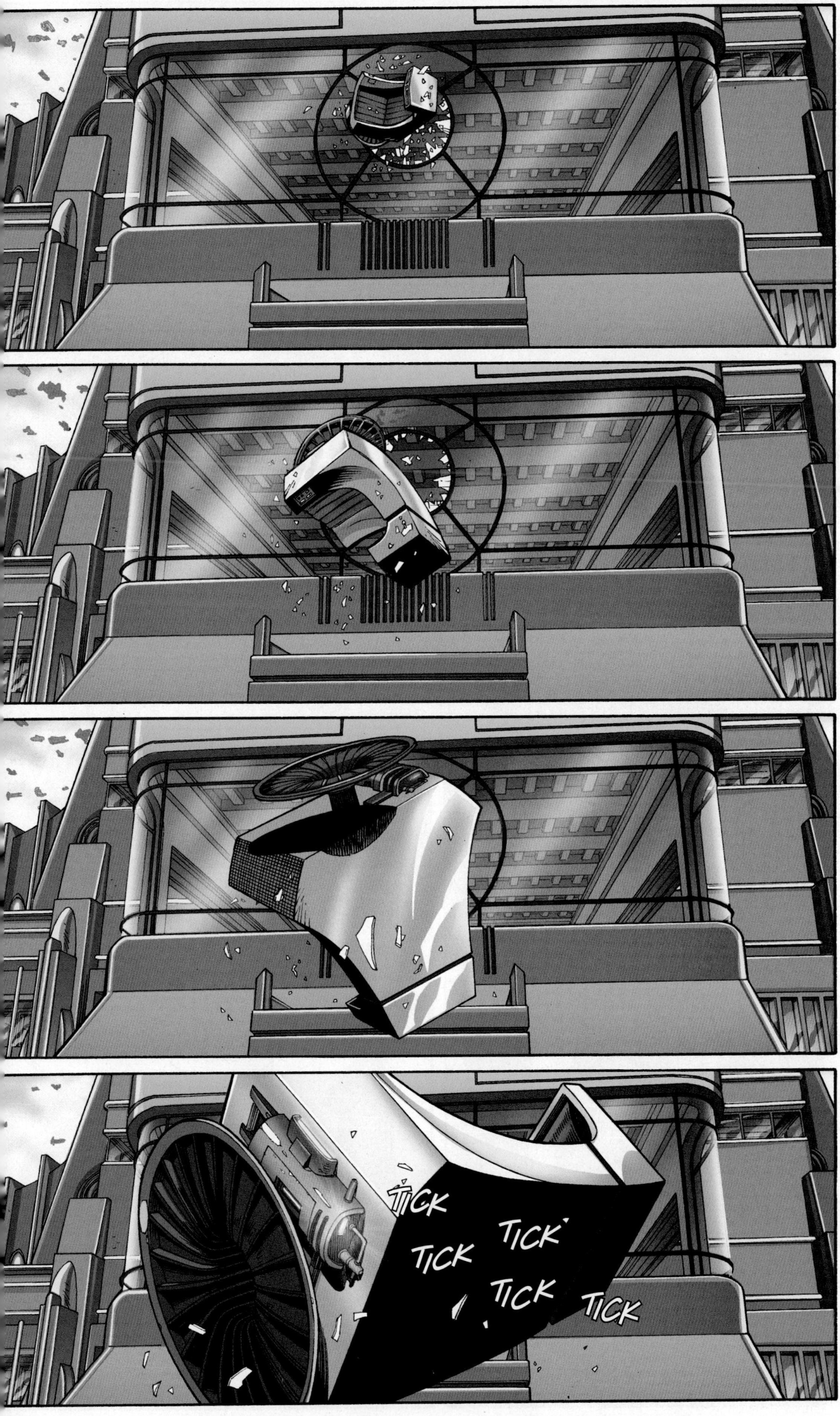
TICK
TICK
TICK
TICK
TICK

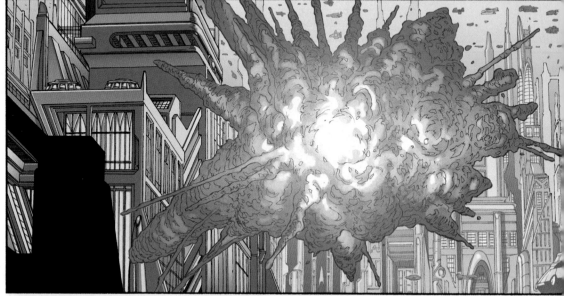

YOU HAVE *FAILED* THE EMPEROR --

-- AND DESERVE TO DIE. *SLOWLY.*

BUT I DON'T HAVE THE LUXURY OF TIME.

NO! NOOOOO...

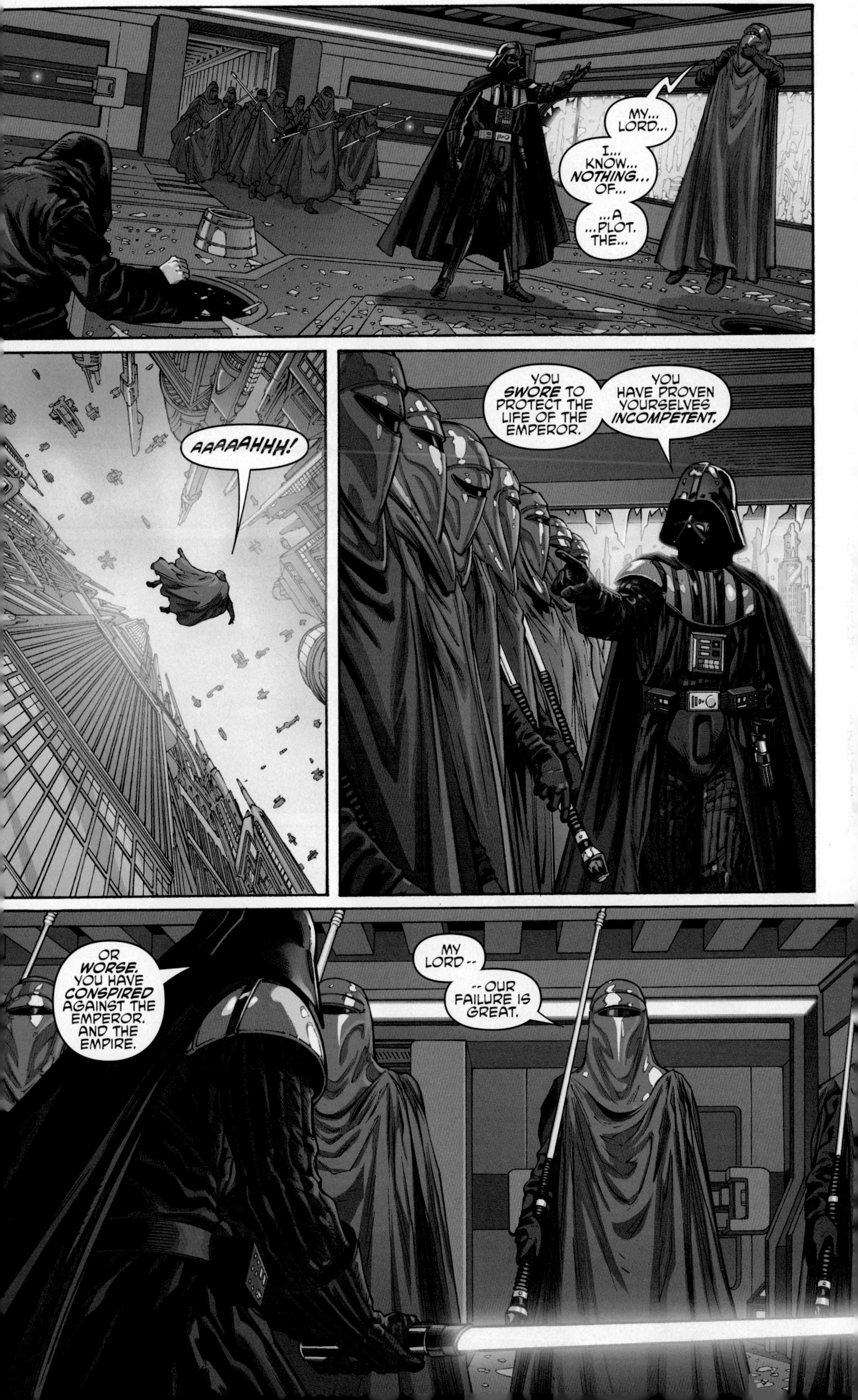
MY... LORD...
I... KNOW... NOTHING... OF...
...A ...PLOT. THE...
AAAAAHHH!
YOU SWORE TO PROTECT THE LIFE OF THE EMPEROR.
YOU HAVE PROVEN YOURSELVES INCOMPETENT.
OR WORSE. YOU HAVE CONSPIRED AGAINST THE EMPEROR. AND THE EMPIRE.
MY LORD --
-- OUR FAILURE IS GREAT.

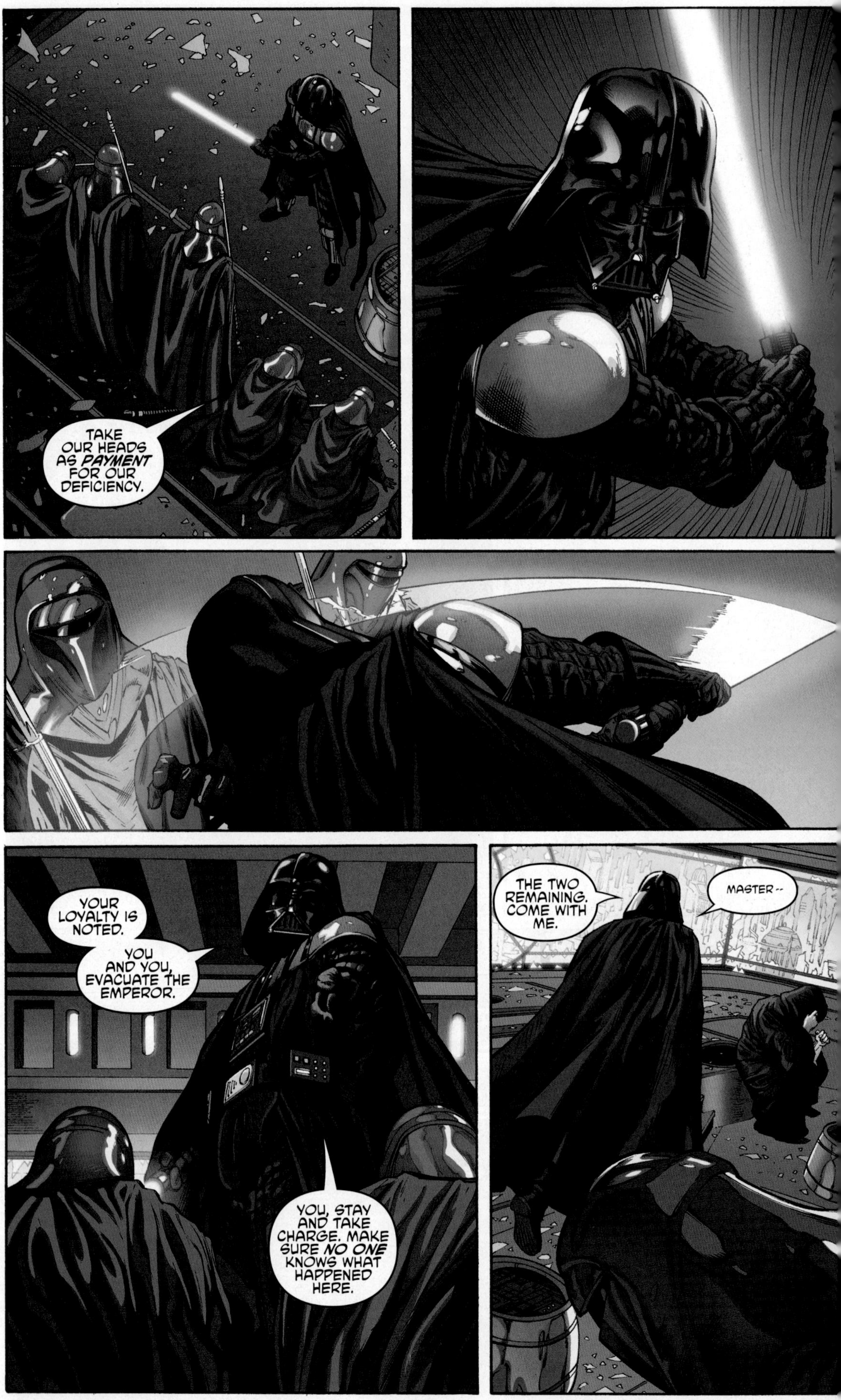
TAKE OUR HEADS AS *PAYMENT* FOR OUR DEFICIENCY.
YOUR LOYALTY IS NOTED.
YOU AND YOU, EVACUATE THE EMPEROR.
YOU, STAY AND TAKE CHARGE. MAKE SURE *NO ONE* KNOWS WHAT HAPPENED HERE.
THE TWO REMAINING. COME WITH ME.
MASTER --

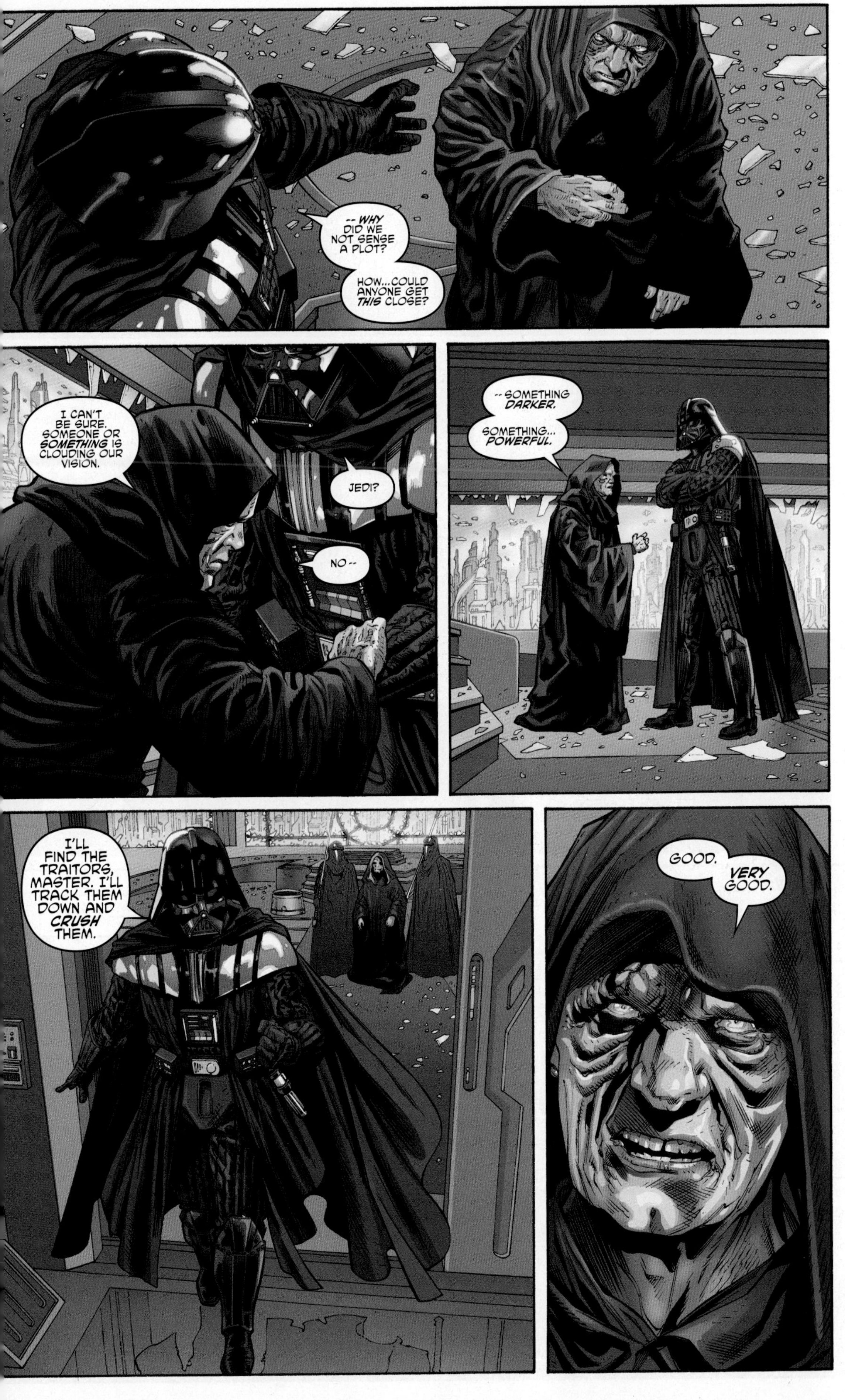
-- WHY DID WE NOT SENSE A PLOT?
HOW...COULD ANYONE GET THIS CLOSE?
I CAN'T BE SURE. SOMEONE OR SOMETHING IS CLOUDING OUR VISION.
JEDI?
NO --
-- SOMETHING DARKER.
SOMETHING... POWERFUL.
I'LL FIND THE TRAITORS, MASTER. I'LL TRACK THEM DOWN AND CRUSH THEM.
GOOD. VERY GOOD.

"BUT BE CAREFUL, LORD VADER.

"YOU ARE DEALING WITH POWERS YOU *DON'T* UNDERSTAND.

"I AWAIT YOUR RETURN --

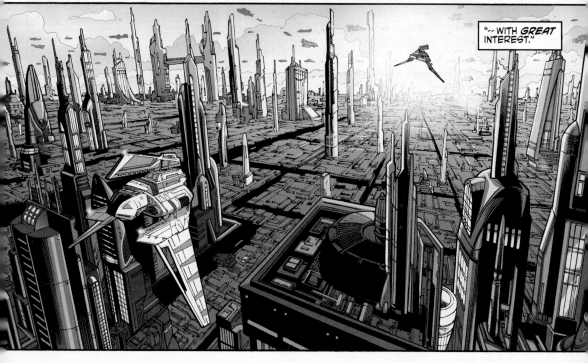

"-- WITH *GREAT* INTEREST."

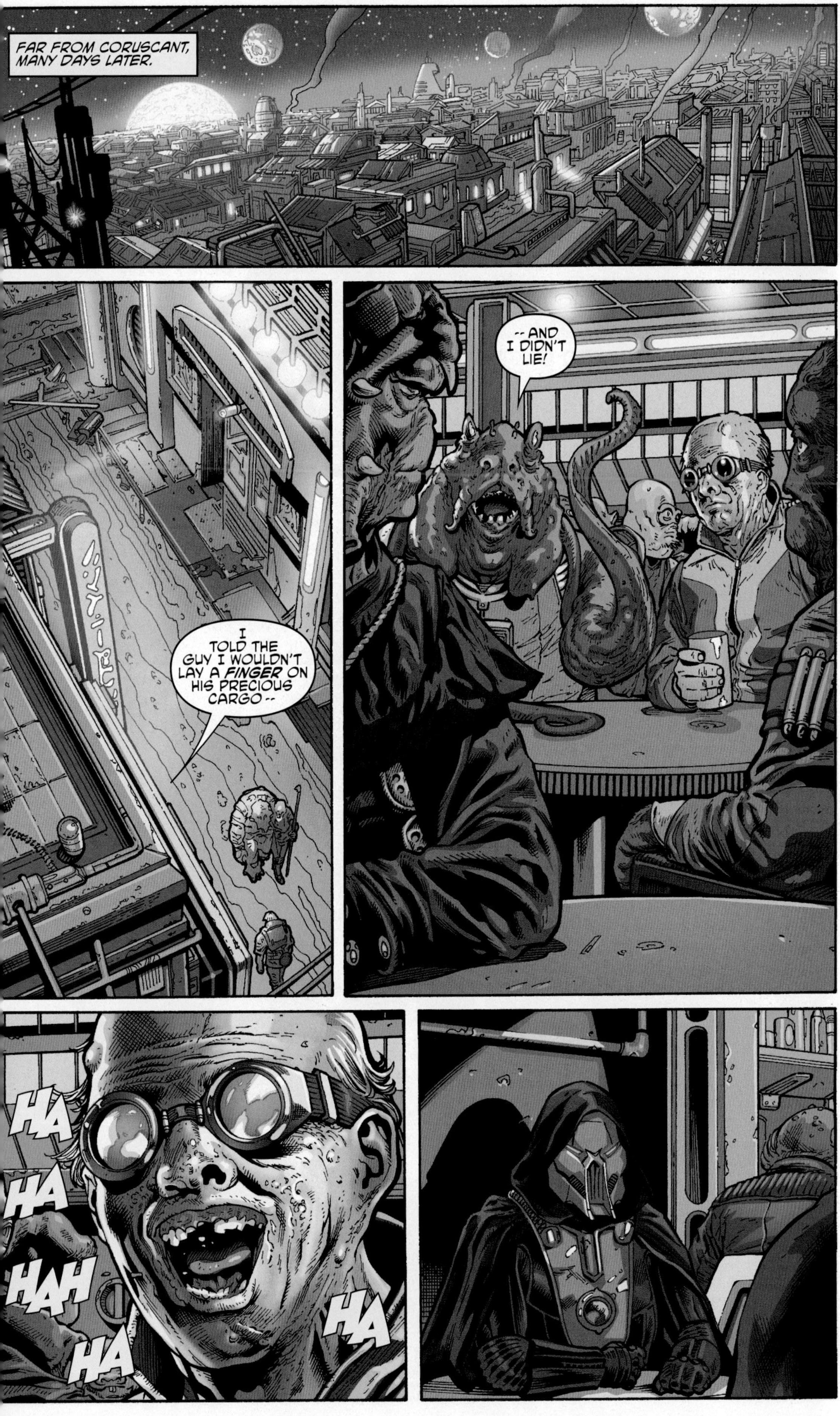

FAR FROM CORUSCANT, MANY DAYS LATER.
I TOLD THE GUY I WOULDN'T LAY A *FINGER* ON HIS PRECIOUS CARGO--
--AND I DIDN'T LIE!
HA HA HAH HA HA

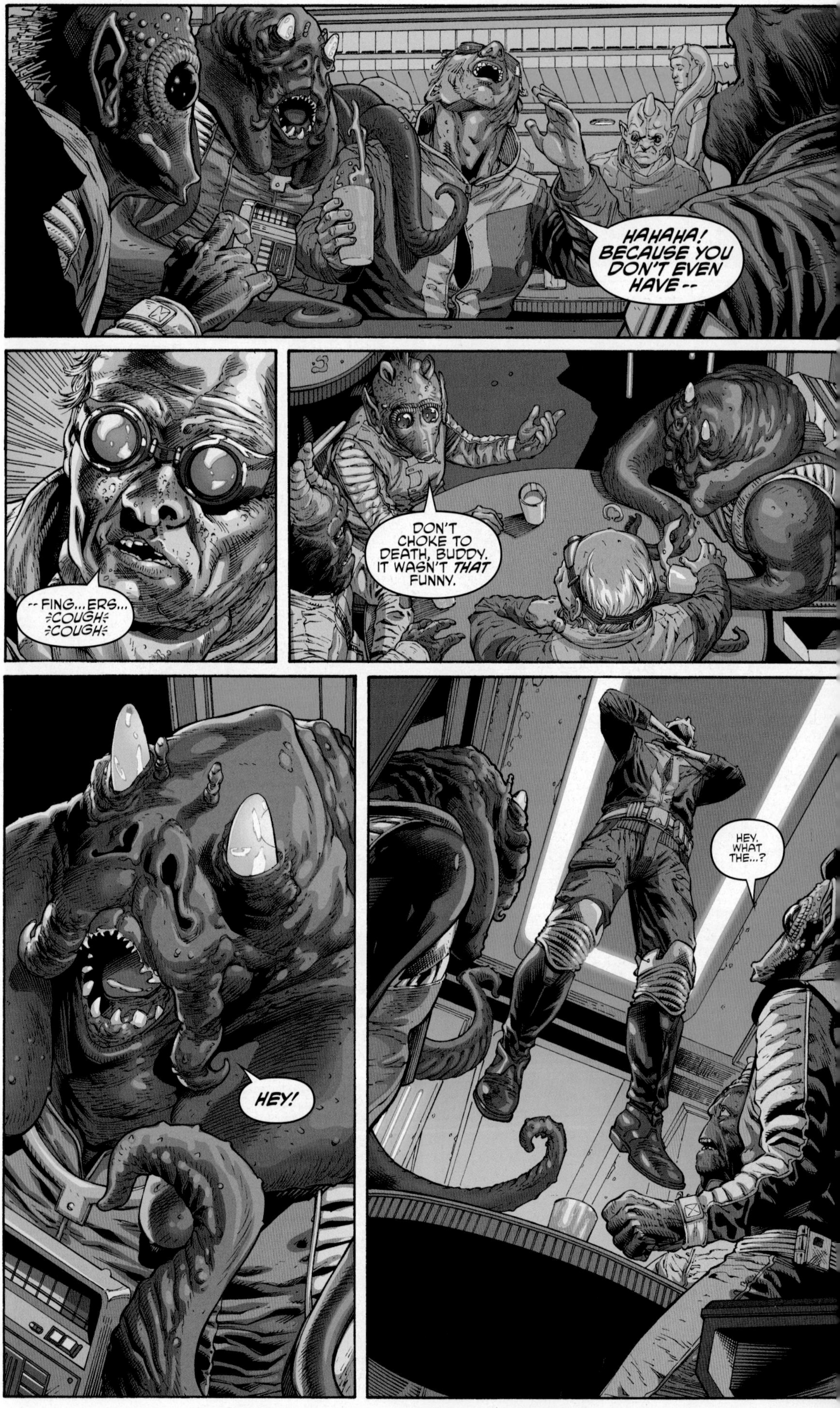
HAHAHA! BECAUSE YOU DON'T EVEN HAVE --
-- FING...ERS... *COUGH* *COUGH*
DON'T CHOKE TO DEATH, BUDDY. IT WASN'T *THAT* FUNNY.
HEY!
HEY. WHAT THE...?

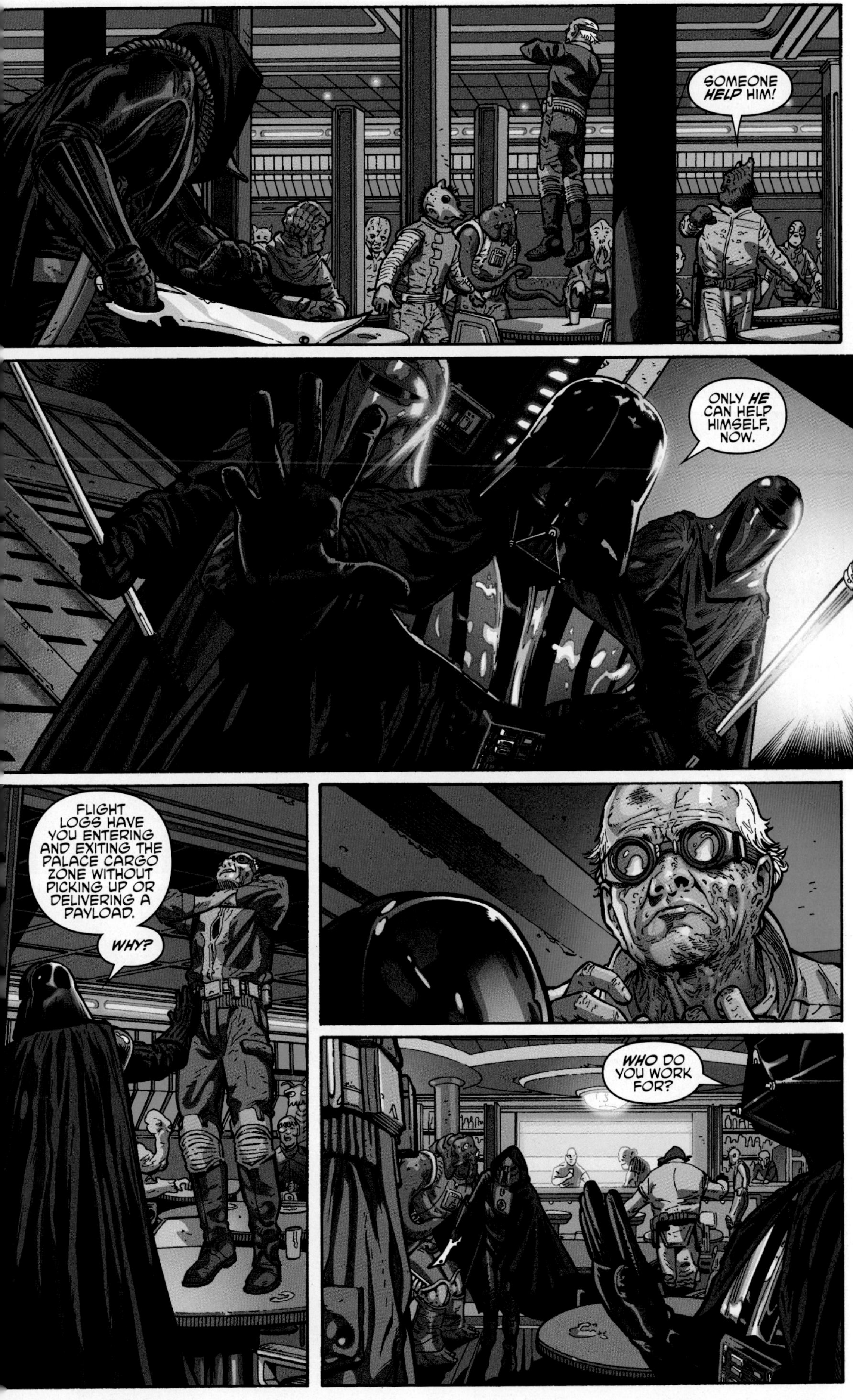
SOMEONE HELP HIM!
ONLY HE CAN HELP HIMSELF, NOW.
FLIGHT LOGS HAVE YOU ENTERING AND EXITING THE PALACE CARGO ZONE WITHOUT PICKING UP OR DELIVERING A PAYLOAD.
WHY?
WHO DO YOU WORK FOR?

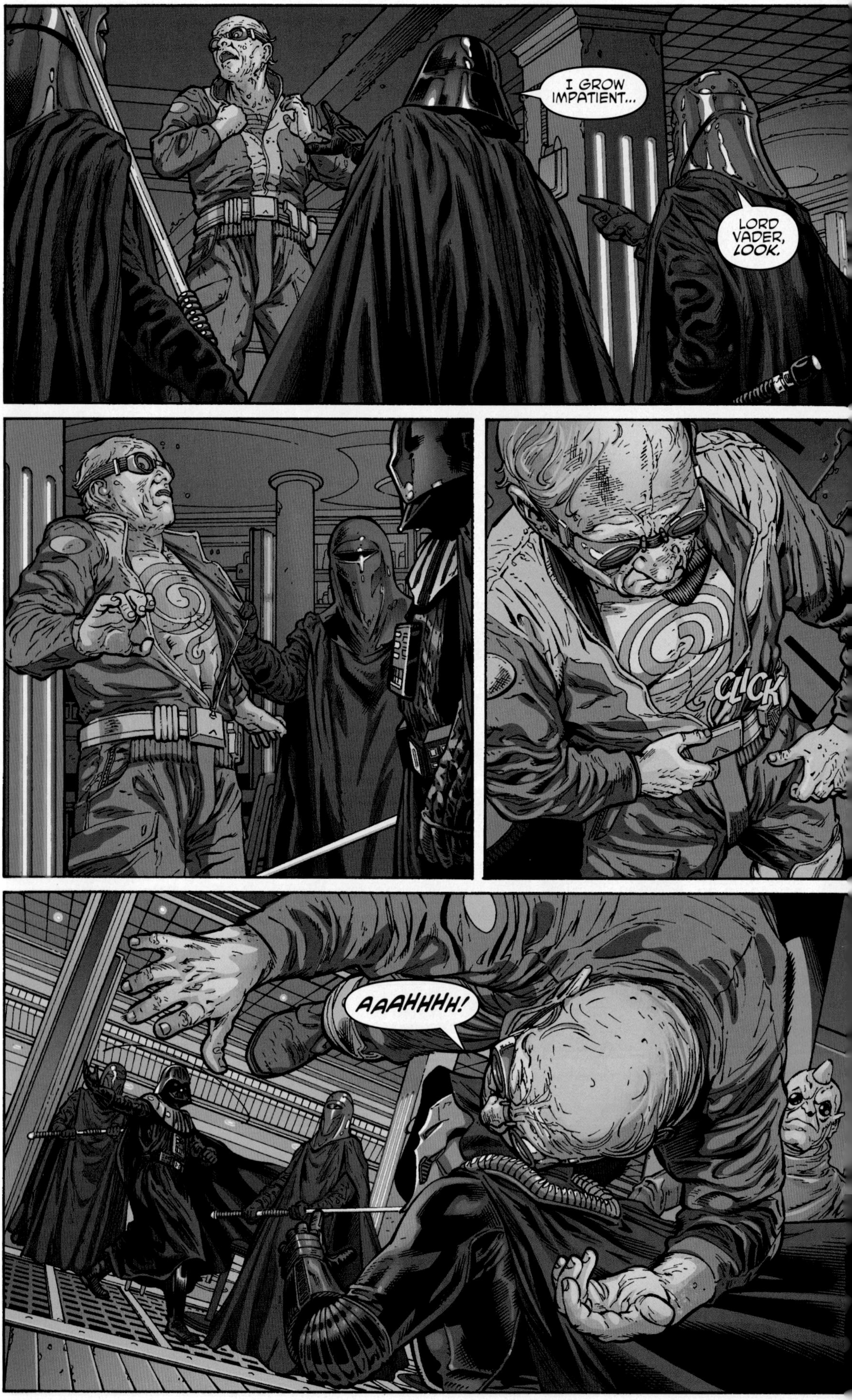
I GROW IMPATIENT...
LORD VADER, LOOK.
CLICK
AAAHHHH!

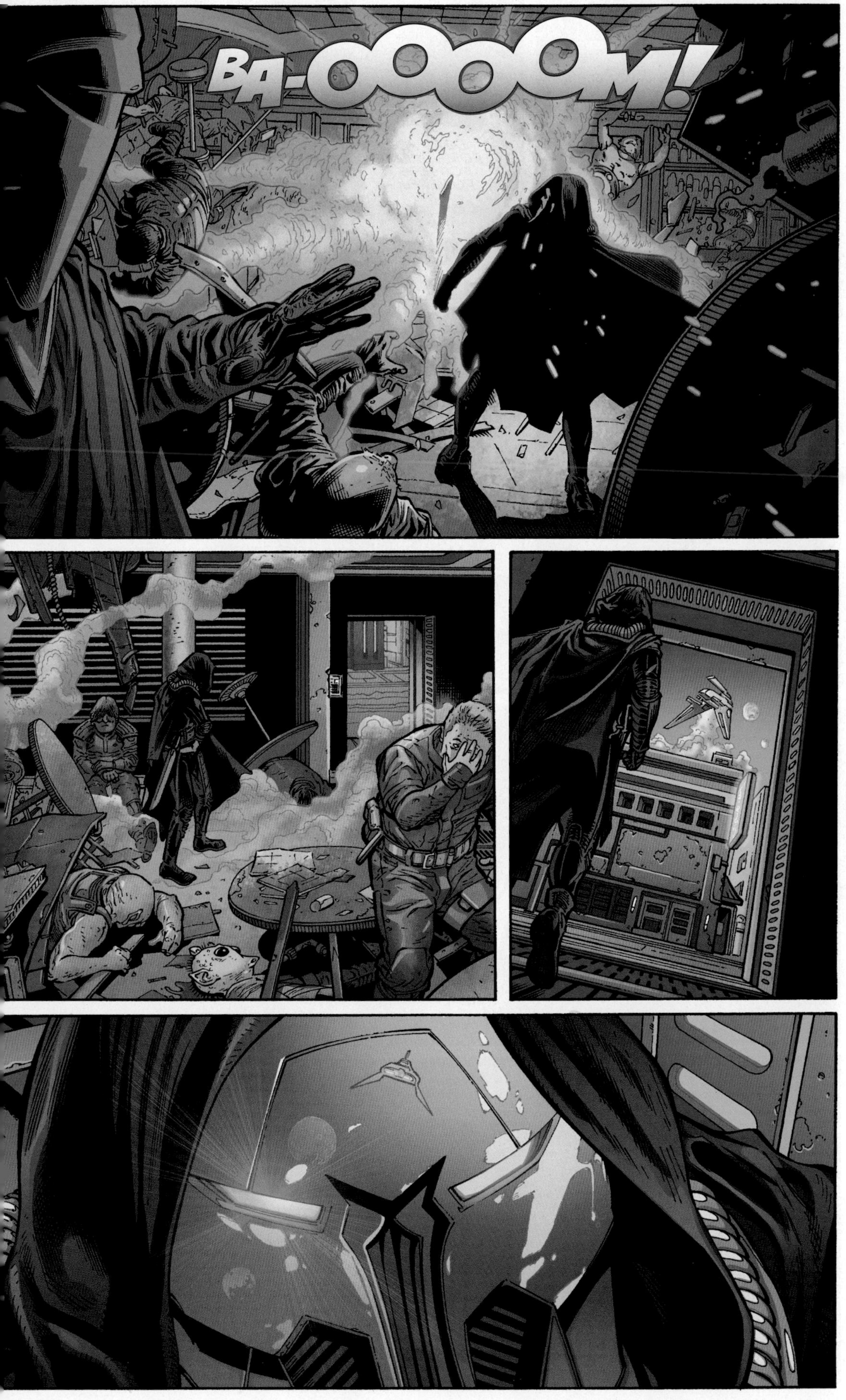
BA-OOOOM!

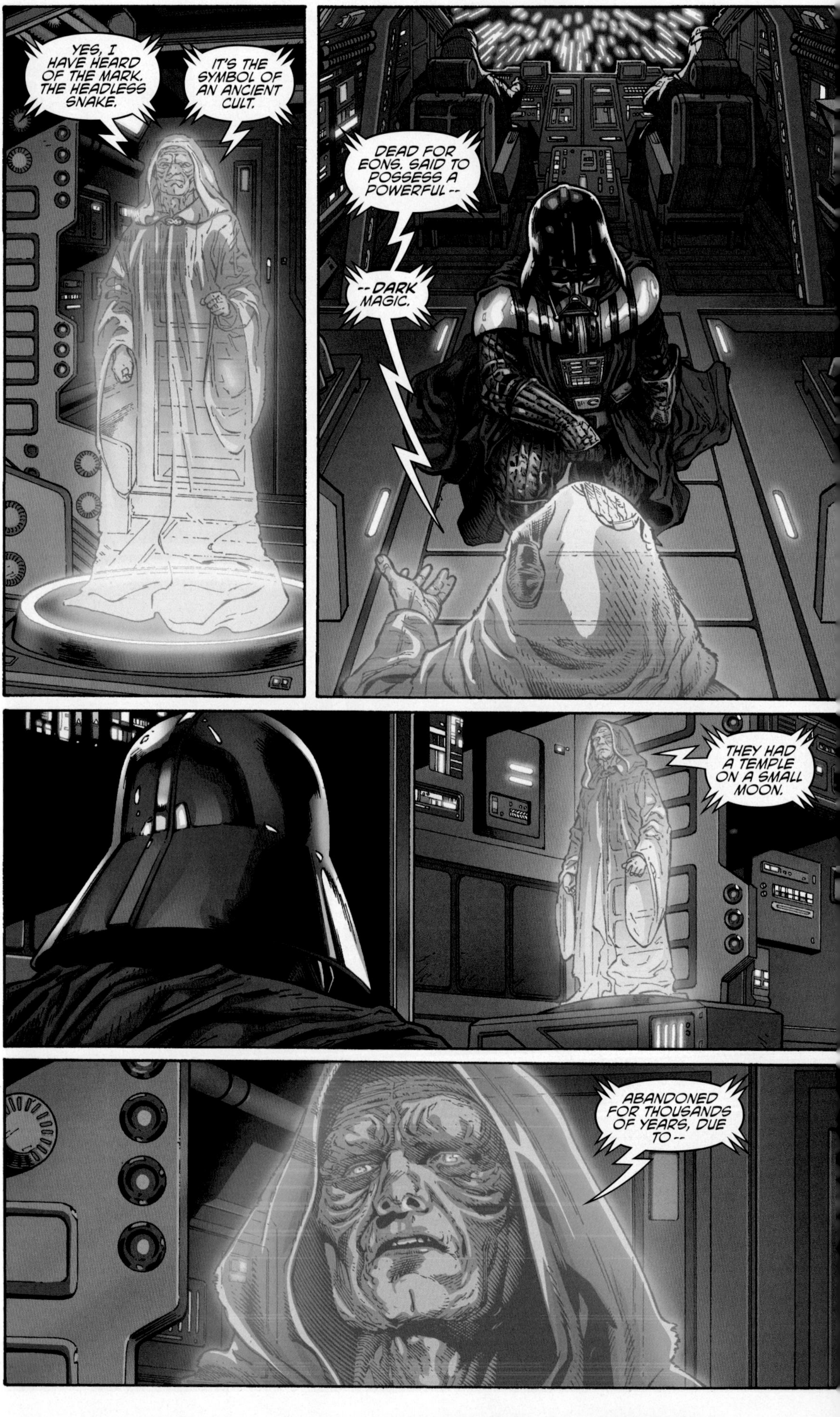
YES, I HAVE HEARD OF THE MARK. THE HEADLESS SNAKE.
IT'S THE SYMBOL OF AN ANCIENT CULT.
DEAD FOR EONS. SAID TO POSSESS A POWERFUL--
--DARK MAGIC.
THEY HAD A TEMPLE ON A SMALL MOON.
ABANDONED FOR THOUSANDS OF YEARS, DUE TO--

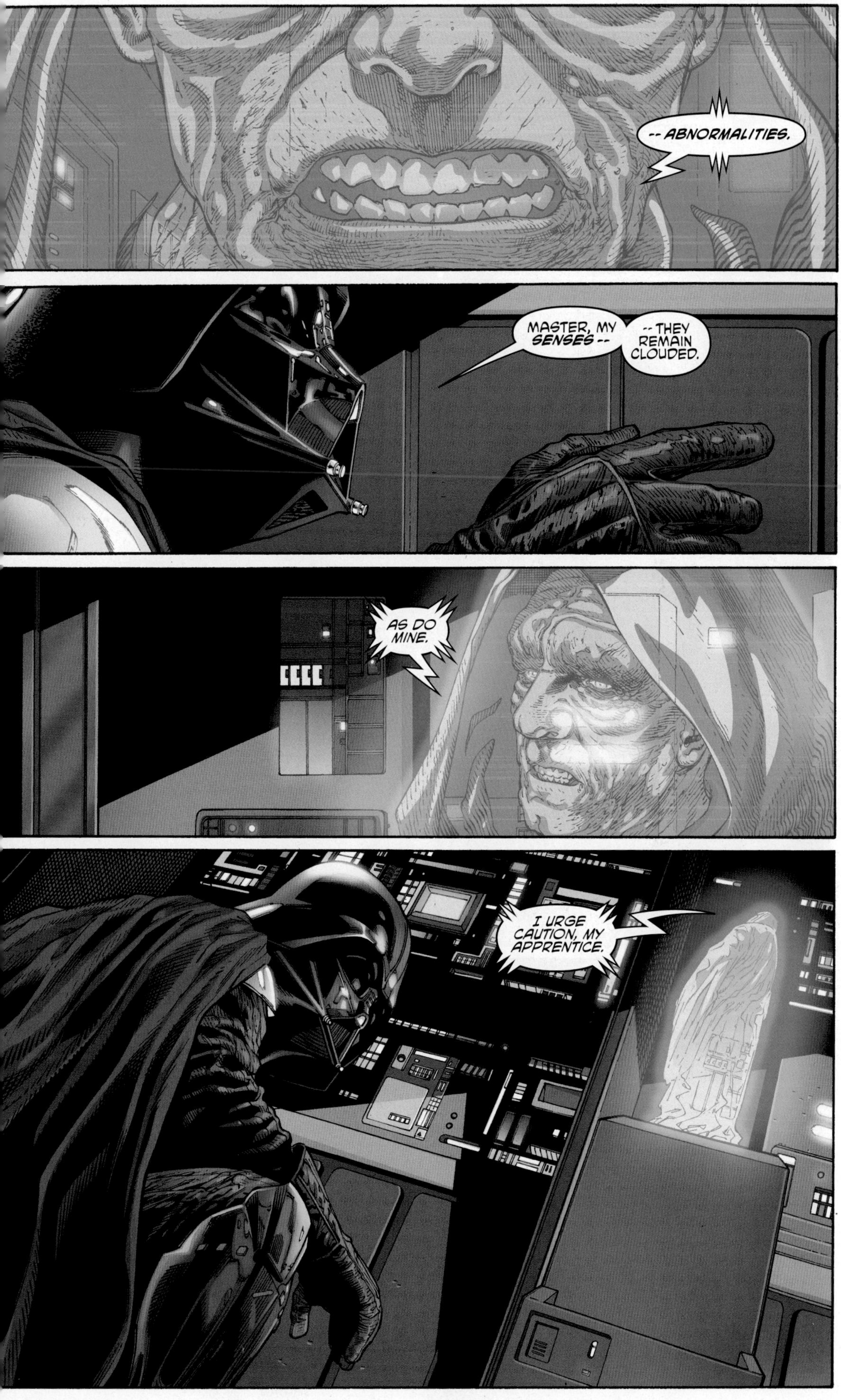

-- ABNORMALITIES.
MASTER, MY SENSES --
-- THEY REMAIN CLOUDED.
AS DO MINE.
I URGE CAUTION, MY APPRENTICE.

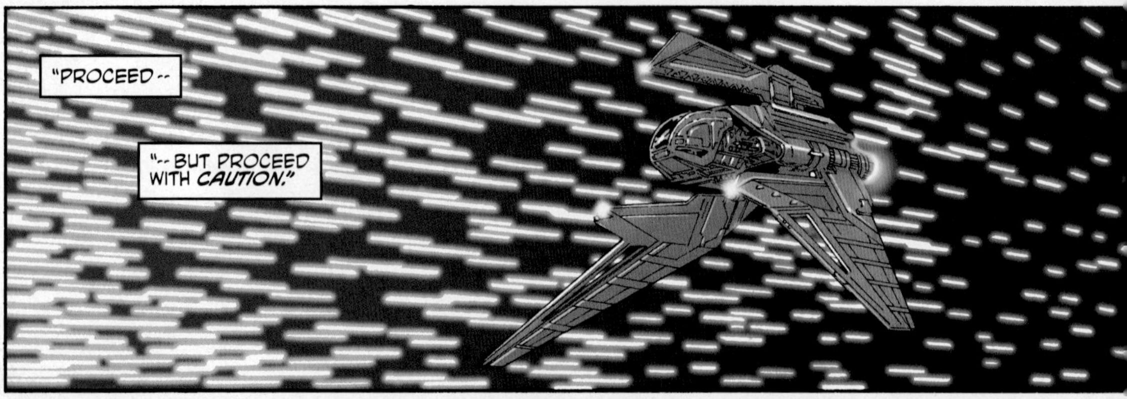
"PROCEED --
"-- BUT PROCEED WITH CAUTION."

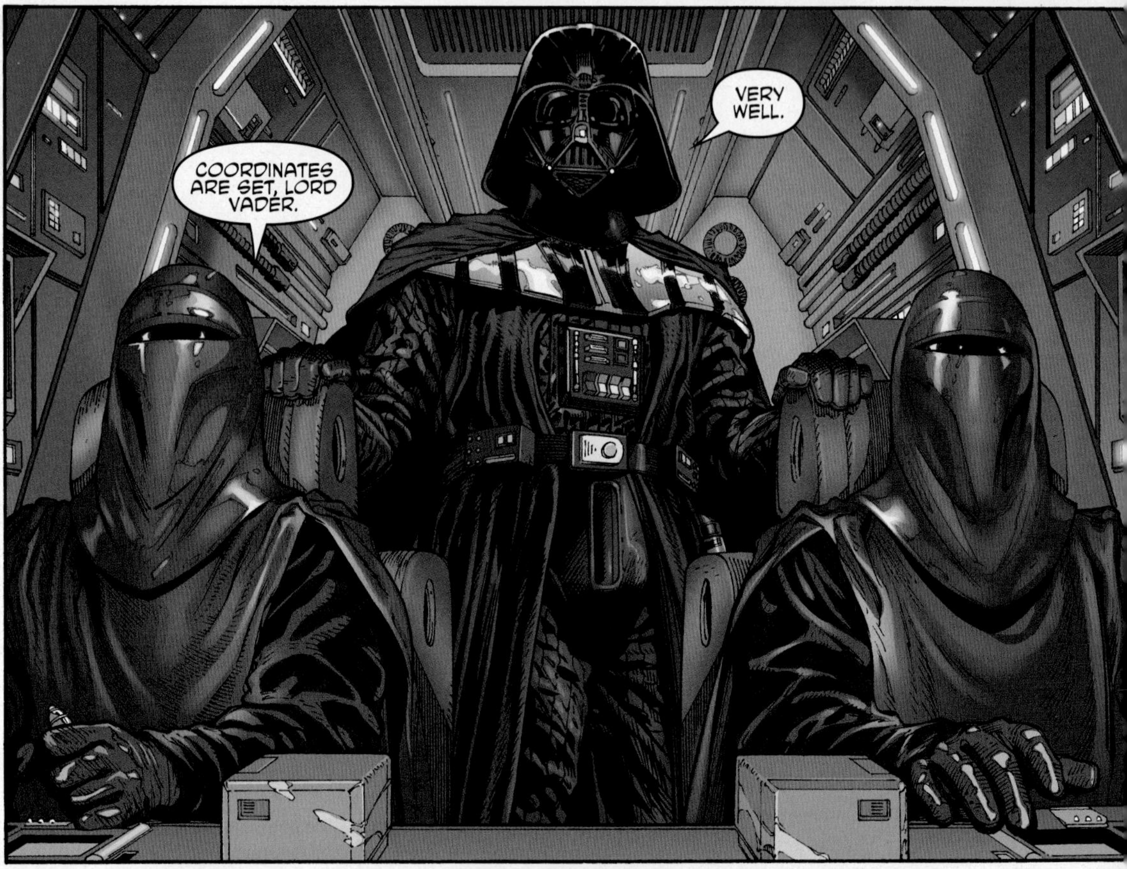
COORDINATES ARE SET, LORD VADER.
VERY WELL.

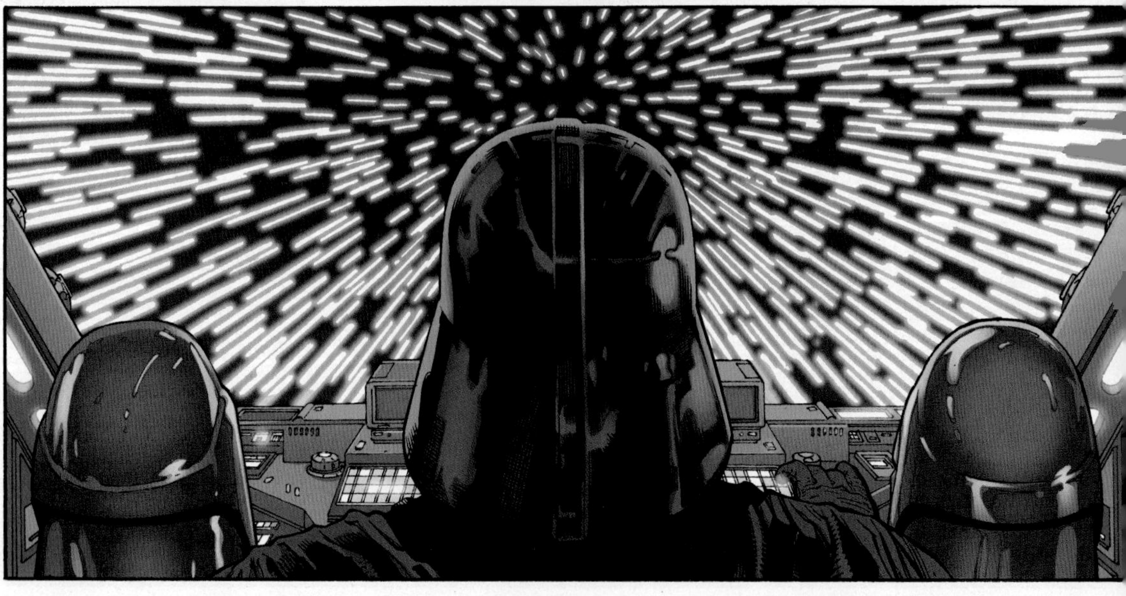

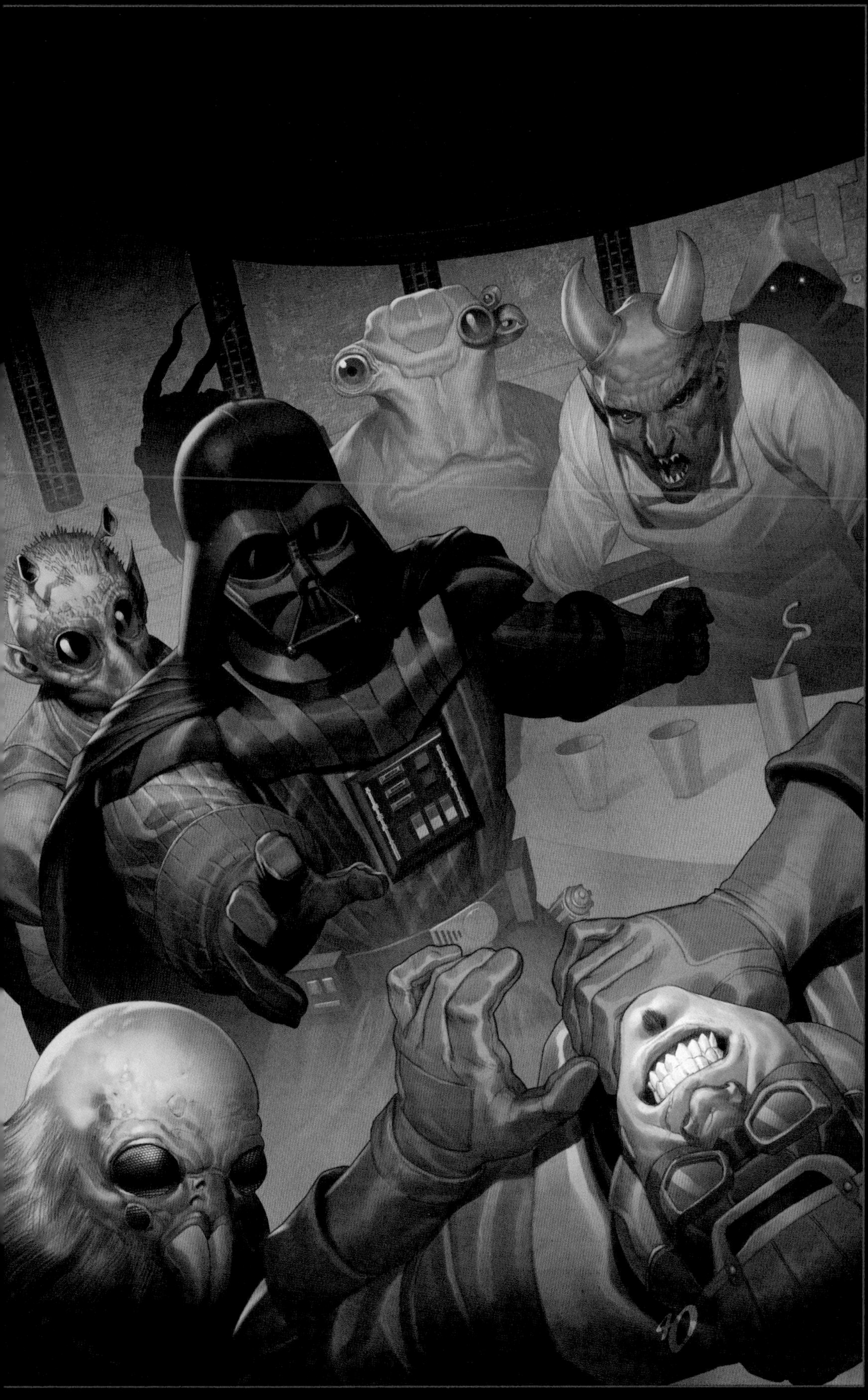
40

*STAR WARS: DARTH VADER AND THE NINTH ASSASSIN #3*

WRITER: TIM SIEDELL • PENCILER: IVÁN FERNÁNDEZ • INKER: DENIS FREITAS • COLORIST: MICHAEL ATIYEH • LETTERER: MICHAEL HEISLER
ASSISTANT EDITOR: FREDDYE LINS • EDITOR: DAVE MARSHALL • COVER ARTIST: ARIEL OLIVETTI

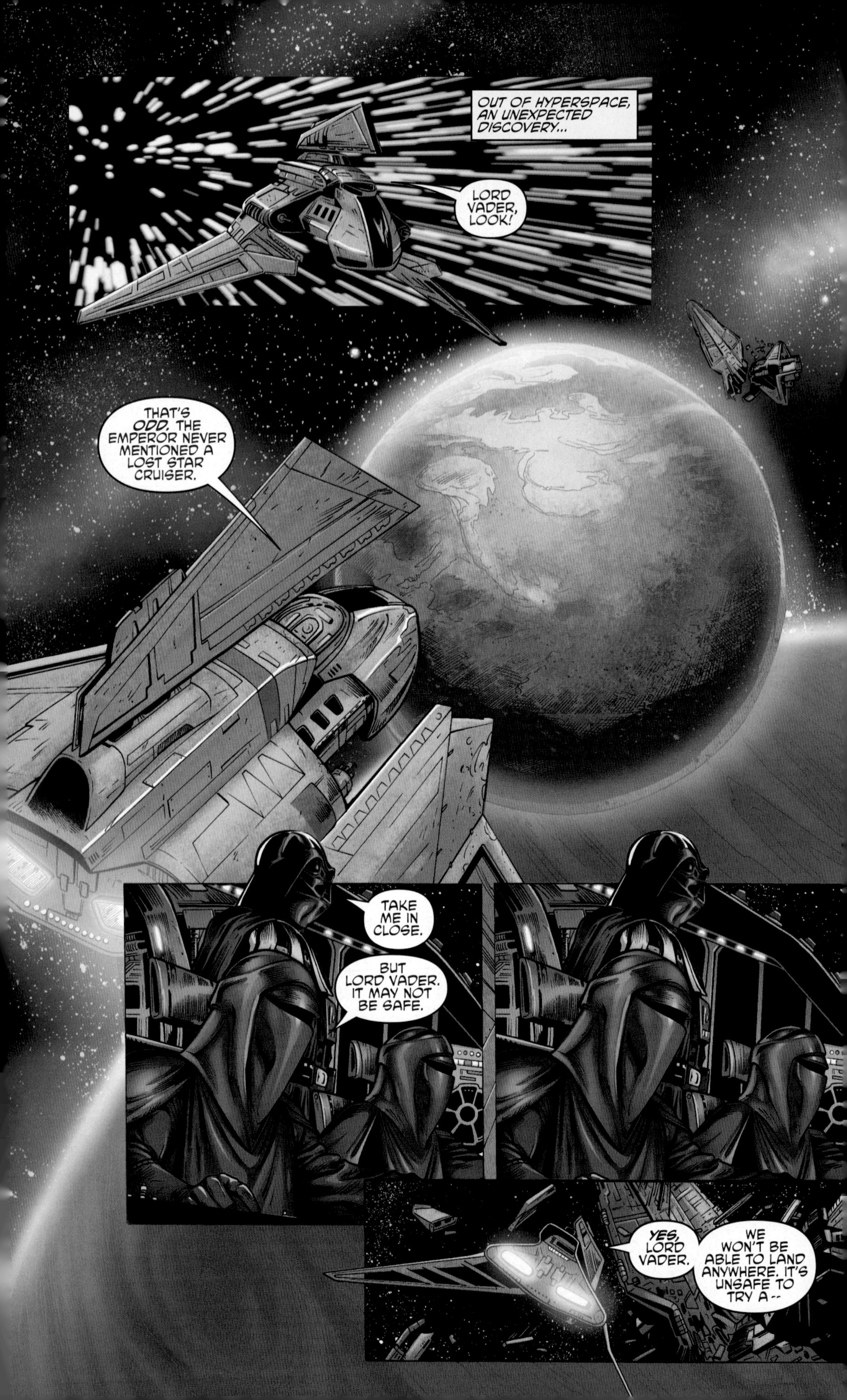
OUT OF HYPERSPACE, AN UNEXPECTED DISCOVERY...
LORD VADER, LOOK!
THAT'S ODD. THE EMPEROR NEVER MENTIONED A LOST STAR CRUISER.
TAKE ME IN CLOSE.
BUT LORD VADER. IT MAY NOT BE SAFE.
YES, LORD VADER.
WE WON'T BE ABLE TO LAND ANYWHERE. IT'S UNSAFE TO TRY A--

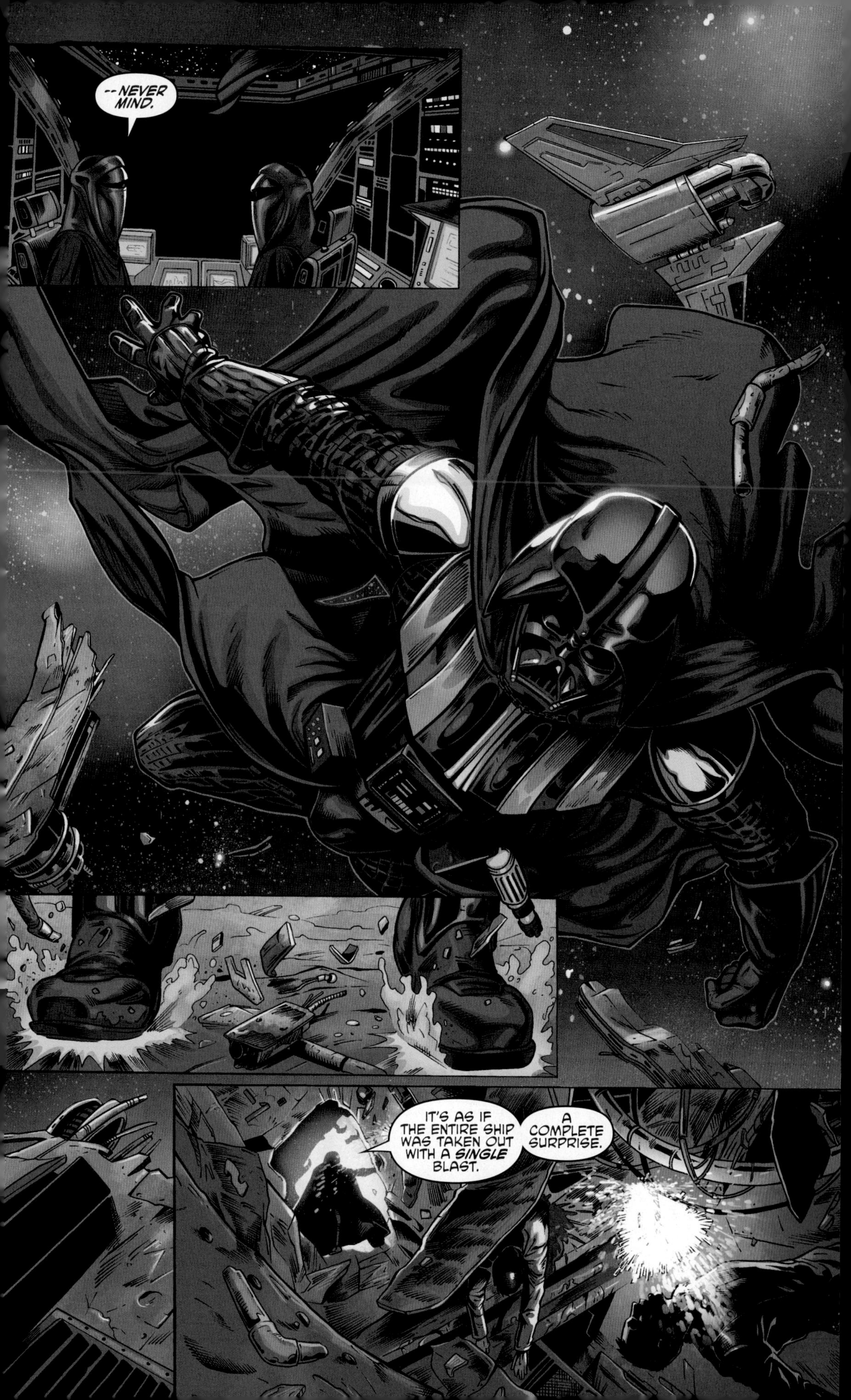
--NEVER MIND.
IT'S AS IF THE ENTIRE SHIP WAS TAKEN OUT WITH A *SINGLE* BLAST.
A COMPLETE SURPRISE.

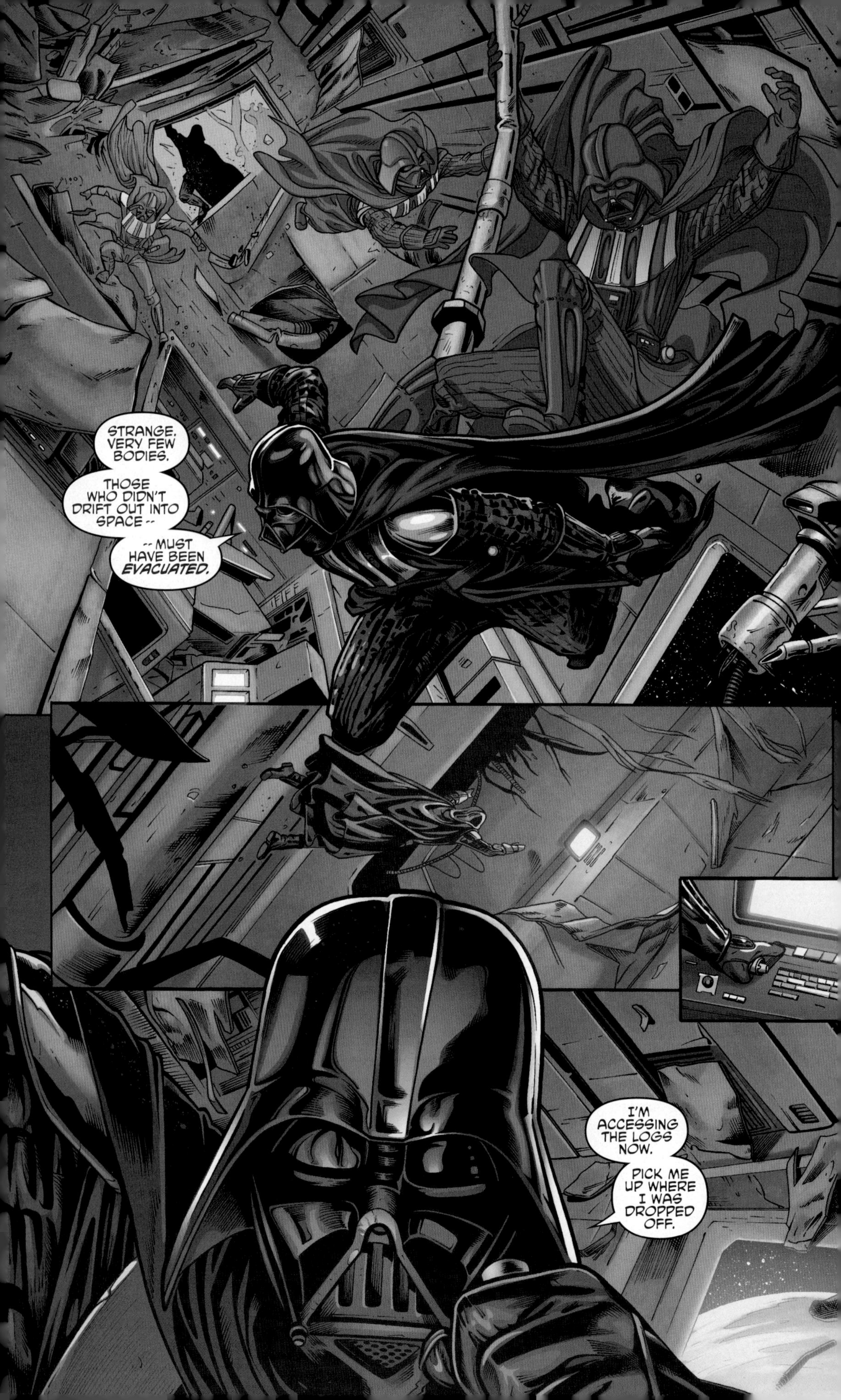

STRANGE. VERY FEW BODIES.
THOSE WHO DIDN'T DRIFT OUT INTO SPACE --
-- MUST HAVE BEEN *EVACUATED.*
I'M ACCESSING THE LOGS NOW.
PICK ME UP WHERE I WAS DROPPED OFF.

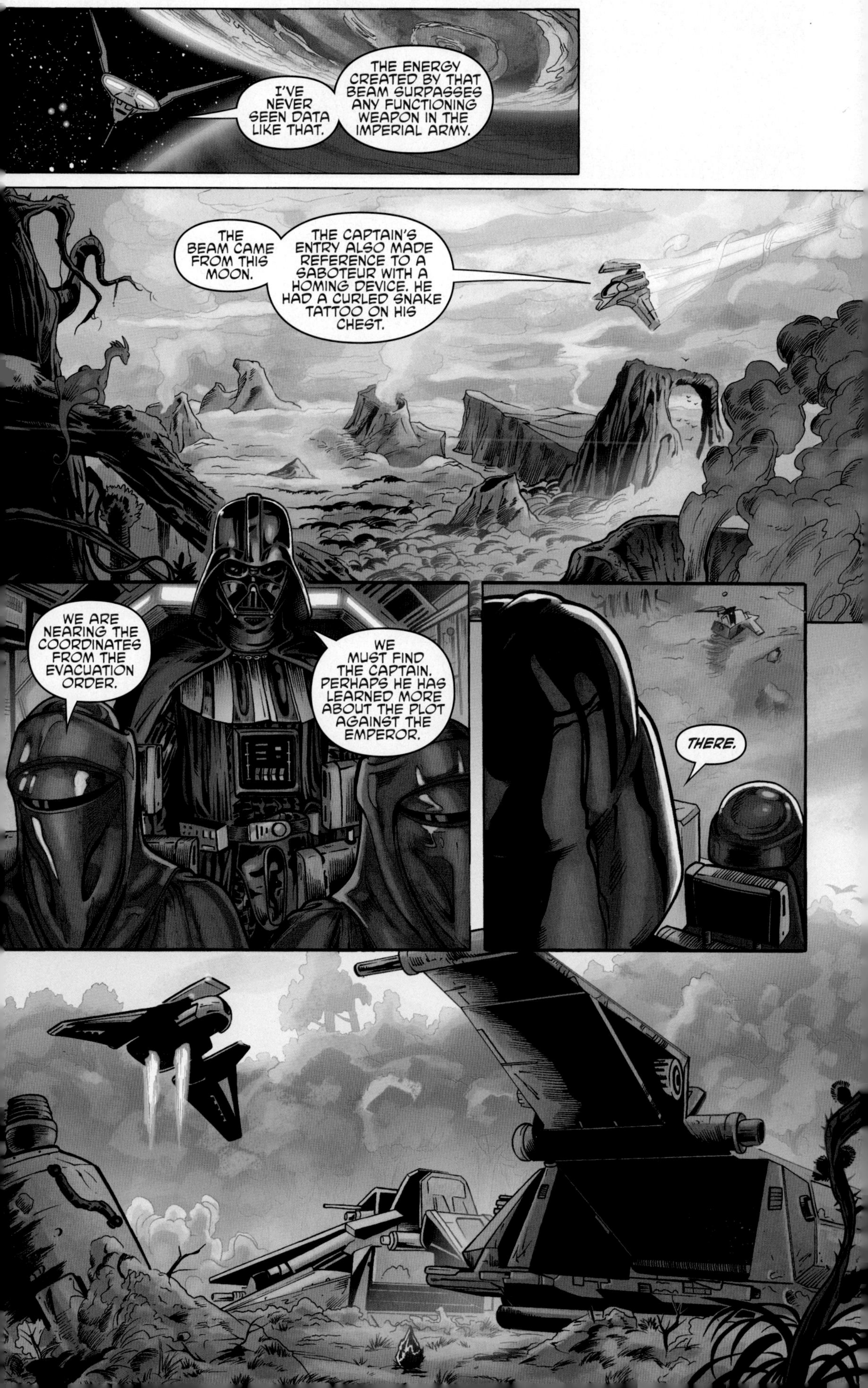
I'VE NEVER SEEN DATA LIKE THAT.
THE ENERGY CREATED BY THAT BEAM SURPASSES ANY FUNCTIONING WEAPON IN THE IMPERIAL ARMY.
THE BEAM CAME FROM THIS MOON.
THE CAPTAIN'S ENTRY ALSO MADE REFERENCE TO A SABOTEUR WITH A HOMING DEVICE. HE HAD A CURLED SNAKE TATTOO ON HIS CHEST.
WE ARE NEARING THE COORDINATES FROM THE EVACUATION ORDER.
WE MUST FIND THE CAPTAIN. PERHAPS HE HAS LEARNED MORE ABOUT THE PLOT AGAINST THE EMPEROR.
THERE.

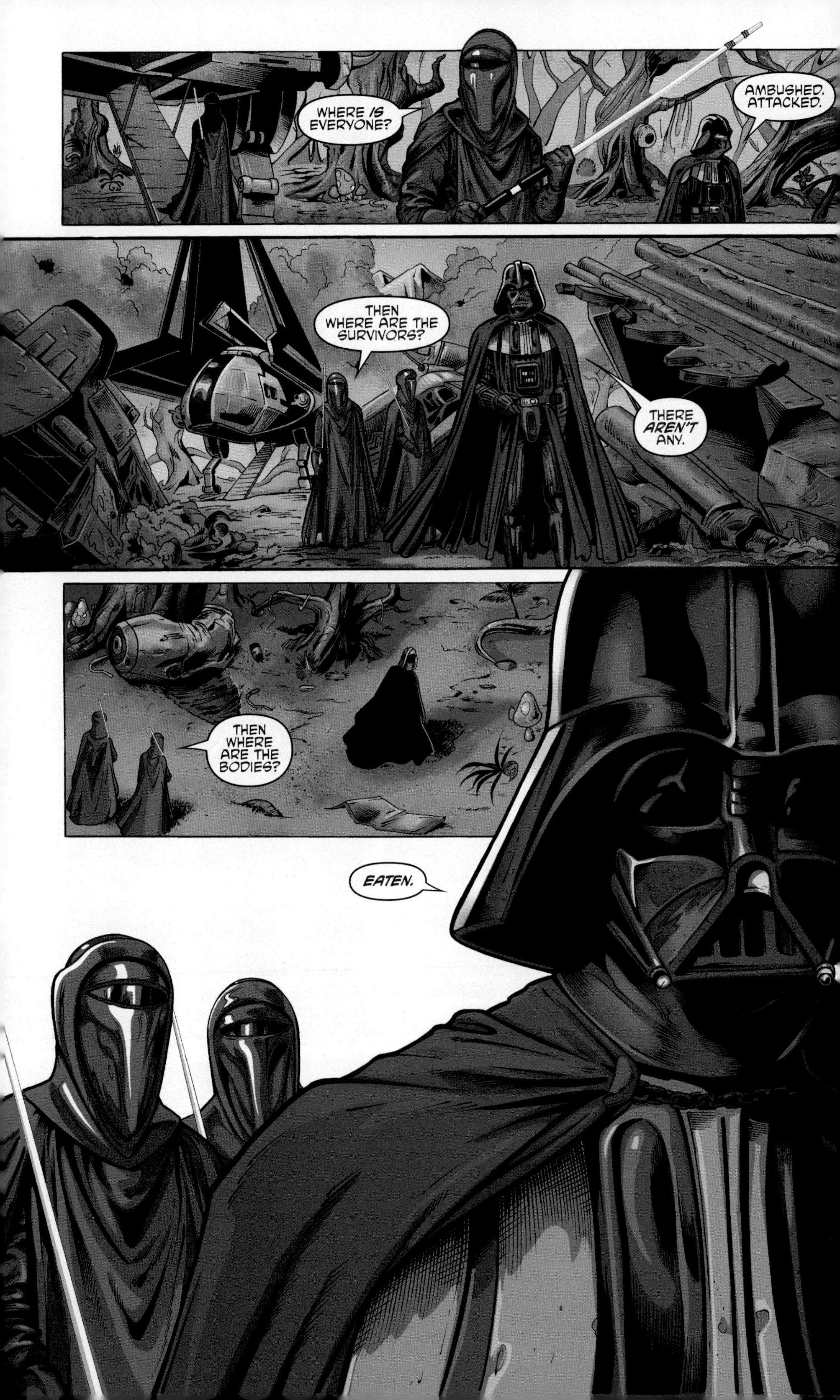
WHERE *IS* EVERYONE?
AMBUSHED. ATTACKED.
THEN WHERE ARE THE SURVIVORS?
THERE *AREN'T* ANY.
THEN WHERE ARE THE BODIES?
*EATEN.*

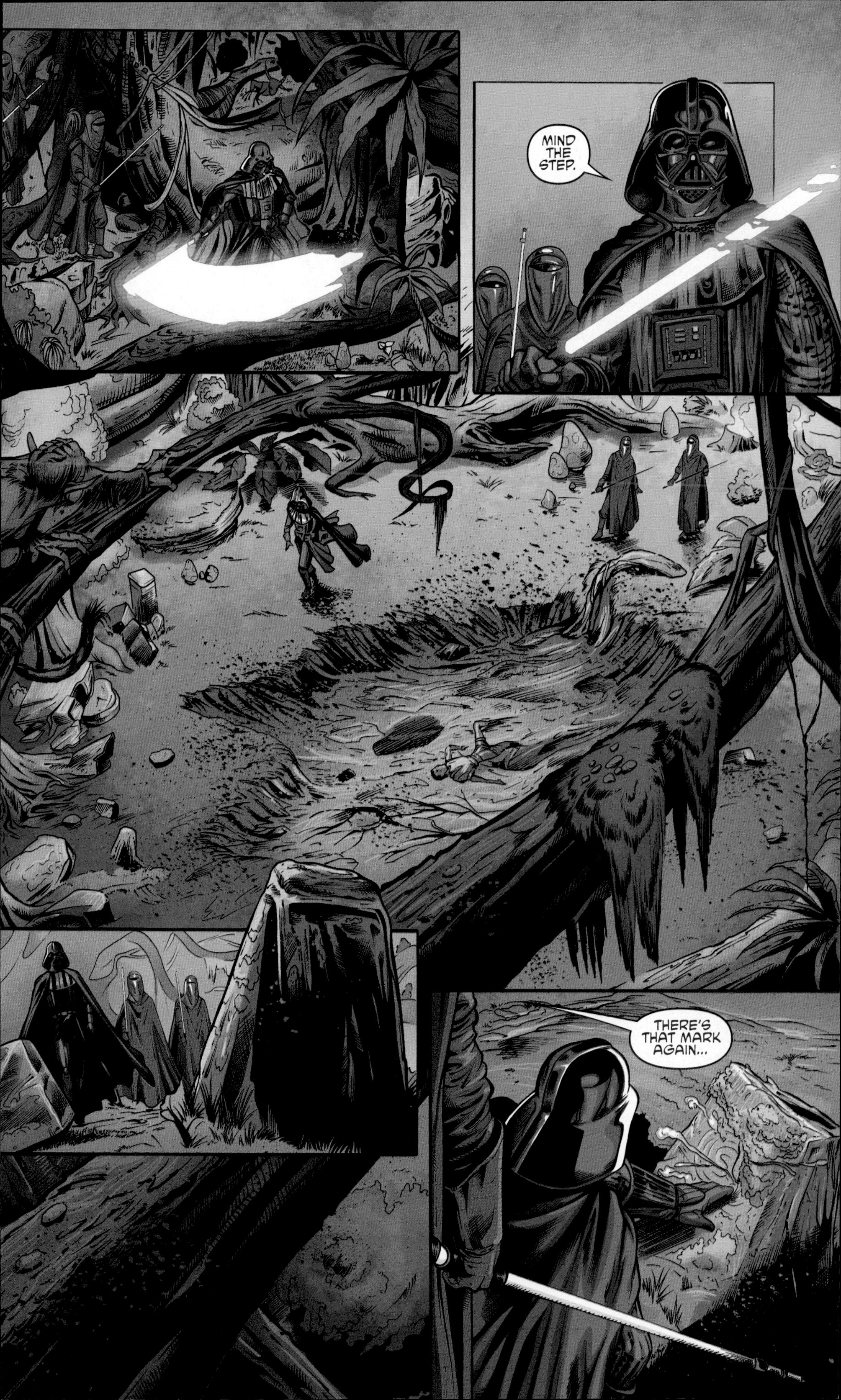
MIND THE STEP.
THERE'S THAT MARK AGAIN...

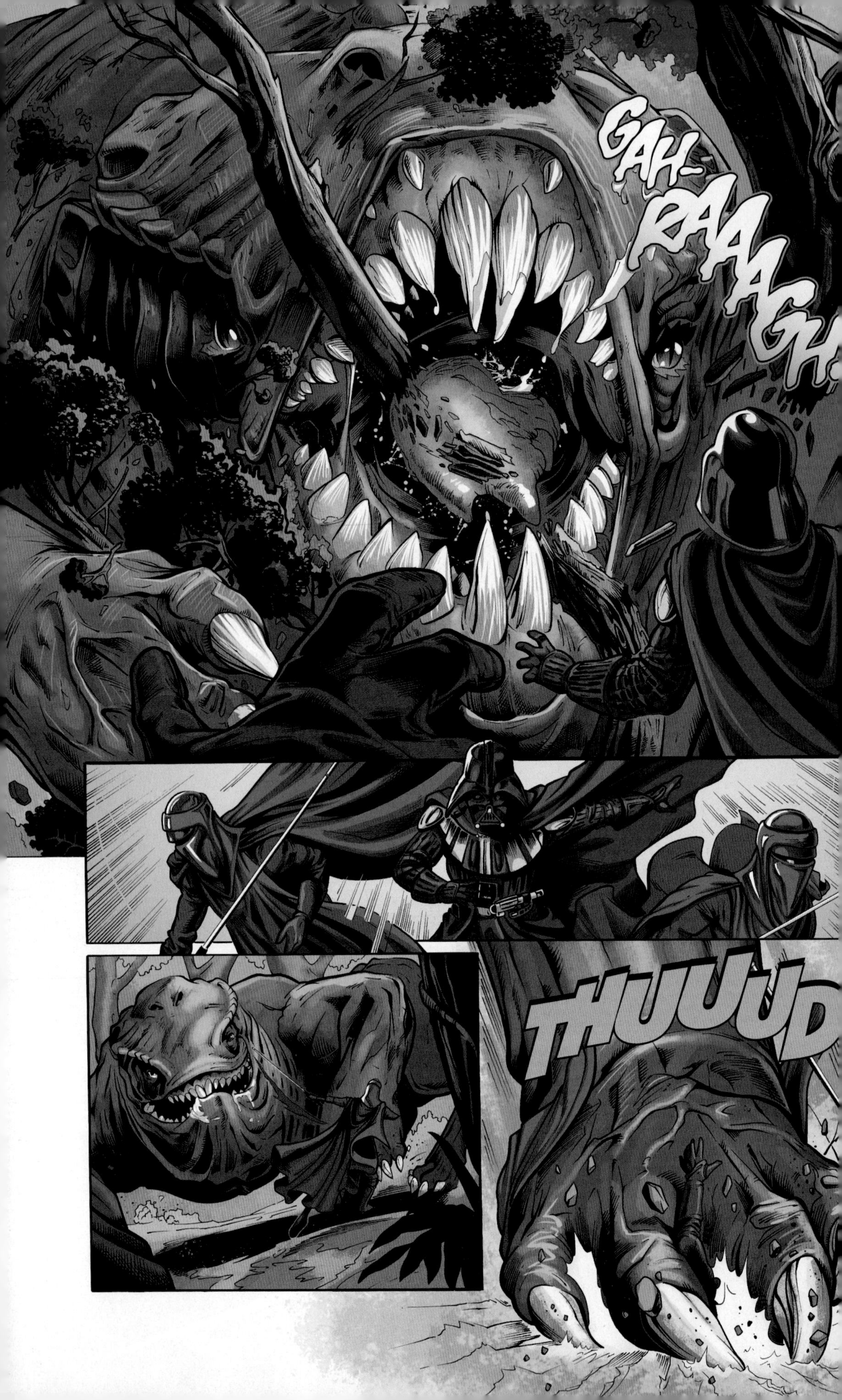
GAH-RAAAGH!
THUUUD

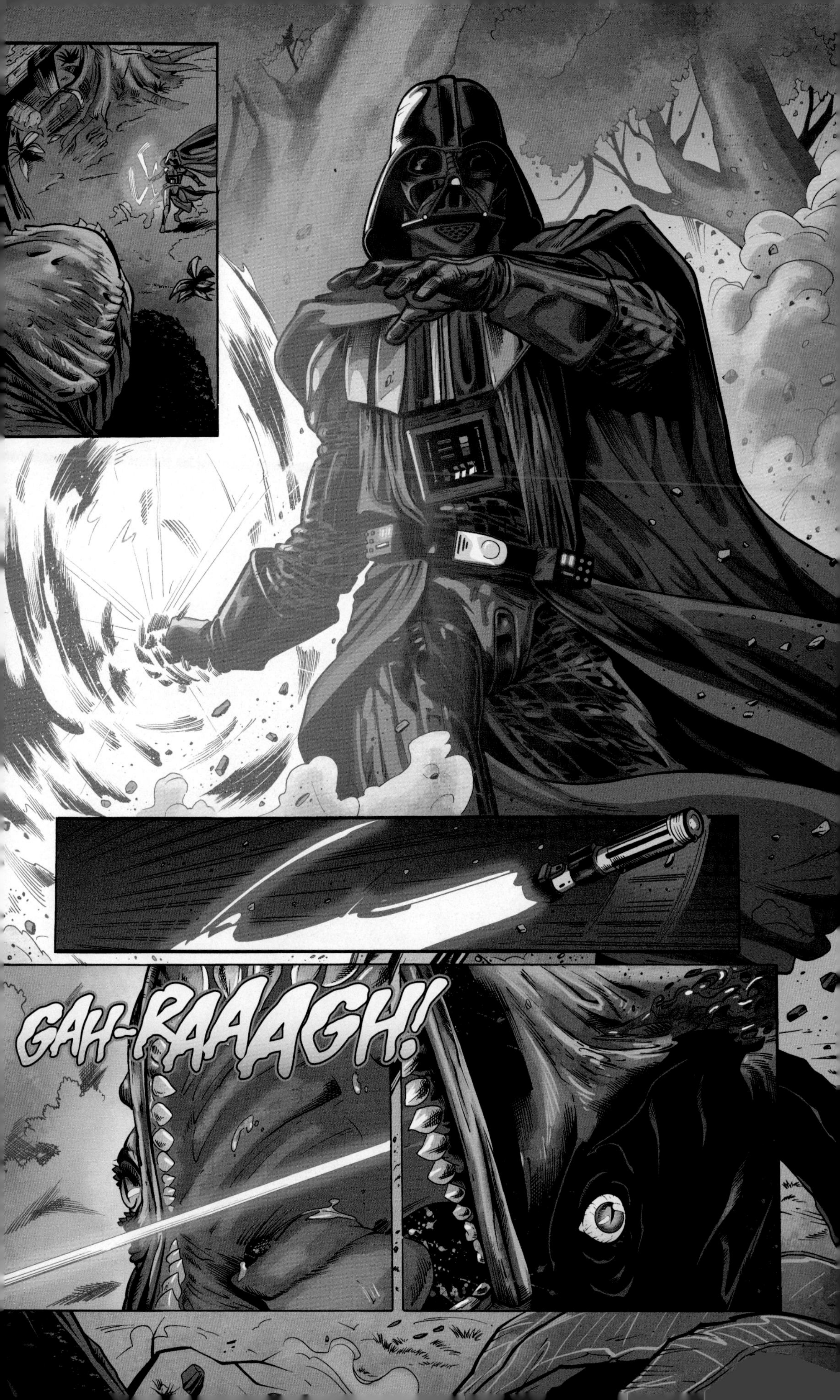
GAH-RAAAGH!

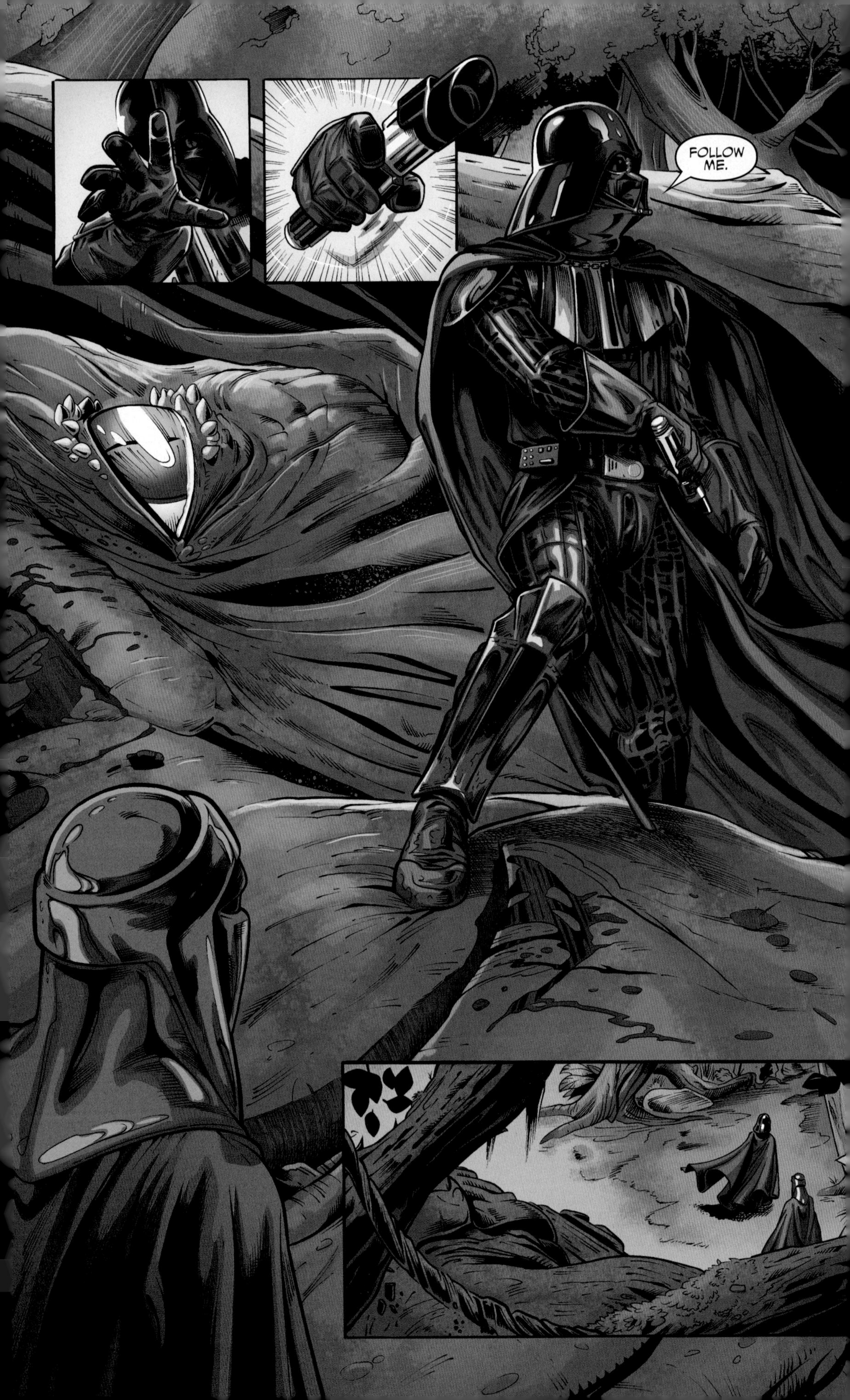
FOLLOW ME.

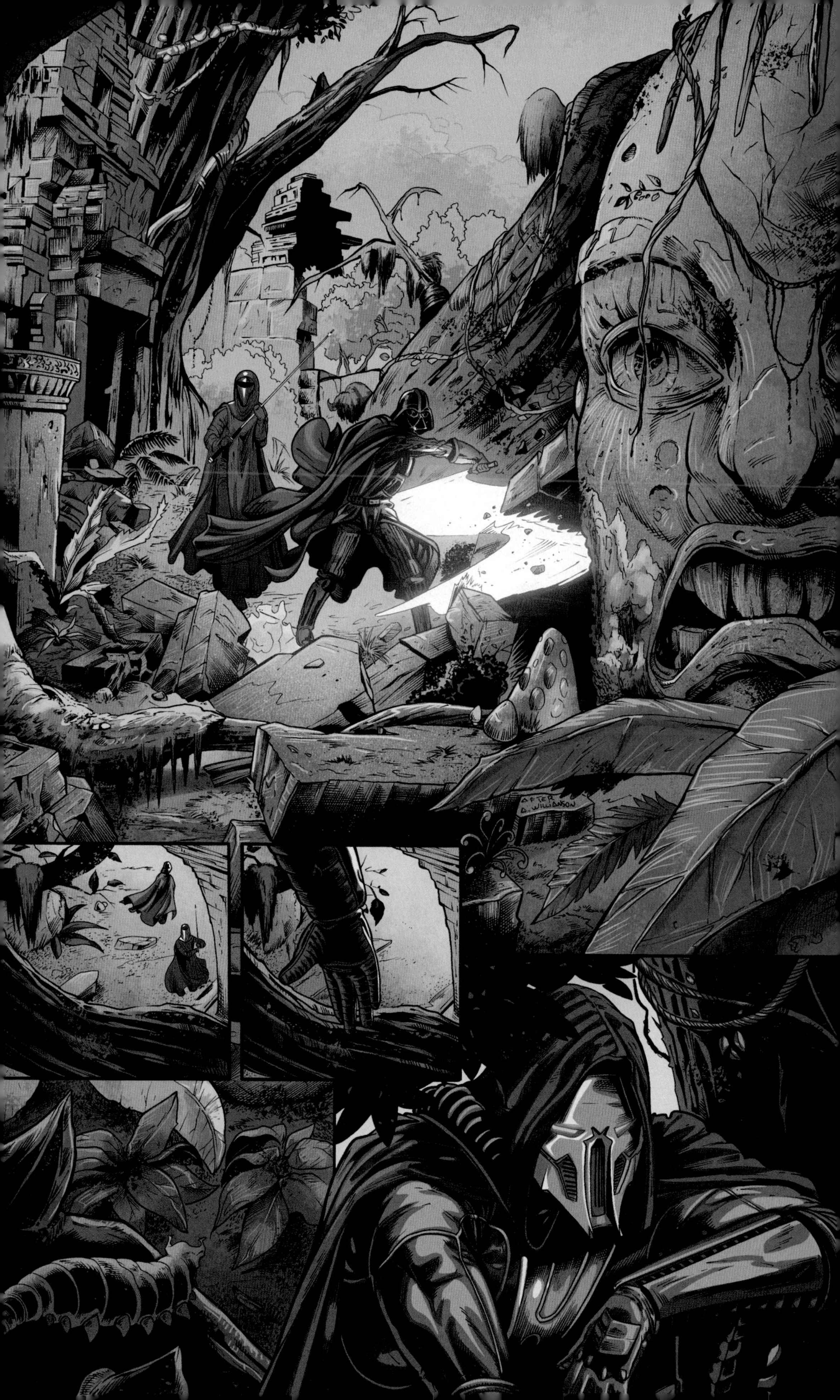
AFTER D. WILLIAMSON

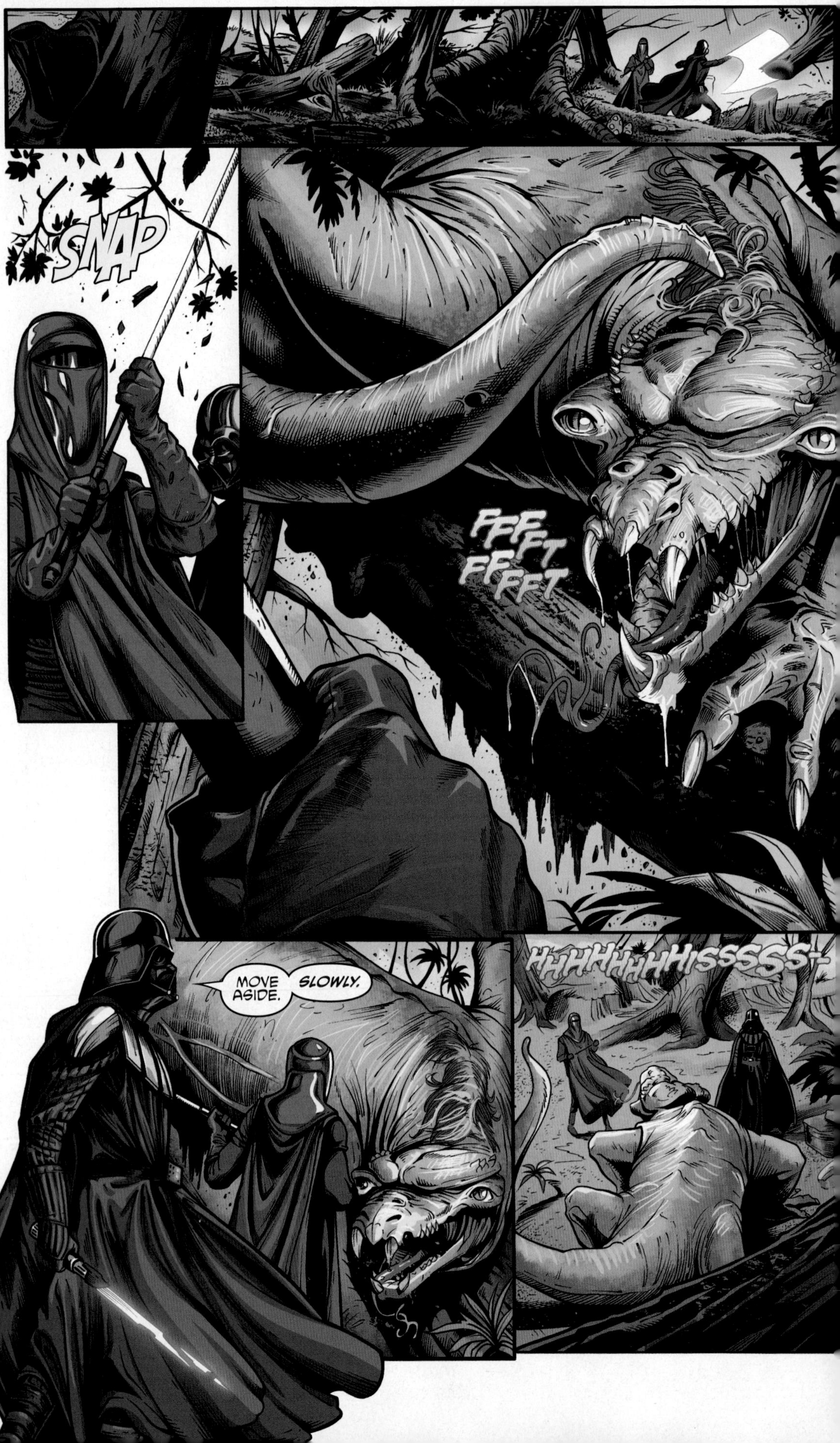
SNAP
FFFFT FFFFT
MOVE ASIDE.
SLOWLY.
HHHHHHHISSSSS-

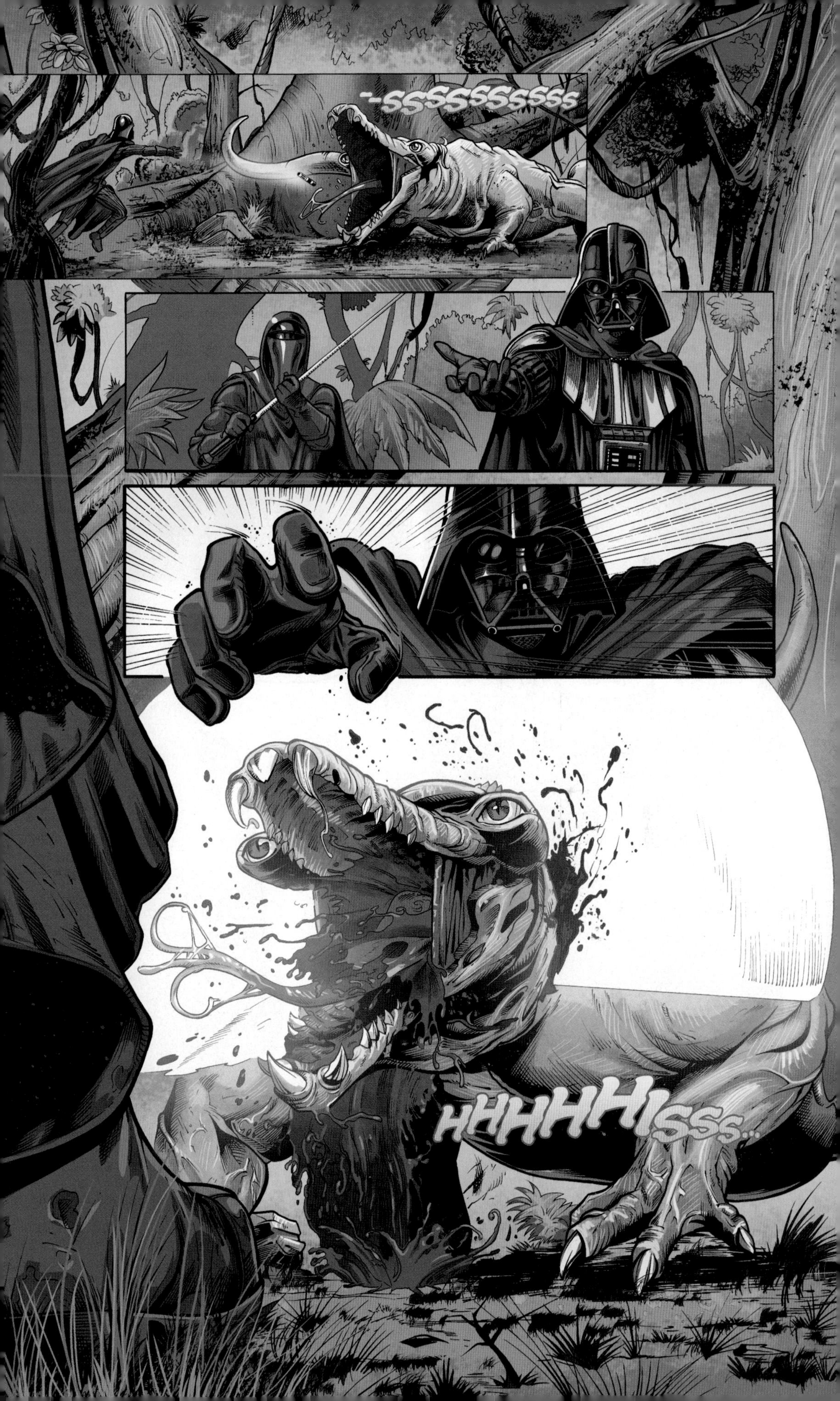
--SSSSSSSSS
HHHHHISSs...

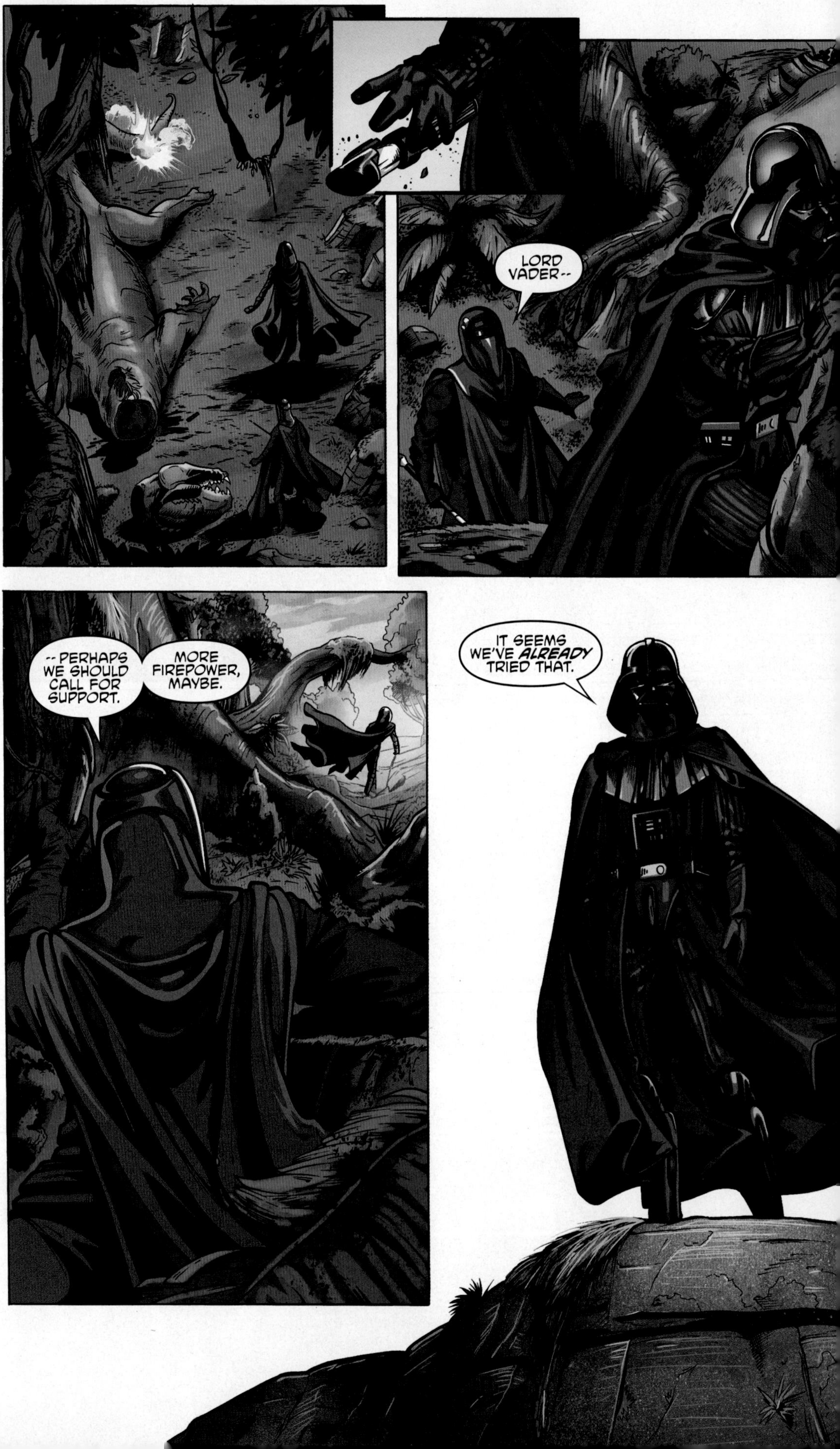
LORD VADER--
--PERHAPS WE SHOULD CALL FOR SUPPORT.
MORE FIREPOWER, MAYBE.
IT SEEMS WE'VE *ALREADY* TRIED THAT.

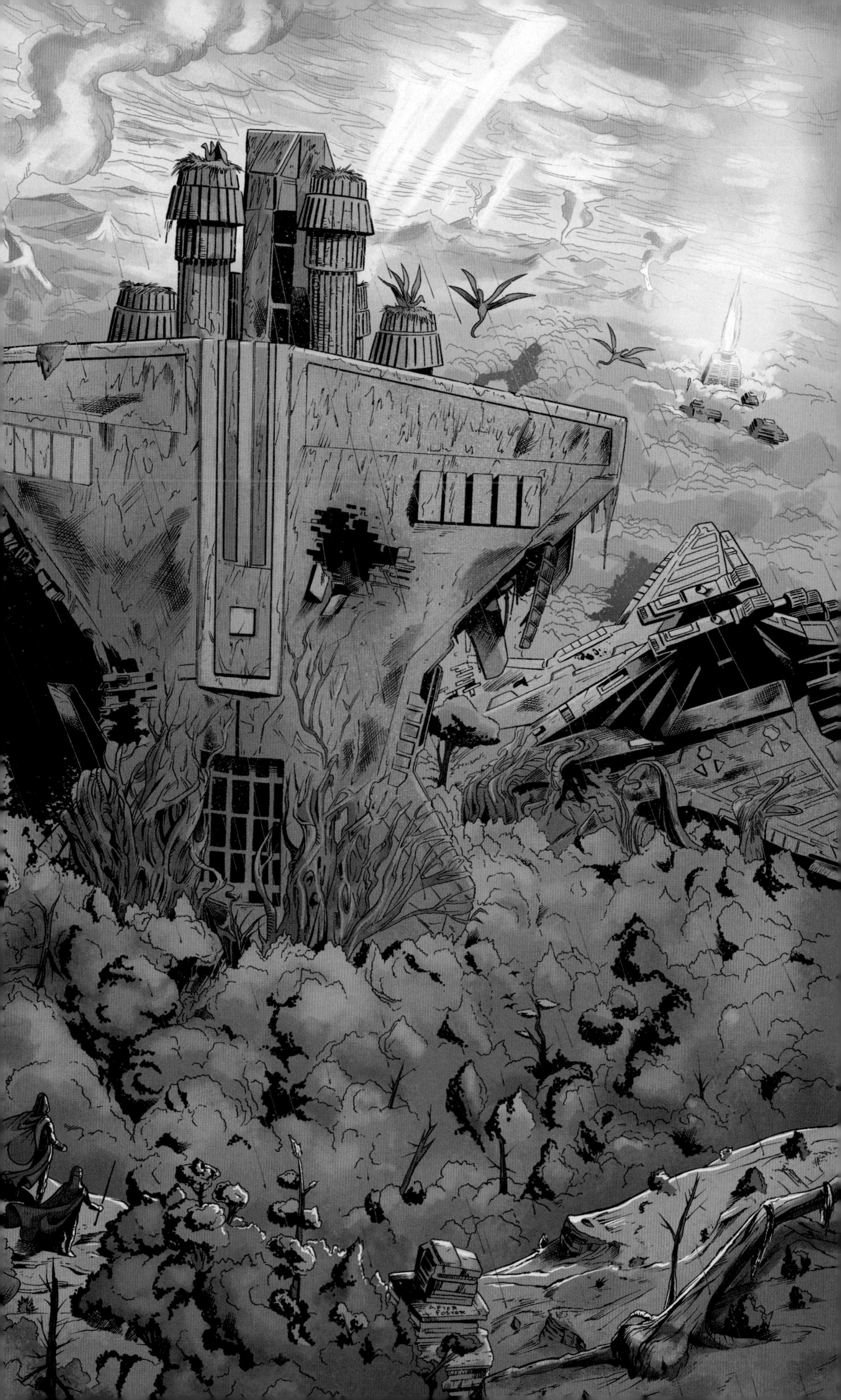
AFTER FOSTER

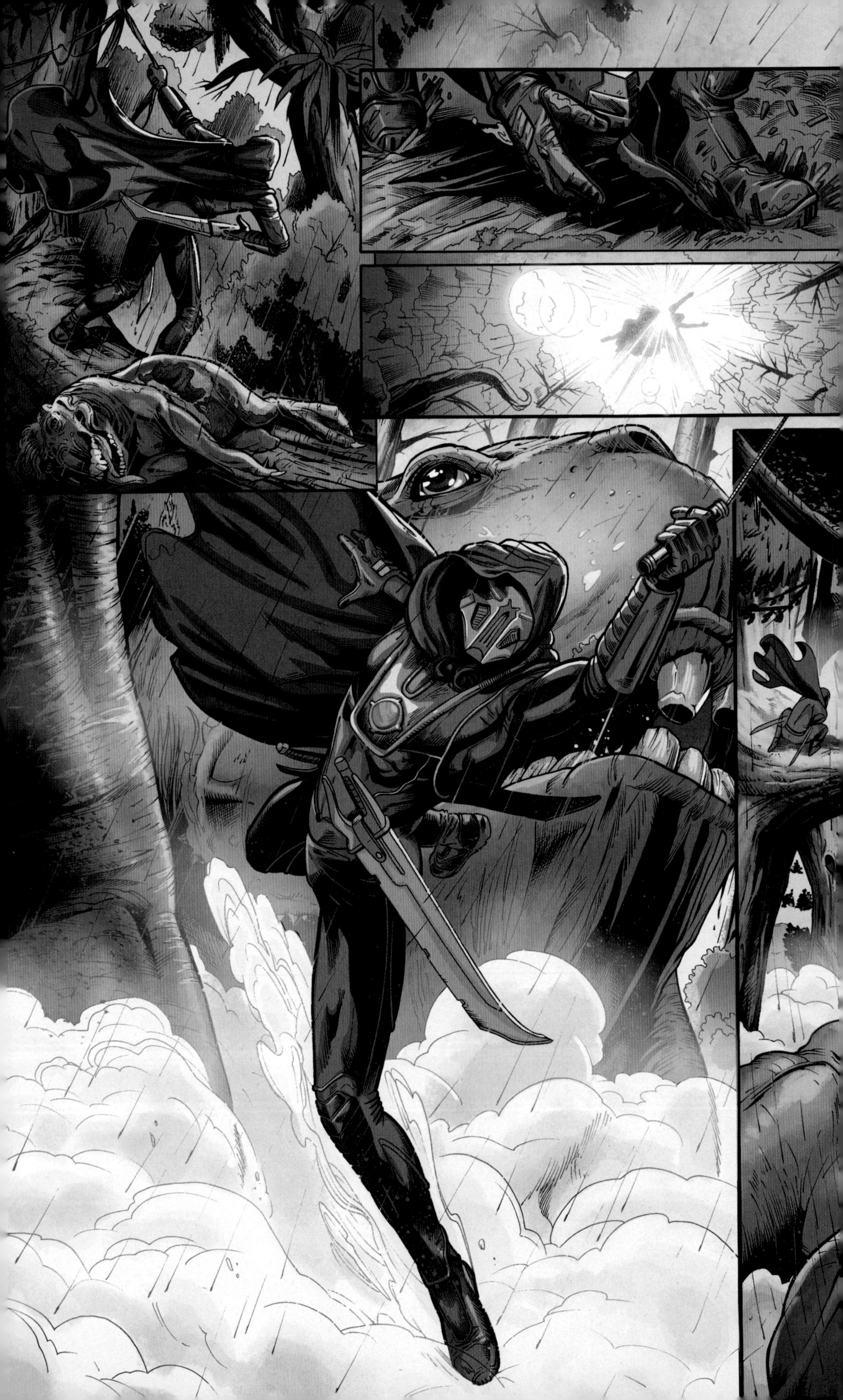

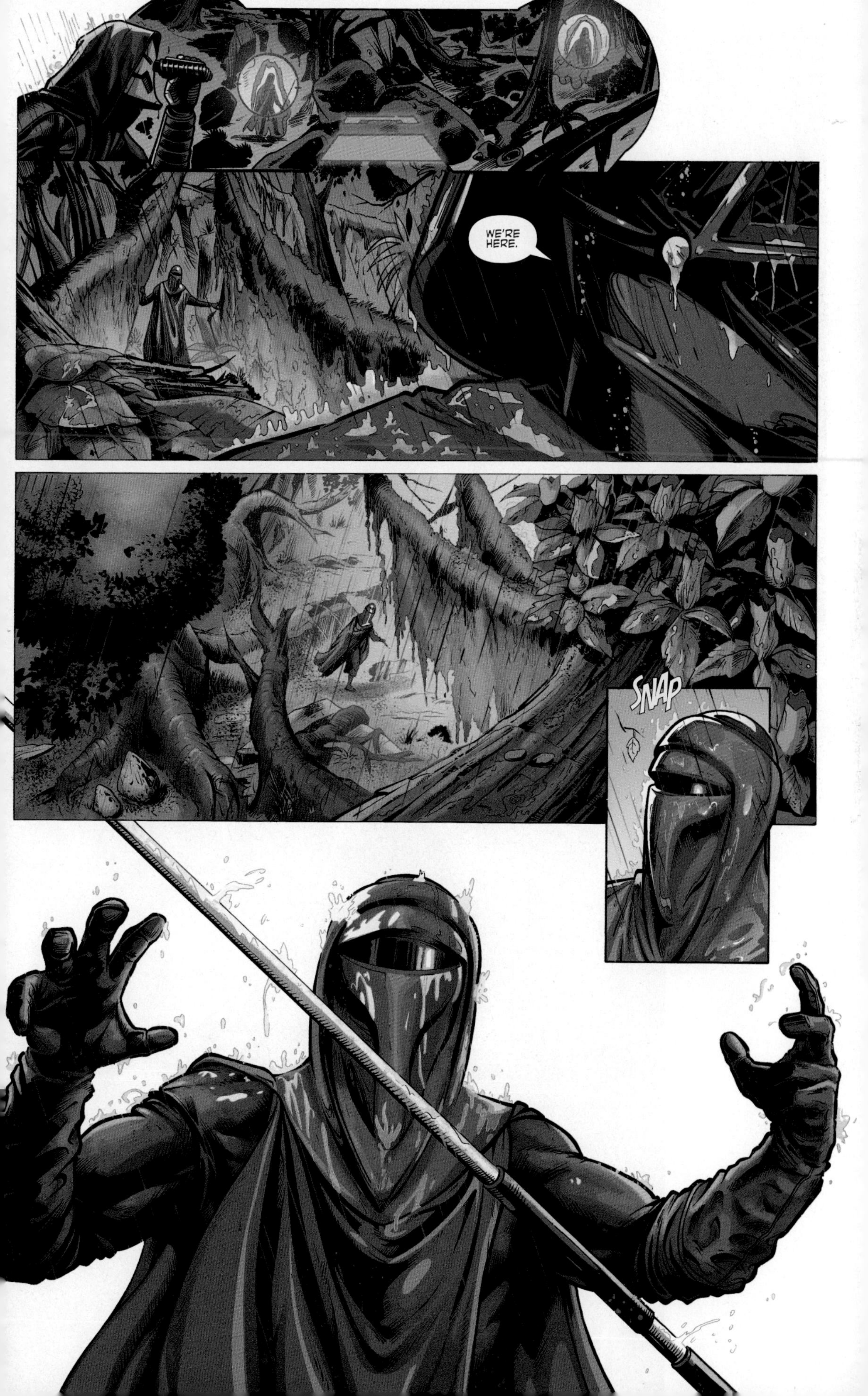
WE'RE HERE.
SNAP

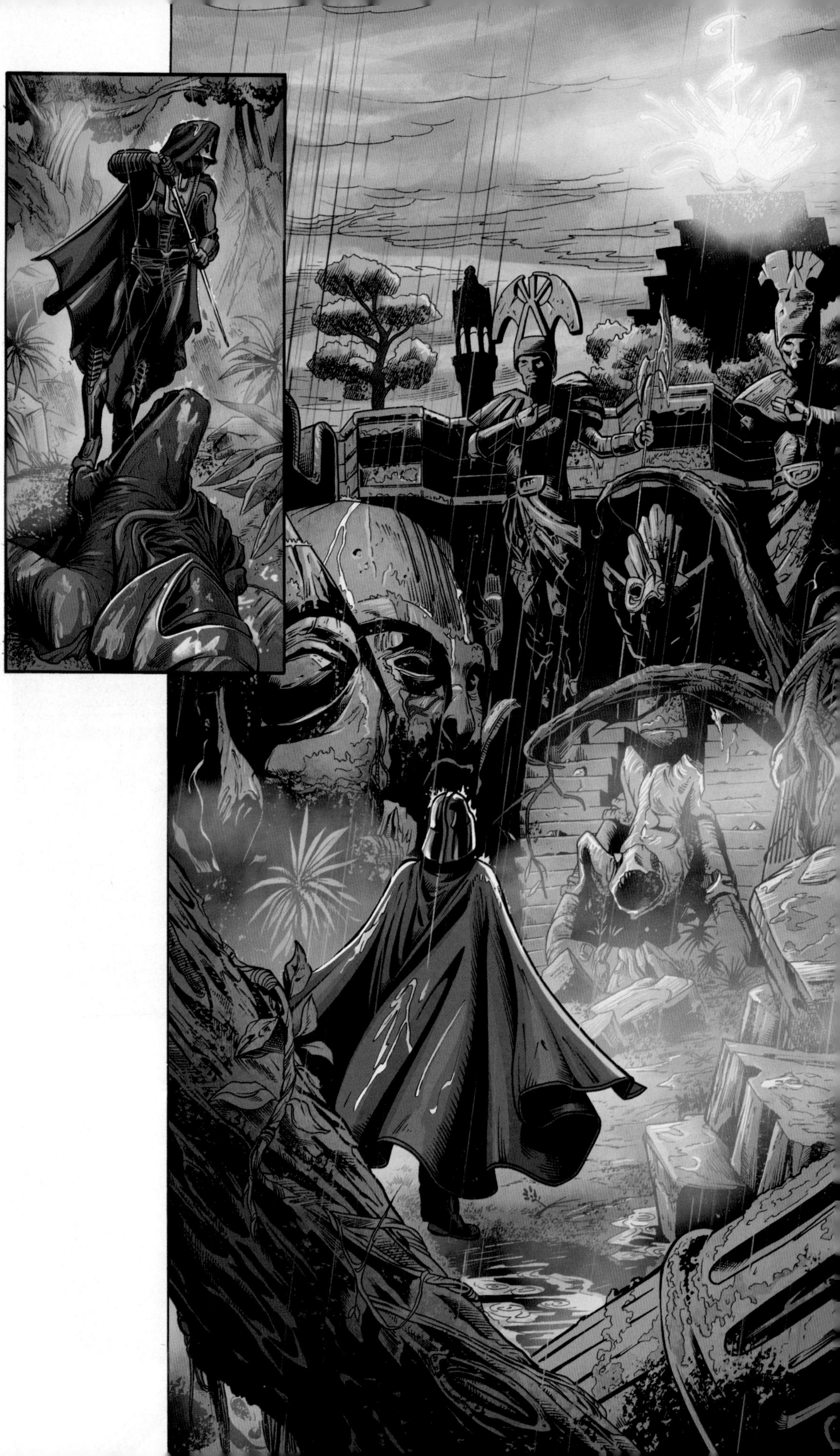

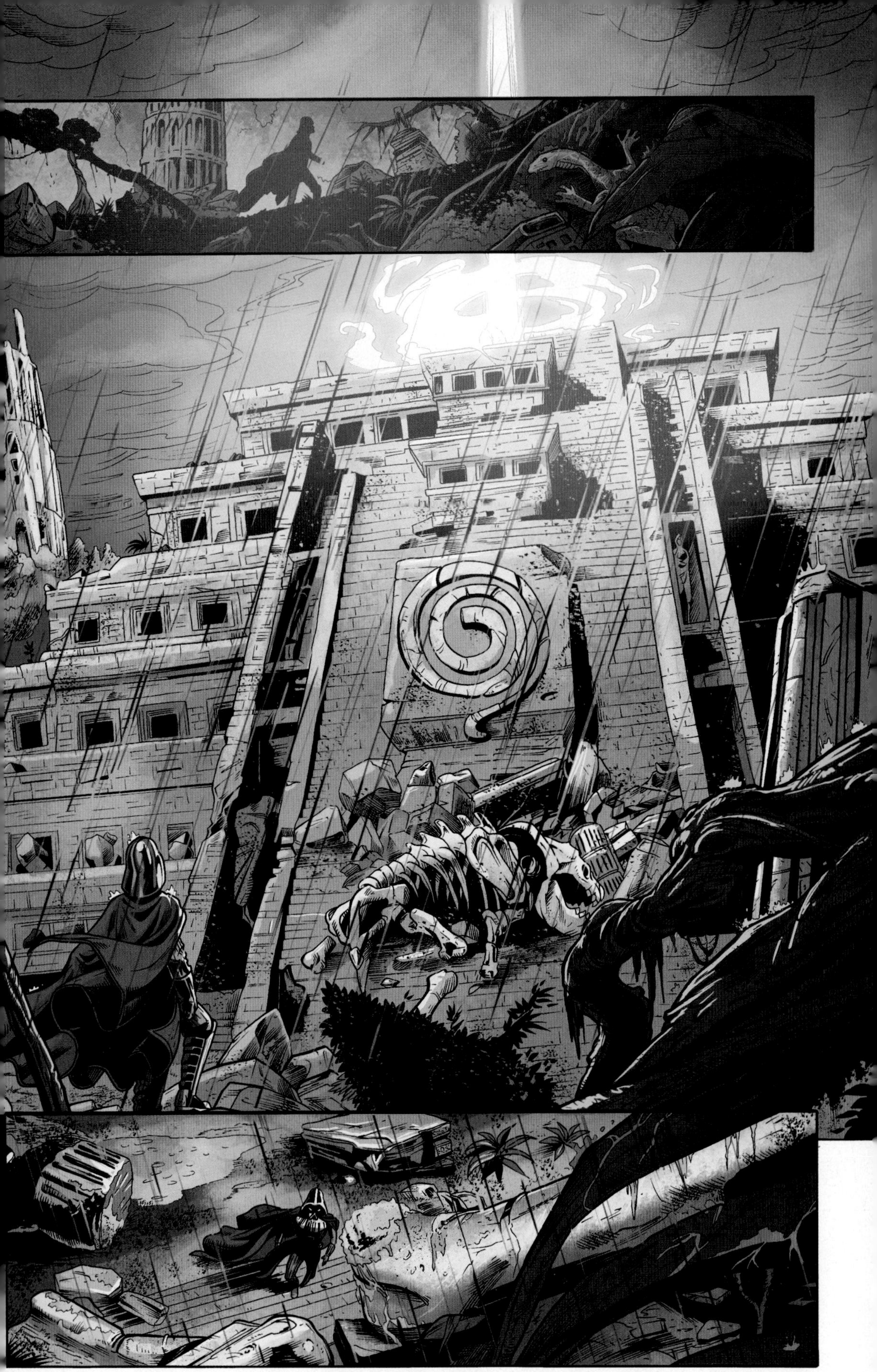

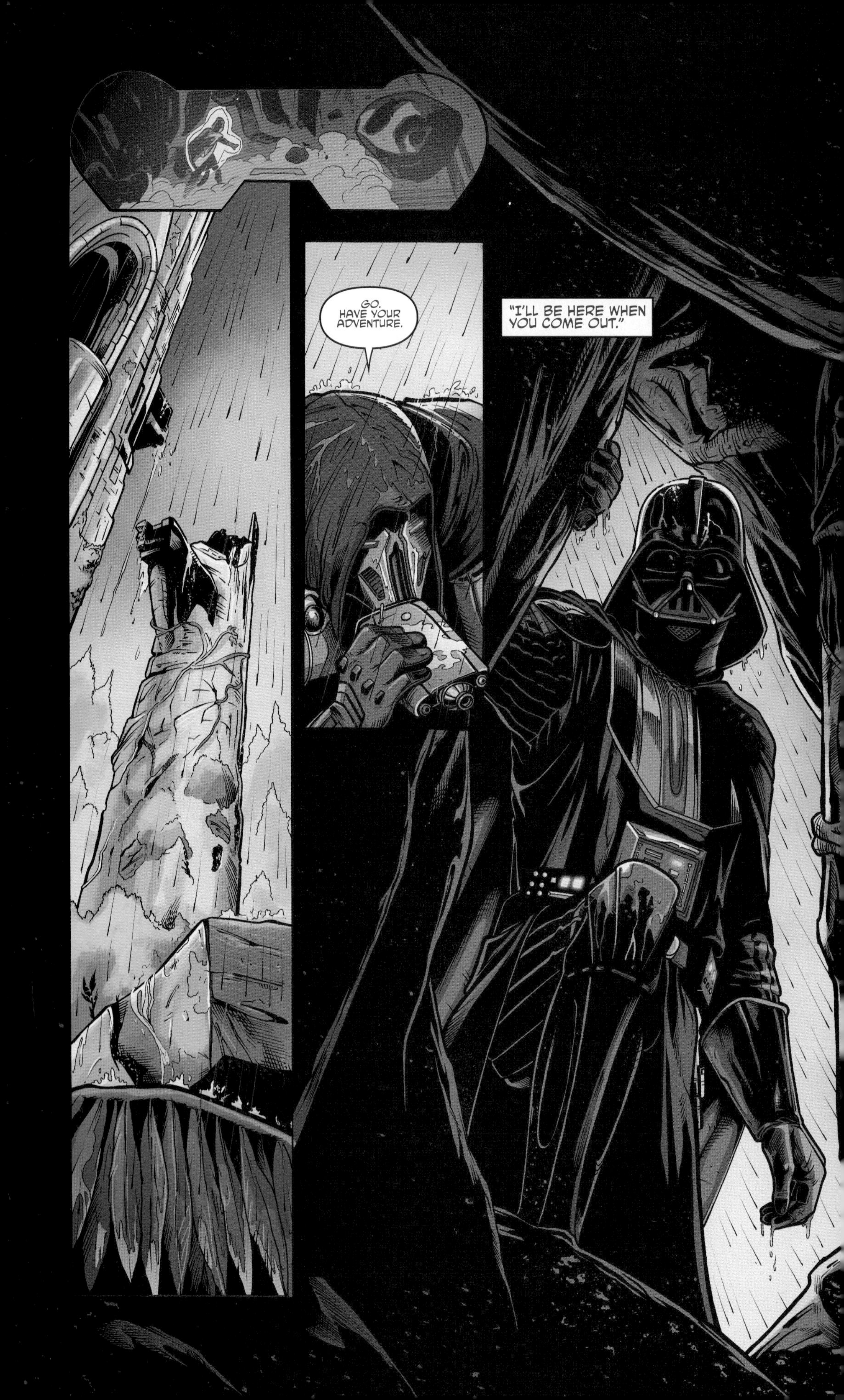
GO. HAVE YOUR ADVENTURE.
"I'LL BE HERE WHEN YOU COME OUT."

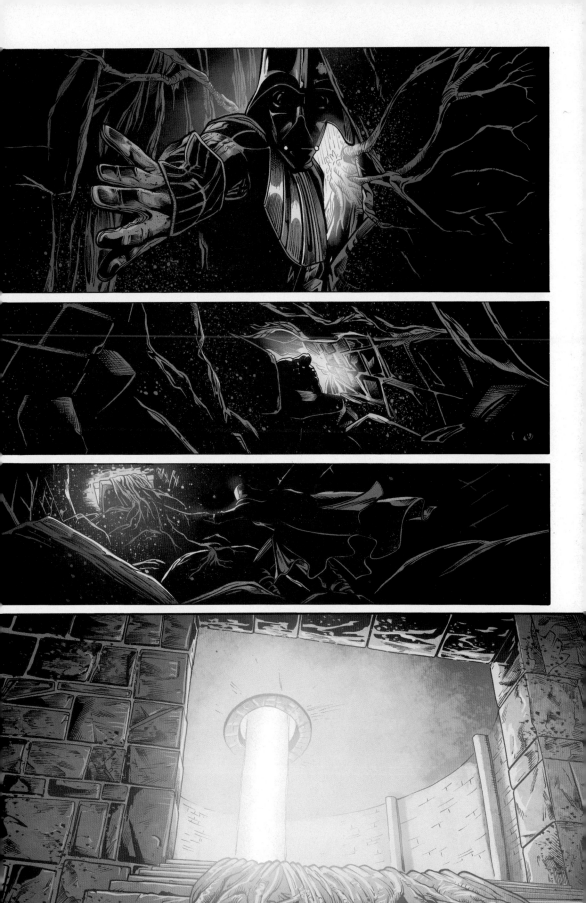

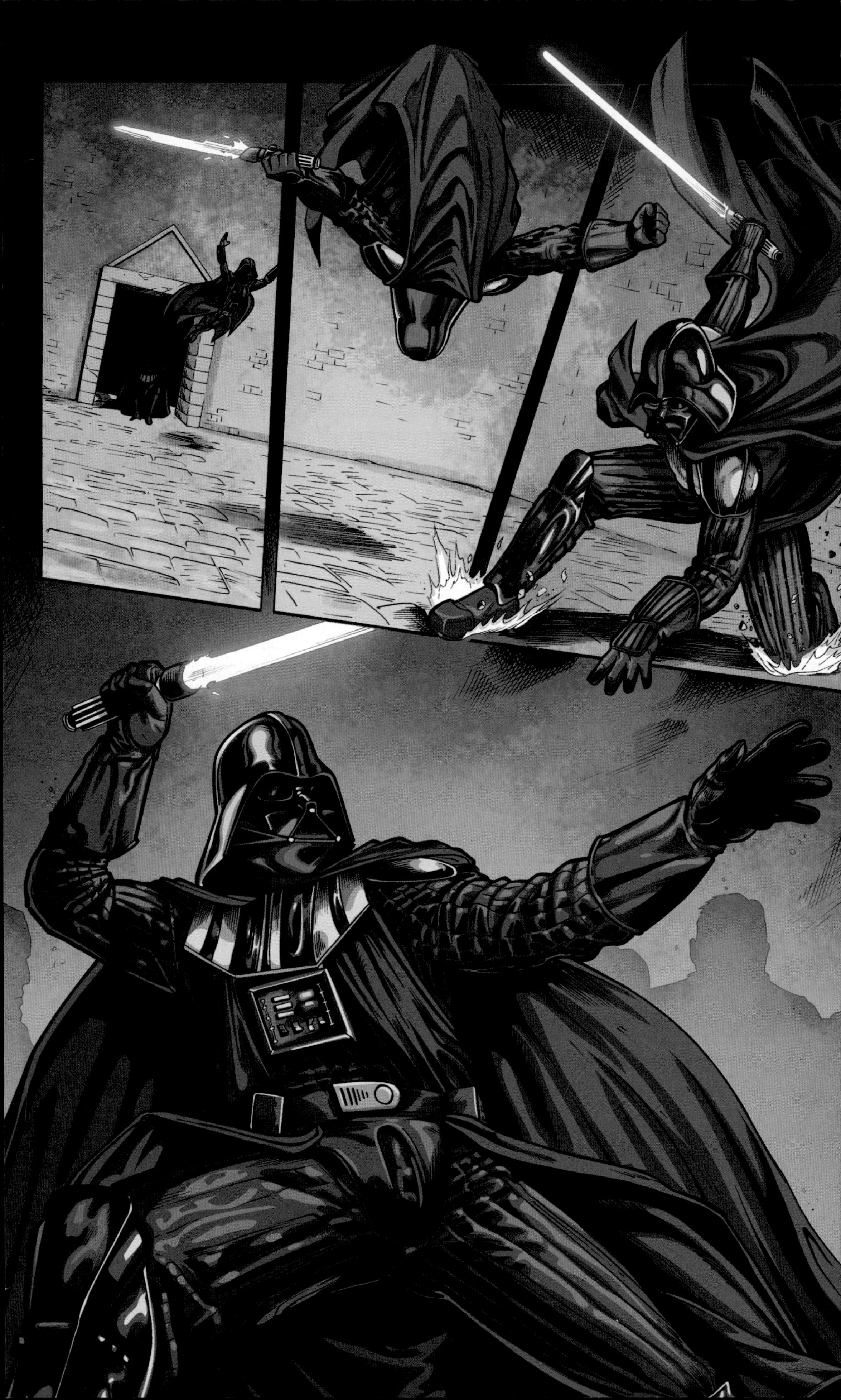

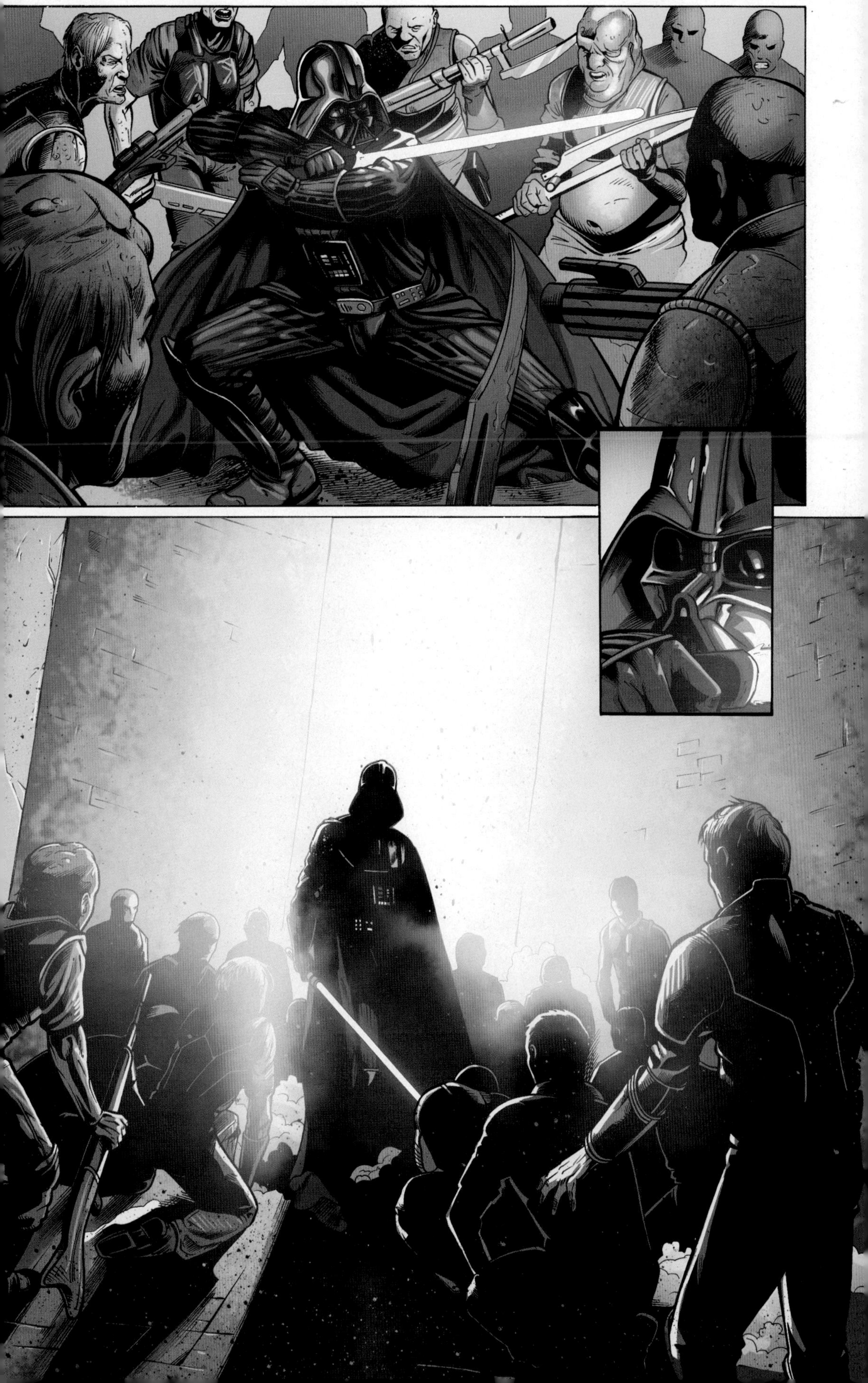

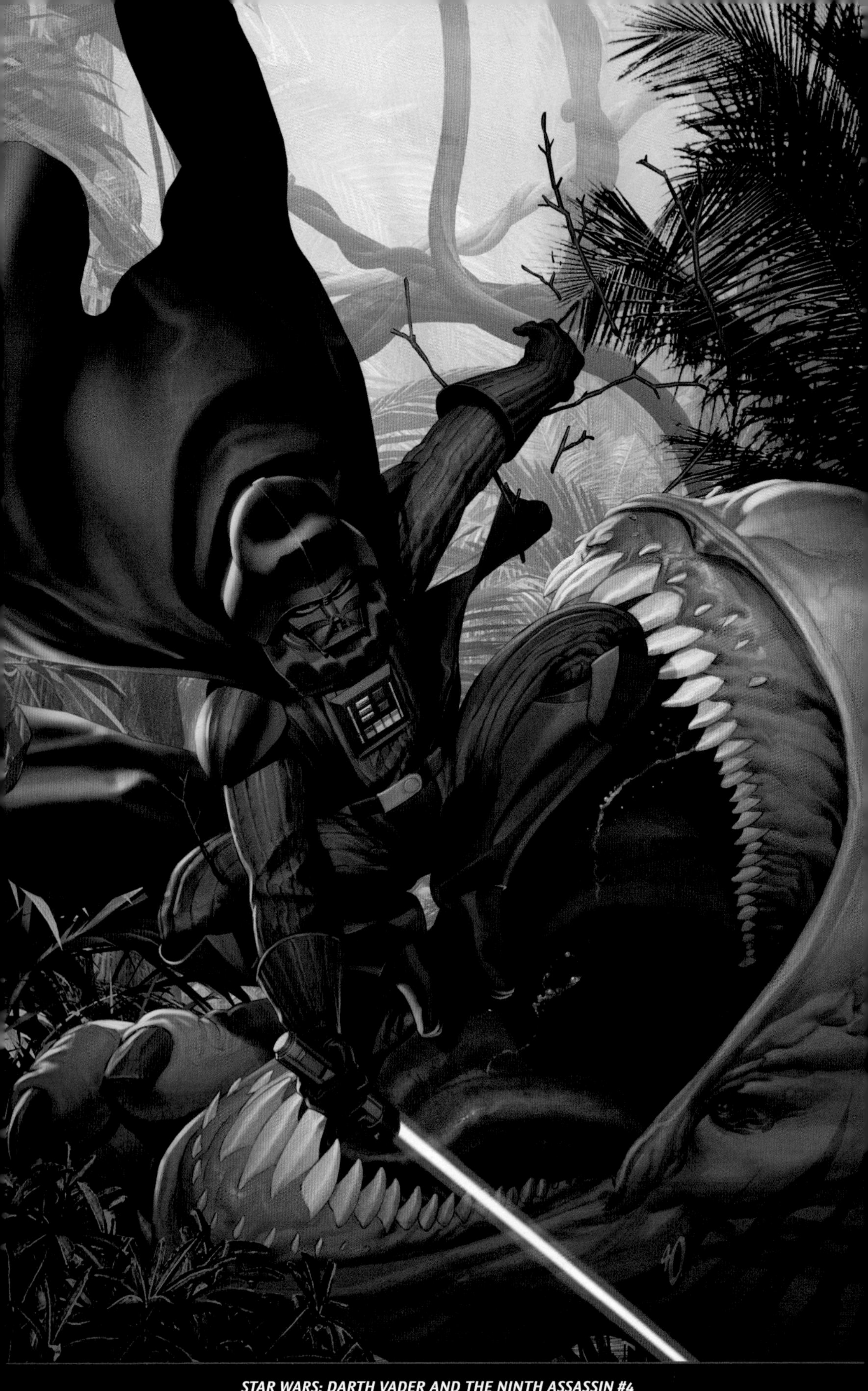

***STAR WARS: DARTH VADER AND THE NINTH ASSASSIN #4***

WRITER: TIM SIEDELL • PENCILER: STEPHEN THOMPSON • INKERS: MARK IRWIN, DREW GERACI & JASON GORDER • COLORIST: MICHAEL ATIYEH
LETTERER: MICHAEL HEISLER • ASSISTANT EDITOR: FREDDYE LINS • EDITOR: DAVE MARSHALL • COVER ARTIST: ARIEL OLIVETTI

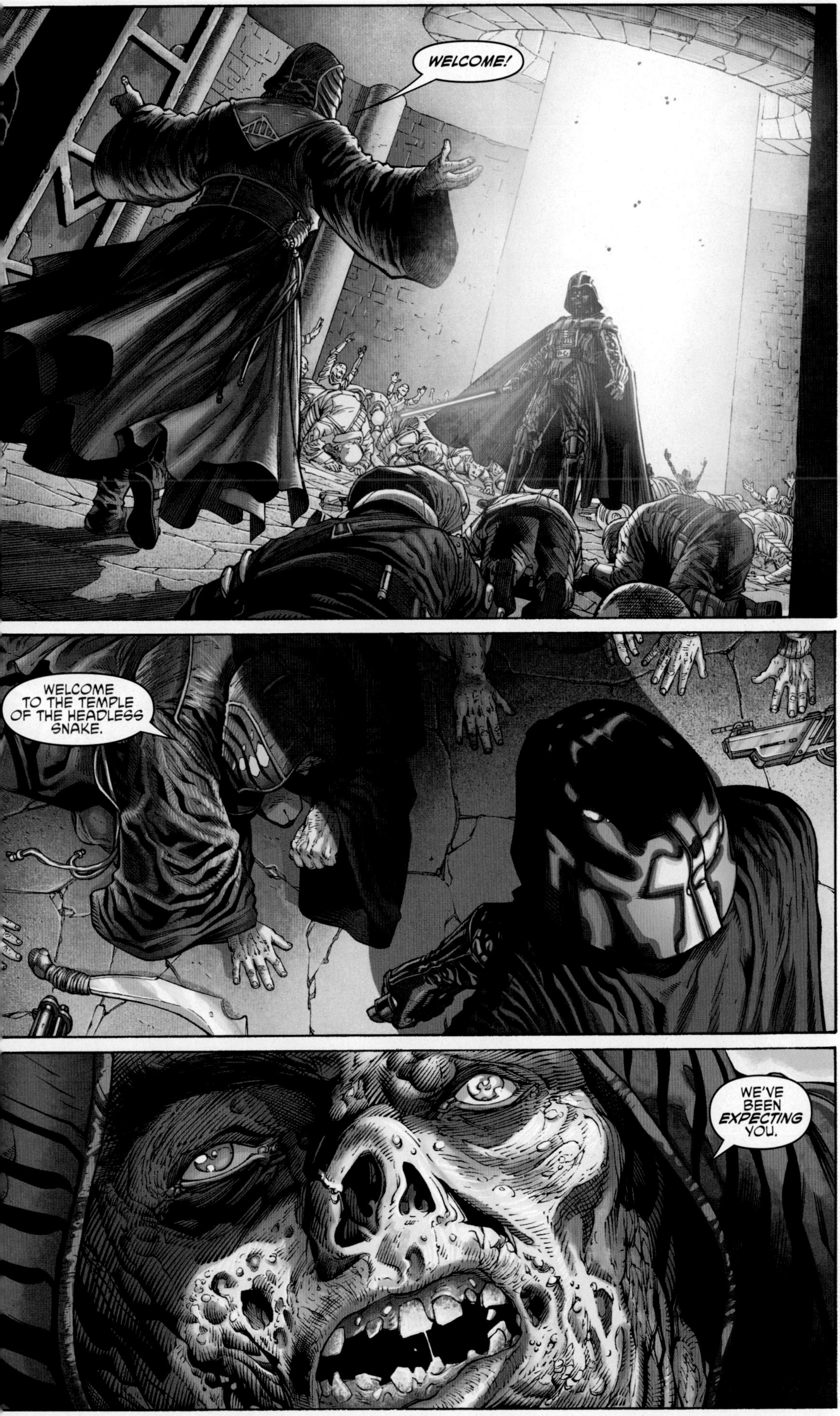
WELCOME!
WELCOME TO THE TEMPLE OF THE HEADLESS SNAKE.
WE'VE BEEN EXPECTING YOU.

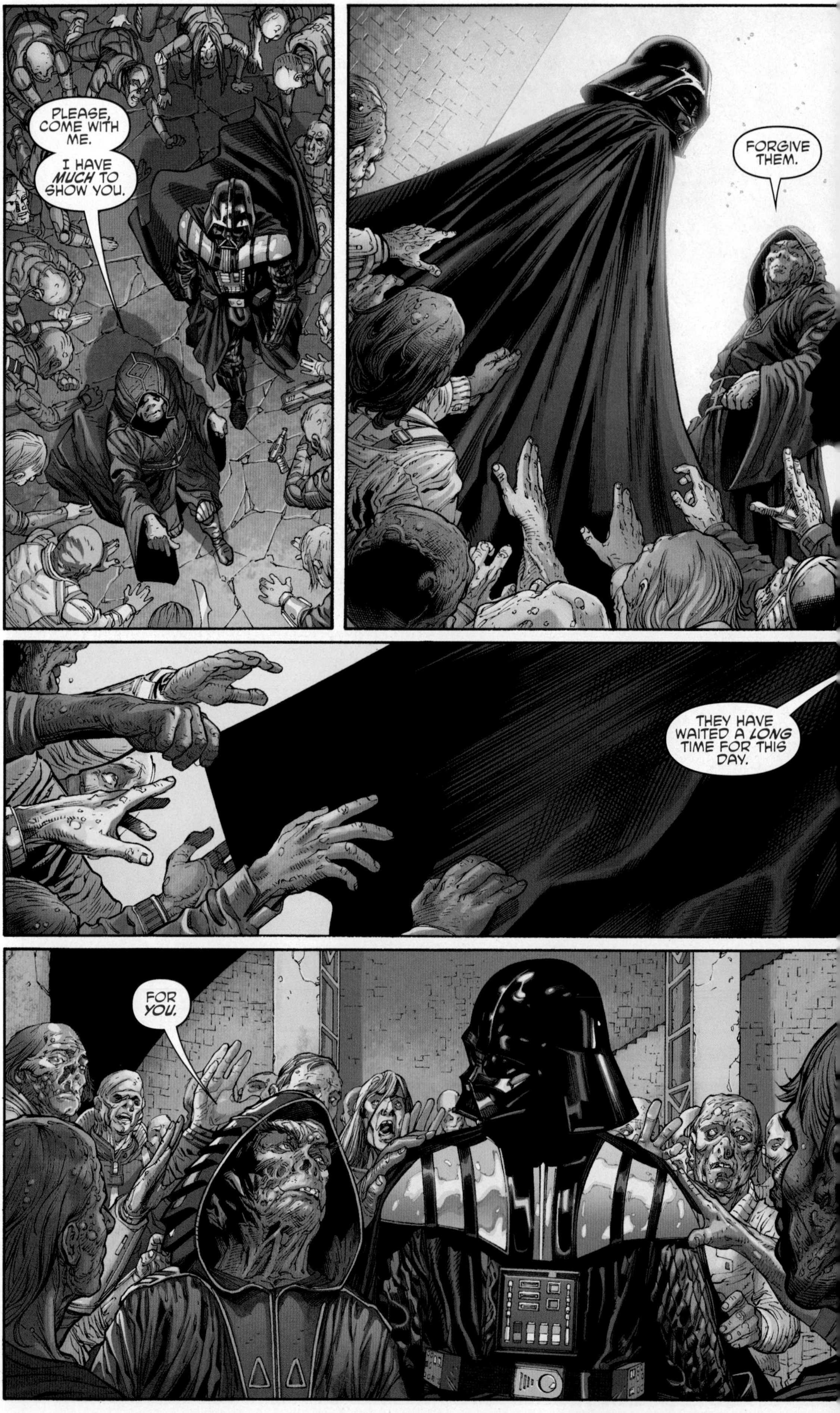
PLEASE, COME WITH ME.
I HAVE *MUCH* TO SHOW YOU.
FORGIVE THEM.
THEY HAVE WAITED A *LONG* TIME FOR THIS DAY.
FOR *YOU.*

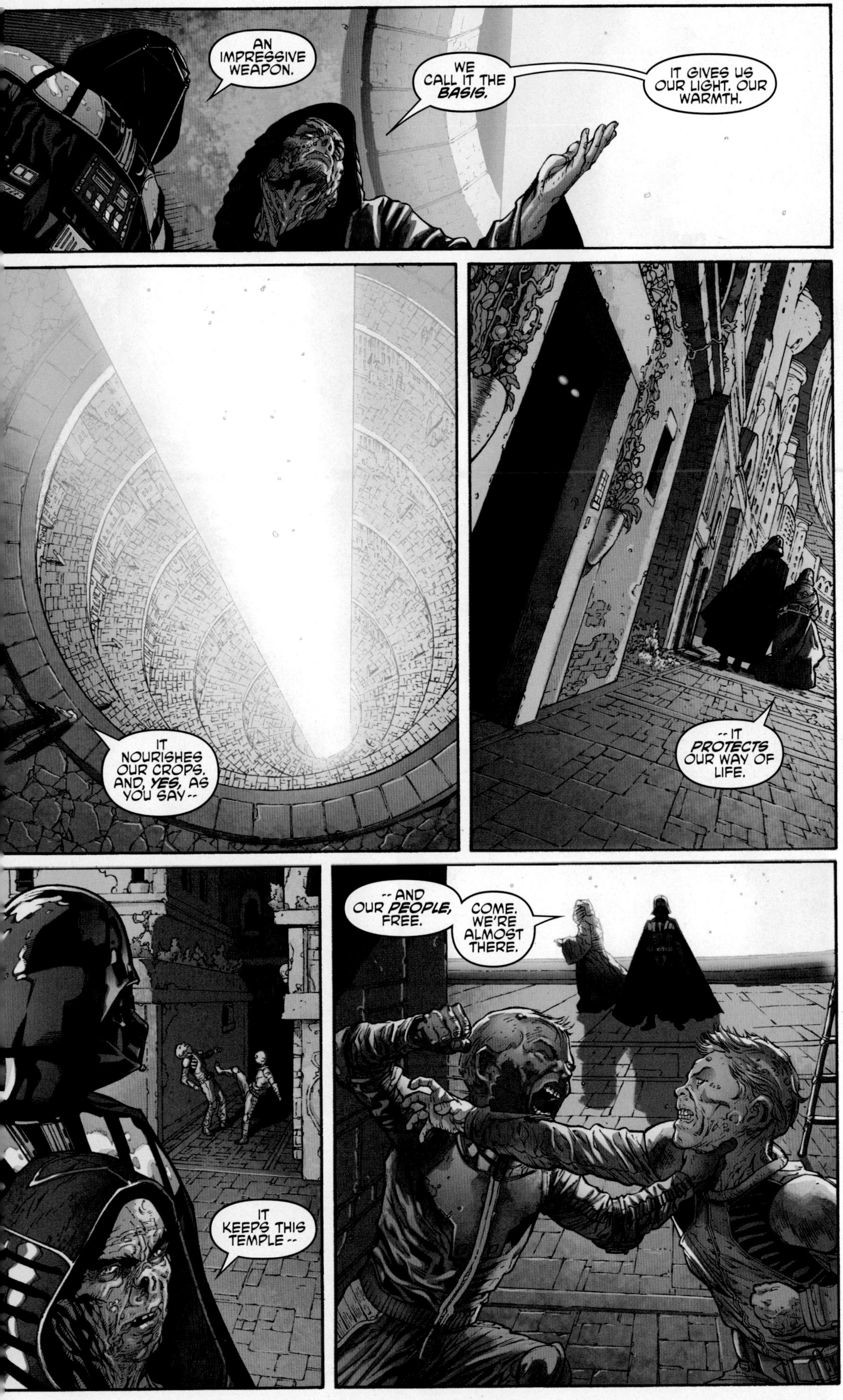
AN IMPRESSIVE WEAPON.
WE CALL IT THE *BASIS.*
IT GIVES US OUR LIGHT. OUR WARMTH.
IT NOURISHES OUR CROPS. AND, *YES,* AS YOU SAY --
-- IT *PROTECTS* OUR WAY OF LIFE.
IT KEEPS THIS TEMPLE --
-- AND OUR *PEOPLE,* FREE.
COME. WE'RE ALMOST THERE.

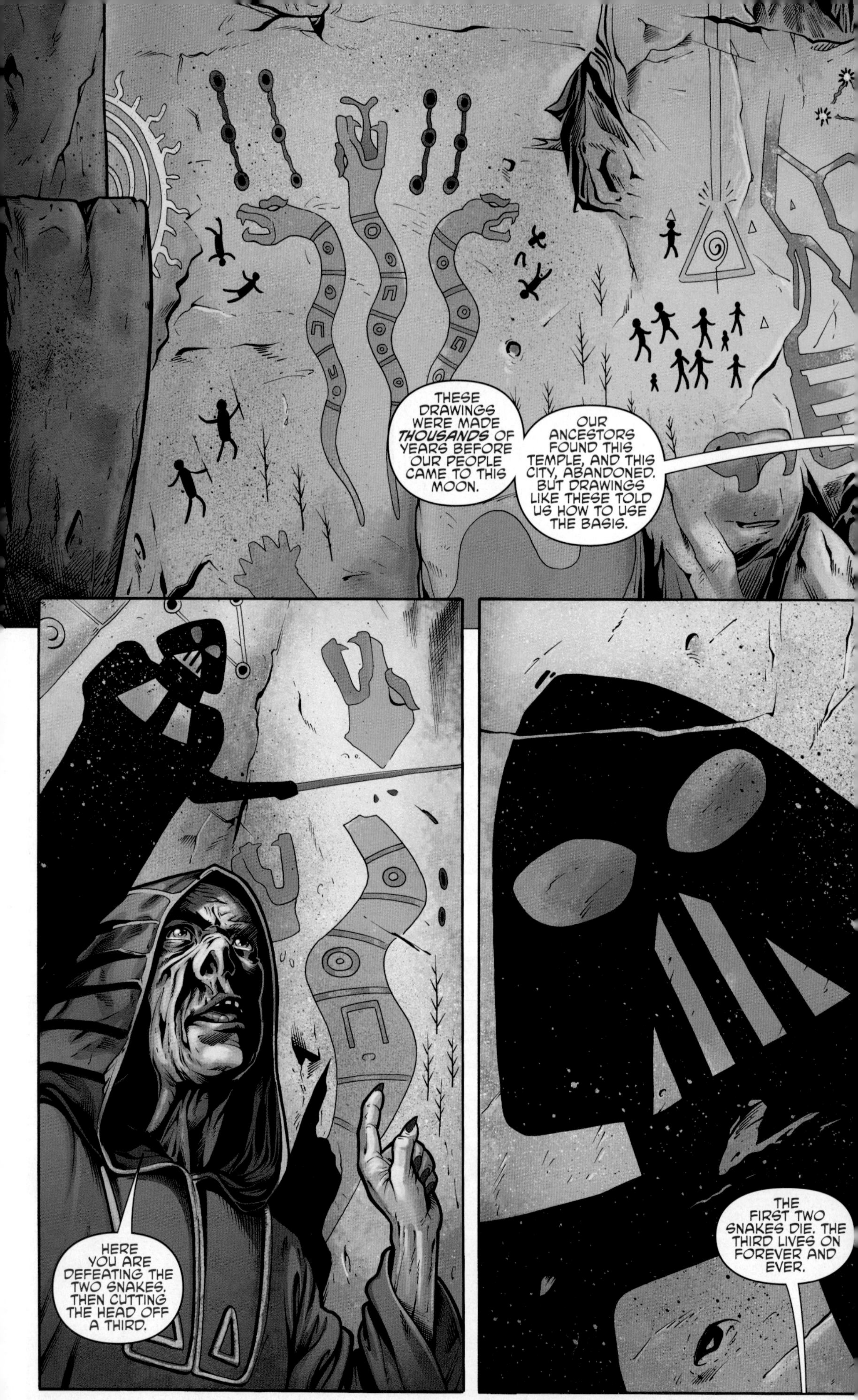
THESE DRAWINGS WERE MADE THOUSANDS OF YEARS BEFORE OUR PEOPLE CAME TO THIS MOON.
OUR ANCESTORS FOUND THIS TEMPLE, AND THIS CITY, ABANDONED. BUT DRAWINGS LIKE THESE TOLD US HOW TO USE THE BASIS.
HERE YOU ARE DEFEATING THE TWO SNAKES. THEN CUTTING THE HEAD OFF A THIRD.
THE FIRST TWO SNAKES DIE. THE THIRD LIVES ON FOREVER AND EVER.

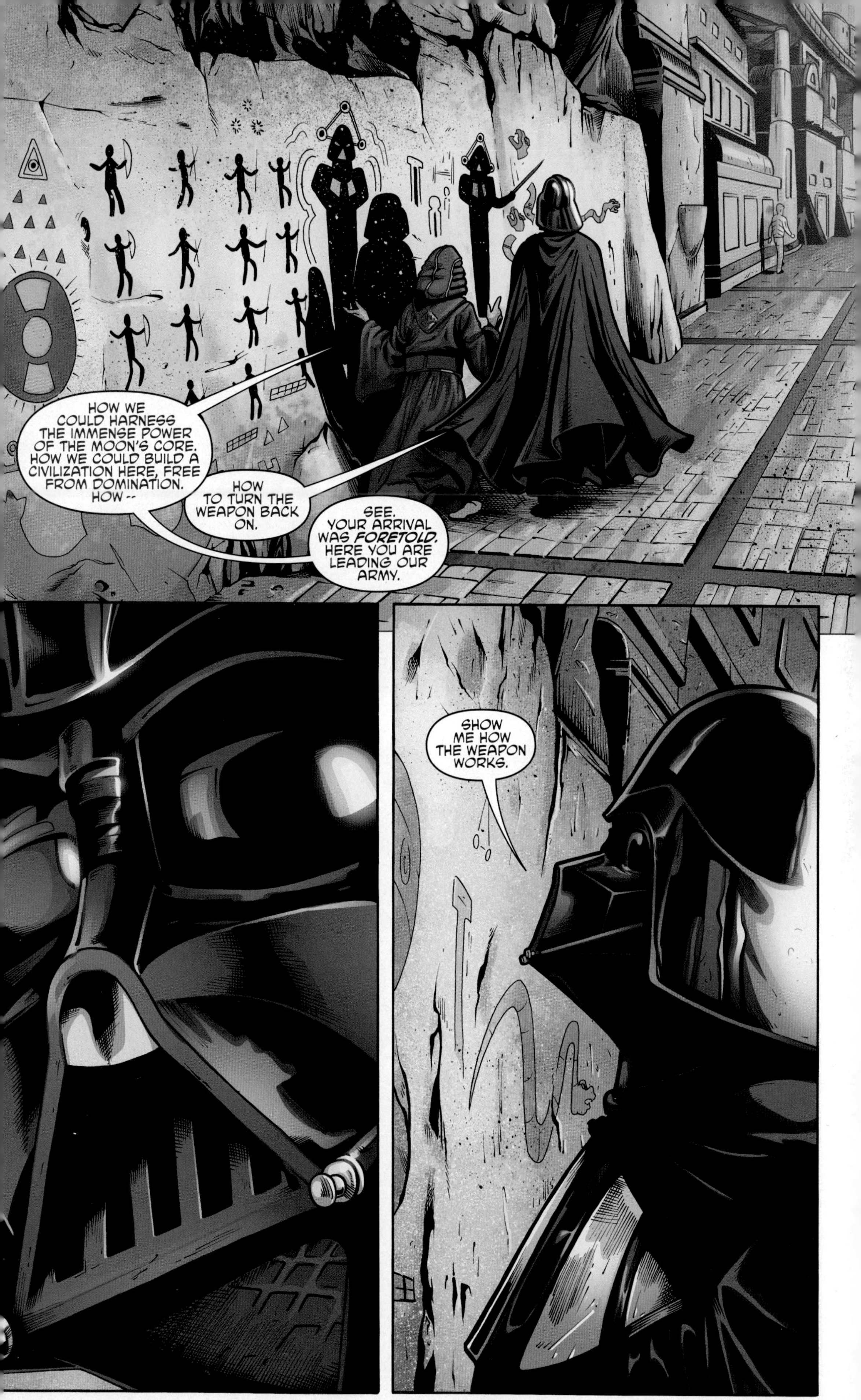
HOW WE COULD HARNESS THE IMMENSE POWER OF THE MOON'S CORE. HOW WE COULD BUILD A CIVILIZATION HERE, FREE FROM DOMINATION. HOW --
HOW TO TURN THE WEAPON BACK ON.
SEE. YOUR ARRIVAL WAS *FORETOLD.* HERE YOU ARE LEADING OUR ARMY.
SHOW ME HOW THE WEAPON WORKS.

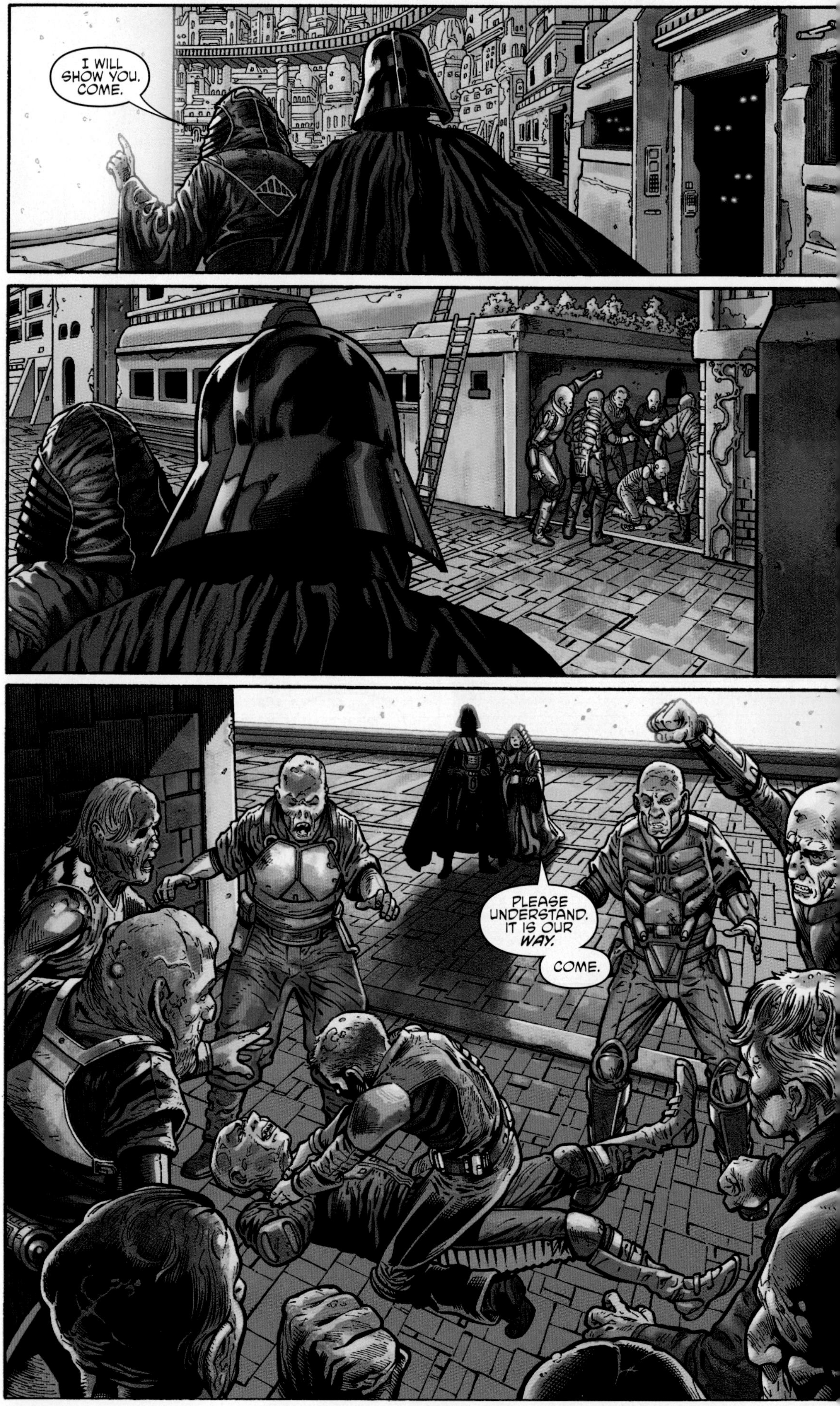
I WILL SHOW YOU. COME.
PLEASE UNDERSTAND. IT IS OUR *WAY.*
COME.

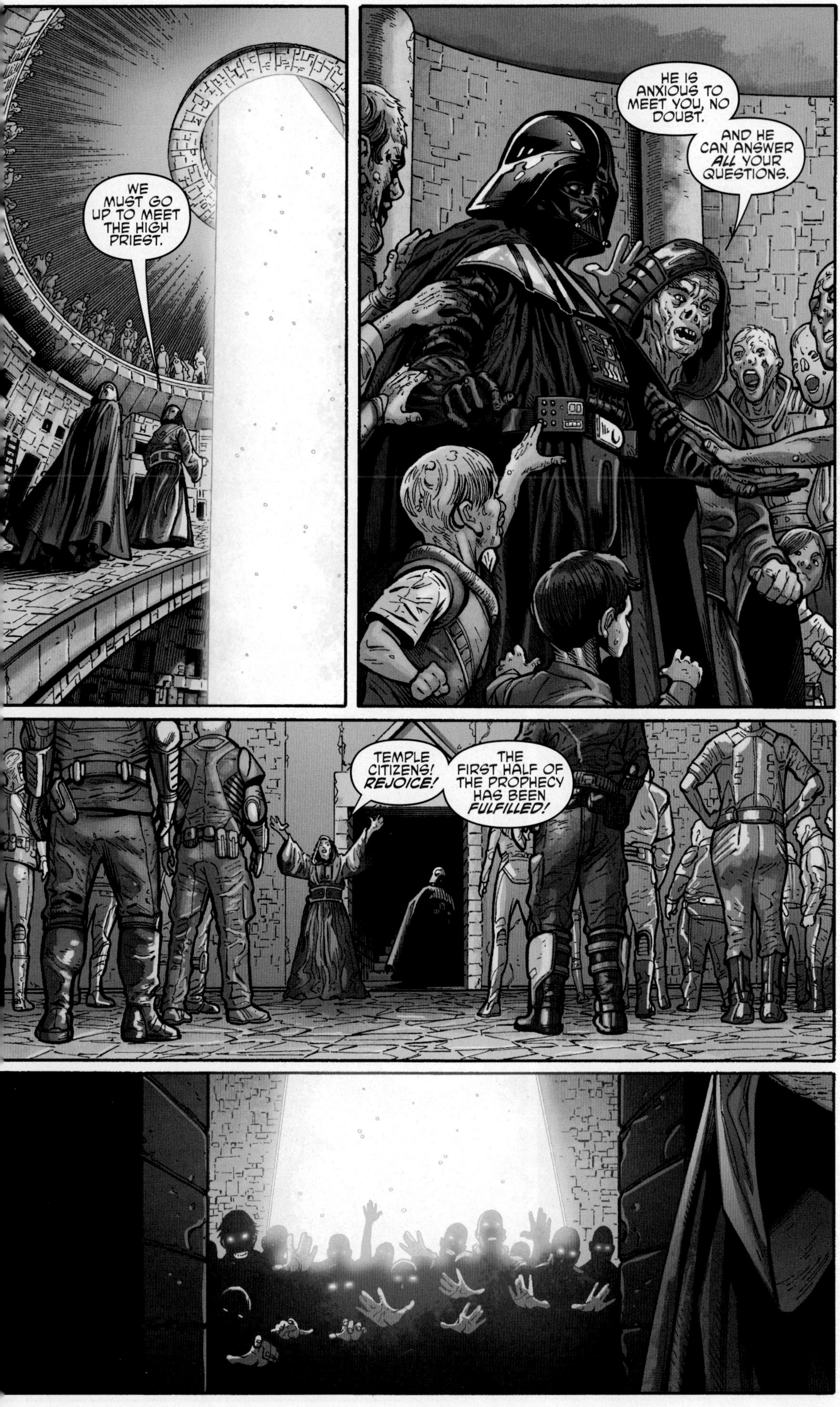
WE MUST GO UP TO MEET THE HIGH PRIEST.
HE IS ANXIOUS TO MEET YOU, NO DOUBT.
AND HE CAN ANSWER *ALL* YOUR QUESTIONS.
TEMPLE CITIZENS! *REJOICE!*
THE FIRST HALF OF THE PROPHECY HAS BEEN *FULFILLED!*

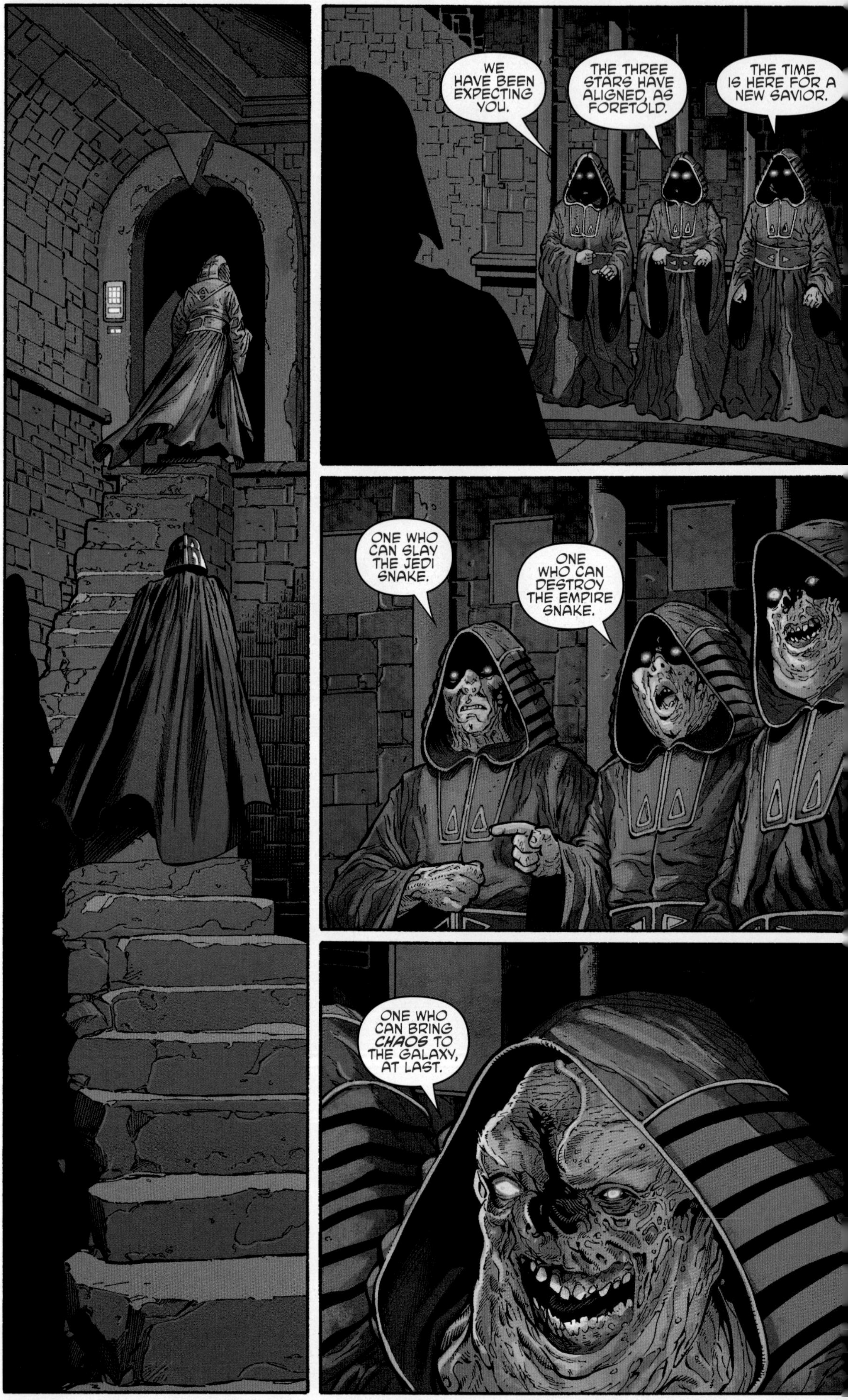
WE HAVE BEEN EXPECTING YOU.
THE THREE STARS HAVE ALIGNED, AS FORETOLD.
THE TIME IS HERE FOR A NEW SAVIOR.
ONE WHO CAN SLAY THE JEDI SNAKE.
ONE WHO CAN DESTROY THE EMPIRE SNAKE.
ONE WHO CAN BRING *CHAOS* TO THE GALAXY, AT LAST.

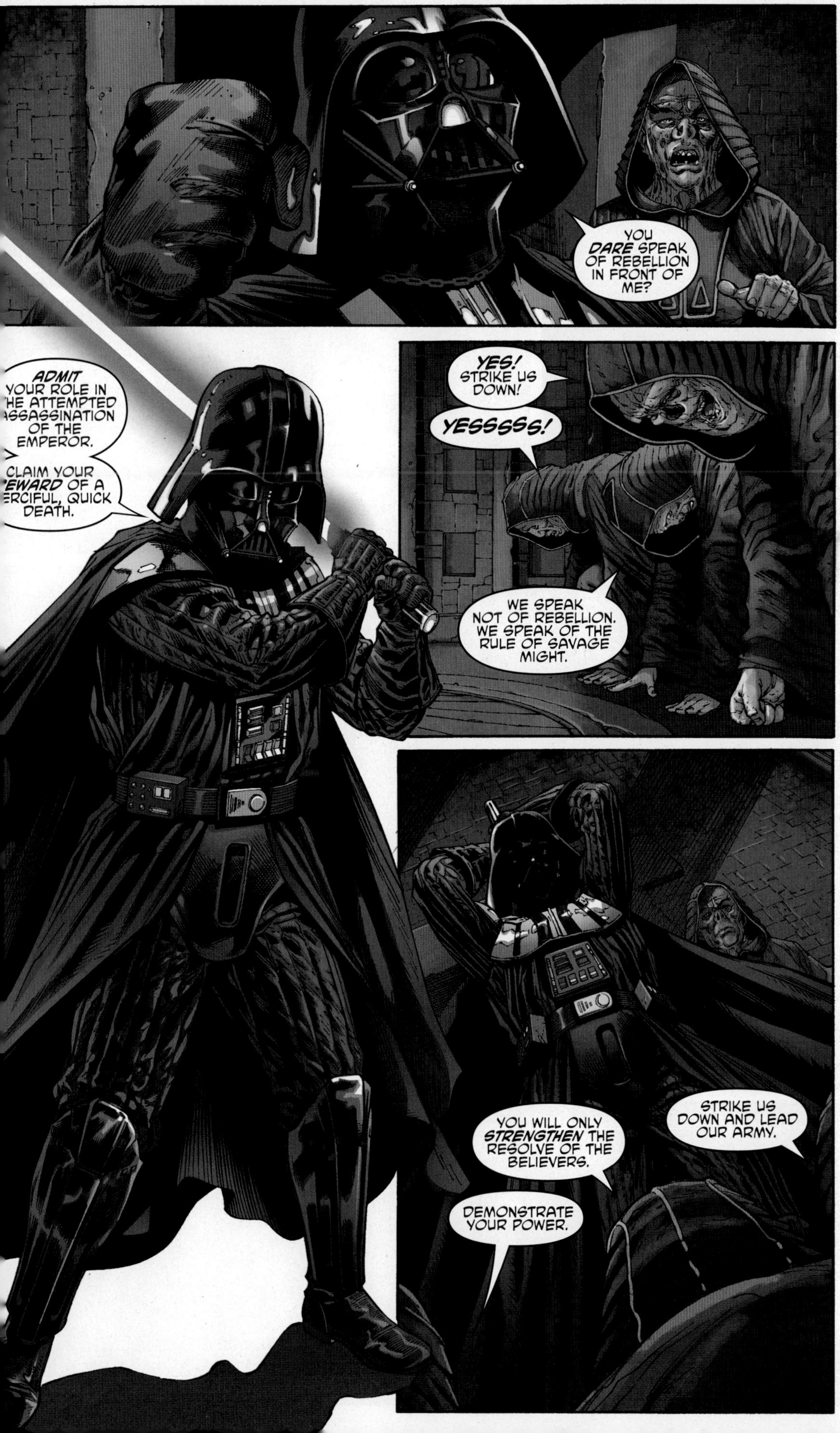

YOU *DARE* SPEAK OF REBELLION IN FRONT OF ME?
*ADMIT* YOUR ROLE IN HE ATTEMPTED ASSASSINATION OF THE EMPEROR.
CLAIM YOUR *EWARD* OF A ERCIFUL, QUICK DEATH.
*YES!* STRIKE US DOWN!
*YESSSSS!*
WE SPEAK NOT OF REBELLION. WE SPEAK OF THE RULE OF SAVAGE MIGHT.
STRIKE US DOWN AND LEAD OUR ARMY.
YOU WILL ONLY *STRENGTHEN* THE RESOLVE OF THE BELIEVERS.
DEMONSTRATE YOUR POWER.

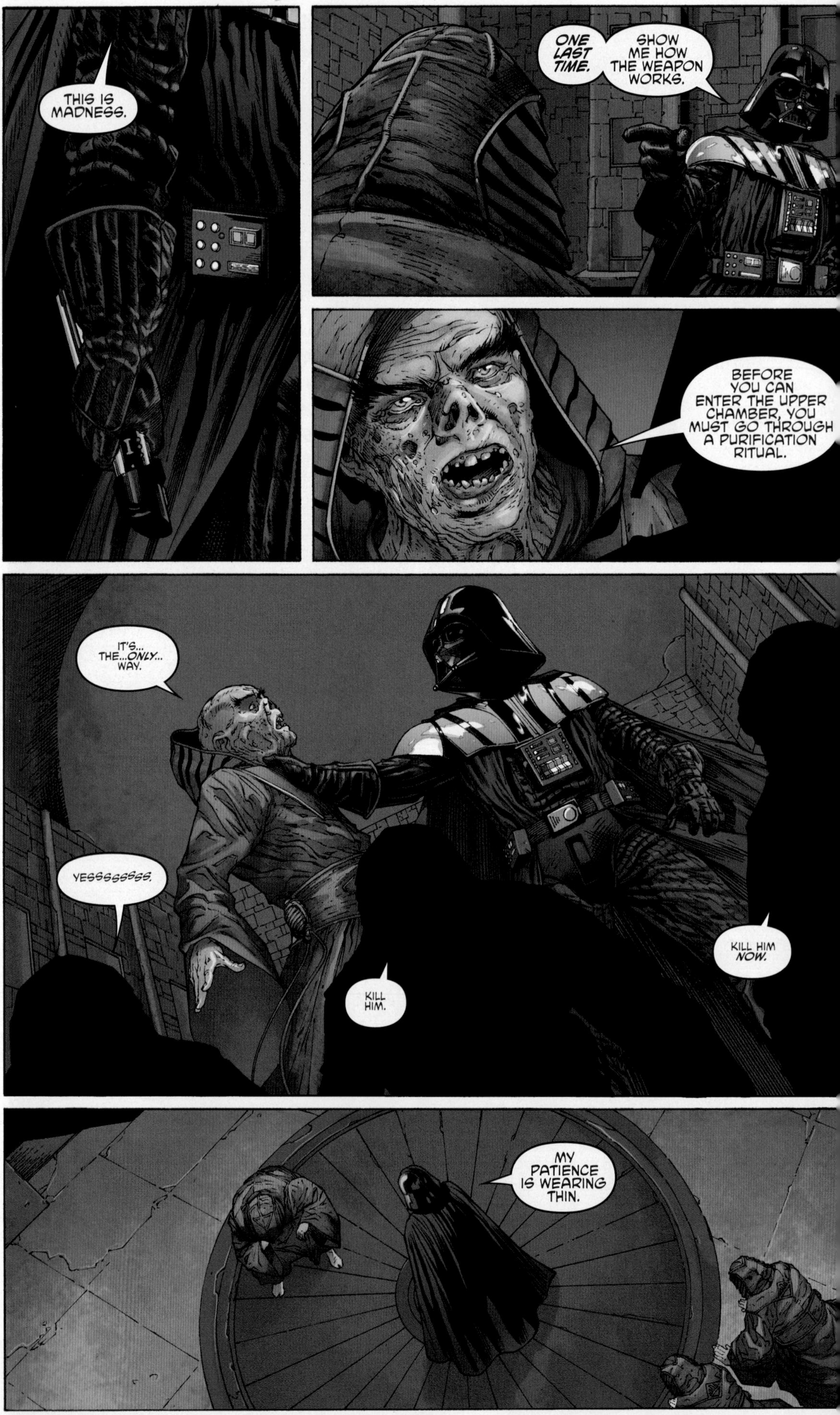
THIS IS MADNESS.
ONE LAST TIME.
SHOW ME HOW THE WEAPON WORKS.
BEFORE YOU CAN ENTER THE UPPER CHAMBER, YOU MUST GO THROUGH A PURIFICATION RITUAL.
IT'S... THE...ONLY... WAY.
YESSSSSSSS.
KILL HIM.
KILL HIM NOW.
MY PATIENCE IS WEARING THIN.

JUST LOOK --
=COUGH=

--THAT'S ALL YOU NEED TO DO.

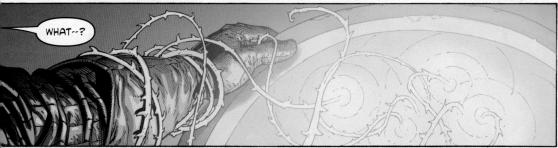

WHAT--?

CAN'T... BREATHE...

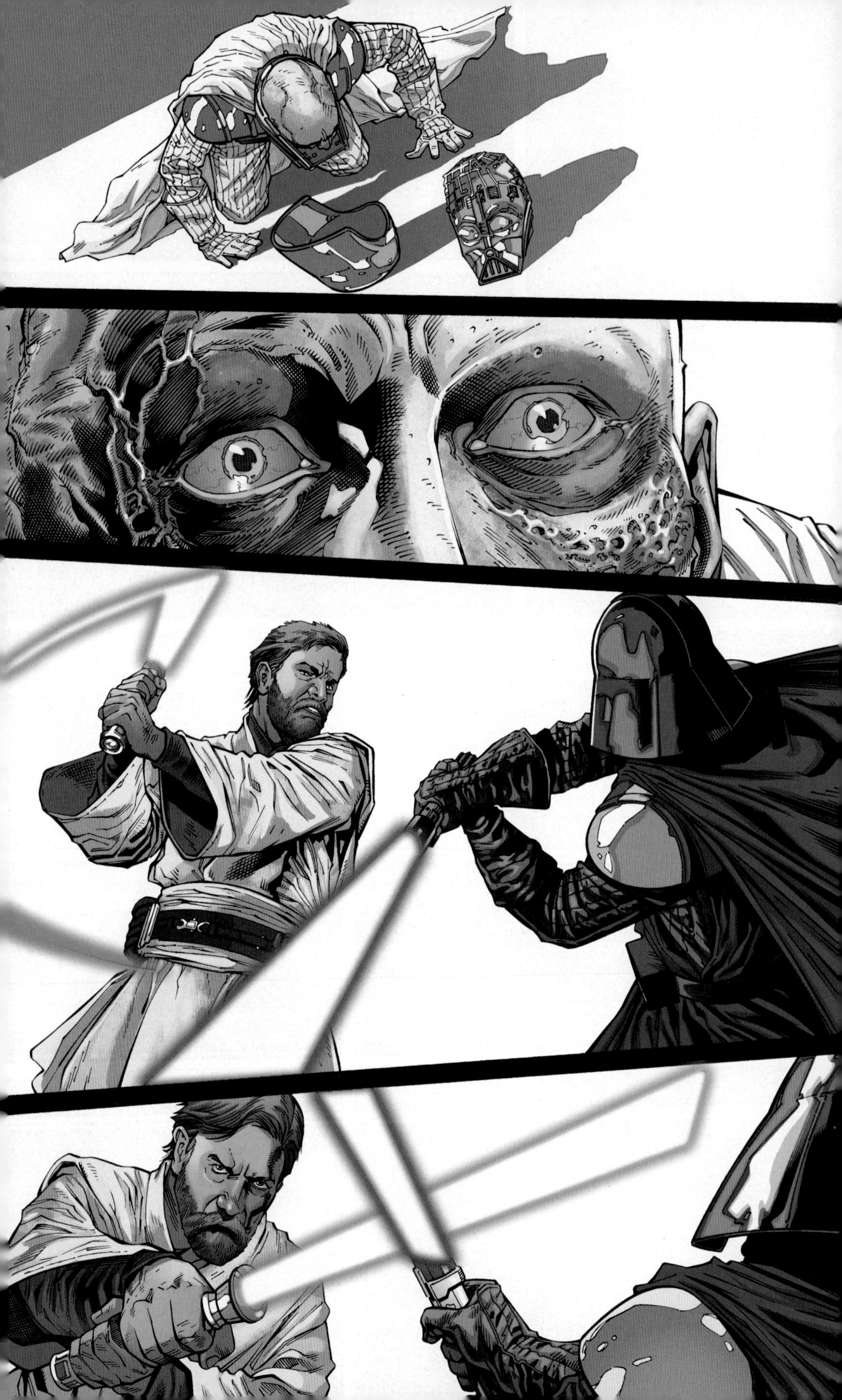

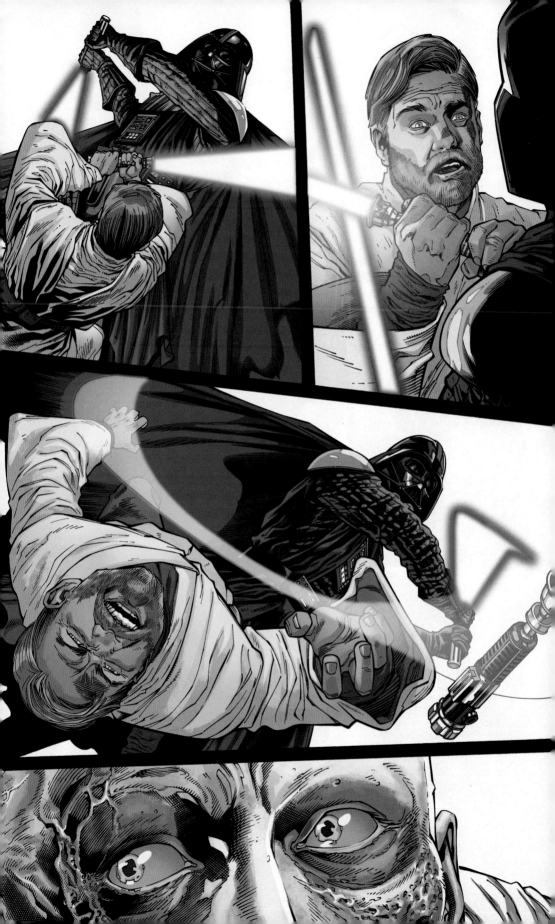

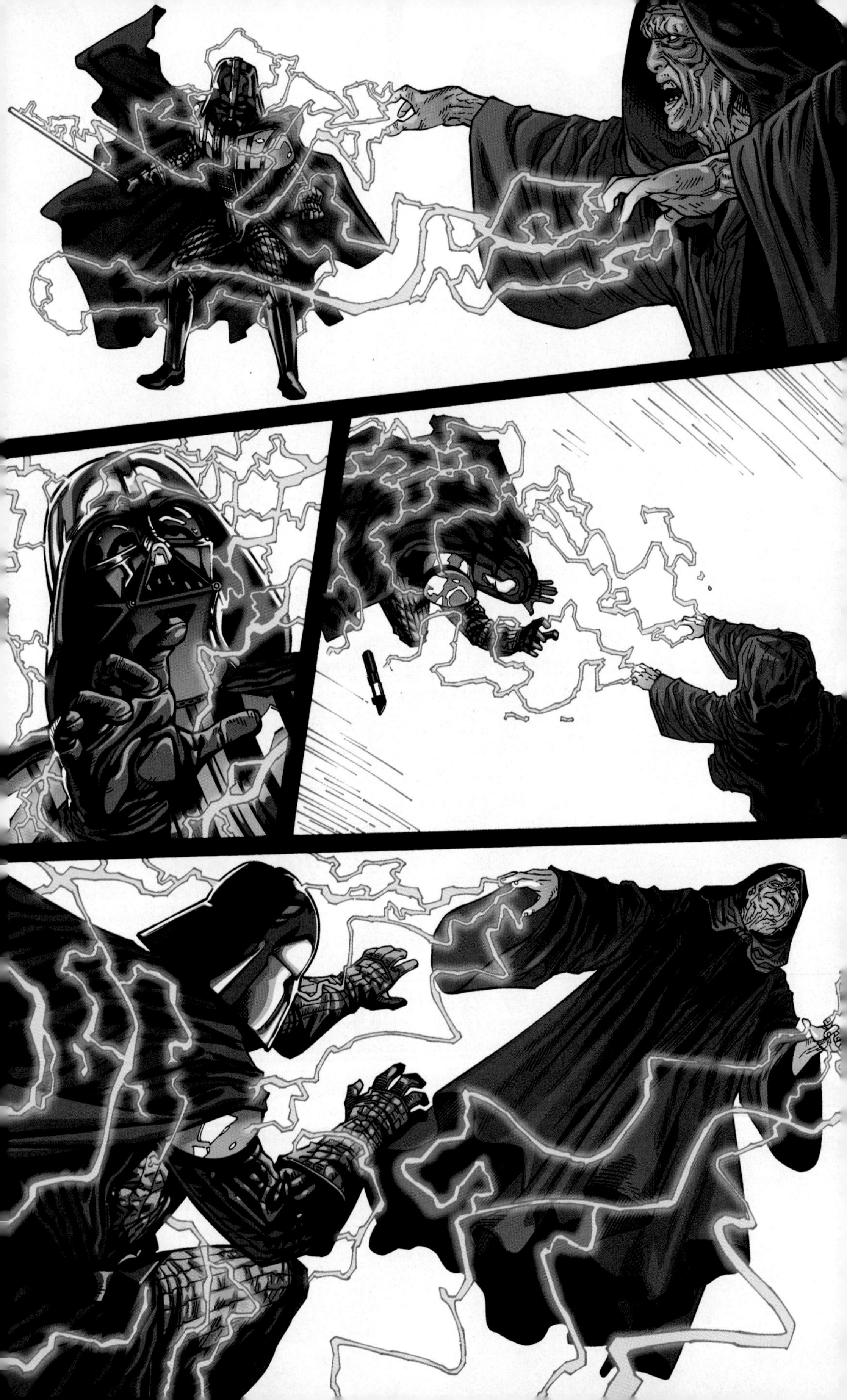

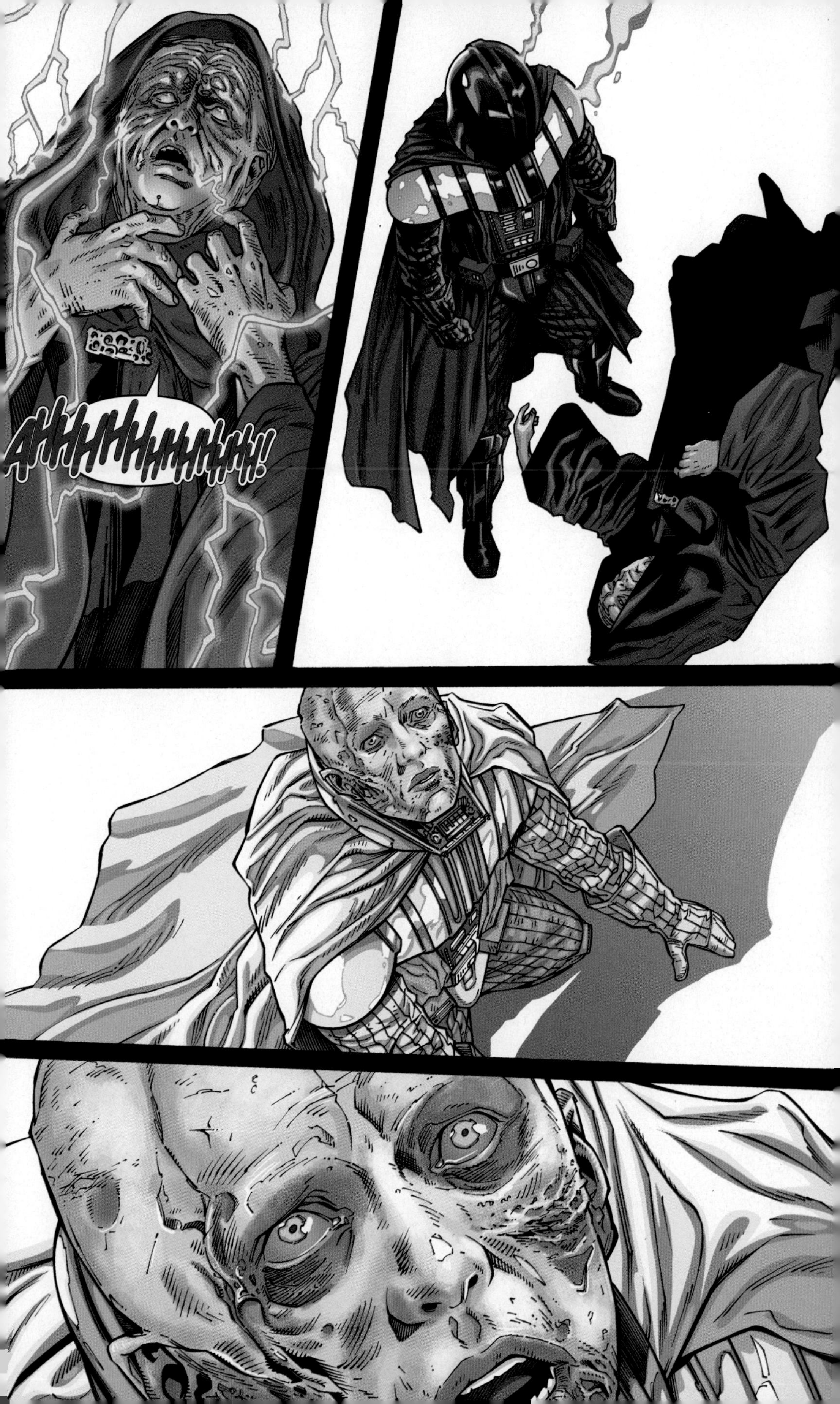
AHHHHHHHHHHHHHH!

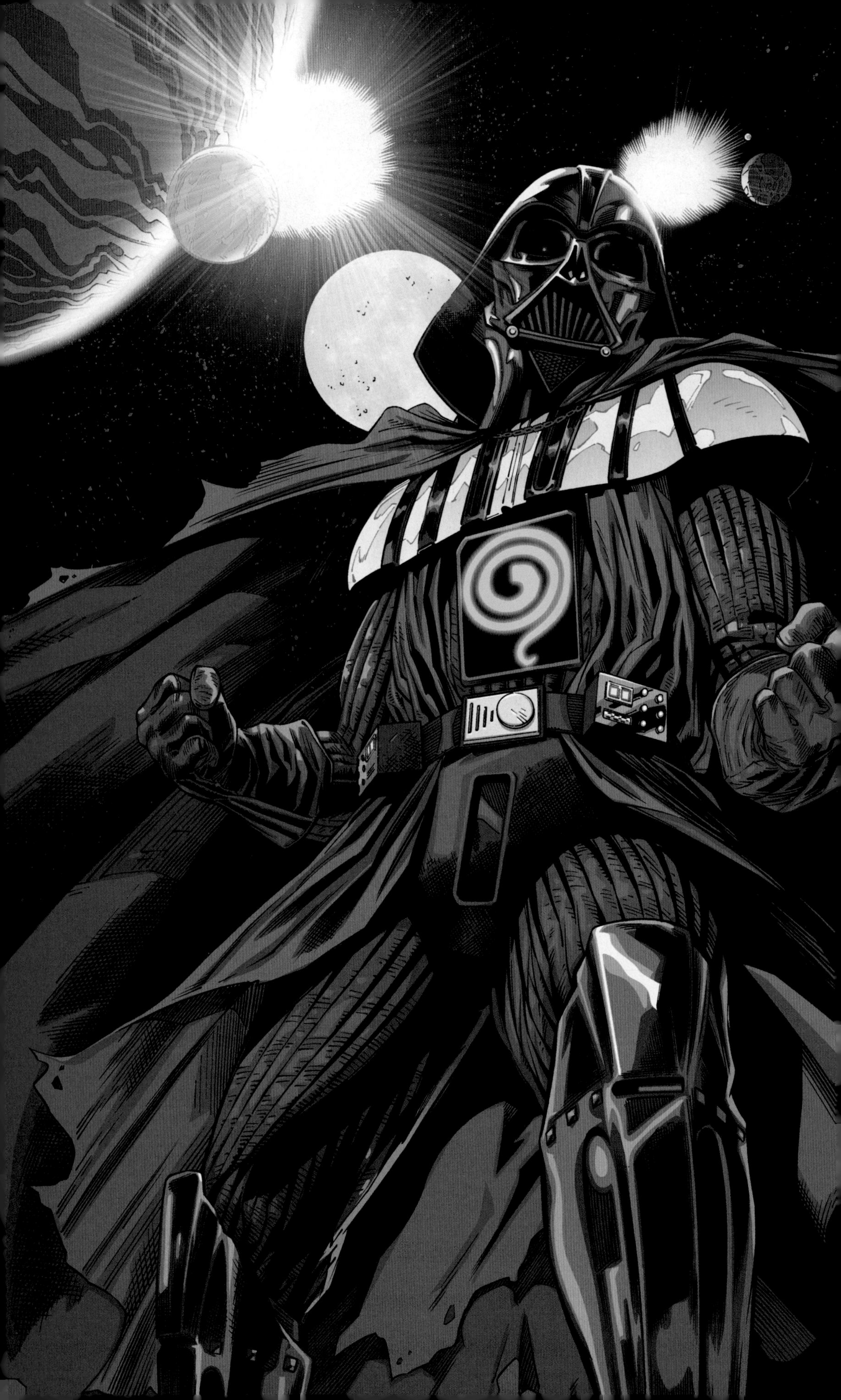

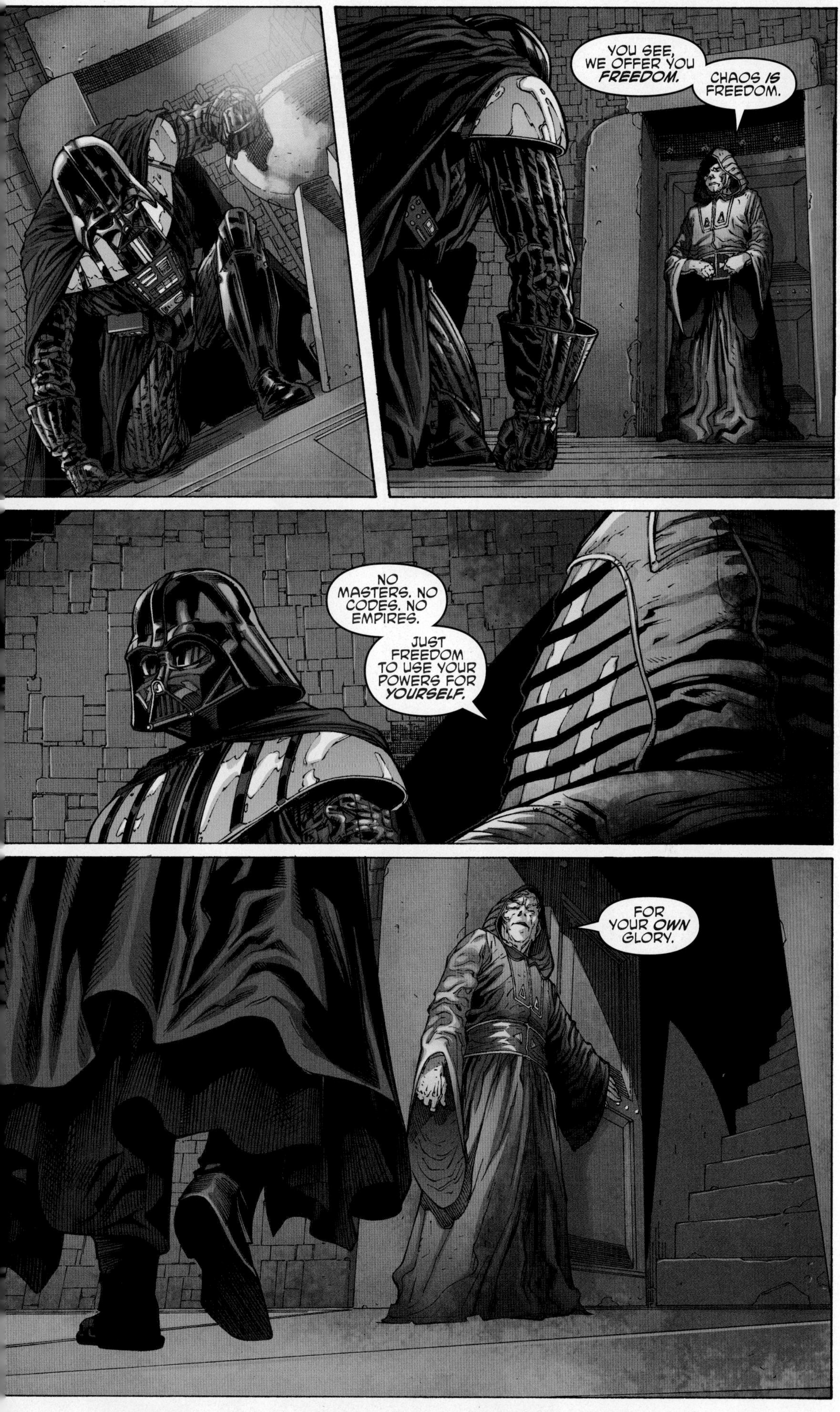
YOU SEE, WE OFFER YOU FREEDOM.
CHAOS IS FREEDOM.
NO MASTERS. NO CODES. NO EMPIRES.
JUST FREEDOM TO USE YOUR POWERS FOR YOURSELF.
FOR YOUR OWN GLORY.

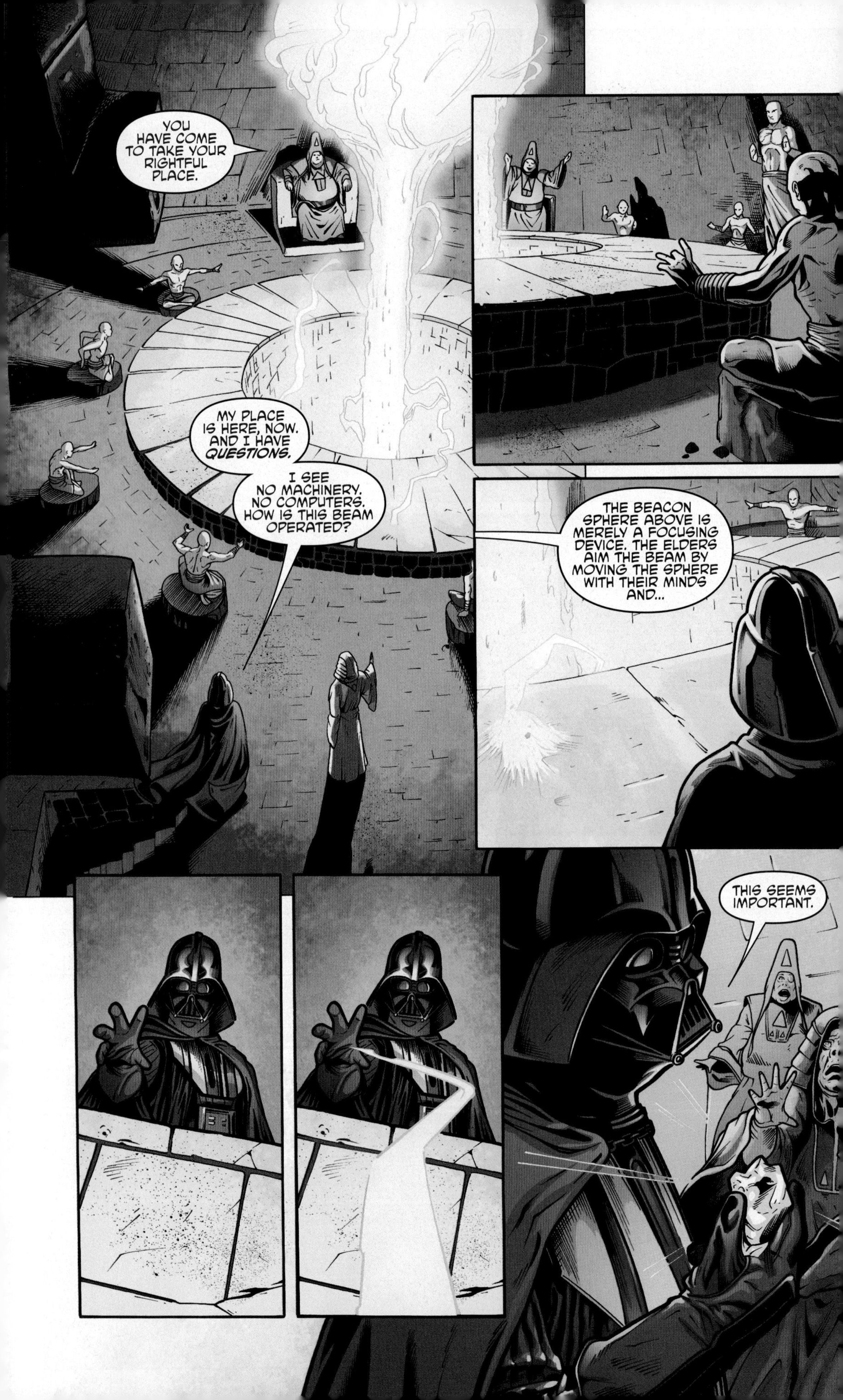
YOU HAVE COME TO TAKE YOUR RIGHTFUL PLACE.
MY PLACE IS HERE, NOW. AND I HAVE *QUESTIONS.*
I SEE NO MACHINERY. NO COMPUTERS. HOW IS THIS BEAM OPERATED?
THE BEACON SPHERE ABOVE IS MERELY A FOCUSING DEVICE. THE ELDERS AIM THE BEAM BY MOVING THE SPHERE WITH THEIR MINDS AND...
THIS SEEMS IMPORTANT.

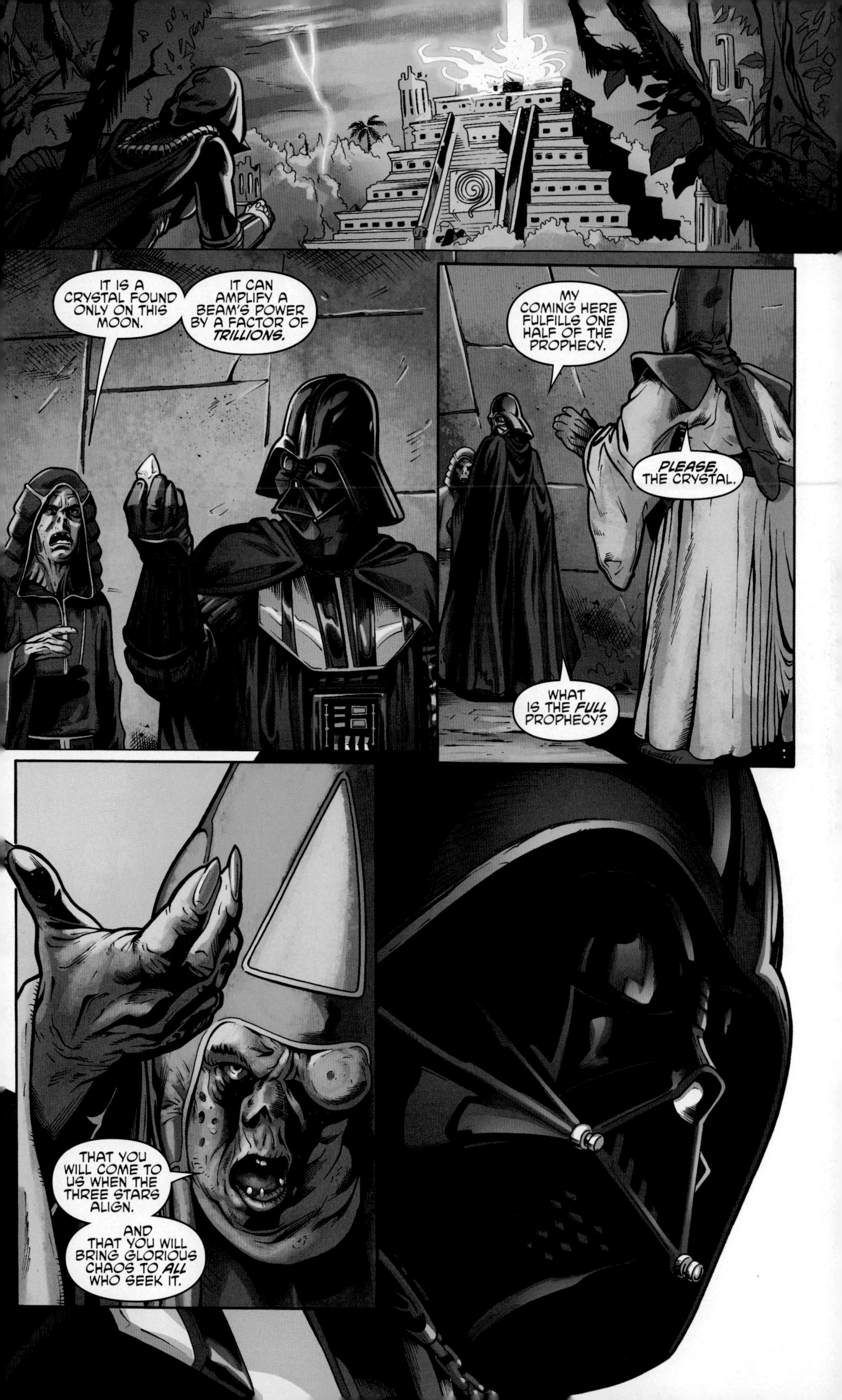
IT IS A CRYSTAL FOUND ONLY ON THIS MOON.
IT CAN AMPLIFY A BEAM'S POWER BY A FACTOR OF *TRILLIONS.*
MY COMING HERE FULFILLS ONE HALF OF THE PROPHECY.
*PLEASE,* THE CRYSTAL.
WHAT IS THE *FULL* PROPHECY?
THAT YOU WILL COME TO US WHEN THE THREE STARS ALIGN.
AND THAT YOU WILL BRING GLORIOUS CHAOS TO *ALL* WHO SEEK IT.

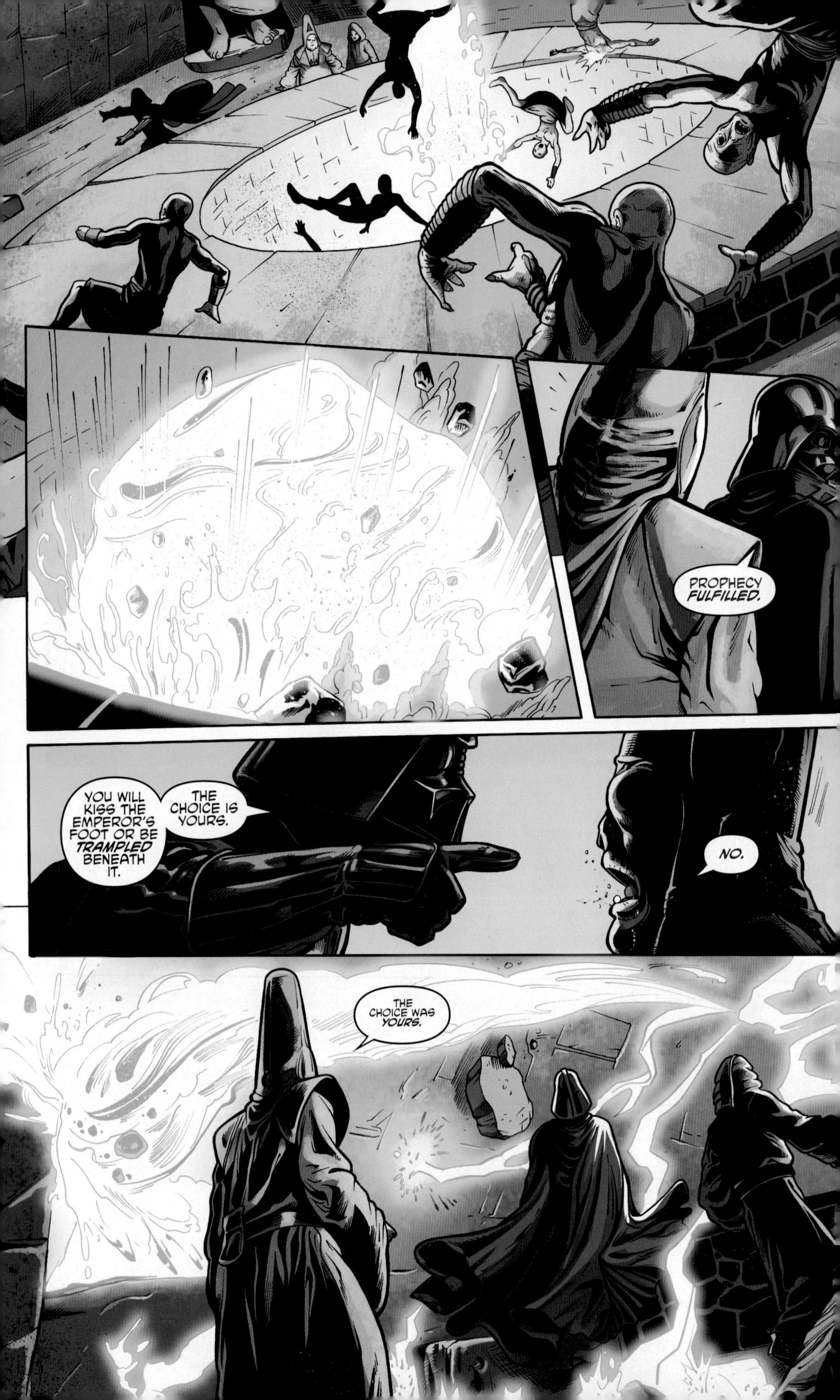
PROPHECY FULFILLED.
YOU WILL KISS THE EMPEROR'S FOOT OR BE TRAMPLED BENEATH IT.
THE CHOICE IS YOURS.
NO.
THE CHOICE WAS YOURS.

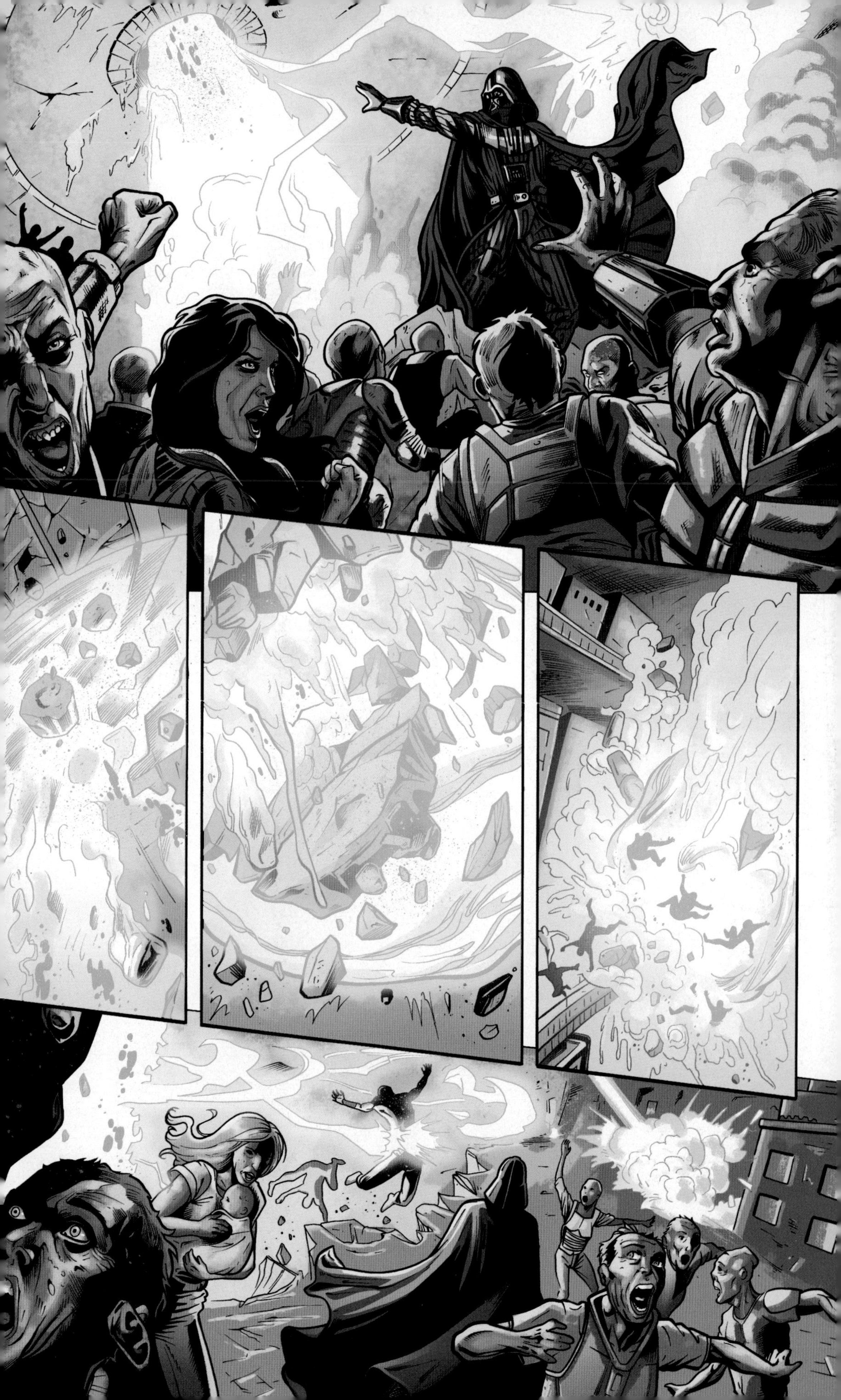

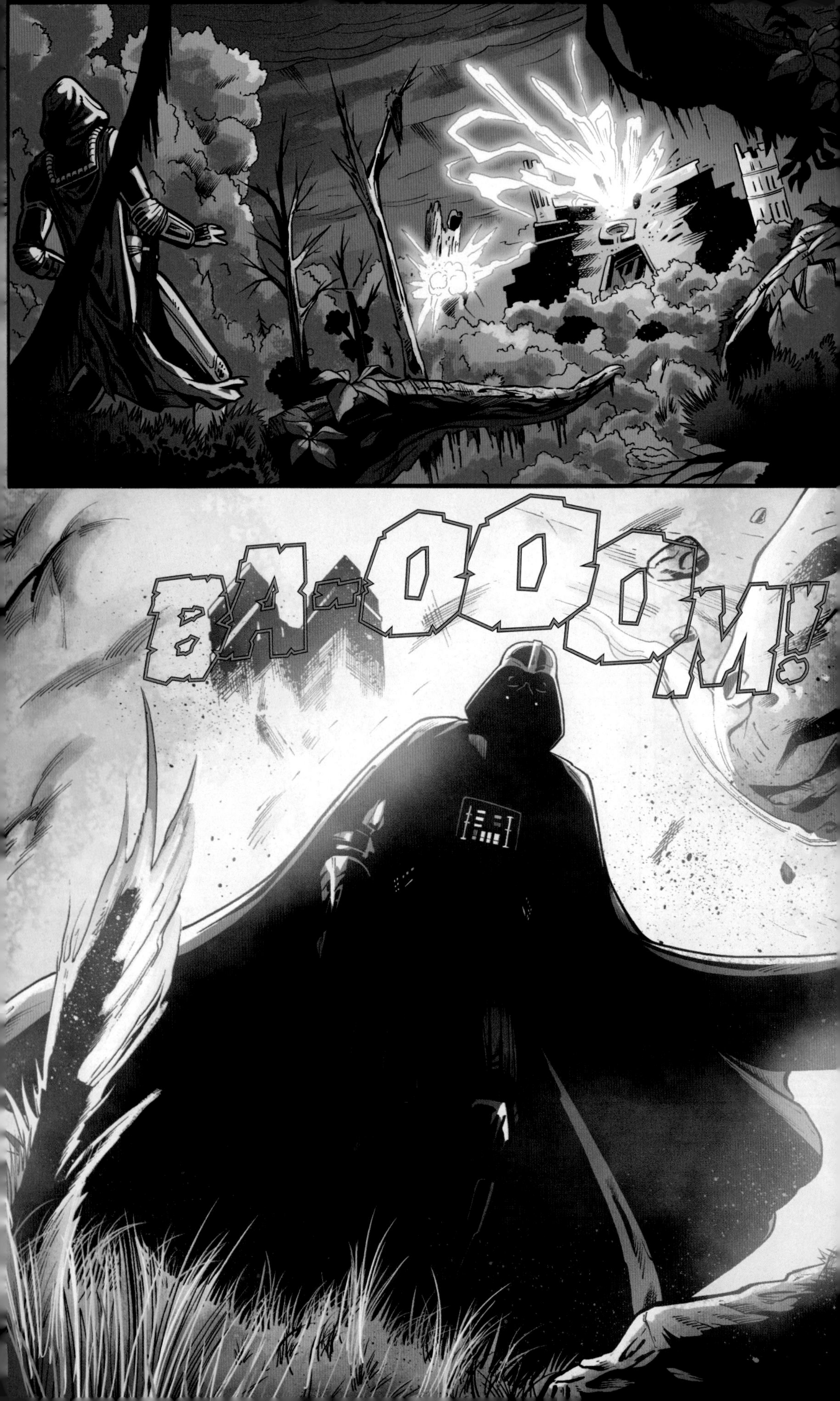
BA-OOOM!

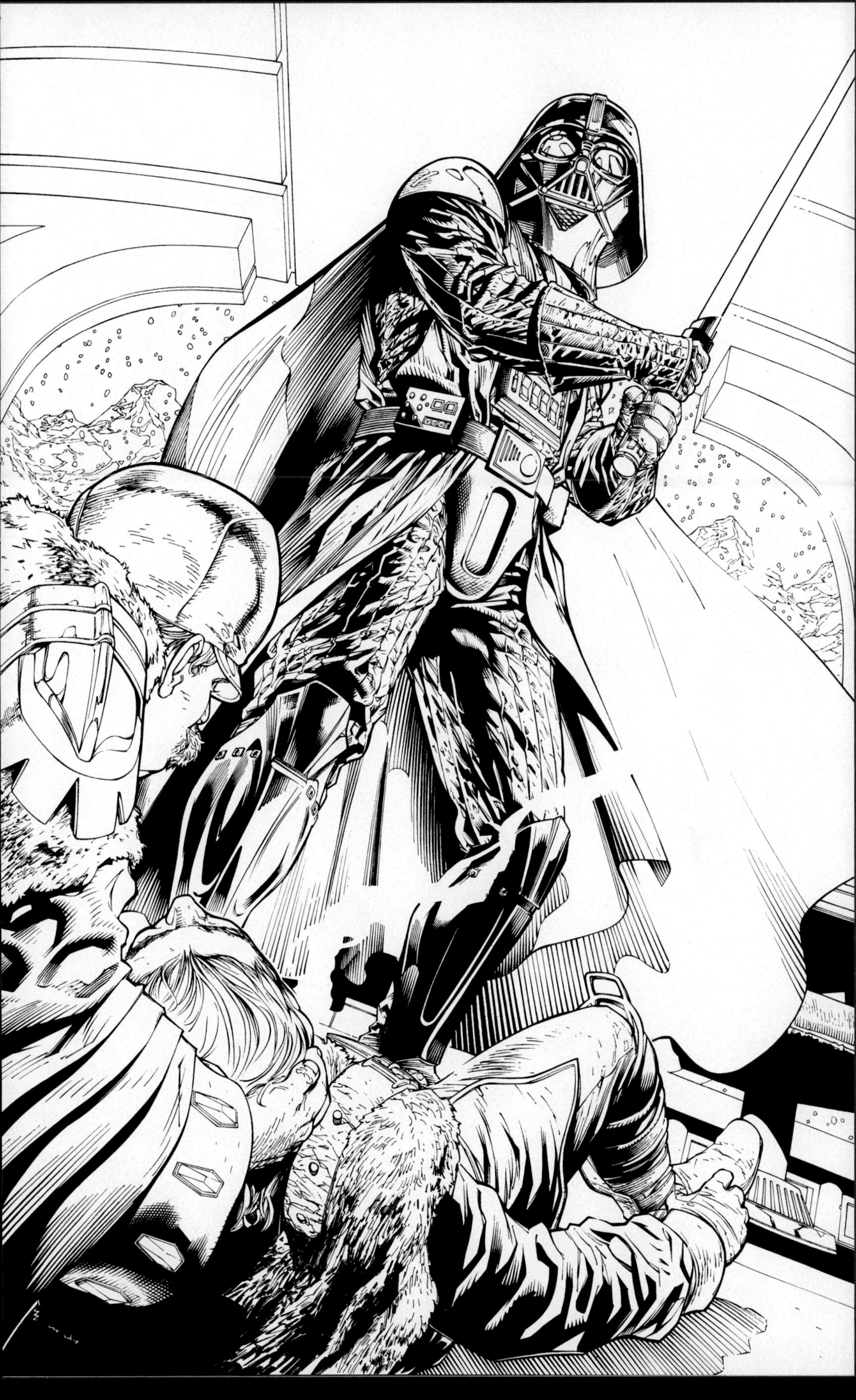

*STAR WARS: DARTH VADER AND THE NINTH ASSASSIN #1*
DIAMOND RETAILER VARIANT BY STEPHEN THOMPSON & MARK IRWIN

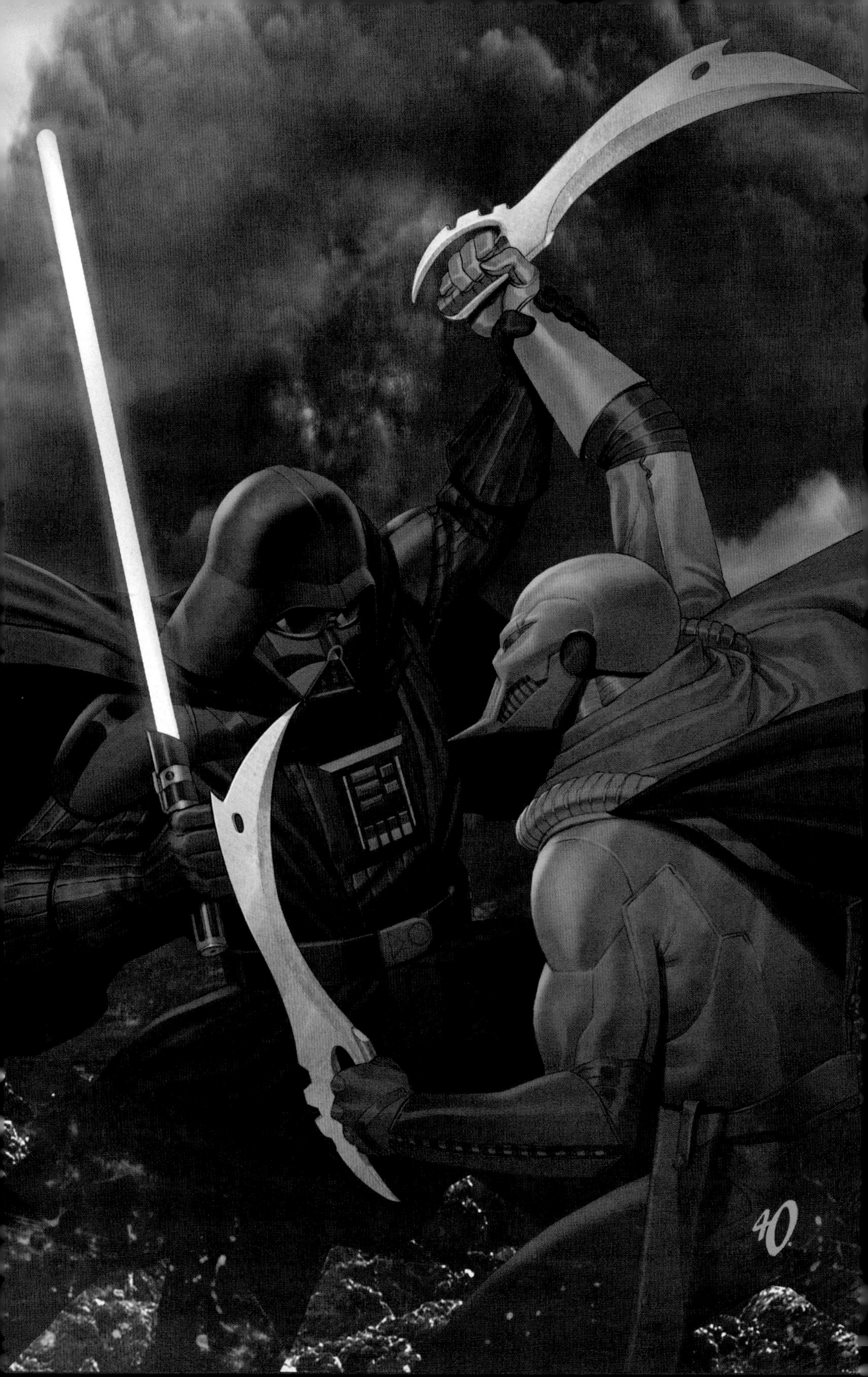

*STAR WARS: DARTH VADER AND THE NINTH ASSASSIN #5*

WRITER: TIM SIEDELL • PENCILER: IVÁN FERNÁNDEZ • INKER: DENIS FREITAS • COLORIST: MICHAEL ATIYEH • LETTERER: MICHAEL HEISLER
ASSISTANT EDITOR: FREDDYE LINS • EDITOR: DAVE MARSHALL • COVER ARTIST: ARIEL OLIVETTI

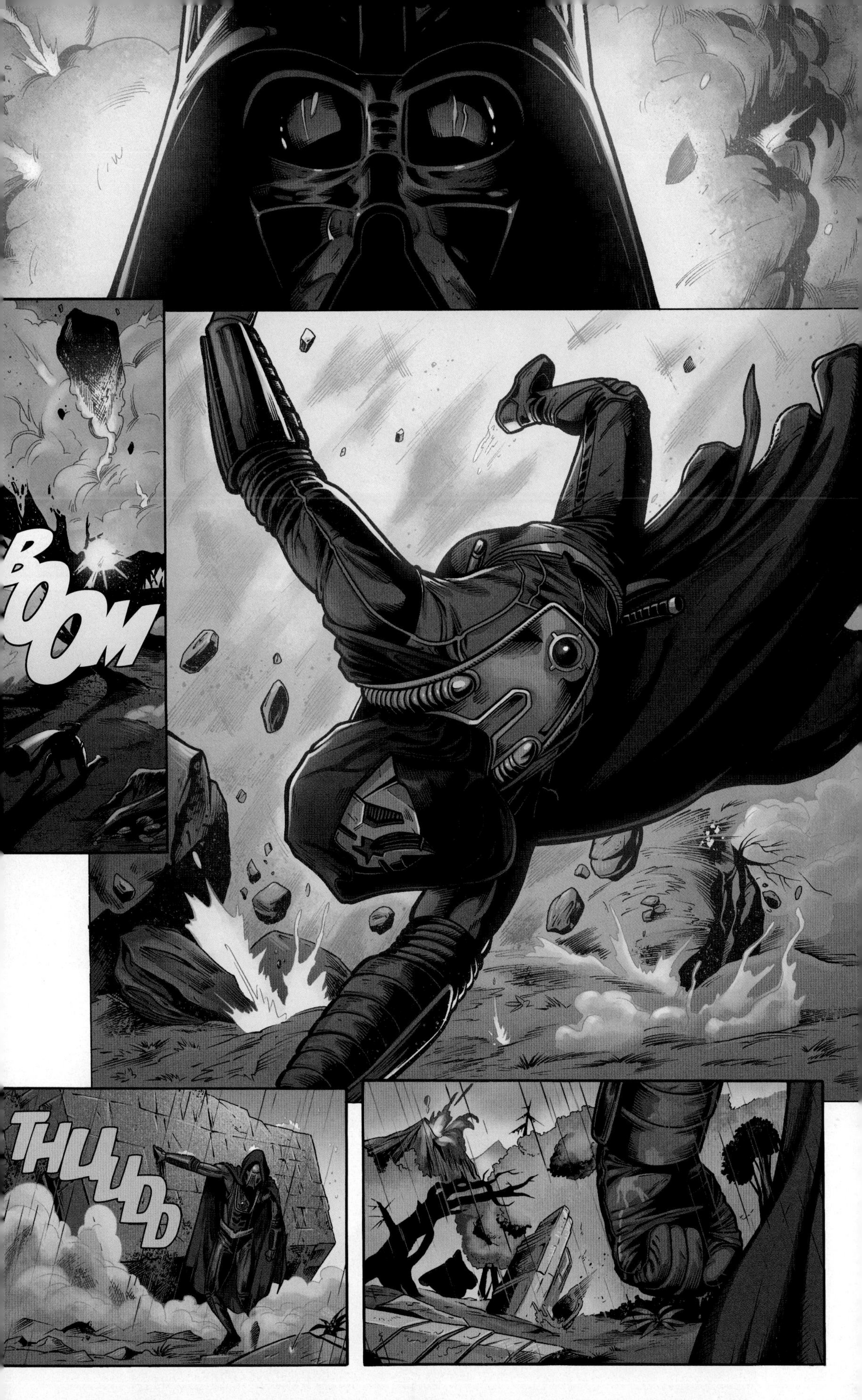
BOOM
THUDD

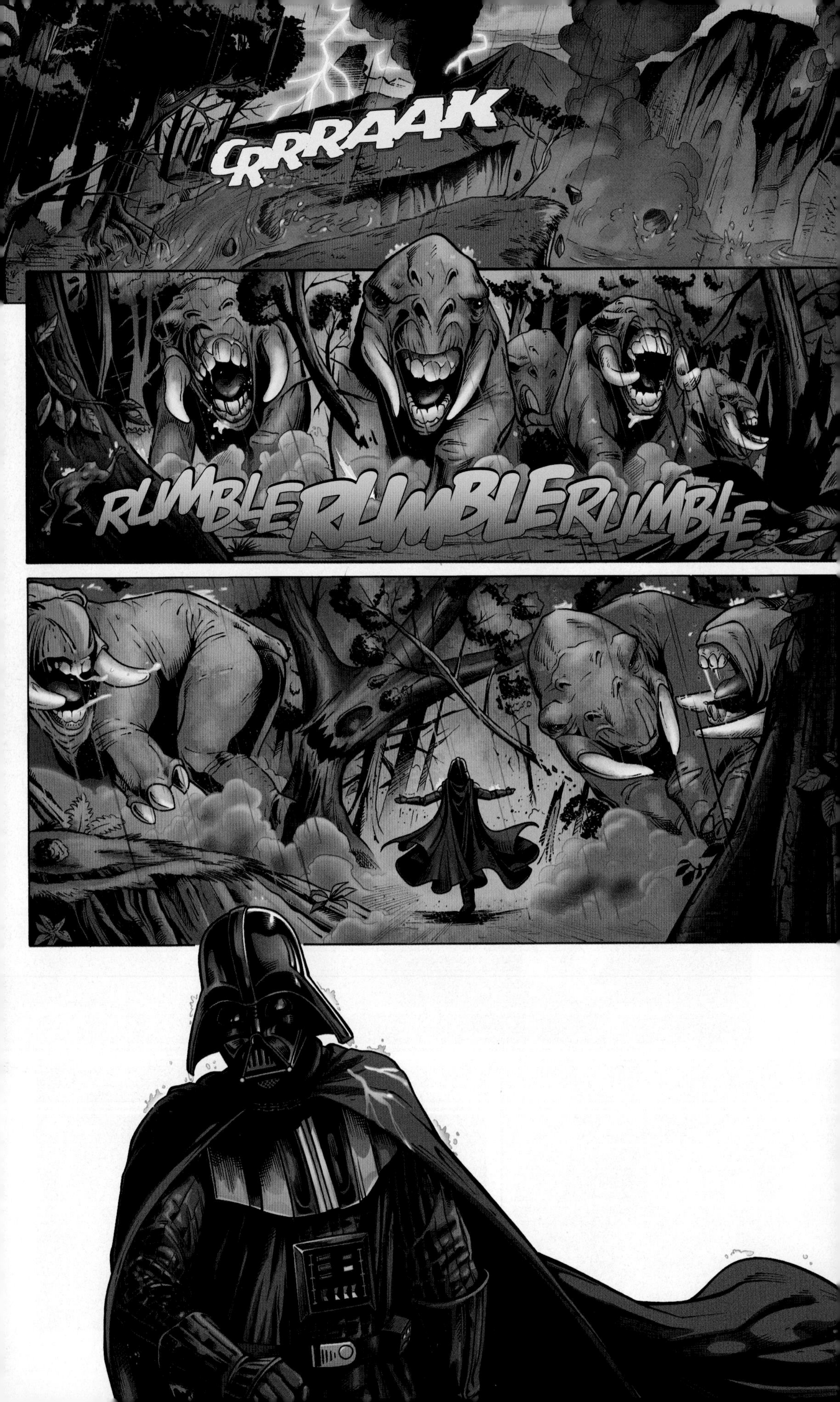
CRRRAAK
RUMBLE RUMBLE RUMBLE

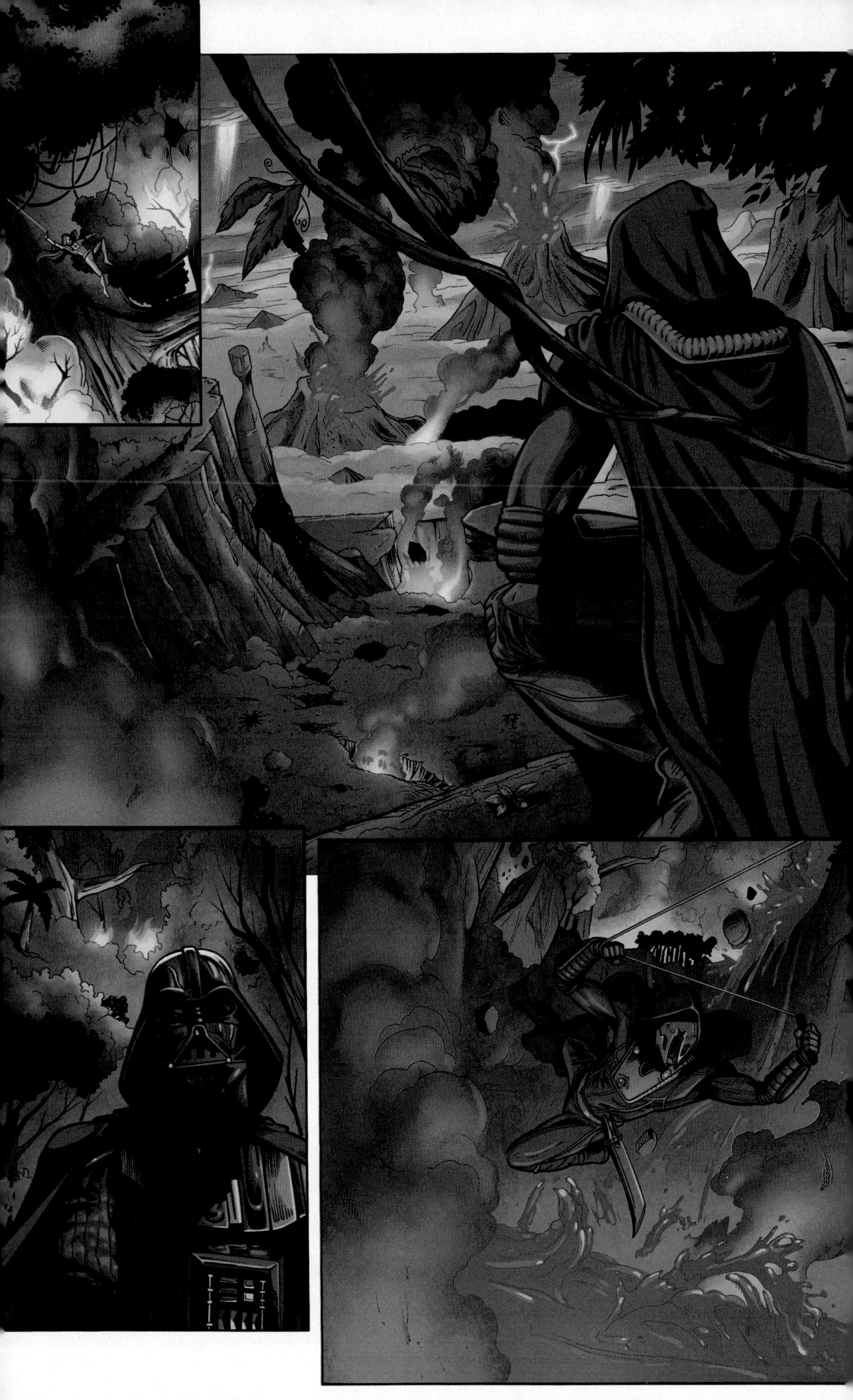

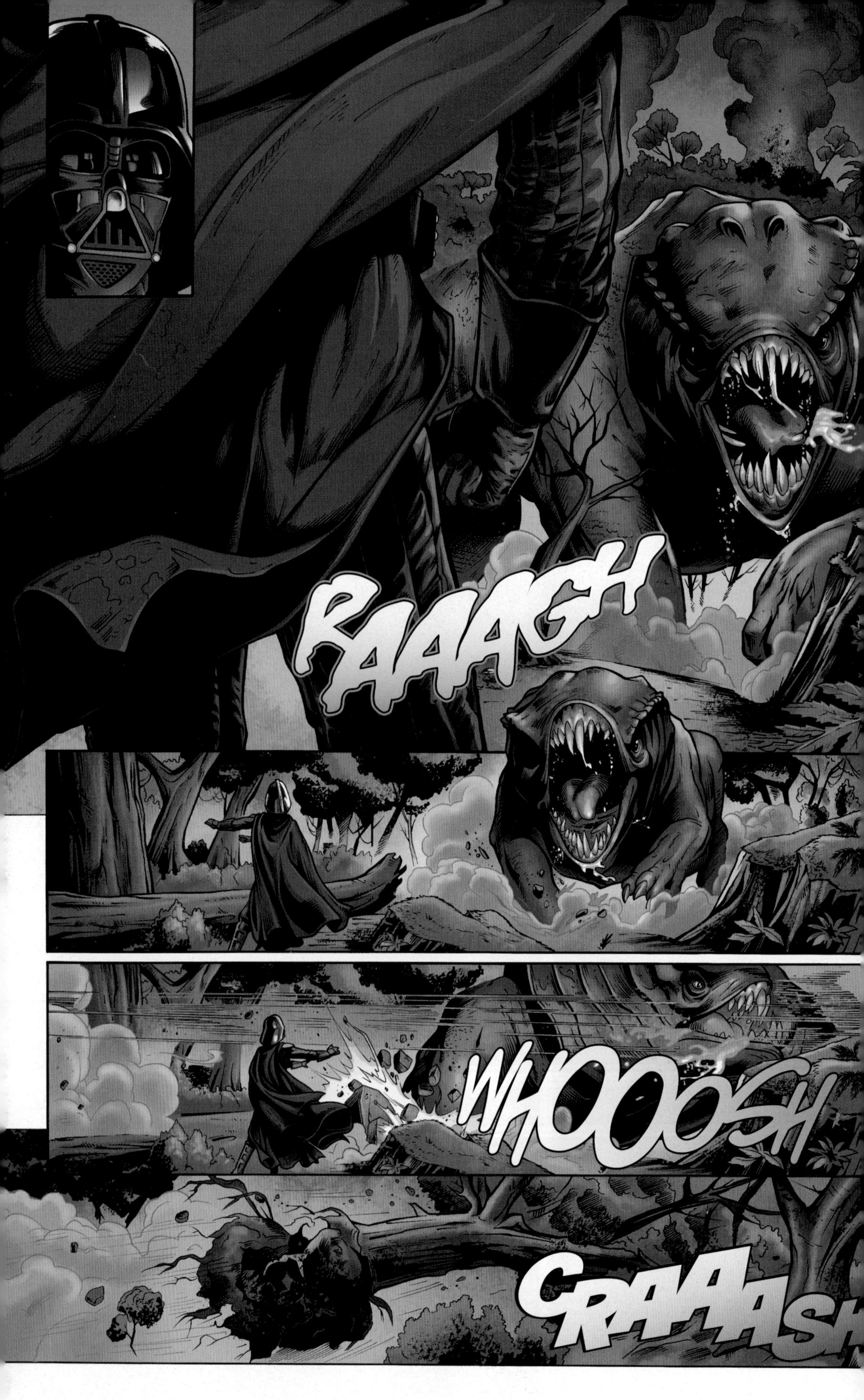
RAAAGH
WHOOOSH
CRAAAASH

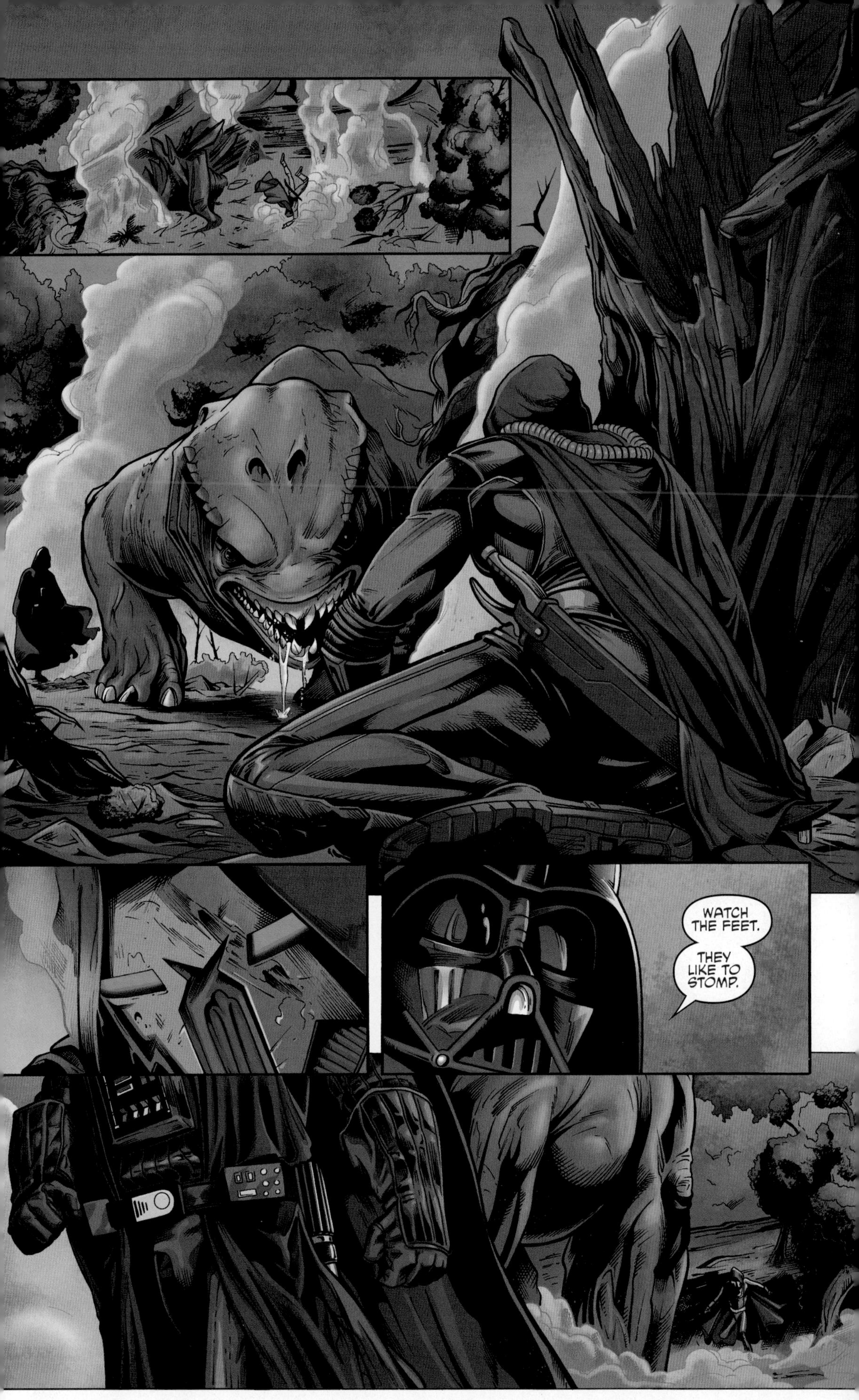
WATCH THE FEET.
THEY LIKE TO STOMP.

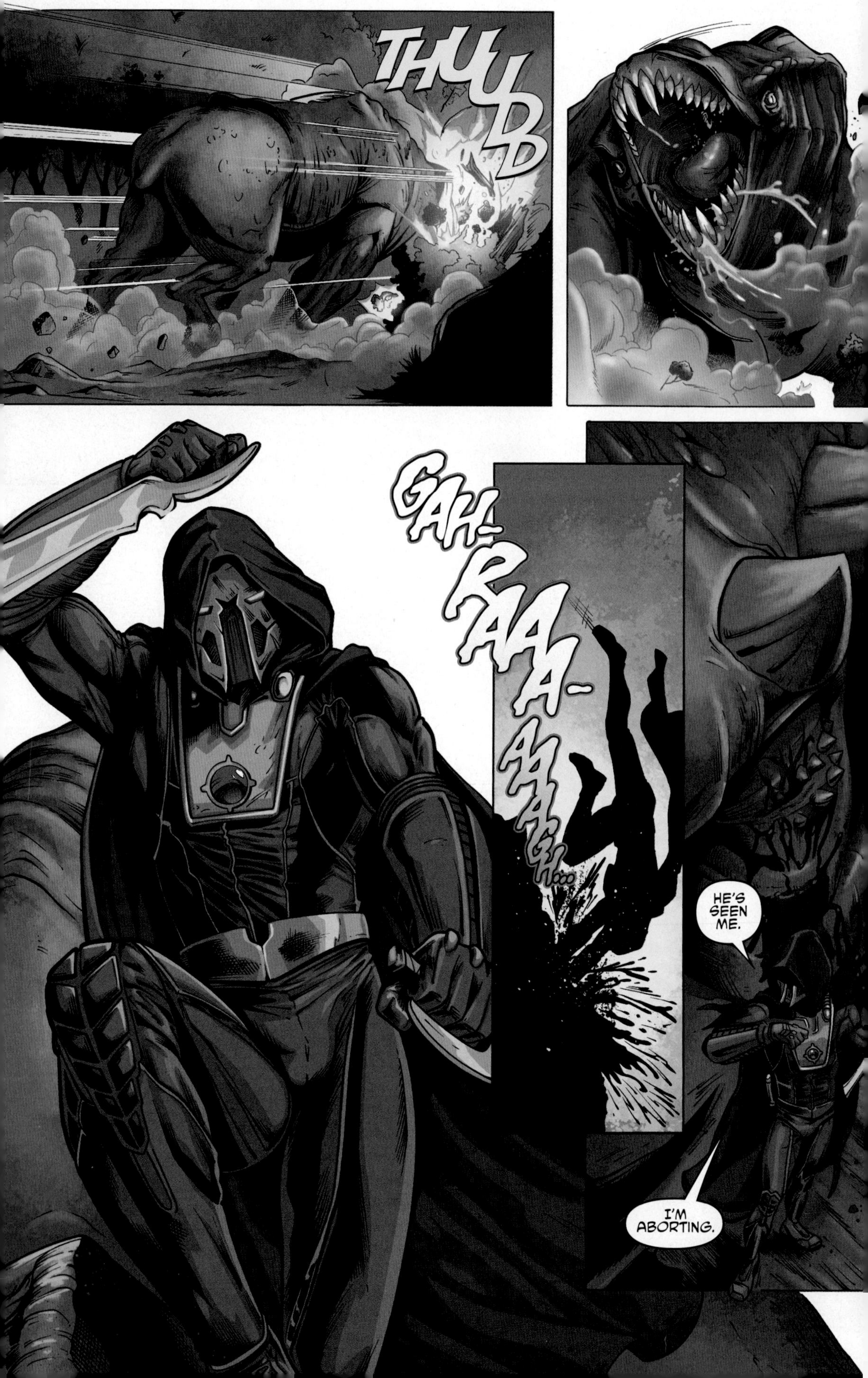
THUUDD
GAH-RAAA-AAAAGH...
HE'S SEEN ME.
I'M ABORTING.

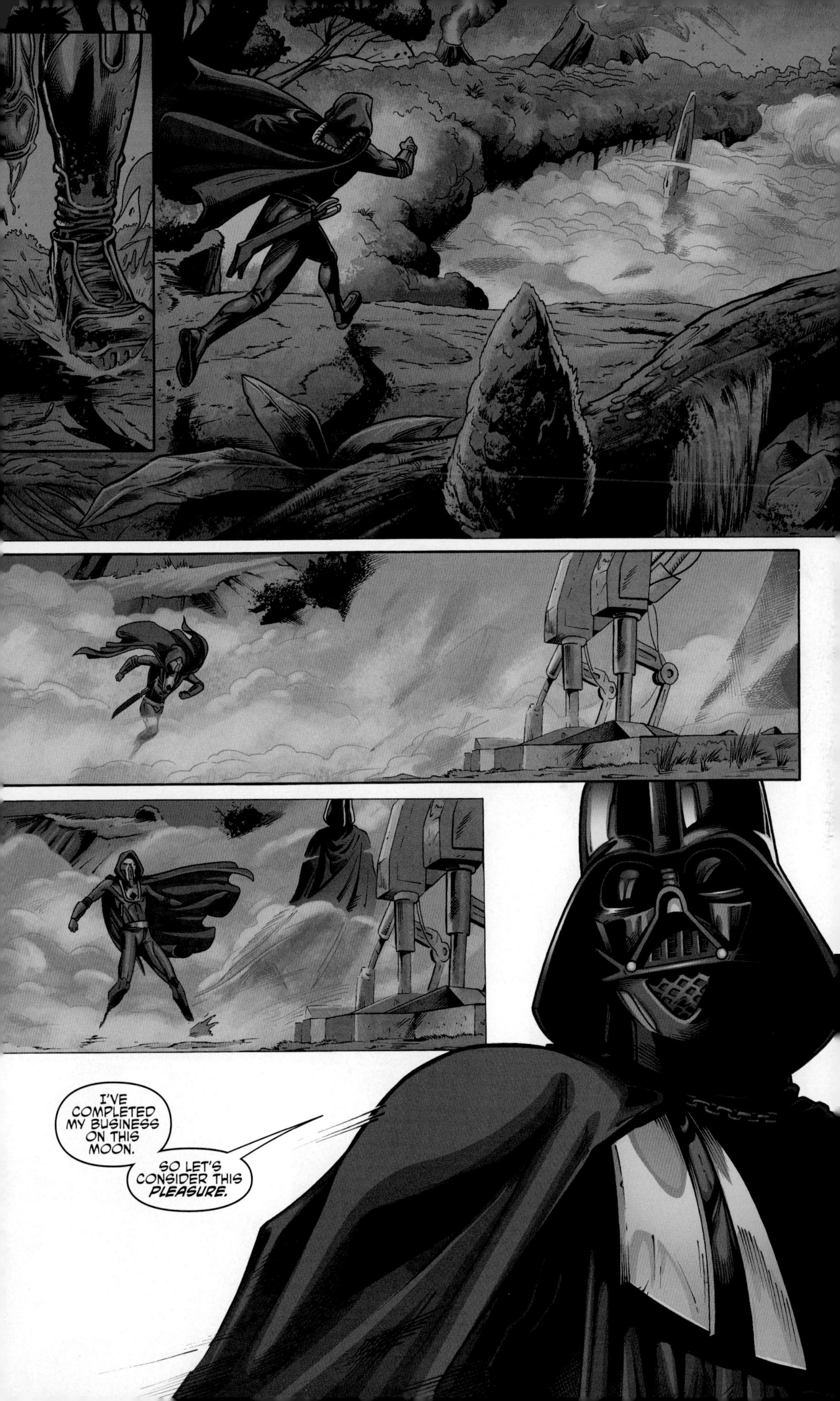
I'VE COMPLETED MY BUSINESS ON THIS MOON.
SO LET'S CONSIDER THIS *PLEASURE.*

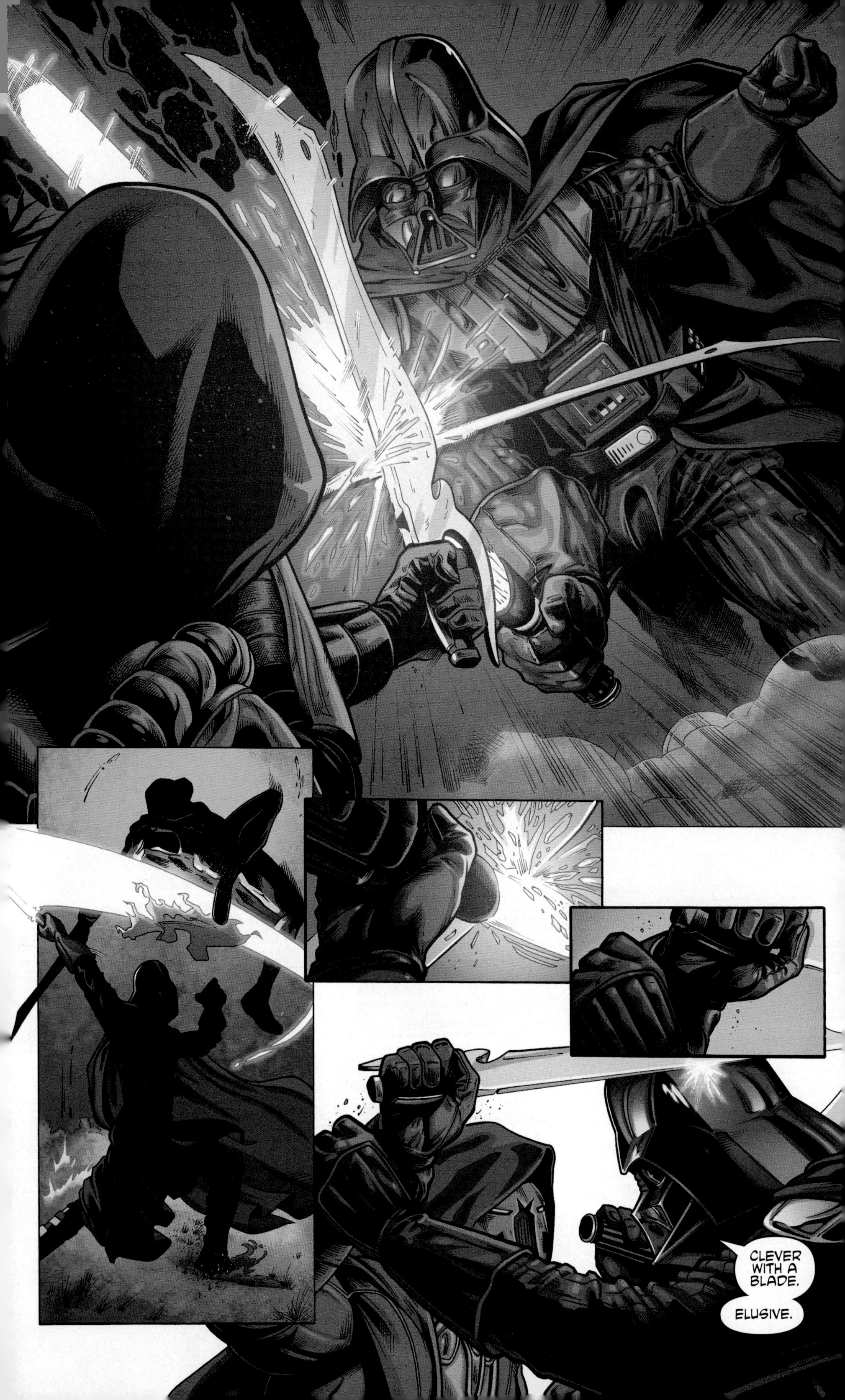
CLEVER WITH A BLADE.
ELUSIVE.

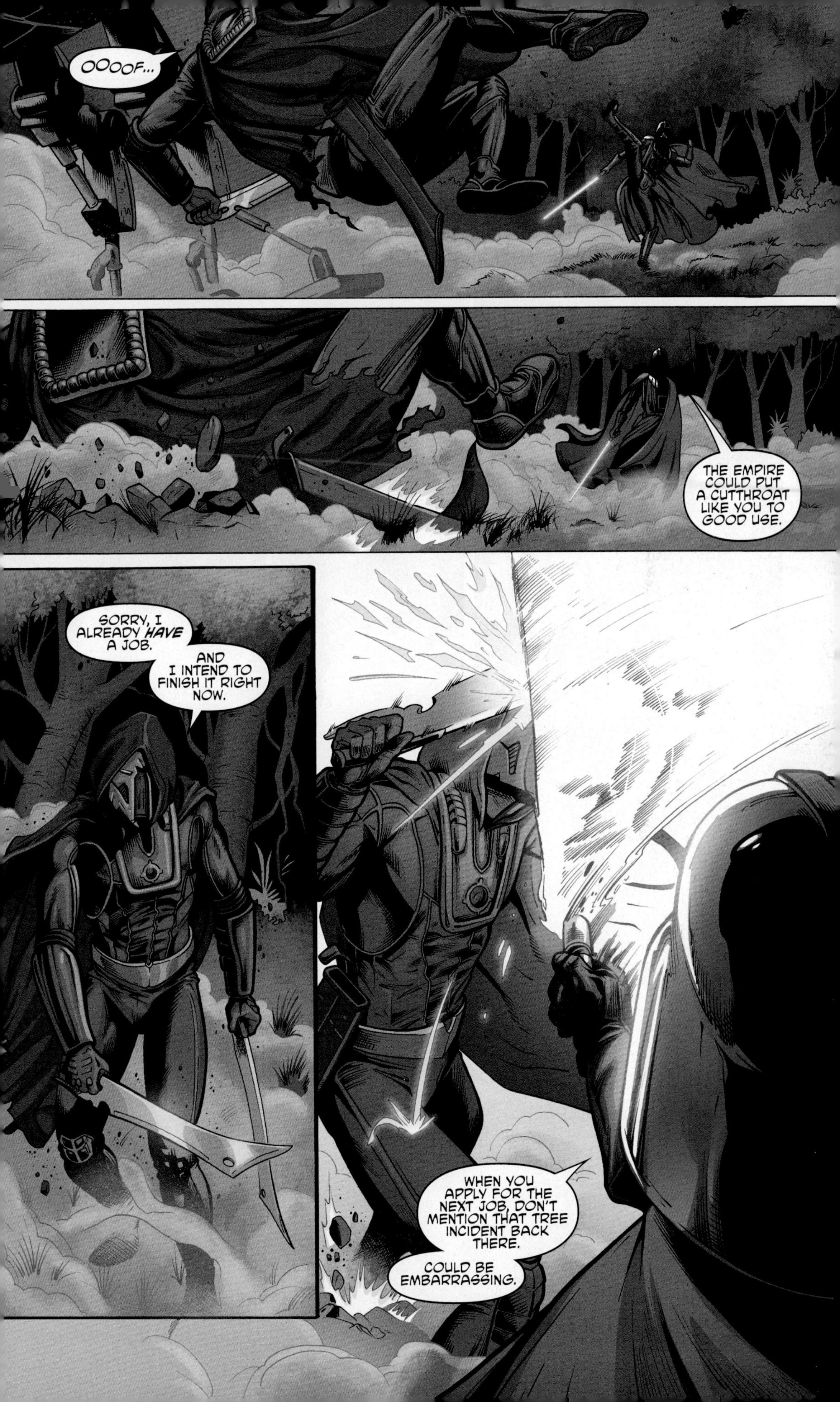
OOOOF...
THE EMPIRE COULD PUT A CUTTHROAT LIKE YOU TO GOOD USE.
SORRY, I ALREADY *HAVE* A JOB.
AND I INTEND TO FINISH IT RIGHT NOW.
WHEN YOU APPLY FOR THE NEXT JOB, DON'T MENTION THAT TREE INCIDENT BACK THERE.
COULD BE EMBARRASSING.

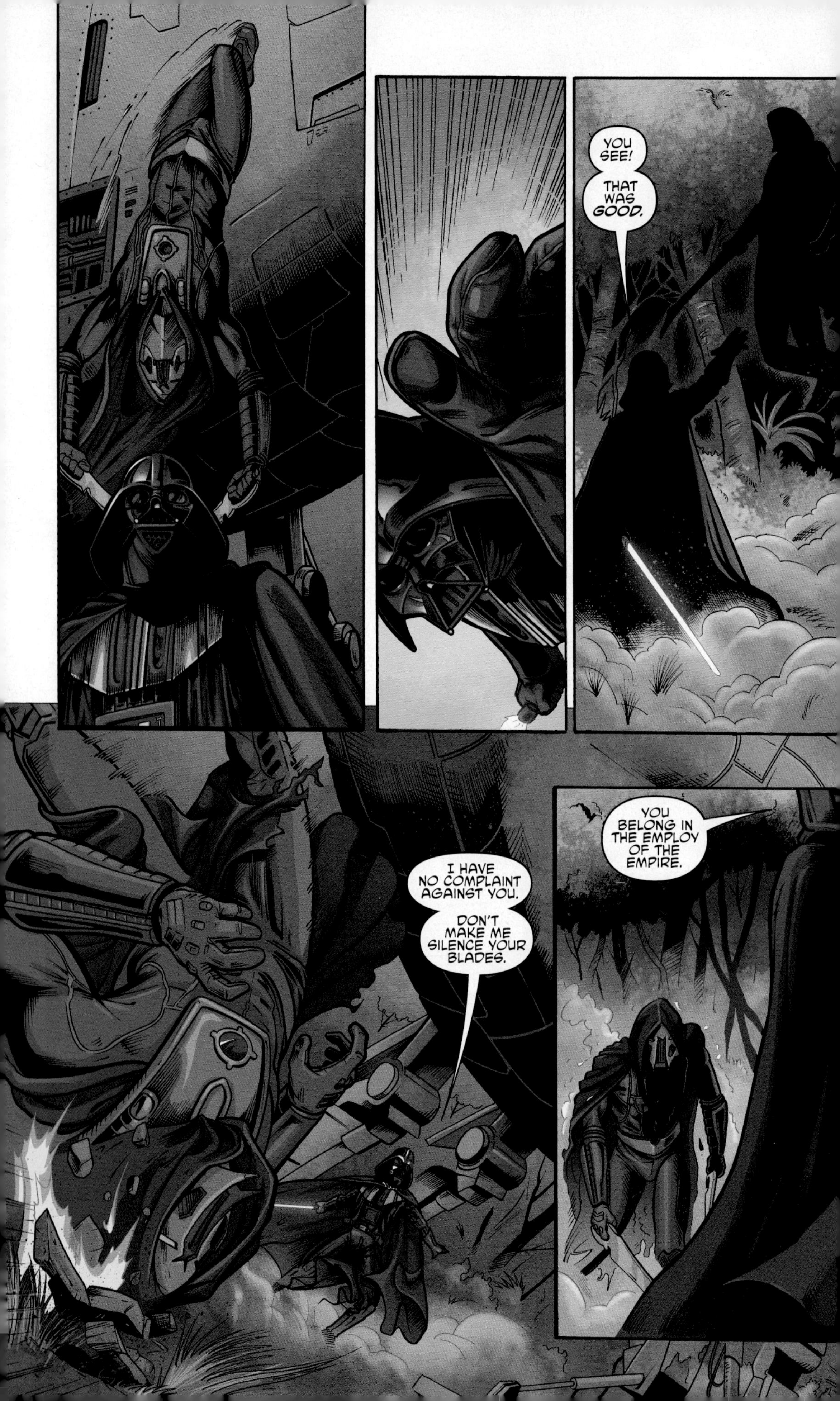

YOU SEE!
THAT WAS GOOD.
YOU BELONG IN THE EMPLOY OF THE EMPIRE.
I HAVE NO COMPLAINT AGAINST YOU.
DON'T MAKE ME SILENCE YOUR BLADES.

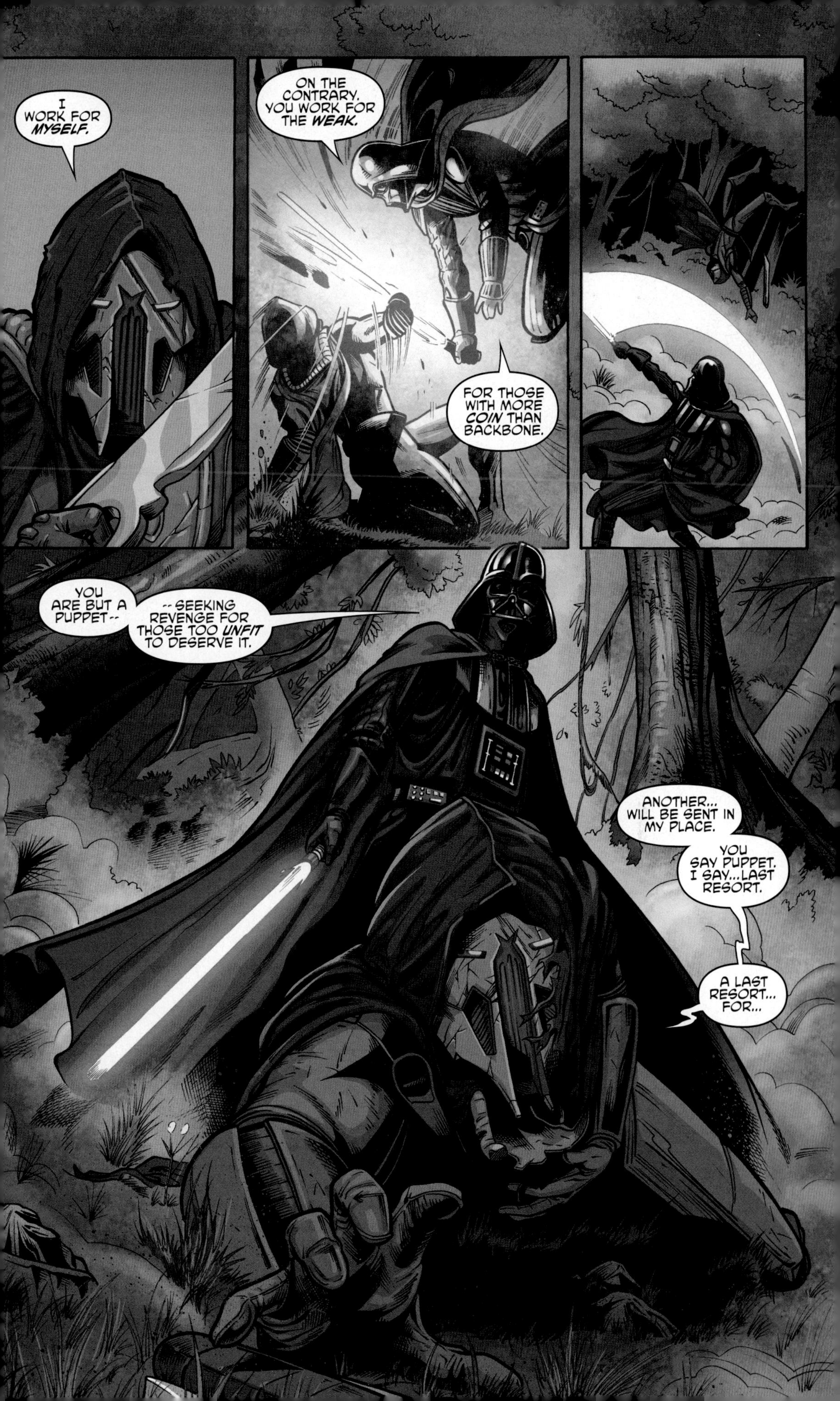
I WORK FOR MYSELF.
ON THE CONTRARY. YOU WORK FOR THE WEAK.
FOR THOSE WITH MORE COIN THAN BACKBONE.
YOU ARE BUT A PUPPET--
--SEEKING REVENGE FOR THOSE TOO UNFIT TO DESERVE IT.
ANOTHER... WILL BE SENT IN MY PLACE.
YOU SAY PUPPET. I SAY...LAST RESORT.
A LAST RESORT... FOR...

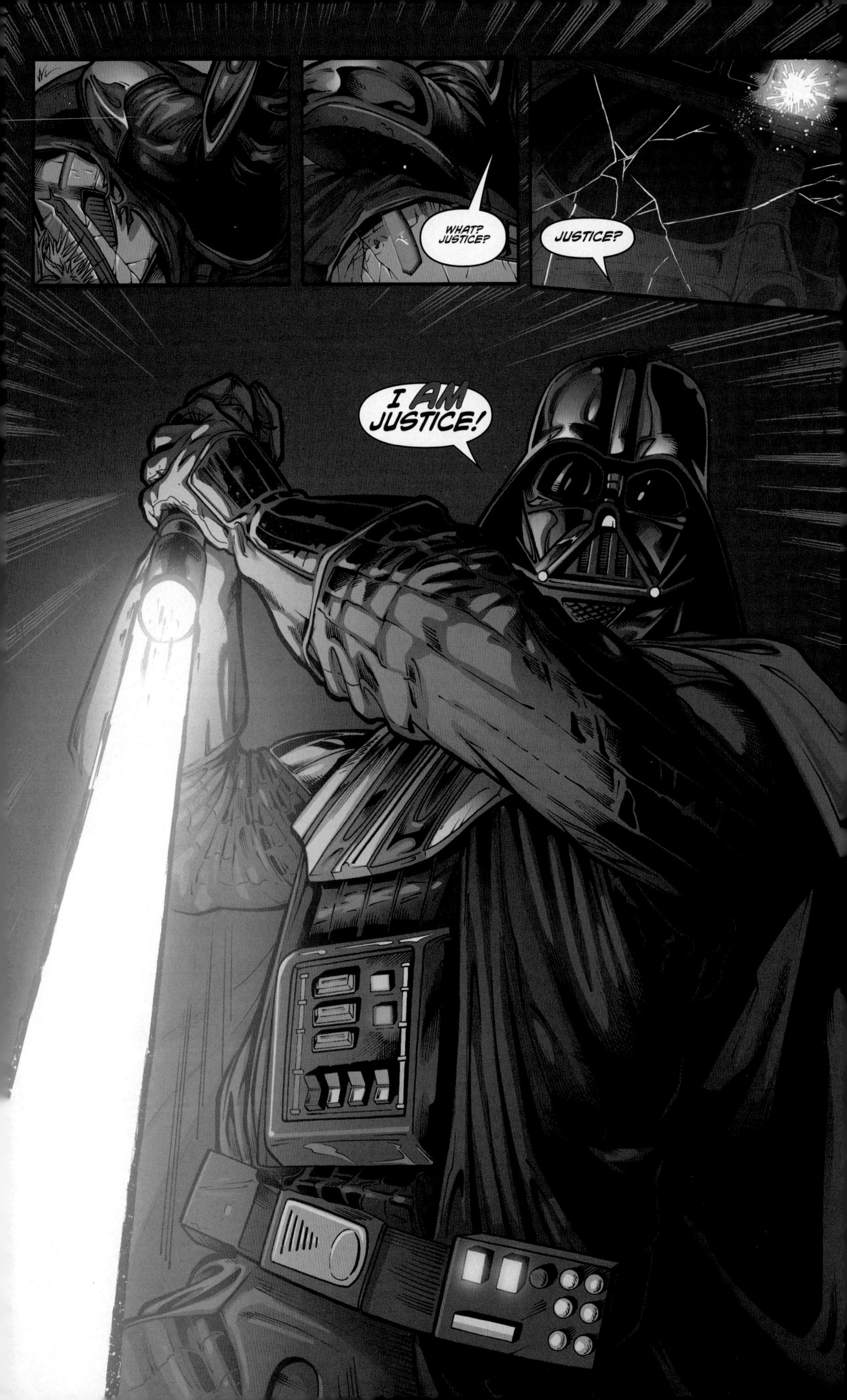
WHAT? JUSTICE?
JUSTICE?
I AM JUSTICE!

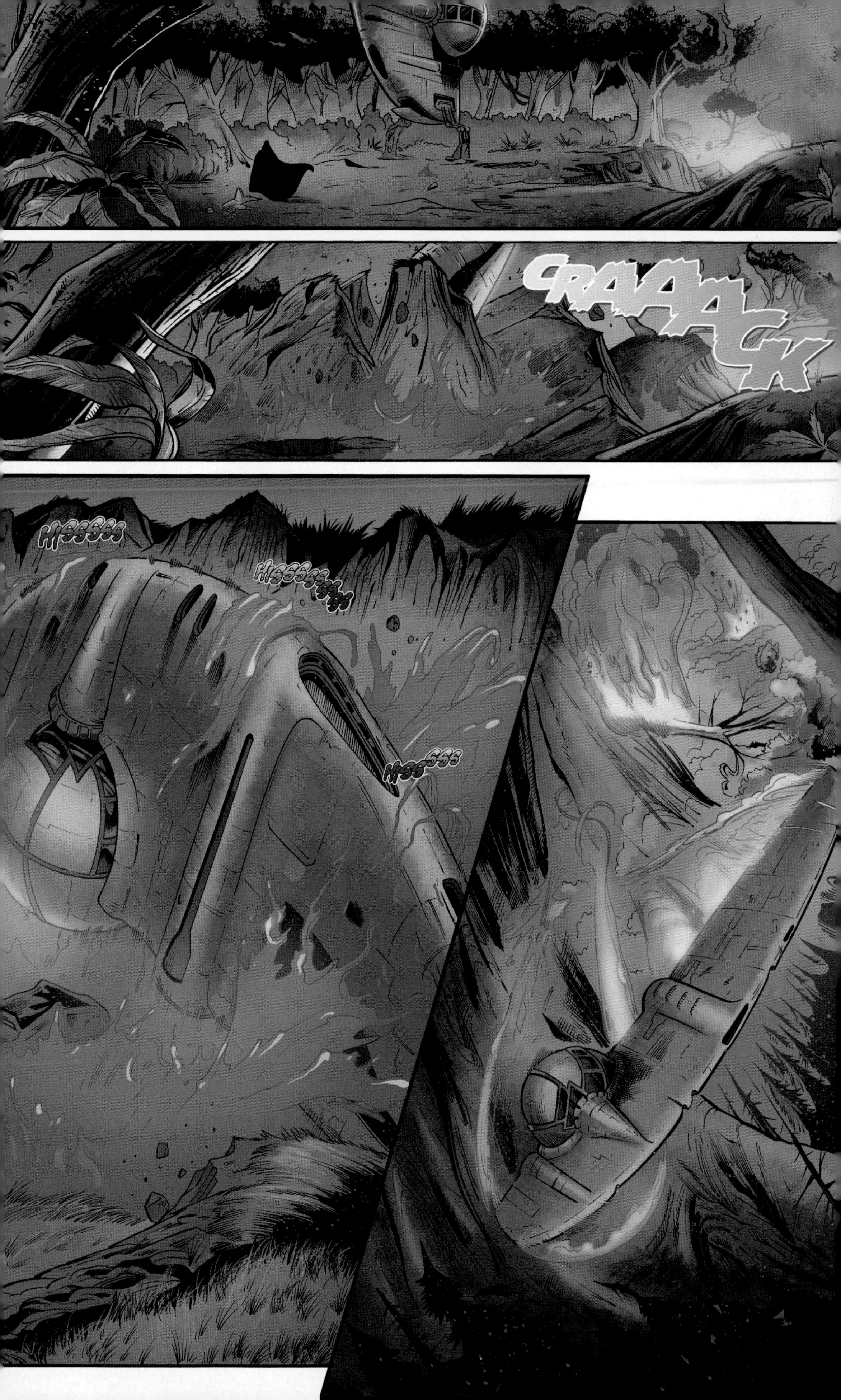
CRAAAACK
HISSSSS
HISSSSSSSSS
HISSSSS

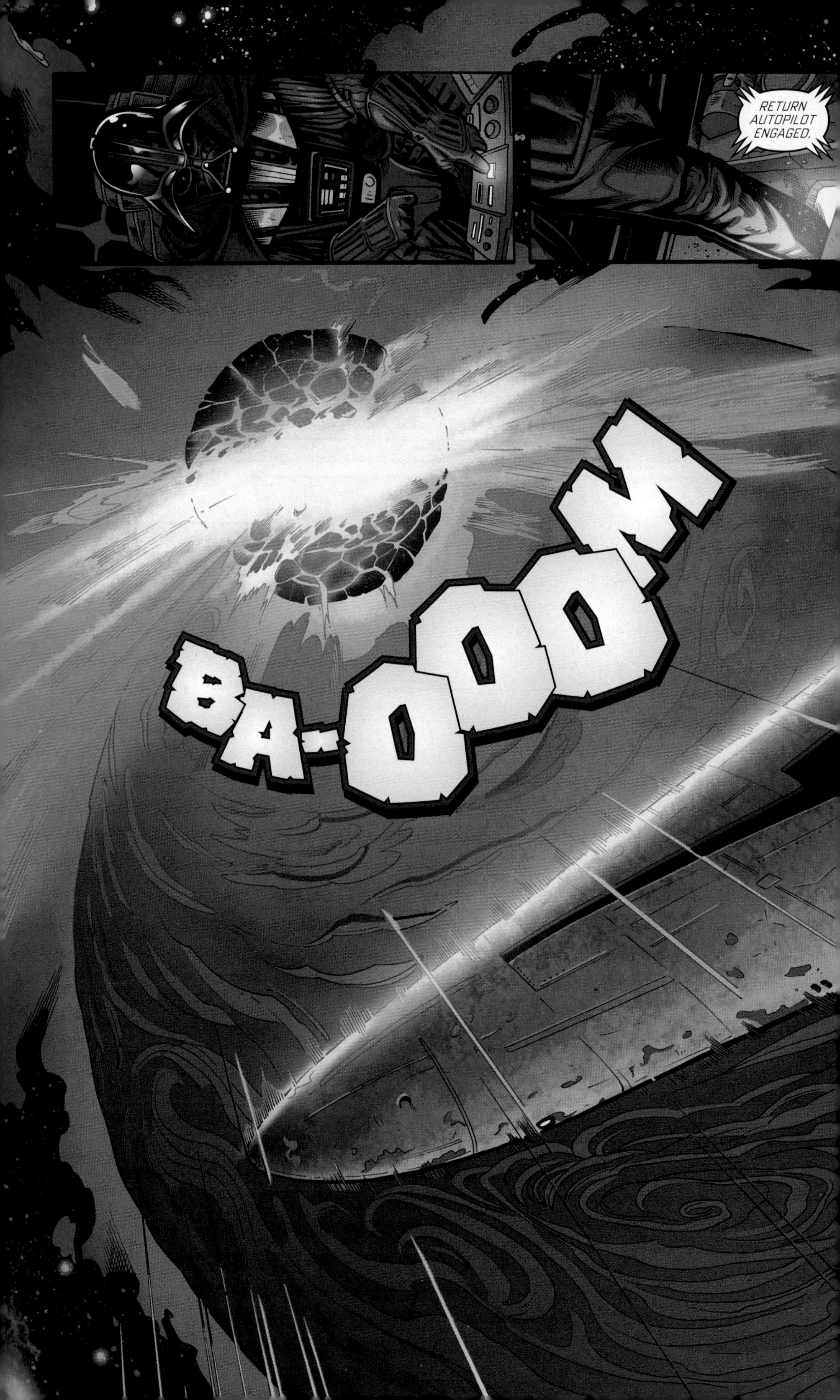
RETURN AUTOPILOT ENGAGED.
BA-OOOM

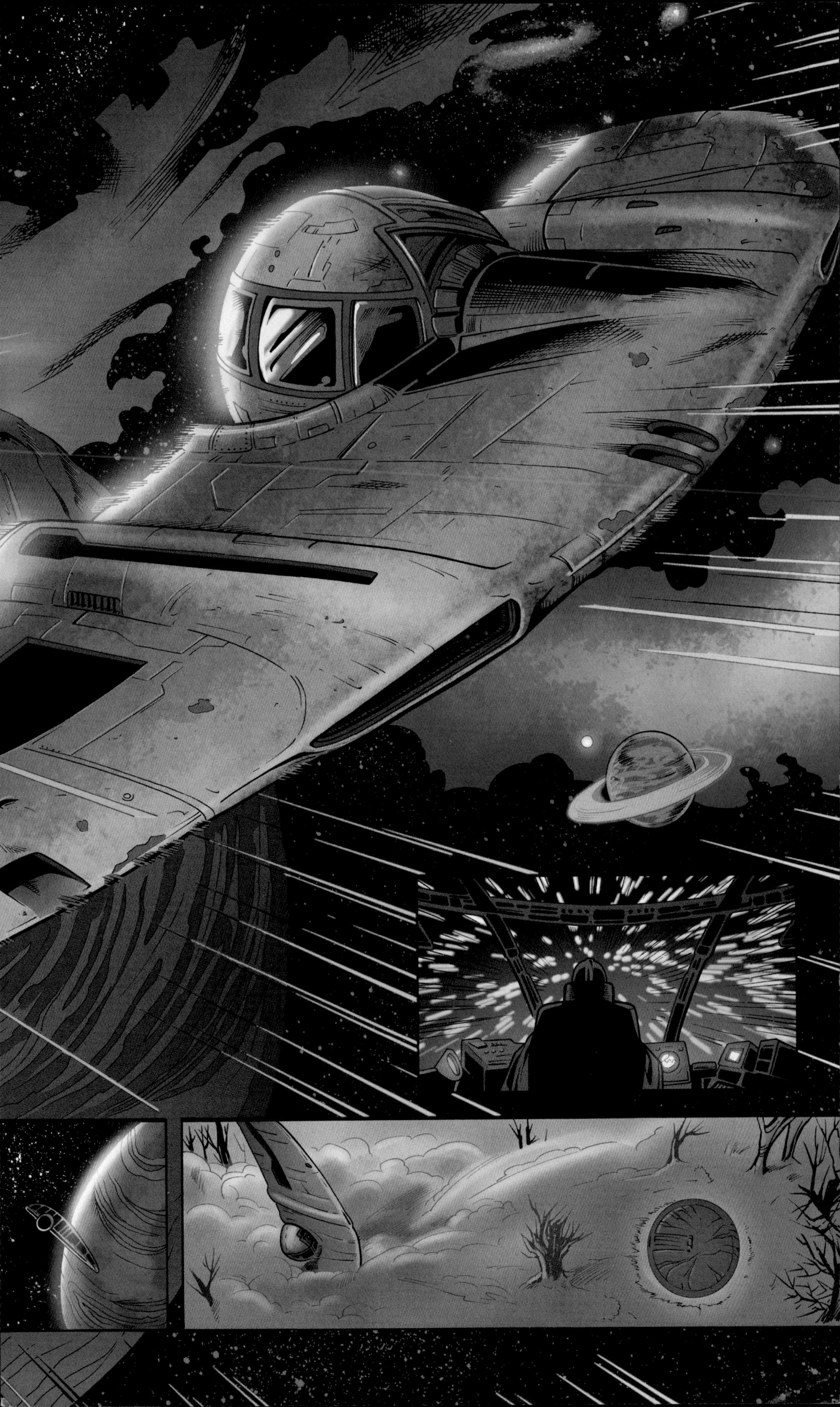

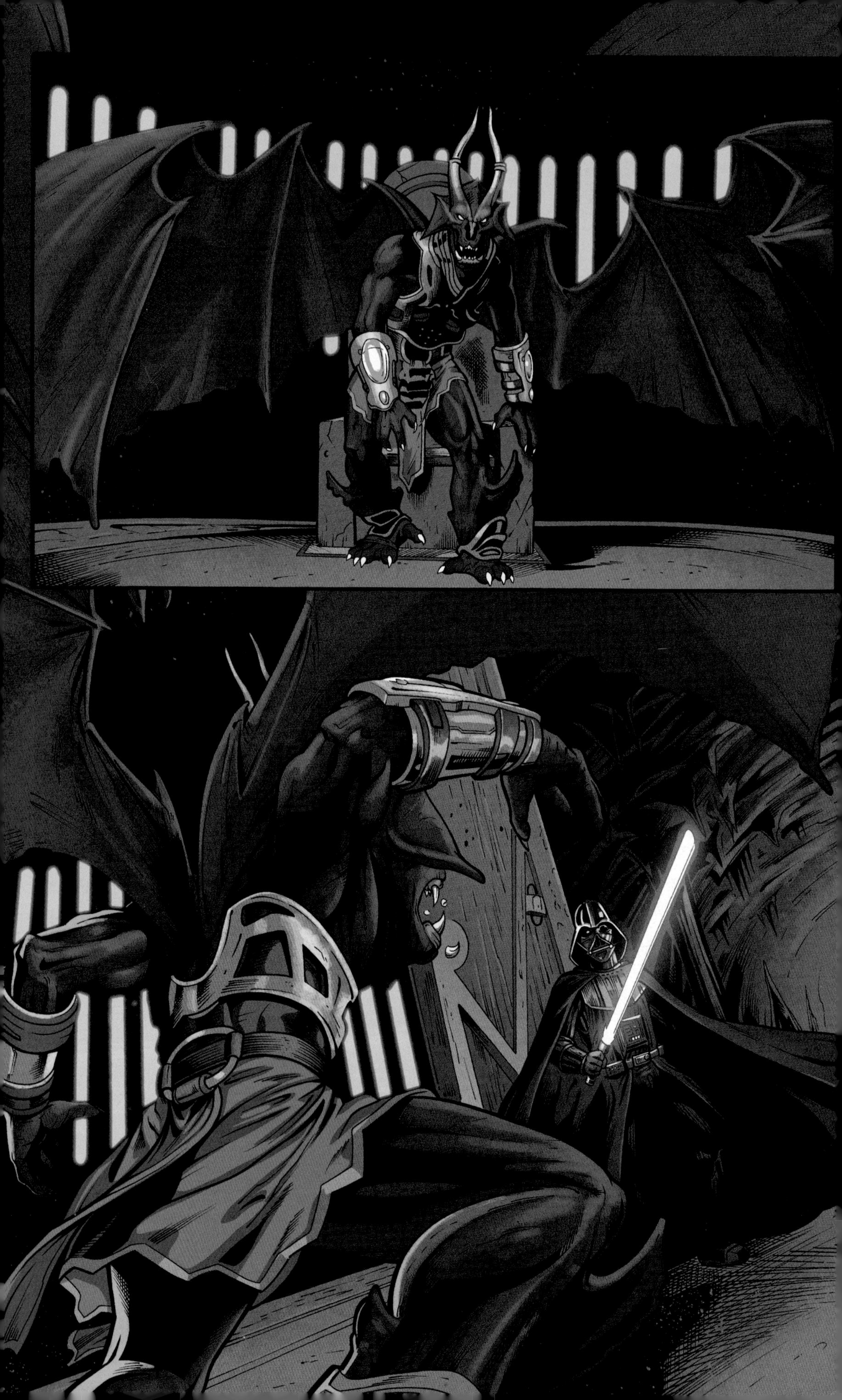

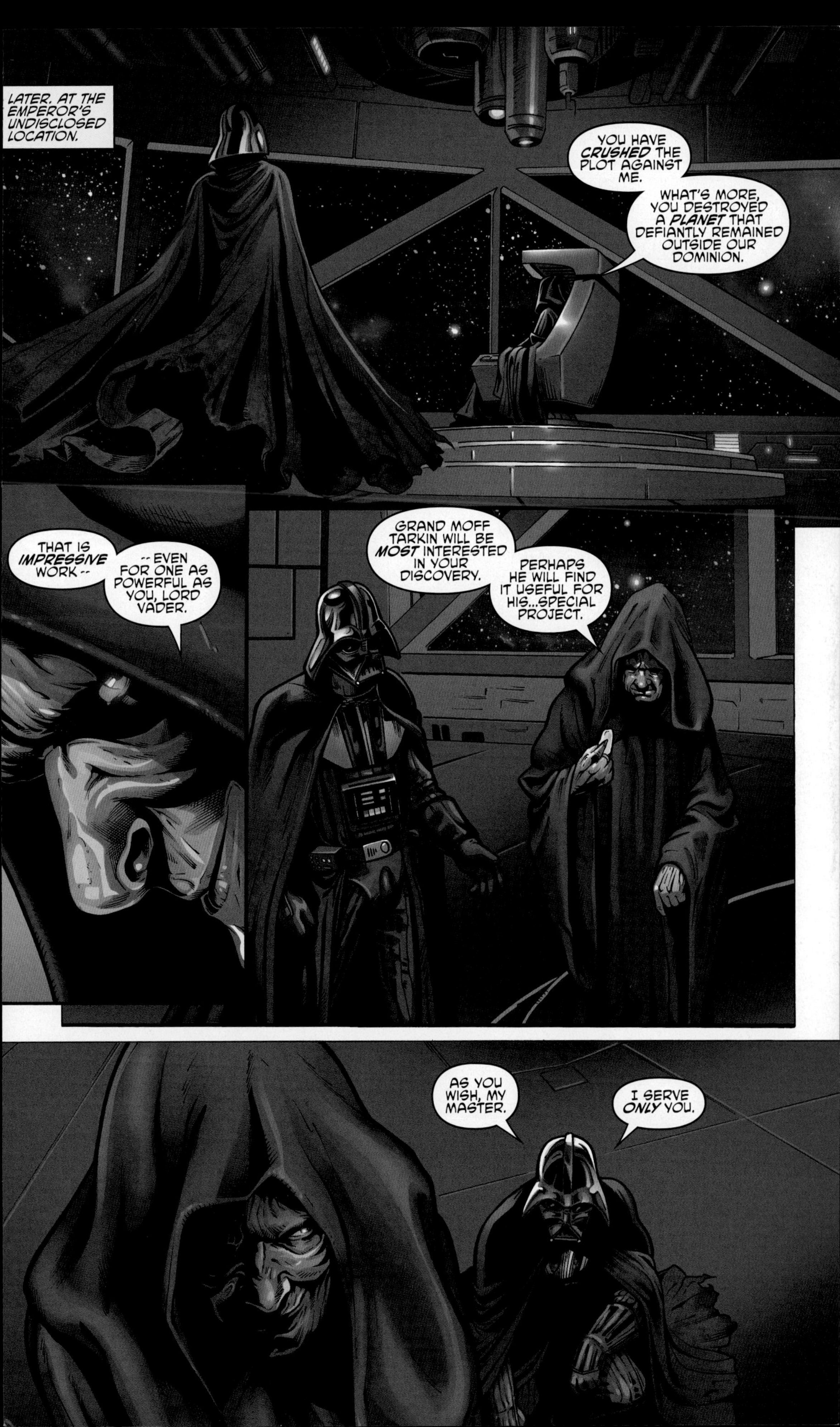
LATER. AT THE EMPEROR'S UNDISCLOSED LOCATION.
YOU HAVE CRUSHED THE PLOT AGAINST ME.
WHAT'S MORE, YOU DESTROYED A PLANET THAT DEFIANTLY REMAINED OUTSIDE OUR DOMINION.
THAT IS IMPRESSIVE WORK --
-- EVEN FOR ONE AS POWERFUL AS YOU, LORD VADER.
GRAND MOFF TARKIN WILL BE MOST INTERESTED IN YOUR DISCOVERY.
PERHAPS HE WILL FIND IT USEFUL FOR HIS...SPECIAL PROJECT.
AS YOU WISH, MY MASTER.
I SERVE ONLY YOU.

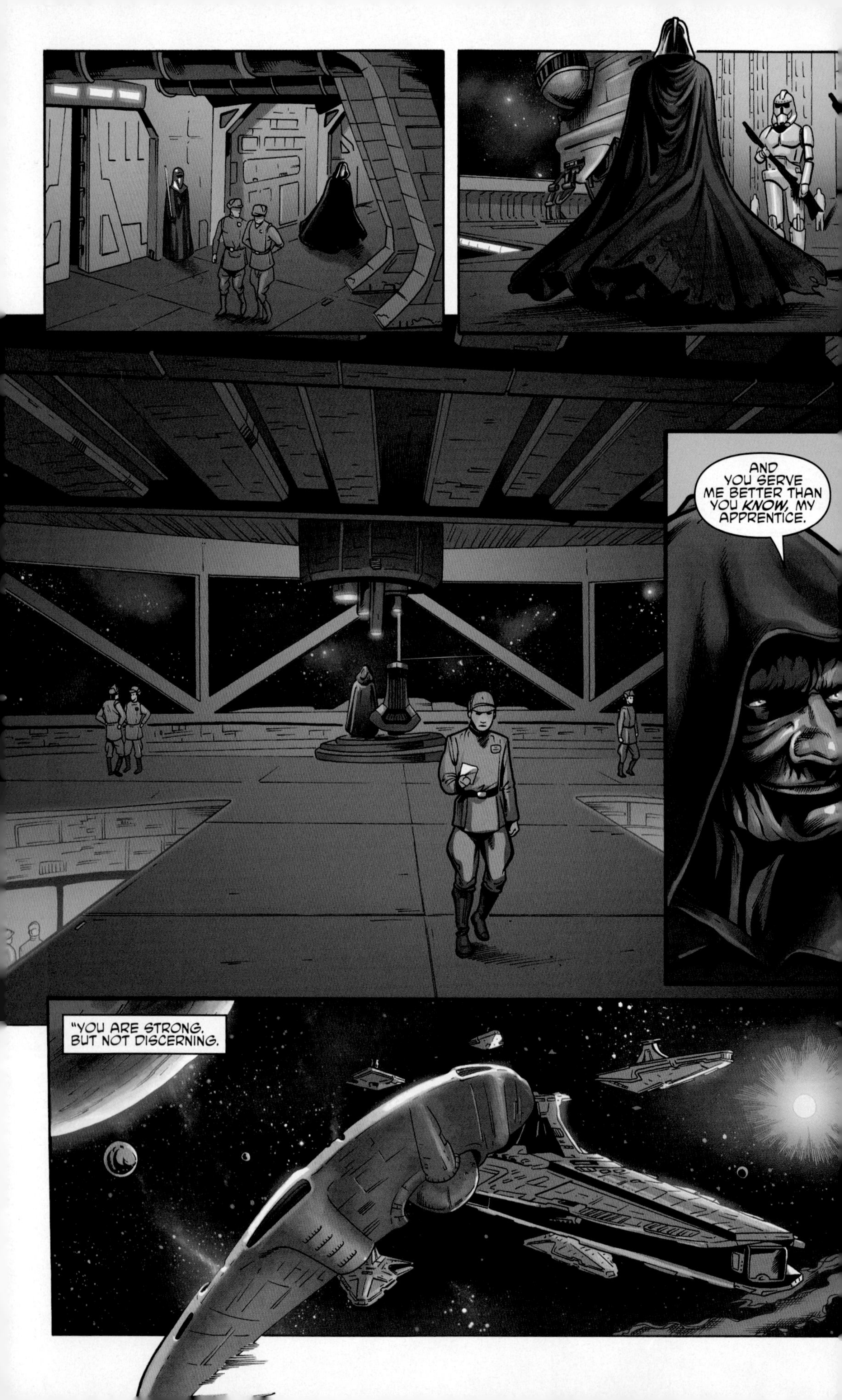
AND YOU SERVE ME BETTER THAN YOU KNOW, MY APPRENTICE.
"YOU ARE STRONG. BUT NOT DISCERNING.

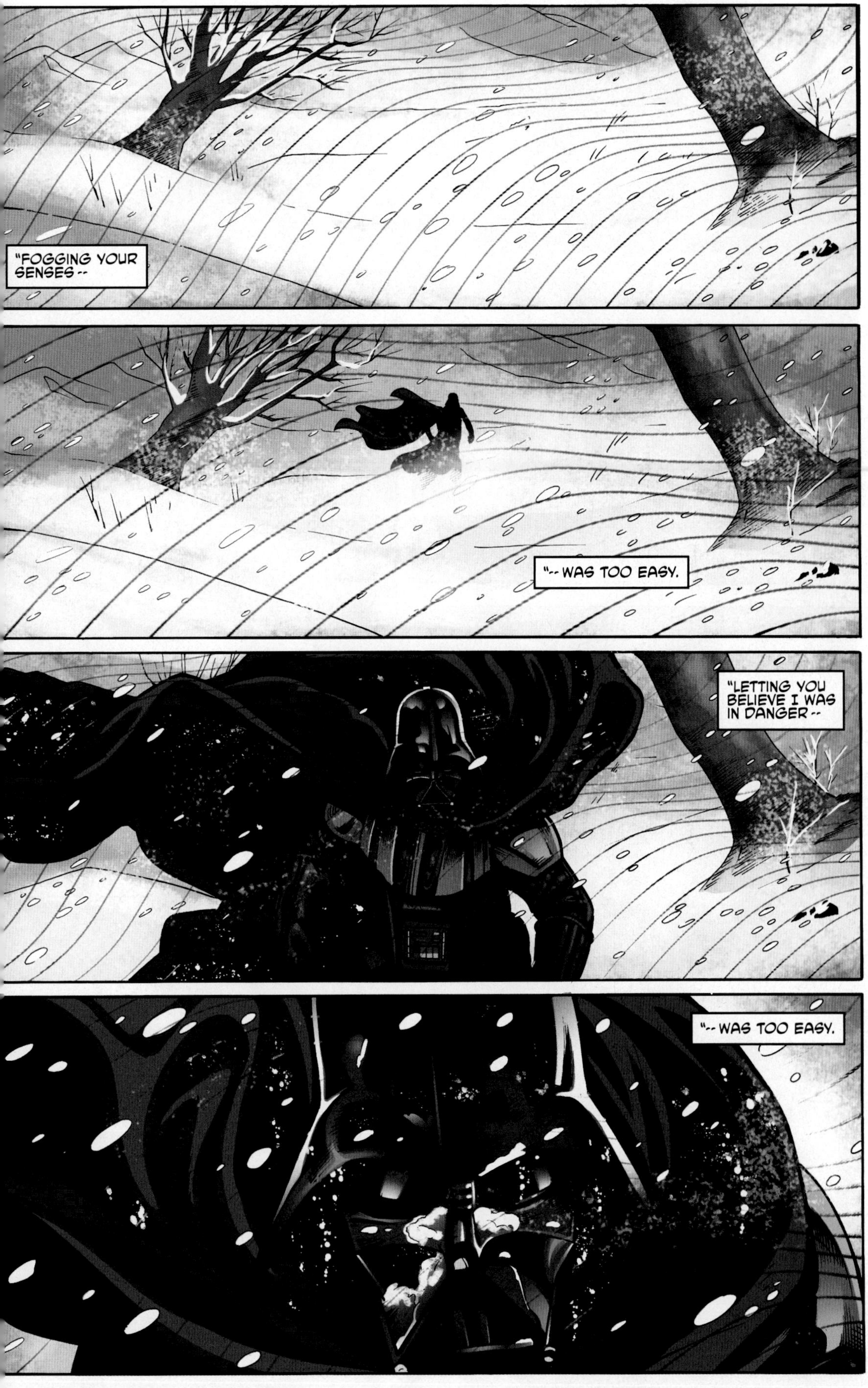
"FOGGING YOUR SENSES --
"-- WAS TOO EASY.
"LETTING YOU BELIEVE I WAS IN DANGER --
"-- WAS TOO EASY.

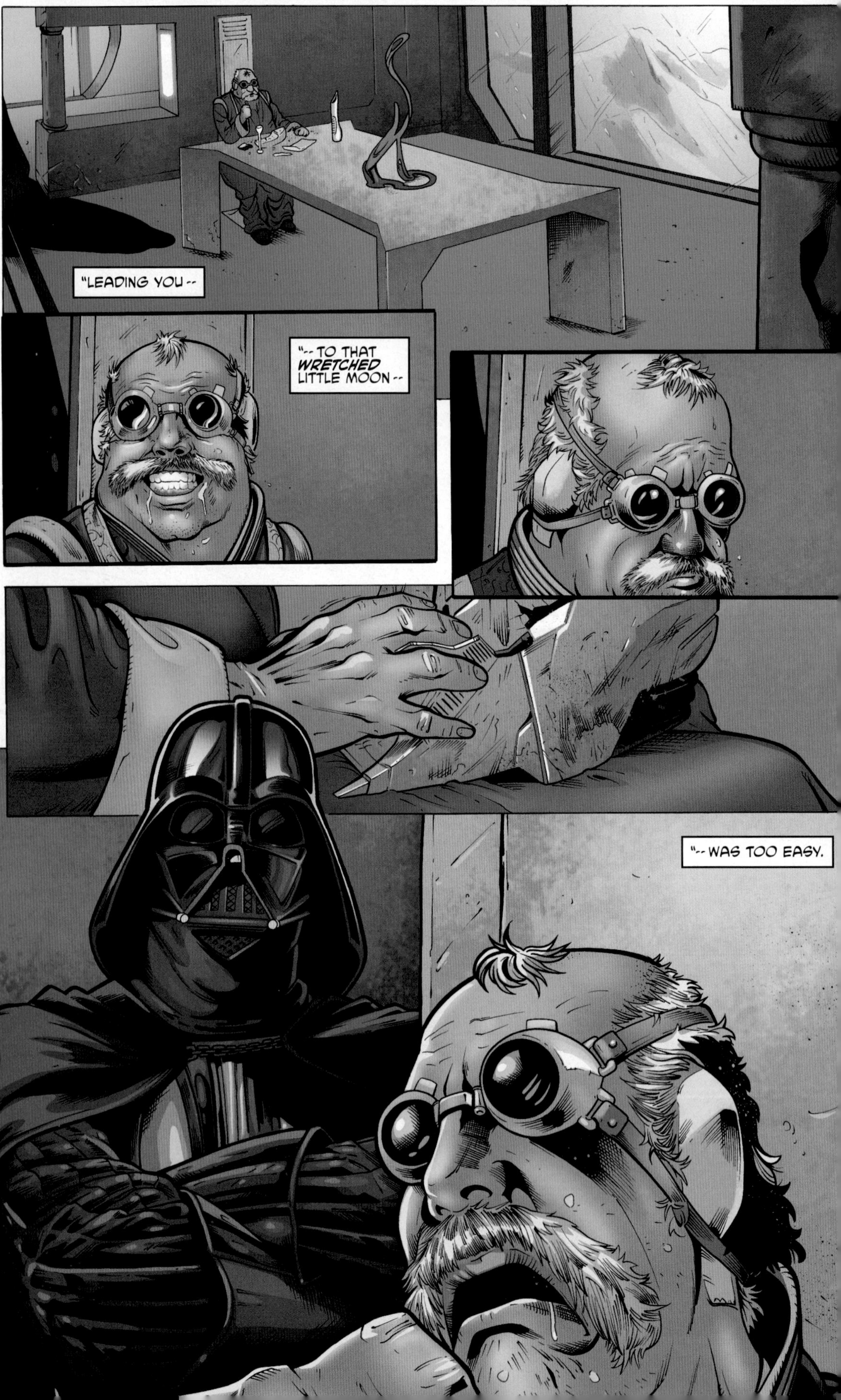
"LEADING YOU --
"-- TO THAT *WRETCHED* LITTLE MOON --
"-- WAS TOO EASY.

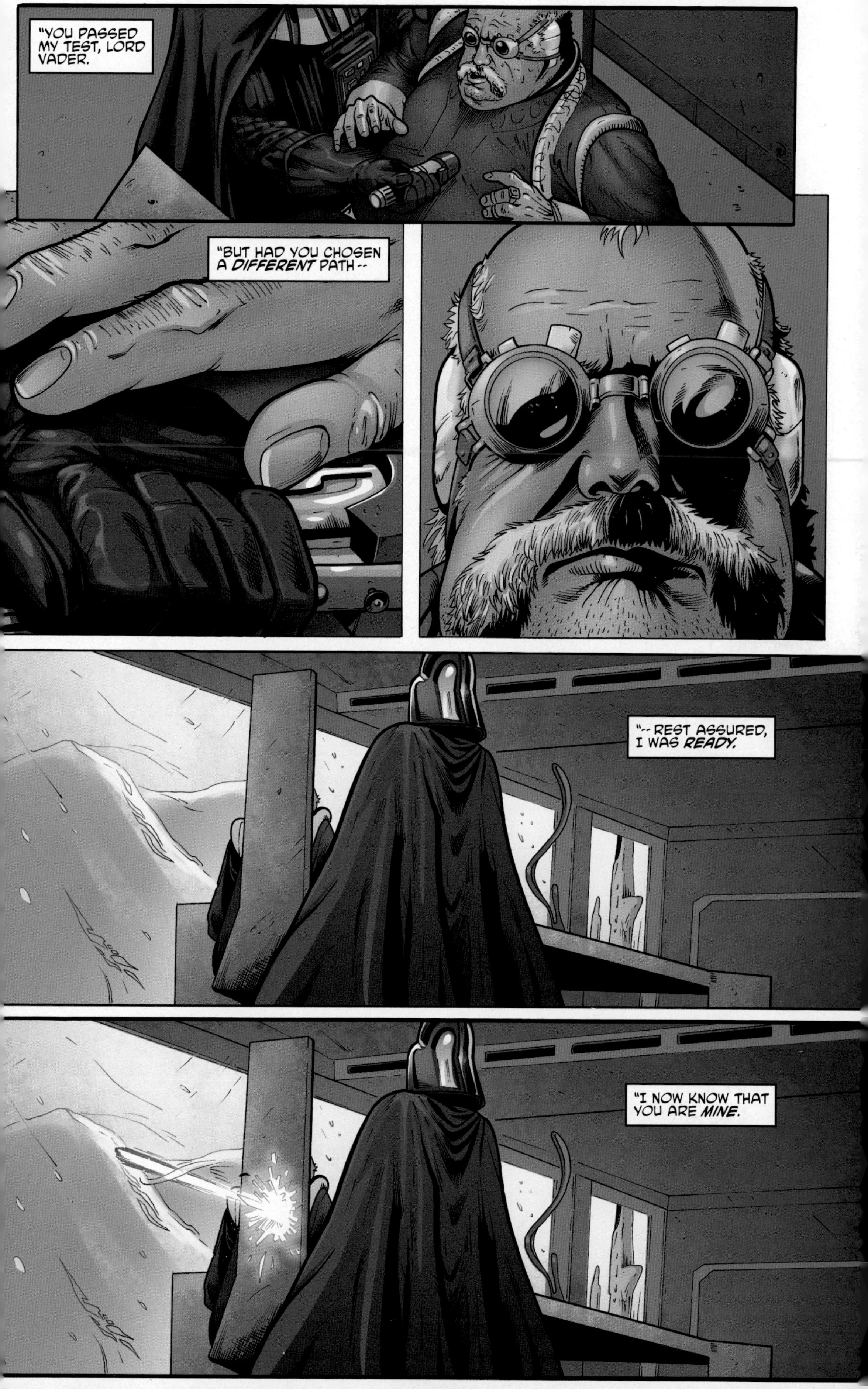
"YOU PASSED MY TEST, LORD VADER.
"BUT HAD YOU CHOSEN A *DIFFERENT* PATH --
"-- REST ASSURED, I WAS *READY*.
"I NOW KNOW THAT YOU ARE *MINE*.

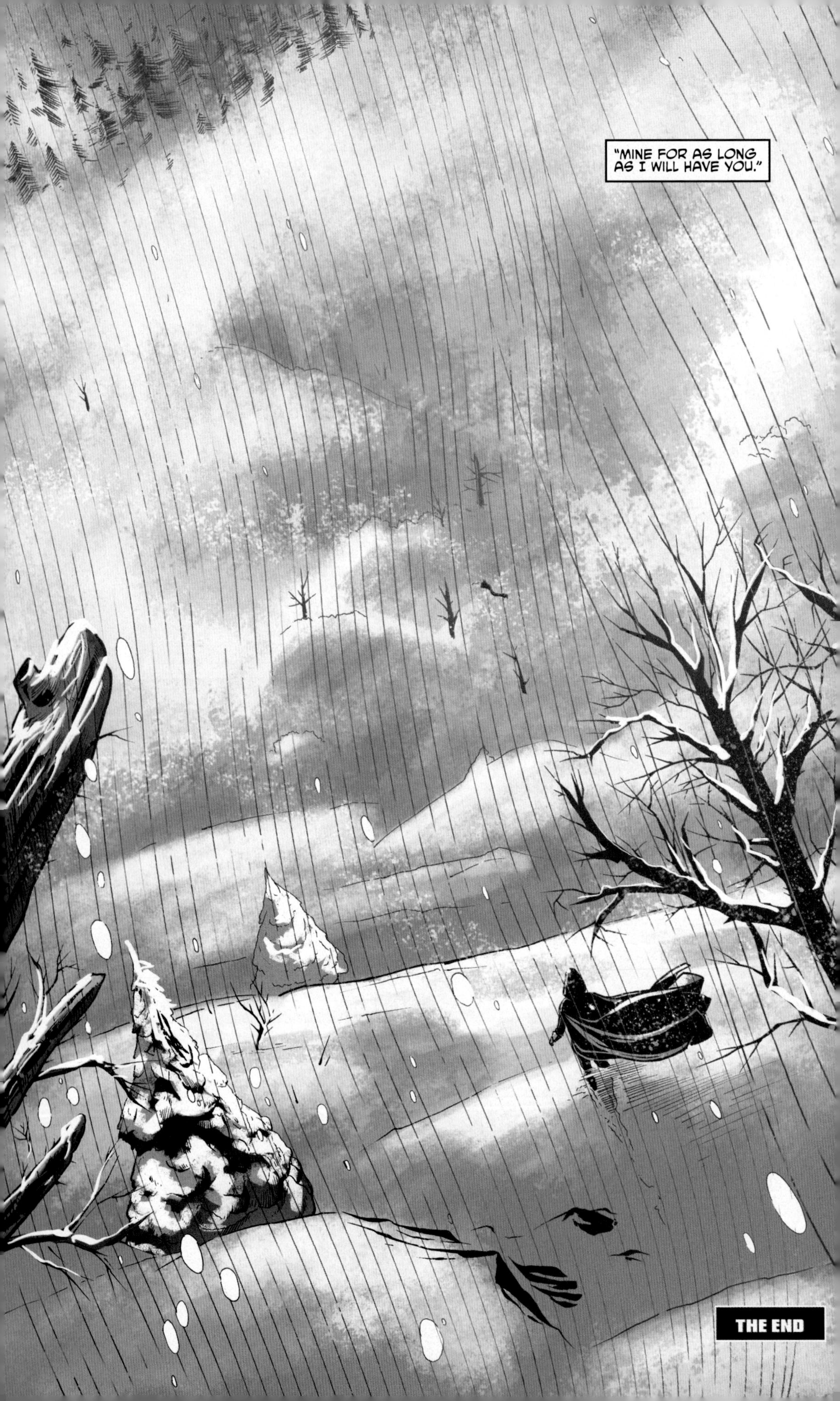
"MINE FOR AS LONG AS I WILL HAVE YOU."
THE END

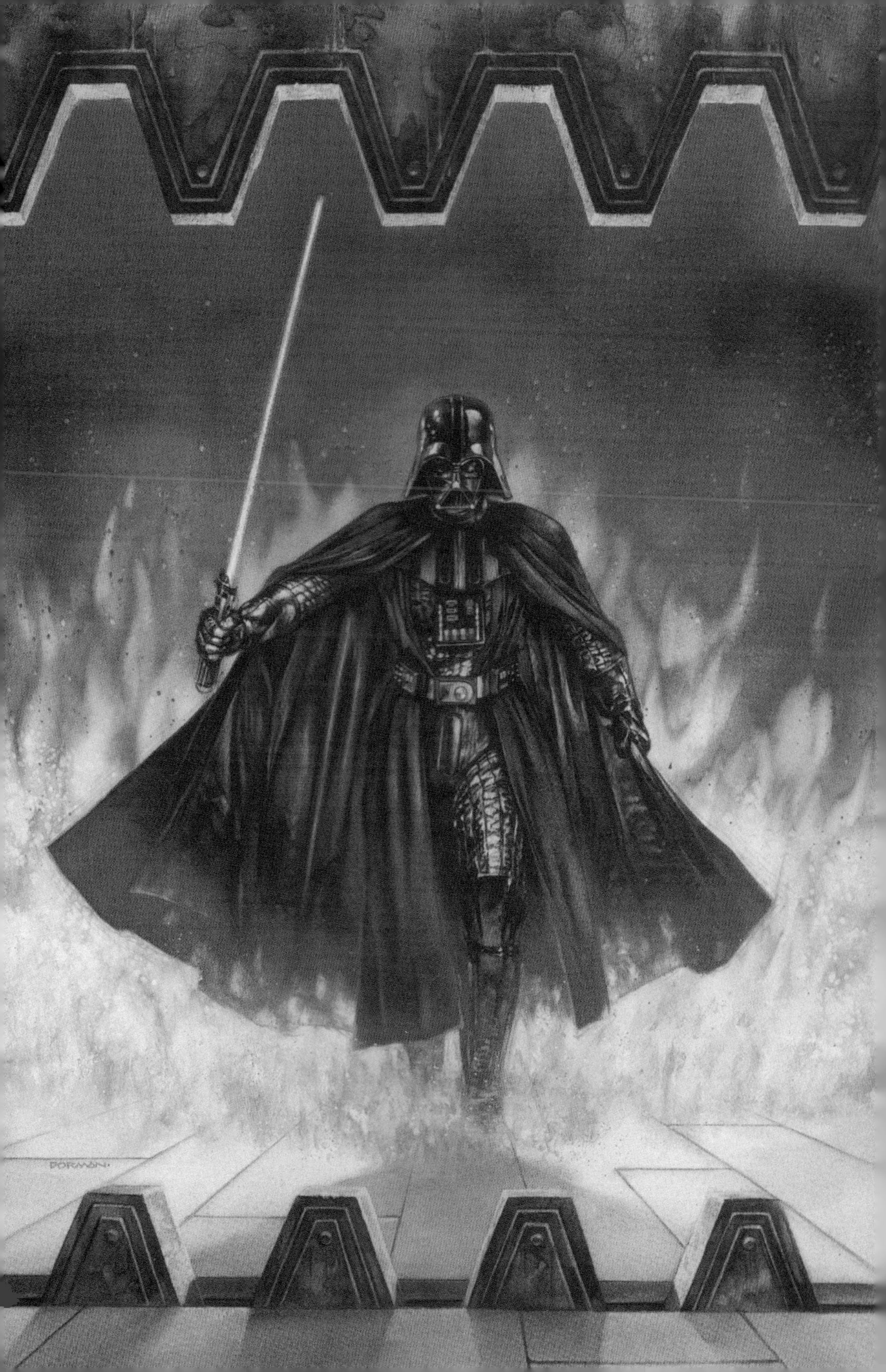
DORMAN

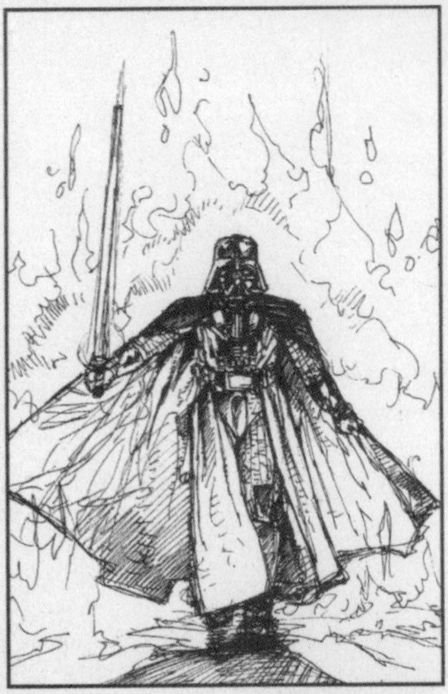

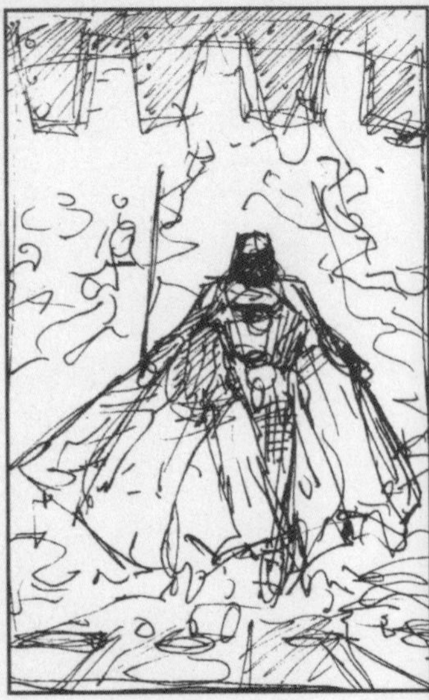

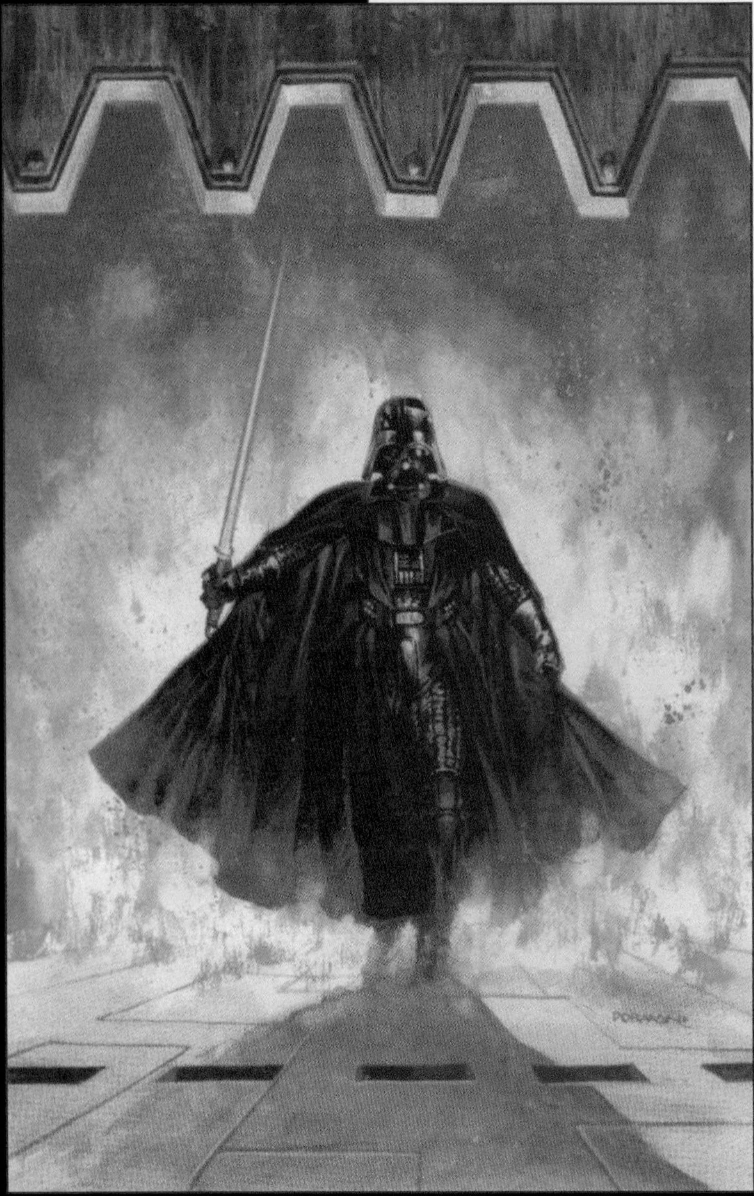

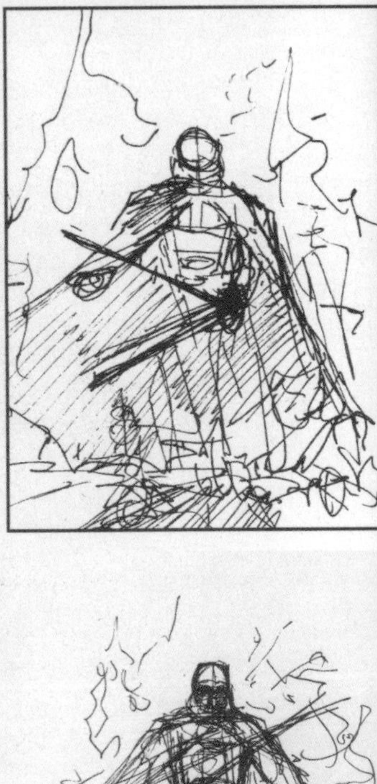

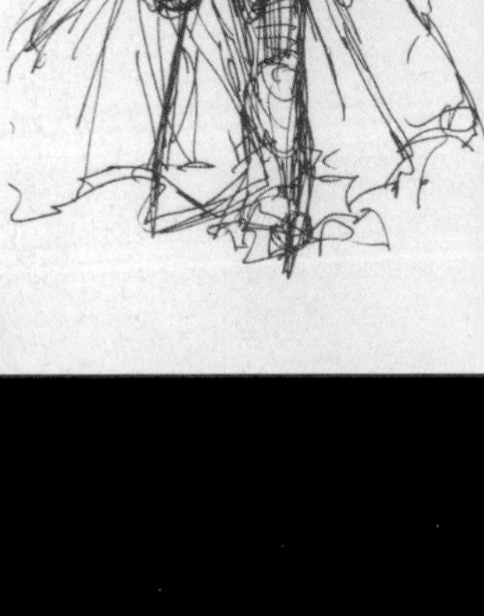

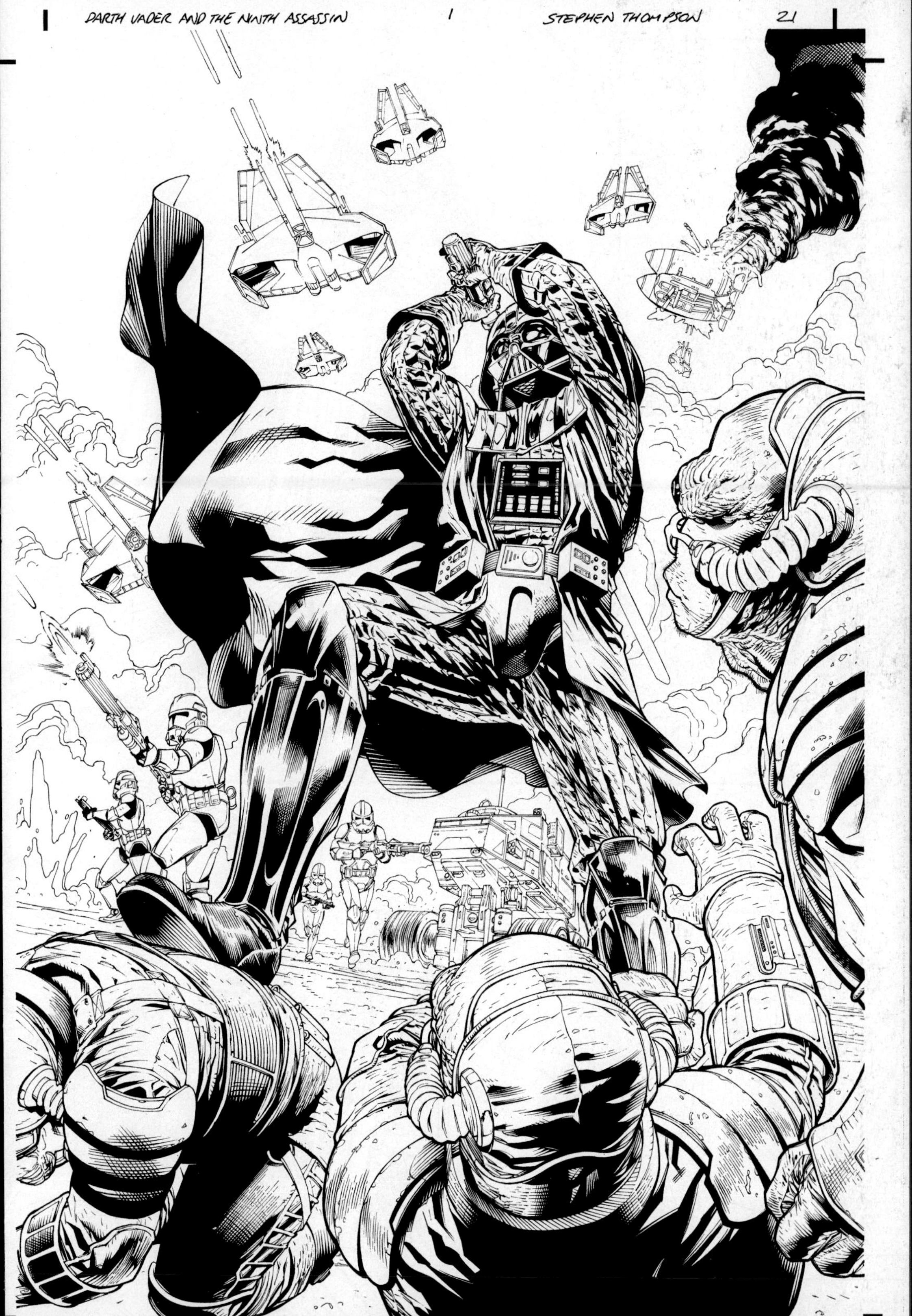
DARTH VADER AND THE NINTH ASSASSIN
1
STEPHEN THOMPSON
21

**STAR WARS: DARTH VADER AND THE NINTH ASSASSIN #1, PAGE 21 ART BY STEPHEN THOMPSON & MARK IRWIN**

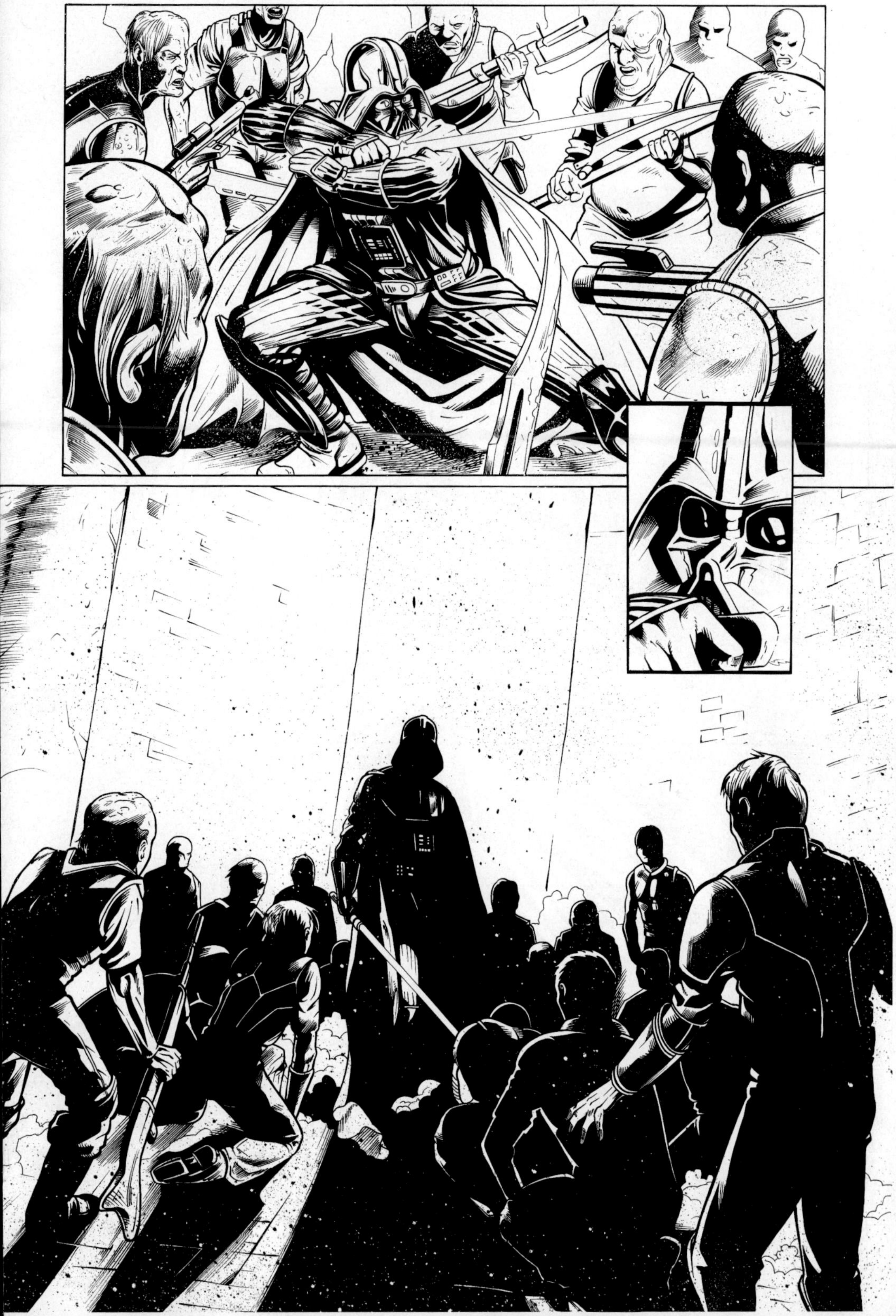

*STAR WARS: DARTH VADER AND THE NINTH ASSASSIN #3*, PAGE 22 ART BY IVÁN FERNÁNDEZ & DENIS FREITAS

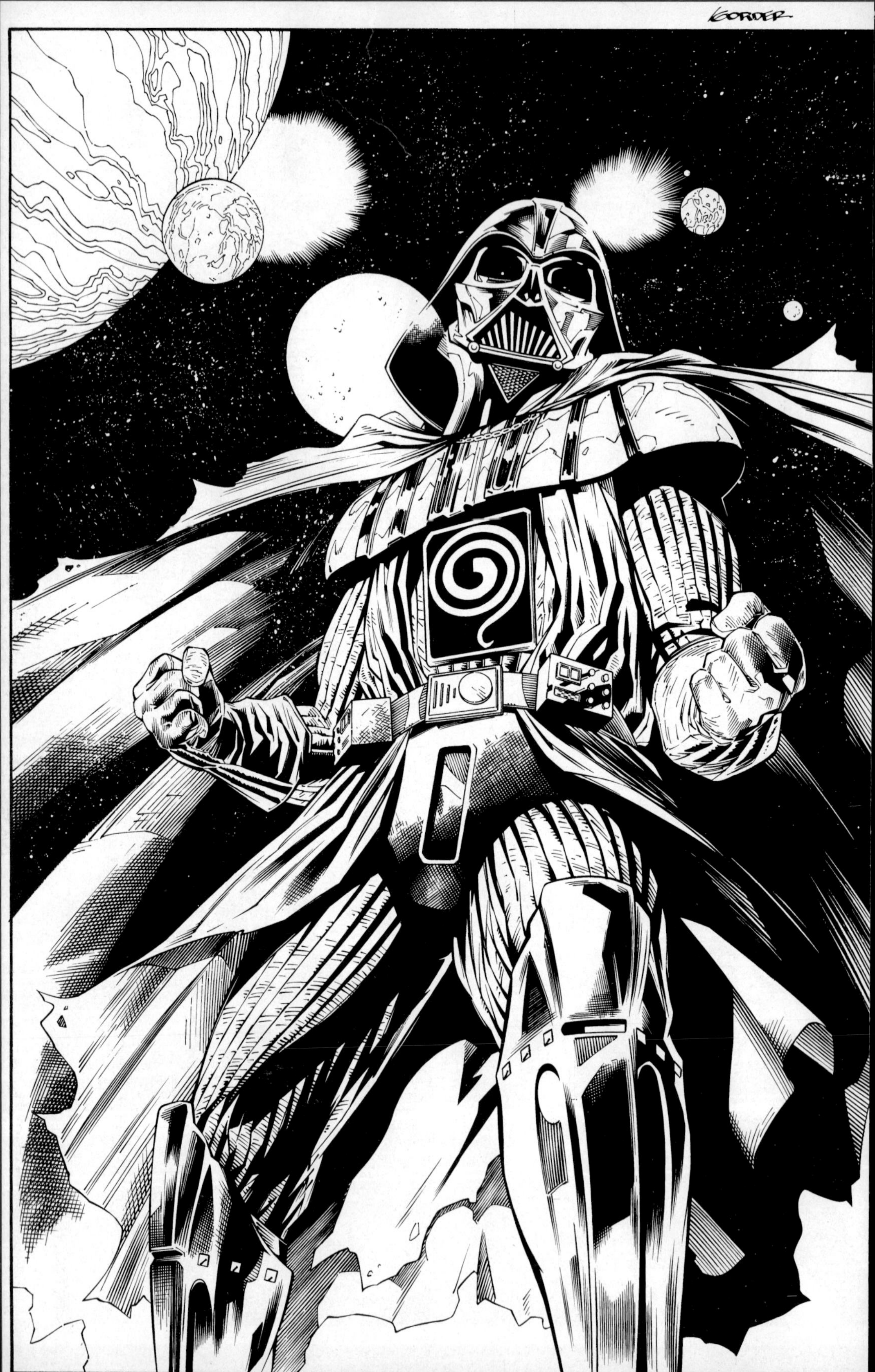

*STAR WARS: DARTH VADER AND THE NINTH ASSASSIN #4*, PAGE 16 ART BY STEPHEN THOMPSON & JASON GORDER